George Eliot

Books by Frederick R. Karl

Franz Kafka: Representative Man (1991)
William Faulkner: American Writer (1989)
Modern and Modernism: The Sovereignty of the Artist 1885–1925 (1985)
American Fictions: 1940–80 (1983)
Joseph Conrad: The Three Lives. A Biography (1979)
The Adversary Literature (1974)
An Age of Fiction: The Nineteenth-Century British Novel (1964, revised 1972)
C. P. Snow: The Politics of Conscience (1963)
The Contemporary English Novel (1962, revised 1972)
The Quest, a novel (1961)
A Reader's Guide to Joseph Conrad (1960, revised 1969)

EDITED:

Joseph Conrad: A Collection of Criticism (1975)
The Collected Letters of Joseph Conrad: Volume I, 1861–97 (1983),
Volume II, 1898–1902 (1986), Volume III, 1903–1907 (1988),
Volume IV, 1908–1911 (1990), Volume V, 1912–1916 (for late 1995)
(general editor and volume coeditor—8 volumes in all)
The Mayor of Casterbridge by Thomas Hardy (1966)
The Portable Conrad (Morton Dauwen Zabel's edition, revised, 1969)
The Signet Classic Book of British Short Stories (1985)
The Secret Agent by Joseph Conrad (1983)
Chance by Joseph Conrad (1985)
The Moonstone by Wilkie Collins (1984)
The Woman in White by Wilkie Collins (1985)
Victory by Joseph Conrad (1991)

COEDITED:

The Existential Imagination (1963)
Short Fiction of the Masters (1963, 1973)
The Shape of Fiction (1967, 1978)
The Radical Vision (1970)
The Naked i: Fictions for the Seventies (1971)
The Existential Mind: Documents and Fictions (1974)
The Fourth World: The Imprisoned, the Poor, the Sick,
the Elderly and Underaged in America (1976)

George Eliot

Voice of a Century

A Biography

FREDERICK R. KARL

W·W·NORTON & COMPANY

New York   London

The text of this book is composed in Goudy Old Style
with the display set in Goudy Cursive with Swash.
Composition and manufacturing by
The Maple-Vail Book Manufacturing Group.
Book design by Jacques Chazaud

Library of Congress Cataloging-in-Publication Data

Karl, Frederick Robert, 1927–
George Eliot, voice of a century : a biography / Frederick R. Karl.
p.   cm.
Includes index.
1. Eliot, George, 1819–1880—Biography.   2. Women novelists,
English—19th century—Biography.   I. Title.
PR4681.K37 1995
823′.8—dc20
[B]   94-37436

ISBN 0-393-03785-1

W. W. Norton & Company, Inc., 500 Fifth Avenue, New York, N.Y. 10110
W. W. Norton & Company Ltd., 10 Coptic Street, London WC1A 1PU

1 2 3 4 5 6 7 8 9 0

To my daughters
and all those, like them,
who became George Eliot's children.

Contents

———————

Acknowledgments

As the first biographer of George Eliot to have access to the full range of research materials concerning her life and work, I find my debts are considerable. Above all, I want to express my gratitude to the memory of that most dauntless of Eliot scholars, Gordon Haight. In preparing the first authoritative biography of Eliot (1968) and in editing the monumental nine volumes of her letters, Professor Haight established Eliot studies on a sound basis; all future biographers, critics, and scholars are indebted to him. Without his sleuthing, his chronologies, his meticulous notes to the letters, my own biography instead of taking four years would have needed at least double that time. Starting back in the 1930s, Haight was even more heroic than we might grant; for as a later generation of English writers had emerged to displace the high Victorians, Eliot studies were more or less stagnant. Since Haight's study, the sole other biographical effort that discusses Eliot's life and work with both close attention to detail and a critical voice is Ruby Redinger's *George Eliot: The Emergent Self* (1975). Richly textured and trenchantly argued, Professor Redinger's book stops short of being a full biography; but more than Haight planned to do, she integrated the work with the life. I am indebted to her study.

In the case of my primary research, I wish to express gratitude to the major holders of Eliot materials: the Manuscript Room of the British Museum/Library, which holds all the manuscripts of Eliot's long fiction, except *Scenes of Clerical Life*. The keepers and curators there showed me the utmost courtesy and provided materials with marked efficiency; and the same is true of the Morgan Library in New York, which holds the manuscript of *Clerical Life*. I am also indebted to the curators of the Humanities Research Center in Austin, Texas; the Beinecke Library at Yale University; the Berg Collection of the New York Public Library; the Princeton University Library; and the Pforzheimer. At these collections, one finds—besides Eliot letters—her notebooks, the letters of John

Chapman, the papers of Charles Bray and Charles Hennell, George Henry Lewes's diary, and proofsheets of Eliot's novels. The Bodleian Library at Oxford University was also helpful, as was the National Portrait Gallery in London with its collection of portraits of Eliot and her contemporaries. The Folger Library in Washington, D.C., warrants mention for its help, and also several offices, museums, and libraries in England: the Nuneaton Museum and Art Gallery, for the Bray and Hennell Papers, and Robert Evans's diary; the Warwick Record Office, for the Newdigate Papers, including letters of Robert Evans and Isaac Evans; and the Castle Howard Archives. One of my most profound debts is to the George Eliot Fellowship, Mrs. Kathleen Adams, the Honorable Secretary; and to Mrs. Kathleen Porter, Vice-Chairman, who personally took me and my wife around to all the important Eliot sites in Warwickshire and saved me much time and difficulty. In several ways, their help has proven invaluable.

I wish to thank my daughter Deborah, for having suggested George Eliot as a topic for a biography; and my wife, Dolores, for having reread all of Eliot's fiction for purposes of discussion with me; Professor Leon Higdon, for having sent on a photocopy of his article on Eliot's use of epigraphs; Professor Bonnie Zimmerman, for sharing with me an unpublished paper on Eliot and Edith Simcox; Professor Jerome Beaty, for his groundbreaking exploration of the *Middlemarch* manuscript; Professor Ira Nadel, for his critical discussion of early biographies of Eliot; Barbara Hardy, for one of the first mature studies of Eliot's fiction; Professor U. C. Knoeplmacher, for his several discussions of Eliot's work; the various editors of the Penguin editions of Eliot's novels, for their attempts to establish authoritative texts, introductions, and notes, especially Andrew Sanders and Andrew Brown (*Romola*), Peter Coveney (*Felix Holt*), David Lodge (*Scenes of Clerical Life*), Stephen Gill (*Adam Bede*), and Q. D. Leavis (*Silas Marner*); and also Gordon Haight's edition of *Middlemarch* in the Riverside edition. However able the Penguin editions, Eliot still needs, badly, a reasonably priced definitive edition, perhaps on the order of the ongoing Cambridge University Press edition of Joseph Conrad. This is, in part, being met by the ongoing Oxford Clarendon edition. Other acknowledgments to scholars and critics appear in the Notes.

I am grateful to New York University for having granted me a year's leave of absence and a year's sabbatical, so that I had almost two unencumbered years to work on the book. I also wish to thank the librarians at the University of Hawaii Library and acknowledge their excellent collection of secondary Eliot materials. It was a great help while I was visiting Citizens' Professor at the university.

As always, I owe a debt of gratitude to my agent, Melanie Jackson, for her support during this four-year period; and to my editor, Amy Cherry, for her close reading of the manuscript and her helpful suggestions.

Introduction

In speaking of George Eliot as the "voice of the century" in England, that is, the spirit and mind of the nineteenth century, we are making great claims for her as a writer and as a person. But perhaps more than anyone else in the period—others like Dickens, Carlyle, Arnold, and possibly Tennyson—she seems most representative, most emblematic of the ambiguities, the anguish, and divisiveness of the Victorian era. Born before railroads, when the great migrations to the cities were just beginning, when England could still look to Wordsworth, Byron, and Shelley, born into a post-Napoleonic age when stability seemed assured, she lived into an era which made the early part of the century seem like another geological age. That she was an independent woman is intrinsic to her representative nature; for as a woman she became part of the spirit of change and progress for both sexes, however reluctantly she at times played that role. Her life and fiction, together, speak of the entire century. She assimilated thoroughly its humanistic and scientific ideas, she understood more than any other figure what was happening to ordinary people, and she found ways to express in her own person and her work the density, texture, and aspirations of the period. Perhaps only Dickens and Carlyle join her here, but their genius was eccentric, often wild and extreme, whereas hers was in the main balanced, stable, and cognizant of human limitations. Without losing sight of man's (and woman's) aberrations, she was, all in all, reasonable.

Yet in her most characteristic pose, caught by the painter Sir Frederic Burton in 1865, when Eliot was turning forty-six, we sense how complicated that balance was. Despite the elegance and even self-confidence of her pose, she was a deeply divided woman, a deeply divided thinker, and, as part of this, an artist desperately trying to hold together many disparate and even contradictory forces. What helps to make Eliot the voice of the century is that recognition, projected from herself, of the uncertainties, the destabilization, the wobbling center in Victorian life. Added to this was her realization of the ambiguous, even precarious, role of women. In those areas which later became the prerogative of feminists, she was caught between the daring of her private life and her difficulty in putting that daring into public policy, or public statements. But far more than even this, she was deeply divided as a person, full of contradictory impulses. Profoundly religious when growing up, she moved toward a rationalism and secularity that never completely replaced her earlier Calvinism. Her humanitarian impulses, her avowed humanism, her earnestness as to individual duty and discipline were all calculated responses to a religious or spiritual life she could no longer experience; and yet the substitutes proved unsatisfactory. She wanted a Christianity with her own kind of Christ; she wanted not a church but an individual who was his or her own church; she found in reason, logic, and intelligence a replacement for a God she could no longer believe in or accept. And yet none of this was easily resolved, as we will observe in her best fiction. Like most great artists, she left a good deal open to interpretation.

Beyond these complexities which preoccupied her, the divisions in her emergence as woman and writer were profoundly psychological. What made her perhaps the first psychological novelist in English was her awareness of feelings of fear, dread, doubt, and anxiety in ordinary situations. Unlike Dickens, she wanted to discover how the individual can define himself or herself in a community or society and yet still honor what belongs to the single self. She recognized the need for authority, something she carried over from her early worship of her father, and yet she saw how authority could have crushed her at the very time she felt her powers building. She knew from her own feelings and from her extensive reading that she had to develop into herself, and yet she also knew that her duty was to obey her father and his commandments. She suffered from terrible fears of frustration and anxiety, and she felt that despite her early vision of something great, she might be hobbled from achieving anything. She sensed some mission, but she was not certain what it was until well into her thirties. Her overriding intellect gave her tools which, until she was past her twenties, her immediate life gave her no opportunity of utilizing. She felt bottled up intellectually and emotionally; a sexual life, furthermore, seemed distant, although to what extent that was a major consideration for her we cannot be sure.

She recognized the major divisions of the age because she recognized them in herself, as did Carlyle, whose depressions, ill health, and sexual anxieties all helped nourish a view of nineteenth-century England as oppressive, spiritually starved, and, inevitably, destructive. Eliot did not go so far ideologically, but she knew from her early twenties that she was different; and she knew, further, that her differences might not ever find an outlet. The splits and schisms within herself over her abilities, her course of action, and her fears of being frustrated created in her an almost lifelong sequence of illnesses, headaches, and annoying ailments which until the end had no clear physical etiology. And in this vein of alternating hard work and malaise, she had perhaps the thinnest skin of any major nineteenth-century figure. Unable to handle criticism, she made sure her companion, George Henry Lewes, screened all comments on her work, and she conditioned her publisher, Blackwood's, to suppress anything that might not prove entirely positive.

Although her fiction attempted to show stability, reason, and responsibility, she was, personally, a series of contradictions. Her fears and anxieties, her worries that her books were useless and her efforts in vain, her inability to feel fully in control of her life, her frequent statements about illness and death all enervated her in her most professionally successful years. Yet in those ways, also, she was the voice of the century. For between her life and her work, she caught the ironies and paradoxes of that time: that compromise the Victorians made to achieve balance, alongside those destabilizing elements undermining that very world of appearances. Eliot asked the great questions of herself and crafted the literary means to respond to them. In an era of enormous and radical change, she posed, what occurs to the individual voice? What are one's responsibilities as well as one's rights? In a period of shifting moralities and dubious ethics, how can one hold on to a sense of community? In a century which lavished rewards on those who could exploit it, how does one preserve a moral and ethical sense? In a time of great cheapening of values and of urban life, how does one maintain the standards needed for a self-respecting life? In such a period, what worth can be placed on mind, on spirit, and on values when it is impossible to believe any longer in a divine being, when evolutionary ideas seem to have subverted an entire country? With God essentially gone or dead—that is, with God ceasing practically to function for a sizable part of the population—what happens to morals, community, individual action? Is a functioning society even possible now that community has been so undermined?

As an older contemporary of Nietzsche—a very different writer in a different culture—Eliot asked many of the same questions he posed; and while her answers are wildly distinct from his, she became the voice of England in the nineteenth century as much as he expressed the inner, potentially explosive voice of Germany. Any new biography of Eliot must see her both as a woman and as an artist attempting to grapple with these and related questions. She moved in a large, expansive world. She was literary in the most ambitious sense, that of becoming a seer, a visionary, a voice. And yet none of it came easily to her; none of it poured out, as her books made it seem that it did. She paid heavily for her anxieties and decisions, for her "difference" from most other women of her time; and yet, withal, she found the surface stability that permitted her to nourish her creative talent and to turn her own divided, troubled self into the highest levels of achievement.

Her elopement and twenty-four-year relationship with George Henry Lewes, a man with a very messy marital arrangement, were by no means the whole story of her personal life. She had to experience the entire range of divisions common to a woman in the nineteenth century. She considered herself physically unattractive, at a time when a woman's appearance in middle- and upper-middle-class circles was deemed paramount. Her intelligence clearly set her off from the common run of women, and men, except a few like Spencer, Mill, and Carlyle. But her intelligence went further than the accumulation of book knowledge.

She experienced or intuited the cultural reshaping taking place, changes which threatened every aspect of Victorian life; and this ability was another form of her difference from others. From an early age, as she assessed the capabilities of those near her, she had begun to move to another level of awareness. And yet her circumstances persisted in disallowing any opportunity for her differences to emerge. Thus, from an early time, she lived divided, one part seemingly devoted to her conventional father and his world while the other, her own intellectual world, lay fallow. The split came in her late teens when she started to move away from all the commonalities of bourgeois life—religious, marital, and professional. She began to chart a future for herself that, at the time, she felt she could not sustain. She feared being wasted in the hinterlands of farms, farmers, and artisans—people she admired but did not wish to emulate.

The change of birth name is a way of breaking away, and yet Eliot, even as she reshaped herself, remained what she was. She never *became* George Eliot; no one referred to her as George or as Miss Eliot. George Sand, on the contrary, was George, was Madame Sand. Eliot appears so representative of her age because even with decisive change—and renaming is critical—she seemed to mirror a period which altered rapidly while it hung on to what was no longer available. She reflected such yearning, but looked backward as well as forward. When she insisted on calling herself Mrs. Lewes, while the legal Mrs. Lewes was alive and well, she signaled traditional values within a radically new kind of family situation. In her every act, she found in her own split needs and divided personality those coordinates of the era which marked her as its voice. When she found her voice, she captured a culture.

A kindred spirit, Virginia Woolf, in *Three Guineas* (1938), expressed how women were omitted from the social and political scene, omitted in fact from history and, indirectly, denied their own language. What does patriotism mean to a woman who cannot defend or serve her country? What do the country's finances signify when a woman is denied membership in the stock exchange? Women do not negotiate treaties, nor do they run the educational establishment. They do not fire weapons, control the press, run the church, or litigate in the courts. Eliot's awareness of these omissions in the public area almost a century earlier helps explain her philosophy of duty and sacrifice, her sense of discipline and social comity, her desire to locate women on higher ground where men could not exert control. In her way, she cleared a space for women, even as she vacillated on important women's issues.

We emphasize how she found in the contradictions of her own personality and needs the tensions and polarities which nourished her fiction. We can, of course, say this about any major author: that he or she discovers conflicts or contrasts and then uses fiction as a way of resolving, suppressing, or triumphing. But in Eliot's case, the situation becomes more intense inasmuch as she helped pioneer a new path for women at the same time she had to preserve a semblance of social coherence. She was pulled in several directions. In point of fact, her role as a woman made it all the more possible for her to confront these contradictory impulses, since as a woman she had to deal with them in ways men could finesse or ignore.

The commitment to Lewes was not Marian Evans's only flirtation with the strict morality of her day. Almost from childhood, she began to take on qualities—emotional and psychological as well as intellectual—which would transform her from a country girl into a figure of universal renown: from a young girl deeply attached to the land, to flowers, to natural elements into a sophisticated woman who made all knowledge her domain. Her entire life from late childhood on was a process of transformation, reshaping herself, or, as an earlier biographer put it, emerging.

The monumental 1854 decision to go off to Germany with Lewes must be viewed as the pivotal move which provided stability in Eliot's personal life at the same time that it created the conflicts which ultimately nourished her fiction; this choice of paths ultimately defined who and what she was. It did not make her "happy" in any conventional sense, but, like most choices she made, it moved her along to a world she would create in her own image. It helped to remove her from the dead end of reviewing and translating to something she had only subconsciously thought of doing—writing fiction.

In retrospect, the biographer sees a steady accumulation of creative energy, peaking perhaps in *Middlemarch,* a decade and a half later. But for the subject herself, there was no perception of the eventual success of her endeavors. Eliot took herself to the edge—as she so frequently did in other matters as well—and plunged. The resulting scandal, the proximity to a volatile figure like Lewes, a man known for his philandering and for his open marriage, the fact that the relationship was possibly short term, the chance that Eliot would be far worse off when she returned to England and was very possibly cutting herself off—all of these factors, or even some of them, could have aborted her career well before it had had an opportunity to emerge.

To an extent, Eliot deconstructed her life at each decisive point, since she moved the center of it to uncertain and ambiguous places: renouncing the religion of her father, moving up to London to carve out a career, going off with Lewes, then attempting fiction. She was opening herself up to potentialities without any assurance that what she was doing would turn out correctly for her. This very cautious young woman had become a less than cautious mature person. She chose courses she could not rationally defend, and yet rational defense became the cornerstone of her humanistic impulses, the basis of her secularism. In effect, she split herself as a further means of renewal.

Her use of the name George Eliot only three years after she started to call herself Mrs. Lewes indicates how she was redefining herself as a woman with her own language and her own story. She was not to be discouraged from her own sense of herself, even when that sense was itself full of irreconcilable elements. The use of pseudonyms, incidentally, while well known with the Brontës and Eliot herself, extended to a broad number of nineteenth-century writers; even men took to the name-change fashion, with William Sharp, for one, becoming Fiona Macleod. Among women, Pearl Craigie (she wrote the article on Eliot for the tenth edition of the *Encyclopaedia Britannica*) became John Oliver Hobbs; Mrs. Mary St. Leger Harrison, daughter of novelist Charles Kingsley, became Lucas Halet; Violet Page became Vernon Lee; and of course, in France, Lucie Aurore Dupin Dudevant became George Sand. In each instance, the woman writer had a different motive, not solely to ease publication; but the common factor in all was to reclaim her own life, relocate it within her own space, away from direct male pressure—all of this achieved, paradoxically, by taking on a male name.

Eliot reveled in such contradictions, paradoxes, and ironies, and like many Victorian novelists she had an arsenal of literary weapons which included secrets and threats. Her focus was often on blackmail, either direct or implied. Its incidence is remarkable given this retiring woman of gentle disposition and orderly habits, inasmuch as blackmail carries with it menace, threat, a corruptible world, an underclass of creatures harboring anger, hostility, and aggression, and even murder. Outright blackmail occurs in *Silas Marner*, *Felix Holt*, and *Middlemarch*; indirect or implied blackmail is seen in *Romola*, with Baldassarre's vow to turn up murderously in Tito's life, and in *Daniel Deronda*, with Lydia Glasher's threats to Gwendolen when the latter is contemplating marriage to Grandcourt.

When we seek some reason for Eliot's fascination with what would seem inappropriate topics for her, it is insufficient to say she was a writer of her times and, therefore, someone who utilized what was at hand. The reasons are more personal. Behind the public topics was her abiding secretive self: her fear, then, of the revelation that behind George Eliot was Mary Anne Evans or Marian Lewes or Mrs. Lewes, as if the disclosure of *that* woman behind her books could frustrate her writing career at any stage. She played out her fears, and then shadowed them throughout her fiction. The gentle Eliot was full of such contradictory impulses, so that layered behind names and decisions, she could well understand the larger sense of blackmail, threat, menace. She knew something of the great disorder which lies beyond seeming order.

Her impulse to undermine or destroy, in contradistinction to the ostensible moral message of her fiction, goes to the heart of women's ambivalent role in society. In retrospect, we tend to make historical roles fit general patterns, and yet clearly there were women who did not fit into any part of the Victorian compromise on acceptable public display. Such women abounded in the upper circles of society as well as in England's intellectual life. Eliot met many of these women, although even in those instances only a few, in defiance of restrictions, really carved out something unique for themselves, as Eliot had done. Yet for most women, submission was the rule, not the exception; and it was through submission, ironically perhaps, that Eliot made her strongest statements. The women who submit most, such as Lydia Glasher and Gwendolen Harleth (to Grandcourt in *Daniel Deronda*) or Hetty Sorrel (to Arthur Donnithorne in *Adam Bede*), but, most strikingly, Dorothea Brooke (to Edward Casaubon in *Middlemarch*), have all found retribution in their destruction of the men they submit to. The conditions differ from novel to novel, but for each woman *submission becomes the weapon* by which she triumphs, even at the expense of her own well-being or life.

The difficulty here is not primarily in assessing what Eliot accomplished, but in trying to determine what in her life led her to become such a seeker of female retribution in her fiction. Her childhood experiences appear, at least superficially, normal. She admired and respected her father, Robert Evans, although seriously disagreeing with him when she became a young woman. She had her disagreements, also, with her brother and half-brother, but these did not at the time appear traumatic, or even problematic. It is true that her plain appearance did not draw many admirers, but over the years she did encounter men who found her excellent company and, in some cases, very possibly desired intimate relationships. As we have seen, some who paid court to her were celebrated and attractive.

In any final assessment, we would be hard pressed to cite definite or particular elements in Marian's life which would lead into George Eliot's fictional attitudes toward men. There appears to be a gap—part of that divided self—between her personal experiences and her fictional attitudes. What we see, instead, is not a narrow personal side developing in her, but a social position about women generally overtaking her personal experiences and driving her toward certain conclusions. We can say that her social sense of women's roles, added to her apprehension about what occurs to women who, like her, possess plain or even unattractive looks, drew her into a radical personal position, even while she maintained in her public statements a neutral attitude about women's issues such as the franchise and divorce laws.

This still further division of self into parts was a corollary of her vision of what roles were relegated to women, and how they would respond. In this respect, Eliot became a representative woman of the nineteenth century: keenly aware of the menu offered women, aware of the restrictions on their role—legal, medical, personal, wary of any extreme action which would change it; and yet, conscious of how a woman must navigate in order to make the most of her position. Eliot's strong women never just "settle." They may offer submission, but they struggle for more, they insist on their own needs, they defer only so much as is necessary to preserve a social polity. Eliot walked a very thin line, in her own life as in her writing; and in this way she reflected not only women of that century, but life as well. For even as she defines roles for women, she also redefines them for men—this point must be emphasized; and in the process, she became one of the few writers of any age who could depict both genders. She was, in this regard, a complete social being, and in the slow working out of her own liberation, her greatest fiction reflects that social vision.

In the last two decades, we have formed very different ideas about biographical studies from what prevailed in the past. We need not promote a psychoanalytic treatise on a long-dead person, which is always problematical and subject to potential excesses; but, instead, we expect a psychological analysis of potentialities and possibilities in the person's life which we have gleaned from certain patterns, repetitions, and perhaps obsessions which recur in the work. The dearth of workable marriages in Eliot's fiction, the large number of grown children without mothers, and the often hostile lines drawn between a child and his or her parent are all elements which must be linked to Eliot's early years and to her later development as a person and as a writer.

Well beyond the need for critical psychological analysis, there is the larger question of biographies which scant Eliot's work, especially when that work made her, along with Dickens, the preeminent novelist of the nineteenth century. What great significance does Eliot's life have if we scant the fiction? Inevitably, the question must be: How did that person write those books, and, reciprocally, how did those books get written by that person? Eliot was in several ways a great and admirable woman; yet while history is full of such women, it contains only a relatively few who wrote great books.

We must also reject the point stressed by previous biographers that Eliot "depended" on men. Instead of depending on them, she assimilated their power before moving on to the next, from Bray and Brabant to Chapman and Herbert Spencer, and finally to Lewes. Accordingly, her relationship to each man was a form of absorption into herself of their place in the masculine world denied to her directly. And from that, she could gather her forces, then move on: not dependent on them, but rather like the warrior who consumes his adversary's flesh in order to ingest his strength. As a corollary, the very first biography of Eliot, by the poet Mathilde Blind, in 1883, as part of the "Famous Writers" series, does not emphasize her dependence. Blind, who says she relied on information from Eliot's brother, Isaac, as well as on the Brays and other friends, stresses inner conflict accompanied by her transcendence of problems. Perhaps surprisingly, given her closeness in time to the subject, she is acute in seizing on Eliot's ability to resolve profound internal struggles through personal decisions.

In addition, a good deal of new material has surfaced, not the least the powerful and troubling letters to Herbert Spencer. With the release of these letters by the Trustees of the British Museum, we observe a far more complicated woman than we receive in most previous biographies. We can now chart her strangely plaintive relationship with that bizarre but highly intelligent man, one of the founders of the discipline of sociology. We may cringe at Eliot's pleas for his love or even his friendship, but that note does not necessarily diminish her. It humanizes her and prepares us for her major decision to go off with Lewes and to find in him a personal shield behind which she could write her fiction.

Other new material includes a fuller sense of Eliot's role as the shadow editor of the quarterly *Westminster Review,* and the possibility of a more realistic view of that prestigious journal and the people involved in it. The surfacing of the letters of George Combe, the phrenologist with connections to Eliot, Chapman, and the *Review,* reveals a viper's nest of rumors, infidelities, philandering, and related matters. In her own long letters to Combe, Eliot opened up her ideas at the very time we want to know more about her, when she was indeed emerging from Mary Anne Evans, or Marian, to become George Eliot. This background material is supplemented by the availability of Eliot notebooks located at various sources. While these notebooks do not appreciably alter our view of the main lines of her life, they do fill us with awe at what she knew. Her intellect was all-consuming, as we see not only in her novels but in these notebooks.

Furthermore, we now possess more diverse ways of observing her role as a strong woman and, in the eyes of her gossipy contemporaries, as an "avenging angel" devastating bourgeois Victorian values. Although Eliot's devotion to women's issues could be vacillating and hedged with qualifications, her relationship to several female leaders needs to be redefined. Previous biographers have scanted her associations with Barbara Bodichon and Edith Simcox, among others. The point cannot be that Eliot failed to resolve thorny feminist issues, or that she attempted to maintain a low personal profile after going to live with Lewes. The point is not even that she fell short in her commitment to the issues—women's rights in divorce and marriage, female education, the franchise, career and professional opportunities—but, rather, that she devoted much of her writing life to an attempt to work through the multifold dilemmas of young women (and the confusion of young men) in a mainly patriarchal society. Her fiction gave her greater freedom than did her life, and surely highlighted the very split in her personal and public life.

But alongside the gender war and its various battlefields, Eliot is significant to us now because she had a functional view of society or community which encouraged individuality at the same time that it enforced moral commitment. Neither gender was exempt. She was working along the lines of the later German sociologist Ferdinand Tönnies and his distinction between *Gemeinschaft* and *Gesellschaft*. The first is a society based on inherited values, on custom and tradition, on historically proven solutions or compromises. Such a society is town or village oriented, anti-urban, certainly anti-industrialization. The second type of society, what Tönnies called *Gesellschaft*, is founded on individualism, a society in which its members lack cohesion with each other since their sole bond is to their own self-interest. Reason, which is individualist, prevails here, whereas in *Gemeinschaft*, there is the precedence of community values. Without sharing Tönnies's romanticism and ethnic view of the "Folk," with its potential for racial cleansing and religious hatred, Eliot outlined a moral and ethical value system distinctly connected to a balance between the individual and the community. While she might not have recognized present-day America—so far has it leaned toward *Gesellschaft*—her efforts to find social linkage for the individual still have considerable cogency. Her morality is rarely too constrained, her ethics only infrequently too vindictive for us to ignore her plea for the individual's social role. This was, very possibly, the great subject of the nineteenth century, in the major fiction writers as well as in Carlyle, Ruskin, Tennyson, Mill, Arnold, and others.

We now take for granted the high literary quality of Eliot's fiction, but several earlier commentators dismissed her (David Cecil) or found her work more like treatises than fictions (William Ernest Henley) or mocked her elaborate apparatuses (Edmund Gosse). Her reputation after her death in 1880 declined precipitously, exacerbated by critics who have themselves disappeared into literary history. Yet once her work was, as it were, rediscovered, we find that the newer forms of criticism catch some of her strategies, uncover other levels of disclosure, and seek in her responses to social ostracism an entire array of countering weapons. Reading Eliot now, we can assume, is far more intense than it was even for her most sympathetic contemporaries. Even Henry James, who maintained a problematic relationship to her work, tended to slight elements which did not fit his pattern of fiction. Now in our eclecticism, we can glory in her wide range and not restrict her to any one tradition, not even to F. R. Leavis's "great tradition" of the English novel.

In broad cultural terms, we have tended to reembrace the major Victorians: their largeness, their density, their textured social sense. The so-called old-fashioned novel has suddenly seemed attractive amidst contemporary minimalism, loss of character and story line, and innovation. Since several recent efforts at nineteenth-century realism have proven little more than pastiches or bouts of nostalgia, we are moved to return to the real thing. We seek that older sense of coherence, cohesiveness, and deliberation. We can even tolerate moral fervor. We have, accordingly, made the previous era into a historical pattern that seems less threatening than ours, more soothing. Much of this is obviously a misreading of Victoria's era, whose smoothness and stability were only superficial; but, nevertheless, in hindsight, and contrasted with our own century, it appears more conducive to civilized existence.

In this embrace of the previous century, however, there is a necessary caution: we must not misread Eliot culturally. Her work is full of the incoherence that any period contains. She was fully aware of rage, anger, and hostility; she recognized how the individual and society pull against each other and often appear inimical to the needs of the other. Nevertheless, despite these destructive forces playing through her work and, as we shall see, through herself, Eliot was able to quiet rage, calm anger, and play down hostility. This she did without recourse to traditional forms of belief. She remained a secular humanist once she broke with Anglicanism and rejected Methodism. She offered no institutional resolutions, only her own form of fallible humanism. What makes her so engaging in these terms is her skill in finding some leverage even when human behavior becomes uncivil, when it borders on anarchy, and when society itself seems threatened. She does not dismiss these elements; she identifies them and finds ways of containing them. We may in the long run reject her ideas, even her tentative resolutions of profound individual and societal problems, but within her fictional means she sought closure on a society's worst dilemmas.

Eliot was an essential part of that condition critics have labeled the feminization of the nineteenth century. By this we mean that through her female protagonists she insisted on the sensibility of women as part of larger cultural values, however much her individual women settled, ultimately, for traditional roles. Her women have a sensibility which impacts on social and community values and resonates in the lives of the men who encounter such women. The latter rebel against being conventional players and they insist on perception, duty, and discipline, which put to shame male ego, profligacy, and a God-given right to power. In this context, the men must reexamine and in some instances transcend themselves. Along with Mrs. Gaskell, the Brontës, later Thomas Hardy, and several others, Eliot insisted on making gender issues the crucible for self-examination.

Her struggle to assert her will was an uphill battle against mid- and later-Victorian evolutionary and medical thought about women and their capabilities. Among several others, Darwin and Spencer undermined women's hopes for more rapid social, political, and educational advancement. Yet in some strange chemistry, Eliot's frequent bouts of depression—which one contemporary medical writer, Sir James Crichton-Browne, attributed to lack of motherhood—gave her not only strength but insight into "another land." The depressed woman has glimpsed a different territory, or as Julia Kristeva writes, "the magnificent land of Death, of which no one could ever deprive her." In effect, anguish and melancholy give the sufferer a unique weapon, and in Eliot's case as a writer, it was a reinforcement of her need to transform herself.

In what is perhaps her best-known poem, "O May I Join the Choir Invisible," written at the height of her fictional powers, she voiced in a few lines her sense of the transformational self. Her secular humanism called for the highest level of behavior, or anarchy would reign. That "choir invisible" is the transformed self, the reshaped individual, the best that is known to man, or woman. "O may I join the choir invisible / Of those immortal dead who live again / In minds made better by their presence. . . ." To become part of that choir invisible, one must reach for the better self, really for a self one might never have known to exist. "May I reach / That purest heaven, be to other souls / The cup of strength in some great agony." The language is traditional religious terminology, but the thought is purely secular, asking the ever-present Eliot question: How can we overcome our failings without calling on some Great Being which we can no longer believe in? And if we try to achieve ourselves in some greater way, how can we prevent ourselves from becoming destructive selves in that desire for achievement? In that quest to overcome ourselves and yet become what we are, we find ourselves having become part of that "invisible choir." This was not advice, but a caution. Eliot expected her life and work to make as great demands on us as they had on her.

George Eliot

PART ONE

In Coventry

1

The Youngest

"No mind that has any *real* life is a mere echo of another."*

G eorge Eliot was born into Jane Austen's England and died in Thomas Hardy's. Although she lived only sixty-one years—as against the four score of several other Victorian writers—she spanned perhaps the most important years of the nineteenth century. One reason she set so many of her novels in earlier eras was her desire to return to those younger years before the railroad, for one, began to change how England lived and fared. Overall in her work, there is resistance to those very elements and forces her life spanned. Before the railroad, England's internal trade and transportation came through an intricate series of canals, and canals called up something of Eden. The water, the more leisurely pace, the colorful men who handled the barges, all tended to create nostalgia for a simpler life. What was forgotten was how hard life was, how unjust it proved for most people, and how unhealthy it basically was despite the appearance of a hale and hearty atmosphere.

England was, in 1819, still recovering from the long years of the Napoleonic Wars; England emerged a victor, and yet a country somewhat traumatized by how close it had come to invasion and, very possibly, defeat at the hands of the Man of Destiny. English patriotism remained intense, and the Tory Party, with the Duke of Wellington its hero, rode high. But the injustices of the society at virtually every level of existence, except the top, were palpable. Just three months before Eliot's birth on 22 November 1819, a terrible event seemed to capture the unfairness of life in this still tradition-driven society. On 16 August,

---

* All epigraphs for individual chapters derive from George Eliot, from her letters, fiction, and essays.

a group of men, women, and children gathered in St. Peter's Field, in Manchester, to petition Parliament for the repeal of the Corn Laws (taxes on grains) and to seek parliamentary reform. Their leader, Henry Hunt, was a radical politician whose support came mainly from the laboring classes, who, however, lacked the vote.

Hunt favored electoral and other reforms, less out of a desire for personal advancement than for the improvement of the lower economic classes. Something of his spirit and stubbornness reappears in Eliot's Felix Holt, also a Radical, or Liberal, a proponent of reform in most areas of society. The meeting in St. Peter's Field had every appearance of moderation and was legal within the English system. It was in the great tradition of the petition, what had become part of a legal process which lacked a formal constitution. But the magistrates ordered the group to disband, and when it failed to do so rapidly enough, it was charged by cavalry and attacked by a large body of yeomanry. The result was eleven deaths on the scene and over four hundred injuries, with many of those injured later to die. The incident became known as the Peterloo Massacre, whereby Waterloo was the ironic model, and it rang down through nineteenth-century English history as the shame of the country. The government, apparently, had given its full approval to the magistrates, and this loosed professional troops as well as local yeomanry on the helpless crowd. Children were trampled, pregnant women were shot, and men who had no opportunity to defend themselves were struck down. Hunt was held culpable, his trial loaded and unjust.

The import of all this was that at the time of Eliot's birth, England was deeply still a tradition-directed society. Forms of behavior, one's attitude toward state, government, and church, were governed by traditional values based on lineage, birth, educational achievement, and family status. History, rather than individual responses, was the measuring rod. Society was honored as part of a contractual agreement made long ago between those who served and those who governed, with God and state supreme. Embedded in this traditional society was a rigid class system which, for the most part, disallowed mobility, although the advent of industrialization would slowly loosen class lines.

Yet for the time, in 1819, the linkages were almost tribal in their clan loyalties and in the fixedness of social groups. A tradition-driven society emphasizes conformity, but conformity based not on social acquiescence; rather, on historical precedent, on family and community loyalties, and on certain agreed-upon assumptions about God, country, state, and history itself. Contemporary generations were ruled by forms of behavior established and fixed in previous generations. History was repeatable, and, therefore, accessible to those who sought the accepted shape of behavior. Etiquette and protocol called for established modes of speech, behavior, dress, attendance at church, and response to family needs. Individual qualities of enterprise might be prized, however, so long as they did not depart from or threaten to undermine social standards. Eliot would portray brilliantly just this seeming contradiction or division: that no-man's-land between the individual need for expression and the social inhibition which acts upon departures from social norms. Many of her female characters are shaped by such matters: Dorothea Brooke in *Middlemarch* is the most prominent, but also Maggie Tulliver in *The Mill on the Floss*, Esther Lyon in *Felix Holt, the Radical*, Romola in that novel; and some of her males, Will Ladislaw in *Middlemarch* and Felix Holt in that novel.

The nature of such a society, in which individual need presses for expression against social sanctions, is built on certain conformities; and if the individual is to survive, he or she must find ways in which expression can take on a social role. Individuals must play institutional parts. Eliot, of course, recognized this: Dorothea as a reformer within acceptable modes, Romola as a nurse ministering to the sick, Felix Holt as a Liberal who renounces the extremes of radicalism. It is clear from such a tradition-driven society that individualism, even when tolerated, is not rewarded, and that energies cannot be abided so long as they remain outside the given social history. Nostalgia for this kind of turn-of-the-century world, or before, touched several nineteenth-century writers, not least Carlyle, Ruskin, Morris, and even Dickens, all of whom saw in older ways a certain stability where everyone knew his place and role. But there is no reason to believe that such a society, simply because it resisted change, was necessarily more emotionally and psychologically accommodating to its people. Privilege reigned, and those born out of privilege served: thus the Hobbesian chain of being which traditional culture called for.

The society into which Eliot was born often seemed to her as parallel to Eden, especially in her early growing-up years when her father administered large properties and the Evans family lived well indeed in rural terms. But the reality in more urbanized areas—Birmingham, Notthingham, and Manchester to the north—was quite different. What had occurred was that Eliot, born Mary Anne Evans on 22 November 1819, grew up in one of the most historically fixed societies possible, where rules established almost as far back as Henry VIII dominated. Her father, Robert Evans, was definitely a link in that noblesse oblige which dictated social policy; and while he made a good deal of himself as an estate manager and administrator, he was a Tory among Tories, a worshipper of the Church of England, a man of the strictest proprieties. Although on a lower social level because he worked for others, he nevertheless took on all the beliefs and behavioral qualities of those above him socially; and he looked askance at any deviation, as Eliot would herself discover when she decided to forsake regular church attendance. What we find, then, is the traditionalism of the system penetrating well below its rulers into the lives of the ruled. Change was almost impossible in this context until industrialization created a sufficiently large middle class of business and commercial interests; and then the threat to traditionalism came through the economy itself.

It is particularly pertinent to recognize that Eliot was born into and grew up in a society which most emphatically would discourage the very kind of life she chose to lead. Her mother, Robert Evans's second wife, was typical of what was expected of a woman: a strict disciplinarian in the home, a person who was efficient with her children and husband and brooked no opposition in her domestic role. She assumed a hierarchical world: the child in his or her place, the wife in hers, the husband in his, and then the further hierarchy of those who owned property, who governed, and, over all, the bishops of the Anglican Church with a Church of England God above them.

Such a society had its own kind of rewards, although for most it meant a life of drudgery. But for a female child, it had special significance, since it permitted so little mobility. And for a female child of extraordinary intelligence and sensitivity, it meant an imprisonment of sorts. For someone like Mary Anne Evans, it proved problematical: while she worshipped her father and lived a life of privilege as the daughter of a very successful man, at the same time she became increasingly aware of the constraints placed upon her. The gender gap here was enormous, in terms of educational possibilities, expectations, and ultimately in terms of quality of life and performance. Whatever positions Eliot eventually held on women's causes can be discovered in the ambiguities of her own position. As the youngest daughter of Robert Evans's second family, she was privileged, but also constrained. Little was expected of her, and that was linked to conventional roles. Although Evans was indulgent and permitted a much higher degree of education for his obviously intelligent daughter than most young women received, he was traditional in the way he perceived her and her future.

All of this was played out against a strange development in the kingdom. England was ruled by a king who addressed remarks to trees, and although he may have been one of the first environmentalists, public opinion tended to see him as mad. Mad George! The same George who had lost the American colonies to a ragtag army. He would die the year after Mary Anne's birth and the Peterloo Massacre, but in 1819 he was in some respects representative of the strangeness of the English system. A parliamentary form of government paid its tribute to a demented king.

In a real sense, George III—in 1820 he was succeeded by his eldest son, George IV, noted for his extravagance and dissoluteness—foreshadowed the strangely divided country England had started to become in the fifty or so years after Mary Anne Evans's birth. On the one hand, there was the rapid expansion of large cities as we know them today, accompanied by extraordinary progress in technology and transportation. On the other hand, almost none of this—what we would term "progress"—was accompanied by social reform, or even a clear recognition that reform was necessary to keep the people from rebelling. Not until Napoleon's succession to the imperial throne of France and eventually of continental Europe was there the sense that the English system might be under sustained attack internally. The church lay stagnant in terms of social reform, more concerned with its prerogatives and authority than with possible change. It held to its Tory line, and its bishops, who sat in the House of Lords, failed to respond to the demographic changes which would alter England so significantly in the nineteenth century. Methodism moved into factory and mill towns, and its sympathy for the underdog and underprivileged subverted the Church of England, which in some forms was moving closer to Rome. The government itself, dominated by Tory traditionalists, those devoted to crown (now mad), the landed gentry and aristocrats, and the Church of England, was unwilling to move or to forsake its privileges for greater balance of power and justice. Under George IV, not much would change, although the Catholic Emancipation Act, of 1829, would open up public office to Catholics.

Until the Reform Bill of 1832, which was more symbolic gesture than substance, both crown and state, with the approval of the church, agreed to hold to the status quo, *even while* enormous changes were occurring in society. We catch some of this division in Eliot when she sets her novels in an earlier time, some of them in and around the period of the Reform Bill, when the franchise was opened up to a new property class, and the rotten boroughs, or unpopulated areas which regularly sent members to the Commons, were eliminated. If we look at England between the end of Napoleon's threat, in 1815, and the beginning of the First World War a century later, we find an almost unparalleled surface of what appears to be development and progress. Peering down the century, we see a kind of cumulative history, with energy and initiative combining to take England to the forefront of the world's nations. Yet the lived life for most people was not like that, and nearly all of the century's major writers attacked one aspect or another of this success, from Carlyle, Ruskin, and Arnold to the novelists Dickens, Thackeray, Mrs. Gaskell, and Meredith. Eliot was never a praiser, never a jingoist, never a nationalist, but, rather, a prober of areas even the above-mentioned writers had neglected or failed to see. She was concerned with how the more ordinary lives of men and women proceeded without regard for state, progress, or wealth itself. In this and so many other respects, she was a true daughter of Robert Evans, whose own surging career was made possible by his energies and the need that developed for able men. The career, not money alone, was the reward.

Robert Evans became a perfect example of upward mobility within a tightly constructed class system. Possibly of Welsh origin, the Evans family, after the Civil War of 1688, split into two factions, one of them moving to Staffordshire, the other to Derbyshire. There, on the Derbyshire side of the Dove River, Eliot's paternal grandfather was born, in 1740. This Evans, George, prospered and instilled in four of his sons his own enterprising manner. Unfortunately, we know nothing of Eliot's paternal grandmother, Mary Leech, except her dates, 1738–1803. Eliot's father, Robert, was born in 1773, the second youngest of eight children in all (five sons, three daughters), at Boston Common, three miles from Rochester in Derbyshire. He would in time cross the Dove into Staffordshire. George Evans and his wife passed on a profound work ethic, a desire to succeed, and a sense of self-discipline and denial which permitted little flexibility. All but his eldest son, George, learned how to prosper without leaving their social class. William Evans was a builder and received large commissions. Thomas became county surveyor for Dorset. The youngest, Samuel, married a Methodist preacher (shades of Eliot's own Dinah Morris) and became head of a ribbon manufacturing mill, that being a major enterprise in and around Coventry.

Long before we find any evidence of the Evans family, however, another clan, which would insinuate itself into every part of the Evans fortunes, had established itself. The Newdigate–Newdigate family in Warwickshire presided over Arbury Hall, since 1586 its seat, bringing them back to the middle and later years of Queen Elizabeth's reign. In 1750, Sir Roger Newdigate restored parts of Arbury Hall, transforming its inner core into a piece of Gothic splendor, with turrets, castellated battlements, and oriel windows. In 1806, on Sir Roger's death, the estates and Arbury Hall came into the possession of Francis Parker of Kirk Hallam, Derbyshire, his cousin, but only for use during his lifetime. Francis Parker assumed the arms and name of Newdigate, but, more important, installed Robert Evans as agent. In *Adam Bede*, Eliot shadows this with Arthur Donnithorne convincing his grandfather, the old squire, to install Adam as master of the woods. By the time of installation, Robert Evans was thirty-three, married, with two children; he came to live at South Farm, located between South Lodge and Astley Castle, the latter the home of Francis Parker Newdigate's eldest son.

This new situation allowed Evans to blossom, since it gave him access to over seven thousand acres. Through his talents in measuring, figuring, and administering, he had the same desire for success in his business as overseer that his daughter would eventually develop in her career as a writer. He was, as he well knew, the perfect Englishman, in that he believed in what he was doing, did it well, and rarely if ever questioned the order of things around him. Having begun as a carpenter, he would have never settled for the minimal comforts Adam Bede strove for. He surveyed roads, measured stands of timber for the lumber they could yield, assessed land; like Adam, he developed the practicalities of character and performance needed for a solid reputation, but, unlike Adam, he wanted far more.

It was an excellent time for a man of energy and skill who accepted his place in the hierarchy. Evans knew how to maximize whatever he knew, and he was fortunate in coming along when the English population was surging and all kinds of products were moving from luxuries to essentials.* Even the way in which he came to know Francis Parker Junior became part of the Evans legend. Evans was not well educated, but he saw in education one of the ways in which a man might succeed; and rather than settling for the few years of elementary school which would ordinarily have been his lot, he attended evening school, something like Bartle Massey's classes (in *Adam Bede*) in accounting, handwriting, and a rudimentary version of mechanical drawing. The latter enabled him to work from plans and to draw up his own. The desire for upward mobility within his class marked every aspect of Evans's young manhood. Having learned carpentry, he worked for a time in the nearby village of Ellastone, and while going out on a commission he met Francis Parker, who was impressed with Evans's energy and initiative. Parker told his father about the enterprising car-

---

* At the turn of the century, when Robert Evans was making his mark, the population of England and Wales was almost 9 million, with the average household figured at three children. Derby had 11,000 people, Coventry 16,000. By the time of Eliot's birth, the overall population had grown by 3 million. Derby went to 17,000; Coventry gained 5,000. The major cities—Birmingham, Manchester, Liverpool, not to speak of London—gained exponentially.

penter, and this led to Evans's assignment as agent for the Arbury Estate.

The two younger men, however different their stations in life and divided by an unbridgeable class distinction, had nevertheless found common cause. Robert Evans's unwavering Toryism, his sense of work and honor, and his devotion to crown and God (as a member of the Church of England) impressed the aristocratic Parker, as these qualities would impress nearly everyone who met Evans. How much he calculated his role we cannot tell, but speculation would hold that he saw in his friendship with young Parker something to pursue carefully, since on the older Parker's death, this eldest son would become owner of this vast property. Evans had discovered his chance, and he pursued it with the single-mindedness he demonstrated in all his activities.

George Eliot would catch her father in her portrait of Adam Bede, or in an even more loving portrait in Caleb Garth in *Middlemarch*. Her father figures largely in several other characters in her novels, who offer up values she carried from her childhood. For even as Adam is flawed by a bad temper and a certain rashness of outlook, he remains a romanticized portrait. Robert Evans could in fact be quite otherwise than merely hardworking and disciplined. He no doubt looked out for his chances, he was ambitious, and he was inflexible in his pursuit of those goals he had set for himself. The temper in Adam is a recasting of a more serious defect in Evans, a rigidity which disallowed dissent. He was the type of person so set on realizing his aims in life he sees weakness or deviation as disasters which will undermine and destroy all purpose. He was a completely tradition-driven man whose rigidity meant he would never question the authority and authenticity of received wisdom, whether it came from the church or the crown. A mad king and a church which served mainly the needs of the upper classes did not make him hesitate in his allegiance. We in fact receive the impression that Evans derived considerable satisfaction from holding views which, while separating him from many members of his own class, associated him with landowning gentry and aristocrats. Inevitably, this rigidity would clash with his loving but also strong-willed daughter.

If we carry this argument further, we can say that his ambition and desire for success blinded him to the fact that while he prospered, most members of his class remained an underclass, almost indentured in their dependence on their masters. Eliot's idealization of her father disguised the fact that unemployment and low wages, added to poor living conditions, even in relatively prosperous Coventry, condemned most of his, and her, class to bare subsistence levels. Eliot was not so concerned with the abject poor as was Dickens, but she was not blind to their condition; yet when it came to giving certain contexts to her novels, the economic condition of her characters is rarely a significant factor. In the background only, we may catch echoes of people who are in difficulty, as in some of the crowds of *Felix Holt* or tenant farmers in *Adam Bede*. Forms of behavior were more important to her than how people survived; and in this, somewhat ironically given her rebellion against her father's rigidity, she mirrored that basic value.

Before he moved to the Arbury property, Robert Evans had acquired a wife and fathered two children: Robert, born in 1802, and Frances, or Fanny, born in 1805. Having deemed his opportunities good, Evans had married Harriet Poynton in 1801; the two children followed shortly, along with a third who died in 1809, when Harriet herself also died. He was twenty-eight at marriage, she was thirty-one, and her death at thirty-nine shortly after premature childbirth, just before Christmas, was an indication of how precarious pregnancy was for women, especially when they began as late as she did. Harriet Poynton was a local woman, and she had served as a lady's maid to the senior Mrs. Francis Parker (the second one). As a consequence of this connection, she had become something of a gentlewoman herself, who, at the same time, brought Evans into close contact with this prominent family. In 1806, when he took over the Arbury properties, Evans had already proved himself as manager of a small estate at Kirk Hallam and supervisor of the wooded lands at Wootton Hall.

He did not seem like the type of person who would let personal matters interfere with his career plans, and when Harriet died after eight years of marriage, he remarried, in 1813. This time he entered into a socially more upward class than his own, the Pearsons. Christiana Pearson was the daughter of Isaac Pearson, yeoman farmer and church warden, and she was one of four sisters. In the fine gradations of the lower class, a yeoman farmer was an independent landowner and, in that respect, "higher" than a man who worked as someone else's estate administrator. As a freeholder, Pearson fell below the gentry, but as a church warden, he reached out to the next rung in the social system. Later on, in *The Mill on the Floss*, Eliot created her own four Dodson sisters, with Christiana and Robert Evans somewhat shaped as the Tullivers. As for the rest, the bride's three sisters fitted well into Aunt Deane (Ann Pearson, wife of George Garner of Astley), Aunt Pullet (Elizabeth Pearson, second wife of Richard Johnson of Marston Jabbett), and Aunt Glegg (Mary Pearson, second wife of John Everard of Attleborough). Eliot's portrayal of the Dodsons is tinged less with affection than with criticism of their foibles, their pretensions to respectability, their desire to rise socially, their overall vanities. A good part of this negative perception derives from Eliot's general dislike of the Pearson family, but even more likely from her lack of affection for her mother. The highly efficient and disciplined but cold Christiana is shadowed in Maggie Tulliver's less than warm mother.

Already with two stepchildren—Robert, aged twelve, and Frances (or Fanny), aged nine—Christiana gave birth to Christiana, or Chrissey, in 1814; to Isaac Pearson, in 1816; and to Mary Anne, on 22 November 1819, at South Farm, Arbury, two miles from Nuneaton.* She was christened at the Chilvers Coton parish church (destroyed in a World War II air raid and then rebuilt by German prisoners of war). Less than eighteen months later, on 16 March 1821, twin boys were born to Christiana and Robert Evans, but they lived for only ten days.

The death of the twin boys would have come too early in Mary Anne's life to

---

* Nuneaton is 10 miles north of Coventry, 20 miles east of Birmingham, and 107 miles northeast of London, just south of the Midlands and not far from Shakespeare and Robin Hood country.

have affected her deeply, especially since the presence of four other children would have forced Christiana and Robert to put their grief rapidly behind them and get on with raising this large family. But we are concerned with her place in the family, as the youngest, with the five children divided into two distinct age groups. Seventeen years old when Mary Anne was born, Robert was considered ready for work, and Fanny at fourteen was almost at marriageable age. Mary Anne would inevitably be thrown back on her full siblings, Isaac and Chrissey, as her true family. When she became George Eliot, she described the early relationship with Isaac as of more importance to her than anyone else except possibly her father.

While Robert Evans was fathering a succession of children, there was considerable turbulence of another sort in the Parker–Newdigate family. The situation will recall the Jarndyce vs. Jarndyce case in Dickens's *Bleak House,* an endless series of lawsuits that occupied the Court of Chancery. At stake was the Newdigate name and the succession of the Arbury Estate within the family. As part of the agreement which allowed Arbury Hall to pass to Francis Parker Senior, he had to take the name Newdigate, which he did; so did his son, who lived at Astley Castle and was also a colonel in the army. Yet the will that came down from Sir Roger Newdigate—he who had had Arbury Hall renovated and who had died in 1806—did not permit the estate to go to Colonel Newdigate, Francis Parker Senior's son. This would have been the direct line, but the will stipulated that the estate was to pass on to a different branch of the family upon the senior Parker's death. The succession, such as it was, became as entangled as a royal succession, complicated by the fact that the terms of the will gave several members of the family the rightful use of the estate during their lifetimes. But this, too, was regulated further by restrictions. The result was a classic Court of Chancery case, one that in fact went to the House of Lords for eventual determination. Such entanglements Eliot transformed into the background legalities of the Transome estate in *Felix Holt.*

Evans's duties and the Newdigate contretemps over land rights crossed when the estate manager was needed to work out details having to do with disputes over various parts of the property. As repairs became necessary, and Robert Evans oversaw them, it became a question of who in the family was responsible for expenses. As woods were cut and timber divided, as stands of trees for sale or for appearance were considered, he had to deal not only with the supervision of work but with the lawyers representing various members of the Parker–Newdigate family. Mary Anne grew up in this atmosphere. It continued throughout her childhood and, until she left Warwickshire, she absorbed the torturous and often oily dealings implicit in the legal system, as lawyers and their clients maneuvered for position in an estate case that would last until almost midcentury.

What this dispute, among others, created in her was a suspicion of all legal matters; but more than that, it made her suspicious of and even antagonistic toward what she considered to be city practices. Many of her ideas were shaped as she followed the contortions of the Newdigate affair and her beloved father's role in it. She perceived him as straight as an arrow; she saw the others as dealing in subterfuges or outright lies and deceptions. She associated such legal matters with urban life, even when they were practiced in the country, and she associated her father's more open life with what she perceived to be best in rustic or laboring-class life. Frequently, her professionals—doctors, lawyers, bankers—either walk the edge of propriety or have fallen over into actual deceit. Theirs is the unexamined life: Lydgate, for example, the onetime idealistic doctor in *Middlemarch,* or the banker Bulstrode, a religious hypocrite, as against the straight laboring man, Caleb Garth. Eliot rarely became simplistic in her equation of city as evil and country as salvational; but like Jane Austen and Dickens, she tended to link urban ways with inner corruption and country modes with a more open, more honest way of life.

Her early childhood was, in most respects, idyllic. There are, however, cautions. If we accept *The Mill on the Floss* as having at least a shadowy relationship to her own childhood, then we must conclude that all was not quite so perfect as the surface seems. The surface provided her with one fine residence after another, with a father whom she doted upon and who recognized her precocity, a standard of living which was always sufficient, early years which were not socially or economically threatening, and a family which seemed to shield her from whatever ills were affecting many of those around her. Yet while we must beware of letting her later fiction overdetermine our view of her early life, we would be naive to dismiss the fictional re-creation as lacking in emotional veracity.

Within five months of her birth, on St. Cecilia's Day, a day honoring music, Mary Anne (later Mary Ann, then Marian, and also known as Polly in Warwickshire) moved to Griff, on the edge of the Arbury Estate, close to Nuneaton, the nearby town. Griff House was a lovely rustic residence of some solidity, located at the back of a lawn, set off by two firs, with the farmyard and outbuildings situated behind it. Covered with ivy, leafy from a yew in front, with green fields surrounding it and a pool (Round Pool) nearby, Griff House was an ideal place for a child to grow up. It was, in many respects, the Wordsworthian dream or fantasy of Eden. Here a child's heavenly preexistence found its counterpart in the actuality of a place she could always return to in memory. Griff House remained as the quintessential place for her, sacred in its potentialities for human development and happiness. In her memories, she transformed it into a temple; and if she removed herself or her characters too far from this ideal, they fell into incoherence, or worse.*

---

* Although this is looking ahead, we would perhaps expect that Mary Anne, as a consequence of her childhood, would become a pantheist of sorts; that is, someone who believes that God is in everything, and everything is God, in which all things are infused with spirit. Yet pantheist she did not become, and even when she had passed through various religious phases, this was not one of them. In a fascinating exchange of letters with Harriet Beecher Stowe, by then the famous author of *Uncle Tom's Cabin* as well as numerous other books, Eliot spelled out her views: ". . . that a religion more perfect than any yet prevalent, must express less care for personal consolation, and a more deeply-awing sense of responsibility to man, springing from sympathy with that which of all things is most certainly known to us, the difficulty of the human lot. I do not find my temple in Pantheism, which, whatever might be its value speculatively, could not yield a practical religion, since it is an attempt to look at the universe from the outside of our relations to it. . . ."

At Griff, she recognized the interdependence of all things. She looked at the universe, to use her words, from within, and from that point of vantage she saw responsibility, duty, deference to the lives of others. Griff House haunted her memories, which became the cornerstone of her existence, as much as did ideas. The beginning of *Mill*, for example, is a journey back in time—Proustian, it has been called—in which memories themselves become the stuff of the novel. Eliot transformed Griff into her own form of religious experience; for when spiritual matters infused her work, it was the spirit of place, a particular place.

We can also see her political views shaped here, for even as she came to reject Robert Evans's extremely conservative outlook, she held to her own sense that radical or extreme action was an unholy part of the body politic. These were feelings she assimilated at Griff House early on. As for radical politics, she lived only a short distance from a Nuneaton center for silk weaving and, therefore, was very sensitive to any agitation coming over from France or homegrown. Peterloo and its massacre of innocent protesters was never distant from the thinking in Nuneaton, and when silk weavers found their incomes being slashed, they protested and were put down just short of the Peterloo violence. Such potential violence was always present, since the Nuneaton (and nearby Coventry) economy was changing as a result of the Napoleonic Wars and from the growth of industrialization. There was considerable worker discontent based on real grievances, and the authorities were quite prepared to suppress any incipient revolt. Workers who advocated better working conditions and protested salary squeezes were arrested and jailed, although often they were provided bail, so as not to inflame the mob further. But heads were cracked, and violence on a large scale was barely averted.

Robert Evans looked upon the Nuneaton unrest as something that should be suppressed rapidly and, if necessary, bloodily. Whatever sympathies the young Mary Anne might have developed for workers essentially exploited by a system that benefited few—with Robert Evans an exception—were counterbalanced by the strong stand her father took. These were essentials of her beliefs, not to be overcome later by reading or by intellectual growth. She saw all life, whether country, village, or larger towns, as part of a comity in which each contributed his or her share.* Such conserving views did not leave much space for rapid change, although they clearly conflicted with her own plans to reshape virtually every aspect of her life.

Griff House was truly commodious. Besides the spaciousness of the surroundings, providing pleasant views in all directions, it consisted of eight bedrooms, four reception rooms, and several attic areas. While sanitary facilities were primitive, the hygiene remained good and Mary Anne and her siblings reached adulthood healthy. In one respect, Griff House became known as the home of gentry, although once one left the vicinity, there was a rundown community

---

* In *Adam Bede*, the wise Reverend Irwine establishes the essential point: "Men's lives are as thoroughly blended with each other as the air they breathe: evil spreads as necessarily as disease. . . . every sin cause[s] suffering to others besides those who commit it." An act of vengeance or of blind fury "would leave all the present evils just as they were, and add worse evils to them." Irwine sounds less like a Church of England man than like Eliot's secular humanist.

which housed numerous looms, one of the main supports of the area. Eliot would take up this aspect in *Silas Marner* and *Felix Holt.* The area had the dingy look of a mining town, since coal was another mainstay of the region. Along with the dinginess came the usual assortment of drinking establishments, public houses, and supply shops for servicing horses and carriages.

Although the Newdigate estates seemed to indicate farming as a major occupation, in reality agriculture took a far third to mining and looming. Nearby pools of water attested to the fact that pumps were kept going day and night to clear the water from the colleries; and a canal that crossed the Evans farm was used to transport coal. Mary Anne grew up in close proximity to water, whether deposits or canals, and this liquid imagery remained with her as a writer. Several of her characters are tested by water, and many fail the test. Among her fictional drownings are Maggie and Tom Tulliver, in *The Mill on the Floss,* a book dominated by water; Grandcourt in *Daniel Deronda;* Mirah, an attempt, also in *Deronda;* and Tito Melema in *Romola.* It is not an aberration but a constant in her work, a kind of summation of her fear of "going under," whether the image is physical or psychologically oriented.

There was a problematic factor, already referred to, which is that soon after Mary Anne's birth there followed hard the birth and death of twin brothers, christened William and Thomas. The mother, apparently, had wanted only sons. What all this meant to Mary Anne cannot, of course, be determined. But we do find evidence to support the fact that she was a disappointment to her mother, especially when the twins died. To her father, however, as the youngest daughter, she was someone special. She found herself with divided loyalties, and this may, in her perception of her role, have contributed to feelings of anxiety or dread or fear of the unknown. The possibility is worth pursuing.

A dualism appears in her character which must have been shaped early: the intelligence and pursuit of goals, which she found in both her father and brother; but, also, a certain self-destructive quality. As a woman growing up, she had learned to be extremely sensitive to what men were saying and doing: we observe this in her female protagonists. Women are the bowstrings; men play on them. Women listen; men speak. Yet this was not to be accepted unconditionally; the women rebel, they make fateful decisions, and they suffer the consequences of their decisions. We think of Dorothea Brooke, Gwendolen Harleth, Romola Bardo, among several others.

This other element, then, was a rebellious side which nearly always led to intense unhappiness. In Eliot, however, this danger does not always fall to women alone. Lydgate is an excellent example of a man who self-destructs, but precisely because he did not listen to what Rosamond was saying; he becomes carried away by what he sees or thinks he sees. Yet it is chiefly women who listen to men and, while dutifully carrying through this kind of ritual self-sacrifice, gravitate toward men who are unacceptable, whether personally or in moral and ethical terms. We have, so far, a sense of Mary Anne's responses: respect, even awe, but internal rebellion. Fear and dread are never far behind.

Yet there is more. The pressure of dominant males, whether a much-admired father or a brother who creates ambiguous feelings of respect and hostility, can result in the strengthening of female resolve. In Mary Anne's case, once she found her footing, in religious and social terms, she insisted on her own feelings, even when they ran directly counter to social sanctions. The very presence of tough, stubborn males reinforced a strong response: to be worthy of their regard on the one hand and yet to stand up to them on the other.

If we follow these leads, then we see her at Griff House responding in a very complicated way: surrendering to what she felt was called for, and yet isolating a part of herself which she refused to sacrifice. One paramount part of Mary Anne's development was her holding back, and her insistence on some dimension of personal isolation which gave her time to develop, grow, and emerge in her own way. But we cannot ignore the toll.

In her early years, Mary Anne's relationship with her half-siblings, Robert Evans's son and daughter from his first marriage, was apparently of little consequence. When she was still small, Robert Junior began to work for his father, as a subagent, but was absent most of the time. By the time she was five or six, the pattern of Mary Anne's life at Griff House was set. Robert Evans was occupied with a myriad of tasks and assignments, and he often took along his youngest daughter, leaving her with servants at various houses as he made his rounds. This was, of course, an enormously satisfying experience for the child, since as the daughter of the chief estate administrator she would be treated with deference and kindness, as if gentry. Left with kitchen or housekeeping help, she could observe and listen, but as someone special and above. Chrissey, by now, was off in boarding school, Miss Lathom's in Attleborough, about two and a half miles from Griff. This threw Mary Anne back on her brother Isaac, and together they attended a day school kept by a Mrs. Moore, an establishment just across the road.

Several early biographers have emphasized how Mary Anne found in Isaac that male support she always sought in later life. John Cross in his adulatory biography stressed this point: that Isaac was the first in line, a person who meant everything to her, and, conversely, to whom she meant everything. Certainly, we receive something of this in *Mill*, and we might quote from a deleted passage of the novel where Maggie fantasizes (or daydreams) about Tom's overwhelming love for her, where he thought her clever and wanted her to be at his side. ". . . Tom never went to school, and liked no one to play with him but Maggie; they went out together somewhere every day, and carried either hot buttered cakes with them because it was baking day, or apple puffs well sugared; Tom was never angry with her for her forgetting things, and liked her to tell him tales; . . . . Above all, Tom loved her—oh, so much,—more, even than she loved him, so that he would always want to have her with him and be afraid of vexing her; and he as well as every one else, thought her very clever." The import of this, and similar passages, is Eliot's transformation of Tom into a benevolent father figure. Surely more than brother and more than close friend, he is protector and shield. In this setting, of fantasy and daydreaming, we have a Wordsworthian idyll, the Garden.

In this fantasy, which also indicates Maggie's fierce yearning for love and affection, Eliot has structured a deeply conflicted person, who sees in childhood a time when one refuses to grow, or when growing up is traumatic. Such a passage—and others like it—recalls several other writers later in the century (Dickens, Lewis Carroll, James Barrie) whose characters would prefer not to become adults. The cult of childhood (culminating perhaps in Peter Pan) was not so much to preserve innocence as it was to avoid adult problems, not the least sexuality. Such an attitude, embodied in Eliot's constant hearkening back to the time of her early childhood, has interesting ramifications in Mary Anne's adult life.

This suggests that despite the maturity of her vision, the balance she brought to her ideas and to her social needs, the reasonableness of her outlook, the largeness of her moral and ethical perspective, there remained unresolved attitudes and a residue of terrible fright; and that these unresolved attitudes, which cannot be neglected, are what make her fiction so rich and textured. In reading Eliot, we often emphasize those elements which come together, whether this or that marriage, this or that resolution of antagonistic forces; and yet so much more richly textured are the uncertainties, the mysteries of behavior, the nuances of another life which can often be self-destructive. Eliot's distinctive voice often derives from what remains inexplicable.

She sensed how close she was to those characters she created who slid away into self-wounding attitudes. She recognized that extreme individual behavior was not the opposite of acceptable social modes, but part of a continuum, an overlapping of phenomena. Those divisions and fears which split her earlier life were underscored in the sonnet sequence "Brother and Sister," which Eliot wrote in 1869, when she was beginning *Middlemarch*. Seemingly seeking a reunion with brother Isaac, she reveals in the sonnets considerable uncertainty, hostility, and ambiguity.

That she chose to write about her early life so feelingly in 1869 is not accidental. Her elopement with Lewes had cut her off from her family, but most of all from Isaac, who remained the epitome of Mrs. Grundy respectability and outrage. By 1869, Mary Anne was the famous George Eliot, with a wide readership and a huge income. She was entering upon her most ambitious book, a signature novel that would associate her name with Dickens and Thackeray, her version of *Bleak House* and *Vanity Fair* in ambition and breadth. Yet during this time, she decided to write poetry about a period forty-five years earlier, almost coinciding with the era in which *Middlemarch* was set. The sonnet sequence takes place when Mary Anne was four or five, in 1823 or 1824; *Middlemarch*, on the eve of the First Reform Bill, begins in 1831. And yet the idyllic sonnets, as suggested, are not merely paeans to life in an earthly paradise, under the tutelage of an older brother. There is the anger the poet once felt and still feels for the one whom she respected and who now rejects her. Eliot wrote them to recall, to recover, to reenter a period when she could count on familial shielding, support, and recognition even while she experienced complete familial rejection in the present.

The seeming adulatory sonnets and *Mill* became the bookends of Mary Anne's childhood yearnings. In one episode in *Mill*, after Maggie has sought out her attic hideaway, Tom relents and takes her fishing with him. The morning becomes idyllic, and it becomes one of those "spots of time" Wordsworth referred to, when love of the earth enters into us and helps shape us. Yet there is another side to this, part of the dark world Maggie inhabits. In the great attic—huge Griff House had several attics—Maggie retreats amidst worm-eaten floors and shelves and dark rafters covered with cobwebs—a refuge, but also a hellish place. Here she keeps a "Fetish" which serves as an object she can punish for her misfortunes. The Fetish is a large wooden doll, now defaced by three nails driven into the head, each signaling a crisis of suffering in Maggie. The last nail was directed at Aunt Glegg, "driven in with a fiercer stroke than usual." Maggie would like to drive even more nails into the doll, but she fears she might not be able to comfort it. Nevertheless, she knocks and scrapes it against the wall. When her anger finally abates, she poultices and embraces the remains. Alone in the attic, cradling the Fetish, she sobs.

Although the scene lasts less than a page, it is extraordinary, its potentialities immense. The rage is more than a child's recognition of injustice in the world. It involves an innate anger, a refusal to accept one's role, an anger that demands nothing less than the demise of the offender, whether Aunt Glegg or someone closer. Murder is there, but also the desire for severe self-punishment. As Maggie's vicarious sufferer, the Fetish can take the horrible injuries she would assume herself for some form of guilt, or as some need for repentance.* There is alternating anger at others—the desire for their death or torture—intermixed with her own sense of unworthiness and wish for punishment. As we pursue the implications of this brief but telling episode, we observe Maggie's revelations, a nine-year-old (sometimes eight, sometimes ten in the manuscript) who has not accepted her role and who responds to its limitations with potential for murder or for suicide. If we carry through the possibilities of the episode, we see in it violence done not only to the detested Aunt Glegg but to the entire family, wherein the aunt is an acceptable stand-in for the murder of parents and, most of all, Tom.

In 1824, Isaac left for a school near Coventry, and Mary Anne joined Chrissey. Miss Lathom's was a boarding school, not a day school, and Mary Anne possibly felt misplaced among girls in the main much older than herself. Although the school was less than three miles from Griff House, the distance came to seem greater during the week when she was on her own; on weekends and holidays, she returned home, with Chrissey. What also was occurring was a shift of emotional ties—from Isaac, now out of sight, to Chrissey, and to her father, who came for her and brought her back. We find this, also, in *Mill*, in Maggie's

---

* We cannot ignore, for example, Dorothea Brooke's identification with St. Theresa, or Romola's with the need to sacrifice herself for others, or even, on different grounds, Gwendolen Harleth's sacrifice of self for her mother and sister.

attachment to Tulliver, whereas the mother is cold and distant, or else critical and chiding. We are rightly cautious about judging the fictional mothers against Mrs. Evans; but it is hard to ignore how Mrs. Tulliver handles Maggie, not with benevolence, charity, or generosity, but as a duty. Maggie's hair, her pinafores, her general appearance all become distressful chores for the older woman, as she contrasts Maggie with Lucy Deane, the pinnacle of young girls. Mrs. Tulliver is described as not being the brightest of women; in fact, Tulliver chose her among the four Dodsons so that she would not compete with him. Her daughter is quite the opposite: book oriented, wide awake, perceptive, her ears and intelligence missing little.

In *Mill*, Eliot creates Maggie as a steady and perceptive reader, using Maggie's knowledge of Daniel Defoe's *History of the Devil* as a way of establishing her separation from both Mr. Riley, a pretentious auctioneer, and her father. But Mary Anne had access to other books in the Evans household, as well: the ever-present *Pilgrim's Progress*, the picture-filled *Aesop's Fables*, and the ubiquitous *Vicar of Wakefield*, Goldsmith's overwhelmingly popular novel which accommodated religious readers.

It is not the books she might have read, however, that reveals the ambiguities of Mary Anne's childhood, but the hair-cutting scene in *Mill* (Chapter 7). We move circumspectly, aware of the dangers of reading back from fiction to life, but the episode so establishes isolation, strangeness, and difference that it calls out to be linked to Eliot's own development. It is, at least, a shadowy intimation. The context is quite significant, for Maggie finds herself among the Dodson sisters, each vying with the other for social advantage. The unbearable one is Aunt Glegg, whose views of propriety and of her own position make her a severe critic of any anomaly. She notices Maggie's long, unruly hair and, in her blunt, unfeeling way, comments upon it adversely. In her less emphatic way, Mrs. Tulliver also remarks that Maggie should not have appeared before her aunts before having had her hair brushed and smoothed out. Yet the true catalyst in the situation is Lucy Deane, Aunt Deane's daughter and Maggie's first cousin, a model of the kind of propriety the family celebrates. Lucy is perfect, with every blond hair in place, a small smile on her mouth when it is appropriate, a model of decorum and deportment. She is the "other" against whom Maggie can be found wanting. Maggie is dark-skinned, with dark hair that will not sit smoothly, and an unruly streak which permeates her manner. Lucy has, as Eliot puts it, a "natty completeness." She says "it was like the contrast between a rough, dark, overgrown puppy and a white kitten."

Lucy is quite kind and of generous spirit, but Eliot cannot let her go easily, for she needs the civility of the one against the deep sensitivity and intelligence of the other. She is re-creating, we feel, her own growing sensibility, as a girl beginning to measure herself against those who seemed prettier, more acceptable because of their ingratiating manners, and, overall, more socially desirable. Mary Anne was not a "pretty" child, since the pronounced features which dominated in later years were already apparent.

Within this context of a critical Aunt Glegg and a standard set by a perfect

Lucy Deane, Maggie commits an act which puts her on the side of the boys: the cropping of her hair. Her act, in which brother Tom helps, is fraught with complications and potentialities, for it is a form of sex change, a demonstration of her dissatisfaction with her gender identiiication, a desire not to become more attractive but more acceptable by presenting herself, in some perverse way, as a boy. Tom enters the situation with some glee, not only because of his own predilection for mischievous and even sadistic acts, but because in some way a cropped Maggie ceases to be his sister. There is, further, his desire for revenge, for by making her unpresentable, he can regain some of the "face" he lost when Maggie let his rabbits die or broke his kite. Together, they hack off the offensive curls, and with this Maggie hopes she can eliminate the Medusa-like look and become not like Lucy—whose role model she resists—but like some indeterminate sexual being, or like a boy.

Maggie's rage in defacing herself with scissors contains a murderous streak that does not stop at herself, at Lucy, or at Aunt Glegg. It expands into an impulse which would like to see the entire Dodson clan dead, including her mother. In her act of rage, Maggie unconsciously reveals what her priorities are: to kill them all, so that she remains alone with Tom, or with Tom and Mr. Tulliver. If we judge the hair episode at its fullest, what it signifies is a desire to crop away the family, so that only those whom she feels close to remain. Yet even here, there is a furtive, undisclosed motive; for her act, while aided by Tom, is also her effort to become the "boy" in the family, somehow to displace Tom. Her act, in reality, is an effort to give herself that equal standing with him which both society and her family have denied her.

Any such rebellious act, whether hair cropping, pushing the sanitized Lucy into the mud, or running off to the gypsies, has still another component: Maggie's opening up of herself, her emergence into some indeterminate newness. In opening up, where will she go? In transforming herself, what will she become? In emerging, what shape should she take? What does she leave behind, and what does she take with her? In these brief episodes, related with both insight and wit, Eliot has located Maggie in ambiguous terrain: grateful to be rescued by her father when the episodes turn sour, and yet making her first efforts at transformation, or at least recognizing that transformation is necessary.

2

Finding Herself Outside

". . . he felt very much like an uninitiated chess-player who sees that the pieces are on a peculiar position on the board, and might open the way for him to give checkmate, if he only knew how."

Mary Anne's reading was quite eclectic and depended in the main on books she found at home or could borrow. By eight or nine, she was reading from *Joe Miller's Jest Book* and from Sir Walter Scott's immensely popular *Waverley*, which a neighbor had lent to Chrissey. Scott remained a large presence in her, although as George Eliot she deflected Scott's romanticism into her own brand of "ordinary" realism. Nevertheless, Maggie Tulliver reflects Scott's *The Pirate*, and several references to Scott appear in Eliot's fiction.

The gravity we have perceived in Maggie Tulliver seems, by ten or eleven, to have been clearly present in Mary Anne. Although we may think of her as quicksilver and precocious, she was not; she developed slowly and on her own terms. She insisted on whatever internal prerogatives she sensed, and she refused to be rushed or sidetracked. Commenting on her behavior at a party when young, Eliot says she first suffered headache and then hysteria. A note in Sara Hennell's hand—Sara would become one of Eliot's closest friends—indicates that at a children's party when Mary Anne was nine or ten, she sat by herself, apart from the main body of the party; and when asked why she didn't seem happy, she replied: "No, I am not. I don't like to play with children. I like to talk to grown-up people." Apocryphal or not—and Sara could have come by this only from the much older Mary Anne—the story rings true.

This gravity or yearning for a life that leaped beyond childhood into adulthood—not at all an unusual expectation for a child whose conflicts could not be resolved in children's terms—moved closer to reality when Mary Anne, at nine, in 1828, was transferred to Mrs. Wallington's boarding school in Nuneaton. Such schools were part of a system which existed outside the state schools and were, really, for privileged children. They fell between the local schooling, which ended early, and the upper-class public schools, for rich and well-placed boys. Many of these private schools were run by women, as was the case with the Wallington Boarding School. Begun by Mrs. Wallington as a way of educating her own four children—she was a widow—it grew until it took in thirty or more boarders, its most famous being the future George Eliot. One of the teachers at the school was Maria Lewis, a warmhearted, generous, and crusading Christian. Although Church of England, Maria Lewis was evangelical, which meant a much more spirited form of religious belief than Mary Anne was accustomed to at home. The major difference between what Robert Evans practiced and what Maria Lewis proclaimed came in their emphasis: His was the church of formal worship, with little if any stress on doctrine. Miss Lewis presented a church saturated with messages, doctrines, and scriptural communication from the life and sayings of Jesus to the individual experiencing them. Hers was a far more personal religion than any Mary Anne had experienced, and it was to influence her enormously until she decided, much later, that formal religion held little significance for her.

Maria Lewis was influential in other ways as well. She was the first person to have an intellectual impact on Mary Anne. Attached though the young girl was to her father and brother, she nevertheless had not established any intellectual link to them, nor could she, given their own predilections. Her father was fixed, immovable, kind, but narrow and provincial in his beliefs; and Isaac was clearly moving away from intellectual endeavor and curiosity into business and other tradional male occupations. Lewis became, then, Mary Anne's first real support. Her evangelicalism derived from the Reverend John Edmund Jones, of Nuneaton, where he preached the gospel to both Dissenters (Methodists and others) and churchmen (Church of England Anglicans). Needless to say, church authorities found this tantamount to rebellion, even treason, since evangelicalism was regarded as a threat to the established order. It appeared to question the formalism of the established church, and in social terms it undermined the authority of the bishops, the church's backbone. Evangelicalism had within it more than religious dissent; it created a crisis with class and caste overtones, and it appealed to emotions, always a dangerous procedure in the eyes of the middle and upper classes.

Robert Evans would have been horrified if he had recognized what an influence Maria Lewis was having on his youngest child. And influence she surely had: to the degree we can say that the first stage of Mary Anne's evolution toward becoming George Eliot came here in 1828, an influence that endured for almost fifteen years. The break came only when Mary Anne had moved beyond a religious position into a secular humanistic one. But the initial opening up was so important because for the first time she was exposed to something beyond family influence—exposed, in fact, to something subversive of family beliefs and practices. Her growing sense of marginality and difference found intellectual support.

There would be other dimensions as well. Although Eliot's relationship to her father is usually viewed as loving, deferential, and worshipful, her fiction presents quite a different view of fathers. They are either absent or lacking in leadership. Adam Bede's father is a drunkard and dies in a stream while coming home from a pub. For years, Adam served as the man in the house while his father deteriorated. In *Silas Marner*, Squire Cass is a self-centered man who does not begin to enter into the lives of his sons, the decent Godfrey and the wastrel Dunstan. Marner himself becomes a father only after he has lost everything else. In *Romola*, the older Bardo uses his faithful daughter as little more than an indentured servant. As a consequence of her relationship to Bardo, Romola misjudges the man who courts her and makes a dreadful marriage. In *Felix Holt*, Felix's father is missing, and Harold Transome's father does not recognize his son; in the meantime, the man who is ostensibly Harold's father is senile. Only Esther Lyon has a real father, although his head is in the clouds. In *Middlemarch*, the Brooke sisters are the wards of their uncle, a silly man who is presented as possessing fatuous views. Because of this lack of mature guidance, Dorothea makes a disastrous marriage to Edward Casaubon. Mr. Vincy in the same novel is too distracted by business matters to pay attention to his children. In *Daniel Deronda*, Daniel is kept from his past by his foster father who, although kind, has little understanding of his foster son. The entire novel is the search for a father on Daniel's part; and as for Gwendolen Harleth, she lacks a father. In most of these instances, mothers, while present, are not much better. They are nags, indifferent, irritants, lacking understanding, hostile, trapped in their own worlds, or else, like so many fathers, missing. Only Maggie Tulliver has a father who dotes on her and takes her side; but when he dies, her brother, Tom, becomes the father figure and he circumscribes Maggie in ways that suffocate her. She drowns in restraint before she literally drowns. The fictional fathers force us to reevaluate Eliot's psychological response to a male-dominated household.

The entire Wallington Boarding School milieu is reproduced in Eliot's works, especially in "Janet's Repentance," the third novella-length piece in *Scenes of Clerical Life*, her first published book of fiction. One of Maria Lewis's disciples was Nancy Wallington, married to J. W. Buchanan, a Nuneaton lawyer, and himself opposed to the Reverend Jones's evangelicalism. The Dempsters of "Janet's Repentance" are usually attributed to the Buchanans, although Eliot told her publisher, John Blackwood, that the originals were far "more dispiriting" than here, and the real town "was more vicious than my Milby." Jones is himself resurrected as Mr. Tryan, whose self-mortification recalls St. Francis. Whatever the exact representation, we sense the intensity of the situation which Mary Anne witnessed in the reexperiencing and portrayal of it twenty-eight years later.

It is to Robert Evans's credit that when he was told in 1832 that Wallington's had nothing more to offer his daughter and that she should move on to another level, the Miss Franklins' School in Coventry, he acceded. This was a level of education not often offered to females, unless their parents (usually fathers) believed sufficiently in education to pay the costs for a daughter who would, eventually, be swallowed up in marriage. Robert Evans apparently observed something exceptional in Mary Anne, or else he feared that her lack of physical beauty would make it difficult for her to marry and, therefore, an education was in order.

The Miss Franklins' School was a combination of finishing school and educational establishment. A good deal of the instruction was cosmetic, particularly the emphasis on pronunciation. Girls like Mary Anne, with a rustic Midlands accent, were transformed into speakers of upper-class English; not the aristocratic drawl, in which the lips remain immobile, but the more exacting speech that Rebecca Franklin taught, in which vowels and consonants received a different, more precise sound. John Cross in his biography of Eliot points out that her low intense voice was probably the result of the Franklin method, of toning down everything so that it sounded soft and socially accommodating.

The Franklins' School particularly prided itself on its teaching of French; for like the Brontë sisters, Rebecca Franklin had spent a year abroad, in her case in Paris, to return with a Frenchified manner and the semblance of a true accent. Now ensconsed in Warwick Row, Coventry, Mary Anne was the beneficiary of this effort to raise the students socially and to give them some grasp of real education, especially in music, French, English language and literature, history, and arithmetic. It is not generally known that Mary Anne was considered a very able pianist, to the extent that had she wished she could have—like Mirah with her voice, in *Daniel Deronda*—eked out a living by performing at wealthy people's homes. At the school, she was frequently asked to perform, and, according to Cross, she did so despite a pronounced diffidence and then would rush off afterward in a state of turmoil, or in tears.

Whatever the sensitivity of her inner life, Mary Anne was quite dogged in her pursuit of pianistic excellence, and she left a record of exercises that indicate her diligence. She also painted watercolors of floral arrangements. But music and art were not her only interests. She began to gain that fluency in French at the Miss Franklins' School which proved so useful when she arrived at the *Westminster Review* and took charge of continental literature and philosophy. She won the first-year prize in French at the school, a copy of Pascal's *Pensées*. We will discover a good deal of Pascal, intermixed with Spinoza, in her more mature philosophy, although secularized to suit her own non-religious taste.

Her progress in all fields of study was rapid, not only in music, French, and arithmetic, but in the area where she would make her mark, composition. In a notebook she kept, and signed Marianne Evans, is a composition of about a thousand words, and it is prophetic. For while in her young teens, she was contemptuous of "conceit" and "affectation." Her description of what constitutes conceit, for example, foreshadows how that characteristic runs through an entire range of her fictional characters. Women of "this foible" set "great store by their personal charms" and in their youth they consider their charms "sufficient to (create) secure the admiration and worship of the whole world and safe in this belief they flutter, on the flattered of the one sex, the envy of the other. . . ." They live in a whirl of excitement and vanity—so we observe Hetty Sorrel, Rosamond Vincy, Gwendolen Harleth. When they grow older, their conceit becomes transformed into affectation. Since they have learned no graces of mind or intellect, their whole thoughts are on "how they shall best maintain their empire over their surrounding inferiors. . . ." These qualities in men, incidentally, are even more contemptuous, as we note with Arthur Donnithorne, Tito Melema, Grandcourt. Their affectation leads to crimes against humanity.

By thirteen or fourteen, Eliot had a theme that held together the various divisions of her self: that authenticity preempted all other designs and desires. Also marked in the young girl was a Calvinist streak of "get thy house in order," or else become afflicted with conceit and affectation: ". . . take care to cast away the love of it [conceit] upon all occasions, that are not in themselves praiseworthy. . . ." Become, in brief, a better person and then you will not have to fear the invasion of demonic forces. Prepare yourself, live steadily, be disciplined. She was hortatory and not a little priggish. In this, we have the earliest stages of Eliot's categorical imperatives, her necessitarianism, her secular humanism, her recurring theme of self-responsibility. This was to become her "voice," and we begin to pick it up in 1836, when, at seventeen, she began to correspond regularly with Maria Lewis.

It was apparent Mary Anne's compositional talents did not depend on instruction, but came with her when she entered the Miss Franklins' School. Of interest is how this talent appeared or became shaped; it seems she had made some inner resolution, that she would make her mark, if possible, through an intense application of her organizational principles. Music, composition, and mathematics all required a degree of order. Evidently by fourteen or so, she was a "writer," although how and what she should write would not emerge for some time.

She was also, as expected, an intense reader, chiefly of English poetry from Shakespeare through the Romantics. Milton would figure largely in her thought, his high seriousness, his disciplined style, his controlled but still decorative language. The orotund manner, not the flights of the Romantics or their aesthetic mythmaking, would become part of her own stylistic development. In one of the anonymous poems she copied into her notebook, "The Forsaken," we discover in its warning of a man's guile a vague foreshadowing of the seduction of Hetty Sorrel in *Adam Bede* and even the marriage of a young woman to a much older man, as in *Middlemarch*. But these are not only foreshadowings: they are the stuff of fiction itself, part of that body of plots on which Eliot would draw in her novels, available to anyone who read. Mary Anne's reading was broad enough to include a good deal of second-rate fiction and poetry, as "The Forsaken" reveals. We should not see her as perusing only serious books. Her tastes were eclectic, including Southey's vapid poetry, Bulwer-Lytton's light fiction (*Devereux*), Scott of course (being read with more intensity by the Brontës at about the same time), and even the now forgotten G. P. R. James, the historical novelist of *Richelieu, Darnley,* and *Mary of Burgundy.* Such books, however light or trivial, actually proved valuable for Mary Anne, for they shaped her taste in terms of opposites; when she came to write her own fiction, she set herself quite firmly against anything that might smack of James and Bulwer-Lytton, and even Scott.

England on the verge of Queen Victoria was, in part, new territory. The Reform Bill of 1832 had extended the franchise, although not significantly; it had, however, begun that cleaning up of governmental excesses which would continue throughout the century. The Factory Act of 1819—banning children under nine from the mills and regulating the hours of those nine and older from sixteen to twelve hours a day—showed that some reform, however minimal, was possible. Even life expectancy rates demonstrated improvement, going to fifty-five for the gentry in some places, while hovering between twenty-five and thirty-eight for laborers (with high infant mortality rates factored in).

England thought of itself as Tory (now softened to Conservative), despite Whig prime ministers in the 1830s: Earl Charles Grey from 1830 to 1834, then Viscount Melbourne from 1835 to 1841, with the Tory Robert Peel from 1834 to 1835.* It considered itself deeply religious, even while moving to become the most industrialized nation on earth. Church attendance, prohibitions against Sabbath work, and similar disciplines were the outward signs of the Englishman's compliance with what was already Victorianism, before Victoria. Her ascension to the throne in 1837 coincided with an enormous push on England's part to assume a world role, not only for economic and political purposes, but for reasons of humanitarianism. The explorations and acquisition of lands in Africa and the Far East had always been associated in the English mind with "doing good," however much the consequence of such acquisition had been the rape of the land under the guise of law and order. Joseph Conrad's Marlow sees the English red on the map of Africa and feels comfort. It was an age ripe for hypocrisy and economic cruelty, since good intentions served as a shield for terrible inequities, most of all within England itself. While Eliot in *Silas Marner* and *Felix Holt* was aware of injustices and inequities, she stood her ground elsewhere, more with the responsibility of the individual than with that of the state or government. Her belief—almost diametrically opposed to Dickens's—was that if individuals behaved with a sense of their social role, then the society would improve; Dickens believed that the society was more or less unimprovable, and only individuals of character might possibly emerge, or be destroyed in the attempt.

The youthful Victoria—virtually the same age as Mary Anne—of course brought with her ascension a sense of hope. The old men of the eighteenth century were finally put to rest, including two unpalatable kings, George III and George IV, and now a delicate, pretty young woman would rule what was deemed to be the greatest nation on earth. Yet as we reflect on Victorianism, we should see it as Janus-faced: on one side there is a series of consistent

* Tory values (reliance on landed gentry, respect for Church of England bishops, honoring king and aristocracy, suspicion of any franchise concessions) continued and permeated the society, the way a conservative strain may persist in the American government and people despite the election of a Democratic president.

thought, but on the other side there are innumerable departures from anything clearly defined and innumerable excesses and imbalances. These divisions and schisms became the very stuff of Eliot's voice.

Under the surface, there was considerable dissent, as evidenced by the Chartist movement in the 1830s and 1840s. There was enormous anxiety in the face of revolutions on the continent in 1830, the presence of revolutionary elements in England, the aftermath of the Peterloo Massacre, and foreign and domestic groups eager to bring the country down in the name of social justice. The demand for universal franchise (for men, and sometimes for women as well) remained a source of dispute until the next Reform Bill, in 1867. As a consequence of the Corn Laws, bread prices were high enough to justify a rebellion. Enclosures of public lands had struck at the heart of the independent farmer and were another source of dissent. The General Enclosure Act of 1801 and the Act of 1845 marked the decline of the small farmer (who had counted on cultivating open land for extra income) and accelerated migration to the cities. Cities were themselves becoming open sewers for the majority of inhabitants: only the upper 5 to 10 percent avoided the filth, pollution, disease, stink, and general misery of unplanned neighborhoods.

Of great concern to large landowners was the violence taking place in counties all around Eliot's Warwickshire: the "Captain Swing" phenomenon that followed the widespread introduction of machinery into farming. Riots in the southeast counties (Kent and elsewhere) led to the smashing of threshing machines by farm laborers demanding higher wages from landowners and large farmers. The breaking of the newly introduced machines was characteristic of this movement, led by several men, the best known of whom became "Captain Swing." Letters from Swing went to landowners and farmers warning them of the coming destruction if they did not alter their ways. The threats—to overseers, owners, farmers themselves, and even magistrates and justices—took several forms. The demands were not only for higher wages, but for reductions in rents and a lessening of tithes or taxes. The movement spread north to other parts of England, in and around Derbyshire and Warwickshire, and also featured arson. The usual demand for male farm labor wages in the southeastern counties was 2s. 3d. per day in winter, 2s. 6d. in summer. This gave the workers barely enough to purchase necessities, and was less than half of what a skilled artisan like Adam Bede might obtain, which was upward of a pound and a half a week.

Arson proved to be a far greater threat than the destruction of machines. A map of incendiarism in 1830 shows few incidents in Mary Anne's area, only one or two compared with over sixty in other places; but to the east of Warwickshire, we find forty-seven incidents registered. One reason Warwickshire may have been spared is that it was identified more with industry than farming. But the threat was always present and became part of that generalized fear of serious disruption of a way of life.

In religion, the Church of England was under attack from the Oxford Movement, and many promising young men were going over to Rome. The church was itself rent by high-church and low-church divisions and threatened from the outside by a growing body of Dissenters and chapel people (as we see in Trollope and in Eliot herself). Forces eager to preserve the status quo or for conserving traditional values or for opposing facile progress—as in Carlyle— were coming up against those eager for scientific and technological advances, as well as for individual freedoms. And all this was occurring well before Darwin's *Origin of Species,* in 1859, split intellectual, religious, and social thought even further. Mary Anne absorbed it all. She read more, knew more, had considered more than nearly anyone in the mid-Victorian period; she was its repository and voice. Only Carlyle and Mill rivaled her.

Mary Anne made her notebook debut as a fiction writer with a scene that could have been taken from G. P. R. James's romantic fiction, although her direct working source was William Coxe's *An Historical Tour of Monmouthshire.* It is a youthful, not at all precocious piece of writing—what we might expect from any young woman slowly emerging from the care of her family and indulging her fantasies about the male world. A historical drama of sorts, it carries the reader back to the days of Cromwell, right after the execution of Charles I, in 1649. Edward Neville, after whom we can title the story, is the nephew of Henry Marten, a real person involved in the regicide. The story shifts suddenly from Neville to Marten when the former visits the jailed man in the Castle of Chepstow. Some of their conversation covers Cromwell's campaign, and from this we learn that Neville and Marten are both fanatically anti-royalist. Banned from all respectable society except that of Sir Verner Mordaunt (shades of *The Faerie Queene*), Neville falls in love with Sir Verner's daughter Mary. Amidst all this intrigue and hatred, their relationship is idyllic until, when they reach the dangerous ages of eighteen and fifteen, respectively, they are separated. Eventually, Henry Marten is himself banned from Sir Verner's home when he reaffirms his hatred of the crown and insists he would commit regicide again if given the opportunity. Both Neville and Marten having been expelled from society, the story ends abruptly.

While the story does not gush, it is not well controlled, either. It is clearly part of the Romantic revival, James and Scott, with not a small touch of Byron. Of real interest, however, is that Mary Anne's fictional effort is of a historical nature, for if we look to the future we observe how little Eliot wrote about contemporary life, how frequently she set her fiction not very far removed from the date in the early 1830s when she wrote this brief piece. Almost her entire corpus of work is set historically: *Adam Bede, Mill, Middlemarch, Silas Marner,* and, most markedly, *Romola.* Further, we note how the romantic posturing of Mary Anne Evans, which might have put her on a course with the Brontës, was abandoned once she became George Eliot. Emergence meant transformation.

At about the same time, in 1834 or so, Mary Anne made a large religious commitment to evangelicalism. Her religious "opening up" is not particularly unusual, given the influence of Maria Lewis and given the renewal of interest in religion as a consequence of the Oxford Movement, begun in 1833, but foreshadowed by other events. The Catholic Emancipation Act of 1829, giving political rights to Catholics, was an influential force in bringing religion to the political forefront. But the Oxford Movement was decisive, and while it did not call for the enthusiasm we associate with evangelicalism, it did accelerate religious polarities. People who might have been indifferent suddenly took sides. The movement was as much social and political as religious, although the latter came to dominate. As a political movement, it posed a threat to the established church and the established order.

The Oxford Movement was not at first a Catholic endeavor. It started quietly enough, with Lord Grey's assertion of state control over the English church. That was denounced by John Keble, a well-regarded Anglican clergyman and author, in an 1833 sermon called "National Apostasy." Thus, the still inchoate religious movement was perceived in political terms. John Henry Newman entered the fray in an effort to strike down liberal tendencies and practices within the Anglican Church. *The Tracts for the Times*, many of them written by Newman, attempted to demonstrate that the apostolic succession—that line from the early apostles to the later clergy—had been passed to the Anglican clergy of the nineteenth century in some mysterious transmission of divine guidance and empowerment. This order of priesthood, so Newman argued, formed a church beyond the power of the state, and any effort to suppress or control it was sacrilegious. Newman's attempt here was deeply divisive, since it appeared to establish the church as an empowered social and political entity owing nothing to the state, to democratic forms, or to the governed will of the people. For England, without a fixed constitution to turn to and heavily dependent on tradition and precedence, Newman's *Tracts* were inflammatory. And he was hardly finished.

As the *Tracts* continued, Newman's researches and conclusions eventually led him from the Anglican Church toward Rome, culminating in the famous *Tract 90*, which demonstrated that nothing in the Thirty-nine Articles of Anglicanism—the very bedrock of the church's teachings and beliefs—was contrary to Roman Catholic dogma. Driven home with his own brand of inexorable logic and graceful prose, Newman's point was that the apostolic succession led to Rome, not Canterbury. With this, the Anglican authorities came down on the Tractarians as heretics who were contaminating English youth. The Bishop of Oxford halted the publication of the *Tracts*, and Newman himself, drifting free of the Anglican Church, joined Rome in 1845. The movement which had started at Oxford ended with a Pyrrhic victory at Canterbury, but also with a strange kind of triumph for Newman and the Catholics. An entire generation of young men (only men, of course, could be ordained) was stirred.

The overall consequences went far, revealing deep social divisions in the society, elements that entered as deeply as evangelicalism into questions of class and caste. The final outcome of the Oxford Movement in the established church was a split between high and low churchmen, with the triumph of the latter and the opening up of Oxford and Cambridge Universities finally to Dissenters and even to nonbelievers. In spiritual terms, the movement awakened both clergy and flock to a new sense of tradition, reverence, and devotion that was to keep religious belief central in Victorian concerns. One of the key documents of the period to catch the religious hopes and doubts of a "typical" Victorian was Tennyson's *In Memoriam,* started during the peak of the Oxford controversy.

At fourteen, Mary Anne was caught up by the religious swirl, not in direct regard to Roman Catholicism, but in relationship to her own Church of England and to the possibilities of an evangelical response to its formalized and subdued ceremonies. Anglicans now had to maneuver both within and outside Catholic doctrine. Exposed to the quiet influence of Maria Lewis and the religious atmosphere of the Franklins' School, with her own background in the Anglican Church firmly in place, she was open to all spiritual impulses. That she became an avid believer in the religious life as a cure for a sinful soul was an important stage in her development as a young woman, and a significant stage toward her later emergence. At the Franklins' School, the atmosphere encouraged a quiet, disciplined belief and actively discouraged enthusiasm or evangelicalism. Mrs. Francis Franklin's brother was secretary of the Baptist Missionary Society, an organization charged with the conversion of the heathen; her daughter Rebecca had served as a missionary in India, and her son had died while preparing for a missionary career.

As part of this establishment, the girls organized prayer meetings—Mary Anne was apparently one of the leaders—and on Sunday they attended the nearby Cow Lane Chapel where Francis Franklin preached. He did not advocate a hard line of Baptism, certainly not the thunder-and-brimstone variety of evangelicalism we associate in this country with Elmer Gantry in Sinclair Lewis's novel of the same name and with the figure of Billy Sunday, on whom Gantry was modeled. Mary Anne, nevertheless, took very readily to ideas of conversion, sinning, and the desperate need for salvation. Very possibly, the young woman, who had few things to repent of personally, saw in the Mammon-driven Robert Evans a semblance of sin, and through her sudden fervor hoped to compensate for his pursuit of the golden calf.

This would not be an extraordinary attitude, in that the fear of the pursuit of Mammon was ever present in the society. One way to counter it was through a relentless Calvinism. The golden calf, or the molten calf, was perceived in sermons as providing the greatest threat to religious life—veritably the embodiment of Lucifer. Material advancement was a Faustian pact, and the fact that Robert Evans remained a devoted church member did not mitigate his pursuit of riches. Warnings about Mammon that started in the 1820s and 1830s continued throughout the middle and later decades of the century. While novelists condemned the materialism of unchecked laissez-faire—in Dickens, most noticeably, but also in Charles Kingsley, George Gissing, and others—several nonfiction writers established entire careers on these cautions: Thomas Carlyle in nearly everything he wrote, as well as John Ruskin and Matthew Arnold.

Although several of these works carry us well past the mid-1830s when Mary Anne was experiencing her spiritual regeneration, they do capture the flavor of the times. And they do provide the context for her sudden adventure in salvational politics. While her Calvinism based on self-denial and on preservation of one's soul would appear to be directed at her father, it may also have been part of her hostility to what she saw developing in Isaac. John Cross quotes her as saying that she disallowed her brother Isaac many of his pleasures and that she offered a kind of ghoulish presence to the household when she returned from school.

Mary Anne's evangelicalism extended into the kind of poetry she copied into her notebook, and into the poetry she was writing. One of her own pieces begins: "A Saint! Oh would that I could claim / The privileg'd, the honor'd name / And confidently take my stand / Though lowest in the saintly band!" Such lines, however youthful, must be relegated to the bathetic school of poetry, something only a biographer can quote without blushing. Eliot later did not develop her poetic talents much beyond a certain limited accomplishment, but here we observe an adolescent girl trying to discover her center or identity through some linkage to a sacred world, as well as a young woman seeking some way in which she can sacrifice herself or become a penitent for the sins of the world. The martyrdom which is both explicit and implicit in so many of her female protagonists is already heralded here. Later, self-denial would become a shield behind which she could hide frustration and depression.

Yet despite her seeming dissent from Anglican worship, Mary Anne remained within the Church of England and simply grafted onto it her own brand of sin, suffering, and penance. She in fact bridged the no-man's-land between traditional Anglicanism and the Dissenters who worshipped not in cathedrals and even in open fields. Yet other events were occurring in 1835 which would affect her life, not questions of worship only, but of life and death. In July, Mrs. Evans was declining rapidly and was forced to go around in a wheelchair, a helpless figure, and in December the seemingly indestructible and indomitable Robert Evans began to suffer from a severe kidney stone attack. Treatment was primitive. In effect, little was directed at the source of the pain, and a so-called curative was applied externally in the form of bleeding with leeches. Two doctors, Bucknill and Mellor, treated Evans, applying leeches to his arm and to the kidney area. Remarkably, he recovered for the time being, a sign of his otherwise good health rather than the benefits of "medication." In the meantime, Mrs. Evans declined further, and she died, probably from cancer, on 3 February 1836.

The consequence of this on Mary Anne was not grief—she had never been close to her mother, or even sympathetic toward her—but the assumption of a new role in the household. This was her opportunity to become "wife" to a father she still respected, and it was this role she began to play, with household chores and other duties as well. It was, as the youngest daughter, a way to establish herself in the family. The tie Mary Anne formed with Evans meant she was shaping herself, now sixteen, in several ways. This close association with her father meant she would measure men by his standard: someone hardworking and disciplined, but also limited and provincial.

Mary Anne was caught by a paradox, part of that division of self which both fed her talent and brought her misery. For even as she embraced her father's conventionality, she was developing those attitudes and beliefs which would pull her from his world. Her enthusiasm for evangelicalism would, in time, be transformed into different ideas of order which put her on a collision course with Evans. That the association with Evans was valuable there is no question, since it imbued Mary Anne with a value system she never lost sight of, even as it became translated into her own version of secular humanism. But it was valuable in another way, too: it gave her something to rebel against in her own choice of men.

Her assumption of household duties and her generally tagging along with her father on his errands or on trips to find materials for decorating the house had not been long in place before her sister Chrissey married, on 30 May 1837, to Edward Clarke. It was an event auspicious in another respect, for in signing the register as bridesmaid, Mary Anne dropped the "e" and became Mary Ann, the first of several such name changes. Clarke had a medical practice at Meriden and was a member of the Royal College of Surgeons; at the time, such a licensed medical man also dispensed drugs and medications. * This now gave Mary Ann three married siblings: besides Chrissey, her half-brother, Robert, with Jane Attenborough, and her half-sister, Fanny, with Henry Houghton. These marriages would later become dramatic elements in Mary Ann's life, since her family—except for Chrissey—created for her considerable anguish and heartbreak.

The name change, however, is of a different order. It would seem that her transformation into a zealous religious person would be accompanied by some change, however small, in how she perceived herself. The dropping of the final "e," while minor compared with her later changes to Marian or Mrs. Lewes or George Eliot, is an indication of an internal change. While we know that after her return to Griff House from the Miss Franklins' School her religious enthusiasm intensified, it is incorrect to see it as isolated from what was occurring in her family. With the death of her mother, she sensed she now had an opportunity to establish a model, on the order of the saint she described in her notebook. Also, such fervor could signal her individuality: she could order the household according to strict principles and, at the same time, demonstrate how different she was.

With Chrissey gone, Mary Ann's role in the Evans home grew; she was now mistress. Three enormous changes had occurred in the life of the young woman: she had suffered (however indifferently) the death of her mother, followed by her assumption of a new role in her family; as a result of her religious commit-

---

* Eliot would draw on Edward Clarke for her portrait of Dr. Lydgate in *Middlemarch*, but she presents a rosier picture of Lydgate's practice than existed in the late 1820s. While outstanding discoveries were being made—Jenner and the smallpox vaccine, Caventou's and Pelletier's development of quinine for containing malaria—tuberculosis, like other virulent diseases, was a dreadful killer for which there was no treatment. Further, anesthesia would not be introduced until 1842 (nitrous oxide gas), so surgeons were successful to the extent that they could get in and out of a body rapidly. A strong patient might stand fifteen minutes of carving. Surgeons like Clarke had a somewhat higher reputation than physicians, since with the former, results could be judged; with a physician, even when a diagnosis was in order, treatment was leeches and beef tea, before the patient died.

ment, she had experienced Holy Communion for the first time; and she had, at
her sister's wedding, changed her name slightly. Mary Ann was, in some limited
respects, a new person, all of this coinciding with her need, at seventeen, to
begin to think of where her life would eventually go. As we note in her portray-
als of women in her novels, her options were few. In 1837, one could, if rightly
placed, become queen of England at eighteen, but most young gentlewomen
would have to choose among governess, teacher (at a school like the Miss
Franklins'), marriage and the production of babies, or spinsterhood. If the latter,
the young woman would live at home, take care of an aging, sick parent like
Evans, become the babysitter for numerous nieces and nephews, and be treated
generally as an otherwise useless bit of human machinery.

Mary Ann was at just this crossroads. Since she was not physically prepossessing—her features had formed, with a large, fleshy nose and a dominant chin,
albeit an attractive smile—marriage became problematical, even if she desired
it. As for becoming a governess or teacher, that was possible, although with her
developing intellectual powers, she would have felt wasted. As the real possibility of spinsterhood developed (when marriage at fifteen or sixteen was ordinary),
she began to dig in, intensifying in two areas. In her religious devotion—her
commitment to experience, to holiness, to potential sainthood, and to the idea
of "optimism of grace"—she was, indeed, God's being. The other area was in
her desire for learning, which she reinforced with intense periods of reading. In
her religious role, she became increasingly puritanical, and her reading of religious works picked up: the Bible, obviously, as well as *History of the Jews* by
Josephus. But she also revealed a harshness in regard to music, which had once
been a joy for her. After having attended a concert that included Haydn's *Creation*, Mendelssohn's oratorio *Paul* (sung by John Braham), and Handel's *Jeph-
thah*—none of them irreligious or secular—she denied the experience of
exaltation. She told her friend and schoolmate Martha ("Patty") Jackson that
no composer should use the sacred words of Scripture as a means to entertainment, as "a rope dancer uses her rope." She also wrote to Maria Lewis that she
would abjure all oratorio, especially when lines such as "we are ambassadors for
Christ" are put in the mouth of "such a man as Braham (a Jew too!)."

She was, clearly, becoming an impossible, intolerant prig; but none of this
should be dismissed as merely the growing pains of an extremely sensitive young
woman whose intellect has as yet no focus. We must see it as part of the forma-
tion of aspects of her character which remained unyielding even in later years.
She was to be strangely divided, for while the narrowness and intolerance of
these ideas would be transformed later, they did not disappear. They became
part of the bedrock that grounded her efforts when she moved out into an
entirely different world, a world which, in time, would revile her while making
her famous. The early austerities were an essential dimension of Mary Ann's
need for certainties.

She transferred her moral strictures on music to literature as well, reviling the
popular entertainment provided by novels. She was now hard put to distinguish
between literature which she enjoyed and literature which she felt was mere

indulgence. Even Shakespeare is suspect: "Shakespeare has a higher claim than this on our attention but we have need of as nice a power of distillation as the bee to suck nothing but honey from his pages." Books, she stresses, can have a malign influence on us. She offers herself as a case in point. "I am I confess not an impartial member of a jury in this case for I owe the culprits a grudge for the injuries inflicted on myself. I shall carry to my grave the mental diseases with which they have contaminated me."

She chides herself: "When I was quite a little child I could not be satisfied with the things around me; I was constantly living in a world of my own cre-ation, and was quite contented to have no companions that I might be left to my own musings and imagining scenes in which I was chief actress. Conceive what a character novels would give to these Utopias." These remarks, however, cannot be seen as mere adolescent moralizing. She is being priggish, of course, but she is moving toward "high seriousness," that loftier ground on which she can justify herself and her newly found fervor.

She was, clearly, remaking herself: denying what energized her in the past so that she could justify what was meaningful to her in the present. "When a person has exhausted the wonders of truth," she writes Maria Lewis, "there is no other resort than fiction; till then I cannot imagine how the adventures of some phantoms conjured up by fancy can be more entertaining than the transac-tions of real specimens of human nature. . . ." More than twenty years later, as part of her literary realism, she wrote in *Mill:* "The pride and obstinacy of mill-ers, and other insignificant people, whom you pass unnoticingly on the road every day, have their tragedy too; but it is of that unwept, hidden sort, that goes on from generation to generation, and leaves no record. . . ." These comments are an extension of the remarks to her friend in 1838: realism or truth, as she calls it, opposes fiction, or romanticism. But she zeroes in on something even more personal in *Mill* than in her correspondence: ". . . such tragedy, perhaps, as lies in the conflicts of young souls, hungry for joy under a lot made suddenly hard to them under the dreariness of a home where the morning brings no promise with it"—such tragedy can be a "slow or sudden death." The next line is dramatic: ". . . they ['certain animals'] can only sustain humiliation so long as they can refuse to believe in it, and, in their own conception, predominate still."

This is not the view we ordinarily have of Mary Ann's childhood, but it fits *her* perception of it as early as 1838, when she was writing to Maria Lewis. Her rejection of fiction in such harsh and moralistic terms indicates a rejection of at least that part of childhood linked to her sense of difference. She speaks like an Old Testament prophet, a Jeremiah or a Savonarola: "They [religious novels] are a sort of Centaur or Mermaid and like other monsters that we do not know how to class should be destroyed for the public good as soon as born." The rigidity from a distance seems amusing, but Mary Ann apparently had to narrow herself before she could expand and emerge; and yet when emerging, as we shall see, she did not completely forsake the implications of these views. In *Adam Bede* and *Mill,* her views of fiction as depictions of the ordinary and even trivial are continuous with the religious strictures presented here. Troubled by fictions which allowed the imagination too much free play or toyed with the reader's sense of probabilities,* she even rakes her once beloved Sir Walter Scott over the coals. As a consequence of his writing romances and novels, he "sacrificed almost all his integrity for the sake of acting out the character of the Scottish Laird, which he had so often depicted."

Except for her high intelligence, Mary Ann, in 1838, at close to nineteen, sounds intolerable. To bolster her views, she went on a rampage of reading: religious works (in her letters she mentions biographies of Wilberforce, Sir Richard Hill, Mrs. Mary Fletcher of Madeley, all of them evangelicals); poetry (Milton, Shakespeare, Young's *Night Thoughts*); volumes of letters (Hannah More); even missionary accounts. She read heavily in commentaries on the Bible: Archbishop Leighton's *A Practical Commentary upon the Two First Chapters of the First Epistle of Peter* (1693), also his *Theological Lectures,* as well as Joseph Hoppus's *Schism as Opposed to Unity of the Church* (1839) and Joseph Milner's *History of the Church of Christ* (1794–97). Fiction writing went by the wayside with a vengeance. All of this helped nourish her evangelical fervor, and she began to formulate a plan to compile a Chart of Ecclesiastical History, a forerunner, perhaps, of Casaubon's Key to All Mythologies in *Middlemarch.* Mary Ann's plan was to show parallel movements among Roman emperors, the political and religious condition of the Hebrews, the early bishops, the sequence of patristic writings, the heresies and divisions, and whatever else accrued, from the birth of Jesus through the Reformation. For the material necessary for this large enterprise, she required a large library, and one was provided by Mrs. Charles Newdigate, who had controlled the vast Arbury Estate and its enormous library since the death of Francis Newdigate four years earlier.

Without knowing that someone else was planning almost precisely the same project, Mary Ann worked ahead on her great chart. When that other project was completed and published, she forsook her own, whose profits were to go to a new church in Attleborough. Through this period, when Robert Evans saw his daughter moving in dizzyingly untraditional and seemingly unfeminine ways, he nevertheless gave her valuable support. He funded her considerable book purchases, and he paid for a tutor, Joseph Brezzi, to give her lessons in Italian and then, in March 1840, German as well. In a short time, she achieved sufficient fluency to read both Italian and German, which served her well in later years when she wrote *Romola* and translated Strauss and Feuerbach.

In reporting her latest reading to Maria Lewis, who becomes the repository of the "new" Mary Ann, the young woman displays her learning with apparent relish. In one respect, she is instructing her former teacher in the ways of God and man and refining what both believed in. A good deal of Mary Ann's insistence on what she was reading—and how it supported her evangelicalism—was

---

* Eliot's "Silly Novels by Lady Novelists," in the October 1856 *Westminster Review,* pulls together most of her objections to such fiction. She was also, by this time, indebted to Lewes's insistence on realistic fiction. We discover how well read Eliot was in "silly novels" and how knowledgeable she was about "silly novelists."

perhaps connected to her brother Isaac's increasing interest in the *Tracts for the Times* and in what were then still considered high-church views, where ceremonials and traditions were favored over immediate experience and holiness. She particularly cites Hilner's *History* because it expresses "the tenets of those who deny that any form of Church government is so clearly dictated in Scriptures as to possess a Divine Right, and consequently to be binding on Christians." This is a direct strike in the religious controversy over the church's insistence on a government presided over by its bishops. Mary Ann's point was that individual experience preempted formalities, a mode of worship which brought her perilously close to Methodists and other Dissenters. This is followed shortly by a snide blow at the authors of the Oxford *Tracts* who attempt to "give a romish colour to our ordinances" and refer to Rome "as a dear though erring Sister." One cannot avoid the hostility not only to Rome, but to those, like Isaac, who followed the Tractarians, many of whom would eventually end up in Rome.

Mary Ann presented herself as something of a recluse, but in actuality she was socially active; she was not without friends and traveled with her father to London, in November 1839. But in one significant respect, she was hermetic, in that she maintained a secret life that no amount of socializing or traveling could touch, not Maria Lewis, or Martha Jackson, a friend and correspondent for several years. In a canceled passage in the manuscript of *Mill*, we find how that "secret self" was organized: "A girl of no startling appearance, and who will never be a Sappho, or a Madame Roland or anything else that the world takes note of, may still hold forces within her as the living plant-seed does, which will make a way for themselves, often in a shattering violent manner." Eliot has just demonstrated that Maggie is yearning for something "that would link together the wonderful impressions of this mysterious life," in which she could achieve her "eager, passionate longings for all that was beautiful and glad, thirsty for all knowledge; with an ear straining after dreamy music that died away and would not come near to her. . . ." This creature experiences such a deep contrast between outward and inward that painful collisions result.

This was the inner life of a woman experiencing those painful collisions. The pain and suffering she wrote of so often, feelings that became the cornerstones of her secular philosophy, were old friends to her. Her early years, placid as they look on the surface, were full of turmoil once she recognized that her external and internal lives were not parts of a whole, but warring selves.

In July 1839, Mary Ann composed some verses which she sent on to Maria Lewis and which were published—her first publication—in January 1840, in the *Christian Observer*. Cast in traditional devotional terms, the poem relates that she will bid farewell to her familiar loves, including natural beauty and books, all but that "Blest volume," which she will carry with her to heaven. The poem is lacking in any felicities of phrase or any intensity except purpose, but it is still another guide to the inner Mary Ann struggling to break out—from herself or her small world, from her chosen duties in the Evans household, from the grip of frustration.

In another revealing letter to Maria Lewis, in 1839, Mary Ann demonstrates a confusion of mind and purpose, but does so in language which is quite compelling. Her scientific metaphors and images indicate how deeply involved she was becoming in such matters even as the matters themselves were assuming increasing importance in English thought prior to Darwin. The early part of the century was a remarkable time for scientific progress, with inventors like Charles Babbage (an early form of the computer), Michael Faraday (his work in electricity and physics), Humphry Davy (his synthesizing of pioneer work in chemistry), John Dalton (lesser known, but an important figure in atmospherics and chemistry), and Jonathan Otley (also lesser known, but an important geologist and geographer). Yet nothing was more significant in English intellectual life than Charles Lyell's *Principles of Geology*, published in 1830, with further parts in 1832 and 1833. Lyell laid much of the groundwork for Darwin and for later evolutionary theory. Eliot demonstrates that she has not been ignorant of the latest developments:

> I have lately led so unsettled a life and have been so desultory in my employments, that my mind, never of the most highly organized genus, is more than usually chaotic, or rather it is like a stratus of conglomerated fragments that shews here a jaw and rib of some ponderous quadruped, there is a delicate alto-relievo of some fernlike plant, tiny shells and mysterious nondescripts, encrusted and united with some unvaried and uninteresting but useful stone.

Having established the seeming chaos of nature, she then speaks as possessing a mind of "just such an assemblage of disjointed speciments of history, ancient and modern." She speaks of scraps of poetry she has picked up from Shakespeare, Cowper, Wordsworth, and Milton, morsels of Addison and Bacon, Latin verbs, newspaper topics, geometry, entomology and chemistry, reviews and metaphysics "all arrested and petrified and smothered by the fast thickening every day accession of actual events, relative anxieties, and household cares and vexations." Her concern with being "smothered" is compelling, to the extent her religious vocation might not emerge. She senses that too much is evanescent and that it is important for her "to be anchored within the veil, so that outward things may only act as winds to agitating sails, and be unable to send me adrift."

As she moved toward and past twenty, she wasn't sure whether things were coming together or failing to cohere. Her education was itself now under siege for having been disorganized; but more than that, she was becoming another female possibly sacrificed on the altar of male needs. Although she was hugging her religious fervor as the sole constant in her inner life, what was in fact occurring was a dissatisfaction that arose when she attempted to join inner and outer. Those images of drowning which are so particularized in her work as George Eliot are already foreshadowed here, however unready she still was to confront them.

What was a typical day for Mary Ann as she turned twenty in November of 1839? Outside Griff House itself, she worked among the poor, having organized a clothing club to help the families of unemployed ribbon weavers. Unemployment in and around Coventry would become more common and even ruinous, what with imports from the continent and changes in taste in fashion. On the domestic side, her half-brother Robert was increasing his family, naming his children Isaac, Robert, and Mary; and Chrissey was rapidly building a family, eventually giving birth to nine children. When they visited, Mary Ann's household duties—supervision of cleaning, meals, and the like—of course increased. Also, since Robert thrived as a moneylender, there was a stream of doctors, lawyers, and businessmen to see him; included in this enterprise were clergy, who borrowed for themselves or for the administration of their churches. Robert was further involved in parish relief: the injunction to perform good works as well as maintain faith. As church warden of Chilvers Coton, he wore many hats: as accountant for church funds and as administrator of the workhouse (called, euphemistically, the Chilvers Coton College of Industry) and several other trusts and funds, including the Bedworth Hospital Trust. As if this were not sufficient, he helped administer the Sunday School, some day schools, and a dispensary which the Newdigates supported with an endowment. All of these activities meant a large number of people came to the house. Later, when Mary Ann became famous as George Eliot and her identity was finally revealed, people recalled her kindness and her generosity with her time. She most certainly was kept occupied.

In a 22 November letter to Maria Lewis, written on her twentieth birthday, Mary Ann is clearly on edge. She announces, after a week in London, that she has "emerged from a slough of domestic troubles" and is only now beginning to "take a breath in my own element." She is mortified that her faculties "have become superlatively obtuse" during her banishment from that element. She feels guilt at having indulged herself by reading in the first three volumes of the six-volume Wordsworth published in 1836–37. Self-indulgent she may have felt, but Wordsworth would in time fill her mind and replace her formal religious spirit with his own brand of nature's spiritual qualities. Overall, she sounds undirected, uncertain of what lies ahead for a young woman of no beauty but of considerable sensitivity and learning. She senses an abyss, but cannot locate or define it.

In the spring of 1840, young men flit in and out of her letters, but are dismissed for fear they will upset her life's plan, which we assume is to religious duty and devotion. A particular young man was not suitable, in any event, not being evangelical; but another man loomed, her Italian and German tutor, Joseph Brezzi. He assumed a more solid place in her affections; she tells Maria Lewis she has found him "anything but uninteresting." Then in a telling phrase, she indicates that "Cease ye from man" (from Isaiah) is "engraven on my amulet." With that strong statement about her rejection of intimate feelings, she admits she feels "involuntarily isolated, and without being humble, to have such a consciousness that I am a negation of all that finds love and esteem as makes me anticipate for myself—no matter what. . . ." She emphasizes that she needs "rigid discipline."

She will later tell Martha Jackson that she senses foreboding, that she or Martha must "be widowed from the world, or you will never seek a better portion. . . ." This may be rejected as the Weltschmerz of a basically lonely young woman attempting to assume a romantic pose—too much Byron, insufficient Goethe, perhaps. But we would be mistaken not to observe the call for help implicit in these lines, help that must derive from within.

Even while she fervently pursues her evangelicalism, it is, apparently, not satisfying her needs deeply enough. The romanticism remains, but one that projects disappointment and frustration: "In this vestibule of life's theatre," she tells Maria Lewis, "we must be content to accomplish all our projects and realize all our hopes imperfectly." Some of this sadness, as of July 1840, was connected to the fact that when Isaac married, she and her father would have to leave Griff House, to which she was profoundly attached. She would also lose Isaac. "Troublesome," she calls it, but it was clearly more than that.

Now moving toward twenty-one, she found herself little different from what she was earlier. Her resolution not to consider men, to engrave that message on her amulet, was making a virtue of necessity, although we should not ignore her desire for sainthood and martyrdom. But her dedication to spinsterhood at this age seems disingenuous when we note her drift in other respects. She tells Martha Jackson, "I take too much mental food to digest without more of the exercise of conversation." She coins a word to suggest her condition: she is nonimpartitive, unable to impart what she is absorbing. She receives, but does not give, or "make."

The young woman, who as a nine- or ten-year-old indicated she did not like to play with children but instead liked to talk with grown-ups, did find herself at a party, at the home of Mrs. Thomas Bull, a neighbor near Nuneaton. But the tumult within, the contrast between her abnegation of amusement and the "oppressive noise that accompanied the dancing" and other activities, created in her an illness of such intensity that "I regularly disgraced myself." She says that the situation made it impossible for her to "maintain the *Protestant* character of the true Christian. . . ." The consequence was headache, "and then that most wretched and unpitied of afflictions, hysteria." After that, she vows, she will reject "all invitations of a dubious character."

The headaches, which continued with varying degrees of severity for her entire lifetime, are some indication of a tense, nervous, or, as she says, hysteria-prone person. Yet the headaches cannot be identified merely as the result of tension or conflict, or of unresolved elements in her character—however significant such matters were. The headaches also served some positive function, in that they gave her a reason to retreat. If the headaches were truly migraine, they were often severe enough to send her into retirement for long periods of time. Suffering excruciating pain, she felt transported into another dimension, not only of pain but of experience, in which she became ultra-sensitive to sound, light, movement. Given the opportunity to retreat, she became secretive and arcane, as she wished. She experienced a life *there*.

One mistake, however, would be to see Mary Ann as having her nose perpetually buried in books. While she did absorb enormous amounts of print, she also cleared time for her household duties, some of which she found quite rewarding. She was an expert maker of butter and cheese, a talent she attributed to the breadth and general largeness of her hands. She celebrated this activity in the dairy scenes of *Adam Bede*. She was quite able in supervising the kitchen, making pies and jellies, and related accomplishments. At holiday time, she was forced to work exceptionally hard to keep up with the festivities, and here she balked, since holidays rubbed badly against her religious scruples. An evangelical, she felt, must celebrate her soul first.

The years 1839–40 were to become turning points. Although Mary Ann was still deeply involved in her Calvinistic evangelicalism, she was beginning to respond to other elements. While she rued aspects of her life, she was slowly changing it. While she upheld her stern ideas on predestination and the determinism of the elect when her Methodist aunt, Mrs. Samuel Evans, came to Griff, she was also reading more openly and more imaginatively. Further, she seemed to have been impressed by a story passed on by Mrs. Evans about a young woman sentenced to death for infanticide. We know she was moved because twenty years later the story of Hetty Sorrel, similarly sentenced, threads through a good part of *Adam Bede*. What was particularly touching about the story was that the young woman died repentant—even a hardened Calvinist had to soften at that.

But there are other indications of Mary Ann's slow defection. She was reading steadily and compellingly in English poetry, centered on the turn-of-the-century Romantics. Surely Byron, especially his *Don Juan*, did not fit a Calvinistic pattern; and her immersion in Wordsworth, as noted above, was carrying her along to conclusions somewhat different from her formal strictures. She continued to read in religious literature, the *Lyra Apostolica* and *Tracts for the Times*, although her tendencies were to reject the Anglo-Catholic identification of the apostolic succession. When she read Isaac Taylor's *Ancient Christianity*, she noted that the Catholic Church of the fourth century, on which the Tractarians based many of their premises, was not pure, as they asserted, but full of superstitions: a religion already contaminated by other elements and not at all that "clear line" of succession claimed by the Tractarians.

Even more important in her development as she read religious books seeking the truth was her growing certainty that the geological explanation of the earth's beginnings sounded more compelling than the religious position. Even when she read Reverend Harcourt's *Doctrine of the Deluge*, which was a defense of the scriptural account of the beginning, she found it "allusive and elliptical," not at all convincing for those who were leaning toward geological explanations. What makes all this so significant is that she was preparing herself for the German Higher Criticism of the Bible which would reduce miraculous events to rational explanation, a movement in which she played no small role because of her translations of Strauss and Feuerbach, those German critics who created such a radical revision of biblical theory.

The conflicts were all there by now: the evangelical hold on her beliefs

remained long after the basis for it had been undermined. Her readings of
Romantic poetry alone would have created a variety of different feelings, not
the least a rebelliousness of spirit and an animistic awareness of nature which
clashed with her Calvinistic determinism and strictness. But co-equal with that
were the stirrings of her own body and blood, her growing consciousness that
something was seriously lacking, and that the missing element was affection,
sympathy, displays of warmth. Mary Ann was growing (or had grown) into a
very sensate person who needed affection and love in demonstrable ways. Below
the surface of her narrow sense of pleasure and her hard sense of duty was a
womanliness which translated into strong needs. She was neither martyr nor
saint nor ascetic. She may have wished to be perceived that way out of some
sense of superiority—what we find in Dorothea Brooke in *Middlemarch*—based
on her ability to deny herself what others embrace. But that wish was giving
way to other realities.

In the family, Isaac was becoming adept enough to learn the tricks of the
trade from his father. At twenty-four, in 1840, he planned to marry Sarah Rawlins, daughter of a Birmingham merchant. Mary Ann was clearly to be left alone
with an aging father. Her half-brother Robert was prospering, having himself
gone the route from artisan to middle class which Tom Tulliver in *Mill* dreams
of doing. But even more, Robert Evans Senior planned to move from Griff
House, leaving it to Isaac and Sarah, while he and Mary Ann lived in a new
house at Foleshill, in Coventry. At sixty-seven, Evans was now ready to retire.
In mid-January of 1841, the new house was approved, and in March, once ownership was established, Isaac and Mary Ann prepared it for their father to move
in. This occurred on the evening of 17 March. Isaac and his bride, married on
8 June, settled into Griff for the remainder of their lives and produced four sons.
As for Mary Ann, to add to the disruption she was feeling emotionally and
intellectually, she was now living in new quarters, having given up her beloved
Griff to her older brother and still older sister-in-law (Sarah Rawlins was ten
years older than Isaac).

On the surface, everything seemed to be proceeding smoothly for the Evans
family; they were even becoming closer to playing the role of gentry. Beneath,
however, were real tensions. In such a move, as we observe from Maggie and
Tom's experience in *Mill*, there is an exodus modeled on the expulsion from the
earthly paradise. The old house, and especially the Griff area for Mary Ann,
had the whiff of Eden. While she had been undergoing several emotional highs
and lows, Griff House was itself the repository of good memories. We have
noted how Eliot lovingly describes even humble abodes, such as Silas Marner's
rough and primitive cottage, how she turned the home into a sacred place, a
touch of the Garden. When the home is not like that, she indicates that the
divisions run very deep, not only into an unhappy family and unhappy marriage,
but into the very fault lines of character, and from that into society itself. She
writes in Mill: "They [Maggie and Tom] had entered the thorny wilderness, and
the golden gates of their childhood had for ever closed behind them." This
ended the first volume of the three-volume edition. Since Eliot was very careful

how she ended a volume, this close is especially meaningful as the Gates of Eden close on them.

The new house at Foleshill was by no means a slide down on the social scale. While its land area was less than at Griff, it was a most pleasant place. Known as Bird Grove because of its abundance of trees and birds, it was located back from Foleshill Road, quiet and private. Mary Ann's room was a small study with a fine view of Coventry's twin spires. In terms of family life, the new house was well located: only five miles from Griff; two miles from half-sister Fanny and her husband, at Badington; five miles on the other side were Chrissey and her husband and their three children. Mary Ann became particularly close to Chrissey's children, and she often took the two oldest home with her. Although she enjoyed Chrissey's family, Mary Ann observed her sister's domestic situation becoming increasingly difficult, since money was always short and she was overworked and exhausted. We get something of this in *Mill* in Tulliver's sister, Mrs. Moss, and her eight children—hardworking but going nowhere and dependent on a large loan from her brother. The closeness of the family and the round-robin of visits brought home to Mary Ann even more forcefully her isolation and difference.

Although she may not have been fully conscious of the changes already occurring within her, by this time, in 1841, she was reaching a crossroads. There was a tendency to let things move along at their own pace: country life, planting, seasonal beauties could deceive her into thinking there was little reason for change, little sense of loss. But rather than being calmed, she was, if anything, more torn between her inner and outer life, in ways she reflected better in her fiction later than in her contemporary letters. In writing about Silas Marner—a very personal and intimately conceived book—Eliot probes into the phenomenon of loss and how that removes the protections we have built up which ensure our survival. She is aware of how even dead objects (Marner's treasure trove) can become a shield behind which one hides; and she is conscious of the fact that even the most hidden, secretive lives have purpose and perhaps eagerness in them. She is, as it were, imaginatively re-creating her own condition twenty years earlier.

If nothing else existed to make Mary Ann feel unsettled, there was the condition of Robert Evans, deteriorating steadily, not having fully recovered from his severe kidney stone attack in late 1835 despite spurts of good health. Now sixty-eight, he bridled at his enforced idleness and still thought of himself as vigorous, even while declining. Evans was visited by his family, children and grandchildren, but it was Mary Ann on whom he depended. As he grew older, he became more convinced than ever that any departure from Tory principles would lead to revolutionary action in England. He protected the past as something sacred, his role in it as priestly. His journal indicates he depended on Mary Ann's reading to him, but it was his church activities which filled most of his time. While he hewed to high-church principles, he was not immune to evangelical enthusiasms, and to this we might suggest the influence of his daughter. The sermons and evening lectures of John Edmund Jones (Perpetual Curate of the Chapel of Ease at Stockingford), Evans indicates in his journal, did touch him. He and Mary Ann followed church sermons in Coventry and Kenilworth, although it is clear the father did not assume the religious fervor of the daughter.

Mary Ann was still, on the surface at least, a strict and ungiving person. But something was coming together internally which would lead to the first of her huge decisions to emerge as her own person. In the next year, in early January of 1842, she refused to accompany her father to church. And despite heavy family pressure, she continued to refuse. This first stage of her rebelliousness was essential, obviously, to self-definition; but it was not a question of her rejection of religion, rather of the formalities of worship. The core belief remained. She divested herself of the church, not the spirit of Jesus Christ. In this respect, she was establishing her frame of mind for her translation of David Friedrich Strauss's *Life of Jesus* begun in 1844. Strauss's predecessors in Bible study were anguished over the question whether any historical meaning of Jesus would remain as a foundation for religion if they applied the idea of myth to that life, whereas Strauss was quite confident that Jesus would nevertheless remain, as would Christianity. In the same sense, Mary Ann did not feel she was negating the Christian spirit by forgoing church attendance. John Cross reports that in 1841 Mary Ann still was upset by the rich dress of churchgoers and of those attending consecration ceremonies at St. Paul's, in Foleshill. She sounds very much like Dorothea Brooke with her distaste for ornamental jewelry and other finery.

Meanwhile, her letters to Maria Lewis, in particular, but also to Martha Jackson, are filled with intellectual endeavors—her reading, for example, of the first three volumes of *The Life and Times of Louis the Fourteenth*, by G. P. R. James, and her eagerness to see the fourth volume. She sets forth her notion that England's need for purgation of a putrid body politic might come only in a foreign war; and while she admits that once she was not so martial in spirit, now she is not at all certain that such a war would be harmful. *

Except for Maria Lewis, whose intellect she was fast outgrowing, Mary Ann had no one in her immediate circle who could keep up with her desire for intellectual stimulation. In Coventry, she saw the Miss Franklins, but they were more concerned with a patina of culture than with the real thing. To her credit, however, Rebecca Franklin spread the achievements of her pupil far and wide, including to the Sibrees. John Sibree was a minister of the Independent Chapel in Vicar Lane and had two children, a son heading for the ministry and a daughter of sixteen, who became attached to Mary Ann. Another family whom Mary Ann came to know was the Pears, the husband a middle-class ribbon manufacturer well known to Robert Evans. Pears's wife was Elizabeth Bray, an evangelist

---

* So that we don't think the lack of a large war after Waterloo in 1815 meant England was not fighting any wars, we need only cite the "minor war" in Burma in 1824. English casualties came to 15,000, most of them deaths from disease (cholera, malaria, dysentery, and scurvy, nearly all preventable). The Burma wars foreshadow the disastrous British campaigns in the Crimea, the enormous casualties there also deriving more from disease than from enemy gunners.

and also from an old ribbon manufacturing family. Clothes, ribbons, and the like had long been the mainstay of the region. The Bray connection was to prove fortunate for Mary Ann and was to backfire on Robert Evans, who at this time was eager to find friends for his solemn and studious daughter.

We get some sense of how Mary Ann sought intellectual sustenance from a particular scene in *Mill*. Eliot has created a multifaceted scene, imaginatively conceived, but it is difficult not to reach back from this plaint into Mary Ann's life in and around the early 1840s. Having recognized the limitations of her current life, Maggie "rebelled against her lot, she fainted under its loneliness, and fits even of anger and hatred towards her father and mother, who were so unlike what she would have them to be. . . ." Maggie finds solace in Thomas à Kempis's *The Imitation of Christ*, but it is dubious and temporary. She gravely hears the words of withdrawal, resignation, internality. She understands that the language in *Imitation* was the chronicle "of a solitary, hidden anguish, struggle, trust and triumph. . . ."

As part of Mary Ann's own opening up, she suffered grave doubts and split herself into segments, only to be steadied by ideas of resignation and renunciation. In *Mill*, the test for Maggie's new resolutions comes in her scene with Philip Wakem at the Red Deeps, when he attempts to undermine her resignation by pointing out that it leads to narrowness and constriction, not to fulfillment: ". . . you are shutting yourself up in a narrow self-delusive fanaticism, which is only a way of escaping pain by starving into dullness all the highest powers of your nature." Yet while the words carve deeply into Maggie, they derive from a sexually neutral or even negative situation. Philip, of course, has his own agenda, which is his love for Maggie, both spiritual and physical. But to her, he is a crippled young man of considerable achievements who lacks all physical appeal for her. While not repelled by his crooked back, she cannot possibly find him attractive; and yet her fascination with him derives from her need for intellectual support, for sympathies she cannot find in her immediate circle. The two, then, are moving on quite different playing fields, although the scene resonates with Mary Ann's hope in the 1840s for salvation.

In Mary Ann's immediate circle, there were eruptions everywhere. Chrissey's husband, Edward Clarke, while prolific in making babies, was less prolific in being able to support them. As a country surgeon, he was not making his way against older and more settled competition. Eliot later caught this aspect in Lydgate's effort to become established in Middlemarch. Robert Evans was himself not at the top of his game anymore: creating work for himself in church activities and other social and political matters, but clearly on the shelf, too old and not feeling full strength. Mary Ann herself, whatever the internal struggles, had not, by 1841, found any way out of her dilemmas. Like Maggie once again, her resignation was merely a narrowing of possibilities leading to her application to study.

Mary Ann did read, heavily and seriously, studied Italian and German until she became fluent in reading, attended chemistry lectures—what would become part of her intense interest in the physical sciences long before she met George

Henry Lewes, himself an amateur scientist of considerable talent. She kept up with her Latin. Her range was extraordinary. While maintaining her interest in languages and in chemistry, she also read steadily elsewhere: in Isaac Taylor's *Physical Theory of Another Life*, a study published in 1836 that anticipated a life after death in which individual duties would be commensurate with newly developed powers. Such reading would seem to reinforce even further personal divisions, since she had to assimilate supernatural materials into her own rational explanations of human behavior. She read in astronomy: John Pringle Nichol's *The Phenomena and Order of the Solar System* and his *View of the Architecture of the Heavens*, books of particular interest because while Nichol was now a professor of astronomy, he had earlier been a minister who had changed his mind about man's and the earth's origins. Mary Ann's reading was clearly in works which attempted holistic views of life, its origins as well as its development. She sought "meaning."

Her letters indicate she also read John Pye Smith's *Relation Between the Holy Scriptures and Some Parts of Geological Science*, published in 1839. As her reading was focusing clearly on contemporary books and problems, she positioned herself for some of the most critical intellectual events of the next twenty years: the geological assault on the religious explanation of the earth's origins; the attack on biblical miracles and other extraordinary events, the so-called German. Higher Criticism; and, finally, Darwin's *Origin of Species*, the culmination of all preceding arguments about fossils, man's origins, and the earth's beginnings. But before she came to the groundbreaking studies which reinforced her growing rationalism, Mary Ann tried out alternate theories, as in the Smith book mentioned above. She was not by any means closed to creationist theory, nor was she as yet prepared to open herself to the new ideas which would effectively question, and subvert, her earlier views.

She kept up, at the same time, her reading of derivatives of Thomas à Kempis, little self-help books such as those she mentions to Maria Lewis: *Thoughts Preparative or Persuasive to Private Devotion* and *The Test of Truth*. Such books were clearly for the less imaginative and less intellectual than Mary Ann, and they offered little in the way of argument beyond surrendering oneself to a greater power. She read, also, with great interest, Thomas Carlyle's *Sartor Resartus*, that stinging attack on ostentation, cultural decline, and individual deterioration in the face of a progressive society. Like so many others, including Dickens, she was deeply impressed by the vigor and fervor of Carlyle's evangelical-like pleas for man to change before he is utterly corrupted. Carlyle's words surely reinforced her own ideas of *Gemeinschaft*, or community, as the ultimate repository of individual needs.

Yet possibly the most significant event of Mary Ann's life at this point was her meeting with Elizabeth Bray, wife of Abijah Hill Pears. Through Mrs. Pears, she would meet her brother, Charles Bray, and his wife, the former Caroline Hennell. On 2 November 1841, Mrs. Pears took her young friend to visit the Brays at their Rosehill home, with its view of Coventry, and its level of culture which extended well beyond Coventry into the entire range of English and continental ideas. Through the Brays, Mary Ann would come into contact with Caroline Hennell's older brother, Charles, author of the enormously influential *An Inquiry into the Origins of Christianity*, published in 1838. While the Brays and the Hennells did not change the course of Mary Ann's life themselves, they did insert their views into hers and challenge what was already beginning to waver.

Their influence might have proven negligible if Mary Ann had not herself, however glacier-like, been opening up toward new ideas and shown dissatisfaction with renunciation. As she writes later in *Mill*, Maggie meditates on what has been her "negative peace," and the dissatisfaction it has brought, even while it controlled her emotions and intellect: ". . . the battle of her life, it seemed, was not to be decided in that short and easy way—by perfect renunciation at the very threshold of her youth." And just as Maggie's life opens up when she comes to stay with Lucy Deane and Stephen Guest, so did Mary Ann's when she became a frequent visitor of the Brays at Rosehill. "Rosehill" became, in its very imagery, that house on the hill which provided new vistas for her intellect.

3

Discovering Herself

"A woman can hardly ever choose in that way; she is dependent on what happens to her. She must take meaner things, because only meaner things are within her reach."

In biography, we always seek those moments which are critical in the development of a creative figure, since it seems that those moments offer change, perspective, and development, qualities which lie at the very core of a biographical pursuit. And yet the moments the biographer creates for such judgments are often subjective and, of course, unproven. The highlights, such as we find here with Mary Ann's meeting with the Brays and Hennells, are somewhat arbitrary. Some moments are, of course, more meaningful than others; but can we tell precisely what those moments are when we look back 150 or more years? Mary Ann appears to have been coming close to an edge, and in looking over the side, she seems to have observed other factors besides those which had governed her life so far.

Every commentator on George Eliot sees in the Brays and Hennells a major turning point in her intellectual and emotional development. Unquestionably, these people were important, but we must also cite Mary Ann's own reading, her movement toward poetry, Romantic poetry at that, and the vague unhappiness she experienced through renunciation. We must not neglect the evidence of her novels, in which renunciation leads, usually, not to satisfaction but to an uncertain and unsettled condition. Before meeting the Brays, she had already assimilated entire philosophical and theological systems, from Thomas à Kempis and his imitators to those who challenged it all in their scientific and poetical writings. She was, in herself, a battleground, a divided personality. The Brays and Hennells acted as catalysts.

Charles Bray, the son of a ribbon manufacturer, was only eight years older than Mary Ann, and was hardly an intellectual, having received a spotty education and spent much of his adult life thus far in the ribbon trade. Yet through marriage and then the death of his father in 1836, he came into an income of £1,200 a year, which made him very comfortable. Bray passed through several religious phases before he rejected all formal Christian beliefs in favor of a secular humanism based on scientific principles. The matter which made up the things of the world, he concluded, was subject to the same elements which made up the mind. With the two areas working according to the same principles, it was only necessary to make the right choices. Implicit in such ideas is a kind of determinism, since man's mind and external matter were composed of certain rules or principles.

This determinism George Eliot later defined as a form of necessity. She herself quoted the German philosopher Novalis that character is destiny; but when she places her own gloss on it, she observes that character is not the whole of our destiny. It needs other coordinates, as she illustrates with Hamlet, whose character, she wittily speculates, could have taken a number of other directions. But determinism was not something she easily gave up. In *Mill,* Maggie's destiny is fixed by water, is "at present hidden, and we must wait for it to reveal itself like the course of an unmapped river. . . ." Mary Ann's early Calvinism dissolved into secular humanism, but its determinism remained a working principle for her throughout her creative life.

Bray fell into several kinds of alternatives to formal Christianity, including a nineteenth-century favorite, phrenology, the pseudo-science which attempted to identify character through head shape and skull protrusions. While this study has its amusing side, it became less amusing later in the century when physical appearance was used by Cesare Lombroso and his followers to predict criminal behavior. It was all part of a positivistic approach to human life, an approach that at one time appealed to George Eliot. None of this pseudo-intellectuality, however, prevented Bray from making a strikingly good marriage, to Caroline Hennell, known to Mary Ann as Cara, in April of 1836. Caroline Hennell was in several respects a good example of the young woman who should have been educated as well as the males in her family, but who, as the eighth child, enjoyed no such benefits. She was clever, insightful, and refined in her arguments. As a Unitarian, she rejected much of what Bray presented to her as fact.

When Cara's brother, Charles, examined the biblical evidence in order to substantiate Unitarian beliefs,* in his *An Inquiry into the Origin of Christianity,* he began that critical analysis of Jesus Christ which led him, and eventually Mary Ann, to move outside of formal religious belief. Particularly striking about Hennell's examination was not that he undermined Jesus, but that he viewed miracles and all extraordinary events as little more than mythological occurrences. Such acts were not divine revelation or divine intervention, but explicable in natural terms, explicable as all other phenomena are to be explained. In

---

* Caroline was instrumental in requesting that her brother make this investigation, since Charles Bray's positivism seemed, to her, to undermine the New Testament. While overshadowed by Bray and then Mary Ann, Cara eventually published six books for children as well as a kind of handbook on personal hygiene.

this regard, the specialness of the divine experience was subverted, and what Hennell came away with was a good man, Jesus, who was little different from the heroes of classical mythology.

While Hennell's conclusions could still support Unitarianism, they simply reinforced Bray's growing agnosticism. He considered himself heretical, and, as a badge of pride, pursued several social and political ideas which were anathema to most of his contemporaries. He believed, for example, that schools should be nonsectarian, that is, not responsible to the established church, and that Dissenters and all faiths should have access to public education.

Since a good part of the Coventry children—perhaps half—fell outside the Church of England, they were in effect barred from schooling after a few years. From Bray's interest in universal education and related ideas, Mary Ann saw that agnostics and Dissenters were far more involved with helping the poor and eradicating widespread illiteracy than were devout Church of England worshippers, including her father. As she began to turn against her hard-held ideas, the influences on her were as much social as religious. Her sympathies were with the "ordinary people" (as she reminds us repeatedly in *Adam Bede, Silas Marner,* and *Felix Holt*), and yet the people with whom she had been associating before the Brays were less interested in the ordinary than with maintaining sharp class distinctions. As we see her ideas shifting in this critical period, we come to understand that she was shaping for herself a holistic view of people and life. In her Calvinistic, narrow outlook so far, she had segmented ideas constrictedly; as she developed and grew away from formal religious belief, she tried to see society as an entity. And while she never viewed herself as a reformer, certainly not as any kind of radical or extremist, her social ideas were leveling and democratic. Hers was a voice of sanity.

Bray's *Philosophy of Necessity* (1841) had been recently published, and one reason it attracted Mary Ann was that it eliminated uncertainty. It appealed to her desire for inevitability, for if we stretch her Calvinism somewhat, we can see that a move from predetermination to necessity or inevitability is not a great distance. None of this implies that Mary Ann read Hennell and Bray and then suddenly shifted her ground. More likely, she was caught in a center of indifference, hostile before ideas she already found wanting, uncommitted to anything else, and therefore open to new ideas and to change. As for the Brays, they were delighted with their new acquaintance, quickly recognizing the superiority of her mind and the textured quality of her ideas. They felt, for their part, that she might prove beneficial to them, as Bray later revealed in his *Autobiography*.

What Mary Ann had to sort out was how morality could be reinforced if religion were removed; or, conversely, without religion, how would it be possible to live a moral life? The question was a profound one for the entire nineteenth century, culminating in the efforts of John Stuart Mill and Matthew Arnold to envisage a society or a body politic in which a moral state is possible without recourse to formal religious worship. The idea would come down to us in Nietzsche's "God is dead," a famous statement which is often misunderstood, since Nietzsche's point, like that of the others, was not the celebration of this death but to question what would happen to a society morally if the idea of God were removed from it.

Mary Ann was ready to enter that dangerous ground where feelings, family ties, moral ideas, ethical principles, and religion came together, or else fell apart. In the meantime, Maria Lewis came to spend the Christmas holiday in 1841. The relationship superficially seemed as close as ever, for Mary Ann asked Maria to return to Foleshill and to remain as long as she wished. Maria had left for a few days to observe her new school at Nuneaton. Mary Ann's letter to her on New Year's Day, 1842, however, ended with some hint of her changing opinions: she speaks of everyone who does his work faithfully and "lives in loving activity" as blessed. This defines a moral character and needs little in the way of formal religion to sustain it.

The next stage was rapid and indicates that Mary Ann had been undergoing considerable conflict without directly expressing it to friends or family, although she may, possibly, have tipped off the Brays as to what she was planning. On 2 January, a Sunday, she chose not to accompany her father to Trinity Church, an event which Robert Evans noted in his journal. He indicates, quite simply, that Miss Lewis went with him, but "Mary Ann did not go." On 16 January, he made a similar announcement: "Went to Church in the forenoon Mary Ann did not go to Church." Robert Evans was not the only one taken aback by Mary Ann's decision. Maria Lewis apparently attempted to dissuade her from this recent course of action, but did not achieve her aim, and when she left, the friendship and correspondence were hanging by little more than memories.

Robert Evans had a more immediate problem at hand, since he was living with a now disobedient daughter, and one whose course of action, in his mind, would prove scandalous. It was, Evans felt, a direct blow at his high standing in the church, as someone in charge of the collection plate. We can, if we project, see Mary Ann's act as having in it not only a religious dimension but a considerable amount of hostility toward her father and his position. It was a bid not only for her own religious freedom, but for the freedom of a woman held in thrall to male domination. The images of father, of God, of God-Father, of the male dominion all suggest she was rebelling on a broad front, and rebelling as much against family as against church.

Robert Evans could not bring himself to plead: he felt that a daughter owed obedience to her father. He wanted the surfaces of life to appear unruffled, and he turned to his other children to put pressure on Mary Ann. What she had to remember was that she had no income or home of her own, nothing she could call property; in this respect, she was subject to the whims and largesse of others.* If she left home, she would have to become a teacher at some low level

---

*Her position was spelled out legally: she was considered little more than chattel. William Blackstone, the renowned jurist (*Commentaries on the Laws of England*), stated that a wife was deemed her husband's common property, under the common-law doctrine of coverture. Since husband and wife were a single body in the eyes of the law, the woman was subsumed under the man, who was empowered to speak for them. Alleviation did not come until the Divorce Act of 1857, which gave rights to married women and, by implication, to single women as well, whose fathers had taken on the same prerogatives.

(she had little formal education). Her position was not enviable, unless friends were willing to take her in; but then she would be considered an outcast, sent to the allegorical "Coventry" or an isolation ward, as it were. That Mary Ann lived near Coventry was prophetic, for that city had been so named by the Cavaliers (Royalists) because so many Roundheads (Cromwellians, those opposed to Charles I) lived there, and it became synonymous with banishment or ostracism.

As family pressure on her mounted, she found herself entering unknown territory. Mary Ann was still far from becoming George Eliot, but the process by which she defined herself as distinct from others was already in motion. Robert Evans was not subtle: become dutiful or face censure. Mary Ann's half-sister Fanny told her to put up a good front: comply, but retain her own beliefs, as Fanny herself did. Chrissey was so wrapped up in family problems and childbirth as to have virtually no opinions except the offer of spiritual support. Isaac, prefiguring Tom Tulliver at his narrowest, warned that Mary Ann would become a pariah and lose all opportunity to snare a husband if she continued her actions.

Later, in her fiction, George Eliot wrote repeatedly about how personal decisions, of whatever kind, were not morally valid if they hurt others, or led to a chain of events which might injure others. We glimpse the intensity of the conflict in her at this time from how she shaped the relationships in her books which reveal how personal decisions may set off disastrous sequences of events. When Maggie Tulliver thinks only of her own feelings—she does so in a kind of reverie in which she is treated like a grown woman for the first time—she goes off rowing with Stephen Guest. Her temporary disappearance leads to widespread gossip, scandal, and, inevitably, enormous pain to Lucy Deane, Stephen's fiancée. Yet Mary Ann's "rebellion" was far more complicated. It was not only her soul she was conflicted over, but the very nature of her role as a daughter—and, by implication, the very nature of her place in the Evans family.

When Mary Ann's close relatives failed to persuade her—she was set in her rebelliousness—friends were called in. In a letter to Mrs. Abijah Hill Pears (Elizabeth Bray), Mary Ann alludes to Mrs. Pears's effort to dissuade her from her course. She says she enjoys conversation on this subject, but cannot bear "blank silence and cold reserve," which she is apparently receiving from her father. She is very insightful about herself and her situation: "Do not fear," she writes, "that I will become a stagnant pool by a self-sufficient determination only to listen to my own echo; to read the yes, yes, on my own side, and be most comfortably deaf to the nay, nay." Yet she is certain of her course. "For my part, I wish to be among the ranks of that glorious crusade that is seeking to set Truth's Holy Sepulchre free from a usurped domination." Her choice of language is compelling: she will join a "crusade," not to affirm the supremacy of God, but to liberate higher truths from the dominion of the church. Still, she assuages Mrs. Pears, she has no intention of becoming godless. She will act in conformity "with the will of the Supreme; a continual aiming at the attainment of that perfect ideal, the true Logos that dwells in the bosom of the One Father."

Other friends received similar sentiments. The lines were drawn, for the inexorability of Evans's strategy did not break his daughter's determination. She wrote to him on 28 February 1842 to try to lay out her objections. At first, she attempts to relieve her father's fear that she will join the Unitarians, the sect of the Brays. Then she moves to her view of the Christian and Hebrew scriptures, which she regards as "histories consisting of mingled truth and fiction." She adds salt to Evans's wounds by saying that while she admires and cherishes "much of what I believe to have been the moral teaching of Jesus himself, I consider the system of doctrines built upon the facts of his life . . . to be most dishonourable to God and most pernicious in its influence on individual and social happiness." Admiringly, she cites Benjamin Franklin to support her conviction.

She says she would be bowing miserably "to the smile of the world" if she professed to join in worship of which she wholly disapproved. She insists she will not do so even for his sake, but "anything else however painful I would cheerfully brave to give you a moment's joy." She adds that her sole aim is to walk in "that path of rectitude" which is the only path to peace, and even the prospect of contempt and rejection "shall not make me swerve from my determination so much as a hair's breadth until I feel that I *ought* to do so." Her words indicate she is in a war and she will fight as long as her strength remains.

As additional pressure on Mary Ann, which she refers to in this letter, was Evans's intention to remove himself from Foleshill, chiefly to escape his daughter's scandalous conduct. He explained that expenses at Foleshill were high and could only be justified as giving Mary Ann "a centre in society"; but since she has placed "an insurmountable barrier" to her prosperity in life, the object of that expenditure has been removed. She has, meanwhile, positioned herself as a willing martyr: "I am glad at any rate this is made clear to me, for I could not be happy to remain as an incubus or an unjust absorber of your hardly earned gains which might be better applied among my Brothers and Sisters with their children."

Her fury contained, she added she would be glad to live with her father at Packington, a cottage of much reduced circumstances. She hopes to be able to minister there to his comfort. But she is also willing to leave him and rely on her own feeble energies and resources, as she describes them. The martyr complex is never distant: "So far from complaining I shall joyfully submit if as a proper punishment for the pain I have most unintentionally given you, you determine to appropriate any provision you may have intended to make for my future support to your other children whom you may consider more deserving." She says she will follow her duty wherever it may lead.

The battle lines were drawn—martial metaphors seem applicable. She has decided to put into a permanent form feelings which have poisoned the family, and she has promised to remain faithful to a father whom, obviously, she can no longer obey. The underlying motif for her is the need to explain herself, to create some individual territory, to define where she can step and where the other, the father, must retreat. Like Antigone, one of Eliot's favorite historical characters, she insisted upon her prerogatives despite the outcome.

Her letter came before eyes which refused to acknowledge it or her. Evans remained silent, and, if anything, her words reinforced his determination to marginalize her until she relented. The terms of their relationship are those of a proud God-like figure and a Lucifer-like villain who has vowed disobedience. Evans consigned Mary Ann to his own version of hell for acts of pride and disobedience; and she remained disinclined to surrender her first real statement about herself. It is a marvelous struggle not only between father and daughter, but between male and female: the male insisting on his traditional rights, the female demanding to be heard. A son could have moved away and made his own living, especially with the high standing of the Evans name in the region. As a woman, Mary Ann had taken herself to the edge.

With her show of rebellion and her defiance of authority, this was not an easy period for her. Her attempt at self-definition did not bring exhilaration; she considered it more of a duty to herself. And she brought to it considerable guilt about her father's life as a consequence of her actions. She had now taken on her own cross, which was to justify her actions against the pain she caused. She was moving toward what Dinah Morris preaches in *Adam Bede*, a form of martyrdom. When Mary Ann considers leaving Foleshill for Leamington and a teaching position, her uncertainty surfaces; her desire for martyrdom wavers. She tells Mrs. Pears not to interfere, not to seek an interview with Evans, since, apparently, he was offering only silence in the face of arguments. She admits she suffers from woes, but one primary woe, that "of leaving my Dear Father." She says she does not fear "doleful lodgings, scanty meals," or reproaches and afflictions. The latter image (from Hebrews) calls up something of Job and his troubles; like him, she hoped to endure.

Robert Evans put Foleshill up for rent and sent Mary Ann to live with Isaac back at her beloved Griff House. Isaac had himself relented somewhat and had opened his home to her, admitting she had been treated harshly. For her part, Mary Ann insisted she only wanted to act on her own principles of liberty. Friends such as Mrs. Pears and Rebecca Franklin persevered with Evans, suggesting that by letting Foleshill he would be perceived by everyone as driving out his daughter; to which Evans responded that Mary Ann was under the thumb of the Brays, especially Cara. But he let himself be convinced and withdrew his offer to rent, at the same time approving Mary Ann's departure to Griff. What had occurred was not a resolution, but a postponement.

The strange situation would be repeated several times in Mary Ann's (and George Eliot's) life. She found herself within skewed alignments. She joined Isaac, who, while bending for the time, would prove to be an inflexible foe in later days. She found herself in virtual noncommunication with a father whom she professed to love, and whom she would portray sympathetically in her fiction as Adam Bede and Caleb Garth. She had left herself almost no position in the family, since she could not return to her home, and she had no means of supporting herself. She had even offered to forgo whatever her father might leave her. While Chrissey remained loyal, she was in no position to be of help, since her own fortunes were taking a financial downturn. Mary Ann's half-sister

Fanny had suggested compliance and was not supportive of open rebellion. The family, which once considered itself solid, compact, coherent, was strangely disjointed as a consequence of the youngest's actions. Yet by choosing to be Antigone, Mary Ann had consciously rejected becoming Iphigenia.

Her challenge to male authority lasted exactly four months. It was a campaign in which, eventually, both sides compromised. Robert Evans relented to the extent that he permitted Mary Ann to return if she agreed to attend church with him, regardless of whether or not she believed in what she heard there. For the Creon-like Evans, it was a way of averting further bloodletting. It was an amusing compromise, in that while all along he wanted appearance more than substance, his daughter insisted that substance was more important than appearance. None of this, however, was easy for her. Writing to Mrs. Pears, we note her reluctant return to the fold; she says she is increasingly "impressed with the duty of *finding* happiness," but only when "we have a peace whose munitions are not to be shaken by the small artillery of circumstances, we may begin our self-catechizing afresh."

Her expression of a *duty* to find happiness is quaint, but happiness in the nineteenth century was a commodity. The aim of life was not simply getting through the days, and people even as intelligent as Mary Ann believed in the "happiness principle." But her way was barred. The martial images, of munitions and artillery, indicate she saw the struggle as a war, the "house" as a battlefield, and herself and her father as generals trying to outmaneuver each other. As one seeks the higher ground for attack, the other finds himself on the defensive. She tells Mrs. Pears she regrets nothing "so much as my own impetuosity both of feeling and judging." She feels she has to "*worm* out the intentions" of others, and she is uncertain of Evans's plans since she has heard he was commencing alterations at Packington. * She fears her father has acquiesced only temporarily to Isaac's advice not to hurry things. She adds: "I must have a *home*, not a visiting place."

Less than two weeks later, she wrote at length to Francis Watts, professor of theology at Springs Hill College, Birmingham, indicating her desire to peruse a book by the Swiss theologian Rodolphe Alexandre Vinet. This text, she hopes, will reinforce her own position. She writes:

It is no small sacrifice to part with the assurance that life and immortality have been brought to light, and to be reduced to the condition of the great spirits of old who looked yearningly to the horizon of their earthly career, wondering what lay beyond; but I cannot think the conviction that immortality is man's destiny indispenable to the production of elevated and heroic virtue and the sublimest resignation.

---

* He had, in fact, done so, noting in his journal that he showed Lord Aylesford his plans for renovating the cottage, and the lord agreed to them. This was on 23 March, late in the third month of the stalemate with Mary Ann.

She is quite clear that she is not rejecting Christianity; she is abandoning revelation, immortality, and formal worship of God and religion, whether Church of England or Dissent. Yet by forgoing her belief in the divinity of Jesus Christ, which she would eventually do, she was, in effect, putting Christianity behind her.

Her letters while she was staying at Griff House indicate her pleasure in being back, although the shadow of not having a home of her own is always present. Isaac's wife intervened and convinced Evans that he was, in effect, driving his daughter further from the church by his obduracy; and with this, he agreed she could return, although he was still set on leaving Foleshill and seeking, now, a new place at "Fillongley (!)," to the surprise of Mary Ann. Fillongley was six miles northwest of Coventry and was the home of Evans's brother-in-law Isaac (Christiana Pearson's brother, a farmer). Mary Ann says she will write her father and "request his decision," although she fears he may remain indecisive for weeks on end, leaving her in a kind of limbo. While she has been made most comfortable at Griff, she says there are "feelings which are incommunicable that render it impossible for me to continue long an adjunct to a family instead of an integral part."

She returned, Evans compromised, and, as mentioned above, Mary Ann agreed to attend church while withholding belief. Much later, she told John Cross—her future husband—that she felt this period was one of the most painful in her life, that while she had not felt herself to blame, she regretted putting herself on a collision course with her father, and that "a little management" might have alleviated the confrontation. This is George Eliot in retrospect, or else it is John Cross in his usual way turning a hostile and antagonistic situation into a small domestic flurry. In the long view, she had not as yet found the correct medium for rebellion.

By the end of April, she was back at Foleshill, and by 15 May, she was attending church with her father. The working-class Evans, like the middle-class families in *Mill*, could only hold his position by virtue of his manners, behavior, attitudes, and appearance. His conservative Tory views (he paid no heed to the "radical Tories" of Disraeli's Young England movement) coincided with his pride in having risen socially. Since this positioning was something Evans had carried out with great care and discipline, he was not about to see it tarnished by a daughter pursuing her own selfish ends. And yet through it all, he did miss her, his companion on many a trip, the one who had remained to take care of him now that he was ill and aging rapidly. Mary Ann is the heroine of this episode, but Robert Evans is not quite the villain.

Meanwhile, his daughter's dependence on the Brays intensified. Since their own lives were not conformist, they supported their friend and displayed a kind of independence that made Evans distrust and dislike them. Charles Bray was a free spirit, philanthropic, supportive of all social and voting reforms. He was, in several respects, a less intellectualized John Stuart Mill. Cara Bray was quieter, steadier, less impetuous, but nonetheless interested in social reform. She thought and worked on a smaller scale, but in practice probably did more good than her more extravagant mate. She was interested in the education of the poor and taught in a school organized by Charles. Her love for children coincided with those sympathies of Mary Ann's, and her feeling for helpless things, whether children or animals, provided a softer side to the marriage than Bray's big sweeping ideas.

Cara Bray was more than a quiet teacher, however, more than a perfect foil to her husband. She was part of a fairly large group of middle-class women who carved out social roles within marriages that allowed them some movement and choice. She was bright, open, an accomplished pianist (fitting in perfectly with Mary Ann's intense interest in music), and a painter as well. Her 1842 portrait of Mary Ann, a watercolor, now hangs in the National Portrait Gallery in London. It deserves some attention, since it indicates that even in a friendly portrait, Mary Ann could not be considered attractive, especially in repose. At twenty-two, she already looks like the classic stereotypical image of the spinster, a woman who has settled in upon herself. The clasped arms suggest someone enclosed and unapproachable.

Similarly, the attire, a frilly gown, seems like a coat of armor which shields her and demands that pensive gaze. The collar-tied neck with a brooch seems to close out as much as it closes in. The embroidered sleeves also appear like armor plating. The face is itself dominated by a large nose, made to appear even larger because of the tight upper lip. The hair, done in typical nineteenth-century fashion, seems perfectly set, parted neatly in the middle, with arranged curls along the side. Like the pose itself, the face suggests a virginal innocence which insists upon itself—we must try to see this portrait as Mary Ann, not as George Eliot. The slightly pursed mouth, with the fuller lower lip, appears to offer more suggestion of opening up; but overall the portrait does not bespeak warmth or sympathy. In an 1850 portrait (by François D'Albert-Durade), eight years later, Mary Ann is transformed into a sophisticated Frenchwoman; but this is an idealized portrait which catches her in a pose that neutralizes the long fleshy nose. Mary Ann at twenty-two and then at almost thirty-one seemed pleasant, withheld—although less so in the later portrait—and quite consciously untouchable in manner and dress.

She spent a good deal of time with the Brays at Rosehill, which reminded her of Griff House with its lawns, fine trees, and quietude—its distance from the outside world. Some of the self-contained world we associate with Eliot's fictional places surely derives from the houses she inhabited as a child and young woman, the sense of them as enclosed societies. Rosehill, however, was visited by several renowned figures, among them Robert Owen, a socialist who influenced Charles Bray; men like Carlyle's friend George Dawson; the phrenologist George Combe, who also had an unduly large influence on Bray's becoming an ardent advocate of that pseudo-science; Combe's wife, the daughter of the great actress Sarah Siddons; and not the least, Ralph Waldo Emerson. Mary Ann met these people, impressing nearly all of them, and they obviously influenced her desire to emerge. They surely revealed a world she could not have suspected to exist from her associations with Griff and Foleshill; and even her reading could not have prepared her for their broad, open discussion of ideas, many of them socially and politically unacceptable to her at this time.

A whole range of religious beliefs passed through the Bray household, not as forms of belief but as materials they could either assimilate into their variegated views or reject as unsuitable. Mary Ann's association with the Brays and the Hennells helped her develop that synthesizing power which enabled her to discover analogies from every branch of learning, including the physical sciences. Some of her characteristic passages, such as with Arthur Donnithorne and the Reverend Irwine in *Adam Bede,* would be based on analogies, in which she could go from human nature to nature, to the physical sciences, then back to the Bible or to the poets and the classical writers. The seemingly endless fund of knowledge she was accumulating in this period was part of a storehouse of images, metaphors, and analogies she could deploy later on.

While Mary Ann's life had taken on a more forward-looking direction, her sister Chrissey was undergoing the travails of a woman with too many children and a husband unable to support them. As mentioned above, Tulliver's sister in *Mill* comes to mind as a working-class reenactment of some of Chrissey's troubles—and, incidentally, one of the very few occasions when Eliot showed anyone completely on the edge of financial ruin. Even Tulliver is saved from that. Chrissey's third child, Mary Louise, died on 5 May 1842 at the age of three months. Mary Ann's response to this was curious, revealing more her old religious attitude than her newer developing ideas. While she says such a death is "like the breaking off of a sweet melody to poor parents," nevertheless the "meltings of sorrow on such occasions are to the harder sex one of the surest means of subduing and refining the spirit." Thus, tragedy for the parents can be turned into a means of making the male better. The Calvinism is there: since all is predetermined, we must make use of what occurs in order to improve ourselves.

But the death of a child was only one part of Chrissey's problems. Her husband found his practice floundering, he was not well (so Robert Evans's journal reports), and the Clarkes needed a large infusion of money, in this instance £800. Clarke gave Evans a bond for the sum, an enormous amount for the time, with the proviso that if it were not paid during Evans's lifetime, it would come out of Chrissey's inheritance. Since there was little chance of its being repaid, Chrissey's fortunes continued to decline. Mary Ann was deeply involved, because despite the psychological and intellectual differences between herself and her sister, she felt close to her and was especially sympathetic and affectionate with the children. We tend to think of Mary Ann / George Eliot as all brain, mental activity, and book learning; but she had deep feelings for children, was excellent in their company, and understood their problems well when they grew older. She surrounded herself with other people's children: Chrissey's now, and later Lewes's sons, and even Lewes's wife's children by Thornton Hunt.

As Mary Ann's circle of friends increased with the addition of Sara Sophia Hennell, sister of Cara Bray, and herself a woman of considerable accomplishments, her letters reveal she was attempting to find her way amidst this morass of new ideas. Writing to Francis Watts, the professor of theology she had confided in before, she outlines feelings which indicate she is moving away from formal worship even as she grasps remnants. The conflict was torturous, an intellectual battleground. She can accept nothing as truth, she writes, "but the principle that that which is best in ethics is the only means of subjective happiness, that perfect love and purity must be the goal of my race, that only while reaching after them I can feel myself in harmony with the tendencies of creation." As she moves toward undertaking the translation of David Friedrich Strauss's *Life of Jesus,* for her a turning point, she writes as though a huge weight were removed from her. "It seems to me that the awful anticipations entailed by a reception of all the dogmas in the new Testament operate unfavourably on moral beauty by disturbing that spontaneity, that choice of the good for its own sake, that answers my ideal." She is ridding herself of a strict Calvinistic sense of a pervasive, burdensome evil. She is coming to feel she can achieve a state of grace through her own choice of the "good," the ideal, a moral life. Finally, her well-being, she reveals, rests in herself, not in some outside force which instructs her to be good by way of threatening her with awful consequences if she is not. Although Mary Ann would not become George Eliot for another fifteen years, she was extricating herself from all those elements which would have made George Eliot impossible.

Like still another young woman who would shortly join Mary Ann's circle— Elizabeth Rebecca Brabant ("Rufa")—Sara Hennell was part of that middle- or upper-middle-class segment of women who, under different circumstances, could have had satisfactory professional careers. But with virtually everything closed off to them, they fell into teaching small children or becoming governesses. Nearly eight years older than Mary Ann, Sara Hennell had been a governess, to the daughters of a prominent man, John Bonham Carter, a member of Parliament, and themselves first cousins of Florence Nightingale. At the time the latter became famous, Hilary Bonham Carter (the eldest daughter) was one of Sara's closest friends. Sara was fluent in German, conversant with art and music, well read in literature, knew some Latin, and was far more than an amateur in philosophical and theological matters. Her entrance into the circle gave Mary Ann a whiff of the really great English houses, not only in terms of manners but in terms of a wider cultural reach than she was familiar with.

"Rufa" entered Mary Ann's life in October, daughter of Dr. Robert Herbert Brabant—at one time physician to Coleridge and to Thomas Moore, the poet; but also a scholar of German and a man fearlessly interested in the new theologies. The latter, based on so-called scientific principles, became part of the "Higher Criticism" which forced a serious reevaluation of biblical studies. Rufa met Charles Hennell, who proposed, but was rejected as unsuitable by Dr. Brabant because of his weak lungs. Rufa, however, stayed in touch with Charles, who told her that a translation of Strauss's *Das Leben Jesu* into English would find a small but eager audience. Once at Rosehill, the Brays' house, Rufa stayed on for three weeks, with Charles as a visitor also.

The circle of extremely bright, intellectual, and accomplished young women and men around Mary Ann had now formed: the Brays, the Hennells, and the

Brabants. They became quite a contrast to Foleshill and the Evans group. Mary Ann did not take to Rufa at first, thinking of her as unsuitable for friendship, but then she changed her mind and Dr. Brabant's daughter became an important element in her life. Her days and weeks had now settled into something of a pattern, one that while satisfactory for the time being could not possibly hold. An explosion or change was imminent.

With both male and female friends who could reinforce her own intellectual interests, it was easier to make her peace at Foleshill with Evans. Church attendance was now a regular event for her, and she maintained silence on the inner changes. She was doing at almost twenty-three (in 1842) what many young people do rather earlier: transferring their deepest interests from family to friends when family members are clearly ignorant of the relations, uninterested, or incapable of responding. Mary Ann's family was lacking in all three areas, with the separation from family and the consequent embrace of friends exacerbating the dualism in the young woman between public and private. The element which created most dissension was the presence of the Brays. For not only were they threatening in the religious area, they maintained an open lifestyle that could be, the Evanses suspected, dangerous for a virginal and unworldly young woman. Would Bray possibly attempt to seduce her? Would she acquiesce, unsophisticated as she was? Upwardly mobile families in the 1840s did not ignore such dangerous matters.

Until she married, Isaac and Robert Evans intended to be the men in her life and to shield her from anyone who might come between them and her. Charles Bray was known for his impetuous and tempestuous interests, and such a man was not to be trusted sexually. But more than that, brothers and father were traditionally the guardian of the vestal flame; daughters were their property until they married suitably and passed over into another male domain. Surely Isaac's relentless isolation of Mary Ann throughout most of her adult life once she went off with Lewes was his revenge on a sister who rejected his protective shield. She was cast as Eve, Bray as the serpent.

The plan was clear: Evans would remove his daughter to Meriden, where she would be beyond Bray's influence. Mrs. Pears tried to intervene with Mary Ann's father, who in turn insisted it was not his doing but Isaac's. This was probably accurate, inasmuch as Evans wanted only appearances and seemed to look no further. Isaac, however, contemplated a whole range of possibilities, including the need for his sister to marry. Under the influence of the Brays, she might indeed marry, but it could be to someone who would disgrace the family: a Chartist, a Radical, a wild Dissenter, a Unitarian, even an atheist. His idea was that if she were separated from the Brays, she would attract a more agreeable sort who would fit in with the Evanses' plans. In his drive to fulfill his scheme, Isaac remained completely ignorant of what his sister was going through emotionally and intellectually, ignorant as well that such a thing as ideas or culture or artistic endeavor could have meaning in one's life. As it turned out Evans chose not to leave Coventry. Mary Ann's father in fact became more lenient once he saw that she did not voice any rebellion.

With Charles Hennell having returned to Rosehill ill, probably with incipient tuberculosis, all parties formed plans for a restorative five-day trip to Malvern and Worcester, with stops coming and going at Stratford on Avon. Somewhat inexplicably, Evans gave his permission for Mary Ann to accompany them—Cara and Charles Bray, and Sara and Charles Hennell, now well enough to travel. This occurred in May of 1843, Mary Ann having turned twenty-three the previous November. In July, the same group took a three-week trip to Wales, with Rufa Brabant joining them. Rufa and Charles became reengaged, which made the circle even tighter. The July holiday proved to be more than just intellectually exciting for Mary Ann; she appeared to be having fun, even going so far as to attend a public ball (unescorted, however). With Rufa's and Charles Hennell's marriage now set for 1 November, Mary Ann was asked to be a bridesmaid. Before the event, she left for London with Dr. Brabant, Rufa's father, then stayed at Hackney with Sara. Remaining in London past the marriage, she attended the theater, went sightseeing, and enjoyed herself with these friends far more than she ever had with her family.

The letter Mary Ann wrote from Foleshill to Sara Hennell (on 30 August 1842) indicates how her spirits had been lifted by these female associations, well before the trips she made with them. She mocks herself for speaking only of her own well-being: "Do I not live with myself and tire of myself until I have no need of metaphysics to make me believe that there is nothing certain but that *self* exists? And you after all your philosophical lectures to me, would keep me on a spot where I have already pirouetted until I am giddy, until I am one of the egotistical speakers and writers in this world of egotists." In another letter two weeks later (16? September), she comments on the portrait Cara made of her: "I should think it is like, only that here benevolence extends to the hiding of faults in my visage as well as my character." She adds that she wishes to kiss and talk to Cara, but "is afflicted with a sort of bashfulness in the early stages of correspondence, and dare not say what I would on paper." Once this bashfulness passed, she wrote voluminously, so that we must conclude her letters were becoming ways of trying out her powers of expression well before she expressed herself fictionally.

As she corresponded increasingly with Sara Hennell and Cara Bray, her letters to Maria Lewis and Martha Jackson dropped off. Her later associations began to nourish the more mature Mary Ann. This entire phase will culminate in another one of those dramatic moments in her life, when she agreed to take over from Rufa (now married to Charles Hennell) the translation into English of Strauss's *Das Leben Jesu*. While superficially this could be viewed as a piece of busyness, it was in reality part of a long movement Mary Ann made toward eventual emancipation from her father and the Evanses in general. By following this path, of associating herself through Strauss with the latest in biblical theory, she was able to practice a kind of substitute liberation, aside from the money she earned.

When we regard the Victorian age retrospectively, we tend to observe an era in which troubles, anguish, and anxieties are brushed away or somehow resolved.

The surface seems quite negotiable, at least for those who have achieved middle-class status. Yet outward signs are misleading. And while even artisans and laborers appeared to have a place, in many instances they lived without any sense of security. For example, the smallest rise in the price of bread, a staple, or a lowering of wages (when machinery was introduced) could wipe out entire families, even entire villages. The headlong dash to the cities continued,* while country people—laboring and agricultural—found themselves torn, holding on to the land even as the younger people fled for industrial jobs. The lower classes filled the huge need for servants. Migration from rural areas to towns and cities, rising prices for foodstuffs, periodic cycles of unemployment, and financial downturns made the times turbulent. While religion appeared to have played a calming role, the uncertainties and difficulties could not be disguised. As Disraeli, Carlyle, Ruskin, Dickens, Mrs. Gaskell, and several other commentators would note, society was slowly becoming dualistic, made up of haves and have-nots: the "two Englands" that Disraeli wrote of in the 1840s. And while continental and, especially, French-style revolutions were not the order of business, there were cycles of violence, as we saw in the preceding chapter with the Peterloo Massacre, then with Captain Swing's attacks on farm machinery, the burning of property, and even earlier the Luddite attacks on industrial machinery; and there were cycles of warnings from political leaders that the lower classes were explosive. The Chartist movement in the 1830s and 1840s mainly to gain the (male) franchise was just such a potentially explosive movement.

Reading England through Mary Ann's eyes, we can perceive how fragile and frail the Victorian balancing act really was. Public policy and private needs did not by any means coordinate; and England's preeminence, until the emergence of the Prussian state after the Franco-Prussian War of 1870, disguised a badly divided body politic and a class-ridden, caste-conscious society of enormous inequalities and injustices. The position of women in this society, as legally second-class citizens in virtually every respect until well after the middle of the century, is only one area where injustice ruled. A few middle- and upper-middle-class women escaped and flourished, but one cannot extrapolate generally from that, as some commentators have done. The control exerted by the Church of England and its bishops sitting in the House of Lords, the continued election of a disproportionate number of upperclassmen to the House of Commons, the still closed-off Oxford and Cambridge to women candidates, the required swearing to the Thirty-nine Articles of the Church of England for graduation from the universities, the presence of dual justice systems in the courts, one for the rich and well placed and another for the poor—these and several other factors all pulled the country apart, of which Church of England adherents and Dissenters were only the most visible divisive elements. Going far deeper than a break from the established church, Dissent entered into every area where injustice reigned in favor of landowners and their representatives in the Commons.

---

*Manchester gained 66,000 people in the decade from 1821 to 1831; by mid-century, it had quadrupled from what it was in 1801 (75,000). Coventry more than doubled between 1801 and 1851; the same was true of Nottingham. Birmingham tripled, and Liverpool increased about fivefold. These figures were well ahead of the general population increase, which was twofold.

All this was paraded before Mary Ann as eminent men visited the Brays' household, and talk ranged over the entire state of English life. Technology was not ignored. While England publicly gloried in its technological advances—with the Great Exhibition in the Crystal Palace in 1851 as a most conspicuous example—technology was a divisive force. Inexorable, it could not be reined in, of course. Yet it was a force to break up stable communities and subsocieties, in small villages and towns. It did lead to extremely squalid conditions in urban housing, to poor sanitation and hygiene, to urban malaise. It led to armies of prostitutes, an unbalancing of social elements, the creation of a permanent underclass. Its uncertainties and anxieties led to large numbers of people who could not adapt, who self-destructed, whether in alcoholism or in crime.

Crime was itself a growth industry in the larger towns and in the cities, and streets in urban areas were as prone to violence as we now say American cities are. Technology was a revolution which required a revolution in social planning; but when that was not forthcoming, England by the 1830s had begun that long retreat into subcultures, into unbalanced and unequal forces determined by birth. Class and caste distinctions which in the past had defined one's place now defined one's disadvantages. The ethics of work itself, so nostalgically portrayed in Adam Bede or in Caleb Garth, or even in Felix Holt's watch repair and Silas Marner's weaving, had to be found in past eras. By mid-century, Disraeli identified the split: a disaffected, potentially explosive lower class; an uncaring, indifferent upper class; and a self-serving middle class embracing the very technology that was proving so culturally divisive.

Eliot's role here was conservative and, to some limited extent, regressive. As we observe Mary Ann moving toward her own emancipation and emergence, we must also note how conservative she was becoming in her social and ethical attitudes. Her aim as a writer was not to embrace the new, *but to make the reader see how the new could seduce and corrupt.* She introduced moral decisiveness as a way of controlling a society in which self-interest was veering out of control, while the church remained indifferent or ignorant. Even though she recognized how change made the old ways increasingly difficult, her goal in all her books was to conserve. Early on, however, as she associated herself with the Brays and the Hennells, she found herself riding with the new, the uncertain, even the trendy. But while she identified with their quest, certainly in their desire for an open, more just society, she still insisted on individual responsibility, the social contract, the orderly state.

The key was Charles Bray, physically attractive, full of sweeping ideas, and at thirty-one far more worldly than the studious Mary Ann. And yet we must emphasize that she dug in her heels and refused total acceptance of his world. She hung back, as she did later when she was infatuated with the dashing, interesting publisher John Chapman. Although she insisted on duty, she knew none of it would come easily; none of it did come easily to her, since personal gratification was never distant from her mind.

Mary Ann's development in the early 1840s was taking her into seemingly contradictory worlds. Like Dickens and Ruskin, she was appalled at a mechanistic view of society, although she eschewed blunt satire or burlesque. She saw that man's best instincts, attitudes, and outlook are associated with nature. Once her Calvinism began to recede, she held to the Rousseauistic belief in natural man: not a primitive, not a noble savage, but a man who textures his existence with natural phenomena in mind. While antithetical to her early views of man's innate evil, her more mature outlook carried her into another kind of awareness. Her gradual shift was surely led on by her associations in the Bray home and by her reading of Rousseau's *Autobiography* and, of course, the English Romantic poets.

All this, in 1843, was in the making. In the meantime, Mary Ann had formed several relationships of considerable weight in her life. Charles Bray remained fascinating, perhaps one of her "early loves," and surely a man she enjoyed being close to. In his darting way, he was a different creature from the stolid Mary Ann; but he was interested in such a variety of social and personal improvements that she had to race in order to keep up with his ideas. Then still another man confused and expanded her life, a man only ten years younger than her father—Rufa's father, Dr. Brabant, Charles Hennell's father-in-law. He was himself married when Mary Ann met him, as were nearly all the men she came close to for the next four decades.

4

<hr>

Who Was She?

"Deep, unspeakable suffering may well be called baptism, a regeneration, the initiation into a new state."

When Mary Ann started to become familiar with Dr. Brabant, she was in
the middle of her rebelliousness against traditional explanations of God
and religion, although outwardly conforming to them. During the trip she took
with Rufa and Sara Hennell to Wales in July 1843, Dr. Brabant joined them in
Swansea. The entire question of Mary Ann's relationship to Dr. Brabant, married, with Rufa as his sole child, is inconclusive and problematic. Both Cross
and Haight feel that there was nothing intimate between them, certainly understandable in Cross's case. But the indications are that while their relationship
may well have stopped short of physical consummation, they were often in a
husband-and-wife understanding. Dr. Brabant was a retired medical doctor who
was now free to pursue his real interests: investigations into the origins of Christianity and other theological matters. It was, in fact, this intense interest which
brought him together with the author of *An Inquiry into the Origins of Christianity*, Charles Hennell, and that in turn led to Hennell's marriage to Rufa. Mary
Ann was entreated to stay with the Brabants, husband and wife, in Devizes (in
Wiltshire, not far from Stonehenge) after her trip to Wales.

Dr. Brabant complained that having become used to the presence of his
daughter, he was lost without her, implying that he felt rejuvenated by young
people and Mary Ann could help him to live. She agreed to join him as a
research assistant. The implication so far is that she was foreshadowing her portrayal of Dorothea in *Middlemarch*, who with her desire to devote herself to some
higher calling focuses on Edward Casaubon, a parchment-dry scholar, as her
form of self-sacrifice. But Casaubon proves a very old forty-seven, and Dorothea's quest for martyrdom and service brings unhappiness, disappointment, and
sexual frustration.

Brabant, however, was a very young sixty-three, full of energy and bounce, and not a model for Casaubon. Evidence of Mary Ann's association with the doctor indicates considerable pleasure. She listened to his every word, and although later she perceived his lack of weight and high seriousness, for the time she entered eagerly into his ideas. There is another side, which is that as Robert Evans declined in health and seemed intellectually so far removed from his daughter, she responded to an older man who, as it were, spoke her language. The doctor was seeking at least a daughter; the daughter was seeking another father figure whom she could respect.

What makes the relationship so problematical—and Mrs. Brabant perceived more was at stake than a research assistant with her mentor—was that Mary Ann craved affection from or closeness to a male figure. When she was with Brabant, they apparently closed out the world; they walked with arms or hands clasped, conversing in German. For Brabant, the appearance of Mary Ann, with her high intelligence and enthusiasm for knowledge, gratified a sizable ego.

While Brabant doted, his (now blind) wife fumed, and Mary Ann was driven from the house and led to believe she could not return. Mrs. Brabant threatened to leave if the young woman ever reentered. What the older woman felt remains in shadows; but apparently the intimacy between Mary Ann, seeking affection, and the older man, whose ego was being stroked, took on the semblance of something far more than daughter figure and father figure. Given her need for passionate attachments, her exclusion from her father and brother and their world, and Brabant's susceptibility to his young companion, it is possible that a physical union was contemplated or even took place. But the opposite could also be argued: that Mary Ann with her sense she could not injure another, the fact she was the Brabants' guest, her awareness that her act could set off an entire chain of unacceptable consequences, all would mitigate against anything as socially rebellious as a sexual union with this man. That both flirted with the idea seems quite possible; that they went ahead will always remain unclear. Whatever occurred, Mary Ann became persona non grata.

John Chapman noted the episode in his diary (27 June 1851):

> . . . his [Brabant's] Sister-in-law, Miss S. Hughes, became alarmed, made a great stir, excited the jealousy of Mrs. Brabant. Miss Evans left. Mrs. B. vowed she should never enter the house again, or that if she did, she, Mrs. Brabant, would instantly leave it. Mrs. Hennell [Rufa] says Dr. B. acted ungenerously and worse toward Miss E., for though he was the chief cause of all that passed, he acted towards her as though the fault lay with her alone. His unmanliness in the affair was condemned more by Mrs. Hennell than by Miss Evans herself when she (a year ago) related the circumstances to me.

Lacking Brabant, she still had Charles Bray, also married. We observe a definite pattern beginning, in that her deepest associations with men, except with Herbert Spencer, were with married men, continuing past Bray and Brabant to

John Chapman and then to Lewes. Married men were older and had a more settled quality to their lives, and were, in the case of Bray and Brabant, more focused on ideas. But the attraction seemed to be located on other grounds: we must not exclude the possibility of danger. Part of this pursuit of married men, or deep attraction to them, can be ascribed to Mary Ann's dualism: that abiding desire to follow the rules, defer to traditional values, forge ahead with a personal morality, as against the pull toward an as yet unfocused rebelliousness, a still unshaped self-definition. Each married man became a stage in that dual movement, carrying her closer to the point at which she discovered what she could do best.

In *Middlemarch*, Dorothea becomes an apt pupil of Mary Ann's earlier twin selves. She throws herself into a marriage with a much older man, not ever married, but even worse, a man who is not marriageable. This she does for the sake of connecting herself to someone who, she believes, will achieve greatness. But there is also the part of herself which can become attached to Will Ladislaw, who through no fault of his own is not socially acceptable and who is perceived as dangerous and unsuitable. The suppression of feeling in her marriage to Casaubon runs parallel to her desire for release and liberation that would come in a union with Will. Although Dorothea is a fully fashioned character, one possible criticism we can make of her is that these two disparate selves are not psychologically connected. They were, apparently, "halves" Eliot found difficult to resolve personally; and in this respect, she reflected nineteenth-century ambiguities, the surface of respectability, the subsurface of quite anomalous behavior.

In the world of 1843, Charles Bray remained endlessly fascinating. Besides his extraordinary, handsome appearance—his features made him look Byronic, so that he was known as the Don Juan of Coventry—he had an inquiring mind. His pursuits were more superficial than Mary Ann would eventually respect, but his sheer range was dazzling. In 1841, just before he met Mary Ann, he had published a very ambitious study which intended nothing less than to locate man's place in creation, to measure the qualities of his mind, to discover where he had gone and where he would head. The title was as ambitious as the contents proved to be: *The Philosophy of Necessity: or, The Law of Consequences, As Applicable to Mental, Moral, and Social Science.* By the time of this publication, Bray was already the author of two books on education, *Address to the Working Classes on the Education of the Body* (1837) and *The Education of the Feelings* (1838). With seemingly unlimited energy, optimism, and idealism, added to his reputation as a philanderer, he roamed the economic and social face of England seeking change.

Bray had been profoundly influenced by the social philosophy of the reformer Robert Owen. Owen was a British social planner, not unlike what Bray was himself to become. His most famous innovation was an attempt at cooperative living in New Lanark, Scotland, in 1800. He bought mills there, reconstructed the community, instituted cooperative economic and social life, established schools, and treated workers as equals, not as industrial slaves. Owen also demonstrated that such cooperative ventures could be capitalistically valid, and his fortunes waxed. Once New Lanark became famous, it was extended to New Harmony, Indiana, but it failed there because of disagreement among the workers. Owen became increasingly "radical," as perceived in early-nineteenth-century terms, and opposed religion and religious teaching. Seeking more than reform, he wanted to transform society, in some ways an early Marxist who saw in inequality and in a poverty class the signs of a corrupt society. His advocacy, however, was peaceful, not part of the sporadic violence which entered into British society. He believed that broader environmental change would bring about individual change. A society of good men, in this regard, could be created through cooperation, and class and caste differences would be effaced.

When Mary Ann met Bray, the latter was very clearly an Owenite, holding ideas that were anathema to Robert Evans and the entire Evans clan, as well as their immediate circle of middle-class successes and churchgoers. In several ways, the Owen experiments were adaptations of Christian principles aimed at democracy, justice, cooperation, and social and economic evenhandedness; but in practice, Owen and his ideas were viewed as dangerous threats to a Christian society, as secular subversions of church doctrines. Bray's co-opting of Owen's ideas came in his attempt to base the silk-ribbon factory he inherited from his father on principles of worker equality and profit sharing. Profits, however, fell, and Bray's plan failed, as did his factory.

Another of Bray's reforms was to wean workers away from the local pubs and into a Working Men's Club, which featured a reading room and a temperance bar; but the workers were not to be tempted from their traditional pleasures, and that idea went under also. Bray, however, was undiscouraged by failure, and he tinkered with Owenite principles trying to find a successful mix. One of the reasons he failed, while Owen succeeded, was that Bray was primarily an idea man, not an administrator or manager, and not someone who would follow up on a given plan. In several respects, he foreshadowed another idea man in Eliot's life, the publisher John Chapman.

Bray next established the Coventry Labourers and Artisan's Co-operative Society. He recognized that weavers in this cloth-oriented city had few opportunities for leisure which did not lead to personal destruction; and to them he offered a garden club, an opportunity to take advantage of the outdoors in their free time. That failed to work also, since the weavers and their like—as Eliot showed in *Silas Marner*—were so enervated by the end of their workweek that gardening was viewed as simply another chore. Then preceding by one year another Owen enterprise, the establishment of a cooperative store on Toad Lane in Rochdale, Bray created one in Coventry. The idea was splendid and timely, but it required management; and while Owen's Lancashire enterprise entered history, Bray's Coventry venture went bankrupt when the city's merchants united against what they perceived as a threat to their own business. Bray's plan was to offer workers merchandise at far lower prices than the local merchants, to enable the worker to hold on to more of his money.

Spinning off still another scheme, Bray organized an infant school, and this succeeded, possibly because it did not require the degree of management associated with moneymaking enterprises. In each of the failures, incidentally, Bray picked up the bill. When he turned to writing books, in 1837 and 1838, they too were ignored. The books, we note in retrospect, were part of that very popular nineteenth-century genre called self-help (in America, Horatio Alger), culminating in the treacly but enormously influential books of Samuel Smiles: *Self-Help, Character, Thrift,* and *Duty.* Bray's aim, while he attempted to change the environment in which workers lived, was paralleled by his effort to alter individual lives through books and education, as well as giving them more social and economic opportunities.

For all of Bray's philandering—perhaps as much by reputation as in practice—Mary Ann saw him as a good man. His ideals for a better society crossed with her own still-forming plans for bettering individuals. But Bray had other interests which were less sound. While even his ameliorative ideas made him seem a crackpot to those outside his circle, his other interests, such as his growing preoccupation with mesmerism or hypnotism, really made him suspect. Bray had always been interested in the physical sciences, but here, as part of that scientific world, he held a mystical belief in fluids flowing from the stars into supervised subjects. The fluid which energized the universe, he believed, could be directed, by a trained practitioner, into the hand of a subject, who would then fall asleep and awake recuperated from whatever afflicted him or her. Dickens, as we know, was also caught up in mesmerism.

It appealed to Bray for a variety of reasons: it gave him a source of power which he could manipulate; but even more, it permitted him access, he thought, into a person's mind, into what later came to be called the preconscious (subconscious) or even the unconscious. The so-called restorative power of mesmerism he left to others to determine; but he felt that if he could gain access to others' minds, he could with intimate examples reinforce his philosophical ideas. When Bray attempted to practice this "new science" on Mary Ann, he could not get past her strong character and needed an expert to put her to sleep. Cara reports that Mary Ann asked to be awakened and found the entire experience so unpleasant she never again permitted it.

Then Bray fell into phrenology. Once again, he became an enthusiast—Mary Ann would eventually tire of his childlike glee at each discovery—and thought that if he could read the skulls of children he could educate them more effectively. He also thought, like the later Italian criminologist Cesare Lombroso, that criminals could be more readily identified in their pre-criminal days. Toward this end, Bray, not one to shrink from practical knowledge as well as theory, had his head shaved and a plaster cast made of his skull, thus using the person he thought he knew best. Once he had established some knowledge of phrenology, he became an advocate of the pseudo-science and gave several lectures in and around Coventry. He even gathered some criminal heads together and rode around the countryside offering them as evidence of how bump reading could be translated into character reading, and eventually into social policy.

While Bray's intentions seem to have been good, to identify slower children so that their education could be improved and to identify criminal types before they committed crimes, the overall effect of such typecasting was pernicious. In another sense, the use of phrenological evidence reveals how Bray, despite his interest in mesmerism, sought empirical knowledge, and how he subverted mystery and tried to replace it with what he thought was something conclusive. It was this tendency which also eventually alienated Mary Ann, as she insisted that mysteries lay at the heart of every act, every choice, every interaction between man and environment.

Just as Mary Ann had agreed to be hypnotized, so she agreed to have her head examined for bumps. Bray apparently welcomed visitors to Rosehill with an examination of their skulls. She entered into it quite willingly, becoming for a time an advocate of phrenology. She attended phrenology classes with Bray, sessions taught by Cornelius Donovan, who had set himself up as an organologist. She also agreed to have her head cast, * without the shaving, and her cast turned out to be particularly large. Imaginative powers, moral regulating faculties, protective faculties, domestic affections, observing faculties, knowing faculties, and reflecting faculties were all assessed and a diagnosis made.

Part of her willingness to subject herself to this mishmash was connected to Bray's enthusiasm. Part was associated, we can speculate, with her uncertainty as to what she believed as she moved from earlier certainties toward unknowns. We must never underestimate the central place religion held in English life, or in Mary Ann herself; its loss left a huge vacuum. Another part was her desire to become involved in what appeared to be an exciting new discipline. Still another part, however, was mysterious, in which, despite her intellectuality and seeming caution, she was daring and even audacious below the surface. Bray and his concoctions represented that other side to her, which wanted to throw herself into events, movements, people themselves, which demanded new territories and the exploration of possibilities for the unusual woman she believed herself to be.

She underwent Bray's examination, and much later, near the end of his life, he reported his findings. But his revelations, which he insisted were contemporaneous with the casting, were surely based on his retrospective knowledge of Mary Ann's transformation into George Eliot. He cited her as having a dominant intellect, with a balance between her moral attitudes and her sexual feelings and needs. From this reading of her character, Bray concluded that without a succession of men, culminating in Lewes, Mary Ann would not have been transformed into George Eliot. The glimmer of truth in this should not blind us to the fact that she had started on a course of rebellion and liberation well before she met a series of (married) men, who did indeed reinforce what she was.

In these early 1840s relationships, Mary Ann was experiencing the different ways marriages were constituted, the perils embraced or denied. Bray and Cara had what we would now call an open marriage. He said that each must find his

---

* If we wonder how the future George Eliot could tolerate such hocus-pocus, we must remember, as touched upon above, that medical science as a whole in the period—and extending well beyond— was mainly hocus-pocus. No serious illness could be treated except in a general way, with no real connection between diagnosis and treatment.

and her own mode of life; what was suitable for one did not carry over to the other. Self-expression was all. Cara agreed, but in the nineteenth century when the woman agreed, it usually meant the man was freed, while she remained faithful and understanding. Not so here, as we shall see. With all his talk of equality, justice, and fair play, Bray was also a man of his times, and he formed a liaison with the Rosehill cook, who proceeded to bear him six children. But there was more to come, and we might find it remarkable how Bray's actions foreshadowed what occurred with George Henry Lewes, Lewes's wife, and her liaison with Thornton Hunt, whom she bore four children. Since Cara could not get pregnant, Bray convinced her to "adopt" his daughter by Hannah, named Elinor Mary, into their household, with Hannah herself retained now not as cook but as nursemaid. Cara accepted this, but was not receptive when Hannah subsequently gave birth to a son, named Charles, after Bray himself, who was then introduced into Rosehill. With this, Hannah was expelled from the house, but not from Bray's affections. She was established nearby, as Mrs. Charles Gray, whose husband was a traveling man. The disguise fooled few, but it fulfilled the conditions of marriage Cara decided to live with.

But while many Victorian wives tolerated this situation, Cara took Bray's words to heart and had her own liaison, although exactly how far it went we cannot determine. Although Bray was known as the Don Juan of Coventry, Cara found someone who was actually related to Byron, Edward Henry Noel. Noel had a consumptive wife and three children, plus an estate on a Greek island; he was well traveled, a poet and a translator (from German). When the consumptive wife died, Noel looked increasingly to Cara, who helped him with his children and, possibly, became intimately involved with him, if she had not already done so earlier. While Bray had Hannah and their six illegitimate children, Cara had Noel, himself illegitimate, and his three children.

What all this meant to Mary Ann was that she observed alternate forms of marriage, clearly precursors to her own "marriage" to Lewes. She was, by now, very fond of Cara, and especially of Bray, and discovered in their socially unacceptable style of life something very attractive. Their relationships fitted into the side of Mary Ann which rebelled, the side which demanded a reshaping of self and an identity of its own. It was that other side which connected to imagination and gave her the material that would nourish her later work.

Bray's influence, then, extended deeply over Mary Ann not only in terms of feeling, but in style, enthusiasms, ways to live. How far their intimacy went we cannot tell; and not unusually, John Cross turns the "affair" into a learning experience for Mary Ann. But there are some indications, from Cara and others, that the relationship went further, especially since all letters from Mary Ann to Bray before 1848 have vanished. Yet the argument against a consummated affair involves Mary Ann's regard for Cara and her desire not to exacerbate an already painful situation. It was not easy being married to the Don Juan of Coventry, leaving aside Hannah's six children. Further, there is the fact of Bray's own silence on the matter when he was a man who talked openly of all aspects of his life. We do know that he spoke of his sex life to George Combe, the author of the study of phrenology which so impressed him. Bray opened up his background, starting at twelve, when, like any well-placed young man, he was "seduced" by a servant; and from there on, except for some periods of abstinence, he indulged what was to be an active sexual life. His not having mentioned Mary Ann, who would have been considered in retrospect a considerable conquest, leads us to assume Bray's relationship with her stopped short of sexual intimacy. Combe, incidentally, kept track of all this material in a secretly coded notebook, whose arcane notations were only recently broken.

If we assume no such intimacy did occur, it was very probably on the minds of both parties. By now, in 1843, when Mary Ann was twenty-four, she may have still been a virgin, but she was not innocent. Having observed her friends and having experienced her own conflicting passions with Dr. Brabant, she may not have been a combatant, but she was prepared for whatever might arise. The year 1843 was a time of magnificent turmoil for the young woman, and we could, if we wished, see it as one of those pivotal years in the life of a creative artist. For not only was she being initiated into attractive alternate lifestyles, not only was her tolerance being opened up, not only was she herself acting out some of her newly found ideas, but she was taking up political positions that were anathema to the male Evanses. One of the most controversial and divisive issues was concerned with prices placed on bread, which was at the heart of the Corn Laws. It was divisive because it called into question nearly every dimension of a class- and caste-oriented society. It was, for many, quite simply a life-and-death issue*; for others, it became symbolic of an ordered, traditional society which assumed class privileges.

As the issue developed and became more intense in the 1840s, Mary Ann opposed the Evans position on the Corn Laws and sided with Bray and with his friend, the social reformer Robert Owen. Owen, Bray, John Bright,† and Richard Cobden were all actively part of the Anti–Corn Law League, with Bray becoming chairman of the local branch. The question was the price of bread, which by the Act of 1815 was kept unusually high. The plan of the Tory government was to maintain an artificially inflated price to forestall an economic downturn when the Napoleonic Wars ended. This artificially maintained price severely hurt consumers, especially the working classes, and benefited those at the upper end of the economic scale. But manufacturers themselves saw that such prices were in effect a subsidization of agriculture and this undermined industrialization. Under the pressure of such forces and the opposition of the Anti–Corn Law League (founded by John Bright), the Conservative govern-

---

* Bread was the staple of most farm laborers and working people, with consumption at about 2 pounds a day (based on 1862 figures of 14½ pounds a week). With bread so central, butter also, more than meat, became very important, even as urbanization led to a decline in milk production. The working classes, then, were suffering from high bread prices and reduced butter production, the loss of basic sustenance.

† Bright's career is instructive because it followed inner dictates, not political expediency, and, like Eliot's own positions, contained several seeming contradictions. A laissez-faire capitalist, he advocated parliamentary reform, for example, which eventually extended the male franchise at a time when he was himself opposed to government intervention to help the poor.

ment of Robert Peel worked to repeal the Corn Laws, although men like Disraeli and Lord George Bentinck in the Conservative Party did not really accept Peel's large gesture. While the immediate situation was alleviated somewhat with the repeal of the Corn Laws, the price of bread nevertheless remained a political issue throughout the century and into the twentieth century as well.

Mary Ann's positioning of herself here was highly significant for her later development, in that she became a novelist of the working man (not of the marginally poor, however), at least in her early fiction and then in *Felix Holt*. Those who see George Eliot in the line of Jane Austen ignore the enormous difference in emphasis between the two writers. Austen came from gentry, Eliot from the working class which reached into the middle range. When Austen in *Emma* values a farmer, he becomes suitable as the husband of the lesser character. Eliot revelled in farmers and workers—the Bedes, Tullivers, Garths, Marner, and Felix Holt, among others.

Mary Ann absorbed this Rosehill euphoria for social change in the company of some of the leading reformers of the day, Richard Cobden and John Bright, not to mention the egalitarian Jacob Bright, John's brother, an M.P. who favored an entire range of women's issues. Without accepting everything, she entered into the Corn Law agitation and agreed with several proposals designed to ease the condition of women: marriage rights, divorce rights (under existing law, a divorce had to go through parliamentary procedures), and birth control— a woman's right to insist on birth control measures, at a time when death during childbirth for the mother was a phenomenally high statistic.

One issue that caught Mary Ann's imagination—and was almost as volatile as marriage and divorce—was the temperance movement. Many social reformers believed that alcohol was preventing the laboring classes from advancing their interests, and that the government favored free access to spirits as a way of controlling the lower classes. Bray was also involved in this movement, as in everything else, although he did not himself abstain. But so passionate were the meetings, so compelling the arguments for abstinence and for social improvement through denial, that Bray worked up great enthusiasm, as did Mary Ann in short bursts. After a particular lecture, she signed the register indicating her support of the temperance movement, even though, like Bray, she had no intention of giving up alcohol when it pleased her to drink. She never took the pledge of abstinence, but, unlike the Irish home-rule issue, this one took sufficiently strong hold of her that her major characters rarely drink. Even on family occasions and in holiday celebrations, there is little if any alcohol consumed in her novels, and then almost never by key figures. *

Mary Ann was not seeking suppression, but release. While she was moving toward full rebellion from her background, she nevertheless began to perceive that Bray's social reforms were inadequate, especially in terms of individual

---

* Molly in *Silas Marner* and Dempster in "Janet's Repentance" (*Scenes of Clerical Life*) are not central; nor is Adam Bede's father in that novel, or any of the characters who hang around the pubs during election time in *Felix Holt*. Only in *Middlemarch* does alcohol become pivotal, in Raffles's death, but he, too, is minor.

change. Much of what he stood for could be called noblesse oblige, in which upper-middle-class people like himself became involved in philanthropies and charities. His change would come from the top, or from changing the environment. Mary Ann wanted deeper, more internalized action. As a convert of sorts, a rebel, an anti-Evansite, she sought out European solutions, such as Strauss's in biblical studies and then Comte's in social and political areas. Ever fervent, she transferred her evangelical enthusiasms, although these phases, too, would pass and she would become a considered moderate. Her final resting place was the individual who internalized everything.

As she focused more clearly on Bray, it became evident that in her relationships with men, she had to triumph, as it were, over each before emerging as her own woman; and in each instance, she had to do so while outraging traditional social norms. Like Jane Eyre in the Brontë novel, she "used" men as signal posts for moving on, from Bray and Brabant to Chapman, to Herbert Spencer (whose uncle, the Reverend Thomas Spencer, had lectured at the temperance movement meeting that so moved Mary Ann), and, finally, to George Henry Lewes. That all the men were "outside" in one sense or another is additionally compelling.

Near the end of her stay at the Brabant home in Devizes, after Rufa's wedding to Charles, Mary Ann wrote (on 24 November 1843) to Cara in somewhat compromising terms. She told her friend: "Dr Brabant spoils me for every one else, and the Trennung [parting or severing] from such a companion will be very painful. . . . Beautifully sincere, conscientious and benevolent and everything besides that one would have one's friends to be." Just before writing those lines and ruing the severing, she says: "I shall miss, too, being told [by the phrenologist Cornelius Donovan] that I have some very bad propensities and that my moral and animal regions are unfortunately balanced, all which is too true to be heard with calmness." There is little question the forced departure upset her, although she appears to have recovered rapidly once she began to translate David Friedrich Strauss's *Das Leben Jesu* into English.

The translation work came about in January 1844, as an exchange among friends.* The groundbreaking Strauss book established a fairly lengthy trail in England. Its translation was first advocated by the Radical politician Joseph Parkes, who later on, despite his reformist politics and advanced views, did not take kindly to Mary Ann's morals. Parkes asked Charles Hennell (then known as the author of the *Inquiry*, which fitted well into Strauss's "natural" view of Jesus) to find a translator, and he, Parkes, would contribute to the cost. The Strauss effort to demystify Jesus took on political implications with the introduction of Parkes into it, inasmuch as the latter was not concerned with religious interpretation but with an undermining of belief itself. Charles in turn asked his sister Sara, who found it too difficult, and she then asked Rufa Brabant to try it.

* At this time, Mary Ann was translating Latin passages from Part I of Spinoza's *Ethics* for Charles Bray, for use in his *Autobiography*. She also considered translating Rodolphe Alexandre Binet's *Mémoire*, whose subtitle was "In Favor of the Freedom of Cults," considered an important book then. Mary Ann did not proceed with this project.

Rufa felt that the translation could be a collaboration, with her father helping and even Sara pitching in when the going became thorny. Sara did agree to revise the final manuscript. Rufa was also to find the project too much for her, and she had recently been married as well; so she suggested to Sara that Mary Ann take over the entire translation, which was two very hefty volumes in what was a very thickly textured German. Rufa had worked through 257 pages before turning to Mary Ann. Both Sara and Cara believed their friend would "do it admirably," as Sara wrote. "She will require correcting in a few words and minor matters, but she will give the meaning faithfully and spiritedly. . . . And she will get on fast, which is a great thing."

Strauss proved a daunting but most valuable experience. His attempt to find a way between a miraculous interpretation of Jesus' deeds and a rationalistic one which denied their divinity brought him to a mythological explanation. Through this, he could preserve the "historical Jesus," but also place him in perspective and thus subject him to an evolutionary process. We should not underestimate the impact of Strauss, not only on Eliot, but on following generations.

At the time of her undertaking, Mary Ann's German was not fluent. Later, with her additional translation of Ludwig Feuerbach and further application to the language, her fluency increased. Of some importance is her willingness to undertake a long and difficult project in which she could foresee problems—not only with vocabulary but with intricate, convoluted constructions and passages that did not lend themselves to translation. Her receptivity to the project, which could potentially prove tedious and unrewarding, must be connected to how she saw herself at the time. Even as her ideas were shifting and broadening, she found herself drifting intellectually, without any firm anchor in achievement. Moving toward twenty-five, she had only proven her ability to absorb and synthesize enormous amounts of difficult material. The translation, whatever her shortcomings in the language, gave her the opportunity to prove herself to herself, and also helped her understand her own changing attitudes toward religious belief.

We note that while Mary Ann was prepared to move rapidly into the new and explore unknown territories socially and theologically, she was not altogether comfortable with innovation, experimentation, or even change. As part of the dualism in her, she felt the strong tug of custom, and she remained suspicious of process and progress, without being able to resist them. Questioning technological wonders which led to individual leisure, she wrote in *Adam Bede* one of her most caustic lines: "Even idleness is eager now—eager for amusement: prone to excursion-trains, art-museums, periodical literature, and exciting novels; prone to scientific theorising, and cursory peeps through microscopes."

Not unusually, she saw her world as "words." She would write later of those ordinary words we must fall back upon, what she calls "unimposing words," such as *light, sound, stars, music*—"words really not worth looking at, or hearing, in themselves, any more than 'chips' or 'sawdust'. . . ." In their ordinariness, however, they happen to be "great and beautiful" because they stir "the long-winding fibres of your memory" and enrich "your present with your most precious past." The foreshadowing of certain elements in Proust which blend past and present is uncanny, but not because Eliot was as artistically self-conscious as Proust. Instead, she sensed that words carry deep meanings which go well beyond their sense in a particular context. She experienced language as profoundly linked to a whole range of feelings which carry us back into our personal histories. Such moments reach deeply into the preconscious and unconscious, into those areas where language and experience become inextricable. Eliot conjures up those key words as part of a human history which only the fiction writer can recall—or, at least, until analysis brought such words out in a therapeutic setting.

This, too, was part of Mary Ann's and Eliot's dualism. The conjunction of these two sides of her was particularly acute as she poured over the 1,500 pages of Strauss's German, inset with quotations in Hebrew, Greek, and Latin—at a time when she did not know Hebrew. To bring the material under control, she needed a rigid disciplining of her time and of her day. Having set six pages a day as her goal—she figured an hour or two per page—she could not keep up the pace and eventually took two years to complete the translation. While not a pleasant task, it represented something she could not forsake. Not only had she taken it on trust from her friends, she was now doing something that would see print. Her correspondence becomes sparser, much of it devoted to the translation itself. She did find time to attend the Daniel O'Connell demonstration, on 18 March 1844, in favor of Irish home rule, a demonstration which got so out of hand the Coventry police were called in.

During 1844 and 1845, she sent on pages of the translation to Sara and Rufa for their judgment and was encouraged by their support and praise. She also found time to have dinner with the Brays, where she was introduced to Harriet Martineau, a distant cousin of Cara's by marriage. George Eliot would have an on-again, off-again relationship with Martineau, as the younger woman came to outdistance Martineau in fame and influence. But at the time of the meeting, Harriet Martineau was established as a journalist and novelist, her fame extending to America. Her journalism was progressive and socially oriented, manifesting her interest in several of the popular and controversial issues of the day: population control, working-class education, and trade unionism. Martineau advocated broad education so that unmarried women, like herself, could be self-sustaining. She was best known in the 1840s, however, for her work in economics. In 1832–34, she published nine volumes of *Illustrations of Political Economy*, and in 1834, *Illustrations of Taxation*, which explained to the layman various theories of political economy.

This was only part of her output by 1845, when she was forty-three, since she also wrote extensively about travel,* a novel (*Deerbrook*, 1841), for which she

---

* Her eight-hundred-page *Society in America* was deemed by Dickens to be the best book written on America, and strongly affected his own views when he came to write his study of American mores.

had little talent, and four volumes of children's tales (*The Playfellow*, 1841). She would also write on mesmerism and then do a critical examination of the positivist Comte (who in time had a considerable influence on Mary Ann), a study called *The Positive Philosophy of Auguste Comte* (1853). Her *Autobiography*, in 1877, contained commentaries on several contemporaries, like John Chapman, who crossed Mary Ann's life. Her circle of friends and acquaintances included, among others, Charlotte Brontë, Florence Nightingale, Darwin, John Stuart Mill and Harriet Taylor, Coleridge, and, of course, Eliot.

Martineau showed herself to be a woman of considerable determination, for she came from a provincial background, was self-educated, and suffered from almost total deafness. She could barely hear even with a large trumpet at her ear. This ungainly device, thrust into people's faces, guaranteed that suitors would be frightened off—a point worth mentioning because all of these qualities, including spinsterhood, finally endeared her to Mary Ann, who felt she was in the presence of true greatness. Further, Martineau's interest in mesmerism, the major topic of that particular dinner party at Rosehill, reinforced Bray's application to it and even led Mary Ann, as mentioned above, to be mesmerized. Martineau's extensive medical problems had been gynecologically associated, and these, she asserted, had been cured by mesmerism.

Bray had immediately wanted to check Martineau's skull phrenologically, and, reports have it, came away disappointed that her head revealed nothing special. Mary Ann's major interest was less in bumps than in what was inside the skull, and particularly what made Martineau so successful in journalism. For it occurred to Mary Ann at this dinner party, fateful in its way, that journalism might provide a source of income and, with that, a measure of independence. Martineau had written articles for the *Monthly Repository*, a publication of little standing, but then moved to the *Westminster Review*, one of the premier periodicals of the nineteenth century. This part fascinated Mary Ann, especially Martineau's assessment of her career, that to make it work she had had to leave her native Norwich and head for London. The younger woman heard a way out, really for the first time, but she was also committed to an old and failing father. As the sole unmarried daughter, she was responsible.

There were events after this, in the year following, 1846, that would draw her along toward her goals. Bray purchased the local Coventry *Herald* and turned to Mary Ann as his assistant. But well before that, each day she confronted the labyrinth of Strauss's German, starting early in the morning and continuing frequently until late at night. Breaks in the routine were welcome, in fact necessary, for Mary Ann felt her routine was wearing her down. Writing to Sara (April 1844), she attempted to be jaunty, but the Sisyphus-like burden comes through. "When I can work fast I am never weary, nor do I regret either that the work has been begun, or that I have undertaken it. I am only inclined to vow that I will never translate again if I live to correct the sheets for Strauss." She did live to translate the Feuerbach book on Christianity and also Spinoza's *Ethics*, from the Latin, which never saw publication.

As early as June 1844, she mentions a book, in a letter to Cara, that sounds suspiciously like Feuerbach's, calling it Bauer's *Wesen des Christenthums,* which is the title of Feuerbach's study and not of anything by Bauer. She was, then, already aware of her next labor. While working on Strauss's attack on conventional biblical studies of Jesus—with his mythicizing of Jesus' story, his treatment of the Gospels as simply a narrative, not revelation, his denial of the historical validity of all supernatural matters in the Gospels, and his interpretation of primitive Christianity in Hegelian terms—Mary Ann did not lose her belief in the spiritual value of the Bible, but compared it to poetry and the arts in general. After asserting that no dogmas, like the canons of the Council of Nice, or the Confession of Augsburg, or even the Thirty-nine Articles of Anglican faith, are suggestive of poetry, she admits that Christianity *is.* "But surely Christianity with its Hebrew retrospect [a remark which suggests she accepted the contemporary belief that the Old Testament's value was that it led into the New] and millennial hopes, the heroism and Divine sorrow of its founder and all its glorious army of martyrs might supply and has supplied a strong impulse not only to poetry but to all the fine arts." With this, she stated an attitude or impulse which would provide a foundation for her later fiction, a belief she never lost, however much her faith wavered and dropped away.

Mary Ann needed a break from her labors, and the Brays, ever ready to help their friend, took her north to Lake Windermere for two weeks, where they stayed at Bowness. On their return, they stopped at Manchester to visit Cara's cousins, the Hollands, whose bachelor sons, Philip and Frank, were most cordial. The Brays' aim, surely, was to give Mary Ann the opportunity to meet men of her own age. But it failed to work. She was still exhausted from her labors, did not appear in an attractive light, and fell back into her usual diffidence when in the company of eligible young men. The trip continued, with a stopover in Liverpool, Mary Ann still in tow, where they spent several nights at Richard Rathbone's and saw still another cousin of Cara's, Mrs. James Martineau. Rathbone was also deeply interested in mesmerism and entertained two guests who were mesmerists, one of whom almost took a reluctant Mary Ann under. This was no charlatan, but a figure of some stature in British education, William Ballantyne Hodgson. Although he did not completely mesmerize Mary Ann, he was apparently very impressed with her, and cited her proficiency in Greek, Latin, French, Italian, and German.

When she returned to Foleshill, she began to tutor nineteen-year-old Mary Sibree in German. Young Mary was the daughter of the Independent minister at Coventry, and at first there was some resistance from Mrs. Sibree because of Mary. Ann's reputation of having slid away from her faith. But the Reverend Sibree said there was no fear of indoctrination, and Mrs. Sibree after meeting Mary Ann agreed. Both were wrong. Mary Sibree on her own was uncertain of her beliefs and leaning toward apostasy. What she apparently received, according to John Cross much later, was Mary Ann's developing humanitarianism, her growing sympathy with suffering and with the human struggle as evidence of a religious spirit. The tutor was gradually becoming less impressed with

Calvinism and predetermined behavior and far more concerned with the actualities of expression which evolved from every individual's choices.

The two women became quite close, the difference in age not being that immense, even though Mary Ann was by far the better read and more thoughtful. The Sibrees, according to Cross, spoke of personal matters with Mary Ann, expressing regret that she might in time find herself "tied to a being whose limitations you could see, and must know were such as to prevent you ever being understood!" They were probably referring to a young artist Mary Ann met at Baginton, near Coventry, in March of 1845, and, in circumstances we cannot unravel—even his name remains unknown—he proposed to her, after only two days in her company. She refused an engagement, but did promise to exchange letters. The situation was unusual, not only in the rapidity with which the proposal came but in the fact that Mary Ann was in the position whereby a young man felt sufficiently emboldened to propose.

Since we have no firsthand information, we must rely on letters between Cara and Sara, one on 30 March (1845) being especially revealing. Cara writes: ". . . she [Mary Ann] wished me to tell you and has often said 'How I wish Sara were here, for she knows what would be for my good.' I may as well say at the beginning though that it has all come to nothing. She says she was talking to you about a young artist she was going to meet at Baginton." She continues: "Well, they did meet and passed two days in each other's company, and she thought him the most interesting young man she had seen and superior to all the rest of mankind; the third morning he made proposals through her brother in law Mr. Hooten [Houghton]—saying, 'she was the most fascinating creature he had ever beheld, that if it were not too presumptuous to hope etc etc., a person of such superior excellence and powers of mind,' etc., in short, he seemed desperately smitten and begged permission to write to her."

As retold, Mary Ann's version was that she "granted this, and came to us so brimful of happiness;—though she said she had not fallen in love with him yet, but admired his character so much that she was sure she should; the only objection seemed to be that his profession—a picture-restorer—is not lucrative or over-honourable." Cara says, "We liked his letters to her very much—simple, earnest, unstudied," indicating that Mary Ann revealed personal correspondence to the Brays and sought their guidance. She said she would like him as a friend. But there is quite a good deal more with the young man: Mary Ann's quandary about marriage itself and her subsequent suffering from grave headaches which virtually incapacitated her. The next stage arrived when the young man presented himself again to Mary Ann, apparently at Foleshill, and "owing to his great agitation," Cara writes, "from youth—or something or other, did not seem to her half so interesting as before, and the next day she made up her mind that she would never love or respect him enough to marry him and that it would involve too great a sacrifice of her mind and pursuits." Consequently, she wrote him, breaking off the relationship—"and there it stands now." Cara adds: "Poor girl, it has been a trying, exciting week to her and she seemed quite spiritless this morning. . . . one does not know what to advise."

One would like to think Mary Ann rejected the first serious suitor in her life because she felt in herself stirrings of a great calling which she was unwilling to jeopardize. That may have been true, but there were other, complicating circumstances. There was, of course, her ailing father and his feelings about her becoming engaged to a "picture-restorer," not precisely a prestigious profession in the eyes of the upwardly mobile. But more than Robert Evans's response was the fact that she had been exposed for some time to extremely intelligent and highly achieving men, and, in comparison, the picture-restorer, however gentle and courtly, could only lose. Mary Ann was surely waiting for something "larger," like Dorothea Brooke with Casaubon. While the doubling of older and younger is only shadowy, it does reveal Mary Ann's embrace of those who offered achievement and her rejection of an attractive but younger man who seemed, in contrast, lacking in gravity or prestige.

Writing to Sara Hennell a week after Cara's letter to Sara, Mary Ann guardedly revealed her feelings. "I have never yet half thanked you for taking an interest in my little personal matters. My unfortunate 'affaire' did not become one 'du coeur,'* but it has been anything but a comfortable one for my conscience. If the circumstances could be repeated with the added condition of my experience I should act very differently. As it is I have now dismissed it from my mind of reference. . . . So now dear Sara, I am once more your true Gemahlinn, which being interpreted, means that I have no loves but those that you can share with me—intellectual and religious loves." Her use of the German term of endearment, *Gemahlinn*, wife or spouse or consort, is quite revealing of the intimacy she felt; an intimacy which she may have suspected would be disrupted by the intrusion of this young man with his plans for matrimony.

Yet Mary Ann's statement that she has put it all out of mind is belied by her admission ten days later (16? April) that she had a severe headache, for four days, relieved only by leeches. Part of the desire to display an undisturbed mind was to allay any of Sara's fears that work on the Strauss might suffer, something Mary Ann was quite sensitive to. But our suspicion that the headache was derived from anxiety in general and this episode in particular comes in a 21 April letter to Martha (Patty) Jackson. "What would you say to me becoming a wife? Should you think it a duty to ascertain the name of the rash man that you might warn him from putting on such a matrimonial hairshirt as he would have with me? I did meditate an engagement, but I have determined, whether silly or not I cannot tell, to defer it, at least for the present." Her mockery serves her as self-deprecation. Later, in 1846, she will repeat the raillery when she relates to Charles Bray the mock proposal of Professor Bücherwurm, a Casaubon type.

The payback for the episode was the "dreadful headache" mentioned above. In the same passage where Mary Ann asserts that the only salutary medicine for her is application to the job, she indicates that she and her father "go on living and loving together as usual, and it is my chief source of happiness to know that I form one item of his." The juxtapositions are compelling: rejection of suitor,

---

* Her casting key words in French is a way of making the situation somewhat arch, even comic; as though she can speak of it only by slightly mocking it, or by puncturing holes in her feelings.

subsequent dreadful headache, followed by description of her life with Evans as blissful. In some conscious way, she perhaps did see it as blissful and did reject the suitor so as not to disturb her father's last years or elicit his censure. But the undertow to this is something quite different, with the headache as manifesting some hostility toward what she was doing for Evans's sake; or else some aggression directed against herself for guilt feelings that with engagement and marriage she would be deserting Evans; or even some unfathomable frustration she could not begin to sort out.

While she suffered regularly from headaches throughout her life, they became particularly severe, it seemed, when she was confronted by choices which exacerbated her uncertainties. Engagement would have provided her with what most other women of twenty-five or twenty-six took for granted, what would have brought her into mainstream society. And this acceptance was to be important for her, as we will see subsequently. The divisions in Mary Ann were rarely more manifest, as she attempted to explain away her strong indifference to what occurred. The temptation to pass into female adulthood in the approved way through engagement, marriage, and children was a great challenge, as was the young man himself. But the other side of her nature called, too.

Strauss rolled on, headaches or not, and served as anodyne. The money for publication (not for Mary Ann) was set up by Parkes, £300, a large sum for those days. Her letters to Sara indicate her need for accuracy, castigating herself for errors or omissions. In June of 1845, the Brays provided some relief with an excursion to London, and then she accompanied them to Birmingham to see *Julius Caesar*, with Maccready as Brutus, on 12 June. Once back at Foleshill, with Strauss and Robert Evans as companions, she was bent over the German, and tells Sara that, despite her distaste for it all, she wants to have the correcting of her own proofs and revisions. She must overcome suffering: "With a most awful pain in my *Eingewelde* [the German sounds more delicate than bowels or guts] which scarcely leaves me the power of thinking," she then launches into a possible translation for two problematic words. On 25 September, she begins to see some of her work as it will appear in print, with the first sheet of type very encouraging.

Intervening in her plans, however, was something now becoming familiar: domestic difficulties. Evans was well enough to leave alone, but her sister, Chrissey, was in even deeper trouble. Her husband, Edward Clarke, the physician, had gone bankrupt. Chrissey and the four surviving children came to stay at Bird Grove, Foleshill, and Mary Ann felt responsible for them. Chrissey had a particular hold on her affections, despite her desire to break away. Yet Bray, once again, came to the rescue and cautioned Evans that Mary Ann was so run down and looked so poorly, a trip would prove a tonic. Evans agreed. Bray could now leave with his harem, Cara, Sara, and Mary Ann.

Yet on the very evening of their departure, Evans broke his leg, and Isaac sent on a letter to Mary Ann telling her to return, the letter following her from Glasgow and catching up on 24 October. The Brays, however, would not permit her to travel the three hundred miles alone, as she insisted on doing, and insisted in turn that she continue, especially since the letter indicated Evans was doing well. The "sacrifice" of Mary Ann within the family is clear: Chrissey and her need for help, with four children; Evans incapacitated just as his daughter was seeking relief; the brother calling her home, although there was money for servants and plenty of family help.

The journey left them all in ecstasies, Sara wrote Mrs. James Hennell (James was the sixth Hennell child) the day after their return. The Brays had given Mary Ann relief and now she was ready for another long pull. Obligated to remain in bed, at a time when a broken limb could lead to deadly complications, Evans made demands on his daughter's time. Besides the leg, his general health was declining, as his kidney malfunction became apparent. Mary Ann spent a good deal of time with him, reading—he particularly enjoyed her grave, resonant voice—and keeping the once active man occupied. She plugged along, interruptions and all, but Cara told Sara that Mary Ann was "Strauss-sick—it made her ill dissecting the beautiful story of the crucifixion, and only the sight of her Christ-image and picture [a twenty-inch cast of Thorwalden's *Risen Christ* and an engraving of Delaroche's *Christ*] made her endure it. Moreover, as her work advances nearer its public appearance"—publication was on 15 June 1846, in three volumes—"she grows dreadfully nervous. Poor thing. I do pity her sometimes with her pale sickly face and dreadful headaches, and anxiety too about her father. This illness of his [has] tried her so much, for all the time she had for rest and fresh air, she had to read to him. Nevertheless she looks very happy and satisfied at times with her work."

The last one hundred pages of Strauss tried Mary Ann's patience; as she says, it was "totally uninteresting to me." In April 1846, she sent a section of *The Life of Jesus* to Strauss for his approval, and he wrote a preface, in Latin, praising the translation for its accuracy. Needless to add, Mary Ann was quite pleased at this reception of her first serious work in print. With the front matter completed in May, the three volumes appeared in June, * and Mary Ann received £20 for her two-year effort. The money was small recompense, although it brought at the time a good deal of spending power; the real recompense was her ability to finish a difficult task and to do it with the praise of the mighty Strauss himself. She was, in this respect, on her way. Yet she did reveal she would like to "fleet the time away" with Sara, and after "all their toils to lie reclined on the hills (spiritually), like gods together careless of mankind."

Once the Strauss was off her desk, she went on nothing less than a reading binge, as though all her desire to "know" had been dammed up while she was working. References in her letters to her reading indicate a breadth of interests, and we must keep in mind that she read books in their original languages. Among English writers and books, she went through Dickens and Thackeray, but she also read Milton, Wordsworth, Richardson (whose *Sir Charles Grandison* she inexplicably thought was "worth much"), Carlyle, Goethe, St. Simon, Frederika Bremer (a nineteenth-century Swedish novelist and feminist, now vir-

---

* Translated from the fourth German edition, published by Chapman Brothers. Her name did not appear as translator; only after she became famous as George Eliot was her name connected to editions of Strauss, and that as Eliot, not Mary Ann Evans.

tually unknown, whom she did read in translation), Lamartine, Disraeli (whose *Tancred* she felt was more detestable than anything that "ever came from a French pen"), several novels by George Sand (with whom she would be compared later in life, the "two Georges"), and Rousseau (whose *Les Confessions* deeply impressed her, as did his *Émile* and *La Nouvelle Héloïse*). Mary Ann had to defend her reading against both Cara and Sara, who thought Rousseau and Sand to be poor, even corruptive, influences.

Saying she might admit that even if Rousseau's views of life, religion, and government were miserably erroneous, even if he was shown to be guilty of a baseness that has degraded civilized man—even with that,

> it would be not the less true that Rousseau's genius has sent that electric thrill through my intellectual and moral frame which has awakened me to new perceptions, which has made man and nature a fresh world of thought and feeling to me. . . . It is simply that the rushing mighty wind of his inspiration has so quickened my faculties that I have been able to shape more definitely for myself ideas which had previously dwelt a dim "ahnungen" [misgiving or presentiment] in my soul. . . .

With George Sand, she had to be more circumspect, since Sand was the scarlet woman of the era, and her way of life was held to be representative of a Frenchwoman, not of an English lady. All the English Grundyish prejudices against the French centered on the profligate, "mannish" Sand. Mary Ann: "I should never dream of going to her writings as a moral code or text-book. I don't care whether I agree with her about marriage or not [in *Jacques*, the protagonist deems marriage to be a barbarous institution]—whether I think the design of her plot correct or that she had no precise design at all but began to write as the spirit moved her. . . ." She says it is sufficient for her as "a reason for bowing before her in eternal gratitude to that 'great power of God' manifested in her— that I cannot read six pages of hers without feeling that it is given to her to delineate human passion and its results. . . . with such truthfulness such nicety of discrimination such tragic power and withal such loving gentle humour that one might live a century with nothing but one's own dull faculties and not know so much as those six pages will suggest." Mary Ann decided not to pursue further Sara's criticisms about the immoral nature of the characters and of the book. George Sand was clearly *there* as a lesson, even as a beacon. *

---

* Besides her appropriation of "George" from George Sand and her extensive reading of the French author's books (*Jacques, Indiana, François le Champi, Lélia, Consuelo,* and *Spiridion,* among others), Eliot was thought to look like her. After a visit to the Priory, the American Charles Eliot Norton, in 1869, found a "strong likeness." Eliot, however, comes out second best, as possessing a head and face "hardly as noble as George Sand's," although the lines of both are "strong and masculine," the cheeks heavy, the hair dressed similarly. But Eliot's eyes, like her complexion, are dull; Norton seems fixated on her "heavy features," as though he cannot accept that she is a woman. Henry James saw much the same thing, but fell in love with it. As for name changes, George Sand, born Amandine Aurore Lucie Dupin, became Aurore Dudevant when she married at eighteen. When she began her literary career, she signed her first book (*Rose et Blanche*) as Jules Sand, after her collaborator, Jules Sandeau. Jules Sand evolved into George Sand. She was also known, by her own naming, as Piffoël, a play on the French colloquialism *pif,* for nose, and probably based on her aquiline nose.

PART TWO

Interim

5

Limbo

"O the bliss of having a very high attic in a romantic
continental town. . . ."

The Rousseau and Sand remarks came in 1849, when Mary Ann was ready
to plunge into London life and put behind her one part of the Evans background. She even changed the spelling of her name, to Marian, in 1850,
although she reverted to Mary Ann in 1880 when she married John Cross and
became a "respectable" woman. The second name change, however slight, does
indicate a shift of person, for in 1849–50, she was altering her position radically,
as in 1880 she again altered it by returning to someone she was before she took
on London life. Name changes followed hard on life changes.

But back in 1846, well before any of this occurred, she was still attempting to
find herself, once the Strauss translation was behind her. She nevertheless hung
on that, telling Sara she wanted the title to include "Critically Examined" after
"The Life of Jesus." Her remarks suggest she wanted it known that the Strauss
was criticism, not history, or perhaps not revelation.

Now, in the summer of 1846, she was ready to write, even though it would
be only reviews. In a comment which cannot be clarified, Sara wrote her mother
that Mary Ann looks "brilliant" and "must be writing her novel." If she was
indeed working on a novel, it is a manuscript now lost; or else it was simply
something associated with a diary or journal or chronicle. The sole writing we
know she did at this time came in reviews for Bray's recently purchased Coventry *Herald*. The newspaper was precisely Bray's kind of enterprise, having been
started some forty years earlier as an answer to Tory politics, represented by the
Coventry *Standard*. The *Herald* had the reputation of being radical, and Bray
intended to maintain that with his own brand of iconoclasm, starting in June of
1846. Mary Ann's duties included book reviewing—excellent preparation for

the much higher level of reviewing she did later for Chapman's *Westminster Review*—and the writing of a weekly column. These articles, which could be on any subject, were anonymous, and thus gave her the opportunity to range anywhere she wished without danger of divulgation. It was these articles Sara may have meant by Mary Ann's "novel," inasmuch as they were fictions of a sort, such as one on snubbing.

The articles are lightweight, but her aim was primarily to entertain, not instruct. Despite her light treatment, Mary Ann already showed her ability to take on heavy subjects, such as Quinet's and Michelet's *Christianity in Its Various Aspects* and the latter's *The Jesuits and Priests, Women and Families*. Her choice of books by Michelet (Jules Michelet, the renowned nineteenth-century French historian, famous for his *History of France*) is noteworthy, since he was notorious for his anti-clericalism and his attacks on both nobility and monarchy. The rebel residing in Mary Ann found solace in Strauss and now in Michelet, until it could emerge in its own way in her life. Between June and December, she wrote several short essays or sketches, apprentice work often little more than intelligent meanderings. She called them "Poetry and Prose from the Notebook of an Eccentric," the form she returned to near the end of her life, with *Impressions of Theophrastus Such*.

In July–August, she spent two weeks with her father in Dover, an indication of her continuing closeness to him even while intellectually she was rapidly pulling away. On her return, she wrote, on 4 November, a short commentary on Gilbert à Beckett's *Comic History of England* and five pieces mentioned above as "Poetry and Prose." She also brought to a conclusion her relationship with Maria Lewis. Cara and Sara now both represented the kind of women she felt she could address with understanding and sympathy. From remarks made after the writer's death by Edith Simcox, a later Eliot friend, it seems some of the conflict with Maria Lewis came from Lewis's jealousy of Mary Ann and Bray.* Both Cara and Sara agreed on calling the friend "stupid Miss Lewis," and we can assume that in indirect remarks they encouraged the break. When the end finally came over Christmas of 1846, it foreran an entire series of far more painful breaks Mary Ann would have to negotiate in order to seek her own direction.

Her relationship with Sara Hennell was never closer. In a mid-September letter (1846), Mary Ann addresses her as "Dearly beloved spouse," and signs off as Pollian, which she used as a term of endearment. She refers to Bray as that "dear unmanageable male unit in our quaternian," who has been ill. Her phrasing indicates she sees him as the center of a kind of court, with the three women in the quaternian circling around him. The intimacy of the letter in its address

---

* The reader is forewarned to be wary of all of Simcox's remarks concerning Eliot or her relationship to the writer. Simcox's love for her friend was obsessional, and while she was highly intelligent and prolific, she was volatile, spiteful, and self-serving. Nearly all previous biographers quote from Simcox's (unpublished) autobiography and tend to accept her views. In no way can she be deemed a reliable witness, however interesting she was as a person. Her perceptions are just that, *her* perceptions.

and farewell and in its contents suggests a breakthrough, some new consciousness.

Her letters to Sara are "love letters" of the sort we have become accustomed to among nineteenth-century women. Although there can be female bonding without overt sexuality, or without the participants even being conscious of it, there is no disregarding an undertone. It may be impossible to separate what is conscious from what is preconscious or unconscious; but there is little question Mary Ann gained emotional strength from female bonding. Her referral to Sara as her spouse and her use of "meine liebe," or "my love," as a farewell indicate that the two had forged an intimacy which made them indivisible emotionally. The intensity of such friendships for the future writer was absolutely necessary, since through her female friends she could express herself in ways that would be impossible with men.

Her recognition of her female friends led her to reevaluate her onetime closeness to Dr. Brabant. She tells Sara:

Pray convince her [Rufa] and every one concerned in the matter that I am too inflatedly conceited to think it worth my while to run after Dr. Brabant or his correspondence. If I ever offered incense to him it was because there was no other deity at hand and because I wanted some kind of worship pour passer le temps. I always knew that I could belabour my fetisch if I chose, and laughed at him in my sleeve. Even that degree of inclination towards mock reverence has long since passed away and ridiculous as it may seem to every one else, I looked on my renewal of correspondence with him as a favour *conferred* by me rather than *received.* I shall certainly take an opportunity of certifying him on which leg the boot was. You see I am getting horridly vulgar as well as proud.

The passage is revelatory. It suggests splits and divisions. On one level, it is the admission of a young woman in need of affection that she made a fool of herself. On another level, it signals her emotional immaturity or pride that she does not recognize her role as submissive and attempts to make it seem she dominated. On still another level, her rejection of Brabant in these terms cements her female bonding, an indication no man such as this could ever fill the role of her female friends. On still a further level, however, she reveals there is a hole that waits to be filled, an affection seeking linkage; a disclosure that while Brabant was not the right man for this, surely the wrong man altogether, nevertheless the need remains. For his part, Brabant, fool or not, did not consider himself "rejected" and invited Mary Ann to accompany him to Germany the following August, along with a Miss Taylor and Mr. and Mrs. Murch of Bath. She refused, although thanking him for his consideration. Brabant was, in effect, history.

Yet in a kind of fantasy of the man she could attract, a spin-off of Brabant, Mary Ann in October of 1846 conjured up Professor Bücherwurm of Moderig University. He comes courting her because he needs a wife-slave. In ways, he foreshadows Casaubon, but of greater interest is the way Mary Ann presents herself at this time. Her handling of the apparition is both novelistic and cuttingly intimate. The professor is a "tall, gaunt personage with huge cheek bones, dull grey eyes, hair of a very light neutral tint, un grand nez retroussé, and very black teeth. As novel writers say, I give you at once what was the result of a survey carried on by degrees through a long interview. My professor's coat was threadbare enough for that of a first-rate genius, and his linen and skin dirty enough to have belonged to the Emperor Julian." He announces his new project, "a system of metaphysics which I doubt not will supersede the latest products of the German philosophic mind." He needs a translator and a wife. "I have," he says, "made the most anxious and extensive inquiries in London after all female translators of German. I find them abundant, but I require, besides ability to translate, a very decided ugliness of person and a sufficient fortune to supply a poor professor with coffee and tobacco, and an occasional draft of schwarzbier, as well as to contribute to the expenses of publication. After the most toilsome inquiries I have been referred to you, Madam, as presenting the required combination of attributes, and though I am rather disappointed to see that you have no beard, an attribute which I have ever regarded as the most unfailing indication of a strong-minded woman, I confess that in other respects your person at least comes up to my ideal."

Her response: ". . . I require nothing more in a husband than to save me from the horrible disgrace of spinster-hood and to take me out of England. As negative conditions, my husband must neither expect me to love him nor to mend his clothes, and he must allow me about once in a quarter a sort of conjugal saturnalia, in which I may turn the tables upon him, hector and scold and cuff him. At other times I will be a dutiful wife. . . ." Mary Ann's burlesque of marriage cannot completely disguise her fears—at best she can expect a Bücherwurm.

As Mary Ann moved past her twenty-seventh birthday, in 1846, we note how little she reacted to external events in the worlds of politics and the military. While she was intensely intellectual in her interests, she does not appear to have a response to contemporary events. Even most social conditions pass by her direct observation in her letters, although we know that when she came to write her novels she had been and was an acute social observer, of class, caste, individual rights, and related matters.

Mary Ann was not indifferent to war and death; her concerns lay elsewhere. She concentrated on broader social factors, on how society structured itself and then demanded modes of behavior by which it could be perpetuated. War was distant from this, virtually a separate dimension in her eyes. She was concerned with the assimilation of *all matter* into social behavior, into moral and ethical principles which guaranteed conservation and preservation of humanitarian values. Community was for her a microcosm of the entire society, presumably of the entire country, including its foreign policies and military successes and defeats. In her dissection of community, Eliot caught what she perceived as the fullness of life in the England of her time, and earlier. She was particularly sensitive to changes of style, to new orders of life, to alterations in daily living, to shifting modes that were transforming moral and ethical behavior. With these as her interests and focus, it is clear that wars, military adventures, even great successes abroad took secondary place in her imagination.

Mary Ann gained as a correspondent the brother of Mary Sibree, whom she had been tutoring in German. John Sibree, at twenty-four, was now studying at Spring Hills College, Birmingham, and proved useful in helping Mary Ann with classical Greek. Yet even with Strauss out of the way, her headaches prevailed, "grievously tormented," as she put it. John Chapman, who would figure so significantly in Mary Ann's life once she left Foleshill for London, turned up in a typical dispute, one that foreruns Eliot's own disagreements with her publishers. Here she disputes the relegation of copies of Strauss and the number of books to be printed by Chapman, whether it should be 1,000 or 2,000. Then in a passage she intended as private (not to be read by or to others), she wrote Sara: "I hope Mr. Chapman will not misbehave, but he was always too much of the *interesting* gentleman to please me. Men must not attempt to be interesting on any lower terms than a fine poetical genius." Her comment needs translation: men are tedious, unlike women, who can be "interesting" on any level.

As she was maneuvering into her own mode and distancing herself from her family's views, Mary Ann reread Charles Hennell's *An Inquiry into the Origins of Christianity*, which impressed her now even more than in her two previous readings five years before. Excepting some material in the introductory sketch, she says "there is nothing in its whole tone from beginning to end that jars on my moral sense, and apart from any opinion of the book as an explanation of the existence of Christianity and the Christian documents I am sure that no one fit to read it at all could read it without being intellectually and morally stronger. . . ." She adds: "I think the Inquiry furnishes the utmost that can be done towards obtaining a *real* view of the life and character of Jesus by rejecting as little as possible from the Gospels." She calls many things "shining ether," by which she means that the embroidery of so-called facts has been made into a kind of luminous anesthesia. "Subtract from the N[ew] Testament the miraculous and highly improbable and what will be the remainder?" That question, posed when Mary Ann was almost twenty-eight, would occupy her for the remainder of her life and become the subtext of virtually all of her fiction. Those biblical "miracles" became, increasingly, part of "shining ether."

Spending some time with her father, Mary Ann followed up the trip to Dover in the summer of 1846 with a trip to the Isle of Wight in September of 1847. Evans was sinking, and she knew he was nearing the end. When they were at home, he attended services at Trinity Church, his rebellious daughter at his side, filled with contempt even while dutiful. As she told Sara, "My soul is as barren as the desert; but I generally manage to sink some little well at church, by dint of making myself deaf and looking up at the roof and arches." Headaches, of course, accompanied the travesty, as did, in time, severe toothache.

On the return trip from Wight in September, Mary Ann, closing in on twenty-eight and still unfulfilled, stopped at Brighton. She sounds guilty at the time she is frittering away and at the waste of her life in general. She speaks of the "demon of procrastination" having taken hold of her for the past three weeks, which she has attempted to exorcise with action. She has already told Sara she was planning a possible work on the "superiority of the consolation of philosophy to those of (so-called) religion." This is, as Gordon Haight states, probably a work later advertised (in July 1854) as "The Idea of a Future Life . . . by the Translator of Strauss's Life of Jesus," a manuscript, if written out, never published or found. From her cursory remarks on her situation, we sense her uncertainty, her fear she has no sizable project in hand or even in mind—"The Idea of a Future Life" was only a stab at work. She knows that as twenty-eight approaches (more than half the expected life span at mid-century) she has done little to justify her great hopes. She was going down as a domestic slave.

John Sibree surfaced, now as the reader of Mary Ann's translation of Strauss and enthusiastic about the ideas the book presents. She welcomes the shift in belief the book has forced on him—he had been studying for the ministry—and she revels in the radicalization of his ideas. "I confess," she writes, "to a fit of destructiveness just now which might have been more easily gratified if I had lived in the days of iconoclasm—for now alas! men's idols are to be demolished only by wit and wisdom and divine enthusiasm." Later in this letter to Sara, she employs an image out of the book of Daniel, the prophetic warning of the coming beast: "All those monstrous, rumbustical beasts with their horns—the horn with eyes and a mouth speaking proud things and the little horn that waxed rebellious and stamped on the stars seem like my passions and vain fancies which are to be knocked down one after the other. . . ." Her inner life, she suggests, is filled with torments and hellish nightmares, while on the surface she says she is "growing happier."

The reacquaintanceship with John Sibree brought forth from Mary Ann some of her most probing and revealing letters. At this stage in her life, lacking poetry or fiction, she found in the epistolary form ways in which she could manage and direct her ideas. Talking to a slightly younger man, and yet respectful of his intelligence, she indulged the range of her knowledge while also maintaining a light tone of badinage and teasing. After assuring Sibree she won't consider him one of those "amiably silly individuals" to whom she writes nothings, she engages him in a discussion of Benjamin Disraeli and race. Although Disraeli was nominally a Christian—his father had him baptized when he was twelve*— he was, for one and all, *the* Jew. Mary Ann praises his attacks on liberal (as opposed to popular) principles, but focuses mainly on race, *his* race. "As to his theory of 'races' it has not a leg to stand on, and can only be buoyed up by such windy eloquence as 'You chitty-faced squabbly-nosed Europeans owe your commerce, your arts, your religion to the Hebrews—nay the Hebrews lead your

---

* Isaac D'Israeli (the original spelling) remained a Jew after his son had been baptized just months short of when he would ordinarily have been bar mitzvahed. The aim was to make him eligible for political life when he reached adulthood.

armies—' in proof of which he can tell us that Messena, a second-rate general of Napoleon's, was a Jew, whose real name was Manasseh." Her solution: "Extermination up to a certain point seems to be the law for the inferior races— for the rest, fusion both for physical and moral ends."

In language that sounds fatefully like the racial views set forth shortly after by the Comte de Gobineau, the French diplomat and racial theorist, she says, "It appears to me that the law by which privileged classes degenerate from continual intermarriage must act on a larger scale in deteriorating whole races." She admits, however, that the so-called pure races, however handsome, "always impress me disagreeably." She says, "The negroes certainly puzzle me—all the other races seem plainly destined to extermination or fusion not excepting even the 'Hebrew-Caucasian.' But the negroes are too important physiologically and geographically for one to think of their extermination, while the repulsion between them and the other races seems too strong for fusion to take place to any great extent."

Mary Ann's racial theories, which make us wince, were part of that reevaluation of race which was occurring toward mid-century when geological and evolutionary theories were creating an upheaval in the way people looked at themselves and at others. In this regard, the growth of uncertainties in individuals reverberated throughout the society into reevaluations of the Hebraic-Christian tradition; and this, inevitably, led into theories of race. Gobineau, an influential force, saw degeneration occurring when people wear down and societies no longer hold the values they once held. Mixed blood is a source of degeneration, although, paradoxically, Gobineau admitted it can also be a source of strength. Mary Ann uses the word "inferior" for certain races, and this is of course part of Gobineau's "rabble," the result of miscegenation, and that in turn derived from mass urbanization. She sees "fusion" or "extermination" not in the later German sense, but as the result of intermarriage or the gradual dying out of certain races.

Implicit in all this, so far, is a distinct anti-Semitic flavor, since she mocks Disraeli's claims for the Jewish race by degrading Judaism itself. But while she agrees with him that the Oriental races are superior, her agreement seems based more on their munificent clothes ("their clothes are beautiful and ours are execrable") than on their achievement. Yet she is not finished with the Jew-Gentile issue and goes after Disraeli—a position she will reverse when she writes *Daniel Deronda* thirty years hence.* The entire passage is of interest, not only because it describes Mary Ann's views in 1848, but because it was altered so completely later on when she chided herself for her earlier anti-Semitism.

The fellowship of race, to which D'Israeli exultingly refers the munificence of Sindona [in his *Coningsby*], is so evidently an inferior impulse which must ultimately be superseded that I wonder even he, Jew as he is, dares to

---

* Also, in *The Spanish Gypsy*, her long poem in the late 1860s, Eliot rethought her racial ideas and began that reversal which culminated in *Deronda*.

boast of it. My Gentile nature kicks most resolutely against any assumption of superiority in the Jews and is almost ready to echo Voltaire's vituperation [his diatribe against Jews in "A Christian Against Six Jews"]. I bow to the supremacy of Hebrew poetry, but much of their early mythology and almost all their history is utterly revolting. Their stock has produced a Moses and a Jesus, but Moses was impregnated with Egyptian philosophy and Jesus is venerated and adored by us only for that wherein he transcended or resisted Judaism. The very exaltation of their idea of a national deity into a spiritual monotheism seems to have been borrowed from the other oriental tribes. Everything *specifically* Jewish is of low grade.

Moving away from race and religion, Mary Ann roves over questions of art, denying, for example, that music—in which she was quite proficient—is "to supersede the other arts." She adds: "I cannot recognize the truth of all that is said about the necessity of religious fervor to high art. . . . Artistic power seems to me to resemble dramatic power—to be an intuitive perception of the varied states of which the human mind is susceptible with ability to give them out anew in intensified expression." This is a romantic notion of the artist's mind as composed of intuitions, natural talents, and an innate imaginative power.

Personal matters intrude into these lofty thoughts about life, the future, and the nature of art. She comments on the mental derangement of Harriet Hennell, one of Sara's older sisters, now confined at Northampton after several "trying scenes and thoughts." Even closer to home, however, Chrissey's nine-month-old son, Leonard, has died, probably of whooping cough, and Mary Ann rues the fact she cannot be with her sister because Evans has been absent with the carriage.

But in her correspondence with John Sibree intellectual matters dominate. As we read her responses to his queries and then her own sallies, we observe how still indecisive she was intellectually, even while being very inquiring and manifesting broad reading. She was unformed in the sense she had as yet no synthetic or fully coherent pattern of belief—as she would have when she began to write fiction. We note, however, some smaller, scattered patterns: the early stages of her moral beliefs, her sense of the interconnectedness of things, her recognition of the need for choice, her concentration on individual independence or emergence but not at the public expense. When she matured intellectually, her thinking became a synthesis of Ruskin, Mill, Carlyle, Dickens, and others: reshaping their ideas into her own unique response, but still very much part of a nineteenth-century pattern of hopes, expectations, fears, and uncertainties.

Impressing upon Sibree that she is arguing positively, that hers is not "a mocking pen," Mary Ann sallies forth with her own fervent belief that the intellect "by its analytic powers" restrains the fury with which the passions and senses "rush to their own destruction." She stresses that "the moral nature purifies beautifies and at length transmutes them." When the French revolution of March 1848 broke out and it appeared to many it would spread to England—

Sibree for one was happy about the prospect—she tells him he is "not one of those sages whose reason keeps so tight a rein on their emotions that they are too constantly occupied in calculating consequences to rejoice in any great manifestation of the forces that underlie our everyday existence." She had little but contempt for Louis Philippe, who, she knew, had to be overthrown if France was to enjoy the "Rights of Man"; but she also refused to see the revolution as some panacea for man's ills or as a direction which would make a better life for the English if the revolution could be exported:

> I should not hope of good from any imitative movement at home. Our working classes are eminently inferior to the mass of the French people. In France, the *mind* of the people is highly electrified—they are full of ideas on social subjects—they really desire social *reform*. . . . . The revolutionary animus extended over the whole nation, and embraced the rural population—not merely as with us, the artisans of the town. Here there is so much larger a proportion of selfish radicalism and unsatisfied, brute sensuality (in the agricultural and mining districts especially) than of perception or desire of justice, that a revolutionary movement would be simply destructive—not constructive [as in Captain Swing's activities].

Much of this is unfocused and overreactive and sounds more like Robert Evans than someone seeking emancipation. Mary Ann simply ignored peaceful working-class movements, like the Chartists, which showed considerable sophistication in their demands. She continues with her attempt at realpolitik.

> Besides, it would be put down. Our military have no notion of "fraternization." They have the same sort of inveteracy as dogs have for the ill-drest canaille. They are as mere a brute force as a battering ram and the aristocracy have got firm hold of them. Our little humbug of a queen [Victoria Regina] is more endurable than the rest of her race because she calls forth a chivalrous feeling, and there is nothing in our constitution to obstruct the slow progress of *political* reform. This is all we are fit for at present. The social reform which may prepare us for great changes is more and more the object of effort both in Parliament and out of it. But we English are slow crawlers.

Sympathy for Ireland, she says, is only "of the water toast kind." She does warn of the Glasgow riots—when thousands of unemployed workers rioted and broke into gun shops, until the cavalry put them down—"but one cannot believe in a Scotch Reign of Terror in these days." She dismisses the possibility of such insurgency in England, although she would welcome it in Italy, if the Italians rose up and "chased the odious Austrians" out of beautiful Lombardy, an action which occurred a little more than a week later.

Mary Ann is full of fervor, full of insights—the "humbug" queen, the sense that the army will do the will of the aristocracy—but also cautious, feeling that the English political system, as apart from the social mechanism, was sufficiently flexible to bend when the winds of political revolution blew upon it. The system did indeed work slowly, for not until 1867 did another Reform Bill add to the franchise and correct other abuses. She understood very well that England was not a democracy, that justice was not available for the majority of people, that workers had valid complaints which were not redressed; and yet she viewed most of it, from her village outside Coventry, as lacking high moral seriousness.

Throughout these letters, with their stabs at public policy, Mary Ann winds back to what she really knows best, those elements of a personal nature where she is clearly more coherent. "No mind," she says, "that has any *real* life is a mere echo of another." When perfect unison does occasionally come, as in music—which she now revalues—"it enhances the harmonies." It is, she asserts, "like a diffusion or expansion of one's own life to be assured that its vibrations are repeated in another, and words are the media of those vibrations." She says that the universe is itself a "perpetual utterance of the One Being," a way of suggesting there is coherence somewhere if we can discover it, or if it will reveal itself. She asks Sibree to burn her letters, which she describes as good for nothing. Perhaps she sensed a flirtation, on both parts.

Even the slightest improvement in her father's condition, reported on 26 April 1848, for example, brings "a gentle dawning light after the moonlight of sorrow." The imagery may be romantic, but the sensibility is depressive. When Sibree announces he is returning to Germany, she is happy for him, and sad for herself. His parents apparently felt she was a poor influence on their son (and daughter) and forbade further communication with Mary Ann, especially when John gave up the ministry. What she longed for was a room of her own: "O the bliss of having a very high attic in a romantic continental town, such as Geneva—far away from morning callers dinners and decencies; and then to pause for a year and think" of other things, and "to return to life, and work for a poor stricken humanity and never think of self again."

Solicitous about caring for her father, she accompanied him to Derbyshire, which proved to be his final trip. In deep decline, Evans developed cardiac problems, and his food, drink, rest, and general activities required constant monitoring. Mary Ann fulfilled all those duties. She read Scott to him (*The Fair Maid of Perth*, among others) and herself read *Jane Eyre*. Her comments on the novel are especially significant because it was a book which reverberated in her imagination and became a touchstone for fiction in Lewes's thought as well. "I have read Jane Eyre," she wrote Bray, "and shall be glad to know what you admire in it. All self-sacrifice is good—but one would like it to be in a somewhat nobler cause than that of a diabolical law which chains a man soul and body to a putrefying carcase. However the book *is* interesting—only I wish the characters would talk a little less like the heroes and heroines of police reports."

"I feel a sort of madness growing upon me," she had written Sara just a week earlier, but "the opposite of the delirium which makes people fancy that their bodies are filling the room. It seems to me as if I were shrinking into that mathematical abstraction, a point—so entirely am I destitute of contact that I am unconscious of length or breadth. . . ." The imagery (coming in May 1848) strikes close to limning temporary madness, describing a shrinkage so profound she cannot conceive of any spiritual existence. She has become a drudge, but intensified in her instance because she long feared her twenties would drift away in personal meaninglessness. Robert Evans hung on, was difficult even when well, and needed full-time attention.

This was a poignant moment, in which all of Mary Ann's reserves and inner strength were called upon, and she became most conscious of her female role in society: a sacrifice for what was considered a worthy duty. Her complaints did not diminish, for she wrote Bray on 5 June in terms that recall Spenser's *Faerie Queene* or some other Renaissance or late medieval allegory. "I possess my soul in patience for a time, believing that this dark damp vault in which I am groping will soon come to an end and the fresh green earth and the bright sky be all the more precious to me. But for the present my address is Grief Castle, on the river of Gloom, in the valley of Dolour." She is using descriptions that actually derive from Scott's *Tales of a Grandfather*. She speaks also of madness. "Truly for many seasons in my life I should have been an appropriate denizen of such a place, but I have faith that unless I am destined to insanity, I shall never again abide long in that same castle."

Amidst this personal lament, she turns outward and sympathizes with the Frenchman Louis Blanc, a leader of the 1848 revolution, and she awaits the day when there will be some memorialization of every man or woman who had a presentiment or a clear vision "of the time when this miserable reign of Mammon shall end. . . ." The combination of Mammon and Blanc leads directly back to herself. Borrowing from Carlyle, she yearns for some guiding principle in an age when man pursues only treasure, and she praises Blanc, who established workers' cells or workshops and fought for ideals.

Her remark overlaps her own yearning for something finer and grander. "I have not half the time to write what I wish. . . ."—and the suggestion is that the moment may be prolonged until she never has time. Yet her "heart is bleeding for my poor Father who is suffering as badly as ever." But even as she writes this to both Mary Sibree and then to Sara, she can add to the latter: "All creatures about to moult or to cast off an old skin, or enter on any new metamorphosis have sickly feelings. It was so with me, but now I am set free from the irritating worn-out integument. I am entering on a new period of my life which makes me look back on the past as something incredibly poor and contemptible." This is accompanied by something of a disclaimer for such a rush of energy: "I am enjoying repose strength and ardour in a greater degree than I have ever known and yet I never felt my own insignificance and imperfection so completely."

This new rush of energy would be reinforced when, on 13 July, she met Ralph Waldo Emerson: "I have seen Emerson—the first *man* I have ever seen." The Brays had already met Emerson, having attended his lectures in London and in Birmingham, and when the American was on his way to Liverpool to return home, Bray convinced him to stop at Foleshill. Mary Ann was not at all bashful

when presented to the eminent visitor and immediately engaged him in conversation. She told him that Rousseau's *Confessions* had first introduced her to
profound thought, and Emerson indicated that Carlyle had said the same thing
to him. Carlyle, however, had to fight his way through Rousseau, rejecting the
temptations the French writer offered in education and the emotional life. For
Mary Ann, Rousseau was not part of the opposition, but a personage, and the
iconoclastic *Confessions* something she had to assimilate into her own growing
philosophy of duty and social commitment.

Emerson and the Brays, along with the Brays' friend Edward Flower, all drove
to Stratford to see Shakespeare, and on this trip, Emerson was full of praise for
Mary Ann—"That young lady has a calm, serious soul"—and regretted he did
not have more time to stay with her and the Brays. She remained behind to
nurse Evans, whose nights were becoming increasingly wretched. She recognized he was declining in all his organs, and she asked Robert to come before it
was too late. Her father's condition now required her constant attention: mus-
tard plasters, a calming presence, reading to him when he was alert. She warns
Cara that the doctors expect him to die suddenly, since his chest is now filling
with water. Cara tells Sara that Mary Ann "looks like a ghost," that she "has
the whole care and fatigue of nursing him night and day with this constant
nervous expectation."

In an allegory of Mother Nature, Mary Ann wrote a remarkable little parable
about herself, but thinly disguised within natural terms. Her point is that Nature
does her work through deputies. "The vulgar may not know it, but she [Nature]
in fact leaves the creation of her plants her animals and her homunculi to a
whole herd of sprites and genii some of whom make but laughing work of it."
She cites just such a sprite who over a quarter of a century earlier turned from
some toads and lemurs and marmosets to "try his hand on the human article and
on 22d of November [Mary Ann's date of birth] he presented to Dame Nature
at her evening levee a rough though unmistakable sketch of a human baby."
Mother Nature was snappish at the product and asked some of her satellites to
smother it. But the father spirit cried that he wanted his first human experiment
to live, and his "brother genii" were so touched with pity they interceded with
Mother Nature. And so she was saved by these bright and good mortals, "and
they pitied and helped it, so that at last it grew to think and to love." This little
parable is full of self-pity, but also survival instincts: the split, once more,
between yearning and dutifulness.

Her litany of complaints continues. She has been unable to touch the piano
for two months and has suffered "unutterable headache," backaches, and vomiting, which could have resulted from migraines, or, in another regard, a kind
of sympathetic parallelism to her father's condition. She became so sick that to
take care of him was a further source of martyrdom; or, in a reversed role, taking
care of him made her so sick she had to overcome her own ailments for the
greater good. Such contraries, of course, play into her fictional heroines.

"My life is a perpetual nightmare," she tells Sara, despite the brave words and
the parable of survival. Her time is "always haunted by something to be done—

which I have never the time or rather the energy to do." Traditional women's work is destroying her. All she can do is think, since the day's duties are laid out for her in service; each morning the boulder comes rolling down. In this letter (9 February 1849), she tells Sara that the writers who have profoundly influenced her, Rousseau and George Sand, for example, are not necessarily oracles for her.

In March, she did find time to review James Anthony Froude's *Nemesis of Faith,* an early version of spiritual autobiography, in which the typical apprenticeship novel is underscored by severe spiritual crises which determine the fate of the subject. Later one of the century's most famous historians, Froude wrote of a young man who, after becoming acquainted with the Tractarians and their writings, becomes so confused he loses his faith and must wander the world without any clear direction. So far is he lost that he commits adultery with the wife of a friend. Froude's general story would become a common one as the Tractarians threw into disarray an entire generation of young men. Froude was himself a Fellow of Exeter College at Oxford, and his fellowship depended on his ascribing to the Thirty-nine Articles of the Anglican Church. Faithless, he would also be fellowshipless. His book was burned in the Hall of Exeter College, an indication of how the religious wars had heated up only a couple of generations after Catholics gained legal rights in England.

Mary Ann, identified as the "Translator of Strauss," had been sent a copy by Froude, through Chapman. The book was made to order for her at this stage, and after the review appeared in the Coventry *Herald* for 16 March 1849, Froude wrote her a letter of thanks, having recognized her hand, he said, in the anonymous review. He says she might help him rise, since he feels he has been dipped in the Styx, the river of hell. Froude apparently wanted to continue the correspondence and see what developed, but Mary Ann withdrew temporarily, since she had begun to translate Spinoza's *Tractatus Theologico-Politicus* from the Latin. In an intimate letter ostensibly about Froude and her review, she tells Sara that she should not be jealous or take this instance as "lawful for you to take a new husband [on the model of Mary Ann and Froude]—therefore I come back to you with all a husband's privileges and command you to love me whether I shew you any love or not, and to be faithful though I play you false every day of my life. . . ." Since their "union" cannot be destroyed, their marriage to each other is safe. Her later words in the same letter indicate how she needs the consolation of their love. "I have nothing to tell you, for all the 'haps' of my life are so indifferent—I spin my existence so entirely out of myself, that there is a sad want of proper names in my conversation and I am becoming a greater bore than ever."

In April, within a few weeks of her liberation, she tells Sara she is in bed, worthy of being put into a coffin. From now on, her comments indicate how Evans is weakening, although in his feebleness his mind remained clear and rational. He had already made his will, with Mary Ann to receive £2,000 in trust and the household items not already disposed of, to the sum of £100, although that bequest was later altered to be a money, not a household goods, allotment. Her brothers, who had contributed nothing to their father's welfare for all these years, received the far more valuable properties: Robert getting the Derbyshire lands, the ones around Nuneaton going to Isaac. As intimate family items were bequeathed, Mary Ann seemed omitted: her mother's Bible went to Chrissey, the silver and the set of Scott to Fanny, Hume's *History of England* to Robert. The will dated from 25 September 1848, so that for the eight months in which Evans deteriorated and his youngest daughter cared for him, she had to live with the knowledge that nothing special would come her way.

Evans's final say on Mary Ann's apostasy appears as an act of small revenge: even the set of Scott she so assiduously read to him in his declining years should not be hers. Mary Ann made no external sign of dissatisfaction. The £2,000 in trust would provide an income, however small (under £100 a year), for an independent life if she could supplement it with reviewing or editing. Her other consolation was her immersion in Thomas à Kempis's *Imitation of Christ*, which conveyed to her some sense of balance between herself as an insignificant speck on earth and the immensities she could not hope to comprehend.

As the end for Evans drew near, Mary Ann tried to find some rationale for her expenditure of time. She tells Bray of Evans's weakness, but adds "Strange to say I feel that these will be the happiest days of life to me." Her explanation of this seemingly paradoxical statement is: "The one deep strong love I have ever known has now its highest exercise and fullest reward—the worship of sorrow is *the* worship for mortals." By 30 May, she knew the end was imminent, as well as the end of her sorrow. "I sat by him with my hand in his till four o'clock, and he then became quieter and has had some comfortable sleep. . . . What shall I be without my Father? It will seem as if a part of my moral nature were gone. I had a horrid vision of myself last night becoming earthly sensual and devilish for want of that purifying restraining influence." Robert Evans died sometime in the early morning of 31 May, and was buried at Chilvers Coton on 6 June.

Liberated though she finally was, Mary Ann's explanation of why her father meant so much to her is compelling. That she feared certain strains in her nature without his admonitions suggests she saw him as some Old Testament God waiting to punish her, and she eagerly sought out the punishment as a way of chastising herself. The degree of self-denial here is intense: she was prepared to burst out into joy, happiness, physical indulgence, and only the presence of that omnipotent God-figure curbed her excess, a curb she welcomed as fit punishment for her having even entertained such feelings. By June of 1849, when she went abroad with the Brays, she was a bundle of contradictory impulses. She would not escape free.

The European trip had been planned before Evans's death as a way of providing Mary Ann with some relief from her duties. Burying her father on the 6th, she met Froude on the 7th, and departed from Coventry with Bray on the 11th, for London, to join Cara. At first, Bray had thought Froude might accompany them to the continent, but that piece of possible matchmaking did not work out. Froude was already preparing to marry. The journey of the three friends was open-ended. Mary Ann needed to recuperate, although her subsequent letters after she settled in Geneva did not indicate undue grief. Further, mourning did not preclude a hasty departure.

Cara Bray does indicate her friend was still depressed, although Mary Ann's letters, when they do pick up, are not grief-stricken or revelatory of low spirits. Nevertheless, Cara felt it might have been a mistake to carry off Mary Ann like this. Some of the places they visited afforded spectacular views. They traveled the Grand Corniche through Nice to Genoa, and then through Milan to Lake Como and Lake Maggiore. It is true that in 1860, when she revisited some of these places, Mary Ann, now George Eliot, revealed how wretched, peevish, and "utterly morbid" she had been, and how sympathetic and kind Cara was. The travelers ascribed this wretchedness to Mary Ann's feelings for her father, and no doubt that was partly the reason. But deeper causes suggest that her peevishness and morbidity, such as they were, were associated with other, unresolved feelings which dipped more profoundly into her condition.

There is the question of an emptiness she was not prepared to fill. She was bereft now of her closest family friend. Her function having ended, she had, at close to thirty, no one to attach herself to. With that removed, the very liberation she had achieved felt directionless, without a goal. She now had time, a small income, good friends, even, possibly, grand thoughts; but the lovely sights could not themselves fill what she sensed she needed: this was, after all, the woman who in ten years would be a famous author. The depression Cara mentions indicates Mary Ann was on the edge of great decisions, which at her mature age must be final ones. To remain at Geneva while the party returned to Coventry was the first stage of that decision to transform herself; but reshaping of self did not come easily, and for a woman of her time it was a momentous undertaking.

Mary Ann wrote Mrs. Henry Houghton (Fanny) from Vevey that she hoped her stay in Geneva would "do more for my health and spirits than travelling has proved able to do." With her stay at Geneva, at the pension Campagne Plongeon, she would finally have her own little room, and her independence was assured. Half a century later, when Virginia Woolf's father died, she and her siblings moved from their Kensington home to Bloomsbury. Mary Ann's Geneva pension, while more tepid, served much the same purpose: in Woolf's words, to try something new, to be different, to put everything on trial. Financially, however, Mary Ann needed help if she was to exist apart from her Coventry life.

By remaining in Geneva, she signaled she was cutting herself off from her family, whom in any event she did not want to depend upon. Even while she had achieved the first step of what she had been yearning to do, her dilemma was still acute. She could not count on marrying, probably ever; she needed some position as a teacher or governess; she could, possibly, write, like Harriet Martineau, but she did not as yet know what or for whom. She did start a notebook in Geneva, in which she wrote about herself and her impressions, eventually running to 1860. But the most significant parts, from 1849 to 1854, forty-six pages of what we must assume were intimate details—the period covering her Geneva stay, her *Westminster Review* work with Chapman, and her meeting with Spencer and Lewes—were destroyed by John Cross after he selectively used them for his whitewashed *Life* of his now dead wife.

The Campagne Plongeon was a fortuitous stop for Mary Ann: located near the lake outside Geneva, on the present site of the Restaurant des Eaux-Vives, and run by Jeanne Madeleine Eleonore Adline de Vallière, a woman worthy of her name. Madame de Vallière was seventeen years older than Mary Ann, living with two sons, one twenty-one, the other eight. She and her husband had run a pension in Lausanne, where he remained with their other six children. She was a woman of some culture, well read, and her pension attracted people of quality, including many refugees from various European revolutions. The political atmosphere was clearly conservative, since the lodgers were people on the run. Mary Ann soon found herself drawn into a circle of women who, while quite different from her in virtually every way, provided that female companionship which was so valuable at this stage of her development. In one regard or another, these were women who fell somewhat outside ordinary or traditional roles, and they provided excellent contrast with the domestic situation she had left behind in Coventry.

Writing to Bray and signing her name as Pollian, Mary Ann reports how settled in and comfortable she is only two days after arriving. She has nothing but praise for Madame de Vallière, calling her a woman of "feeling and language, evidently accustomed to the society of superior people." Mary Ann fell easily into others' company, mentioning to Cara "an elderly English lady," who was Mrs. Nagle Lock, the widow of Captain Nagle Lock of the Royal Navy. At some point, Mary Ann wrote notes for a novel which included the names of several of these women encountered at the pension. Although at first she thought Mrs. Lock had a waspish look, she took to her—"she is just the sort of person I shall like to have to speak to—not at all 'congenial' but with a character of her own." Mary Ann mentions two American ladies: "They are very rich, very smart, and very vulgar—just a specimen of Americanism according to the Tories." She calls the daughter "Miss America" and says she bragged of being presented at court. We feel we have entered a Henry James novel.

Mary Ann chides Mme. de Vallière for saying things "so true they are insufferable," but she recognizes such talk is necessary to create a community of the disparate group at the pension. "She has been very kind and motherly to me. I believe she has found out already that I do not know how to look after my own interests—but I am sure she is a straight forward person. I like her better every time I see her." The last few sentences reveal a more tolerant Mary Ann, suddenly able to see beneath the trivialities of conversation to the decency of the person. This would become her strength when she turned to writing *Scenes of Clerical Life.*

Just two days after arriving, Mary Ann found she could enter a foreign arena and define her place in it. She was also writing, not only the immensely long letters to Cara and Sara but in her notebook; and she was observing, seeking out physical and other details, learning to measure people who passed in and out of the pension, giving herself an education outside of books. More than this, she was taking on the persona of a female living an independent life, clearly an adventure for a woman of those times. Whatever trepidation and misgivings she may have felt in the past, she was undertaking a mysterious journey.

The relationship with Mrs. Lock deepened. "She is quite a mother to me— helps me buy my candles and do all my shopping—takes care of me at dinner and quite rejoices when she sees me enjoy conversation or anything else." She finds the St. Germains delightful: the marquise "with kindness enough to make the ultra-politeness of her manners quite genuine." The "vulgar Americans" have left, and in their place is a lady from Frankfurt with her daughter and governess. She comes to know the young German, the Baron de Herder—"the veritable grandson of the great Herder.* I should think he is not more than two or three and twenty—very good-natured, but a most determined enemy to all gallantry. I fancy he is a Communist, but he seems to have been joked about his opinions by Mde. de Vallière and the rest until he has determined to keep a proud silence on such matters."

Withal, Mary Ann recognizes she would not be such a sharp observer if she had her books with her. One of the things she had to do to transform herself into a writer of fiction was to rethink and redo her style of writing. What could be heavy and ponderous in her letters or in her reviews had to be lightened. Her powers of description had to be broadened; her very notion of language and vocabulary had to change, to include more ordinary and everyday words. One way she was able to do this was by means of analogy: creating the trivial and ordinary, but comparing or contrasting it to the larger world of nature or the cosmos. Her experience in the Geneva pension reassured her that she had an eye for detail and the trivial. While she would continue to develop intellectually, she also evolved on a parallel track of intensive observation and perception on the small scale that would become her fictional standard.

In talks with the marquise, Mary Ann is advised that she has isolated herself by her studies, "that I am too cold and have too little confidence in the feelings of others towards me. . . ." She is witty about two young Germans who stay at the pension. "Prussians . . . the eldest odious, with an eternal simper and a mouth of dubious cleanliness. He speaks French very little and has a miserable

---

* Johann Gottfried von Herder (1744–1803), a philosopher who developed the "folk theory" of races, which later became transformed into racial theories and into the Aryan concept of German superiority under Hitler. Herder stressed feeling, language, history, and uniform laws as ways of defining a folk, in a paradoxical way not too different from how Eliot evolved in her own thinking.

sputter between a grunt and a snuffle so that when he begins to speak to one one's brain begins to twist and one feels inclined to rush out of the room. His brother frowns instead of simpering and is therefore more endurable." The descriptions are excellent preparation for those characters George Eliot would dislike; one sees in these distasteful brothers some of the mouth movement of Grandcourt in *Daniel Deronda*.

Yet within all this apparent warmth, Mary Ann's discomfort pokes through. She tells Cara and Sara she does not know if she likes the pension sufficiently to stay on during the winter. "I have been under the disadvantage of wanting all on which I chiefly depend—my books, etc." She says she will give it another month, and then decide. Part of the difficulty is that the pension was getting away from Madame de Vallière; with the illness of the housekeeper and house-maid, Madame "is not the best manager in the world." But more than that, Mary Ann says there "is just as much 'world' here as in England—just as many eyes are on you—and one requires the utmost flexibility of mind and feeling to render intercourse tolerable." Even in this small world, Mary Ann finds herself caught up in crosscurrents and intrigues; and while it would prove beneficial for the fiction writer, it was slowly becoming too intrusive on the intensely private twenty-nine-year-old.

Other elements poke through: her family writes little, and she complains that her half-sister Fanny writes not at all. "I shall be ready to write to every one when every one has written to me, but I require *warming* up by letters first." She now finds she is completely dependent on friends, and this disturbs her, espe-cially the neglect of Isaac, who is for her something of a stand-in for the now deceased Robert Evans.

She is, of course, sad to hear that Chrissey's Clara has died, at less than four months old. "However I cannot regret that I am not there, for I am really good for nothing yet, and I feel that my future health and actions entirely depend on my recovering thoroughly my strength and spirit." She has to decide whether to remain at Plongeon or go on, perhaps, to Paris, which would be more expensive. One major reason for leaving is that she prefers to be the starer rather than the one stared at; further, people have told her she is not old enough to "ramble about at will." She adds: ". . . I confess I am more sensitive than I thought I should be to the idea that my being alone is odd. I thought my old appearance [i.e., unmarriageable state] would have been a sufficient sanction and that the very idea of impropriety was ridiculous. . . . As long as people carry a Mademoi-selle before their name, there is far less liberty for them on the Continent than in England."

Yet even the beauty of her setting, which she cherishes, has its countereffect. And it is all connected to her feelings of drifting. "The perpetual presence of all this beauty has somewhat the effect of mesmerism or chloroform. I feel some-times as if I were sinking into an agreeable state of numbness on the verge of unconsciousness and seem to want well pinching to rouse me." If anything, the scenes of "perfect enchantment" create guilt that she is wasting her time. Not unexpectedly, her health was affected. "I have had," she says, "a bilious attack, partly I believe from the way of living here—long fasts etc.*—indeed I have never been well since I came."

She considers shifting her lodgings, Plongeon having outlasted its usefulness. Her first thought was of private lodgings in town, but money is a problem, and she inquires about selling her *Encyclopaedia Britannica* at one-half price, and her globes. The first cost the enormous sum of £42 and the globes £8.10, so that half of that would give her enough money for several months in private lodgings, if she factored in income from her trust.

Mary Ann's extensively detailed letters, incidentally—an extraordinarily long one to the Brays followed on 20 September—were a way she could connect herself to her home, and another means by which she could turn her friends also into maternal figures. She reports to them her observations, but in some deeper way she is as well seeking their approval, or through their advice trying to find her way. We do not need their letters to observe how they encouraged her and reinforced her attempt at independence, how they wanted to think well of everything she did. The bulk of the 20 September letter concerns possible plans, whether to stay or leave, and if she leaves, to go to Thimoléon Labauche's so as to be with Mme. de Ludwigsdorff.

But of equal importance are Mary Ann's novelistic observations of this friend, her attempts to penetrate an arranged surface in order to probe the person beneath. "Her character," she writes to the Brays, "is really remarkably destitute of animalism and she has just the sort of antipathy towards people who offend her refined instincts which we know so well in another person." As for still another family, the Forbeses, she is precise: "Mr. Forbes with a fine moral and intellectual head but spoiled by immense pride and vanity, which betray themselves in his thin affected-looking lips at the first glance." His daughter, Elizabeth Jane, sat by Mary Ann's side at dinner and thought to herself—as she told the older woman—"That is a grave lady. I do not think I shall like her much," but then as soon as Mary Ann spoke to her the young woman looked into her eyes and felt she could love her. Meanwhile, Mme. de Ludwigsdorff pets Mary Ann. "She sends me tea when I wake in the morning, orangeflower water when I go to bed, grapes, and her maid to wait on me. She says if I like she will spend the winter after this at Paris with me and introduce me to her friends there—but she does not mean to attach herself to me, because I shall never like her long. I shall be tired of her when I have sifted her etc."

Under these seeming trivialities of social intercourse, several aspects of Mary Ann's character were shaping themselves in a final way. Her need for affection, here female affection, was overwhelming. Perhaps because of a distanced mother, her emotional life had not as yet developed, and she relied on these

---

* The "long fasts" remain a mystery, since Mary Ann did not appear to have any food peculiarities. One possibility is that in seeking her privacy, she abandoned the pension dining room, preferring to fast rather than be sociable.

mothering women, as well as on their expressions of affection and love. She would, in time, replace these women when she did tire of them with a series of men—Chapman, Spencer, and finally Lewes. Much of the society she preferred in her maturity was male, and it, too, came to be adulatory of her. Even Spencer deferred to her intellect.

The significance of the Plongeon stay was that she was considered special: grave, of enormous intellectual capacity, a person in the process of developing and reshaping. Mme. de Ludwigsdorff's insight that Mary Ann would tire of her is prescient, not only of the immediate situation but of her friend's overall needs: the pressure to move, to keep replacing pieces as she moved on, always gaining emotional support even as she began to outgrow the admirer.

For Mary Ann, the Plongeon was a miniature society, a form of subculture, of the kind she would later write about; eschewing the whole, she concentrated on just such miniatures. She notes a Mrs. Wood, a guest at the pension: "Mrs. Wood a very ugly but lady-like little woman who is under an infatuation as it regards her caps, always wearing the brightest rose-colour or intensest blue, with a complexion not unlike a dirty primose grove." We hear the cadenced descriptions of the Dodson sisters in *Mill* beginning to march in. Mary Ann is amused that one woman thinks she is an amiable, sweet creature—"which will give you a better opinion of her [Mlle. de Phaisan's] charity than her penetration."

She sadly misses the "solidity of mind" and "expansion of feeling" of her Coventry friends. She is witty about her situation. "I am still thin and my hair is falling off—so how much will be left of me by next April I am afraid to imagine. I shall be length without breadth—quite bald and without money to buy a wig. . . ."* She nevertheless plans to remain in Geneva until spring, when she will return to England.

Lodgings at an apartment in the house of M. François D'Albert-Durade, at Rue des Chanoines No. 107, would become her new address in early October. M. and Mme. D'Albert-Durade were a family of four, he an artist, with two male children. Mary Ann paid 150 francs a month, including meals and light, and would be the sole lodger, as Mme. de Ludwigsdorff had been the previous year. She sounds cheerful at the prospect, although we cannot be certain why the Plongeon became suddenly so inhospitable to her. Mismanagement was, of course, becoming clear; but more probably Mary Ann was seeking artistic company and saw in the Plongeon a dead end. Sara in the meantime had apparently revealed fears about her friend's welfare, but Mary Ann tells the Brays she would prefer encouragement to warnings and checkings.

As we read in the interstices of her words, we see that while independence was a blessing, it was decidedly mixed. We recall how in Casaubon in *Middlemarch* she defines pleasure by its absence, even when the middle-aged (but old in spirit) clergyman is prepared to seize happiness. Like Mary Ann in Geneva, even as she struggled to release herself: "Here was a weary experience

---

* At one point, Mary Ann's friend Martha Jackson called her Clematis ("mental beauty"), a flower-like label that would hardly fit someone lacking both breadth and hair.

in which he was as utterly condemned to loneliness as in the despair which sometimes threatened him while toiling in the morass of authorship without seeming nearer to the goal." The very thing he had waited for proves to be sinister and filled with dread. Eliot is extraordinary in plotting out Casaubon's feelings, in capturing the crosscurrents of a spirit attempting to open up even while it recognizes there is only fear in flexibility.

Yet in creating this scene, which communicates so well her own fears at liberation of a self caught in contradictory impulses, Eliot is not finished. The other side to Casaubon and his cautious foray into possible enjoyment is Dorothea Brooke herself. She is moving, as it were, in the opposite direction: castigating pleasure, joy, and sensuality in favor of closing down. Her life hitherto had been a sequence of small pleasures, like riding, and now she has chosen to reject them in favor of dedication. Even as Casaubon contemplates the other side of his scholarly pursuits, Dorothea opts for duty and dedication. If we put the two together, a ballet of contradictory impulses, we have a good sense of Mary Ann poised in 1849, very much caught up in her own conflicting impulses. When she confesses the following to the Brays, she is seeking some way to bind the two selves. "I believe I am so constituted that I shall never be cured of any faults except by God's discipline—if human beings would but believe it, they do me most good by saying to me the kindest things truth will permit. . . ." Failure always beckoned. As she told John Cross during their brief marriage, when he asked her to write her autobiography: "The only thing I should care much to dwell on would be the absolute despair I suffered from ever being able to achieve anything. No one could ever have felt greater despair, and a knowledge of this might be a help to some other struggler. . . ." The nightly fears she later ascribed to Gwendolen Harleth, in *Deronda,* she told Cross were hers—fears of failure and impending disaster, visions of death.

Her need for money became acute. Selling off some of her possessions would provide funds for lessons "and other means of culture." She recognized she could live more reasonably at other pensions, but decided to pay the extra money to enjoy the company of "intelligent respectable people even at the sacrifice of not saving £8 or 10." At this stage, there was little of the Bohemian in Mary Ann; she feared falling into disreputable or scruffy company, although later that would change when she moved to London and lived with the Chapmans. Then she directly scorned the morals of her family.

The move to the new lodgings, however, did not assuage her disquiet over finding her own direction; we observe the drift, the uncertainty. "When people who are dressing elegantly and driving about to make calls every day of their life," she writes, "have been telling me of their troubles—their utter hopelessness of *ever finding a vein worth working in the future life* [italics added]—my thoughts have turned towards many whose sufferings are of a more tangible character, and I have really felt all the old commonplaces about the equality of human destinies. . . ." Once at the new place, she did nevertheless find satisfaction. The house was exceptionally well run by Mme. and M. D'Albert. Although physically deformed, D'Albert was a man of considerable charm and energy. Even the sons seemed quiet and well-behaved. Her schedule was set: breakfast in her room at 8:30, lunch at 12:30 (the major meal of the day), supper at 4, and tea at 8. Her reflections at the start of her stay: "It would really have been a pity to have staid at Plongeon out of reach of everything and with people so little worth talking to." She admits she hasn't as yet discovered the "disagreeables" here and knows she will, but she thinks they will not be too numerous.

She suddenly, however, becomes particularly harsh in writing about Mary Sibree, probably because the latter had shifted her faith. Clearly, the remarks have some application to herself, possibly to feelings of guilt that she has forsaken "the hardships of the new Protestantism" now taken up by her onetime friend. Mary Ann seems to be describing caustically a fictional character, Rosamond Vincy, Gwendolen Harleth, or even Esther Lyon. "Sibreeanism is that degree of egotism which we call bad taste but which does not reach to gross selfishness—the egotism that does not think of others, but would be very glad to do them good if it did think of them—the egotism that eats up all the bread and butter and is ready to die of confusion and distress after having done it." About her host and hostess, she is no less precise, although far kinder.

> For M. D'Albert I love him already as if he were a father and brother both. You must know he is not more than 4 feet high with a deformed spine— the result of an accident in his boyhood—but on this little body is placed a finely formed head, full in every direction. The face is plain with small features, and rather haggard looking, but all the lines and the wavy hair indicate the temperament of the artist.* I have not heard a word or seen a gesture of his yet that was not perfectly in harmony with an exquisite moral refinement—indeed one feels a better person always when he is present.†

M. D'Albert sang and played a little on the piano, activities after Mary Ann's heart. As for Mme. D'Albert, she was enchanting in her own right: ". . . [she] has less of genius and more of cleverness—a really lady-like person, who says everything well. She brings up her children admirably—two nice intelligent boys. . . . I have not said half I feel about these good creatures because I am afraid you will laugh at me." Their whole behavior, she says, is as "if I were a guest whom they delighted to honour."

These observations were, in part, nourished by Mary Ann's desire to justify her move, as well as to find a "family" which would replace, temporarily or not, the strictures of her own. All of her moves—to pensions in Geneva, to the

---

* The details are very close to those used to describe Philip Wakem in *Mill*, including the accident in childhood, the deformity of the spine, the fine head on a stunted body. The face: a "melancholy boy's face; the brown hair round it waved and curled at the ends. . . . This Wakem was a pale, puny fellow, and it was quite clear he would not be able to play at anything worthy speaking of; but he handled his pencil in an enviable manner, and was apparently making one thing after another without any trouble."

† M. D'Albert-Durade translated George Eliot into French, doing *Adam Bede, Silas Marner, Romola,* and *Felix Holt* during her lifetime, and *Scenes of Clerical Life* in 1883, after her death.

Chapmans in London, then to Lewes and his large brood—were actions that brought her into surrogate families. She entered other people's lives as she had entered Robert Evans's as the youngest surviving child of two sets of children. In some way, she was replicating her own placement in the family, introducing herself into the affairs of others as someone they would watch over, maintain, even worry about. In every stage of her opening up, she used family groups as a means of educating herself to aspects of life different from her own family. We should not ignore the fact that Sara and Cara Hennell were the youngest of eight children, and Bray himself fathered six. These foreshadowed the large Lewes establishment. One cannot conceive of a man motivating himself in this way, since he would *acquire,* whereas Mary Ann's method was *to be acquired.* "Mde. D'Albert anticipates all my wants," she wrote the Brays, "and makes a spoiled child of me. . . . I like these dear people better and better." In time, Mary Ann referred to her hostess as "Mamam."

There is little question she had entered a household with an inviting hearth. Her room was pleasant, with a view of the street, looking out on a convent built on the site of the house where John Calvin had died. The food was uniformly good, as she reports to her friends, "two kinds of meat thoroughly well-cooked, nice vegetables and pudding." She rented a piano by the month, and enjoyed the company of the D'Alberts' musical friends. She was permitted an unlimited supply of candles. The friends did not pass down into history, but they were sufficiently renowned to leave a trail: Clara Luce Adèle Herpin, daughter of a well-known Geneva physician and herself a fine pianist; Jean François Chaponnière and his father, the younger a physician, writer, and scientist, the father a onetime art student, a poet, and a playwright. Amidst all these reports of delightful people, Mary Ann sounds a note with personal reverberations: "I am beginning to lose respect for the petty acumen that sees difficulties. I love the souls that rush along to their goal with a full stream of perpetual negatives, which after all are but the disease of the soul, to be expelled by fortifying the principle of vitality."

This last sentiment suggests how the change in atmosphere has strengthened her resolve, even though she would backslide and rue her lack of direction. Also implied in her remarks is the fact she was getting on well with strangers: that she had communicated to them she was special. Her remarks become less satirical or cutting, more generous and accepting; all of which indicates a person more apt to settle into her own sense of things without the need to wound others in order to define herself. This acceptance comes in her assessment of the D'Alberts' religious beliefs, an assessment of considerable significance in Mary Ann's development of her later novelistic philosophy. Rather than opposing or mocking their evangelicalism, she almost accepts it, since she finds it to possess greater breadth than the practitioners in England.

Expenses, as ever, remained a problem. The Coventry *Herald,* Bray's paper, was arriving with an exorbitant price of over a franc, and Mary Ann felt she must renounce the "too costly pleasure of seeing it." Husbanding her money, she took local excursions to the Salève, a 3,000-foot mountain with views of the lake, the town, and the Jura on one side and Mount Blanc on the other. She found the walks around Geneva "enchanting." She describes her life to Sara as that "happy situation." There is, she writes, "an indescribable charm to me in this form of human nest-making. . . . One is so out of reach of intruders, so undiverted from one's occupations by externals, so free from cold rushing winds through halldoors, one feels in a downy nest high up in a good old tree. I have always had a hankering after this sort of life and I find it was a true instinct of what would suit me." Given this idyllic picture of her urban nest, it is curious that George Eliot failed to write about cities or city life, that she did not even indirectly use Geneva in her novels. Rural life so dominated her earliest years, probably, that these pleasurable urban months were effaced, at least as far as fictional purposes were concerned.

As for her more intellectual activities, these she outlines to the Brays in early December (the 4th), having now passed her thirtieth birthday. Perhaps the proximity of her birthday, on 22 November, brought home to her that she was not using her brain sufficiently or she owed some explanation to the Brays that her life was not becoming all creature comforts or sensuous pleasures. "Spinoza and I have been divorced for several months. My want of health has obliged me to renounce all application" on the *Tractatus Theologico-Politicus*. In this connection, Chapman had indicated his willingness to publish Mary Ann's translation and had asked Bray about her progress; thus this letter, that all progress had stopped. Her "want of health" was not the real nub here, since her well-being had picked up considerably at the D'Alberts' home. "I take walks, play on the piano, read Voltaire, talk to my friends, and just take a dose of mathematics every day to prevent my brain from becoming quite soft." She therefore absolved Chapman from any obligation to her. She turned away from the Spinoza, she tells the Brays, because what is needed is "a true estimate of his life and system." She stresses his solitary life, someone who "says from his own soul what all the world is saying by rote. . . ." The bringing together here of Spinoza and Mary Ann herself as "solitary lives" speaking from the soul cannot go unnoticed. As noted, the translation was never completed.

Intellect, however, is not all. She loves being mothered. "She [Madame D'Albert] kisses me like a mother, and I am baby enough to find that a great addition to my happiness." As for the rest, "I am careful for nothing. I am a sort of supernumerary spoon, and there will be no damage to the set if I am lost." Although she voices how she misses her loved ones, England for the moment does not beckon: ". . . I can only think with a shudder of returning to England. It looks to me like a land of gloom, of ennui, of platitude, but in the midst of all this it is the land of duty and affection, and the only ardent hope I have for my future life is to have given to me some woman's duty, some possibility of devoting myself where I may see a daily result of pure calm blessedness in the life of another." This last remark is curious, and it appears she was dissembling to her friends. The suddenly expressed desire to be dutiful to another is not the drift of her attitudes. Although in a holding pattern, and seemingly enjoying moments, she was preparing for a dramatic move, not toward service but toward self-expression.

Hardly pursuing service or duty, she was attending a course of lectures on experimental physics given by M. le professeur Arthur Auguste de la Rive, at the Athénée and Hôtel de Ville, with an audience mainly of women. Quite distinguished in both chemistry and physics, de la Rive had been a professor of physics at the University of Geneva, and had invented a process of gold plating that won him an award from the Paris Academy of Sciences. Mary Ann attended twice a week, and we can assume the lectures were at a high level, not condescendingly directed toward a nontechnical audience. She also sat for a portrait by M. D'Albert,* and, as one observer remarked, even with her new coiffure and the painter's generosity, "she is no beauty." What the portrait lacked was the animation which gave her face a different look, as well as her voice, low and modulated, which created the sense of great inner strength and, therefore, of a beauty radiating outward.

She attended the opera to hear Marietta Alboni, the Italian contralto, whom Mary Ann labeled "a very fat syren"; as well as comedies acted by D'Albert's friends. These she praised, as superior to professional actors. Her spirits seem high here, as in her general remarks to her half-sister, Fanny Houghton. While admitting homesickness, she nevertheless says she will experience real grief "at parting from the excellent people with whom I am living. I feel they are my *friends*—without entering into or even knowing the greater part of my views, they understand my character, and have a real interest in me." Yet amidst these positive comments, especially her attachment to Mme. D'Albert as "Mamam," she reveals that the severe winter has proven a drawback in her recovering her strength. She has lost, she says, weeks from headaches, although she is better than when she was at the Plongeon pension. She now, in a reversal, or else in uncertainty, longs for England in the winter: ". . . at least for all except those who are rich enough to buy English comforts everywhere. I hate myself for caring about carpets, easy-chairs, and coal fires—one's soul is under a curse, and can preach no truth while one is in bondage to the flesh in this way; but alas! habit is the purgatory in which we suffer for our past sins."

In her newsy letter the following week to the Brays, she still complains of ills. But she also praises the beauties of the Jura, and admits to walking all day after rising as late as ten. "I have had no discipline, and shall return to you more of a spoiled child than ever. Indeed I think I am destined to be so in the end—one of the odious swarm of voracious caterpillars, soon to be swept away from the earth by a tempest." Her fears of a slothful life are apparent, and surely this is affecting her health. "I am getting better—bodily. I have much less headache, but the least excitement fatigues me. Certainly if one cannot have a malady to

* D'Albert painted at least three copies of the original, done in 1850, with the original itself going to the National Portrait Gallery in 1905. Mary Ann received a copy, 13¾ × 10½ inches, which remained with her manuscripts until all were sold at auction in 1923, from the estate of Mrs. Charles Lee Lewes, George Henry Lewes's daughter-in-law.

carry one off rapidly, the only sensible thing is to get well and fat, and I believe I shall be driven to that alternative."

She was, because of money and health problems, planning to return to Rose-hill, and she thought D'Albert might accompany her to Paris; but she says he cannot afford the journey. Yet when she did travel to England—they left on 18 March 1850—he did accompany her all the way. In her excitement at leaving Geneva, she repeats that she has become "an idle wretch." During the Alps crossing the snow was so deep they went by sledge, then crossed the Channel from Calais, which made Mary Ann ill. On 25 March, she left D'Albert in London and returned to Rosehill. This shift in her life now became as important as the original plan to remain by herself in Geneva. As her letters indicated, she feared becoming slothful and idle, losing purpose in the sheer pleasure of being taken care of. But other changes were also taking place. Her letters are signed Polly and Pollian, and in 1850 she also adopted Marian as an alternative for Mary Ann.

We must assume that even as she describes herself in unflattering terms, the internal Mary Ann was shifting into something new but still undefinable. Some resolve was taken, or some act of determination was present, none of it apparent as yet—certainly not the direction any of this would eventually take. Coming home, however, was a catalyst, even while she described herself to Sara as "idle and naughty—on ne peut plus—sinking into heathenish ignorance and woman's frivolity. . . ." Her need to describe herself repeatedly in these terms indicates she has sunk to the lowest estimate she could make, but was readying herself for the climb out. The next decade would prove to be a remarkable one for her, remarkable for any person in the nineteenth century, but especially astonishing for a woman. For even as she perceived herself as idle, naughty, and slothful, she was steeling herself, in her way, to become George Eliot. Not ripeness, but reshaping was all.

6

London at Mid-Century, and the Westminster Review

> "Fancy what a game at chess would be if all the chessmen had passions and intellects, more or less small and cunning: if you were not only uncertain about your adversary's men, but a little uncertain also about your own; if your knight could shuffle himself on to a new square by the sly; if your bishop, in disgust at your castling, could wheedle your pawns out of their places; and if your pawns, hating you because they are pawns, could make away from their appointed posts that you might get checkmate on a sudden. You might be the longest-headed of deductive reasoners, and yet you might be beaten by your own pawns."

Marian's siblings seemed pleased to have her home, and she went to Griff to stay with Isaac. Yet apparently even while she was welcomed, she did not find England totally congenial. To Martha Jackson, a little more than a week after her return, she said she was becoming uncertain about her plans, whether to remain in England or to return to Geneva. Now that she had conditioned her family to her type of life, she could stretch her possibilities and try for London alone. For good or for ill, her family must have recognized that the Marian who returned was not the Mary Ann who had left several months before; that she had made steps which went beyond them. She refers glancingly to the past: "I have seen much trial since we met," she tells Martha, a statement stronger than anything we know about her.[*] "My return to England is anything but joyous to me, for old associations are rather painful than otherwise to me. We are apt to complain of the weight of duty, but when it is taken from us, and

---

[*] Whether this meant an involvement with D'Albert or not, we cannot determine. A case could possibly be made that their closeness, including their trip together to England, had created an "understanding," but how emotionally involved this was we do not know. Marian in writing to him in French did use the familiar form, and these letters D'Albert destroyed, fearing that the wrong interpretation might be made of them after his death. The circumstantial evidence seems to point toward something more than regular friendship, but we cannot go beyond that.

we are left at liberty to choose for ourselves, we find that the old life was the easier one." Her doubts are apparent.

As she made the rounds of her siblings' homes, first Griff with Isaac and then Meriden with Chrissey and her remaining brood, she saw them through changed eyes. When she visited Chrissey, she was happy with her, and dependent on her sister's sweetness, but she recognized that she was of no importance in their lives. Caught up as the Clarkes were in their loud and active family, with finances precarious, they were too concentrated on themselves to display more than kindness. As a result of these experiences, Marian began to consider lodgings with Chapman in London. On 11 April, even before visiting Chrissey at Meriden, Marian asked Sara to inquire about Chapman's prices for lodgings, and to ask further about other London boardinghouses. Chapman kept a large house on the Strand, formerly a hotel, and he managed his businesses in the same building. He had prepared a prospectus for potential lodgers on both sides of the Atlantic (Emerson and Greeley, among other Americans, visited), offering his residence for short or long stays for ladies and gentlemen, a combination of the advantages of a hotel and the quiet and comfort of a private residence. It was a curious establishment, as Marian would discover.

Chapman drew prospective lodgers with more than quiet surroundings and all the comforts of home. The central location of the house, midway between the City and West End, within brief walking distance of the theaters and House of Parliament, close to steamers and buses, was an added attraction. But Chapman was not finished with his pitch; he was, after all, a publisher,* with his American agent Little and Brown, Booksellers. He offered Americans desirous of adding to their libraries aid "from his long experience as an extensive purchaser of all kinds of Old and New Books for Exportation. . . ." This was one side of his prospectus; on the other, Mrs. Chapman listed rates for board and residence at 142 Strand. For first-class accommodations, £2.10 a week, which was a good deal of money, and far more than Marian could afford; for second class, 5 shillings a week less, still a considerable sum; for an additional person in any of the rooms, an additional £1.10. Fires were extra, at 3s. 6d.; boots cleaned and other attendance, the same fee. All this was exclusive of wine, spirits, and malt liquors, in effect, a cash bar. The lodgings, clearly, were not for struggling artists; no "La Bohème" this. Hours for meals were posted: breakfast at 8:30 A.M., luncheon at 1 P.M., dinner at 6 P.M., tea at 8:30 P.M.

It all sounded like a well-organized, efficient operation; but it was more *Fawlty Towers* than the prospectus made it seem, and, in fact, the lodging house did not turn a profit unless it was nearly full, which was rare. On paper, the Chapman establishment *seemed* like an ideal business, combining book publishing, magazine editing and publishing, and a respectable lodging for respectable visitors. As Marian discovered, the reality was different, although the place did possess distinct charm.

---

* He was also a dim forerunner of Eliot's Felix Holt, in that Chapman was a watchmaker, a future student of medicine, and the son of a pharmacist, all later reproduced in Felix.

In the meantime, while she waited on costs before departing, she invited M. D'Albert to visit Rosehill on 7 May, where he stayed for three days and she showed him Kenilworth and Warwick. They would not meet again for ten years, by which time she was George Eliot and on her way to becoming famous. Owing to her feeling that she was supernumerary in the presence of her family, Marian decided, after visits to half-siblings Robert and Fanny, to remain at Rosehill for the next seven months, until November of 1850, when she lodged with the Chapmans. There would be tragedy in the small circle of friends, when Charles Hennell, at forty-one, died of tuberculosis on 2 September; but Marian's grief was mitigated by the fact that his widow, Rufa, was not her closest comrade, surely not so close as Sara, whom she repeatedly referred to as her spouse. Mary Ann was now firmly Marian—the French form—but also Polly and Pollian to her friends. Pollian was either a female version of Apollyon, the destroyer in Revelation, or else Apollo, god of light and music. How much was disguise, how much self-expression, how much transformation, how much process, unfortunately, cannot be gleaned from her letters, which in the period were few. Nevertheless, momentous changes were coming.

We do know that John Chapman, now twenty-nine and married to a woman fourteen years older, Susanna Brewitt, an heiress to a Nottingham lace manufacturing fortune, came to Rosehill in October. His companion was Robert William Mackay, someone who might have been suitable for Marian had the two of them found each other more sympathetic. Mackay was a bachelor and an author (*The Progress of the Intellect, As Exemplified in the Religious Development of the Greeks and Hebrews*, a book heavy enough even for her), with some income from property. He was evidently "a catch," but Marian saw him differently, not as a suitor, but as part of a collection: someone whose qualities she would store up to create that composite, Edward Casaubon, in *Middlemarch*. Mackay was Casaubon's exact age, forty-seven, and he was interested in myths and mythologies, especially in nature cults, and of course drawn to Strauss's conception of the Holy Book as a sequence of myths. Chapman asked Marian to write a review of the book for the *Westminster Review*, which he now edited.

Just after the middle of November, Marian finished the review, delivered it to Chapman in London, and lodged with him for two weeks. The review, while not definitive, does reveal Marian's philosophical-theological concerns at this critical time when she decided to make her way as a writer. Now committed more or less to Auguste Comte's positivism, in which society, treated scientifically, is viewed in progressive stages of development, Marian also held that historical examination can be useful in shaping contemporary society. But in examining the past, while we should see how each race has its own needs and stages of development, we should not in succeeding generations hope to retain the spirit as well as the forms of the past. That is futile. Marian was arguing for certain absolutist ideas, which are amenable to the development of all races in all ages—some scientific container for all myths, allegories, and even memories. This meant jettisoning some of the vulgar and condescending racial ideas she had expressed earlier.

With a vengeance she was going after her previous religiosity and spiritualism. Not that Comte's so-called scientific thought was absolutist; but it did permit a given society to find what best served its needs for growth and progress. It was absolutist only in its insistence that past certainties had given way to new needs. Marian could ascribe to Comte's Law of the Three Stages, in which man passes from theological interpretations (where the supernatural is guide) through the metaphysical (in which fundamental energies or ideas seem to drive natural phenomena) to the positive, or final, stage, in which observation and experimentation explain natural phenomena. Such a "sociology" (Comte coined the word), further based on succeeding forms of science, could lead to man's harmony, happiness, and comfort. Comte's positivism should be viewed as one of those overarching nineteenth-century philosophies that, like utilitarianism in England under Bentham and Mill, attempted to find some replacement for the loss of religious belief and, at the same time, to provide a new religion, as it were, for a new age. Marxism ran a slightly later parallel course.

Marian found herself caught up in Comte's philosophy of man and society for much of her life, although it was qualified by her own sense of sadness, even tragedy, as man always confronted a fate or destiny seemingly larger than he could comprehend. If we had to cite one of the decisive moments in her intellectual and personal development, it came in November 1850, not only in the review of Mackay's book but in her decision to lodge with Chapman, whose reputation for personal irregularities had already preceded him. Chapman was a man for all seasons, although spring would seem more suitable for him than winter. He lacked a deep inner sense, but had a flair for living beyond his intellectual resources. He was, uncannily, able to find those with greater intellect, like Marian, and use them to advance his own fortunes.

Even in rough mid-century reproductions, John Chapman comes through as a ruggedly handsome man, very masculine, even charismatic. His marriage to Susanna Brewitt gave him the money he needed for his various enterprises; she was, however, plain and fourteen years his elder. She was just one of a series of women he charmed, although in Marian's instance he proved a positive intrusion in her life. The Chapmans had had four children, two of whom lived with them; a third surviving one, a deaf mute, lived with an uncle. There was, though, one other resident of the large house, Elisabeth Tilley, thirty years old, and seemingly the governess for the children (aged six and five) and a helper in the household. In reality, Tilley's main function was to serve as Chapman's mistress; more physically appealing than his wife, she was, until Marian appeared, apparently secure in her position.

By 8 January 1851, Marian was at the Chapman house. She found herself in a very different environment from anything remotely connected to her previous experience, even to her pension life in Geneva. For here, she was truly on her own, an independent woman, forced to evaluate herself against others. Mackay, whose book she reviewed, was apparently still on the scene, having given her a ticket for Faraday's lecture at the Royal Society. Michael Faraday was one of the leading scientists of the century, best known for his development of the dynamo, his discovery of electromagnetic induction, and his research on electrolysis, which became known as Faraday's law. This was heady stuff. Mackay appeared to pursue Marian in several ways, inviting her to dinner, and showing himself far more amiable, she recognized, in his home than elsewhere. She was impressed with some of the sketches of Italian scenes he showed her. Marian also attended lectures on geometry given by John Henry Newman's brother, Francis William Newman, one of the founders of Bedford College for women. And in some indirect way she became entangled in the Eliza Lynn impasse with Chapman. Lynn's last book, *Realities,* about the lower depths of London theater, was deemed by Mrs. Chapman as going too far beyond respectability for her husband to publish (the same Mrs. Chapman who tolerated her husband's mistress in her home). When Lynn refused to make revisions and deletions, and Chapman continued to refuse to publish, she sought another outlet, in Saunders and Itley. Marian did meet Mrs. Lynn, who said she found her a "loveable person." But the real significance was that Marian realized if Lynn could be a novelist, she, too, could write.

After spending Christmas at Rosehill, she took up lodgings at Chapman's on 8 January 1851. In the interim, Elisabeth Tilley, Chapman's mistress, as well as Chapman's wife, Susanna, were beginning to become suspicious of this woman who moved so independently. Chapman noted in his *Diary* that Marian was "studied," which probably means she had been warned off. While she found her dark room high up in the house comfortable and accommodating, she had entered into a highly charged emotional situation. It is unclear at precisely what point she recognized that she was deemed an interloper and a threat to the two women living in the house; and it is, further, unclear whether she was going to let them bother her. Chapman seemed devoted and attentive, and even helped her select a piano for her room—it was later moved to the drawing room, so that her playing, with the publisher in attendance, was not so private. However, he found another way to remain close to his new boarder, by seeking German lessons from her; and to this, she added Latin. Elisabeth Tilley found herself less and less in Chapman's presence, as her physical attractions gave way to Marian's obvious intellectual superiority.

The pattern was by now familiar. Her apprenticeship was to attractive men who were her intellectual inferiors, and she was able to engage their attention not through physical attraction but through her vastly superior mental abilities, her knowledge of languages, and her grasp of material which went from theology and philosophy to mathematics and physics. * There seemed little she could not grasp, as we note in the analogies she uses in her novels, drawn as they are from a multitude of sources and disciplines.

The procession of people at 142 Strand makes us wonder how Chapman

---

* The journal of the phrenologist George Combe (especially the entry for 29 August–1 September 1851, at the National Library of Scotland) attests to her effect on such men: ". . . with the exception perhaps of Lucretia Mott [an American abolitionist and feminist], she [Marian] appeared to me the ablest woman I have seen, and in many respects she excells Lucretia." We recall this is before Marian had made her mark in any area.

found time for his business enterprises. Among the crowds passing through the house was Thornton Leigh Hunt, who came and went without meeting Marian. The son of the poet Leigh Hunt, he would play a huge role in her life, when it became clear he was fathering children with Lewes's wife, leading to the separation of the Leweses. Another who turned up was the good Dr. Brabant, from whose home Marian had been chased; also Dr. Hodgson, who had once attempted to mesmerize her. Marian was now doing odd jobs for Chapman, in addition to her review of the Mackay book, none of it providing income or, for that matter, satisfaction. We have to emphasize that in these early years of the 1850s, when she was becoming established at the Chapmans', there was still a good deal of intellectual wastage. Chapman attempted to find some use for his new protégée, but he lacked funding for the *Review*; and when he attempted to obtain something for her at the prestigious *Edinburgh Review*, he was turned down.

Part of the difficulty was that his attention was so divided. With three women living in the house, each competing for his attention, he was trying to balance himself on a tightrope. His attention had turned toward his bright new star, Marian, and if we read back from his *Diary*, we can see her hesitation in accepting his invitations, even while she wanted to ingratiate herself with him. There was, all in all, the making of a British country house farce, with bedroom doors slamming, people in bad humor, assignations, and the rest; although it is unclear how far things went between Chapman and Marian. Even an invitation from the publisher to go for a walk led to confrontational sexual politics, as Marian at first was noncommittal, then accepted, then declined when it turned out she would be walking with Susanna. Words were exchanged, followed by rudeness and accusations, although both Chapman and Marian apologized to each other. In the shadows, Elisabeth Tilley did not enjoy what she saw, and Chapman was himself becoming somewhat isolated as the women alternated not speaking to him. Marian apparently did not lie quietly, but spoke out with agitation and temper. Several pages of Chapman's *Diary* were deleted, so that it becomes impossible to determine how he soothed all these angry feelings. *

A good deal of energy was going into these farcical scenes—farcical in retrospect, but probably painful for Marian, who had a somewhat different agenda from what Susanna and Elisabeth had in mind. What was becoming clear, however, was that she would be forced out, with the two other women allied against her. From Susanna's point of view, the presence of Elisabeth, while not ideal, created a kind of stability she could accommodate; whereas Marian was a malig-

---

* In his biography of Eliot, John Cross attempted to solve the Chapman–Eliot problem by ignoring it. Except for marginal references to the publisher, Cross in effect deleted Chapman from Eliot's life. In the index to his three-volume biography, there is no citation for Chapman, and the entire episode which consumed two years fades into shadows, even though Chapman survived Eliot by fourteen years and could have been interviewed if Cross wished. The latter preferred not to know, or else distrusted whatever Chapman might say. Gordon Haight, in *his* biography, was too cautious in assessing Marian's role in this ménage à trois. It is quite possible she and Chapman were intimate, although we will probably never have definitive proof one way or another.

nancy that could lead to the possible loss of her husband. Mrs. Brabant had, once before, reached this conclusion. According to Chapman's *Diary*, the two women agreed he and Marian were "completely in love with each other—E. being intensely jealous herself said all she could to cause S. to look from the same point of view. . . . E. betrayed my trust and her own promise. S. said to me that ever I went to M's room again she will write to Mr. Bray, and say that she dislikes her. . . ."

The back-and-forth was surely connected to a good deal of indiscreet behavior on Chapman's and Marian's part. The German lessons, in which the publisher had suddenly showed interest, did not inspire confidence, nor did the intimate piano sessions. Susanna was protecting her territory, as was Elisabeth; whereas Marian was seeking affection along with a foothold in the London literary world.

Chapman's *Diary* records the ups and downs of his relationships, of alternate warmth from Elisabeth, then freezing cold; of angry outbursts from Marian; of Susanna's insistence that he forgo the German lessons after she opposed them. The alternating attitudes can be attributed to shifting balances of power, with Susanna and Elisabeth at one time allied against Marian, and then Susanna driving a wedge between Chapman and Elisabeth by supporting Marian. Only Elisabeth, in this ongoing charade, seems to have driven hard to rid the house of the new woman; only she appeared not to countenance compromise, and that is understandable. As the unmarried woman in the house, she had the most to lose, and she had (by thirty) in one respect given her life over to Chapman. When Marian and Elisabeth became increasingly bitter, Kate Martineau, a new friend, took Marian to Highbury for the weekend. This was, of course, only temporary relief. The arguments became more frequent, and Susanna and Elisabeth, now allied once again, finally ganged up on Marian and forced her from the house. Déjà vu. This carries us into early March 1851—yet the very entries in Chapman's *Diary* which could have illuminated the recent outbursts were excised, from 25 February to 3 March.

Chapman did not succumb to the nasty drama right away, but accompanied Marian to several events—theater, concerts, opera, and a viewing of Turner watercolors; and even Susanna took her to a Bach concert. On the Saturday before her 24 March departure, she and Chapman attended *Lucia di Lammermoor*. During this latter period, there is a falling-off in Marian's correspondence, except for a very brief letter to Cara Bray and another brief one to Elinor Mary Bray, the Brays' adopted daughter, then six years old. In just the area we would like more information, we discover a gap. Chapman tells of accompanying Marian to the railway, of her sadness at parting, and he indicates she pressed him for some expression of his feelings. "I told her that I felt great affection for her, but that I loved E. and S. also, though each in a different way. At this avowal she burst into tears." Chapman says he reminded her of her dear friends, but "the train whirled her away very sad." Before Marian's departure, Susanna had spoken "very bitterly" about her, and the house became filled with recriminations, machinations, plots, conspiracies, and denials; not at all what we might associate with George Eliot, and perhaps not what we might associate with mid-century England.

At thirty, Marian was understandably starved for affection, and Chapman was a very attractive presence. Unfortunately, she was only one of several women in his life. Beyond these immediate three, he took advantage of his extraordinary good looks and dashing intellectual manner to gather in a number of conquests; and while there is little question he was truly devoted to Marian, he was a man for many occasions. Haight tells the story that the writer and editor T. P. O'Connor was walking along the Strand with Chapman in the 1890s, long after Marian's death. As they passed number 142, O'Connor brought up the rumor that Marian had once been in love with Herbert Spencer. Chapman, relates O'Connor, squeezed his arm and whispered, "You know, she was very fond of me!" The publisher said no more, and the story is thirdhand, from O'Connor; and it is forty or more years after the fact. What we can derive from it is both simple and complicated: Marian sought affection, she needed love, and there may have been sexual consummation. But whether consummated or not, the relationship was, in her eyes, that of lovers.

Marian lost no time in writing to Chapman, on 4 April, but it was purely a business communication. Nevertheless, both the business matter and the single reference to personal details are of interest. Chapman, with his usual indiscretion and feeling of invulnerability, had sent on to Marian a packet of letters he had received from Susanna (now in Truro) berating him for their seeming alliance against her. Also, the publisher had come up with a new idea which kept Marian linked to him, even when she was in Rosehill, a project called *An Analytical Catalogue of Mr. Chapman's Publications.* Published in 1852, these summaries enjoyed Marian's hand. When the idea was first broached, Susanna felt she was further being shut out and read different motives than scholarship into both her husband and his friend. Because of this, Marian had refused to work on the *Catalogue* at first, but then sent the 4 April note saying that she would undertake the venture.

The tactics and strategies going forth from each combatant are worthy themselves of fictional or dramatic treatment. It is difficult to see Marian as a home-breaker, siren, husband-stealer; and yet in some way she was, probably because of her intense need for emotional support, affection, sympathy, even sensual satisfaction. Unlike most other women of her class and time, she acted on her feelings and she suffered the outrage that ensued, as she would later endure the outrage created by her attachment to Lewes. Chapman's *Diary* indicates that the anger seemingly dissipated by Marian's departure was present whenever she communicated with him. For example, on 28 April 1851, his *Diary* reads: "I had a short simple note from M. this morning, which E read and then flew into a great passion, and begged me not to speak to her." Withal, Chapman hoped that Marian, who was writing to Susanna, would become "better friends" with his wife. It was all completely self-serving, since Chapman had resumed sexual relations with Elisabeth while planning a truce between Susanna and Marian.

He even wrote Marian about his hope that all could be soothed over. "I begged her [Susanna now] to be calm and not to let recent circumstances agitate and needlessly pain her. I told her that I feel even in the midst of the tumult of grief, and in the very moment of excitement the most intimate essence of my being, or some element of it. . . ."

Chapman's own feelings preempt all considerations of the domestic scene he had helped to create, and, in the right hands, he could have been magnificent fictional material. George Eliot never tried to catch him directly, but spread him out among several egoists: Grandcourt in *Daniel Deronda,* Tito Melema in *Romola,* Harold Transome in *Felix Holt,* and Arthur Donnithorne in *Adam Bede.* While none is Chapman, who had broad intellectual pretensions, and a few which were realized, they have some of his movement, his energy for intrigue, his delight in the messes he created around him. They are all self-servers, ranging from egoism to narcissism. Chapman's flightiness in personal and business matters, however, should not lead us to conclude he was utterly superficial or simple. Although a person at the opposite end from Marian, he was, possibly, as complicated in his way as she in hers. One such complication came in the use of letters, alluded to above, wherein Chapman read Marian's letters to Susanna and then, in turn, sent duplicates of his letters to both of them. Meanwhile, he was observing and noting much of this in his *Diary.* As a fictional character, he was close to an epistolary Lovelace, perhaps, recalling Richardson's *Clarissa;* and if Eliot later had wanted to capture him in print, she might have done so best in an epistolary novel.

One other dimension (at least): most probably, Marian's letters also ended up before Elisabeth's eyes, those letters written to Susanna as well as those to Chapman. There is malice in Marian's comment to him: "I should think you are right glad to have Mrs. Chapman again to enliven you all." Susanna had returned from Truro on 2 May. Marian's irony could be pointed at herself as well, for when Chapman moved into her former room at 142, she spoke of it as having been "duly exorcised" since she left it, so that he would not be bitten by the devil. But while all this may seem persiflage, Chapman was engaged in a transaction which would have profound reverberations in Marian's life.

A wealthy landowner named Edward Lombe, with an annual income of £14,000 a year—an amount equivalent now to in excess of a million dollars— was a free thinker and a champion of his own causes. Anti-religious, he was interested in every aspect of the secularization of society, including secular education, and in this regard he was a man of enormous democratic potential, despite his vast income and the noblesse oblige in his way of life. Lombe wrote to Chapman in April that he wanted the publisher to reprint Theodore Parker's *Discourse on Matters Pertaining to Religion,* or if not that, then Hennell's *Inquiry,* or else Marian's translation of Strauss's *Das Leben Jesu* in an abridgment of the three volumes. All of these were, in one respect or another, attacks on religion or on religious interpretations of forms of life.

Lombe, however, was not finished; he was willing to subsidize a quarterly review reflecting his views, which were not too dissimilar to those of Chapman and Marian. Lombe had already contributed £200 a year to the *Westminster Review* for special contributions; and now Chapman found himself in the position to buy the *Review* from W. E. Hickson, for £300, and start a new series. The amounts seem ridiculously small in the light of present-day transactions, but the *Westminster Review,* despite its high quality and prestige, was not a source of income and could prove, as it eventually did, to devour subsidies. Almost from the first, when editorship became a possibility, Chapman recognized that he needed an assistant who could handle complicated material, especially that flowing in from the continent. Most people took England's intellectual isolation for granted, but for an advanced few it was no longer possible, not with so much about religion, philosophy, and politics crossing the Channel, especially from France and Germany. Marian came to mind as the perfect assistant who could fill in intellectually for Chapman and yet defer to him on questions of salary and position. There is little question that whatever other designs he had on Marian, he had the highest regard for her intellectual capabilities, her critical judgment, and her ability to write clearly and succinctly on difficult, complex matters.

Chapman sought further support from a group already known to Marian: Brabant, Francis Newman (brother of the priest, and later cardinal, John Henry Newman), Mackay, Joseph Parkes, and others who wanted to see the *Review* shaped into a vehicle for their secular, pragmatic views.* Bray, in fact, invited Chapman to Rosehill, where he stayed for two weeks and, of course, mixed with Marian, as well as Mrs. Thornton Hunt, Sara Hennell, and Cara. The purpose of Chapman's visit was, possibly, to see Marian, and although he noted in his *Diary* that he found her "affectionate," his interest was probably interwoven with professional aims. For whatever reasons, Marian was becoming entangled in a web of feelings and counterfeelings cutting across several of the people whom she had felt close to. As we observe her movement here, alternately sad and pleased with herself, we recognize that even the future George Eliot had to move circumspectly. She realized that whatever she did, she still did not have the mobility of a Chapman or a Bray; that her feelings, however powerful and directed, had to be held somewhat in check; that appearances for a woman of nearly thirty-one were all. Yet behind all this circumspect action was her overwhelming desire to get on with her life, and the *Review* in Chapman's hands would be her opportunity.

---

* Chapman's pragmatism did not lead to any "bleeding heart" humanitarianism. He opposed measures that would hinder industry, even legislation that would protect workers in certain sectors. He was, in these respects, a true Liberal, like Nassau Senior, the economist whose wife corresponded with Eliot over social welfare. Senior said cotton mill work was a soft touch, with the women sitting around most of the day watching the machinery. This justified workdays of sixteen or more hours. Similarly, Harriet Martineau, a reformer and ameliorist, warned against legislation to aid factory workers in a paper entitled "Factory Legislation. A Warning Against Meddling Legislation" (1855). Chapman, nevertheless, refused to publish it in the *Westminster Review* (his letter of 6 November 1855; MS: Martineau Collection, Birmingham University). For her, reform took second place to free manufactures and the free flow of goods. A solid part of this work force, incidentally, was female, with three-quarters of unmarried women working, according to the 1851 census; 21,000 were governesses, the remainder in factory and mill work, until they were replaced by machinery.

Chapman, meanwhile, pursued Marian and walked with her at every opportunity. One series of remarks indicates that he and she may have discussed a break with Elisabeth. Chapman, in his *Diary:* ". . . told her the exact condition of things in regard to E. whom on every account I wish to stay at the Strand. She [Marian] was much grieved and expressed herself prepared to atone in any way she could for the pain she has caused, and put herself in my hands prepared to accept any arrangement I may make either for her return to the Strand or to any house in London. . . ." The wording suggests a final decision had been made, that Chapman felt he was tied to Elisabeth, perhaps as some curious way of maintaining a stable situation. In any event, Marian agreed she was ready to write an article on foreign literature for each number of the *Westminster Review.* Chapman gave her the prospectus* to read over and polish, since he knew his own powers of expression were not strong.

At the end of May, Chapman and Marian went for diversion to Leamington and came home by way of Kenilworth Castle. His *Diary* entries on this and related matters are compelling for what they reveal of Marian, himself, and his way of juggling disparate matters. When he dwelt on the ruin of Kenilworth and on its "incomprehensible mystery and witchery of beauty," Marian was disturbed and "wept bitterly." Chapman attributes this to her consciousness of "her own want of beauty," but he probably read her shallowly. It was not want of beauty, it was her sense that *her kind* of beauty had no outlet; or a corollary of that, that only external and superficial forms of beauty were admired. He recognizes she is not fit to stand alone; but this conclusion leads him into a related, self-serving area, of how to shape his life so that all his women can be brought together. "I find it," he writes, "of great difficulty to determine what can be done in regard to M's return to Town. Both Susanna and Elisabeth oppose her return to the Strand, and I suspect they would be equally opposed to her residence elsewhere in London, and yet as an active cooperator with me in Editing the *Westminster Review* she must be in London much of her time."

He wishes for the return of trust—whose? under what conditions?—and laments his loss of confidence. "For my part I do not feel in raptures with any woman now, and my passionate moods are exceptional and transcient [sic] and are rather *permitted* as a means of according the strongest evidence of *affection* than storms wh: I cannot controul [sic]." He tries to get behind his disappointment and to return to his first love, Susanna. "The beneficent affection, and pleasure of social intercourse, which I experience, seems to be equally distributed towards Susanna E and M, but in regard to *passionate enthusiasm*, my 'first love' will I believe also be my last. I wish I could make her happy!"

Chapman's remarks in this *Diary* passage reveal the kind of man he was. Decent, when his own needs were not contravened; frettish and peevish, even solipsistic, when he felt he was not being satisfied; needful of the women circling him, but finding them insufficient in some passionate area; hoping to be just, but also aware of his use of Marian's mental abilities; trying not to betray his wife, or his "first love," but betraying her nevertheless. If we assess these words

*See Appendix A.

for what they do not say as much as for what they say, we can build a case for physical consummation between Chapman and Marian. His guilt, his desire to do the right thing by his wife, and his grouping together of the three women as not providing satisfaction all suggest that while unequal as life partners, they were somehow equal as bed partners.

Meanwhile, at Rosehill, the evenings were spent on music, with Marian singing or playing. Her musicality surfaces into every aspect of her life, not merely at such gatherings—into her regulated, paced speaking voice, into her stately prose, and into the very rhythmic structures of her longer works, built as they are on point and counterpoint, or on the balance of elements which recall longer works of music. The choral music she occasionally heard in the concert hall, or the operas she attended, all appeared to affect her novelistic sense, since she worked hard to create structure based on parallels, repeats, and dualism.

Quite unmusical in structure, however, was the relationship of Marian and Chapman on the *Westminster Review,* which was vague in its outlines of authority. Chapman was nominally the editor—he and she both felt it was better for one person to represent authority, or at least she so stated that—but in the actual running of the quarterly, Marian was the key figure. Besides the writing of articles on foreign literature and other subjects, she was editorially involved in all decisions, and for this she apparently was not paid. Just what the arrangement was we have to piece out: room and board at the Strand lodging house in exchange for editorial work; the promise of some monies for extra chores, like the abridgment of Strauss for which Lombe offered £100 (nothing came of this); small payments for particular articles; and the largest payment of all, the experience of subediting or managing a well-known quarterly and the presence of Chapman, who was a conduit to many famous and interesting people.

Beyond these duties, assigned or otherwise, lay a gray area of combat between the two, a certain jockeying for positions of power, a mutual need which was frequently expressed in overlapping and opposing forces. Marian recognized that Chapman was an undisciplined, loose writer; that as a thinker, he was superficial, although a good idea man; and that as a contributor to the *Review* he would lower its quality. In her letter to Chapman of 15 June (1851), where she corrects his language directed at John Stuart Mill about the prospectus for the *Review,* she is relentless in altering his choice of words. We receive the impression that in recognizing her own intellectual superiority, she was also beginning to withdraw some of her admiration for Chapman, even as she depended on him for her chance to gain a foothold in London literary life. Chapman's *Diary* provides insights into the power struggle that was going on, although disguised as matters that are best for the *Review.* Chapman: "Miss Evans thinks I should lose power and influence by becoming a writer in the Westminster Review, and could not maintain that dignified relation with the various contributors that she thinks I may do otherwise."

In a chatty letter to Chapman, the same 15 June one in which she altered the wording of his letter to Mill, Marian mentions several of the men who will prove significant in her life: Herbert Spencer, subeditor of the *Economist,* and later viewed (by her) as a potential husband; Thornton Hunt, who would play such a large part in her relationship with Lewes; and Lewes himself, part of a dissolving partnership in the Leader Newspaper Company and soon to be considered by Marian and Chapman as the writer on "Modern Novelists" for the *Review.* She also mentions Edward Henry Noel, Cara's close friend, and closes with comments on an "Independent Section" which would allow those who disagreed with published stands in the *Review* to voice their disagreements. The "Independent Section" lasted for the first two numbers, and thereafter appeared only sporadically as the *Review,* having found its own voice, insisted upon it.

Meanwhile, while Marian was still pondering the prospectus, Chapman was once again engaged in his own maneuvering, attempting to relocate Marian to 142 Strand so that they could collaborate. But Susanna, who had learned to deal with previous situations, saw the literary collaboration as a mere cover for something else; or so we derive from Chapman's stalwart efforts to get beyond her arguments to the needs of the quarterly. He finally attempted a finesse of the situation by inviting the Brays, Sara, and Marian to stay, together, at his lodgings for a week in August. Marian was pressing Chapman, by letter, to settle on a writer for "Modern Novelists," little anticipating that what occurred in that area would change her life. "There would be," she wrote her publisher, "the same objection to Miss Bronty as to Thackeray with regard to the article on Modern Novelists. She would have to leave out Currer Bell [Charlotte Brontë's pseudonym], who is perhaps the best of them all." When Lewes came to write the article, he laid out certain ground rules for fiction which, in his view, should prevail, ground rules that proved extremely influential in the kind of fiction Marian would herself write.

That August week was another stage in Chapman's choreography of the women in his life, although it took place while Marian was worried about Chrissey and her very ill husband. Marian went with Cara to visit Cara's friend Noel, at Bishop's Teignton, in Devonshire; and Chapman, thinking he could lure them all to London for the Great Exhibition in the Crystal Palace,* and in this way get to see Marian, invited them and the Brays to 142 Strand. On their way

---

* That architectural wonder and sign of progress in which the English vaunted their technological superiority to the rest of the world. Victoria's Prince Albert turned the exhibition and palace into, virtually, a religious experience, infused with nineteenth-century Christian worship of divine materialism. That shaper of middle-class taste and morality, the poet laureate Tennyson, weighed in with hymnlike words: "[Victoria] brought a vast design to pass, / When Europe and the scattered ends / Of our fierce world were mixt as friends / And brethen, in her halls of glass." Ruskin, however, was negative about the enterprise, calling the palace not crystal but glass and labeling the exhibition "paltry arts" boasting of "fashionable luxury." London itself in most of its neighborhoods was a sinkhole. While Victoria and Albert celebrated technology, the streets were open drainages for sewage, the Thames was the recipient of London's waste, pure water was almost impossible to obtain, housing was putrid, filth was everywhere, children were dying of starvation and disease, prostitution was a rapid growth industry, street crime in most areas was a way of life, the smell of the city was overpowering, and the life expectancy of the Londoner averaged out to under thirty, with the working-class average close to twenty. The medical census just before mid-century indicates that one-quarter of London's 2,100,000 population was infected with typhus; and for a child to reach ten years of age was an achievement against overwhelming odds. Metropolitan London was in the main one vast graveyard. Only the rich could isolate themselves from the general malaise. Unlike Dickens, Eliot did not at this time respond to these aspects of the city. Except in parts of *Daniel Deronda,* she would not react to urban London at all.

back from Devonshire, Cara and Marian, along with Bray, went to stay with Cara's friend Mary Marshall, in St. John's Wood. Chapman joined them on 13 August, and then on the next day took Susanna to call. On the 15th, as part of this strategically organized ballet, the group visited the exhibition and then returned to the lodging house. Chapman presented this as an opportunity for Susanna to see Marian under normal conditions, and to give himself the chance for an editorial conference. But as he reports in his *Diary*, his plans did not quite work out: Susanna had a bad headache, and the next day, with Elisabeth in tears, Marian departed for Rosehill.

Chapman returned to Coventry twice and needed help over the article James Martineau was to write on "Christian Ethics and Modern Civilization," an article Lombe insisted upon. Marian was the one delegated to answer Martineau's questions about what was required. Once Chapman had her guidelines, he repeated them to the writer as his own comments. After the weekend with Marian, discussing the prospectus for the first number under his editorship, Chapman returned to the arms of Elisabeth at 142, only to find his wife in a miserable, vengeful mood. She vented her unhappiness—she had just turned forty-three—on the thirty-one-year-old Marian. Chapman laments in his *Diary* how both women upbraided him, and yet by September, through some kind of masculine magic or deception, he was able to placate them sufficiently so that they agreed eventually to accept Marian's return to the lodging house. With this, she was on the edge of something both precarious and rewarding. Having been disappointed by having her own article on Greg's *The Creed of Christendom* deflected in favor of Martineau's, she nevertheless saw her immiment return to the Strand as triumphant; and, furthermore, she was entering into one of the great journalistic ventures of the century, the rejuvenation of the *Westminster Review* and whatever that would bring. For a woman at mid-century, it was a distinct triumph, a significant way station on her path to complete liberation from her Coventry background; a repudiation—as we shall see in her prospectus—of nearly everything theologically and philosophically she had held ten years before.

By 29 September, Marian was back in her former room, having rented even the same piano. Several leaves are missing from Chapman's *Diary* in and around this time, so how the various wars among the several women and the one man were going remains shadowy. In the ascendancy because of her importance in the functioning of the *Review*, Marian tried sympathy and generosity with both women, and in Susanna's case she apparently prevailed. Elisabeth, who was now truly marginal, would become the sacrifice. In time, she was pushed out, which is not to say Chapman stopped altogether having relations with her; but although she hung on until May of 1854, nearly another three years, she found her days numbered.

We note a letter from Elisabeth to the now famous George Eliot in 1878, after Lewes's death, a letter written in sorrow at Eliot's bereavement. The letter seems a sincere attempt to settle once and for all their wars of the past, and parts of it are quite affecting. "Since I saw you last," Elisabeth wrote, "I imagine your life has been a very happy one, and your domestic peace and comfort per-fect. I have enquired a few times when I could do so quietly. . . . it has not been my fate to meet such [this is the sole bitter thrust in the letter]. I must not now speak of your exalted position and the pleasure I have had in reading nearly all—not the latest yet—of your books, these things are as nothing to you now and possibly the gap in your affectionate nature can never be repaired. . . . May God help you to bear your loss as He only can. I wish you could return to the simple faith of your youth for consolation in your time of distress." Writing from a pension in Heidelberg, Elisabeth speaks of being "amongst strangers." "If you blame me [for writing, or for the past], then pray forgive the mistake only believe that I am grieved for you from my heart and that I hope and trust you have some gentle loving friend with you to soothe and sustain you. . . ."

Now lodged with the Chapmans and Elisabeth at the end of September 1851, Marian was ready to put her full plans to work. An open question remains whether her arrangement with Chapman precluded intimacy. That the physical side—whatever form it took—was minimized may be possible, since with the quarterly they had moved to another level, but that it ended altogether is open to speculation. Certainly, she did not put behind her ideas of intimacy and marriage itself. She would soon become deeply involved with Herbert Spencer, a relationship that gave her considerable anguish and one that demeaned her, until she recognized he was a bachelor who feared any intimacy. But her major concern now was the *Review*, the first number, and an exciting prospect that was.

The first issue in the new series of the *Review* was to appear in January 1852, less than four months after Chapman officially took over the purchase. There was urgency now, for Marian, like Chapman, was under extreme pressure to make the quarterly distinctive and significant from the first issue. The competi-tion was fierce and by the end of the decade would grow fiercer. In the earlier part of the century, the most prestigious quarterlies were the Whig *Edinburgh*, the Benthamite *Westminster*—the precursor of Chapman's journal—and the Tory *Quarterly*, not to mention the stately *Athenaeum*, all soon to be joined by the monthly magazines: Blackwood's *Edinburgh Magazine* (known as *Black-wood's*) and *Fraser's Magazine*. But then came the popular periodicals such as *Punch* and Dickens's *Household Words*, succeeded by *All the Year Round*. The *Cornhill*, established in 1860, would prove later competition, as would *Macmil-lan's Magazine*. The reinvigorated *Westminster*, then, would face competition on every front, from the established quarterlies and monthlies, the intellectual *Athenaeum*, the popular magazines, and those which mixed a broad appeal with the serialization of serious fiction. Chapman and Marian planned nothing less than to make the *Review* indispensable in English intellectual circles; to have it become a leader of thought and to provide the English reader with everything of significance occurring within the larger (and more sophisticated) European world. The quarterly, like its hidden assistant editor, was making a new start. For both, it would be auspicious.

Chapman wanted to court the leading figures of his day, and toward that end he pursued Carlyle and John Stuart Mill (whose father, James Mill, had founded the original *Westminster Review* in 1824), for an article on the peerage, on the assumption, one can speculate, that sparks would fly, although one could not predict in what direction. Carlyle held off Chapman for a while and then refused, even when Chapman indicated he had an "able Editor," whose name he did not divulge. Mill, likewise, refused.* His entire response to the quarterly was ambiguous, since he had grown up with its presence in its earlier form. Some of the other topics and assignments were less inflammatory, and some were especially English, such as an account of shellfish, by Professor Edward Forbes. On more central topics, W. R. Greg wrote about labor relations; James Anthony Froude discussed Mary Stuart, of particular interest since the Catholic issue had become intense over the Oxford Movement and Newman's conversion to Roman Catholicism. Newman's brother, Francis William, wrote about rejecting any plans for direct legislation by popular vote, what we would call a referendum. George Henry Lewes hove into view with an article on a Russian pietist, Julia von Krüdener, who tried to influence politics through religion. James Martineau weighed in with "The Ethics of Christendum," the piece which displaced Marian's own on the subject and which, further, displeased the *Review*'s patron, the radical Lombe.

The general tone and outlook of these pieces were reformist, without being alarmist. Disraeli's "Young England" movement had called for radical reform within the Tory Party; while here, in the *Review*, we see not real radicalism, but a gradual reformist spirit, a secularity which downgraded pure religion, a democratic spirit which was not rebelliously populist. Marian's hand was heavy, not only in the editing, but in the assignment of articles. By designating pieces in the ten numbers she edited, she could more or less control what would be produced in print; although in the Martineau case, the results seemed to fall outside of all desirable positions.

Marian's personal life, in the meantime, appeared to be on hold, almost completely sublimated to her professional interests and the intellectual effort required to launch a major journal. Her health was not so good as she had hoped—work did not solve her problems. "I have hardly been well a day since I came." She wishes she were rich enough to have a holiday at the seashore "and have some plunges in the sea to brace me." But she assures Bray she is enjoying her stay, that she gains satisfaction from seeing new people and may find country life dull after this.

Crossing Marian's path was the Swedish novelist Fredrika Bremer—and perhaps not unexpectedly, Marian's response was, at first, to her appearance. She sees a mirror image. She thinks she is old (Bremer was fifty), "extremely ugly—and deformed. . . . Her eyes are sore—her teeth horrid. . . ." This attention to looks, while putting Bremer's achievements (the "earthen vessel") secondary,

* William Johnson Fox, far less known and less talented, agreed to write the piece; he also wrote for the very first issue of the *Review*, twenty-eight years earlier.

was precisely how Marian felt people judged her. She continues in this vein: "She is to me a repulsive person, equally unprepossessing to eye and ear. I never saw a person of her years who appealed less to my purely instinctive veneration. I have to reflect every time I look at her that she is really Freda Bremer." In time, Marian's view of the novelist changed, just as people's view of *her* looks changed when they saw her animated or deep in conversation.

Marian observes the parade of people passing through 142. For someone who wanted an antidote to Coventry boredom—or "country living," as she called it—the lodging house was perfect. Its one drawback was that she had little time left over for work, or thought, of her own, whatever shape it might have taken. With extremely heavy reading for the reviews she was editing, the coming and going of visitors, the need for consultation with Chapman, and the fending off of Susanna and Elisabeth as the instance arose, she had a full day. Furthermore, in October and November, leading up to the first issue of the new series of the *Review*, she was worried about the reception of the prospectus. Intermixed with all is "headache, headache."

Marian was encouraged by the money contributions coming in, as well as subscriptions, but Chapman apparently used Edward Lombe's money in ways that did not satisfy the benefactor. What belonged to the *Review* and what to the publishing house was not always clear in Chapman's accounting. Marian was also collecting articles for future issues, and was pleased to have on assignment Professor Edward Forbes, on "The Future of Geology," which would appear in the July issue.* Although to the late-twentieth-century reader the future of geology is not of primary concern, in the mid-nineteenth century, in the years preceding Darwin's *Origin of Species*, geology was the giant that could topple the church. Geological findings, with Lyell's *The Principles of Geology* as a central document in 1830–33, then his *Elements of Geology* in 1838, seemed to hold the fate of the validation or subversion of biblical thought. Darwin's publication in 1859 was deeply indebted to Lyell's theories of geology, which stressed uniformitarianism against the catastrophic theory (creationism) advocated by religious thinkers.

One of Marian's duties, apparently, was to court rich subscribers or contributors, foreigners as well as native-born, whom she called "men of literary tastes and fat purses both." References to Thomas Carlyle, now positioned as one of the most important men of the century, recur in her letters, along with foreign citations. She was reading his life of Sterling, not so much for Sterling as for Carlyle himself. Strikingly, she sees the biography in virtual fictional terms, with its rapid characterization and "racy bits of description." Writing to Sara, she observes her table covered with books—"all to be digested by the editorial maw"—and foresees "terribly hard work for the next 6 weeks." She adds: "My table is groaning with books and I have done very little with them yet—but I trust in my star which has hitherto helped me to do all I have engaged to do." Consistent with her supercharged duties is the fact that her letters are far briefer.

---

* See Appendix B for the issues of July and October 1852.

Still filled with protestations of her affection for and dependence on her old friends, she is, nevertheless, creating another life for herself; and its separation from Coventry is clear in that her letters now are closer to news reports or communiqués from the front rather than the deeply felt missives of before.

Not that she lost her satirical eye or bent for burlesque, which we saw earlier in her "wedding proposal" from Professor Bücherwurm. She is quite amused at a group, including Brabant, Mackay, and a disciple of Robert Owen's, who sat in Chapman's first-floor front shop and discussed socialism, all the while posing in an aristocratic manner and putting handkerchiefs to their faces. Marian was suspicious now, as later, of all ideological stands, especially when people advocated one thing while experiencing something else. Her eye, already being trained as a novelist, picked up incongruities; and, further, she could turn them into witty phrasing. Herbert Spencer began to enter her life, asking her and Chapman to attend the theater with him, and she "ended the day in a godless manner, seeing the Merry Wives of Windsor." She had just turned thirty-two, and the tickets served as a birthday present. Spencer, who from a personal point of view was worthy of a satirical portrait, did not fall into Marian's witty column. As he appears and becomes closer, she treats him seriously.

The first issue of the *Review* was looming, and while monies had been generously contributed, the quarterly was not so well funded as it might have been. Chapman considered that he had sufficient money for four years of publication, but he was optimistic about any project he was involved in.* In a letter just before the first issue was to appear, Marian tells Cara she has been ill for the past three days with racking headaches—"Just when I ought to have been working the hardest. . . ." Three days later, on 23 December, she tells the Brays that work is "so heavy just for the next three days—all the revises being yet to come in and the proof of my own article—and Mr. Chapman is so overwhelmed with matters of detail that he has earnestly requested me to stay till Saturday." Her article was "Contemporary Literature in England," which included books on theology, history, physiology, and poetry as well as fiction; it was a composite review in which she linked several reviews by others. She had planned to return to Coventry for the Christmas holiday, but her heavy work carried her through the 27th in London; after that, she visited Rosehill.

The contents of the first issue were to set the stage of Marian's editorship. Under her watchful eye, the mid-century reader could become aware of vast stretches of English life. These early numbers were intellectual masterpieces. The major issues were all paraded: education, government policy, prison reform and stagna-

---

* With about 1,000 subscribers in 1851, the *Review* under Chapman and Marian rarely went much over 1,500 in the following years. The issue cost 6 shillings, a considerable sum, and low sales guaranteed that it would always be financially behind. Contributors alone claimed £300–400 per issue, plus paper and printing costs. We can understand how little was available for payment to the subeditor. Chapman projected he would need £2,000 to run the *Review* for four years, but that was a conservative figure, and the sponsors could well see it all go down the drain. If they had penetrated Chapman's accounting procedures, they would have run.

tion, questions of charity, the state of industry—its future and its effects on English life, the thorny question of labor relations and their place in a society hell-bent on "progress"—issues surrounding progress itself, and foreign relations and the spread of the empire. Added to these were those questions concerning the sciences, especially in geology, botany, biology, and early evolutionary theory, the issue of catastrophism versus uniformitarianism, and the early atomic theories in chemistry, as well as pseudo-scientific matters like vegetarianism, astrology, the occult, homeopathy (a popular form of medical practice), the water cure, and other aspects of what passed for medical treatment during a still primitive phase of the discipline. Herbert Spencer was a frequent contributor, with his theory of evolution eventually taking up four issues.* In foreign relations, the British position vis-à-vis France, Italy, Turkey (the Crimean War was not too distant), Russia, Ireland, and the colonies was examined and reexamined, together with books on travel. Of particular interest was the Irish question (the Great Famine was running its course, and millions of surviving Irish were emigrating to America), as well as the occupation of Jamaica (where a rebellion would occur in the next decade and be put down brutally).

This listing suggests the nonliterary range of Marian's interests, and it has not even touched upon questions of philosophy and theology which were pursued more intensely. History, also, in Froude's articles probing Tudor England, was well represented. In philosophy, Arthur Schopenhauer was introduced to English audiences by John Oxenford, who, unfortunately, did not read German; and in theology, we have already noted James Martineau, but there were also examinations of religion and religious questions in Catholic countries like France and Italy, as well as analyses of less familiar offshoots of Christianity such as the Quakers and the Mormons. Very little appeared on Jews or the role of Jews in English life, possibly because so few of the contributors to the *Review* were themselves Jewish; or else it simply was not considered a burning issue, although increasing Jewish attendance at English universities and participation in political life could not be ignored for long. Disraeli, for one, was not going to vanish.

The literary section devoted most of its space to contemporary subjects: Lewes's piece on Shelley, also articles on Matthew Arnold (as poet, not as critic), De Quincey, Thackeray, Charlotte Brontë, Mrs. Elizabeth Gaskell, and Balzac, among others. Marian had about 1,000 books reviewed during her tenure as subeditor. The range was enormous, and we must proceed carefully in trying to disentangle what she wrote and what she helped to commingle among the reviews. Most evidence suggests she probably coordinated many of the reviews, wrote "bridge" material, and linked shorter reviews to create longer, more comprehensive ones. It is doubtful that she wrote several of the reviews often attributed to her. We will get to those below.

The reviews were themselves gathered together into four large groups, as the

---

*Spencer argued that nature, physically, metes out what he called "pure justice," a biological division of labor and needs that remained fixed. Eliot's "moral law" would be her response.

contemporary literature of America, Germany, France, and England. Other countries were not completely ignored, but those four were considered the major arenas for new work. With close to a hundred books reviewed in each issue— truly a remarkable undertaking and clearly beyond the scope of Chapman to coordinate—we receive some idea of the breadth of Marian's interest and how much she had developed in literary sophistication. Lewes handled French material in the first seven issues.

As for Marian's direct contributions as reviewer apart from her bridging the work of others, we find references to Carlyle's *Life of John Sterling* and Macready's *A Sketch of Suwarow* in the first issue; and in later issues a few more, including Kingsley's *Westward Ho!* Direct attributions are difficult to determine since all contributions remained anonymous. By this stage in the development of the quarterly, Marian was a jack-of-all-trades: editing, helping to select both subjects and suitable contributors, making abridgments when articles ran over, as they frequently did, making cuts and then joining elements for continuity, proofreading, and even supervision of the press run when the issue was completed. More than anything else, this illustrates the size and scope of Marian's career before she became involved with Lewes and before she became George Eliot. Although she worked in the shadow of Chapman, she had created an identity for herself as article writer, editor, reviewer, proofreader, and the like— a career not too different from that of many notable men in publishing at that time. What all this lacked, however, was any sense of where it would lead and what further shape her life would take.

In her review of Carlyle's *Sterling*—to cite one instance of how reviewing for the *Westminster* moved Marian toward fiction writing—she emphasizes the need for good biography. Instead of the "dreary three or five volume compilation of letter, and diary, and detail," the reading public could use a "real Life." In her description of this life, she comes close to a fictional portrait: "personal intimacy, a loving and poetic nature which sees the beauty and the depth of familiar things, and the artistic power which seizes characteristic points and renders them with life-like effect."

In another area, in her position of choosing contributors for subjects agreed upon by her and Chapman, Marian was becoming not only a judge of experts but an observer of character. She was measuring a topic against the individual's capabilities and reach; she was able to make decisions which ranged across a broad spectrum of ideas, personal qualities, matters of temperament, and suitability.

There was a further bonus in that several of the writers came to 142 Strand to discuss their topics or reviews, or to attend parties given by the Chapmans. Personal contact gave Marian the opportunity to match the physical appearance of guests to intellectual and emotional capacities: a further stage in developing her powers of observation. Many of the people who attended were of considerable intellectual prowess, including Thomas Henry Huxley, Sir Richard Owen, and the physician Sir David Brewster. We note that the society in which she mixed, in these and later years, was male, the educated establishment. She was meeting renowned men as part of the *Review* circle; later, when she was denounced as a scarlet woman, it was mainly men who felt "safe" in her company. The corollary of this is that despite the strictures placed on women as far as education, morality, and achievement were concerned, despite the accepted "code" that women were the lesser sex and, therefore, fit only for certain duties, despite all this, Marian because of her enormous intellectual achievements was able to move freely among men who would have sought a conventional life for their wives and daughters.

The so-called scientific evidence accumulated by male doctors in the nineteenth century was simply a reflection of Victorian mores: that because of their physical machinery, women were destined by nature for secondary roles. Scientific "evidence" was drawn from a variety of fields: physiology and anatomy, of course, but also psychology, physical anthropology, and sociology. All of these disciplines were deeply indebted to evolutionary theory which, in the Darwinian stage of its development, "proved" that woman's difference from man relegated her to an inferior position. Darwin and his followers even attempted to make a virtue of this necessity, since woman's lack of intellectual development meant her energies were conserved for childbearing, and this strengthened the race. As one contemporary commentator points out, women were perceived as inferior to men in the way primitive people were inferior to civilized races; since women were childlike in those areas of development which required reason, logic, and imagination, they were dependent on men. As a consequence of such pseudodata, scientists in these various disciplines made it clear that women could never match men in either intellectual or artistic matters. The legal system followed suit, so that until the Married Women's Property Acts of 1870 and 1883, women were under the protection of their husbands, which was called coverture, and their property belonged to their spouses.

Many of the visitors to 142 left with distinct impressions of Marian. Despite her unprepossessing looks, they found solace in her voice and recognized the intelligence of her comments, political and otherwise. It should be made clear that whomever Marian met, her own political views would not be radicalized. While she sympathized with reform and felt compassion for the needs of the lower economic classes, she was representative of the century in that she was a gradualist. More than that, she looked to other areas, not to the political or economic arena but to questions of personal morality and ethics. She was the century's "voice" precisely because she could assimilate the particulars of the body politic into large human issues.

There is no clear evidence that Marian encountered Karl Marx, although it is believed Marx passed through Chapman's, brought there by Chapman's friend Andrew Johnson, a clerk in the Bank of England's Bullion Office. Johnson, in turn, was close to Ferdinand Freiligrath, a poet of the French Revolution and himself a friend of Marx, who offered to write for the *Review*. Johnson indicated he would translate Freiligrath's pieces into English, but Marian did not seem happy about this. Louis Blanc was more to her taste, the reformist who combined ethical considerations with better working conditions for the laboring classes. Mazzini, the writer who was attempting to unite Italy, was another one she favored, and she looked forward to his contributions to the *Review.*

More frequent visitors to the Strand were the phrenologist George Combe, * a great admirer of Marian's intellectual accomplishments, and Harriet Martineau. Martineau's current belief, which she held to intensely, was mesmerism or hypnotism; she felt it had helped her recover from a near mortal disease. Much of what passed for science at mid-century was, as mentioned, pseudo-science, some of it outright fraud, although even intelligent people put trust in it. Marian held back from the excesses of Martineau's material sciences—mesmerism, phrenology, and the like—while she herself took more readily to the scientific possibilities of Darwin's evolutionary theories. One could argue, in fact, that well before 1859, Marian was a Darwinian and an evolutionist, although not wholeheartedly.

For the time, she almost rejected Martineau as well, revolted by the "vulgarity" of her looks and gestures and her interest in fads. Marian viewed knowledge as something sacred, not to be abused for personal interests; and, in fact, she learned languages, the scientific method, and the uses of history as ways not solely to inform herself, but to liberate herself from the ignorance of others. The abuse of knowledge defined even people like Martineau as no better than the ones she had separated herself from. As noted, she revised this opinion of the quite remarkable Martineau, a woman of enormous determination and resolve, although the body of her work has fallen into neglect.

Phrenology, however, would not go away. In his journal (an entry for 29 August 1851), George Combe notes how he worked his phrenological magic on Marian. He is quite firm about the results.

> She has a very large brain, the anterior lobe is remarkable for length, breadth, and height, the coronal region is large, the front rather predominating. . . . Love of approb, and Concentrativeness are large. Her temper is nervous lymphatic. She is rather tall, near 40 apparently [she was thirty-one], pale, and in delicate health. . . . She shewed great analytic power and an instinctive soundness of judgment.

With her acceptance of the position at the *Review,* the normally socially reserved Marian found herself in the center of an intellectual brew. Surely her friendship with several doctors—not least, Sir James Clark, physician to the queen—gave her an easy familiarity with medical men, several of whom appear in her novels and stories. Through these and other acquaintances, who included political personages like Joseph Parkes, the radical who funded the publication of her translation of Strauss, she learned the distinctions among societal figures:

---

* As we shall see, Combe was forming very negative views of Chapman ("a dreamer and a schemer") while enjoying his hospitality. Based on a phrenological examination, he was forming very favorable views of Marian, until she left London with Lewes, and then Combe recognized that phrenology in her case had failed. Instead, he fished around to see if there had been insanity in the Evans family.

that peculiar manner of observing which allowed her to limn individuals so sharply while also insisting on their social roles.

She made more than acquaintances, however, in that continuing emergence from her Coventry background. Joseph Parkes's daughter Bessie (Elizabeth Rayner Parkes) became a particular favorite, a feeling shared mutually. Not all was merely "learning." As her letters in the early 1850s indicate, she desperately needed validation of her person from supportive men and women; and women comforted her mainly as counterpoint to the heavy male world in which her position took her. The feminine side of Marian, as she insisted, was not to be slighted. Bessie's description of her friend emphasizes the womanly Marian, not solely the mental giant. One of the burdens Marian had to live with was that her face in repose seemed heavy, even morose; she suffered from thick features which only softened when she smiled or became animated. Bessie Parkes speaks of her brow, blue eyes, and upper part of her face as having great charm, the lower half being disproportionately long. This gave her the hangdog look which characterized the few portraits of her which went untouched. She enjoyed abundant brown hair and a countenance, Bessie says, which "was certainly not in any sense unpleasing." She cites it as noble in outline, sweet in its expression. Bessie indicates her figure seemed supple and agile, having "an almost serpentine grace." She says Marian's characteristic bearing suggested fatigue, and thought that even when she was younger she could hardly have been animated. But this was counterbalanced by her eyes filling with laughter when she was amused.

Although Bessie lacked Marian's intellectuality, this did not hinder the growing friendship. However much several of her female friends were women of considerable distinction and potential leaders if given the opportunity, Marian did not require of them the same qualities of intellect she demanded of her male friends. But even here she was not consistent, for some men, like Brabant, Combe, and Chapman, were hardly intellectual giants; in fact, they seemed like a curious mix of achievement and mountebank sensibilities. The Parkeses were a very close group, with Bessie's father insisting on including Marian in any dinners with prominent figures, including Thackeray. Bessie has described how Marian would appear on Parkes's arm, the sole woman with the exception of his wife and daughter permitted in the presence of the great men. Bessie adds that Marian would look admiringly into Parkes's face as she was led into these distinguished meetings. All this strengthens one's view that Parkes considered her "his property," and explains why he, despite being a radical, became vindictive and nasty when she went off with Lewes.

Invitations to Marian extended to balls, but she lacked proper expensive dresses for an appearance. As she noted, at a dinner party good conversation was expected, but at a ball a dowdy appearance in black velvet must give way to elegance and freshness. She had read her Jane Austen, as well as having looked deeply into her own feelings. She did not intend to crucify herself by appearing "like a withered cabbage in a flower garden." Her characterization leaves little doubt about her assessment of her appearance. As she moved toward her mid-thirties, her self-evaluations were darkening, becoming more hopeless.

The association with Parkes's daughter proceeded slowly, part of it created by

Marian's reticence when confronted with Bessie's insistence on her views. Bessie, for example, intended to publish a volume of poems based on her reading and on her political and feminist enthusiasms. Through Marian—who, apparently, had a rather dim view of the quality of the work—the poems were published by Chapman in November of 1852, as *Poems* by B. R. Parkes (the initials disguising female authorship). Lewes reviewed the volume in the *Leader,* along with Matthew Arnold's important volume *Empedocles,* and was kind to Bessie while being dismissive. Marian warned her not to shock people with her radical ideas or else it would be said her views were shaped by Marian's "bad influence" over her. Bessie, meanwhile, said "Marian is so great."

As George Eliot noted on several occasions in her fiction, the reshaping of a human being was a wondrous thing to observe. In 1852, she found herself in this position, observing herself in the process of change. One of the most significant moments came when she found herself forced to confront women's questions, and one of the earliest times for this occurred when Bessie Parkes introduced her to the granddaughter of the abolitionist William Smith, Barbara Leigh Smith. The latter was part of an extraordinary family, illegitimate on the one hand and yet connected on the other to several distinguished figures. Her father was himself a member of Parliament and a Radical (Liberal), like Parkes, on most issues, including repeal of the Corn Laws. But Barbara's father was exceptional in another way, in the impetuosity of his personal life, a radicalism which rubbed off on his daughter. Member of Parliament, a bachelor in his forties, a man seemingly settled in for life in English clubs, where his type was legion, he made a move which changed his life dramatically.

As the story goes, Benjamin Leigh Smith observed an extraordinarily pretty girl on the streets—she was seventeen, a milliner's apprentice, uneducated, and nearly helpless—and proceeded to enter her life, with the inevitable seduction following. But the story lacks the usual ending. Smith did not desert her when she became pregnant, but remained supportive of her and the child, as well as the next four born to her. Barbara was the oldest, and she remained quite close to her father, especially after her mother died of consumption in 1834. Her life, like her mother's, seemed to play in and out of a Dickens novel. Smith turned out to be a good father and an attentive companion for his children's mother, but he refused marriage—which would have compromised him socially. Barbara, then, was the product of a situation which was curiously Victorian: Smith could move among English society as long as he did not marry a lower-class woman; she remained in the background, bearing his children, but having no social identity. We catch glimpses of Lydia Glasher in *Daniel Deronda.* Fortunately for all concerned, Smith, unlike Glasher's Grandcourt, remained devoted, attentive, and caring.

When Marian met Barbara in 1852, the latter enjoyed an income, had trained as an artist (with William Henry Hunt), and was an independent thinker. Her cousins included Florence Nightingale and the Bonham Carters, but as an illegitimate daughter she was not welcomed in public by these august figures. Nightingale, incidentally, had not yet achieved fame, but the Crimean War was soon to provide her with the bodies on which to work her procedures.

With £300 a year to live on, Barbara had precisely what Marian lacked: the means to keep herself while she pursued those female-oriented goals she began to set for herself.

Marian was struck with Barbara from the beginning and told Bessie the young woman would soon make an indelible impression. But while Barbara was full of certainties, Marian was caught up in conflicting ideas and propositions, caught between contradictory impulses about the very nature of life. She was not a quick study, nor was she easy to decipher even in these deep, loving friendships with other women. What they saw was not what was there. Marian hid layers and layers of personal doubt, conflicting yearnings, and uneasy decisions about her future behind a fairly accessible social manner.

One major conflict for Marian manifested itself in her relationship to the incipient women's movement. With Barbara Leigh Smith (later she married Eugène Bodichon), women's causes had a supporter which they only intermittently had with Eliot. Before 1850, the movement for female social and judicial equality was fragmented. In 1848, however, Queen's College for women in London was established to improve the training of governesses, a small step but one that hardly broke new ground. In 1849, Bedford College was co-founded by Elizabeth Jesser Reid to allow women an opportunity for secondary education, another small step. Several women who attended these institutions later went on to become active in political campaigns concerning marriage and divorce laws, education for women, the franchise, and related activities. From 1850, a rudimentary franchise movement began. But higher education for women was more actively pursued than the franchise, especially since in the 1850s most men could not vote either. Those active here were, like Barbara Leigh Smith, often women whose husbands or fathers were rich and sufficiently advanced to want the best for their wives or daughters. Also, religious views often drove the movement, based on ideas of equality and justice. Evangelical, Quaker, and Unitarian churches were in the vanguard here, the major enemy among churches being the established Church of England, with its bishops sitting (or dozing) in the House of Lords.

Despite differences on such questions, Marian and Barbara became so close that when Lewes and Marian decided to live together in 1854, they asked Barbara for advice. Lewes did not have sufficient funds to petition Parliament for a divorce, the then requisite process. Smith had herself recently written *Laws Concerning Women* on just this point, the injustices which made divorce possible only for the rich and well placed. *

If we skip forward a few years, to September 1856 and Eliot's first fiction, "The Sad Fortunes of the Rev. Amos Barton," we note a passage canceled from the printed text which catches some of the contradictions playing through Marian

---

* As part of her emancipation, Barbara became one of Chapman's many mistresses. The publisher as lover can be judged from one of the exchanges he had with her when he urged the young woman "to pay especial attention to your bowels" and advised her on how to have a regular menstruation (hip baths and horsehair socks). At this time, Chapman was considering a medical career, which he did take up later. His nostrums were typical.

earlier in the decade. By 1856, she had of course made a profound life decision in going off with Lewes, and she had made another profound decision in her attempt at fiction, at Lewes's suggestion and at the prodding of something within herself. She had, then, by 1856, begun to settle some of her deepest problems, those associated with her personal life and those linked to her inner need to express herself in some mode other than reviewing and translation. Yet the following passage suggests how caught she still was, between the very advanced material she helped commission for the *Review* in her days there and her desire for a simpler kind of life which brought her back to childhood and innocence. This conflict remained a considered part of Marian's writing life, and it was this very tension between two different kinds of existence which helped make her a voice for the century. If we accept the validity of the passage, we can perhaps also understand why she hesitated on women's issues. Such issues, while socially just—and she never denied *that*—were disruptive of a particular memory she could not shake.

The occasion comes near the beginning of "Amos Barton" (only a short way into the first chapter), and concerns changes which are occurring in church music. The canceled passage recalls another time.

> Oh that happy time of childish veneration! It is the fashion to regret the days of easy merriment, but we forget the early bliss of easy reverence, when the world seemed to us to be peopled with the great and wise, when the old, weather-prognosticating gardener was our Socrates, and our spirits quailed before the clergyman without needing to be convinced of the Apostolic Succession [referring to the turbulence of the Oxford Movement].

Eliot rhapsodizes about the choir and the bassoon player in those times, a man whom she venerated as an Olympian deity in disguise. The schoolteacher, despite flaws, was a person of command.

> Alas! if the truth must be known, he was an old soldier of aberrant orthography and disordered liver, whose pedagogic functions brought on a premature death from *delirium tremens*. But he carried himself military-wise, and looked round with an imposing air of authority; and when he cuffed reprovingly the head of some too communicative schoolboy, I dreaded the implicit censure he might be passing on my own devotional bearing.

This goes beyond nostalgia and bald sentiment. It drives to the heart of what Marian and then Eliot saw as happening to England: that as the mighty march of progress continued unabated, there was terrible personal loss. But even more than this is at stake; for Eliot saw in "Olde England" some glimpse of a mode of communication, a common language, a means of living decently, and forms of behavior which demanded restraint and social balance. All three of the long fictions in *Scenes of Clerical Life* are made up of this same sense that certain values must be retained if a society is to remain civil and civilized; and yet these very values are either passing or in short supply. For Eliot, these matters were so contradictory because she was herself on the cutting edge of a newer kind of society, and at the same time she recognized that if everyone were new, society would lack coherence. Those who want to see her as always moving ahead, emerging toward some future direction and goal, must note the abundant passages of retreat, withdrawal, backward glances, and concern for the very liberation she herself embodied.

Yet her expression of these sentiments would have to wait while she wrestled with internal problems at the *Review,* problems created by Chapman's overcrowded schedule and his lack of organization plus the intrinsic nature of a magazine and its highly charged contributors. There was a litany of difficulties as Marian and Chapman prepared for the October 1852 number. The people involved were clearly not to be palmed off with platitudes. This is the real world of authors' egos. She will give Froude his twenty-six pages; she will let James Martineau have his way—his "self-interest" will ensure that; John Stuart Mills' name comes up as someone who will counter Martineau, and that creates immediate questions about how to label a discussion that is certain to be passionate. Martineau also suggested what he thinks a quarterly should be, but Marian says caustically that it cannot be realized at the *Westminster.* There is a note to be forwarded to "Miss Bronty," Marian's preferred spelling of Charlotte Brontë's name. Combe, the phrenologist, writes that an article by D. S. Brown, a philosopher, expected for the October issue, will not be forthcoming, a "defection" which Marian regrets.

She has noted the advertisement for the *British Quarterly* and is much impressed, but also worried about competition, especially from one piece called "Pre-Raphaelitism in Painting and Literature," a subject which the *Review* has neglected because of the lack of a suitable writer. She wonders if they should go after David Masson, author of an article on Patagonian missionaries which Marian thought "very beautiful." She also cites a piece on Margaret Fuller, the American writer and feminist, and rues the fact that she, Marian, has not written an article on her. And so it continues, all headache-inducing. This is still only one aspect of the situation, each element fraught with possible tempers, anger, losses, maneuverings, and decisions about what to include, what to omit, what writers to engage, which ones to dismiss, how to calm raging egos.

She feels insufficient to the entire enterprise, calling herself a "wretched helpmate." She can be witty. "If you believe in Free Will," she tells Chapman, "in the Theism that looks on manhood as a type of godhead and on Jesus as the Ideal Man, get one [an editor] belonging to the Martineau 'School of thought,' and he will drill you a regiment of writers who will produce a Prospective on a larger scale [Martineau's grandiose plan for a quarterly], and so the Westminster may come to have 'dignity' in the eyes of Liverpool." She then follows with a passage that can be offered as a blueprint for her fictional works to come. "If not—if you believe, as I do, that the thought which is to mould the Future has for its root a belief in necessity, that a nobler presentation of humanity has yet to be given in resignation to individual nothingness, than could ever be shewn

of a being who believes in the phantasmagoria of hope unsustained by reason—
why then get a man of another calibre and let him write a fresh Prospectus. . . ."

In brief, if Chapman believes in her secular humanism, in the historical and
personal qualities of necessity, in reason and not merely hope, then they may
be in accord. She then assesses what and whom they have: Martineau, warts
and all; Newman; Mill; Froude. But she indicates they are a fitting group for the
Westminster: "among the world's vanguard, though not all in the foremost line."
They need a place to speak out, and since they can't each have a journal for
themselves, the *Review* is ideal for them. But the editors should make it clear in
the prospectus that they are not responsible for everything that might be said.
As to Lewes, she wishes to pursue his work on Lamarck, the evolutionist of will,
not of natural selection. "Defective as his articles are, they are the best we can
get *of the kind?*" This is Marian's first candid assessment of the man with whom
she would spend almost the rest of her life. A little later in this same revealing
letter, she comments: "I thought Lewes's criticism in the Leader very poor and
undiscriminating."

As they slogged their way through the muddy prose and ideas of the prospectus, we observe Marian trying to create a distinctive profile for the journal, and,
at the same time, carve out beliefs which would be reflected in it. The prospectus served at least two functions: to establish what the *Review* would be, and to
define or outline what Marian could herself hold to. Her intensity of purpose
here can only be explained by the fact that the prospectus had taken on a deeply
personal meaning. The *Review* would be, for her, heuristic; while she was ostensibly working for Chapman, she was, also, working for herself.

Shortly after the auspicious first number appeared, in January 1852, even
while the second issue was being readied for the printer, funding for the *Review*
began to falter. Lombe, who had funded several articles, and indirectly the first
issue, died. The finances of the quarterly were thrown into chaos, especially
since its monies were not separated from Chapman's other enterprises, his publishing company and bookselling business. The hard facts became even harder
when Dr. Brabant urgently called in his £800 loan to Chapman. Expenditures
were clearly out of proportion with income and subsidies once the delicate balance was shattered. The editors were caught in a familiar bind: to obtain the
best writers they had to offer high fees, and yet a journal of this kind had such
limited appeal it could not survive only on subscribers.

Marian, accordingly, was ensnared in financial matters which went to the
heart of the kind of quarterly she wanted to be associated with. In the background was another financial trap, the fact that Chapman needed to break out
of the price regulations set by the Booksellers' Association. The association's
plan was to prevent booksellers from exceeding certain limits on discounts—
what we see now with the large bookstore chains, which offer sharply discounted
books that smaller stores cannot match. The idea was to keep bookselling as a
gentlemanly profession within limits, so that both sellers and public were held
in balance. Price fixing was in, competition out. Chapman had agreed to these

guidelines, which kept discounts to 10 percent or less; but he had agreed under protest. He felt, withal, that no matter how the English market was regulated, such guidelines should not extend to the American market. In 1852, he created a storm by announcing he would sell imported books at little more than cost, and this act led to his losing his right to buy books; in effect, he was put into Coventry. Chapman decided to act, probably not without drawing in Marian. He placed pressure on every source of influence he possessed—on members of Parliament, cabinet members, prominent political figures not in government, well-known authors—who stood to gain from cracking open the publishers' monopoly on price setting. In the April issue of the *Westminster,* with Marian's aid and very possibly her words, he wrote on the evils of price setting, "The Commerce of Literature." The title was itself punning, virtually an oxymoron. The Booksellers' Association, hitherto impregnable, began to back off and permitted an impartial committee to be established, whose decision would be final.

Chapman, however, was not appeased. He may not have been the heaviest of intellectuals, but when he grasped a cause, he proved tenacious; and Marian sailed these shoals with him. She left a record of the next step, a meeting of famous authors called by Chapman on 4 May. The writers were indeed renowned, including Dickens as chairperson, along with Wilkie Collins, Herbert Spencer (who jumped at the chance to break the Booksellers' monopoly), F. W. Newman, George Cruikshank (the famous illustrator), Henry Crabb Robinson, Lewes, and several others. Letters from those who could not attend were read to the group by Dickens, and these included encouragement from Carlyle, John Stuart Mill, Cobden, Leigh Hunt, Gladstone, George Combe, and several members of Parliament. "Dickens in the chair—a position he fills remarkably well, preserving a courteous neutrality of eyebrow, and speaking with clearness and decision. His appearance is certainly disappointing—no benevolence in the face and I think little in the heart. . . . he is not distinguished looking in any way—neither handsome nor ugly, neither fat nor thin, neither tall nor short."

Chapman, however, looked distinguished and refined, and read his statement well. Marian cites how the speeches went, surely a good observation post for the novelist looking to see how men negotiate tight situations, whether they come through with reasonable statements or fall back into peevishness. Her reference to Spencer, now looming in her life, comes at the beginning of the letter to the Brays, when she says she saluted Chapman on the piano at midnight with "See the Conquering Hero Comes"; for not until then "was the last magnate except Herbert Spencer out of the house." In the spring and summer of 1852, he was rarely out of mind.

7

---·◦•◦·---

Herbert and George:
The Two Voices

"But for the present my address is Grief Castle, on
the river of Gloom, in the valley of Dolour."

I n her movement among male company, Herbert Spencer was probably the
most distinguished man Marian came close to. He was, in most respects
except creative imagination, her intellectual equal. Emotionally, however, he
was lacking what we might call "affect," since he appeared to be so self-contained, so self-absorbed, so narcissistic—a term apparently made to order for
him—that he could not relate to anyone except on the intellectual level. When
Marian came too close, Spencer retreated in fear and horror that she might be
seeking a permanent union; a lifelong bachelor, he seemed to have no sexual
needs, or else repressed them for the sake of his work. Perhaps part of his self-
centeredness can be attributed to the circumstance that he was the sole surviving child of nine. Attention was lavished on him by his schoolmaster father and
his mother, the daughter of a craftsman. Both parents were devout Methodists,
of the Wesleyan wing of the faith, and both recognized early their son's proficiency in science and mathematics.

Spencer was sent to live with his uncle, Thomas, at Hinton Charterhouse,
and the older man's influence proved significant. Thomas Spencer was a Wesleyan who had abandoned the faith and was a firm believer in liberal causes, in
eliminating the Corn Laws, and in denouncing slavery such as it still existed in
the colonies and in America. He was also a fierce leader of national temperance,
edited the *National Temperance Chronicle,* and lectured widely. Marian heard
him lecture in Coventry, in 1845, and was deeply moved by his sermon against
demon rum and gin. The temperance movement for him went profoundly into
the social and political process, since he, like many other reformers, believed
that alcohol was undermining the working man and that the upper classes
encouraged the lower class to drink as a means of control.

In this atmosphere, Herbert Spencer developed, showing little enthusiasm for literature or the classics—the sole way into a university then—and instead turned to drawing, engineering, and mathematics. These subjects foreshadowed his later career as a founder of the discipline of sociology based on "scientific" principles. By 1845, when he was twenty-five, he had turned also to social subjects and became subeditor of the *Economist*. He had already met John Chapman, who published his uncle's *Temperance* journal. When he was subeditor of the *Economist*, Spencer found himself living across from Chapman's Strand boarding and publishing house. In 1850, Chapman published the first of Spencer's books, *Social Statics, or the Conditions Essential to Human Happiness Specified, and the First of Them Developed*. Despite, or because of, the title, Spencer was launched on a spectacular career which eventually comprised psychology, biology, statistics, ethics and philosophy, and sociology—the latter the broad term under which he identified his aims. After Darwin published *The Origin of Species* in 1859, Spencer became, along with Thomas Henry Huxley, an enthusiastic supporter of evolution, and it was he, not Darwin, who coined the phrase "survival of the fittest." His plan for a vast *Synthetic Philosophy* (shades of Casaubon's Key to All Mythologies) was to apply evolutionary ideas to all areas of knowledge, a plan which he acted upon from 1855 to 1893. *

Marian had met Spencer in August 1851, shortly after he had published his first book; but when she came to know him better in 1852, he had begun to settle into a passionate attachment to his ideas and to prolific writing. His assignments on the *Economist* included the unlikely job of reviewing theater and opera, and he asked Marian to accompany him. They attended, among others, a play called *The Chain of Events*, an adaptation from the French by Lewes—a strange convergence of triangular lines, Marian, Spencer (whom she would have married), and Lewes, her eventual life companion. Her criticism of the play is quite severe, as having "a very long chain" and as dragging "rather heavily." "No sparkle, but a sort of Dickens-like sentimentality all through. . . ." She wrote this to Bray, but just before, she told Cara she had "two offers last night— not of marriage, but of music"; one of them being a proposal from Spencer to take her to hear Rossini's *William Tell*. The juxtaposition of events, couched in terms of proposals, suggests quite strongly that Marian even this early, in March of 1852, was sizing up Spencer as possible marital material; or else, she was so anxious about marriage that the words suggesting "offers" were part of her daily thought. She was, she feared, on the edge of spinsterhood.

---

* His "social Darwinism," as suggested above, used the biological model for all aspects of life. In this scenario, the socially strong survive in the way the biologically fit come through, and a laissez-faire social and economic structure is justified on the example of nature. The best government is no government; the best society is one uncontrolled by forces outside nature. The influence of Jeremy Bentham's and James Mill's utilitarianism, wedded to Comte's positivism, all underscored by Darwin's natural selection, seems apparent. Not to be neglected in this mix is Malthus's *An Essay on the Principle of Population*, an argument for a laissez-faire struggle for existence. The confrontation between Eliot and Spencer was set: he arguing against man and for nature, she arguing that man was more than merely a creature controlled by nature.

She was very conscious of her appearance. When announcing she was going to see *The Huguenots*, on 1 May, she says it is "a fine thing to pick up people who are short-sighted enough to like one." She may mean Spencer or men in general. If she did mean Spencer, he was not "looking" at her, but assessing her brain power. In his *Autobiography*, he writes of her as "the most admirable woman, mentally, I ever met. . . . I am frequently at Chapman's, and the greatness of her intellect conjoined with her womanly qualities and manner, generally keep me at her side most of the evening." As we shall see, Spencer meant no more than this. Marian, too, came to observe that admiration and respect for her intellect did not lead to love, although she suffered great pain and eventually demeaned herself. Spencer had a plan for his life—he lived until 1903, dying at eighty-three—which did not include any intrusion on his own formidable intellect.

Marian told Cara (27 April), "we have agreed that we are not in love with each other, and that there is no reason why we should not have as much of each other's society as we like." She adds: "He is a good, delightful creature and I always feel better for being with him." This is not what she had written Spencer, however, on 21 April, perhaps responding to his fear that people might consider them a couple. "I felt disappointed [from his note] rather than 'hurt' that you should not have sufficiently divined my character to perceive how remote it is from my habitual state of mind to imagine that any one is falling in love with me. But perhaps I still misapprehend you, so I will run no risk of blundering further. I will only say, that I value your regard very highly, and that the more strictly truthful you are to me, both explicitly and implicitly, the better I like you."

It is clear, nevertheless, from Marian's subsequent letters to Spencer that had he demonstrated more interest in the emotional and sexual side, she would have complied; and if he had proposed, there is little argument she would have accepted. Given his lack of emotional resonance and his self-absorption, this would have proven a marriage made in hell, and he perhaps foresaw it more clearly than Marian.[*] A very candid letter Spencer wrote in February 1881, after Eliot's death, outlined to E. L. Youmans why any intimacy was impossible. He tells of how he and Marian went to the theater together, how he enjoyed her company, and how they were colleagues at the *Review*.

> After a time I began to have qualms as to what might result from this constant companionship. Great as was my admiration for her, considered both morally and intellectually, and decided as was my feeling of friend-

---

[*] Or in line with several Victorian marriages based on curious relationships: unconsummated between Thomas and Jane Carlyle, unconsummated in Ruskin's marriage, madness in Thackeray's wife, Dickens's public disclaimer of his wife's incompetence after she had borne him ten children, the maiden / death worship of several pre-Raphaelites, the fleeing from marriage of George Meredith's wife, John Stuart Mill's relationship only to women named Harriet. This brief list prepares us for later in the century, for someone like Lewis Carroll, who abjured marriage but photographed little girls in the nude (with their mothers' permission). Spencer and Marian might well have fallen somewhere betwixt and between.

ship, I could not perceive in myself any indications of a warmer feeling, and it occurred to me that mischief would possibly follow if our relations continued. Those qualms led me to take a strange step—an absurd step in one sense. I wrote to her indicating, as delicately as I could, my fears. Then afterwards, perceiving how insulting to her was the suggestion that while I felt in no danger of falling in love with her, I wrote a second letter, apologising for my unintended insult. She took it all smilingly, quite understanding my motive and forgiving my rudeness. The consequence was that our intimacy continued as before. And then, by and by, just that which I had feared might take place, did take place. Her feelings became involved and mine did not. The lack of physical attraction was fatal. Strongly as my judgment prompted, my instincts would not respond.

Although almost thirty years after the event, Spencer's retelling fits the letters Marian wrote pleading for some consideration. He says he found it very painful as the episode continued through the summer and autumn of 1852, and even thereafter. "She was very desponding and I passed the most miserable time that has occurred in my experience; for hopeless as the relation was, she would not agree that we should cease to see one another. So much did I feel the evil that I had done involuntarily, or rather against my will, that I hinted at the possibility of marriage, even without positive affection on my part; but this she at once saw would lead to unhappiness."

The appearance of Lewes was salvation, and increasingly Marian and this man-about-town became a couple, much to Spencer's "immense relief." But before this occurred Marian suffered the harrowing of hell. Her letters to Spencer in the summer of 1852 are despondent and bitter. Clearly, he had raised her expectations, or she had so misjudged his intentions that she could not control herself. By early July, there was ice between the two. As she wrote, with both wit and self-pity: "No credit to me for my virtues as a refrigerant. I owe them all to a few lumps of ice which I carried away with me from that tremendous glacier of yours. I am glad that Nemesis, lame as she is, has already made you feel a little uneasy in my absence [she was now outside London at Chandos Cottage], whether from the state of the thermometer or aught else. We will not inquire too curiously whether you long most for my society or for the sea-breezes." After these metaphors of heat and cold, Marian comes to her main point, which is an invitation for him to come. He apparently did spend some time with her, on 10 July, rebuffed her, and this led to an even more desperate letter in which she sounds almost suicidal. First the letter leading up to that: "If you decided I was not worth coming to see, it would only be of a piece with that generally exasperating perspicacity of yours which will not allow me to humbug you. . . . But seriously and selfishness apart, I should like you to have the enjoyment of this pleasant place. . . . Do come on Saturday [10 July], if you would like it."

Behind the somewhat lightened tone of the invitation to Broadstairs, Marian surely had other intentions—to try to pin Spencer down to some understanding; surely not to give him an either / or choice. Her letter of what is possibly 16

July, after his visit of the 10th, suggests that "either / or" did indeed arise, and he made it clear he was not in love with her, nor did he intend any intimacy. Her letter is personally demeaning and reveals how fragile she was, despite her march toward some position in London literary life. We can understand why this and similar letters have been held back until recently.

> I know this letter will make you very angry with me, but wait a little, and don't say anything to me while you are angry. I promise not to sin any more in the same way.
>
> My ill health is caused by the hopeless wretchedness which weighs upon me. I do not say this to pain you, but because it is the simple truth which you must know in order to understand why I am obliged to seek relief.

But the worst was to come.

> I want to know if you can assure me that you will not forsake me, that you will always be with me as much as you can and share your thoughts and feelings with me. If you become attached to someone else, then I must die, but until then I could gather courage to work and make life valuable, if only I had you near me. I do not ask you to sacrifice anything—I would be very glad and cheerful and never annoy you. But I find it impossible to contemplate life under any other conditions. If I had your assurance, I could trust that and live upon it. I have struggled—indeed I have—to renounce everything and be entirely unselfish, but I find myself utterly unequal to it. Those who have known me best have already said, that if ever I loved any one thoroughly my whole life must turn upon that feeling, and I find they said truly. You curse the destiny which has made the feeling concentrate itself on you—but if you will only have patience with me you shall not curse it long. You will find that I can be satisfied with very little, if I am delivered from the dread of losing it.
>
> I suppose no woman ever before wrote such a letter as this—but I am not ashamed of it, for I am conscious that in the light of reason and true refinement I am worthy of your respect and tenderness, whatever gross men or vulgar-minded women might think of me.

Such a letter, morbid as it appears to have been, was momentous in the evolution of Marian's feelings. For the future novelist, it gave her insight into vulnerability, the way a terrible illness or personal disaster might. It opened her up in other ways, also, not only to female vulnerability but to male frailty. By the end of July, she could tell Spencer she had reached a different conclusion about their relationship, although the latter remained wary. In her 29 July letter, she addresses the man she wanted to marry as "Mr. Spencer."

> It would be ungenerous in me to allow you to suffer even a slight uneasiness on my account which I am able to remove. . . . The fact is, all sorrows

sink into insignificance before the one great sorrow—my own miserable imperfections, and any outward hap is welcome if it will only serve to rouse my energies and make me less unworthy of my better self. . . .

If, as you intimated in your last letter, you feel that my friendship is of value to you for its own sake—mind on no other ground—it is yours. Let us, if you will, forget the past, except in so far as it may have brought us to trust in and feel for each other, and let us help to make life beautiful to each other as far as fate and the world will permit us. Whenever you like to come to me again, to see the golden corn before it is reaped, I can promise you such companionship as there is in me, untroubled by painful emotions.

The headaches were relentless. Surely, they resulted from tension, now intense because of Spencer's inability to love, but also the consequence of dissatisfaction with the way her life was going, part of a frustration of will which had still not found full direction for its energies. In a more speculative view, one could interpret the headaches as modes of expression, as part of the complex building within for some personal emergence which was being frustrated by her need for attention to detail at the *Review*.

She carried on, and in a curious way, Spencer became a friend who replaced, in London, the close relationship she had had with the Brays and Hennells. They attended all varieties of activities, even flower shows, not something we would associate with the pragmatic Spencer. But one of his interests was biology, and the excursions, wherever they led, gave him ample opportunity to discuss deeper matters with Marian. At this stage, she was more of a sounding board for his ideas than he was for hers. He was moving toward a period of intense activity, whereas her work was mainly administrative, not expressive. Spencer held several theories about plants and their place in the evolutionary cycle, and the flower shows were not mere indulgences for him. For Marian, with her keen interest in all aspects of nature, they were indeed pleasure; but she, also, was slowly forming her views of nature as fitting well into evolutionary theory. On a more personal note, she met Spencer's father, who made an excellent impression, "very pleasing," she told Bray. Externally, her life seemed on an even course: days filled with *Review* activities; evenings with the famous and near-famous; weekends on jaunts with Spencer to plays, operas, shows, or on long walks; other evenings of concerts or opera. It seemed, externally, as though her plan to emancipate herself had fully succeeded. Yet as we have observed, the external view was not close to the internal one, which was full of dissatisfaction even apart from the Spencer fiasco.

The Brays told Marian they would invite Spencer to Rosehill while she was there, in July, if she wished. As we have seen, Spencer, ever fearful of being considered a suitor, was near panic. "We certainly could not," she writes them, "go together, for all the world is setting us down as engaged." She says it makes one uncomfortable. " 'Tell it not in Gath' however—that is to say, please to avoid mentioning our names together, and pray burn this note, that it may not lie on the chimney piece for general inspection." But the plot thickens when both Spencer and Lewes enter into her correspondence with Bray, and then Chapman. The publisher, she says, will await an invitation to Rosehill when she is present; and if Lewes should not accept an invitation now, she asks Bray not to press it. "Not that I don't like him," she tells Bray, but she feels he is too "Londonish" when she plans to "enjoy the fields and hedgerows. . . ." In that agonizing time before she and Spencer agreed on "just friendship," her social planning had become hectic.

Professionally, she alternated between some hope for the quarterly, in terms of funding, and despair about Chapman's anxieties. She feels the third issue will be capital. As we know, Spencer's two visits were extremely disquieting, so that she found herself holding on personally, very uncomfortable with herself as Spencer made his position absolutely clear. He later confided to friends he could not be tempted by any woman who lacked physical attraction.

But Spencer had turned down at least one other woman, a beauty. Not the most discreet of men when it came to his relationships with women, he wrote a piece for the *Leader*, in 1854, called "Personal Beauty." In this, he speaks of those physical qualities which contradict the ideal of beauty, which is the classical Greek head of harmonious proportions. With typical lack of tact, he condemned prominent or fleshy noses, prominent jaws, sizable mouths and upper lips—all the qualities Marian possessed and which made her recognize she was growing to look, in her own perception of herself, like an "old witch" or an "old hag." If the ideal was the classical Greek head, then she saw herself increasingly as Medusa. Yet, despite this emphasis on physical beauty, Spencer kept a photograph of Marian in his bedroom throughout his entire life, including the more than two decades he outlived her.

The relationship had so many complexities it is tempting to speculate on matters for which we have no direct evidence. Spencer, irrationally, also held that physical ugliness was a manifestation of inferior intellect and even character; that physical beauty meant beauty of intellect.* Yet while all of this was in direct contradistinction of Marian's qualities of intellect and character, it is clear she held a large place in his mind and even affections, such as they were. Here we speculate that perhaps Spencer experienced a certain feminine element in his personality which was repelled by Marian's *supposed* masculine qualities— lack of physical beauty, powerful intellect, and desire for independence. We find here something difficult to unravel: that in Spencer's eyes, Marian, in playing a role he approved of, nevertheless fell far outside the stereotypical view of women he had cultivated; and that failure to fit into the stereotype made her seem masculine in his view. Feeling this, his own delicate masculinity was troubled,

---

* Spencer's own appearance, incidentally, was hardly Don Juanish, nor was it part of the classic Greek ideal: balding by his mid-thirties, facial hair surrounding the sides and chin, no mustache, but fairly regular features. While not prepossessing or distinguished, he was pleasant enough looking, whereas a photograph of Marian taken in 1858, and retouched in an 1884 etching by Paul Adolphe Rajon, shows a woman whose features, except for lovely eyes, seemed too heavy for the feminine look she was trying to achieve.

and he recoiled; or else his sexual proclivities were so low-keyed—"borne out" by a phrenological study of his head in 1842—that he withdrew when confronted with any threat to his carefully composed self. In his *Autobiography,* Spencer finessed all such deeper significance.

By the summer of 1852, probably at Broadstairs, Spencer was confronted with all these contradictory elements, and since they did not resolve themselves, he withdrew from active contention for marriage with some final statement which made Marian feel more unsettled and uglier than ever. By this time, and surely by October, when he joined her at Rosehill, it was clear that Spencer, for all his qualities, was not marriageable material; that Marian's need for reciprocated affection could not be satisfied by this thinking machine.

Her stay at Chandos Cottage in Broadstairs extended into August.* Whatever her complaints—insects, isolation, boredom—she found it like paradise, especially in comparison with her hectic schedule in London. But by the end of August, she had returned to London with "a violent headache and sickness." The headaches persisted, and she characterized herself to Sara as being in "the worst spirits, under the influence of blue devils. . . ." In another letter, also to Sara, she says she is in a "croaking mood." In this 2 September communiqué, she indicates she is inundated by articles, quarterly business, and other matters which give her little opportunity to catch her breath; not to mention the aftereffects of the Spencer rebuff and her futile pursuit. Along the way, she defends Lewes against an attack on him by Harriet Martineau, whose views she calls "incomprehensible ignorance"; the point being Lewes's introduction of psychology as a science into his comments on the French sociologist and positivist Comte. Marian says she fears that whatever she says will become gossip at Rosehill and get back, somehow, to Lewes.

All this is a kind of holding action, part of a personal pause. She was reading American fiction, Hawthorne's *Blithedale Romance,* Stowe's *Uncle Tom's Cabin,* and others. She would later carry on an extensive correspondence with Harriet Beecher Stowe. She was, possibly, reviewing for the quarterly these very books. Missing her friends from Coventry, she tells Bray she is counting the hours until she can see his kind face. She seeks their complete acceptance of her, their belief, but, foremost, their maternal care, their fussing.

To Sara, she comments on the October issue as "respectable," nine articles, two or three of them good, the rest not bad. For January, she has lined up Froude, Harriet Martineau, Theodore Parker, and others, on topics as diverse as Ireland, the Mormons, atomic theory, and Mary Tudor. She sees this as making a good start on the new year. But her manner of stating this lacks enthusiasm or intellectual excitement. She still lacks vocation.

Spencer was on her mind, even when it became clear the relationship would

---

* The American reader may not be aware of Broadstairs in literature, but the English reader will probably identify it as the place where Dickens wrote a good deal of *David Copperfield.* After this became known, Broadstairs (located on the Channel midway between Margate and Ramsgate, a few miles east of Canterbury) gained greatly in popularity among English tourists. Dickens himself was a frequent visitor.

be friendship or nothing. The philosopher king, meanwhile, adamantly denied they were about to be married when Lewes hove into view. He wanted to publish this disclaimer shortly after her death, but was dissuaded on grounds the words made him sound like a cad. As a consequence, Spencer decided to ask Cross in his biography to handle the matter circumspectly and to make it clear that he, Spencer, and Marian were no more than good friends. Spencer's letter, dated 3 April 1881 (four months after Eliot's death), first asks Cross to contradict statements of closeness and then states "that high as was my admiration for her, and great as my feeling of friendship, yet my feeling did not grow into a warm one—or something to that effect." Later, when Cross's biography was nearing completion,* Spencer had not forgotten his request and added that the two had not been in love with each other. He dictated the wording *he* preferred: "The intimacy naturally led to rumours. It was said that Mr. Spencer was in love with her. This, however, was not true. I have the best possible warrant for saying that his feeling did not pass the limits of friendship."

Inasmuch as Cross was rewriting the past to fit a laundered view of his now dead wife, Spencer's "rewriting," and Cross's dissatisfaction with Spencer's proposed wording, was in itself ironical. But this duel over what was now a sanitized past was not finished; we must also keep in mind that Spencer did not destroy Marian's pitiful letters to him. The historical record was still available, although not to any outside reader until 1985 (one hundred years after Cross's biography appeared). Cross rejected the "rumors" ploy of Spencer, and so the latter came back with another try. This now spread out toward the end of 1884, the battlefield taken up with Spencer's desire to protect his past—but against what?—and Cross's desire to protect Eliot's past—but against what? Spencer's 21 October 1884 disclaimer was possibly the least discreet of all: "Of course the intimacy caused speculation. After some time it was concluded that Mr. Spencer was in love with her and that they were engaged. But I have the best possible warrant for saying that this was not true."

Cross countered with the possibility of a note which denied that Marian had jilted Spencer, a point equally lacking in tact. In an earlier age, a duel might have ensued over each one's honor. Spencer of course rejected this latest effort and said that no note was better than that, since it opened him up to ridicule either way. Cross nevertheless went ahead and deleted Spencer's words "We are not in love with each other," and left the statement that they decided to enjoy each other's company nevertheless. Spencer persisted and continued the battle into 1885 (2 February) saying that Cross's account now makes it sound as though he were jilted for Lewes. "I cannot say that I have been fairly used." But a week later he wrote to soften his words and to admit that Cross's version as it stands is probably the best way to handle it, convinced as he was by his friend Potter's daughter, Beatrice Webb. Spencer had admitted to her that he was

---

* John Cross's three-volume biography, mainly related by way of Eliot's letters and journals, appeared in 1885 (Blackwood); and then, revised and with new material, appeared in a one-volume edition in 1887 (Blackwood). The 1887 volume, incidentally, involved the deletion of several passages and entire pages, thus having provided Spencer with an additional opportunity to influence Eliot's biographer.

never in love, the "never" meaning not only with Marian but with anyone; that so focused was his mind on perfecting his ideas he had no feelings left over for anything else. So ended this bizarre episode, with two men fighting over Marian's life well after her death, each writing and rewriting a scenario whose precise truth we may never know.

Marian's response to events beyond her circle or beyond intellectual arguments about issues was minimal. News as such did not attract or distract her. The death of the Duke of Wellington on 14 September 1852 elicits no immediate comment from her, although the event may have been stored away as possible background for a novel later on. The duke's death ended not only an era of great military triumph for England at Waterloo, but also, more immediately, an era linked to the passage of the Catholic Emancipation Act in 1829 and then the jockeying for political position during the first great Reform Bill of 1832. His involvement in those momentous days possibly fixed that period in Marian's mind, although the duke's death in itself did not appear to stir her. When it came time for her to settle in to write her masterpiece, *Middlemarch,* she set the novel during the high days of this political activity, when Catholic emancipation and reform were very much in the air.

With the October issue put to bed, Marian spent that month in a variety of activities which provided a break in her routine. She visited the Combes in Edinburgh, on 5 October; she went to Craigcrook Castle, the home of Francis Jeffrey (founder and editor of the *Edinburgh Review*); and she stayed with Harriet Martineau at Ambleside in the Lake District (near Windermere, with views of Grasmere and Rydal Water from Loughrigg Fell), while there visiting workers' cottages with Martineau, as part of the latter's Cooperative Building Society— which may have planted the seed of Dorothea Brooke's intense interest in workers' cottages in *Middlemarch.* Near the end of the month, on the 26th, Marian left Ambleside for Rosehill, where Spencer was coming to spend a long weekend. Her stay at the Combes' in Edinburgh was idyllic, and her comments to the Brays indicate she was being indulged and mothered, just the circumstances to "nourish her sleek optimism" and convince her, momentarily, that this is the best of all possible worlds. She is critical, however, of the conversation, "pleasant enough, though of course all the interlocutors besides Mr. Combe have little to do but shape elegant modes of negation and affirmation like the people who are talked to by Socrates in Plato's dialogues." But the paucity of good conversation cannot undermine the beauty of the place, "not an ugly object to be seen." She says that when she wakes up, it is as though she were in utopia.

The idyll either continued or ended when she arrived at Rosehill: "continued" because she was home, as it were, but "ended" because she was faced again with Spencer. Despite the July rejection, she was building up that alternation of expectation and disappointment, so painful for her personally, but later so significant in her fiction: that sense of possibility dashed by actuality. It would be as if the experience of the whole century—that tension between hopefulness and reality—was encapsulated in her responses.

Her relationship with Spencer was by circumstance delicate, although he did find useful a particular line she suggested for his book *Psychology*, the line going: "Things which have a constant relation to the same thing have a constant relation to each other." It is possible Marian contributed more than what Spencer was ready to admit to. The long weekend at Rosehill indicated the finality of any hopes she may have had for intimacy. Although her letters are spare, she does tell Bessie Parkes that her week so far among affectionate friends will make her "feel brave for anything that is to come after. . . . that being extremely comfortable I am resigned." She adds that her resignation always flourishes best in that familiar soil. We should not, however, underestimate her suffering here merely because she had put a good face on it. Surely she had figured that mixing as she did in intellectual circles she would find a suitable male, a companion, a suitor, even a potential husband; and yet, except for Spencer and Mackay, she moved among married men.

Haight speaks of her powers of renunciation, but rather than renunciation here, we observe that suffering, headaches, and other ills possibly linked to menstruation were all part of that mechanism which, in her, led to creative work. Whereas the woman may have been unhappy, even enraged by her fate (those tension headaches), the potential novelist was not wasting moments. All of these rebuffs, these implicit attacks on her appearance, the disappointments which followed upon her perception of liberation were matters she was squirreling away for later forays into fiction. Be someone on whom nothing is lost, Henry James later advised all budding writers.

Marian moved unsteadily toward her thirty-third birthday. Upon her return to London, Spencer visited and "spent the evening with me." In his biography, Cross omitted the "with me," since it apparently carried the intimation of something closer than he thought suitable for print. The topic of conversation was possibly world population statistics, or another one of Spencer's pet projects. The remainder of 1852 left all the uncertainties in place. Her days were filled with activities which did not cohere: incidental reading, such as Kingsley and Thackeray; editing of articles, one on taxation by Greg and a related piece by Hill; social events at 142. It all sounds very distant, even in her half-joshing, half-self-pitying tone. Her comments to the Brays carry some of this weary spirit: "When I had got some way into this *magnum mare* [Greg's or similar pieces], in comes Mr. Chapman with a thick German volume. 'Will you read enough of this to give me your opinion of it?' Then of course I must have a walk after lunch, and when I had sat down again thinking that I had two clear hours before dinner—rap at the door—Mr. Lewes—who of course sits talking till the second bell rings. After dinner another visitor—and so behold me at 11 P.M. still very far at sea on the subject of taxation but too tired to keep my eyes open." A typical day, very possibly.

Marian notes that Disraeli has for the second time committed plagiarism in his eulogy on the Duke of Wellington, lifting several passages from Thiers's funeral oration on Marshall Couvion St. Cyr, what she calls "cool impudence" in her tone of glee at having found him out. So much for Wellington, so much for Disraeli! In one of her few political comments, she says she could tolerate even Louis Napoleon if only he could help pick up Coventry trade. The clothing industry was sliding badly, and Coventry was suffering unemployment and unrest.

In family terms, Marian was grieved to hear on 20 December that Chrissey's husband, Edward Clarke, had died after a long illness. His death left Chrissey and the children in poor financial straits, so that Marian felt she had to find some way to help. She believed there should be a family summit with her brother Isaac, although because of his disapproval of her way of life she was now on very cool terms with him. When she arrived at Meriden, Chrissey's home, at Christmas, she found that while money matters were not critical, something had to be done. When she decided she could not help Chrissey by remaining another week, Isaac flew into a rage that she had failed to consult him before deciding to leave. She tells her Coventry friends he wound up saying "that he desired I would never 'apply to him for anything whatever'—which, seeing that I never have done so, was almost as superfluous as if I had said I would never receive a kindness from him." Clarke's practice was sold for £1,200, so that independent of aid from her siblings, Chrissey would have less than £100 per year, insufficient for a family. Marian offered to help, although her limited resources did not permit substantial support at this time.

The year 1853 was a decisive one for Marian. It was more a personally significant year than one of professional triumph. Although she did translate Feuerbach's *The Essence of Christianity*, the main area concerned her relationship with Lewes. Now that it was clear that Spencer was not suitable for an intimate relationship, Marian and Lewes gravitated to each other; and toward the latter part of the year she and he came to some kind of understanding, although they would not live together openly until July of 1854, when they left for Germany.

Marian, however, was not the only sufferer in her rebuff by Spencer. He underwent several changes of fortune in 1853. Having inherited a legacy of £500 from his uncle, he was financially free to marry, if he had so chosen; but clearly that was not in his thinking. Yet even his iron will was unsettled; the man suffered. He may have rejected Marian's desire for intimacy, but he himself appeared to be undergoing some inner turmoil. Resigning from his post at the *Economist*, he left for his first trip to the continent. Physical changes were undermining his health, an ailment diagnosed as a cardiac disturbance, an enfeebled heart, which suggests numerous possibilities both bodily and metaphorically. Curiously, Eliot gives Casaubon that disturbance in *Middlemarch*, as diagnosed by Lydgate—leading us to believe Spencer was himself one of the models for that unfeeling man, although clearly not the sole model. Unhappy with his foreign travel, which included the British tradition of great walks and mountain climbing, he returned to his parents' home and completed in a few months his book *Psychology*.

While writing the segment on "Reason," he felt his nervous system give way, something akin to what John Stuart Mill also records in his autobiography, the result of his force-fed education at the hands of his father. Spencer's breakdown, however, was of a different kind, coming well in his thirties and clearly associated with his abnegation of an intimate emotional life in favor of a life of reason. Neither the heart condition, such as it was, nor the nervous collapse was life threatening—Spencer lived for another half century and became an amusing hypochondriac.

He was intelligent enough and sufficiently perceptive to know what the trouble was—and that Marian almost filled the bill. But he also knew that "moral and intellectual beauty" did not by itself attract him; and that because of the limitations of the British educational system he could not find such moral and intellectual qualities connected to "a good physique." He characterized himself as a curmudgeon of sorts, a "melancholy Coelebs" (a bachelor seeking a wife, after the character in the Hannah More novel), what he knows he will be to the end of his days. He did become a reliable and supportive friend.

This carries us well into 1853, when Spencer's eccentricities multiplied, as he recoiled from his close call with Marian. She herself seemed to disengage emotionally, although with her recurring ailments it is difficult to assess. Perhaps her intense work on the *Review* was a way in which she could find an outlet without breaking down over Spencer or other disappointments. Her letters early in the year, nevertheless, describe her as miserable and dejected. She finds she must defend Lewes to Sara, who was becoming increasingly moralistic, by saying her friend should not lay the sins of an article on atomic theory—one in which the author attempts to associate developments in chemistry with those in religion—on Lewes, since the author was not he but Dr. Samuel Brown. Marian says she dislikes the article intensely and is amused that Harriet Martineau finds it beautiful and poetical.

Her response to Martineau's remarks is quite in keeping with the way she judged people. Marian sharply distinguished between what she felt about the person—Martineau was modeling cottages, something close to Marian's heart—and what she felt about that person's intellectual activities. Even Lewes had fallen under these strictures: his wit and the amusing quality of his person were not an excuse for mental slackness. On that Marian showed no mercy, made no concessions.

Her return to the Strand and the *Review* at the end of the year brought more controversy, mainly between Chapman and George Combe. Furthermore, in her absence, the January issue contained several mistakes, factual as well as typographical, which she felt she might have caught. She was interpreting her role at the *Review* as indispensable, and this led, in turn, to her overdetermining everything. Having become almost fanatical about details and anxious about errors, she fell back on herself; only illness could provide a respite. When at the end of January 1853 she was racked by pain in her right shoulder, she identified it as rheumatism. Packed in wadding, she took to her bed, ill, and only felt better when she learned that Bray was coming to London to whisk her off to Rosehill. The Strand had become for her the poisoned place.

Intrigues of all varieties, soothing huge egos, Chapman's haphazard business affairs, insufficient funding for the *Review*, failure to gain sufficient subscribers, fractious contributors (not all of them first rate), constant misunderstandings—these are some of the elements thrust upon Marian, apart from her own unsettled personal life.

In early 1853, Marian used the time away from the Strand to visit Chrissey, now settled at Attleborough, Isaac's former house. The visit was hardly joyful, however, for Marian was quite attuned to her sister's plight. With six children to care for in a small, pokey house—and Isaac keeping her on a tight budget—Chrissey was just beyond falling through the cracks. When one of Clarke's former patients offered to send Chrissey's oldest boy to Australia, Marian toyed with the idea of accompanying the entire clan there, getting them settled, and then returning—a suggestion she made to Bray. Nothing came of this, and it takes some concentration to see Marian helping a family of seven to get settled in Australia. She really feared that Chrissey would succumb psychologically to the meanness of her existence, although Marian interpreted her sister's life in her own terms of intellectual growth and accomplishment. Chrissey's goals were quite different. Nevertheless, her situation was intolerable; besides the lack of money, she was living, in Marian's view, amidst "ignorant bigots," a condition Marian says would be "moral asphyxia" for herself. She thinks of removing her sister and brood from this mean little cottage, but fears Isaac will then cut them off, and she, Marian, might not enjoy sufficiently good health to support them.

Her next comment, to Cara, is telling at several levels: "Yet how odious it seems that I, who preach self-devotion, should make myself comfortable here [in London] while there is a whole family to whom, by renunciation of my egotism, I could give almost everything they want. And the work I can do in other directions is so trivial!" Her precise meaning is not clear, but her sentiment suggests that while her pursuit of *Review* activities is trivial, she could do other work which, while not nourishing her ego, would enable her to support Chrissey's family. While the particular activity is not spelled out, it is possible to read into these words some sense that journalistic writing might offer the income which would support Clarke's widow and children. Her concern here only deepened the divisions in the way her life was taking her.

Marian's interest in Chrissey's children was part of her lifelong attention to children. Although we do not know how much she wanted children of her own—by now, at thirty-three, it was becoming remote—she was always devoted to them, both in the flesh and as embodiments of something fine. Later, when she became "stepmother" to Lewes's three surviving sons, we note from their affectionate letters how they cherished her. Her comments on Chapman's little ones, now suffering from whooping cough—an often fatal disease—indicate how closely she identified with them: ". . . from having been quite beautiful with healthy bloom they have become pale as death." She says she has an increasing respect for Mrs. Chapman and feels that Cara underrates both of them.

Lewes also enters into the equation. From the unattractive figure she had described when they first met in October 1851, he has now gained greatly, to become "kind and attentive and has quite won my regard after having a good deal of my vituperation." He is, she says, much better than he seems, "a man of heart and conscience wearing a mask of flippancy." From these words, we see the shadow of Will Ladislaw in *Middlemarch*, and the way in which Eliot develops him from a figure of flippancy and seemingly little substance into someone who, with kindness and attentiveness, becomes more focused for Dorothea.

Marian's letters at the end of April and beginning of May activate the theme of illness once again. She has embraced ailments. Obviously, for a woman of thirty-three, who would live nearly another three decades, none of these ailments was organically serious. Overall, her health seemed sufficient to carry her well past the average age for mortality of women who did not bear children. But a cough now joined other conditions, with a pain in her throat making her "quite hysterical" that afternoon. Four days later, she has been "very ill again" and her sole hope for improvement is a change of air. What strikes us is not only how psychologically induced these ills were, but how much she needed mothering from her Coventry friends, who received the full litany of ailments in letter after letter. On 13 May, she wrote Chapman that he may put her project "The Idea of a Future Life" on his list; but this work was never completed and possibly never even started. Chapman, however, did announce it in the *Leader* for 18 June (1853). On 15 May, she told Bessie Parkes she has been an invalid for more than a month, with the bad cough giving her the most concern. Incidentally, Marian was not consumptive; when she died, it is generally believed a kidney ailment or some complication from kidney stones led to her final illness. No symptoms of this condition would appear for some time. On 30 May, she suffered headache and backache, although she recovered sufficiently to attend the opera *Ernani* with Bray. Trouble with her teeth took her to a dentist, Henry Barclay, who put an end to her pain "by stopping my hollow tooth." The ailments sound as though she were a somewhat lesser-scaled Job.

She revived, to see Rachel, the famous French actress whose greatest role was in Racine's *Phèdre*. Marian says she fails to see that Vashti in Charlotte Brontë's *Villette* owed anything to Rachel. She mentions, in a generally light vein, going off to a party to meet Mrs. Caroline Francis Cornwallis, whose early education recalls John Stuart Mill's. As a child, she learned Latin, Greek, Hebrew, and German, came to know Egyptian hieroglyphics, and became an expert on Tuscan criminal procedures. She wrote two articles for the *Review*, one on married women and property, the second on the capabilities and disabilities of women. She was in her way as remarkable as Marian in hers, and Marian's lightness of tone in referring to her suggests she knew she had met her equal. But even this momentous meeting of two enormously accomplished women, about which we have no further evidence, takes second place to an examination by Sir James Clark, physician to Queen Victoria herself. Clark told Marian she had a perfectly sound constitution, sound heart and lungs, but was "a soft pulpy individual, certainly not fit for a Strand life." This was a most astute diagnosis, made even more perceptive by the fact that Marian's health picked up when she left England with Lewes.

Lewes does not play a large role in her letters at this time, in the spring and summer of 1853, but he was much in mind. Having overcome his unprepossessing looks, Marian peered into the man; just as he, once he had confronted Marian's own plain appearance, could judge the woman beneath. She seemingly forgot him as she traveled from one vacation spa to another once the July issue was completed; but she carried with her, apparently, an interest that would intensify upon her return to London. She had moved from Bray and Brabant to Chapman and Spencer, and now Lewes was ready to take his place, another married man who seemed possible for her. In 1853, he was a combination of some professional achievement on a broad range of subjects with a personal life which seems bizarre even by present-day standards. As we examine what had occurred to him, and what he tolerated in personal terms, it is hard to avoid the conclusion that part of his appeal *lay in the very danger he presented.* Marian was not attracted to run off with him despite his messy family problems, but because he offered himself as someone badly wounded.

Her ultimate act of hostility to her dead father and her ultra-respectable brother was to become a scarlet woman. Not that she entered this role without trepidation, since it could of course have ended quite badly; but she entered with the realization that her first step in refusing religious instruction had as its final step a renunciation of Mrs. Grundy and her Victorian strictures on propriety and respectability. Put another way, Lewes was the worst possible choice she could have made; the man was, from this angle of vision, beneath contempt.

In *Middlemarch,* Eliot wrote a passage which seems not only a fictional drama but something dug out of personal experience. After Casaubon has died and Dorothea learns of the codicil to his will which forbids her to marry Will Ladislaw on penalty of forgoing all inherited money, she undergoes what is called a "convulsive change." "She might," Eliot writes, "have compared her experience at that moment to the vague, alarmed consciousness that her life was taking on a new form, that she was undergoing a metamorphosis in which memory would not adjust itself to the stirring of new organs. . . . Her whole world was in a state of convulsive change." What occurs to Dorothea is her recognition that the world is shaped differently from the way she had conceived it; but more than that, the "convulsive change" indicates that her choices for herself had been faulty and that she needed to vault into another kind of life with other kinds of feelings and responses. There is almost a Lamarckian leap here into the world, whose contours she is still unaware of, but which she senses to be out there awaiting her. She must confront "the beast in the jungle." The parallel to Marian's experience in 1853–54 leading to the elopement with Lewes seems of this kind: not just an alteration in her pattern of living, but a jump into another form of life, whatever its perils.

The man who was considered contemptuous by those who held to a particular set of moral values was quite charming, debonair, and perhaps more French than English in his manner and style. All contemporaries who knew him—even Carlyle, who could not be considered part of Lewes's social and political world—testified to what a fine conversationalist he was, how he appeared knowledgeable in several fields, how he sparkled when in company. Lewes was not a university man, nor was he a graduate of one of the great public schools, although he did attend a fine seminary at Greenwich, Dr. Charles Parr Burney's school, which had an excellent scholastic reputation. Lewes there gained his foothold in respectable English education, which meant he became well grounded in Latin and Greek; and he learned to write clearly and directly. Lewes's prose lacked the complications of Marian's, but in its way it was effective. After finishing at Dr. Burney's, with few prospects, Lewes went out into the world. Even by this time, he had already knocked around: born in London, he had lived in Boulogne, then Jersey and Brittany as a child—thus his command of French—and then at thirteen came to Greenwich. Once let loose in London, he became a jack-of-all-trades, working in the business world at low positions, then studying medicine—which gave him a good grounding in chemistry and a penchant for the physical sciences—before applying himself to literature. He had languages, the aforesaid Latin and Greek, French from childhood, and he would later acquire German, in Germany, where he gave English lessons. He was a quick study, not only able to absorb information rapidly, but capable of using it just as rapidly. Like Will Ladislaw, whom he resembled in several ways except for appearance,* he had quick insights which could seem somewhat superficial.

Once he had applied himself to literature, he showed enormous energy. Novels, biographies, blank verse tragedies—some of them produced, all of them forgettable—poured forth with a fluency which immediately made them suspect. But Lewes could be a careful researcher. In his biographical work and in the several articles he wrote on multifold subjects, he demonstrated responsibility. But all this only suggests his versatility. He had been an actor, a teacher of English, a reviewer of books, plays, concerts, and art exhibitions. And he was occupied on other fronts as well, as a ladies' man, where he seemed successful despite his less than ladies' man's looks. Jane Carlyle admitted she and her social circle referred to him as "Ape," although she found him charming and amusing. Always lively, he was a good storyteller, a man who could take all the parts in a complicated story and turn it into a theatrical event. We find here considerable accomplishment, without much left for eternity; and his appeal to Marian was not profundity, which she had demanded in others, but the sense he was good company, a strong conversationalist, and, strangely, dependable. More than anything else, he believed in her.

At twenty-three, Lewes had married Agnes Jervis, daughter of the member of Parliament for Chatcull, Straffordshire. How they met is not quite clear, although probably when Lewes came to the house as a tutor. What made Lewes acceptable to this family is also not clear, since at twenty-three his prospects were uncertain and he was not an imposing figure in other respects. Agnes was nineteen when she married, on 18 February 1841, and their first child, Charles

---

* Will is described as radiant, as being part of the sun. He brings light into dark rooms, and when he meets Dorothea in Rome on her honeymoon, she is cast in shadows, whereas he sends forth beams of brightness. Lewes, on the other hand, had a puckered-up face, reminiscent of a monkey's—according to contemporary descriptions—with a weak, receding jaw, and thick lips; all in all, a pitted face that with its hollowness of cheek seemed the opposite of Will's. If the latter radiated light, Lewes seemed to absorb it.

Lee Lewes, was born in 1842. Agnes was considered a beauty, creating a beauty-and-the-beast coupling, her blondness setting off Lewes's pinched, set-in face. But she was no stereotypical blond pushover. Besides a strong mind and will of her own, she was accomplished in languages, translating from French and Spanish articles which Lewes sold when their funds were low. With babies coming rapidly (besides Charles Lee in 1842, Thornton Arnott in 1844, Herbert Arthur in 1846, and St. Vincent Arthy in 1848), the Leweses desperately needed money. Lewes was a whirling dervish as a writer, producing the four-volume *A Biographical History of Philosophy*, in 1845–46, when he was only twenty-seven. The volumes were based on lectures he delivered at W. J. Fox's Finsbury Chapel; but even so, they required research, extensive reading, revision for book form, and considerable organization. The energy expended here was prodigious and would mark everything in the future about Lewes, in both his professional and his social life.

Although contemporary witnesses found the couple happy—Carlyle among others testified to this—there were rumblings in the background which would affect the marriage. Soon after the ceremony Lewes went on several trips abroad for long periods of time. On one trip, he went to France and, through Mill's letters of introduction, met Comte, de Tocqueville, and Michelet; in Germany, he came to know a cast of intellectuals, in Berlin alone, August Boeckh, Friedrich Schelling, Ludwig Tieck, and Brentano (Bettina von Armin). This was in 1845; and in 1847, he returned to France, ostensibly to meet George Sand, who was to play such a large role, later, in Marian's life. He traveled extensively around England lecturing, in Manchester in the spring of 1849, on the history of philosophy, and earlier in the year at the Liverpool Mechanics Institute. Many of these institutes or their like were alternate educational establishments for adults who lacked the opportunity to enter into the very restricted upper-class education the elite enjoyed. Lewes also appeared as an actor in his own play *The Noble Heart*. He repeated the lectures in Edinburgh and there acted in *The Merchant of Venice*.

Having met a dazzling array of accomplished writers, philosophers, and other intellectuals, Lewes was ready to found a journal of his own, the *Leader*, along with Thornton Leigh Hunt, an old friend, in 1850. By then Lewes had written extensively for the *Westminster Review*, from 1840 to 1847. When Chapman took over, he found Lewes very useful for long, inclusive articles on French literature and other cultural matters. Lewes was not restricted to French, but covered German and English as well. Marian correctly thought he was hasty and often superficial, but at this time Lewes was more interested in coverage—and profitable copy—than in profundity.

The trips away from London were beneficial for Lewes's career, but accelerated the demise of what would have been a difficult relationship under the best of conditions. Agnes had been raised by her father, Swynfen Jervis, as a free-thinker, and her idea of marriage was not Victoria's or Mrs. Grundy's. If Lewes believed in the freedom of the male in sexual matters, Agnes believed in the freedom of the female. If Shelley was his model of profligate behavior, George

Sand could have been hers. Her father, the M.P., did nothing to discourage her; and both she and Lewes felt that one's emotional life dictated social life, not the other way around. This could lead, as both recognized, to what we call an open marriage, which gave freedom to one or both to pursue other romantic interests. Our first evidence of the openness they agreed upon came on 16 April 1850, when she gave birth to another son, this one the child of Thornton Hunt. *

As mentioned above, Lewes and Hunt had started their own journal in 1850, the *Leader,* a weekly whose duties they divided; Lewes handled the arts or cultural side (theater, exhibitions, concerts, books), and Hunt covered political, social, and other such news. The division of labor suited both, for Hunt was a journalist and Lewes aspired to something higher, although reviewing was not precisely higher. Because the *Leader* office, on Wellington Street, was so convenient to the Strand, Lewes and Spencer, who wrote for the weekly, came to see Marian and, of course, Chapman. Spencer cited one of these visits as the beginning of Lewes's and Marian's interest in each other; but, more likely, the interest grew as each assessed his and her own future. Lewes torpedoed any chance of divorce for adultery by accepting Hunt's child by Agnes as his own, his fifth son, and registering him as Edmund Alfred Lewes.

Lewes's acquiescence to this arrangement had some rationale. His own youngest son, St. Vincent, had died only three weeks before, on 23 March, at two years old, from whooping cough. This was in a sense a replacement son. Further, the first issue of the *Leader* had only just appeared, two weeks before Agnes gave birth, and Lewes may have been so caught up in this venture he did not wish to create volatility in his household or with his business partner. But still another reason is compelling, which is that Lewes, an inveterate philanderer, kept up his familiar ways while he was on the road. And being an honest man when it came to sexual equality, he could not condemn his wife when he was himself guilty of the same behavior. Still further, that the man was Thornton Hunt, his co-editor and partner on the *Leader,* created the possibility that if he insisted on a divorce, his professional life would suffer. Surely, the *Leader* could not survive a co-respondent suit by one editor against the other.

This was, however, only the beginning. Once Lewes accepted one child, he put himself in the position to accept all. He had placed himself outside of commonly accepted morality, as had Agnes and Hunt; the consequences were that by English law he had to forgo any opportunity to sue for divorce based on adultery, unless he petitioned Parliament, a very costly and elaborate procedure. Matters did not remain static, however, and the acceptance of the new son did

---

* Haight quotes from Jane Carlyle's *Letters to Her Family,* in which she has noted some change in Agnes's attitude, a change which would indicate that while Lewes was away, she let her feelings and emotions direct her elsewhere. "I used to think these Leweses a perfect pair of love-birds, always cuddling together on the same perch—to speak figuratively—but the female love-bird appears to have hopped off to some distance and to be now taking a somewhat critical view of her little shaggy mate!" Jane Carlyle noted the changes in the February–April 1849 period, just one year before Agnes gave birth to Hunt's son. We can date the liaison from at least that point.

not bring harmony. The marriage was leaking badly, and it would soon founder. Although Lewes continued to live with his wife and children at 26 Bedford Place (the Lewes residence from 1846 to 1855, with Agnes remaining after he departed), the rift was there, whatever the moral principles involved. Agnes was a baby-making machine, as was Hunt—he had ten children by his wife, plus eventually four by Agnes—and they produced a daughter merely eighteen months later, on 21 October 1851. By this time, however, Lewes had recognized the unworkability of the marriage.

Lewes did not walk away from the marriage—on this point Marian was careful to learn the facts. He remained responsible, even as Agnes continued to have children by Hunt, including on two occasions giving birth within weeks of Hunt's wife also giving birth. * Hunt was planting a good deal of seed, and there is always the possibility he had other children as well. As the son of Leigh Hunt, a member of the Shelley / Byron circle, he was raised to be uninhibited and to flout social rules as arbitrary matters not applicable to people who felt differently. And since he continued to have cordial relations with Lewes on the *Leader,* Hunt considered the growing family as a kind of community.

Lewes broke from the marriage in late 1851, but supported Agnes and the assorted children. This continued until his death, and by his later years, Marian as George Eliot earned huge amounts of money and contributed to Lewes's children's welfare as well as the children of Agnes and Hunt. Lewes, in fact, was quite close to his own sons, and both he and Marian enjoyed seeing them.† The boys, strangely, did not appear to suffer from this unusual arrangement and grew up without ostensible emotional wounds. Later, they came to accept Marian as their stepmother quite readily. Lewes kept in touch with Agnes by mail when he was away, so that "support" went further than the dispatching of money.

By the time Lewes met Marian, he had altered some of his ideas about flouting social forms. He was, in fact, steadfast in his attention to Marian, and we must assume he was loyal to her sexually and emotionally for the rest of his life. Some slim "evidence" and some speculation on possible infidelities will appear in later chapters, but it is all circumstantial. Once their union became fixed, it remained more principled than the unions of others who charged Lewes and Marian with outrageous behavior and shunned her.

Marian was finally attracted to Lewes for several reasons. That her relationship with Spencer had gone under was surely a factor in her shift to Lewes.

---

* Agnes and Hunt brought forth, besides Edmund Alfred Lewes on 16 April 1850 and Rose Agnes Lewes on 21 October 1851, Ethel Isabella Lewes on 9 October 1853 and Mildred Jane Lewes on 21 May 1857. The breeding season lasted over seven years, with one son and three daughters. By 1857, Agnes was thirty-five and probably felt she was at the end of her childbearing years. She had produced eight children (four with Hunt, four with Lewes) and Hunt had fathered fourteen (four with Agnes, ten with his wife). No wonder London population figures were rising exponentially.

† Quite unlike his own father. Lewes's family background had been hazardous. Although it is unclear if he knew it, he had been illegitimate. His father, the would-be poet John Lee Lewes, abandoned Lewes's mother, with three children, as he had previously abandoned another family to take up with Lewes's mother. Brought up by a stepfather he disliked, Lewes was informed his own father had died when the boy was two.

Further, Lewes was an admirable talker, a man of considerable knowledge, however thinly spread out, and, more significantly, "present" in the flesh as a contributor to the *Review*. But as suggested above, possibly more than any of the other explanations was the fact that he represented the final stage of Marian's move toward independence. He embodied all the dangers in her emergence. Once she was sure he was responsible in family matters, the fact of his messiness was not a negative but, in this perverse way, a positive factor. He could, like Dorothea and Will in *Middlemarch* under somewhat different circumstances, become the furthest reaches of her break with repressive respectability.

We must take into account other considerations. Depressed about her lack of positive achievement, moody because she was standing still, and unable to make sufficient money through Chapman to support Chrissey's family, Marian needed some way to break out. An entire stage of independence and liberation was stumbling to an end, and she had achieved less than what she had predicted for herself, or felt herself capable of doing. She would tell Chapman shortly (in March 1853) that after the July issue was published, she was planning to leave the *Review*. But this was not a hard and fast decision, and what she probably had in mind was an eventual move from 142 Strand into lodgings less frantic. Yet even there she equivocated, moving into Chapman's own room (he vacated it), which she found so pleasant she began to doubt if she would leave at all.

The problem was clear. Each year seemed a replay of the previous year. When she put an issue to bed, she would crawl out of London to travel to some spa or to see friends, or to recover at Rosehill. Her life had acquired a predictable pattern which was not encouraging: tremendous expenditures of energy followed by the need to recuperate, heights of activity followed by valleys of depression, moodiness, and illness. When the July issue was ready for the printer, Marian joined her usual crowd, the Chapmans and Sara Hennell, to spend a weekend with Bessie Parkes and Barbara Leigh Smith at Ockley, Surrey; and this was followed by two weeks in Tunbridge Wells, on the western borders of Kent, but as she told Bessie, while it was beautiful it was too dear for her. She says the place was full of Blanche Amorys, the epitome of the affected social being in Thackeray's *Pendennis*. She knows she does not fit. From there, she went on to St. Leonard's, in Sussex, near Hastings, and she seemed genuinely touched by the scenery: "a delightful hill looking over the heads of the houses on the main road, and having a vast expanse of sea [the Straits of Dover] and sky for my only view." The fact that she was not seeing Lewes did not appear to concern her, since the main thing was her removal from the hothouse atmosphere at 142 Strand. Her stay at St. Leonard's stretched through August.

Lewes might have joined her at some point during the summer, the evidence based mainly on Marian's sudden interest in Goethe and the fact that Lewes was an authority on the German sage. But whether this was true or not, Lewes did find an opportunity during this general time to reveal his marital situation and to seek Marian's sympathy or rejection. He must have felt fairly certain of her to make such revelations, or else he assumed she had heard through the rumor mill about his marriage and subsequent separation. It is hard to believe that what Lewes told Marian was a complete surprise, since whatever occurred in the small world of London literary life was generally known to all, especially when the news was scandalous. Lewes was by now a central London personage, well known in many literary salons and even better known as a theater, art, and book critic and reviewer. Marian would have known also from Chapman, who kept his ear strikingly close to the ground, much of the time listening for reverberations from his own scandalous behavior. However she heard the news, from Lewes for the first time or from other sources, she was not without compassion; and she was, apparently, prepared to move to another level in the relationship.

Marian returned to London in September and immediately tried to find new quarters. Money was of course an obstacle. As she informed the Brays, "I find it difficult to meet with anything at once tolerable and cheap. My theory is to *live* entirely—that is, pay rent and find food—out of my positive income [the £100 a year], and then work for as large a surplus as I can get." The rub was where that surplus from work would derive from, with reviewing and article writing as the most likely source. Before the first week in October was over, Marian was located at 21 Cambridge Street, Hyde Park Square. Since her return from holiday, she had grumbled, complained, and felt sorry for herself. Bray said he found her letters uninteresting, and the high-toned Sara made her ashamed for grumbling; but Marian tried to excuse herself by claiming other concerns besides moving.

Her attitude toward the move was ambiguous. She tells Cara she likes her lodgings, her housekeeper cooks "charming little dinners for me," and she has nothing disagreeable to complain of at present. "Still, I shall not be at all surprized to find myself in the Strand again at the end of November." Her health definitely seemed to improve, as though she had moved herself to a better climate. Yet her words suggest she is lonely without Strand activity, without the give-and-take of evening conversation. To Bray, two weeks after writing Cara, she indicates relief: ". . . certainly when I put my head into the house in the Strand I feel that I have gained, or rather escaped, a great deal physically by my change." The alternating attitude about the Strand can only be explained if we see it as a microcosm of Marian's entire adult life up to this point. Since she still had not defined her aims or pointed herself toward some identifiable goal, she could not decide whether the Strand or private quarters were preferable. This was no small matter, for if this assessment of her uncertainty is valid, then we see her vacillations as quite dangerous in terms of her development; with sufficient unrelieved uncertainty, she could have continued along present lines, as an unacknowledged and unpaid subeditor, as a reviewer, and as an intellectual resource on whom Chapman relied, but without any clear achievement for herself. It is precisely that uncertainty or divisiveness—that imbalance between inner and outer—which characterizes so many of her female protagonists and which Eliot diagnosed as endemic for women in that era. From it developed neurasthenia, depression, morbidity, and ultimately wastage.

In her 22 October 1853 letter to Sara, there occurs a line which has become famous in Eliot lore. "Will you tell Cara," she writes, "that I left a small gold brooch on the table in my room with my Father's hair in it." Because her father seems to be left behind or "lost" in a hostile act, it might appear she is experiencing guilt at her present course of action: Robert Evans as conscience; her Strand activities as indulgence. There is, in fact, no evidence that leaving the brooch with her father's hair in it was anything more than an inadvertent act. To emphasize an *isolated* slip, without a pattern or rhythm, is ludicrous. If Marian made a habit of leaving brooches, or other family treasures, or if she were generally forgetful or inattentive to detail—none of which was true—then we could speak of unconscious hostility.

Despite her uncertainty about the Strand and the *Review*, Marian was keeping herself occupied with a multitude of activities. Cross, perhaps on evidence from Marian's journal—pages no longer extant—thought she was correcting Lewes's proofs for the *Leader*, as early as the spring of 1852. But her help for Lewes extended into the present time, the summer of 1853, when she possibly helped him to write, or actually wrote, some of the pieces for the weekly. If so, she wrote under his nom de plume, Vivian. It is doubtful that with his other activities—one of them being to adapt and even write plays for the Lyceum under the name of Slingsby Lawrence—Lewes had time to do the reading necessary for the book reviews, or even to see the plays he wrote about. Once again, Marian found herself as a kind of subeditor, or subwriter—doing some or much of the work, but receiving no credit except in terms of Lewes's gratitude. As for her other large enterprise, a translation of Ludwig Feuerbach's *Das Wesen des Christenthums (The Essence of Christianity)*, which Chapman advertised on 18 June 1853 as being prepared for his new "Quarterly Series," even this was based on the work of someone else.

Her accomplishments, as she moved toward her thirty-fourth birthday, had been for others whose work she revised, edited, or rewrote. It is no wonder she quoted Comte favorably, to the effect that our true destiny is made up of resignation and activity. "I seem more disposed to both than I have ever been before. Let us hope," she tells Sara, "that we shall both get stronger by the year's activity—calmer by its resignation. I know it may be just the contrary—don't suspect me of being a canting optimist. We *may* both find ourselves at the end of the year going faster to the hell of conscious moral and intellectual weakness."

These self-depreciating remarks were possibly responses to another birthday, which came and passed without an appreciable alteration in her situation. In personal terms, she had, so to speak, traded in Spencer for Lewes, and that seemed more emotionally satisfactory. But if we pick up from the self-mockery in her words, we observe under the persiflage a chronic depression, not to be lifted by anything less than a drastic act.

Marian, meanwhile, found she had to defend Lewes against attack. When he brought out his book on Comte (*Comte's Philosophy of the Sciences*), Thomas Henry Huxley became the *Westminster's* reviewer of this and of Harriet Martineau's less ambitious abridgment of Comte's *Positive Philosophy*. Huxley attacked Lewes's work, praised Martineau's slighter effort, and caused Marian no end of personal difficulty. She tried to have Chapman postpone the review until she could work on it—probably to soften it—but Chapman was himself caught in a ticklish situation and the review appeared unrevised. Lewes responded with a letter in the *Leader*, attempting to refute Huxley's charges. The position Marian found herself in was not isolated, but endemic to the type of work she did and the people she was meeting. There were bound to be conflicts of interest, though few of them so embarrassing as her subediting a publication which allowed an attack on Lewes, while she and Lewes were becoming increasingly close and possibly already intimate with each other. Huxley's comments, incidentally, were well taken, for Lewes's work by necessity in this period was hasty, on occasion inaccurate, and somewhat slapdash.

In her personal life, even without residence at the Strand, Marian was still popular, and her new lodgings brought the usual array of visitors: Lewes of course, but also Harriet Martineau, Bessie Parkes, Barbara Leigh Smith, even Mrs. Chapman, accompanied by her husband, and old friend Robert Mackay, now married. If she had sought privacy at her lodgings, she did not find it; but more likely she needed the steady infusion of social activity to alleviate her loneliness until Lewes began to occupy most of her free time. She was invited out a great deal, and she went often, even to the home of Sir James and Lady Clark.

Although her health seemed generally improved since her move, she still suffered chronic ailments which sometimes became acute, apparently part of a generally nervous or anxiety-ridden temperament. How she responded to Lewes's increasing attentions could have created great tension that this relationship, too, might come to little or could have shaped another kind of anxiety, that if the relationship did work, she was committing herself to something that was indeed a convulsion. A woman in her situation was twice cursed. For if the affair succeeded, she might have to contemplate moving to the continent to escape the calumny of a hypocritical society.

On 24 November, she told Chapman she wanted to give up any connection with the editorship of the *Review*. "He wishes me," she wrote Sara, "to continue the present state of things until April, but admits that he is so straitened for money and for *assistance* in the mechanical part of the business that he feels unable to afford an expense on the less tangible services which I render." Those "less tangible" services went far beyond editing or writing, and fell under her attention to the details of every part of the publication. She admits she will be glad to be done with that affair, but she does need money, since she expects little from her translation of Feuerbach. She still holds out hope for "The Idea of a Future Life," the book she never wrote, but even there she doubts if Chapman will be able to pay her anything for it. At the least with Lewes, they could pool their resources and save on one residence.

By 2 December, she reported all kinds of ailments: liver or stomach, she surmises, "or some other agglomeration of cells" has been striking her. By this time, Lewes and she were a couple—more than friends, perhaps less than lovers. Meanwhile, she plugged along on the Feuerbach translation, with an ultimate

£30 from Chapman as the monetary goal. Feuerbach seemed to have perceived someone precisely like Marian when he wrote his study, for the essence of Christianity to him was the way in which human love could be separated from narcissistic love. The latter she had recently experienced with Spencer. Human love, in Feuerbach's terms, derived from self-sacrifice, from compassion, from the way one individual is willing to defer, even sacrifice herself, to another person. Duty, discipline, and a martyrdom of sorts loom large in Feuerbach's conception of the individual self, and such qualities fitted well into what Marian was developing for herself. This would be her voice warning against a materialistic, secular, self-serving century.

But there was far more in Feuerbach which at this time spoke directly to Marian. A passage like the following, in her translation, suggests her own yearning for that "essence": "Religion being identical with the distinctive characteristic of man, is then identical with self-consciousness—with the consciousness which man has of his nature." Since religion is generally consciousness of the infinite, then it is nothing less than the consciousness man has of his own infinite nature. This reach would carry Marian, in her fictional application of it, beyond the harsh realities of necessity, or at least mitigate that sense of determinism. The meeting of that infinitude and of harsh necessity comes at the conclusion of *The Mill on the Floss,* when Maggie and Tom, locked forever in each other's embrace, suffer the inevitability of a natural event, the flood, but at the same time can become part of an infinite expression of love, devotion, and sacrifice. That the embrace is orgiastic in its nature—they find final love by killing each other—does not subvert Eliot's expression of how necessity can link with something beyond, some "essence."

In this representative passage from Feuerbach, we find Eliot weaving her own tapestry for the future, a kind of Penelope spinning out a verbal plan which will not take effect for the next few years. "Consciousness is self-verification, self-affirmation, self-love, joy in one's perfection. Consciousness is the characteristic mark of a perfect nature; it exists only in a self-sufficing, complete being." Man sees that perfection in the mirror, but what, Feuerbach asks, distinguishes man's vanity from that sense of perfection itself? Vanity arises when man admires himself as perfection of the individual form—like Grandcourt in *Daniel Deronda* or, earlier, Arthur Donnithorne in *Adam Bede* and Tito Melema in *Romola;* but it is not vanity when man admires himself as a specimen of human beauty in general. Man (woman) must always transcend himself even while seeking himself in perfection.* If he fails to transcend himself, then he defines his qualities as Spencer defined his. In undertaking the translation, Marian was, in one respect, undertaking a critique of Spencer, his self-love and his inability to tran-

---

* As we see in Mirah in *Daniel Deronda* (her character possibly based on Phoebe Marks, a Jew married to a Christian, W. E. Ayrton, and a protégée of Barbara Leigh Smith) and in *Romola* in her novel, and perhaps closely based on Barbara and her devotion to others. But Eliot went only so far with Smith, for this relationship became strained over questions of immortality: Barbara needing it, Eliot believing in "utter annihilation." Eliot chose to live perilously, Barbara more within mainstream Christianity.

scend that to some more general posture. Spencer's sense of love and marriage was based to a large extent on power: the power of the male to gain beauty, to appropriate another, to build his own self-esteem. She had moved away from that. In seeking infinity, where Spencer denied it, she was seeking her "choir invisible," that conjoining of voices beyond the outstretched reach of man.

Feuerbach came into Marian's life in this intense way just when she was convinced she wanted to retain the morality and ethics of Christianity but not its expressions of faith, its humanistic reach without its theological grounding, its optimism about man and his possible salvation or redemption without counting on God's revelation, its possibilities for the structuring of family and society without its celebratory aspects. In these respects, from the church's point of view, she was that most dangerous of non-practitioners or non-worshippers: the person who retains religion's essence while rejecting the trappings and even the God who promises grace and providence for believers. Like Feuerbach, Marian preferred "understanding" to religious practices and to God's immanence. "A man without understanding," Feuerbach writes, "is a man without will. He who has no understanding allows himself to be deceived, imposed upon, used as an instrument by others." Such remarks link up with similar comments which speak of marriage as a union of souls, not as a social or state contract. Marriage, then, such as the union Marian was contemplating with the married Lewes, could be "holy" or celebratory despite its lack of legal standing.

Love becomes the real linkage: not romantic love, not love in the popular sense, but love which is transcendental without being directed at God. Feuerbach asks the essential question: how can man, who has separated himself from God, bring about a separate, isolated existence, adrift in a world which lacks coherence? Feuerbach: "Now, by what means does man deliver himself from this state of disunion between himself and the perfect being, from the painful consciousness of sin, from the distracting sense of his own nothingness? How does he blunt the fatal sting of sin? Only by this; that he is conscious of *love* as the highest, the absolute power and truth, that he regards the Divine Being not only as a law, as a moral being of the understanding; but also as a loving, tender, even subjective human being (that is, as having sympathy even with individual man)."

These expressions of love, linkage, union, and ethos were not novel for Marian. Long before she came to translate Feuerbach, she had reached these conclusions herself; such ideas, in fact, were implicit when she refused to attend church services with her father. Beginning then, however inchoately, she was carving out a mode of life which combined love with the progress of the individual. She was not alone in this, since we find strong aspects of such ideas in George Meredith, Thackeray, Dickens, and others. But they were men, and when they flouted the sacred bonds of Victorian society, connected as these bonds were to church and state, they were not severely damaged. Thackeray could quietly visit prostitutes and brothels; Dickens could take a mistress. But the point is not merely that Marian had company, but that as a woman she broke free of restraints, and did so well before Feuerbach's words (really her

words) sanctioned such thoughts. As a corollary, there is little question that
Feuerbach helped support her views in the 1850s, coming at just the time when
she needed such reinforcement, since she was on the edge of convulsive change
in her personal life. She was to form a union that helped heal that profound
divisiveness she felt between public and private, in this her thirty-fifth year; a
union, further, that allowed her, finally, to express her sense of the century.

PART THREE

The Web Begun

8

One George, One to Go

> "But even while we are talking and meditating about the earth's orbit and the solar system, what we feel and adjust our movements to is the stable earth and the changing day."

While Marian was still involved in the translation of Feuerbach, Agnes and Thornton Hunt had another child, announced in the *Leader* as the birth of a daughter on 9 October 1853 to G. H. Lewes. This put Marian in an extremely difficult situation, since Strand people knew what was happening between Hunt and Agnes, and she had to defend Lewes against what seemed an outrage. Lewes, meanwhile, maintained a mocking, nonchalant manner, disguising his real feelings and presenting himself, still, as a debonair man of the world for whom real trouble does not exist. It was her job to penetrate to another layer of feeling, which Lewes did have.

A Lewes review, of *How to Make Home Happy*, expresses his own unhappiness at home—that, in fact, he has no home; he wonders what the secret of a happy home is. He had nevertheless contributed his bit to this condition, to the disaffection of Agnes and to her coupling with Hunt. What Agnes had done, however, was to create a vulgar situation, in which what should have remained hidden was open to everyone's mockery. In the eyes of literary London, Lewes was a cuckold of the worst kind, a man who acquiesces to his wife's concupiscence and its products. Since Hunt's background was in the West Indies, and he was himself dark, the children Agnes had by him were themselves dark, "sooty-skinned children," according to Carlyle, who was always ready with some racially tainted remark. Nevertheless, the so-called sootiness was another source of mockery, since it seemed Lewes's wife had linked up with a Moor—such being the implication of the description.*

---

* Haight quotes from Lewes's review of Coyne's *The Hope of the Family*, in which the hapless husband of the fertile Agnes interpolates his own experience into the play, citing that once when he was on the Gold Coast, in Africa, he thought he saw a boy who was his "indirect heir." Here

Given the circumstances, Marian's position was very delicate. She could not ignore the situation, of course, and at the same time she had to try to strike the right note of sympathy and understanding, along with the preservation of her own feelings. The birth drama going on in Lewes's family would become shadowed in several instances in Middlemarch, with Will Ladislaw: under different circumstances and with different moral factors, there is nevertheless a profound concern with who belongs to whom, and the consequences deriving from that. Similarly, in Daniel Deronda and in Silas Marner, once again under very different circumstances, we find birth dramas. Whatever her personal difficulties in dealing with Lewes's feelings, Marian assimilated the situation and, much changed, re-created it fictionally. While such birth dramas were standard Victorian literary fare, for Marian they were intertwined with her life.

Marian did believe in Lewes and apparently did penetrate his veneer of cynicism and seeming unconcern. But she did not do so without personal suffering, instanced by her signing "Pollian," destroyer, subverter, in her letter to Cara of 2 December. "Pollian" here suggests something desperate because of its connection to Apollyan, a breaker and underminer. She sees herself as some subverter of ordinary life, a perception borne out by decisions she was making about her future. In her letter to Chapman on the same day, she allows a truculent tone, one which indicates she is struggling to retain some civility in a relationship breaking down. "You seem to be oblivious just now," she writes, "of the fact you have pledged yourself as well as me to the publication of another work besides Feuerbach in your Series [a reference to her "The Idea of a Future Life]." All comes back to money, since Marian needs research tools, which she says are indispensable, but she has no money to subscribe to the London Library; and she depends on Chapman, in the absence of payments to her, to provide such books as she requires for the historical part of the Feuerbach. She adds she "bitterly" regrets having allowed herself to be associated with Chapman's series. She says she would much prefer he publish it and not pay her than not publish it; although it was possible it could end up that he would neither publish nor pay. Chapman and the Review were in desperate straits. "I don't think," Marian continued, "you are sufficiently alive to the ignominy of advertising things, especially as part of a subscription series, which never appear. The two requests then which I have to make are first, that you will let me know whether you can, as a matter of business, undertake to supply me with the necessary books, and secondly, that you will consider the question of Feuerbach as one which concerns our honour first and our pockets after."

The tone suggests that the honeymoon, such as it was, is over; that acrimony had surfaced not only because of money but because of promises not kept. The comments also indicate how negatively Marian felt toward the Review, that Chapman was a handy victim for her feelings of frustration at the quarterly and her work on it. In this letter and its acerbic manner, we observe Marian turning away from this stage of her life. From her lodgings, she still handled Review

---

Lewes plays with Carlyle's characterization of "sootiness," and he even says that while one is always the son of somebody, not everyone is the father of somebody.

business, but it had become far more difficult than when she lived at the Strand and everything was contained in one building. Whenever problems arose, she had to run back and forth, and she had to waste endless time in discussions with Chapman himself or the contributors. She had written to George Combe frankly about her position, as a subeditor and as a woman. "If I were sole editor of the *Westminster*, I would take the responsibility on myself, and ask you to send them [testimonials from experts as to Combe's accuracy in stating that 'prison discipline must be based on physiology of the nervous system'] through me, but being a woman and something less than an editor, I do not see how the step you propose could be taken with the naturalness and *bien-séance* that could alone flavour any good result."*

The internal maneuvering at the *Review* kept her in a perilous position in dealing with contributors; thus, the elicitation of her woes that she is not solely in control of the quarterly. Also, we must reckon with her realization that as a female she is lacking in power. Combe was a monetary supporter of the *Review* and a contributor, and he could not be chided too heavily without jeopardizing the money. Yet Combe's piece here, on phrenological applications to criminal legislation and penal reform—a topic so full of pitfalls and speculations that he succumbed to them all—was not acceptable in Marian's terms. Weakly argued, diffuse, scientifically suspect, Combe's article needed heavy revision, and it was postponed while Marian was expected to edit it for publication. Caught between Chapman's needs and her own standards, she had nowhere to turn, so that postponement of the article was the sole solution. When Combe, in anger, decided to publish it in full privately, in a pamphlet, Marian's task was to edit it to article length; for any appearance in the *Review*, she would have to cut it virtually to a third of the original length. While we may say that this is indeed the work of a serious editor, it was not satisfactory work for her, not least because she received no credit and no monetary reward.

But all was not simply articles which, even when revised, were unsuitable or poorly argued. There were other experiences, some of them positive. She could congratulate herself on the January 1854 issue, despite her unhappiness with Huxley's treatment of Lewes.† The issue contained pieces by both Martineau siblings, Harriet and James, Huxley, Froude, Lewes, and several other distin-

---

* If we take only Marian's correspondence with Combe in the last months of 1853 and in early 1854 as an example, we can observe the complications of her work at the *Review*. Combe kept her letters; countless others did not, but we can multiply her letters to him by a large number to others and come up with a stupefying, and basically arid, correspondence. Nearly everything about her intellectually remained on hold. The Combe–Chapman interchange here became so ugly that Marian was in danger of being crushed; to that extent she warned Combe not to make her a referee in matters pertaining to Chapman's private life (3 March 1854).

† Huxley's comments on Lewes appeared in the "Science" section of the January 1854 issue. Marian found Huxley wrong on several counts, since Lewes knew continental theories of which Huxley, the great proponent of Darwin in later years, was still ignorant. Marian felt no qualms about attacking Huxley while writing to Chapman, but despite her objections to what she felt were inaccuracies, the review appeared. Lewes's rejoinder in the *Leader* demonstrated Huxley's ignorance of certain facts which French scientists had developed; and in this respect Lewes, with his knowledge of French and German, was actually better informed than Huxley. It was, of course, the professional Huxley who eventually won the day over the gifted amateur.

guished writers; and the issue following, in April, in which Marian also had a hand, was strong, with several of the same authors making repeat appearances: Spencer, Huxley, Froude, Harriet Martineau. Some parts, however, were less distinguished, especially "Belles Lettres," which Marian quickly dismissed as not her work but Mrs. Edward Sinnett's, who apparently needed whatever pittance Chapman offered her. Chapman suggested that Marian take it over, for payment of £16.16 a quarter, a ridiculously small amount. It is doubtful if Chapman could have paid her for her services even if she had agreed to edit the "Belles Lettres" section, for his finances were in disarray. He was, in fact, on the brink of bankruptcy, with debts accruing to £9,000, an estimable figure, well over half a million dollars in contemporary spending power. But just as bankruptcy seemed the only way out, Harriet Martineau put up £500 and some others came through with sufficient sums so that Chapman could pay off a third of each pound, which for the time being kept his creditors at bay.

As 1853 ended, Marian at thirty-four found her condition, as in past years, unsatisfactory. She was feuding with Chapman, as part of an endgame. She was overspending at her new lodgings, exceeding her inheritance. She was worried about Chrissey's family. The Feuerbach translation was moving, but she knew she was involved in a project that would pay her little and consume much time. The relationship with Lewes seemed promising, but it was edging scandal and would, if they came together, translate into outright disgrace. She was, as always, caught up in the minutiae of the *Review,* trapped also by Chapman's messy finances and messy personal life (while floundering, he would soon start an affair with Barbara Leigh Smith). She passed Christmas Day alone at her lodgings, an indication that Lewes spent such holidays with his children.

Although the Feuerbach would be completed in the spring of 1854, Marian was so unsure of her abilities she checked with Sara over the translation, as she had done with the Strauss. She also needed support over the book itself: the fact that even though Feuerbach was the man of the hour in Germany, with his unorthodox views of God and Christianity he might be attacked in England. "People here are as slow to be set on fire as a *stomach,*" she writes Sara. "Then there are the reviewers, who set up a mound of stupidity and unconscientiousness between every really new book and the public." During the reading of proof in the spring, she worried incessantly about the press and its reception of the book. *Essence* had become more than a translation exercise; it had become a focus of belief. Proofs were ready in early June, and in the final proof of the title page Marian Evans's name appeared for the first time. The book was published as July, Number VI of Chapman's quarterly series.

Sara was a steady support, and Marian was grateful, but she cast her gratitude in a way that reveals her distaste for Chapman: "It is such a comfort to have at least *one* person who can appreciate one's work. The dreariness of giving such a translation to Mr. Chapman who neither knows what is in itself good English nor what is the difficulty of truly representing German!" With these words, the romance with the *Review* and its handsome owner was finished. More particularly, certain parts of the Feuerbach troubled Marian through the spring and right into the proofs. The preface she found indigestible, and yet she felt it must be read. The appendix, also, needed modification for the English reader, and Marian was anxiety-ridden about its inappropriateness. Dripping with irony, Feuerbach asserted that only in name has the modern Christian anything in common with the old, claiming that you can rip the heart from the body and still be a good Christian as long as you do not meddle with the name itself. Such irony, while suitable for German skeptics, would simply raise English hackles, Marian felt, probably based on her perception of the English church as composed mainly of hypocrites.

April brought Lewes's severe illness, and he was ordered not to write for a month, leaving the duties of the *Leader* with Marian. She was herself once more out of sorts, most likely from the pressures put upon her hard after the completion of the translation. She now suffered the entire range of her ailments, so that her letters sound like hospital reports: headaches, as always; tooth problems, a new constant; ringing in the ears, which may have been emotionally induced; occasional digestive problems, possibly from migraines; and a general disaffection and malaise, which were most certainly linked to her emotional and psychological frame of mind. In another respect, her ailments gave her leverage with Lewes; not only could she match ills, she could continue to work while afflicted.

She knows it is time with "no fun," which means no opera or concerts, but also no supportive company. Lewes went off to see his good friend Arthur Helps at Vernon Hall in Hampshire, but even upon his return he was incapable of work and filled with ennui. It is unclear what his ailment was, but some of it, we can assume, was connected to the contemplation of profound changes in his life, as he and Marian moved closer to some permanent attachment. Lewes was not immune to the enormity of what he was attempting, and the monetary pressures on him had not relented. He was responsible for a very large household, as well as for his own upkeep. With Marian, he would gain a companion, but also someone who could barely support herself. They could end up being poor together rather than separately. Lewes seemed to be suffering a nervous collapse. His illness did not allow for optimism, since his condition could linger and, of course, recur (as, later in his life, it did). "I expect to see Mr. Lewes back again today. His poor head—his only fortune—is not well yet, and he has had the misery of being ennuye with idleness without perceiving the compensating improvement."

With Lewes returning, but not yet recovered, some other cure was necessary; and he went back to the country, this time to try a water cure at Halvern, just north of Gloucester. Since he was to live almost another twenty-five years, the present ailment cannot have been seriously organic, however intense it seemed. Lewes's health did not remain good—like Marian he suffered on and off for the remainder of his life.

As noted above, Lewes's pen name at the *Leader* was Vivian, and as Vivian, Marian filled *Leader* pages as best she could. She also may have reviewed Ruskin's lectures on architecture which he gave at Edinburgh University, although

validating this is difficult. Further, she may have done an article on Sydney
Smith, clergyman and wit, defender of the poor, a satirist often compared to
Swift, and one on Wilkie Collins the following week. It is quite possible she
linked together pieces of work by other hands so that only the patterning is
hers, not the prose or thought.

Whatever the case, she managed to fill in more than adequately, and this
alone should have assured her that a woman was as well prepared as any male to
edit a major journal. Yet such was not to be. The fact that England had a
popular queen did not change its assumption about what women could do. Sex-
ist notions were still medieval—and still embodied in the law—except in the
most advanced circles: John Stuart Mill, Lewes himself, some remarkable
women like Barbara Leigh Smith and Bessie Parkes. A good example of how
repression could come from the first rank of English intellectuals is revealed in
the Carlyles. As we know from her letters and other comments, Jane Welsh
Carlyle was a woman of considerable distinction: witty, insightful, ironic, the
possessor of a wickedly trenchant prose style. Yet such was her relationship to
Carlyle that she was afforded no opportunity to emerge from his shadow. For
her, the unconsummated marriage was a smothering act, and the evidence is
the incidence of illness the two suffered, her headaches and other ailments close
to neurasthenia, his lifelong digestive problems.

Under duress, Marian was reaching another level of understanding herself in
this critical period before she made her major move. There is desperation in her
words as well as in the move itself. She speaks of herself as an island, which is
an expression of depression unless one can discover some mode of using isolation, as in fiction. But she knows she can no longer pine away, as a person does
when young. She writes poignantly to Cara:

> When young we think our troubles a mighty business—that the world is
> spread out expressly as a stage for the particular drama of our lives and that
> we have a right to rant and foam at the mouth if we are crossed. I have
> done enough of that in my time. But we begin at last to understand that
> these things are important only to one's own consciousness, which is but a
> globule of dew on a rose-leaf that at mid-day there will be no trace of. This
> is not high-flown sentimentality, but a simple reflection which I find useful
> to me every day.

The tone and language speak of an acceptance of self; but the apparent calm
should not mislead us. Even if her words to Cara reveal a new breakthrough in
maturity, Marian was not ready to acquiesce to ordinariness. Despite this seeming revelation of a new self, still dogging her was her sense of failure more than
midway through her life.

There is danger, possibly, in placing too much emphasis on the association
with Lewes. Without in any way depreciating the significance of his attachment—his affection and support *were* of great importance—Marian's lack of
achievement at thirty-four was stronger and more intense than any other experi-

ence. Lewes gave her emotional support and perhaps sexual satisfaction, but her great intellectual abilities had not found a suitable outlet. While Lewes's presence was needed, so was some record of accomplishment which could satisfy the enormous demands she made on herself.

Associated with her desire for achievement was something seemingly dissimilar—where she should live. But the two were linked, for how she chose to live would affect her free time, her connection to the *Review,* and the demands made on her by others. In May 1854 she had a tempting offer which would have saved her money, to live with the Chapmans at 43 Blandford Square, near the southwest corner of Regent's Park. The Chapmans were giving up their Strand address, and they immediately thought of Marian as a combination friend / boarder. But her acerbic tone with Chapman cited above was an indication of her desire to break from this now unfulfilling relationship. As she told Bray: "I have finally decided not to live with the Chapmans. The consideration that determined me was, that I could not feel at liberty to leave them after causing them to make arrangements on my account, and it is quite possible that I may wish to go to the continent [with Lewes?] or twenty other things. At all events, I like to feel free. Apart from the comfort of being with people who call out some affection there would be no advantage in my living with the C's—at least none that *I* take into account." What she failed to inform Bray was that her life with Lewes was reaching the point of permanent commitment and that, intellectually, she was disenchanted with Chapman and all his enterprises.

The plan Marian had concocted was quite different from lodging once again with the publisher. She soon told him, probably his wife as well, and the Brays that she had decided to live openly with Lewes, first on the continent and then together in London. They gave her the usual warnings, but did not discourage her. Whatever Chapman lacked in business acumen or in intellectual substance, he was a supportive ally, and the Brays, as always, wanted only the best for their friend. Of course, Marian did not escape without payment for this decision, since as she tells Sara on 3 June, at the decisive time, "Brain and legs and fingers all move heavily with me. I do nothing well but idling and the consciousness of this is like a garment of lead about me. If I could only fancy myself clever, it would be better, but to be a failure of Nature and to know it is not a comfortable lot. It is the last lesson one learns, to be contented with one's inferiority—but it must be learned."

The meeting with Bray came on 11 June, and it was, she told Sara, accompanied by "more than my usual headache and other evils." Turning down an invitation from the Combes to travel with them for part of the summer, she focuses on Feuerbach proofs and her assessment of Chapman's fate. Despite her intellectual break with him, she is still concerned.

Chapman produced a journal of considerable quality that despite its small circulation (now under 1,000) was considered a benchmark of opinion. It made its mark. He was a shrewd enough judge of character to have picked Eliot as subeditor, and to have given her leeway in running the journal. Further, he was shrewder still in seeing that he did not have to pay her commensurate with her abilities and hours spent, so avid was she to enter London intellectual life.

Marian was now on the edge of her great decision, an act of daring on her part which, outside the upper classes, has few equals in Victorian annals. She visited the Brays at Rosehill in late June (17–26), and together they went through all the arguments against her running off. Like most people who knew Lewes superficially, they were not impressed. Lacking gravity, he did not seem earnest enough for Marian, plus of course he carried the freight of a domestic situation known to all London. The Brays probably told her what she already knew, that social punishment was swift and cruel, as she could see readily from contemporary fiction and life.

The men who kept mistresses were called philanderers, but the women who were kept were called whores. The Brays reminded Marian that she was making a decision that would be irreversible. It would create a permanent taint. Marian's argument was that she apparently had little to lose; she was already tainted, from her stay at the Strand. In the end, she had not gone to Rosehill for advice that would change her mind, but for the hospitality which made her feel she could do whatever she wanted and still count on the Brays. Their support in any event was firm.

But even amidst this intense personal decision, the most critical point of her life, there remained the question of Feuerbach's *Essence*. She tries to explain that the book might justly be called a natural history of Christianity, but that by *Wesen* Feuerbach meant *essence*, with its association to something fundamental as well as to a state of being: ". . . anyone who has read Feuerbach . . . will be aware that this title corresponds perfectly or rather *uniquely* to the author's mode of statement." Her insistence on this suggests her integrity as a translator, but perhaps, and more so, the accuracy of her perceptions, her demand that one read correctly. In the same letter to Sara, she provides high praise for Spencer, whose article on the genesis of science had just appeared in the 20 July issue of the *British Quarterly Review*; she follows this with a brief note on "Vivian," or Lewes, whose head, she says, will not be up to a review of the Feuerbach. Marian expected the reception of the book to be so explosive that she hoped Lewes's review of it in the *Leader* would be one way of defusing the situation. On the eve of her departure, her professional life still called and was heeded.

On 20 July 1854, she and Lewes left London and reached their destination of Weimar on 2 August. Marian kept a record of their life together in a personal journal; earlier segments are no longer extant, but the part beginning 20 July remains. She planned to go as Mrs. Lewes, and that was how she represented it to her friends, Cara and Sara. Mrs. Agnes Lewes did not sue, nor did she appear to care for such trifles. Marian continued to present herself as Mrs. Lewes while the legal wife lived on (and on and on, until 1902).

Marian arrived first at the steamer, the *Ravensbourne*, and then waited anxiously, she says, for Lewes to arrive. The great adventure of her life was now to begin, as was the calumny she was to experience once the fact of what she had done spread in London. Her ties to her family, except to Chrissey, were now sundered. If she had meant to plot one thing to cut herself off effectively, she had succeeded. She was now on the edge, trusting in Lewes, who was her shield against the world, and trusting her own instincts and intellect to keep herself on an even keel.

On board, Marian and Lewes found Robert Ralph Noel, brother of the Noel she knew from London, and he—married to a German baroness—was full of useful information about Weimar and suggestions for their stay there. As a descendant of Byron and himself the topic of some scandalous behavior, he was not shocked at Marian's situation. Her journal records the couple's arrival at Antwerp, where they made their way to the cathedral, observed the Rubenses, and in good spirits enjoyed their own company and freedom from England. As a writer so distinctly English, so much its hortatory voice, Marian on numerous occasions nevertheless viewed her country as a prison house from which she must escape to maintain her equilibrium. Although she and Lewes traveled economically, they were obviously privileged people, sightseeing while others worked, touring freely without regard to obligations. Her itinerary now was entirely aesthetic and intellectual, worlds apart from what she had known as a young woman.

After two days in Antwerp they left for Brussels and walked the park and perhaps the Basse Ville, recalling Charlotte Brontë's *Villette*. They enjoyed simple things like sunrises and sunsets; they indulged in tea in their rooms; and once the heat of the day was dissipated, they roamed at will. They made their way, still with Weimar as their final destination, to Liège, staying in the Hôtel de l'Europe. With its palaces, churches, and art, Liège proved so attractive they stayed on, and then took the train to Cologne. Inveterate sightseers, they tried to take in as much as their energies allowed—Marian had particular praise for the flamboyantly Gothic Church St. Jacques in Liège, but also found beautiful everything they saw. On the platform as they awaited their train for Cologne, they encountered Dr. Brabant, who entered their carriage and talked and talked, so Marian reports. Brabant had a number of useful and interesting connections, including the famous Strauss himself, whom Marian had translated. Brabant arranged an interview for them at nine the next morning. The meeting was somewhat farcical for a variety of reasons, not least that Strauss's English translator did not really speak German—hers was book learned. But that was not all; Strauss's poor condition cast a pall. "It was rather melancholy," she wrote Bray on 16 August. "Strauss looks so strange and castdown, and my deficient German prevented us from learning more of each other than our exterior which in the case of both would have been better left to imagination."

The farce heightened: Strauss also had some differences with Marian, which were probably muted at this session because of their failure to communicate clearly in German. He had by now, after eight years, softened his theological position, and yet Marian's translation, from the fourth edition of his life of Jesus, made his attitude seem harder and more sharply focused than he wished. All the compromises and concessions he had restated in earlier editions had been washed away in the fourth, where he had shown anger at the attacks upon him. The consequence was that the fourth edition, manifesting his most extreme and hostile views, was now the standard English translation. So even without any further communication, Strauss, old and worn, could not have looked with favor on the woman who presented him to the English in ways with which he no longer agreed. Yet the two iconoclasts stood aside as Dr. Brabant, who could handle spoken German, did most of the talking.

The main goal of the journey was Goethe's Weimar. Goethe had been dead a little more than two decades, but Weimar was redolent of the man considered Germany's greatest poet and literary figure. Lewes was also interested in other aspects of Goethe, the literary man as naturalist, biologist, and botanist, the man of science, amateur though he was. In some ways, Lewes had modeled himself after Goethe, whose biography he would write and which would be for many years the standard study in English. Lewes admired Goethe as a man for all seasons, and from that, Lewes attempted to pursue a comparable multitude of projects in both literature and science. He, too, as an amateur scientist was quite effective—able, as we have seen, to hold his ground with Thomas Henry Huxley in the early 1850s.

Before getting to Weimar they stopped in Frankfurt, where Goethe had once lived. Lewes was interested in all aspects of the city which concerned the poet, and they themselves lodged near the house where he had been born. They visited Goethe's house twice, as Marian observes in her journal, and they walked the Judengasse ("Jew-Street"), which became memorable enough to appear in *Daniel Deronda* more than twenty years later, as the locale for the meeting between Daniel and Joseph Kalonymos. They caught the paintings in the local museum and whatever other sights they could before leaving for Weimar on the 5 P.M. train, for arrival between three and four in the morning.

The trip fatigued them both. Each suffered from ailments which lay close to the surface and could be activated by either fatigue or discomfort, but they recovered at an inn in the heart of town. Their first sense of Weimar was disappointment. Marian observed in her journal that she did not know how Goethe had lived in such a "dull, lifeless village." And she wrote Bray, on 16 August: "A ten hours' railway journey from Frankfurt brought us to Weimar—the 'Athens of the north' was a considerable surprize to us. We had expected something as stately as your little statue of Goethe and lo! we found a huge village rather than a town—a place so sleepy that it had no gas and its shopkeepers do not think it worth while to put up their names at their doors." But they had come for several reasons, and they quickly found lodgings at 62a Kaufgasse.

The high point of their visit early on was not the local people they met, not even Gustav Schöll, director of the Art Institute, but the renowned Franz Liszt, who seems to have captivated Marian. When they met, Liszt, apart from his fame as pianist and composer, was director of the Court Theatre and the duke's Kapellmeister, a position once held by Johann Sebastian Bach. Liszt was also living openly with a married woman, Princess Caroline Sayn-Wittgenstein. In such circles, Marian and Lewes—whatever rumors floated in—ran into no moral strictures, or any suspicion of impropriety. In both her journal and her letters to Bray, Marian reveals her deep admiration for the musician. In one letter, she waxes eloquent; she virtually purrs. "Liszt is the first really inspired man I ever saw.* His face might serve as a model for a St. John in its sweetness when he is in repose but seated at the piano he is as grand as one of Michel Angelo's prophets. When I read George Sand's letter to Franz Liszt in her 'Lettres d'un voyageur,' I little thought that I should ever be seated tête-à-tête with him for an hour, as I was yesterday and telling him my ideas and feelings."

But if she allows herself to get carried away in her letter to Bray, she is no less enthusiastic in her journal.

> Then came the thing I had longed for—Liszt's playing. I sat near him so I could see both his hands and face. For the first time in my life I beheld real inspiration—for the first time I heard the true tones of the piano. He played one of his own compositions—one of a series of religious *fantasies*. There was nothing strange or excessive about his manner. His manipulation of the instrument was quiet and easy, and his face was simply grand—the lips compressed and the head thrown a little backward. When the music expressed quiet rapture or devotion a sweet smile slitted over his features; when it was triumphant the nostrils dilated. There was nothing petty or egoistic to mar the picture.

There is, of course, hero worship in this, Marian seeking an ideal or a philosopher king. She would put some version of the experience to use in *Daniel Deronda*, where Klesmer's ideal of music fits well into this portrait Marian makes of Liszt. But there is more here than hero worship. She has a glimpse, perhaps for the first time, of someone reaching for the highest level of performance, transcending himself and his instrument of expression. She found not only an ideal in Liszt, but an ideal for herself here. The meetings with the pianist and composer, which subsequently became quite frequent, were high points for Marian.† He was the source, also, of a considerable social context for Lewes and Marian, introducing them to the very young Anton Rubinstein, the Russian composer and pianist, and giving Marian the opportunity to attend several Wagner operas, including *Lohengrin*, *The Flying Dutchman*, and *Tannhäuser*. She

---

* In her remarks to Bray, Marian indicates that Liszt and his princess were married, but this was not the case. Perhaps Lewes had so informed her. In fact, the princess was only recently separated from her husband, who had hesitated to recognize the obvious relationship with Liszt and only now was about to divorce her. The Sayn-Wittgensteins, a German aristocratic family, were not related to the Wittgensteins of whom Ludwig was most famous.

† Marian's view of Liszt should be contrasted with the more general English view, which saw him as mixing too much personal shoddiness with his virtuoso musical brilliance. As Ernest Newman (*Life of Wagner*, II, 465–66) says, Liszt's "name stank in the nostrils of thousands of quiet, sober people because it had so often been associated with the escapades of the boudoir and the bedchamber." Marian, however, was not concerned with that, since the same words could have been applied to George Eliot.

had mixed feelings about Wagner, finding *Lohengrin* wearisome, the declamation too monotonous, but citing *Dutchman* as an opera she wanted to rehear. Also, *Tannhäuser* struck her as "remarkably fine." They attended as well Weber's *Der Freischütz* and Flotow's *Martha,* both of which disappointed her; she called the Flotow opera "trash."

Meanwhile, Marian tried to get on with spoken German, tutored on occasion by Hofrath Schöll, the new director of the Free Art Institute in Weimar, formerly a theology student and professor, a man heavily influenced by Strauss at one time and, therefore, interested in Marian. She found her work in German hampered by her need to work heavily in French, the mode of communication with Liszt and Sayn-Wittgenstein. All in all, she considered her stay in Weimar "a little island of repose between the fortnight's journeying which was full of more exciting pleasure, and the stay at Dresden and Berlin to which I am looking forward." Liszt, once more, is lauded, this time to Bessie Parkes, as a "glorious creature in every way—a bright genius, with a tender, loving nature, and a face in which this combination is perfectly expressed." She says he has that divine ugliness ("laideur divinisée") "by which the soul gleams through it, which is my favorite kind of physique."

The words here and the expression of taste are of interest. First of all, Liszt was hardly the person Marian described. She heard something heroic in his music and interpreted the man by the touch in his fingers or his compositions, which are lofty, but, for most late-twentieth-century ears, pretentious and self-dramatized. What she omitted was a ruthlessness which lay in his character, a disregard for others' feelings, a philandering nature, an anti-Semitism which could be as virulent as Wagner's, and, overall, the qualities we associate with a man profoundly ambitious rather than the one described by Marian as having reached the mountaintop. As for his "divine ugliness," that was a way of coming to terms with Lewes's appearance, not to mention her own, an ugliness through which the soul poked through.

Furthermore, her "quiet happiness," as she described it, was surely the fact that she and Lewes found themselves compatible; that, still further, they were a good sexual match. Marian's temperament was sensual, even passionate—we catch this in the feelings which lie just beneath the repressions of her female protagonists, not the least Maggie Tulliver. That passionate nature must have found itself fulfilled with the experienced Lewes.

Lewes, meanwhile, was occupied with researching and writing his biography of Goethe, on which he depended for income—he had seven people to support in Bedford Place: Agnes and their six children by himself and Hunt. Also, he had to contribute toward his and Marian's expenses. Marian was herself preparing an article for the *Review* on Victor Cousin's *Madame de Sablé: Études sur les femmes illustres et la sociétié du dix-septième siècle,* which explains her heavy work in French at this time. As we observe Marian and Lewes here, his work centered on Germany, hers on France, we note how she put herself at his service, in somewhat the same way Dorothea puts herself at the service of Casaubon in

Middlemarch. This deference is continuous with her article on Mde. de Sablé in the seventeenth century.

This is a strange piece, full of contradictory impulses which perhaps can be explained by Marian's own contradictory position, and by the fact she was not working in a mode which fulfilled her needs. Articles were important for income—and she did several for Chapman in the next couple of years—but they were ephemeral, high-class journalism, not the permanent work which she knew established a career. In the article, she writes of a large treasure trove of works authored by women, to the sum of 32,000 volumes, collected by a Count Leopold Ferri, and which *she* would assign, for the most part, to the flame. The exceptions, she says, would be the works of French women. "With a few remarkable exceptions, our own feminine literature is made up of books which could have been better written by men. . . . when not a feeble imitation, they are usually an absurd exaggeration of the masculine style."

That is for openers. She cites Richardson and his *Sir Charles Grandison* as having a feminine sensibility. She does, however, admit there is such a thing as gender in literature: ". . . in art and literature [as opposed to science], which imply the action of the entire being, in which every fibre of the nature is engaged, in which every peculiar modification of the individual makes itself felt, woman has something specific to contribute. Under every imaginable social condition she will necessarily have a class of sensations and emotions—the maternal ones—which must remain unknown to men. . . ." From this difference, as well as from differences in physical strength, "will come a psychological difference and will not vanish before woman's intellectual and moral nature. . . ." She felt that under these circumstances, in France alone "woman has had a vital influence on the development of literature; in France alone the mind of woman has passed like an electric current through the language. . . . in France alone, if the writings of women were swept away, a serious gap would be made in the national history."

Her disregard of Fanny Burney, Jane Austen, and the Brontës seems unusual, and placing them below Madame de Staël and Madame de Sévigné is not so much an act of criticism as a disregard for literary values. By taking this stand, in August of 1854, when she was deferring to Lewes's tastes, she was either being masochistic or else trying to carve out some role for herself by diminishing the contributions of other female English writers.

One other possibility arises, that in French literature she found a less harsh morality, a less constricted sense of human freedom, a more liberal attitude toward female behavior when it fell outside of accepted standards. George Sand would be the standard-bearer here. Marian would be very sensitive to this, particularly now when her position in Weimar really depended on Lewes's connections and the fact of his work on Goethe. She does touch on this in one part of her long article, sent off to Chapman on 8 September. She links what is in her present life and what exists in French fiction as she interprets it: ". . . it is undeniable, that unions formed in the maturity of thought and feeling, and grounded only on inherent fitness and mutual attraction, tended to bring women into more intelligent sympathy with me, and to heighten and complicate their share in the political drama." She is seeking some justification not only for her way of life but for women in general, who, she felt, must be roused beyond "embroidery and domestic drudgery."

The single cause of the superiority of feminine culture in France over that in England comes in the influence of the *salons*. Here, of course, Marian is speaking of Parisian culture, or that of other large cities, little of which filtered down to the countryside in the way she means. She perceived the salons as so effective because they brought together men and women where "conversation ran the whole gamut of subjects. . . ." She tried this herself, in her Sunday afternoons, when she was George Eliot, although men dominated. Women thrive in this atmosphere, she believes, because they are fitted to the combination a salon provides: ". . . first, from their greater tendency to mingle affection and imagination with passion, and thus subtilize it into sentiment; and next, from that dread of what over-taxes their intellectual energies, either by difficulty or monotony, which gives them an instinctive fondness for lightness of treatment and airiness." Marian did not mean this to be an attack on women—although the contemporary reader may cringe—but a way of demonstrating that when these feminine qualities were brought into touch with the great masculine minds (she cites Corneille, Balzac, Bossuet, among others), women can shine forth. In this respect, she reveals her strategy: within the confines of a masculine society, which she takes for granted, women must find their own space. England, she observes, allows no such process, if we keep in mind she is thinking of women like herself.

She closes with what is clearly a plea for her kind of woman.

> . . . Women become superior in France by being admitted to a common fund of ideas, to common objects of interest with men; and this must ever be the essential condition at once of true womanly culture and of true social well-being. We have no faith in feminine conversazioni, where ladies are eloquent on Apollo and Mars; though we sympathize with the yearning activity of faculties which, deprived of their proper material, waste themselves in weaving fabrics out of cobwebs. Let the whole field of reality be laid open to woman as well as to man, and then that which is peculiar to her mental modification, instead of being as it is now, a source of discord and repulsion between the sexes, will be found to be a necessary complement to the truth and beauty of life. Then we shall have that marriage of minds which alone can blend all the hues of thought and feeling in one lovely rainbow of promise for the harvest of human happiness.

Chapman accepted the article without comment—annoying Marian in this respect—and paid her £15 for her efforts. In the next few years, Marian wrote a series of long articles for the *Review*, partially to keep busy, but mainly to generate income. Hard pressed, she and Lewes had to forgo a journey to Dresden because of lack of funds. Liszt inadvertently provided some work, having written a lengthy piece on Wagner and Meyerbeer; Marian translated and abridged it, and it appeared in the *Leader* as "The Romantic School of Music." It was not exactly the kind of work she envisaged for herself, but it did help to bring Liszt, Meyerbeer, and especially Wagner to the English public. English music, in this pre–Gilbert and Sullivan era, was rather a wasteland. Yet even though the work she was doing was not of the high kind she wished, she was at peace with herself, apparently, if we can believe her midsummer letters to Bray and Bessie Parkes. Her words to Chapman when she sent her article are characteristic: "I am happier every day and find my domesticity more and more delightful and beneficial to me. Affection, respect, and intellectual sympathy deepen. . . ."

But that would soon end; all was not well on the home front. We get some premonition of how George Eliot used rumor and gossip as a backdrop for her narratives when we observe rumor and gossip speeding across literary and intellectual England, with Lewes and, by implication, Marian reviled. Even Carlyle wondered about the scandal, but more direct was a letter from the sculptor Thomas Woolner to William Bell Scott, who turned out to be a friend of Lewes's. Writing on 4 October, Woolner was narrow and nasty: ". . . have you heard," he writes, "of . . . two blackguard literary fellows, Lewes and Thornton Hunt? They seem to have used wives on the ancient Briton practice of having them in common: now blackguard Lewes has bolted with a ———— and is living in Germany with her. I believe it dangerous to write facts of anyone nowadays so I will not any further lift the mantle and display the filthy contaminations of these hideous satyrs and smirking moralists . . . these Mormonites in another name—stink pots of humanity."

Having identified the serpent, Woolner later became quite fond of Marian when he met her as George Eliot, although her rising fame could have been a factor. She was no longer a "————." He also became a fairly frequent visitor when Marian and Lewes set up at the Priory. On 11 October, in a journal entry, Marian noted that a painful letter arrived from London, from Carlyle, a letter which has disappeared but which apparently brought up the scandal as it was enveloping the couple. Lewes responded, and that brought a sympathetic reply from Carlyle. Lewes's answer to that, probably on 19 October, was a sense of gratitude and relief that not everyone had turned aginst them. His answer was part of a two-part response—his to Carlyle, hers to Chapman and Bray in an effort at damage control. Weimar, then, was not unsullied, since news from London proved unsettling. Marian would live with this gossip, some of it quite open, until she died; for even her marriage to Cross in the final year of her life disturbed proprieties. Lewes, to Carlyle, suggests the poisonous atmosphere.

> Your letter has been with me half an hour and I have not yet recovered the shock—delightful shock—it gave me. One must have been, like me, long misjudged and harshly judged without power of explanation, to understand the feeling which such a letter creates. My heart yearned towards you as I read. It has given me new courage. . . . So much in gratitude. Now for

justice: On my *word of honour* there is no foundation for the scandal as it runs. My separation was in no-wise caused by the lady named, nor by any other lady. It has always been imminent, always *threatened,* but never before carried out, because of those assailing pangs of anticipation which would not let me carry resolution into fact. . . . At last—and this more because some circumstances into which I do [not] wish* to enter, happened to occur at a time when I was hypochondriacal and hopeless about myself, fearing lest a chronic disease would disable me from undertaking such responsibilities as those previously borne—at last, I say, the crisis came. But believe me the lady named had not only *nothing* whatever to do with it but was I solemnly declare, ignorant of my own state of mind on the subject. She knew the previous state of things, as indeed others knew, but that is all.

Particularly insidious was the response of the once-friendly George Combe, the thwarted phrenologist. Combe wrote to Bray on 15 November 1854.

An intimate friend of Mr. Lewes's in this city, wrote to him begging of him to contradict the reports of an improper connection with Miss Evans. He gave ample explanations about his wife, denied that Miss E. had written to Miss Martineau [more on that below]; but in regard to the main question, he said that he is not answerable to his correspondent for his conduct. He has written in precisely similar terms, in answer to a similar request, to Mr. Carlyle. The conclusion, then, is irresistible that the reports are too true.—They are spread everywhere, and we now meet them in society.

Combe assesses Marian: "We are deeply mortified and distressed; and I should like to know whether there is insanity in Miss Evans's family; for her conduct, with *her* brain [impervious to his phrenological methods], seems to me like morbid mental aberration." He is by no means finished.

I have no right to dictate to you, but I esteem you too much not to state frankly to you my convictions. T. Hunt, Lewes, and Miss Evans [Agnes is not factored in] have, in my opinion, by their practical conduct, inflicted a great injury on the cause of religious freedom. "The Leader" has become disagreeable to Mrs. Combe and me as the recorded thinking of minds that can act in such a manner, and when my subscription expires I shall give it up. "The greatest happiness of the greater number" principle [Bentham's and Mill's utilitarianism] appears to me to require that the obligations of married life should be honourably fulfilled; and an educated woman who, in the face of the world, volunteers to live as a wife, with a man who

---

* Strikingly, in the very sentence indicating the crisis which led to Lewes's act to separate, he miswrote "do wish," which he may have really meant, for the "do not wish" he consciously intended to write. Lewes was putting the best possible face on what looked like scandalous behavior all around.

already has a living wife and children, appears to me to pursue a course and to set an example calculated only to degrade herself and her sex, if she be sane. —If you receive her into your family circle, while present appearances are unexplained, pray consider whether you will do justice to your own female domestic circle, and how other ladies may feel about going into a circle which makes no distinction between those who act thus, and those who preserve their honour unspotted.

Bray defended Marian, saying he does not judge, and doesn't believe she is mad. He speaks of a natural law which preempts conventional law, and within this frame of reference he says he does "not think that Miss Evans would admit that Lewes had a wife now, or has had for some years, and they may both of them intend to fulfill all the conditions that belong *naturally* to the marriage state." In the background, of course, was Bray's own second family, part of "natural law."

There was also the question of another rumor, mentioned in the Combe letter, that Marian had sent on to Harriet Martineau a letter or message of explanation which was supposed to be circulated at the Reform Club. Lewes denies—as does Marian with Chapman—that any such letter was sent, asserting, in fact, that Marian had not communicated with Martineau for the last year: ". . . in short this letter," Lewes tells Carlyle, "is a pure, or impure, fabrication—the letter, the purport, the language, all fiction. . . . Thus far I give you a solemn denial of this scandal. Where gossip affects a point of honour or principle I feel bound to meet it with denial; on all private matters my only answer is *silence*." Carlyle's note on the letter was supportive, but also wary of something so close to pure scandal. *

Marian had preceded Lewes's letter, on 15 October, with her own to Chapman. We observe how Germany's playground atmosphere had been sucked into England's marital requirements, and how Marian was fighting not only for her reputation but, in some way, for her life. Everything suddenly seemed at stake. "I am sorry that you are annoyed with questions about me," she wrote. "Do whatever seems likely to free you from such importunities. About my own justification I am entirely indifferent." Quite the opposite: she was in turmoil. As we can see in her later fiction, she used the devastating and often unjust quality of rumor and scandal to bring down some of her characters. But further than that, she used town choruses and other means to demonstrate how rumors can spread into injustices; that moral issues become so intertwined with scandalous reports that accuracy is impossible. Truth suffers, even when guilty people—like Bulstrode in *Middlemarch*—are punished. This sense of rumor, scandal, and gossip followed her, like collective furies, into every crevice of her fiction. As in Greek classical drama, they are implacable forces.

* Carlyle's letter to his brother, however, was less than supportive, saying that after Agnes had produced those "dirty sooty-skinned children" by Hunt, Lewes "has certainly cast away his wife here. . . ." Carlyle's words make Lewes into a victim or cuckold who has indeed cast out his wife.

The heart of the problem, she informs Chapman, is the gossip that Lewes has run away from his family. "This is so far from being true that he is in constant correspondence with his wife and is providing for her to the best of his power; while no man can be more nervously anxious than he about the future welfare of his children." Marian supports this by citing Agnes's letters, revealing that his conduct as a husband "has been in the highest degree noble and self-sacrificing."

After denying she had sent any message to Martineau—"one of the last persons to whom I would speak as a confidante"—Marian continues:

> You ask me to tell you what reply you shall give to inquiries. I have nothing to deny or conceal. I have done nothing with which any person has a right to interfere. I have surely full liberty to travel in Germany, and to travel with Mr. Lewes. No one here seems to find it at all scandalous that we should be together. . . . But I do not wish to take the ground of ignoring what is unconventional in my position. I have counted the cost of the step that I have taken and am prepared to bear, without irritation or bitterness, renunciation by all my friends. I am not mistaken in the person to whom I have attached myself. He is worthy of the sacrifice I have incurred, and my only anxiety is that he should be rightly judged.

This is as explicit an explanation of her position as Marian would make, but she still had to deal with the divided dualistic role she was acting out—as a traditional woman, on the one hand, and as a woman who did indeed "run away," on the other. She wrote at considerable length to Bray (not Cara), on 23 October, going through the entire matter with possibly her most devoted friend. Bray had defended her, although with some equivocation; but she had to be certain he knew the truth as she perceived it. Ostensibly her letter was to tell him that her income from her father's estate, of which her brother Isaac was co-trustee, was to be paid directly to Bray, who could then forward it to Marian wherever she was. Although this sounds innocent, it was an indication of her wish to be free of encumbrances and her recognition of Isaac's hostility to her position.

The bulk of the letter is filled with news of her and Lewes. She unravels the entire equation. She says she has seen all the correspondence with Agnes and is convinced Lewes has acted honorably. She adds she has known him long enough to offer the opinion "that he is worthy of high respect." About herself, she says that if Bray hears anything about what she has done beyond the fact of her attachment to Lewes, he is to believe it false. She adds she is not exerting any influence over her companion, except to stimulate "his conscientious care for them [his family], if it needed any stimulus." Then she arrives at a difficult point, what all this means to Cara Bray and the moralistic Sara Hennell. "I am ignorant how far Cara and Sara may be acquainted with the state of things, and how they may feel towards me. I am quite prepared to accept the consequences of a step which I have deliberately taken and to accept them without irritation or bitterness. If I do not write, therefore, understand that it is because I desire not to obtrude myself."

Nor were *her* explanations all there were. In the background, Chapman and Bray, among others, tried to keep the record straight with their own explanation of what Marian had done. In a series of letters to George Combe, one of which was noted above, Bray attempted damage control in a hopeless case. In an 8 October letter—that fall of 1854 was abuzz with activity—Bray told Combe about Agnes's disaffection, and with that Lewes sought out someone of "a mind like Miss Evans, and the more, from the want of sympathy from his wife." But even Bray falters and tells Combe he would have preferred it if Marian and Lewes had traveled with others in the party—a risible idea, since their very plan had been to isolate themselves to test their compatability. He tries to explain their elopement as Marian attempting to help someone in need. Two weeks later, Bray repeated this—Marian acting as a good samaritan, as it were. Still going strong, on 24 October he quoted liberally from Marian's letter to him, about how she did not turn Lewes against his family.

On 28 October, Bray added a new note, that he has been imploring Marian to separate herself from Lewes. Writing once again to Combe, Bray reports Marian's words to him, Bray, from a letter now lost: "So far as my friends or acquaintances are inclined to occupy themselves with my affairs, I am grateful to them and sorry that they should have pain on my account, but I cannot think that their digestion will be much hindered by anything that befals a person about whom they troubled themselves very little while she lived in privacy and loneliness." Marian's remarks evince bitterness, and beleaguerment as well, besides not a little unfairness. Many of these friends were concerned with her loneliness, and Combe, for one, had repeatedly invited her away with him and his wife during summers. Unlike Dr. Brabant, his concerns were intellectual, not romantic. From her tone, we observe her nerves becoming frayed; the situation as related from London had gotten through. If anything, advice and attacks made her more resolved to go her own way and created an even stronger hold Lewes and she had on each other. Combe, however, was not convinced by Bray's explanations and retorted nastily.

The scandal continued well into the next year, as we learn from Charles Kingsley, who referred to Marian as G. H. Lewes's "concubine." He was writing to Frederick Denison Maurice, who had recently been unfavorably reviewed in the *Westminster*. "The woman who used to insult you therein [either as reviewer or as editor of the *Review*]—who I suppose does so now—is none other than Miss Evans, the infidel esprit forte," that remark followed by the concubine designation.

Marian's firmness toward her decision, however, should not deceive us as to how deeply she felt about cutting herself off. She knew, of course, that she had taken possibly the most significant step a woman in Victorian England could take. The sole more scandalous move would have been if she, too, were married and then left the country with another married person. Her decision placed her in that category of scarlet woman, home-breaker, creator of discord, like those women in classical mythology who must be avenged. Worse, she had taken on the role of a woman who defies all conventions because of an overpowering passion or sensuality in her nature. She had not suppressed her feelings for the sake of conventional standards, and she had demonstrated defiance for the worst possible motive: gratification of her sexual impulses. She had revealed a sexual nature, and instead of denying and burying it, she had dared to indulge it. Physicians and men of science denied that women were even capable of orgasm. Marian was, quite simply, enjoying herself, becoming Lilith, who was worse than Eve, and doing so without regard for family or friends.

In the next year, Marian did not abandon the matter, but brought it profoundly into her reviews, especially one she did on a collection of John Milton's writings, edited by Thomas Keightley. She was consumed by the inadequacies and injustices of the divorce laws, and she cites, as well, one of the most famous divorce cases of the nineteenth century: the Caroline Norton suit against her husband for his refusal to pay her an allowance. This case was fresh in Marian's thought, since it came in August 1853, when Norton refused to pay one of his wife's creditors. Mrs. Norton did not take it quietly, but wrote *English Laws for Women in the Nineteenth Century,* in May 1854, and then her even more sensational *Letter to the Queen,* in December 1855. With attacks and counterattacks creating a scandal and forming the background, Marian reviewed Keightley's volume on Milton, but emphasized, not unusually, Milton's *Doctrine and Discipline of Divorce.* Her words on this are a blueprint not only for Lewes's marriage but for the marriages of several of her fictional characters.

Her point throughout, in this *Leader* review (4 August 1855), is how young people walk blindly into a union in which there is no way of knowing the other person's potential. She writes of a husband who finds himself "bound fast to an uncomplying discord of nature, or, as it oft happens, to an image of earth and phlegm, with whom he looked to be the copartner of a sweet and gladsome society; and sees withal that his bondage is now inevitable; though he would be almost the strongest Christian, he will be ready to despair in virtue, and mutiny against Divine Providence." In effect, she sees such a marriage as making men "the bondsmen of a luckless and helpless matrimony." Strikingly, her remarks are oriented toward the unfortunate man, although Mrs. Norton's case stank in every liberated woman's nostrils.

Despite protesting her "lack of concern," the phrase she uses in several places, Marian stored up her anger and revealed it not only in reviews but full blast in her fiction. While this period was painful, we should not neglect how much of a breeding ground it was for George Eliot. But since she was writing fiction and not autobiography, she disguised herself with several literary devices. One of the most repetitious and insistent is her use of dualism: dual characters, dual situations, dual choices, dual natures. This use manifested the split within Marian herself, and the most illuminating of such intimate details comes in *Middlemarch,* not surprisingly her most fully fashioned and mature work.

Middlemarch abounds in divisions, although not always of the most symmetrical kind. The one emphatic point is that unconventional action is measured against conventional; so that, in one way or another, Eliot is working through contraries she herself experienced as Marian Evans, especially those months and years when she was with Lewes just prior to her writing of fiction. In the novel, the dualisms are of several types: Dorothea Brooke and Tertius Lydgate, but also Lydgate and Edward Casaubon, Dorothea and Rosamond Vincy, Lydgate and Will Ladislaw, Will and Casaubon, Rosamond and Mary Garth, and others. Working across gender lines, Eliot paired Dorothea and Lydgate in the very structuring of the novel. We could argue that in Eliot's way of approaching this long novel we have biographical data embedded in a structural concept. As we know, she wrote the Lydgate part first, without thought of incorporating Dorothea Brooke; and then, only later, as the Lydgate material proceeded slowly, she decided to bring in and blend together with Lydgate a character named Dorothea Brooke. This joining together of the two is structural, but it is also part of the idea of the novel, immediately establishing them as co-joined, commingled, overlapping, and also opposing figures. *

Equally compelling is the split between Dorothea and Rosamond, with Will Ladislaw as the connective tissue. Superficially, Rosamond Vincy is a typical Eliot creation, the embodiment of everything the author despised in a young woman: physical beauty, lack of moral depth, self-centeredness based on her physical attractions, her consideration of herself as the object of every male's desire, her failure to achieve any intellectual depth or even self-recognition—the list could go on. This is our first glance. But as Eliot develops Rosamond into her first instance of self-awareness, when she admits Will does not care for her and worships Dorothea, we have Eliot's recognition of other qualities in her character: that she, too, this lovely physical specimen, is entrapped by her role as a woman. Possibilities here are multidimensional, including Eliot's realization that Rosamond, with her conventional societal tastes, is little different from all women who must toe the line; and that Dorothea, with her desire for martyrdom to the right man, is the other side of that role-playing, the woman who, while moving outside convention, is forced back into conventional female strictures. We have, in the two, the blending together of the Marian Evans of the mid-1850s: that meeting of seemingly very different qualities, which in effect turn out to be qualities associated with women, whether they are entrapped by marrying a Casaubon or a Lydgate, or running off with a Lewes.

That is, however, only the beginning. In the novel, we observe in Lydgate—but also in Dorothea—a process which we have long traced in Marian, the need to project herself into the future as an achieving, successful person. Eliot writes: "We are on a perilous margin when we begin to look passively at our future selves, and see our own figures led with dull consent into insipid misdoing and shabby achievement." Lydgate was "groaning on the margin." Yet it is also Dor-

---

* As we see with Daniel Deronda and Gwendolen Harleth later. The two parts of *Daniel Deronda* must be viewed not as disparate elements but as segments of a dualism which runs through all of Eliot's major works.

othea's worry, leading up to her decision to marry Casaubon. Her anxiety is based on the fear of ending up with a wasted life, a life without anything to show for her evident attributes. We have, in this, Marian's shadowy presentation of self, of one career (Lydgate's) frustrated by wrong choices; of another (Dorothea's) baffled also by a wrong choice. The fictional version is a dimension of the dilemma Marian faced when she left England with Lewes; but even more than that, her decision to stick loyally to him—when everything about her seemed threatened with ruin. Just as rumor and scandal are going to bring down Lydgate—until Dorothea's intercession on his behalf—so the same gossip could have destroyed Marian's world during or after these Weimar weeks.

But we still have not adequately penetrated that complicated world in which the fictional achievement manifests what is hidden in the writer's emotional and psychological life. Eliot's strong identification with Lydgate, despite her evident disapproval of his moral laxity and his gender miscalculations, is an indication of how she sympathized with his goals and with the frustration of these goals. In Chapter 73, when the good doctor finds himself immersed in all the crosscurrents of a situation which will lead to his eventual ruin, and he must confront the crumbling of his idealized marriage, he tries to avoid the consequences of his choices. Eliot is not unsympathetic, merely caustic. "Lydgate thought of himself as the sufferer, and of others as the agents who had injured his lot. He had meant everything to turn out differently; and others had thrust themselves into his life and thwarted his purposes." He has truly lost his bearings, since he identifies himself as the victim; and even his tenderest feelings are an enemy to his nature, because he fears tenderness will lead to further decline. "Lydgate's tender-heartedness was present just then only as a dread lest he should offend against it, not as an emotion that swayed him to tenderness."

The shadow of nearly everything in Marian's life is caught here, although we could find comparable examples in *Daniel Deronda*, *Romola*, *The Mill on the Floss*, and her long undigestible poem *The Spanish Gypsy*. The situation is so intimate because it demonstrates that Eliot has discovered how disorientation can enter into personal relationships. Her own feelings were disoriented to the extent that while she wanted her friends to understand her, she was prepared to accept the consequences of their rejection, even Cara's and Sara's. The move with Lewes had at once centered and decentered her world: centered it in giving her a focused companion at the age of nearly thirty-five, but decentered it in that she opened herself up to all kinds of hostile reactions. She had, as it were, thrown the dice and she had not, as the Mallarmé poem would have it, abolished chance, but abetted it. In that throw of the dice, she had made her life all possibility; she had negated restriction. But rather than bridging disparate elements in her life, she had made them more threatening.

The immediation situation climaxed when Marian heard from Sara Hennell, who felt Marian had treated her shabbily by not revealing the true sequence of events. Sara was not angry at Marian's departure with Lewes, but at not being trusted to hear the truth and accept it. Sara applauded independent action by women, but felt deserted here. Marian's letter, of 31 October, still from Weimar, was yet another effort at damage control, and an attempt to explain her actions. "When you say that I do not care about Cara's or your opinion and friendship it seems much the same to me as if you said that I didn't care to eat when I was hungry or to drink when I was thirsty. One of two things: either I am a creature without affection, on whom the memories of years have no hold, or, you, Cara and Mr. Bray are not the most cherished friends I have in the world. It is simply self-contradictory to say that a person can be indifferent about her dearest friends; yet this is what you substantially say, when you accuse me of 'boasting with what serenity I can give you up,' or 'speaking proudly' etc." To this she gives an unequivocal denial, and then explains. In point of fact, she walked a fine line, saying that if she had to, she would stick with Lewes even if it meant losing her most cherished friends. But Sara, while moralistic, valued her friendship with Marian. Later, when it flattened, it was on other grounds.

Marian's words reveal her difficult situation and suggest her conflicting impulses about past and present. She adds that everything between her and Lewes is now in the open, and that she is under "no foolish hallucinations about either the present or the future and am standing on no stilts of any kind." She shrinks, she says, from divulging profoundly personal and intimate details; but now that she knows she may do so, she is considerably brightened. She repeats that she, Sara, and Cara and her own sister are the three women who are connected to her heart by a cord that can never be broken. "My love for you rests on a past which no future can reverse, and offensive as the words seem to have been to you, I must repeat that I can feel no bitterness towards you [for Sara's reproach about Marian's silence and her assumption that Marian felt strongly enough to give up her closest friends], however you may act towards me." Marian adds she has been "miserably ill," and closes with her undying love to her and Cara. The miserableness did not appear to affect her travel with Lewes, for shortly after this, they left Weimar for Berlin.

This phase of the journey more or less closed with Marian's letter to Bray on 3 November, before her departure for Berlin. In this, she says her personal life is closed to all except Bray himself and those "who are one with you" and to Chapman, ostensibly also to Mrs. Chapman, who has now become almost a confidante. Sara, incidentally, papered over this disruption in the friendship, but was permanently affected. Her response arrived at about the time of Marian's thirty-fifth birthday, and it could not have created everlasting joy. She swore fidelity, but she also noted changes in the relationship. "I am glad," she wrote Marian, "you feel it will be a pleasure to tell us some of the things you are now enjoying. . . . But I have a strong sort of feeling that I am writing to some one in a book, and not to the Marian that we have known and loved so many years. Do not mistake me, I mean nothing unkind."

If we extrapolate from this particular situation, we find Marian once more moving toward some of her most intense fictional themes: the secrets her protagonists harbor and the arcane lives they carve out for themselves, and the disguises they create for their real selves. So much of Eliot's fiction is based on hidden lives which eventually emerge, or secret selves which lead to decline or disaster, that all of it seems wedded to her inner divisions. In one respect, Marian had become a fictional character in Sara's view because she was moving behind disguises; but from Marian's point of view, disguise was all. Sara had no awareness that there were things which must remain secret; and in her insistence on complete openness she not only misread her friend but also misjudged the enormity of what her friend had done.

Withal, Marian stabilized her friendship with Sara, but Cara Bray, having written once and only once, stopped altogether. She disapproved of Lewes and, by implication, of Marian's departure with him; and she possibly felt disloyalty on her friend's part, or even desertion of principle. The cuckolded journalist was not liked by any of the Coventry crowd, in part, perhaps, because he had stolen *their* Marian. Having discovered her, they very possibly wanted to keep her. Even Bray (but especially Combe) was hostile to Lewes's stated amusement at those who considered phrenology to be scientifically based. But hostility went further than Cara's silence; it extended also to M. P. Joseph Parkes, whose radicalism ended when he thought social proprieties were being flouted. Parkes was one of those typically hypocritical men Victorian ethics created: insane with rage, apparently, over what Marian had done with that philandering Lewes and yet himself unfaithful to his wife—all the while, however, advocating radical ideas about man and society.

In most instances, while the couple headed for Berlin from Weimar, Lewes was held responsible. Termed a seducer, he was marked as a cad who had led virginal Marian into sin. But others knew better, perhaps none better than Chapman, who was aware of Marian's passionate nature and her desire to experience reciprocal feelings and to find emotional support. Bessie Parkes, incidentally, defied her father's attitudes and remained a correspondent. Harriet Martineau, however, felt quite otherwise, and perhaps out of both professional and personal jealousy, she became part of the rumor-spreading group, more virulent than most, tarring both Lewes and Marian with her brush of sin, immorality, and breaches of propriety. Martineau wrote to several of her friends to try to poison the London literary atmosphere against Marian, but especially against Lewes, who had reviewed negatively her *Letters on the Laws of Man's Nature and Development.* The response from her quarter did not appear to upset Marian, perhaps because it was literary politics. Martineau was liberal and a supporter of women's issues, but, like Parkes, her public views made little difference when her private needs were exposed.

Martineau remained one of the great haters. Yet at a point in 1856, when Martineau thought she was going to die of an incurable disease, probably cancer, Marian nevertheless responded with considerable compassion. She also indicated to Chapman that if she, Marian, outlived Martineau and the latter's memoirs were published, she would like to write a favorable review of them. These were droll stories from the deep, but Martineau did not die, living up to the time almost of Marian's own death. Even when the latter as George Eliot compelled everyone's admiration, Martineau did not let go. Her hatred for Lewes—for the above reasons and also possibly because he published a competing book on

Comte—did not lessen, and she even revelled in the news when he was truly ill and she could anticipate his death. Her virulence toward the couple went beyond literary competition, fierce as that was, into an anger which could not accept that plain-looking, unattractive Marian Evans had landed a companion, and was riding out the scandal. One looks in vain in Eliot's fiction for a portrait of Harriet Martineau, for she would have made a tremendously interesting character.

Bad news poured in. Chapman reported that the *Review* was now a battleground, with Harriet and James Martineau attempting to wrest control from him; and Chapman further reported the death of his cousin, John, a supporter of the quarterly. Between deaths and the imminent demise of the journal, there seemed little good news. The scandal-mongering, of course, picked up momentum. Once in Berlin, Marian asked Bray again about her income, controlled by Isaac, who was now playing a nasty game with his sister. Isaac wrote Marian he would pay her income when he received it, which meant he could do whatever he chose. She tells Bray about their arrangement: "But I will take care in future not to involve anyone else in the annoyance resulting from his disinclination to accommodate me." There was a further wrinkle, that some £1,500 of her money had to be reinvested in another fund, which meant for the time being a reduced income, starting in the summer of 1855. This could possibly explain the outpouring of review articles from Marian's pen which appeared in 1855 in the *Westminster* and the *Leader*. Chrissey was also suffering from money worries, and two of her sons were causing particular difficulty, one of them ill, the other "very naughty" so that he had to be sent to sea. This son, Robert, was shipwrecked and lost in 1855.

Fortunately, Marian had other matters at hand, since everything associated with Coventry was depressing. She writes in her recollections about their departure from Weimar, their sorrow at saying farewell to the "grand, fascinating Liszt" and the others. Her life was bustling with activities, breakfasts, invitations, and the like—a social side we normally do not attribute to Marian. On Friday, 3 November, she and Lewes reached Berlin, which in time disappointed them. They lodged their first night at the Hôtel de l'Europe and, though the next day they moved into lodgings at 62 Dorotheenstrasse, they took their meals at the hotel for four months. Lewes had several connections in Berlin, including Karl August Varnhagen von Ense, a scholar and biographer of Goethe, among others. Von Ense proved quite useful, lending Lewes books and serving as a sounding board for ideas as Lewes worked steadily on his Goethe biography. The social circle was set almost from the beginning: Lewes was much better received in Berlin than in London. Fräulein von Solmar's salon was opened to them, almost a daily event. Marian and Lewes attended Lessing's play *Nathan the Wise*, a plea for religious and racial tolerance which Marian found exhilarating. "It thrilled me to think that Lessing dared nearly a hundred years ago to write the grand sentiments and profound thoughts which this play contains. . . . In England the words which call down applause here would make the pit rise in horror." Overall, her assessment of Germany gained high marks. While she misses some of England's creature comforts, she finds that Germans "know better how to use the means they have for the end of enjoyment." Despite some egregious behavior (putting their dinner knives in their mouths, for example), they are "happy animals."

For the October 1854 issue of the *Westminster,* Chapman asked James Martineau to review Marian's translation of Feuerbach's *The Essence of Christianity.* It was a poisonous review, not of Marian, but of the enterprise itself, revealing how ill-suited the reviewer was for the task at hand. After praising her translation—even "better than her Strauss"—Martineau states that "we are only surprised that, if she wished to exhibit the new Hegelian atheism to English readers, she should select a work of the year 1840, and of quite secondary philosophical repute in its own country." This is a complete misreading of Feuerbach, which is hardly "Hegelian atheism," but an effort to put Christianity on grounds whereby people like himself and Marian could remain associated with the faith—an effort to find coordinates in Christianity for a more modern world in which the claims of the clergy and the church might be examined in the light of a rational discourse. Martineau could have disagreed with this, of course, but he distorted the contents, causing Sara Hennell to call his review "disgraceful." One could, in fact, argue that Feuerbach's work was most appropriate at a time when Darwin's evolutionary theory was in danger of sweeping away everything in Christianity except blind faith.

In Marian's eyes, the English scene was corrupted, and she looked to Berlin for respite. Lewes sought out a friend from earlier Berlin days, Professor Otto Gruppe, whose *Gegenwart und Zukunft der philosophie in Deutschland (The Present and Future of Philosophy in Germany)* would be the subject of Marian's review in the *Leader* on 28 July 1855. She found him very attractive, very learned, with books on all subjects and a charming family of a much younger wife and two small children. In the review, Marian reveals her sympathy for Gruppe's renunciation of metaphysics, his rejection of all efforts to form theories of the universe and to derive first principles. Philosophy, he says, must be concerned with determining logic and methods; and it should apply its methods to the investigation of psychology and to its subordinate, aesthetics. She is pleased that "at last we have a German professor of philosophy who renounces the attempt to climb to heaven by the rainbow bridge of 'the high *priori* road' "—that is, by the Kantian and Hegelian road—and is instead content "humbly to use his muscles in treading the uphill *a posteriori* path," which is the way of logic and the scientific method.

Marian and Lewes formed friendships with a variety of people. One of them was an interesting woman named Fanny Lewald, a novelist who was living openly with the literary scholar Adolf Stahr, whom Marian described as lacking "scarcely any moral radiation." Fanny Lewald was eager to meet Marian, whose social position was similar to her own. In time, however, Lewald and Stahr married. Lewes and Marian met in rapid succession the portrait painter Eduard Magnus and his chemist brother, Heinrich Magnus, both of whom Marian found sympathetic for their willingness to criticize the Germans. The sculptor

Christian Rauch, now in his mid-seventies, made an enormous impact on Marian, next to Liszt the most impressive man she had met so far. Rauch had stories about Goethe to tell Lewes, especially Goethe's manner of relating his experiences. While many of these budding friendships were just that, there was never distant from the couple's minds the imperative that Lewes had to research and complete his biography of Goethe.

Yet except for those pieces Marian would write that appeared in 1855 in the *Leader* and the *Westminster,* she had little to do. She was looking for something that could engage her, while at the same time she tried to help Lewes. Something finally did emerge, although the income produced was hardly commensurate with the effort. In her 22 November 1854 letter (her birthday letter) to Sara, she edges into her plan: "I should be very glad to have my pen employed in something that would yield immediate profit, and there are plenty of subjects suggested by new German books which would be fresh and instructive in an English review. But I cannot bring myself to run the risk of a refusal from an editor. Indeed I cannot for several reasons make any proposition at present. So I am working at what will ultimately yield something which is secured by an agreement with Bohn [a publisher]." This was a daunting project, a translation of Spinoza's *Ethics* from the Latin, which she began on 8 November and continued until she and Lewes left for England. At the same time that she was working on this Latin text, she was also translating passages from German which appeared in Lewes's *Goethe.* Given Lewes's need to hurry along, Marian quite possibly contributed to several aspects of the biography; we know definitely of her translation of the genealogical tables. An added point which the contemporary reader might find amusing: when Lewes's book did appear, Marian reviewed it in the 3 November 1855 *Leader.*

Marian's translation of Spinoza's *Ethics,* incidentally, never appeared. For financial reasons, Bohn withdrew from the agreement to publish it, and Lewes subsequently tried to peddle the translation and life to A. and C. Black, but nothing came of that either. The manuscript of the translation is now at Yale, with some pages of notes in Lewes's hand. Marian was desperate to generate some income, and she made a number of suggestions to Chapman for articles for the *Review,* as the year became 1855 and she was still not established in any kind of writing rhythm or pattern. She suggested "Ideals of Womankind" for the quarterly, and when Chapman discouraged that topic, she moved to another called "Women in Germany," which was never written either.

Chapman was himself out of sorts, ill, having more or less lost his direction in both the *Review* and his personal life, although we should not underestimate his resilience. His philandering, including his affair with Barbara Leigh Smith (summer 1854 to September 1855), occupied a good deal of his time, as did the emotional turmoil in which he lived. His publishing firm was still near bankruptcy, and he was practicing economic triage in order to hold things together. Without Marian's active support as subeditor, the *Review* was foundering or, more accurately, lacking in the firmness such an enterprise requires. Marian finally wrote, for the April 1855 number, a piece called "Memoirs of the Court of Austria," based on Karl Eduard Vehse's voluminous history of the Austrian court (eleven volumes of a projected twenty-eight having appeared). She padded out the piece with long excerpts from Vehse, along with some marginal comments by herself to hold the article together. Chapman paid her £20 for her contribution, which amounted to one-fifth of her annual income. It was effort, but not real work.

9

Facing Up

"There comes a terrible moment to many souls when
the great movements of the world, the larger destinies of mankind, which have lain aloof in newspapers,
and other neglected reading, enter like an earth-
quake into their own lives. . . ."

On 11 March 1855, Marian and Lewes left Berlin for England, first traveling
to Cologne and Brussels. In assessing her eight months abroad, John Cross
felt she did not waste her time; that her enormous amount of reading, chiefly in
German literature (Goethe, Schiller, Lessing, Schlegel, and others), served her
well when she came to writing fiction. In addition to the German writers cited
above, Marian noted in her journal the delightful long evenings she and Lewes
read Shakespeare, Macaulay, Heine, and countless more. Surely, this bout of
heavy but enjoyable reading enlarged Marian's purview, providing her with that
ready fund of literary references which so fill her novels, as epigraphs and as allusions.

Yet there is another, not so positive, side which Cross as well as Haight slide
away from; and that is the drift which occurred as Marian "served" Lewes's needs
while snatching for herself whatever came to hand. While Lewes was quite
focused at this time, her projects made no consistent or coherent sense. Her
career, such as it was, was as a high-level freelance journalist; and that meant
she had projects, but no direction to her work. In just these last months, we
observe a hodgepodge of half of her Spinoza translation, the long piece on the
Austrian court (padded with quotations), and proposals for articles on women
she did not write. She was spinning out ideas to generate income and to enable
Lewes to complete his Goethe biography without interruption. She was allowing
her own plans for a career to splinter.

As she moved into her thirty-sixth year she had not appreciably advanced in
career terms from several years before; but this is not to say she was personally
miserable. On the contrary, all indications are that she was less ill than usual

and that, while trying to put the scandal behind her, she did not regret her situation. Yet she had not realized her potential. Like Joseph Conrad three decades later, she was passing well into her thirties without having found her métier; and like Conrad, who stored up images during twenty years on and off at sea, Marian warehoused ideas, without being at all sure how she would use them.

One other aspect should be noted: during their stay in Weimar and then in Berlin, she and Lewes were meeting (mainly) men who had forged serious careers. Lewes, too, had established something of a reputation, and his current project on Goethe gave him professional validity. In this atmosphere, Marian had to measure her own relatively small forays into seriousness against larger careers; and for lack of anything else to distinguish her, she had to accept being known as the translator of Strauss and Feuerbach. Those suggestions for articles made to Chapman in early January of 1855 are poignant: small stuff amidst the larger achievements of the men in their social circle or those they met at Berlin salons.

Marian's last letter to Sara from Berlin is newsy, full of public utterances about operas attended (*Fidelio, Orpheus and Eurydice*), people met and made into friends, but little to indicate the closeness of the couple's relationship to each other. She does send her love to the now uncommunicative Cara. Before departing from Berlin, they became conventional tourists, visiting artworks in particular, especially the Titian, two Corregios, and a Jan Steen at the Old Museum. In Cologne, they went to see the cathedral and then made their way to Brussels, where, by chance, they sat across the table from Hector Berlioz at the Hôtel de Saxe.

By 14 March, Marian had lodged at 1 Sydney Place in Dover, England, while Lewes continued on to London. Although she put a good face on their situation—she explained to Sara, in a 16 March letter, that Lewes had "some arrangements" to attend to—her real reasons remained unstated; most likely, she was unable to face the scandal directly as Lewes's companion. Lewes could, so to speak, prepare the ground, or at least deflect some of the slings and arrows of slander directed against the couple. In her farewell to Berlin, in her journal, Marian says Germany "is no bad place to live in, and the Germans, to counterbalance their want of taste and politeness, are at least free from the bigotry and exclusiveness of their more refined cousins."

The short time she announced for her stay in Dover stretched out, and she remained apart from Lewes for five weeks. She worked on the Spinoza, but one thing above all else must have preoccupied her: whether or not Lewes would honor the relationship and remain loyal once he had returned to London and confronted the scandal thrust upon him and Marian. Writing to Bessie Parkes, she plays the stoic, but even a calm passage turning on the scandal suggests her anxieties. She assures Bessie, first, that no one knows the truth of what occurred, and that if she, Marian, told everything no one would disagree with her, least of all faithful Bessie. Then: "My mind is deliciously calm and untroubled so far as my own lot is concerned, my only anxieties are sympathetic ones."

This was hardly the case. Nearly everyone expected Lewes's solitary arrival in London to mark the breakup. Even the Chapmans and the Brays had their doubts, and Bray, subject to his own demons, was rather curt in his letters to Marian; she chided him by saying she would rival his curtness with brevity of her own. But she did make one of her rare political comments, with a reference to the Crimean War, although only in connection with how it would affect the Coventry cloth and textile trade. Marian slid away from it immediately, into questions of her income. In the meanwhile, in Dover, with the Spinoza on her desk, she waited for the day when she and Lewes would be reunited; she did receive regular letters from him, and trusted in his constancy. She viewed the arrangement as temporary, until Lewes could find lodgings, and having made no friends in Dover, apparently led a solitary life. Lewes, in the meantime, had turned into a huckster, with himself as product. His chief preoccupation was to generate income by selling his Goethe biography, and to drum up monies from any sources which could use his hackwork. As we observe Lewes writing plays for small sums here and there, we can begin to understand that his suggestion to Marian the following year that she try her hand at fiction was based not only on her potential talent but on the more immediate need for income.

The *Leader* articles Marian wrote, as well as Lewes's contributions, brought little more than a pittance. Lewes's main concern was support of his still growing family—three of them his (Charles at thirteen, Thornie at eleven, and Bertie at nine) and three Agnes's by Hunt. The latter himself was not so well fixed he could afford to support two large establishments (ten by his wife); and for Lewes, there was now the question of private schooling for his sons at Dr. Pearce's Bayswater Academy. Actually, he wanted them to continue and finish their schooling on the continent. We do know he was responsible for Agnes's debts, which were heavy, and which Hunt dallied in paying, if at all. In any given year Lewes barely got beyond what he paid out for Agnes and his sons. * We recognize how thin was the line for Lewes and Marian between living decently and falling slowly through the cracks. The domestic situation for Lewes was not over, either, since Agnes would soon have another child by Hunt. There was an amusing side to this: Lewes scrambling to raise sufficient income so as to support children who seemed to pour from Hunt and Agnes like water flowing from a faucet.

With her companion still in London, Marian was both monetarily and emotionally being drawn into the triangular relationship of Lewes, Agnes, and Hunt, since whenever the latter two got together a child could possibly be conceived, thus adding to the costs Lewes incurred. He was caught in a Malthusian equation, his expenses rising exponentially, his income by slow degrees. For Marian, some little respite came from her reading of Shakespeare, but then more

* In the Berg Collection, we find Lewes's literary receipts, and in 1855 there is a notation that he owed £300, which we can assume was for Agnes's debts. In Eliot's handwriting, the amounts indicate a "minimum of yearly payments to others at £250 for 23 years," or £5,850; to this is added the 300 for a total of £6,150, with complete earnings for these twenty-three years coming to £9,363, leaving a positive balance of £3,213. This carries the entire account through Lewes's death in 1878.

comfort from Chapman's offer to her to oversee the "Belles Lettres" segment of the contemporary literature reviews in the *Westminster;* each segment would bring her £12.10, or £50 for the year. Suddenly, such small sums looked attractive.

This invigorated her enough to work on the Spinoza, but she also paid heavily for the worry and anxiety of the previous days, with nausea and debilitating headaches that once again sound like migraine. One, on 28 March, left her too ill to climb from bed for two days. It was shortly after that she called Bray to task for writing curt letters, one of the few times when annoyance surfaced between them.

In the same letter she mentions that Lewes had gone to Arthur Helps's at Vernon Hill for a week or ten days, an indication that his nerves and general health were cracking under the pressure. We tend to think of the scandal from Marian's point of view—and hers was clearly the heavier burden—but it was also a terribly difficult time for Lewes. He had to deal with the scandal, of course, but he also had to respond to the other scandal, which was by now known to everyone in literary London, the "sooty children" that Agnes was bearing Hunt, the cuckolding Lewes acquiesced to, the shame of it all. There is a further dimension, and that is his commitment to Marian, who was emotionally involved in every part of the relationship, and dependent socially on him. He had to live up to her expectations of him, an ideal she had created for him. This somewhat superficial individual, with a philandering, bantering background, had to transform himself into a very different kind of man.

Given these pressures, he needed a rest cure to calm his nerves and provide some breathing space. Marian told Bray that when Lewes returned to London from Vernon Hill, she would rejoin him—which occurred on 18 April—and they would set up in London until "the big books are fairly through the press. . . ." With this, she hopes their funds will be restored sufficiently for a new journey to the south of Germany and to Italy. The "big books" were Lewes's *Goethe* and her Spinoza translation, which was never published. In that two-week period, before she and Lewes went to live at 8 Victoria Grove Terrace in Bayswater, just north of Kensington Park, Marian had a difficult time, as everything bad seemed to converge. Her journal entries are now full of trepidation and anxieties. The whole question of her relationship to Lewes came into play: not necessarily his loyalty to her, but how the future would be unrolled in his triangular relationship to Marian and his wife. Was Agnes willing to give him up? Was the marriage really over? Was Lewes to be reclaimed now that he had returned? Just what commitment did he have to the mother of his sons, and what was her commitment to the man who accepted her children by Hunt? The entanglement and scandal could seem distant when one was wining and dining with Liszt in Weimar or visiting salons in Berlin, but now in Dover, by herself, Marian could retrace all the possibilities of her position and was forced to confront dimensions she had avoided.

In Edith Simcox's autobiography—Simcox became very close to George Eliot at one time and remained, throughout her life, a devoted emotional slave—we note Cara Bray referring to the situation. Cara told Simcox that Marian before returning to London wanted to know if a reunion between Lewes and Agnes was possible, for if such was the case, her position became completely untenable. Then she would move from lifetime companion to mistress, and she could not possibly sustain the calumny that would follow. There had to be a definite understanding, not only from Lewes's side, but from Agnes's. It was a peculiar quartet; for in the arrangement of bodies, Marian now considered herself Mrs. Lewes even while the legal wife flourished. And the legal Mrs. Lewes, Agnes, was in fact Hunt's wife, not legally, but in point of relationship. There was, of course, off in the shadows, the legal Mrs. Hunt, now ignored. What Marian wanted, in effect, was to be known as Mrs. Lewes without interference, with only the legal barrier standing between her and respectability. According to Simcox, Agnes was more than willing to give up Lewes and hoped Marian could indeed become Mrs. Lewes by marrying her companion. With that assurance, in whatever form it came—Marian's journal is circumspect on the entire episode—she returned to London, to the Bayswater lodging house Lewes had rented; and, on 18 April, she and Lewes set up house as husband and wife. It had been a terrible period.

The Bayswater lodgings remained suitable only as temporary quarters, for two weeks, and then the couple were on the lookout for something more accommodating in location and comfort. One problem with a residence was the question of who would dare to visit in the face of a still growing scandal; a private location was preferable. They found such a place in East Sheen, a suburb near Richmond Park, in Surrey, at 7 Clarence Row—moving there on 2 May 1855—but before that received Chapman in Bayswater on 26 April and Rufa Hennell two days later. Rufa, we recall, was the widow of Charles Hennell and sister-in-law of Cara Bray, who refused to countenance the new state of affairs. Rufa herself had to confront the calumny attached to anyone who dared to run the gauntlet of public opinion.

When Chapman visited, he offered Lewes the chance to write on "The Psychological Errors of Teetotalism," which appeared in the July issue of the *Review*. As a journalist, Lewes could assemble these articles quite rapidly, with some hasty research into physiological matters; but such pieces, while adept, had little medical standing and came around to stain his reputation when he attempted more serious work. At this time, Marian completed "Three Months in Weimar," on 28 April. The two were clearly grasping at anything that would generate income. In an intimate letter to Bray, Marian looks forward to his visit and to a resumption of their close ties. She suggests her condition: "We are panting to be in the country and resume our old habits of undisturbed companionship and work. Mr. Lewes has been much worse since he returned to town and the other evening he alarmed me terribly by fainting. Imagine that I had never seen any one faint before, and that I thought he was dead! You will be able then to understand my condition for three or four minutes until he returned from consciousness." Her hope was that the changed conditions would allow Lewes's nerves to recover.

Before leaving Bayswater, Marian received Bessie Parkes, a clear rebellion on Bessie's part from her father's strictures, and in return Marian dispatched a letter to Bessie the next day to an address Joseph Parkes would not discover; in it she said her friend should address any mail to Lewes at East Sheen. Marian made it clear she would not be addressed by Bessie or Bray, or anyone else, as Miss Evans. That name became anathema.

But the implications go much further for Marian Evans / Marian Lewes. Nothing was simple for her. The need to become a wife has profound reverberations in Marian's background, going back to her indifference to her own mother and her early worship of her father. When Mrs. Evans died, Marian became Evans's wife in all but bed—as domestic manager, companion, reader, tender of the sick man. This position as "wife" was then denied her when he died, and she tried to find equivalents for it in the relationship to Lewes, when at first she served his needs as she had served Evans's. Her assumption of the title "Mrs. Lewes" was so necessary *because* it expressed her feminine side even while her assumption of the name "George Eliot" as nom de plume would express her other, "masculine" side. In that division which cut through every part of her, she insisted on both with equal intensity. *

The East Sheen lodging brought Marian into the kind of setting where she could flourish, recalling the idyllic scenes of her childhood and providing the couple with quiet walks, streams, natural loveliness. All of this encouraged their frayed nerves to recover. While they both enjoyed concerts, operas, and museums, they received their chief sustenance from rural settings. Here they hoped to make the kind of income they needed to live well and to support Lewes's large and still growing family. In 1855, Marian noted in her journal an income of £119.8—which with her trust fund gave her a little over £200 a year. Lewes's earnings came to £430.13, which included £250 for the first thousand copies of his *Goethe*. This was an encouraging improvement over 1854, when he earned a little less than £329. The 1855 total would stabilize in subsequent years, going over £500 in 1856, but dipping below that for 1857–59. In the 1855–56 period, then, Marian and Lewes could count on an income of £600 to £700 a year, more than adequate, if they kept churning out copy (Dorothea Brooke in the late 1820s has £700 a year), but far below what they needed once Lewes's domestic expenses were factored in. † He was, in fact, borrowing heavily to cover Agnes's debts, which he considered his obligation.

With her responsibility for the "Belles Lettres" segment of the *Review*, Marian was suddenly turned from general reviewer into something of a literary critic, an event fortunate for her in the light of her future activities. Increasingly, she

---

* Not unrelated to that, she had to remind Bray not to mention (she says "misquote") anything disparaging that she, Marian, had said about Lewes before she became his companion. She says her remarks have been converted, by Bray, into "a supercilious impertinent expression of disapprobation" on her part. She fears he might let something slip when he is in Lewes's company, and must protect not only her present but her past.

† This is a far cry from Marian's earnings in 1860, with over £4,200 from *Mill* alone. In 1860, Lewes's earnings were one-seventh of hers. Their monetary "collaboration" proved his salvation.

would devote herself to literary subjects, culminating in a long piece for the *Westminster*, "Silly Novels by Lady Novelists," written just as she was attempting her own first fiction. This article appeared in the October 1856 issue, and it was both a departure for Marian and a summation of points she had already made about the "failure" of female novelists. The implication is, of course, that her type of fiction will be different and will not replicate what she perceived as female failings. But all this came later, more than a year away, when Lewes had already been strongly suggesting that she try her hand at fiction.

In other critical comments, Marian criticized Kingsley's *Westward Ho!* for being too "parsonic," an amusing remark given her own penchant for sermonistic writing. She also rides moralism hard in her comments on Geraldine Jewsbury's *Constance Herbert, a Tendenz-roman*. She found Matthew Arnold's sadness and renunciation more appealing, in his *Poems: Second Series*, especially in poems such as "Empedocles on Etna" and "Resignation." As for Tennyson's *Maud*, one of the poet's favorites, her comments in the October 1855 *Review* were scathing. She did not find Tennyson's views on women pleasing—they embodied everything condescending and vindictive that a mid-century Victorian male was capable of—and she found equally unpleasing his saber rattling, his belief that wars (the Crimean War, for example) were regenerative. The Crimean War was, in fact, a triumph of British fumbling and bumbling, a squandering of life on a large scale, and an act of deception toward the British people, who in the main were ignorant of what was going on. Despite her lack of focus on national issues, Marian was not duped by Tennyson's war cries, the male song of blood and sacrifice.

Her taste is revealed in her approval of Thoreau's *Walden*, which she reviewed in the January 1855 issue of the *Westminster* and found quite sympathetic. How could she not have found a receptive voice in Thoreau's paean to solitude and to natural splendor! She found particularly gratifying his joining of a clear eye with a poetic strain which allowed him to turn realism into imaginative prose. But she also found Longfellow's *Hiawatha* sympathetic, and recommended it; that she failed to object to its childish moralism cannot be explained, except that she may have been carried away by the fluidity of the lines and its accessible verse. Her comments on Charlotte Brontë's *Villette*, however, are mature and deeply appreciative, saying she would prefer to read *Villette* for the third time than other novels for the first. We contrast this with Lewes's pronouncement in "The Lady Novelists" (in the July 1852 *Westminster*) that Jane Austen was the greatest artist who has ever written fiction—the perfect master (mistress?) of means and ends. Lewes's insistence on sharply focused social realism would come to have a large influence on Marian's fiction, but she managed, as we shall see, to break away, finding middle ground between Austen and the Brontës. In all, she covered over 150 books in her seven contributions to this segment of the *Review*, including favorable comments on Harriet Beecher Stowe's *Dred*, in October 1856.

Marian had also found, in the 1855–56 period, a way to "double dip," to review in the *Leader* some of the books she had noticed in the *Westminster*. She

had become an avid journalist, with reviews in both of the above journals and
articles in the *Westminster* (five), in *Saturday Review* (four), and in *Fraser's*
(two). One that she prepared as she and Lewes settled into East Sheen was
"Evangelical Teaching: Dr. Cumming" (in the October 1855 *Westminster*), an
article suggested by Chapman as a way of earning some money for Marian. It
was a case of the lamb being exposed to the teeth of the tiger, for Marian simply
ate Cumming up. In this very long piece, she took apart every aspect of Cumming's evangelical beliefs, as though she had been waiting for someone to reexamine her own past beliefs so that she could devastate their fallacies. The review
became less a notice of a particular book than a justification for Marian of the
direction her own life had taken, somewhat on the order of Newman's *Apologia*
after Kingsley's attack on his integrity. Needing to justify her reshaping of herself, Marian found Cumming a handy tool.

Published anonymously—she felt that a female reviewer would be dismissed—
her review demolished the strange ideas Cumming offered up, including the one
that the seventh vial of the Apocalypse was to be poured between 1848 and
1857: the kind of biblical prophecy which disgusted Marian as well as many
other Victorians who held religious beliefs. Prophecies and pronouncements
about the millennium, the age of the world, and the like poured forth in and
around the time of Darwin's book, in 1859. One brief passage near the beginning of the review suggests the tone of the whole: "Let such a man [with a
smattering of science and learning] become an evangelical preacher, he will
then find it possible to reconcile small ability with great ambition, superficial
knowledge with the prestige of erudition, a middling morale with a high reputation for sanctity." The caustic tone undercuts every dimension of Cumming's
ideas on predestination, on the External Being, and on the coming of the millennium—that seventh vial of the Apocalypse, for example. She finds in his
comments an imprisonment, not liberation, of the intellect. His views hamper
the free search for truth. Her conclusion is equally devastating. Cumming's
creed "often obliges him to hope the worst of man, and to exert himself in
proving that the worst is true; but thus far we are happier than he. We have no
theory which requires us to attribute unworthy motives to Dr. Cumming, no
opinions, religious or irreligious, which can make it a gratification to us to detect
him in delinquencies. On the contrary, the better we are able to think of him
as a man, while we are obliged to disapprove him as a theologian, the stronger
will be the evidence for our conviction, that the tendency towards good in
human nature has a force which no creed can utterly counteract, and which
ensures the ultimate triumph of that tendency over all dogmatic perversions."
Although Bulstrode in *Middlemarch* is more complicatedly presented, this portrait of Dr. Cumming provides good foreshadowing.

Not only was Marian shaping her secular ideas, she was also defining her
prose. Her comments have some of that whiplash wit she was able to focus on
her fictional characters. But more than that, she was struggling to achieve a
clarity, which was for her always a difficult matter. Many passages in her fiction
are so dense as to require a hermeneutical reading, what we associate more with

biblical language than with prose fiction. If the *Westminster* pieces involved a sharpening of skills, little engaged her more than theological dispute.

She and Lewes kept mainly to themselves in their rural retreat, the kind of life they hoped to establish permanently. Chapman, of course, visited, and on 8 June brought with him proofs of "The Position of Women in Barbarism and Among the Ancients," an article he had written which in Marian's judgment required considerable revision. First she went after language: ". . . certain old faults reappear—inexactness of expression, triads and duads of verbs and adjectives, mixed metaphors and a sort of watery volume that requires to be reduced by evaporation." She then analyzes particulars. She questions words, precision, or lack of it. She chides him for not demonstrating correct emphasis of points. And then after this onslaught, she adds that the article is "very interesting and able."

Chapman took it well. By this time, he knew her ferocity for detail and for apt expression. When he wrote back inquiring whether to scrap the entire enterprise, Marian responded (on 27 June) that she had commented as she had because she believed the article "worth publishing." She becomes Chapman's mentor: "There is no reason for you to be desponding [sic] about your writing. You have made immense progress during the last few years, and you have as much force of mind and sincerity of purpose that you may work your way to a style which is free of vices, though perhaps you will never attain felicity—indeed, that is a free gift of Nature rather than a reward of labour." She emphasizes she has written merely from "personal and intellectual sympathy." She also made it clear who had the brains.

This period in Surrey was restorative for Marian. Her anxieties about Lewes had been resolved: he remained true and loyal. She had entered into a situation almost entirely of her own shaping, having broken completely the hold upon her of her brother and, before that, her father. Her life as a nightmare, as she described it to friends while she cared for Robert Evans in his last days, had passed into something personally constructive. Certainly, she was still seeking outlets for her talents and her intellectual powers—that was a continuing source of anxiety; but work for the *Review* and *Leader* gave her at least the semblance of having discovered such an outlet. She would, eventually, have to confront what lay beyond East Sheen in the London world of scandal and gossip, but that, too, was possible given the solidity of her companionship with Lewes. She could, in fact, think of herself as Mrs. Lewes. But most of all she had entered that peaceful time, more or less, when reverie and fantasy could work their way through her mind, when imagination could be activated, when potentialities and possibilities were ahead, even if still shadowy and uncertain. This was not the calm before the storm in her life, but the calm that preceded an imaginative leap on her part. Like Crusoe on his island, she had stocked her goods, and this restorative period, even if temporary, was a further source of storing, shaping her imagination, and allowing her knowledge to cohere into something distinctive. All the rest having been preparation, she was on the edge of pulling together the pieces.

Rosehill was much in her thoughts. It was not only friendship she felt nostalgic about, but the source of energy she felt radiated out from the Brays and from her earlier days when they supported her. Although she declared she could if necessary go it alone, she was much frailer than she allowed to be seen. Even in her best times, depression and headaches came on too regularly for us to accept completely her assessment of herself. She hoped to see at least Bray, and he agreed to visit on 10 July, which she looked forward to. When he did arrive, the situation was not particularly congenial to all three: Lewes was ill, with a cold, headache, and facial abscess, ailments that afflicted him for much of his life, and Marian was herself struck with a cold. And there seemed to be a contentious air, indicative of changing positions and loyalties. When the subject turned to phrenology and to George Combe, Lewes went on the attack, finding in that pseudo-science everything contradictory to his early studies in human psychology. Marian sided with Lewes, and this led Bray—who still hung on loyally to Combe's views—to feel she was a turncoat. After Bray left, Marian felt obliged to write a letter to repair the friendship.

Her 16 July letter is almost all apology. She excuses herself as having been ill, the reason "for the very imperfect companionship and entertainment I gave you." She disclaims that Lewes had written a nasty notice of a friend of Bray's, a man named James Silk Buckingham, whose Autobiography was satirized in the Leader when Buckingham was terminally ill. But her chief effort was to mend phrenological fences. She denies she has rejected the "physiological basis," apparently a defection which Bray assumed came from her partisanship of Lewes's psychological basis for behavior. Marian continues: "I never believed more profoundly than I do now that character is based on organization. I never had a higher appreciation than I have now of the services which phrenology has rendered towards the science of man. But I do not, and I think I never shall, consider every man shallow or unconscientious who is unable to embrace all Mr. Combe's views of organology and psychology—especially as some of the ablest men I have ever known are in that position of inability." Nowhere more do we see her positioning of herself for the kind of fiction she would write: that territory where physiology and psychology meet, an area that became so clearly a nineteenth-century battleground and where her voice was so distinctive and commanding.

If we follow some of the articles published later in the century, we see how "physiological" was slowly turning toward "psychological." Staid journals like Cornhill Magazine, Fortnightly Review, and Nineteenth Century included pieces called "Having Two Brains," "Genius and Insanity," "Is Insanity Increasing?," and even "Animal Intelligence." Such articles went against the grain of Victorian optimism and ideas of perfection, which were, in large part, based on physiology.

Marian has walked a tightrope: not embracing Combe, not rejecting Bray completely, and yet leaning toward Lewes's psychological man. Having let Bray almost get away, she needed to reel him back in. They even disagreed, she and Bray, over her caustic review of Lord Brougham's book, mentioned above. "I

consider it criminal in a man," she writes, "to prostitute Literature for the purpose of his own vanity and this is what Lord Brougham has done." She says
that Bray is incorrect in thinking her review was mere "word quibbling": ". . .
Literature is Fine Art, and the man who writes mere literature with insolent
slovenliness is as inexcusable as a man who gets up in a full drawing-room to
sing Rossini's music in a cracked voice and out of tune." In matters of language,
Bray was quite defenseless, given his own infelicities of style, his lack of ear,
and his disorganized sentences. But even at the peril of jeopardizing a friendship,
she insisted on her standards.

Lewes's ailments continued. On 21 July, Marian reported to Sara that he was
tormented with toothache and face pain. "This is a terrible trial to us poor
scribblers, to whom health is money as well as all other things worth having. I
have just been reading that Milton suffered from indigestion and flatulence—
quite an affecting fact to me." Marian herself suffered from indigestion, and she
might have been gratified to know that Carlyle, who lived to a mighty old age,
suffered from that ailment and from flatulence for his entire life. But none of
this was real consolation. Lewes's ailments were painful, and in the primitive
state of medication hardly able to be alleviated. Aspirin, the magic painkiller,
was still some years off. The sole relief came from heavy drugs, like morphine
and opium, cocaine somewhat later.

Normally, Lewes went up to London on regular visits, to see his sons and his
mother, as well as to deliver manuscripts and catch up on London events or
rumors which might affect him and Marian. The boys were kept from knowing
about a second Mrs. Lewes, although they must have been aware of Hunt, the
father of several of their half-siblings. Although Lewes apparently said nothing
to them about his arrangement with Marian, it is quite possible that the pregnant Agnes did, in her effort to be completely open. She did not seem to be
embarrassed by the situation, or else Hunt's magnetism was so powerful that
nothing else mattered. In any event, Lewes took his sons off to Ramsgate for a
week's vacation in August. Marian was left alone, to work on one project or
another, and to mend fences back in Coventry, with both Sara and Bray. Sara
was slowly slipping away, Bray was annoyed by his visit on 10 July, and Cara
had stopped writing.

Repairs were in evidence all around. Marian tried to propitiate Sara by send-
ing on autographs, Sara being an avid collector: Liszt and Currer Bell (Charlotte
Brontë), among others. Sara even visited in early September, but did not find
the couple at home. While working on her scathing review of Dr. Cumming,
Marian wrote the Brays and addressed Cara after a year's silence. Her letter of 4
September is truly an *apologia pro vita sua*, or at least posing as one. Part of
Marian's defense is that she has changed and that Cara more than anyone
should be tolerant of change, since she herself had supported Marian when religious change was altering her mental condition. The latter attributes Cara's
coldness and remonstrative letter to her ignorance of Lewes's true character.
This was easy to do, since he, too, had changed. "If we differ on the subject of
the marriage laws, I at least can believe of you that you cleave to what you

believe to be good, and I don't know anything in the nature of your views that should prevent you from believing the same of me."

She tried again to state her position, and we must be clear she was not merely attempting to convince Cara but to defend this entire period of her life.

That any unworldly, unsuperstitious person who is sufficiently acquainted with the realities of life can pronounce my relation to Mr. Lewes immoral I can only understand by remembering how subtle and complex are the influences that mould opinion. But I *do* remember this, and I indulge in no arrogant or uncharitable thoughts about those who condemn us, even though we might have expected a somewhat different verdict. . . . We are leading no life of self-indulgence, except indeed, that being happy in each other, we find everything easy. We are working hard to provide for others better than we provide for ourselves, and to fulfil every responsibility that lies upon us.

She assures Cara—whom she would not see for another four years—that if there is one subject on which she feels no sense of levity, it is marriage and the relations of the sexes; and if there has been any one act of her life which can be called serious it is her relation to Lewes. She apologizes further for perhaps seeming cold and self-asserting, but her aim, she assures Cara, is to demonstrate her love for her and her desire to relieve her friend of the pain she says she has suffered. She assures her, still further, that she has not forgotten the words and deeds of kindness shown her in the past. "But if we should never be very near each other again, dear Cara, do bear this faith in your mind, that I was not insensible or ungrateful to all your goodness, and that I am one amongst the many for whom you have not lived in vain."

Diplomatic, assertive, apologetic, ungiving: Marian's letter is all of these, but it is also deceptive. For the grand issue behind the entire episode, for Cara and Sara and for others, including men, is about sex. Sex with Lewes might not seem like much to those who found him ugly, even repulsive, but nevertheless it remained a considerable factor; and it is, of course, given her reticence, the very point Marian omits. She writes of a relationship, of their working together without self-indulgence; but what was also apparent was that they were physically compatible, the experienced Lewes and the less sophisticated, but possibly not unknowing, Marian.

In one respect, Marian's relationship to Lewes, the sexual side of it, not the question of her having broken up a marriage, became the test of those who could abide the situation and those who could not confront it rationally. As we can see, Cara could not confront it, especially since her handsome husband himself had a wandering eye—however much she had agreed to an open marriage. This ongoing drama of alternating candor and disguise, incidentally, would serve Marian quite well when she came to write fiction, even though she transcended sexual questions by posing them in different terms.

Despite the general contentment at Surrey, all of this shadowy play had some physical effect on the Leweses, making them ill, headachy, out of sorts. Lewes returned from his week with his sons, but by then he and Marian decided East Sheen had worn out its welcome, and they moved for two weeks to Worthing, six miles west of Brighton, in West Sussex, on 19 September. At Worthing, they took a fortnight's lodgings, and the holiday seemed to do them good. They bathed, walked the beach, sought out some geological data which Lewes stored up for future articles or books. On 3 October, they returned to Surrey and settled into lodgings at 8 Park Shot in Richmond, just south of London. They would remain there for three and a half years—a fine location, with easy access to the city and the Thames; but, of course, they were lodgers, with the presence of other guests in the house, owned by a Mrs. Croft. Marian posed here as Mrs. Lewes and was quite insistent, indeed fearful, that no one call her Miss Evans. "We find it indispensable to our comfort," she writes Bessie Parkes, "that I should bear Mr. Lewes's name while we occupy lodgings, and we are now with an excellent woman that any cause of removal would be a misfortune."

Marian's insistent tone here with "Mrs. Lewes" further resonates in her name change to George Eliot a year and a half later. That she took Lewes's first name, after assuming his last name, is more than symbolic, it is symbiotic; and it is further connected not only to her desire to be thought a male author for personal and commercial reasons, but to put aside, finally, the whole question of what to call herself. The name changes, in a respect not to be neglected, also gave her the ability to effect a gender alteration and to take on the masculine power she had always coveted—as a name change did with the French author George Sand, another "George" whose name lay in the background of Eliot's choice. The masculine power meant freedom of maneuverability, a matter, really, of free expression and liberation. It did not mean she forsook her femininity—on this she was quite clear—but it suggested she could add another, the masculine, side.

Behind all the women who came to worship her, Edith Simcox being the most obvious, was their feeling she had taken on the mantle of masculinity and all its strengths in the nineteenth century. It is uncertain whether they adored her as a female turned male—despite her feminine appearance—or as a male; whether they worshipped her as a strong woman, or as a woman who had crossed over. In some ironical way, as Marian settled in as Lewes's wife, she transformed herself with a male disguise. She was not only competitive, she was reshaped.

Reports as though from a hospital continue. Spencer, we learn, suffered a nervous collapse and was resting in France. Lewes was moving in and out of ailments, as was Marian, although in somewhat lesser degree—since she had settled down, her health had improved. Chapman was on the edge of dangerous pulmonary problems, probably the onset of tuberculosis. But work they all did, Lewes and Marian toiling away at their Surrey lodgings. By September of 1855, Lewes had completed his biography of Goethe, which was to appear in two volumes on 1 November as *The Life and Works of Goethe, with Sketches of His Age and Contemporaries*. The work was dedicated to Thomas Carlyle, who had pioneered the English interest in German literature and was himself established as a biographer. Carlyle was genuinely pleased with the book. It is perhaps Lewes's most solid piece of work, indicating that his skills lay not in fiction—his two novels are quite weak—but in biographical narrative and historical reconstruction of a period.

As noted earlier, Marian gave the book a long review in the *Leader*, really a notice rather than a critical review. The book enjoyed splendid notices and was reprinted in America and translated on the continent. It brought in steady monies—comprising the larger part of Lewes's income for 1855 and 1856 and far outdistancing the sums any of his other work brought.

Marian's own "Cumming" piece made a strong impression, although published anonymously. Her old friend Mary Sibree (now Mrs. John Cash) was much taken with it, and she and Bray were certain it was by Marian, which brought Marian's request to Bray for the authorship to be kept secret. We see in this, of course, still another foreshadowing of her position later when she published her first fiction. Far more important than the "Cumming" piece, which was really left-handed work for Marian, was her immersion in an immensely long study on the German poet Heinrich Heine. Chapman, once more, provided the impetus for this, suggesting she write on Heine for the *Westminster*, an article which appeared in January 1856 and filled thirty-three of its large pages. Marian called it "German Wit: Heinrich Heine," and it was really the first serious treatment of the poet and his work in English, preceding Matthew Arnold's more famous piece on Heine in 1863.

Marian has not received her full credit for introducing German literature and thought into England, Carlyle seemingly having preempted that role, with Lewes a somewhat distant second. She was more than equal to their efforts. The couple had met Heine's friend Varnhagen von Ense in Berlin and, as we will see later, Marian's literary sympathies fitted well with Heine's caustic wit and ever-present irony. Her piece was published just one month before the German poet died, in February 1856. We get some sense of her approach when she writes of him as having "a real voice," calling him "one of the most remarkable men of this age: no echo, but a real voice. . . . a surpassing lyric poet. . . . a humorist, who touches leaden folly with the magic wand of his fancy, and transmutes it into the fine gold of art. . . ." Not the least, Marian provided large chunks of Heine's poetry in her own translation and thus made available to the English reader the work itself.

At Christmas, she went, alone of course, to visit Chrissey and her children at Attleborough. She went with secrets, not mentioning Lewes or her "married" situation, and probably not seeing Isaac, who lived at Griff. She had sent a copy of Lewes's *Goethe* to Bray, but did not see him either on this visit, very possibly because of the friction existing between her and Cara. We can judge, from her letters, that she recognized she was intellectually superior to everyone she had left behind in Coventry, including Bray and all the subsidiary figures, and that this knowledge was affecting her relationship to them. From her London vantage point, Coventry seemed narrow, provincial, a far-removed miniature world. By New Year's she had returned to Richmond and sent Bray holiday greetings.

In her New Year's letter to Bray, she explains why she could not accept his invitation to visit. She says, quite frankly, that she was "not likely to take a journey twice as long as necessary and walk all through Coventry in order to make a call where I had only the invitation of the master of the house." Cara's continuing coolness kept her away, or so she pretends, and her words to Bray clearly separate husband from wife as her friend. But more than that was involved: Marian was preparing herself for a new life, and she was settling her affairs with her old friends, not through outright rejection, but through placement of them just outside her interests.

Lewes had gone for the holiday to Arthur Helps's, and Marian's journal indicates she kept herself occupied, almost frenetically, so as to pass the time until his return. Her frenetic pace reinforces the fact that she now considered herself incomplete without Lewes's presence; that she needed his emotional support for her endeavors. We can see from her Christmas / New Year reading list what variety she was capable of, from George Meredith's satiric *The Shaving of Shagpat* to Kingsley's *Greek Heroes*, Kahnis's *History of German Protestantism*, and most recently Peter Von Bohlen's *Introduction to Genesis*. Much of this reading went into the "Belles Lettres" section of the *Westminster* or into individual reviews in the *Leader*.

At this time, she was revising her translation of Book IV of Spinoza's *Ethics*, while moving along with Book V. Leading up to this time, as 1855 turned to 1856, she had been reading steadily in the classics: the *Iliad*, in Greek, then a progression through Greek drama, Sophocles' *Antigone*, *Ajax*, the Oedipus trilogy, *Electra*, and *Philoctetes*, followed by Aeschylus, the Oresteia trilogy. This love for classical Greek and its literature she maintained through her years of fame and fortune, and she drew heavily on the Greek myths for images and passages in her fiction. As always, she remained on familiar terms with the Latin writers: Virgil, Cicero, Horace, Tacitus, Plautus, and others. She kept up with this solid reading even when she was occupied with her own writing.

The heavy reading schedule may be attributed to the enormous amounts of time she found herself with because of social ostracism, when Lewes was invited alone to dinner and apparently went, or else to the long evenings when the two of them remained by themselves. But the reading probably derived from something deeper than the need to occupy herself; it went to the heart of how she felt about being a woman who had not had the opportunity to study at a public school where the classics were made available to the sons of the privileged, or to study at Oxford or Cambridge when she felt more than equal to those who attended. The vast reading gave her an edge over most of the men she did meet socially, or whom she edited or reviewed. Her reading went to the heart of her personal pride, that she was capable of anything, that hindrances placed on her because of gender (and, even, because of social ostracism) would not impede the advance of one thing she knew she had, capacious intellectual powers.

Reading, in Latin and Greek, in French and German, and later in Spanish, Italian, and Hebrew, gave her a personal, self-perceived stature that no society could blemish. Reading, also, served a somewhat unfortunate function in that it revealed to her how far she had outdistanced her Coventry friends; indeed, how she had removed herself from the run of well-known people who had frequented Chapman's Strand location. Even Lewes was far outdistanced, as both of them were implicitly aware.

Lewes's work on Goethe made him resolve to delve more deeply into scientific research, since one chapter of his biography was called "The Poet as Man of Science." Lewes was more an intuitive scientist than the kind who worked with scalpel and microscope. Thus comes Huxley's nasty charge that he was a "book-scientist," a charge, incidentally, which ignored the fact of Lewes's early medical training. In any event, Lewes decided to focus more thoroughly on the nuts and bolts of science; not merely on methods, but on actual investigation. Marian, in fact, enjoyed entering into this activity. She had always been interested in scientific processes, had attended lectures in advanced physics, and seemed capable of digesting whatever matter was presented in book or lecture. Together, they decided to explore seashore and mountains for aspects of inorganic matter which, later, might become part of a scientific theory.

She also became peripherally concerned with women's issues—"peripherally" because such matters came and went in her correspondence and life without fully engaging her. For her real involvement, we must turn to her fiction, where her responses to women's issues are everywhere. But the case of Mrs. Caroline Norton involved Marian's sympathies. Mrs. Norton could not get support from her separated husband and eventually brought on a petition, circulated by Barbara Leigh Smith, to be sent to Parliament. The petition asked that "married women may have a legal right to their own earnings, as a counteractive to wife-beating and other evils." Despite her usual hesitation about being drawn into such matters, Marian signed it and then told Sara that if she and Cara were interested, she would send it on for their signatures. She characterizes the petition (which appeared in its entirety in the *Review* for October 1856, along with the names of a twenty-four-woman committee) as "well and soberly drawn up, and has been signed by Mrs. Gaskell, Harriet Martineau," and many others. Adding to her comments, Marian says that Harriet Martineau—still badmouthing Lewes and, by implication, Marian—is doing valuable work, even though the *Review* rejected her article on the "factory question" because she so violently attacked Dickens.

Now on the virtual eve of Marian's turning to fiction writing, however intense the inner coordinates, she gave little *overt* indication of the dramatic transformation which would take place. She was still much involved in *Review* affairs, full of comments on recent or current articles, always on the edge of the latest literary gossip, ready to discuss nearly any issue, reading steadily, yet not giving any intimation of what was to come. Scandal—both known and unknown to her—still whirled around her: in the background a letter from Mrs. Anna Jameson, a writer, to Ottilie von Goethe (Goethe's daughter-in-law) which acknowledged Marian's first-rate intellect and achievements, but "considered [her] also as very *free* in all her opinions as to morals and religion." Mrs. Jameson says she does not "well understand how a good and conscientious woman can run away with another woman's husband. . . ." Smacking her lips, she says she fears all the stories of Lewes and his wife are true. Although Marian pretended not to care, there was, she recognized, no protection against such a misreading of what had occurred despite her efforts at explanation. All she could do was to put such gossip to good use fictionally and insist even more firmly on being called Mrs. Lewes.

The Brays, meanwhile, were suffering from the economic depression in Coventry, the result of a sharp drop in textile manufacturing, and they would soon be forced to leave Rosehill as too expensive for them to keep up.* With their troubles in mind, Marian reports more communiqués from the hospital: Lewes's head still infirm, poor Herbert Spencer unable to read more than a quarter of an hour together, and herself "a croaker." There were questions about what to do with Lewes's two older boys, matters of schooling and in what country, and how much tutoring they might need. The Hofwyl School, north of Berne, Switzerland, became a distinct possibility; Hofwyl enjoyed considerable renown and had a distinguished group of alumni. In April, Spencer was capable of coming to London, and he took Lewes and Marian to the reestablished Crystal Palace, now in Sydenham. Spencer spoke of the coast—he had been to Tenby, on a wild peninsula in southern Wales—and although he disliked it, as he disliked every place he went, he did report enthusiastically about the marine life there. This appealed to Lewes and his scientific interests, and whatever seemed to make Lewes happy Marian accommodated. They both agreed that she could continue to write for the *Westminster* and the *Leader*, while Lewes carried out his researches. Still stung by Huxley's characterization of him as an amateur, he was eager to prove him wrong.

The couple set out for Ilfracombe, on the Bristol Channel, the north shore of Devon, on 8 May, hoping to combine all their interests. Marian left a long description of their experience in her journal, from 3 May to 26 June. They carried with them a hamper of tall glass jars, which they meant for their seaside vivarium. Marian suffered from her usual headache, a typical affliction when she made a move, even a desirable one. They found a lovely spot at Northfield, for a guinea a week in May, a guinea and a half in June. She had plenty to do, a review for the *Westminster* of Wilhelm Heinrich Riehl's *The Natural History of German Life*, which she had not yet read (in German), and the article for the "Belles Lettres" section of the *Review*. Ilfracombe town she found ugly, but the

---

* Although Bray was an unlikely businessman, and appeared to spend little time on his enterprises, his ribbon manufacturing firm was going under through no fault of his. Coventry was caught in a general falloff in cloth, textiles, and related industries. He and Cara did have an income to fall back upon, about £400 a year, which enabled him, barely, to devote himself to his writing and to his social reforms. Within a year, the Brays had moved from Rosehill, and that, too, became for Marian only a memory, part of that effacement of the past she had been experiencing for several years.

surrounding areas enchanting. As they extended their walks, Marian began to think in geological and zoological terms. As the following passage demonstrates, her thinking here will become part of her permanent "analogous mind." Those repeated passages in her fiction linking man to nature, her use of man–animal parallels, and her man–plant associations all seem to become fixed here. She was focusing on a world Darwin would develop and explain in far greater detail, but the accommodation of man and nature was already implicit for her well before Darwin, as we can see from her comments in her journal.

> . . . when one sees a house stuck on the side of a great hill, and still more a number of houses looking like a few barnacles clustered on the side of a great rock, we begin to think of the strong family likeness between ourselves and all other buildings, burrowing-house-appropriating and shell-secreting animals. The difference between a man with his house and a mollusc with its shell lies in the number of steps or phenomena interposed between the fact of individual existence and the completion of the building. . . . Look at man in the light of a shell-fish and it must be admitted that his shell is generally ugly, and it is only after a great many more "steps or phenomena" that he secretes here and there a wonderful shell in the shape of a temple or palace.

Her remarks on sea life nearly all contain descriptive aspects which move from biology or zoology to human attributes, as though she were searching on this trip for some way of expressing herself through a world beyond. The fact that she and Lewes were seeking diversity, not uniformity, is another indication of how the stay in Ilfracombe fed into Marian's fictional needs. While not forsaking generalities, she learned to identify specifics, "the pale fawn coloured tentacles of an Anthea Cereus waving like little serpents, in a low tide pool."

By 17 June, her articles were dispatched, an indication of her discipline: observing, reading, writing, organizing, and revising. Before leaving for Ilfracombe, she had completed her translation of Spinoza, and when Lewes saw it was not to be published, he went into a rage. Her journal omits this unpleasant development. With the articles out of the way, she announces: "I felt delightfully at liberty and determined to pay some attention to sea-weeds which I had never seen in such beauty as at Ilfracombe." With that, Marian revelled in the flora of the shoreline with the enthusiasm of a budding zoologist. She even consulted a reference book, David Landsborough's *A Popular History of British Sea-Weeds* (1849). The indications are that her mind took so many turns it is possible that if she and Lewes had not needed income, she might have turned to other fields where observation of detail prevailed, not the least zoology. She and Lewes took prodigious walks, one to Chambercombe, a wooded area. She noted carefully what appeared before them and what a more casual eye might pass over: brooks, lanes, bridges, tufts of fern, a donkey path, leafage of all kinds. She was structuring her realism, not unlike the way Darwin was building his arguments for evolutionary theory based on keen observation.

On 29 May, England publicly rejoiced at the commemoration of the peace with Russia, on 29 April 1856, the formal end of the Crimean War. The celebration, held one month after the signing, brought to a close a terrible war for the British, most of whom were unaware of the disasters, the losses, the miscalculations, the unnecessary victims of illness and disease. Neither the war nor its termination seemed a large matter to Marian or to Lewes. Their meanderings were the main event, for here she could focus on the ordinary and trivial elements which fill rural life.

These rural observations were reinforced by her reading and review of Riehl's *Natural History of German Life*, for the July 1856 *Westminster*. She had already praised the third volume of Ruskin's *Modern Painters* in the April 1856 *Review*, having found that in him, as in her own observations, all truth and beauty were to be achieved through a faithful study of nature. All of her faculties were coming together and becoming more than "observation"; rather, they were being shaped into a point of view, a style, a way to proceed into her unique kind of realism. A further point: the Wordsworthian presence is powerful here, and it remained, with its belief in the people, its faith in the natural order, its devotion to the observation of the ordinary and the trivial, although on occasion Marian could be caustic about Wordsworthian excesses.* Not the least, her strong attachment to history and memory became part of this Wordsworthian desire to conserve, and we are not surprised to find that nearly all of her fiction is associated with previous historical eras, especially those in and around the time she was born or being brought up.

In one particular passage from her journal about Ilfracombe, we see her looking at nature with the eye of a realistic painter. In speaking of the Ilfracombe "lanes," she says one should know the names of all the flowers clustered on their banks. "The desire [to know the names of all things] is part of the tendency that is now constantly growing in me to escape from all vagueness and inaccuracy into the daylight of distinct, vivid ideas." She knows that merely to name an object "tends to give definiteness to our conception of it—we have then a sign that at once calls up in our minds the distinctive qualities which mark out for us that particular object from all others."

Here, clearly, was a statement about her literary method, what she repeats in different terms in that passage at the beginning of Book Two of *Adam Bede*: her theory of the ordinary as heroic in its way, even while the author eschews the heroic itself. In the review of Riehl's *Natural History*, she said much the same. We have, here, the thrill of self-discovery. She is careful to avoid Wordsworthian sentimentality: peasants are not joyous, they are not rosy and merry,

---

* Among poets, her use of nine epigraphs from Wordsworth was exceeded only by the thirty-one from Shakespeare; overwhelmingly, however, such epigraphs as appear in her fiction derive from herself.

their lives are not idyllic. If tempted by a pocketbook, they may not even be honest. She says that the painter, under the influence of idyllic literature which exalts, expresses the "imagination of the cultivated and town-bred, rather than the truth of rustic life." She then defines, in this review of Riehl, her own world, as against that of her imaginary "idyllic" painter:

> Idyllic ploughmen are jocund [for such painters] when they drive their team afield; idyllic shepherds make bashful love under hawthorn bushes; idyllic villagers dance in the chequered shade and refresh themselves, not immoderately, with spicy nut-brown ale. But no one who has seen much of actual ploughmen thinks them jocund; no one who is well acquainted with the English peasantry can pronounce them merry. The slow gaze, in which no sense of beauty beams, no humour twinkles—the slow utterance, and the heavy slouching walk, remind one rather of the melancholy animal the camel, than of the sturdy countryman.

Similarly, a group of haymakers: from a distance, they toss up the hay, the sun shines brightly, and you pronounce the scene "smiling," the workers bright and cheerful, the work handily accomplished. "Approach nearer, however," Marian writes, "and you will certainly find that haymaking time is a time for joking, especially if there are women among the labourers; but the coarse laugh that bursts out every now and then, and expresses the triumphant taunt, is as far as possible from your conception of idyllic merriment. That delicious effervescence of the mind which we call fun, has no equivalent for the northern peasant, except tipsy revelry; the only realm of fancy and imagination for the English crown exists at the bottom of the third quart pot."

This recalls Coleridge's hard-nosed response to Wordsworth's sentimentalized preface to the second edition of the *Lyrical Ballads*, his much more realistic view of common people and the tawdriness of their ordinary lives. Marian is more sympathetic than Coleridge, but she insists on the truth of observation, not the idyllic eye of poet or painter. Fidelity to truth lies on another level of existence. Then in an extremely significant passage, she takes on the one writer who will be her competitor when she turns to fiction. Charles Dickens had for the past twenty years commanded the English fictional scene; but with Eliot's work in the 1860s and then in the 1870s, after Dickens's death, she became the "other" novelist of the period. In this same piece, she must locate Dickens, to indicate her homage and her difference. Dickens (unnamed) is the "one great novelist who is gifted with the utmost power of rendering the external traits of our town population; and if he could give us their psychological character—their conception of life, and their emotions—with the same truth as their idiom and manners, his books would be of great contribution."

The distinction she draws is psychological, her own great contribution and what she finds lacking in Dickens: ". . . he scarcely ever passes from the humourous and external to the emotional and tragic, without becoming as transcendent in his unreality as he was a moment before in his artistic truthfulness."

The next lines are self-serving, although ostensibly still about Dickens: "But for the precious salt of his humour, which compels him to reproduce external traits that serve, in some degree, as a corrective to his frequently false psychology, his preternaturally virtuous poor children and artisans, his melodramatic boatmen and courtesans, would be as noxious as Eugène Sue's idealized proletaires [Marie Joseph (Eugène) Sue, best known for *Les Mystères de Paris*, 1842–43] in encouraging the miserable fallacy that high morality and refined sentiment can grow out of harsh social relations, ignorance, and want; or that the working-classes are in a condition to enter at once into a millennial state of *altruism*, wherein everyone is caring for everyone else, and no one for himself."

The onslaught is not restricted to those who idealize peasants or other laboring classes, but includes those who, like Herbert Spencer, catch up social views in larger, abstract efforts and call it science. "The tendency," she writes, "created by the splendid conquests of modern generalization, to believe that all social questions are merged in economical science, and that the relations of men to their neighbours may be settled by algebraic equations,—the dream that the uncultured classes are prepared for a condition which appeals principally to their moral sensibilities,—the aristocratic dilettantism which attempts to restore the 'good old times' by a sort of idyllic masquerading, and to grow feudal fidelity and veneration as we grow prize turnips, by an artificial system of culture,—none of these diverging mistakes can co-exist with a real knowledge of the People, with a thorough study of their habits, their ideas, their motives." Here she sideswipes Carlyle's feudal ideal, but primarily goes after Disraeli's so-called Young England movement, an effort by a few in the upper classes to forge an alliance with the lower classes in order to restructure England. This political movement was, amusingly, characterized as radical Toryism.

Marian wishes that English writers could capture the natural history of the English social classes as well as Riehl does for the German; then Britain would have the basis for real social reform—reform based on the truth of observation rather than on some idyllic vision or cooked statistics. This enormously long essay must be viewed along with her article "Silly Novels by Lady Novelists," which appeared in the October 1856 *Westminster*. Both pieces establish her on the edge of her fictional writing career, when she needed to define not what she was, but what she believed; when she sought to find coherence in her reading and thinking as preparation for creative work. The first of the *Scenes of Clerical Life*, "The Sad Fortunes of the Rev. Amos Barton," was begun on 23 September and completed on 5 November, paralleling neatly the review of Riehl and the writing of the "Silly Novels" article. More and more pieces were coming together.

The thorny question of who influenced whom in novelistic theory—whether Lewes influenced Eliot or she him—probably cannot be disentangled. After we sift the chronological order—Lewes's 1852 "The Lady Novelists," Eliot's 1856 "Silly Novels by Lady Novelists," Lewes's 1858 "Realism in Art: Recent German Fiction," Eliot's comments on realism in *Adam Bede*, her 1859 novel—we should not speak of influence, but of parallel ideas. Lewes's realism was not based on verisimilitude but on a "representation of Reality," with character altered by circumstance or cultural context. While Eliot did follow many of Lewes's ideas on realism, some of which she was familiar with before she met him, in several novels she enlarged on his ideas with abundant psychological analysis and somewhat sensational scenes which fall outside of his sense of representation.

Implicit in Eliot's realistic presentation of commonplace life was not a small amount of determinism, although her naturalism, as the French critic Ferdinand Brunetière indicated, was different from more rigid French naturalists like Balzac and Zola. Her deterministic, naturalistic component derived from several areas: the ideas of Charles Hennell, then Strauss and Feuerbach, given further validity by Comte, and, finally, Darwin. But more than that was a certain degree of finality in Eliot's moral ideas, and not unrelated was her experience of periodic depression, which convinced her that certain things do not change whatever their external appearance. As a figure of change herself, she doubted that fundamental change was universally possible—and this, too, reinforced her belief in a determinism that gripped, like depression.

A clue to Eliot's own artistic development perhaps comes in her *Westminster* notice (July 1855) of Matthew Arnold's *Poems, Second Series*. She speaks of his "deep thought" linked to an "exquisite sensibility," and from this we can see how thought or ideas—in Arnold's case pessimistic ideas which ran against public Victorian optimism—would overtake her earlier reliance on commonplace realism. Her attack on female "Silly Novels" was based on her belief that such authors lacked moral and intellectual stature, the very qualities she found in Arnold.

Coinciding with these two momentous pieces of writing—"Amos Barton" and "Silly Novels"—was a sequence of journal entries which indicated her commitment to an emerging self, the life of a fiction writer. These entries came in July; but before this, she and Lewes left Ilfracombe, on 26 June, for Tenby, on the Welsh coast. During the long trip—a Swansea boat, a train, then a coach to Tenby—Marian was alive to observations. Two cockle women caught her attention, and she notes the lines of their faces, the majesty of their carriage, the impress of heavy work in their countenances. Tenby itself proved felicitous, for five weeks, of tramping, searching for mollusks and other matter, reading in science and in Shakespeare. When Barbara Leigh Smith spent four days with Lewes and Marian in July (the 12th through 16th), she gained a real sense of how the couple got on. Smith wrote Bessie Parkes, who intensely disliked Lewes, that she, Smith, had nothing but good feelings about him; that he was excellent for Marian; and that their relationship, which was highly sexual, seemed to make them happy.* But this news was no more than what we already

---

* The material for this was accessible only to Gordon Haight, who was informed about Smith's letter to Bessie by Bessie's daughter, Mrs. Belloc Lowndes. Mrs. Lowndes had destroyed the letter, and told Haight about it in 1942. The fact that the letter was destroyed suggests it was quite intimate; Haight himself says that Smith "explained that the Leweses practiced some form of birth control, and intended to have no children" (Haight, p. 205).

suspect: the relationship to Lewes was not solely mental compatability but physically satisfactory as well.

Yet transcending all this is the beginning of a new tone in Marian's journal. She says she does not wish to do an article for the *Westminster* for the coming quarter. "I am anxious to begin my fiction-writing, and so am not inclined to undertake an article that will give me much trouble. . . ." Toward September of 1856, this became consolidated into a firm commitment. All the pieces were now in place, including, as we shall see, Lewes's strong urging. In her journal, Marian appeared certain of her intentions, in a segment called "How I Came to Write Fiction" (written on 6 December 1857).

It had always been a vague dream of mine that some time or other I might write a novel, and my shadowy conception of what the novel was to be, varied, of course, from one epoch of my life to another. But I never went farther towards the actual writing of the novel than an introductory chapter describing a Staffordshire village [perhaps part of that 1846 effort which came to nothing] and the life of the neighbouring farm houses, and as the years passed on I lost any hope that I should ever be able to write a novel, just as I desponded about everything else in my future life.

The last line indicates how associated fiction writing was with Marian's general feelings; and it suggests that until she put her skewed personal life into some order she was incapable of delving deeply into her imagination for whatever was required for fiction. Novels, for her, insisted on a probe into childhood or young adulthood which only on the surface seemed happy; beneath the surface were unresolved or even traumatic experiences she could not face as long as her present personal life offered no respite. By "traumatic," one does not mean large-scale events—none of these appears to have existed—but those events which became traumatic to the sufferer by virtue of her sensitivity to what might be minuscule to someone else. Marian's ultra-sensitivity very likely made her more aware of life around her than we can probe from this distance; and that awareness, bottled up within her extraordinary intelligence, but without release or compensation, created in her a blocked or entrapped body of material which only a more resolved future life could release. We can say, accordingly, that her ordering of her life *in rebellion* against virtually everything socially restrictive in her upbringing was as much a release as was the attention from a man like Lewes.

In her explanation of why she waited so long, she puts the causes more in technical than personal terms. "I always thought I was deficient in dramatic power, both of construction and dialogue, but I felt I should be at my ease in the descriptive parts of a novel." To work her way through this feeling of inadequacy, she made sure her early novellas, in *Scenes of Clerical Life*, were more descriptive by far than dramatic. Drama, such as it is, is mainly held in the past, or assimilated into a narrative process. We need only look at the first pages of "Amos Barton" to observe how description was dominant in her mind—the sense of place, the awareness of time as caught in history and memory, the studied avoidance of dramatic detail.

Still offering her explanation of how and why she went forward, she says she pulled out that earlier, aborted effort, from 1846, and read it to Lewes. "He was struck with it as a bit of concrete description, and it suggested to him the possibility of my being able to write a novel, though he distrusted—indeed disbelieved in, my possession of any dramatic power. Still, he began to think that I might as well try, some time, what I could do in fiction." When they returned from Germany, in March 1855, Lewes observed what great success she had in other kinds of writing: ". . . his impression that it was worth while to see how far my mental power would go towards the production of a novel was strengthened." He urged her to try to write a story, and in Tenby he prodded her to begin at once. She says she deferred it, but one morning when she was lying in bed, "thinking what should be the subject of my first story, my thoughts merged themselves into a dreamy doze, and I imagined myself writing a story of which the title was—'The Sad Fortunes of the Reverend Amos Barton'. I was soon wide awake and told G." He agreed it was a "capital title" and from then on, Marian decided it should be her first story.

When we read a passage like the following in "Amos Barton," we see how it blends in with her earlier observations, so that there is an unbroken line between her experiences and her fictional beginnings. She did not, as her journal suggests, suddenly plunge in and, caught by reverie, decide to write fiction. She had *been there* before she actually arrived. By Chapter Five, she is eager to demonstrate that her Amos Barton is no ideal or exceptional figure, and she wonders if she is trying a bold thing by attempting to interest the reader in such an ordinary fellow. Anti-heroic, Amos is an indication of Marian's more general effort to demystify the heroic, turn it inside out. Most of her English countrymen are of this "insignificant stamp."

> At least eighty out of a hundred of your adult male fellow-Britons returned in the last census are neither extraordinarily silly, nor extraordinarily wicked, nor extraordinarily wise; their eyes are neither deep and liquid with sentiment [a swipe at the popular upper-class "silver fork" novels], nor sparkling with suppressed witticisms; they have probably had no hairbreadth escapes or thrilling adventures; their brains are certainly not pregnant with genius, and their passions have not manifested themselves at all after the fashion of a volcano.

Instead, they are men of a different complexion, "more or less muddy, whose conversation is more or less bald and disjointed." Yet, "these commonplace people—many of them—bear a conscience, and have felt the sublime prompting to do the painful right; they have their unspoken sorrows, and their sacred joys; their hearts have perhaps gone out towards their first-born, and they have mourned over the irreclaimable dead." They have by their very insignificance gained pathos—"in our comparison of their dim and narrow existence with the glorious possibilities of that human nature which they share."

How, then, would Marian avoid the kind of stifling realism which closes down imaginative activity? Would she become a Zola, a depicter of small lives caught in a destiny they cannot control, a cataloguer of facts? Would she close down even more, like the character Biffen in George Gissing's *New Grub Street* somewhat later? As himself a novelist, Biffen portrays only the most trivial details, without comment or assessment. Such fiction—and to this we could add much of George Sand's—concerns the ordinary, the quotidian, and it would of course be "realistic." If we accept Marian's comments on the ordinary fellow and his ordinary mate, such would appear to be her plan. Yet she was not going to do this at all. Like Flaubert, she planned to heroize the insignificant until it radiated importance. Adam Bede, her first novelistic (as apart from novella) protagonist, works at ordinary things, as a master carpenter, but Adam strides with larger than trivial steps. He thinks with more than low thoughts, and he acts with large swings of personality and temperament which raise his stature far above the ordinary fellows in Marian's theories. Clearly, she worked fictionally at other levels of enlargement and expansion. For she omits in her description here how her own commentary would intensify the level of discourse; how by introducing herself through external commentary, just outside the narrative, she would intensify the lives of ordinary characters, transforming them into more universal figures and, thereby, conveying to them increased stature. In still another respect, she gave her characters ambitions and hopes for the future. Their daily lives may have been ordinary, but they have plans which raise their energy levels or reinforce their desire for personal change. Even when they are caught in the trivial run of life, they have thoughts which run on intensely. Like Sisyphus, a frequent reference for Eliot, they may push the boulder eternally, but their minds cannot be enslaved.

Marian would have a good deal more to say about her fictional efforts in her journal remarks in December of 1857, but now, in the foreground, in the fall of 1856, she started to write. Theorizing came afterward. More immediate was her life with Lewes and her writing of an article / review for the *Westminster* which was another stage in her movement toward fiction. "Silly Novels by Lady Novelists" was completed on 12 September, and her writing of "Amos Barton" was begun on 23 September. The background for Marian's article is interesting, since it started with her desire to attack the idea of "compensation"—that one is compensated for good deeds with passage into heaven—as a false moral or religious doctrine. At one time, she admits, such ideas gave her a sense of superiority; she believed they might lead to some future heavenly triumph. Now she is on the attack, and her article on silly novels and their equally silly authors focuses on those artificial ideas as presented in, among others, *Compensation: A Story of Real Life Thirty Years Ago*, by Henrietta Georgina Marcia Lascelles, Lady Chatterton (1856, two volumes).

What Marian aimed at was the exposure of an entire spate of religious novels, fictions which had as their primary function a didactic purpose, with thoughts expressed in high-flown language but fundamentally vacuous. She was not in the main imitating Lewes's own article "The Lady Novelists" in the July 1852 *Westminster*, although it was rarely distant from her mind. Most important, we should *not* view her attack on female novelists as an attack on the gender or on their endeavors; it was, rather, her effort to call forth from women the same standards and demands for quality she made for men. As she points out in her article, "Fiction is a department of literature in which women can, after their kind, fully equal men. A cluster of great names, both living and dead, rush to our memories in evidence that women can produce novels not only fine, but among the very finest;—novels, too, that have a precious speciality, lying quite apart from masculine aptitudes and experience." She mocks the "silly" aspects of the books under review: the "mind-and-millinery" species of novel, in which the heroine is usually an heiress, or the oracular species in which the writer expounds her theological, philosophical, and moral theories without knowing what she is talking about.

Diction and content are Marian's twin points of attack. She makes a compelling scientific parallel, revealing how she herself synthesized knowledge, whether literary or physical. "By a peculiar thermometric adjustment, when a woman's talent is at zero, journalistic approbation is at the boiling pitch; when she attains mediocrity, it is already at no more than summer heat; and if ever she reaches excellence [as in Harriet Martineau, Charlotte Brontë, and Elizabeth Gaskell], critical enthusiasm drops to the freezing point." It was, all in all, a tour de force: sweeping out the stables of contemporary muck so as to clear the stage for her entrance into the literary life; part of that transformation of herself, of which the name change was only one ingredient. As she tells Chapman, her article on "Silly Novels" might be made "the vehicle of some wholesome truth as well as some amusement."

After the first week in August, the couple left for Bath, spent the night, and then returned to Richmond on 9 August. Lewes took his sons to Hofwyl in Switzerland, leaving Marian alone from 25 August to 4 September, but in somewhat better spirits than when she had been alone before. The two had entered deeply into the study of zoology, and upon their return from the coast, they carried with them some unknown marine animal species for further investigation. They had had a most satisfactory time, with Marian entering into Lewes's activities and he into hers. Also, some of the future had shaped up; heading toward her thirty-seventh birthday that November, she saw a direction for herself. She still had a pile of books to work through for the October "Belles Lettres" and history segments of the *Westminster*. She did tell Bray she hoped to have some solitary time for Chapman's work, but she suddenly suffered from torturous toothache, coming from seven spots, she thought. The doctor diagnosed neuralgia and dosed her with quinine. But that was of little use, and the dentist finally went to work, putting her under chloroform and extracting a wisdom tooth. After this, she wanted to forgo the piece for Chapman, but that man—involved in time-consuming personal affairs, his health failing, and under the gun financially—insisted that she not desert him at this time. "So here am

I on this blessed 1st of September," she writes Bray, "with this odious article to write in a hurry and with Mr. Lewes coming home to reduce my writing time to the minimum."

As she was beginning to find her medium, even Lewes's presence was perceived as an interruption. She insisted to Bray, nevertheless, that despite all the pressures, they must see him on the 6th, but her context for saying this casts doubt on her desire to have his stay further interrupt her concentration. She writes four days later that she is glad he postponed his visit—Bray surely found in Marian's words a distinct ambiguity. She says that in a fortnight they will be freer; but this was hardly the case, for on 23 September, Marian Evans or Marian Lewes or Mrs. Lewes would start to become, with "Amos Barton," George Eliot.

10

Becoming
George Eliot

"So our lives glide on: the river ends we don't know
where, and the sea begins, and then there is no more
jumping ashore."

M arian's journal records, simply, on 23 September 1856: "Began to write
'The Sad Fortunes of the Reverend Amos Barton,' which I hope to make
one of a series called 'Scenes of Clerical Life.' "* "Amos Barton" burrows deeply
into Marian's past; and her use of materials in and around Barton, an evangelical
minister of no pretensions, reveals how close her own religious background still
was to her. It existed solidly, not as faith or belief, but as a structured existence,
a substratum society. Here she had not at all changed, and we catch her desire
to maintain a stable, highly structured society which replicates what she experienced twenty and thirty years before.

At first look the story appears slight and even seems to bear out Lewes's doubts
about her ability to manage dramatic presentation, which he deemed essential
for the highest fiction. Yet appearances are deceptive, for Marian was not
attempting to display her full array of talents. "Amos Barton" is a trying out,
and it, along with the other two novellas in the collection, would become the
rock on which her fiction would rest. We must view Eliot's unfolding literary
career as a series of building blocks: the deceptively solid *Scenes of Clerical Life*;
the still tentative foray with her first novel, *Adam Bede*; the movement toward
achievement with *The Mill on the Floss*; the deeply personal *Silas Marner*, a

---

* Even as she began to write, Lewes's activities were very much in mind. As she tells Sara, Lewes
had written an article on physiology for *Fraser's Magazine* and, as usual, signed only his initials,
G.H.L. A letter from George Combe came back, addressed to G.H.L. by way of Fraser, praising the
article for having revealed much sounder views on physiology than he usually found. Combe had in
the past castigated Lewes as "a shallow, flippant man," and Marian was much amused when Combe
realized who the author was.

confessional of sorts; the overdetermined and overwrought *Romola;* a period of faltering which included her long dramatic poem, *The Spanish Gypsy,* and the now neglected *Felix Holt, the Radical*—all of them leading to the best work of her career, *Middlemarch,* and ending with the enormously ambitious *Daniel Deronda,* an attempt at summation and recapitulation.

Central to all of Eliot's fiction is that stable, structured society which made her politically and socially conservative, without, however, blinding her to the terrible abuses and hypocrisies of the age. In this respect, she joined the other "conservers" of the period: Thackeray and Trollope, Dickens himself, Meredith, Elizabeth Gaskell; and, outside fiction, Carlyle, Tennyson, Ruskin, and Matthew Arnold. We are speaking of more than a literary stance, but of something she desperately needed, without which, despite her prodigious gifts, she could not confront life. Scandal, gossip, backbiting, possibly fears of Lewes's ultimate loyalties—all of these increased her need for stability, for conserving history and memory.

The opening of "Amos Barton" indicates that world of stability, and it sets the pace for her fiction as historically oriented, nearly all set back into an era before railroads, before "progress" was the shibboleth of the day. The very rhythms and tones of Eliot's prose suggest her hostility to vulgar progress or her antagonism to the machine as the harbinger of a better life. Her response was slow, stately, processional-like rhythms, the very opposite of anything mechanical. Her language, too—with its heavy literary overlay, its use of classical references, and its meditative pace—suggests how she opposed the rapidity and the finality of the machine.

As "Amos Barton" begins, it goes back twenty-five years—to the time when Eliot was twelve—and we come across Shepperton Church, based on her own Chilvers Coton,* near Nuneaton, Warwickshire; and the reverend, Amos Barton, is based solidly on John Gwyther, the Chilvers Coton curate from 1831 to 1841. Eliot was now back in her evangelical childhood, when she was most impressionable, and when society seemed to stand still. The time was just before the Reform Bill of 1832. This becomes Eliot's "fantasy" return. She goes back to pre-scandal, virginal time before ambition and difference had taken firm hold of her imagination. The beginning of "Amos Barton" is concerned with the virtues of fixity and the demons of change. Eliot emphasizes chiefly how progress has not brought improvement, though it has brought change: in the use of the church organ, for example, instead of the string and wind instruments which earlier had provided the sacred music. It is a small matter, not at all theological, but the substitution does not seem for the better, although some will call it "immense improvement." The "improvement" will further include all the fancy new circumstances in society: the newly formed police force under Sir Robert Peel ("bobbies"); the Tithe Commutation Act, which turned the payment of 10

---

* All that remain of All Saints, Chilvers Coton, are the tower and the "Benefactors' Boards," on the west wall. Eliot refers to the boards telling of the benefactions to the poor of Shepperton. Some additional bells were installed in the church belfry in 1908 as a tribute to Eliot.

percent of income, or tithe, into a fixed amount—which either hurt or helped people, depending on their incomes; the advent of the penny-post, introduced in 1840. All of these, she says caustically, have made it possible for "dear, old, brown, crumbling, picturesque inefficiency" to give way to "spick-and-span new-painted, new varnished efficiency, which will yield endless diagrams, plans, elevations, and sections."

After that—recalling Wordsworth looking back on London from Westminster Bridge to seek its original beauty before industrial filth fogged it over—Eliot turns to what she finds endearing in old things: ". . . I recall with a fond sadness Shepperton Church as it was in the old days. . . ." Then in a twist of the narrative, she moves back even further, when the narrator was much younger than Eliot herself. There follows a description of the church as it was near the turn of the century. The narrative device is itself of interest. At first, one may think that the narrator is Eliot herself, since she places the first moments when she was twelve; but the narrator is not Eliot—it is a created person, someone much older than she, whose childhood goes back perhaps fifty or more years. We have, with this, a question of telling, in which the author has provided a surrogate "teller," yet at the same time someone who overlaps her own experience.

Furthermore, we assume the narrator is male, since the name eventually associated with the novella will be George Eliot—in February of 1857 she called herself by that name. She has, accordingly, created a double- and triple-layered form of narration: seemingly using many of her own experiences in the past, but ascribing them to another, and turning from her own female identification to that of a man not only in the naming of the author but in the assumptions of the narrator. None of this is worked fully through; we do not have as yet the self-conscious narrator who winds everything back to himself or herself (yet he does say he is considered a "blockhead"). But there is some sense of strategical method, to disguise the author on the one hand, and to thicken the tale on the other.

In this respect, the Reverend Gilfil is mentioned—he will form the material of the second novella in *Clerical Life*—but he is bypassed for Amos Barton, who comes to Shepperton long after Gilfil's death. We note how Eliot layers the material: pastness is preceded by still further (fictional) pastness; the protagonist of this story preceded by the one who will become the protagonist of the second. Gilfil's older period was much simpler, for unlike him, Barton must deal head-on with the world of evangelicalism and the Catholic question.* The layering, then, involves different historical questions, different religious and theological assumptions, and, therefore, different social and political issues. The evangelical movement was in itself ticklish, since it drew the Church of England toward its Protestant basis, whereas the agitation over Catholicism in the 1820s and then over the Tractarians in the 1830s would pull the Anglican Church toward certain origins in the Catholic Church.

---

* That is, with the split within Anglicanism between high and low church and the increasing role of Catholics, which created a threat to the Anglican Church; in effect, a triangular conflict.

What now seems a quaint struggle between high and low church—issues which permeate all three novellas in *Scenes*—was a matter of deadly seriousness. As the young Mary Anne Evans grasped, more than theological doctrines were at stake: the split indicated a social dimension and a political one. Low church tended to be more democratic, more politically open; high church was Tory, socially restrictive, hierarchical, politically conservative. The evangelical movement was an effort to breathe life into a stodgy Anglican Church, offering up preaching over liturgical doctrine, the "call" which derived from personal conversion, the freeing up of the clergy from church and hierarchal duties, the justification by faith rather than deed, without slighting social duties, the fundamentalism of the Bible over church historicism—in all, a more individualized expression of faith and one far less dependent on structures and authority (bishops and lords, for example).

Most of all, however, evangelicalism lay close to the lower classes, as well as to the slowly emerging middle class. It was anathema, for the most part, to upper-class society and to the aristocracy, neither of which Eliot had much use for. We can say, then, that beginning with "Amos Barton," Eliot was displaying a political as well as a social and theological self. However much she vacillated over particular reforms, her sympathies were clearly with lower-class and lower-middle-class life. All three novellas can be viewed as describing injustices which needed redress, and often failed to obtain it.

There is something almost formulaic about this first novella, as if Eliot had to prove to herself she could run through the "ordinary" events of life and present them with sufficient dramatic éclat to satisfy Lewes and her own doubts about her ability. As she wrote in her journal in December 1857, she tried out on Lewes Milly's death—Milly was the long-suffering wife of Amos, hobbled by six children and a husband who barely scraped out a living—and he responded positively. "One night G. went to town on purpose to leave me a quiet evening for writing it [Milly's death]. I wrote the chapter from the news brought by the shepherd to Mrs. Hackit, to the moment when Amos is dragged from the bedside, and read it to G. when he came home. We both cried over it, and then he came up to me and kissed me, saying 'I think your pathos is better than your fun.' "

Despite the reservations of others in the community, the narrator considers Barton to be a good person. But the narrator is called a "blockhead" by a neighbor. By revealing different perceptions of Barton held by the townspeople, Eliot is attempting some confusion of realms, and not by chance. Out of this emerges a man who is deemed not to have "refined sensibilities," but who does make an effort, always, to do the right thing. If we project Barton somewhat and examine his dilemma more personally, we can see, carefully shaded, glimpses of Marian Evans in the good reverend, embodying others' perception of him (not favorable) along with what he actually is (a good, weak man). The agent of his downfall is the Countess Czerlaski, who comes to live with the Bartons when her brother decides to marry their maid. She is undeniably beautiful and elegant, especially as set off against Milly, and her beauty is of the kind that Eliot would henceforth present with intimations of the sinning Eve or the demonic Lilith: the woman who while falling will bring down others with her, or the woman whose surface is all disguise. The sins of the countess are not huge, and her background is fairly close to what she claims. But, Eliot writes, she "was a little vain, a little ambitious, a little selfish, a little shallow and frivolous, a little given to white lies.—But who considers such slight blemishes, such moral pimples as these disqualifications for entering into the most respectable society." Since the most severe ladies in Milby would not consider these qualities as extraordinary, they had to invent far worse things to justify their own distance from the countess. Eliot was orchestrating one aspect of her own position, that of being judged a home-breaker.

Compared with the countess, the Reverend Barton is one of those ordinary souls who come and go without glowing. Their sorrows are there, and no one cares, and their joys arrive also without fanfare. Such people are the overwhelming majority, and yet they remain, in novels at least, almost invisible. They may have six children, as the Bartons do, matching almost precisely Chrissey's large number. Off in the distance, as further shadowy models for Milly and Amos, are Chrissey and her now deceased doctor husband: people who attempted to make their mark, failed, and fell back into the interstices. This, too, had been Marian's fear.

The psychological implications of the countess moving in with the Bartons, eating their scarce food, creating expenses which they can ill afford, and gradually causing rumors about Amos's relationship to her are all of considerable biographical interest. It is insufficient to assert that the Bartons are typical victims and that the countess, a parasite, preys upon them as people likely to succumb to her charms. This is only partially true. More complicated than that, the situation evolves out of profound needs within Eliot to view herself as pure but also to perceive herself as someone whose reputation is unjustifiably besmirched by rumors and scandals swirling around her. Not by chance does her first story involve a character and his family brought down by virulent rumor, an innocent protagonist simply unaware of what is occurring until it is too late to respond, even if he could. The "clerical brethren," as Eliot characterizes them, become the chorus-like background which will lead to Amos's demise.

But the psychological need goes still further than Eliot's suggestion of her own situation through the Bartons'. The nature of the relationship between the family and the countess is based on class and caste. The countess assumes certain privileges because of her upper-class status, treating the Bartons as her servants. Class distinctions here are part of the psychological process working in Eliot, and it is complicated. The injustices she sees as a result of class are for her an intensification of injustices she perceives at the personal level. Reinforcing the unfairness of what occurs to the Bartons at the level of their ordinary lives— doomed as they are by a caste system as well—is the complex question of how that injustice is generated at large in the society. Eliot is already developing her distinctive voice.

Beyond her own scandal, she sees further than personal invective into an entire society out of kilter in its evaluation of a given situation. The demise of the Bartons is caused by their inability to handle larger social questions as much as by their ineptness with personal matters. Amos is simply worn down, as is Milly, whose poor health is exacerbated by her need to minister to the countess's whims. When Milly dies, Amos must face that "oppression of the blank interval in which one has nothing left to think of but the dreary future—the separation from the loved and familiar, and the chilling entrance on the new and strange. In every parting there is an image of death."

Forced to leave his post at Shepperton, then Milby itself, Barton and his six children are isolated, little more than waifs. By giving them no place for support, Eliot has carried to the extreme her own situation as an outcast, and has acknowledged that, if anything happened to Lewes, she would face the same "blank interval" as Amos. The details and overall pattern of the novella are profoundly autobiographical, in terms of time and place, for example, but more so in the shaded way Eliot has presented the case for Marian Lewes. In fictional terms, she has begun her long association with her own predicament.

With this work, Eliot entered the considerably fierce world of literary competition. The great literary figure of the 1850s was Dickens, with *Bleak House* and *Hard Times* near the beginning of the decade, *Little Dorrit* after the middle, and *Great Expectations* at the end. Thackeray had almost kept pace after the triumph of *Vanity Fair* in the late 1840s, with *Henry Esmond, The Newcomes, Pendennis,* and *The Virginians.* Trollope had begun his Barchester series with *The Warden* and *Barchester Towers.* Not to be ignored were Bulwer-Lytton (an ongoing career), Charles Kingsley (*Alton Locke, Yeast, Westward Ho!*), Wilkie Collins (*The Woman in White,* 1860), Charles Reade (*It's Never Too Late to Mend*), and George Meredith (*The Ordeal of Richard Feverel*). On the female side, there were Charlotte Brontë (*Villette*), Charlotte Mary Yonge (*Cynevor Terrace, The Heir of Radclyffe*), and, most of all as the decade continued, Mrs. Elizabeth Gaskell, with *Cranford, Ruth,* and *North and South.* These were the serious writers. On the more popular side, we find fiction full of didacticism and jingoism, with a strong reformist spirit—a fiction of social commitment; but alongside was a trivial, high-society novel, an afterglow of the "silver fork" fictions of the 1820s and 1830s, satirized by Thackeray and others. It was not easy for Eliot, or anyone else, to create a distinctive voice, since high and low society seemed accounted for, as did humor, horror, and sermonizing.

Yet her beginning was auspicious. Lewes was much taken with the work of his companion and submitted the manuscript of "Amos Barton" to the publisher John Blackwood on 6 November 1856. Lewes's letter to John Blackwood, who ran *Blackwood's Edinburgh Magazine* (or *Maga*), part of the Blackwood publishing enterprise, recalled previous business dealings.* The *Magazine* was extremely

---

* The ever-busy Lewes had submitted work to *Blackwood's Magazine* in the past, a story called "Lesurques," in January 1843; and a piece just recently rewritten and published in three installments in May–June 1856, a play of his reworked as a novella, called "Metamorphosis." In August, the *Magazine* started to publish Lewes's findings at Ilfracombe, called "Sea-side Studies," which included several descriptive passages from Eliot's journal. Lewes's own reputation with Blackwood's was very much on the line in his submission of Marian's work.

prestigious, reaching out to the British intelligentsia and to many literary people as well. To be published there was a coup. Lewes wrote his letter one day after Eliot completed the novella, and it permits us to be present at the creation. This particular exchange with Blackwood set the stage for much of Eliot's future publishing life. Lewes's hand, of course, was restricted by the fact that he had to invent a "clerical friend," hide that his friend was a woman, and, further, disguise the fact that this woman was the scandal of London, or else Blackwood, as a conservative and high-minded Scotsman, might have balked at what he was getting into.

Lewes eased into the situation: "I confess that before reading the m. s. I had considerable doubts of my friend's power as a writer of fiction; but after reading it those doubts were changed into very high admiration. I don't know what you will think of the story, but according to my judgement such humour, pathos, vivid presentation and nice observation have not been exhibited (in this style) since the 'Vicar of Wakefield' [Oliver Goldsmith's often stultifying picture of clerical life]—and in consequence of that opinion I feel quite pleased in negotiating the matter with you." Lewes then tells Blackwood what he has been commissioned to say, that the book will consist of

> tales and sketches illustrative of the actual life of our country clergy about a quarter of a century ago; but solely in its *human* and *not at all* in its *theological* aspect [theological questions do poke through, especially the favoring of evangelicalism], the object being to do what has never yet been done in our literature, for we have had abundant religious stories polemical and doctrinal, but since the 'Vicar' and Miss Austen, no stories representing the clergy like any other class with the humours, sorrows, and troubles of other men.

Lewes says his friend begged him to add that the tone throughout will be sympathetic, not antagonistic—perhaps a sly swipe at Trollope, whose portraits of the Anglican clergy mock their worldliness. Lewes thinks that some of these stories in the offing, or all, may prove suitable for *Maga*. "If any are sent of which you do not approve, or which you do not think sufficiently interesting, these he will reserve for the separate republication and for this purpose he wishes to retain the copyright." Here we have the experienced Lewes plotting publication strategy so that Eliot could maximize whatever income the stories brought.

Blackwood responded almost by return mail, on 12 November. He showed a perceptive sense of Eliot's "over-determining" her characters, telling rather than suggesting. "I am happy," Blackwood wrote, "to say that I think your friend's reminiscences of clerical life will do. If there is any more of the series written I should like to see it, as until I saw more I could not make any decided proposition for the publication of the Tales in whole or in part in the Magazine. The first specimen Amos Barton is unquestionably very pleasant reading. Perhaps the author falls into the error of trying too much to explain the characters of his actors by description instead of allowing them to evolve in the action of the story; but the descriptions are very humourous and good." The publisher's point does reveal he shared Lewes's doubts that Eliot, at this stage, had sufficient dramatic power. This was something Eliot, as the most intellectual of novelists, would grapple with for the rest of her writing career.

Even on the ending, in which Eliot brings Amos and his daughter back to visit Milly's grave in Milby, Blackwood is incisive, calling it "the lamest part of the story." He says the defect results from "the specifications as to the fortunes of parties of whom the reader has no previous knowledge [Eliot supplies lists, simply ages or activities] and cannot consequently feel much interest." The publisher goes on to say he hates sneers at real religious feeling, and he comments that while he senses the author is of the same persuasion, the clergymen in the novella with one exception are "not very attractive specimens of the body." He sums up by saying he will have a more decided opinion of the piece once he has reread it. There is no definite acceptance of the entire series for publication, although there are congratulations if the author is a new writer, on "being worthy of the honours of print and pay." Blackwood's caution, as befitting the editor of *Maga,* a highly conservative, establishment publication,* was over accepting a series, still unwritten, from a stranger.

Marian was launched, but anonymously, and mainly through the intervention of Lewes with someone he knew and in a publication that did not really represent her views. While she had impressed Blackwood, there is the question of acceptance if she had come in "over the transom," unsolicited and unknown. Certainly Blackwood would have hesitated about publishing a series in which he had only the first part. "I am sorry," he wrote Lewes on 18 November, "that the author has no more written but if he cares much about a speedy appearance I have so high opinion of this first Tale that I will waive my objections and publish it without seeing more; not, of course, committing myself to go on with the other tales of the series unless I approved of them. I am very sanguine that I will approve as in addition to the other merits of Amos I agree with you that there is a great freshness of style. If you think also that it would stimulate the author to go on with the other Tales with more spirit I will publish Amos at once. He would divide into two parts." Blackwood published "Amos Barton" in January and February 1857.† He goes on to say, "I am glad to hear that your friend is as I supposed a Clergyman. Such a subject is best in clerical hands and some of the pleasantest and least prejudiced correspondents I have ever had are English clergymen."

---

* *Maga,* founded in 1817 by William Blackwood (father of John), was in content quite the opposite of the *Westminster Review.* Like the *Review,* it was an outgrowth of a publishing firm, William Blackwood & Sons, founded in 1804 in Edinburgh; but there resemblances on social, religious, political, penal, and scientific issues ended. Despite having traveled abroad as a young man, in Italy and France, John Blackwood remained a Tory all his life, although, as we shall see, he was able to bend. His *Maga,* withal, was the conservative answer to the more liberal and Whiggish *Edinburgh Review,* which represented the other side of Scottish politics and religion and had its English parallel in the *Westminster Review.*

† In manuscript, "Amos" runs to 111 pages; Eliot canceled only one long passage, appearing in Folios 4 / 5: "Oh that happy time of childish veneration . . . my own devotional bearing."

We recognize Lewes was playing a dangerous game, for in one respect he was making a fool of Blackwood while protecting Marian. Not only had he disguised the gender, he had also deceived about the occupation, so that in all his initial dealings with Lewes and Marian, the editor of this prestigious magazine—and someone in a position to make professional difficulties for Lewes—was being hoodwinked. Lewes had disguised a writer whom Blackwood would not have approved of at all: a scandalous woman, as well as someone who had deserted the church for natural theology, positivism, and the demon evolution.

Blackwood closes by saying that even without a second reading, he is deeply impressed by the tone of the piece, its character, and its incidents. This was a good birthday present for Marian, who now as a male cleric had turned thirty-seven. The parodic correspondence continued with Lewes's follow-up of 22 November. "Your letter," Lewes writes, "has greatly restored the shaken confidence of my friend, who is unusually sensitive, and unlike most writers is most anxious about *excellence* than about appearing in print—as his waiting so long before taking the venture proves. He is consequently afraid of failure . . . and by failure he would understand that which I suspect most writers would be apt to consider as a success—so high is his ambition."

He was now involved in several dimensions of disguise, deception, and out-right lies. He had to justify Eliot's postponement of another tale on grounds quite different from the real one, her *Westminster* work: the "Belles Lettres" section, as usual; the segment called "History, Biography, Voyages, and Travels"; and the very long and important essay called "Worldliness and Otherworldliness: the Poet Young"—Edward Young, famous mainly for *Night Thoughts*. In all, these contributions would come to one-quarter of the entire January 1857 issue and would involve a prodigious amount of reading for the first two sections. As for the Young article (well over 20,000 words), Eliot did have a version of it written in April 1856, and when Lewes said he thought it was the best article she had written, she completed it and sent it to Chapman. Even so, there was a mountain of work for her to get through before turning to "Mr. Gilfil's Love-Story."

All this ferocious activity was hidden behind Lewes's deceptive words to Blackwood. Eliot's companion went on: "He will be gratified if you published Amos Barton in January, as it will give him ample time to get the second story ready, so as to appear when Barton is finished. He is anxious, however, that you should publish the general title of 'Scenes of Clerical Life'—and I think you may do this with perfect safety, since it is quite clear that the writer of Amos Barton is capable of writing at least one more story suitable to Maga, and two would suffice to justify the general title."

Lewes now began to see that his misleading statements needed correction. "Let me not forget to add that when I referred to 'my clerical friend' I meant to designate the writer of the clerical stories, not that he was a clericus. I am not at liberty to remove the veil of anonymity—even as regards social position. Be pleased therefore to keep the whole secret—and not even mention my negotiation or in any way lead guessers—(should any one trouble himself with such a guess—not very likely) to jump from me to my friend." Lewes has recognized that "the friend" would become "his friend," and then the game would be over. His caution to Blackwood to keep the entire proceedings secret now has the editor caught up in the umbrella deception, under which were an entire web of other deceptions. All of this became amusing when the guessing game began—and people in Coventry came to suspect Marian Evans, and Dickens penetrated it all and perceived that a woman was writing these tales.

Marian's incidental letters to friends, to Sara and to Bray, for example, give away none of the drama occurring in her life and work. So far has she moved from that world of Coventry that she has undergone a veritable sea change in her life and yet it must remain undisclosed. She has, in effect, become another person: literally taking on another identity, somewhere between male and female; somewhere between Lewes's "clerical friend" and not being a cleric; somewhere between Lewes's closest companion, his "Mrs. Lewes," and not Mrs. Lewes. She has become, in these respects, fiction itself, part of the imaginative process in which transformation is key. She was, in fact, tunneling deeper and deeper into divisions even as her writing career augured healing.

Her piece on Young, the poet of her youth, fits this new terrain, a measured response to what she is no longer. The *Night Thoughts* of her youth are now the lies and deceptions Young has perpetuated on his readers. The argument is over religion and questions of immortality. She again attacks the idea of compensation, the sense that the individual's virtuous life derives from his or her desire for immortality. This is, as Eliot realizes, a denial of everything she has worked toward since her translation of Strauss in the mid-1840s. Her attack on Young, then, is a kind of apologia, at the very time she is writing about clerics and their values.

When Eliot decided to probe the literal value system of Young—leaving aside the poetry—she found little but slipshod views, outdated or sensationalized points about mortality and immortality. Once an admirer, she now has come to see his work as pernicious and intellectually flaccid. Young is the opposite of Amos Barton, and the two are juxtaposed somewhere in the shadow of Eliot's imagination. For the creature in the poem is impressed not only with death but with burial fees, and he has a "fervid attachment to patrons in general, but on the whole prefers the Almighty."

The vitriolic nature of the attack—later in her article she puts the poetry of Cowper in opposition to Young's, the real against the meretricious—derives directly from Eliot's need to justify her attitudes in *Scenes of Clerical Life*. In "Amos Barton," she attacks the type of worldly cleric whom she describes in Young's career. But further than that is the personal need to justify her break with Young's deceptive, greasy, uncentered world. This article was more than a contribution to the *Review*; it was a cry which attempted to set the world right. In its intent it was heuristic and pedagogic: give up your Young and all those fantasies of heavenly reward. Virtue is its own reward; compensation is sophistry. And virtue must be won, not simply requested. Priggish or not, Eliot was honing her intellectual and moral weapons, for this would be the ground she would defend.

For her exposé of Young, Marian earned a good sum, £20, to which Chapman added another £5. With the other contributions she made to the January issue, she brought home a little over £44, to which must be added the 50 guineas paid for "Amos Barton." Her income was now beginning to climb—her total earnings in 1856, for example were £192.11 (not £254.3 as she noted in her journal). This meant that with her annual fund she had close to £300, which, while not munificent, was enough for her and Lewes to consider living better.

As her fiction writing took hold, her involvement in *Review* matters and her contributions would end. Chapman soon learned that his most valued subeditor and contributor would no longer need his small payments; the additional £5 he sent on for the Young article was an indication of how he feared her defection. Lewes's and her income, however, was not free and clear, since he was deeply in debt. Part of it was Thornton Hunt's continued failure to support Agnes, so that Lewes had to assume the burden. The matter was confrontational. Lewes's journal indicates a near duel-level situation with Hunt over what Hunt called Lewes's offensive charges. Lewes was amused, and yet somewhat taken aback, and he offered to have a court-appointed arbiter hear out his charges of Hunt's defalcation. Hunt would not agree, but a third party did work out some compromise in which Lewes did not have to withdraw his charges against Agnes's lover. This running argument coincided with Christmas 1856 and may have explained why, once again, Eliot found herself alone while Lewes went off to Arthur Helps's for two weeks to recuperate. She notes "alone" in journal, possibly the sign of resentment. In any event, she took the time to start "Mr. Gilfil's Love-Story."

On 29 December, she received a letter from Blackwood, addressed to "My Dear Sir." The deception was working so perfectly that Blackwood seems to have swallowed everything. Demonstrating delight in "Amos Barton," he says it will begin the January number. His words are full of overkill—"It is a long time since I have read anything so fresh"—for in an age of Dickens, Thackeray, the Brontës, Trollope, and Meredith, freshness was all. But the editor / publisher was truly pleased to have a new voice, and he may have discerned that however slight the story, the tone is witty and yet sympathetic, the material surrounding the characters completely authentic. He sends on the most welcome part of all, the £52.10, which comes to 50 guineas. He looks ahead to separate book publication and an arrangement for the monies from that to be divided, or else as an outright payment to the author. In all their dealings with Eliot, the Blackwoods were absolutely aboveboard, generous, and understanding, while not neglectful of their own financial needs.

Marian, meanwhile—as Marian and as Pollian—continued to write to Sara and to Bray as if nothing had happened. Having distanced herself from them, her huge secret moved her even closer to Lewes, who was her only contact with the truth—even while he was the conduit of the deception to others. It was a curious situation which overtly did not seem to affect Marian, but it did influence her work, for "Mr. Gilfil's Love-Story" is based on a secret. "Such was the locked-in chamber in Mr. Gilfil's house: a sort of visible symbol of the secret chamber in his heart, where he had long turned the key on early hopes and early sorrows, shutting up for ever all the passion and the poetry of his life." To further the more amusing side of the secretive life Eliot had chosen, she heard from Blackwood on 30 January 1857, a letter addressed to "My Dear Amos," to which she responded on 4 February and signed George Eliot, thereby establishing her new name. In an earlier letter to Blackwood just after the new year (on the 4th), Marian had signed her letter "The Author of Amos Barton." In that letter, she expressed her gratitude; and she has noticed the payment—guineas indicated a higher level of accomplishment than would an equivalent amount in pounds.* It was a sign of a benevolent and thoughtful publisher. She says she is sure they will agree on reasonable terms if *Scenes* appears as a volume. She indicates she hopes to send the second story by the beginning of February—by 7 January, she had completed Chapters 1 and 2 of "Gilfil."

In the "My Dear Amos" letter, Blackwood admits that critics are a good deal divided about the first part of "Amos," but "they generally are about anything of real merit." Some of his friends, he says, praise it; others condemn it. He adds that the first two men who had seen "Amos" after publication spoke out against it, and "it required all the self reliance, without which an Editor would be the most miserable dog alive, to make me feel easy and satisfied that I was right." One of them, a Colonel Hamley, felt the style "obscure and laboured" and thought the author very possibly a man of science; and Blackwood agrees, that this had also occurred to him. The other negative critic was W. E. Aytoun, renowned for his satirical portraits of the poets who made up a loose group called the Spasmodics. Thackeray himself was presented by Blackwood with a copy, and looking over a page or two, said he would have liked to read more. But Thackeray did not otherwise comment.

In her reply, using George Eliot as her nom de plume, the writer made a sharp distinction between those whose adverse opinion arises from "a dislike to the *order* of art rather than from a critical estimate of the execution. Any one who detests the Dutch school in general will hardly appreciate fairly the merits of a particular Dutch painting," an analogy well taken since Eliot presented herself on occasion as a writer in the Dutch painterly tradition of intense, almost verisimilitudinous, realism.† "And against this sort of condemnation, one must steel oneself as one best can. But objections which point out to me any vice of man-

---

* Payment in guineas carried an upper-class caché; pounds were for wages. Guineas symbolized an entire class / caste world.

† In an essay called "The Progress of Fiction" (in the October 1853 *Westminster*), which Eliot may have written or at least cobbled together, the question of suitable subject matter arises. The critic condemns Wilkie Collins's sensational *Basil* and indicates that some subjects are appropriate only when treated in certain ways. Although Eliot would soon move to a broader view of what was fictionally tolerable, she did hew to the nature of "treatment" as paramount, even when her own subjects were otherwise considered unacceptable according to Victorian mores.

ner or any failure in producing an intended effect will be really profitable." Here she seems to welcome criticism which can help her write more effectively; later, she had to be protected against both advice and criticism, a practice which Lewes followed throughout her entire career.

For her choice of name, Haight mentions several other "George Elliot"s, spelled with two els, which might have entered our George Eliot's mind. His best suggestion is the name Jane Eyre gives to the Rivers family when they take her in, Jane Elliot. Whether this actually registered on Eliot we cannot know. The simplicity of the name made it all the more difficult for anyone to penetrate it; it was truly nondescript. And even the fact of the "two Georges" would distract people, never thinking that one George was the companion of the other. Yet it is this very point which has grasped our imagination: the fact that Marian Evans appropriated the name of the man she was living with; that she also became his "wife," another appropriation; and that by these moves she had made herself more than companion to Lewes. She had brought him into a secret he could not reveal without doing injury not only to her but to himself. If we probe Marian's motives here, it is clear her use of a male nom de plume must signify more than empowerment as a masculine writer; after all, by now it was apparent that women who signed their own names had no trouble getting published or finding a market.* The motive went deeply into her needs, to surround herself with mystery, to prepare scenarios in which she took herself to the edge, to test out unresolved possibilities.

The guessing game was on. With the scandal dogging her in London and in Coventry, Marian Evans had created another "scene" for herself with the enigma of authorship. As the plot thickened and Blackwood began to look obtuse, his London manager, Joseph Munt Langford, wrote with what seemed to be inside information. "I heard a curious thing about Amos Barton, namely that it is the actual life of a clergyman named Gwythir who at the time the incidents occurred lived in a place called, I think, Coton in one of the midland counties and who is now a vicar of a small parish in Yorkshire. Indeed his daughter wrote to a lady, a friend of mine, telling her to be sure to read the story as it was their family history." Despite errors, Langford was coming close; Coton was indeed the place. So, too, in "Gilfil," the use of Cheverel Manor would recall Arbury Hall, near where Mary Anne Evans grew up. And Gilfil himself was based on the vicar of Chilvers Coton, the Reverend Bernard Gilpin Ebdell, who had baptized her at a week old. If Eliot were to be revealed, it would be because of the details of her stories, which were becoming recognizable to an ever-growing number of people.

On 10 February, for example, Blackwood told Eliot—now addressed as "My Dear George Eliot"—the piles of letters from readers were lying on his "groaning table." He was also looking forward to the next installment, telling her that the

---

* By the 1860s and thereafter, women writers, in fact, flooded the market. By a decade or two later, about three-quarters of the published novels were by women, a trend that started as early as the 1850s.

second should come rapidly so as to capitalize on the interest in "Amos." "Do not," he cautions, "of course hurry yourself to the detriment of the story; the perfecting of that must always be the first consideration, but it would be a serious disadvantage to baulk the public expectation now fairly raised." He suggests that everyone feels the author is new to writing, which implies not rawness "but that invaluable quality *freshness.*" He cites the popular author and lecturer Albert Richard Smith as surprisingly having taken the story to heart, and that together with him "the luminaries of the Garrick [the upscale London private club] generally seem to have mingled their tears with their tumblers over the death bed of Milly." Shades of Little Nell in Dickens's *The Old Curiosity Shop!* Blackwood repeats that he and others thought the author had a scientific background because of the "precision of expression or illustration." This was, of course, a recognition of Eliot's type of realism, which rarely was as close to Dutch genre painting as she made out or as Blackwood felt it to be.

By 11 February, Eliot had sent off the first two parts of "Gilfil," much cheered, as she says, by Blackwood's supportive letter. Lewes, meanwhile, carries deception. He calls Eliot—his George—"a sensitive doubting fellow. You would never believe the work I have had to make him credit his own genius," he tells Blackwood. "He (very judiciously!) looks up to my critical opinion as oracular; but in spite of confidence in me he is so diffident of himself that I had to *bully* him into acquiescence with the fact that I had discovered a genius. I cackle over my hatched chick; and so may you."

We observe in the making a fiction which appears to have engaged Lewes as much as his companion, and with an engine and energy of its own. With each letter to Blackwood, Lewes carries the editor / publisher further into the deception, until the deception becomes part of the entire enterprise—not merely Eliot writing, but writing within an artificial situation with its own "fictional" significance. Very possibly Eliot's ability to present material so easily and so rapidly to *Maga* was based on her disguise of self, freed up even while hidden. She was now Lewes's "hatched chick," before that his "clerical friend," always a protégée looking up to his "oracular" presence. The web was being spun ever thicker and more intricately.

Yet some of what Lewes asserted is not altogether deceptive; Eliot was diffident and retiring, and she did need Lewes's critical opinion. Her journal for 2 January 1858 reveals her uncertainties as she proceeded. "I wonder how I shall feel about these little details [about the author of *Clerical Life*] ten years hence, if I am *alive.* At present I value them as grounds for hoping that my writing may succeed and so give value to my life—as indications that I can touch the hearts of my fellow men, and so sprinkle some precious grain as the result of the long years in which I have been inert and suffering. But at present fear and trembling still predominate over hope."

Blackwood meanwhile decided to start publishing "Gilfil" without seeing the conclusion, a procedure the firm did not ordinarily adhere to. By 16 February, with the kind of alacrity in publishing and in the mails which seems extraterrestrial to our own times, Blackwood was sending back to Eliot the proofs of the first part of "Gilfil." "Many men," he says, "write well and tell a story well, but few possess the art of giving individuality to their characters so happily and easily as you in both these stories." He does make some suggestions, such as giving Caterina—Gilfil's love—more dignity, but he immediately abjures any real criticism. He says he looks forward to "the picture of her half-broken heart turning to Gilfil," a remark which indicates what sentimentalists and weepers even hardened readers were in Eliot's time. Not only Dickens opened the flood-gates. In her response, Eliot stressed that she must be true to her characters, insisting that weaknesses are not untruths but the very matter of her fictional efforts. With this, Blackwood stood back and told Lewes he had heard Thackeray was an admirer, the ultimate accolade.

Eliot's work on "Gilfil" includes a pastoral setting, a cleric, and his love for a woman not long for this world; but the real substance of the tale is closer to opera, Italian opera. We cannot ignore Caterina's fine voice, which expresses the stream of passion she feels for the unconcerned, uncaring Anthony Wybrow. We are involved in a version of *Cavalleria Rusticana*, or a Verdi opera, in which a hopeless love plays out while the truly worthy man looks on and pines away for his lost opportunity. In its working through, we expect arias, duets, choruses. But co-equal with this development we also note Eliot working increasingly with narrative. She has her intermediary narrator once more, and she uses flashbacks into previous eras; she was evidently trying to open up the fictional form somewhat even as her material remained traditional, even intractable. As the tale progresses, its melodramatic, sensationalized dimension gains momentum, with its fruitless love affair between Caterina, the Italian adopted child of Sir Christopher, and Anthony, the well-born English captain, who seems hardly aware of her intense passion. We perceive here the dim foreshadowing of Hetty Sorrel and Arthur Donnithorne in *Adam Bede*, although Caterina is more sympathetically presented than Hetty. When the Italian adoptee, whose chief asset is a beautiful and powerful voice, finds that Anthony cannot be hers, she plots to kill him with a dagger; but the captain suffers a fatal heart attack before his tormented admirer can get to him: an English rather than an Italian resolution. At that point Caterina, crushed, agrees to become Gilfil's wife, and then, after a few months, wastes away and dies, like the tubercular Violetta in *La Traviata*.

The operatic dimensions make the piece sound more sentimentalized than it actually is; but the conception took some real characters from Marian's background and transformed them and their stories into emotionally charged situations. As noted, Gilfil was apparently based on the Reverend Bernard Gilpin Ebdell, whom she knew as the vicar of Chilvers Coton and of Astley until he died, when she was nine. Caterina was someone taken in and educated by Lady Newdigate, a collier's daughter, Sarah Shilton. She was not a waif, but did possess a singing voice. She married Ebdell, and the union endured for twenty-three years, not a few months. In nearly every instance, Eliot took the basic facts and not only transformed them into fictional events, but altered them so as to fit a dramatic scenario. Even in the scene between Caterina and Sir Christopher, the helpless young woman and the kind but powerful master, we have that staple of opera in which the woman's pleas fall on the deaf ears of a ruling male party. Eliot, incidentally, seems to have taken over the scene from Austen's *Mansfield Park* when young Fanny Price, given a home by the Bertrams, must explain to Sir Thomas Bertram why she has rejected Henry Crawford; and, obviously, she cannot make an adequate explanation, except to express her feeling that he is the wrong man for her. Similarly, Sir Christopher cannot understand why Gilfil is not suited for Caterina, who is bedazzled and tormented by her love for Captain Anthony Wybrow.

In still another phase of the novella, Eliot was sharpening her knives for later work and at the same time working the conventions of melodrama. In her description of Anthony's love, Miss Assher, we have the first instance of what will become a George Eliot staple: the handsome, sometimes blond, splendidly put-together young woman as against the darkish or sallow, less physically prepossessing gypsy-skinned adversary. The physical attributes are not always the same—Dinah Morris in *Adam Bede* does not fit—but the basic contrast is there. "Miss Assher was tall, and gracefully though substantially formed, carrying herself with an air of mingled graciousness and self-confidence; her dark-brown hair, untouched by powder, hanging in bushy curls round her face, and falling in long thick ringlets nearly to her waist. The carmine tint of her well-rounded cheeks, and the finely-cut outline of her straight nose, produced an impression of splendid beauty, in spite of commonplace brown eyes, a narrow forehead, and thin lips." Overall, she conveys the impression of robust health, but also qualities of self-possession and self-love, a narcissistic type.

The "other woman" possesses qualities which are like those of a vise. She grasps the man in a deadly love (intimations of Medea) which promises a much greater degree of attachment than a Miss Assher could possibly experience. The dark, possibly unhealthy woman, such as Caterina, is the vengeful figure in opera, the gypsy or witch who mixes deadly potions, or else she is someone who burns out from her inner flame. She focuses all her energies on her goal, here a man, and she has no other life except what she foresees with him. A Miss Assher is a commodity for the marketplace, shopping around for a suitable match, seeking someone who will fulfill her social plans, an embryonic Rosamond Vincy or Gwendolen Harleth. She has few emotional needs, or else her needs can be easily transferred as part of a larger plan. She may even be kind—Miss Assher tries to befriend Caterina—but she simply lacks the emotional depth of any commitment. Only the image that peers back from the mirror conveys love.

Blackwood worried about Caterina's devotion to a "Jackanapes," his designation of Anthony. He worried that Eliot was pushing an agenda concerning Caterina at the expense of making her more palatable to his readers, who, he feared, would be upset by the intensity of her hopeless passion. The publisher was cautiously attempting to move Eliot's characters into the mainstream, so that his mid-century readers could identify with a sympathetic Caterina. Eliot, however, was interested in the intensity itself, not in whether Caterina met conventional expectations or whether Captain Wybrow fitted traditional male heroic roles.

This highly charged situation has all the intensity which she, Eliot, felt in her relationship to Lewes, and implied in that intense emotional attachment—the focus of her life, and of Caterina's—we have the potential of killing the person who might slip away. Blackwood had no way of knowing Eliot's subtext, but the autobiographical element is there; not only in terms of the characters who reappear from Marian's background, but in more intimate terms, as part of Eliot's own feelings of possession. The point is not that Eliot would plunge a dagger into her George if he defected, but that she was pursuing a passionate and possibly fatal attachment without pulling back and without redress.

For these and artistic reasons, she had to resist Blackwood's suggestions, however cautiously offered. She insisted on psychological truth, but also the truth of her own feelings. In the meantime, she found "Gilfil" running longer than expected and recognizes it will need three or four parts. Blackwood did run it in four parts, in the March through June 1857 issues of *Maga*. * Meanwhile, in her "other life," Eliot helped Lewes write and revise a 28 February 1857 *Leader* review of Sara Hennell's *Christianity and Infidelity*. What Eliot did was to make sure that Lewes, who was antagonistic to Sara's ideas, did not savage the book; instead, what emerges is a quite sympathetic and even enthusiastic notice. Eliot tells Sara that Lewes is one of those people who cannot disguise their feelings, and cannot "say or write what they do not believe, either *for* a friend or *against* an enemy." She did not, of course, mention her softening touches. Sara had trotted out all the old arguments for the influence of Christianity on moral behavior and the need for Christianity to achieve social balance, matters Eliot had now forsaken.

Money was coming in, £21 for the first part of "Gilfil," more to follow when Eliot submitted copy and installments appeared. Eliot's letter to Blackwood and his to her are part of a love fest: that early stage in an author–publisher relation-

---

* In January 1858, the three novellas ("Janet's Repentance" ran from July to November) were published by Blackwood, in two volumes. Although Eliot went over the text and made minor corrections, the book text is basically the same as the serialized text. The following year another edition appeared, and the year after that, in 1860, a third. Three years later, Blackwood issued a corrected text—minor changes all—along with *Silas Marner* in a single edition of Eliot's work, a 6-shilling cheap edition which was to capitalize on her growing popularity. This 1863 edition then became the basis for the illustrated edition of 1867, when Eliot had become a best-selling author. *Scenes of Clerical Life* was Volume IV in this 1867 edition and itself appeared in 1868. One more edition, the Cabinet, appeared in Eliot's lifetime, in 1878 (the Cabinet edition went from 1878 to 1880). Eliot had corrected three versions of *Clerical Life:* the first book publication; then the 1863 edition as part of the 6-shilling offering; and then, finally, the version for the illustrated edition. None of these editions, incidentally, shows more than minimal corrections; here and there, we find an alternate or deleted passage. The manuscript is in the J. Pierpont Morgan Library in New York City.

ship when each dotes on the other, before financial positions harden or other considerations set them at each other's throats. The sending of checks created a small ripple, however, since Lewes had to back all checks made out to Eliot with his signature; and he suggested that, instead of the mailing back and forth called for, Blackwood send the amount with the proof of Part III. He assures the publisher that "Gilfil" in this third part "improves greatly"; he even calls the development "exciting," and the "subtle truth in delineation of complex motives is better than anything he has yet done in that way."

In return, on 11 March, Blackwood sent on £45 for Parts II and III, a sum sufficiently large to allow Eliot and Lewes to take a vacation in the Scilly Isles, twenty-eight miles southwest of Land's End, Cornwall, of King Arthur fame. They planned to leave by mid-March. But things were bothering Blackwood, off in Scotland, and one of them was Caterina with a dagger and murder in her heart. "I have grave doubts, about the dagger," he told Lewes, "beautifully as the impossibility of her using it is indicated. I daresay George Eliot will kick furiously at the base idea of altering a syllable at this point, but I am pretty sure that this dear little heroine would be more sure of universal sympathy if she only dreamed or felt as if she could stab the cur to the heart and I think it would be more consistent with her character than the active step of getting hold of the lethal weapon." Blackwood's suggestions, directed at Eliot, had to pass through Lewes, who once more indicated how diffident and sensitive his friend was.

As the publisher surmised, Eliot rejected his idea of a "dream sequence": ". . . it would be the death of my story to substitute a dream for the real scene. Dreams usually play an important part in fiction, but rarely, I think, in actual life." Eliot was, all in all, defending her kind of realism, which meant not flinching from something as unpleasant as a dagger. She makes a strong point, that many people feel a criminal impulse even when they are guarded by their entire constitution from committing a crime. The comment is, of course, personal as well as fictive, and suggests how deeply Marian and then Eliot intended to protect her territory. Of equal significance is her insistence that she wished "to retain my incognito for some time to come, and to an author not already famous, anonymity is the highest *prestige*." Besides, she adds, "if George Eliot turns out a dull dog and an ineffective writer—a mere flash in the pan—I, for one, am determined to cut him on the first intimation of that disagreeable fact." With this, we glimpse still another side of the nom de plume. It gave Marian an opportunity to evade possible disaster as a writer and afforded her an escape from something she knew she could not confront directly.

Lewes's journal records the couple's departure for the Scilly Isles, via the Great Western Hotel in London and then Plymouth on the southern coast of Devon, where they arrived after a seventy-one-hour trip from London. They found lodgings, and Lewes's description is amusing. "Everything rickety in the house. Bedpole fell as I drew aside the curtain. Teapot with wobbley top; fender without rests; chairs with yielding back etc." He sounds Dickensian. Not until the 26th were they able to take the packet boat. Since they were exhausted by their journey so far, Eliot feared the extra seasickness of a rocky trip. The journey to St. Mary's, the largest of the Isles, as it turned out, was not easy. They were the sole passengers, perhaps an indication of their courage. *

The Scilly venture, despite the ardors of the journey itself, was important for Eliot. In this quiet and isolated place, by early April, she completed "Gilfil," and entered into a reading program, mainly of fiction, a change from her usual fare of heavy, nonfiction books. Even more significantly, the fiction she read was of the kind which would enter into her own work, although she was already familiar with some of it. After reading Mrs. Gaskell's *Cranford,* she took up her life of Charlotte Brontë, then Brontë's *The Professor.* She reread Hawthorne's *The Scarlet Letter,* Elizabeth Barrett Browning's *Aurora Leigh,* and then focused on the work of Jane Austen, reading all but *Pride and Prejudice,* which she already knew. Lewes was, as he had shown in his 1852 article "The Lady Novelists," a great admirer of Austen, having lauded her as a model writer for having achieved complete control over her material. In "Gilfil," in the unequal audience between Caterina and Sir Christopher, Eliot had already incorporated a scene from *Mansfield Park.*

Her reading helped establish Eliot in a tradition of powerful female novelists. Healing some of the divisions within herself, it surely gave her a kind of confidence. When, after Charlotte Brontë's death in 1855, Lewes corresponded with Mrs. Gaskell and praised her life of the writer, he suggests that her *Brontë* has application to the still novice Eliot in her fiction, providing perhaps some guidance and certainly associating her with her female predecessors and contemporaries. "The book will, I think," he writes, "create a deep and permanent impression; for it not only presents a vivid picture of a life noble and sad, full of encouragement and healthy teaching, a lesson in duty and selfreliance [vide Eliot]; it also, thanks to its artistic power, makes us familiar inmates of an interior so strange, so original in its individual elements and so picturesque in its externals—it paints for us at once the psychological drama and the scenic accessories with so much vividness—that fiction has nothing more wild, touching, and heart-strengthening to place above it." Unlike Charlotte, Emily Brontë is viewed as "une bête fauve in power, splendour, and wildness." On 16 April, Lewes sent on Part IV of "Gilfil," completed on the 8th. He was himself preparing "New Seaside Studies" for *Maga,* for the June issue.

As a consequence of her sister's latest disaster, with typhus, Eliot wrote her brother Isaac to transfer to Chrissey £15 of her, Marian's, next half-year income, to be used for a holiday or change of air. She asks Isaac, in fact, to advance the

---

* Coinciding with their departure for the Scilly Isles was a series of tragedies befalling Eliot's sister Chrissey, who seemed dogged by misfortune. One of Chrissey's daughters, Frances, died at the age of seven, from typhus; another daughter, Catherine, now five, almost died from it; and Chrissey herself barely recovered from it. The nature of the illness suggests some carelessness in Chrissey's way of life, since typhus, except among the very poor and destitute, was not at mid-century a major killer; it suggests, further, that she was so harassed by life she had lost control over it. Eliot mourned the loss, since she was attached to the children; but, curiously, the incident does not appear to have upset her as much as we would have expected, the reason probably being her distancing of herself from all such events connected to her past.

money if it cannot be freed up as yet. He had apparently written recently, but Eliot's letter is quite formal and stiff, part of her general distancing of herself from Coventry. A stranger in name, she was truly a stranger in fact.

Another part of the Coventry world Eliot had to confront was Sara Hennell's *Christianity and Infidelity*, whose very title made her brain rattle. She writes to Sara of the couple's reading and reveals that Sophocles is her latest love. "I rush on the slightest pretext to Sophocles and am as excited about blind old Oedipus as any young lady can be about the latest hero with magnificent eyes." She also mentions reading Mrs. Gaskell's *Charlotte Brontë,* and she comments on Branwell Brontë in a way which recalls her own fictional processes, perhaps in her forthcoming portrait of Dempster in "Janet's Repentance." "She sets down Branwell's conduct entirely to remorse," Eliot tells Sara about a wayward brother, "and the falseness of that position weakens the effect of her philippics against the woman [Mrs. Edmund Robinson] who hurried on his utter fall.* Remorse may make sad work with a man, but it would not make such a life as Branwell's was in the last three or four years unless the germs of vice had sprouted and shot up long before, as it seems clear they had in him. What a tragedy—that picture [at the end of Gaskell's Chapter 13] of the old father and the three sisters trembling night and day in terror at the possible deeds of this drunken brutal son and brother!" In "Janet's Repentance," which Eliot would soon begin, this is very close to Janet's response to Dempster as his drinking and choleric temper intensify. In some dark corner, Eliot was perhaps also thinking of Isaac—brothers are problematic in her fiction.

Even now, in mid-April, she had not heard from Isaac about Chrissey's condition, which was still serious, even critical. She commented to Sara about Barbara Smith, her activist friend, who was planning to marry Eugène Bodichon, which did not "satisfy" her and Lewes. Bodichon was one of those undefinable nineteenth-century figures, a less warrior-like forerunner of T. E. Lawrence, a mixture of social conscience and a desire to disguise himself. Born of a well-placed bourgeois Brittany family, he became a physician who practiced in Algiers, where he met Barbara. An early cultural anthropologist, he also had very liberal views and worked to abolish slavery in the Arab countries. As he aged, he grew more caught up in his own designs and in idealistic causes, and yet at forty-seven he decided to marry. Along with his other personal eccentricities, he took on Arab and other peasant clothes and manners even when in London, giving him the reputation of a crackpot. For Barbara, after Chapman, Bodichon perhaps seemed "normal." Allowing for vast differences, Barbara and

---

* Mrs. Gaskell's assertion that Branwell was seduced by Mrs. Robinson and asked to elope with her—Branwell was her children's tutor—was never proven, and she was forced to withdraw it from the English edition. But the next part is even more compelling for Eliot's own use: the Reverend Robinson changed his will so that if his widow ever saw Branwell again, she would forfeit her entire bequest. With this, Mrs. Gaskell says, Branwell descended into his own version of the snake pit. This detail, of changing the will to forbid contact with a particular person, is precisely what Casaubon does in *Middlemarch* to discourage Dorothea and Will Ladislaw from marrying. Eliot's point with Branwell is that he was deeply infected by vice, and that, not remorse, did him in. She argues for something intrinsic as against the biographer's more sentimental remorse.

Marian had each made bizarre choices. As much as anyone, as we shall see, Barbara Bodichon was a model for Eliot's Romola in that 1863 novel.

Lewes and Eliot stayed on Scilly for seven weeks, mainly as a retiring place where they could work. Whereas Lewes had more or less exhausted his researches into marine specimens, Eliot was beginning to write "Janet's Repentance," which she completed on 30 May, the work of perhaps a month. "Janet's Repentance" takes on more significance in her career than the previous two novellas since it really begins her characteristic style. Her insights deepened, her prose became more trenchant, her powers of characterization intensified, her philosophical ideas broadened, and her fictional powers overall became less constricted. This third novella in Clerical Life becomes distinctive Eliot. Like the others, the novella is a return to her childhood, to the period when England was calmer and less "progressive." But the correlation between actual people and fictional re-creation is less obvious, although the Reverend Tryan was apparently based on the evangelical curate at Nuneaton, John Edmund Jones. Milby, the town in "Janet's Repentance," is a description of Nuneaton, but by virtue of unique details it becomes Eliot's own. Although Milby now is enlightened and modern, the town of Janet's time was a slow-moving, gossipy place; withal, a town which considered its life to be delightful. It was anything but.

Eliot's method is to circle around Milby and its people before focusing on Janet and her angry, drunken, choleric husband, the lawyer Robert Dempster. We are made to endure several portraits of minimal concern in order to locate Janet as part of this milieu, and then to see how she fits and interacts. It is a method Eliot would prefer, providing long, often dull, scenes of gossipy townspeople, a kind of Greek chorus, but with a distinct purpose in mind. Combining both memory and immediacy, the procedure turned the novelist into a kind of biographer. That latter role fitted her well since she was trying to bring to life a mutant form linking fictional matters with history, politics, social questions, and, most of all, moral and ethical issues. As biographer, she could break free of standard narratives and characterization into newer forms, their embryo in "Janet's Repentance."

As history and memory, this novella, like the others, is concerned with how the present has changed, and how the past is either receding or failing to penetrate into contemporary consciousness. The vicious Dempster states the point incisively when he attacks the evangelical Tryan as the embodiment of all negative change. Eliot may have forsaken her earlier beliefs, but she wanted to keep the record clear; an attack by the villainous Dempster was one way. "The pulpit from which our venerable pastor has fed us with sound doctrine for half a century is not to be invaded by a fanatical, sectarian, double-faced, Jesuitical interloper." He continues: "We are not to have a preacher obtruding himself upon us, who decries good works [not true of Tryan], and sneaks into our homes perverting the faith of our wives and daughters!" Dempster sees the young as demoralized and corrupted as an outgrowth of Tryan's Sunday evening lectures. He alleges that nothing less than the breakdown of society will occur, a society which he sees based on common interests that disallow individual expression.

He also foresees political dangers. "We are not to be poisoned with doctrines which damp every innocent enjoyment, and pick a poor man's pockets of the six-pence with which he might buy himself a cheerful glass after a hard day's work. . . ." The lawyer's implied point is not reformist, but that the worker be kept in line with his glass of beer; that our "innocent enjoyments" are part of a social polity, not to be endangered by intrusive ideas. A drunk worker is a safe worker.

Like the other novellas in *Clerical Life*, this one is controlled by an "I," a narrator who otherwise plays little role. But the "I" provided Eliot with a witness and further strengthened her idea of a document or historical record of what occurred. Furthermore, the "I" allowed her to maintain a persona within the narrative which added to the persona she maintained outside of it, as George Eliot and as Mrs. Lewes. Hidden, secured, shielded, she could manifest her awareness that in a world which does not validate divine creation and in which heavenly reward cannot be found in faith, there is an implicit melancholy in all human endeavor. No longer was her voice buried.

Yet even as she probed into the most narrow, even cruel, motives, she attempted to discover where a particular life went wrong, where some balancing element may be revealed, where human qualities still poke through the venial self. Even Dempster, now plotting to bring down Tryan, still has enough humanity to take a walk with his old mother. Overall, however, her subject is "loss," and loss leads inevitably to sadness, decline, death. "Our habitual life," she writes, "is like a wall hung with pictures, which has been shone on by the suns of many years: take one of the pictures away, and it leaves a definite blank space, to which our eyes can never turn without a sensation of discomfort. Nay, the involuntary loss of any familiar object almost always brings a chill as from an evil omen; it seems to be the first finger-shadow of advancing death."

She finally gets to her subject, which is the plight of a woman who has made the wrong choice in marriage. This is the fate of Janet Dempster and her effort to survive what was not an unlikely Victorian marriage.* Dempster is the ultimate male chauvinist, choleric both outside and inside the home, and someone who must punish his wife for his own mistakes. The portrait of Dempster reveals Eliot at her most hostile to married men, to the institution of marriage itself. It is a portrait etched in venom. One night, Janet is thrown from her home, in her nightgown, into the chill, and she has virtually no one who can understand her or her position. She is no working-class woman with a drunken husband, but a genteel, well-bred, attractive middle-class figure, whose divestiture of everything is unexpected. Her own property is controlled by her husband, under

---

* Although Janet seems based on Mrs. Nancy Wallington Buchanan—of the Wallington School, where Mary Anne had boarded from 1828 to 1832—Eliot took considerable pains to reconfigure the story. About the only element which was true to the original was Mr. Buchanan's accident that shattered his legs, which is duplicated when Dempster has his accident and dies. Buchanan did not die, nor was the marriage with Nancy Wallington, the daughter of the school's owner, drunken or violent. The Reverend John Edmund Jones, the model for Mr. Tryan, was persecuted, but not by Buchanan. Another point: Mrs. Buchanan actually predeceased her husband, with Eliot of course changing the chronologies so that Janet survives Dempster.

the Married Women's Property Act; and even if she had it, it was barely sufficient without his aid. He has in effect put her out of life as well as home, since
all her energies have gone into her marriage—helpless within it, as circumstances proved, and helpless without it. Her options now are few, and she seeks
out Tryan, whom earlier she had conspired against with her husband. The married man destroyed; the single man might save.

Tryan receives the bulk of Eliot's compassion. His is a secret, quiet, sad life,
an early version of Silas Marner. When Janet confesses to him her horrible
existence with Dempster, he must control his own feelings in order to comfort
her. As a man who tries to equate inner and outer life, he lives according to
what he believes are Christian principles. "In this artificial life of ours," Eliot
writes of Tryan, "it is not often we see a human face with all a heart's agony in
it, uncontrolled by self-consciousness; when we do see it, it startles us as if we
had suddenly waked into the real world of which this everyday one is but a
puppet-show copy." Tryan's quiet life has gone on at the opposite end from
Dempster's tempest, so that Dempster's violent hostility is a real threat. Yet,
withal, the man of God lives only in his faith; for the rest, he is sunk into his
own kind of depressed living, hardly taking care of himself, letting himself sink
into illness through poor food, poor hygiene, and poor sanitation, a man seeking
martyrdom through self-neglect. Even as he fades, he must cater to Janet's
needs, especially when Dempster dies, from his own excesses.

Janet must now face the desperation of widowhood; for despite the horrors of
her marriage, she fears the lonely years ahead. Eliot knows loneliness and such
fears, whether spinsterhood or widowhood, and knows how women are isolated
by their social conditions. Widowhood for them is often the same as death itself.
"It is such vague undefinable states of susceptibility as this—states of excitement
or depression, half mental, half physical—that determine many a tragedy in
women's lives. Janet could scarcely eat anything at her solitary dinner: she tried
to fix her attention on a book in vain; she walked about the garden, and felt the
sunshine melancholy." Life in this respect ends. When Tryan himself dies, Janet
has been sufficiently strengthened to go on—we see her with children around
her in her later years. The point, however, is not the ultimate triumph over
despondency, but the difficult path for the woman who does not quite fit or the
woman whose marriage goes badly. Janet's tale reaches out to nearly all of Eliot's
future fiction.

It is clear that had Eliot so chosen she could have spun out such tales or novellas
for some time to come. They paid well, they came forth almost effortlessly, and
they derived from the abundance of her own past. Instead, she stopped and
became more ambitious. What was at stake was something profoundly linked to
her sense of herself: that the real challenge in imaginative writing was the novel,
especially in the late 1850s and early 1860s when Victorian fiction blossomed.
If nothing else, the novel had overtaken English poetry and become, with Dickens, Thackeray, Trollope, Meredith, the Brontës, Mrs. Gaskell, and several
others, the voice of mid-century and thereafter. If Eliot was to make her mark,
it must be in longer fiction.

This, however, was still in the future: *Adam Bede,* her first novel, began to emerge only in late 1858, with the first four chapters by early January of 1859. In May of 1857, when she had just begun "Janet's Repentance,"* the couple, on the 11th, left the Scilly Isles for Jersey,† another idyllic place which required a good deal of travel. Lewes was familiar with Jersey, since he had attended school there, St. Helier's, a fully twenty-eight years before.

Their stay on Jersey was idyllic, but there were other elements in the background which could not be ignored. While Eliot's writing was going well, and Blackwood was responding to Lewes about it with enthusiasm,‡ she was not quite free of her past. There were several levels of anxiety: Chrissey's hard time in the "fever-stricken house of Attleborough"; thoughts of Cara and Sara, now becoming shadowy and distant; and, most of all, her own position vis-à-vis her brother, Isaac. He was displaying the cruel hardness Eliot later associated with Tom Tulliver in *The Mill on the Floss,* but she also found she could not easily give him up. Actually, as her journal descriptions of Jersey reveal, the grassy aspects of the terrain made her temporarily homesick for Nuneaton and conscious of her separation. This awareness of being cut off not so incidentally coincided with career decisions that would increase the division even more.

Writing from Gorey, on Jersey, Eliot told Sara of her nostalgia. But more significant than that, her train of thought led her to write Isaac and to put their relationship on a new footing. The letter is signed Marian Lewes, calculated to prod her brother one way or another. Dated 26 May, the letter could have been the result of the birth of another child to Agnes by Thornton Hunt, a daughter born on 21 May and registered as Mildred Jane Lewes—a connection between a young female child and *her* brothers. But more likely the letter to Isaac was motivated by a host of other factors, a leading one being her need to make sense of naming itself. Another was her feeling of homesickness for her early years with Isaac, the past as evidenced in the three novellas she had written and which would reappear in *Adam Bede* and *Mill.*

It seems almost certain that even as she transformed her past into fiction, she had to decode the fiction back into some form of emotional past for herself. The letter to Isaac, a dramatic point in her emergence and liberation, was full of such conflicting feelings. Another interpretation of her motives for writing is that she was so strengthened by the success of her fiction, felt so secure with Lewes—even to using him as her agent—and had so turned around her life, she felt sufficiently self-assured to write Isaac about personal matters. Yet given her

---

* "Janet's Repentance" appeared in five issues of *Maga,* July–November of 1857.

† Located in the bay of Mont St. Michel, Jersey is the largest and most southerly of the Channel Islands. The couple settled in a small village, Gorey (in Rosa Cottage), about four miles from St. Helier, on the coast facing France. Jersey was a dependency of the British crown, but French was the language of choice.

‡ Blackwood wrote Lewes once all of "Gilfil" was in: "I am very anxious to see the next story. Tell George Eliot that I hope he will be in a very great form as he will run along side of a new series by Bulwer [Lytton] and I should like our Clerical friend to come out well in such company. Sir Edward is I think first rate." Little did Blackwood or Eliot herself realize she would leave Bulwer in the dust; his work is of interest now only to historians of period fiction, and best known for *The Last Days of Pompeii* because Hollywood made it into a successful motion picture.

vulnerability to scandal, and to Agnes Lewes's faucet-like productivity, it might seem more a defensive move on Eliot's part than an act of bravura or a display of self-confidence. In this most important area, her motives remain enigmatical.

She starts with "My dear Brother." Then: "You will be surprised, I dare say, but I hope not sorry, to learn that I have changed my name, and have someone to take care of me in the world. The event is not at all a sudden one, though it may appear sudden in its announcement to you. My husband has been known to me for several years, and I am well acquainted with his mind and character. He is occupied entirely with scientific and learned pursuits, is several years older than myself, and has three boys, two of whom are at school in Switzerland, and one in England." As we shall see, Isaac gave his solicitor the pleasure of responding and sending for the facts of the case. In the meantime, Marian plowed on, now presenting herself to her family, as to Blackwood, as someone she was not.

She tells Isaac of the couple's plan to stay either in Jersey or in Brittany for some months to come, because of her frail health. Was this an effort to gain his sympathy? She asks Isaac to pay her income, from the fund, directly into Lewes's account at the Union Bank in London. This was, of course, inflammatory. She repeats her request that Chrissey be given £15 from her, Marian's, half-year income. She encloses a letter to her half-sister, Fanny Houghton, in Leamington, to be forwarded. She signs: "Your affectionate sister, Marian Lewes." It was a valiant effort which proved futile. Like Tom Tulliver, Isaac fell back on his rigid respectability and, in effect, routed his sister to the allegorical Coventry. *

The letter to Fanny was one of several in which she presented herself as Mrs. Lewes—even while writing "Janet's Repentance" as George Eliot and signing one letter to Fanny as "Marian Lewes *alias* Polly." Writing to Fanny, she says she hopes the latter has sufficient sisterly affection for her to accept her "kind husband"—something more of a plea than a statement. On 27 May, Marian wrote Chapman, who had now become a medical doctor. The conferring of medical degrees was not too finely tuned or supervised, and after only a few months of study, Chapman received his degree from St. Andrews University. In any event, Marian informed Chapman she had taken the step to inform her family she was married. Chapman of course knew the true story of Lewes and Agnes. But he had been Marian's post office address, and with this in the open, he no longer had to function surreptitiously. In his way, he had remained loyal to his subeditor, although part of his support came from the knowledge that he desperately needed her help on the *Review*.

In this frenzy of confession—coinciding with these three novellas touching on her past—Marian wrote, still further, to Sara Hennell. She says she has informed her family "with what is *essential* in my position, and if any utterly

---

* In March of 1856, in the *Leader*, Marian had published "Antigone and Its Moral," and it is hard not to believe that the tale of Antigone and her brothers reverberated personally for her. Her argument there is not reverence for the dead or the significance of sacred burial rites, but sisterly feeling versus the legalities of the state. By arguing this way, she brought Sophocles' play into line with her own sibling problems.

false report reaches them in the first instance, their minds will be prepared not to accept it without reserve." She assumes that Chrissey will not give up correspondence with her even after Isaac applies pressure. "If I live five years longer [Eliot was now thirty-seven], the positive result of my existence on the side of truth and goodness will outweigh the small negative good that would have consisted in my not doing anything to shock others, and I can conceive no consequence that will make me repent the past." This letter is signed "Pollian." It is both defiant and wistful, manifesting her twin selves of open rebellion alongside a desire to be accepted back. She was tough, but also ready to pick up any link offered her.

Fanny's response came and was helpful, although it is doubtful that she knew the whole story. Fanny sent on, amusingly, some information on stories in *Maga* about Chilvers Coton and Arbury, written by a Mr. Liggins of Attleborough, so she had been informed. Marian then pulled her magical vanishing act, disappearing within the swirl of her words to her half-sister in explaining why Liggins could not be the author and creating still another confusion of realms in the information she was conveying to her family. "You are wrong," she wrote, "about Mr. Liggins or rather your information is wrong. We too have been struck with the 'Clerical Sketches,' and I have recognized some figures and traditions connected with our old neighbourhood. But Blackwood informs Mr. Lewes that the author is a Mr. Eliot, a clergyman, I presume. *Au reste*, he may be a relation of M. Liggins or some other 'Mr.' who knows Coton stories." This letter is signed "Marian Lewes *alias* Polly," which links present and past.

The division into selves and the explanations going forth to clarify her position *even while* she throws further confusion into the plot characterize Eliot in this period. Her response suggests extreme agitation which had no way of emerging except in the violence of "Janet's Repentance": physical brutality, psychological cruelty, drunkenness, the expulsion of Janet. The story contains several extremes, the aforesaid violence and cruelty, bonded to great injustice, but also the opposite, a gentle world which can also be Janet's. It is difficult to know if Eliot's own internal agitation found sufficient re-creation in what she was writing; but it is also possible she internalized these "confusions" and then intensified them to violence when she heard from the family solicitor in lieu of Isaac. This sequence of letters led to precisely the opposite of what she had consciously intended when she wrote her family that she was married: they cut her off. But there is another line to the story: she may have decided to precipitate this response, forcing them to make the move, acceptance or rejection. Still another possibility is that in order to justify *her* dismissive view of them, she wrote her family fully knowing their response would be negative. Flush with professional success, she felt bravado; but becoming George Eliot, or Mrs. Lewes, was not proving to be easy.

Before hearing the devastating news of Isaac's rejection from the solicitor, Eliot wrote Cara a long newsy letter full of future plans for herself and for Lewes, including his need to take Bertie, his youngest son, to join his brothers in Switzerland. This 5 June letter contains an amusing description: "You wonder how my face has changed in the last three years. Doubtless it is older and uglier, but it ought not to have a bad expression, for I never have anything to call out my ill-humour or discontent. . . . and I have everything to call out love and gratitude."

She also received a letter from Blackwood with his most incisive critique yet of her writing, this concerning the first four chapters of "Janet's Repentance." He found it drawn out and wished she had gotten to the "powerful and pathetic story" sooner rather than later. "The first scene especially," he writes, "I think you should shorten. It is deuced good but rather a staggerer in an opening scene of a Story of Clerical Life. Dempster is rather too barefaced a brute and I am sorry that the poor wife's suffering should have driven her to so unsentimental a resource as beer." He says he cannot comment further until he sees more. Blackwood was not as yet attuned to Eliot's slow pacing, which was more suitable to longer fiction than to a novella or tale. But he does admit that he and his brother liked it better after a second reading. What he objects to, this voice of Victorian mediation, is the roughness Eliot displays, what he calls the "harsher Thackerayan view of human nature. . . ." He wanted a more harmonious view, even if it was not true. This is, of course, precisely what Eliot was struggling against. Her realism heightened truth, did not deny it. Yet some of Blackwood's strictures are well taken. Dempster is an unrelieved brute, one of the few in Eliot's works, and suggestive of a boiling center internalized within her which could only become manifest in a character full of violence and cruelty. Blackwood's letter about her "new life" as a fiction writer came just one day before the solicitor's, which carried her back into her "old life." The solicitor's letter deserves lengthy quotation.

> I have had an interview with your Brother in consequence of your letter to him announcing your marriage. He is so much hurt at your not having previously made some communication with him as to your intention and prospects [i.e., obtaining his permission to go ahead, heeding his advice] that he cannot make up his mind to write, feeling that he could not do so in a Brotherly Spirit. . . . Perhaps you will not object to make some communication to me which I may convey to them [brother and sister]. Permit me to ask when and where you were married and what is the occupation of Mr. Lewes, who I think you refer to in your letter as being actively employed, and where his residence is as you request a remittance to be made to his Bankers in London by the Trustees under your Father's Will.

The solicitor is writing to a woman of thirty-seven, but the tone is that of an adult addressing a child, an indication of where women stood in financial and legal matters.

Eliot was now engaged on two fronts: dealing with her family through the solicitor, Vincent Holbeche, whose business went back to Robert Evans, and responding to Blackwood, who, for the first time, had been frankly critical of her submission to *Maga*. It was a double crisis, and it surely contaminated the otherwise idyllic nature of Jersey in the spring. Her 11 June response to her publisher's misgivings was an immediate denial she was wounded by his remarks. She says she is grateful to be allowed entrance into an editor's frank judgment. While she cannot make any but superficial alterations in her proofs, she will attempt an explanation—which suggests that Blackwood misread what she wrote. "The collision in the drama is not at all between 'bigotted church-manship' and evangelicalism," she explains, "but between irreligion and religion. Religion in this case happens to be represented by evangelicalism, and the story as far as regards the *persecution* is a real bit in the religious history of England that happened about eight-and-twenty years ago." She says that in fact she softened everything; the reality was much harsher. "The real town was more vicious than my Milby; the real Dempster was far more disgusting than mine; the real Janet alas! had a far sadder end than mine. . . ." She says she has had an intimate knowledge of these people, with close observation of them in their real lives. If she undertook to alter Dempster's language or character, she would be playing to "what may possibly exist in other people's minds, but has no existence in my own."

She has, of course, fallen back on her sense of truth and reality, truth to her feelings and the reality of ordinary lives which need no embellishment to offer up a rich texture. She continues: ". . . as an artist I should be utterly powerless if I departed from my own conceptions of life and character. . . . I am keenly alive, at once to the scruples and alarms an editor may feel, and to my own utter inability to write under any cramping influence, and on this double ground I should like you to consider whether it will not be better to close the series for the Magazine *now*. I daresay you will feel no difficulty about publishing a volume containing the story of Janet's Repentance, though you may not like to hazard its insertion in the Magazine, and I shall accept that plan with no other feeling than that you have been to me the most liberal and agreeable of editors and are the man of all others I would choose for a publisher." She repeats that if he thinks she has failed with "Janet," then "Gilfil" should close the series.

Then came the measured response to Vincent Holbeche, on 13 June. The other half of Eliot's life was closing, and she wanted to avoid being crushed. She tells the solicitor she is glad her brother did not write if he felt unfriendly, the very point Maggie makes about Tom in *Mill*. She understands, she says, the need of a third person as an intermediary, although that device pained her as creating an enormous distance. She then enters thickets when, after identifying Lewes as a well-known author, she admits "Our marriage is not a legal one, though it is regarded by us both as a sacred bond. He is unable at present to contract a legal marriage, because, though long deprived of his first wife by her misconduct, he is not legally divorced."

The admission would become Isaac's means to distance himself from her, as Tom emotionally disowns Maggie when her behavior with Stephen Guest in *Mill* upsets his sense of propriety and male control. Eliot repeats she has been Lewes's wife and has borne his name for nearly three years, "a fact which has been known to all my personal friends except the members of my own family, from whom I have withheld it because knowing that their views of life differ in many respects from my own, I wished not to give them unnecessary pain."

Suddenly, the letter becomes caustic, even surly, in tone. "It may be desirable to mention to you that I am not dependent on any one [her assertion of adulthood], the larger part of my income for several years having been derived from my own constant labour as a writer. You will perceive, therefore, that in my conduct towards my own family I have not been guided by any motives of self-interest, since I have been neither in the reception nor the expectation of the slightest favour from them." With this, she was already distancing herself emotionally for their rejection.

Then, officiously, she speaks of Lewes's account at the Union Bank of London and presumes, she says, that she has the right to appoint the payment of interest "due to me to any person I may choose to name." The import of this gives the appearance she was supporting Lewes; or, to see it from the Evans point of view, that she was passion's child. In any case, she could not have her own account without revealing her cover. She ends in more of a conciliatory manner, saying she recalls Holbeche's friendship with her father, and also that the solicitor gained for her some £100 after Evans's death in lieu of household goods. She signs her letter "Marian Lewes." Holbeche then forwarded her letter to Isaac, with a note saying that he, the solicitor, need add no further comment. Isaac never responded, and he put pressure on Chrissey and Fanny, also, to sever all correspondence with their wayward sister. With consequences she had foreseen and even sought, Eliot had now cut herself off. Having tried to justify her outcast status, she had lost all but her £100 annuity.

Lewes himself, ever supportive, wrote Blackwood a long letter saying he was "in raptures" over "Janet." He says Blackwood's comments, therefore, staggered him, and two readings later of the novella have still left him in the dark as to the publisher's objections. Here Lewes is pitting his literary judgment against Blackwood's. He says Dempster is a marvelous creation, although Blackwood seemed more on target in thinking the lawyer lacked the nuances that might strengthen the story. Then Lewes opens up an entirely new tack: "I had set my heart on breaking through the incognito, and bringing you and Eliot together [Blackwood was leaving town], feeling sure that if you once saw and conversed with him and found the sensitive, shrinking, refined creature he is, you would have your opinion of your new contributor considerably modified." Lewes had hit upon a strategy, for he had no intention of introducing Eliot, since he was still speaking of a man. The plan was to mollify Blackwood and keep him open to Eliot's work, to offer him entrance into the inner sanctum. However much Lewes believed in his companion's work, the payment of another £22.10 into his account could have alone nudged him along, since, as we have seen, this money made the difference between living frugally and being free to travel.

Blackwood, meanwhile, was spelling out his meaning to Eliot. "I do not fall in with George Eliots every day, and the idea of stopping the Series as suggested in your letter gave me 'quite a turn' to use one of Thackeray's favourite phrases." He says he will not hesitate to publish it. On the contrary, it is impossible to read it without being impressed by the truth of individual pictures. He says he did not fear that his talented author was wasting his power by sketching in figures who would prove excessive or extraneous—not recognizing yet that Eliot was pointing toward length and breadth. He does admit he feels the first part will not be much liked, but every author needs his way of proceeding. He agrees he is writing in the dark, since he has not seen the whole manuscript. Of course, behind the Blackwood reaction was his own high-church sympathies and a certain religious, and perhaps social, disdain for the Tryans of the world, living in squalor and preaching an evangelicalism which snapped at high-church Anglicanism. But Blackwood was enough of an editor and publisher to move beyond his own prejudices, and he did not wish to lose George Eliot. His letter is in almost every respect a retreat. He ends by saying he would have liked to shake hands with the author.

Eliot was obviously gratified at this response from a man she truly respected. She says she made several minor revisions which would help to bring the manuscript closer to his criticisms, although his major objections would not be met. Her revisions, incidentally, were not extensive, more often a phrase or passage than anything substantive.* She assures Blackwood that as the story proceeds he will see how everything fits, this slow development heralding the novelist more than the writer of tales. She indicates she looks forward to many years of happy and friendly exchanges between them. (Such would be the case, until, in a moment of weakness and greed, she broke with the faithful Blackwood and went elsewhere, only to return repentant.)

These intense and feverish exchanges calmed down at the end of June, and on the 28th, Eliot entered into her journal her recollections of the Scillies. We have already noted her trip, but of interest is the fact she could finally turn to her journal only when she had settled both her personal and professional lives. She was running so many varied lives that the journal was simply another level; if anyone wanted to get at her, it would prove an archeological dig, or the search for a palimpsest. Layered and re-layered, she was burrowing in: the letters, the fictional efforts, the journal observing her journey and her life with Lewes, the name changes, the deceptions about her personal life, her opening up finally about her "marriage," her attempt at damage control with Blackwood on the one hand and with her family on the other, the need for compensatory happiness through writing while holding tight to her secret. It was, all in all, an

---

* The following passage from Chapter Two, on drunkenness, the longest deletion, may have been excised in response to Blackwood's concern. After some remarks on virtue, Eliot comes to the point: "Drunkenness was indulged in with great candour; no one put on very charming manners to his wife when in company; neighbours on the best of terms imputed boastful lying and spiteful detraction to each other without affectation of disgust; and other sins prayed against in the litany were the subject of very free allusion and were committed with considerable openness. Dempster's life, to be sure, was thought too flagrantly irregular; his drinking was out of bounds, and he often abused his wife beyond what was reasonable. Still he was one of those valuable public characters in whom society has at all times tolerated an extra amount of private aberration; he was very well received in most houses, and there were several ladies rather proud of 'knowing how to manage Dempster,' or of jocosely twitting him with being a sad husband" (Morgan Library manuscript, Folios 22 / 23).

enormously rich time, a spur to her imagination, giving her little time to indulge in illness or depression. Her health throughout seemed relatively strong, and she had created identities even if she had to lie about them.

Blackwood's remarks on Part II, in proof, reveal that he was still struck by negative aspects of Eliot's characterizations. Yet while Blackwood could ask for gentler fictional treatment, in life he could be quite assertive, as he showed during the famous Madeleine Smith trial. Smith was on trial, during the first week in July, in Edinburgh, for the arsenic poisoning of her lover, Emile l'Angelier, who refused to return the love letters written to him during their affair. Blackwood hoped she would be acquitted, saying she was a nice young woman and he doubted if she really "did poison the beast." In any case, he deserved it, he says. "I wish the dog had died and made no sign. . . ." It is an amusing comment for the staid publisher, but his sense of honor had been piqued, and it was this sense of honor, transferred to literary matters, which would characterize his publishing history with Eliot. He even admits that George Eliot had become a celebrity of sorts by way of being a "mysterious author."

In response to further manuscript objections by Blackwood, Eliot had become more accommodating, admitting to small changes in the conclusion. In other cases, she stood firm. Blackwood argued that the placard—the indictment of Tryan cast in broadly satirical terms—was too long and he suggested it be cut down. He is, he says, eager to have the story get on with Janet. Eliot answered that she did not intend the placard (or playbill) to have "Attic wit," but rather Milby wit. Fine sarcasm, she says, would not be fitting; broadness is. Falling back on "truth" as justification for her method, she cites that in the real situation such a playbill was printed and circulated. Her comments on her art were now recycled for Blackwood's sake, not for eternity; she did not precisely hold to what she told him:

> Art must be either real and concrete, or ideal and eclectic. Both are good and true in their way, but my stories are of the former kind. I undertake to exhibit nothing as it should be; I only try to exhibit some things as they have been or are seen through such a medium as my own nature gives me. The moral effect of the stories of course depends on my power of seeing truly and feeling justly; and as I am not conscious of looking at things through the medium of cynicism or irreverence, I can't help hoping there is no tendency in what I write to produce those miserable mental states.

This was the basis for Eliot's career, but it was not cast in stone. While all her work thrusts toward the real and the concrete, her psychological probing creates another dimension which moves her close to the "ideal," if we take the ideal to mean not something romantic but metamorphic. It is in just this area that she becomes the distinctive voice of the century. Through psychological probing, patterns of doubling, manifestations of her own dualism, Eliot moved well beyond her own characterization of herself, significant as that description is in defining her conscious sense of her powers. But she was not Gissing in her realism, just as she was not Dickens. She was not even Thackeray, although we can observe affinities. She was not Jane Austen, either. Her affinities to Charlotte Brontë, however, are often clear, especially in their ability to intensify the real to the point that it becomes multidimensional, that is, transformational.* Her riot scenes in *Romola* or in *Felix Holt*, for example, have something of the phantasmagoria we find in the surreal, celebratory scene in *Villette*. Eliot did not have Brontë's romantic overdetermination of events, but she forced the concrete to vibrate with mysterious aspects. Henry James, later, became a secret sharer with her, until he distanced himself; but even then her voice can be recognized submerged beneath his.

In response to Blackwood's comments on the Madeleine Smith case, Lewes took quite a different tack. Blackwood rallied to the injured party and attacked the man as a dastard who deserved to die. Lewes—and, possibly, Eliot—saw a more varied case with different circumstances. That Smith was a Scot and her victim French gave her a court chance; otherwise, she would have been hanged. Lewes finds no sympathy for her—a hideous case all around. As for Angelier, the victim, he surely did corrupt Smith; but she was also willing to give him what he wanted. Lewes's broader sense of how a woman is tempted to defy society is clear, as against Blackwood's monolithic view of men and women: evil men, pure women. As for the question of who corrupted whom, Lewes finds that Smith probably corrupted Angelier as much as he did her. He thinks Smith guilty, and says the sympathy shown this woman is incomprehensible to him. The evidence was clearly against her, and yet the audience cheered her acquittal. "Unless that cheer meant a condemnation of capital punishment altogether, it has a hideous sound in my ears." Lewes's angry words surely reveal a personal stake in the verdict: his sense of himself being victimized by Agnes, his shadowy equation of Angelier with Thornton Hunt, Agnes with Smith, these views supported by Eliot.

Lewes's final comments, however, were of a different, more immediate kind: that unless Blackwood has serious objections to Eliot's work, he is not to voice any criticism, since his friend is so easily discouraged he will close the series and perhaps write no more. "I laugh at him," Lewes writes, "for his diffidence and tell him it's a proof he is *not* an author. But he has passed the middle of life without writing at all, and will easily be made to give it up." He says all this must be kept confidential.

Lewes may have been exaggerating, but there is little question Eliot, now as later, was not receptive to criticism; and part of that was not simply "diffidence," but her implied recognition that she was intellectually superior to editors and publishers, and even readers. This gave her confidence to find her own voice in

---

*The anonymous reviewer in the *Atlantic Monthly* (May 1858) picked up some of Eliot's method in these remarks: ". . . these stories give proof of that wide range of experience which does not so much depend on an extended or varied acquaintance with the world, as upon an intelligent and comprehensive sympathy, which makes each new person with whom one is connected a new illustration of the unsolved problems of life and a new link in the unending chain of human development."

fiction rapidly. By the end of "Janet's Repentance," however much she later deepened and broadened, her voice and method were already there. What came across as "diffidence" to Lewes may have been the opposite: her disallowing negative criticism because it was coming from people whose literary opinions she could not fully respect, whatever she felt about them personally.

She tells Sara that she never expects to hear from Isaac again. She says that "will be a great relief to me. So now there is nothing to be concealed from any one, and the greatest service my friends can do is to tell the truth in contradiction to false rumours." Isaac, in the distance, was becoming physically punier as writing gave Eliot confidence; but we also cannot accept her words as she states them. If Isaac had relented, she would have been immediately reconciled. Chrissey's defection of course wounded, but Isaac's she could not let go of. It entered her fictional persona.

As Eliot wrote her recollections of Jersey in her journal, beginning on 26 July, we wonder with what persona or self, with what voice. Was it George Eliot keeping a journal, or Marian Evans, or Mrs. Lewes? We suspect that consciously it was the latter, since Lewes is very much part of the contents. But it is also George Eliot, someone who, even while holding his name, had in part broken away from his world into her own. And yet the observations and "innocence" of the writing suggest it is still Marian Evans.

One thing the journal validates is how she and Lewes were completely absorbed in each other and in their work. When they weren't taking long walks together, they read, either separately or together, and they wrote. Lewes's own journal also cites their long, idyllic walks through the labyrinthine paths inland, as well as on the shore. Their reading was diverse and seemingly directionless: Austen's *Sense and Sensibility*, Samuel Smiles's *Life of George Stephenson* (the builder of the first locomotive in England), Draper's *Psychology*, Charlotte Brontë's *The Professor*, two lighter books on marriage, and for Eliot alone, a "smattering," as she calls it, on botany from Spencer Thomson's *Wild Flowers*. As they left Jersey on the 24th of July, they brought with them, apparently, good memories of a rewarding and calming extended holiday; given the anxiety produced by her attempt to explain herself to her family, it was fortunate Eliot could fall back on Jersey to absorb her disappointment.

When she came to the journal after their return to Richmond—Eliot went right to it while memories were fresh—she had been restored. But one part had to pay, and now back near London she suffered from "one of her terrible head-aches," as Lewes reported to Sara, who decided to postpone her visit. Since Lewes's entry on 26 July coincided with Eliot's long entry in her journal about Jersey, it is questionable if the headache was so intense, but instead an excuse to give them breathing space before Sara appeared. Quite possibly Sara, while a dear friend in correspondence, was somewhat of an intrusion in person; so closely allied were Lewes and Eliot that other people were unnecessary in their now self-absorbed lives. Marian Evans was being absorbed into the "two Georges."

PART FOUR

The Voice

11

Becoming
an Author

"Our deeds determine us, as much as we determine
our deeds; and until we know what has been or will
be the peculiar combination of outward with inward
facts, which constitutes a man's critical actions, it
will be better not to think ourselves wise about his
character."

On her return to Richmond, with "Janet's Repentance" on her desk, along
with her journal, with her family finally undeceived, with her nom de
plume firmly in place with Blackwood and her growing reading public, Marian
Evans had passed into another level of her life. Jersey had become something of
a dividing line, where all the elements leading up to the present joined; she had
both undeceived and continued to deceive. Mrs. Lewes had been explained, but
George Eliot remained; and yet all of this had a kind of finality. Whatever the
unconscious residue, she had cleared her desk of the past.

Now back at 8 Park Shot, Lewes and Eliot began to pick up their regular
routine. Sara came and went, for one night. Lewes had to be in London for his
"Sea-side Studies," now being prepared for republication with illustrations. He
and Eliot attended several operas: *Lucrezia Borgia, Macbeth,* and *Medea.* Money
was coming in from Blackwood, another £24 for "Janet," dutifully acknowledged
by Lewes, the couple's accountant. When the publisher had Part III ready in
proofs, on 12 August, he sent them on with warm praise for Eliot's accomplishments, and he in fact apologized for having at first expressed any doubts. Lewes's
advice not to discourage his clerical friend had taken hold. Just before that,
Barbara Leigh Smith with her husband, Dr. Eugène Bodichon, came for dinner,
on 4 August. Rufa Brabant, remarried to Wathen Mark Wilks Call, a *Westminster Review* contributor, invited Lewes and Eliot to dinner. Rufa had broken
through the scandal and was one of the few women to invite Eliot.

Eliot's life did not appear to be going through any extreme phases, and her
steady work on "Janet"—copy against payment—occupied her days, while reading filled her evenings. Some readers, however, were trying to zero in on the

author of these *Scenes*. Eliot's use of actual people, however transformed, was putting older readers on the alert, for they caught resemblances. William Pitman Jones, for example, Perpetual Curate at St. Thomas in Preston, thought he recognized his long-dead brother in Tryan. Some slight parallels exist, mainly in their long, lingering deaths, but Jones died in his thirty-fourth year and Tryan at a considerably older age. Eliot responded to Blackwood, who was intermediary here, that Tryan was "an ideal character," indebted to no one, living or dead. This gives her the opportunity to restate her position on the use of real people and real history, which she continued to do throughout her career.

> I should consider it a fault which would cause me lasting regret, if I had used reality in any other than the legitimate way common to all artists who draw their materials from their observation and experience. It would be a melancholy result of my fictions if I gave *just* cause of annoyance to any good and sensible person. But I suppose there is no perfect safeguard against extraneous impressions or a mistaken susceptibility. We are all apt to forget how little there is about us that is unique, and how very strongly we resemble many other insignificant people who have lived before us.

Explanation and fiction were at odds: first, she maintained that her real models were undifferentiated from other people; second, she differentiated.

Lewes commented to Blackwood that he was affected by the characters in "Janet," but felt "the want of a larger canvas so as to bring out those admirable figures"—an indication he was beginning to prod Eliot into starting a novel. She would do just that in less than two months after this 23 August letter. Bessie Parkes, now editing a publication called the *Waverly Journal*, swam back into Eliot's life. While Bessie's father remained adamantly opposed to seeing Eliot, Bessie sought out her friend, although she indiscreetly addressed her as Miss Evans. Eliot showed interest in the *Waverly* and said it needed something special, but she did not think that the inscription "Conducted by Women" should be the specialty. She suggests more business, more statements of philanthropic enterprises, for example, than literature. "Not because I like philanthropy [while admitting she has done no good works of her own] and hate literature, but because I want to *know* about philanthropy and don't care for second-rate literature. However I am a wretchedly bad judge of what a newspaper should be—a person who dislikes wine can never be a good 'taster' and I only read newspapers as a hard duty."

But Eliot's real ammunition was saved for more than three weeks when she and Lewes, in London for dinner at the Calls', visited the *Waverly* offices and she was introduced as Miss Evans. Eliot was unequivocal about how she wanted to be presented. She says she has renounced "Miss Evans" and does not mean to be known by it in any way. It is Lewes's wish, she says, for her to be addressed as Mrs. Lewes, and even her father's trustees send her receipts marked Marian Lewes. "There is not much probability of such a chance as that of your having to introduce me should occur again. But I think it better to write on the subject to you while it is in my memory, to prevent the possibility of a future mistake." She further tells Bessie that she should not expect an invitation to Richmond, since it would compromise her.

George Eliot, meanwhile, was still known to no one except Lewes; but with the success of *Scenes* in *Maga*, she was beginning to waver in her secrecy. This reinforces our suspicion that she did not take the male name solely to make publication easier, but as a way of taking on power and protection she did not feel; once that power began to flow to her, she was tempted to reveal who she was. This she did, to Herbert Spencer in the fall, and little did she realize what a gossipy mouth this straitened man had. Dr. Chapman was all the while prod- ding her to write for the *Review*, this time a puff piece on Francis W. Newman, defending him from several attackers. Eliot held him off. Blackwood sent on another £21 for Part III of "Janet," and by October she was ready to send on the conclusion.

Either John Blackwood or his brother William—or both—was beginning to find the George Eliot disguise a little weak. Nothing was said in October when she announced her preparation for a longer work, started on the 22nd. Corre- spondence over "Janet's Repentance" was kept at the most superficial level of sympathy and accommodation, John having declined further interference. He was apparently not happy with Janet's drinking, finding it untoward in a hero- ine, but he withdrew by saying it was a legitimate subject for a writer because of its misery. He was also troubled by the length of Dempster's delirium; he suggests greater impact through shortening, but does not insist. All in all, the love fest was ongoing. Eliot wrote back, on the 17th, to indicate that her new story haunted her, that it would be a country story, about cows and hay! She said she would send on manuscript copy only when she had a volume or more, and then Blackwood could judge whether to serialize it in *Maga* or publish it as a separate novel upon completion.

He told Eliot he was sorry *Scenes* was not long enough to fill the statutory three volumes—the so-called three-decker, which would have made it more attractive for the lending libraries—and would issue it in two volumes, to sell for 21s. or a guinea. The first edition would be only 750 copies, not 1,000, because he feared being left with several hundred copies; and for this, he offered £120. Copyright would remain half and half, the standard policy unless the author is so well established as to ensure a large sale.

Despite this assessment, not 750 but 1,050 copies were printed, a goodly number for a still unknown writer. Eliot was pleased with the terms, but warned Blackwood not to be too hopeful about the book's success. She also acknowl- edged the final payment, £30, for Part IV of "Janet." After a brief visit from William Blackwood to the Lewes household, she felt her disguise was pierced, although nothing was said. The disguise in any event was beginning to fall apart, especially since Warwickshire scenes were recognizable, and people began to speculate as to who knew this material so intimately. Blackwood was not eager for divulgation, since with the book publication of *Scenes* imminent, he looked for high sales by a mysterious male author. Liggins is a name which appeared, incidentally, in "Gilfil," but in the book text it was altered to Higgins, to avoid further identification of Eliot with Liggins. If Eliot had wanted to create a context for her work through hiding her real name, she had succeeded, and London played a guessing game.

With her denials flowing in to Blackwood that no real persons were the models for her characters—she was especially forceful in denying a model for Tryan—plans for publication moved along. Eliot felt secure enough in her achievement to ask copies to be sent to Dickens, Thackeray, Ruskin, Tennyson, Faraday, Jane Carlyle, and others of almost equal magnitude. The book would be published on 4 January 1858, with 350 copies ordered by Mudie's, the most prominent of the circulating libraries. The circulating libraries were a number of firms which took copies of books, not primarily for sale, but for subscribers. The latter might pay a pound or two for a year's access to the collection, which included all the newest acquisitions. This gave the libraries enormous control of publishing, since by refusing to accept a book for their members (on grounds of religious, political, or sexual unacceptability), they could effectively kill it, or else stifle its sales. Books were themselves in the main too expensive for most people to buy, so that subscription was the sole means for many readers. It was a workable arrangement, except that it could prove deleterious to any author who left the beaten track. Even *Scenes* did not provide enough of an attraction to make Mudie's interested unless the library received a significant discount from Blackwood, in this instance 10 percent off list price.

The circulating libraries began to fade later in the century when cheap editions, of 5 shillings or less, brought books down to manageable prices, and that, in turn, led to somewhat shorter books, since the three-decker novel* was clearly aimed at subscribers, not buyers. By the time of publication, Eliot had started her first novel, *Adam Bede*, which also drew heavily on personal experiences: among other things, a story told her by her aunt, and the re-creation of some aspects of Robert Evans in Adam himself. Moving from novella to novel did not dilute the past, but intensified it. As for her publisher, whatever his suspicions, he wanted to keep her identity hidden; in his mind, George Eliot and Marian Lewes were incompatible.

Quite welcome was the income. When Blackwood increased the first edition of *Scenes* to 1,050 copies, he gave Eliot an additional £60, and this raised her income on this single book to almost £450 in 1857. With Lewes's income for that year only a trifle less, the couple had ample money for their needs, although Lewes's expenses remained high. It was during this general time, on 6 December 1857, that Eliot turned to her journal to write "How I Came to Write Fiction." This entry has already been referred to in some detail, but it is well to recall that it coincided with her first efforts at longer fiction; it was perhaps an indication that she needed some personal apologia to explain her defection from nonfiction writing for the *Westminster*, the *Leader*, and *Fraser's*.

---

* Eliot was herself fearful that two volumes instead of the standard three would hurt her in the "eyes of the librarians."

As Christmas approached, one full of imminent excitement because of the book publication, Lewes was off to visit his friend Arthur Helps for the holiday, and Eliot spent it alone, as was usual. It was a strange arrangement, but quite probably associated with the space each allowed the other as far as traditional matters went. Lewes was away until January, but she did not appear to miss him, since her life seemed so full. On New Year's Eve, she writes in her journal of her life deepening "unspeakably during the year." "I feel," she says, "a greater capacity for moral and intellectual enjoyment, a more acute sense of my deficiencies in the past, a more solemn desire to be faithful to coming duties. . . ." She speaks of a "perfect love and union," which grows daily. She says her real trouble has been anxiety about permanent separation from her sister (Chrissey), but she appears to be able to shake that off. "Few women, I fear, have had such reasons as I have to think the long sad years of youth were worth living for the sake of middle age. . . ." Yet this middle-aged mellowness was not quite so firm as she thought, for her fiction reveals several elements she had by no means reconciled.

When Lewes returned, he brought with him a quite favorable review of *Scenes* from the prestigious London *Times.* * Suitably encouraged and buoyed by friendly correspondence from Blackwood, Eliot moved very rapidly on *Adam Bede*. The manuscript indicates how easily the story and words came to her. It is remarkably clean, suggesting quite a sure hand. What she did later was to simplify the local dialect to bring it closer to standard usage, but even this was only lightly done. Unfortunately, when deletions do occur, Eliot drew a broad band of black so that they are undecipherable. By 6 January, her journal indicates four chapters. As she wrote Blackwood, "My new story goes on with a pleasant andante movement. I have read the early chapters to Lewes. . . . and he pronounces them to be better than anything I had done before. That is the best thing I have to tell you about it, and the next best is, that my heart is in the story. But I fear that this last has been the case with very poor writers and very poor stories."

What created suspicion that Marian Evans was George Eliot was that she no longer produced any articles or reviews; as she tells Chapman, she has not done anything on the F. W. Newman piece. She admits hopelessness in the matter and says she will send on the books to him, for someone else to do the writing. She adds she is "disgusted" with herself and unhappy with her article. Yet since this was so unlike her, particularly since she and Lewes needed income, her excuses seemed hollow. No fool in personal matters, Chapman did not fail to notice. Unless one believed she suffered from writer's block, every sign pointed toward other activities.

Exposure was imminent. "When I wish to drop my incognito, I will take a few intimate friends into my confidence, but not till then; and I shall not feel that wish for a long time to come." This is, as far as we know, the first time

---

* Unsigned, but by Samuel Lucas (2 January 1858). Lucas stressed Eliot's forcefulness in handling the ordinary in scene and character. Other reviews which followed struck a similar note.

Eliot had spoken seriously to Blackwood about her nom de plume; but of course she kept her gender secret behind this admission that one day she would appear. With *Adam Bede*, however, it would become impossible to carry on the secrecy, with recognizable characters as the major reason. In the meantime, she was very pleased with the appearance of the two-volume *Scenes*, whose arrival reinforced what she was now writing. *Adam Bede* was also a "clerical scene," intended and then developed as such. Tryan of "Janet's Repentance" undergoes a gender change to become, with suitable modifications, the Methodist preacher Dinah Morris. Their message is comparable, and their sense of mission makes them sharers of the same Christian duty.

Where the novel differs radically is in the story Eliot had heard from her paternal aunt, Mrs. Samuel Evans, the Methodist who had broken with her brother's Anglicanism. Mrs. Evans told the young Mary Anne about her visit to a prison to see a young woman condemned to hang for child murder. So moved was Mrs. Evans she accompanied the condemned woman to the scaffold, attempting to raise her spirits in the face of her terrible suffering and the punishment to come. When Eliot related this story to Lewes, he saw in it dramatic possibilities, and with this she decided not to go on with purely clerical scenes. She had one such scene, "The Clerical Tutor," in mind for *Maga*. As she had told her publisher earlier, her new story would not be a clerical scene as such, but would contain a larger country canvas—a country novel, in fact.

This brought Eliot into Wordsworth territory, and since he was one of her favorite poets, she worked through her material with his salient values in mind. Further, since her chief male character was loosely based on Robert Evans, she could link Wordsworthian rural qualities with the work ethic represented by her father, as well as the Methodism she knew about from her earlier days (and reinforced by further extensive reading). *Adam Bede* became, as we shall see, the perfect transitional novel for Eliot, taking her from the clerical scenes of her first literary effort into a broader sense of life, and yet at the same time solidifying values she could hold to. It enabled her to develop her type of realism without forgoing that sense of suffering and redemption already established in the three tales.

But as she began reading heavily for this book—Southey's *Life of Wesley*, for example, and *Gentleman's Magazine*, on different flowers—she was also trying to maintain some part of her former life. We are caught by her effort to grasp the past even while moving out so forthrightly into another career. Her correspondence with Chapman, Bray, and Sara Hennell, while not so intimate as before, came regularly, even as Coventry and the *Westminster* faded. To Sara, she cites an article Chapman printed called "The Religious Weakness of Protestantism" (in the January 1858 issue) and moans the tribulations of an editor who must publish such stuff. She also attacks a January piece on Shelley, as full of crudities of thought and expression. In a more tolerant mood, she mentions seeing Spencer, and having had a sparkling talk with him on monetary theories.

She cites Ruskin's book *The Political Economy of Art* as possessing magnificent passages intermixed with "stupendous specimens of arrogant absurdity on some economical points." Nevertheless, she says she venerates him as one of the great teachers of the day. "His absurdities on practical points do no harm, but the grand doctrines of truth and sincerity in art"—which she would take to heart in *Adam Bede*—"and the nobleness and solemnity of our human life, which he teaches with the inspiration of a Hebrew prophet, must be stirring up young minds in a promising way." She also cites the final two volumes of Ruskin's *Modern Painters* as containing some of the age's finest writing. She sees him as linked to the best in Wordsworth, whom, she says, she is rereading now "with fresh admiration for his beauties and tolerance for his faults." These remarks indicate her own contexts: truth and sincerity, realism of manner, adherence to certain empirical truths, and a distinctive voice that can capture the essence of the country and its people. She was widening her sweep.

Meanwhile, events were catching up with her. On 18 January, Dickens wrote full of praise for the first two tales of *Scenes*, which she had asked Blackwood to send to him. He lavished praise before arriving at his real subject: that only a woman could have written these tales. And in his covering letter, asking that his note be sent on to George Eliot, he said that if these two volumes, or parts of them, had not been written by a woman, then "should I begin to believe that I am a woman myself." In his letter proper, Dickens says he is obliged to accept the name selected by the author of *Scenes*, but if left to his own devices he would address him as her. "I have observed what seem to me to be such womanly touches, in these moving fictions, that the assurance on the title-page is insufficient to satisfy me, even now. If they originated with no woman, I believe that no man ever before had the art of making himself mentally, so like a woman since the world began." Dickens apologizes for seeming to poke into such private matters, but he says it is of great interest to him, to the extent that if ever George Eliot finds it suitable to show him the face of the man or woman who wrote these tales, it would be for him a memorable occasion.

Writers dreamed of receiving such a letter from Dickens. He was, in 1858, at the very summit of his popularity and powers. Considered England's greatest writer, he was also probably the most famous writer in the world. His readings, his acting in amateur theatricals, and his editing of a succession of journals all gave him a fame and a cachet which probably no other writer since has had. For two decades, since *Pickwick*, the country bowed to him. Writing to Blackwood, Eliot can barely contain her glee. At first, she tells her publisher not to permit any specific allusion to the letter, by which she means the speculation about gender. But she wants the letter known. "There can hardly be any climax of approbation for me after this, and I am so deeply moved by the finely-felt and finely expressed sympathy of the letter, that the iron mask of my incognito seems quite painful in forbidding me to tell Dickens how thoroughly his generous impulse has been appreciated." Then in sinuous fashion, she tells Blackwood that if he can communicate these sentiments to Dickens, she would feel obliged. Her comments are on the edge of revelation, gender and all, but she pulls back.

The publication of *Scenes* in book form intensified the search for the author. Speculation went from rumor to real efforts to uncover the writer and, above all, to determine gender. For the biographer, the gender deception is the most compelling, since a nom de plume in itself was not unusual, but the gender crossover, far more than with the Brontës, had deeper meaning. Jane Carlyle, always inquiring and sharp, tried to ferret out some authorship details, wondering why George Eliot, someone she did not know, would have a copy sent to her. She thought it was sent so that Jane would give it to her husband, "he being head and ears in *History.*" But even he, who never reads novels, "has engaged to read this one. . . ." Then Jane focuses on the authorship, an amusing groping for clues. "I hope to know someday if the person I am addressing bears any resemblance, in external things to the Idea I have conceived of him in my mind [this addressed to 'George Eliot']—a man of middle age with a wife from whom he has got those beautiful *feminine* touches in his book, a good many children and a dog that he has as much fondness for as I have for my little Nero! for the rest, not just a clergyman, but Brother or first cousin to a clergyman!—How ridiculous all this *may* read, beside the reality!"

Ridiculous, yes; but the guessing game was inspirational to Eliot. Not only was she a new author, with considerable success, with letters from Victorian notables attesting to her skill, she was accomplishing this while disguising herself from probing eyes. That secretive, hidden, elusive part of her character was fulfilled even as she started to become a public figure. And as a "man," she reinforced her divisions; she was for the time Janus-faced. Putting off Chapman on the Newman article, she could not account for her expenditure of time— simply that she could not write this or other pieces. Even this deception was a notable success, since Chapman, whatever his suspicions, still honored Eliot's disguise. Operating behind her wall of secrecy, she received warm praise from the great scientist Michael Faraday. He said he looked forward to pleasure from the book as a relief from his other mental occupation. None of this praise went to Eliot's head, or at least did not inhibit her work on *Adam Bede,* whose Chapter 8 she reached by the end of January. *

Dickens, meanwhile, pushed ahead with his investigative plans. The man who had learned the mysteries of detective work from Wilkie Collins and from his own researches was not to be put off. Writing to Blackwood on 27 January 1858, he repeats he is certain a woman has created scenes that no man could: Mrs. Barton sitting up in bed to mend the children's clothes, the selfish young fellow with heart disease in "Gilfil," the fact that nearly all the female characters are more alive than the men, "and more informed from within." As for Janet, Dickens says he knows of no man who could have described her—her eyes and form and height—as Eliot does. The scene in which Janet is cast out by Demp-

---

* For this novel, Eliot's notebook contains information on Wesley and Methodism—as background for Dinah Morris's preaching—and then lists costumes in the late eighteenth century, as well as "facts in 1799." The list of facts includes theatrical productions, the publication of the major Romantic writers, and social and political events (the suppression in March of habeas corpus). She extends that to "facts from Gents. Mag. 1800–1802," which lists even preachment against bull baiting; also, information on the seasons, from July through October. Much of the information is technical, indicating Eliot's ability to absorb such diverse materials. Such accumulation of information and detail could, at times, sink her, as in *Romola.*

ster, Dickens emphasizes, could only have derived from a woman's point of view. "If I be wrong in this, then I protest that a woman's mind has got into some man's body by mistake that ought immediately to be corrected."

The big moment, however, came when Blackwood visited Richmond on 28 February and asked Lewes if he was finally to see George Eliot. It was clear he knew who this was. Lewes asked her privately if she wished to be revealed, and she said yes, but to make it spontaneous. Eliot notes she left the room, Blackwood was informed, and acted kindly. He came the following Friday to chat and take a look at the new fiction on his author's desk, and he pronounced "This will do." Gossiping, he said that Thackeray had declared *Scenes* was not by a woman; also his, Blackwood's, wife had the same opinion, and the novelist Mrs. Oliphant was sure it was no woman author.

Blackwood did inform his wife by letter, but said the identification was "a profound secret." He went on: "She is a most intelligent pleasant woman, with a face like a man, but a good expression." The publisher was pleased it turned out to be as he suspected, Mrs. Lewes. At this latest meeting, Lewes flattered Blackwood that, as the publisher wrote his wife, he would do ten times the work for him that he would do for any other editor, adding that "he does not think any other editor in the world would have been able to induce George Eliot to go on. It was very flattering, as his experience of editors is great, and he is a monstrous clever fellow."

Eliot's career as a fiction writer, which seems so solid, so well nourished, so fixed and balanced, so wise, intelligent, and logical, was in actuality a somewhat chancy thing. Although the desire was there to express herself in different forms, she needed support. She was unable to take hard criticism, she did not have the rock-hard solid ego biographers over the last century have given her, and she did not, despite her intellectual superiority, have that overwhelming belief in herself which could have overcome all external obstacles. She required ingredients: Lewes to settle her personal life and a publisher who believed in her virtually without qualification. It is quite possible that even after her successful beginning, Eliot might have thrown over the career, despite her need for money and despite her consciousness of powers within. This is not to suggest she would have stopped dead, but that her development as a writer depended on more than the single factor of her talent. Just as earlier she had depended on certain men to help her out of her domestic situation into the larger world, now she needed very different conditions to help her. If she had put aside fiction, non-fiction was always there as a source of some income.

Lewes and Eliot were planning an excursion abroad, including a long stay in Munich. As the departure neared, on 7 April (they reached Munich on the 11th), she told Blackwood she would dispatch the fourth part of *Adam Bede*, although serialization in *Maga* had not been decided upon. Her work on the novel brought her back to her "other" family, especially when a somewhat repentant Cara, after four years of silence, invited her to visit Coventry. She declined, with the offer of kisses instead. And she warned Bray not to spread "false rumours, or any other rumours afloat about me." She even denies bringing out "a supposed novel." In a follow-up letter, two days later, she says there is "no undertaking more fruitful of absurd mistakes than that of 'guessing' at authorship, and as I have never communicated to any one so much an intention of a literary kind, there can be none but imaginary data for such guesses." She tries to explain herself to Bray, who has been open with her in the past. "I can't afford to indulge either in vanity or sentimentality about my work. I have only a trembling anxiety to do what is in itself worth doing and by that honest means, to win every necessary profit of a temporal kind." Then, quoting Matthew: " 'There is nothing hidden that shall not be revealed'—in due time. But till that time comes—till I tell you myself 'This is the work of my hand and brain'—don't believe anything on the subject. There is no one who is in the least likely to know what I can, could, should or would write."

This is, in effect, if not an admission of authorship, then a confession of secrets to be revealed later. With Blackwood, Spencer, and probably Chapman knowledgeable about the mysterious author's identity, Eliot was splitting the recipients of the information. Her "new world" was informed; her "old world" kept guessing. And, strikingly, all the people who knew were men. Blackwood's response to 219 manuscript pages of the new novel, meanwhile, was enthusiastic. Along the way, he made brief, discreet suggestions for clarification—spotting the description of Chad's Bess as too brutal. Eliot called her "that unsoaped lazy class of feminine" character. Blackwood's comments, as with his earlier suggestions concerning *Scenes*, were toward softening; and he hastens to add that he worries a little about the excess of dialect, especially with Adam's mother, Lisbeth.

As we might have expected, Eliot made none of the changes suggested by Blackwood, except for minor dialect alterations here and there and in the offending Chad's Bess passage. Blackwood also feared that the Arthur Donnithorne–Hetty Sorrel affair would end very badly, and he hoped that Eliot would not come "to the usual sad catastrophe!" While still speaking as the "typical" Victorian reader, he says he has never read anything quite like *Adam Bede*, and he thinks of the characters as real personages, which he considers a good thing. He indicates it will grace the pages of *Maga*, but it would not, when Eliot requested he publish it only in book form.

Yet even as matters seemed to be going Eliot's way, the material of *Adam Bede* indicates a large number of unresolved internal problems. The novel speaks for her more trenchantly than can her letters or even her journal. In this novel and in its successor, *The Mill on the Floss*, Eliot revealed far too much for us to take her at her word as happy, satisfied, fulfilled, and at peace. The novel suggests several subversive dimensions of her life which, consciously, she appeared to dismiss; or at the least, the novel suggests much she omitted from public utterance. One of the key dimensions of this personal side comes with Dinah Morris. Although Eliot sees her as triumphant, supportive, and sympathetic to human suffering, she is, also, anti-life in many of her pronouncements. And she represents a broad-based Methodism which depends strongly on a God figure and on Jesus the redeemer.

Dinah's figure manifests several contradictory impulses—contradictory not within the character only but between the character and her creator, Eliot. In order to promulgate her message of sacrifice, suffering, and inner pain, Dinah must sacrifice life—not only sensual life, but enjoyment of life itself. She represents in her creator, now moving toward her fortieth birthday, someone still unsure of pleasure or a broader range of feeling. Eliot does not chide Dinah, but gives her message full thrust; and we can only conclude from this that she was, herself, still caught in a puritanical code which feared or suspected self-expression: in effect, a perfect articulation of mid-century Victorianism. We catch this stance even as late as *Middlemarch* more than ten years later, in Dorothea Brooke's continuing desire for sacrifice and for suppression of sensory satisfactions in favor of more socially based fulfillment.

Yet we cannot view the preacher woman in isolation. Eliot uses her both as a foil and as a double of Hetty Sorrel; and in the play between the two, we find further elements which Eliot has not really resolved. Many have read Eliot's presentation of Hetty as an unrelieved attack on the young woman for her naive guile, her petty affectations, her lack of intellectual content, her vain prettiness, and her willingness to forgo Adam's sincere love for the vapid Arthur Donnithorne, who seems to offer position and riches. As opposed to Hetty's insistence on catching someone with her pretty childlike looks and divine little figure, *Eliot speaks of the importance of insignificant people in her portrayal of a society, and yet she does not extend that importance to Hetty. *Her* insignificance becomes the source of a virulent attack on her lack of principle as well as her appearance—whose blooming prettiness is merely a disguise for a heartless, mindless, affected, simpering young thing. She is a flower, with its short burst of life and its transient qualities. She becomes not part of the "ordinary folk" who make up Eliot's world, but someone extraordinary by virtue of her superficial beauty. Eliot harasses Hetty.

In "The Dairy" scene—which Thomas Hardy would imitate in *Tess of the D'Urbervilles*—Eliot pins Hetty to the wall. The dairy background, which promises purity and cleanliness, becomes the context in which Hetty's "spring-tide beauty" can attempt to attract Captain Donnithorne. It is all surfaces and affectation, the dairy as a dispossessed, polluted Garden.

There are various orders of beauty, causing men to make fools of themselves in various styles, from the desperate to the sheepish; but there is one order of beauty which seems made to turn the heads not only of men, but of all intelligent mammals, even of women. It is a beauty like that of kittens, or very small downy ducks making gentle rippling noises with their soft bills, or babies just beginning to toddle and engage in conscious mischief—a beauty with which you can never be angry, but that you feel ready

---

*If we compare Eliot's handling of Hetty with Thackeray's portrayal of Becky Sharp in *Vanity Fair* in their common pursuit of an upper-class husband, we are enlightened. Eliot's treatment is vindictive; Thackeray's is cynical and witty. Eliot seeks to humiliate Hetty; Thackeray casts Becky as an amoral survivor, an embodiment of the way the world works.

to crush for inability to comprehend the state of mind into which it throws you. Hetty Sorrel's was that sort of beauty. Her aunt, Mrs Poyser, who professed to despise all personal attractions, and intended to be the severest of mentors, continually gazed at Hetty's charms by the sly, fascinated in spite of herself; and after administering such a scolding as naturally flowed from her anxiety to do well by her husband's niece—who had no mother of her own to scold her, poor thing!—she would often confess to her husband, when they were safe out of hearing, that she firmly believed, "the naughtier the little hussy behaved, the prettier she looked."

That childlike beauty which catches both male and female eyes is then further explored and excoriated. Little or none of Hetty's description has anything adult in it; she is cublike, a fuzzy little animal, or an object opening up prettily like a flower. The description is unrelenting; not only is there hatred for what Hetty represents, but *deep, abiding attraction.* Eliot can't keep her eyes off her. The hostility is so trenchant because of Eliot's fascination with this childlike woman who represents everything Marian Evans had set herself against. Hetty was not just a girl, but a representative of an entire society Eliot wished to sink. The threat she poses comes in her attraction to men; but more than that, in her ability to establish a standard by which men measure women. If Hetty is the standard of all things beautiful in the female world, then where does that leave the intellectual, plain-looking (Blackwood's "face like a man"), sober and serious woman, like Eliot herself? Yet what is loathsome is also seductive.

With her presentation of Hetty—and with her placement of self-denying Dinah against her—Eliot was protecting her world. No matter her successes, she felt that social values still did not provide a valid context for someone like her; that a Hetty, or some other version—Gwendolen Harleth, Rosamond Vincy, Esther Lyon at first—could turn a man's head and thus create a standard. Her inexorable persecution of Hetty, in excess of what she does with any of her other affected females, indicates that in 1858 Eliot was still struggling with those demons which had tortured her early in childhood, and was fighting, further, with her role in a society which vaunted superficial beauty.

This is, however, only part of Eliot's internal struggle. Beyond Hetty lies Arthur Donnithorne, the "pretty male" equivalent of the dairy girl. Arthur, also, must be destroyed, or else through pain and suffering be made to change direction. He is one of Eliot's "gay" people, males or females who have face and manner, but little substance and few fixed principles. A hollow man, he desires to be liked, to cut a good figure. That he is so young does not give him license, just as youth does not allow Hetty to make mistakes. Arthur has some democratic tendencies, but his fundamental value is noblesse oblige: to dispense favors from high to low and to gain gratitude in return. That both Arthur and Hetty are headed for disaster is clear; but not so clear is how inexorable their punishment will be, how unrelenting Eliot will prove to be in her pursuit, disallowing happiness or even any equitable life. They are to become outcasts, Hetty a criminal punished almost with execution and then with transportation out of England.

Beyond the creation of characters lies another division within Eliot, a division which reflected some of the uncertainties that lay within Victorian society as a whole. By 1858, the perception was unmistakable that one type of society was encountering another, and that the shift taking place was not necessarily for the better, although progress seemed unstoppable. The mid-Victorian years were critical, because England was undergoing a profound sea change, the Great Exhibition of 1851 being only one major manifestation of this shift. The modern element, reinforced by science and technology, was altering the way people perceived their lives. But more than this, as Eliot well knew, changes in value systems and beliefs were being personally altered, to be further threatened, even undermined, with the publication in 1859 of Darwin's *Origin of Species.* Darwin's work meant little to most people in its scientific aspects; but in its social, religious, and political consequences, it had a vast effect, forcing a rethinking of all the old nostrums. For some, like Charles Kingsley, a naturalist *and* Anglican minister as well as a prolific author, Darwin's *Origin* would valorize God's plan, whether one of creation or of intervention in the development of species. For him and for others (including some bishops), evolutionary theory confirmed, not denied, a divinity at work. With Lewes's investigations into natural objects, with her own vast knowledge of the shifts in religious and social beliefs, with information accumulating in geology and in other natural studies, Eliot saw as a possibility the disintegration of the society she cherished. She would help save it.

For the twentieth-century reader, some of the implications of Darwin's book should be spelled out. Eliot saw in it all the old questions arising: between free will and determinism, philosophical realism and nominalism, spirit and matter, ideas of progress and traditional values, individual and society or community. As she entered into fiction, her job, as she conceived it, was to present as much of this conflict in literary terms as Darwin had in scientific terminology. Her recognition of the importance of his book, after some initial hesitation, came when she perceived how he had created a context for the reexamination of such vexing problems, nearly all of them continuous with what she had found in Strauss and Feuerbach earlier. Added to this was the paradoxical and troubling fact that Darwin's findings could be accommodated to a conservative view of the world, such as Eliot eventually came to share: his reliance on the hereditary past, on vestiges of creation or vestigial structures, on the significance of time itself, on slowness, minuteness, a crawling history—in all of these he paralleled the Burkean conservative view of society, rather than the more radical one linked to ideas of progress and development. Yet, and here is the paradox, in still another area Darwin was anathema to Eliot, in his disregard of the individual life, as against the species—for here Eliot sharply departed from him, however much she marveled at the largeness of the enterprise.

Near the conclusion of *Adam Bede,* we find a long passage on such changes,

presented in Eliot's typically down-home images. She derides newer forms of
labor-saving devices, and she writes nostalgically about the old forms of leisure.
Eliot's former time is curious, since it suggests not intellectual effort, but a slowly
moving society sure of itself and of its future. At present, with novelty, people
are frantic, society is uncertain, the future is clouded. We see the slow making
of a particular kind of conservative.

Only by understanding Eliot's fear of such changes—and she was herself, as a
powerful female, paradoxically an avatar of this newness—can we fully understand her negative response to Hetty and Arthur. Part of her response to them
was, obviously, personal; but her full persecution of them comes only when she
recognized that they are hollow people born seeking amusement and lacking
societal values which would restrain personal sensations. In standing only for
sensationalism, they are subvertors of a society which depends on Poysers,
Bedes, Garths, Tullivers, and others who, like Atlas, support the earth.

That Eliot by 1858 had not made her peace with these changes in society
which envelop Hetty and Arthur indicates that going from Marian Evans to
George Eliot was by no means a complete transformation. She emerged, but
longed for the cocoon. Further evidence of her uncertainties comes in her shift
of the novel's narrative to an earlier age—from 1799 to 1801—a procedure she
would follow with all her major fictions except *Daniel Deronda*. She evinces here
a hesitancy to relinquish the past, a desire to reacquaint herself with what she
knows best, and the wish to return to years she wanted to find happy. But Eliot's
letters, as we have seen, belie her statements in her fiction about those "happy
years." At stake is not deception or self-delusion, but some of the uncertainties
Eliot shared with other Victorians, not the least Dickens.

On many issues, the two were in much the same position, most of all in trying
to find some hand or foothold on a society slipping away. She could not, like
Carlyle, actively campaign for a return to medieval times; nor could she, despite
her admiration for Ruskin, speak of the virtues of Gothic or other earlier times
when he believed art was functional and meaningful. She was not a romantic
even in the Wordsworthian mold, although there was much of Wordsworth in
her attitudes. These uncertainties of how and where to position herself are
revealed in *Adam Bede* and in the novel succeeding it, *The Mill on the Floss*. She
demanded self-knowledge even when it brought pain, anguish, redemption, or
perhaps charity, and she found these qualities only in earlier times, or thought
she did. The present offered only self-gratification. She sought stable social com-
ities, but perceived, instead, society splitting into any number of subcultures, a
process that would continue right through the century. Perhaps these uncertainties lasting throughout her career help to account for her failure to publish more
than one novel (*Daniel Deronda*) in the last ten years of her life.

Even in her development of certain narrative forms in *Adam Bede*, we can
observe her uncertain frame of mind. Her shift to narrative complications three-
quarters of the way through the novel has biographical resonance. It heralds, in
part, some hesitation as to what can actually be stated or presented; it questions
where she is going. The part in question comes when Hetty must stand trial for

her infant's death. In Chapter 43, these four narrative strands come together: Adam's sense of the story from what he has heard—none of it final or certain; the rumors circulating which go beyond the story itself to Hetty's evil crime, already judged; the court hearing, in which an effort is made to get at what occurred, although details remain shadowy; and, finally, Hetty's own story, which Adam and the court hear for the first time. Those four levels are a sophisticated narrative device, for they serve not only the function of the internal story line, but the external purpose of making the events available. We as readers come into the material as Adam does, although our sense of the evidence is not the same as his. Adam wants to believe in Hetty, as her erstwhile husband-to-be; whereas we, as Eliot's manipulated readers, have less regard for her, so much has Eliot set us against her. Yet the four-layered narrative now takes on its own life, and it turns Adam as well as the reader toward Hetty, as the author finally allows narrative to replace persecution.

While serving a functional purpose in the story line, such a strategy does reveal Eliot's uneasiness in reaching a finality. Her presentation of the court scene is that of a process, where truth, rumor, witnesses, and the victim all come together with various versions of a single story. That single story has proliferated into many, and the sense of absoluteness or finality is shattered. We must see this, surely, as more than a fictional device—in fact, as a biographical dimension, the way in which Eliot revealed her reception of the material, and the uncertainty that lies at its heart. This does not, obviously, mean she lost sight of right and wrong. It does signify she recognized the variability of human behavior, the uncertainties at the basis of that behavior, and the impossibility of ever arriving at precisely what happened or what the motivations were. While this strengthened her position as a fiction writer, it also revealed her willingness to forgo absolutes and accept process.

We spot this attitude in many of the descriptions of characters who turn out to be different from what we thought, or from the way they have been presented. Speaking of Mrs. Poyser, for example, when the Hetty Sorrel scandal hits home, Eliot says: ". . . Mr Irwine was struck with surprise to observe that Mrs Poyser was less severe than her husband. We are often startled by the severity of mild people on exceptional occasions; the reason is, that mild people are most liable to be under the yoke of traditional impressions." Eliot's recognition was clearly a fictional and imaginative advance over her work in *Scenes*. She had begun to observe that depths lay well beneath behavior, and that these depths often dictate attitudes more than do the gestures or words of the individual. Withal, Eliot did not forsake her earlier belief in suffering and anguish as self-revelation; but she did realize that every act and its accompanying pain or pleasure had consequences. As she says of Adam:

There is no sort of wrong deed of which a man can bear the punishment alone; you can't isolate yourself, and say that evil which is in you shall not spread. Men's lives are as thoroughly blended with each other as the air they breathe: evil spreads as necessarily as disease. I know, I feel the terrible extent of suffering this sin of Arthur's has caused to others; but so does every sin cause suffering to others besides those who commit it. An act of vengeance on your part against Arthur could simply be another evil added to those we are suffering under; you could not bear the punishment alone; you would entail the worst sorrows on every one who loves you. You would have committed an act of blind fury, that would leave all the present evils just as they were; and add worse evils to them. You may tell me that you meditate no fatal act of vengeance; but the feeling in your mind is what gives birth to such actions, and as long as you indulge it, as long as you do not see that to fix your mind on Arthur's punishment is revenge, and not justice, you are in danger of being led on to the commission of some great wrong.

These are the words of Mr. Irwine, a liberal somewhat dilettantish preacher who is a reader of Aeschylus in the deluxe Foulis edition; but such sentiments reveal a core of meaning repeated by Eliot. They present an individual behavior that cannot be separated from a social polity; and that, in itself, indicates how Eliot was struggling to shape the one with the many, the private with the public. If we project this into her personal life, not directly but imaginatively, we can see her working through, still, her own action of running off with Lewes. As she agreed with the utilitarians that the one and the many cannot be divided, that the actions of the one must be multiplied several times over to achieve a society of the many, that the individual is free to indulge his or her behavior as long as it does not restrict another's freedom—as she pondered these questions and attempted to find some solid hold on human and social behavior, her chief asset was her own action. The most daring move of her life could not have been settled since it became the problematic situation of her fiction, beginning here: to what extent, like her refusal to attend her father's church, do one's acts hurt others; to what degree does individual behavior affect the social polity; in what respect can one act with impunity, without trespassing on others? While these are all questions of broad behavior, they are also matters suggesting uncertainty. As Eliot attempted to answer these questions, her understanding of human behavior deepened well beyond the Calvinism of her earlier days. More than anything, she needed fictional re-creations of these personal dilemmas and struggles.

Eliot's statement of realism helped her become a novelist. In passages already cited above, she needed to reconcile several elements. In her plea for suffering and anguish as a form of baptism—what she calls the "initiation into a new state"—she comes very close to Greek tragedy. She was throughout this period dipping into such work, especially Aeschylus's *Eumenides*, with its theatricality and cosmic revenge. What Eliot sought was some form which, while it did not take her into the high theatrics of Greek tragedy, provided suffering, pain, and the inevitable downfall of hubris-ridden individuals. Bringing them down gave her great satisfaction, not in the religious sense of the Greeks but in the personal sense of a woman who felt something of Medea in herself. Her introduction of her kind of realism, in the beginning of Book II of *Adam Bede,* "In Which the Story Pauses a Little," was her way of measuring classical drama for Victorian consumption.

The definition of realism Eliot uses is seemingly opposite to the cosmic qualities of Aeschylus and his *Eumenides.* Yet *Adam Bede* has within it many of the characteristics we associate with the Greek dramatist's presentation of revenge and how it can be contained. It has been insufficiently emphasized how much Greek drama influenced Eliot, not the least in *Adam Bede,* adapted of course for a Victorian audience. Eliot's "bloodletting" comes in the typical Victorian tale of the murdered child, or the kidnapped child, or some variation of this, a derivative of Euripedes' *Medea* and the revenge motif of Aeschylus. As the era became increasingly child oriented, in Dickens and others, the idea of a dead child through violence or through natural means became a typical subject for fiction. For a variety of reasons, the topic appealed to the Victorians: as a measurement of injustice, as an indication of frequent infant and child mortality, but also as a source of inquiry into types of violence and asocial behavior which flouted all traditional rules of conduct. Victorian piety was often at odds with Victorian obsession with aberrant behavior; Dickens's popularity is testament to that, but also Wilkie Collins's, and other sensationalist writers. Further, beyond the infant-murder theme, Eliot has elements of a revenge motif, more indebted to classical drama than to Renaissance English revenge drama. In the latter, the stage becomes something of a slaughterhouse, whereas in Greek drama, violence occurs behind the scenes. But it is not any the less intense; Adam's desire for revenge on Arthur Donnithorne is part of that *Eumenides*-like theme, just as Hetty is a Medea figure in her alleged destruction of the child she has by a man who abandons her. *

In creating her realistic terms for the novel, Eliot found a means by which she could temper her theme of violence and vengeance with more socially oriented actions. Her realism stresses the ordinary, the everyday, the trivial, even the ugly and unseemly. There is little of the high and low we associate with the Greeks; and when hubris does appear, as in Arthur—whose downfall is imminent even as he preens himself for his finest moments—it comes in miniatures. No kings and princes, no emperors, no dictators and tyrants, no rulers of the world or masters of the universe—none of that enters into Eliot's realism. Yet in the shadows of these trivializing realistic details, there is the "fallen prince" in Arthur, whether Victoria's or Guinevere's; the emergence of a heroic mold in Adam (Adam!); the self-sacrifice of brother Seth (son of Adam after Cain slays Abel); the queenly behavior of Dinah (daughter of Jacob and Leah). Such developments strengthen the classical and biblical dimensions of the novel even as Eliot argues for a trivializing or miniaturizing set of characters.

Eliot cited her delight in Dutch painting as the basis for her kind of realism. But if by Dutch realism she meant Vermeer, there is something heroic in Ver-

---

* After Jason deserts Medea to marry Glauce, a princess, Medea murders her own children by this faithless man.

meer's interiors, in his maids, servants, flower girls, and others like them; something uplifting and extraordinary by virtue of the intensity with which they are perceived. Eliot, too, created a supra-realism through intensity of perception and through persistent commentary about her characters. The latter are rarely permitted to define themselves through dialogue, that is, through their own words alone; they are subjected to repeated authorial remarks which help us see the characters even when they fail to see themselves. Thus, her claims for realism—some of which she borrowed from Lewes and his distaste for the extraordinary in fiction—are belied by her procedures. This, too, is part of the dichotomy we observe in her in this period: the statement of one thing, the practice of another; the positioning of herself in one theoretical set, the use of fictional techniques to subvert that very theory.

By 1858, Eliot had become a very complicated person: not only an author on the edge of broad fame and monetary reward, but a human being of several kinds of potentiality. Near the end of *Adam Bede,* she speaks of change. Like so many Victorian novelists, she addresses the reader. "It would be a poor result of all our anguish and our wrestling, if we won nothing but our old selves at the end of it—if we could return to the same blind loves, the same self-confident blame, the same light thoughts of human suffering, the same frivolous gossip over blighted human lives, the same feeble sense of that Unknown towards which we have sent forth irrepressible cries in our loneliness." Change is not only inevitable, it is desirable. Eliot was becoming a novelist, which meant she lived in her created work as much as she did in her life, and the blending of the two was transformational. She says our sorrow still lives in us, but changes its forms. Those "forms" were now the new person, not only Marian Evans, or Mrs. Marian Lewes, but George Eliot, the maker of master fictions.

Little in Eliot's description of how she came to write *Adam Bede* indicated the complexity of her responses. In her explanation, she stresses certain autobiographical elements, while at the same time denying any strict adherence to personal history or to actual persons. It is, in fact, her usual procedure: to have definite sources, but to deny she hewed closely to personages or events. The time was 1839–40, when she was, she says, in need of someone to talk to, and Aunt Samuel (the wife of Robert Evans's younger brother) proved a sympathetic listener as her niece explained rapid changes in her own inner life. Aunt Samuel's story of infant murder, we recall, became the basis for Hetty's episodes. *
When Eliot repeated this story to Lewes, she was just starting to write *Scenes of Clerical Life* and thought of extending the three tales with another one about this girl. But after "Janet's Repentance" closed the volume, she decided to make what she called "My Aunt's Story" into the subject of a novel.

---

* The Nottingham County Library has in its collection a broadsheet on "An Account of the Experience and Happy Death of Mary Voce," executed for child murder on Tuesday, 16 March 1802. Although the story became the basis for Hetty's ordeal, in the original, Mary Voce is, indeed, executed. But similarities exist in that both condemned women are brought to self-recognition, to acceptance of God's mercy, and to understanding the enormity of their sin. Each in her way accepts her fate.

Her aunt remained a strong figure in Eliot's memory, and she decided to build Dinah Morris on certain aspects. Physically, they were quite different: Dinah, commanding and beautiful beneath the severity of her look, her aunt small and unprepossessing except when she preached. When Marian Evans came to know her better, Aunt Samuel had mellowed from her preaching days, and her niece found she could "talk to her about my inward life, which was closely shut up from those usually round me." This was the critical period when she found herself drifting from the religious beliefs of her father, and her ability to express herself to someone like Aunt Samuel provided that support she needed at certain periods of her life.

As for Adam, she says one or two incidents were suggested by her father's early years. But, she insists, "Adam is not my father any more than Dinah is my aunt." She says that Adam is a composite character, with no single portrait in him; but she is disingenuous in asserting he is not structured on Robert Evans and his type. Incidents differ, yet the basic character fits closely what we know of Evans: a dogged, dedicated, fully committed worker, a man caught up by a rigid sense of right and wrong, a conservative who feared change and hewed to conventional ways, a person who insisted on his way of seeing things, the result of a certain strain of self-righteousness. Adam's doggedness at work is an extension of a character which permits little flexibility.* His stubbornness and belief in the righteousness of his ideas bend only somewhat under the advice (and beauty) of Dinah.

Eliot's final remarks on the origin of *Adam Bede*: "When I began to write it, the only elements I had determined on, besides the character of Dinah, were the character of Adam, his relation to Arthur Donnithorne [a composite, but based mainly on Robert Evans's employer], and their mutual relation to Hetty— *i.e.*, to the girl who commits child-murder—the scene in the prison being, of course, the climax toward which I worked. Everything else grew out of the characters and their mutual relations." Eliot altered Hetty's fate, as we know, by staying her execution with a last-minute writ brought by Arthur Donnithorne—a typical Victorian "escape" mechanism. She continues: "Dinah's ultimate relation to Adam was suggested by George, when I read to him the first part of the first volume: he was so delighted with the presentation of Dinah, and so convinced that the reader's interest would centre in her, that he wanted her to be the principal figure at the 1st." This, she says, she accepted immediately, and from the end of the third chapter worked with that in mind.

The entrance of Lewes into the equation is interesting, and his suggestion about making Dinah Morris a central figure has possibly some personal intimations. It is speculative, but entirely plausible, that he saw in Dinah the shadowy version of Eliot herself. When he perceived the relationship of Dinah to her preaching and to other people, he understood how Eliot in one of her phases

---

*A notebook entry suggests, perhaps incongruously, that Eliot also shaped Adam on George Stephenson, the pioneering railway engineer—from what she had gleaned from Samuel Smiles's biography of him. Besides physical and temperamental similarities, they both attended night school and excelled in mathematics, showed their affection for a favorite dog, and indicated a willingness to use their fists when provoked.

was Dinah. The Eliot of 1858 was not Dinah Morris, but Marian Evans at one time had the fervor and conviction the preacher communicates. Still further, it is possible that in Adam Bede Lewes saw something of himself; obviously not in the physical aspect, where Adam is strong and sturdy, but in the way in which Lewes found his life turned around by his association with Marian Evans, roughly comparable to changes in Adam's life with the advent of Dinah. In a revealing journal entry, Lewes speaks of how his life was on a treadmill before he met Marian. He writes of how much he owed to Herbert Spencer, their acquaintance being "the brightest ray in a very dreary, *wasted* period" in his life. He says he had "given up all ambition whatever, lived from hand to mouth, and thought the evil of each day sufficient." But Spencer's contribution was not only long talks and his intellectual theorizing, but the fact he introduced Lewes to Marian, which is "another and deeper debt." It was through him, Lewes says, that he came to know and love her, and "since then my life has been a new birth."

As the novel proceeded, Blackwood wanted to know the rest of the story, but Eliot refused, noting the fact in her journal on 1 April, without explanation. It is apparent, however, she feared some inhibitions placed on her story by Blackwood, with his sensitivity to Maga readers. What was acceptable in a book was often unacceptable serialized in a journal; and Eliot finally decided not to publish Adam Bede in Maga, but to go directly to book form. Although there was no rift here, Eliot's secretiveness about her work ran up against Blackwood's understandable desire to see what he was getting.* Blackwood immediately acquiesced and indicated he would publish the novel at once, certain that in whatever form it was issued it would prove excellent both in earning power and for the author's reputation. Eliot received £800 for a four-year copyright, very generous terms for a first novel, and a considerable amount of money when we consider that a working-class family in the 1850s earned only a little over £50 a year. A middle-class family might figure on close to £100.

Flush with the prospect of a large sum, Lewes and Eliot left for the continent on 7 April, for a stay of five months. Before departing, Eliot told Cara Bray she still held cherished feelings about her and Sara and that they "always will be the women I have loved best in the world—the women I have had most reason to love and admire. . . ." Nevertheless: "It is impossible ever to revive the past, and if we could recover the friend from whom we have parted we should perhaps find that we could not recover precisely the old relation. But that doesn't hinder the past from being sacred and belonging to our religion." She sent along a photograph of herself taken in late February by Mayall, with the inscription "to my sisters Cara and Sara." "I can't say much that is good of her," Eliot wrote Cara, "but I am confident that she will not misconduct herself in your society."

---

* Writing to Lewes, not Eliot, Blackwood said he understood "his" decision not to reveal the story, for Eliot had said to him, Blackwood, that the essence of art is the treatment of the story, not the working out of the plot. The publisher was so taken with her argument that "any subject being suitable entirely depends upon how it is handled," he planned on using this expression any time someone proposed a paper based on a particular subject.

In this poignant scene, there is a valedictory, even to the "sisters" touch. Only memories exist. And this stance is quite appropriate to the time, when in her fiction, in *Adam Bede* and in the forthcoming *Mill*, she was probing the past and reliving it. As she speaks of her feelings and of the difficulty or impossibility of regaining them in their fullness, she suggests how painful this journey into the past will prove. Even the trip to Germany, starting in Munich, will be a reliving of the past, recalling the first trip she took to the continent with Lewes, when Weimar was, in one respect, their honeymoon. Eliot had entered a period of intense pastness, of troubling memories, of things she simply could not put beyond her even as she moved outward. Becoming a novelist meant for her just this jousting with the past.

12

Arrival

"... the passions of the past were living in her dread."

In his biography, John Cross omitted material from Eliot's journal where she spoke of Agnes Lewes as being ungrateful for her help. Agnes was again deeply in debt, for £184 (equivalent to perhaps $5,000–10,000 in present buying power), and this had to be settled before Lewes and Eliot went abroad. While the couple seemed flush with new money, Agnes was a hemorrhaging body into which they poured funds, some of it Eliot's. The trip to Munich was chiefly to enable Lewes to research his *The Physiology of Common Life*. Eliot would work on *Adam Bede*, which did not require any particular location. They did not head directly for Munich, a place selected because it was reasonable and, they hoped, quiet. Stopping off in Lille, then Cologne, Frankfurt, and Nuremberg, they walked the cities, and found Nuremberg especially enchanting. Eliot praised the music at Frauenkirche and felt a glow from the appreciative audience around her. Her experience in the church had little to do with God and a lot to do with the organ and chorus—an aesthetic rather than a pious moment. They reached Munich on 11 April and soon found suitable lodgings at 15 Luitpoldstrasse, what Eliot described as two elegant furnished rooms. The cost was only 10 shillings a week, justifying their trip to Munich as a way of holding down costs.

They almost immediately established their routine, which meant work in the morning, a meal at one o'clock, followed by a walk. Because of his life of Goethe, Lewes was well known, and the couple fell into an intellectual circle of scientists, historians, and poets. On the evenings when they did not attend the opera or theater, they stayed in and read a mixture of books: Mrs. Gaskell's

Mary Barton (which may have planted some ideas for Eliot's *Felix Holt*), Emily Brontë's *Wuthering Heights,* some Wordsworth and Tennyson.

The acquaintances they knew through introductions were, in the main, scientists: the anatomist and zoologist Karl Theodor Ernst von Siebold, professor at the University of Munich, and, also at the university, Baron Justus von Liebig, the professor of chemistry. They met Friedrich Martin von Bodenstedt, a poet and journalist, and another professor. The preponderance of scientific friends proved very valuable: obviously for Lewes with his researches into physiological processes, less obviously for Eliot. We observe in her fiction increasing reference to the physical world—anatomy, physiology, geology, physics—especially after Darwin's *Origin of Species* appeared in 1859. As Eliot solidified her agnosticism, she became ever closer to naturalism in her fiction; she believed as much in environmental factors as in individual will. She did emphasize a sequence of events as determining individuals' lives as co-equal with choice, and she did see deepening human tragedy as a continuum with grapplings for happiness. She did not make her characters victims of fate or destiny, or of scientific determinism; but determinism is rarely distant from her contexts, and, as she aged, she tended to seek out more and more deterministic patterns. Her *Daniel Deronda* tells somewhat the same story as Hardy's *Tess of the D'Urbervilles* (1891). Her sense of personal choice, however, remained—she needed that as a cornerstone of her moral and ethical view—but it became confused with constraints from other areas, especially from that inexorable scientific world where determinism and causality ruled. *

Eliot was not fond of Munich, and she only agreed to their long stay because of Lewes's scientific needs. Only a short time after their arrival, she filled her long letter to Sara with disappointment. She measures Munich against Nuremberg, which she appreciated as an authentic medieval town that "has grown up with the life of a community as much as the shell of a nautilus has grown with the life of the animal. . . ." Every house there, she says, has physiognomy, and its variety is like nature's itself. Her points of reference are strongly scientific; her guiding images are those of animal and plant life. In this, we find intimations of her next work, not yet announced, *The Mill on the Floss:* naturalistic in its insistence on the power of the river Floss, full of animal and plant analogies to human life, and deterministic in many of its patterns of behavior.

Back in London, what we may call the authorial recognition game was proceeding. The unlikely Joseph Liggins was the candidate of choice, although Barbara Bodichon soon penetrated the disguise, and Eliot would reveal herself to the Brays and to Sara the next year. In Munich, however, she was beginning to find the social rounds oppressive. Part of it was that it interfered with her working time, but co-equal was her disgust at the Bavarian wives of these promi-

---

* She fitted loosely, but not exclusively, into what was called "scientific naturalism," a belief held by Lewes, Huxley, Spencer, Frederic Harrison—the follower of Comte—and other scientists and writers that man can be understood only through nature. In this view, nature is a valid way of gaining "truth." It was this fixedness on moral elements as a way of responding to nature's pressure that led Nietzsche to condemn Eliot and her kind as "little bluestockings," as moral fanatics. Nietzsche, of course, urged personal confrontation, not social comity.

nent men. They could be kind when she was ill, but intellectually she found them wanting, and yet often she was obliged to sit with the women while the men congregated on the other side of the room.* "It is quite an exception to meet with a woman who seems to expect any sort of companionship from the men, and I shudder at the sight of a woman in society, for I know I shall have to sit on the sofa with her all the evening listening to her stupidities, while the men on the other side of the table are discussing all the subjects I care to hear about." She writes this to Sara, but she is not finished. "I think I was going to say that the stupidity of a Bavarian woman has not the virtue of German cabbage—it is not copious, liberal, abundant—it is stingy, feeble, barren of propositions." She cites North Germans as perhaps providing some modification of Bavarian stupidity.

The scientists were truly kind, interrupting their researches to take the Leweses to various exhibitions of scientific processes. Liebig, for example, gave them a tour of his laboratory and explained the process of silver mirror manufacture, and entertained them in his home as well. As the biographer of Goethe, Lewes had entrée into nearly every leading home, and his relationship to Eliot was not questioned. They were taken as husband and wife, although even if not, it would not have mattered in this circle.

She and Lewes spent many hours at the museums. She developed an enormous admiration, even adoration, for Rubens, who was well represented at the Pinakothek.† She says that more than anyone else, he makes her recognize that painting is a great art. She finds his men and women moved by real passions, not posturing and posing, as she does in the German painter Wilhelm von Kaulbach. She sees the men as ready to do the work of the world, the women "such real mothers"—a comment neatly dividing the world in ways Eliot's own life belied. She and Lewes also looked intently at the collection of Dutch paintings: Breughel, Metsu, Teniers; no Vermeer, however. And yet it is Vermeer-like interiors she cites in that segment of *Adam Bede*, "In Which the Story Pauses a Little," she was writing at this time: that praise of the ordinary and the everyday. None of this fitted with Rubens, the painter of the heroic; but Eliot knew her own gifts lay not in heroical figures—despite the classical backdrops—but in the people she had experienced as a child and young woman.

Questions of authorship followed her to Munich, in the form of John Blackwood's revelation of Mr. Newdigate, a descendant of the Newdigate who helped Robert Evans in his youth. The family heir had observed that Sir Christopher Cheverel in *Scenes* was based on old Sir Roger Newdigate. Newdigate detected

---

* Some exceptions might be, as Haight indicates, Frau Martius, Frau Bodenstedt, and Frau von Siebold; but it is unclear whether they are exceptions because of their kindness—helping Eliot when she was ill for a week—or because of their intellectual distinction from the common run of Bavarian women. Eliot seems generally disdainful, but she was also contemptuous of English women. Only the French seemed exceptional—knowledgeable, expansive, capable of dealing equitably with men of distinction. As an exceptional woman, Eliot tended to be intellectually harsh on those who were less gifted.

† The Munich Pinakothek contains Rubens's *Large Last Judgment, Rape of the Daughters of Leucippus, Battle of the Amazons, Massacre of the Innocents,* and several other major works.

a clear identity with Sir Christopher's ward, Caterina. This brought forth from Eliot her usual disclaimer, that her characters are composites and that readers who discover certain points of concidence with something they recognize will deceive themselves that they have a key to the whole. Her comments foreshadow Henry James's dictum for fiction: minute observation, inner experience, and transformation of all into artistic forms. Amusingly, Newdigate told Blackwood that the family facts must have been communicated by that ever-present Eliot alter ego, Joseph Liggins. As she rose, so did he, Liggins as much an invention as Eliot.

She was rapidly tiring of Munich, despite the ministrations of a wide circle of friends and acquaintances. Her paramount job was *Adam Bede;* she was now, toward mid-June 1858, writing about Arthur Donnithorne's birthday feast, the celebration before his fall and Hetty's entrapment in a web of terrible events. Lewes had left to visit his sons at Hofwyl, although they knew nothing of his relationship to Eliot and apparently did not inquire. There was, here, simply another deception, in fact deceptions within deceptions. For if and when Lewes told his sons about his new "wife," what name would he use, who would she be, how could he transmit the confusion of realms? Was she Mrs. Lewes, as she called herself, when their mother was Mrs. Lewes? Was she Marian Evans, a name she had forbidden everyone to address her by? Was she George Eliot, who was known only to a very select few and certainly not to young people at school? All the while, Blackwood was still addressing her as "Dear Sir," although he knew her identity.

The role-playing was not debilitating. Both Eliot and Lewes seemed to ride its strange course, although frequent illnesses, headaches, and attacks of nerves and anxiety may have resulted from emotional strain. As Eliot harrowed her background for experiences and observations, she reentered a particularly divisive, multi-leveled kind of reality: what belonged to her as Marian, what as Mrs. Lewes, what as George Eliot! The gender change was most compelling, since to all the world except a few she was achieving her fame and fortune as a man. Where did that leave the woman? And how would that influence her presentation of women? or men? From what we have so far gleaned, women wield power and eventually survive, not at all surprising given the fact that, with the male name, Eliot had in some respects taken on what belonged to the male world.

As with previous Lewes absences, whether to visit his sons or to spend the holidays at Arthur Helps's, Eliot made use of the quiet. Although the two did get along quite well, there were petty annoyances which could build, as each heard the other's pen scratching along, or as they ran into each other during working hours in a two-room lodging. Withal, there appeared to be no overt competition, perhaps because they were working in different areas and because each took such interest in the other's work. Eliot became an amateur scientist of sorts, and Lewes remained something of a literary critic, with two novels to his credit, one of them *(Ranthorpe)* almost readable.

By the end of June, Eliot had completed Chapters 23 and 24 of *Adam Bede.* Disruptions, worry about Lewes during his trip to Hofwyl, and social obligations did not appear to send her off course, although she would pay later. So sure was she in her writing that it flowed. The almost clean manuscript* indicates the steadiness and certainty of her fictional plans. On 7 July, they left Munich. Their itinerary took them on a whirlwind tour of Salzburg, Vienna, Prague, and Dresden, where they expected to remain for a few weeks. With the help of the physiologists in their social circle, Lewes's work had gone very well. During their final days in Munich, Strauss came to visit, and Eliot had a quarter hour's chat with him, which she found very pleasant. Strauss had mellowed, and her spoken German had improved since their last meeting.

Eliot described their journey from Munich to Dresden as a "fortnight's unspeakable journey." In addition to the above stops, they added Ischl, which meant they arrived in a place, unpacked, repacked, caught another train, and repeated the process almost every other day until they reached Dresden. Not surprisingly, Eliot was ill for the week before their departure, but found it almost "a luxury because of the love tended me." The illness was one of several she suffered from, and not relieved by either fame or fortune. Her description of that intolerable fortnight should be contrasted with Lewes's, which is full of delight, almost idyllic. He calls the Tyrol part of "an exquisite tour," and Prague "the most splendid city in Germany." But Eliot had disdained Munich, and her illness could be linked to that, or else to anxieties about her first novel, despite the smoothness with which it seemed to proceed. Their jammed itinerary, she could foresee, would leave her little opportunity for sustained writing, and now that she was closing in, she could well have responded with illness.

Vienna was well known to Lewes—he had spent six months there before marrying Agnes. They did the usual sights: the museums, the famous St. Stephens Cathedral, and Lewes's old digs in Kärntner Tor. They then took an overnight railway to Prague, where Eliot, like Lewes, was most impressed by this magnificent city. The Old Jewish Cemetery, with its Mondrian-like tombstones, particularly moved her, as did the old synagogue. "Then came the sombre old synagogue with its smoky groins, and lamp forever burning." Prague remained

---

*The British Museum Library possesses not the manuscript but the fair copy, which we would expect to be cleaner than the working pages. In Eliot's explanation, in a note, of the progress of composition, however, we see how even alternate parts were barely changed. "The first volume was written at Richmond, the second at Munich & Dresden, the third at Richmond again. The work was begun on the 22nd October 1857 & finished on the 16 November 1859 [the '9' is overwritten an '8']. A large portion of it was written twice, though often scarcely at all altered in the copying, but other parts only once, and among these the description of Dinah & a good deal of her sermon, the love-scenes between her & Seth, 'Hetty's world,' most of the scene in the Two Bedchambers, the talk between Arthur and Adam, various parts in the second volume which I can recall less easily, & in the third, Hetty's journeys, her confession & the cottage scenes."

Affixed to the manuscript is the dedication: "To my dear husband, George Henry Lewes, / I give this M.S. of a work which would / never have been written but for the / happiness which his love has conferred on / my life. / Marian Lewes / March 23, 1859." The first edition did not contain this dedication, but did feature an epigraph from Wordsworth, about those who fall and whether they may be forgiven. "So that ye may have / Clear images before your gladdened eyes / Of nature's unambitious underwood / And flowers that prosper in the shade. And when / I speak of such among the flock as swerved / Or fell, those only shall be singled out / Upon whose lapse, or error, something more / Than brotherly forgiveness may attend."

with her, becoming the place in *Daniel Deronda* where Mirah escapes from her parasitical father; and also referred to in "The Lifted Veil," Eliot's bizarre story of shifting identities, hidden motives, and disguised sensibilities.

On 17 July, they journeyed to Dresden, now on the last leg of their trip which would see them back in Richmond on 2 September. Like Prague, Dresden was a jewel of a city. Lewes was working along on his physiological studies, having completed and printed "Hunger and Thirst," "The Food We Eat," "The Blood and Its Circulation," and "Respiration and Suffocation." He had also finished "Digestion and Indigestion," "Why We Are Warm and How We Keep So," and "Feeling and Thinking in Relation to the Nervous System," plus three other pieces he says he did not intend for *Maga*: "Sleep and Dreams," "The Qualities We Inherit from Our Parents," and "Life and Death." Several of these topics were on the frontiers of physiology (and would later become part of psychology); and while Lewes did not make his mark as a great original scientist, he was far more than a journalist poking into still esoteric subjects. His work was pioneering, particularly on inheritance, sleep and dreams, and the nervous system.

The Physiology of Common Life (in two volumes, 1859–60) might have had a far greater impact if not for the almost simultaneous publication of *The Origin of Species,* which became the central document for that and future years. But physiologists who were not particularly taken with evolutionary theory saw in Lewes's study the enormous significance of his contribution, especially in areas where he could apply animal experimentation to human behavior. Even more compelling for us is that Lewes as physiologist and his companion as psychologist were like two sides of the same problem: each coming to an understanding of what the other was doing, but, in effect, working different areas with very different results.

After the social bustle of Munich, the couple was ready to settle down to a more work-friendly atmosphere. Lewes tells Blackwood they were living like hermits—Eliot herself writes of each one sitting in his or her place working, with doors closed—and their sole outside communication is with the magnificent Dresden collections of Raphael, Titian, Corregio, and Veronese. He admits that in Munich they had too much society, and that it interfered with work. With "the affections engaged," it is amazing how well one can do without others.

At Munich, while Lewes mentioned the great Venetian painters, Eliot noted in her journal the Dutch: the Vermeers, * as well as Holbeins and Titians. She was, however, especially taken with Raphael's *Sistine Madonna,* which gave her, she says, a sense of awe. *The Sistine Madonna* is spectacularly dramatic, with the Madonna, infant Jesus in arms, coming through heavenly curtains pulled aside for her figure. Kneeling before her are the martyred Pope Sextus II and St. Barbara, who starved to death for her faith. At her feet are two cherubs, eyes drawn upward. The grayish-white background of clouds gives the magnificent

---

* Two in particular, *Girl Reading a Letter* and *The Procuress;* a third, *View of Sandhills on the Dutch Plain,* meant less to her.

vestments of the Virgin, the pope, and St. Barbara a shimmering, magnetic quality. When the couple returned to look at it, Eliot records she felt "quite hysterical." Very possibly, all that martyrdom in one concentrated place! They returned repeatedly, to make their viewing of this painting their final event each day. She was now heading toward the end of Book II of *Adam Bede,* having completed Chapter 34, "The Betrothal," of Adam and Hetty. The novel was a little over two-thirds completed. She was moving so well that when she and Lewes returned to Richmond, she had Book II in hand (through Chapter 35) in a few days and sent off the manuscript to Blackwood for his comments. Before leaving Germany, however, they went to Leipzig, where they met the famous Julius Viktor Carus, the professor of comparative anatomy who thought enough of Lewes's forthcoming book on physiology to translate it into German for Brockhaus Verlag. Carus became even better known as the translator of Darwin.

Back in Richmond on 2 September—after a combination of carriage, railway, and boat travel that occupied almost two full days—Eliot sent off the manuscript on 7 September. Her letters indicate that despite the richness of their travels and experiences, she was pleased to be back in familiar surroundings. Some of this was surely connected to her desire to get on with her book. When she submitted the *Adam Bede* manuscript, she explained to Blackwood that the book is so tightly organized she wishes he could have read it in one piece, but since she is behind, she wanted him to see what she had written. She was hurrying along now not only from internal imperatives but from the desire to catch the Christmas season. She assumed that the three volumes could be printed in six weeks! Blackwood did not respond for a month, not until 4 October, but despite the delay, he was, quibbles and all, quite enthusiastic.

James Anthony Froude, at the beginning of his career as a historian of England, wrote to Eliot thanking "him" for the copy of *Scenes,* but inquiring further about the author, so touched was he by the book. Eliot was moved by his enthusiasm and by his desire to penetrate the disguise, and she asked Blackwood to respond that she had sent the book because she admired Froude, but for her own reasons she would maintain her incognito.

Blackwood wrote Eliot his full impression of the two books of *Adam Bede.* Hetty he sees as pure triumph, but he misreads the relationship between her and Arthur; he sees her as a "little villain" and Arthur as someone who can only escape by taking to his heels. This is hardly what Eliot meant, for she saw in the encounter Hetty's and Arthur's weakness, their youthful ardor creating massive self-deception. The violent encounter between Adam and Arthur disturbed the publisher, possibly because it became coarse, or possibly because he felt Eliot had not made Adam sympathetic enough. Once again, Blackwood misread: Adam is oaklike, but he does have feelings, and this scene in which he knocks the squire down is the first intimation of how deep his feelings can run. He becomes sympathetic to the extent that Arthur deserves to be punished, and Blackwood's inability to understand Eliot's depiction of the squire blinds him to this roustabout scene.

Blackwood feels the novel will be successful, but that much depends on the third book. He wants to leave final matters as to publication, numbers printed, price, and the rest until the entire manuscript is at hand. He sees no reason for her to start on proofs now. On 3 November, the publisher followed up with warm praise for the final segment. He liked everything, even the touches concerning Hetty's trial and travail, Adam's support of her at the court, and Dinah's and Hetty's clinging to each other; he now seems to get Arthur straight as someone bursting with self-importance just as the bomb explodes upon him. Completely satisfied, Blackwood offered £800 for four years' copyright. Eliot accepted, and later on Blackwood tendered an additional £400 as an earnest of his pleasure in being her publisher.

Possibly, he should not be blamed for his misreading of Arthur and then his hesitation about the scene between Arthur and Adam. In an unsigned review in *Saturday Review,* which is quite admiring, the critic questions Eliot for moving into violence and melodrama: Adam's fighting, Hetty's crime, a series of events built on trials, scaffolds, and pardons. Behind the reviewer's comment is the sense that the novel is about ordinary people—Adam is cited as the special creation of a writer who has observed common people—and not about "dramatic or stirring" incidents. Taking for granted that the author is a man, a man who has, indeed, sat at the feet of the novelist Charles Kingsley, the reviewer chides him for introducing "the startling horror of rustic reality. We do not expect that we are to pass from the discreet love of a well-to-do carpenter to child-murder and executions, and the shock which the author inflicts on us seems as superfluous as it is arbitrary."[*]

The comments are astute, and they go to the heart of what might seem to be a problem in Eliot's first novel: that sudden violence which flares up and which leads to self-destruction or death. What the reviewer has missed is that she has prepared the reader for this: Adam has a violent, almost uncontrollable temper, Arthur is building up dangerous illusions about himself, and Hetty is foolishly seeking a higher social position through Arthur; the ominous pregnancy—standard Victorian fare—is not at all unlikely, and the disposal of the baby equally likely. But there are other factors the reviewer could not at the time know. In every novel of Eliot's, except *Middlemarch,* there is brutality and death. In "Janet's Repentance," we have already seen Dempster die a violent, self-inflicted death. In *The Mill on the Floss,* Maggie and Tom die in the destructive, vehement flood. In *Felix Holt, the Radical,* Felix is accused of murder. In *Romola,* Tito Melema is savagely murdered and tossed into the Arno. In *Daniel Deronda,* Grandcourt drowns, while Gwendolen feels she might have saved him and is,

---

[*] With more psychological insight, the critic might have been troubled by other things as well. The astute reader is tempted to see Adam's and Dinah's happy ending enjoyed at the price of Hetty's sacrifice. Is she an Iphigenia figure, martyred so that the principals can accomplish their destiny? Eight years after having been transported abroad for her guilt in the death of her infant, Hetty dies on the way home—making possible the novel's closure on an Eden-like scene. Henry James saw Hetty as the central figure, by virtue of her calamitous fortunes. None of this, however, should be cast in stone, for Dinah may be central: a double of Hetty and the sole character who has mobility and maneuverability without paying a heavy price. She is a vision of the "free woman," although Eliot finally grounds her.

accordingly, a murderer by intention. The violence done major characters in Eliot's fiction—and we should not neglect *Silas Marner*—calls for comment. It is insufficient to see it as misplaced; it is part of her vision.

We do not think of Eliot as a violent writer, unlike Dickens, for example, who is full of mayhem. Part of Eliot's vision of common life included a perception of the violence that lay beneath ordinary existence; but more than that, there was a part of her nature or moral character which saw in death some final sacrifice or final redemption. Although she had dropped the formal trappings of religion, Eliot still believed in the organizing quality and order religion brings: the fact that it can act as a check on people's base instincts, on their individual acts of greed and self-serving ways, on their desire to explode into possibly forbidden areas of conflict. When it waned, violence erupted.

This does not mean Eliot saw man as basically evil; quite the contrary. Yet she recognized how frail the moral life can be, how fragile the individual's hold on right action; and while she wanted to believe in man's innate goodness— even given her knowledge of man's potential for temptation and self-serving acts—she also perceived that some "higher power" was necessary. That higher power was not God, not formal church teaching, but the spiritual power which emanates from institutions that have traditionally served to organize man's behavior around good acts. In some part of her agnostic self, Eliot still held to hierarchical assumptions about mankind, that linkage of responsibility in which power is transmitted from above and goes along a kind of chain until it reaches down to the lowest levels.

Too much of a republican to believe wholly in such an arrangement, she nevertheless reached for harmony in social and political life which gave man, individual man, his place; and once he found that place he was morally safe. Yet beneath the safety of that "place," there was the potential for violence, the need to protect one's territory, or to assert one's needs which did not quite fit into that organizational principle. And violence must be dealt with, since society's cohesiveness depends on how acts of violence (vengeance, brutality, cruelty) can be confronted and assimilated into a moral structure. Eliot's position was delicate. That she embraced Comte's positivism at one time was, as we shall see, a mark of her uncertainty, her need to grasp absolutes. She greatly feared the runaway individual, and yet she could also be a fierce republican and democrat. This, too, was the troubled voice of the century.

When Sara asked about *Westminster* contributions, the clue to Eliot's identity was there. Either she had stopped writing or she was writing elsewhere. Eliot told her not to "guess at authorship." Chapman's name pops up. He is in poverty, not well, his various enterprises having fallen into disarray. He had now become embroiled in a nasty row with James Martineau, Harriet's brother, and a regular contributor to the *Westminster*. Martineau had broken with Chapman and, having established his own journal, the *National Review*, demanded the copyrights of his articles in Chapman's quarterly. When Chapman refused— copyrights were always considered part of any contributor's arrangement—Martineau threatened suit in bankruptcy court. Chapman tried to counter this with an effort to ruin Martineau. Eliot felt sympathy for her onetime friend, although in the not so distant future she would break with him over his flippancy about her identity.

Specimen pages of *Adam Bede,* in proof, looked "shabby" to Eliot, and Blackwood immediately agreed to new pages. This and other circumstances (the fact that the printing office was tied up with a long Bulwer-Lytton novel) meant postponement for Eliot's book, a circumstance which troubled her.

Bray, Sara, and members of her family had followed her career with varying degrees of attention; suddenly, it had stopped completely. When Bray asked, she even joked with him that she was indeed writing a novel, amusingly leading him astray. Eliot clearly wanted the freedom to be who she was, without interference, the way Sir Walter Scott had denied all authorship of Waverley. But as Eliot showed in so many novels, gossip and rumor were the way of the world. Even Lewes intruded into the situation with a letter to Blackwood. He agreed that the delay of the book might compromise Eliot's identity, or somehow introduce matters that would distract from the book's rightful reception. "He thinks," Lewes writes, "that *mystery* as to authorship will have a great effect in determining critical opinion. . . . The evil consequences of the mystery being disclosed before the book seems to him [GE], and to me, far greater than any disadvantage of contemporaneous appearance" with the Lytton novel. He asks Blackwood to "crowd all sail." Lewes cites the fact that when *Jane Eyre* was "finally known to be a woman's book, the tone noticeably changed. Not that I believe in the possibility of anything adventitious permanently hurting a *good* book, but there is always something temporary in the success of a novel, and one may as well secure all adventitious aids."

Adam Bede missed the Christmas season by a wide margin, not appearing until 1 February 1859. All of Eliot's and Lewes's fears seemed unnecessary, for it was successful both critically and commercially. Their stated fears, in fact, reinforce the sense that shielding Eliot was as important, at least, as the book itself; that she needed the disguise in order to work well; and that this need was connected to her ability to capture her earlier experiences *while appearing to be someone else.* A strange kind of transference occurred: she could write well about Marian Evans's experience as long as she was George Eliot; or else she could continue writing well only if she had the shield of obscurity before her. In this view, Marian Evans was such an unpleasant association—those memories of everything depressing and unhappy—that she could keep going only as long as she suppressed her name while utilizing her experiences. In this "doubling" we observe the rejection of nearly everything connected to Marian Evans, so that protestations of a "happy childhood" are belied by the miserable adolescence and young womanhood, to the extent these years had to be expunged. The implication is that if she were to survive as a writer she had to be left to mine her earlier experiences while denying who she was.

The break with Chapman came with Herbert Spencer's statement to Marian that the publisher had asked him point-blank if Marian had written *Scenes of*

Clerical Life. On 5 November 1858, the outraged Eliot sent off an angry letter to her former mentor.

I have just learned that you have allowed yourself to speak carelessly of rumours concerning a supposed authorship of mine. A little reflection in my behalf would have suggested to you that were any such rumours true, my own abstinence from any communication concerning my own writing, except to my most intimate friends, was evidence that I regarded secrecy on such subjects as a matter of importance. Instead of exercising this friendly consideration, you carelessly, certainly, for no one's pleasure or interest, and to my serious injury, contribute to the circulation of idle rumours and gossip, entirely unwarranted by any evidence. . . . Should you like to have unfounded reports of that kind circulated concerning yourself, still more should you like an old friend to speak idly of the merest hearsay on matters which you yourself had exhibited extreme aversion to disclose?

Chapman did not answer for three weeks, and Eliot considered the friendship closed. When Chapman did reply, Eliot wrote to ask if any part of her letter was a misstatement. Chapman responded that he would like to come to appeal his case; Eliot refused, using as an excuse that she and Lewes were house-hunting. The real reason was that Chapman had worn out his welcome. But he did not consider himself finished. In February of 1859 he wrote again, intimating that he knew her identity, firmly, as the author of *Scenes*. This time Lewes answered, with a very sharp rejoinder. He told Chapman that, as previous correspondence had shown, his effort to impute these works to Mrs. Lewes might have been meant as a compliment but was really an offense against delicacy and friendship. "As you seem so very slow in appreciating her feelings on this point, she authorizes me to state, as distinctly as language can do so, that she is not the author of 'Adam Bede.' " Eliot was not happy Lewes wrote this, for he had turned a disguise into a lie, which eventually would be revealed. With Chapman, what she appears to have missed is that, with all his schemes failing, he needed reflected luster, and that his attempt to identify Eliot was not malicious, as she felt, but his need to associate himself with someone achieving fame, someone he had helped to put on her feet, literarily speaking. It was an unpleasant episode. Lewes called Chapman an "impertinent fellow."

Despite this diversion, there was still a good deal of detailed work to do with *Adam Bede* before their next move, to Holly Lodge, at Southfields, Wandsworth.* Blackwood had written of his pleasure at the conclusion, and he even bent enough to accept the provincial dialect, something he usually asked to be cut. Meanwhile, proofs had to be read, and Eliot herself suggested toning down

---

* In an unfashionable, semi-industrialized part of London, south of the Thames, across the Albert and Battersea Bridges. Eliot told Sara (19 February 1859): ". . . you must not imagine it a snug place. . . . Imagine it, rather, as a tall cake, with a low garnish of holly and laurel." The move finally took place on 5 February 1859, but the couple remained there only nineteen months.

the dialect, by which she meant the spelling and perhaps some of the expressions. Lewes, who knew no dialect, was willing to go over the proofs for that purpose. She was, of course, cheered by Blackwood's kind words about the ending. Bray, meanwhile, visited at Richmond, and in writing to Cara of the visit, Eliot revealed how precarious was her feeling of happiness, indeed her stability. Her words and tone reinforce our sense of her need for disguise, for she was, she recognized, a dual person—giving one impression, feeling quite differently. Although we jump ahead, a minor story, "The Lifted Veil," a tale of considerable psychological import for Eliot, written in the spring of 1859, contains several clues to the fragility of her inner self even as she was poised for great success.

"The Lifted Veil," strikingly, fits almost perfectly between the publication of *Adam Bede* and the decision to start pulling steadily on *Mill.* It also coincides with the death of Chrissey, from tuberculosis, in March of 1859. The story, one of Eliot's very few of this length, does not appear to be her kind of tale; it is almost Poe-like in its nightmarish features. But involved in the Gothic elements is something else, a passive, almost helpless, but compelling narrator. This young man, Latimer, has clairvoyant talents, an "abnormal sensibility" which enables him to read others' thoughts, ideas, and emotions. This clairvoyance occurs only fitfully, and he feels relief when the souls of his companions are closed to him. Yet when the feeling comes on him not with trivial acquaintances but with those near him, he experiences great pain and grief. He says this happens when "the rational talk, the graceful attentions, the wittily turned phrases, and the kindly deeds, which used to make the web of their characters, were seen as if thrust asunder by a microscopic vision, that showed all the intermediate frivolities, all the suppressed egoism, all the struggling chaos of puerilities, meanness, vague capricious memories, and indolent make-shift thoughts, from which human words and deeds emerge like leaflets covering a fermenting heap." Under the social graces, like an artist, he sees into the real human debris. But with all his powers, Latimer cannot make use of them. He is not an artist, but a sufferer. He lacks true expression. He has taken on the depressed, unhappy, sadness-prone qualities Eliot wrote about so much in her letters, but without the saving grace of her creative abilities.

Eliot's dip into such an unhappy life comes right after Chrissey's death, her favorite sibling, and somehow reveals guilt feelings. Just before her death, Chrissey conveyed how sorry she was that she listened to Isaac and did not write to her sister. Eliot immediately forgave her, but then Chrissey died. All this caught Eliot in several levels of psychological and emotional response which revealed how fragile her hold on her role really was. For even as Chrissey's death returned her to those earlier years she wanted to forget or transform, she was perpetuating several layers of deception: as Mrs. Lewes, as George Eliot, as an author. Furthermore, with her ideas for *Mill* set, she was entering into that childhood period which clearly shadowed her own years with Isaac; and in *Adam Bede,* she had revisited the earlier time most intimately. The confluence of all this was to strain her emotional life, to make her aware of how fine her edge was, and to make it possible for "The Lifted Veil," with its series of disguises and deceptions, to emerge. It was not, characteristically, an "English" tale. *

Despite his clairvoyance, Latimer finds himself drawn to a sarcastic, cold, calculating young woman, Bertha Grant. Her physical beauty does not blind him to her qualities of serpentine nastiness; on the contrary, he is drawn to her because he knows how cruel she might be. But more than anything else which makes her attractive, she is to be engaged to Latimer's hated older brother, Alfred; the engagement has taken place just before Alfred falls from his horse and is killed. Latimer's relationship to Alfred is fierce, for Alfred is everything his passive, weak brother is not: handsome, full of overwhelming confidence, competent, his father's favorite, not at all studious, a man without doubts. As his name implies, Alfred is a conqueror, and he never suspects the hatred Latimer feels for him and his type. Alfred is more a type than a fully fashioned character, a narrowed-down male equivalent of later figures like Rosamond Vincy and Gwendolen Harleth. Bertha does not foreshadow these female characters, since she is calculating in a far more evil fashion, looking ahead, perhaps, to Tito Melema in *Romola* or Grandcourt in *Daniel Deronda*. She is the Lamia Keats wrote about in his poem, the Lilith-like creature who tempts men and sucks their life from them. Not surprisingly, Eliot used Charlotte Brontë's Bertha, a madwoman.

What Eliot created is a family of terrible schisms, where some tragic outcome must develop. Latimer's and Alfred's father is a very rich banker who sees in his older son a successor and in his younger—Latimer is known as the poet—a wasted life. While he is kind to Latimer, he has also written him off as unproductive, a dreamer who will never succeed. Latimer bears out this assessment, never achieving anything until his end approaches, the result of angina pectoris. But in one respect he exceeds his father's expectations, and that occurs when Alfred dies and Latimer marries Bertha—for the father sees that as the salvation of the family, when it is, in actuality, its demise. Bertha marries Latimer out of complete cynicism. As she has told him earlier, she will marry Alfred but not for love—love would only complicate her life; and she then marries Latimer out of a desire to have a husband she can control, while he would, apparently, sustain her contempt for all men. Since she has money of her own, her aim is not pure self gain, as with Gwendolen, and since she already has social position, it is not to rise, as with Rosamond. She lies deeply buried in hatred and contempt, a Medusa figure, a would-be Medea. Eliot fails to give her one redeeming quality; we do not know what has provoked her. Caustic, mean, calculating, ungiving, she is a figure of complete deception; only after marriage does Latimer begin to understand the full range of her weaponry. Despite his clairvoyance, he had insulated himself from believing the worst about her.

* For its time, that is, since later on it fits into a genre of *Dracula, Dr. Jekyll and Mr. Hyde,* and the like. Even Dickens and Wilkie Collins—who come to mind as sensationalists—did not probe so deeply into madness. A curious contemporary novella, however, is Mrs. Gaskell's *Lois the Witch.* Although the two stories are dissimilar in details and levels of madness, they both foreran the developing genre of sensationalist fiction. *Silas Marner,* incidentally, is not to be discounted as part of this "mad" literary scene.

What he does not perceive, however, is that she is planning to poison him. In a Grand Guignol finale to this story—grand opera more than tale—Bertha's maid, whom Latimer detests, has fallen mortally ill with peritonitis. Latimer's friend, a famous doctor, is visiting, and he suggests waiting until the maidservant dies and then, by way of a blood transfusion he has perfected, bring her back to life. She returns to life for moments, long enough to state that Bertha has put poison in the cabinet, intended for her husband. With that Bertha stands indicted, without recourse, and the two separate, both of them sworn to silence.

No direct relationship to Eliot's life is apparent; but there is a shadowy representation of all kinds of fear about her place in society, her work, her relationship to herself, and the entire question of identity.* Coming as it does at the confluence of so many significant elements in her life, this story manifests her erupting in ways she controlled in her longer, more seriously considered fiction. The fact that she draws on all her travels—Basel, Geneva, Prague (where Latimer is drawn to the Old Jewish Quarter), and Vienna—indicates the deeply personal nature of this story of transference. Into Latimer she pours all her doubts and fears, and by making him a poet and a passive creature, along with his clairvoyance, she has tied together everything that has developed in her since she left Coventry. She is drawn back and forth, into her life as an intense creative person, back into the life she left behind. And submerged in this Gothic tale of operatic climaxes is her relationship to Lewes: on the surface, happy, stable, and balanced; beneath, full of possibly unconscious deceptions, disguises, and calculated positionings of herself.

In another respect, "The Lifted Veil" is a quarry for later work. What Latimer comes to see in Bertha is an exaggerated version of what Lydgate in *Middlemarch* will eventually see in Rosamond Vincy. The latter is not evil, but if Lydgate projected her calculations and lack of emotional response, he would see something akin to evil; and even in the poisoning potential of the story, we foresee Lydgate's shadowy relationship to his first love, the French actress who deliberately kills her husband on stage, although it is deemed an accident. With Gwendolen Harleth, we have an even more developed instance of the Latimer–Bertha situation. Here there is some gender reversal, for Gwendolen as she gazes deeply into Grandcourt's soul sees almost what Latimer perceives in Bertha—not simply deception, but evil itself. Even further, with that insight, Gwendolen perceives her own "evil heart," her own calculations, and the injustice she has done Grandcourt's earlier companion, Lydia Glasher, and her children. The perception now cuts both ways, an indication of Eliot's deepening as an artist. "The Lifted Veil," then, becomes more than a curiosity. It affords a path into Eliot's fictional thinking for almost the remainder of her career, and yet the tale

---

* And not least her ambiguous feelings about writing itself, since Latimer's "previsions" are a creative gift which leads *not* to achievement, but to passivity and otiosity. The "lifted veil" does not, as in the way art is usually presented, lead to illumination or enlightenment, but to loss of illusions and to withdrawal. Art, then, is not in itself a true vision, but a despoiled spiritual experience. This does not signal a rejection of art on Eliot's part so much as her uncertainty about the very course she was following.

might not have existed at all if she had not experienced the linking of so many elements which could be resolved not in life but only in fiction.

From still another perspective, Latimer is the acquiescent "female," the eventual renunciatory Madonna figure whom we shall see in Romola and more immediately in Maggie, whereas Bertha is the "masculine" figure. Eliot usually proceeded so that the renunciation of the female is a form of vengeance upon the aggressive, predatory male. On occasion, the female needs a doubling figure to carry out her revenge, as Baldassarre fulfills Romola's wish to eliminate her husband, Tito. In this way, through assuming a Madonna-like pose, the female, as we shall see, gains empowerment.

In a related area, Hetty Sorrel was obviously troublesome for Eliot, not only because of her beauty but because of her challenge as an outcast, even a demonic figure, who stretches social proprieties. In a sense, Hetty "gets away" from the author precisely because, while she is treated so unsympathetically, she still stands for so much Eliot had to deal with. Despite her harsh handling of the young beauty, Eliot could not quite control her: Hetty seeks to raise herself not by intellect but by physical wiles, and this does not fit easily into the author's frame of reference. As a fallen creature, Hetty, with all her posturing and simpering manner, becomes a subtle yet demonic double of Eliot's own desire to rise, achieve, emerge. *

Near the end of the story, Latimer experiences a great moment of revelation, almost an oceanic vastation.

> The terrible moment of complete illumination had come to me, and I saw that the darkness had hidden the landscape from me, but only a blank prosaic wall; from the evening forth, through the sickening years which followed, I saw all round the narrow room of this woman's soul—saw petty artifice and mere negation where I had delighted to believe in coy sensibilities and wit at war with latent feeling . . . saw repulsion and antipathy harden into cruel hatred, giving pain only for the sake of wreaking itself.

Here we have the artistic experience in all its ambiguity, and it comes just as Eliot was to dig deeply into her earlier experiences in Mill and seek equity in the relationship between Maggie and her brother Tom, with linkages to Eliot's father, to the coldness Eliot felt toward her mother, and all the rest. Something akin to Latimer's revelation is involved here, something close to a shutting down of innocent hope, the consciousness of something both impenetrable and frightening. One thinks of Emily Dickinson's "soul" closing "the valves of her

---

* In still another respect, Hetty is a modern version of the Medusa figure—first a beauty, then punished by Athena and transformed into a monster who will punish men. Hetty's despairing journey (in Chapter 37) suggests her as having suffered Medusa's fate: Eliot even refers to her as having a "Medusa-face, with the passionate, passionless lips." Much of the Medusa material derived from Adolf Wilhelm Theodor Stahr's Torso: Kunst, Künstler, and Kunstwerk der Alten (1854), which Eliot reviewed in the Leader (Volume I, 17 March 1855; Volume II, April 1856).

attention / Like stone." In such fear and trembling, Eliot proceeded into 1859.

We catch the edge of her feelings when she wrote to Cara Bray, on 26 November 1858, as she was heading into the juncture of elements which gave expression to "The Lifted Veil." She was a Victorian depressee, part of that large number of both male and female figures who lived close to depression, madness, and breakdown—Tennyson, Dickens, John Stuart Mill, Carlyle, Rossetti, and Emily Brontë among others. "I am," she writes, "of a too sordid and anxious disposition, prone to dwell almost exclusively on fears instead of hopes, and to lay in a greater stock of resignation than of any other form of confidence. . . . I know there are incommunicable feelings within us capable of creating our best happiness at the very time others can see nothing but our troubles. And so I go on, arguing with myself." That "arguing with myself" is almost precisely what occurs in the telltale story of a dual character: passive on the exterior, boiling within; a doubling figure who is a poet and yet someone *who needs danger*, represented by Bertha Grant. *

Not incidentally, Eliot wrote "History of *Adam Bede*" during this unquiet time (her journal entry for 30 November 1858). We have already commented on this gloss on the novel, its origin with her aunt's story and other personal elements. If we wished, we could see this calm assessment of her novel as a need to control inner disruptiveness. She had also turned thirty-nine, past middle age for her time. Anxieties piled up: divulgation of her identity; fear about delay in publication of *Adam Bede*, and trepidation about its reception; further fears about her ability to go on as a novelist now that the couple depended on her income—the fact that *Mill* did not form coherently in her mind until the next year; and a more generalized uneasiness, that everything which had happened to her had not brought the calm she had hoped for. She felt "resigned," which is not happiness; and she felt depressed and often ill, with undiagnosed ailments. Lewes, too, was not well over the Christmas holiday.

In December, Lewes mentioned to Eliot he thought a preface to *Adam Bede* was in order. She wrote one, called "Remonstrance." But she felt it was "written against the grain . . . for I have a strong disinclination to place anything in the shape of preface or personal speech with the public, before my novels." In response, Blackwood advised against its publication. "It might raise a nest of hornets about you. Consider that probably one-half of the small deer who will sit down to review you are constantly guilty of the very crime you reprobate and

---

* We could make something of naming here. Despite Brontë's Bertha in *Jane Eyre*, Rochester's mad wife, Bertha Grant is hardly the name for a Lamia-like figure. Eliot was always careful with names, and her characters' names almost equal those of Henry James in their class and caste particularity: Gwendolen Harleth, Hetty Sorrel, Daniel Deronda, Rosamond Vincy, Bulstrode, Caleb Garth. These are names with some reverberation. Bertha Grant denotes solidity, wholesomeness, not at all what the character represents. The question is why Eliot used such a name, and the sole answer would seem to be that deceptive wholesomeness was her purpose: wholesome in social terms, but privately demonic, the inner self belying the name. Naming, then, was part of the problem Eliot faced, Janus-like, since she chose George Eliot as a nom de plume precisely for its solidity and wholesome Englishness—while "Mrs. Lewes" lived on the edge.

would consequently come to the book with highly irritated feelings after seeing themselves so justly shown up." Among other literary crimes, Eliot had taken reviewers to task for their narrowness. Eliot removed the preface. She told Blackwood: "I had myself anticipated the very effects you predict. The deprecatory tone is not one I can ever take willingly, but I am conscious of a shrinking sort of pride, which is likely to warp my judgment in many personal questions, and on that ground I distrusted my own opinion."

Lewes left on his usual holiday trip to Arthur Helps's, although this would be the final time he and Eliot separated at Christmas. With that, she awaited publication of *Adam Bede* and the move to their new lodgings, at Southfields, Wandsworth. On 15 January 1859, she read final proofs. One problem was in putting off the insistent John Chapman, who, having been rejected by Eliot's letters because of his indiscretion, was now trying to visit. Eliot's excuse once again was their busyness with their imminent move. Her words are peremptory, cutting. Blackwood, meanwhile, was involved in a little price war with Mudie's, the bellwether of the circulating libraries, over Mudie's insistence on a 10 percent discount whether he took 500 copies or not. Blackwood demanded 500 copies with that discount. Mudie's threat was to take no copies of *Adam Bede*, or else to tell his customers he had no copies on hand. The bookseller retreated.

Yet while business matters swirled about her, Eliot was concerned with more mundane affairs, such as finding a servant for their new quarters, which they were to take possession of on 5 February. Like a conventional matron—a side she did not reject—she had to furnish the place as well. Lewes accompanied her as they shopped for crockery, furniture, and the rest. At a wholesale house on Watling Street, they purchased rugs and carpets, visited St. Paul's while they were in the area, and generally forgot about literary and scientific fame as they splurged on creature comforts. This is a side to Eliot we normally do not credit— the dutiful housewife (with servants' help, of course). This would be, at least temporarily, their real home, after so many years in lodgings whether in England or on the continent. Eliot eagerly awaited delivery of the bookcases, so that she and Lewes could arrange their sizable collections. Lewes himself had to pack up his quarters at 26 Bedford Place—books, pictures, and other items. It was, all in all, the kind of move one expects from a young couple, not one where the woman is closing on forty and the man just over.

Blackwood was quite enthusiastic about the publication of *Adam Bede* and, with characteristic interest in his unusual author, tried to pick up her spirits. "Whatever the subscription [at the lending libraries] may be," he writes, "I am confident of success, great success. The book is so novel and so true. The whole story remains in my mind like a succession of incidents in the lives of people whom I know." The publication was, at first, hardly auspicious. In all, 730 copies were subscribed, only 50 of them, initially, by Mudie's. That canny businessman was apparently awaiting reviews before committing himself to an offbeat novel. A novel about a carpenter was, for him, not quite the stuff of a bestseller. Even Lewes was circumspect, although he did predict future success. "I continue to have faith in the *ultimate* triumph of the book," he wrote in his journal. But he confesses "to being a little shaken as to the immediate success. Literature is such a strange thing. In Fiction readers love to see a reflection of their own egoism. They like to fancy themselves doing and feeling what the heroes and heroines do and feel. Now in Adam Bede there can be but slender gratification of this desire." Lewes says few men yearn to be an upright carpenter who rises only to be a master builder, and few women care to be Dinah.

What Lewes intuits is that Eliot was redirecting fiction, away from the heroic she mocked to the heroically ordinary; and she was tempting people not to identify with her characters as either too low or too strict (Lewes cites Dinah's "mob cap" as a sign of fervor, or as moral tightness). Although in retrospect such fiction does not seem radical, in its time it was deemed a threat to the establishment, a new voice. Even Dickens leavened his stories of low life with scenes of people of quality; and while he may have blasted some of them—the Dedlocks in *Bleak House,* for example—he nevertheless presented for an eager audience scenes of how the rich and mighty lived. While there was always some break in his presentation of street creatures, in Eliot the presentation is unrelieved. She is unrelenting in her insistence on the life of a carpenter, a female Methodist preacher, a dairy farmer. We see mighty little of Arthur Donnithorne's comfortable life. He is disengaged from that and shown in interaction with his subjects, not in his higher element. With this, Eliot was attempting a good deal, although when we look back the novel seems to fit its time and place. To its contemporaries, it was daring, even threatening, as any new voice is.

While Carlyle dismissed the novel as the work of a woman who knew nothing about carpentry—even while a carpenter was saying the author knew his business thoroughly—Jane Carlyle wrote a long Virginia Woolf–like letter praising the book. She sidesteps carpentry. One cites Woolf because Jane Carlyle moves around with intuitions and impressions; hers is almost a stream-of-consciousness letter. It is a lovely tribute; she calls it a "beautiful most *human* book. . . . I found myself in charity with the whole human race when I laid it down. . . ." The letter was a tonic Eliot needed. Besides Jane Carlyle, she had sent copies to Dickens, Thackeray, Froude, Charles Kingsley, and other eminent figures. Thackeray did not read it and, in fact, admitted he couldn't read *Adam Bede* or any of that author's books. Eventually, others weighed in with praise. Dickens waited until 10 July, and then gave the kind of encouragement a first novelist could only pray for. "*Adam Bede,*" he wrote, "has taken its place among the actual experiences and endurances of my life. Every high quality that was in the former book, is in that, with a World of Power added thereunto. . . . The whole country life that the story is set in, is so real, and so droll and genuine, and yet so selected and polished by art, that I cannot praise it enough to you. . . . You must not suppose that I am writing this to *you.* I have been saying it over and over again, here and elsewhere, until I feel in a ludicrously apologetic state for repeating myself on this paper."

Dickens then made two requests: that one day Eliot might become "a fellow labourer" with him, meaning the author would join him on *All the Year Round,* which Dickens edited; and the other was a desire to come to see "him," who

Dickens is convinced is a "her." He wants to tell Eliot that "you were a woman, and for the absolute and never-doubting confidence with which I have waved all men away from *Adam Bede,* and nailed my colors to the Mast with 'Eve' upon them."

But it was not this commentary which "created" George Eliot. The review in the *Times* (unsigned, but by Eneas Sweetland Dallas, on 12 April 1859) gave credence to the fact that Dickens now had a rival, or else there were now three: Dickens, Thackeray, and Eliot. The reviewer says that with this novel "the author takes rank at once among the masters of the art." After a review of great length, he crowns his praise with the final tribute:

> Nobody seems to know who is Mr. George Eliot, and when his previous work appeared it was even surmised that he must be a lady, since none but a woman's hand could have painted these touching scenes of clerical life. Now, the question will be raised, can this be a young author? Is all this mature thought, finished portraiture, and crowd of characters the product of a 'prentice hand and of callow genius? If it is, the hand must have an extraordinary cunning, and the genius must be of the highest order.

The notice in *Bentley's Quarterly Review* (in July, by Anne Mozley, an expert on Cardinal Newman and an essayist) is a well-reasoned critique of the novel. It gives a great deal to Eliot's acumen and to her art, but at the same time, it does not slight the excessive moralizing. Inevitably, the moral fervor is swept up into "universal assent and sympathy." The reviewer senses an author who is not young, but one who has learned from experience, from "real contact with trouble." In all, it was the kind of review which wins readers for a book by way of making it sound compelling, but without the enthusiasm which can fit into blurbs. *

The weekly newspapers were lavish in their praise and respect for the novel and author. In the influential *Athenaeum,* Geraldine Jewsbury called it a work of genius, a fiction of the highest order. Even the slightest demurrer in any of the reviews, however, sent Lewes into a rage. Even the word "delighted" was insufficient for Lewes, who thought it lightened what should be a more serious reception; "genius" was more to his liking. He may have feared that the slightest discouragement could lead to Eliot's halting—so delicate did he deem her sensibilities. The reviewers, meanwhile, speculated wildly: that Eliot had sat at the feet of the novelist Charles Kingsley; that she had the pregnancy material wrong—it was either indelicate or incorrect, in that no premature infant would bawl like that; and several other theories or disclaimers which had little to do

---

* While most contemporary reviews were admirable, some that came later were considerably different, often hostile on ideological grounds. One in the *London Quarterly Review* (in July 1861, two and a half years after publication) attacked Eliot's presentation of Methodism. Since the *Review* was a Methodist periodical, this could be expected, although one is struck by how the reviewer (anonymous) has distorted the book in order to make his or her condemnation.

with the actual novel. It was, nevertheless, a splendid reception, calculated to make George Eliot both famous and rich.

The Liggins attribution went on: the more Eliot wrote, the more famous became Joseph Liggins. One writer, John Gwyther, zeroed in on the actual people in *Scenes* and applied the knowledge to Liggins, never thinking of Marian Evans. Amusingly, intermixed in this clownish stunting is Eliot's difficulty in quite another area, finding a suitable servant. We gain some insight into the Lewes household, as she tells Cara she wants ". . . a servant who will cause me the least possible expenditure of time on household matters. *Cooking* is a material thing, not because Mr. Lewes is epicurean (for he is stupid of palate) but because he is, among his other eminences, eminently dyspeptic. I am anxious therefore to have a cook who is not only honest but soupmaking and full of devices. . . . Honesty and cleanliness are the other two emphatic requirements and a not unimportant one is a power of keeping simple accounts. . . ." Some of her needs sound very much like the housekeeper Marian herself was for Robert Evans in his final years. She adds she wishes she was not "an anxious fidgetty wretch, and could sit down content with dirt and disorder. But anything in the shape of an *anxiety* soon grows into a monstrous vulture with me, and makes itself more present to me than my rich sources of happiness, such as too few mortals are blessed with."

This and a following letter to John Blackwood about the "wretched weakness" of her nature and her inability to confront criticism are revelatory. In the Lewes household, clearly all matters of running it, from cleanliness to kitchen, were her domain, whether she liked it or not. It was a typical Victorian arrangement, and she and Lewes, so extraordinary in other ways, were conventional here. Lewes's time was allocated for his work, whereas she was expected to do her writing and also keep the household functioning. The servant problem appears to have been her problem. But we also learn she was obsessively clean and orderly, in that she built up her anxieties to the point she could not bear untidiness and dirt. She was, in her words, a compulsive personality, a condition often linked to a general sadness and depression—the reach for perfection would always be disappointed. Her inability to tolerate criticism was associated with her sense of an ideal she knew she could never achieve. As she told Blackwood, she puts her best heart and soul into her work, and how can she be expected to be hardened to the result? Anxiety would, inevitably, run away with her and disallow her that calmness and placidity she knew she should experience from her newly achieved position.

Amidst the publication of her book and the appearance of reviews, her anxieties seemed to be a harbinger of really bad news, the poor condition of Chrissey, as she headed toward death. This brought back Coventry and Warwickshire to Eliot, for in her response to this situation she wrote not only Chrissey but Sara Hennell and signed her letter "Pollian," the old style. Chrissey had written "Mrs. Lewes" apologizing for not having corresponded before and asking if Marian were well and happy. Eliot, as noted, responded immediately. "The past," she told Sara, "is abolished from my mind—I only want her to feel that I love her and care for her." A little earlier, Eliot told Cara that news from Chrissey and her illness had "ploughed my heart." She informed Bray she would come to see her sister as soon as she could leave Lewes, who resisted her departure as long as the present servant was in the house. The question of loyalties here is of interest, but Eliot did not elaborate.

The servant question was still dogging them, even though Eliot says her anxiety and despondency have lessened. Blackwood communicated that while he thought some newspapers were not being kind, their coverage and publicity would be good for the book. A few newspapers proved to be nit-picking and pretentious, their reviewers often ignorant of literature and what they were reading. In any event, Eliot postponed her plans to see Chrissey, even though the Brays offered their home to her. With the servant problem still looming and her own disinclination to make the journey, Eliot failed to see Chrissey before she died, on 15 March 1859.

Eliot's role here is both explicable and mysterious. Chrissey was definitely from the past, which she had protected herself against with layers of new roles, new names, new skins. Had she gone to the funeral she would have seen Isaac and been forced to defend herself against his accusations concerning her style of life. This part is explicable, connected as it is to Eliot's desperate need to emerge as her own person. The mysterious part concerns how deeply, or not, she felt Chrissey's loss, and how much was diluted by her sister's place in the depressing and unachieving past. We can speculate that her feelings fell into the very dualism we have observed throughout her life: sorrow at the loss and sorrow at Chrissey's hard existence, but with that, rejection of that kind of life except as it offered fuel for her fictional efforts. Below the surface lay an inferno of emotions.

By this time, as periodical reviews succeeded weekly reviews, as Blackwood planned a new edition of *Adam Bede* (in March 1859), and as Chrissey lay dying in the north, Eliot was preoccupied with the ever-present servant problem and her plans for a new novel, in the formative stage since January. In her journal, she noted that she and Lewes went into town to look into the *Annual Register* for cases of inundation, death by drowning. The servant problem, however, would not resolve itself. Eliot was considering a woman who periodically became ill, Ann Overton, and she was worried she would have to nurse her without help from neighbors in this "undestroyed Babylon" where they lived. The terms of employment are mentioned: £15 a year, all the foods she may wish as her favorites (tea, sugar, beer, etc.), and simple orders only from Eliot herself; and as for the washing, it would all go out except the maid's own.

It was not an onorous job, but one has the impression that in her quiet way Eliot was demanding of a certain standard, and this was difficult to find in the untrained farm girls who flocked to the city to find work. Meanwhile, she speaks of herself as someone who lives in unconsciousness of what is occurring in the world. "I am like a deaf person, to whom some one has just shouted that the company round him have been paying him compliments for the last half hour."

Some of Eliot's remarks are disingenuous. She was hardly a deaf person, she thrived on laudatory comments, she needed constant reinforcement, and she was not ill informed or insulated or isolated. Lewes was himself a very political fellow, and there was no way that in their close personal intercourse she would be ignorant of his interests, or he would be dismissive of hers. The insulated person she presented to Blackwood was merely another of her roles, part of that larger role-playing by which she could disguise something of herself behind a shield of protective layers.

13

---·—·---

There

"Will not a tiny speck very close to our vision blot
out the glory of the world, and leave only a margin
by which we see the blot? I know no speck so troublesome as self."

With the publication of *Adam Bede* and the early stages of *Mill* forming in
her head, Eliot had arrived "there." Whatever her anxieties and even
disclaimers, she was not only a writer but an author. An author is someone who
is recognized as a professional; authorship is a career, whereas writing is often
considered a stopgap. Until this point, Eliot was a writer who had found in
fiction some way to earn a good deal of money; but with *Mill,* she entered fully
into a career for the next two decades. Authorship also established her routine.
She set aside a period of time when she could work, and she insisted on her
priorities. Lewes, who had always been supportive, except in household matters,
respected her position in the family as the major breadwinner and, in time, as
the consummate artist.

Chrissey's death brought sad lines from Eliot, directed at Sara. She had heard
of the death the day after it occurred; and she noted that the oldest daughter,
Emily, writes good honest letters. Emily was now fifteen; Edward, the oldest
boy, twenty-one; Christopher, fourteen; and Catherine, seven. Once money
poured in from her writings, Eliot would do what she could for them.* Emily,
incidentally, lived until 1924, into the age that had forgotten Eliot for the most
part as it embraced another Eliot, the poet, and writers as diverse as Joyce,
Woolf, Yeats, Conrad, and Lawrence. The days succeeding news of Chrissey's
death are blank in Eliot's journal; but however she felt, she seems to have been

---

* As we shall see, Eliot's earnings supported not only herself and Lewes stylishly, but also Lewes's
sons by Agnes, some of Agnes's children by Thornton Hunt, Agnes herself, and, in part, Chrissey's children.

able to carry on with her affairs. Her life was now her own, not part of the Evans world. The day after the funeral, she received the bound manuscript (in red russia leather) of *Adam Bede,* which she inscribed to Lewes as her "dear husband" and signed "Marian Lewes."

The notice of *Adam Bede* in the April 1859 *Westminster* was more like an article than a review. Even with Eliot cutting him off for his inability to keep a secret, Chapman showed he had not learned discretion. At the end of the prodigiously long article, he said that while he referred to a masculine author, who would ever believe it was really a "George Eliot"? Too much in the book was the result of a female sensibility. Chapman was, of course, drawing on privileged information, gleaned from Spencer, and making believe his observation was insightful. As far as Eliot was concerned, it was still another nail in his coffin.

Adam Bede sales had started slowly, but as the quarterlies weighed in with their admiring reviews—some of it orchestrated by Blackwood himself, especially in *Maga*—the numbers picked up and Mudie's increased its order to 1,000. The second edition of 750 also sold, and another impression of that edition, 500 copies, was made. This was still in the expensive 31 / 6 (31 shillings 6 pence) edition; when the cheaper one went on sale in June, at 12 shillings for two volumes, more than 10,000 copies were sold. The novel eventually appeared in a 6-shilling one-volume edition, and it sold in America and in many European countries in translation. In Russia, Tolstoy read it in translation and located it among "the highest art." Blackwood sent Eliot an additional £400 because of the book's success and as a sign of his appreciation for such an author. In all, she earned £1,942 in 1859, virtually all of it from *Adam Bede.* The remainder of her income came from a second edition of *Scenes* and from the sale of "The Lifted Veil" to Blackwood for *Maga.* In 1859, that pivotal year, Lewes's income was £353, about one-sixth of Mrs. Lewes's. Clearly, she carried the household.

Yet, as we have seen, Eliot was not overwhelmed by success. *Adam Bede* was cited as the premier novel of the period, taking precedence over Dickens's *A Tale of Two Cities* (1859) and Thackeray's *The Virginians* (1857). When the *Times* came in with its influential long review, George Eliot was the talk of the town. She was, however, writing "The Lifted Veil," her tale of anti-success, which she mentioned to Blackwood on 31 March: ". . . I have a slight story of an outré kind—not a *jeu d'esprit,* but a *jeu de melancholie,* which I could send you in a few days for your acceptance or rejection as a brief magazine story—of one number only. I think nothing of it, but my private critic [Lewes] says it is very striking and original, and on the strength of that opinion, I mention it." Blackwood was being finessed; had an unknown author submitted such a melancholy and morbid piece, he would have rejected it outright for *Maga.* But now the famous George Eliot commanded the firm, and Blackwood would publish against his better judgment.

Sara Hennell embarrassed herself with a letter about that still present figure Liggins, the "real" author of George Eliot's work. She sent on an account which amused Eliot and possibly made her squirm. Sara wrote:

> I want to ask you if you have read "Adam Bede" or the "Scenes of Clerical Life," and whether you know that the author is Mr. Liggins. . . . a deputation of dissenting parons went over *to ask him to write for the Eclectic,* and they found him washing his slop-basin at a pump. . . . The son of a baker, of no mark at all in his town, so that it is possible you may not have heard of him. You know he calls himself "George Eliot." It sounds strange to hear the *Westminster* [reviewer] doubting whether he is a woman, *when he here is so well known.* But I am glad it has mentioned him. *They say he gets no profit out of "Adam Bede," and gives it freely to Blackwood, which is a shame.*

Sending this on to Blackwood, Eliot asks him to imagine the real George Eliot's feelings—"not washing his own slop-basin, and *not* giving away his M.S.!" As for Sara herself, Eliot wrote that Lewes had read *Adam Bede* and was so "dithyrambic about it" that "*I* must refresh my soul with it now, as well as with the Spring tide." Eliot's fun-making suggests considerable hostility.

The chase continued in earnest, reviewers wondering about the author, others writing directly to Blackwood, some like Barbara Bodichon aiming at Eliot. She had read excerpts of *Adam Bede,* and she knew, she said, that it was Marian Lewes, "her great big head and heart and her wise wide views. . . . It is an opinion which fire cannot melt out of me." This Eliot could not pass up, and she revealed herself graciously and thankfully. "You are my first friend who has given any symptom of knowing me—the first heart that has recognized me in a book which has come from my heart of hearts." She asked her friend to keep the secret "solemnly till I give you leave to tell it. . . . You have sense enough to know how important the *incognito* has been, and we are anxious to keep it up a few months longer." She cites Liggins as having screened her from friends possibly recognizing her as the author. "I am a very blessed woman, am I not? to have all this reason for being glad that I have lived, in spite of my sins and sorrows—or rather, by reason of my sins and sorrows. I have had no time of exultation; on the contrary, these last months have been sadder than usual to me, and I have thought more of the future and the much work that remains to be done in life than of anything that has been achieved." She singles out Lewes as the "prime blessing that has made all the rest possible." In a postscript, Lewes calls Barbara "a darling" and says he has always felt that, but modesty prevented him from expressing it.

Legions of hangers-on now flocked around the strange Liggins. A Reverend Henry Smith Anders stated assuredly that Mr. Joseph Liggins of Nuneaton was the author of *Scenes* and *Adam Bede.* Since he expressed it in a letter to the *Times,* it received a good deal of attention. Through Lewes, Eliot wrote to the *Times* saying Liggins never saw a line of those works and complaining bitterly that the newspaper had tried to deprive him, Eliot, of all privacy, all the "courtesies usual among gentlemen." One's name, she writes, is one's own concern, meant to be withheld; all the rest is unconscionable rumor. Itself of some interest, the letter reinforces the mystery, and while speaking of "herself" as "himself," Eliot uses Lewes as her mode of communication. It is difficult to see anything less than an extraordinary effort to hide, to deny herself by presenting herself in so many guises, to divide herself among varied personas—and to alter gender expectations, or else to experience both genders: "wife" and male authorship. She was both consciously and unconsciously inhabiting a house of games.

The Liggins matter did not fade. Anders said his information derived from a Reverend James Quirk, curate of Attleborough. Quirk reported that Liggins showed him a manuscript which purported to be *Scenes of Clerical Life;* and then after *Adam Bede* appeared, Liggins told Quirk he had written it ten or twelve years ago, sent it to Blackwood's, and was paid nothing for it. Quirk then trumpeted this in the *Manx Sun* (Isle of Man newspaper), a piece of news which obviously troubled Blackwood. When Quirk insisted Liggins was the man, only a sample of Eliot's handwriting convinced him he was wrong. Eliot caustically said she was fond of Liggins compared with Quirk. The latter, while admitting defeat on *Scenes,* did not withdraw gracefully. He said that Liggins, when he published a future work, would clear up the mystery—of Quirk's making! The Quirk matter did not go away. A delusion is harder to dismiss than a lie. Eliot wrote to Bray in September saying there was no getting rid of Quirk. But she felt some obligation to answer because he had introduced himself (by letter) as a friend of Chrissey's, apparently when she lay ill. Eliot is resigned: ". . . Quirk will go to his grave believing in Liggins. Resquiescat in pace!"

Quirk, unstoppable, had communicated his "facts" to a magistrate, Charles Holte Bracebridge, a friend of Florence Nightingale's. He, too, took up the cudgels for Liggins and wrote extensively to people in and around Eliot's and Lewes's circle: the Brays, Harriet Martineau, Mrs. Gaskell, and others. As the story fanned out, the name became Higgins, as printed in the *Literary Gazette.* Although painful to Eliot, there was a farcical side to these delusions, compounded by misinformation, typographical errors, and miscommunication. Another contestant in the George Eliot sweepstakes was the Reverend W. H. King, former curate of Nuneaton—this was the name thrown out to Blackwood by a Yorkshire preacher. When passed this letter, Eliot sent on her usual denial, by way of Blackwood. Mrs. Gaskell, for another, possibly believed George Eliot to be Gilbert Elliot, dean of Bristol, although "Elliot" to "Eliot" does not seem much of a disguise.

We cannot fully assess to what degree the need for denial and negation had affected Eliot, although we know it did deepen her need for disguise. * Her denials extended to friends, and that would hurt when they discovered the truth. And the truth had to emerge soon, since Chapman's inability to keep secrets meant that all of literary London was learning some part of the truth. The editor of the *Times,* John Thadeus Delane, wrote Blackwood he had heard the books were written by a lady who lives with Lewes. Another notices how the Leweses' style of living had changed; and now Spencer was saying he knew the authoress.

---

* She admitted that the Liggins affair did annoy her, but only because it subjected the Blackwoods "to the reception of insulting letters and the trouble of writing contradictions." Otherwise, she says, "the whole affair is really a subject for a Molière-comedy." She mentions a letter from Mrs. Gaskell in which the latter has had the compliment paid her that *she* is the author of *Adam Bede.*

Still another said that Lewes's eyes lit up when *Adam Bede* was mentioned. Sara tells Eliot that Isaac stated that only his sister could have written *Adam Bede*, and that he felt the same about *Scenes*. This was said to a local farmer in Griff, a John Loake Gill, and the news was spreading like the rumors in an Eliot novel.

The rumors referred to George Eliot as Miss Evans, bypassing her designation of herself as Mrs. Lewes and returning her close to her birth name. By this time, Sara knew her friend was the author, but was forced to parry a whole sequence of queries. The Coventry friends had learned only a few days earlier, when Eliot revealed herself to the Brays and Sara. But even with the knowledge, they had to play the game, as though doubling their gullibility. Eliot felt that, having caught her friends in a web of deceit, she had abandoned them "to gather the truth amidst an inextricable mixture of falsehood." Feeling guilty, she tried to excuse herself, saying that to hear remarks or compliments from friends, she would "lose the repose of mind and truthfulness of production without which no good healthy books can be written." What had put Isaac on the trail was his recognition of facts about Robert Evans that only a family member could know.

Eliot's explanation is disingenuous. Her secrecy was part of her pattern of profoundly internal needs connected to the precariousness of her situation as a female. If she had been able to settle "Mrs. Lewes," then the general pattern of secrecy, while not removed, would have been less significant. But as she achieved fame, she had to confront several dimensions of her situation. The Blackwoods did not look forward to her emergence as the author since it would put them in a strange position. Who could they say she was? She insisted on Mrs. Lewes, which, legally, she was not. She insisted on Marian Evans Lewes, which combined both the legal name and one she was not entitled to except de facto.* All this intensified as she tried to put the Liggins affair behind her, and she wrote the *Times* editor that Liggins is an imposter if he says he wrote a word of George Eliot's books and received any money for them. The editor, Delane, was taken aback by the force of the letter—he felt Eliot should be more benevolent toward Liggins, who was obviously a fool—and asked Blackwood to prevail on her to take the sting from her language. But she was not placated by Liggins's playing the fool, since the purported manuscript of *Scenes* was being circulated as authored by Liggins, without his denial. Eliot told Blackwood, in language that suggests considerable disturbance, "The thing will soon come to a pitch that would oblige me publicly to declare myself the author," this coming on 28 June 1859.

At this point the Blackwoods felt they were headed into a dilemma whose resolution could be unpleasant for them. Curiously, we find little in their files to suggest they had foreseen the ultimate divulgation would create unhappy consequences. They knew that the legal Mrs. Lewes was not the woman living

---

* The British Museum Library Manuscript Room was, apparently, equally diffident in identifying the author. When the reader seeks her manuscript under George Eliot in the main index, the citation shifts one to Cross, née Evans, Mary Anne. In the end, only her married name, Cross, carried weight, and the twenty-four years with Lewes, among other things, are wiped out. Even "George Eliot" is effaced. The citation returns her to the nineteenth-century view.

with Lewes, and yet carried away by two clients they appreciated, and from one of whom they were making good profits, they let this go. Now the possibility of Eliot stepping forth as the woman who lived with Lewes was disquieting to the ultra-respectable Scots house. To muddy the situation, Blackwood was reading the opening chapters of *The Mill on the Floss*, 110 manuscript pages in all, which he predicted would be a "grand success." He was correct in his estimation, not only of success, but of a growth in Eliot's maturity. While deeply personal, *Mill* is one of her most accomplished works, manifesting a fluency and fluidity in her narrative quite superior to her first two books.

In the meantime, while the Blackwoods were pondering how to handle their end of the secret, *Adam Bede* was selling sufficiently well to require another edition, the fourth, in two volumes, with an additional 3,150 copies. Since a novel could be expected to sell 500–750 copies, the number of *Adam* was extraordinary.* Blackwood feared that once Eliot's identity was revealed, sales of her essentially family novels would fall off in the ensuing scandal. This, too, had not escaped Eliot.

The Blackwoods—both John and William—had to prevail on Eliot not to publish her bitter letter to the *Times* calling Liggins, among other things, a swindler. Her angry words bear repeating: "What he may have done to abet and keep up the delusion, I cannot say, but I am forced, in justice, to say: That if Mr. Liggins, or any one bearing a name at all resembling Liggins [like Higgins], has in any way stated, or suggested, or by implication of smile, shrug, or tone, allowed any one to believe he wrote the 'Scenes of Clerical Life' or 'Adam Bede'—or even contributed a single detail to those works—or ever saw a page of the MS.—*he is an imposter.* And if he received money knowing at the time the money was intended for the author of those works—*he is a swindler.*" This is the letter the Blackwoods finally convinced Eliot to suppress.

In Blackwood's office, the hand-wringing continued. John wrote William that he had just visited the Leweses: "It is impossible not to like her excessively. She gives irresistibly the impression of a real good woman. It is impossible not to like him too. It is most melancholy that their relations cannot be put straight." Having informed her closest friends, Eliot was still insistent on keeping her incognito: ". . . things must take their course," she told the Brays and Sara. "We can't help people saying *now* that the books are mine, but the one point to secure is that we and our friends make no categorical statement, which can be taken as absolute authority." She says if Liggins is annihilated, others will assume his place. "The only safe thing for my mind's health is to shut my ears and go on with my work." But if she thought the matter would eventually fade

---

* Measured, however, against the real best-selling novels, Eliot's figures were minuscule. *David Copperfield* reached 25,000 in 1849–50; *Bleak House*, 35,000 in 1852–53; *Little Dorrit*, at least 35,000 in 1855; Stowe's *Uncle Tom's Cabin*, in England alone, 150,000 in 1852 and over a million by the succeeding year, including the colonies; Bulwer-Lytton's *Pelham*, 46,000 from 1853 to 1858; Hughes's *Tom Brown's School Days*, 11,000 in 1857, more than double that in the next six years. Earlier in the century, Scott's novels went into the tens of thousands, before the circulating libraries had taken hold.

away, events proved her wrong. If anything, it intensified. With John Blackwood working the *Times* and others, Eliot was forced to deal with statements
coming in from friends, like Barbara Bodichon, who presented the full blast of
gossip as it swirled in her circles. Lewes attempted to explain to Barbara that
the concealed authorship was not due to any fear of scandal, but to avoid pre-
judgment of the work as a woman's, or of that of a particular woman (which
suggests scandal). But the worst was yet to come, and on 2 July it did.

It came in an *Athenaeum* gossip column from William Hepworth Dixon, the
editor, and even considering its source, it was brutal: a mixture of gossipy comments with snide slaps at Eliot's artistic achievements.

> It is time to end this pother about the authorship of "Adam Bede." The
> writer is in no sense a "great unknown"; the tale, if bright in parts, and
> such as a clever woman with an observant eye and unschooled moral nature
> might have written, has no great quality of any kind. Long ago we hinted
> our impression that Mr. Liggins, with his poverty and his pretensions, was
> a mystification, got up by George Eliot. . . . Vanish Eliot, Nicholas Lig-
> gins,—enter, (let us say, at a guess,) Miss Biggins! . . . The elaborate
> attempt to mystify the reading public, pursued in many articles and letters
> at the same time, but with the same Roman hands observable in all, is itself
> decisive of the writer's power. No woman of genius ever condescended to
> such a *ruse,*—no book was ever permanently helped by such a trick.

Dixon had evidently forgotten Currer, Ellis, and Acton Bell, the Brontës.

All serious authors face contemptible notices and reviews. Eliot had just gotten hers, a mishmash of such contempt—and, under its persiflage, attack on
gender—that she could only recoil in pain, which is what she did. Even Lewes
could not protect her here. As she wrote to Barbara Bodichon, "If one could be
glad at any baseness, one would be glad this is so bad—it will carry no sympathy
with it." But behind her dismissal was the consciousness that if the editor of the
Athenaeum could stoop like that, then once her identity was revealed, she was
in for revilement, contempt, ridicule. Exactly what the Blackwoods feared could
come to pass: the gossip-mongers, with their contempt for anything of achievement, would party. The focus would be deflected from Eliot's books to her personal life and to her motives for concealing her identity; literary discussion
would pass into gossip. She would be a celebrity, not an author.

The burden of revealing her identity to her Coventry friends, finally, made
Eliot more preoccupied than usual in her dealings with Sara; and when the
earnest Sara visited with the Brays in June, bringing with her the manuscript of
her *Thoughts in Aid of Faith,* Eliot overshadowed it with her own startling news
as the author of *Scenes* and *Adam Bede.* This was an epiphany that created a
crisis in their relationship. Sara wrote, on 26 June, that she now realized she
had lost "the only reader in whom I felt confident in having secure sympathy
with the *subject* (not with me) whom I most gratefully believe—believed in—
that she has floated beyond me in another sphere and I remain gazing at the

glory into which she has departed, wistfully and very lonely." To this plaint, Eliot answered with an apology, saying she had erred in her discussion of Sara's manuscript, the truth being she was too agitated with her own problems to feel sympathy for her friend's continued religious devotion.

Even when smoothed over, the confrontation with Sara was a portent. Herbert Spencer was another who recognized the change and, apparently, could not deal with it on a personal level. Lewes notes in his journal entry for 24 March that Spencer had visited and was distinctly cool. "He used to be one of our friends on whom we most relied; but jealousy, too patent and too unequivocal, of our success, acting on his own bitterness at nonsuccess, has of late cooled him visibly. He always tells us of the disagreeable things he hears or reads of us and never the agreeable things. His jealousy of me has been growing these last two years; and it is more excusable than his jealousy of her.—His visit was one we were glad to see the end of."

The June visit of the Brays brought things to a head, for they were then told of Spencer's poisoning of the atmosphere. They became virulent in their attack upon him, to the extent Eliot felt it necessary to warn Bray he was to maintain silence both to Spencer and to others about what he was told. "We shall be doubly careful to speak only of what we admire in him to the world generally." But it is clear they had misjudged Spencer. The man was so self-oriented and self-serving that he could be friends with someone like Marian Evans only as long as he felt mental superiority. His side of the friendship depended on his more meritorious achievement; and when that achievement was not demonstrable, he could not hide his hostility, whether jealousy, envy, or something stronger.* Having been displaced, further, by Lewes, toward whom he also showed competitive antagonism, Spencer could only respond with betrayal; an effort, somehow, to do Eliot harm without directly attacking her. It was a ploy she would have to deal with on several occasions in her professional life, but coming as it did from Spencer, she could only cry "O I am sick!"

All these developments had proven disquieting, and yet despite Eliot's protestations of unhappiness and misery at events, she did not suffer blockage in her writing of *Mill.* Once she saw what she could accomplish in fiction, she moved along as if on a separate motor from what kept her going personally. Her professional life had, by now, taken on a distinctly other self, as though she could split herself between public and private. The private was often ill—she speaks of herself and Lewes taking care of each other in some interwoven bedside scenario—but the public voice was producing books of considerable length at a rapid pace. Money was some consolation: the additional £400 from Blackwood from the runaway sale of *Adam Bede,* then £50 from the German firm of Tauchnitz and £37.10 for the sale of "The Lifted Veil."

The story created a disturbance at *Maga,* not only for its distasteful contents,

---

* We must also take into account, as Spencer's *Autobiography* makes quite clear, that he considered fiction a frivolous enterprise: that is, women's work. Men dealt in science or scientifically oriented projects. But even this assessment did not lessen his jealousy.

but for the fact that John Blackwood suggested George Eliot's name be attached to the story, instead of remaining anonymous. This opened up the firm's fears at divulgation; his brother, Major William, felt that the prestigious name should not be frittered away on a mere story, but should be kept fresh for a new novel. Yet both brothers shared misgivings about the deception. Withal, they wished the best for her, while also hoping to make the most of the situation in terms of publicity and sales. But they did not consider her as a mere commodity or product and treated her with sincere consideration for her welfare. Everyone, now, was puzzled about what to do.

Coming up in her life was something strikingly new. She would, for the first time, accompany Lewes on his visit to his sons at Hofwyl in Switzerland. The boys had acted quite maturely, after having recently learned about her from their father, and were excited to meet "Miss Evans," the author of an exciting new novel. With plenty of funds in the bank, Lewes and Eliot now traveled in more elegant style. On 9 July, they departed, stopping at Paris, passing through Basel, and arriving in Lucerne on 12 July. They settled in a luxurious hotel, with a view of the lake, and Lewes, alone, went on to Hofwyl. Lewes told his sons about Agnes—although how much they learned of their several half-siblings we cannot determine—and all about Marian Evans and his arrangement with her. He apparently mentioned she was the author of *Adam Bede*. Lewes then returned to Lucerne to bring the happy news about his sons' acceptance of the situation, an acceptance surely predicated on the fact that their own lives would not be disturbed and on their acquisition of a famous author as a friend. Eliot was, of course, gratified at their enthusiastic reception of everything, and together the couple returned to Holly Lodge.

Blackwood had nothing but good news: more sales of the novel, money promised to them whenever they needed it, and a pug dog—purchased for the prodigious sum of 30 guineas and proffered as a gift. Eliot said it filled the "void left by false and narrow-hearted friends." She adds: "I see already that he is without envy, hatred, or malice—that he will betray no secrets, and feel neither pain at my success nor pleasure in my chagrin." These are tough words, indicative of the extent to which she had been hurt.* She clearly had Spencer in mind. The pug delighted her, a new, loyal friend. Like most English, she romanticized animals and turned them into great sources of love and devotion.†

---

* She saw her betrayers as perfidious creatures waiting for her to fall. Writing to Barbara Bodichon, she exalted in the sale of 500 more copies of *Adam Bede,* saying that such results "give one fortitude to endure one's enemies—even to endure one's friends. I will not call you a friend—I will rather call you by some name that I am not obliged to associate with evaporated professions and petty egoism."

† To some extent, the pug was a sign of having arrived. By mid-century, pets had become a cult for the English middle and upper classes, and no pet more than the dog. The cult led to a veritable industry of breeders, traders, collar makers, kidnappers (dogs held for large ransom), product makers (dog cakes, combs, houses, even articles of clothing and ornaments in addition to brass collars). Books on pets were not far behind. Thirty guineas for a pug was almost a working-class family man's annual wages, but some breeds went for ten times that. There was an additional industry of those who cut, trimmed, combed, washed, and walked the dog. Eliot and Lewes were now definitely part of the bourgeoisie.

Upon their return, on 21 July, Eliot and Lewes began to think of different residences, where they could be further from neighbors, less given to possible gossip. Also, Eliot had now reached the point of affluence where she wanted to give up housekeeping. Even with a servant, she felt tied down with the management, although there is some evidence Lewes would occasionally help out when she felt ill. The trip to Hofwyl, even though for some personal reason she did not see the boys, led her into correspondence with Charles (the oldest, and the only one to survive Lewes and Eliot), a letter which establishes just the right tone for the young man. She says she looks forward to playing duets with him— he on the violin, she on a grand piano which the couple hoped to afford. Without condescension to her young reader, she speaks of Lewes's recently published *Physiology of Common Life*, the first volume; and then asks him to keep them informed about his planned walking trip. Particularly gratifying was that "Charlie" addressed her as "Dear Mother" and referred to her as "loving mother." Throughout her life, she remained deeply devoted to the three sons, especially to Charlie, even after Lewes's death.

The time was approaching for publication of "The Lifted Veil" (July 1859), and Blackwood requested that Eliot remove the use of the blood transfusion at the end. The transfusion, we recall, revives the maid sufficiently so that she can identify Latimer's wife as a potential poisoner. Blackwood felt it was pseudoscience; and when Eliot changed nothing, he wrote her that he wished she was in a happier frame of mind. William Blackwood told John that he did not like the story, that it did not fulfill the fine opening, and he could not understand how George Eliot could have written it. Publication was anonymous, but some breach in the relationship had appeared.

For Eliot, the depressive nature of the story was continuous with her personal feelings, as she recognized George Eliot would be generally revealed. She wrote Sara:

> The weight of my future life—the self-questioning whether my nature will be able to meet the heavy demands upon it, both personal duty and intellectual production, presses upon me almost continually in a way that prevents me even from testing the quiet joy I might have in the *work done*. Buoyancy and exultation, I fancy, are out of the question when one has lived so long as I have. . . . I thought then how happy fame would make me! I feel no regret that the fame, as such, brings no pleasure; but it *is* a grief to me that I do not constantly feel strong in thankfulness that my past life has vindicated its uses and given me reason for gladness that such an unpromising woman-child was born into the world.

In some respects, her exploration of Maggie Tulliver in *Mill* was linked to this "unpromising woman-child," a description of herself in which sadness passes into melancholy.

Meanwhile, Eliot sought a female friend and formed a close relationship with Mrs. Richard Congreve, who lived close by. Maria Congreve was the daughter of the physician who tended Robert Evans in his last years, Dr. John Bury. At only twenty-two, Maria turned out to be a charming, intelligent young woman with some memories of Foleshill. She had apparently observed Marian carefully, her piano playing, her bookish tastes, her commitment to learning. The man she married, Richard, was older than Eliot and was an ardent positivist. He had been at Rugby and Oxford with Matthew Arnold and Arthur Hugh Clough, and, like them, had come to disbelieve in formal Christianity. He moved to Comtean positivism, a position sympathetic to Eliot. He had been a master at Rugby after his graduation from Oxford (with a first) and then a Fellow at Wadham College, Oxford; when he resigned, he made his living by tutoring private pupils. It was an existence predicated not on worldly success but on sincere beliefs that the Christian church no longer held the key to human progress; rather, Comtean "sociology" did. Comte offered science, reason, and an order to society—the answer to those who questioned the church.

Maria Congreve recorded her thoughts when she found herself near Eliot and Lewes.* She had heard her father speak well of them, disparaging the gossip and rumors which scandalized Marian's actions in running off with Lewes. At first, she says, Eliot refused to meet Dr. Congreve "as being a clergyman." When he converted to positivism, this objection was removed. But still she doubted if the couple would care to know them. Yet her inducement to call, she insists, "was the scorn we both had of the unfairness with which a connection like theirs was visited on society—the man cut off from scarcely anything, the woman from all she most values. . . ." When they met, the couples immediately took to each other, although Lewes and Congreve were not so intense. The differences may have been over Comte himself—Lewes had separated himself from the French thinker, whereas Congreve was a fervid follower and had turned Comtism into a new religion. It may have been more personal, however, with a whiff of displeasure on Congreve's part, the former clergyman, at the arrangement between the two Georges. Or it may have been even nastier, as Haight implies, with Congreve the more well-bred university man, and Lewes the cosmopolitan, witty, obviously not well-bred, non-university man. Caste differences as well as possible class distinctions may have played a part.

With Maria and Eliot, however, there were no such differences, except age. Maria analyzed her friend as cherishing "all the pieties of her early life, even towards those who had ceased all intercourse. . . ." Beginning in February 1859, the visits back and forth jumped to twice or more a week, and Eliot recorded how happy she was in Maria's company. When the Congreves left for the continent, Maria corresponded with great intensity of feeling, her remarks revealing amorous undertones. "You must have a very strong influence over me," Maria wrote. "I usually wake so entirely mistress of the situation, but you make such a difference to me in my rising and lying down and in all my ways— now I actually know you, and that you will let me love you and even give me some love too. . . . Sometime I should like to talk over my difficulties, past

---

* She left extensive recollections, now at the Bodleian Library, Oxford (MS Eng. let e.).

though they are, with you. I have such a perfect confidence in you. I do not think I should venture to write this though but for what you said to me once about your requiring to be told that people love you. . . ."

Whatever the ripple flowing between the husbands—at one point Congreve said he wished Lewes and Eliot were not so inseparable—the friendship flowered. Despite her closeness to Lewes and her commitment to a writing career, Eliot was lonely for the kind of friendship she had once had in Coventry; and she could not reject a disciple, someone who believed fervently in her and offered her devotion. She saw the Congreves when she went to Lucerne, at the time Lewes visited his sons. There, she revealed her identity as the author of the two books and presented Maria with a copy of *Scenes,* with an inscription indicating how the friendship had enriched her own life. This was heady stuff for the young woman and, of course, intensified her devotion.

But there was more than the friendship of a young worshipper; there was, of course, Comtism itself, the religion of humanity which cut closely across beliefs Eliot held. Comtism was for disbelievers who yet wished to maintain Christianity's sense of order, its principles of behavior, its moral and ethical views. It offered morality and order without God, surely without a religious hierarchy and church, at least at first. It was, furthermore, rational, and it eschewed a future life. We can find strong positivist elements in Eliot: the religion of humanity, the negation of an afterlife, the rational restructuring of a society in which religion withers away, the emphasis on social reform, and the progression of society from theological through metaphysical to scientific, which insisted on empirical observation, on hypothesis and experimentation.

What is likely is that while Eliot did not accept any formalized system of beliefs, within positivism—as we see in her letters to Maria Congreve—she found enough sympathetic material parallel to her own beliefs to make her a believer of sorts. Critics of Eliot who feel her positivistic concerns have been "greatly exaggerated" are judging on the basis of her denials, not on her practices. It is true that she told Benjamin Jowett, the great classicist, that she was never a Comtist, and equally true that she was reported as saying she would never submit to an unqualified acceptance of it; it is also true that Congreve himself said she was not a convert, but an acceptor of certain general ideas. But her denials were part of the Eliot intellectual game: in her mature years, she denied all formal commitments to any sect or group. Nevertheless, in positivism she had found that empirical and rational approach to human existence which satisfied her. She, too, had advanced from theological to metaphysical to scientific or rational, the very steps Comte had recommended for society as a whole.

Despite her attachment to Maria and her husband, Eliot wanted to leave Wandsworth. * She was desperate for something more private, although exactly what she and Lewes wanted would not be clear until they bought the Priory. Both felt unsettled about where and how to live, most probably the result of

---

* The couples had become close enough so that the Congreves became witness for the wills Lewes and Eliot signed on 21 November 1859.

their unmarried condition, but also because of Eliot's own varying identities and the ensuing rumors and gossip. Ideally, they would find a place that proved a fortress, insulating them against English provincialism, yet accessible to the continent, where more social sophistication existed.

In late summer, they were beginning to think of traveling again, for research on mills, rivers, floods, and the like for *Mill.* In the winter Eliot had copied into her commonplace book (scrapbook) several scenes of flooding which she had found in the town *Annual Register,* scenes she reproduced in the last pages of the novel. Dorlcote Mill clearly was based on her fond memories of Arbury Mill—the details and particulars of description, but not the imagined life around it. What she required in her research was some river which could explode into the flood that inundates all, something clearly impossible for the stream by Arbury Mill.

In the spring of 1859, after a three-day visit to the Isle of Wight, Eliot worked over the first two chapters of *Mill,* which she called in manuscript "The Tullivers." She also thought of "St. Ogg's on the Floss," a title so lacking melody it might have, alone, sunk the novel. She also thought of "Sister Maggie," as she notes in her journal. But that was only the beginning. Writing to Blackwood (3 January 1860), she suggested "The House of Tulliver; or, Life on the Floss," which she says Lewes prefers to "Sister Maggie." " 'The Tullivers; or, Life on the Floss,' has the advantage," she thinks, "of slipping easily off the lazy British tongue." She also considers "The Tulliver Family; or, Life on the Floss." She asks Blackwood for his advice. When, eventually, Eliot simplified the title, she set the practice of clear, unencumbered titles for all her books. All but *Scenes of Clerical Life, Mill,* and *Middlemarch* were named after the chief character.

Before leaving on the Lucerne trip, she was able to send Blackwood nearly seven chapters of *Mill.* Even with her unhappiness at Wandsworth and other intrusions on her peace of mind, she carried the novel along, if not in actual pages, then in mental plans for its working out. When we consider she wrote by hand and that she interrupted her writing to read voraciously—plus the traveling she did with Lewes—she produced manuscript copy quite rapidly.

She and Lewes decided to travel to Wales to search out isolated places to walk, a location where they would be uninterrupted by the outside world. They were not well, either, with each one's ailments seemingly acting symbiotically on the other; the trip, calculated for a fortnight, was to give them a respite, in the hope they could return refreshed, find new lodgings, and get on with their respective books.

The trip proved both rewarding and tiring—they found it difficult to land lodgings. After some wandering, they left Wales on 31 August for Weymouth, in Dorset, in the south. Along the way, they stopped at Lichfield, near Birmingham, to see Chrissey's two daughters, Emily and Catherine (Katie), who were attending Miss Eborall's School (tuition paid courtesy of their paternal uncle, Henry Clarke).

The purpose of the trip was to find streams Eliot could use for her novel. Having returned to Wandsworth for ten days, on 16 September they set out again, still seeking a suitable river. This piece of research, in which a real river and setting had to be found, validates one aspect of Eliot's realism, something which looks ahead to Zola's researches for his novels. Yet despite her attention to this kind of actuality, she turns the Floss, its mill, and its potentialities into something well beyond realism, into mythical proportions, like Zola's mine in *Germinal.* Her Floss becomes a great river of vengeance, a force well beyond rational life, an element recalling Noah's Flood; and it transforms surrounding areas into wastelands of water. On this latest journey, they traveled to Newark and Gainsborough, in Robin Hood country, rowing down the Idle. After that, they continued on foot and walked back to Gainsborough. This was it: she had found her river and her setting. *

———

Looming soon beyond their own endeavors was an event of the greatest importance and one Eliot grasped as momentous. By December, she and Lewes were reading Darwin's *Origin of Species.* Eliot recognized it made "an epoch." Its lack of illustrative facts, she felt, would make it less popular than the now very famous *Vestiges of Creation,* but, she says, "it will have a great effect in the scientific world, causing a thorough and open discussion of a question about which people have hitherto felt timid. So the world gets on step by step towards brave clearness and honesty!" Then she intrudes with her own contribution, which slides beyond Darwin's touch: "But to me the Development theory and all other explanations of processes by which things came to be, produce a feeble impression compared with the mystery that lies under the process." That mystery lying under the process would be *her* material. Although she and Lewes perceived the greatness of Darwin's book, despite the fact that it was "ill-written," she recognized he did not poach on her particular world; and, if anything, the publication could reinforce her own resolve, that what she was pursuing could not be caught in any other way.

The rewards of growing fame were several, including an offer from the *New York Century* to write a story for £1,200, an astonishing figure. Dickens himself would come calling, on 10 November 1859, offering Eliot his periodical for her next novel, after *Mill* was completed, and when the serialization of Wilkie Collins's *The Woman in White* ended. The periodical, *All the Year Round,* was eventually to find competition in *Once a Week,* a magazine begun by the booksellers Bradbury and Evans, designed as adversarial to Dickens. The booksellers, who figured later in Eliot's life, even asked Lewes for a fictional contribution. The requests were indicative of how fierce the competition had become, and not the least how favorably Dickens looked upon Eliot as someone who would give him

---

* The mythological dimensions of the river are accompanied by numerous classical allusions—to Ajax, Hecuba, Troy, and others—so that the "Flood" is reinforced as an element with a recognizable pedigree. Eliot's notebook reveals some of her research on "Inundations" in the *Annual Register*: the gathering of water, its destructive force, its depth and torrential qualities, its effect on people and livestock. She cites places of such inundations, including her own Derbyshire and Warwickshire.

the edge. She was flattered, but none of these periodicals carried the prestige of *Maga*. By the 1850s, William Blackwood & Sons was an institution, a kind of feudal monarchy, with John Blackwood at the top hobnobbing with royalty and aristocracy, and the political leaders of the Conservative Party. George Simpson, his Edinburgh manager, acted as if he were a factotum in a ducal family.

Besides, Eliot feared difficulty with *Mill*, telling Blackwood that while her stories grew in her like plants, sometimes they are only in "the leaf-bud." She hopes the flower will come. Since she was unsure of her endings, or even her middles, she avoided printing in serial. Several authors, like Dickens and Thackeray, serialized when they were only one or two chapters ahead in the writing. Since there was no going back once chapters began to appear, they had to revise heavily in book form to compensate for what they could not do in the serial. Eliot tried to avoid that, not only as artistically faulty but as something personally too full of anxiety for her.

In the fall, these relatively quiet interchanges with Blackwood took a different turn. Once Eliot decided to drop the incognito with the partners, there was a climate change in the firm. John Blackwood had not yet made an offer for *Mill*, although he asked Lewes how the new novel was getting on. While wondering if they could begin the serial before the end of 1859, he did not stipulate terms. Hesitations and new calculations were beginning to poison the atmosphere. Eliot answered ambiguously, from Weymouth, where she and Lewes were rusticating. She cited that serialization would lose her many book readers, some 20,000, even 40,000. Further, she feared serial readers might be disappointed and that would be reflected, through word of mouth, in book sales. Advertising of the magazine serial would not help the book. She had become a bargainer now, someone aware of her marketability and power, although almost certainly Lewes was tutoring her.* She stressed that money was very important to her. "I don't want the world to give me anything for my books," she told John Blackwood, "except money enough to save me from the temptation to write *only* for money."

This shrewd piece of business was supplanted, however, by another ripple in the relationship, this one a lack of tact on John Blackwood's part about Eliot's dropping of her incognito. His jaunty tone here, as against the solemnity of her feelings, was the consequence of bickering in the office between John and William. William feared the revelation of Marian Evans—*that* Mrs. Lewes—might prove embarrassing, whereas John wanted to cash in on what he saw as another marketable book. He wanted to offer £4,000 for *Maga*, but then compromised on £3,000 for a four-year copyright on *Mill*.

Blackwood failed to heed the seriousness of his client. "In the Magazine," he

---

* Lewes was aware of the changes occurring in publishing, not the least in contracts. In the 1840s and 1850s, most contracts (although not Dickens's) were little more than verbal agreements jotted down, giving the publisher considerable leeway. Publishers kept double ledgers, one for themselves and one for the author, what we now call a royalty report. By the 1850s, this had taken hold: more professional contracts and tighter, more controlled fictions. Eliot was the beneficiary of this, and we observe it in her increasingly hard contract talks. In all this, Lewes may have been the first literary agent.

wrote Eliot, "we would not put any author's name, and it would be great fun [not for Eliot, however] to watch the speculations as to the author's life." Considering the sensitivity of his correspondent, these were heartless words. "The style would be to me easily recognizable but no one, especially of the puffing and publishing order, would suppose that we would throw away such an advantage as putting the magic words by George Eliot at the head of a series of papers. In the long run however ours is the wisest course, as nothing equals the excitement of uncertainty." Eliot read these words as mockery of her position; but even worse, she was being treated as an object. Her personal life was in the balance against marketability.

Her response was hardly friendly. She says she was right in believing they would not compensate her for the loss of book sales if she were serialized. She also says she has no intention of surrendering copyright, but only to give up the edition. "As, for the nature of your offer, I infer that you think my next book will be a speculation attended with risk, I prefer incurring that risk myself." But Blackwood's persiflage was not the sole disturbance. She mentions the pain she suffers from Charles Holte Bracebridge—a magistrate!—and other friends of Liggins. Bracebridge still maintained that Liggins gave her the material, and he had himself taken a trip into Staffordshire to discover Eliot's models, such as the Poysers. In his view, he identified Seth Bede and Dinah Morris as the Wesleyan uncle and aunt of Marian Evans, and the Reverend Irwine as a Reverend George Hole, whom Eliot says she has never heard of. "I hope the world is getting a great deal of good out of Adam Bede—it will signify less, then, that the author gets so much pain out of it." Bracebridge was asked to apologize for the implications he cast on Eliot, but, she says, he is "so nearly an idiot that it would not be safe to predict his mental process."

In a long letter to Bray, who was drawn in through sending on to her Bracebridge's letters to him, she warns him not to take any steps on her behalf. She worries that one deception, made to increase her marketability, has come home to subvert her writing itself. "That these things are painful to me is I dare say, partly due to morbid sensibility," she tells Bray, "but the pain is not the less real—not the less a clog on my mental activity. I am not the first author who has suffered from such annoyances, though they become more intolerable as the years bring with them that increased facility of communication which makes the conjectures and inferences of local ignorance matter for current circulation throughout the Kingdom." So much for Victorian propriety!

Yet intermixed with this was the matter of publication itself, a situation that would prove more problematic than authorship and sources. With the two Blackwood brothers bickering over payments, contracts, agreements, copyright, promises, and other publishing matters, Eliot was drawn into Dickens's vendetta against Bradbury and Evans.[*] Hoping to line up Eliot as a contributor to his new weekly, he finally came to visit the Lewes and Eliot household, at Holly

---

[*] Dickens had broken with the latter because they had refused to publish in *Punch* his ill-tempered and ill-advised statement of why he had separated from his wife (after ten children). He had accused her of being a poor mother as well as an inadequate wife, and that type of thing simply was not publicized, even when the "injured party" was Dickens.

Lodge, on 10 November. As noted, Dickens asked Lewes (not her) for her next book, after *Mill,* and became part of an ongoing drama in Eliot's relations with her publisher.

Equally compelling, she had begun to deal with several parallel developments. There was, most immediately, her growing mastery as a writer, as *Mill* would demonstrate. There was also the removal of her identity via her publisher, resulting in her standing forth as a female novelist named George Eliot. There was, further, the ambiguity of her "Mrs. Lewes" designation, and her use of Marian Evans Lewes in some of her correspondence, especially with Blackwood. There was, still further, the continuation of others' probe into her fictional characters, and a general contemptuous atmosphere among some surrounding her accomplishment—the Bracebridge, Quirk, Liggins ramifications.

Having surrendered certain givens of a traditional woman in the nineteenth century—motherhood and legal wifehood, for instance—and having been deprived by inheritance procedures of the larger part of her father's estate, she had managed to emerge through intellect, will, discipline, and imagination. Yet forces gathering just beyond were interfering, in effect redividing her. It was a time of extreme emotional and professional difficulty, as she reentered her period of childhood and adolescent entrapment in the very novel she was writing, *The Mill on the Floss.*

Perhaps equally significant was her effort to maintain her bearings as a serious writer, a devoted wife, and a committed friend in the face of so much money flowing in, so many temptations beginning to accrue. She had her integrity to think of, and this was no small matter. To be offered £400 on top of the original agreement for *Adam Bede* and then an additional £800 in the next year—this was to find money an enormous factor in her life. The £3,000 offered for *Mill* was another huge windfall. This was three times her entire trust fund, in a time of relatively low inflation.

Eliot weighed in with a further letter, once more to Bray, indicating her anger over another matter: Bracebridge had referred to her father as a farmer, and she felt Bray had spoken that way of Evans. "Now my father did not raise himself from being an artizan to be a farmer; he raised himself from being an artizan to be a man whose extensive knowledge in very varied practical departments made his services valued through several counties." All this was true, but it also had the element of distinguishing in class and caste terms between her father and a farmer. Eliot was the daughter not of a farmer, she insists, but of a man who was of the solid middle class. She also resisted being called a "self-educated farmer's daughter," a term Bracebridge—now zeroing in on Marian Evans—was circulating. As if explaining her sharpness of tone, she says she would not mind being called a tinker's daughter if her father had been a tinker. Her piety toward his memory, she says, calls for no less than this.

She was, she told Cara, depressed. Behind the scenes, the Blackwood brothers were trying to arrange a final strategy to deal with what they now perceived as their cantankerous author. William suggested the extra payment to Eliot, but only after they settled for the new novel: a potential threat, if she balked at their terms for *Mill*. Once large sums of money were bandied about, friendly relationships deteriorated into calculation. The Blackwoods were definitely not pleased with Eliot's exasperated tone, nor were they certain how to deal with her. It had all passed beyond a handshake, and, behind the scenes, Lewes was devising strategies.

On 7 October, in a chain of thought while she was working on *Mill*, Eliot reached back into *Adam Bede* for an extensive review of her relations with the Wesleyan aunt, Mrs. Samuel Evans, who had recounted the tale of the infant murderer. Eliot recounts the past, not as nostalgia, but as something sustaining, a female reinforcement she now seems to require. In retrospect, she sees her aunt as belonging to another era in her "truly religious" soul, in "whom the love of God and love of man were fused together." We recognize that despite her literary sophistication and her intellectual achievements, Eliot still depended heavily on these early experiences—not sentimentally, but in the Words-worthian sense of memories and intimations as stabilizing forces which have enabled her to go on.*

Bracebridge, finally, wrote Eliot that he accepted she had used her material originally, and not derivatively; that Dinah belonged to her, not to the diaries of one Mrs. Elizabeth Evans. Eliot was relieved, but told Sara that Lewes was so sensitive, so used to feeling both glad and angry on her behalf, he has been made unable to work by this Bracebridge affair. "No one is more indifferent than he is, to what is said about himself—but when anything once takes hold of him he is as nervous as a fragile woman, and now that his health is so delicate he has to suffer a good while from what would otherwise be a transient agitation." Although Lewes would survive for another two decades, much of that time pro-ductively, his health was nearly always precarious: nerves, connected to a num-ber of other ailments which made it difficult for him to breathe, digest, or avoid germs. There is a peculiar cycle which characterizes him and Eliot: seemingly as she waxed ever stronger, he became weaker. He did not precisely wane, but in taking second place to her—*consciously* doing so—he appeared to shrink; and this shrinking was part of a general deterioration in his health. Like her, he came alive when they traveled, but on returning to London, he frequently became enervated. Despite her frequent ailments, which were themselves sig-nificant, Eliot rarely stopped working.

After asking Blackwood for greater care in the *Adam Bede* edition—she detected typos and transcription errors in the dialect—her next news was more ominous. Newby would soon advertise a sequel to *Adam Bede*,† and Eliot had

---

* We could argue that the complex of classical allusions in *Mill* and in her other novels was not merely a parade of learning—although in part it was that—but also her need to find a stable, unchanging source. The classics were something she knew early, and they provided both an informa-tional and emotional base, a staging area.

† The *Examiner* announced on 22 October the imminent publication of *Adam Bede, Junior: A Sequel*. It would be one volume, at 10/6. The *Times* advertisement the next day repeated this, to be published by Newby of Welbeck Street.

herself received an anonymous letter asking her to write a sequel in which she "perfects and extends" the benefits Adam has conferred on society. This would include material on Hetty after her reprieve, Dinah's letters to Hetty, and other such matters. This became simply another poaching effort on her property, part of the Bracebridge, Quirk, Liggins thing; she saw clearly now that as a public figure she belonged to a large critical mass "out there," whose ideas of her talent were quite different from her own. She was still unprepared to face this challenge, which came not from within, but from without. When Dickens visited in November, she vowed to discover how he handled such exposure.

Lewes, in the meantime, was connecting himself to the *Cornhill Magazine,* whose editor was Thackeray when it started up in 1860. The *Cornhill* was owned by Smith, Elder & Co., a firm that would figure in Eliot's future. It was a prestigious offer—first to contribute, later to edit—and Lewes was attracted. While his career was not exactly declining—his papers on physiology, for example, were gaining acclaim—he did need some regular position so he could carry his weight financially. Eliot was herself fighting a rearguard action against Newby's advertisement of the *Adam Bede* sequel. She feared most people would not know the difference between Newby and Blackwood's and would not realize that the sequel could not be hers. Her success brought what Dickens experienced with *Pickwick* on a large scale, with imitators, sequels, episodes, and the like. At least the imitation *Pickwick Abroad* was signed; the *Bede* sequel would go unsigned.

But Eliot was still uneasy with Blackwood's, and her letter to John seemed too cool for him, especially her perfunctory expression of gratitude for the promised extra monies. His feeling was that if the "most popular author of the day" left them, the firm should be able to show she was treated with extreme liberality. In a letter from George Simpson, the firm's Edinburgh manager, to Joseph Munt Langford, the firm's London manager, Simpson refers to Eliot as greedy, someone who perhaps expects some magnificant price from another firm and is cold, insensible, ungrateful. He says that both Blackwoods are "utterly disgusted" and thinks they would now "decline the new book if it were offered to them." He adds that John Blackwood has been "most thoroughly hood-winked."

Two people who had had high regard for each other suddenly felt hostility and antagonism emanating from the other. We pick up some of this in Eliot's relationship with her friends, surely with Chapman, then with Spencer, even with the Brays and Sara. As she remade herself, she required reinforcement, and any slight criticism created doubts which she translated into attacks upon her. Her hypersensitivity worked both ways, making her miserable when she felt threatened, however slightly, and yet giving her insights she could use in her fictions. She created an ideal publisher, they created an ideal author, and then each observed that ideal crumble in the face of real people in real dealings with each other. In that fictional re-creation, we have several subsidiary figures, those who act as a kind of chorus, the rumormongers, the scandal-bringers, the ones who get everything wrong. Bracebridge, Liggins, Quirk, and others will reappear, disguised, in Eliot's fiction as part of that background of gossip and rumor which bring down her major characters. Her life provided the poison.

The kind of support she desired came from Elizabeth Gaskell, a fellow practitioner of fiction Eliot admired. Mrs. Gaskell speaks of *Scenes* and *Adam* as
something "complete and beautiful in fiction." She even brings up the forbidden
topic of Marian as Mrs. Lewes, and says she wishes it were so, but since it
cannot be, she agrees that one should not judge others.* The day after, on 11
November, Eliot was quick to respond with gratitude. Eliot raises Gaskell's
praise to another level, saying that she feels that artists who know each other's
pains so well should help each other more; and she is particularly gratified that
an artist of Gaskell's quality has found her work worthy. "You know, without
my telling you, how much the help is heightened by its coming to me afresh,
now that I have ceased to be a mystery and am known as a mere daylight fact."

The letter from Gaskell and Eliot's response came at a time when Spencer
reappeared, and both he and Eliot were ready for reconciliation. In this as in so
many other episodes of Eliot's life, Lewes acted as intermediary, finally getting
through to the self-absorbed Spencer that his gossip-laden comments were
undermining Eliot's confidence. The reconciliation was formalized when Spencer came to Holly Lodge on 23 October. With this and the Gaskell letter a little
later, Eliot was gradually finding a circle who accepted and supported her, not
only personally but professionally. Spencer had even asserted that *Adam Bede*
considerably benefited him.

While the test of friendship was one's response to her books, she seemed more
willing to forgive men than she did women. A reviewer of *Mill* in Chapman's
Westminster picked up some of her indulgence of men. "As with Donnithorne
so here with Stephen Guest, the hero escapes with but qualified reprobation; his
dishonourable abduction of Maggie is treated as the quite natural result of his
passion for her; in George Eliot's eyes he is evidently not disgraced by conduct
that would cause any honourable man to turn his back on him, conduct that
cannot have left him a moment's peace of mind to enjoy that colourless marriage
to which the author at last consigns him." Then the critic (in an unsigned
review) says: "The treatment of Stephen Guest is the rest of that fascination
which men exercise over women even when most intoxicated by them, and
affords a cardinal test and patent demonstration, if it were still needed, of
George Eliot's sex."

The comments were both insightful and a misreading of *Adam* and *Mill*.
Arthur Donnithorne is severely punished; his conscience will not allow any of
his dreams to come to fruition, and he remains something of an exile. Stephen
Guest, it is true, seems to regain his original position with Lucy Deane, but
Eliot's point is that Stephen is not a man of deep feeling. He ignores the more
profound level of suffering and rejection which Maggie experiences; he is

---

* Mrs. Gaskell was careful not to upset Eliot about Lewes, but behind her back, she told the
publisher George Smith "I know he [Lewes] has his good points but somehow he is so soiled for a
woman like her to fancy." It never occurred to Gaskell that Marian might herself have been "soiled."
More generally, the comment indicates how Victorian morality had penetrated into even those who
attempted not to judge, or who thought of themselves as somewhat liberated from Mrs. Grundy's
strictures.

indicted for his superficiality, something the reviewer misses. The latter also misses the point Eliot is making, how men can be caught up again in society, whereas women who err are ostracized or finished.

Yet elements of truth in the critic's remarks remain. Maggie's punishment for her "near adultery" with Stephen is death, and a near incestuous death at that. With Stephen, Maggie does not understand the rules of the game, and the game itself, we note, takes her out into those areas shadowing Eliot's own edgy personal life. With Stephen, the young woman leaves the familiar territory of childhood and adolescence; she is confronted by an adult decision, a dilemma whose terms are unknown and fearsome. Caught between social bonds and personal desire, she flees back into memories, into a past which is sustaining. There, Tom ominously awaits her; their embrace, death.

But there is another critical dimension, one that was taking place in the world of science and pseudo-science and which paralleled Eliot's portrayal of Maggie. We cannot fully comprehend Maggie's frustration without the following medical context. She is doomed not by Eliot but by how medical "evidence" determined women's destiny; the argument being that because of the female sexual and reproductive systems, women's cerebral evolution had been arrested at a certain undeveloped point. In this respect, since her cerebral mechanism was undeveloped, she lacked the element that was thought to contain the "will"—it was the will which gave Victorian males their superiority and which put them at the peak of the evolutionary pyramid. These were the conclusions of Darwin and, in time, of Spencer. This did not require proof; it was accepted as fact, even by the first female doctors, who were cowed by the male establishment and fearful of their own shaky position. Even when young women, such as we see in Eliot, are more perceptive and precocious than their male counterparts, they were stopped from further development by this assumption: that in time they would still finish at a lower level in mental evolution.

The craniologists and phrenologists supported these findings by asserting that the female brain weighed five ounces less than the male and was, by definition, inferior. But even when the craniologists were found to be faulty scientists, their conclusions remained. With their smaller brain, their lack of mental development and will, women were more subject to diseases of excitement; that is, hysteria and related nervous ailments. This, too, was held as "scientific," despite evidence that men outnumbered women in such nervous diseases. Victorian medical science was clearly driven by social and political considerations. The Maggies of the world were clearly doomed. Eliot understood that well.

In the *Adam Bede* "sequel," meanwhile, Dickens saw the makings of a pleasant piece of publishing and personal scandal, and asked Lewes—who declined— to write about Newby and his methods for *All the Year Round*. Eliot did not go public with her feelings of outrage, but turned to her journal, precisely on her fortieth birthday, saying—ominously, as it turned out—that Blackwood's did not feel any urgency here. She implied the firm was so slow to act because it felt less threatened than she did. Still, Dickens was pursuing her full gallop, quite aware he was dealing with someone sensitive and difficult. In a letter that followed the 10 November dinner engagement with the couple, he indicated he wanted to close with terms to be arranged with his subeditor and business manager, Wills. "An immense new public," he tells Lewes, "would probably be opened to her, and I am quite sure that our association would be full of interest and pleasure to me." He continued: "Of my personal feeling and wish in the matter, and of the extent to which I have it at heart as an artist, to have such an artist working with, I have no right to say more in this connexion." By mid-1859, a war was emerging on several fronts: Dickens's *All the Year Round* (having merged with *Household Words*) set against Bradbury & Evans's *Once a Week*, with Blackwood's forming the third point of the triangle. All wanted Eliot, and she began to waver. Langford of Blackwood's London office, meanwhile, stigmatized her as ready to sell herself to the highest bidder.

John Blackwood was himself upset at several things. He thought Lewes was overreacting to the fake *Adam* sequel, and perhaps saw it as Lewes's way to edge Eliot out of the firm. He was disturbed by Eliot's own tone expressed in her response to his generous offer of £3,000 for *Mill*. He suspects, too, that she may have received an "absurd offer" from someone else; and if so, he believes she could have replied more courteously. He senses deception, some behind-the-scenes manipulation. Further, he writes Langford, "Our kindness too in doubling the original price of Adam Bede has been acknowledged in the most painfully unhandsome way with hardly thanks." Blackwood then arrived at the nub of the issue, that possibly his suggestion she publish anonymously is the "crochet at the bottom of it." This is the very point Eliot would emphasize when she replied. Business was important to her, but identity, revelation, and disguise were also; and what Blackwood was doing, further, was fighting her on gender issues, as well as on deeply personal ones.

Langford replied to John Blackwood that he felt some of the extravagant offers may have been more "brag" than real. He says that a little "judicious reticence" may bring the author back to the firm. But he recognizes a crisis situation, one that goes beyond money into personalities, questions of artistic value, even into the eventual worth of the book Eliot was writing. One large question still unanswered was whether or not *Mill* would appear in *Maga* as a serial before publication. Lewes had raised the possibility of much higher payment than the £3,000 offer if the book were to be serialized. Meanwhile, the "sequel" to *Adam Bede* was postponed to 26 November, and an anonymous notice had appeared in the *Daily News* to the effect that the sequel "is not by the author of *Adam Bede*."

Lewes's intervention was beginning to prove counterproductive. In his effort to protect Eliot, he was muddying the waters with something of his own needs. As we sift the correspondence, we suspect that Lewes was gaining power by way of the woman who was becoming famous and rich. Although as far as we can judge she and Lewes remained on the best of terms, his intervention in her life was now an indication of his need to realize personal goals through her reputation. In the Newby affair, Lewes became so insistent he appears overfocused on something trivial. Indiscreetly, he tells the Blackwoods that Eliot has encountered several efforts, assumedly astronomical, to "seduce" her. In the background was the firm's fear that Mudie's might boycott *Mill* once her irregular relationship was freely made public. At Mudie's, someone had referred to *Adam Bede* as having come from a "polluted source."*

The point of all this internal fighting was that, whether she wished it or not, as Eliot became famous she became involved in publishing politics. Lewes may have thought he was doing the infighting for her, but in fact he was creating a good deal of bad feeling. Also, in some psychologically significant way, he was in part taking over Eliot's career, in most respects except the actual writing, and directing her into positions which might have jeopardized her artistic integrity. Dickens's role in all this, as suggested above, was as spoiler, to create as much turbulence as possible and hope the fallout came his way. Bad feeling was intensified, and Eliot, by letting others speak for her, had contributed.

Inevitably, she had to enter the arena. On 26 November, she briskly told John Blackwood: ". . . I am induced to ask you whether you will wish to remain my publishers, or whether the removal of my incognito has caused a change in your views on that point." She continued: "I have never myself thought of putting an end to a connection which has hitherto not appeared inauspicious to either of us, and I have looked forward to your being my publishers as long as I produced books to be published; but various indications, which I may possibly have misinterpreted, have made me desire a clear understanding in the matter."

On the 28th, Blackwood replied. Without at first addressing the question of the incognito, he vows eternal loyalty, but says he would be the last man to stand in her way if she received a more advantageous offer. "But I think," he adds, "I should have been told so frankly instead of having my offer treated as if it were not worth consideration at all." He then comes to the delicate part. "As to the withdrawal of the incognito, you know how much I have been opposed to it all along. It may prove a disadvantage and in the eyes of many it will, but my opinion of your genius and confidence in the truly good, honest, religious, and moral tone of all you have written or will write is such that I think you will overcome any possible detriment from the withdrawal of the mystery which has so far taken place."

While Blackwood's plan was to placate Eliot, his wording *could* be read as quite wounding. For in effect he was suggesting that because her works are highly moral, even spiritual, she will be forgiven her indiscretions. And if she continues to write in a high moral tone, her readers will allow her her personal life. Blackwood's own moral views blinded him to the indelicacy of his phrasing, to the fact he was burrowing into the very areas where Eliot was most sensitive.

She answered immediately, on the 30th, now eight days past her fortieth birthday. After commenting on how serial publication would cut book sales, she gets to the nub: "Your proposition at the same time to publish the story [in

* In just the three-year period from 1858 to 1861, when Eliot was publishing her first books, Mudie's increased its *annual* rate of acquisitions from 100,000 to 180,000 books. Mudie's control over who read what was that much more solidified.

Maga] without the name of George Eliot seemed to me (rendered doubly sensitive by the recent withdrawal of my incognito) part of a depreciatory view that ran through your whole letter in contrast with the usual delicacy and generosity of your tone." She denies she suggested she had other offers—Lewes, however, had strongly suggested this—or stated she was unhappy with a three-volume edition of "Maggie," as *Mill* was still called. She says her first inkling of the firm backing out came when Langford, of the London office, mentioned it to Lewes. But this is disingenuous, since—unless she had blocked everything out—she was aware, through Lewes and her own correspondence with Blackwood, that she and the firm were undergoing a rocky experience.

Then she zeroes in on Blackwood's indifference to the matter of the "sequel" to *Adam,* a certain cavlier attitude, one without any sense of the urgency of the situation: ". . . in declining to write to the Times, to write to the Athenaeum, a paper which has grossly insulted me, to ask them to insert a paragraph without the mention of your name, indicated, I thought, a forgetfulness which implied a very considerable alteration of feeling towards me." Blackwood had clearly underestimated the depth of disturbance the "sequel" created in Eliot; for it was an invasion of her deepest privacy, a rape of her artistic talent.

She says she wishes to keep her publisher, since she prefers permanent solutions to shifting ones. But, she insists, since she is "in a position of anxiety for others as well as myself" her duty is "to seek not less than the highest reasonable advantage from my work." After apologizing for appearing ungrateful for the extra monies, she says she hopes this clears the air. She had, by now, completed about half of "Maggie" and was becoming nervous about its final disposition.

How much this controversy affected Eliot's conception of Maggie and of *Mill* we cannot pinpoint. But of interest is the fact that the manuscript reveals a far more rebellious Maggie than the book text. In the manuscript, Maggie is more of a recluse—she hides under a bed to avoid going to Aunt Glegg's—and more marginal to family life. Part of her rebellion against her parents and their lives involves a fantasy of Tom and her together; he does not attend school, Bob Jakes does not exist, and the two siblings exist as Adam and Eve in an earthly paradise. For the book text, Eliot toned down some of these aspects, especially Maggie's rebel nature.

What comes through, furthermore, in the exchange with Blackwood is Eliot's recognition that a climate change had occurred. For the firm, there was the same feeling. Amusingly, in their internal correspondence William and John continue to refer to the author as "he" and "him," a denial on their part that the incognito has been removed, and an indication that with George Eliot, a man, as their author they could market "his" books without fear of moral retribution from booksellers or readers.

So insistent are these internal memos, in fact, that one receives the impression all activity at the firm had ground to a halt while relationships with Eliot were worked through. In one exchange, William indicates his continuing fear that disclosure of the author's name will "affect the circulation in families of any future work." They see difficulty with Lewes, also, in some way. "Altogether it is a tangled kind of business, and though I feel that we should continue to be publisher for her [finally, not "him"] as long as we have confidence in her other writings, we shall always, I am afraid, have disagreeables attending it in some shape or another. I think too very strongly that we should not bind ourselves until we have seen the new work." Eliot had not yet submitted any of "Maggie" for their perusal.

Both parties were then positioned for John Blackwood's very long letter to Eliot of 2–4 December. As he recognized, this letter could be decisive, and perhaps for strategic reasons he wrote it from Arbury, where he was visiting Charles Newdigate. He admits there has been misunderstanding on both sides, and he adds that he cannot think of any depreciatory comment he might have made about the new novel. He explains that he wanted the story to be anonymous in *Maga* as a matter of policy, but realizes that "the proposition might fall disagreeably upon you and I wish I had said more than I did in explanation." Then he arrives at the critical juncture: naming. "I regretted the partial removal of the incognito but I never thought of ceasing to be your publisher on that account nor did I dream that such an idea would ever occur to you. As to the effect of the spread of the secret on the new book there must be, and I know there are, different opinions. My opinion is that George Eliot has only to write her book quietly without disturbing herself about what people are saying and she can command success." It is doubtful if Blackwood would have written this to a man, since it suggests that all she has to do is to be a good little girl (in her work) and everything will fall into place. As for the contretemps over the "sequel" to *Adam*, he felt that it was better, as he told Lewes, "to let the rubbish die a natural death. . . . You have no idea what a bitter pill it was to me to write a civil note to that hound the editor of the Athenaeum. . . . I wrote it because I thought it might satisfy you and, the advertisement giving the ground, it seemed the most natural place for attaining the object without causing a fuss which I am sure it was desirable in every way to avoid." Blackwood was, of course, wrapping Eliot's needs into his own way of tamping down anything that was disagreeable.

Eliot invited John Blackwood to Holly Lodge on Wednesday, 7 December, so that they could range over the entire relationship. This was a particularly critical time, for while her earlier two books had created considerable stir, her reputation was not yet firm. *Mill* would either establish her as a great novelist—in the line of women like Austen and the Brontës[*] and men like Dickens, Thackeray, and Trollope—or relegate her to a secondary position. A good deal depended, accordingly, on how the new book was handled, and toward that end Lewes attempted various strategies.

We suspect that from his plans for *Mill*, he was seeking not the best possible artistic deal, but the largest possible return. He requested publication in 1-shilling numbers, for example, which he figured would bring £5,000 on 10,000

---

[*] The Gothic genre of "The Lifted Veil" revealed she had read her Mary Shelley, not the least *Frankenstein*. This, too, was part of the tradition.

copies, an enormous return. Meanwhile, Bradbury & Evans offered £4,500 for publication in *Once a Week* and in two further editions. John Blackwood was appalled by the amounts of money under discussion, and he told Eliot so; she assured him she did not wish any comparable sum from the firm. But the ante had been raised, and Blackwood recognized he was negotiating on another level. Lewes had created that shift. The publisher admitted that "Lewes is much the keener of the two," but that was because Eliot deferred to his business sense. The publisher also commented on Eliot's appearance as having much improved since he says she has gotten over her worry and annoyance of the last few weeks.

Perhaps because so much of *Mill* involved a dip into the past, Eliot wrote at length to D'Albert-Durade, her former landlord and friend in Geneva. In Geneva, she says, she was still antagonistic to religion, very unhappy and in a state of rebellion toward her lot. Now she says she no longer harbors any antagonism "towards any faith in which human sorrow and human longing for purity have expressed themselves. . . . I have not returned to dogmatic Christianity—to the acceptance of any set of doctrines as a creed, and a superhuman revelation of the Unseen—but I see in it the highest expression of the religious sentiment that has yet found its place in the history of mankind. . . ." She emphasizes that she believes in "our struggling fellow-men and this earthly existence," which should be the objects of our highest emotions. She speaks, also, of "our eldest boy" coming home from school, and that will make, she says, "a new epoch" in their domestic life. "I hope my heart will be large enough for all the love that is required of me."

Meanwhile, John was writing William that he had brought back with him a volume and a half of the manuscript of "Maggie," which suitably impressed him. "It is wonderfully clever and shows an almost incredible wealth of fun and illustrations and power of painting character." He finds it impossible to read rapidly, but feels this is a disadvantage, arising from the "want of the hurrying on interest of a taking narrative." In plain English, this means the narrative is too slow, since half of the book occurs before the hero and heroine, as he calls them, are not more than sixteen. Yet he praises the genius of the writer, and says that whatever the faults of a slow narrative, the reader will almost certainly go on. He particularly praises the Tulliver mother and the three aunts. Astutely, he sees Tom Tulliver as a "lifelike contrast" to the Tom Brown ideal—Thomas Hughes's idealized portrait of youth in his very successful 1857 novel. An offer would be forthcoming, despite Lewes's effort to gain publication in shilling numbers in *Maga*.

Eliot was herself not taken with the "Nightmare of the Serial," as she called it. The terms would be below what Lewes had counted on, but still generous: £2,000 for an edition of 4,000 copies, selling in three volumes at 31 / 6, and the same rate of payment for every copy sold above 4,000 at the same price. For a possible 12-shilling edition, they offered £150 per thousand and for any 6-shilling edition, £60 per thousand. Within the week, Eliot agreed. If the book sold well, she could make a huge fortune on these terms.

As it turned out, in 1860 alone, Eliot earned £385 from various other editions of *Mill* (including American reprint and German and Dutch translations), all in the expensive edition, plus an additional £600 in a cheap edition. Furthermore, once the negotiations for *Mill* were ended, the firm sent on that extra £800 for *Adam Bede,* as a sign of goodwill. In 1860, then, counting advance monies, Eliot earned about £5,000 from new ventures, plus other monies coming in still from previous publications. Lewes's earnings rose also to £591, not a meager income, but insufficient to sustain their new way of life. When we note the disparity in incomes between the two, we can understand Lewes's efforts to squeeze out every shilling from Eliot's work. He with his business sense and she with her artistic talent had tapped into a Victorian treasure trove. If we add the £2,400 from *Adam* and *Scenes,* the couple had an overall annual income of about £8,000. It was for Eliot, however, only a beginning, as her earnings went much higher for subsequent books.

For the time, negotiations with Blackwood had settled down. The crisis loomed, but was not reached. One element nevertheless remained: Eliot requested that payments be made on publication, which the firm did not like to do. It paid at intervals, but a compromise was struck with £1,000 at six months and another £1,000 at nine months after publication. This was the firm's New Year's gift to their now celebrated author. Lewes's own gift, for Christmas of 1859, was a forty-eight-volume set of Scott's Waverley novels, inscribed: "To Marian Evans Lewes, The best of Novelists, and Wives, These works of her longest-venerated and best-loved Romanticist are given by her grateful Husband 1 January 1860."

The new year brought both money and an expression of "wifehood." It came at a good time, because in *Mill* Eliot had reentered some highly sensitive and intimate areas of her life; and her presentation of these conflicts had not alleviated the pain, but intensified it. She had probed deeply into the very regions that made her uncertain, anxious, and often ill—areas of marginality, feelings of being unwanted, depressive states—and she had set them in a locale that recalled Arbury. Shielded, shadowy, the novel is deeply personal, not with the recall of definite details, but in the presentation of an earlier Marian Evans in different guises, as moving in and out of hostilities and antagonisms she could never reveal publicly or nakedly. Even the early titles—"The House of Tulliver," for example—are of interest because they suggest a family rather than a place, although Eliot then agreed that the place was more appropriate, even if the mill was not really on the Floss but on a tributary. She was torn here between the desire for accuracy—her insistent realism—and her recognition that the story was personal, impressionistic, not starkly realistic. *The Mill on the Floss* captures that impressionism, what we find immediately in the Proustian beginning, a meditation on time, pastness, history, and inevitably on how to be.

Mill is a Bildungsroman: that type of fiction which charts the younger life of a hero or heroine and usually ends with that person's emergence into the larger world, as in Dickens's *David Copperfield.* Such a novel describes the difficulties of growing up, efforts to find one's way in the dense thickets of a hostile or ungiving society, attempts to seek a parent or parent figure with whom to identify, the struggle to find reciprocal love or affection, and the modulations one makes to find balance between individual need and societal demands. It is full of angst, alienation, and isolation, but it is also educational. The protagonist begins to learn how to live, how to modify his or her behavior, how to adapt to external demands without forsaking one's integrity. Maggie Tulliver journeys into forms of recognition; she must balance several conflicts, including deeply feminine ones. She is brighter and more intelligent than her society or even her sympathetic father has room for. Her mind goes wasting, while her emotional life is in turmoil when it confronts narrow restrictions. She is "unwanted" in the sense that her inner dictates find no outside coordinates; in another way, she overdetermines her role because she is unwilling to accept the part assigned to her.

The central autobiographical element of *Mill* seems to be the alternating hostility and affection between Maggie and brother Tom. If we are hasty, we see this as a replay of young Marian Evans and brother Isaac; but such an explanation is too facile. That is not to deny there are resemblances: even with her overwhelming love for her sibling, Maggie manages to show considerable antagonism by destroying his playthings, undermining his activities, and insisting on herself as "different," as a girl with different priorities from his.* This much is clear. Eliot had found a way in which she could relive some of those years; but we do not know how much of it was actually true and how much of the hostility Maggie displays and the rigidity Tom shows are the result of what came *after*, rather than before. We must question whether Eliot was really carried back to an earlier time in memory and feeling, or whether she was manifesting a contemporary antagonism toward Isaac for his rejection of her as an adult woman and a famous writer. In this respect, Tom could be a scapegoat for Eliot's present feelings toward her brother, or, more generally, toward men.

One way out of the biographical dilemma is to see Eliot working through certain generic modes: using Maggie as a young girl and woman who lacks the social support to become something, and using Tom as representative of that male world which cannot allow the girl or young woman to achieve herself. Tom, then, becomes all men; Maggie, all young girls and women. The personal or autobiographical element is subsumed into the larger one, on the scale that human activity is itself subsumed into the larger natural order of a river, a flood, a maelstrom.

The structure of the novel, one of Eliot's tightest,† creates the impression of swallowing or devouring, until that final devouring when, in a *Liebestod*, Maggie and Tom both achieve recognition in a frenzied embrace leading to immediate death. Full love comes only in death; but we are prepared for this, by the title

---

* Later, in the summer of 1869, Eliot would write another version of this in an eleven-part sonnet sequence, "Brother and Sister." Cast in Wordsworthian terms, the sequence opens up all the old wounds.

† The manuscript reveals the sureness of touch. There is little sign of heavy revisions; usually only a word or phrase is altered. Unfortunately, the deletions, such as they are, are heavily inked out and illegible. We cannot in these instances determine what Eliot had corrected.

of the novel and by the edginess of Maggie's "difference." The structure, then, must develop this theme of devouring, and does so through a peculiar kind of grid. If we put the major characters at the top of the grid—Tom, Maggie, Stephen Guest and Lucy Deane, Philip Wakem, Tulliver, and the four Dodson sisters—and the several significant themes running through them at intervals, we can reconstruct part of the grid. The major themes which intersect with the characters are the river itself, the escape or expulsion from Eden, womb images creating alternating security and emergence, nature, the Romeo and Juliet linkage of families feuding, and various forms of success and / or failure. Moving diagonally through all this are two insistent elements: the question of duty versus pleasure, and the question of free will versus determinism.

The texture of the novel derives from this living grid, the linkage of people, ideas, destinies, and natural events all against a background of devouring. This was essential Eliot, her "voice." She may have theoretically rejected in part the evolutionary determinism of Darwin; but in *Mill,* she persists in swallowing her major figures, until the final submergence in the flood. Water images, here and elsewhere, become critical in Eliot's thought, not only as cleansing agents but as deterministic elements. So, too, are the classical references to water, not the least the linkage of Maggie with Hecuba, who for her various deeds was thrown into the sea.

There is little chance for escape. Book Two, for example, ends with the expulsion from Eden of Tom and Maggie; as if they were caught up not only in their own tragedy but in the downfall of man, which no one can avoid. Related to the expulsion from Eden is the presence of several exile images: that emergence into a new experience whose coordinates lie outside what the characters can handle. Similarly, nature itself appears inexorable. Philip Wakem, who is so suited for Maggie intellectually and emotionally, is "anti-Nature" in his physical handicap, so that, despite his sensitivity, he cannot engage her affections. Another dimension of swallowing is the conflict between the Tulliver and Wakem families, so that the young people, Maggie and Philip, are forbidden to see each other. This, too, is a form of determinism in which external forces devour the will of the participants. Finally, another theme, that of the drive for success and the attendant fear of failure, grips nearly all of the male figures and drains them of choice. When his father fails, Tom must allocate all his energies to being successful, to save the family; the Dodson sisters measure success by silverware, furniture, and clothing; Wakem, described in stereotypical Semitic terms, is driven to succeed, however underhandedly, to provide for his handicapped son and to calm his own inner rages. Success is not presented as desirable, since in all cases it is connected not to personal achievement but to material factors, retribution, or compensation. It devours. It denies expansiveness, breadth, revelation, or even a firmer sense of morality and ethics; it is almost entirely an open maw, a swallower.

That such a trope of a devouring destiny finds its most forceful expression in a flooding river indicates how deeply Eliot had meditated on what belongs to the individual and what to the larger elements, on what, in another dimension, belongs to duty and what to pleasure, and how it all comes together not in achievement, as we might expect from Eliot's own career, but in inevitable destruction. With Maggie, Eliot has introduced her characteristic woman: the attractive, intelligent person who finds herself hemmed in on all sides, so that even when she seems to carve out some area for herself, like Dorothea Brooke in *Middlemarch,* she is nevertheless still trapped by social forms and pressures, by a destiny which disallows personal control. If we extend the metaphor, Eliot was riding tremendous waves, very close to elements in the novel, and she saw herself as a figure bobbing along on a tide that might at any time prove destructive.

Once she had received encouragement from Blackwood, she completed the second book (the expulsion from Eden) on 16 January 1860, and the remaining books, astonishingly, within eight weeks. Blackwood suggested the title, *The Mill on the Floss* (Lewes thought "Sister Maggie" sounded like a child's story), which she accepted, and her aim was to clear her desk of the manuscript in time for a spring trip to Italy. It seemed a heady time: the completion of a new novel in sight; a financially secure position, with huge amounts yet to come if the book did well; a trip to Italy forthcoming; health relatively secure; and a sound relationship with Lewes, made even sounder by his financial dependence on her and his sons' acceptance of her position as "stepmother." Yet the novel belies any easy acceptance of personal "happiness." It turns all possible success into contingency, into some outside force dicing with individual lives. It leaves open a multitude of questions for any close reading of the author. It reveals an underlying, unalterable sadness.

With *The Mill on the Floss,* Eliot had arrived "there." Although *Middlemarch* would become her most ambitious and perhaps most characteristic fiction, *Mill* set the context. It indicated her mastery of her subject, her brilliance with detail, her ability to provide backgrounding for her main characters, and her abundant use of allusions and images from her extensive reading. The four Dodson sisters, with their chattering, self-serving, but sometimes generous ways, were the perfect "society" for Eliot's major figures to step forth from. In this respect, she had found her method: a narrative of two or more major figures caught up in a buzz saw of social comments from ordinary people. Linked to this was the firmness of her literary philosophy: the balancing of individual choice with an abiding destiny or fate. Her surety in writing *Mill*—being able to predict, for instance, when she would finish the third volume—indicated she had learned from herself what she could do.

This growth of confidence was significant because it had to carry her past at least one serious misstep in her judgment of her art, the novel *Romola,* and in part in a second one, *Silas Marner.* While these novels fulfilled certain psychological aspects of her character, or gratified certain internal needs, she was unable to find sufficient structural and narrative terms in which to express them. Critically, they sag, even as biographically, they penetrate.

In all, by 1860, Eliot had achieved everything she had hoped for herself. She

had confronted, emerged, become liberated, done it all. And yet enormous bat-
tles remained, not the least because of her position as a woman unwilling to
settle for a woman's traditional role. As we shall see, she would pay and pay—
not on the continent, which was a kind of refuge, but in England, which was a
kind of trap.

ﾞ

John Blackwood hoped to issue *Mill* by the end of March. He had several suggestions about wording in the manuscript, especially passages connected to descriptions of characters. He questioned why Maggie has to be "in love" with a
defective person like Philip—apparently missing the entire nature of the relationship from Maggie's point of reference. He questioned Mrs. Tulliver's lack of
affection toward her husband, but missed that, as a Dodson, she was more interested in position than in the man she married. He created a patina of romance
over a novel which is distinctly not romantic, and he conventionalized and
sentimentalized aspects of the book in which Eliot had created the opposite
effect. His entire attitude about Eliot's identity, and her role as Mrs. Lewes, is
implicit in the kinds of gentle criticisms he made. Every remark has a shadowy
negative connotation. In John Blackwood (as well as in Major William Blackwood) Eliot had the perfect sounding board for what she wrote and for who she
was: men who were frightened by the behavior of an author who was making
too much money for them to think of dropping her, men who feared scandal
and who wished he / she could be a little more conventional, even religious. We
must not forget that the Blackwoods, while honorable, were among the great
reactionaries of the century.

With proofs going back and forth, Blackwood eagerly awaited the final volume; his criticisms notwithstanding, he knew she had written a magnificent
book, and he was weary with anticipation about how she would conclude it. By
the end of the first week in March, he had in hand about two-thirds of the
final volume, and he was not disappointed. During this time of writing *Mill* and
correcting proofs, Eliot also found time to have a will drawn for both herself and
Lewes, by Henry Sheard, whom she also used to work out certain details (the
Mill bankruptcy) in her novel. She again ignored all of Blackwood's serious
suggestions, although she deleted a harmless word like "lymphatic" from her
description of Mrs. Tulliver. After this, John Blackwood did nothing but reinforce Eliot's desire to reach the fulfillment of her aims without interference.
Lewes had told him, once again, how she was different and dependent, so that
constant bolstering was needed. Blackwood wrote that he was "enchanted," and
in a follow-up letter he repeated how solid everything was.

Bulwer-Lytton visited at Holly Lodge and entered his criticism of *Adam Bede*:
the dialect and Adam's marriage to Dinah. Eliot commented she "would have
her teeth drawn rather than give up either." The dialect, which she only barely
altered, was not only part of her effort at realistic portrayal, but her desire to
recapture the language of her childhood. It was more than nostalgia; it was an

attempt to regain that world as it had sounded, not necessarily because it was a better world, but because it was one she saw as coherent and cohesive.

None of this suggests that sentimentality was altogether absent. Lewes informed Blackwood that Eliot had cried over the final scenes as she composed them, her eyes reddening and becoming swollen. Like her readers she believed thoroughly in the efficacy of tragedy in fiction. Dickens, also, had proven that such scenes sell.* Eliot was rushing along, now in early March, waiting eagerly for their Italian journey to become a reality, and willing to "fly" even before she saw the three volumes of *Mill* in print. But she was apprehensive. As she tells Barbara Bodichon, "There is an immense expectation—and of course a very strong predisposition to find that the book is a 'falling off'—second books always have to go through *that.*" Nevertheless, she says, the reading public is agog, and *Adam Bede* continues to sell at 200 copies a month; she even divulges that she refused £4,500 for three editions of *Mill.*

On 21 March, Eliot wrote the final pages, just three days before they left Holly Lodge for Paris. Their plan was to spend Easter week in Rome. She thought final proofs would have to be forwarded to them in Paris, but they arrived at Holly Lodge in time, a marvel of efficiency for printers and mail services. Throughout this period, when she was writing against this self-imposed deadline, John Blackwood kept up a steady stream of letters to encourage her. He says his nephew (William, the major's son, and the editor of *Maga* when Joseph Conrad published *Heart of Darkness* and *Lord Jim* there) felt that a first printing of 4,000 was too small. Actually over 6,500 copies were printed in the three-volume edition; 3,600 alone went for subscriptions.

Even as Blackwood sent on encouragement, Lewes was still trying to squeeze out better terms for the cheap edition: if the novel was priced at 5 shillings, he suggested a larger edition; if it would be a smaller edition, then 6 or 6½ shillings. "The extra sum," he says, "is little to the purchaser, but makes a great difference to us." Rather than a financial ploy, Lewes pushed as some kind of a power play to put the firm on notice it was negotiating with a shrewd operator. The sole delay in Eliot's sending on final copy before their departure came from a siege of headache which lasted two days.

No one can doubt John Blackwood's sincerity as he came toward the end: "No words of mine can convey the feeling of the greatness of the success you have achieved. . . . This book is a greater triumph even than Adam and you may make your mind easy about all Critics. Any mean creature that may venture to carp will only dispute himself." Eliot admitted that this letter helped to inspire her for the final eleven pages. Her concentration on the book was now so total she lay awake at night and made mental notes of three verbal corrections she wished to arrange. She indicates that she planned to send *Mill* to no one except Dickens, and she warns the firm not to send out copies saying "From the

---

* While Eliot may have been getting swollen eyes over her pages, Lewes was active in making foreign publishers' faces swollen and red as he extracted the last possible pounds from them—Tauchnitz in Germany, as mentioned, but also Harper's in America. In each case, Eliot's "agent" held out for more than was offered and gained it.

publisher" lest people think they came from her. Her reasoning here is both curious and expected. Although earlier, with *Scenes* and *Adam*, she was eager to be read, now she is self-contained, sure of herself. But in this gesture there is also competitiveness with other writers and hostility toward critics. If they are to read her, let them purchase the work. While the gesture is a sign of a growing mastery of herself and her talent, it is also a sign of her wariness toward those who might judge her, as well as her recognition she no longer needed them— they may need her. We observe Eliot emerging, scorning others, repaying old debts in which she felt, rightly or wrongly, insulted and injured, playing out the game as she feels it rather than as convention calls for. *

Having dined with the Congreves, Eliot and Lewes embarked for Paris on 24 March. Once in Paris, they stayed at the Hôtel du Louvre, which was then for visiting royalty as well as successful writers. They remained two nights, did some conventional sightseeing (Notre Dame, Sainte Chapelle, the Louvre, the Palais Royal), saw *Otello* at the opera house, and then took the train for Italy.

What is remarkable to us is how such ailment-ridden people were able to withstand the rigors of travel, even with adequate means at their disposal. In going from Paris to Italy, for example, they had to forsake the railroad at St. Jean de Maurienne and take a carriage, which brought them to a sledge that would carry them over the Mont Cenis pass. Since this was late March, Mont Cenis, at about 7,000 feet, was the only pass even reasonably open. There were only minimal stops for fortification with coffee or hot chocolate or tea; they had to wait while mules were loaded with the luggage; and then they were packed into the sledges for the midnight ride over the snow-covered pass. They had to deal with a powerful wind, and had no chance to sleep, except for brief naps. The sledges brought them to Susa, where they caught a train to Turin. They had a few hours there, and then entrained for the five-hour ride to Genoa. They had been traveling for seventy-two hours, on a journey which now takes two. In her journal, Eliot recorded their exhaustion on arriving in Genoa.

Once rested, they toured this beautifully located city—much less industrial-ized and built up than at present, of course, and much more a maritime experi-ence. It was and is a city of magnificent cemeteries and tombs, a city of memorials. After two days there—having walked many of the major thorough-fares and expensive residential areas—they boarded a steamer to head south to Leghorn (Livorno). They attended Sabbath services at a synagogue, foreshad-owing Eliot's interest in Jewish life. They used Leghorn as a base and went to Pisa, returned, and boarded the steamer for Civitavecchia, on the coast not far

---

* To Sara, more than a year later (13 April 1861), she took a related tack. "Don't think about reading Silas Marner just because it is come out. I have obligato reading and obligato talk about my books. *I never send them to any one* and never wish to be spoken to about them, except by an unpremeditated spontaneous prompting. They are written out of my deepest belief, and as well as I can, for the great public—and every sincere strong word will find its mark in that public. Perhaps the annoyance I suffered from Mr. Bracebridge and Co. has made me rather morbid on such points, but apart from my own weaknesses, I think the less an author hears about himself the better."

from Rome. It was now Palm Sunday, and they hoped to reach Rome that day, which they accomplished by noon.

Her disapproval of Rome was keen: ". . . no other feeling than that of disappointment, deep and bitter," upon their entrance into the city. Her early days there seem little more than the occasion for complaints about lodgings and "dirty, uninteresting streets." As they wandered, she found "narrow and ugly streets," and entered their hotel dejectedly. But these first impressions passed, and a drive to St. Peter's, then to the Capitol and the Coliseum, exhilarated her, and she felt "an intoxication of delight, making me long to stay here and study till I know Rome by heart all except those ugly modern streets which are enough to scare away every haunting spirit of the past."

Possibly, Eliot's poor first impressions of Rome led her to dismiss the city in favor of Florence as the location for her next large novel. That novel is mentioned for the first time in a letter to Blackwood near the end of August (the 28th), after their return, where she says their stay in Florence gave her the idea of writing a historical romance, set near the end of the fifteenth century, a period marked by the firebrand religious reformer Savonarola's career. Florence may have won out because in Savonarola she found someone who helped her test out her own moral attitudes, her sense of human conduct, and her need to find flexibility within moral and ethical problems. Through Savonarola she would confront what she had been and what she had become. *Romola* loomed so insistently *because for the first time fictionally she hoped to heal the divisions between public and private in herself* by defining what she was through Romola and the figure of Savonarola.

But, as she tells Blackwood, the Florence novel would have to wait for "my next English novel," which she wanted to write when the Italian one was far enough advanced for it to begin in *Maga*. Her plan, at this stage, called for a start on *Romola* (as yet unnamed), followed by *Silas Marner* (the English novel, as yet undefined), then the completion of *Romola*, which would all along be serialized. Interspersed in this plan was a short novella called "Brother Jacob," but not itself published until July 1864.

She tells Blackwood (from Rome) she has borne the trip not like "an invalided novelist" but like a "muscular Christian," whereas Lewes has not been well, suffering from his usual ailments, lightness in the head, faintness, need for rest. She says she believes Rome will "chase away Maggie and the Mill from my thoughts; I hope it will, for she and her sorrows have clung to me painfully. As for the book, I can see nothing in it just now but the absence of things that might have been there. I tremble rather, to hear of its reception, less high hopes should be speedily checked. But then, I am always in a state of fear, more or less rational; and if any good news comes, it will be the more welcome."

The pain derives from a deep alliance between *Mill* and Eliot or between Maggie and Eliot. The chief imagery of *Mill* is water; early on, Maggie almost drowns, and water pursues her until, finally, she does drown. From the point of view of Eliot's art, water integrates into a general association with the female.

In some complicated way, Eliot has intertwined water with Maggie's own nature: an image in the novel which becomes mysteriously connected to something in the author. Maggie must struggle against water so that it defines her. It is the single element she must conquer if she is to emerge, and yet it is the "destructive element." Whenever she encounters it, she is neutralized or, finally, lost.

Water becomes the test of Maggie's endurance, fortitude, and ability to reach into herself; but if we turn it slightly, it becomes the imaginative element, the artistic force which will enable Eliot to turn around her life once and for all. In some transmuted way, water becomes the way in which Eliot must confront the artistic demons within. By intensifying it in each of its appearances, Eliot had made it something increasingly potent. The final scene in which Maggie is dragged down by Tom and water is a cautionary tale. Eliot's fear of being drawn in or devoured, manifest in so many other ways in her life, is dramatized in Maggie, who is entrapped in a life in which fulfillment—sexually, emotionally, and intellectually—becomes impossible.*

Eliot touched on this when Blackwood sent on to Rome Bulwer-Lytton's criticism, including his negative remarks on the Maggie–Stephen relationship. Her answer is crafted in such a way that we must see the autobiographical elements here.

> The other chief point of criticism—Maggie's position toward Stephen—is too vital a part of my whole conception and purpose for me to be converted to the condemnation of it. If I am wrong there—if I did not really know what my heroine would feel and do under the circumstances in which I deliberately placed her, I ought not to have written this book at all, but quite a different book, if any. If the ethics of art do not admit the truthful presentation of a character essentially noble but liable to great error—error which is anguish to its own nobleness—*then*, it seems to me, the ethics of art are too narrow, and must be widened to correspond with a widening psychology.

Maggie's flirtation with Stephen, and his with her, assumes some shadowy version of Marian Evans's running off with Lewes. In this formulation, Maggie must be stopped or punished by some exterior force symbolic of the inner dictates she feels she has traduced; the novel is saturated with feelings of guilt, alienation, depression, and marginality, all the qualities Eliot continued to describe in her letters and journal. And as for water, she views it as a suffusion, as part of a life always near drowning even when one is alive and seemingly functioning.

Rome was supposed to chase away these demons. That it succeeded to some extent we find in Eliot's astonishment she has suffered no headache since setting

---

* The shadow of Milton and *Paradise Lost* hovers over this formulation, in which the woman as the inheritor of the Eve–Satan myth can never be fulfilled socially or emotionally; any effort to break out is punished.

out from Holly Lodge. But she was ever anxious about Lewes's health, now that he was suffering from a "terrible oppression" of the head, with deafness on one side. She says that is the "dark crow" in their lives, since nearly everything else is perfect.* They were now settled in an apartment near the Piazza del Popolo, in center city. On Maundy Thursday, while at St. Peter's, Eliot knelt, along with everyone else, to receive the pope's blessing. She later spoke of Holy Week as a melancholy, hollow business, and regretted the time was not better spent. She says she does not feel any improvement as a result of the pope's act, and she assumes that the pope's curse—directed toward the king of Sardinia—would have a comparable effect. But on Good Friday, 6 April, the couple returned to hear the Miserere at St. Peter's. In his journal, Lewes comments about the nonsense they felt in being blessed, and at being present when the lodgings where they were staying were blessed by a young priest.

What is striking is that while Lewes and Eliot were enjoying the fruits of their relationship in a country they relished, even the favorable reviewers were hitting at the very relationship in *Mill* which shadows that of the couple—using the Maggie–Stephen incident to indict the author. The principals being blessed in Rome were, of course, quite different; and yet the "temptation," the near fall, the dare to society are parallel to those elements in the novel. In nearly every one of her books, Eliot toyed with the strategies of what she had done: it remained the central move of her life, and while she never regretted it, she also never forgot about it. She knew more about this aspect of life than any other English woman novelist, surely more than her contemporaries, the Brontës, or Mrs. Gaskell, or her earlier master, Jane Austen. Only George Sand, in France, could meet her on this ground, and the more astute reviewers of *Mill* and Eliot's other books observed the similarities.

Innocent of all this, the couple toured Rome, using Liddell's *History* of the city, with the kind of frenetic energy which belied their usual sedentary life. Eliot was interested in improving her Italian, which later on became fairly fluent. In her journal, she indicates how avidly they visited sites, using Coindet's *Histoire de la Peinture en Italie* as a guide to the museum collections. Since they knew nobody in Rome, they were thrown back upon each other and upon the city. In *Middlemarch*, Eliot recaptures some of this sightseeing, with Dorothea moving around without Casaubon, who was buried in his books. In the novel, the honeymoon—which does not appear to have included sexual consummation—proves a cold, gray affair for the young woman. Even St. Peter's, which Eliot found magical when illuminated, for Dorothea is a vast, dullish affair. Eliot and Lewes also visited suburban areas, such as Frascati, Tivoli, and Tusculum; but their desire to see Hadrian's villa was defeated by poor weather. Rome proved an exciting but mixed experience, a blending of the magnificent with the tawdry. Eliot did not see the city whole, as she saw Naples, Florence, and Venice.

---

* Reviews of *Mill* were also part of that perfection, although, except for the *Times*, Eliot was not to see any of them during her trip.

They arrived in Naples on 30 April, learning that Mudie's planned to take a third thousand of *Mill*; with this, the 6,000 copies printed were being brought to the reading public. In Naples, they took rooms at the Hôtel des Étrangers, with its views of the bay and Posilipo; and they used the city as a base from which they went to Pompeii, Salerno, Paestum, and the Amalfi Drive, returning to Naples by steamer. They appear indefatigable. On 13 May, they were back in Naples, and already preparing for the major leg, Florence, via Civitavecchia. Besides taking in the usual sights in Florence—the Uffizi, the Accademia della Bella Arte, Santo Marco (for the Fra Angelicos), Brunelleschi's dome, Giotto's Campanile, the Bargello (for Donatello's *David*), the Duomo, and other famous churches such as Santo Spirito, Santa Croce, and Santa Maria Novella—they made several excursions. These, too, were the usual places—Boboli, the Cascine, Fiesole, and San Miniato. The couple eventually went to Siena, and were suitably impressed by its lovely location and the charm of its streets and main piazza.

They visited the Villino Trollope—Mrs. Trollope was in attendance—on 30 May, but were not overly impressed. In her journal (31 May), Eliot indicates that setting a novel in the time of Savonarola—whom Lewes had been reading about in a guidebook—would test her powers: it would be a "historical romance," quite different from Sir Walter Scott's type, but saturated with the time and place. They decided, as a team, to do some immediate research on Savonarola. At San Marco, Lewes visited the monastery (women were excluded) and took notes for a possible project. They got hold of Savonarola's poems and a book about him, in French, and examined a manuscript of his in the Magliabecchian Library. They viewed a painting by Pollaiulo called *The Death of Savonarola* and saw the Great Hall in the Palazzo Vecchio, which had been built under the spiritual leader's direction. All of this was, of course, superficial. If Eliot were to write of Florence, she would have to return and bury herself in documents—ironically in much the same way as Casaubon on his honeymoon in Rome with Dorothea. *

Throughout this time, Eliot was keeping up a good front. Behind their excursions and sightseeing, behind her sudden glimmer of a new project, was her apprehension about the reception of *Mill*. Pretending to be indifferent, she was, in effect, most eager to hear about it. She asked Blackwood about reviews and gave their address. Commercially, as we have seen, the novel was selling above expectations, having almost gone through 6,000 copies in the early months. In fact, when William Blackwood wrote on 23 May, an additional 500 had been printed. He assured Eliot that except for one or two obscure newspapers, the notices had been favorable, and the *Times* review could be expected to perk up even greater interest. It was, possibly, the single most important review an author could receive, something akin to the present-day Sunday *New York Times Book Review*. When John wrote two days later, he rejoiced in the sales and

---

* The name "Romola" itself possibly came from a hamlet in Italy of that name, just southwest of Florence.

South Farm, formerly known as Arbury Farm, Eliot's birthplace outside
Nuneaton.

George Eliot's baptismal entry (as Mary Anne Evans), in Chilvers Coton
Church, dated one week after her birth on 22 November 1819.

Arbury Hall, seat of the Newdigate family; Cheverel Manor in "Mr Gilfil's Love-Story," in Scenes of Clerical Life.

Griff House, the corner where Eliot had her room when she was growing up.

Griff House, with the contemporary printing above the bottom right window, now a restaurant.

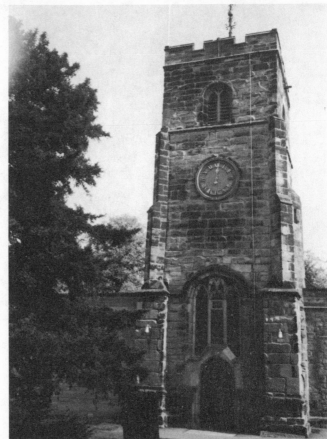

Chilvers Coton, the model for Shepperton Church in "Amos Barton," in Scenes of Clerical Life.

Robert Evans, Eliot's father, in 1842;
in part the model for Adam Bede in that novel
and for Caleb Garth in Middlemarch.

*Two photos of Charles
Bray, the "Don Juan of
Coventry"; Bray and his
wife, Cara, provided the
young Eliot with an intellectual home away from home.*

Sara Hennell and Cara Bray, about 1850, both of them important figures in Eliot's early intellectual development.

George Eliot in 1850,
painted by François D'Albert-Durade
in Geneva, Switzerland.

John Chapman, *editor of the* Westminster Review, *who opened up London's intellectual life for Eliot in the early 1850s.*

Herbert Spencer in 1855, the philosopher and social scientist whom Eliot misjudged as a potential husband.

George Eliot in 1858,
an etching by Paul Adolphe Rajon,
made in 1884 from a photograph.

Emma Gwyther's grave, at Chilvers Coton, used for Milly's grave in Shepperton Church in "Amos Barton."

George Henry Lewes in 1859, Eliot's companion from 1854 until his death in 1878.

Isaac Pearson Evans, Eliot's brother;
in part the model for Tom Tulliver
in The Mill on the Floss.

George Eliot in 1860,
from a chalk drawing by Samuel Laurence,
signed and misdated 1857.

Barbara Bodichon (born Barbara Leigh Smith),
one of Eliot's most loyal friends,
an early supporter of women's rights and
a co-founder of Girton College, Cambridge.

The Heights at Witley, in Surrey, the country home of Eliot and Lewes, purchased at the end of 1876.

George Henry Lewes's tombstone, in Highgate Cemetery, London.

George Eliot's grave in Highgate Cemetery, London,
located in unconsecrated ground next to
her friend Elma Stuart's and George Henry Lewes's.

Two views of the
George Eliot memorial in
the center of Nuneaton,
the bronze statue by
a Warwickshire artist,
John Letts.

mentioned that he thought through the arrangement Eliot would make as much as the most speculative publisher would have offered her.

Yet little of this really settled her, for she feared that disclosure of George Eliot as Marian Evans Lewes would reverberate into attacks on the novel; and she was not entirely incorrect, since some spoke of an immoral work produced, it was intimated, by an immoral woman.* Lewes's journal shared this fear, that the loss of incognito might have a real effect on the book's reception, the implication being that the book could be attacked as a cover for an attack on the author. It was in these creases, some of it anxiety, some of it paranoia, some of it quite real, that Eliot found her fears accumulating. She knew how rumor runs roughshod over explanations and subtleties.

Her ultra-sensitivity surfaces in remarks she made to her old friend D'Albert-Durade. D'Albert-Durade was doing a French translation of *Mill* (he would translate many of Eliot's works), but this was not the occasion of her letter. It was to caution him not to write her again "about criticism or remarks in French journals or reviews." She adds that she has warned her publisher not to forward any newspaper critiques to her, and that the *Times* review should be the sole exception. Writing for the ages about most newspaper reviewing, she says: "Journalistic criticism does good to no author; it is written by incompetent men who are not even doing their best, and it is utterly indecisive as to the ultimate rank of any book."

Having hinted to Blackwood about what she called an "ambitious project," Eliot was so vague about it he was unable to determine anything definite. She says she intends to keep it a secret, and possibly one reason for the secrecy was its personal nature. A young woman, Romola, whose life is given over entirely to her father's needs—a blind father, at that!—a woman who has suppressed all gaiety and passion, was coming close to Marian Evans as she tended Robert Evans. When Romola does emerge, she comes forth in much the same way as Maggie Tulliver. Romola's "Stephen Guest" is Tito Melema, the superficial Englishman reborn in the self-serving, amiable, treacherous Greek who turns up in Florence. And Romola comes to recognize she has exchanged service to a blind father for service to a man who is blind to moral nuances. Her passage is intimately linked to Marian's own as she went from Evans to Chapman, from Coventry to London. That she was writing a cautionary tale, directed not only at women but at herself, may explain her conspiratorial air.

On 1 June, the couple left Florence for Bologna, on their way to Venice. They also stopped at Savonarola's birthplace in Ferrera, then went on to Padua (for the Giottos), and finally Venice. At her hotel on the Grand Canal, Eliot enjoyed with Lewes a Venetian experience she would repeat with her young husband, John Cross, after Lewes's death.

---

* Haight indicates that the *Punch* circle called the book "dreary and immoral," and reports that Langford, Blackwood's London man, heard such remarks at the Garrick Club. The *Punch* group felt that Bradbury and Evans were fortunate in not having acquired it.

Having sampled what Venice offered—led through by a cicerone named Domenico—they went on to Desenzano, Milan, Lake Como, and Bellagio, at the confluence of three lakes, which Eliot found exquisite and magical. From there they worked their way into Switzerland, via the Splügen Pass to Chur, where they entrained for Zurich. Zurich was within a short distance of Lewes's sons at Hofwyl. They came to meet their new "mother" (*Mutter* to them). They were by now sweet, understanding young men, and although puzzled how to respond to their new mother—since their friends had met their other mother, Agnes—they made the transition with a minimum of fuss.

Charles, the oldest, had completed school and accompanied them to Geneva, where they decided to meet the D'Albert-Durades. The Swiss couple had yet to be introduced to Lewes, and the encounter came off with great warmth. Lewes was pleased to observe their happiness in seeing Marian and to note how deeply she had once entered into their lives. Another part of their mission was to find a place for Thornie, the second son, in Geneva, and Eliot's friends agreed to look after him, for 3,000 francs for the year. But Lewes found he could not afford this amount, and, for some reason, Eliot did not contribute. In any event, Thornie was removed from any potential continental apprenticeship as a scientific or medical man and instead was sent to Edinburgh, to be prepared for English examinations under a Dr. Schmitz. The aim was to have him bone up for the East Indian service, where with the right moves and sufficient callousness, a young man could make his fortune. No one considered that these intelligent young men, Thornie or Charles, should try for the university. Thornie, perhaps, was not fully suited for a university career, although he seemed naturally inclined toward the sciences; but Charles was well disciplined, eager to learn, and might have benefited enormously. Lewes, it is true, with his multifold expenses, could not afford the outlay; but with their combined income their lack of larger concern for the boys appears strange. Or else, the way in which their concern was expressed seemed to underestimate the qualities of the boys they evidently loved very much.

Eliot, Lewes, and Charles started the long trip back, to arrive at Holly Lodge on 1 July. Their plan, while Thornie remained on hold, was to locate a position for Charles in the civil service, and this, with his own intelligence as a help, was not difficult. They applied for information to Anthony Trollope, who knew everyone in the postal service, and Trollope wrote to the Duke of Argyll, the postmaster general. Coached by Lewes and Eliot, Charles took the qualifying examination, passed easily, and found a position in the postal service at £80 a year, in the secretary's office.

While Blackwood was attempting to ferret out Eliot's "grand secret" about her new book, she and Lewes were house-hunting. They were disenchanted with Holly Lodge, and Charles needed something nearer for commutation to his office. They could either buy a house—which meant a permanent residence and a commitment of time and money—or continue to rent, which allowed them more mobility. Eliot knew she would have to return to Florence for extensive research, and that mitigated against the purchase of a house. They did, never-theless, offer £1,600 for a residence near Gloucester Gate, which is within a short distance of central London, but their offer was insufficient. There was still another factor, the central one running through Eliot's entire adult career, and that was her uncertainty about living in London altogether, given her irregular relationship with Lewes in the eyes of others.

Instead of the permanent connection to a purchased home, the couple rented a furnished one at 10 Harewood Square, off Kings Road, in the Walham Green section of London, and moved in on 24 September. But Eliot quickly became displeased with its interior appearance, and within three months they were once again house-hunting. This time they moved to 16 Blandford Square, just off Regent's Park, where they could use their own furniture. The lease was for three years, which Eliot figured would give the boys a chance to establish themselves and then she and Lewes could calculate their assets and make a more definitive move. All of this shifting around meant, of course, that she was tied up with household matters—arranging, purchasing, planning, and the like. With her imagination full of plans, and with so much money to be made from these plans, the time lost on household matters was a source of anxiety and anguish.

In the move, her favorite pen was lost, one that she had used for the last eight years. She was disconsolate, perhaps because this loss seemed to connect to other losses, some very palpable. She did not wish to see Sara Hennell, and her comments to her old friend about the latter's books were barely civil. She saw less and less of Mrs. Congreve, her neighbor at Holly Lodge. At 16 Blandford Square, she was close to Barbara Bodichon, who lived on occasion at Number 5 but spent her winters in Algeria. But losses were not measured only in terms of possessions or friends. If we take the ending of *Mill* seriously, she was also getting lost in conflicting ideas.

The major problem comes with her attempt to transform the human conflict in *Mill* by means of a natural event. The structuring of the novel which gave even sympathetic critics pause was associated with her catastrophic resolution of forces. The major thrust, connected to Maggie, was the latter's inability to work through her desire for knowledge and her feelings of suppressed passion within her role as a responsible woman, as a daughter and as a sister. The weight of her burden becomes so great she attempts, in some fantasy, a breakout with Stephen, or at least contemplates it. All of these fictional elements are human, set deeply within Maggie's warring faculties. And yet when Eliot attempts to resolve them, she must do it with a natural disaster which washes away both the problems and the people suffering them. The natural, inexorable force of the flood inundates free will and choice.

The conflict suggests considerable turmoil in Eliot below the surface of her letters and journal. It suggests she had reached a critical period in which her ideology was insufficient for the stories she planned to write; or, conversely, her fiction had an engine of its own which disregarded her attempts to resolve the conflicts.

Writing to Bray about a new edition of his book *The Education of the Feelings,* as well as Cara's *Physiology for Common Schools* (1860),* Eliot veered into personal matters. She says there is so much she wants to do every day that she needs to cut herself into four women: writer, stepmother, wife, housekeeper. She speaks of caring for their "big boy Charley," who was then prepping for the government postal examination. She calls him "the most entirely lovable human animal of seventeen and a half, that I have ever met with or heard of: he has a sweetness of disposition which is saved from weakness by a remarkable sense of duty." Astonishingly, all three boys seemed to have survived their parents' irregular personal lives, very possibly because Lewes astutely sent them far from the scene. By the time they returned to England, they were mature enough to accept Lewes's arrangement with Eliot, who in domestic matters was kindness itself. Just as Lewes had become her husband, so the boys became her sons. Whatever people might say, she had her family.

She sat for another portrait, by Samuel Laurence, the artist who drew the chalk head of Thackeray. Her comment was that Laurence was an interesting man, with "plenty of sadness in his life, like the rest of us." Eliot was moving toward her forty-first birthday.

There was little, overtly, to be sad about. Charles, as noted above, passed his examination at the top of the competition. Lewes had himself come into £256 for his *Physiology of Common Life,* far more than anticipated. *The Mill on the Floss* was about to go into a cheaper edition, generating more income. But news from the firm was not good. Major William Blackwood was ill, as it turned out with an incurable disease. August of 1860, however, was most notable for Eliot's short fiction "Brother Jacob," written while the couple was still at Holly Lodge, before the contemplated move to Harewood Square. "Brother Jacob," while psychologically interesting, seems odd in Eliot's canon even if we agree she was waiting on more significant material to come forth to be shaped into a novel.

It concerns an unscrupulous young man, David Faux, who steals money from his mother's hoard—but only after pacifying his idiot brother (Jacob)—and then runs off to the Indies, returns, opens a confectionary shop in a small town, becomes engaged to a pleasant young woman, and is revealed as a fraud by the sudden appearance of the idiot brother. The entire work, of some forty pages, is done with tongue in cheek; the style is arch, affected, always reaching for something amusing, but missing along the way. It clunks and creaks, all efforts at wit misfiring.

In psychological terms, the story has resonances, since it works on a secret, the hoard hidden by David's mother; then the secret background of David in

---

* Her frayed relationship to her Coventry friends can be picked up in a letter to Sara of 27–28 August. Eliot spelled out that they had parted ways. "I am very sorry that anything I have written should have pained you. *That* certainly is the result I should most seek to avoid in the very slight communication which we are able to keep up—necessarily under extremely imperfect acquaintance with each other's self." Eliot makes her point clear: "You do not know me well enough as I *am* (according to the doctrine of development which you have yourself expended) to have the materials for interpreting my imperfect expressions." They are by now, she insists, speaking different languages.

the Indies, his disguise under a new name when he returns, his reshaping of himself as the owner of a confectionary shop. Secrets and a money hoard would become the substance, also, of *Silas Marner;* but they were already elements in Marian Evans's life—a name change, a reshaping of self, a multiplication of money, and overall a life lived within several reshapings. But there are still other factors in "Brother Jacob" which seem personally connected, shadowy elements which make the work, while not artistically compelling, autobiographically relevant.

The basic situation is itself significant: a young man decides to get his start in life by stealing from his parents, so that his entire later success depends on an act he must hide. In committing this act, he must trick an idiot brother, Jacob, into forgetting that golden guineas are being stolen, and he does this by tempting him with a steady supply of lozenges, a forerunner of the sweets and goodies in David's confectionary shop. David's name is Faux, which, like the other names in the story, has an eighteenth-century farcical element, but also the symbolism of falseness, trickery, hypocrisy. He later becomes Freely, and there are also Palfrey, Towers, a town called Grimworth, and minor figures called Crypt, Prettyman, Fullilove.

Within this basically throwaway piece, Eliot moved in and out of the secret self of her own life. In her perception of her act, she "steals away," she deceives an idiot brother (Isaac?), and she achieves success based, in the world's view, on what is an act of treachery and theft. In order to reshape her life, she has stolen something, is living a lie, is forced to disguise her background. She rakes over the background of a successful man, until he is unveiled, disgraced, and remarginalized. At the end he is deemed a victim of Nemesis herself: the Greek goddess of retribution.

However unsteady the work, it reveals great fears in the author, if we assume this reading of the story. Behind her great success lay a sense it could all collapse, that her shaping powers were given to her only to be taken away, and that off in the not-too-distant future Nemesis awaited her. Her "great secret," however she perceived it, would be uncovered; she would be disgraced, and she would, like David, flee Grimworth (a personal hell), never to be heard of again. It was, we can assume, a condition a woman more than a man might fear. These internal feelings went well beyond any external compensations; they were the very stuff of an existence no popular or critical reward could allay.

We catch some of this in a letter to Mrs. Peter Alfred Taylor, an early feminist and a woman who wrote Eliot very generously and approvingly first in 1856 and then thereafter, when she needed all the support she could receive. After thanking Mrs. Taylor for having written recently when most persons who knew anything of her were disposed to judge her harshly, Eliot gets to the core of her response, which is that she is not to be addressed as "Miss Evans." Her reply (on 1 April 1861) indicates an insistence, even an obsession, about her new life.

For the last six years I have ceased to be "Miss Evans" for any one who has personal relations with me—having held myself under all the responsibilities of a married woman. I wish this to be distinctly understood; and when I tell you that we have a great boy of eighteen at home who calls me "mother," as well as two other boys, almost as tall, who write to me under the same name, you will understand that the point is not one of mere egoism or personal dignity, when I request that any one who has a regard for me will cease to speak of me by my maiden name.

In a follow-up letter on 6 April (1861), Eliot stated unequivocally that in London she never pays visits. She ascribes that to lack of a carriage and her "easily perturbed health." In fact, there was virtually nobody she could visit, carriage or not. In most homes, wives would not accept her. Mrs. Taylor agreed to visit, since Eliot would not. Eliot's insistence here was that she had constructed shifting defenses around herself in order to protect *and justify* the kind of life she was leading. She could never merely "settle in."

On 28 August (1860), Eliot decided to tip her hand to John Blackwood about her literary career. She revealed her plans for *Romola* and *Silas Marner*. She wanted the Florence tale to be published without any name in *Maga* and "subsequently reprinted with the name of George Eliot." She resisted divulgation in *Maga* because everyone knows how a writer who does something unexpected is greeted. By the end of September, Eliot began *Silas Marner*, which became one of her most popular novels. While not a major achievement, it is a treasure trove, not only of Silas's money, but of revelations about its author and her perception of herself. She had found a mythical element, a treasure in which to express profound psychological and emotional matters. Blackwood was taken with her plans, saying that her doubts are better than other people's certainties. He also foresaw large sales following the great success of *Mill.*

The beginning of *Silas Marner*, however, would have to wait until the couple moved from their present quarters at Holly Lodge, the move finally occurring near the end of September. Eliot was characteristically depressed by the situation—the miseries of moving, as she called it. The impending experience of town life did not make her happy, and, as we shall see, several of the familiar ailments returned: not because of the poor London air, but surely because of what she felt was a hostile atmosphere for a woman like her. Eliot's journal now is full of trivial details, mainly logistics concerning a move that would turn out to last only three months. Her misery comes through loud and clear, although she attempted, she says, to restrain her complaints.

Money was coming in from *Mill*, the first payment of £1,000 and another £2,250 still to be paid at intervals. But while funds were plentiful, Eliot missed the regular walks with Mrs. Congreve, back in Wandsworth. She had little company now, although in her next move she would begin to see a good deal of Lewes's mother, who appeared quite proud of her new daughter-in-law. In the evenings, she and Lewes, along with Charles, went to hear a series of ten lectures on chemistry by Dr. A. W. Hofman at the Museum of Economic Geology, beginning on 17 October. Eliot enjoyed this kind of thing not only because of her desire to keep up with the sciences, but as a way of keeping her brain alive;

she learned new languages for much the same reason. She reported to Sara, in still distant but calmer tones than when commenting on her friend's book ideas, that she and Lewes spend most of their time alone, almost always at home, husbanding their energies rather than expending them on social expectations.

Although *Mill* was heading into a fourth edition, Blackwood's report on sales showed a downturn for it, but a continued market for *Adam Bede* and *Scenes*. He assured her that whatever carping critics might say of *Mill* no one could deny the power and "the extraordinary fertility of the author's resources." He hoped she would not bother herself with doubts.

Another contretemps with Sara arose when she planned to come to London and asked to stay with Eliot and Lewes. Needing an excuse to hold off her former friend, Eliot used Lewes's quirky disposition as the vehicle. She says Lewes finds a visitor so incompatible with his ability to do his work that no one is permitted to stay. "He will hear of no one for more than *one* night, except my niece Emily [Chrissey's daughter]." But there is more: Eliot would like Sara to see them in their own house, when they have moved to Blandford Square, not in this "yellow" place. With that, Sara's invasion was resisted.

Eliot admits she feels languor, depression, an inability to confront the demands of life. She senses self-distrust and despair, and only some tonic recommended by the eminent surgeon Erasmus Wilson has brought her around. Her journal for 28 November—just after her forty-first birthday and perhaps somewhat the cause for despair—says it all. "Since I last wrote in this Journal I have suffered much from physical weakness accompanied with mental depression. The loss of the country [home] has seemed very bitter to me, and my want of health and strength has prevented me from working much—still worse, has made me despair for ever working well again."

But amidst these complaints, she asserts her "cup is full of blessings," in that her home is bright and warm with "love and tenderness" and her income is high. She says with possible false modesty that they have enough to keep them from beggary, having just invested £2,000 in East Indies stock, with another £200 to be invested shortly. The move to Blandford Square on 17 December did not relieve her malaise and depression. Although London drew her because of its cultural offerings,* it also made her ill, like some swamp whose vapors slowly overcome those who live near it.

She was gratified to receive D'Albert-Durade's French translation of *Adam Bede*; as for *Mill*, she had a choice of titles, *Le Moulin de Dorlcote* or *Sur le Floss*, but she left the final decision to her friend. As it turned out, the French was far more expansive than the English: *La famille Tulliver, ou le moulin sur le Floss*. Settled now in their new house for the next three years, Eliot could rail against the fates that decreed she must fritter away her time in housekeeping, arranging furniture, shopping, and the like. Her letter to Barbara Bodichon is a litany of complaints: she has been ailing for weeks, has lacked spirit to write, was filled

---

* Such as the concerts at St. James's Hall. Music remained an abiding pleasure for Eliot, as listener and as performer on the piano(s) she and Lewes always kept.

with the anxieties of the move, and was immersed in pots and kettles. But the larger news came near the end of the long letter (26 December) in which Eliot's remarks indicate they have consulted a barrister about the possibility of Lewes obtaining a divorce abroad. The barrister pronounced the chance "impossible."* Eliot: "I am not sorry. I think the boys will not suffer, and for myself I prefer excommunication. I have no earthly thing that I care for, to gain by being brought within the pale of people's personal attention and I have many things to care for that I should lose—my freedom from petty worldly torments, commonly called pleasures, and that isolation which really keeps my charity warm instead of chilling it, as much contact with frivolous women would do."

Eliot's reasoning on this explosive issue is curious. She locates most of her response to the possible divorce, and then remarriage, in the fact that regularization of her position would force her into social intercourse she finds repugnant. She does not present it as a means of settling her affairs or creating a normalized arrangement good in itself, but as something which will lead to further burdens. The curious part of her explanation is that it seems such an evasion: for while we know she might revel in the irregularities of her arrangement, another side of her was not so happy with her secret life, as evidenced by her frequent ailments, headaches, and bouts of depression. What her conscious self was telling her was not what her unconscious was informing her.

On 29 December, as a somewhat belated Christmas present, she received £1,300 from Blackwood: £1,000 for the second installment of *Mill*, £150 for *Adam Bede*, and £150 for the still healthy *Scenes*. More was promised in the spring; and for a person who was now so keyed in to money, Eliot saw this as one of the "blessings" she had experienced in 1860. In a large respect, this and the following year would be dominated by money—and by the doubts and uncertainties such large sums brought with them. Meanwhile, her journal dated the last day of 1860 does record that it had not been a fruitful time for work, and that her inability to sit for a long pull at her desk was the result of poor health and depression.

With the move to Blandford Square, however, she could look forward to three years of relative quiet, and a sudden burst of energy on *Silas Marner*— thirteen chapters would be sent to Blackwood on 15 February—indicates how rapidly she could turn herself around. But even that burst of energy could not disguise the fact that she felt low and feeble, caught in a depressive cycle. So forceful are her complaints that even Blackwood, not usually given to personal intervention, expressed concern. He counsels her that she needs exercise.

Silas Marner, a book which probes profoundly into shadows of its author's own life, finally surfaces. "I am writing a story," she says, "which came *across* my other plans by a sudden inspiration. I don't know at present whether it will resolve itself into a book short enough for me to complete before Easter. . . . it

---

* The matter of divorce was a burning issue through the 1850s, and even though nearly all considerations favored men, Lewes had so compromised his position he fell outside all laws in England and the continent. A Scottish divorce may have been possible, but that, too, involved problems.

seems to me that nobody will take any interest in it but myself, for it is extremely unlike the popular stories going. . . ." Lewes, however, said it was as good as anything she had done, just the reinforcement she required.

*Silas Marner** did not come by "a sudden inspiration." It was a natural progression, embodying in imagined episodes and characters qualities intimately wedded to Eliot herself. Marner's obsession with money is not to be neglected as Eliot and Lewes build up their fortune, including piles of investments, nor is the sudden appearance of a child who saves Marner to be disengaged from the appearance of Charles in Eliot's life. Further, Marner's basic marginality and isolation—his solitary work at his loom, his social estrangement—are not to be ignored in the light of Eliot's own profession at her desk and her own disinclination for social life and fear of scandal. Money dooms, even as one devours it; and the love of a child saves. Work itself is, also, salvational: lonely work, without anyone intruding or criticizing.

Eliot confessed she felt "timid" in her writing, and perhaps that was the result of her worry about houses and servants and the boys. With her energy sapped, she nevertheless hoped her new quiet might bring fictional renewal. *Silas Marner* was written in and around just this sense of living in a trough. Another source of company was Lewes's mother, Mrs. John Willim, who, while she remained on good terms with Agnes,† was proud of her son's second wife. She and Eliot met for the first time in 1860, and then when the couple moved to Blandford Square near the end of that year, they were close enough for her to visit. Her complaints were legion, most of them related to her eighty-six-year-old irritating husband, Captain Willim, whom she often threatened to leave. At one point, Lewes said she could live with them, although we do not know Eliot's opinion about this. The irony was that while Lewes's mother was admiring of her daughter-in-law's fame (and riches, one should add), Eliot's own family remained not only distant but silent.

The portrait Samuel Laurence made of her at this time, in 1860, is pensive, quite sad—as opposed to the more forceful Mayall / Rajon etching, a retouched photograph. The 1860 drawing does bear out Eliot's own dismal assessment of herself, so undefined is the face, despite the dominant long nose. Her lips are not expressive, and there is no hint of animation. Part of the taste in drawing then was based on pre-Raphaelite painting and drawing, which emphasized the pensive, faraway look. Eliot surely has that—she stares into the distance, without clear focus or definition, or even interest. What is so striking about her oval

---

* It appeared as *Silas Marner: The Weaver of Raveloe;* the words "A Story by George Eliot" were originally considered, then deleted. The manuscript, if the one at the British Library is her original and not a clean copy, shows how certain she was of direction and phrasing. The main change: William Waif in the manuscript becomes William Dane in the first edition; Waif, or Dane, is the man who betrays Marner in Lantern Yard.

† Agnes occasionally visited the Eliot household when Lewes was there. An enlarged psychological profile of Lewes based on speculation could be mounted: that while his devotion to Eliot was clear, he relished the notoriety of his position and considered himself, bigamously, wedded to both women. It was surely a boost to his ego that two such different types—and Agnes was no intellectual slouch—were attached to him.

face, pensive eyes, long nose, hair parted in the middle and falling artlessly is the lack of definition such a powerhouse of a person projects. All the tensions and divisions remained securely hidden, part of a secret self.

The month of January (1861) proved so unrelentingly grim that she and Lewes decided to flee the city for the country. With Charles, they went to Dorking,* twenty miles south of London, in Surrey, for an overnight, and then themselves stayed on in the area until Tuesday. The fresh air appeared to energize her, for, as noted, she enjoyed a long pull on *Silas Marner*.

In a completely different area, that of political life, as we survey Eliot's responses in early 1861, we notice she has passed through several years in the 1850s with virtually no comment on the Crimean War or on other issues of the day. Except for a brief notice of the ratification of the English–Russian peace treaty of 1856, her letters and journal indicate no involvement in that larger world, or no desire to set down her thoughts. The Crimean War, in particular, should have created some interest, especially since Lewes and Eliot knew people close to Florence Nighingale; but even in its own right, the war brought forth serious political realignments in southeastern Europe and changed the course of England's political relationship with Russia. England's other movements into North Africa, into central and South Africa, its intermittent wars with Zulus in the south and with Muslims in the north, and its campaigns in India and Afghanistan are all missing from Eliot's correspondence. There is almost no mention of the government, except, perhaps, her note that Queen Victoria was reading *Mill*. The change of prime ministers, the advent of Disraeli (whom she distrusted), his challenge by Gladstone, and the deep policy splits this represented do not appear to have engaged her thought. It is all the more strange because Lewes was himself interested in a broad range of subjects, and their conversation must have taken up political and social ideas. Further, their friend Herbert Spencer was deeply immersed in social issues, and not only theoretically.

There are several explanations, one being that the couple had so turned in on themselves, creating an island impenetrable by the rest of the world, that their isolated state excluded that larger world. Even when Eliot did respond to political life, as in *Felix Holt, the Radical,* and then *Middlemarch,* her focus is localized; whatever national issues are involved are subsumed in a local election. Larger questions of policy and political ideology are marginalized. This leads us to another explanation, that because Eliot wrote so intimately about personal history and related beliefs, projected imaginatively into her fiction, she consciously excluded anything she could not experience directly. Her distinctive voice derived from her assimilation of all policy questions into moral behavior, into ethical decisions, the sole things that counted for her.

On 15 February, she sent Blackwood 230 pages of manuscript, about 100

---

* Dorking was known for its fine walking trails and its Leith Hill, the highest point in southeastern England. Walking such lanes and climbing were a tonic for both Eliot and Lewes. Another great walker, George Meredith, who often visited the couple, is buried in Dorking.

pages under what she estimated would be the final length of *Silas Marner*. She was hurrying along as she wanted an Easter publication—Easter Sunday was 31 March, and *Marner* appeared two days later. Blackwood's response to the first 100 pages was admiring, although he wished the "picture had been a more cheery one and embraced higher specimens of humanity," but, he added, "you paint so naturally that in your hands the veriest earthworms become most interesting perfect studies in fact." He sees the child, Eppie, as restoring Marner to a more Christian frame of mind. He comments further that his sole objection is the absence of "brighter lights and some characters of whom one can think with pleasure as fellow creatures. . . ." He looks forward to this in the remainder of the manuscript. The question then becomes whether he should offer one volume at 12 shillings or two smaller volumes. He assures her, in a remark that makes the contemporary reader breathless, that he can put the whole into type in a very few days.

Eliot agreed it should be one volume, and then tried to explain the tale's somberness. She says Nemesis is very mild here, and the entire purpose of the story is heuristic, to reveal the "remedial influence of pure, natural human relations." She adds: "it came to me first of all, quite suddenly, as a sort of legendary tale, suggested by my recollection of having once, in early childhood, seen a linen-weaver with a bag on his back; but, as my mind dwelt on the subject, I became inclined to a more realistic treatment." She says she wants to publish the story now because she likes her works to appear in the order she wrote them, since they represent successive mental phases. "Brother Jacob," not published until 1864, was an exception.

In response, Blackwood offered generous terms of £800 for an edition of 4,000 copies, payable six months from publication, and a like payment for any copies sold beyond the 4,000. He hoped to sell 5,000–6,000 copies, although the library sale might be smaller than expected because of one-volume (as against three-decker) publication. He was sanguine that would be offset by private purchasers, willing to put out 12 shillings for one volume, whereas they would not spend over a pound and a half for three.

Eliot accepted the terms and asked for an advertisement saying "New Work by George Eliot," and the novel to be called *Silas Marner, the Weaver of Raveloe*. By 4 March, Eliot sent on more manuscript, seeing the end in about thirty pages. Her motto for the title page derives from Wordsworth's poem "Michael": "A child more than all other gifts / That earth can offer to declining man, / Brings hope with it, and forward-looking thoughts." By 10 March, final pages were delivered to the firm. *Marner* emerged as if Eliot had been programmed for it. Lewes told Blackwood he was occasionally made anxious (his word) by her belittling of what she writes. We may assume that only by perceiving her writing as triumphing over her disabilities—ill health, perception of failure, inability to achieve her ideals—could she produce the writing itself. It was a product of a poor self-image, which she could transform into the strength of the word, in some kind of transmutation of self into language. It was a workable arrangement.

By the 18th, proofs had been dispatched to Eliot, read, and returned, with an advance copy in hand a week later. She presented a copy, the sole one so presented, to Lewes's mother. With the original printing expanded to 8,000 copies, income for *Silas Marner,* including reprint rights and translations, came to £1,760 in 1861. On the 18th, the couple left for Hastings, * on the south Channel coast in East Sussex, for a week of walking the beach, looking for mollusks, getting London out of their systems. It seemed on the surface a good time, a book completed, the idea for the Italian novel taking shape, their physical health still able to withstand rigorous trips and excursions. On 26 March, they returned to Blandford Square, to await publication of *Silas Marner.*

Specific biographical similarities between Eliot and Marner are even more compelling than general ones. In one respect, Eliot was interested in regeneration of a lost soul, or in the restoration of spiritual life in someone who had focused exclusively on hard, unyielding matter. In another respect, she was eager to castigate the squirearchy for its dissolution, its thievery, its lack of moral principle, its failure even to recognize its own daughter. By this means, she could laud the working class, who appear as honest, hardworking, and focused. In a third way, she was attempting to reveal how guilt must eventually be confronted: that the really evil are punished—Dunstan in drowning, Molly in freezing during an opium stupor—while Godfrey is saved by facing the truth. In a fourth respect, she was interested in textures themselves: soft versus hard, gullible versus strident, the warmth of the cottage hearth versus the coolness of the large house on the hill. In still a further respect—and here we have the engine that drives the novel—Eliot used the material as a personal myth, as the myth of Marian Evans / Mrs. Lewes / George Eliot: what she believed, both consciously and unconsciously, and how she could emerge in the question of a theft.

The accumulation and then theft of Marner's money has certain intimate overtones for the author. The "theft" does seem linked to Eliot's uncertainty about her work, her inability to listen to even the slightest criticism, her sense of her writing as falling beneath the highest achievement, and her more generalized fear that everything was precarious. The theft, to this extent, is linked to deep inner anxieties that it all might vanish, that something—destiny, circumstance, Nemesis—was waiting to dispossess her of her gifts, and it would all be swallowed up as rapidly as it appeared. This is not too different from the lifting of the veil, in that story, which leads to disillusionment, not clarification.

That could be one area of theft which parallels Marner's loss of his treasure trove, but perhaps not the major one. A more central view would be that Eliot saw herself as part of a "theft." She had "stolen" Agnes's husband; she was the thieving receiver of someone else's children, Lewes's boys; she had stolen a particular kind of life in the face of social opprobrium. This view depends on how

---

* Hastings was notable for being one of the Cinque Ports, five fortified ports constructed in the Middle Ages to protect southeastern England against invaders from the continent. The other ports were Romney, Dover, Sandwich, and Hythe, extending into Kent.

deeply Eliot confronted her position and how much credibility she gave to it. But if we read her remarks and asides correctly, we know she felt profoundly distressed about her social ostracism and isolation and had developed several defenses to protect herself. Her perception is of someone who has stolen what clearly does not belong to her.

Related to theft is guilt and, not distant from that, the "myth" of Eliot, of a person sinking, shaping, and reshaping. Money—the hoard, the treasure, the mystique of a kind of power—is the "other" which provides a false sense of security or an artificial self. Also not far off is sibling rivalry, which by *Silas Marner* had become a constant in her work—here deadly in its implications. * Many of these relationships, as in *Marner*, contain disturbing elements, from mere rivalry to outright hostility and hatred. Intertwined with all in this novel is a not unrelated reaction, guilt.

The fact that this novel is not major Eliot does not lessen the biographical weight. For guilt here is part of the condemnation of money at just the time Eliot and Lewes were becoming particularly greedy about building a fortune, or creating a treasure trove, well beyond their personal needs. The condemnation does not take the form of a Marxist or other social critique of money but is based solidly on a Christian view of Jesus driving the moneylenders from the temple and by so doing condemning the accumulation of a hoard. The classical myths of a warrior chasing after a treasure—Jason and the golden fleece, and others— are brought into play in Marner's humble cottage, and there subjected to a Christian critique. The play of elements in Eliot is compelling: the idea of a treasure as a compensation for past injustices; an absorption in the hard but dead matter of coins, the fascination with the golden glitter; the character's social withdrawal and isolation while the hoard accumulates; the compensatory life which comes, essentially, from fingering dead matter, the despair and depression implicit in this solitary act; the sexual connotations of this lonely activity, the manipulation of piles of coins, of arrangement, the need to keep touching so as to create a "reality"; the perversion implied here, of an unconscious drive to accumulate power even as one's actual position loses it; the perverse act of writing itself, the self-absorption and even narcissism translated into money, whether in piles of glittering coins or in securities and bank accounts.

Much of the activity occurs at the hearth in Marner's cottage—with the hearth taking on its classical role as a holy place where the gods of hearth and home (the Roman Lares and Penates) are honored for their protection. Here Marner fingers and counts his money; here he compensates for the loss of money with the child Eppie; and here he redeems himself as a social being. That Eliot has cast the novel back in the early part of the century, and before that for

---

* The sibling question has been discussed in *Adam Bede* (Adam and Seth), in *Mill* (Maggie and Tom), and is apparent here, in *Marner*, with Godfrey and Dunstan. We will see it play out in *Felix Holt*, between Harold Transome and his wastrel brother; in *Middlemarch*, more benignly between Dorothea and Lydia; and finally in *Daniel Deronda*, between Gwendolen and her four younger half-sisters. Two novellas, "The Lifted Veil" and "Brother Jacob," also fit well into sibling rivalry, a particularly virulent form.

Marner's expulsion from Lantern Yard, is fitting. Also fitting is her use of the Eden myth: the expulsion, the entrance into a wasteland of sorts, the gradual accommodation to the world beyond the Garden, a world full of conspiracy and criminal activity. Within such contexts—the past, the sacred hearth, an innocent child—Marner can transform himself from a falsely accused guilty person and from a bizarre, solitary, almost lunatic-like weaver into someone who can give and receive love.

Since the child Eppie is compensatory for Marner's monetary loss, we must move back into Eliot's shadowy, unconscious response to her position. As she approached her forty-second year, she recognized the impossibility of childbearing; Eliot, in fact, told a friend that she and Lewes decided not to have children and took precautions.* By this time, she may well have been menopausal, in itself a difficult time psychologically for a woman without her own children. But her growing desire to acquire money cannot be discounted as compensatory—in *her* perception—for her failure to fulfill traditional wife and mother roles. Tellingly, Marner becomes as much a mother to Eppie as a father; and, pointedly, the child is female, so that he must assume more of the maternal role than with a male child. In a gender switchover, he serves as father in his earning capacity as a weaver, but as traditional mother in his way of raising Eppie to be a fine young woman. Also, not to be discounted in the equation is Eliot's new role as stepmother—a maternal role she had to balance with her own "work," not at the loom, but at her desk.

Her hortatory, moralistic tone has increased considerably over her previous work. Money, so desirable, has become an evil force. But more than money is involved in this internal struggle for which moral advice seems a palliative. She was reaching, we suspect, a critical point in her writing. Now that she had arrived "there," she found herself on the threshold of a new, potentially perilous venture, the Florentine-based *Romola*. As her first novel set outside what she knew intimately, it would also involve a historical re-creation of an era in which religious values were paramount. Not only was she full of doubts about *Romola*— her letters bear this out—but she was going to force herself to confront the very religious elements she had forsaken. Savonarola was both salvational and demonic, and Eliot's need to get beyond him with her own brand of positivism, evolution, humanitarianism, and realism would put her under enormous strain. That strain emerges in the preliminary to, or first act of, *Romola*, and in the heuristic *Marner*: caution to herself as well as to society.

Not disconnected to the above internal struggle shaping up was Eliot's artistic effort to make *Marner* more than realistic without forsaking realism. She adopted several strategies. Marner's "gaze" suggests a mystery, not only demonic but otherworldly, as though his head and his body moved in separate directions. He also suffers an epileptic fit during a prayer meeting, which associates him with devil worship. Raveloe is itself somewhat shrouded, "a village where many

---

* With the development of vulcanized rubber, condoms became available by mid-century and may well have been the form of contraception the couple used.

of the old echoes lingered, undrowned by new voices." Once in Raveloe, where Marner has arrived in the 1780s, he experiences reveries, part of that "other world" he inhabits. He is described, at his loom, as a spider, a "spinning insect," suggesting his linkage to the natural, rather than human, world. Then in his association with treasure, he takes on the mythical connotations of the keeper of the hoard, like Alberich in the Wagner Ring cycle. And when he emerges into the light—that is, when his life is illuminated by Eppie—he assumes a certain Christ-like quality.

All of this heightens Eliot's supra-realism even while allowing her to maintain, nevertheless, a strong social realism: the townspeople and the tavern scenes, and subsidiary figures like Godfrey and Dunstan Cass, old Squire Cass, Nancy Lammeter (a Lucy Deane figure), the peasant Dolly Winthrop, the doomed Molly, and others. This part is consistent with *Silas Marner*'s Wordsworthian qualities: the unity of people and nonhuman elements is evident. Woods, hearth, quarry, plants, flowers, and seasons are all continuous with human activity, and underscore the interwoven quality of the lives and their environment. Marner weaves, and Eliot encloses him in one woven web after another, nearly all of them connected to lower-class or working-class life. It is fitting that Marner's adopted daughter should marry a gardener. Nowhere else has Eliot tried so determinedly to dramatize the drab life of people for whom startling events are almost unknown, even as these lives push against an "unreal" or mysterious world.

At every stage, she revealed deep inner struggles, most of all personal and artistic conflicts which the novel resolves with Christian humanism. Yet even as she created it, she suspected it didn't suffice; that such humanism by itself fell short. *Romola* would have to carry her forward. *Savonarola would be her test.* Her difficulty with the novel was rooted in this immense struggle.

The couple's return to Blandford Square coincided with the book's appearance, the first reviews, and the death of Major William Blackwood, on 8 April. The reviews were admiring, especially the one in the *Saturday Review* (13 April), whose critic located Eliot in the company of Dickens and Bulwer-Lytton, even Scott, and saw her as possibly superior. Lewes probably read out parts of this to Eliot. The *Economist* (27 April) lauded both book and author. The important review in the *Times*, by E. S. Dallas, was an author's dream, equal to the one in the *Saturday Review*. "To George Eliot," Dallas begins, "belongs this praise—that not only is every one of her tales a masterpiece, but also they may be opened at almost any page, and the eye is certain to light upon something worth reading. . . ." And it ends: "The moral purpose which is evident in her writings is mostly an unconscious purpose. It is that sort of moral meaning which belongs to every great work of art. . . ."

Even the *Westminster Review*, which had savaged much of *Mill*, came around, calling *Marner* her finest, although this may have been left-handed praise. The following year, the reviewer in the *Dublin University Magazine*, as if in some Irish vendetta against British literature, continued with the Eliot bashing that had begun with *Mill*. Withal, Eliot was fortunate in her reviews, for while *Marner* does have its telling aspects, it is small beer among her other fictions—an inter-lude with strong personal baggage, but a limited perspective.

She and Lewes were now trying to arrange their affairs and prepare for another long trip, a return to Italy and to Florence in particular. Possibly, a large check from Blackwood, for £1,350, on 1 April, helped them decide to go at this time; the monies derived from additional sales of Mill starting with the fifth thousand copy. Eliot said she was grateful for the money as protection against the time when she was no longer able to write well. The decision having been made to leave on 19 April, she wrote Samuel Laurence that she did not wish to have his portrait of her exhibited at the Royal Academy; in fact, she wanted the portrait kept within his own studio. In time, Laurence sold it to Blackwood's, where it was framed and hung in the book room of the London office. Amidst this, Eliot found time to comfort John Blackwood in several letters for the death of his brother, although she herself had not been deeply attached to the major.

The couple then began another one of their exhausting journeys, combining complicated conveyance travel with extensive sightseeing, as they worked their way through France on the way to Florence. They stayed in Paris for one day and then entrained for Avignon. John Stuart Mill had built there a tomb to his wife, Harriet, who had died in 1858, and Eliot wished to see it. From Avignon, they headed for Nice, via Toulon. Since they were now flush with guineas, they hired a private carriage for the final leg of the journey, stopping when they wished. After two nights in Nice—where they were outraged by a licentious French play—they continued by private carriage via the Grand Corniche to Genoa, a journey that took four days. In Genoa, they rested, went sightseeing, and then headed for Pisa, arriving on 4 May. This was Eliot's third sight of the city, and in her journal she picked out the cathedral, baptistry, and campanile for special note. They were in Florence by nightfall, and Romola became immi-nent. The book proved both rewarding and torturous, and it forced, possibly more than any other literary experience in Eliot's life, that split of herself into conflicting roles and ideas. Romola awaited her like fate, and she couldn't hide.

PART FIVE

Fathers, Daughters,
and Intruders

14

The Question of Romola

"I would not lose the misery of being a woman, now
I see what can be the baseness of a man."

A lthough for a major writer every year is critical, it appears that 1861–62
was a particularly pivotal time for Eliot. *Romola* did not come easily. She
was still, much of the time, despondent, forced to nurse Lewes when she was
herself not being nursed. She did not feel secure in writing the novel, uncertain
of how it would incorporate her feelings and her beliefs. She would break with
Blackwood over its publication, move to another publisher, and then rue the
decision. She seemed so uncertain that at times, her journal indicates, she
thought of giving up writing altogether. She did not consciously wish to pursue
money, but great offers tempted her. She felt the alien nature of what she was
doing, an Italian novel set in a very distant past. But none of these uncertainties
was the main arena. She was tackling something else: a blind father, a devoted
daughter enslaved to his needs, and an intruder who "steals" the young woman.
She was reentering a terrible drama, her father's death, one that she described
as having left her, in 1849, as despairing, incapable of action, and feeling she
would fail in whatever enterprises she chose for herself. In this curving back,
Romola returned her to Robert Evans, to whom she read, whose house she cared
for, and whose wishes she bowed to. Romola does no less. In fictional tropes,
Eliot reestablished the terms which had given her so much pain, to the extent
she feared for her sanity.

The 1861 complaints were truly remarkable. We recognize she could work
only by creating and overcoming obstacles, real and imaginary. Her journal for
16 June 1861 is typical: "At least there is a possibility that I may make greater
efforts against indolence and the despondency that comes from too egoistic a

dread of failure." Or: "Read little this morning—my mind dwelling with too much depression on the probability or improbability of my achieving the work I wish to do. I struck out two or three thoughts towards an English novel. I am much afflicted with hopelessness and melancholy just now. . . ." Or 23 September: "I have been unwell ever since we returned from Malvern [a lovely spa northwest of London, near Gloucester], and have been disturbed from various causes, in my work, so that I have scarcely done anything except correct my own books for a new edition [a cheap edition for her four books]." On 7 October she registers that she began the first chapter of *Romola*. On 6 November she wrote: "So utterly dejected that, in walking with G. in the Park, I almost resolved to give up my Italian novel."

Early in 1862, on 13 February, she seemed to be reexamining herself and her response to the past. "I think the highest and best thing is rather to suffer with real suffering than to be happy in the imagination of an unreal good." While noble, this thought is the product of a depressed, divided person. Near the end of 1862, with *Romola* still before her, she wrote: "At page 22 only. I am extremely spiritless, dead, and hopeless about my writing. The long state of headache has left me in depression and incapacity. The constantly heavy-clouded and often wet weather tend to increase the depression." Yet in her assessment of 1862, written on 31 December, she sums up her and Lewes's blessings: an abundant independence, satisfactory progress with their two eldest sons, happiness in their work, and an ever-growing happiness in each other. She says she hopes the coming year may be as comforting—but "with trembling because my work is not yet done." She then examines the negatives: she must finish *Romola*, Thornie has to pass his final examinations for Indian service, Bertie must soon leave Hofwyl, and she and Lewes must find a new residence.

The assessment is a kind of Benthamite calculus of plus and minus. What she omits is the heavy burden the novel has placed upon her. Not only was it a matter of reliving her own 1849 period, it was also the presence of Savonarola, to whom she was drawn and who reminded her so much of her earlier self in his insistence on the letter of religion, in his refusal to bend even if it meant his life. Savonarola brought home to her, as he did to Romola, the attractions of a religious impulse in which one surrendered to an external force, in which one was swallowed up by all-powerful elements, whether natural or religious. The attractiveness of authority had, apparently, not completely left Eliot; while she now held to beliefs that rejected an omnipotent God, she had not completely forsaken the reaches of Christianity, including sacrifice, self-discipline, and deferring to a greater spiritual power. She was still divided, dualistic in her responses, split between unconscious and conscious needs. Perhaps most of all, Savonarola appealed to the side of her that sought out pain and suffering as the lot of humanity. For Eliot, pain and suffering were entrances into the higher reaches of experience; without them, the individual remained ignorant of life's intensities and complexities. Savonarola brought her to these extremes.

Having arrived in Florence on 4 May 1861, Eliot spent five days in the Magliabecchian Library sifting through early books for information about Savonarola. She was, however, impeded by ill health, a harbinger of the period to come. To Blackwood, she indicates that she and Lewes both have colds. Their first week was full of chills, grippe, headache, sore throat, fever, and, for her, possibly menstrual pains—a conglomeration of her usual ailments but now intensified. Lewes, further, seemed to be suffering from migraine. Yet they did not want to miss out on Florentine sights, and they visited, bodies sagging, Santa Maria Novella, Giotto's Tower, and the cathedral, plus, of course, the bookstalls. At the library, Eliot was careful to make up lists of elements she might use: costumes, street activities (fairs, exhibitions, jesters, disturbances, criminals), ceremonies and holidays, and other matters relating to everyday life in late-fifteenth-century Florence. She was particularly interested in how people dressed, and toward the end Lewes pencil-sketched several costumes for her.

Their schedule was regularized. They arose at seven, had breakfast, and then read. Lewes enjoyed a cigar. By midmorning they were out, visiting a church or two, some picture galleries, and bookstalls; they enjoyed walking the old streets. Then they headed for the Magliabecchian Library, where they settled in to do research or just to read. At two o'clock or so, they dined, and then took a siesta until five or six; after that they drove out or rambled about, on occasion going to the opera. There was little social activity. Their friend Thomas Trollope, Anthony's brother, was away when they arrived, but they saw his wife and daughter. At the Trollopes', on one of their infrequent social excursions, they met several English people and Italians, including one Tibaldi, who gave them tickets for a grand ceremony to be held in Santa Croce, honoring the Italian heroes of 1848. Eliot reproduced a blind priest's speech on a united and free Italy for Savonarola's speech in *Romola.*

On Trollope's return, he convinced them to stay on beyond the end of May and suggested they see the monasteries at Camaldoli and La Vernia, a three-day excursion. To get there, at a certain point, they had to mount ponies, alternately walking and riding. Their ill health did not seem an impediment. They enjoyed the monkish life, and Lewes's journal is full of monastery routine. By the evening of 6 June, they were back in Florence, preparing to leave the next day. Trollope, incidentally, while he did write a novel in 1861, was a historian, and was preparing a four-volume *History of Florence.* He became an excellent source of historical detail.

The couple wound back toward England by way of Genoa, then went to Hofwyl, in Switzerland, to see Bertie. They traveled by means of train, boat, and carriage, and included in their journey the scenic route along Lake Maggiore and the entire waterway to Lucerne. By 14 June, they were in Blandford Square, and Eliot shortly afterward noted in her journal that she had "too egoistic a dread of failure," an indication she was uncertain of the entire venture. In actuality, the time provided much-needed atmosphere and acquaintanceship with the physical layout of the city.

Eliot, however, ended up doing most of her research outside Florence, especially in working up the historical background, which she found daunting. *

She read voluminously for the project. For the Middle Ages, she consulted the standard works, Gibbon, Hallam, and Michelet; for monastic orders, she used Montalembert, Nardi, and one she indexed in her notebook as Lastri's *L'osservatore Fiorentino*. She read biographies of Savonarola and of the Medicis, plus Vasari's lives of the painters. She also read firsthand works: Machiavelli as a matter of course, Petrarch, Boccaccio, and Politian. Lewes testified to her diligence, telling Blackwood that "Mrs. Lewes is buried in old quartos and vellum bound literature which I would rather not read; but she extracts nutriment, I have no doubt." Costume did not escape her eye: she consulted *Le moyen âge illustré* and related sources. But the Florentine background alone was not sufficient. Since Tito Melema, the "intruder," has a Greek origin, she researched Greece and Greek matters in the late fifteenth century. She used the vast libraries of the British Museum, and checked prints in the Print Room. Her journal indicates she revelled in this immersion.

The very saturation in sources, however, had unfortunate consequences. Long portions of *Romola* do not distinguish between Eliot's vast researches and the fictional transformation of detail. The main thrust was to be imaginative—Romola, her father, Tito Melema, and a fictionalized Savonarola, among others. The drama was personal, set within a particular context she was eager to catch in its details and multiplicity. Yet caught up by the great historians of the time (Carlyle, Macaulay, Froude), Eliot was obsessive about historical veracity. Possibly because the personal dimensions were so intense, she found herself accumulating historical detail to balance out private feelings, or else she thought she could better explain the personal drama by giving it such intense factual bases. It is not that we learn too much, it is that the characters lose definition and the fictional voice becomes muffled. She sought to write a parable for her own time, in that clash of ideologies and historical perspectives; yet the edges are blurred.

The passages cited above about her depression and loss of nerve could also signal she was swamped by history, unable to perceive the fictional line. † During the summer of 1861, her despondence about the book was unremitting. And even when she began the first chapter in early October, it was tentative and had to be rewritten later. Not until December did she begin to have a clearer focus for her story, and she told Lewes of her plans, for which he expressed, as she says, great delight. She made sketches and drafts, apparently, which have not come down to us.

---

* After a lunch at Blandford Square, Blackwood wrote his wife about Eliot's diffidence in writing *Romola*. So meticulous is she about realism, he says, she feels her characters should be speaking Italian, not English. He was particularly taken with her distinction between what is called the real and what is called the imaginative. "Any real observation of life and character must be limited, and the imagination must fill in and give life to the picture." As Eliot moved on as novelist, she journeyed further and further from flat realism, as we see particularly in *Daniel Deronda*.

† To those plaints, we can add her anxiety-ridden letter to Thomas Trollope about the exact origin of the Bardis, her use of colloquial terms such as *in piazza* and *in mercato*, for which she cites sources, and like matters which have overtaken her performance.

Not until 1 January 1862 did the novel have its title. Before that, she referred to it as her "Italian story," or, more plainly, her "novel." Very possibly Thomas Trollope's novel *La Beata: a Tuscan Romeo and Juliet* gave her some formative ideas. In the Trollope, the female protagonist allows her love, Pippo, to desert her. In *Romola*, the peasant girl Tessa bears Tito's child and permits him to move in and out of her life. Although they are not married, Tessa accepts her position as his wife. It was a tale which, obviously, appealed to Eliot, but it also gave her an important subplot; it even gave her ammunition for the negative presentation of Tito, a kind of poisonous intruder. In still another respect, it gave her a foil for Romola, in the ignorant Tessa: two very different women deceived by Tito.

The triangle here—Romola, Tito, Tessa—is compelling and personally intricate, a shielded version of Eliot, Lewes, and Agnes. Romola is married to the faithless young man, Tessa is not; but it is Tessa who bears Tito's child, while he deceives both of them. Tito clearly is not what he appears to be, and as Romola recognizes what he is, her desire for revenge increases. Tessa is too soft and accepting to fight back. But Romola has an avenger in the Florentine shadows, Tito's "father," Baldassarre, who is trying to kill the ingrate. The reverberations are not to be ignored: a faithless husband, son, and lover; a vengeful father figure; a Madonna-like wife who harbors tremendous hostility and anger which she must swallow. Although the equation does not personally play out—Lewes was no Tito—Eliot's perception of the male is telling, and the effect on her of such a drama is clear.

The central problem for the novel is how Romola can maintain her equilibrium amidst a menagerie of male figures all of whom represent forms of power. The sole other female of note is Tessa, but her weakness is so obvious her very presence accentuates Romola's need for strength. The scene, with obvious distinctions, is somewhat reminiscent of Marian Evans's position at the *Westminster Review*, amidst Chapman, Spencer, and Combe; or earlier with Bray, Brabant, Hennell, and, of course, Robert Evans. Father, husband, protector after Bardo dies, Savonarola, all are figures with little use for women except those who can serve. The male function is to use and then discard, some gently, some more brutally.

Romola's response to male power and to male pressure is curious, in the light of George Eliot's own predilections. Having served her father, having been deceived by her husband, having been unable to accept Savonarola's appeal for martyrdom, Romola becomes a nun of sorts. She represses her sexuality, disguises her obvious physical beauty, hides her acquired classical knowledge, and becomes a servant of people in desperate need of help. She buries herself in humanitarian aid, a religious without any definite religion.

We can view all this as a metaphorical journey for Eliot, so that the entire scenario worked out in Florence is itself a metaphor of the author's perception not only of a woman, or of women, but of herself. In this large, played-out conflict, the subject is no less than a struggle for Eliot's soul, in which Romola and the various pressures on her are forms of temptation intermixed with ran-

domness and willed behavior—in effect, all the elements we have associated
with Eliot.

That Romola "resolves" her conflicts in service and in self-effacement under-
scores the author's dilemma, the several pulls and tears in her own effort to
break through. We can speculate that *Romola* caused her such pains not solely
for the usual reasons of difficult imaginative work, but because she was moving
so close to the bone of unresolvable elements. Since she was writing a novel,
which demanded closure, she had to resolve and conclude Romola's predicament. But that it went against the grain of the author's own solution would help
explain Eliot's anguish, and perhaps explain, further, her obsession with detail.
If this were indeed such a personal scenario, then she *had* to get it right.

One other area of the novel indicates even more terrible internal tensions in
Eliot. The long-suffering, even passive Romola has been building up feelings
she cannot express. Her hatred of Tito grows, but to relieve the pressure she
cannot, of course, murder him. Here, Baldassarre serves as her agent of revenge.
Eliot uses a "father figure" to eliminate the intruder, a wandering, deceitful husband; all of it accompanied by water imagery. The Arno becomes a major factor:
Baldassarre is a river rat, and Romola chooses the river as a means to bring about
her own death. Eliot had used such watery contexts for Maggie in *Mill*, and in
Deronda, Gwendolen will let her husband, Grandcourt, drown. We cannot
define these tensions precisely, although they reveal Eliot's recognition that as
compensation for women's weakness other forces must be employed, even if
such forces signify murder.

Cara Bray paid a fast call on or around 22 June, an indication that despite their
vast differences, Eliot welcomed the support of old friends now that she felt frail
and exposed by her hesitancy over *Romola*. In an amusing letter to Cara, she
mentions Sara's advantages in being single, that there are some advantages
"over and above what St. Paul saw." One of them: the power of opening the
window at any hour of the night "without dread of giving a husband sore throat,
and the power of sitting up as long as she likes without danger of disturbing
his rest."

Playfulness, however, was only a temporary respite. Eliot searched for some
way to unify her researches with her imaginative plans; this was made all the
more difficult because she apparently was unsure of what she wished to achieve
fictionally. *Romola* was a much larger effort than anything she had attempted
previously, a true three-decker. Because of the unfamiliar territory, she was forcing herself into ever more recherché researches in an effort to discover some
guiding plan. She settled on the Bardo family as her locus of interest, a family
noted for its power and described in detail in Lastri's *L'osservatore Fiorentino*.
What she needed was a further connection which would bring Tito into the
Bardo circle, and that came through Baldassarre, who adopts Tito. She needed
parallelisms: old Bardo and his dutiful, slavish daughter; old Baldassarre, with
his deceptive ingrate of a son. The parallelism would allow a gender contrast

and, related to that, play in shadowy fashion on her own background: the obedient daughter who remains at home, the prodigal son who is poisoned by ambition. If we tilt the picture, Maggie and Tom from *Mill* reappear as Romola and Tito. In the background, there is always a father. Fathers are a jejune lot in Eliot.

In Berlin, in 1855, Eliot had heard a story (from General Pfuhl) which she wrote down in her commonplace book (at the end of the journals). According to this tale, a man of considerable wealth in Rome adopted a poor street urchin. The boy was all deceit, and in time attempted to gain legal title to the benefactor's property. The outraged man killed the villain—as Baldassarre will kill Tito, after stalking him for years—and is condemned for the murder. In prison he says he wishes to go to hell, so he can follow his villainous adopted son. When Eliot wrote this story in her notebook, she foreshadowed another tale of vengeance. Characteristic of both is "stalking," where hatred is so intense it can last for years until the deed is done. The boy in Pfuhl's story is more conniving and villainous than the weak, ambitious Tito. Nevertheless, Eliot now had several of the elements her book required. What she still lacked was the actual sequencing, the clarity of focus, and the means of blending elements with each other: she lacked the fictional, creative dimension.

The summer of 1861 was pivotal. If these elements failed to come together— and they would not for almost another six months—she had no novel. Although she and Lewes were not hurting for ready money, they had become accustomed to a steady influx from previous books plus the huge advances. We must connect Eliot's hesitation about *Romola,* and its inherent difficulties, with her readiness to accept George Smith's large offer, which meant a break with Blackwood. Although she repeatedly declared she did not want to write merely for money, money was never completely absent from her or Lewes's mind. Having geared themselves to a more affluent way of life, if her "Italian story" was aborted she had nothing on her desk for the foreseeable future. In this area alone, there was reason for anxiety.

For the working writer, the summer became a kind of limbo; not the last such period in her life, but one of the most difficult. Lewes went away for a brief period for the waters, and Eliot felt low during his absence. She looked into Bulwer-Lytton's historical novel *Rienzi* to find out how such fiction was put together, and she also dipped into Scott's *The Pirate.* But she was not following her best instincts. She was grubbing for the last detail, as if in discovering *that* she would have clues to the fusion of history and fiction. Lytton had himself warned that too much history can clog the literary arteries. Lewes saw her obsession with accuracy, but was himself superficial in his own view that a fiction writer had only to skim some Scott and come away with the method. Further, Lewes was caught in his personal version of the *cafard.* On the one hand, he was trying to maximize Eliot's popularity by asking Blackwood to have his salespeople place books at train stalls and the like; on the other, he was attempting to keep his hand in with a science paper, "Discoverers in Science: Marshall

Hall," but was unable to concentrate. While he tried to bolster Eliot's spirits, he was himself fighting off one ailment after another, attacks of nerves, and an undefined high anxiety about the present and the future. Eliot counted on his natural good spirits, but Lewes was finding it increasingly difficult to bubble when he felt himself going under.

This view from the inside is quite different from the way the couple was perceived. Blackwood and other close friends saw riches, fame, achievement, a happy couple more compatible than most married people. For others, it appeared much the same, except for condemnation of the irregular relationship. Few had the sense of a symbiotic misery that periodically flowed back and forth between the two, or of the uncertainties and hesitations which no amount of money or gains in fame could allay. This sadness, which seemed natural for Eliot, but less so for Lewes, bled into her books, becoming part of that sorrowful charity of spirit which infuses her sense of character and event. Sadness gave her psychological insight—in effect, her voice.

There was something else gnawing at her, as she revealed when she wrote to Frau Karl Theodor Ernst von Siebold, a friend from Munich days. She indicates she is staying in London for the sake of her oldest boy, who needs a London residence for his position in the general post office: ". . . we are living in London; a change which is a great sacrifice to me, who care more about the country than about all other outside enjoyments." Although they could walk in Regent's Park and in the Zoological Gardens, which were nearby, these were inadequate substitutes for the "blue sky of Munich." Meanwhile, Lewes was really ailing, becoming thinner, finding it impossible to work, and proving impervious to tonics and drugs. Since he was to live more than another decade and a half, it is difficult to see what his condition might have been; surely cancer or some other killer disease would have finished him before 1878. When he went away to spas or they traveled together for a few days outside London, he seemed for the time to recover; this occurred in the visit to Malvern in September, for the water cure. The temptation is to diagnose Lewes's ailments as psychologically oriented, not organic; to view him as recovering when he left his desk and microscope, and to see him relapse whenever he returned to work or when he could think of his former London life. But this is not quite satisfactory. Some kind of venereal disease comes to mind, the consequence of his profligate days when he was a bachelor and perhaps during his first marriage. But this, too, was not diagnosed. Tuberculosis was another possibility: the loss of weight, the fevers and sore throats, the shivering, the frequent colds; but such sufferers usually did not last another seventeen years, as Lewes did. The fainting spells, however, suggest a possible diabetic condition.

On 23 September, Blackwood sent one of his encouraging missives, a check for £1,600 due Eliot for the 8,000 printed copies of Silas Marner. In a later letter, he offered £3,000 for the entire remaining copyrights of Scenes, Adam Bede, Mill, and Marner, payable in the course of a couple of years from the date of publication of the first volume of the reprint edition. He says this is the best he

can do, an offer Eliot rejected, as she knew her copyrights were worth far more. *
During the final quarter of 1861, Eliot's correspondence dwindled to a few letters, mainly to Blackwood, some to Maria Congreve and Barbara Bodichon, but
lacking any depth or overall interest, an indication of how *Romola,* or plans for
it, had dragged her down.

Blackwood meanwhile went ahead with a cheap edition (6 shillings) of
Marner, that to be followed by others at the same price. All of these schemes
moved along, at least in Blackwood's mind, as part of his continuation as Eliot's
publisher, failing to take into account that both Eliot and Lewes could be
tempted by large sums. The publisher's complacency was reinforced by his
nephew† reporting a long fruitful interview with Lewes, and even showing hope
that Mrs. Lewes would soon start her new novel.

She would, but not for Blackwood. No one understood the complexities of
Eliot's position as she was trapped between malaise and serious artistic intentions, all compromised by the growing desire to make money while she could
still write. On 1 January 1862, she was able to send on good auguries: she had
begun her novel, however tentatively and uncertainly. She also mentions something very close to her heart, her love of dogs. Her beloved pug had died the
previous year, and Blackwood, who had given her the dog, now sent on a Dresden china pug as a memorial of the flesh-and-blood pug. It was a touching gesture, for, as we can see from Eliot's novels, she had the same affection for dogs
as did Dickens: both used dogs as bellwethers for judging people's characters.‡
It was the kind of sentiment linked to Eliot's childhood when farm animals as
well as domestic creatures were an integral part of her life.

Blackwood was clearly pursuing her, finally beginning to suspect she might
pull away. When he came to lunch on 22 December 1861, he even brought his
wife, the first meeting of the two women, and surely a sop to Eliot's feeling that
women had segregated her. He came also on 2 January of the new year, then
again on the 12th, a sequence of visits unprecedented in their relationship. He
was courting her either out of true devotion or fear of losing her. But whatever
else was on Eliot's mind, *Romola* was not coming easily. Overcome by malaise,
she wrote in her journal she had never felt so "unpromising" as now, although
in the 1849–52 period, especially in her despairing letters to Herbert Spencer,
she was even more unpromising and despairing.

---

* She explained to the firm that her idea was to secure a sum of money so that Lewes could work
on his "history of science" without interruption; this sum of money would be invested. But Blackwood's offer was not what she had in mind and would not, in any event, have made much of a dent
when invested.

†The nephew, William, was the oldest son of Major William Blackwood, and he became a partner
in the firm in 1862. After his uncle, John, died, Eliot corresponded with this William.

‡The way in which Victorian writers have their characters treat (mainly) dogs and horses indicates how the reader should respond to that character. But beyond that, animals were imbued with
a kind of purity, somehow connected to a prelapsarian state. The nineteenth-century use of animals
in such a manner suggests that the domesticated beast was a counterbalance to the "undomesticated"
beast of industrialism and headlong progress, William Blake's "mind-forg'd manacles."

Not unusually, physical ailments tormented her. As soon as one cold and stuffiness departed, another began; she reports the endless cycle of feeling unwell. Lewes was constantly ailing, although he was working on his *Aristotle* manuscript, the rough draft of which he completed on 21 February. On 23 January, however, there occurred the first stage of what would prove a sea change in Eliot's life. The publisher George Smith called at Blandford Square. Smith had published in the *Cornhill* some of Lewes's "Studies in Animal Life," before discontinuing the series as possibly too controversial—Lewes had linked his own zoological ideas to Darwin's evolutionary theories. Lewes now wanted to start a new series. Smith's game, however, was only partially Lewes; he took aim at Eliot and suggested to his still disgruntled science author he might make a "magnificent offer" for her next work. Lewes was suspicious and even wrote in his journal it might be better for him not to be rich. Within the month, Smith reappeared, and this time he had a definite offer. The *Cornhill* needed an infusion of new blood; having run two serialized novels—Anthony Trollope's popular *Framley Parsonage* and Thackeray's much less successful *The Adventures of Philip*—Smith saw an opening after April and wanted Eliot's new novel, for £10,000. The enormity of this sum was stunning, the equivalent in spending power today of almost half a million dollars.

This threw both Lewes and Eliot into disarray. Lewes considered the offer: it was for the entire copyright, not merely for serial appearance in *Cornhill*, "the most magnificent offer ever yet made for a novel." Eliot was firm that she would not be far enough along by April or May to begin a serial, and she did not wish it to appear until she had numerous chapters on her desk. She was by now quite aware how serialization could subvert a novelist's conception of her material and undermine at least the novel's structure. Since she was having difficulty even starting, an April or May publication, only two or three months away, was out of the question. Smith was not pleased with this turn of events and suggested that he print "Brother Jacob" split into three numbers, so that the new novel could be postponed until August or September. Eliot agreed to let him see the story—which did not appear in *Cornhill* until 1864.

Smith also had another plan in mind, to obtain Lewes as editor for the *Cornhill*, to succeed Thackeray, who was not happy in the post. Lewes agreed to be a consulting editor, which meant he would select the articles and make suggestions for subjects; and for this he would receive a very generous £600 a year. One suspects Smith wooed Lewes in order to cozy up to Eliot, although the job did seem to fit Lewes's talents well. The serialization of *Romola*, however, was still out of the question. On the Blackwood front, Eliot wrote a curt letter complaining of the firm's method of advertising her books. She was annoyed that Simpson (George Simpson, Blackwood's loyal but tart Edinburgh manager) may have a system he regards as best for their common interests, but the fact that her books have entered a new edition remains "quite a secret." Her follow-up letter of 28 February, however, was something of an apology, since she found Simpson's list "a sufficient vindication of his advertising energy, and I am sorry to have worried him on the subject."

It had meanwhile become clear Eliot could not produce enough copy for a spring serialization, and that Smith could not wait until early fall. The project was abandoned, but Smith still wanted to publish Eliot, and he and Lewes discussed a sixpenny serial, as well as publishing the book at 6 shillings. Lewes admitted he regretted the loss of £10,000 in one bundle. But with such large amounts of money in view, ideas were spinning, and while no one was completely satisfied, everyone made concessions to strike a deal. Smith gave up the idea of selling *Romola* in small weekly portions and instead suggested using large chunks of the novel in monthly installments which would fill forty or forty-five pages of the *Cornhill*; in all, 384 pages of the journal spread out over a year. For this, Smith offered £7,000, and the novel was to begin in July—well before Eliot felt she would be ready. The copyright, including foreign rights, would remain with Smith for six years, and, further, the firm could sell the book until 1905 in any one form they determined—they chose an edition of 2½ shillings.

It was a curious deal and was very probably connected to Eliot's need for visible compensation to balance out her fears of artistic deficiency.* She had somehow cheapened herself and was, furthermore, rushing matters with a July start in the *Cornhill*. But perhaps most damaging of all, she was permitting her work to fall into very cheap editions—although the 2½ shilling edition did not appear until after her death. The deal was consummated in May, after Eliot read Smith several segments of *Romola*. While Lewes's journal reported the event, it also introduced a troubling aspect of their life: Charles was not advanced and was back in his old office at the post office. Anthony Trollope himself inquired into the case and was told that the young man was "not doing well, was careless, slow, and inefficient." Lewes immediately suffered a bilious attack.

Two days later Blackwood was the recipient of bad news, brought him in rather brusque terms by Eliot. The sharpness of her tone indicates she knew she was betraying a trust. She states she has received an offer for her next novel superior to any ever received by a fiction writer. She says she hesitated and contemplated discussing it with the firm. But then a follow-up offer removed her objections, and after further reflection, she realized the terms were "hopelessly beyond your usual estimate of the value of my books to you. . . ." Recognizing that, she felt it would be indelicate to make an appeal to him before deciding. She says that by holding copyright to six years, she will not be impeding any general edition the firm might be planning.

Blackwood put a good face on things. He responded he was pleased she could make such a satisfactory arrangement, and that given the "wild sums" offered to inferior writers he thought it probable such an offer would be made to her. He agrees he could not match such a remuneration. "We have had several most

---

* That she may have been bothered by it comes in her remarks to Sara: "I have refused the highest price ever offered for fiction"—which was for the entire copyright. Yet, amidst this turmoil, in one of her rare comments on contemporary matters, she expressed to Barbara Bodichon her anxiety about "the war with America," and showed sympathy for the queen, who had recently lost her Prince Albert. The American Civil War divided England, and at one point seemed to draw in the country on the Confederate side.

successful enterprises together and much pleasant correspondence and I hope
we shall have much more."*

With this Eliot stepped down into a commercial world she usually deplored.
Whatever her protests, money had become an element in her life, pursued in a
somewhat shady manner. The production of the book was to reflect the expensive outlay—with Frederic Leighton, a Florentine for the earlier part of his life,
as illustrator at £20 an illustration. Leighton left an impression of Eliot: "Miss
Evans (or Mrs. Lewes) has a very striking countenance. Her face is large, her
eyes deep set, her nose aquiline, her mouth large, the under jaw projecting,
rather like Charles Quint; her voice and manner are grave, simple, and gentle.
There is a curious mixture in her look; she either is or seems very short-sighted.
Lewes is clever. Both were extremely polite to me; her I shall like very much."

Is it possible to view Eliot's motives as less than venal, without ruling that
out? We do know she sought after a kind of power. She needed to be assured
she had succeeded, that she had turned her life around. More upscale houses
(the Priory would enter their lives soon), private carriages, first-class hotels, and
all the rest were indications of her power. In still another respect—and this is
speculative—her enormous earning power gave her an ascendancy over Lewes.
Devoted and supportive as he was—and no one questions this—he was dependent on her, even when the *Cornhill* paid him £600 a year as a consulting editor.
While Lewes as her agent and manager seemed to call the tune, she wrote the
words. A good deal of this interpretation of their relationship depends on how
much hostility toward men she carried over from her father and brother. Certainly, *Romola* reveals many layers of such hostility.

After further inquiry, one source of anxiety seems to have been dissipated,
Charles Lewes's performance at the post office. He was not considered lazy or
slack, was indeed well liked, but did demonstrate "slowness of apprehension and
of execution," which could be cleared up. But that was the sideshow. On 17
June, the inevitably unpleasant confrontation with Blackwood took place,
which we learn about not from Eliot or from Lewes but from Blackwood's letter
to his nephew, William. The meeting was not agreeable. Lewes was taken
unwell, probably an attack of nerves. Eliot asserted she could not refuse such an
offer from Smith, although she could not feel toward another publisher as she

---

* Blackwood's remarks to Eliot were one thing, those to Langford in the London office another.
"The conduct of our friends in Blandford Square," he wrote, "is certainly not pleasing nor in the
long run will they find it wise however great the bribe may have been. It is too bad after all the
kindness she has experienced but I am sure she would do it against her inclination. The going over
to the enemy without giving me any warning and with a story on which from what they both said I
was fully intitled to calculate upon, sticks in my throat but I shall not quarrel—quarrels especially
literary ones are vulgar." Blackwood adds, amusingly, "In reality I do not care about the defection
and it has not disturbed me a bit. From the voracity of Lewes I saw that there would be great
difficulty in making the arrangement with them. . . ." For his part, Langford says that Smith was
already announcing the new tale by Eliot and planned to advertise it in *Maga*, what he calls a
"disgusting transaction." The advertisement: "A New Novel by the Author of 'Adam Bede' Will Be
Commenced in the Next Number of the Cornhill Magazine." John Blackwood sent on the ad to
William, his nephew, with strong words: ". . . I am sorry and disappointed in her but with their
extortionate views we could not have made an arrangement so all is for the best. She does not know
how strongly her desertion and going over to the enemy will tell upon the public estimate of her
character and most justly."

felt toward Blackwood's. She added she was unsure if she acted rightly, and she hoped another time would arise when she could show her strong feelings for her old publisher. Blackwood's comment is disbelieving: "I did not wish any *confi-dences* nor in her peculiar circumstances to hit her [that is, openly to question her sincerity], so merely looked her full in the face and shaking hands said, 'I'm fully satisfied that it must have been a very sharp pang to you' and came away." Blackwood's conclusion: he considered her a liar.

If Eliot seemed anxious and tight, she had good reason, for the July number of the *Cornhill* with *Romola* would start when she had only enough for July and August, and this was mid-June. She now found herself in the position of all serial writers, especially Dickens and Thackeray, forced to write rapidly against deadlines. By July, she had three parts ready, but since the segments were quite lengthy, she needed to come up with a great deal of copy swiftly. Yet in some mysterious way, such a tight schedule worked well, and she lost her blockage. Although she never got more than two numbers ahead of the magazine, she did not, henceforth, feel particularly put upon. The fact that Leighton's illustrations were right on target helped; Leighton, in fact, knew Florence far more inti-mately than she, and he was able to question both her use of Italian and her visual images and make corrections.

Eliot and Lewes were not socially active, as she buried herself in this most ambitious project. She did ask D'Albert-Durade to do the translation, saying that the absence of dialect might make his task easier. She is incessantly worried about the artistry of her book, telling Sara not to judge hastily from the early parts, or else she may be disappointed. Eliot admits this novel is addressed to fewer readers than her previous books, and she has no expectation of popularity. "If one," she says, "is to have freedom to write out one's own varying unfolding self, and not be a machine always grinding out the same material or spinning the same sort of web, one cannot always write for the same public." She says she warned Smith before they started publishing, "so I am acquitted of all scruple or anxiety except the grand anxiety of doing my work worthily. Also, I want to do something very much better than I ever *can* do—if fasting and scourging would make one a fit organ, there would be more positive comfort."

Yet her desire to express herself by way of a different kind of book led to an overabundance of self, in the form of an overheated context and a fuzzy presen-tation. It also led her, as Sara noted, to the creation of an unbelievable heroine, a saint or an ideal, as Eliot herself came to recognize; and this, too, subverted her conception of fiction.

Reports from Blandford Square were increasingly like hospital communiqués, as if the couple were defying the fates simply by staying alive. Lewes was plan-ning a spa vacation in Belgium to restore, as he put it, some vigor to his stom-ach. Eliot was herself not well, and she planned to remain behind at her desk. The sparse correspondence in the late summer of 1862 indicates either illness or concentration on her book, not the least the difficulty of putting herself into the novel and then overcoming that personalized element by transforming it into fictional terms. Unquestionably, she resented the very air of London, but it was difficult to separate London from the Florence where her imagination had landed her, even while memories roved back to Nuneaton. She had separated herself into three parts. She and Lewes did take short trips to small villages in Sussex or Surrey, but Eliot begrudged time away from her desk. On one of those excursions, to Littlehampton, in Sussex, she was able to write, accounting for some of Part VI, in September.

As she turned forty-three, she told D'Albert-Durade she and Lewes lived a quiet life, without incidents, absorbed in their work and "our fire-side affections." In this world of "struggle and endurance, we seem to have more than our share of happiness and prosperity . . . in spite of the loss of youth. Study is a keener delight to me than ever, and I think the affections, instead of being dulled by age, have acquired a stronger activity—or at least their activity seems stronger for being less perturbed by the egoism of young cravings." The lines reveal a maturation which would be reflected not so much in *Romola*, which generated too many internal problems, but in her later fiction.

Romola clearly served as a hinge. While it looks back to Eliot's earlier work, to its personalized and privatized elements, in another respect it served as a purging of those intense personal responses and opened her up to more imaginatively conceived fiction, not to speak of most of her major poetry. Eliot in 1862 definitely was looking in two directions. She had been writing fiction for little more than five years, and her development as a writer meant she needed to sort out the miseries of her past, as she perceived them. *Romola* gave her space to do that and proved a painful cathartic. It coincided with her recognition that her youth was over; but since she gave herself a few more years of work, she realized she was now at a pivotal point. That perception helps explain the ailments, the anxiety, the difficulty of getting through each day, despite whatever she might say about blessings. It is not often in the life of a major artist that we can pinpoint a particularly critical time. In Dickens, for example, it would be difficult to find that pivotal time, perhaps between *David Copperfield* and *Bleak House*, where a darkening and hopelessness occurred. But in Eliot, we can be specific, and find such a time in a single work. After *Romola*, she would be a different person and a different writer.

Cross reports her later remark that she started *Romola* as a young woman and finished it as an old woman, a remark which suggests either maturation or a movement toward death. She also spoke of working under a "leaden weight." She told Blackwood that every sentence was written in her "best blood," a comment suggesting a morbid involvement. The frequent trips out of London were respites, although she carried with her the need to complete the novel which the *Cornhill* was devouring so rapidly.

Ironically, even as Eliot was moving out toward a new definition of her work, however difficult the journey, D'Albert-Durade with his French translations of *Mill, Marner,* and others was bringing her back to her younger self, still another form of divisiveness. Although praise for the early chapters in the *Cornhill* was coming to her attention, Eliot felt like a "feeble wretch, with eyes that threaten to get blood-shot on the slightest provocation." Also bringing her back to her earlier fictions was the fact that Blackwood was going ahead with cheap editions of her three previous books, and she had been correcting these volumes—what for most readers has become the standard edition, her final version of what she attempted to achieve.

She and Lewes slipped off to Dorking. Eliot planned another stay there in April, on the 23rd, and while she settled in, Lewes went off to Hofwyl, where Bertie was still a student. Her journal in and around this general period from mid-March to mid-April 1863 groans with complaints, annoyances, and personal disturbances. She worried she was only at page 22 of Part XII (*Cornhill* Chapters 57–61), which meant she had only about a two-serial lead on the magazine. On the 23rd, when Lewes left her in Dorking, she felt "ill and alarmed," fearful the ability to work had deserted her—while the *Cornhill* serial inexorably marched on. After Lewes returned to Dorking on 28 April, they stayed on until the following Sunday (4 May), she with violent headache, and then throughout the week suffering "an incessant malaise from indigestion, producing Hemicrania [pressure on the brain]. . . ." The rest of the journal entries during this period indicate progress, then bouts of anxiety about only getting a few pages done: cycles of accomplishment and backsliding. She did feel picked up by the arrival of the French translation of *Mill,* in two volumes.

In another area, there was strain that she and Lewes had to remain in London because of Charles's post office position. His position picked up with a promotion in 1863. Unquestionably, Eliot looked forward to solitude, despite her expressed devotion for Charles and her pleasure in their duets on the new piano she and Lewes had acquired. At few other periods do we find in her such a driving need to exclude others and reach within.

In her journal for 16 May, she announces with a kind of glee that "in great excitement" she has killed Tito. She couples that act of violence with their plan, in time, to buy or lease the Priory, at 21 North Bank, along Regent's Park Canal, * a house they recently went to see. On 18 May, she mentions beginning Part XIV. On 6 July 1863, the novel was published by Smith. The final *Cornhill* installment appeared in August. Her completion date was 9 June, an indication of how fine the line was between her writing and the serialization, and then how the end of the serial overlapped with book publication. †

Once their preoccupation with Charles and his post office position began to diminish, it picked up again with Thornie, a high-spirited young man. In 1861,

---

* North Bank, on a site now occupied by an electric power station, was bounded by Grove End Road, St. John's Wood, and Park Road and was, at the time, private, even secluded.

† Despite her haste in preparing text for the serial and then her lack of opportunity to revise for the book version, the early text of *Romola* does not differ substantially from the 1878 Cabinet edition. The changes from one text to another are minimal, usually a word, phrase, or sentence which only very slightly affects meaning. More often than not, alterations are matters of tonal variety or emphasis, not substance. The general conclusion is that the manuscript tended to be more overwrought, the *Cornhill* text a little toned down, and the book text more attuned to niceties of expression, as well as manifesting deletions of repetitious passages. The manuscript at the British Museum Library (Add. MS 34027–34029) shows difficulty mainly in Chapters 14 ("The Peasants' Fair"), 37 ("The Tabernacle Unlocked"), 38 ("The Black Marks become Magical"), and 58 ("A Final Understanding"). By Book Two, her changes moved toward simplification: "She started" for "She felt a shock of surprize that made her turn quite cold." Eliot apparently intended to include mottoes or epigraphs at the head of each chapter, but eventually withdrew them—most were in Latin and Italian and beyond her readers' comprehension.

at seventeen, now at the Grange House School in Edinburgh, he did not take kindly to authority, as his classics master, George Robertson, discovered. Robertson was also owner of the house where Thornie lived, and one evening when the boy was locked out—after hours coming from a concert—he climbed into his room through a window. Robertson verbally abused him for his act, then kicked him in the rear; at that, Thornie lashed out and knocked the schoolmaster down, blackening his eye and further bruising him. After an intermediary intervened, Robertson offered an apology which Thornie accepted, and the incident was passed over.

Thornie now, along with Charles, spent summers with the couple, creating a noisy, tumbling atmosphere. Eliot could not really complain, since she cherished the boys, but the commotion made their absence all the more welcome. Also, Thornie needed tutoring to pass his civil service examinations. Once again, there was no effort to prepare him for the university. Having passed his first examination, in June 1862, he took the test for the Indian service, ranked thirty-eight out of several hundred applicants, and began to bone up on Sanskrit and Indian law. He failed, however, his final examination, for he had become more interested in philately than in the charms of the Indian legal system. He even published, with another enthusiast, a brief guide to postage stamps, called *Forged Stamps: How to Detect Them . . . Containing Accurate Descriptions of All Forged Stamps*. Despite Lewes's counsel that he try again, he did not wish to pursue the Indian direction. It would have meant a two-year pull at the books, and instead the Byronic Thornie cooked up idealistic schemes, such as going to Poland to fight the Russians. This would have been during the 1863 insurrection, an insurrection doomed to fail. Thornie had several such schemes, all rooted in boyish derring-do which must have driven Eliot and Lewes into panic. When the young man refused to do anything more acceptable, Lewes had to call on his influential friends about getting him a posting.

Added to this, Bertie came home from Hofwyl, making the Blandford Square house more a dormitory than an office for a serious writer. Eliot's letters pick up her family obligations and her parental chores; she sees herself as an organizer of a suddenly large home. She jokes about it, describing herself as "up to the ears in Boydem," but she also begrudged the time away from her desk as long as *Romola* still beckoned. Furthermore, Bertie, while sweet, could not be pushed like his brothers; he simply was not intellectually up to examinations. He was, accordingly, sent away to learn farming, in Lanarkshire, the area in Scotland south of Glasgow, a position also gained through Lewes's extensive network. As Eliot remarked later, Bertie was a fine fellow, but all he was fit for was farming, and even that required now a kind of skill and enterprise which would test him.

Eliot's journal from 20 May to the completion of *Romola*, on 9 June, is full of physical disabilities, a slight cough, hemicrania, more coughs and headaches. The original twelve installments stretched out to fourteen; and, as Haight remarks, she could have made it sixteen. With the completion, she went to see Rossini's *La Gaza Ladra*. There was some relief, of course, but she was more worried than ever that in the book she had offered too much local color and historical detail and too little imaginative re-creation of character and scene.

As we observe in the manuscript, to the end she was seeking the right word, the correct detail, even the precise color—matters for which Thomas Trollope helped her. Thomas's brother, Anthony, warned her not to aim at a few readers, but at thousands; yet he warmed to her veracity and even to Romola, whom he praised highly as unique in fiction.

Robert Browning also wrote, after having read the first two volumes only; and his praise was lavish, especially for the noble and heroic elements. But with the third volume, he was irritated by Eliot's loss of focus; in his eyes, she should have stuck more to the moral atmosphere created by Savonarola and paid less attention to Tito, whom he found shallow and expendable. What Browning failed to observe, or else did perceive but dismissed, was Eliot's search for a counterbalance to the Savonarola motif, and in that she found Tito and his foster father, Baldassarre. They become the elements of choice for Romola, and in her need to choose one or the other, she realizes both represent extremes she cannot accept.

What Eliot did was to present nineteenth-century polarities in late-fifteenth-century guise. She infused the Romola–Savonarola encounter with her own God-less Christianity. Her positivism, which was based on humanitarian feeling as it emanated from the individual, is contrasted with Savonarola's severe religious attitudes.* Yet Eliot could not completely reject his ideas. She realized that religion enables less enlightened people than herself to manifest their feelings, as well as to control their baser impulses. She plays, so to speak, a double game. Rejecting Savonarola's strictures on self, she presents such strictures as necessary for a functioning society. Surely, she had in mind the state of English belief just past mid-century, a state she had herself reinforced with her translations. The Anglican Church, together with the smaller English Roman Catholic Church, was forced to defend itself from frontal attacks by evolutionists, agnostics, and those, like Matthew Arnold, who offered an "aesthetic life."†

Put most baldly, the argument could match John Stuart Mill against John Henry Newman, or Charles Darwin (personally a believer) against Thomas Carlyle. That split in society between those who took a scientific or rationalistic approach to life and those who argued for more traditional and spiritual forms— a split which has carried without resolution into our century—was what Eliot chose to place in late-fifteenth-century Florence.

On 6 July, the book version appeared. As usual, Lewes kept the reviews (mainly highly favorable) from her, although one, by R. H. Hutton in the *Spectator* (18 July 1863), came to her attention. Hutton had generously called *Romola* one of the greatest works of modern fiction, and he correctly identified Eliot's purpose as tracing the conflict between the aestheticism and scientific outlook of Lorenzo de Medici and the strictures of the Dominican friar Savonar-

---

* Savonarola's followers collected the "vanities" of the Florentines—jewelry, rich robes, and the like—and burned them in bonfires.

† In one of the most insightful (albeit antagonistic) articles written on Eliot, the liberal Catholic Richard Simpson reviewed her career to 1863. Simpson picked up contradictory impulses between "emanations of feeling" and support for a Christianity she did not believe in. He found this a fatal flaw, not in reading her, but in deciphering her results.

ola, who set himself against every dimension of that liberal culture. Hutton also saw the struggle as between superstition and learning which sought an empirical base. He found Tito a wonderful creation, unlike other reviewers; and he described Savonarola as a great triumph. However, he called Romola "the least perfect figure in the book. . . ." Her character is "half-revealed and more sug-gested than fully painted." He closes by declaring that while *Romola* will never be Eliot's most popular book, it is much the greatest she has produced.

On 8 August, Eliot did the unusual, she responded directly to Hutton. She grants he has seized on her ideas with a sympathetic understanding, and she defends her concentration on details as necessary for her artistic purposes. She admits she is not surprised he had difficulty with the character of Romola, because she herself believes that the problems involved in the treatment of such a character cannot be easily overcome. Although unstated, Eliot implicitly reveals that Romola has within her the tensions and conflicts we have associated with the author. She concludes by saying that if she has achieved anything, it is that the "great, great facts have struggled to find a voice" through her.

Like some gigantic hovering bird, Lewes continued to shield her throughout. He suppressed even Sara Hennell's letter (to Eliot) because it contained some gossip which reflected poorly on the serial. He cautions Sara never to tell her friend anything that others may say about her books, whether for good or ill, unless it is exceptionally gratifying. "You can tell me any details (I'm a glutton in all that concerns her, though I never look after what is said about myself [not quite true]) favorable or unfavorable; but for her to let her mind be as much as possible fixed on her art and not on the public."

Lewes's position is suggestive. In his biography, Haight agrees with the state-ment that without such protection it is possible Eliot would have written noth-ing. But that is unacceptable. Lewes became paternalistic, the protector of a grown woman, and in the truest masculine sense became her warrior defending her against a hostile world. In her long dramatic poem, *The Spanish Gypsy*, Eliot would reproduce some of this in Fedalma and her father, Zarca. Possibly Eliot might not have written anything; but in another regard, she was *impeded* from emerging fully by Lewes's hovering figure. He kept her cocooned. He also kept her *his*. Lewes's protection went further than keeping adverse criticism from her; he was her manager, literary agent, chief confidant. He became a father figure in the household; and while we should be grateful to him for providing the conditions under which she could evolve into a fiction writer, we must also see his role as one of control. How less control and more confrontation would have become manifest in her fiction we cannot tell. In *Romola* itself, with different guidance, she might not have let the novel become so clogged or permitted Romola to become so angelic. These are speculative areas. It *is* hard to argue against Lewes's strategy given the enormous career Eliot finally did have, but there is also something distasteful about this remarkable woman being walled in against the outside world by a man who had everything to gain from his protective stance.

As reviewers fought over their interpretations of *Romola*, Eliot's career went on hold. Except for the move to the Priory, on 5 November 1863, she had nothing planned. Not until her idea for a play called *The Spanish Gypsy* (later recast as a book-length romantic, dramatic poem) in May of 1864 did she have any writing ideas. As could be foreseen, *Romola* was a commercial disappointment. Smith took a considerable loss on the book's sales, and he had to console himself with the knowledge that he had acquired prestige, not financial gain. "Brother Jacob" was, in fact, Eliot's gift to the *Cornhill* to compensate for Smith's monetary losses on *Romola*. It is questionable if this story was compensatory or a way of adding literary failure to commercial failure.

The money Eliot garnered, which was invested shrewdly and safely, was the nest egg she needed for herself and Lewes's extensive family. Nearly half of his annual earnings now went to Agnes and her four children by Hunt, about £250, plus extras for clothing and medical expenses. He had other family obligations as well, a widowed sister-in-law and her child. Charles was supporting himself at the post office, barely; but Thornie and Bertie would need an outlay of capital if they emigrated. Even with his earnings as assistant editor, Lewes was still clearly overextended, and one may use this as a way of excusing Eliot's seeming avariciousness.

Yet a good deal of Eliot's emergence or transformation at this stage came as the consequence of her acquisitiveness, and her growing maturity as a writer after *Romola* cannot be disengaged from her ability to earn huge sums. She was careful not to subvert her artistic intentions, and, clearly, she did not write anything just for the sake of income, not since her articles in the *Westminster Review*. Another factor, touched upon above, was that these sizable sums gave her leverage over her family, which still rejected her, and, further, gave her advantage over all those women who would not admit her to their homes.

Robert Browning now became a visitor at Blandford Square, his interest in Eliot quickened by her immersion in Italian matters, his own great love. Her life had become quite domestic making a home for the boys, whom she refers to amusingly. "Conceive us, please," she writes her old friend Mrs. Taylor, "with three boys at home, all bigger than their father! It is a congestion of youthfulness on our mature brain that disturbs the course of our lives a little, and makes us think of most things as good to be deferred till the boys are settled again."

Eliot and Lewes took a break by traveling to Worthing, on the coast of Sussex, on 10 August, returning eight days later; but their most significant venture in August was to purchase the Priory, which would become, finally, a permanent home. The Blandford Square house was filled with boys, and some of their activities were not welcome news, such as Thornie's sense of drift and a rebelliousness which revealed little focus. Unable to stand the bickering, Eliot went off to Richmond alone for a fortnight.* As Eliot told Cara: ". . . we are still in a nightmare of uncertainty about our boys—awaiting one letter here and

---

* Influenced by Barbara Bodichon, Thornie would eventually sail for Natal, South Africa, on 16 October, armed with a long list of recommendatory letters to various notables, a rifle and revolver, and a smattering of Dutch and Zulu picked up from grammars and dictionaries. Bertie ended up in Scotland, in Lanarkshire, a farming apprentice.

another there, and feeling in many ways the wide gap between theoretic longing and possible practice." But she consoles herself with having at her side "a dear companion who is a perpetual fountain of courage and cheerfulness and of considerate tenderness for my lack of these virtues."

Eliot looked forward to being settled at the Priory, for which she had paid £2,000, on a forty-nine-year lease. She left all decorations to Owen Jones, an architect and interior decorator, although she trembled at the cost. Jones did an exquisite job, with new wallpaper, carpeting, and all new furniture, drawing them into what Lewes called "serious expense." To move their possessions into the Priory, including their large collection of books, took an entire week; and even then, Lewes was not able to arrange them, nor was the drawing room habitable. During the move, one of the workers stole Eliot's purse. But the house delighted them. The new quarters were bright, with large windows, and the rooms themselves were expansive. It was clearly a home for people with upper-middle-class aspirations, not luxurious but exceptionally well appointed.

Eliot of course found the move hellish. She singled out the choice of carpets and tables as "an affliction to me and seems like a nightmare from which I shall find it bliss to awake into my old world of care for things quite apart from the upholstery." Despite complaints, by 24 November the Priory was ready for a housewarming, which coincided with Charles's twenty-first birthday. The decorator suggested to Eliot that in keeping with events and the expense already incurred, she should dress up, and she did, in what she called a "grey moiré antique." The house filled with old friends, and included Charles's colleague at the post office, Henry Buxton Forman, later a notorious bibliographer and bookseller. Lewes and Eliot entertained Spencer, Mrs. Peter Taylor, the Robert Noels from old days, and Owen Jones, the decorator; there was music, and it became a festive occasion. Eliot seemed actually pleased with the event and with the results of the decoration.

She had just passed her forty-fourth birthday. Bertie was settled on a Scottish farm, but Thornie, en route to South Africa, was out of touch for another month or two. Nevertheless, she says her parental mind was at rest. As she surveyed 1863, she appeared to be at peace with herself. She had come through some difficult personal and professional moments, or so she thought. Lewes made his own assessment of the year as "chequered."[*]

Thackeray, whose editorship of the *Cornhill* crossed over with Lewes's role, died suddenly, at fifty-two, on 24 December. As part of a large turnout of between 1,000 and 1,500 people, Lewes attended the funeral. As the result of the Thackeray funeral, he reencountered Theodore Martin, an old acquaintance from *Fraser's* days in the 1840s. Martin and his wife, the actress Helen

---

[*] He was the recipient of the *Romola* bound manuscript, with the typical inscription from Eliot: "To the Husband whose perfect Love has been the best source of her insight and strength this manuscript is given by his devoted wife, the writer." Incidentally, when Smith, Elder & Co. published the novel in three volumes, they did so without the twenty-three Leighton illustrations which had appeared in the *Cornhill*.

Faucit, subsequently became friendly with the couple, since she fell outside the circle which ostracized Eliot.

On 29 January 1864, another death occurred, her half-brother Robert Evans. Eliot wrote to his son, also called Robert Evans, and although she extended her sympathy to the son as well as to his mother, her letter lacks warmth. Robert had become so distant she could only recall him as someone who had once been kind and generous toward her. Eliot wrote directly to the widow on 12 February and expressed all the requisite feelings. She tells of her half-brother's "ready kindness," and says she cherishes the memory of how both she and he venerated their "one dear Father." Eliot adds it would be most pleasant to hear from her, as a "very sweet renewal of the past." She offers her blessings after this "supreme loss." The formality of the message is tinged with some sadness that an era has passed and cannot be recalled. To ensure it was not to be recalled, she signed "M. E. Lewes."

A literary piece, an outline of a play, was written in February or March of 1864; apparently by Lewes, it was overscored by Eliot. Called *Savello,* the play is an opera buffa suggested by the Don Juan legend, perhaps more directly by Mozart's *Don Giovanni.* Many parallels are present. Savello is an insatiable lover, he has a faithful servant, he revels in his profligacy and the misery he brings others, and he dies done in by his own impetuous behavior with women. The entire remnant of the play—the play itself is not extant—covers one page; and it sounds, in summary, like dreadful stuff. But possibly it did serve a purpose, for what appears to be Lewes's work entered into Eliot's head as beckoning her to attempt a new form, her own play. This idea would not develop until May, when she and Lewes were in Venice, but the sense is she was worn out with novel writing and needed some respite. In seven years, she had published three novellas, one short novel, and three quite long novels, one of them involving extensive and exhaustive research. *The Spanish Gypsy,* as this latest venture came to be called, was something she could take seriously but not exhaust herself with.

In early March, Blackwood sent on a check for sales of Eliot's four books published by him: *Mill* was not moving, but *Adam Bede* "goes on," and *Marner* was selling slightly. The check for £150 covered mainly the 6-shilling edition of *Mill* from 1862 and the 6-shilling editions of *Scenes* and *Marner.* The accounting for *Bede* would come later. As usual, the check was delivered directly to Lewes. Blackwood was formally correct, but cool. Eliot was herself suffering from ailments which caused considerable bodily pain, to the extent she identifies with Hecuba. "I wish an immortal drama could be got out of my sorrows," she tells Mrs. Taylor, "that people might be the better for them two thousand years hence." Such passages alongside others counting her blessings indicate that the jolly manner Eliot presented on occasion was short-lived or was social papering for the sake of her friends.

Despite the new house, the fact that the three young men were at last on their way (or seemed to be), the financial security now hers for life, and the recognition that she and Lewes were inextricably bound together, she could not rid herself of a chronic sadness which might suddenly become so acute she could not work. Then she sank into reading, not as one reads for pleasure, but as one reads for seeking oneself, as she did with Hecuba. A trip to Scotland, especially to Glasgow, at the end of March helped break the cycle. They saw Helen Faucit, Theodore Martin's wife, in *Cymbeline, Much Ado about Nothing,* and *Romeo and Juliet.* They mixed socially with the Martins, but Lewes was unwell, attributed by him to the smell of paint in the hotel, to the east wind, and to the general noise. Headache and sickness resulted, possibly migraine, with not a little nerves in the mix.

They saw Bertie on this trip and were quite pleased with his situation at the farm and with the owner, Stodart. Bertie had even learned to weave at the loom and was quickly picking up all the skills a successfully run farm involved. Lewes seemed bolstered by the boy's attitude and performance. Furthermore, a long letter from Thornie in South Africa revealed he was in high spirits.

Eliot's proliferation of names at this time indicates some renewed uncertainty, conflict, or reconsideration. In writing Sara, she signs herself "Pollian," the old, familiar name from a very different time. To Barbara Bodichon, she is "Marian." To her half-brother's son, she signs "M. E. Lewes," an aunt distancing herself. Also to D'Albert-Durade, she is "M. E. Lewes," which seems fitting. Within a period of two months or so, she has used three different names, and on some occasions two different names to the same person: to Sara, both "Marian" and "Pollian"; to Cara, both "Marian" and "M. E. Lewes." The names carried her deeply into her past and then forward to her present "married" state. Whatever else they signify, the profusion of names suggests a confusion of realms. Thus, in 1864—to limit ourselves to that year alone—Eliot had become four people, each with its own experience of life. *Pollian* (not Polly) was the name, as mentioned, suggested by a subversive force.* *Marian* was itself a shift from her birth name of Mary Anne. *M. E. Lewes* was a name she was not entitled to. And *George Eliot* was a nom de plume, conjured up by circumstance.

We cannot dismiss this strange conglomeration of identities as merely the choices an independent woman has made for herself. The shifting identities must be perceived as elements of internal confusion: not that she was unaware of who she was, but that unconsciously she had difficulty in identifying which self she was at any given time. This did not lead, apparently, to different personalities for each person; her letters do not bear out that she actually became a different person each time she changed her name. But all this suggests that in

---

*Not lost on us is the juxtaposition of the "demonic" Pollian with the virginal Marian, the name carrying back to the mother of Jesus and caught in the popular imagination as the Maid Marian in Nottingham, not too distant from Eliot's birthplace.

writing under different names she thought of herself as having been divided into segments, each of which meant different things to her. We could speculate that the confusion of realms, if it were indeed that, was linked to her period of inactivity, her lack of a suitable object for her next work, and a general relaxation of intellectual activity. At a deeper level, it suggests she had lost her moorings and was compensating for the loss with a retrieval of name and identities.

What was needed, and it came fortuitously, was a trip abroad. Accompanied by a painter friend named Frederic Burton,* Lewes and Eliot left the Priory on 4 May for Italy, with several stops along the way. Their object was to spend several weeks in Venice, which Burton knew well. From Paris and Chambéry, they traveled familiar territory, through the Mont Cenis pass, then to Turin and Milan, before arriving in Venice. During her stay there, Eliot glimpsed the idea for *The Spanish Gypsy,* which she would not complete for another four years, in 1868, after she had written *Felix Holt, the Radical.* In some related way, her idea for writing about a gypsy girl during the time of the Spanish struggle with the Moors is an overflow from Romola's immersion in Florentine politics at the time of Savonarola's attempted coup. Eliot was to conclude that her idea derived from Titian's *Annunciation,*† in which, as the familiar story goes, a young maiden awaiting marriage "has suddenly announced to her that she is chosen to fulfill a great destiny, entailing a terribly different experience from that of ordinary womanhood. . . . Here, I thought, is a subject grander than that of Iphigenia [Agamemnon's sacrificial daughter], and it has never been used." Then Eliot extends that individual moment to one in Spanish history, "when the struggle with the Moors was attaining its climax, and when there was the gypsy race present under such conditions as would enable me to get my heroine and the hereditary claim on her among the gypsies. I needed the opposition of race to give the need for renouncing the expectation of marriage."

The couple lived in the Hôtel de la Ville, where they had stayed four years earlier, with a salon and three bedrooms, a balcony overlooking the Grand Canal, and only a few steps from the Rialto. Lewes bragged to his son Charles that for this splendor they pay only 9 francs each per diem. It is the tone of a man still seeking a good bargain, but also proud he can afford the best. Leaving Burton in Venice after three glorious weeks there—not a little abetted by the painter's knowledgeable eye—they spent another three weeks of heavy traveling before returning to the Priory on 20 June.

The journey acted at least temporarily as a regeneration of spirits. Yet even

---

*They had met Burton in Munich, and like most of their friends, he was not only a creative person but successful in other ways as well, becoming in time director of the National Gallery in London. In 1865, Burton did a chalk drawing of Eliot which has become one of the most famous and familiar portraits.

†In her notes on *The Spanish Gypsy,* written in 1868. (See Cross, III, pp. 42–43, but more accessible in Haight, p. 376.) Corneille's *El Cid* was another possible indirect source, and Haight suggests Bulwer-Lytton's *Leila, or the Siege of Granada,* in which the heroine is not a gypsy but a Jew.

while traveling buoyed them, Lewes's health seemed delicate, and they were unable to go to Ravenna, which Eliot wished to see. Her words on returning, however, are ominous: "You can imagine," she wrote D'Albert-Durade, "that London does not look pretty after such a journey, and the gratification we get in returning home must be such as comes from the sense of duties to be fulfilled there." But the real surprise was Charles's announcement he planned to marry Gertrude Hill, the granddaughter of Dr. Southwood Smith. * Eliot thought the young woman remarkably handsome, possessing a splendid contralto voice, and seemingly to have been brought up, she says, in a way that has preserved the best of youthfulness while providing her with "much domestic experience." Eliot assumed she would be a housewife, not that she would pursue any professional career with that "magnificent contralto." We sense here the slightest germ of Gwendolen Harleth and her attempts to use her voice professionally. Eliot's view of marriage is of interest: "One never knows what to wish about marriage— the evils of an early choice [Gertrude was almost twenty-seven, Charles twenty-two] may be easily counterbalanced by the vitiation that often comes from long bachelorhood. So Mr. Lewes and I fix our minds on the good we see instead of the possible ills which we may never see." Eliot's position becomes bizarre: not legally a wife, not really a mother, she is now becoming not precisely a mother-in-law, and in time she would have to face becoming not quite a grandmother.

Eliot was sufficiently composed about the coming marriage to joke that she was surprised a woman of twenty-five (really twenty-seven) could "fall in love with our crude bit of human goodness." But she admits parents are not judges in these matters, and she and Lewes rejoice in Charles's happiness. Starting in the summer of 1864, Eliot sat for Frederic Burton, who had asked to try his hand at a portrait. As Haight indicates, she was dissatisfied with photographs of her, which highlighted her large features in uncomplimentary ways, and she was dissatisfied as well with the Laurence drawing, although that had softened some of her facial heaviness. Burton tried several versions, beginning with a sitting on 29 June. He kept at it until what appears to be a final version a full year later, which, after Eliot's death, was given to the National Gallery. Before that, it was Lewes's property. As we have already observed, in the Burton portrait she seems more definitive; she had become herself. The pose is still pensive, and the nose still dominates; but there is a kind of regularity, so that the prominent nose composes rather than bisects the facial structure. Eliot's hair is abundant, parted in the middle and combed fully to both sides, a frame. Her skin looks clear and healthy, her eyes penetrate. The Burton likeness becomes for those

---

* Dr. Thomas Southwood Smith had two considerable careers, as a Unitarian minister and as a practicing physician. He was also something of a literary man, being one of the founders of the *Westminster Review* (in its earliest days, before its reorganization), and contributing an article "The Use of the Dead to the Living," which was not a philosophical treatise but an advocacy for dissection. He had good results, for the body of Jeremy Bentham, the famous utilitarian philosopher, came to Dr. Smith for dissection. When Smith's daughter and her husband could no longer afford their household, he adopted Gertrude, who was born on 28 July 1837. When Smith died in 1861, Gertrude was taken care of by Mary and Margaret Gillies, who had been her mother's bridesmaids. All this reveals a young woman well brought up and completely protected against adversity.

who could never see the woman herself *the* Eliot portrait. She is, while not happy, settled.

With *The Spanish Gypsy* firming, Eliot needed to discover some way of dealing with her subject, which, we have noted, was not unlike the situation with *Romola.* She needed coordinates, tensions, conflicts. As with the novel, she decided she had to know everything about her subject, and toward that end she studied the Spanish language, working hard at both grammar and punctuation. She translated *Don Quixote,* for example, as Lewes read it aloud. She undertook a regimen of reading heavily in history and in ecclesiastical studies of the period, including Prescott's *Ferdinand and Isabella,* Gibbon's *Decline and Fall* (a reread-ing), and works by J. K. L. Gieseler and J. L. von Mosheim. While she advanced with Spanish, she read about the Moors in several languages. In terms of acquiring knowledge and linguistic skills, there was no falling off in her abili-ties as she moved toward her forty-fifth birthday, in 1864; there was, in fact, an avidity for learning which pointed in a straight line back to her earliest days.

Lewes, however, was a continued source of worry—his health was poor, and even riding did not help. They tried Harrogate, a spa in Yorkshire, just north of Leeds, for ten days in September, and then moved on to Scarborough, northeast of Harrogate on the coast, also for the waters. Eliot told Sara there was not much improvement in Lewes's health, but she hoped the chalybeate waters (sul-fur springs at Harrogate, useful for jaundice and skin diseases) would help. But what Lewes was suffering from did not appreciably improve. Lewes's letters to his son Charles remained cheerful and not at all self-serving. But his chronic illnesses did keep him at the center of things, since Eliot worried constantly about him.

On 1 October, the couple returned to the Priory from Scarborough, and Eliot began almost immediately to write the first act of *Gypsy.* She treated it as a play, although she recast it as a long historical-dramatic poem, in blank verse, per-haps as a kind of Shakespearean exercise. When Lewes left in October for the Malvern waters, in Worcestershire, she completed Act II. By this time, Lewes had given up his consulting editorship at the *Cornhill.* Declining circulation made it impossible for the magazine to afford his large compensation. He natu-rally regretted the loss of income, and this might explain why Eliot in the face of such difficulty was moving along on a new project. As an investment in the couple, Smith had suffered a double loss: on *Romola* and now in the *Cornhill* circulation. Strikingly, Smith did not give up on Lewes, and when he started up the *Pall Mall Gazette* a little later, he offered him another consulting editor-ship or advisory position, this time for £500 a year.

Throughout the rest of 1864, as she passed her forty-fifth birthday, Eliot labored on *The Spanish Gypsy.* After Act II, which she read to Lewes, she found herself foundering on the remainder; this brought on the inevitable ailments and headache. She plugged along, however, completing Act III on Christmas Day. Lewes praised the work highly, but her dyspepsia suggested she knew differ-ently. Drama was not her forte, and the subject itself seems to have been played out in *Romola.* Only a more contemporary subject might pull her out of what she called "this swamp of miseries." Her talk is all of malaise and feebleness—clearly psychological and emotional. In her play, the subject of a father demanding loyalty of his daughter while an "intruder" wins her heart was only to bring back the worst of memories and the worst of times. The fact that Lewes "approved it highly" was only a temporary respite. * Even his acceptance of Smith's latest offer did not bring her around. In accepting the *Pall Mall Gazette*, Lewes annoyed Anthony Trollope by turning down—after accepting—the editorship of the new *Fortnightly Review*. He reasoned that an editorship would strain his health, whereas an advisory position was manageable.

Bertie visited from Christmas Day to New Year's, his visit acting as a tonic. Lewes and Eliot celebrated with a family party, which included Lewes's mother, now a great fan of Eliot's. After Christmas dinner, postponed to 27 December, the couple picked up sufficiently so that they headed for Paris on 15 January, ostensibly to give Lewes a chance to establish ties with the editor of the *Revue des deux Mondes*, Eugène Fourcade, with the aim of contributing articles.

They returned from Paris on 25 January. Before assuming official duties at the *Pall Mall*, Lewes knew that his defection from the new *Fortnightly* meant that some compensation from the couple was called for, and Eliot filled the gap with a long, somewhat acerbic analysis (15 May 1865) of William Lecky's *History of the Rise and Influence of the Spirit of Rationalism in Europe*, a two-volume monster mixing history and speculation.† Her willingness to do this resulted from the malaise she suffered in her own work and a desire to help Lewes. The review also gave her an opportunity to reconsider her own philosophy as she was entering a new phase in her career, a reconsideration which takes hold in *Felix Holt*, *Middlemarch*, and *Daniel Deronda*.

Lecky's argument was that rationalism helped save Europe from witchcraft and other fanciful ideas, and that this act of salvation was a sign of "progress" in man's history. Eliot, however, balked at the simplification of history she found revealed in Lecky's discussions of miracles, secularism, moral development, aesthetic and scientific forces in society, and the rest. She felt there was no clear definition of rationalism, no sense of coherence to the argument, no illumination "by a sufficiently clear conception and statement of the agencies at work, or the mode of their action."

She was clearly using Lecky as a way of working through her own skepticism about rationalism as a progressive force in human life. As a novelist, not a historian, she observed a different set of guidelines in society. Without rejecting some forms of rationalism, she concluded that mysteries had to be accounted for as part of human motivation and shapers of lives. As a supporter of the physical sciences, Eliot promulgated an empirical, experiential dimension; but this pro-

---

* The entire project was so antithetical to her talents that after completing Act III, she became anxiety-ridden to such an extent that Lewes actually took the drama away from her in late February of 1865.

† It appeared as "William Lecky's *The Influence of Rationalism*," about 7,500 words.

cess was not merely rationalistic. It involved the senses, some speculation, and an awareness of ambiguities. As a novelist, if she followed Lecky's views, she suspected her work would collapse under ideas of progress.* She signed her review article George Eliot, a break with the previous anonymity found in English periodical writing and probably an attempt to capitalize on her fame.

Just before doing the Lecky piece, Eliot wrote two brief articles for Smith's *Pall Mall,* probably to ease the fact that *Romola* bled him. One piece was on German scholarship, "A Word for the Germans" (7 March), the other on domestic help, "Servants' Logic" (17 March)—neither one more than left-handed work. In the first, she praises German labor and German genius, warning that no one should portray "the typical German" until he had made his acquaintance and seen the thoroughness with which that "typicality" is imbued. The second of the two pieces, on servants, is that they are not to be reasoned with, but ordered. Little democratic sentiment rests in the following: "Reason about everything with your child, you make him a monster, without reverence, without affections. Reason about things with your servants, consult them, give them the suffrage, and you produce no other effect in them than a sense of anarchy in the house, a suspicion of irresoluteness in you, the most opposed to that spirit of order and promptitude which can alone enable them to fill their places and make their lives respectable." With her own servants, Eliot was demanding—she was a demon for order and neatness—but fair.

March of 1865 was a propitious month. On the 20th, Charles was married to Gertrude Hill. Eliot thought again of picking up *The Spanish Gypsy,* but on the 29th of the month she began a novel, duly noted in her journal, which became *Felix Holt, the Radical.* This would prove to be less popular than her earlier fictions, but artistically a distinct improvement over *Romola.* The period of malaise and despair—all the aftermath of *Romola*—seemed relieved; and with this novel, she was primed for the most productive part of her career. Having passed the midpoint of her forties, she could have ended her career on the intractable material of *The Spanish Gypsy.* Had she stopped after less than a decade of fiction writing, she would have been considered a fine but somewhat minor writer. She might have entered the literary canon, but below Austen and the Brontës, perhaps on a par with Mrs. Gaskell, surely below Dickens and Thackeray, and probably below Trollope, Meredith, and Hardy. Without the splendor of her imagination and the broadening of her voice manifested in the later novels, she would be perceived as working, however successfully, in a lesser mode.

Felix Holt became a battleground for the nature of culture itself, ground already surveyed by Arnold, Carlyle, Mill, and Ruskin. Eliot was carving out

---

* If we wish to hear views of progress at their most vulgar, we can cite novelist and clergyman Charles Kingsley's words about the Great Exhibition in 1851. Materialism and God are evoked in a tandem linkage which makes no historical sense. "The spinning jenny and the railroad, Cunard's liners and the electric telegraph, are to me . . . signs that we are, on some points at least, in harmony with the universe; that there is a mighty spirit working among us . . . the Ordering and Creating God."

her own sense of what the larger culture might be: the question of democracy and its values; the role of the political process in preserving a society or changing it; the positioning of the parties as either representational or not; the role of the landed gentry or local aristocracy; the part played by the working man in a class- and caste-ridden society; the state of England—where it is to go, how it is to fare, what it might become. With Felix as her spokesman, she was mainly concerned with the limits of democracy, so that rights become secondary to responsibilities, for both the working man and the landed gentry. We suspect a double standard: order before everything, fear of the working class, an evolution of rights as a response to Marxists and English socialists, the desperate need for an organic, coherent society.

Can we determine precisely what occurred in this general 1863–65 period which gave Eliot the impetus, energy, and imaginative power to transcend her feelings of malaise? We are tempted to say she had hit the bottom, and once there, after considerable writhing, she reached more deeply into herself than ever before; from that, she could exorcise the subjective parts of herself and let a more objective, broader element emerge. In this two-year period after *Romola*, she discovered something in herself which encouraged liberation. We could point to the fact that Lewes's sons were gradually getting settled; the fact of the couple's prosperity and security; and the fact that after years of exploration she had established herself, given herself direction, and proven to her family and others that she was more than capable. All of this is true, but it is not the most significant area. We are also tempted to see climate changes in her, and here we admittedly speculate—a maturation as the result of aging, possibly a hormonal, physical alteration now that she was, for that period, deep in middle age.

All of these explanations possess validity. But the more likely reasons for her transformation were possibly far deeper, well within her imaginative powers where she pursued a life unreachable by Lewes or anyone else. In there, she had created her own world with its own patterns—religious, moral, social, ethical, artistic—and only she could reach it. We might say the same about any major creative artist, but in her instance there were differences. The struggle she had made to establish herself as a female writer by disguise gave her a uniqueness denied others (except the Brontës). The battle she had fought to make her social positioning of herself seem normal and regularized was another unique factor. The enormous financial success she had had, as a writer, was surely out of the ordinary for the author of serious, as against purely popular, fiction.

By 1865, she had played several roles which had separated her from the run of other women. She had carved out something distinct and unique. This gave her a base of operations no other female writer had, and which no nineteenth-century male writer could compare with. From this distinct position of opposition to so much her society accepted—things with which Dickens, Thackeray, Trollope, Meredith, and the others did not have to deal—she had empowered herself; and in some way, it all came together to give her the energies for her final decade of novels, through *Daniel Deronda* in 1876. A good deal of such a theory is speculative, but it is founded on the idea that rather than being weakened by her various struggles, she was ultimately strengthened.* In that two-year period after *Romola* was completed, she had hovered between two extremes: a malaise which could have crippled her for the remainder of her life and a strong recovery which would enable her to work despite periodic returns of depression and other ailments. That she made the recovery is, very possibly, firmly linked to the fact that she had remade herself through other forms of adversity; that she had insisted on her own priorities and prerogatives; and that from this vantage point of having taken on the entire English establishment—with the help of Lewes and several friends—she had uniquely emerged.

---

* Certainly, the "Author's Introduction" to *Felix Holt* suggests a strengthening. For much of its brief length, the introduction is concerned with the contexts of another era, a noncommercial, nonprogressive, organic time. Clearly, Carlyle seems influential here, although we should not discount Eliot's own predilections starting with *Scenes*. The question of when this introduction was written remains thorny: the argument for its having been written before the novel itself is that it does establish social and cultural contexts for what ensues; the argument against is that it is numbered (1–12) separately from the novel—Chapter 1 begins the novel's pagination. The paper itself is also different.

15

Out of the Valley
with Felix

"God was cruel when he made women."

Parallel to this renewal of literary self was a strengthening of Eliot's sense of man's lot. The occasion was the death at twenty of Nelly Bray, an adopted daughter of Charles and Cara Bray, dead of consumption on 1 March 1865, and someone Eliot was quite fond of. Finally, on 18 March, she brought herself to write to the Brays and tried to put the devastating death into philosophical perspective. Her words are directives for her own fictional characters, as well as comfort for the grieving family.

> I don't know whether you strongly share, as I do, the old belief that made men say the gods loved those who died young. It seems to me truer than ever, now life has become more complex and more and more difficult problems have to be worked out. Life, though a good to men on the whole, is a doubtful good to many, and to some not a good at all. To my thought, it is a source of constant mental distortion to make the denial of this a part of religion, to go on pretending things are better than they are. . . . So to me, early death takes the aspect of salvation—though I feel too that those who live and suffer may sometimes have the greater blessedness of *being* a salvation.

These lines are important to remind us that while Eliot had reemerged whole in 1865 she was not a joyous or buoyant person. Her sense of human tragedy had deepened; not that she thought people lived within a circle of doom, but she felt the transitory nature of life made us recognize how puny we were in the plan of things. Her immersion in natural law—and her acceptance of Darwinian evolution—as well as her own experience from young womanhood made her realize that one's wishes and needs play only a small role in the way of the world. *

More astonishing is that just a few days before she entered upon *Felix Holt*, she wrote in her journal that she was "in deep depression, feeling powerless." She complains she has written nothing but beginnings since her piece on servants for *Pall Mall*. Eliot was an intellectual writer in ways we would never ascribe to Dickens, but she was also a visceral author who needed familiar territory. Although her subjects were not limited to country life, as in Jane Austen, she did gain her range from her immersion in such particulars, and only from that could she spread her net. *Felix Holt* served another important function, in that it took Eliot back to the time of the First Reform Bill, also the period of her greatest novel, *Middlemarch*. In *Felix Holt*, the time is just after the bill has passed, from September 1832 to May 1833, with the major activity coming from September to March. The novel returned Eliot to her young womanhood when she was first becoming attuned to English political and social life.† And in still a further sense, it brought her around full circle to *Scenes of Clerical Life*, which hailed the days when life had not been traduced by modern technology.

The period was, in these respects, a kind of Arcady or Eden, even with all the abuses of rotten boroughs, unjust Corn Laws, unrepresented cities (Birmingham, near Coventry, had no member for the House of Commons), and an abundance of pauperism. Homelessness was a way of life. Despite all this—and Eliot mentions these aspects in her "Author's Introduction"—her memories were pure and she could indulge herself in a society which sanctioned slow development. But not for those in different circumstances; for a Dickens character, 1832 might have seemed nightmarish.

What Eliot celebrated in the earlier time was its coherence and hierarchical rightness, in which each unit of society had its place and knew what was expected of it. She emphasizes expectations as part of the idyllic past, a past surely colored by quirks of memory and by the aging process itself: ". . . here and there a cottage with bright transparent windows showing pots of blooming balsams or geraniums, and little gardens in front all double daisies of dark wall flowers; at the wall, clean and comely women carrying yoked buckets and towards the free school small Britons dawdling on, and handling their marbles in the pocket of unpatched curduroys adorned with brass buttons."

It is all very quaint, except that in reality the women were workhorses, enduring drudgery from dawn to dusk, and many died in childbirth either early on or after repeated pregnancies, since husbands insisted on large families; most chil-

---

* That fate could operate in unforeseen ways. The treaty of 1860 with France created a shortage of French ribbon, and this in turn made Coventry sink, as its manufactures closed down. The Brays were deeply affected, and the entire region suffered.

† The manuscript is in the British Museum Library, in three volumes; it contains few alterations, but, as we shall see, there are several passages Eliot decided to delete. As for the time: it comes when Maggie Tulliver was herself passing from twelve to thirteen. Maggie dies in 1839 (she is described as "gone nine" when Catholic emancipation was the talk, in 1829).

dren experienced only a few years of school before they had to help at home or on the farm; while there was usually sufficient food, it was monotonous for most, barely nutritional for the majority, and subject to disadvantageous price changes; and there was catastrophe—loss of job, sudden illness—for which almost no one was prepared. That was the actuality, and yet Eliot in retrospect presents it as a true community, the *Gemeinschaft* mentioned in the introduction, in which a society cohered and resisted capitalistic exploitation. In Eliot's picture, there was little such exploitation, and yet we know that anyone born without certain advantages—hers, for example—could look forward to a life of class and caste injustice, without hope of appreciable change.

Nevertheless, in some way, whether she actually believed her memories or not, she needed them. The past made her expansive. It was not quite the "Edenic dream" we associate with American writers, since Eliot did not see in the past a sense of renewal, rebirth, or resurrection. What she saw, more than anything else, was an alternative way of life, preferable in its dimensions, and probably, she felt, healthier for the individual. Such a vision was the motor that drove her fictions.

Yet Eliot did not misremember or turn *all* pastness into idyllic adventures. As she began to think deeply about *Felix Holt*, she recalled the other side of a coherent, organic life, the unemployment among miners and weavers as the textile trade dipped, the need for soup kitchens for the poor, the injustice of the elections taking place in and around 1832, the way in which such elections could be manipulated by the party in power in local elections (the Tories), so that force would prevent the rightful winner from claiming his reward, the means by which elections were bought, manipulated, and distorted: all of these lessons which establish *Felix Holt* as a very prescient view of human greed, ambition, and perversion of justice, the ingredients of a modern political system.

As she dug in, she picked up many details which fell outside her memories. The activity in the novel revolves around Nuneaton, the Coventry suburb where Eliot gew up, and it centers on an election growing out of the agitation over the Reform Bill. In preparation, she consulted back issues of the London *Times,* transferring several passages into her notebook; a procedure she followed, also, with the *Annual Register* for 1832–33, Samuel Bamford's *Passages in the Life of a Radical,* books by Mill (especialy his *Political Economy,* for the political theory she wanted to introduce), Macaulay's *History,* also a history of the Puritans, a study by Hallam, and work by Fawcett on the British laborer. *

We could also cite the anonymous private journal "Occurrences at Nunea-

---

* In her journal for May and June 1865, she mentions several of these works, along with, unexpectedly perhaps, a rereading of Aristotle's *Poetics.* In fictional terms, parallels to *Felix Holt* appear in Kingsley's *Alton Locke,* Dickens's *Hard Times,* Gaskell's *Mary Barton* and *North and South,* Disraeli's *Sybil, or the Two Nations,* and Mrs. Trollope's *Michael Anthony the Factory Boy,* among others. Fear of violence or being drawn into radical action leads to the individual's need for redemption through innocence. An innocent man (Felix; Alton; Blackpool, in Dickens) is accused of a serious crime, murder, theft, or the like, and the novel is diverted from the strong social issues to the proof of "innocence" of the person accused. Or else, in *Mary Barton,* real radical activity is diverted onto someone mistakenly accused. When the innocent person is exonerated, then the author has redeemed his or her original premise; and all the while the political issues go begging.

ton," for 21 December 1832, as a valuable source. The army was called in to stop an election in which the Radical candidate (Dempster Heming) was likely to defeat the entrenched Tory (Dugdale). The Riot Act was read and when the crowd did not disperse—a crowd obviously favoring the Radical—mounted soldiers cut a swathe through the people in an action reminiscent of the Peterloo Massacre in 1819 or some of the czar's actions against his subjects. Dozens were wounded by sword thrusts, horses trampling them, or simply in fleeing; one man died of injuries. The Tory won, having spent £12,000, a phenomenal amount for a local election.

As soon as *Felix Holt* became implanted in her imagination, Eliot began to perk up. There were the usual headaches—a condition she expected to reconcile herself to—but the malaise lifted. Her journal entries are chatty and involved; she does not indulge that note of disengagement from herself which characterized the entries when depression squeezed her. Lewes's poor health was always a source of worry—they would leave in August for a month's trip to Normandy and Brittany, as a way of clearing their heads and ridding themselves of ills. Visitors came and went from the Priory, some of them, like Browning, becoming regulars. An unusual event came up when Eliot was asked to contribute to the Mazzini fund.* As she explained to Mrs. Peter Taylor, whose husband had just been returned to the House of Commons, she was afraid the fund might mask some conspiracy. Mazzini was an Italian patriot who, when elected to the Italian parliament, refused to swear allegiance to the king, mainly because he, Mazzini, was still under a death sentence the king refused to cancel. Eliot now walked a thin line, trying to be supportive of Mazzini, whom she genuinely admired, but revealing all her old fears about conspiracy, riot, and that imbalance in which society might slide toward anarchy. Avowing a reverence for the Italian, she still refused to contribute to the fund:

> Now, though I believe there are cases in which conspiracy may be a sacred, necessary struggle against organised wrong, there are also cases in which it is hopeless, and can produce nothing but misery; or needless, because it is not the best means attainable of reaching the desired end; or unjustifiable, because it resorts to acts which are more unsocial in their character than the very wrong they are directed to extinguish; and in these three supposable cases it seems to me that it would be a social crime to further conspiracy even by the impulse of a little finger, to which one may well compare a small money subscription.

Eliot, in fact, never deals with the "supposables" that could lead from organized wrongs; and this omission is a key to the fears she had of any chaotic activity which might rend a society. So directed was she to coherence and cohe-

---

* Giuseppe Mazzini was a fierce republican who, having been exiled to England after 1837, wrote revolutionary articles from this base. He was a firm believer in action by the people, the basis of his republicanism, and, if necessary, he recommended revolutionary action. Mazzini appealed to English liberals, as well as to liberals throughout Europe, but his political means were antithetical to the entire English process.

sion that she could not countenance any alternative, even when that society was palpably unjust—a condition not at all unknown to her. All of this enters her fiction in Felix's plea to the working men not to jeopardize stability for the sake of a few temporary promises.

On 10 August, the couple embarked on another of their arduous journeys abroad. Although they planned only a month in France, they did not stint on the number of places they would visit. Eliot's journal lists enough destinations for a couple half their age and in much better health: Boulogne, Dieppe, Rouen, Caen, Bayeux, Vire, Avranches, Dol, St.-Malo, Rennes, Auray, Carnac, Nantes, Tours (by 26 August), Le Mans, Chartres, Paris (29 August–2 September), Rouen, Dieppe, Abbeville, Boulogne, and back to the Priory on 7 September. True, these places are located in only two areas of France, but the distances are considerable, especially in an age when trains moved slowly and carriages were often the sole mode of transportation. What appears as a break in their routine, now that Eliot was writing again, appears like a killing schedule, moving in and out of hotels and lodgings, finding places to eat, besides the touring itself of churches, historical sites, and museums. The places were, indeed, lovely, located in picturesque settings for the most part, and chock-full of cultural interests: in Rouen alone, the great cathedral, the Joan of Arc memorabilia, the museum, the *Madame Bovary* ambience; in Caen, the great churches (which in the main withstood even the savage bombings of World War Two); in St.-Malo, the lovely walks along the walls of the city, the beaches, and the labyrinthine paths. Ill health did not appear to impede their rapid movement or their intense interest in what they saw.

Refreshed and exhausted at the same time, they resettled into their "real" life, writing. She also found a letter at the Priory from Sara, apparently charging her with having fallen out of "love" with her old friend, and we have Eliot's strong denial. With the friendship crumbling, we note her effort to deny the very changes occurring in herself which led to a reevaluation of all her former associations. Careful not to reject entirely the personal past, eager to seem the same old Pollian, she tended to deny she was altogether another woman from the one Sara knew.

As if to make sure her friend did not see her as moving away too distantly intellectually, Eliot produced a flurry of letters, mainly concerning Sara's new book, a two-volume study called, forbiddingly, *Present Religion: As a Faith Owing Fellowship with Thought*. Eliot, and Lewes too, found the title "cumbrous." Sara's argument was rather cumbrous as well, an effort to retain a theistic point of view that can be fitted into an evolutionary doctrine, so that religion and science can be reconciled rather than struggle against each other. It was the main theme in the post-Darwinian era, and the lines were sharply drawn between the church and the scientists. The archetype of the former was Bishop Wilberforce, Bishop of Oxford and then Winchester, and his chief rival was Thomas Henry Huxley, with Spencer also an able defender of the "new ethics" based on evolutionary doctrine.

Eliot could not resist discussing verbal changes with Sara. One such instance arises with her friend's use of man's "subjectivity" to the external world, which Eliot thinks somewhat a falsification, inasmuch as man also exerts control over that world. She was not merely nitpicking. In these and related remarks, she was attempting to sort out her own views; and the question of whether man is subject to external affairs, or in control of them, is related to her inquiries into morality and ethics. Her last three novels—beginning with *Felix Holt*—were deep probes into several aspects of human behavior: not only how people act, but why they act that way. The psychological dimension which becomes so apparent in Eliot's "second phase" of fiction is linked to her need to discover the "why" of action, whereas earlier she had, in the main, been satisfied with the action itself and its relegation to good or bad morality. A character like Tito Melema would no longer appear, nor would Romola Bardo. Later, even a senti-mentalized figure like Daniel Deronda is heavily layered, and a demonic creature like Grandcourt contains disguises within disguises.

Part of Eliot's heavy "layering" comes in her emphasis in *Holt* on parent–child relationships, especially mother–child. She had always been concerned with this relationship: Maggie and her father, or with her less than sympathetic mother; Adam Bede with his mother and absent, dissolute father; Romola with her demanding father, whom she serves as Milton's daughter; Eppie as a bastard taken in by Silas Marner. But by *Felix Holt*, the theme becomes even more insistent, certainly heavier and more ominous. Harold Transome is a bastard, conceived by Mrs. Transome after a long affair with the lawyer Matthew Jermyn, now alienated from both mother and son. Meanwhile, she has had another son (Durfey), a disgrace, like Dunstan in *Silas Marner*. Mr. Transome is senile, a silly, kind old man. Harold has himself been absent, a figure whom his mother barely recognizes, both a wanted and an unwanted prodigal. Esther Lyon has a kind father, but her mother died when Esther was young; and she, too, like Romola, is left to care for her father once she is old enough. Felix himself lacks a father and possesses a quaint, addled mother whom he must parent. She sells drugs and medications as cures, and Felix endeavors to bring her around to a rational, not magic-based, life. She is loyal to her son, but they move in such different worlds that one thinks of young Marian and her mother.

All of these troubling and insistent relationships are part of a larger sense of Eliot probing that familiar Victorian world of orphans, misplaced or displaced children, inadequate mothers, absent or failed fathers, parents who themselves require parenting. Besides the examples cited, Eliot reworks that theme in *Middlemarch*, with Dorothea and Celia, wards of a foolish uncle, and in *Daniel Deronda*, where Daniel's own background is mysterious, so that he believes his guardian is really his father when another man is, and where Mirah lacks a mother and must deal with a dissolute, corrupt, even pandering father. Like Eppie, she is taken in by strangers. In most instances, the young people must develop and shape themselves *despite* parents. Victorian nostalgia for strong family ties is as much belied by Eliot's fiction as by Dickens's. When a relationship does prove successful, such as Eppie with Marner, it is outside the child–parent familial structure; or else, in another format, the child–woman goes off with an intruder—Romola with Tito, Gwendolen with Grandcourt, Maggie with Ste-phen—and almost destroys her life.

The reverberations from all this are intricately woven into Eliot's sense of how development and reshaping can take place. By putting such a burden on young people to break away in order to achieve themselves, Eliot has replicated her own effort at emergence. Yet she also recognized that such activity puts the individual in peril—several of her characters hover on the edge or fall over. There is no guarantee that once the young person rejects family the act will prove advantageous. Mirah in *Deronda,* almost a suicide, falls into good fortune; for Gwendolen Harleth it is quite the opposite. Clearly, Eliot was reworking the dangerous moves toward liberation that can lead to success, as in her own case, or to terrible pitfalls.

One of her problems in dealing with all this, and notable in *Felix Holt,* is structuring how personal morality and ethical notions can remain compatible with the desire for escape and liberation. The individual's sense of freedom must be contained within a moral and ethical context. In *Felix Holt,* for the first time, Eliot has attempted to play off individual need against social requirements, all cast on a rather large stage of an election, political advantage, and jockeying for position between Tories and Radicals (Liberals) as they fought over what England was and was to become. Earlier, in *Mill,* when she revealed the struggle in Maggie, it was self-contained; here, in *Holt,* it is extended.

With *Felix Holt,* Eliot moved to new ground. It perhaps required a long incu-bation period not only because of the research into politics and legal questions but because it was so broad in its implications. One of the temptations for those who cannot abide their parents or who lack parents is the development of a fantasy life, such as Esther Lyon's here or Gwendolen's later, or even Doro-thea's. That fantasy life, akin to what Freud called the "family romance," involves the individual's belief that she or he belongs in another, more favorable family. Esther has fantasies of riches and a fine life, as does Gwendolen, once her own family loses its fortunes; and Dorothea makes a dismal marriage so as to will herself into another kind of person with another kind of background. In all such instances, Eliot is clear that the dangers for reshaping can lead to personal disaster, although Esther catches herself in time.

The first chapter alone of *Holt* reveals Eliot's mastery of her material. It is based on expectation, a great Victorian theme and now Eliot's own. It is, fur-ther, solidly grounded in psychological insights into family relationships. Mrs. Transome waits at Transome Court for the return of her son, Harold, whom she has not seen for fifteen years. Harold is now thirty-four, she fifty-six, her "imbe-cile husband" sixty-seven. Her older son, Durfey, now dead, had been a disaster. The chapter opens with an Eden-like setting for Transome Court, but then Eliot begins to capture the trouble within. Mrs. Transome is herself a figure of lan-guor, indolence, and world-weariness—she *waits,* although supercharged with conflicts. Even as she places a great deal on Harold's return, she fears what he might be or bring. She is full of terrible secrets; the past, as if in some Ibsen play, is poisoned.

Politics immediately come between them once her son enters, as she expects Harold to run for Parliament as a Tory, but he announces he is a Radical. That announcement in a class–caste system such as England's in 1832 (or in 1865, for that matter) indicates a rebellious son, a rejection of his past, and, most of all, hostility toward his mother and her values. Her feelings are of profound disappointment. "The moment [of hope] was gone by; there had been no ecstasy, no gladness even; hardly half an hour had passed, and few words had been spoken, yet with that quickness in weaving new futures which belongs to women whose actions have kept them in habitual fear of consequences, Mrs. Transome thought she saw with all the clearness of demonstration that her son's return had not been a good for her in the sense of making her any happier."

With this, the novel's dramatic tensions are established through *distances*, the main metaphor in the novel. Because of the secrets of the past and the political developments of the present, distancing in all its implications is notable. Even the finale of the chapter is a spatial metaphor, recalling Henry James's beast in the jungle waiting to spring. No one ". . . divined what was hidden under that outward life—a woman's keen sensibility and all dread, which lay screened behind all her pretty habits and narrow notions, as some quivering thing with eyes and throbbing heart may lie crouching behind withered rubbish." With this, Eliot had her novel.

Or did she? Was she, perhaps, hopelessly divided about her real subject matter? For example, it can be suggested that because Eliot was so immersed in classical tragedy (especially Aeschylus's *Agamemnon*) at the time she began *Felix Holt* the novel may have been intended at first as a Greek tragedy. In this view, the fall of the House of Transome would coincide, roughly, with the fall of the House of Atreus. In both instances, Nemesis stalks the families, and of course along the way the Oedipal potentialities are strengthened, with Jermyn as Laius, Harold as Oedipus, and Mrs. Transome as Jocasta. Even with the shift to Felix and his fortunes, the classical lines remain as a dual theme: the fall of the aristocratic line paralleling or shadowing the survival of the working or lower middle class. Was the division here a foreshadowing of that division between the Gwendolen and Deronda segments of *that* novel? Was Eliot's fictional imagination becoming so thick and dense that a novel could no longer contain a single theme but needed intricate interweavings to satisfy both her private and public views? If so, she was edging into Dickens territory, however much she felt he was inferior to Thackeray.

Recourse to the *Felix Holt* notebook or "Quarry" reinforces the sense of division or interwoven material. The quarry suggests that the genesis of the novel recalls Dickens's *Bleak House*, with his Lady Dedlock and her adulterous affair leading up to Mrs. Transome's affair with Jermyn.* But that provocative material is balanced out by the heavy political reading Eliot did, which indicates she

---

* An early biographer, Leslie Stephen (in his 1902 "English Men of Letters" series, *George Eliot*), saw Mrs. Transome—and by implication that part of the novel—as the best thing in *Felix Holt*. He suggested that those segments surrounding her were Eliot's real subject, not the political matter.

intended the Felix Holt and election controversy all along as part of a thickening of her social vision. The manuscript is tantalizing. It reveals Eliot's difficulties in the early pages, especially in connection with Mrs. Transome. The uncertainty here, as Eliot fussed over her portrait, suggests, possibly, an initial focus on the older woman. After that, the manuscript, while steadily revised, is not heavily worked out—the usual deletions, insertions, overwriting, blackening out. Nevertheless, this is the most arduously worked of the manuscripts thus far, an indication not so much of strategic changes as of a desire to get things right verbally. While not conclusive, both notebook and manuscript reveal some initial uncertainty as to the real subject, but then emerges Eliot's large, inclusive plan to divide, interweave, and connect. As for strategic changes, only the insertion of the Chapter 6 material, with its thickening of plot and its introduction of inheritance law, seems a structural change. Chapter 6 alters the numbering of the manuscript and begins that "filling in" of the past and of secrets that shape the novel's substance. It is tempting to argue that only here did Eliot finally grasp *Felix Holt* and its layered materials.

As she was becoming increasingly friendly with Robert Browning, he one day took her to his house, which included a "museum" dedicated to the now dead Elizabeth Barrett, her chair, tables, books, her Hebrew Bible with her notes in it, her copies of the Greek dramatists with her annotations. Eliot was suitably impressed.

Despite doubts and continued attacks of ill health, she moved along on *Felix,* reaching Chapter 7 by her forty-sixth birthday, then reading Chapter 9 to Lewes on 4 December. But she ran into blockage around the holidays, when Bertie returned for Christmas. Part of her problem lay in legal areas, regarding the Transome inheritance and how she could disentangle that and work it in literarily. She studied Blackstone's famous legal *Commentaries* for guidance, but her main problem—like Dickens's in *Bleak House,* with the Jarndyce case—was to blend in legal details with fictional uses of them. These structural decisions, intrinsic to any novel which reaches outside itself for factual material, brought her close to impasse.

Eliot was now most open in her correspondence with D'Albert-Durade, not least because her Swiss friend was translating her books into French. But beyond the translations, there was the sense that Eliot had turned him into a paternal figure; that because she had met him when she was young and drifting, she came to see him and his wife as substitute parents. Then when she became famous, he reentered her life by attempting to bring her work to a French-speaking audience, so that the father–daughter relationship deepened. Her letters to him appear uncensored, without the usual reserve. She intuits his indisposition to write, but excuses both of them by saying that with age, time becomes more precious, and letters are, all in all, just throwaways. She confesses prosperity and happiness in Lewes, but regrets it is marred by ill health.

She is quite proud of Lewes's connection to the *Fortnightly,* a journal, she says, of great dignity which draws valuable writers. After first rejecting its editorship, Lewes became convinced he should accept it, at £600 a year, plus the help of a subeditor and a clerk to do routine work. While Lewes liked the work, they both worried about the commercial viability of the venture. Still to D'Albert-Durade, she indicates she is pursuing her own writing in a leisurely manner— she had just completed Chapter 10 of *Felix*, about one-third through. She also disclaims writing for periodicals, although in recent months she had made contributions, mainly as a support for Lewes. In much the same way, he had taken the editorship as a way of holding up his end of their income.

The question of translation came up after D'Albert-Durade indicated he had trouble placing his version of *Romola*. The problem with all his translations was that Paris publishers hesitated to accept them, although he found Swiss publishers for them. As a consequence, they remained relatively unknown, to the extent that a Mlle. Bohn was inquiring about translating *Romola*, unaware that it had been done.

Eliot reveals her fears about the fortunes of Thornie and Bertie, although Charles's marriage has made him and his parents happy. Thornie wrote of crisis after crisis in the Natal—monetary as well as martial—and Eliot says she and Lewes are wavering in their intention to send out Bertie. Nevertheless, they feel he is more suited for colonial than English life, which means he is fitted to be a farmer and not much else. She feels farming in England now requires, besides considerable capital outlay, great skill, a quality apparently lacking in Bertie. One continues to wonder how these seemingly deficient young men got through a demanding school like Hofwyl.

Now developing in Eliot's life was a valuable correspondence with Frederic Harrison, the journalist whose disagreement with Lewes over Comte almost made him persona non grata at the Priory. But she broke through the frosty atmosphere and invited him to dinner, in January of 1866, along with Huxley, Spencer, and Burton. The mixture had the potential of being incendiary—Huxley having called Lewes a rank amateur in the sciences; and, not forgotten, Eliot's onetime pleas to Spencer—but it all worked out, and Harrison, whom Eliot had met through the Congreves, turned out to be a most felicitous guest. His legal knowledge (he had been called to the bar in 1858) proved invaluable in her writing of *Felix Holt*.

In a 9 January 1866 letter, Eliot listed a number of problems which had to do with entailment of an estate, with a particular focus on who has the best legal claims when an estate's ownership is under a cloud.* Harrison's response indicated he was most interested in the problems she raised, and he tried to answer with a technical discussion that seems almost parodic. Eliot, however, saw it differently, as an "ample and clear statement" which has put her in high spirits, "as high spirits as can belong to an unhopeful author suffering from a bilious attack." Letters now shot back and forth rapidly, a testimony not only to Harrison's sudden loyalty but to the postal system Charles Lewes was hoping to

---

* Entailments or related aspects were the stock-in-trade of nineteenth-century novelists—Austen, Dickens, Thackeray, Trollope, as well as Eliot—as part of that secularization of life and deconstruction of a spiritually oriented, religious world. But even more, the focus on entailments indicated a certain democratization of social life, since traditional or ceremonial forms were suddenly jeopardized.

improve. Eliot had given Harrison the initial volume of *Felix* to read, the first time she had allowed a manuscript to move outside of Lewes or Blackwood's. Harrison read some of it and then excused himself, apologetically, that he could not decipher her handwriting—which, incidentally, is not difficult; and yet he felt, from what he did read, that other men will see in this her "most memorable drama." There is a certain high comedy in this, in which Harrison plays straight man for Eliot's need to be praised; and she strokes his ego by revealing to him her deepest secret, her hitherto unseen manuscript (except by Lewes in smaller segments).

Eliot maintains the comedic aspect when she responds on 22 January. "In proportion as compliments (always beside the mark) are discouraging and nause-ating, at least to a writer who has any serious aims, genuine words from one capable of understanding one's conceptions are precious and strengthening." Eliot proceeds to stage two of this comic drama, and indicates she does not believe "the book will ever be worthily written." She emphasizes no one except Lewes has ever seen her manuscripts in medias res, and now since he, Harrison, has incurred the trouble of reading her written words, she is eager to obtain the "full benefit of his participation." Harrison was hooked, and helpful, and Eliot had not only information but support.

The lawyer–journalist went to work for her, and in an enormously long letter, on 27 January, not only gave her advice on how to simplify the legal side of her novel, but also included a lengthy description of a certain Transome case in the middle of the eighteenth century. The crux of the letter is an attempt to deter-mine how the correct inheritance can be measured and, then, who might be the heir(ess). All of this was encouraging to Eliot, who, with some of her legal doubts removed, or her confusions clarified, moved steadily ahead; by the end of April she had almost the second volume. Without doubt, Harrison's sleuth-ing, which continued unabated throughout January, was shifting some of Eliot's focus in the novel. He suggested making Esther Lyon a Transome (probably on the order of Jane Eyre becoming an heiress), which Eliot said she would con-sider. Her original plan, as suggested above, may have been to make Mrs. Trans-ome central, or else the relationship between Harold and his mother. But slowly the narrative shifted toward Esther and, by implication, Esther and Felix. Another consideration was the large role the election was to play, and the way in which politics entraps Felix. One of the problems with the completed novel is, in fact, the several strands; and we can observe this apparent uncertainty of focus early on as Eliot insisted on the legal areas, possibly to the detriment of the fictional sequencing.

In her letter responding to Harrison's suggestion that she make Esther a Transome, we catch some of her uncertainty: ". . . I have mentioned the matter to Mr. Lewes this morning, and he concurs in my present reasons for disinclina-tion to adopt this additional coincidence. Setting it aside [but only temporarily], the story is sufficiently in the track of ordinary probability. . . ." She says, after this tentative point, that she is satisfied in her plot "which beforehand I had sighed for as unattainable."

Lewes's physical condition, meanwhile, took a turn for the worse. He experienced extreme discomfort, in what may have been a gastrointestinal ailment which at that time could not be either diagnosed or adequately treated. Bad weather did not help, and Eliot reported in her journal and to Sara that he was so enervated no lift-up could be expected. They had for reasons of health made a run to Tunbridge Wells, in Kent, west of Dover, at the end of January, but on the return Lewes showed no improvement; and Eliot herself suffered bilious attacks—an indication of some digestive complication. Eliot saw these excursions as serving little function except to make their return home the chief gain. "You see, to counterbalance all the great and good things that life has given us beyond what our fellows have, we hardly know now what it is to be free from bodily malaise."

No one escapes divine retribution, and everyone pays for good fortune with an equal dose of poor fortune. She worries, implicitly, about suffering from hubris—their money, their happiness in each other, their comfortable style of life relatively free of disaster—and she intuits some external force punishing them with a counterbalancing power, a maker of ills. She does not cite the book of Job, but it, too, is implicit in her remark, as is, most of all, the classical idea of moderation, balance, repayment for any extreme of pride: ". . . we must accept our miserable bodies as our share of moral ill," she tells her journal, and this in payment for their "love and uninterrupted companionship." She did not call down divine retribution on her characters idly, but she did punish hubris, starting with Dempster and continuing to Gwendolen Harleth and Grandcourt.

Meanwhile, as *Felix Holt* was reaching a critical mass, it was necessary to think of submitting it to Smith. It was left to Lewes to market the book, and he asked Smith for £5,000 for the copyright. Although a tremendous sum, it was in keeping with Smith's phenomenal payment for *Romola* and his promises to Eliot that he wanted her on his list. But this was more than Smith could swallow, especially when *Romola* failed to earn out. Smith read the first two volumes to his wife, and then decided it was overpriced. He declined to publish it. Lewes did not inform Eliot about any of this, but went back to Blackwood, hoping to place the novel without causing Eliot any grief. In fact, at this time, in early April, her spirits seemed good, even with liver and stomach acting up. She says she feels cheerful, not because of any great reward, but because "I torment myself less with fruitless regrets that my particular life has not been more perfect." She was feeling better because she had stopped whipping herself, the kind of relief she equated with cheerfulness.* But there was hope, after the completion of *Felix* by June or so, for a contemplated journey back to their beloved Germany.

To Barbara Bodichon, she presented, nevertheless, a jejune view of English society: ". . . conversation more or less trivial and insincere, literature just now not much better and politics worse than either." In politics, she was probably referring to the new Reform Bill of 1867, which was coming into view and would among other things extend the (male) franchise to those with £7 of prop-

---

* One recalls Freud's formula for psychotherapy at the end of *Studies in Hysteria:* that the aim was the transformation of the patient's hysterical misery into everyday unhappiness.

erty rights, down from the previous £10. This was Gladstone's compromise bill, which angered Radicals as still restricting the franchise, *and* Conservatives, who saw this as giving power over to the rabble. Eliot's complaint does not seem to extend to either ideologically, but to be a reaction to the bickering, which she identified as a breakdown of civility and community.

Meanwhile, Lewes's letter to Blackwood gained a response. The publisher was delighted to have the opportunity to regain Eliot as an author, although he said his firm would not permit him to make an offer without first reading the manuscript. But he promised an answer within a couple of days after receiving the manuscript, and if it measured up, he would offer £4,000–5,000 for the copyright for five years from the date of publication. He says that if this falls below Lewes's expectations, then he cannot see any way to make it more. It was precisely the answer Lewes hoped for.

The next day, 21 April, Eliot, with "fear and trembling," sent off Volumes I and II, by registered mail. Blackwood telegraphed arrival of the manuscript. By then, as he wrote Eliot, he had read eighty pages with great admiration. He also indicated he was breaking the Sabbath, no mean trick for the conservative Scot. To Lewes, on 24 April, the publisher made his formal offer for *Felix*, £5,000 payable in equal sums six, nine, and twelve months from publication date, with the firm holding copyright for five years. It was a gracious and generous offer for a book which did not appear to have a considerable popular market.* Eliot was herself delighted to be back with the firm, her letter suggesting, but not stating, she should never have left. Since she found herself with large spaces in the day when she could not write, she asked for proofs as soon as possible. Blackwood sent on proofs of Volumes I and II before Volume III was even on paper. It was a challenge for a publisher, but so much good feeling flowed back and forth that neither side doubted the other.

Blackwood poured on praise as passages struck him which he wished to quote. Mrs. Transome and her maid are "a perfect picture." Esther is charming, and he is eager to learn about her future. The "side scenes are inimitable." Blackwood says little about Felix himself, since he cannot comment until he sees the plot worked through. At the end of his letter, he indicates he nearly forgot to say "how good your politics are." Blackwood, that Tory of Tories, now identifies himself as a "radical of the Felix Holt breed," perhaps because he perceived that under all of Felix's bluster, he was as safe as any conservative Tory.

We shall see this spelled out later when Eliot wrote "Address to Working Men, by Felix Holt," which she completed in December of 1867. Triggered by Disraeli's speech on the 1867 Reform Bill to Edinburgh working men, it was an address continuous with Felix's politics in the novel. As we read the address, it is clear Felix is no Radical, but more closely a Conservative—not even the kind of radical Tory once associated with Disraeli's politics. Blackwood, then, knew his man, just as he knew his author. Eliot now held to a Burkean organic sense

---

* Blackwood admitted as much to Lewes, saying that "there may be a complaint of want of the ordinary Novel interest. . . ."

of creeping slow change, then assimilation, then more creeping, so that at no time is society radically different from what it was. For her the "nature of things" meant things as they were, with their own inherent laws; and such a view determines what will come. All in all, in these areas, she remained both her father's daughter and a spokesperson for Victorian thought.

Comforted by Felix's safeness, Blackwood told one and all that the book was "a perfect marvel." He bragged to Langford, in London, that Eliot's politics "are excellent," and we recognize this could have been a factor in his generous offer of £5,000. But he warns Langford to keep the sum "strictly a secret," an indication he knows he overpaid in order to reclaim her. In a 27 April reply to Blackwood's suggestion of a color for the paper, Eliot says she is delighted with the choice, but then uses the occasion to voice her disdain at present-day fiction. "The tone of the prevelant literature just now is not encouraging to a writer who at least wishes to be serious and sincere. . . ." Not encouraging? Dickens had published *Our Mutual Friend;* Trollope, *Framley Parsonage, The Small House at Allington,* and *The Last Chronicle of Barset;* Thackeray, the posthumous *Denis Duval;* Meredith, *Evan Harrington, Emilia in England (Sandra Belloni),* and *Vittoria.* It was not, in the mid-1860s, exactly a wasteland for fiction, and Eliot seems unduly harsh by vaunting herself over what she considered feeble efforts.

She was possibly speculating that English fiction would suffer a certain loss of focus, in that Dickens was winding down his career (and would be dead in four years). Eliot herself was to write only two more novels; Thackeray was dead; and Trollope, however expert, was predictable. Only Meredith was to write major novels (*The Egoist,* for example), but he was never popular in the sense of Dickens or Eliot. Hardy was still unknown, although with Meredith, Gissing, and a few others he would provide a critical view of the century which might have satisfied Eliot's requirement of high seriousness and morality.

Encouraged by Blackwood's attention and by the generous contractual offer, she moved rapidly, writing the final volume of *Felix* in six weeks. Finished on 31 May, the novel was published, in three volumes, on 14 June. Right up to the completion of *Felix,* Eliot attempted to ferret out details which would make her presentation authentic. As she told Blackwood, she was "in a terrible fidget" about certain details, and she asked her publisher to help out in Edinburgh, if he could find a suitable lawyer and historian. Her questions roamed over a variety of areas: whether in Napoleon's war with England the seizing and imprisonment of civilians was exceptional or it continued throughout the war; whether in 1833 a transported criminal, not sentenced to hard labor, might be at large on his or her arrival. To these, Blackwood dutifully responded—that seizure did take place, that transported criminals became serfs or domestic slaves. He cites authorities for further information, if she wishes it.

As Eliot was writing furiously to end what had become for her another difficult novel, Lewes was working almost as furiously in the shadows trying to obtain as much subsidiary money as he could, from translations and for American rights. As he began negotiations with the famous Baron Tauchnitz in Germany, he told Blackwood to ask for far more than he thought the baron would pay, £500. Lewes thought little of the Tauchnitz series and felt that if the baron overpaid, it would compensate for the "disadvantage of his reprint." Even as Eliot pounded along to finish, now in ill health, she returned to Harrison for help in legal details and about Felix's trial. She incorporated many of his suggestions directly into the manuscript—right up to the point at which she submitted it to Blackwood.

Although distinctly her own novel, *Felix Holt* nevertheless owes considerable debts to Dickens. Mrs. Transome, arguably the most successfully drawn character, recalls Lady Dedlock of *Bleak House*. Felix is himself a composite of some of Dickens's rougher young men who grow more gentle as they mature. The legal intricacies also seem to owe much to the Jarndyce case in *Bleak House*. The political background finds some of its material here and there, in *Hard Times* and even *Barnaby Rudge*. The relationships between parents and children are reminiscent of an entire range of Dickens family scenes, not the least those in *Dombey and Son* and, to some degree, *Little Dorrit*. The nostalgia Eliot elicits in the opening section contains some of the sentiment we recall from *The Pickwick Papers*. The question of legitimacy replicates Esther Summerson's plight in *Bleak House*.

But beyond direct references or literary allusions, the entire cast of *Felix Holt* seems Dickensian, down to its affirmation of certain Victorian moral and ethical beliefs. Eliot flirts with radicalism, as does Dickens, and then retreats, as does Dickens, into mainstream individual behavior. The thrust of her novel is a moral tale on how the excesses or extremities of behavior can be contained, in fact must be contained, in much the same way that Dickens celebrated eccentricities only as long as they remained marginal to the main body politic, which itself held together. For Eliot, even the Oedipal elements, with Harold Transome and his real father, are worked through not in the commission of violence but in the Victorian mode of emotional compromise. Furthermore, despite very strong statements about the victimization of women—women as second-class citizens, women caught in restrictions—Eliot's transformational heroine, Esther Lyon, finds her destiny not as an independent woman but as Felix's grateful helper.

Yet not everything is straightforward. In an interesting development, in Chapter 6, we find traces of Eliot's ambivalence about many elements in the novel, not least how extreme situations must be brought to heel. As noted, Chapter 6 was a later insertion—we can tell from the manuscript pagination that she decided she needed more narrative structure, and the chapter is the result.* Although not part of her earlier plan, it helps establish some of the major details, not least where Esther came from. It also locates her in a manner

---

* The manuscript, at the British Museum Library, is divided into the following chapter segments: Volume I, Chapters 1–14; Volume II, Chapters 15–33; Volume III, Chapters 34–51, and Epilogue. Manuscript page 55 of Volume III is missing, which falls within Chapter 37, pp. 468–69 of the Penguin edition. It is a particularly strong passage (from the phrase "life, rather than part of it" and continuing to "not a young") on how Felix as a typical male avoided disaster or even significant choice by retreating into privation, whereas a woman wishes to worship, to give of herself, only to be sent away.

which helps justify her sense of difference, without forgiving her vanity. Mr. Lyon is not her father, even though he has brought her up after her mother's death, the vagrant, destitute Annette Ledru. The outline of this part of the story is conventional: a "lost" woman; a helpful, lovelorn minister (recalling Gilfil from *Scenes of Clerical Life*); an extraneous child; and a close father–daughter relationship reminiscent of Silas Marner and Eppie. Yet the point of the chapter is not solely to offer significant narrative, but to manipulate the young woman by opening up the Cinderella potential. The "extra" child can now become not so much a strong woman but a player in a genetic game, in which her real father's blood—Annette Ledru's husband—will valorize her upper-class standing. Accordingly, Esther's destiny is not to achieve something in her own right—although she is transformational in her attitudes and tones—but to emerge by virtue of something which occurred before her birth. She becomes a significant player with choices, but by way of circumstance, not of effort; and this, too, is part of that Dickensian world of "miracles," not achievements.

Eliot's extreme ambivalence about the life of a woman not only folds into the Dickensian and more general Victorian typecasting; it nourishes her later fiction in which an apparently independent woman gives herself over to the stronger social and cultural force, the man, as though it were her destiny, genetic or otherwise. We can read this as a melancholy conclusion that no woman has any other choice, or that even such strong women are thus restricted. Another possibility arises, the "Jane Austen solution": that strong women become good partners because they will bring up stable, healthy children. In any event, the woman sacrifices.

Upon the novel's completion, Lewes wrote with relief in his journal: "The continual ill health of the last months, and her dreadful nervousness and depression made the writing a serious matter."

Lewes's judgment was that *Felix Holt*, despite Blackwood's enthusiasm, was inferior to *Adam Bede*, but he considered it a "noble book" which would prove more popular than *Mill*. Coinciding with the completion of *Felix*, Lewes described headaches so bad he had to go to bed before dinner, and then as the condition worsened, he and Eliot boarded a train for Dover. "The train made my head worse," he reported. Their plan, notwithstanding headaches, nerves, and bodily ailments, was to tour Holland, Belgium, and Germany. The idea was to be outside the country when reviews appeared.

They proved generally excellent. Yet a new reviewer with a slightly different critique hove into view, writing in the *Nation*, unsigned. It was Henry James, who, among other things, used Eliot's fiction as a means of coming to grips with his own. Having learned a great deal from her, he then found he had to unlearn it.* James went for the jugular, for the weaknesses he saw in Eliot's plots, which

---

* Not until May 1869 did James finally meet Eliot, on the 9th, a Sunday. His description turns her into a character: "To begin with," he tells his father, "she is magnificently ugly—deliciously hideous. She had a low forehead, a dull grey eye, a vast pendulous nose, a huge mouth, full of uneven teeth and a chin and jawbone *qui n'en finessent pas*. . . . Now in this vast ugliness resides a most powerful beauty which, in a very few minutes steals forth and charms the mind, so that you

he says have always been artificial and clumsy. He also finds her conclusions weak: the flood at the end of *Mill* as irresolute; the reprieve of Hetty in *Adam Bede;* the reconciliation between Tessa and Romola. James was having none of this Victorian tidiness. Other faults are Eliot's slow-moving, lingering mannerisms, with those unsatisfactory conclusions to follow. He sees a disproportion between the meagerness of the whole and the "vigorous character of the different parts."

Faults aside, James now moves to the immense merits, which are so great that the critic, he says, finds it difficult to disengage himself from the spell of "so much power, so much brilliancy, and so much discretion." Such brilliancy makes us forget the rustiness of the plot and the longueurs of exposition. James was, of course, already looking ahead to his own plot design, his own methods of narration, and his own sense of the novel as a complete, self-enclosed unit, rather than as a series of engaging parts.

In faulting the political aspects of the novel, James plays the aesthetic game. "The radicalism of *Felix Holt,*" he writes, "is strangely remote from the reader"; it is presented "simply as a feeling entertained." He characterizes Eliot, furthermore, as more successful in her portraiture of low life than of high life. He sees Mrs. Transome as "unnatural," or as a "superfluous figure." Here James mistakes the crux of the novel, since Mrs. Transome and her ill fortune lie close to the center and are not that distinguishable from some aspects of Felix, with whom she might otherwise have nothing to do.

For his final paragraph, he comes down heavily on his subject, refusing her a place with the big boys of English fiction. He says that neither *Felix Holt* nor *Adam Bede* nor *Romola* has the inspiration, "the heat," or the essential simplicity we associate with masterpieces. Instead, they belong to another kind of writing, to that which is clever, voluble, bright-colored—he cites Maria Edgeworth and Jane Austen. While he agrees Eliot is stronger, she is of their kind. "With a certain masculine comprehensiveness which they lack, she is eventually a feminine—a delightfully feminine—writer." In his citation of gender, James turns it into an attack: she is more masculine, meaning less narrow; but she is also feminine, meaning not strong enough. She is, unfortunately for him, not a hybrid or mutant, since she fails at being either masculine or feminine. Then

end as I ended, in falling in love with her. I don't know in what the charm lies, but it is thoroughly potent. An admirable physiognomy—a delightful expression, a voice soft and rich as that of a counselling angel—a mingled sagacity and sweetness—a broad hint of a great underlying world of reserve, knowledge, pride and power—a great feminine dignity and character in these massively plain features—a hundred conflicting shades of consciousness and simpleness—shyness and frankness—gracious and remote indifference—there are some of the more definite elements of her personality. . . . Altogether she has a larger circumference than any woman I have ever seen." James points out that the sadness of his visit resides in the fact that Thornie Lewes lay writhing on the floor from pain in his spine. As James left, he saw Lewes—"in all *his* ugliness"—come rushing in with a dose of morphine from the local chemist. From this, we can observe James transforming everything about Eliot into fictional terms, and then backtracking to see her in person as a result of his having fictionalized her. It was, nevertheless, a lot better than what he said of George Sand in *her* milieu: ". . . mighty and marvellous George!—not diminished by all the greasiness and smelliness in which she made herself (and *so* many other persons!) at home."

James makes a young man's error, when he cites Charles Reade as "the most readable of living English novelists." This was patently absurd, since Dickens had just published *Our Mutual Friend*—admittedly not James's type of fiction— which towered above any fiction in the mid-1860s and would not be challenged by another novel until Eliot's own *Middlemarch*.

James took away as much as he gave, and his gender distinctions are of such a condescending nature as to condemn the reviewer, *unless* we acknowledge James less as a reviewer than as a young man (he was twenty-three) trying out his own gifts and weapons against a female antagonist. In this respect, by identifying her as "feminine," he neutralizes her power and locates himself higher. It would be not only James's method but the overall Victorian strategy, and suggests why Marian Evans chose originally to write under the solid masculine name of George Eliot.

To cap the spate of fine reviews (excepting James's) was that of G. S. Venables (a lawyer with close literary ties to both Thackeray* and Tennyson) in the *Edinburgh Review*, a competitor of *Maga*. He described the novel as art of the highest type, especially in the depiction of English provincial life. Like several of the other reviewers, Venables was troubled by the "dual" plotting, what he called parallel lines which rarely if ever meet. But Eliot, he says, overcomes these faults through the trueness of its picture of life—in the genre of Teniers and other Dutch painters—and the historical value of the book.

But these reviews were still to come when the couple left for the continent "after days and nights of throbbing and palpitation," as Eliot described her final hours on the novel. She acknowledges also the death of old Dr. Brabant, at eighty-five, the man who seemed to emerge in medieval mists in her life and yet who was, in some way, significant in her intellectual development. She and Lewes went to Brussels first, touring the city and revisiting places they recalled from nearly thirteen years ago.

They traveled to Antwerp and, after mass at the cathedral, the Rubens *Descent* was uncovered. They also saw the large collection of Rubenses at the museum. Lewes thought little of Van Dyck in his religious pictures, but considered him splendid in his portraits, apparently a view Eliot shared. But the big event for them was the Passion Play. The performance was all pantomime, and it exceeded their expectations, Lewes wrote. The Jesus they found excellent, the other actors as bad as bad actors can be. Lewes commented on each scene, but did not note the anti-Semitic aspect of this play, in which through gesture a good deal of Christian fury is whipped up against Jews as Christ killers. Lewes, and we assume Eliot, was interested in the aesthetic aspects of the performance, not its virulent ideological message, although in just a few years, in *Daniel Deronda*, Eliot would focus on just this aspect of Christianity.

From Antwerp, the couple left for Rotterdam, two hours by rail and two more hours by a delightful steamer. Then came The Hague. From there they moved

---

* That "famous" broken nose of Thackeray's when he was a student at Charterhouse came from the fist of Venables; later, they became friends.

on, only to encounter, in Coblenz, the beginnings of Bismarck's notable war against Austria,, which led to the crushing of the latter and the emergence of the German state as a major European power, to be consolidated by the smashing of French forces in 1870–71. Lewes and Eliot seemed unaware, politically, that the European balance of power was shifting from England and France to a new nation, a unified Germany which would devour the continent in a series of deadly wars. It is strange to find them here at the beginning in Coblenz, when the city was being mobilized and filled with troops, and for them not to observe that a new European order was in the making.

Nothing, however, would interfere with their tour. From Coblenz, southeast of Cologne and Bonn, they went to Schwalbach, near Wiesbaden, where they remained a fortnight, still unaware they had walked into a war. Eliot was pleased they knew no one and that they did not have to sit at a table d'hôte full of English guests and presided over by a British chaplain. Her scorn for all that is clear. At Schwalbach, they received Blackwood's letter of 18 June citing favorable reviews of *Felix Holt*. Sales held up, with 3,000 copies going almost immediately, and Mudie's taking 1,500; but since the publisher held copyright, Eliot stood nothing to gain from sales alone, or from a second edition the firm issued in December 1866, in two rather than three volumes. In her response, she assured Blackwood she was making every effort to remain idle.

With the publication and favorable reception of *Holt* behind her, this period in Eliot's life was a quiet one in terms of literary accomplishment. Except for completing *The Spanish Gypsy* (published 1868), she did little work until she began *Middlemarch* in July of 1869, and that desultorily. For a period of three years, in terms of fiction, her imagination seemed to remain fallow. And yet that idleness on the surface was not idleness beneath. *The Spanish Gypsy* had opened up for her a wide range of personal feelings before she abandoned it in its dramatic form after Act III. What she had accomplished up to that point is important in her development, even though she put it all behind her to write *Felix Holt*.

The Spanish Gypsy in its early stages was a working out, in the time of Columbus, of some deeply personal feelings on Eliot's part. Her story is well disguised with a gypsy girl (Fedalma) who, before she discovers her real father (a gypsy chieftain), is to marry the duke, de Silva, and live a life of splendor. Behind the events in Spain at the time when Christian forces were trying to drive the Moors from the country—and the gypsies were pawns in this struggle—is something we recognize as vintage Eliot. The crux of Fedalma's situation is that she is to be married secretly to de Silva and then the marriage will later be announced; the secrecy is the result of her low birth, for de Silva will be considered to have married beneath him. The sudden appearance of Fedalma's father, the gypsy chief who opposes the marriage and says his daughter must undergo a different calling, has profound overtones. Dead set against the marriage, also, is the prior, who in talks with de Silva warns him to abandon his folly. Thus, in the structuring of a marriage which is not to take place, we have the prior acting as a father figure for de Silva, who resists all such advice, and the gypsy chieftain as the real father offering advice which Fedalma accepts. Instead of marriage she must commit herself to opening a secret door to permit the gypsies (and her) to flee.

The centerpiece is the marriage, which is cast in terms of secrecy, opposition, and potential disaster. In the reemergence of the father—and one as strict and stern as Robert Evans—Eliot has relived one of the great traumas of her life. She reentered the drama of father–daughter and intruder. Although Evans was long dead when she ran off with Lewes in 1854, Evans's children—her siblings and half-siblings—were there to represent their father's displeasure. By creating a heroine who chooses familial duty over what might make her personally happy, Eliot was now *reversing* her own dramatic decision. Fedalma senses that her call to duty will end badly, but she is caught in the grip of a demanding father, who is set to destroy everyone in his quest for personal honor and gypsy pride. These were the elements developed by the time Eliot dropped the manuscript to move on to *Holt*.

Intimations of *Holt* waft through *Gypsy*. The degree of autobiography in Eliot's works is palpable, as long as one sees it as shadowed, disguised. While Felix has ideas that might get him in trouble—his radicalism recalls her rebelliousness—he is "saved" from disaster. But it is Esther Lyon who must settle affairs in her life, which recalls Eliot's: her connection to a man, here Felix, an intruder deemed unsuitable as companion or husband. In *The Spanish Gypsy*, the elements are even clearer. The prior, who is adamantly opposed to the marriage, represents public opinion, the force of the church, and the world of class and caste. His role is to prohibit any union which does not fit social need. De Silva himself seeks a secret marriage, hoping to finesse what he knows is socially wrong; and Fedalma is moved to a marriage which is well beyond anything she had ever contemplated, she being a woman of the people. All of this occurs before the appearance of the avenging father.

With Zarca's appearance, all elements consolidate into a mandate for Fedalma's decisions about her future. Eliot toys with her own position, for she took the decisive step with Lewes without knowing how enduring it would prove to be. Fedalma must step into that unknown, Eliot plays with how close Fedalma comes to succumbing to de Silva. Fedalma's following speech, made when Zarca has told her of her destiny, is an archetypal statement made by a daughter to a father when an "intruder" appears.

> I will not count
> On aught but being faithful.
> I will not be half-hearted; never yet
> Fedalma did aught with a wavering soul.
> Die, my young joy—die, all my hungry hopes—
> The milk you cry for from the breast of life
> Is thick with curses. Of, all fatness here
> Snatches its meat from leanness—feeds on graves.
> I will seek nothing but to shun base joy.

The images of food indicate how Fedalma feels herself devitalized, even desexed; her womanliness is a fleshly sacrifice to male needs. The lines recall

Eliot's despair at the time she cared for Robert Evans and saw only divisiveness in her life; they recall her sense of drift and her awareness that her expectations might come to nothing. She gained, then, the conviction that achievement always falls below one's expectations for oneself, and that sorrow is the cup from which she would drink. "Die, my young joy"—the young Marian Evans associated her own development with the "death of" her aspirations, imprisoned unless her father's death released her into life.

When we speak of Eliot's lack of imaginative work in this three-year period, we must take into account how much she had blocked herself with personal memories, even though *Felix* did emerge. Once free of that novel, we could argue, she had to confront the demons she had set loose in *The Spanish Gypsy*. If she abandoned it, she had nothing else on her table, and yet she and Lewes had become accustomed, as we have observed, to a regular infusion of monies from a new work. Although they could live comfortably on current earnings— investments, royalties still trickling in, cheap editions, foreign translations— they had acquired expensive tastes, and they took large sums for granted. While *The Spanish Gypsy* would not bring a great deal—the English edition £350, the American £400—the amount was an expected addition to their income. Without *Gypsy*, Eliot would have suffered both a financial and an imaginative dry period, from 1866 to 1869. Her career, in 1866, as she surveyed it, was a mere ten years old, and somewhat in jeopardy.

Still at the beginning of that dry period, the couple extended their European trip to continue on to Schlangenbad, especially since both began "to lay in a stock of health" and were able to bear a walk of an hour and a half before breakfast. Eliot says they stay away from other people as much as they can, but we are struck, once more, at how their health tended to improve once England receded. Despite the outbreak of the Austro-Prussian War on 14 June, they considered both Schwalbach and Schlangenbad as a kind of paradise, especially with their rows of beech and fir, and the fields. Blackwood wrote on 26 June that the chorus of applause "upon Felix waxes loud and strong," although the Great English Public was as yet unaware of the existence of the book. But the publisher assures her that word of mouth will "get at the monster speedily." Now that she was back in his stable, the careful and somewhat dour Scot was becoming almost playful. He suggested that one way to get the novel known would be to have one hundred fellows go about London carrying a placard and "shouting 'Felix Holt the Radical is published this day.' " Bulwer-Lytton, he says, despite complaints about Mrs. Transome being "too painful," has nothing but admiration for the writing. Blackwood had himself assigned a man, William Lucas Collins, to review the book in *Maga*, and predictably the latter found it, except for Felix's abnegation of wealth, a highly successful novel. And so he went on, Blackwood chirping happily about the return of the prodigal daughter, to bring glory upon herself and the firm.

Like upper-middle-class tourists in retirement, the couple established a leisurely routine. Having decided to remain idle, Eliot practiced it with almost as much control as she practiced sitting at her desk. They were up at six, or before, then after "tub and toilet" walked on the promenade—this at Schwalbach, but part of a general routine. Once there, they drank the sparkling water, on the assumption it would allay their digestive problems, and listened to the band performing overtures, movements from Beethoven's and Haydn's symphonies, waltzes, and medleys. At nine-thirty, they would ramble, sometimes taking books; then walk and talk, sit and muse, read, listen to the birds, before returning to dine in their rooms at three. In his letter to Charles outlining their activities, Lewes indicates that their apartment is quite expensive, but they have sought seclusion because "mother" dislikes the table d'hôte and dressing for it. Also, they can avoid all acquaintance. Then they nap after the midday meal, in the European fashion, and for the evening they dress in their "war-paint" and partake of the splendors of the evening promenade. After that, home early, to bed, reading if they feel like it.

The residue of this is their utter self-sufficiency (given the expense such a simple routine cost at a German spa) and their utter devotion to each other. Now that they could afford to skip the table d'hôte, with its cheaper cost, they could indulge their desire for solitude. Well more than a decade after they came together, they appeared a perfect union of desires and needs. Walking, talking, reading—these are their major comforts, plus each other. Disagreements, if any, appear minimal, although we cannot imagine people this close together without friction or some abrasive moments. But when Eliot was depressed and anguished, as she was when she worked on a book, Lewes either backed off to give her plenty of space or moved in closely enough to provide the support she needed, as the moment required. And when he was ailing, she was there to nurse him; when he needed to do research on his physiological projects, she was there to accompany him. It seems too perfect, but it was probably a relationship set in stone because each had taken such a chance. The popinjay Lewes and the depressed Marian Evans grew into maturity.

Even with the threats of war—Eliot notes that a doctor had indicated a great battle at Frankfurt was inevitable—their visit to the German towns was "indolent, dreamy, languorous." Schlangenbad was the dreamiest of all, with the further advantage of the Schwimm baths, "water as clear as crystal and as soft as milk." The couple stopped at Bonn, then went on to Aix and Liège; they remained for several days in Chaudfontaine, near Liège, in Belgium, then reached Ostend on their way back to London, arriving on 2 August. The trip had served its immediate purpose: it allowed Eliot to recover from *Felix Holt*, it took her out of the country when the reviews appeared, it gave her the sense that idleness was something she could enjoy without guilt, and it appeared to have settled temporarily the health of both of them.

On her return to the Priory, Eliot found awaiting her a lengthy letter from Frederic Harrison with kudos about *Felix Holt* and a curious request. "Are you sure," he wrote, "that your destiny is not to produce a poem—not a poem in prose but in measure—a drama? Is it possible that there is not one yet existing or does it lie like the statue in the marble blocks? I am no fortune-teller but I believe it is in the Stars." The work he has in mind would try to approximate

Comte's ideal state which only "a great comprehensive poem" might capture. He sees this poem—which he hoped Eliot would write—as having the possibility of molding together a society whose ideals have been demeaned. What is needed is a great work of synthesis, in which the "idealization of certain normal relations is eminently the task of all art." He insists: "There is not any one, there never has been any one but yourself to whom we could look for this."

We suspect this tempted Eliot: to write a large syncretic work which would bring together all the elements of her life and thought. One way to regard *The Spanish Gypsy*, despite its exotic subject, is as such a work, which unfortunately failed in its scope because of Eliot's lack of strong poetic and dramatic ability in this form. Harrison: ". . . forgive me for wearying you with a dream—an ever present dream of mine that the grand features of Comte's world might be sketched in fiction in their normal relations though under the forms of our familiar life." He points out that there is nothing in the positivist philosophy which does not lie in "the depths of human nature and civilized society," an idea Eliot would not have disputed. Harrison has come close to her position on the making of a society or community into a set of checks and balances.

We might also observe how close Harrison's positivism and Eliot's humanitarianism come to Mill's utilitarianism. All were efforts to replace God and formal faith with other forms of belief or degrees of social adjustment. Harrison speaks of permitting moral and ethical values to become elevated without destroying individuality; the ideal would blend the individual's desires with a practical society. The idea was tempting enough for Eliot so that in *Middlemarch* she wrote, in part, a true syncretic work which brought together high and low in society and different political points of view. She set the novel on the eve of the 1832 Reform Bill to give it a politically controversial edge; and she moved characters in and out who were both ideological and noncommitted. The aim was a fused society which functioned through interlocking interests.

Yet implanted in her mind in the mid-1860s was the faint intimation of still another work. In *The Spanish Gypsy*, she created the character of Sephardo, a Spanish Jew. Sephardo is a dim forerunner of Daniel Deronda, not in the qualities they share, but in Eliot's recognition that the Jew is a central moral figure in history and deserves more than dismissal as merely a bystander in a Christian divine comedy. Sephardo becomes instrumental for de Silva, who points out that Spanish kings—up to Ferdinand and Isabella—have "found their refuge in a Jew / And trusted in his counsel." Sephardo makes a strong defense of Jews: "Israel / is to the nations as the body's heart." De Silva points out that he is not an anti-Semite; quite the contrary, he is one of many Spanish nobles "who detest / The roaring bigotry of the herd, would fain / Dash from the lips of king and queen [Ferdinand and Isabella] the cup / Filled with besotting venom, half infused / By avarice and half by priests." The lines are unmistakable: in this exchange, Eliot recognized she had an idea or a theme; that she would work against the grain of English anti-Semitism, based as it was more on class and caste lines than on purely religious differences. Of course, what she finally worked out in *The Spanish Gypsy* would pale in contrast with the vast mechanism of Zionism and Judaism she would eventually produce in *Daniel Deronda*.

Despite these intimations of future work, Eliot remained idle, and a good part of it was the psychological trauma she was undergoing with the *Gypsy* material, but part was also a kind of exhaustion or malaise. Even the couple's touring on this particular journey abroad was not well defined. Their travels before had been more specific—research for her or for Lewes, the need to see certain people or visit museums and monuments. This time it was a journey to get away from everything. Although Eliot shows sorrow at the enormous Austrian losses, people whom she identified as her "Tedeschi" or Germans,* she was not put off by the war and its enormous implications.

Back in London, the couple could indulge their fame. Although married women were still wary of this husband-stealer, the Priory became the meetingplace of both close friends and the famous. Spencer was a regular by now, friend to both; also Robert Browning, as noted was by now a frequent visitor. There were also those who had replaced the earlier friendships with the Brays and Hennells: Barbara Bodichon, who accepted Eliot warts and all, the Congreves, Bessie Parkes, Mary Marshall (a Hennell cousin), and Edward Pigott (a *Leader* writer). Lewes was in considerable demand, although he often went alone to gatherings—at Richard Monckton Milnes's, for example—which were intended solely for men. Lewes had met Matthew Arnold there in 1863, among those whom Arnold labeled the "fearful" philosophers: Spencer and Lewes, but including Swinburne, Browning, and Ruskin. Milnes's place—he would soon become a lord, Baron Houghton—was the cultural hub of London male society. In addition to the above at Milnes's, Lewes met Huxley, Holman Hunt, Grant-Duff, Lord Arthur Russell (cousin of Bertrand Russell's father, Viscount Amberley), and others active in scientific, literary, or political life. Milnes himself, the famous collector of pornography, was not of course disturbed by the Lewes–Eliot relationship and had turned up at the Priory as early as June 1864; he now became a regular visitor on Sunday afternoons, when Lewes and Eliot met guests on a weekly basis. As a result of Lewes's associations with the *Cornhill, Pall Mall,* and the *Fortnightly,* other regulars included John Morley, Walter Bagehot, and Alexander Bain.

Yet despite all this excitement, Eliot had wandered once again "into the valley." Whether it would be life or death remained to be seen. It would all become a question of how she could handle her time when she had nothing to force her to her desk. Social life could be as rich as she wished, with Saturday night gatherings becoming Sunday afternoon salons, and much sought after by the famous and powerful. It was, nevertheless, a curious time. We wonder how much of Fedalma's stated depression, in *Gypsy,* was also Eliot's:

> *Oh, I am sick at heart. The eye of day,*
> *The insistent summer sun, seems pitiless*

* The battle of Sadowa (Königgrätz), in the Moravian section of Czechoslovakia, decided the Austro-German War in its earliest phases, with the Austrians losing 40,000 men in the one battle. Eliot notes—for the contemporary reader rather amusedly—that the care the Germans showed for the wounded Austrians is proof "we are slowly, slowly growing out of barbarism." She tells this to Blackwood, who wanted to hear good things about people's motives and actions.

Shining in all the barren crevices
Of weary life, leaving no shade, no dark,
Where I may dream that hidden waters lie;

Eliot compares Fedalma to a shipwrecked man who, gazing from his "narrow shoal of sand," and seeing nothing but blue and more blue, recognizes that "full light is errorless despair." The image is a telling one, of a man secure on his narrow piece of beach, but also stranded by the immensity of things and despairing that he lacks even the saving grace of light. The image, further, casts everything into shadows and darkness, a sign of real depression which cannot be dissipated. This comes from the beginning of Book III, still the part written before Eliot gave up the drama; and while we should not equate her in any direct way to Fedalma, in the young woman's brief hope of happiness as only a sliver of light in a generally dark universe, we do observe an image the author finds appropriate for herself.

In a long 15 August 1866 letter responding to Frederic Harrison's comments about Comte, positivism, utopias, and the rest, Eliot declared her intention to pick up *Gypsy* again. "Now I read it again," she tells him only after swearing him to secrecy about the project, "I find it impossible to abandon it: the conceptions move me deeply, and they have never been wrought out before. There is not a thought or symbol that I do not long to use: but the whole requires recasting, and as I never recast anything before, I think of the issue very doubtfully." By the end of the month (the 30th), she noted in her journal she had taken up the drama again.

Her work on it proceeded desultorily, but by 15 October, she had decided to recast it in a new form, a kind of hybrid combining drama, fiction, and verse. In the main she retained dramatic voices, to which she introduced long novelistic sections, all in verse forms which themselves fall into no set pattern. Much of her verse is, in fact, prose cropped to simulate a poetic line. But the significant part came in her admission to Harrison that she had to use every symbol and thought—an indication the drama had profound personal, rather than purely artistic, interest for her. Not the least of this personal burden is Eliot's use of Fedalma to show lack of focus in her own life. "But now I totter, seeing no far goal: / I tread the rocky pass, and pause and grasp, / Guided by flashes." This is not only Mary Ann Evans in the late 1840s, it is also a sense of George Eliot in the mid-1860s, the internal, struggling Eliot, not the successful, rich, famous woman. When she writes that Fedalma looks toward her father for his "generous hope," she is assailing that hope as an element which will doom her personal life. The mature author is recasting her own dilemmas, hostilities, loyalties, and memories, so that the gypsy woman *becomes the representative of a woman's situation.*

This situation always involves men—father, suitor, male intruder, brother perhaps—and the woman is guided not by her own desires but by decisions men make for her. Fedalma has only foreclosed opportunities. Surrounded by men, her happiness must be circumscribed by their decisions, especially since the time is martial, the situation fraught with male competition. Zarca, the gypsy chieftain, and Don Silva, Fedalma's suitor, become locked in a male struggle; Zarca wins in the short run, but eventually pays the penalty when de Silva kills him. In this kind of struggle, Fedalma can gain nothing. Her options are squashed.

On the domestic front, Thornie had acquired a large tract of land in Natal and asked Bertie to come out. In early September, Eliot and Lewes were preparing Bertie for the voyage to join his brother and become a farmer. Meanwhile, with her decision to take up the Spanish drama again, Eliot found herself "swimming in Spanish history and literature," as she put it to Blackwood. As with *Romola,* she was becoming fanatical about detail. While the project, whatever her attentiveness, was now taking on elements which went beyond her artistic powers, she could not let go. It became her Sisyphean hill.

After a farewell dinner Lewes and Eliot threw for Bertie, the young man headed out for Natal on 9 September. The couple was now free of "big boys," with Charles married and the other two distant farmers. As noted, it was, all in all, a strange dispersement: two sons of Lewes, educated at the prestigious Hofwyl School in Switzerland, ending up as farmers in the colonies; the third, also from Hofwyl, served in the post office. There was, apparently, no intellectual dimension to the three, nothing that would carry them out of the ordinary, despite their highly cultured father and stepmother and their expensive education. None of this seemed to strike Eliot as odd.

The correspondence of the sons with Lewes and with Agnes shows them to have been devoted, accommodating, and understanding. Charles's letters are the most straightforward and sober, whereas Thornie is uninhibited, witty, full of mockery of himself and of letter writing itself. Their letters to Eliot, once they have learned of her role in their father's life, are warm and appreciative of her growing fame; and after they have met her, they are accepting. While their letters do not give us much new insight into Eliot, except for the fact that she was a devoted stepmother and "Mutter," they do suggest why neither Eliot nor Lewes tried to push his sons further. The boys' command of written English often became confused with the German language usage at the school, and they do seem unfocused. Although still only "boys," they have little sense of what they want or where they might go after their years at Hofwyl. This lack of direction or even discipline on their part may well have discouraged their father and stepmother from trying to advance them in more professionally oriented fields. Yet it also must be admitted that while she was a fine stepmother, Eliot did often find three "big boys" more than she wanted to handle and certainly an unwanted interruption on her time and need for intense concentration.

She agreed to Blackwood's proposal for a two-volume edition of *Felix Holt,* at 12 shillings, even though the three-volume edition had not yet sold out. In the background, Langford was uneasy about sales, with 201 of the expensive set still on hand, and foresaw dim prospects for the cheaper edition. He suggested selling as low as 6 shillings, but this proposal Blackwood could not as yet bring to Eliot. In the foreground, domestic sadness struck the household with the death of

Charles and Gertrude's first baby, strangled by its umbilical cord. This would have been Eliot's first grandchild. But before that occurred, on 24 September she wrote one of her characteristically long letters to D'Albert-Durade, now a most faithful correspondent and a sage / father figure for her. She speaks of being happy, this just before the death of her grandchild. As ever, Lewes remains a source of real worry, with his ailments accumulating. She announces that he will soon give up the editorship of the *Fortnightly,* since it ties him down too much. This had personal reverberations, for it drastically reduced his earnings and put the burden squarely on her. On 9 November, Lewes formally submitted his resignation, which Trollope regretfully accepted.

As Eliot's fame spread, even while sales lagged, she and John Blackwood attempted to find some formula for increasing her popularity. She had won the high ground; the middle remained to be claimed. Toward some middle-ground sales, she agreed in principle to an illustrated edition of her books. She indicates she had always objected to illustrated literature, "but abstract theories of publishing can no more be carried out than abstract theories of politics." She said she would be "sturdy" only as far as the *matter* of her books was concerned, but publication, she implies, belongs to another dimension. She mentions that *Romola* will belong to her in another three years, and thus by June 1869 that novel can be included in a series or edition of her books. With that, she turned forty-seven, on 22 November, the news accompanied by the announcement Lewes was in bed with a headache.

His indisposition sent them to Tunbridge Wells in Kent for a week in early December. The year 1866 had not proven much different in texture or quality of life from the previous one, except that Eliot was working, however desultorily, trying to recast *The Spanish Gypsy,* unsure of her direction and caught up in the struggles and conflicts the poem created internally as well as technically. On 13 December, Blackwood sent on the first installment of the *Felix Holt* advance monies, the sum of £1,633.13.4, despite the fact that sales had not lived up to the firm's expectations. Of 5,251 copies printed, several hundred were left and monthly sales in October and November came to only 35 and 25, respectively. Blackwood then issued the second edition at 12 shillings for two volumes, but by early December it had not done much. Eliot, incidentally, was quite pleased with the cheap edition, which she found tasteful.

Blackwood, meanwhile, was working up another kind of offer, which would bring Eliot to the public in a cheap illustrated edition of sixpenny numbers,* with *Scenes, Adam, Mill, Silas,* and *Felix* to make up four volumes selling at 3½ shillings each. Eliot had only begrudgingly agreed to that proposal. The publisher sent on very detailed figures which permitted him to offer only £1,000 for the rights to publish in this way for ten years, with a reward of an additional £500 if the edition sold better than the figures indicated. He expressed regret he could not offer more, but since the 6-shilling edition of the books had proven

---

* Books were broken into parts and sold at sixpence per part. It was a typical Victorian marketplace strategy.

disappointing, his projection of figures indicated he might take a loss on his proposal. He also suggested that "The Lifted Veil" and "Brother Jacob," which he describes as "clever," should not be included in this series. He says there is a want of lightness in them, which is an amusing way of referring to their morbidity. Decisions about *Romola*, when the Smith & Elder copyright expired, would be made later.

What this meant to Eliot, and Lewes, went well beyond the receipt of the £1,000 recommended by Blackwood. She accepted the offer, but behind it was the sense her earning power based on past books was nearly over. Sales were winding down, and even if she did well in the cheap edition, she would not receive more than the additional £500. Current earnings were all they could depend upon, unless she could produce another best-selling novel. Since *The Spanish Gypsy* was not expected to have a large popular appeal, the *Felix Holt* check in 1866 was the last large infusion.

Comparably, Lewes's income dropped dramatically after a high in 1865 (£1,300), much of it connected to his work on the *Fortnightly* and *Pall Mall.* In 1866, his income was down to £865. After that, with his resignation from the *Fortnightly*, his earnings for 1867 were £418, then £162 for 1868, £19 in 1869, none recorded for 1870, another £160 in 1871, £14 for 1872. As suggested above, any effort to understand Eliot's life and her continued emergence in the period after *Romola* must take into account the financial situation. It is not sufficient to declare that the couple was already well located in the bourgeoisie; it is necessary to understand the pressure Eliot felt to produce something to maintain current expenses. Her entire attitude toward life and, by implication, toward society had undergone change, into a more conservative mode, even as, paradoxically perhaps, she felt her own powers of development and growth expand. Both sides of this unequal equation were linked to her earning power; the inflow of money was an indisputable form of empowerment.

None of this implies that Eliot was mercenary. As she explained on several occasions, she would not jeopardize her artistic aims for any sum of money; and her next work of fiction, *Middlemarch*, is certainly not a concession of art for popularity. What it does mean, however, is that she did not perceive herself as a writer above the fray, nor did she turn her back on her audience. In this respect, she was an essential Victorian, a writer who recognized an audience and played to it, not against it. Unlike George Meredith, who challenged his audience to read his difficult and sometimes impenetrable comic prose, she wrote for the intelligent reader who had no special skills except the desire to engage a novel as a refined form of life. Yet working against this desire for an audience—and its monetary rewards—was a certain morbidity, a depression or despair which separated her from those who looked for simple entertainment. In a real glimpse of herself, she describes to Sara Hennell, quite candidly, what she feels.

No, I don't feel as if my faculties were failing me. On the contrary, I enjoy all subjects—all study, more than I ever did in my life before. But

that very fact makes me more in need of resignation to the certain approach
of age and death [at forty-seven, Eliot had reached the statistical mortality
rate for women]. Science, history, poetry—I don't know which draws me
most. And there is little time left me for any one of them. I learned Spanish
last year but one and see new vistas everywhere. That makes me think of
time thrown away when I was young—time that I should be glad of now. I
could enjoy everything from arithmetic to antiquarianism, if I had large
spaces of life before me. But instead of that, I have a very small space. But
I strive to get it. *

Such words suggest quite a different person from the one reaching out
to an audience, or one holding well-received and desirable Sunday salon
meetings. In one respect, Eliot had divided herself, between the self which
feeds upon defeat, resignation, a sense of mortality, and the end of self
itself and the self which produces, develops, matures, emerges, and reaches
out to others either as author or as social being. While this split may be
true of many or most authors, in Eliot's case it was exacerbated by the
struggle she had undergone just to be Mrs. Lewes or George Eliot. Along
the way, she had suffered wounds only her fiction could fully reveal. As
we will see shortly, her various positions on women's issues, on the franchise, on questions of political change, and on matters involving justice
and equality were all influenced by her own struggles. Now that she had
reached a plateau of a stable relationship, fame, a fine home and investments, she was eager to consolidate that divided self, if at all possible;
and like a legion of other writers—Wordsworth coming most directly to
mind—she completed the shift from early radical ardor to more traditional
views based on a barely evolving society, although she insisted on social
justice.

As she began the recasting of *The Spanish Gypsy* from dramatic form to a verse
drama with strong novelistic overtones, she also began to recast her thinking.
Fedalma is still central, of course, the woman caught between unresolvable conflicting forces. In the recast version, Eliot perceived that Fedalma had to be the
sacrifice—that is the way with women, caught up in the politically and militarily
based needs of men. Don Silva and Zarca "duel" over Fedalma's loyalty, and the
sole resolution is that her choices are bypassed. Male dominance prevails, and
de Silva kills Zarca. This occurs only after de Silva has surrendered his own
people, his position, and his warrior status—and yet even that is insufficient.
The showdown must come, and Fedalma must lose. The point is that even while
Eliot would reject most pleas to support female issues socially and politically,
she did not desert women; on the contrary, even in this minor work her long-
suffering Fedalma is the embodiment of female sacrifice in a world run by masculine concepts of family loyalty, racial allegiance, and martial partisanship.

* Her reading certainly did not show surrender or slackness. On a trip to Tunbridge Wells alone,
she read *Astronomical Geography, Spanish Ballads on Bernardo del Carpio,* Lewis's *Astronomy of the
Ancients,* and Ockley's *History of the Saracens.* Much of it was directed at her dramatic poem, but
some of it was simply part of her intense desire to accumulate knowledge.

At the end of 1866, the couple entrained for Paris. Departing on 27 December, they arrived late the next day. Planned as a two-month trip, they would not return until mid-March. Some of the trip's purpose involved research for *The Spanish Gypsy*, but most of it would be a dip into nostalgia, with some new places to record. One aspect of their plan was to improve Lewes's general health. To defray costs, Eliot received two installments of Blackwood's offer, £500 on 15 March 1867, the second £500 on 15 June. This would be in addition to back monies still due on *Holt*.

On 31 December, they met Ernest Renan in Paris. Renan was one of the beneficiaries of the German Higher Criticism of the Bible, and he wrote an eight-volume *History of the Origins of Christianity* over a period of twenty years. The first volume, his *Life of Jesus*, based on historical principles, became his most famous work, and when the couple met him his study had already scandalized a generation. Lewes apparently was not impressed with him, since he said "he talked just as the thousand and one Frenchmen talk—inconsiderately, superficially." He characterizes him as "broad, coarse, suave, agreeable, commonplace." He says Renan spoke of Comte with the usual nonsense; even his appearance is nondescript, a "Belgian priest in aspect." When he spoke of Immanuel Kant, the German idealist philosopher, Eliot discovered he knew Kant only secondhand "and that inaccurately." Renan, however, was taken with Lewes and pressed to see him again, but the latter declined, as did Eliot, and they moved on. Lewes, however, was not getting better. An already slim man, he was losing weight, a condition now suggestive of a tumor.

As they made their way to Biarritz, Eliot's reports on the splendors of this resort for the rich are intermixed with comments on Comte. Writing to Mrs. Richard Congreve, whose husband would later translate Volume V of Comte's *Système de Politique Positive*, she indicated that both she and Lewes were converts. Having written on the French sociologist in the *Fortnightly*, Lewes admitted that his previous opposition to Comte's "sacerdotal despotism" had been changed by someone dear to him, so that now he saw Comtism not as antagonistic to positivism but as a kind of utopia, an ideal rather than a set of doctrines. Eliot herself wrote: "My gratitude increases continually for the illumination Comte has contributed to my life." She and Lewes, she says, passed volumes of Comte from one to the other, with questions and remarks. Positivism was for Eliot a way to shape her secular ideas without surrendering her sense of an ideal (or utopia) which she felt was achievable through sufficient suffering. It was an unlikely combination, *of self and non-self*, but it sustained her; and when she came under fire from women's suffrage groups, her answer was that woman's resignation gave her the high ground.

In Pau, in the south of France, the Leweses saw a good deal of Mrs. Frederick Lehmann. She was part of the rich, exclusive crowd they were accustomed to meeting in London, a crowd which, among other things, collected the famous: writers, painters, composers, politicians, and the like. The Lehmanns almost literally collected Eliot and Lewes. Having sat next to them at Covent Garden, in 1864, the Lehmanns—she was the daughter of Lewes's friend Robert Chambers—invited the couple for dinner the following Sunday, 1 May. They ran a very elegant salon, and Eliot often accompanied Lewes there. In Pau, Nina Lehmann invited the Leweses to tea. Her description of them is compelling: "There is such a gentle graciousness about Mrs. Lewes, one must love her, and she seems to adore him. He is worn out and thin and languid, has lost his old spirits. . . ." Although her husband was away, she invited them to dinner and continued to see them during their two-day stay. Her further comments: "What a sweet, mild, womanly presence hers is—so soothing, too, and *elevating* above all. It is impossible to be with the noble creature without feeling *better*. I have never known any one like her—and then her modesty, her humility. A modesty, too, that never makes her or you awkward, as many modesties do. I am full of her. She makes a great impression on me, and I long to see more of her, and be with her." This was similar to Henry James's response to her two years later. Eliot had transformed her great intelligence into a "presence" so that, for observers and friends, she seemed to be large and full and weighty, even while she was relatively compact, not heavy, or even physically impressive.

As befitting people with plenty of resources, the couple's itinerary was leisurely, the only pressure on Eliot being to work her way through the rewriting of *The Spanish Gypsy* and to acquire a firsthand knowledge of the Spanish scene. From Biarritz they moved on to San Sebastián, staying for three days, and then headed for Zaragoza for two nights, before going on to Lérida, then to Barcelona. Eliot sounds delighted and reports even Lewes appears picked up by Spanish sights and sun. The angle of light, the rugged scenery, the play of rain on the hills surrounding many of the cities: she finds all these magical. The hills flanking the plain of Zaragoza "are of palish clay washed by the rains into undulating forms, and some slight herbage upon them makes the shadows of an exquisite blue."

Barcelona itself does not appear to have meant much to her. She did not pick up on the independent air of the Catalonians. She calls it a "mongrel town" that one can never care for much, except for the splendid climate. But before coming to Barcelona, she is struck by the Spanish people, a combination of goodwill without servility that catches her attention. She is unaware that Barcelona is itself not really the same as the rest of Spain, just as the northeastern Basque region is different. She seems unaware, in fact, of how Spain differs from region to region, even as their itinerary took them to Alicante, Malaga, Granada, Córdoba, and Seville, all of them distinct. In Spain she observed as a provincial Englishwoman, not as an experienced traveler.

In Granada, on 18 February, Eliot heard from Frederic Harrison about a legal point in *Felix Holt*. A reviewer in the *Edinburgh Review* (a rival of *Maga*), obviously playing journalistic politics, had pointed out that she knew nothing about perpetuities. Calling the reviewer an idiot, Harrison sent on the notice. But after having read it, Lewes did not show the details to Eliot. Harrison had arranged to have a friend publish (in an article called "A Mouldy Conveyance") an attack on the critic's error and a defense of the original text. Eliot says she suspected such an attack was bound to come, although she was kept from the brunt of it. What we observe is how Lewes continued to protect her against something even so minor as a possible error in law which Harrison had himself counseled her about; and then how Harrison, to protect her as well as himself, had arranged a quick rebuttal.

When Eliot informed Blackwood about her pleasure in Spain, she finally informed her publisher of her literary interest in the trip. "I began to interest myself [three years ago] in Spanish history and literature, and have had a work lying by me partly written, the subject of which is connected with Spain. Whether I shall ever bring it to maturity so as to satisfy myself sufficiently to print it is a question not settled, but it is a work very near my heart." Not until she returned home did she inform Blackwood what that "work" was. Her strategy, apparently, was to arouse his curiosity before telling him it was a long dramatic poem, not a work of fiction.

The couple's return to the Priory on 16 March 1867 coincided with Eliot's taking up her dramatic poem once again. She told one and all they had had a glorious journey, and part of that gloriousness was surely associated with her ability to work on *The Spanish Gypsy*, if not on the page then in her mind. Seeing Spain over a fairly long period gave her some feel for her material, although unfortunately her poetic gifts were not up to the standard she had set for herself. When Blackwood sent on the sum of £2,166.13.4 for *Holt* and for copyright on all her novels except *Romola*, she took the occasion to divulge her secret. She was full of trepidation, for, as she knew, the last thing in the world any publisher wants to hear is that a valued novelist is writing a long poem. She softened her remarks by prefacing them with comments on the cheap illustrated edition of her novels: she has lowered her hopes so as not to be disappointed by their appearance. She expects the worst of them, a form of surrender which gives her some leverage with Blackwood for her own announcement. She even approves of "placarding" or advertising her novels at railway stations as an effective measure of commercial acquiescence—so that if Blackwood is to make money here, he might be willing to lose it elsewhere.

Having laid the groundwork, she announces: "The work connected with Spain is not a Romance. It is—prepare your fortitude—it is—a poem. I conceived the plot, and wrote nearly the whole as a drama in 1864." She goes through the familiar tale, that Lewes told her to put it aside, with a view to recasting it. He thinks hopefully of it, she reports, but she is *"not hopeful."* But her next comments are also of considerable interest, since they look forward to what might be *Middlemarch*, however dimly Eliot still saw that novel. "Of course, if it [Gypsy] is ever finished to my satisfaction, it is not a work for us to get money by, but Mr. Lewes urges and insists that it shall be done. I have also my private projects about an English novel, but I am afraid of speaking as if I could depend on myself."

She writes of being somewhat dizzy about returning and settling down; but her uncertainty about starting another novel is linked to more than settling back in the Priory. She had the premonition her energies were waning; the ailments, headaches, Lewes's physical problems, and the rest had taken their toll on her determination to see another long project through. Since she was no ordinary novelist—no Trollope, for example, who sat down each morning to write a requisite number of words—she knew any lengthy project involved research, application, long hours of preparation. Dickens reached deeply into himself, as did Meredith; but she not only had to reach deeply, she had to know everything there was to know about her time and place. Every novelistic venture was a scholarly visit into the past, as *Middlemarch* would eventually prove to be.

Blackwood's response to her tentative comments did not come until two weeks later, on 8 April. He put a good face on it, since he was not about to antagonize an author in whom he had invested a good deal of the firm's future. "I shall be very curious to see the Spanish Poem or Drama," he wrote. "That it will be very fine I have not a doubt. . . . If any of the M. S. of the Poem is in such a state that you would not mind showing it, I should feel very great interest in looking at it."

Eliot was at this time, in the spring of 1867, still lying low, somewhat positioned on the outskirts of the valley of death. She had grown wiser, more mature, but work did not come any more easily. Some of the gloom seems to have been dissipated by the Spanish trip; but even the recasting of *Gypsy* was a matter of reworking old materials, not creating anything brightly new. This is the shadow substance of many of her letters. When she writes to close friends, like D'Albert-Durade, she is full of details of her trip, but reticent about her plans for work. It is difficult to see that she could have been satisfied. Even when she felt she would succeed, her distant goals were so mighty she perceived her career as unfulfilled. The uncertainties and ambiguities—not to underestimate the hole left by her loss of faith—fed the malaise.

As she looked out at the literary scene—and we know she was not exhilarated by what she observed—she noted that her major competitors had written long novels (Dickens several since mid-century, Thackeray one, Trollope several), and the only way she was going to emerge from the reviewers' categorizing her as a "female novelist" was to write the long book that Austen, the Brontës, and Mrs. Gaskell did not write. *Romola* had been, by far, her longest novel, but it was clear now that, whatever her aim had been, it had failed. She had been accurate about the setting, but not careful enough about shaping her fictional material. The dissatisfaction that lies under her letters and even her journal in this period derives not from her personal life—she calls herself and Lewes "privileged creatures"—but from a sense of professional incompleteness. Yet she was, after all, only in her late forties, and she had been working at her craft only a little more than a decade. It was time to seek a remedy.

16

Maturity

". . . she was ready for one of those convulsive, motiveless actions by which wretched men and women leap from a temporary sorrow into a life-long misery."

Eliot's climb from the valley of despair in the mid-1860s was not in a straight line. She did not head into *Middlemarch* in some linear fashion. Yet her movement toward conceiving and writing that novel did enable her to emerge still further, for in imagining and then carrying out such a long work she enlarged herself and discovered resources she had not used before. The carrying out of *Middlemarch* meant she had not only to reclaim her old work habits, but to squeeze her imaginative processes more, and also to incorporate personal feelings into fictional shapes. The novel became not only an emergence for her, but a culmination.

Meanwhile, upon their return from Spain, the couple began to entertain on a much larger scale. They also expanded their circle of the rich and successful, and Lewes in particular went out into society—sometimes alone, occasionally with Eliot. His position had increased because of his own efforts as editor and writer, but also because of hers; he was renowned as "Mr. Eliot." It was a typical crossover of their relationship. Lewes's journal for just the brief period of 5–7 May 1867 indicates the intensity of his social activities: the opening lectures by Richard Congreve on positivism brought out George Trevelyan (M.P. and historian), Lord and Lady Amberley (M.P. for Notthingham and father of Bertrand Russell), Frederic Harrison, Lord Houghton (Richard Monckton Milnes), Henry Buxton Forman (the famous book collector, critic, and, as it turned out, forger of literary texts). At this gathering, at the Sussex Hotel, Eliot was introduced to the Amberleys.

The next day, 6 May, Lewes notes he continued to write his *Prolegomena*—the introductory matter to his *History of Philosophy from Thales to Comte*, the third edition, in two volumes. Then he lunched with John Morley at the Garrick, where he also saw Robert Browning, John Forster (Dickens's biographer-to-be and a literary critic), George Meredith (now embarked on one of his most fruitful periods), Anthony Trollope, Alexander Macmillan (chairman of Macmillan and Co., and publisher of *Macmillan's Magazine*), and other successful men such as Fitzjames Stephen (writer for the *Saturday Review*) and Frederick Greenwood (former subeditor at the *Cornhill*). Then on Tuesday, the 7th, Lewes dined at the Amberleys', where other luminaries were present, including several lords and knighted men. Lewes was much taken with Lady Amberley's sister, Lady Airlie, who spoke exceptionally fondly of "Polly." Except for Congreve's public lectures, Lewes attended these social functions alone. At the lectures, Eliot heard a mixed message, so that she found the first good, the second acceptable, the third "chilling," the fourth an improvement; and then the series, which went to nine, drops from her journal and letters. Both Eliot and Lewes were wary of one side of positivism which Congreve emphasized, and that was the authoritarian aspect in which Comte became a kind of ultimate leader. His mission had become apostolic, and this was too much for the couple, who backed off from anything that paralleled formal religion.

Public matters, however, intruded, and Eliot made one of her rare comments on social or political policy. The burning issue was the female franchise, for John Stuart Mill, an ardent supporter, had in May moved an amendment to Gladstone's Reform Bill (the bill which in 1867 would broaden the male franchise) to include enfranchisement of women. John Morley, at the *Fortnightly*, had published articles supporting this amendment. On 14 May, Eliot opened her position to Morley, her remarks obfuscating as much as revealing. She was no advocate. Instead, she saw in the debate some way of discussing the different roles relegated to men and women.

> I would certainly not oppose any plan which held out any reasonable promise of tending to establish as far as possible an equivalence of advantages for two sexes, as to education and the possibilities of free development. I fear you may have misunderstood something I said the other evening. . . . I mean that as a fact of mere zoological evolution woman seems to me to have the worse share in existence. But for that very reason I would the more contend that in the moral evolution we [women] have "an art which does mend nature." It is the function of love in the largest sense, to mitigate the harshness of all fatalities. And in the thorough recognition of that worse share, I think there is a basis for a sublimer recognition in women and a more regenerative tenderness in man.

Apparently, Morley had himself argued along these lines. In an attempt to defend her position, which she admits may be idiosyncratic, she offers a tortured argument that efforts toward a growing moral force might "lighten the pressure of hard non-moral outward conditions." All of this is consistent with her later remarks about women, female education, the franchise, and the condition of the working poor, male and female.

On 30 May, now being pursued on all sides, she told Clementia (Mrs. Peter) Taylor that she agrees women should be socially elevated—"educated equally with men, and secured as far as possible along with every other breathing creature from suffering the exercise of any unrighteous power." Here she softens her position on female suffrage and says she looks toward "much good from the serious presentation of women's claims before Parliament." She praises Mill's speech as "sober and judicious," and in a particularly strong statement calls Sir John Burgess Karslake's comments "an abomination." Karslake treated Mill's amendment to the Reform Bill on women's suffrage as trivial. What seemed to draw out Eliot was not much the issue itself as the idiocy of those, like Karslake, who refused to see the matter debated seriously.

But for those who look for progressive views, there is bound to be disappointment. She was now even less ready to see women move out on their own and take their chances than she was before. She emphasized to Barbara Bodichon she would like to be certain that as a result of higher education for women—"a result that will come to pass over my grave"—there is "recognition of the great amount of social unproductive labour which needs to be done by women, and which is now either not done at all or done wretchedly." What she means may be charity work, or else labor which does not interfere with the male professional world.

She argues an elitist approach. "No good can come to women, more than to any class of male mortal, while each aims at doing the highest kind of work, which ought to be held in sanctity as what only the few can do well." This is a theory of the remnant, also offered by Matthew Arnold: that only the few are qualified, only the few should be encouraged. No one should aspire above one's place. She repeats: "I believe . . . that a more thorough education will tend to do away with the odious vulgarity of our notions about functions and employment, and to propogate the true gospel that the deepest disgrace is to insist on doing work for which we are unfit—to do work of any sort badly." This is Burkean social policy; the opposite, more progressive point would be that education should give the individual the choice to reach beyond himself (or herself). If there is failure, at least the overreach has permitted extension of self. But Eliot's was a top-down, not a bottom-up, theory. She does tell Barbara that since such comments do not come well from her, she would prefer not to see them quoted.

But she had said as much—in fact, more—in her "Address to Working Men," allegedly by Felix Holt, commissioned for *Maga's* January 1868 issue. The form of the address is in itself of interest, for it purports to derive from Felix Holt, himself a fictional character in a novel by the woman George Eliot. Yet however much the address is a fiction—doubly and triply removed from an authentic voice—Eliot believed in these words. Blackwood, of course, loved the article.

Besides representing Eliot's mature views of man and society, the address also laid the ideological groundwork for *Middlemarch*. That novel, which Eliot said had been floating in and out of her mind for years, was a tribute to an organic society in which every element either contributed its share and was rewarded or was revealed as antisocial and, in some way, punished. Now that more working men were about to obtain the vote, Eliot cautioned them about the abuse of power. She demonstrates many of the same fears Dickens revealed, in *Hard Times* and elsewhere. Both looked back at Carlyle. This fear was based on the enfranchisement of a large number of relatively uneducated men who might use the vote as a way of redressing injustice, and in the act create disorder, imbalance, or even injustices of their own.

Like many Victorians, Eliot feared small units of discontent; such subcultures could possibly surface into real social disorder, even anarchy. "Captain Swing" was a memory from her Coventry days. The broad enfranchisement of these men meant they had to know their responsibilities, and they had to recognize their leaders as their betters. Eliot repeats her argument that a society is formed by the top down. In the voice of Felix Holt, she was not even a Tory democrat, not even the type of radical Tory Disraeli manifested in his Young England movement in the mid-1840s. Fortunately, Eliot's fiction was more varied than this, and her description of a woman's lot in her fictional efforts demonstrates a more sympathetic reading of her gender than she gives in her letters or in this address. This is true, also of her handling of the working class.

She downgrades the franchise in itself. What good is the vote, Felix asks, if men cannot show their better side? Had everyone acted more wisely and morally, then better members of Parliament would have resulted, "better religious teachers, honester tradesmen, fewer foolish demagogues, less impudence in infamous and brutal men; and we should not have had among us the abomination of men calling themselves religious while living in splendour on ill-gotten gains."*

Although there is criticism of those ruled, there is no comparable caution to the wealthy, to government officials, or to members of royalty and the upper levels of the crown. On these, Eliot is silent, and yet most of the abuses in her own social contexts were coming from the top down. She warns working men not to think they are "much better than the rest of our countrymen, or the pretence that that was a reason why we ought to have such an extension of the franchise as has been given to us." In a passage that does recognize abuses, she cites them only to pass on to her real message, that working-class morality must be improved.

A society, she emphasizes, is held together not by those who strive to get ahead by virtue of wits or cunning, but by the "dependence of men on each other and the sense they have of a common interest in preventing injury. . . ." A society is made up of pieces wherein each part has learned to fit: ". . . no

---

* This attack on easy religious living may or may not have been a shot at the high churchmen in Anthony Trollope's novels, those who espouse Christian doctrine but live, as Eliot says, in "splendour."

society is made up of a single class; society stands before us like that wonderful piece of life, the human body, with all its various parts depending on one another, and with a terrible liability to get wrong because of that delicate dependence." This is an old, platitudinous analogy, long worn out, perhaps suitable for Eliot now because of her awareness of her own bodily failings, as well as Lewes's. It also signals the softness of Felix's argument, its flabby intellectual content. Offering the body as a fixed point for his argument, Felix hammers away: "That is because the body is made up of so many various parts, all related to each other, or likely all to feel the effect if any of them goes wrong. It is somewhat the same with our old nations or societies." This line of argument, offered as critical, is philosophically baseless, on the analogy of the watch for those who see God as a "maker."

She recognizes that classes or divisions are necessary, and there is no way to rid ourselves of such distinctions; they are, to use her analogy, part of the body politic. But the sole way to improve society—and Eliot here *is* on the side of the ameliorists—is not to do away with existing class distinctions and advantages, "as if everybody could have the same sort of work, or lead the same sort of life . . . but by the turning of Class Interests into Class Functions or duties." She remarks that each class should be responsible for turning the nation toward reason and justice, but her stress is on working men as those who must bear the greater burden of this mission. She sounds increasingly like a voice from Carlyle's *Past and Present*, or an evangelist praising the divine creation.

In a curious passage, she even misrepresents her own novel. The "I" states he has never "forgotten that the election riot was brought upon chiefly by the agency of dishonest men who professed to be on the people's side." This is, at best, a simplification of what occurred in her novel, for the Tory candidate was manipulating his cohorts as much as anyone on the Radical side. The riot was the result of all elements in the election having broken down, not merely the side of the working man.

Eliot then arrives at an inevitable point, that change requires patience on the part of those eager to see progress. Security demands "not only the preservation of order, but a certain patience on our part with many institutions and facts of various kind, especially touching the accumulation of wealth, which from the light we stand in, we are more likely to discern the evil than the good of." The class system must be preserved. "Do anything which will throw the classes who hold the treasures of knowledge—nay, I may say, the treasure of refined needs—into the background, cause them to withdraw from public affairs, stop too suddenly any of the sources by which their leisure and ease are furnished, rob them of the chances by which they may be influential and pre-eminent, and you do something as shortsighted as the acts of France and Spain when in jealousy and wrath, not altogether unprovoked, they drove from among them races and classes that held the traditions of handicraft and agriculture."

The position one takes must be founded on fellowship, not opposition, and from that grow the rules "which gradually shape themselves to thoroughness as the idea of a common good becomes more complete." Ask what your contribution should be, not what you expect in return.* Felix speaks of this as part of the "supreme unalterable nature of things. . . ." We must learn to obey such dictates; ". . . we have to submit ourselves to the great law of inheritance." Darwinism points to an organic society, even to Toryism. Eliot's next comments slice into her view of women and their roles as resigned sufferers who bring higher moral standing to society. "The deeper insight we get into the cause of human trouble, and the ways in which men are made better and happier, the less we shall be inclined to the unprofitable spirit and practice of reproaching classes as such in a whole sale fashion."

Eliot intimates that her arguments, possibly based on personal fears and not universally applicable, are not rock solid. She closes by emphasizing that not all evils can be blamed on others, and there is no guarantee that changes in situations can provide quick remedies. "To discern between the evils that energy can remove," she says, "and the evils that patience must bear, makes the difference between manliness and childishness, between good sense and folly." Suffer, forbear, move slowly, do not rock the body politic, do not form an opposition group, honor the elites who govern: this is Felix Holt's message to the working men of England as many of them acquire the vote (agricultural workers would wait until 1884, women several decades more). As Blackwood recognized, it is a virtuoso performance; but although it is implicit in nearly everything Eliot wrote, it is also a more extreme view than she took in her fiction. What remains ironic is that while her views had evolved into "conserving" social forms, in her fiction she toyed with opposition to her own views, as we will observe with Will Ladislaw, however much he is at heart a bourgeois observer of old values, as safe as Dorothea.

Eliot did see in her novels how her ideas of society and community hobbled women, prevented them from advancing according to their talents, frustrated their chance at achievement. She did not relent on that part of her own experience, in which she felt overwhelmed by circumstance. Maggie Tulliver is a good early example, Dorothea Brooke a good middle figure, and Gwendolen Harleth a good late instance. All are prevented from any sense of full achievement, with Maggie and Gwendolen broken by a social system which disallowed their emergence. And even Dorothea could easily have been squashed had Casaubon not died soon after their marriage. Psychologically abused, she could have ended up like Janet in "Janet's Repentance." In just these three instances, Eliot undermined her argument that an organic community could serve as a model for gradual, progressive development in which all would benefit.

Back in the spring of 1867, in a seeming division of her mind between getting the Spanish material straight and working out her conservative social and political ideas, Eliot was recasting the early segments of *Gypsy*. By 5 June, she had

---

* One could mock this with President John F. Kennedy's exhortation ("Ask not what your country can do for you. . ."), also directed at those who had the most to lose.

sufficient faith in what she was writing to send to Blackwood the first fifty-six pages of the manuscript.

Meanwhile, the Priory was increasing in popularity with guests, including the sister of Lady Amberley and Lady Airlie, a militant champion of women's issues, Rosalind Howard. Her husband, George Howard, came out of a pre-Raphaelite background as a painter, and in time the couple became favorites. Often, however, Lewes went alone to so many lunches and dinners that talk began to form of some rift between the couple. Also, the refusal of many households, still, to entertain Eliot led to further gossip, that she was uncertain of her role, or that the "marriage" was collapsing. Some saw her as under a strain since, after more than a decade, she had not moved to regularize the relationship. For despite the harsh divorce laws, Eliot now had sufficient money to petition Parliament for a grant of divorce for Lewes and Agnes. But to have done that would have created tremendous scandal and opened up all the old wounds, including those with her immediate family. Having called herself Mrs. Lewes for these long years, she could not be expected to endure a long legal proceeding to become Mrs. Lewes. Yet rumors persisted.

The situation seemed one of Lewes being damned for doing what he did, or damned for not doing enough, or damned because he did not regularize his relationship with Eliot, or damned for whatever reason by people who detested him. George Meredith, not the most venomous of men, called Lewes a "mercurial little showman," and others less exalted viewed him as a slimy viper. All this backbiting was beside the point. There is no hard evidence that either Eliot or Lewes regretted their decision to come together; although we may wonder at the continued illnesses each suffered, especially when they were at home. Speculation will always remain that the illnesses were symbiotic or else derived from some aspect of their relationship which lay buried deep within unexpressed wishes, disappointments, or frustrations.

At the midpoint of *Gypsy*, in July of 1867, the couple went to Niton, on the Isle of Wight, for a break from the Priory; they returned to find another large check from Blackwood's, for £2,166.13.4 for the final installment of *Felix Holt* and the second £500 for the ten-year copyright of her other novels in the new edition. With this, Eliot had reached the end of her current earnings (these were actually back earnings), and she could expect nothing more, except perhaps from a translation here or there. Any further income would have to derive from work on her desk, or in her head.

Their social life at the Priory immediately picked up. The couple had become friendly with Oscar Browning—in 1890, he wrote a book on Eliot—who invited them to Eton, where he taught, and then they made him a frequent guest at the Priory. He sent her a reproduction of a chair she had admired at Eton. But she and Lewes now made another decision to head for the continent, for an extended tour of Germany, both familiar and new places. This would take place on 29 July, and Eliot clearly looked forward to this break, chiefly from the recasting of *Gypsy*. Her uncertainty about what she was doing comes out firmly in her letter to George Smith, who had published *Romola*, in which she informs him she is not writing a novel and whatever it is it will "be dead against the taste of that large public which a publisher is for the most part obliged (rather unhappily) to take into account." Her doubts dominate. "Whether I shall ever be able to give the finish to my work which would so far satisfy me as to make me willing to print it, is still doubtful. But if every other obstacle were removed, I believe it would be quite ineligible for publication in the 'Cornhill.' " Yet there was always the hope the journey would transform their ills and perhaps dissipate her doubts. In August, during the trip, she did write her finest poem, "O May I Join the Choir Invisible," which is her poem on intimations of immortality.

Women's issues dogged her right up to departure. Her correspondent was Emily Davies, who was interested in starting a college for women. Eliot pointed out that the physical and psychological differences between men and women cannot be ignored. Apart from gender differences, these include muscular superiority of men, quality of skin, and related matters which enter into the emotional and mental activity of each sex. But her chief argument lies in the moral sphere, where women have a particular influence, despite all the wrongs and mistakes history records. And then she makes her sharpest point: ". . . there lies just that kernel of truth in the vulgar alarm of men lest women should be 'unsexed.' We can no more afford to part with that exquisite type of gentleness, tenderness, possible maternity suffusing a woman's being with affectionateness, which makes what we mean by the feminine character. . . ." This is a real fear on her part: that an *emancipated woman* might stop being a "feminine" creature. Yet she was responsive to female education.

> The answer to those alarms of men about education is, to admit full that the mutual delight of the sexes in each other must enter into the perfection of life, but to point out that complete union and sympathy can only come by women having opened to them the same store of acquired truths or beliefs as men have, so that their grounds of judgment may be as far as possible the same. The domestic misery, the evil education of the children that come from the presupposition that women must be kept ignorant and superstitious, are patent enough.

She was aware that without education women were consigned to lives like Janet Dempster's.

This was part of the intellectual and ideological baggage Eliot carried with her to Germany: a very unsettled creature with an ailing husband started out on a grueling journey both hoped would wash away their troubles and in some way rejuvenate them. The sense of the past was their medium.

On the passage to Calais, the couple met the Ernst Benzons (she Elizabeth Lehmann), members of that wealthy group with whom they were friendly in London. The Benzons were particularly cultured, and in their Kensington home they had a salon popular with musicians, artists, and writers. At such homes, Eliot was of course welcome; she was, in fact, a center of attraction. At Calais, they linked up with old friends, Theodore Martin and his wife, the actress Helen Faucit, and went on together to Brussels. With that, the Leweses were off on their arduous travels. An overview shows that they traveled as hard in Germany as they had in Spain. They visited Ilmenau, Dresden, and Berlin—places they knew from previous journeys—but also took in several new sights: Wetzlar, Cassel, Eisenach, and Hanover. They were drawn to these places because of a cathedral or a museum, or because they wanted to walk certain parts of the city, or simply to check out literary allusions in German literature. By this time, Eliot's spoken German was quite serviceable while Lewes was fluent. Along the way, she continued to work on *The Spanish Gypsy*. In Dresden, for example, she rewrote the scene between Fedalma and Zarca, the pivotal confrontation, in which the young woman is convinced she owes more to her people than to herself.

Wetzlar became a stopping place because of Lewes's interest in Goethe. Surprisingly, he had never visited it when he was doing his *Life*, although Wetzlar was the scene for Werther and Brunnen in Goethe's *The Sorrows of Werther*. The place was also the site of the secretary to the Brunswick legation at Wetzlar, a man named Jerusalem, the original source for Werther and his unrequited love. At Wartburg, also new to the couple, they saw the castle where Martin Luther was sequestered for ten months, and where he translated the Bible into the Vulgate. Many of Luther's accoutrements—bed, writing table, bookcase, handwriting specimens, portraits—were open to public view. They went on to Arnstadt, chiefly for their memories of their visit thirteen years before. Ilmenau was also part of the itinerary they followed for nostalgic purposes. For Eliot, seeing and re-seeing was important.

Eliot put some of these experiences on paper, the private notebook written at some time in 1868 and called "Notes on Form in Art." Her comments on form, which she distinguishes from "merely massive impressions," depend on the recognition of the whole and then the discrimination of the parts. In these remarks she was attempting to moderate somewhat her earlier emphasis on fiction as a purely imitative art based on minutely noted details. Her statements, if we can project them, suggest a larger vision of fiction which she could then apply to her own massive projects yet to come. What we notice is that even as she narrowed politically, conserving rather than spending, she was attempting to open up imaginatively, and to rid herself of earlier limiting fictional ideas. How much the success of the expansive Dickens was in her mind we cannot determine; nor can we ascertain if she wished to take on Dickens directly as her most ambitious competitor.

By using the idea of "form," Eliot was able to expand. Form, she says, is distinct from matter (she capitalized both in the best German usage), and from this "every difference" is form. Her example: ". . . with this fundamental discrimination is born in necessary antithesis the sense of wholeness or unbroken connection in space & time: a flash of light is a whole compared with the darkness which precedes & follows it; the taste of sourness is a whole & includes parts or degrees as it subsides." And knowledge "arrives at the conception of wholes composed of parts more & more multiplied & highly differenced, yet more & absolutely bound together by various conditions of common likeness or mutual dependence." Yet even as "wholes" denote largeness, expansion, a broader social and political base, Eliot has not completely forsaken her earlier views. For she perceives fiction, still, as an "arrangement of events or feigned correspondence according to predominant feeling."

She sees poetry as having superiority over all the other arts because "its medium, language, is the least imitative, & is in the most complex relation with what it expresses—Form begins in the choice of rhythms & images as signs of a mental state, for this is a process of grouping or association of a less spontaneous & more conscious order than the grouping or association which constitutes the very growth & natural history of the mind." Eliot did not make the leap into that seamless web which exists between form and matter, but in her view of poetry she moves toward that very modern idea. She almost sees form as "making" matter, and matter as "demanding" a certain form; but she stops short. Poetry, she says, "begins when passion weds thought by finding expression in an image; but *poetic* form begins with a choice of elements, however meagre, as the accordant expression of emotional states." She perceives form at first as being a conscious decision, not allowing that perhaps form might also be a product of "emotional states." But then in her closing remarks, she shifts: "A Form being once started must by & by cease to be purely spontaneous: the form itself becomes the object & material of emotion, & is sought after, amplified and elaborated by discrimination of its elements till at last by the abuse of its refinement it preoccupies the room of emotional thinking. . . ."

In some respects, these remarks, merely private musings, foreshadow ideas articulated by Walter Pater, then by Henry James in his "Art of Fiction" and Joseph Conrad in his preface to *The Nigger of the "Narcissus"* near the turn of the century. In all three, poetry is replaced by the binding power of music, where form and matter become indistinguishable; in this, Eliot has come close. Whatever else, these ideas moved her along to new considerations which could provide grounding for long fictions.

As Eliot had expected, work on *The Spanish Gypsy* moved slowly. She was not in any respects a natural poet, and she had imposed on herself a blank-verse form. Her thoughts were of Wordsworth in his longer poems, but Wordsworth's natural language was blank verse, whereas hers was prose. The strain we sense in the dramatic poem derives from Eliot's intelligence trying to impose itself on a language she did not possess. Her frequent use of historical analogy, for example—from Homer, or from the Greek tragedians—was a means by which she could disguise her lack of lyric line; also, she frequently fell into platitudinous, often-heard modes of expression because her ear, so sharply tuned to prose rhythms, was not tuned to fresher poetic ways of expression.

Before they went to Dresden, Ilmenau—halfway between Frankfurt and Dresden—proved refreshing. Yet it was not the city so much as the "pure beloved pine forests" which caught Eliot's attention. For both of them, the real Ilmenau was in the silence of the pine woods, "far out of the reach of 'Slap Bang' and lying after-dinner political speeches." This city they viewed in retrospect as a kind of paradise, and even Lewes's health was "regenerated." Weimar they glimpsed only from the train, since their destination was Dresden, where they took up their former lodgings, at 5B Waisenhausstrasse. Dresden was part nostalgia, part an effort to visit galleries and attend operas and concerts. They fell into their familiar routine, which meant a good deal of reading, at this time Tennyson.

By 1 October, the couple had returned to the Priory. Three years into the effort, there was no avoiding *The Spanish Gypsy*. Eliot told William Blackwood she was having trouble writing and was dependent on outward conditions, whereas once pen, ink, and paper sufficed. Meanwhile, Lewes's health had sufficiently improved so that when Spencer suggested a walking expedition into Surrey, Lewes agreed with alacrity. The two men went by rail to Weybridge, stopped at the inn, and there encountered friends of Spencer's, the Cross family. The family consisted of Mrs. William Cross and her ten children, of whom John Walter was the third. At the time Lewes met the group, the twenty-seven-year-old John—Eliot's future husband—was working as a banker in New York and was home temporarily. Lewes was very fond of the family, and discovered they knew his books and also worshipped Eliot. His journal describing the brief, but historic tour is full of good cheer; no sign of indigestion, headache, biliousness, indisposition. Once again, he recovered when he left the Priory.

When John Blackwood wrote Eliot on 7 November, asking to see more of "Fidelma"—his spelling—she was beginning Part II, "Silva Marching Homeward." Blackwood also suggested, generously, that perhaps she would like to see some of the drama in type, to get an idea of how it would look. The type followed, 122 pages, and with that Eliot continued. But even this gesture made her feel uncertain not only about its look but about the project as a whole. She asked Blackwood on 9 November to keep the thing private, locked up in the printing room and not "set afloat." She added, "I want to keep myself free from all inducements to premature publication; I mean publication before I have given my work as much revision as I can hope to give it while my mind is still nursing it. I could no more live through one of my books a second time than I can live through last year again. . . . If you thought it possible to secure us against the oozing out of proofs and gossip, the other objection would be less important."

When she was uncertain about variant readings of the same passage, Blackwood accommodated her there also, by setting variant readings one above the other. Fear of failure here is immense, and it is understandable, since she was in over her head. She had as examples all the closet dramas of the nineteenth century—Tennyson's and Browning's, whose work she often found unintelligible. Hers would be a closet drama as well, intended not to be performed but read. Perhaps in the shadowy distance was Goethe's *Faust*. More immediately, she disliked what came to be Browning's 21,000 lines of *The Ring and the Book*, another kind of drama, and her aim was to avoid both his length and his prolixity. She set herself a limit of 9,000 lines. But fear of failure took a much more personal note, since *Gypsy* was digging ever deeper into her most intimate conflicts, the traumas of the past where the divisions she had had to confront seemed insurmountable.

Eliot's earlier books—*Adam Bede,* in particular—were not doing well in their cheap editions. Blackwood could only throw up his hands, feeling that any attempt to predict the fortunes of a book was like entering a lottery. Eliot herself showed surprise, not, she says, from vanity, but because so many people told her of their fondness for her books, especially young men, "who are just the class I care most to influence." But the uncertainty of the poem possessed her, so that when Lewes at Christmastime planned a trip to Germany for research (on his *Problems of Life and Mind,* a study of psychology and the nervous system), she remained behind to work on *Gypsy.* She was even fearful of sending the poem in the mail; as soon as the "precious manuscript" arrived, Blackwood responded immediately. On her birthday, Eliot saluted herself and Sara (who shared 22 November) with the line from *Othello* that "chaos is come again." She was now two years short of fifty, what was considered at that time old age.

By December, Eliot had in hand proofs of her "Address to Working Men," to be published as the lead article in *Maga.* Blackwood was beside himself with agreement, which should have warned the less conservative Eliot she was forsaking her background to some extent and giving comfort to enemies of the working man. Blackwood: "According to my knowledge of working men, which is not inconsiderable [almost nil], the good among them are thoroughly up to the useless self-seeking character of their own noisy demagogues, and I think you may say something more on that head." Fearful of continental revolutions, Blackwood saw rampaging hordes, a new storming of the Bastille. Eliot was being hoist with her own petard.

But her response the next day showed no retreat, or even full awareness of her publisher's direction. She was heuristic, and, like any missionary, sure of her plan for others' salvation. Sharing Blackwood's fear that "any workman believed himself a future master," she said he might write an explanatory note begging off any "over-trenchant statements on the part of the well-meaning Radical." He did not write such a note, but Eliot's decision revealed how completely enwrapped she was in her "good message" without seeing how potentially damaging it might be to an entire class. *

After announcing to Blackwood that Lewes's plans called for a trip to Bonn and Heidelberg to consult some professors of physiology, Eliot reports to another acquaintance she was suffering from an indisposition, perhaps connected to Lewes's upcoming absence. The new friend was Mrs. William Henry Brookfield,

---

* A very different kind of address to working men was given by Thomas Henry Huxley, in his opening address as principal of the South London Working Men's College. His address was called "A Liberal Education, and Where to Find It." It became quite famous and was taken up by Matthew Arnold for rebuttal in various essays. Huxley's point was that a "liberal education" was the means by which the working class could find itself—the opposite of Eliot's point about subjecting oneself to an existing class system.

wife of the Reverend Brookfield and herself an author (*Our George*, published in 1864); Eliot had met her at the Benzons' salon and in turn invited her to her own, on Sundays between 2 and 5:30. On 27 December, Lewes left for Germany for a fortnight. The day before, Spencer came to the Priory; and three days before his departure, Lewes and Eliot visited the Benzons, to see their children with their Christmas tree. Lewes also went to see his mother. Blackwood sent on £25 for the Felix Holt "Address," with a comment that if only the masses could rightly appreciate such words and sentiments, "what a grand nation we could become." Eliot complained of dyspepsia to Mrs. Congreve and said she felt "like a leaden struggle under the leaden sky." Her mood: "I object strongly to myself as a bundle of unpleasant sensations with a palpitating heart and awkward manners."

Frequently, Eliot's career is viewed as one consistent spiral into success after success. Quite the opposite was true, as we observe in the above paragraphs where no continuity is apparent. She was not only full of self-doubt and had to be protected against adverse criticism; she was often barely able to get through the days without falling into depression and anguish. This was a constant that ran through her life, a quality impossible to derive from anything specific, except possibly that in her intense effort to transform herself, she had forsaken what could give simple joy.

Even her many successes made her feel not triumph, but how transitory it all was, even how unworthy she was; or, in another respect, how her achievement fell well below her ideal. Whatever the reasons for her shakiness—and they will remain both multifold and shadowy—she did not proceed in any linear way. Trollope did, going from one stage to another with relatively little worry that, once he had transformed himself from great poverty to great success, he would ever fail, or that his powers would suddenly end. Eliot could not be Trollope, nor could she experience Dickens's manic flights. Neither could she fully share the firm belief in the saving grace of nature that Meredith expressed, a kind of natural agnosticism he happily believed in. Her learning had made her too aware of the limitations placed on a person's happiness or pleasure: she was aware of classical hubris, of the classical mean, of the ideal of thought and feeling which combined to produce not joy but the temperate and balanced life. For her, that translated into chronic depression.

However tentative, she was hopeful about her poem, especially since Lewes was "in an unprecedented state of delight" with it. He seemed particularly pleased with its "variety," testimony she cherished the more because it was Lewes who asked her to put it aside in 1865 on "the ground of monotony." She even applies the adjective "exultant" to describe his pleasure with it. Lewes had discovered the way to make Eliot work, in a blaze of praise and flattery. He would return from Germany on 8 January, and Eliot admitted she felt low because of bad weather, poor health, and solitude.

Having met several influential and famous scientists in Heidelberg and Bonn, Lewes was full of his study. In Heidelberg he spoke to Hermann von Helmholtz, professor of physiology; the physicist Gustav Kirchhoff; Georg Gottfried Gervinus, the critic and historian; several physicians from the Matthew Arnold family; the psychologist Wilhelm Wundt; as well as pathologists, botanists, and historians of science. At Bonn, the group was almost as prestigious: Wilhelm Thierry Preyer, physiologist and psychologist, supporter of Darwinism and evolutionary theory, now sweeping through continental Europe; Veit, the gynecologist and professor; Max Schultze, his primary contact in Bonn; and several medical doctors and physiologists. It had been a heady experience, and Eliot cited it as a "brilliant time."

In Lewes's absence, she had refused to attend a positivist meeting with Mrs. Congreve, offering as an excuse that Lewes "objected, on grounds which I think just, to my going to any public manifestation without him, since his absence could not be divined by outsiders." Her reason, on the one hand, made sense, since Eliot seen alone could start gossip the couple had separated, or that Lewes was slipping away; but on the other hand it made no sense, since they purported not to care what people thought. In still another way, her refusal reinforced her desire for reclusiveness.

Although January 1868 started well, the month brought more ill health—so that she and Lewes went off to Tunbridge Wells, in Kent, for two days, returning on the 29th. Her physical discomfort, she tells D'Albert-Durade, did not hinder her intellectual curiosity; in fact, mentally, she says, she feels younger than ever, with a keener interest in all subjects. She adds that their family is prosperous, with Charles promoted and happily married, and the two farmers in Natal doing well. But in one of her still rare references to political affairs, she is distressed by the position of England and the "hideous prospect" of a European war—what would become the Franco-Prussian War. England was not drawn in but was profoundly affected, since with its overwhelming victory, Germany would begin to overshadow the rest of Europe. An arms race would soon be on.

In mid-March, the couple went on another excursion, this time for a month, to Torquay, on the coast in southwest England. Here Eliot could think about *The Spanish Gypsy* without interruption from callers in their social circle. They left the Priory on 17 March and stayed at the Queens Hotel on the Strand; Torquay was chosen so that Lewes could do work in zoology in preparation for a series of articles on Darwin in the *Fortnightly.* *

Eliot knew she had to rethink Fedalma's role. In her original plan, the drama had no satisfactory close; but in her recasting, she decided on several developments: Fedalma must lose de Silva, once he killed her father; de Silva is not avenged, but will depart for Rome to gain a pardon so he can use his sword once again; and she, in compensation for having been squeezed between father and suitor, now assumes the gypsy leadership, a Pyrrhic victory. At one stage, Eliot had considered having both Fedalma and de Silva die—the Verdian solution—

---

* What began as two long articles on Darwin extended into four, the first appearing on 1 April, the others in June, July, and November. In the background of Lewes's intense work on Darwin was Eliot's increasing interest in Darwinian determinism, which she both used and fought against in her fiction.

but now there is no great scene of revenge; penitence and hope for pardon replace theatrics. "The poem will be less tragic than I threatened," she told Blackwood. It is in keeping with *Romola:* what seems like a martial drama is transformed into a personal one.

Blackwood planned on publication at the end of May, but the actual publication came slightly after this, in early June. He maintained the barrage of flattery, indicating the beauty of the lines, now that Parts II and III were set in type. He worried about the title; should it be something vague, he wondered, such as "a poem" by George Eliot? In the revisions, she had called it *The Spanish Gypsy,* but the publisher thought she might use "Filema." Eliot insisted on Fedalma, *her* spelling; but for the title she agreed with Lewes that the firm should first announce it as "a poem," then later as "The Spanish Gypsy." "Fedalma" as title might be mistaken for an Italian name, she says, and create an incorrect expectation. By 16 April, they were home, and Eliot could tell Mrs. Congreve that Lewes received more zoological experience than health from their extended stay. On 21 April, she sent on Book IV, which like the other books would be set in print before she actually finished the drama; that occurred on 29 April.

The psychological dimensions of *The Spanish Gypsy,* apart from the difficulties posed by the writing, are compelling. Eliot leaves at the end a grieving, but powerful woman, a broken man hoping to regain some of his male empowerment through repentance, and a division between the sexes that, in this case, cannot be bridged. It was all part of a psychological manifestation of her own fears about gender roles. True, Fedalma becomes the chief of the gypsies, but it is almost a consolation prize Eliot confers on her, a compensation for having lost de Silva. Further, within this view, the suitor has killed her father, an act of several complications. In killing the father, de Silva has claimed Fedalma, but at the same time made it impossible for her to accept him. In this respect, by killing her father, he has liberated her from Zarca's tyranny and given her considerable power; whether she wanted it or not is not the question. Yet in another sense, de Silva has acted for her: killing the father who stands in her way. According to this reasoning, Zarca has to be eliminated because he remains the obstacle to Fedalma's self-expression. But obviously she cannot herself kill him, so she watches de Silva do it; and then, with that, she can sacrifice herself, exchanging love for a chieftain's power.

While complicating factors reside in this psychological scenario, we also observe the shadowy presence of Eliot's own conflicts: from Mary Ann Evans with Robert Evans; to the death of her father, who is replaced by Lewes, who protects and shields her; to her being liberated by this new development; all leading to her emergence as a famous writer, a "chief." But none of this implies a perfect Eden; quite the contrary. For within this, there is still the serpent— the personal equivalent of the slaying in the drama—and that is the sacrifice Marian Evans made in not becoming Mrs. Lewes in fact. Had Eliot been at ease with her own situation, then Fedalma would have had both the power as chieftain and as de Silva's wife. But Eliot has created a tragedy of choice, a kind of Spanish *Antigone;* and while Fedalma gains a considerable reward, she loses what she really wishes. The allegory of self is unmistakable. Eliot as usual sees the negatives in choice, which is part of her tragic vision; and this she perceives primarily in her female characters. They may not be, for her, creatures who should rise on the world stage, but they are creatures done in again and again by a male world.

The end of *The Spanish Gypsy* was indeed the end of an era for Eliot. Henry James saw it as poor poetry, as something seen through "a glass smoked by the flame of meditative vigils." By this, he meant too much intellect, not enough divine talent. But apart from its lackluster versifying, the dramatic poem had tied up Eliot for three years, and it had become for her a transitional work which cleared out the *Romola* mentality and left her open to an English novel. We judge in hindsight, but there is a rightness and pattern to a large and major career; and the rightness here is that Eliot had to wrestle with unmanageable material (for her talents) and come away with a product which convinced her she had exorcised it from her system.

Blackwood liked it sufficiently to offer £300 for an edition of 2,000, with an additional 3 shillings per copy for whatever sold beyond the 2,000 at the same price and size. It was a generous offer, made more to retain an author than in expectation of profits. But *The Spanish Gypsy* unexpectedly did well, so that a small second edition (of 250) was issued in August. The price was held at 10½ shillings. This edition, which incorporated some minor revisions, also sold out; and in November a cheaper edition was published, 1,000 copies, priced at 7½ shillings, from which Eliot derived a royalty of 1½ shillings per book. Another 1,000 were printed to cover sales for the next few years. In America, the prestigious firm of Ticknor & Fields sold more than 8,000 copies, paying Eliot 1 shilling for each. She was pleased to be dealing with such an "honorable" firm, inasmuch as many American publishers simply pirated what they wanted, and the author received no royalty. From the first, she felt that Blackwood's offer of £300 outright might lose him money if the book did not sell its 2,000 copies, so she offered to take a straight royalty. In this way, Blackwood would not be paying her for copies left unsold. But after an explanation of financial needs by the publisher, she accepted his terms. In these negotiations, where sums were small compared with what Eliot was accustomed to receiving, we note the maneuvering: her consideration for him, his desire to keep her. It was part of a publisher–author "romance," in which each played the other superbly: Blackwood with flattery and support, Eliot with consideration for the firm's profits as measured against her desire for more income.

She writes Cara about precisely this matter. "Don't you imagine how the people who considered writing simply as a money-getting profession will despise me for choosing a work by which I could only get hundreds where for a novel I get thousands." Her reasoning is lovely: "I cannot help asking you to admire what my husband is, compared with many possible husbands—I mean, in urging me to produce a poem rather than anything in a worldly sense more profitable. I expect a good deal of disgust to be felt towards me in many quarters for doing what was not looked for from me and becoming unreadable to many who have hitherto found me readable and debatable."

As she and Lewes prepared for their May departure for a two-month stay in Germany and Switzerland, she emphasizes how feeble she is, how "flaccid and piteous to behold"—this from a woman with another twelve years to live and with no discernible malfunction. "I try to avoid all unnecessary writing, as a matter of hygiene," she tells Mrs. John Cash (Mary Sibree).* Also, Lewes had been "headachy" since their return from Torquay, with a lowered pulse. Their plan, apparently, was to leave England before *Gypsy* reviews appeared. They were mixed, with the most favorable coming from expected sources, where Blackwood had influence, but also from the reviewer in the *Spectator*, who found it the greatest long poem ever *by a woman*—not quite what Eliot wanted to hear. In Henry James's flat review, cited above, he observed that she did not have a genuine poetic voice, and he located that failure in some of his typically convoluted prose when he wanted to wound without appearing a villain. The *Pall Mall Gazette*, from which one might have expected more, was not moved and called the work melodramatic. But most of all, the positivists, including Frederic Harrison, were angry Eliot had betrayed their doctrines. Harrison's objections came six months after publication in an extended letter in which he questioned the entire matter of *The Spanish Gypsy*. What he picked up was something deep within Eliot which created ambiguities: that shadowy but very personal scene in which father and suitor struggle for the loyalty of the young woman.

Harrison was disturbed by such characters. What he and the positivists could not accept was that Fedalma had surrendered to "blood," to the needs of her people, instead of commanding her own life. Zarca, in turn, speaks of the need to sacrifice oneself for one's people: another indication for the positivists of someone who has given up his identity and direction. As for de Silva, he was utterly contemptible, heading off to the Vatican to seek salvation and the right to bear arms again, as though a man had to appeal to the pope in order to make his own decisions. Harrison touched on virtually every failing in the work,† and because of his own point of vantage, he gained insight into the strange contradictions of the plotting. He did not perceive how psychologically important the story was to Eliot, but by applying positivist ideas, he had unraveled some of the ambiguities which resulted from her personal stake in *Gypsy*.

Just before leaving for the continent, Eliot had corresponded furiously with Harrison about *Gypsy*. In his reply, later, he repeated an idea he felt only she

---

* There is an intimation here that Eliot accepted an insidious Victorian medical view of women: that because of their small brain capacity, women should not think too hard or else they will suffer illness.

† William Blackwood was writing quite the opposite to both Eliot and Lewes. To Lewes, he spoke of the poem as having "perfected form" and "matchless depth and power." But even he wonders how a public attuned to Dickens or to earlier Eliot will take to it. He looks forward, nevertheless, to her being placed as high among poets as she is among novelists.

could do justice to, "the idealisation of the Positivist vision of society as a whole, especially to typify the great institutions and social functions of the future. How far this accorded with ideas already present to you, how you judged it I do not exactly know." What Harrison looked forward to—and Eliot would be his vehicle—was a devotee of Comte who could turn a distant philosophy into an accessible and accommodating fiction with a large popular audience. It was a grand scheme, and about the furthest thing from Eliot's mind. While she did not reject Comte's synthesis of the various stages in human development, her own view of fiction was quite different.

On 26 May the couple left on their trip. Their plan was twofold, to retrace their previous visits and in some instances to see the very people Lewes had encountered in his January visit to Bonn. They also met several other scientists of note along the way. Their itinerary, which was not firm, took them to Bonn, then to the southwest to the spa at Baden, which they found lacking, and on to another spa in the Black Forest, called Petersthal. Baden was too fashionable, Petersthal more modest. At the latter they remained for a fortnight, where among other things they read aloud to each other William Morris's *The Earthly Paradise*. Eliot was possibly interested in how a verse saga, recalling hers, could be written.

At Petersthal, which enchanted the couple, their schedule was leisurely— there seemed less of that frenetic need of earlier trips. According to Lewes's journal, they rose at six, drank the waters and walked until seven, then break-fasted in the open air, rambled around the walks, read William Morris, bathed, drank waters, and rambled some more until the one o'clock table d'hôte, then rested until five, walked again until seven, ate a light supper, rambled some more, and were in bed by nine. In terms of health, none of this seemed to do much good, since Lewes continued to suffer from headaches, possibly migraines.

Their next stop was Freiburg, near the French-Swiss border in the southwest corner of Germany, for an encounter with another group of well-known scientists, Funcke, Manz, Ecker. From there, they went on to another spa, St. Märgen, where they stayed four days, moving on for a week at Interlaken, in the Swiss Bernese Oberland, before their departure for London, arriving on 23 July. While the trip was mainly to allow Lewes further consultation about his project linking physiology and psychology, it also provided material for Eliot's poem "Agatha," the outgrowth of her visit to a peasant cottage in St. Märgen.

As the couple moved around, Blackwood kept in touch with them, and his news was encouraging: he reported good sales of *Gypsy* to Lewes. When the news was good, as it was here, Lewes relayed it to Eliot, who felt encouraged that people seemed to care about the poem. But we suspect people purchased or subscribed to *Gypsy* because of their expectations of Eliot as a novelist; or else they were lulled into purchasing a title by George Eliot, only to discover it was not fiction. One such reader, the actress Mary Frances Scott-Siddons, suggested the poem be recast for dramatic presentation; and Lewes responded by saying he recognized how eminently suitable it was for opera, but eminently unsuitable for an acting play. This was a shrewd remark, since the Verdian overtones of the plot were clear, and, in fact, one can see *Gypsy* edging in and out of themes Verdi covered in *Il Trovatore, The Masked Ball,* and, later, *Don Carlos.* In any event, Lewes finally took the authority to squash the idea of a dramatic presentation. By 2 July, Blackwood could report the disposal of 1,500 copies; and in attempting to assess the reviewers, he concluded something big had come into the world.

Eliot fell ill about ten days before their return, so that they decided to cut short their more ambitious plans. She admitted they had stayed out of touch with "home sayings and doings," and she actually seemed pleased to be home. If we can believe her later remarks, then she was already, by midsummer of 1868, beginning to think of an English novel, the eventual *Middlemarch.* There was, as yet, no definite plan or pattern, or any note or definite indication of what she would do. *

It was now clear *The Spanish Gypsy* would prove profitable, which did surprise Eliot. The poem had, in some way, struck a nerve among readers. Over a period of years, it provided a small annuity, with continued sales in cheaper editions and in the American edition. Eliot eagerly corrected typos and other errors for the reprint. For his part, Lewes was pleased to hear from Darwin that his articles on the latter were excellent work. Lewes had himself gone off to a meeting of the British Medical Association, held at Oxford in July, where he met, among others, Charles Eliot Norton, editor and art historian, and friend of Carlyle, Ruskin, Emerson, and Lowell. What was encouraging to both Lewes and Eliot was that his career had picked up, and he was being treated seriously as a researcher into new areas, not characterized as a journalist of the moment.

Eliot wrote to Dr. Thomas Clifford Allbutt, whom Lewes had just encountered at Oxford, a letter not remarkable in itself but compelling nevertheless because Allbutt was one possible model for Dr. Lydgate in *Middlemarch.* Although Lydgate does not appear to be based on one particular figure, Eliot's brother-in-law Edward Clarke and Allbutt seem likely models for some of Lydgate's characteristics: his being well born and above the social status of other doctors (Clarke) and his broader sense of the field than most doctors held (Allbutt, who combined interests in art, Comte, and science). Eliot engaged Allbutt in a discussion of religion, which made her feel uneasy, she says, since "hasty discussion" can lead to misrepresentation. She indicates that her "inspiring principle" which encourages her to write is her "conviction as to the relative goodness and nobleness of human dispositions and motives."

She admits that the bent of her mind is more conservative than destructive, "and that denial has been wrung from me by hard experience—not adopted as a pleasant rebellion." Each of us, she adds, must be heroic and constructive about

---

* The manuscript at the British Museum Library (Add. MS 34034-34037, the final volume on microfilm) suggests a troubled beginning. Chapter 1, "Miss Brooke," is very fussy, full of insertions and deletions. It caused Eliot a good deal of trouble, although unfortunately the deletions are too heavily blocked out to be legible. Possibly, the Chapter 1 epigraph from Beaumont and Fletcher's *The Maid's Tragedy* suggests some of Eliot's unease or ambiguity in her relationship to women's roles: "Since I can do no good because a woman, / Reach constantly at something that is near it."

ourselves like those other strong souls who lived in eras of religious decay. It is possible, she speculates, that in such a period of low moral requirements the highest possible religion has not yet evolved. This leaves open, as she suggests, the question of just what that religion should be—here we find links to humanitarianism, her substitute for formal religion, and to Comtism, based on science, rationalism, and one's control of oneself and the environment, itself a kind of religion. She distinguishes very succinctly between her veneration for the great religions of the world, which have mirrored mankind's struggles and needs, and the "shifting compromise called 'philosophical theism.' "

Skeptical, a conserver, a worrier about gender roles, a denier of many current moral ideas, a believer in the remnants of old religions, a partial positivist, a Darwinian of sorts—in all of these guides and beliefs Eliot had built up something she could hold to. She seemed quite aware that there were cracks everywhere in her intellectual shield, but she also became aware that this collection of emotional and intellectual baggage could provide material for a long novel. Even though *Middlemarch* was not yet in view, these remarks to Allbutt provide some of the grounding for the novel: that mix which became Eliot's distinctive voice.

On 14 September, Eliot and Lewes visited Allbutt in Leeds, in Yorkshire, for a planned three days. The university specialized in science and technology, and had a particularly well-stocked library. From Leeds, they traveled to Ilkey, still in West Riding, and to Bolton, part of Greater Manchester, then to Newark, on the Trent River, northeast of Nottingham. They strolled in the walks, looked up favorite places, enjoyed the quiet of the banks of the river, and were back at the Priory on 19 September. Eliot was still troubled by her being closed out by certain kinds of people, especially women, but at the Priory they entertained intellectuals—mainly bachelors—who were unconcerned with the Lewes arrangement. One of them was the kind of person Eliot particularly enjoyed, Emanuel Deutsch, an acquaintance from their evening with the Lehmanns. Deutsch was a polymath, extraordinarily learned in languages, one of those talented young Germans who were remaking archeological and biblical studies. He knew most of the European languages, plus Sanskrit, but his main area was in Chaldaic, Aramaic, Amharic, and Phoenician. He had just written a well-received piece on the Talmud for the *Quarterly Review,* and he may have provided Eliot with a glimmer of the world of Daniel Deronda, or even served as some kind of shadowy model for her creation of Deronda.

Another young favorite was W. R. Sheeden-Ralston, also a bachelor, an assistant at the British Museum, whose speciality was Russian and Slavic languages and culture. A pair of brothers, John Burnell Payne, a teacher and journalist, and Joseph Frank Payne, a physician, became spirited regulars. Allbutt was a steady visitor, and he became quite famous for his invention of the clinical thermometer. Other young bachelors followed, some in journalism, others in bookbinding and printing, several of them young men who had left the church over doctrinal disputes; few if any visitors were still deeply involved in church activities or held strong religious views.

One of the more renowned guests was Edward Burne-Jones, who first came to the Priory in February 1868, with his wife, Georgiana. Burne-Jones was a well-recognized pre-Raphaelite painter, part of a group which included William Morris, Holman Hunt, and the Rossetti clan (painters, poets, and dabblers in strange rites). The Burne-Joneses were much younger, but carried with them the glamour of their artistic world and an enormous admiration for Eliot. The painter and his wife were probably led into the Priory salon by Frederic Burton, the friend from their 1858 Munich trip. Burne-Jones was struck with Eliot's high intelligence, the depth of her knowledge, and, at the same time, her sympathetic attitude. The young couple saw Lewes and Eliot at their Sunday afternoon salons, but also at other times, for lunches, dinners, or just for visits. In turn, the Leweses would visit them in Fulham, a posh section of London where they kept a far greater establishment than did Eliot and Lewes. Eliot particularly liked their two young children. Through the Burne-Joneses, she met William Morris, and, at a later date, Rossetti came to the Priory. But neither of them became regulars or intimates.

Charles Eliot Norton, whom Lewes had met in Oxford at the British Medical Association conference, came to live near the Priory. A Henry James character, Norton arrived with a large entourage of mother, wife, children, and two unmarried sisters. He is significant here because he left portraits of both Lewes and Eliot, in January 1869. He viewed Eliot in particular, but also Lewes, the way we would expect Lambert Strether, in James's *The Ambassadors,* to observe them *before* his revelation matures him. Norton carried over the worst of American (Boston) puritanicalism and narrowness. "She [Eliot] is not received in general society, and the women who visit her are either so émancipée as not to mind what the world says about them, or have no social position to maintain." Norton's use of the French word is perfect; only the French could countenance such immorality.

After noting that Lewes dines out a good deal and that some of the men he mingles with come without their wives to the Leweses' Sundays, Norton says: "No one whom I have heard speak, speaks in other than terms of respect of Mrs. Lewes, but the common feeling is that it will not do for society to condone so flagrant a breach of hers of a convention and a sentiment (to use no stronger terms) on which morality greatly relies for support." Norton surely means "adulterous," but cannot bring himself to write the word. He continues:

I suspect society is right in this;—at least since I have been here I have heard of one sad case in which a poor weak woman defended her own wretched course, which had destroyed her own happiness and that of other persons also, by the example of Mrs. Lewes. I do not think that many people think Mrs. Lewes violated her own moral sense, or is other than a good woman in her present life, but they think her example pernicious, and that she cut herself off by her own act from the society of the women who feel themselves responsible for the tone of social morals in England.

Mrs. Grundy had voyaged over from America.

From this assessment, there was no recourse. When a man of Norton's supposed intelligence could not get at the truth of the relationship and could not understand how much more moral it was than those marriages socially sanctioned but in practice dysfunctional, Eliot could only walk away. But Norton was not finished. His description of Lewes is that of a popinjay, and a French popinjay at that. Like an innocent Lambert Strether, Norton is comfortable with thinking the French are the lax ones of the world.

> Lewes received us at the door with characteristic animation; he looks and moves like an old-fashioned French barber or dancing-master, very ugly, very vivacious, very entertaining. You expect him to take up his fiddle and begin to play [now more Italian than French]. . . . His acquirements are very wide, wider perhaps, than deep, but the men who know most on special subjects speak with respect of his attainments. . . . But he is not a man who wins more than a moderate liking from you. He has the vanity of a Frenchman; his moral perceptions are not acute and he consequently often fails in social tact and taste. He has what it is hard to call a vulgar air, but at least there is something in his air which reminds you of vulgarity.

When they go to lunch, in the study, Norton's attention is caught by a "staring likeness and odious, vulgarizing portrait of Mrs. Lewes [actually a magnificent portrait made by Frederic Burton in 1865]. Indeed all works of art in the house bore witness to the want of artistic feeling, or good culture on the part of the occupants," with the single exception of a "common lithograph" of Titian's *Christ and the Money Lenders.* In comparing Eliot's portrait to Couture's drawing of George Sand, Norton found the former wanting; not so much the result of the artist's poor hand, but because of some flaws in the subject. The face is not so noble, the eyes not so deep, there is less suggestion of positive beauty. "Indeed one sees a plainer woman; dull complexion, dull eyes, heavy features."

Even Eliot's talk was found wanting. "Her talk was by no means brilliant. She said not one memorable thing, but it was the talk of a person of strong mind who had thought much and who felt deeply. . . . Her manner was too intense, she leans over to you till her face is close to yours, and speaks in very low and eager tones. . . . It [her manner] is a little that, or it suggests that, of a woman who feels herself to be of mark and is accustomed, as she is, to the adoring flattery of a coterie of not undistinguished admirers." When Norton leaves, he asks his wife, Sue, if she wished to come again, and she answered, "No, I don't care much about it." But come she did, in two weeks, when several other women were present; and then Lewes dined at the Nortons', and in still another visit Mrs. Norton brought her two children. So much for Norton's effort to quarantine Eliot and her French barber companion. It was high Boston disdain at its best, full of moralistic fervor but without any spine supporting it. *

* "Boston" continued to arrive at the Priory, a little later in the person of the daughter of James Russell Lowell, Mabel Lowell. At about the same time, Harriet Beecher Stowe wrote Eliot, and that began a warm, instructive, and often compelling correspondence between one of America's most famous women and one of England's, although as it turned out they agreed on little. In all, Stowe wrote fourteen (extant) letters, and Eliot responded with eleven, with many long gaps in the correspondence over a period of eleven years, from 1869 to 1880. The gaps suggest missing letters.

Eliot had been experiencing another of her slack periods, although by 1869 she came out with a list of several new projects: a novel called *Middlemarch*, several poems, and a long poetic effort—perhaps another dramatic work—on Timoleon, a Greek statesman and general who fought the Carthaginians.

By August 1868, Eliot began two notebooks (now at the Folger Library and the Berg) which contained reading material deeply influential in her development of *Middlemarch*. In that impressive list—including George Gote's *A History of Greece*, in eight volumes, and Max Müller's *History of Ancient Sanskrit Literature*—were several books which especially held her attention and appear to have affected her overall sense of *Middlemarch*. Two were more significant than others: Lucretius's *On the Nature of Things* (which she read in the H. A. J. Munro translation, 1864) and Sir Henry Maine's *Ancient Law: Its Connection with the Early History of Society and Its Relation to Modern Ideas* (1861).

Lucretius's philosophy of man—and his downgrading of the gods—was attractive to Eliot; but so also was the Roman poet's emphasis on nature as the binder for all individual matters, the so-called atomistic composition of things. Lucretius held that the soul was material, associated with, not separated from, the body, so that the universe came into being not through some miraculous event but by means of natural laws. There is no immortality of the soul; there is no consciousness beyond death. There is only natural law. Eliot cites his remarks on time, which coincide with her sense of history: "Time also exists not by itself, but simply from the things which happen the sense apprehends what has been done in time past, as well as what is present and what is to follow after."

Sir Henry Maine's views on the individual and the group work well within Lucretian lines as Eliot developed them for *Middlemarch*. Maine argued that the individual has emerged from the group in early history, so that questions of free will, necessity, guilt, and the rest have led away from absolutes to matters of relativity. Without any final arbiter, individual perception and behavior lie with the individual. All overarching explanations—including Casaubon's "key"—are no longer valid. This particular reading carried Eliot into the fall of 1869 and helped to establish the lines of thought of *Middlemarch*: not any radical departure for her, but a considerable reinforcement of where her mature ideas had been steadily heading. With this intellectual buttressing, she could use her fiction to close the personal gaps and divisions; or so she tried.

Her letter to Cara Bray on 11 October 1868 speaks more of a retiree than of someone preparing for a long haul on a difficult and complicated book. She rambles through the last few months of her life as though she and Lewes were just an old couple living on a pension and enjoying themselves with occasional jaunts here and there. She insists, however, that she will keep to her plan of visiting no one; if friends wish to see her, they must come to her. Although she offers ill health as the reason, the real motive was to make certain she did not meet a social snub.

Blackwood proposed that the third edition of *Gypsy* be put into a cheaper issue, at 7/6, with a printing of 1,000 and a "lordship" (or royalty) of 1/6 on each copy sold. After comparing price, size, and other matters with Tennyson's *Idylls of the Kings*, Eliot accepted that. She reports to her publisher unusually poor health since her trip abroad. She says most of her time is spent dealing with her malaise, but she indicates she is "brooding over many things, and hope[s] that coming months will not be barren."

She was now aware of some of the criticism of Gypsy, and she was shaken by the negative comments. "In spite of my reason and my low expectations, I am too susceptible to all discouragement not to have been depressingly affected by some few things in the shape of criticism which I have been obliged to know. Yet I am ashamed of caring about anything that cannot be taken as strict evidence against the value of my book." She assumes that different reviewers take completely different tacks in order to earn their guineas "by making easy remarks on George Eliot."

On 4 November, she and Lewes set off for Sheffield (between Nottingham and Leeds), visiting the ironworks and going over sights she had viewed over twenty-five years before with her father. Although we have no firm evidence, it is quite possible this return to the past, to the late 1830s, helped her focus on time and place for *Middlemarch*, or at least pointed her in the general direction of the novel. Reporting to Barbara Bodichon on her pleasant trip to Matlock, south of Sheffield, Eliot repeated one of her constant plaints: "I drove through that region with my Father when I was a young grig [cricket]—not very full of hope about my woman's future. I am one of those perhaps exceptional people whose early childhood dreams were much less happy than the real outcome of life." It was the kind of revelation, under different circumstances, she transferred to several of her heroines.

The Leweses were seeing a good deal of Spencer. He was, as we know, a special type, intellectually Eliot's equal in many respects, but a man of such neurotic tendencies as to defy definition. Eliot mentions he looks younger than ever, but almost always he returned from trips dissatisfied with the living conditions, unable to eat the food, incapable of tolerating new noises, and suffering from headaches and chills and strains of flu. Despite their differences, his friendship with both Leweses wore well, as Eliot recognized. She cites his truthfulness "that makes amends for many deficits." There is affection in her negatives.

Eliot was fully aware that her life, while placid, was not productive.* In her journal, she notes she is not engaged in any work which "makes a higher life" for her, although she was meditating the subject of Timoleon. The point of the latter was to be a direct application of positivism, which would demonstrate how Timoleon's character influenced destiny; in one respect this is a direct blow at the Marxist interpretation of history. She went at this project with her usual research skills, reading in Sicilian history and following a detailed chronology

---

* Perhaps this explains her carping letter to Blackwood about the weak advertisement for Gypsy. "In justice to the book," she writes, "it seems to me that there should be a distinct, prominent announcement of the Third and Cheaper Edition. . . . I have no superstitions about these things, but the practice of duly acquainting the public with the appearance of a new, cheaper edition commends itself as reasonable. The routine of a large business often involves some inadvertence to specialities, and on this ground I mention the point to you." The tone is sharp. Blackwood responded that he was shocked and hastily assured her he would make certain the slip did not recur.

of Carthaginian history up to the time of Timoleon's death in about 336 B.C. The project apparently never progressed any further than this. Several poems, however, derived from ideas in her journal.

Now in its third edition, *The Spanish Gypsy* by the end of 1868 earned Eliot £333.18, with 2,362 copies disposed of, including 122 sent to reviewers. While not on the scale of royalties for her novels, the sales brought her the present-day equivalent of well over $25,000. Eliot was naturally pleased with sales and with the physical appearance of the third edition.

She and Lewes were reading Browning's *The Ring and the Book* aloud. Here her critical faculties failed her when she indicated Browning's choice of subject does not justify the elaboration of his treatment. "It is not really anything more than a criminal trial," she writes Blackwood, "and without any of the pathetic or awful psychological interest which is sometimes (though very rarely) to be found in such stories of crime. I deeply regret that he has spent his powers on a subject which seems to me unworthy of them." She failed to perceive in Browning's Pompilia several of her own ideas, as well as several of her own female figures: going back to Janet Dempster, or to Hetty Sorrel and Romola; or, more generally, those women she portrays as trapped in marriage, like the looming Dorothea Brooke or the later Gwendolen Harleth. And her dismissal of the psychological import of the dramatic poem is equally surprising, since *The Ring and the Book* reminds us of some of Eliot's fiction in its psychological reach. Blackwood had earlier said he read Browning with more attention than admiration. It was these remarks which, apparently, set off Eliot's own comments, although she warns her publisher she does not want them bandied about. Browning was, after all, a regular visitor at the Priory.

It was, all in all, a regressive time for her. As she tells Clifford Allbutt, all the devices of mankind under the title of consoling truths cannot dissipate the fact that "*absolute* resignation" is the sole course open to us; but even she has gained no more than a "fitful exercise of such resignation." She adds: "So if I seem austere, please to interpret that seeming as the result of an unwilling conclusion that a human lot in which there is much direct personal enjoyment must at present be very rare." She says this to Allbutt, the positivist who believed in man's control of his destiny, who trusted that society can transform itself.

Quite another level of depression, resignation, pity, and suffering, however, was developing. At the very beginning of the new year, 1869, the couple learned that Thornie was ill, with what they thought was a kidney stone. As he wrote from Natal, his suffering was so great Lewes suggested he should return to England for further advice and for possible surgery. Toward that end, Lewes sent on the considerable sum of £250. A kidney stone was, of course, extremely painful, but it could be helped, and if the correct medical treatment followed, it did not have to prove fatal. But Thornie suffered not from a stone but from tuberculosis of the spine, an agonizing disease which was always terminal.

Once the news arrived, with the assumption that the condition was only a stone, the Leweses returned temporarily to their normal life. Eliot notes in her journal that she wrote a long poem, "Agatha." She cites extensive reading, despite ill health: Book 24 of the *Iliad,* the first book of the *Faerie Queene,* Clough's poems, some Italian things read aloud to Lewes, Ben Jonson's *Alchemist* and *Volpone,* and John Bright's political speeches, besides the first four cantos of *Don Juan.* The reading seems unfocused, but this she blames on her seeming "to live under a leaden pressure—all movement mental or bodily is grievous to me." But on 25 January, she began to write still another long poem, "How Lisa Loved the King," intended for *Maga.* Blackwood offered her £50 for it, and proofs arrived in time for Eliot to take them with her when she and Lewes left for Italy, in early March.

Completed on 23 January 1869, "Agatha" had some special meaning for Eliot, although for the contemporary reader it seems treacly. Based on a peasant woman she visited near St. Märgen, a German spa, the poem traces the final years of a modern-day saint. Agatha (Greek for "good") is a country woman who serves others, gains their respect and support, and lives entirely within the confines of a true religious life. When she is visited by an angel, in the form of "Countess Linda," she indicates she is prepared to meet her heavenly fate. We can only read this piece of verse as an effort on Eliot's part to will herself or her perceptions back into a simpler Wordsworthian time, in which, like Agatha, she divests herself of all earthly riches and hopes. Psychologically, it reveals a very depressed person seeking not expression, but escape. If literarily the poem is a Christian parable, psychologically it is a disheartening case history.

"How Lisa Loved the King" is based on a tale in Boccaccio's *Decameron* (X, 7). It is an awkward work, about a young woman, Lisa, daughter of a drug merchant, who falls in love with Pedro, king of Aragon and currently master of Sicily now that the French have been driven out. The dramatic poem appears made up of leftovers from *The Spanish Gypsy* and even *Romola.* It has few reverberations either as poetry or as part of Eliot biography. Once Lisa gains the love of the king (a pure love, since he is happily married), she recovers her health, which had become precarious, and is betrothed to someone of her own class. It seems as if Eliot merely wanted to keep her hand in, and this poem is the result.

Was Eliot always in a state of depression? Did she feel joy or pleasure beyond the moment? Henry James's neurasthenic and reclusive sister, Alice, thought Eliot lived without joy. Calling her features "dank" and "moaning," she says she makes "upon me the impression, morally and physically, of mildew or some morbid growth—a fungus of a pendulous shape, or as of something damp to the touch."

Alice James was judging Eliot on the basis of early biographies of her, after her death, and from her reading of Eliot's books, intermixed perhaps with envy that someone could transform morbidity into achievement and fame. There is, however, a large omission in her assessment. A morbid strain in Eliot did exist, that sense of absolute resignation, but there was also the pleasure she gained from the writing itself when it was going well. We tend to stress her morbid qualities because she emphasized them in her letters, and her books are somber, but they are somber because she felt life was not to be trifled with. She recognized, with classical sense of balance, that pleasure and pain in equal doses are implicit in every act; that all life is choice; and that choice is not in itself a guarantee of rightness. It is true that once she threw off formal religion, she looked around uncertainly for something to replace it, but she did not see in her humanitarianism a total abnegation of life. Dorothea Brooke finally makes a decision which may disappoint us, her contemporary readers, but it is one which seems to satisfy her, *given her choices*. Daniel Deronda is set on his way, with a certain joy of spirit, or joy of discovery. In another area, Eliot found real pleasure in her travels, especially when she stopped at small towns and could ramble on forest paths. Those moments were, for her, revelatory, part of that recapturing of the earliest years of her life when she was not yet in a quandary about her future, or caught in personal confusions.

That acknowledged, Eliot was not overall a happy person. She had had too much internally to overcome, and her life did not fit into regular patterns in an age that demanded regularity. She was always conscious of what an anomaly she was. And there was still another dimension: as she gained fame and presence as one of England's greatest writers, she felt the burden of other women's expectations. Pressure came from several sides: from women's movements, from individuals who looked up to her for moral and ideological guidance, from politicians with questions for which she was supposed to have answers, and from those who thought her very presence was a stain on all womanhood. She recognized in the late 1860s that whatever she said or did created a ripple in English life; people were immensely interested in her, not only for the obvious reason of possible scandal (still!), but also became she had achieved hieratic fame.

With Dickens ceasing to publish any long works after *Our Mutual Friend* in 1865, Eliot was virtually at the center of English fiction—not the most popular, but the most prestigious. But connected to all was her role-playing as a man, the submergence of private Marian Evans into public George Eliot, and that added to the ambiguity and dualism of her position. Further, her daring exploration of what a woman of will and determination could do was thrust alongside a growing conservatism which offered up a shaped, virtually predetermined society. As a consequence of all these seeming contradictions and ambiguities, as a result of her position of extraordinary fame, along with her irregular union with Lewes, she had taken on almost guru-like qualities. She was both honored and chided, admired and attacked, but no one in London intellectual life, or close to it, could ignore her. All this created burdens and pressures which, shy and diffident as she was, drove her further back into herself and intensified what was already an introspective, highly isolated sense of self.

In the 1860s, Eliot had to struggle to be herself. The expectation to be "another" was so high she could feel it palpably at the Priory. Each work she published was expected to be, if not a masterpiece, then superior to the previous book. Lewes had helped to create this awareness in her, through his high praise and through his shielding of her from adverse criticism. This, too, threw her back into herself; and in that region of self, she moped, pitied herself, regressed to the times when she feared her entire life would come to naught. These memories and experiences were close to her; and while at times they served as therapy—making her aware of the full range of human frailty—they also acted to depress her. That shaping of "absolute resignation" which she offered as the bedrock of her humanitarian impulses was a sign of maturity, but also the symp-tom of a severely depressed person. If we add up all the negatives and link them to the positives, we have a woman of enormous contradictions who held it together with a depressive personality, but this personality allowed into itself long moments of pleasure, from the work itself, from Lewes's company and devotion, from their travels. As for the rest, she shared Hamlet's lament:

> O God! God!
> How Weary, stale, flat, and unprofitable
> Seem to me all the uses of this world,
> Fie on 't! ah fie! 'tis an unweeded garden,
> That grows to seed; things rank and gross in nature
> Possess it merely. That it should come to this!

In that, too, lay maturity.

PART SIX

❧

Reaching Out

17

Toward Middlemarch

"Men and women make sad mistakes about their own symptoms, taking their vague uneasy longings, some-times for genius, sometimes for religion, and oftener still for a mighty love."

In the month before Eliot and Lewes left for Italy (for two months), she spent the time reading, going to concerts, and generally experiencing one of those seemingly unfocused periods we have noted so frequently in her career. She read Matthew Arnold's poetry and concluded, as most readers have, that his earlier work was superior to his later. She heard Clara Schumann play Mendelssohn and Beethoven, in a chamber group and as a soloist. She read John Bright on Ireland, then read aloud portions of Manzoni's *I promessi sposi*. These barren periods, in which she appeared to be standing or sitting still, were quite possibly periods in which she allowed her brain to wander freely until it caught up the integuments of a story which could become her next work. While she seemed idle, or even absent, in reality she had learned how her personal cycle worked. And she waited out patiently the fallow periods, until the material began to shape itself. As we see in the *Middlemarch* "Quarry," a notebook* Eliot kept in which she jotted down medical information, political events, and, most of all, ideas on how to shape the material into a fictional whole, that novel grew in just this way.

On 14 February, the Leweses entertained a glittering gathering at the Priory: Browning, Palgrave, Burton, Barbara Bodichon, Mark Pattison (the rector of Lincoln), and many others. Four days later, Blackwood wrote admiringly of "How Lisa Loved the King," a letter so supportive we recognize the publisher was, like Lewes, protecting his client. Despite his praise, Eliot did not wish to

---

*Located in the Houghton Library of Harvard University. We will take up the "Quarry" when *Middlemarch* becomes more shaped in Eliot's mind; when, in fact, it blends with the novel.

publish the poem in the March *Maga* since it was unrevised and she planned to take proof with her to Italy. In her same response, on 19 February, she indicates she means to begin her novel, "having already sketched the plan." She says she is uncertain about the portions between the middle and the end, but ". . . various results of the novel have been soliciting my mind for years—asking for a complete embodiment." She recognizes this novel would be her fullest statement. Its gestation period was the longest of any of her works, and it would have the furthest reach. While her preparations for other novels had been extensive—one thinks of *Romola*—here she was concerned not only with details and historical and medical veracity but with shaping itself. The growth of the artist is implicit in *Middlemarch.*

In still another way, her position on women's issues would come to a head. Her Dorothea Brooke would be the spokeswoman for Eliot's fullest sense of the female role in society, and Dorothea's acts would lead, in time, to much controversy. * One point we should establish: Eliot's view of what was open to women in those days—around 1832, the time of the First Reform Bill—led them into marriage as a career. Implicit in Eliot's presentation is her awareness that even such an attractive, rich young woman as her heroine cannot find achievement in any way except attachment to a man, one old and desiccated, the other young and somewhat unproven and unconvincing. If marriage is fate for Dorothea, then what about women who do not come close to having her accomplishments and physical beauty?

On 3 March, with her head filling with *Middlemarch* and plans for an early beginning, Eliot and Lewes traveled to Italy by way of the French Riviera. In Florence, they ran into heavy rains, and although they stayed with the Thomas Trollopes, whom they genuinely liked, Eliot had a miserable time of it, in bed much of the visit with flu-like symptoms, sore throat, and general indisposition. Although the trip was planned as a nostalgic return to the past, because of the poor weather they barely had time to see the cathedral, baptistry, and Giotto's Tower. From Florence, they entrained for Naples, only to find the same dismal weather. They left Naples for Rome, which proved significant, but not for purposes of sightseeing. In the Pamfili Gardens, they encountered the eldest daughter of Mrs. William Cross, and this led to the latter visiting the Leweses on 18 April, accompanied by her handsome twenty-nine-year-old son, John Walter. This was Eliot's first sight of the man who would become her husband after Lewes's death. Young John Cross was upright-looking, striking with regular English features, a successful broker and banker just back from New York in order to enter soon the London office of the family business. The scene foreshadows in some respects Dorothea's meeting with Will Ladislaw in Rome on her ill-fated honeymoon with Casaubon.

Except for this, their Italian trip, which they undertook with so much expec-

---

* At the George Eliot international conference in 1980, for example, panelists fought over the soul of the writer, and not the least over her attitude toward characters like Dorothea Brooke. There were those who considered her a traitor to female causes and others who defended her as a feminist manqué. As Dorothea went, so went her creator.

tation, proved disappointing. Lewes was anxious not only about the poor weather but about his elderly mother, his recurring ailments, and his inability to bring back old memories. He was also feeling the lack of work, and perhaps also sensed that Eliot, too, was eager to return to her desk with her new project. After a return trip to Florence and the Trollopes, they came back to London by way of Paris. On 5 May, they were back at the Priory, exhausted, enervated, and without any of the exhilaration previous trips had given them.

Their arrival home coincided with the beginning of the nightmare with Thornie. The young man arrived on 8 May, a wasted figure, having lost fifty-six pounds since they last saw him. He was unable to sit, and only by lying down and being heavily dosed with an opium derivative was he able to bear the agonizing pain. His spine was, in effect, rotting away under the disease. On the day after his arrival, there was still another caller, the twenty-six-year-old Henry James, uncertain of his reception but eager to meet the famous George Eliot, on whose work he had already written three review articles. Lewes was out when James came, trying to find medication for his son. The moment was dramatic in more than one respect, since after Eliot's death, James would emerge as one of the leading novelists in the English language (along with Conrad and Hardy). James attempted to assist the writhing Thornie, kneeling beside him and asking if he could help in any way. James apparently thought it was merely an injury— an accident, perhaps—and having himself suffered from back ailments, he felt he knew something of the condition. By this time, Lewes had returned with the medication, and James offered to run off to find the surgeon James Paget.* He left a message at Paget's house, and that ended his first visit to the Leweses. We have already noted James's description of Eliot, citing her as "magnificently ugly—deliciously hideous," but indicating to his father he nevertheless had fallen in love with her.

For the next five months, Lewes and Eliot had to watch Thornie die. While morphine occasionally relieved the pain, it was not always effective. What possibly kept the couple from going mad was their unawareness of the seriousness of the ailment, which continued to go undiagnosed. The very inconclusiveness brought with it some hope it would vanish as rapidly as it had appeared, although the day-to-day agony Thornie suffered could not be ignored.

Lewes's diary for 8 May through 15 May suffices to show what was occurring at the Priory. Sunday, the 9th, is entered as a "dreadful day," with Thornie rolling on the floor in agony. Lewes administered morphia four times in the night. Monday continued the suffering, and the surgeon John Henry Roberts came. Then for two nights in a row, Lewes is grateful Thornie has been quiet, without pain. Lewes took time to visit his mother, now eighty-two and a source of worry. During the day, he tried to read (he mentions John Stuart Mill) but

---

* Although Paget (surgeon to Queen Victoria) was deemed the best in England, he could do little except prescribe morphine for Thornie's pain. He did not diagnose the case as spinal tuberculosis, but even if he had, it was incurable, even with surgery. After failing to diagnose the ailment, he called in another authority, who suspected tuberculosis of the glands. He, too, prescribed morphine. For both doctors, the prognosis seemed to be either death or miraculous recovery.

spent most of his time with his son. The sole break in the clouds, as he calls it, is an offer from Ticknor & Fields for a uniform American edition of Eliot's work and a further offer of £300 for "Agatha" to appear in the *Atlantic Monthly*.

At this time, Eliot was herself writing Blackwood that Thornie's disability resulted from a wrestling injury to the spine suffered four years ago. She recognizes the injury has now developed into something very grave, complicated by a hardening of the glands. She understands from Paget that it derives from some constitutional weakness. If Thornie can lie prone on an inclined couch, she foresees a cure. She concludes: "By and by we shall get more used to our trouble"; that conclusion was based on her prognosis of a cure. Writing to Cara Bray, Eliot gives some sense of how their daily routine was going. "We have been suffering much in seeing his suffering and our days have been broken into small fragments."

Yet she and Lewes attempted some normal routine. Eliot was herself compiling the "Quarry" for *Middlemarch*, which she had started sometime after September of 1868 and continued to add to until 1871, when most of the novel was concluded. It should be noted that *Middlemarch* was not conceived of in the way it finally appeared, for at first Eliot saw the stories of Dr. Lydgate and Dorothea Brooke as separate. When she started to write, in midsummer (July 19) of 1869, she planned to begin with Lydgate's story, but this material formally enters the novel in Chapter 15.

The Dorothea Brooke material, which was now in hand, was *not* considered part of the novel until November 1870, when Eliot indicated she was experimenting with a story she had not thought of carrying out to any great length. "It is a subject which has been recorded among my possible themes ever since I began to write fiction, but will probably take new shapes in the development." She titled this segment "Miss Brooke." Throughout 1870, she worked on "Miss Brooke," the material probably from the beginning of the novel up to Chapter 15, when Lydgate enters fully. Then in early 1871, she joined the two elements, glancingly in Chapter 10, with the dinner party Mr. Brooke gives for the Vincys and for other townspeople.* In the latter part of Chapter 10, Lydgate's presence in Middlemarch† is introduced with several comments by Brooke himself, then by Lady Chattam and by Bulstrode. It was a masterly way of bringing him in without his being physically present, since it links him with nearly everyone of importance in the town. The structural method indicates how Eliot has mastered the technical aspects of her craft and leaped beyond the earlier novels.

---

* Evidence suggests that Eliot had completed the first eighteen chapters by 19 March 1871. Jerome Beaty (*Middlemarch from Notebook to Novel*; Urbana: University of Illinois Press, 1960, p. 5) also argues that Chapter 23, the beginning of Book Three, "Waiting for Death," falls into that time period.

† Initially, Middlemarch referred to the county and then gradually evolved into the name of the town. By Chapter 10, when we assume Eliot joined the "Miss Brooke" and Lydgate stories, Middlemarch was firmly established for the remainder of the manuscript as a town. The point is a small one, but suggests how tentatively Eliot proceeded in her conception of characters and place.

The "Quarry" reveals extensive research on medical matters as they were practiced in the late 1820s. Further, Eliot had access to the numerous medical scientists Lewes had consulted in his work on physiology. The "Quarry" demonstrates she was reading the British medical journal Lancet for a variety of reasons. As Eliot wrote in her journal, she needed all of this information so that she could imagine her hero, Lydgate, the sole occupant of the novel as yet. Her reading involved several kinds of information: how medical reform was being carried out; how a medical candidate was selected for a particular position; how medical associations were formed, how a dispensary was established, and how the amounts were set for charges (patients were doctored for a penny a week); how a doctor was trained—Eliot had Lydgate educated at Edinburgh, London, and Paris, all three places cited in Lancet as best; how medical jurisprudence was arranged, the division into police and forensic medicine, with a court of examiners; how poisons were treated; how one might buy a diploma—perhaps with John Chapman in mind; how practitioners were remunerated—the complex settlement of fees; how bodies might be obtained for dissection; how cholera had spread in certain sections of England and how it was guarded against and even stopped in others.

But that was only a beginning. Eliot probed deeply into aspects of medical research, with her analysis of how the microscope had revealed cell theory and blood problems. Much of her work was historical, going back to Leeuwenhoek's work on the microscope and Malpighi's discovery of the capillary system. She went into questions of how surgeons came to perform their duties—the historical record of medical practitioners beginning with Henry VIII. She examined the charter of James I as it referred to medical practice. The College of Physicians was established with the charter, and she was interested in how the college was itself organized. After several pages of research materials, she moved to questions of particular diseases, including how lunatics were treated at Bethlehem Hospital (with purges, vomiting, and bleeding). She was also interested in dissections and postmortems, matters she would pick up later in cases of poisonings and other causes of death. She wanted to distinguish between typhus and typhoid, in terms of treatment and related matters. She delved into questions of anatomy, the "structural elements" which make up life. Then after a short break for "Mottoes" (from Goethe, Chaucer, G. D. Rossetti) and "Political Dates," she focuses on cholera, which by the end of 1831 had extended to Newcastle in the north, then swerved into Scotland, reaching as far as Edinburgh, where special attention was paid to halt it.

From cholera, Eliot moved into "History & Treatment of Delirium Tremens," more directly applicable to Middlemarch in its later pages. She was interested in aspects of it which create a paroxysm of poisoning by alcohol, followed by a critical sleep. Sleep, however, does not mean the end of the paroxysm, since the condition can repeat itself for several days. Withdrawal of accustomed stimulants does not end the condition, and the condition may recur in individuals who have not given up the stimulants. This was, for her, valuable information.

The second part of the "Quarry" is more directly related to the shaping of *Middlemarch*. It will be taken up in its proper place, since it was evidently a working plan for the novel and something Eliot consulted regularly as she wrote.

Not at all directly related to this dramatic development in Eliot's life (beginning to settle in on a monumental novel) was a letter from Harriet Beecher Stowe, the famous American novelist and an admiring reader of *Adam Bede*, *The Mill on the Floss*, and *Silas Marner*. At the time of her letter, 15 April 1869, Stowe was already a legendary figure because of *Uncle Tom's Cabin*, the book Lincoln said had caused the Civil War. She was fifty-seven, although as early as forty-two she had described herself to a friend, Mrs. Elisa Follen, as "withered and dry as snuff." Eliot enjoyed Stowe's modesty in saying she was a "used-up particle." With this, the two seemed like silent partners. They never met, but their (extant) correspondence extended to twenty-five letters. One other linkage was that Eliot had reviewed Stowe's novel *Dred* in the October 1856 *Westminster*, a mixed notice at best.* In 1869, although *Uncle Tom's Cabin* remained her masterpiece, Stowe was known as a prolific writer of twenty-four other volumes; and yet even as she reached her apogee, she sank into decline shortly after, not only in popularity but in quality.

Stowe wondered about Eliot's soul, and felt that their souls could commune. Their husbands, she points out, are similar, even to their common interest in Goethe; it is an open question if she knew of Eliot's and Lewes's arrangement. Eliot was touched and responded at considerable length, especially since Stowe's "spirituality" gave the English writer an opportunity to clarify several matters. Eliot is quick to establish what she means by a new stage of religion, not so far from what positivists were asking for:

> I believe that religion too has to be modified—"developed," according to the dominant phrase—and that a religion more perfect than any yet prevalent must express less care for personal consolation, and a more deeply-awing sense of responsibility to men, springing from sympathy with that which of all things is most certainly known to us, the difficulty of the human lot.

She says she denies pantheism, since it is not practical and looks at the universe from the outside of our relationship to it. "As healthy, sane human beings we must love and hate—love what is good for mankind, hate what is evil for mankind. For years of my youth I dwelt in dreams of a pantheistic sort, falsely supposing that I was enlarging my sympathy."

If nothing else, the Stowe correspondence allowed Eliot to hone her views as preparatory for *Middlemarch*. The letters fall into four distinct time frames:

---

* *Dred: A Tale of the Great Dismal Swamp*, based on the Nat Turner rebellion of 1830; the book is an indication that even after the unprecedented success of *Uncle Tom's Cabin* in 1852, Stowe was still pursuing examples of racial injustice in America.

1869–72, the period of *Middlemarch;* 1874–76, the time of *Daniel Deronda;* 1876–78; and finally 1878–80, when Eliot died. The two seemed to have entered a sisterhood which overcame the breaks in the continuity of the series, so that one or the other could pick up even after two years had elapsed. That Eliot took the correspondence seriously can be seen from the length of her letters, as well as from her candor with this American she would never meet. In terms of *Middlemarch,* the early part of the correspondence allowed Eliot to confirm her view that human happiness is assimilated to the wholeness of society, that community values must prevail over individual ego.

In another area, Eliot was gratified at the idea of a possible uniform American edition, especially since *The Spanish Gypsy* was doing so well there. Among others, Longfellow and Lowell in the "Boston set" were taken with it and even knew lyrics by heart—so Lewes told Charles and Gertrude. In August, "Agatha" was published in the *Atlantic Monthly.* * In the spring and summer of 1869, when *Middlemarch* was incubating and the "Quarry" was proceeding, Eliot carried on a fairly extensive and interesting correspondence with several people who were significant in her personal and literary life. We can say nearly everything becomes compelling when a large book like *Middlemarch* is in the offing. It is the kind of novel which sucks up everything in its wake: revelatory experiences, scenes recalled, research painstakingly done, and real people encountered who could be transformed.

Mrs. Pattison, married to the rector of Lincoln College, Oxford, had visited the Priory in January 1869 and returned often with her husband. Mark Pattison has often been cited as the model for the faux scholar, desiccated Casaubon, and Mrs. Pattison (the daughter of a bank manager) as a model for Dorothea. Charles Dilke, Mrs. Pattison's second husband, denied that his wife had anything in common with Dorothea, but felt that the religious side of his wife was taken from her letters to Eliot and grafted onto Dorothea. He also observed that Casaubon was shaped from Pattison's words, transformed into the terms of Dorothea's defense of her marriage to Casaubon and Casaubon's version of his marriage to her. Dilke cautioned that the matter ends there. Yet the only real point of contact between the Pattisons and the novel's characters is that the rector's wife, like Dorothea, was twenty-seven years younger than her husband. The Pattisons, in fact, never seemed to feel they were the models for the *Middlemarch* characters.

If we seek models for Casaubon and for Dorothea, there is no end of speculation. Haight himself offers up Eliot's old friend, Dr. R. H. Brabant, for Casaubon, and others have suggested Mr. and Mrs. Robert William Mackay, a

---

* In an amusing aside, T. J. Wise and Henry Buxton Forman (Charles's colleague at the post office) misrepresented the printing of an edition of "Agatha," asserting it was a second issue of the first edition when it was actually a second edition, since the type had been reset. This amounted to forgery and a much higher price for the poem. Forman had, earlier, written an admiring piece on "Agatha" and Eliot, although it is impossible to pinpoint when the actual forgery occurred and to what extent Wise was involved in it. (See John Carter and Graham Pollard, *An Enquiry into the Nature of Certain Nineteenth-Century Pamphlets,* 1934, the great work on sleuthing into the extensive Wise and Forman forgeries and their attempts to produce invaluable first editions.)

bachelor until forty-eight and Eliot's friend from *Westminster* days. * While
Casaubon can be located in still others, the point remains that Eliot had a wide
selection of older men whose careers had not matched their expectations; and
Dorothea, with her youthful idealism, was not unlike the young Eliot with hers,
or even Barbara Bodichon. If we must keep seeking, Casaubon could even be
patterned on someone as professionally successful as Herbert Spencer. For while
Spencer produced *his* work, he was old before his time, unneedful of a woman
except as a reflection of his own ego, wrapped up in immense projects, and
seemingly impotent in everything except his own work. Even Frederic Harrison
comes to mind, not because he is Casaubon, but because he pecked away at
grand ideas and projects. After all the debris has been cleared away, Mark Pattison remains, mainly because he wrote a biography of Isaac Casaubon, the eru-
dite and scholarly French-born intellectual of the seventeenth century. But
Pattison's own broad published works do not make him a likely model for the
sterile and failed Casaubon of *Middlemarch*, and this leads to the inevitable conclusion that the latter was, like most of Eliot's later characters, a combination
of acquaintances, experiences, and inner dictates.

   In her next response to Stowe, Eliot indicated how pleased she was with
the portrait of the older generation in *Old Town Folks*, and also with Stowe's
interpretation of Calvinism. Once again, we note how Eliot was moving back
and forth from her plans for *Middlemarch* into her letters to the American writer.
For there is strong Calvinism in the portrait of Dorothea, especially in her phase
leading up to her marriage to Casaubon. Duty, discipline, even her playing an
inferior role as female helper are all aspects of Calvinism assimilated into her
character. Eliot says she is cheered by Stowe's awareness that a dogmatic system
presents to society a mixed moral influence. In this, we have a few of Eliot's
most firm beliefs: that any given system sends out mixed, often confusing signals;
that information deriving from dogmatism can be misinformation, or at best
misleading; that a moral system can be built only on eclectic principles; and
that good and evil, if such distinctions are made, cannot be discovered by any
dogma.

   But Eliot was not sympathetic to Stowe's emphasis on spiritualism, which the
latter said was sweeping American thought. On the contrary, spiritualism (by
which Stowe meant spirit communication, such as séances) appears to Eliot to
be "degrading folly, imbecile in the estimate of evidence, or else as impudent
imposture." Eliot's next statement, while convoluted in her later almost Jamesian style, is condemnatory of all such efforts at understanding the universe
which fall outside of verification.

   So far as my observation and experience had hitherto gone, it has even
   seemed to me an impiety to withdraw from the more assured methods of

---

* Richard Ellman, for example, in "Dorothea's Husbands" (in *Golden Codgers*, 1973), cites
Mackay as a possible candidate, suggested also by an early commentator, Frances Power Cobbe, in
her 1894 autobiography (*Life of Frances Power Cobbe*, by Herself). Some similarities aside, Mackay's
industry and achievement disqualify him as a model for Casaubon.

studying the open secret of the universe* any large amount of attention to alleged manifestations which are so defiled by low adventurers and their palpable trickeries, so hopelessly involved in all the doubtfulness of individual testimonies as to phenomena witnessed, which testimonies are no more true objectively because they are honest subjectively, than the Ptolemaic system is true because it seemed to Tycho Brahe a better explanation of the heavenly movements than the Copernican.

Eliot's implication is that once one disregards science, Darwin, geological studies, and related matters, one falls into an area where anything is possible, and from that subjectivity, nonsense emanates. This discussion of spiritualism and spiritual conflicts will characterize a good deal of the Stowe–Eliot correspondence.

Thornie was of course always present in the couple's thoughts, but Eliot more than Lewes looked for an optimistic prognosis. On 5 August—when the young man was two and a half months from death—she told Blackwood he was out of "visible danger." Possibly her optimism was linked to her beleaguerment, for by this date in 1869 she had completed the first chapter on Lydgate and was trying to clear away hours for her new work. Very possibly, the lack of overall structural conception Henry James was to critique in *Middlemarch*—which he otherwise admired—derived from Eliot's inability to concentrate fully at this time.†

Just three days after Eliot thought Thornie was out of visible danger, he became paralyzed from the waist down, and this, in the strange way of disease, helped ease some of the pain. Although paralysis was his destiny until his death, Thornie did recover use of his legs now and then, contrary to the expectations of his physician, Sir Henry Holland. When his suffering was less intense, he maintained an equitable, even cheerful manner. A whole array of people came to try to ease his pain. His brother Charles, who fainted on first seeing his condition, helped take over his care, along with his wife, Gertrude. Thornie's mother, Agnes, came, probably more frequently than the single time recorded in Lewes's diary. The young man actually was able to talk about his African experiences and to sing Zulu songs; and when Barbara Bodichon came, at least once a week, she brought fresh country produce and spent entire afternoons with him. Mrs. Nassau Senior—he was the economist—not ordinarily considered a member of the inner circle, visited with flowers and other gifts; and Edward Pigott, from Lewes's *Leader* days, came to play cards with Thornie. Eliot

---

* The phrase derives from Goethe and Carlyle ("The Poet as Hero") and indicates that Eliot had stationed herself so solidly in Victorian thought that its significant phrases had become part of her own common stock of expressions.

†James's point was that once one forms the inevitable conclusion that Dorothea and Will will come together, the novel slims down. "We can well remember how keenly we wondered, while its earliest chapters unfolded themselves, what turn in the way of form the story would take—that of an organized, moulded, balanced composition, gratifying the reader with a sense of design and construction, or a mere chain of episodes, broken into accidental lengths and unconscious of the influence of a plan." He felt that Eliot's failure here meant she had not achieved "the first of English novels."

herself entertained him with piano sonatas of Beethoven and Schubert, while he lay on the lawn. Although there was an organized effort to keep up his spirits, after 8 August, when the paralysis started, it was recognized he was doomed. Even as Thornie attempted to keep his composure, Eliot saw, finally, what was occurring. She recorded, to Mrs. Nassau Senior, that his face was becoming more and more the visage of a wizened being which denotes a slow withering. But even then Eliot says she was encouraged by Lewes's prediction that the emaciated look might disappear once a more "rapid assimilation" set in. As Eliot herself moved toward her fiftieth birthday, she noted that death resided in the very areas where she had hoped to see life.

Even Thornie's nurse, Charlotte Lee, broke down, either from observing his deterioration or from overwork. Until his death, it was clear that the Priory as a temple of isolation where Eliot and Lewes could work had become quite the opposite: with helpful guests coming and going, with the need for constant medical attention, and the need, further, for the Leweses to stay up at night to administer morphia, not to mention the emotional drain. The death watch was on. All of this requires emphasis, for Eliot had chosen this period to begin *Middlemarch*. Further, we do not know how much this extended episode with Thornie made her see Lewes differently, especially when she drew on aspects of him in her ennobled portrait of Will Ladislaw; or, in other respects, how much this influenced her desire to create Ladislaw at all. Although we cannot identify precisely how Thornie's condition and death on 19 October affected the creation of this particular book, it cannot be neglected as a factor; and it cannot be ignored, either, as an element in Lewes's relationship to Eliot, however little we can pinpoint any possible guilt. This was, after all, Lewes's second loss of a son. They might have thought it a form of punishment.

All the while Thornie was sinking, in the early autumn, Eliot tried to keep up a good face about it, especially with friends who came to the Priory. She protected them against the worst. Even to Sara, who was distant, she sounded an encouraging note—that the paralysis was not total. But as death approached, she began more openly to express her fears. To give some run to her imagination about life and death—with her own approaching birthday not an idle thought— she wrote the poem "The Legend of Jubal." The poem, one hundred lines of which were written before Thornie died, is a celebration of how art can triumph over death itself, a traditional idea carried into the poetry of the time by Keats, Tennyson, and Browning, among others. Death was certainly on her mind, and when Thornie died, with Eliot at his side, she recorded in her journal: "This death seems the beginning of our own."

We might see "The Legend of Jubal" from several sides. Jubal (from Genesis, 4:21) was a direct descendant of Cain, and the poem was Eliot's effort to comfort the dying Thornie and to find meaning for herself in the face of the young man's personal tragedy. Having composed that small part in October before Thornie's death, she continued writing this long poem into January of 1870. Cast in epical terms, "Jubal" is the story of the triumph of art over Cain's world of death ("Death was now Lord of Life"). Jubal is himself the father of musical instruments, especially the lyre, and his insistence on creating music suggests that in the face of death only art can offer salvation. His is the sole triumph "in the home of Cain." He cries, " 'I am Jubal, I! . . . I made the lyre!' " With this, he finds "new passion and new joy." In this poem at least, Eliot's god is not God, but music and art as ways of transcending human tragedy.

The sole way out of individual catastrophe was through the reshaping of life in art—precisely how Eliot had attempted to transform herself and to emerge as a different form in nature. The entire idea fitted not only her sense of art, *her* art, but also her sense of the natural order, of evolution and reformation, of mutational forms, and everything she had carried away from Hennell, Lyell, Darwin, Lewes, and others. She was reaching toward some explanation, and she perceived how indifferent any religious or even philosophical analysis was to human tragedy; only in art can some meaning be revealed which would permit her to go on. "Jubal" served, in part, that purpose. These lines were both a final resting place for Thornie and a consolation for Eliot:

> This was thy lot, to feel, create, bestow,
> And that immeasurable life to know
> From which the fleshly self falls shrivelled, dead,
> A seed primeval that has forest bred
> It is the glory of the heritage
> Thy life has left, that makes the outcast age:
> Thy limbs shall lie dark, tombless on this sod,
> Because thou shinest in man's soul, a god,
> Who found and gave new passion and new joy
> That nought but Earth's destruction can destroy.
> Thy gifts to give was thine of men alone:
> 'T was but in giving that thou couldst atone
> For too much wealth amid their poverty.—

Her models were Keats's "On a Grecian Urn," perhaps Milton's "Lycidas," and the entire genre of elegy, but also the nineteenth-century growing sense—through the pre-Raphaelites and then Pater—that only art can transform death into something positive. In that regard, God had died.

Thornie's fate was significant in still another way. Besides the grief, the sense of injustice, the recognition of loss, there was also an end of something in Eliot's own life. With the young man's death, she could start up again. As "The Legend of Jubal" implies, it was not an irony lost upon her. She not only wrote a good deal of poetry, and completed "Jubal," but she found time to plan *Middlemarch.* The introduction had come in July, but it belonged to Lydgate, and somehow Eliot knew she had to recast it. She wrote the first chapter in early August, but that, too, could not remain in this order, as she later recognized. Accordingly, the work she had done so far, except for the research in the "Quarry," would have to be reworked. In that reshaping of the novel after Thornie's death, we have something of a reshaping of Eliot's own life. As if following her poem of

Jubal, in which the children of Cain thrive after Cain has committed his terrible fratricide, Eliot reemerged from one of her fallow periods. Some kind of exchange had been made.

With her journal words still ringing in her ears—that Thornie's death seemed to her the beginning of their own demise—she attempted some recovery after the funeral, by going to Park Farm, Limpsfield, in Surrey. Even though *Middlemarch* was moving through her mind,* she could not quite shake the young man's end, "shattered" she calls herself; and even though she had, as it were, exchanged death for some new kind of life, in both poetic and fictional form, she was overwhelmed by the injustice of it all. Since something like Thornie's death assumed a randomness in life that fell outside of her need for control, or even linkage, she was shaken in her own beliefs. Duty, discipline, deference, social obligation, moral and ethical behavior—*her* modes of control—all seemed irrelevant when a young person could be taken in such great pain and anguish. The "life" of her novel was born in the recesses of an inexplicable death, and the mature somberness of its tone and content cannot be separated from the biographical context.

During the death watch in July 1869, she had also written the eleven sonnets which made up "Brother and Sister," recollections of childhood which somehow compensated for her present expectation of loss. She took up a Wordsworthian style and tone—quite suitable for someone who in her novel would return to the years of her youth.

The eleven sonnets making up the sequence are notable for their dip into *The Mill on the Floss* and into Eliot's past. But most significant is how she turned that past into an idyllic tome between a brother and a sister when, in fact, her brother was ignoring her deliberately, and she was suffering the loss of a stepson. We noted how Eliot needed some compensatory experience for her loss, and how that need coincided with a return to the experience of the Garden of Eden before the fall from grace: that is, before she gained adulthood and that relationship of brother and sister was shattered. In the sequence, she omits the hostile scenes between Tom and Maggie in *Mill*, when Maggie errs and Tom is irate. Instead of bringing disaster to his enterprises, this updated Maggie brings triumphs. While she is fishing, a lucky chance turns a dismal failure into the landing of a perch and her brother's praise.

More than anything else, however, the Wordsworthian lines offer a celebration. This return to the past is more than nostalgia; it is an indication of how much Eliot's conserving spirit required memory:

> Thus rambling we were schooled in deepest lore,
> And learned the meanings that give words a soul,
> The fear, the love, the primal passionate store,
> Whose shaping impulses make manhood whole. [Sonnet V]

---

* On 2 August, she began the Vincy and Featherstone parts, but by 1 September, she observed she was standing still in Chapter 3. Ten days later, she wondered if anything would ever come of the novel, the implication being she might put it aside.

The need to reenter the "Garden" and to put behind her "the dire years whose awful name is Change" is so powerful she needed support from another poetic voice, the Wordsworth of her childhood years. Once brother and sister went away to school, they entered into a "divorce" and elements "shaped them" so that they were two forms with their "life's course" severed. As a sister, she put all her energy into worshipping her brother: "His sorrow was my sorrow, and his joy / Sent little leaps and laughs through all my frame; / My doll seemed lifeless and no girlish toy / Had any reason when my brother came" (Sonnet X).

Psychologically, this sequence served several functions, not all of them beneficial. Primarily, it allowed Eliot *to move from her present situation* and to project herself into a past that memory had turned, however falsely, into bliss. She cuts herself away from Lewes and his dying son, from her fame and riches, from her irregular union, from her separation from family—and having "regressed" she can find joy. This was beneficial in that it soothed her; but it was disadvantageous because it strengthened her fixation with death and distorted the past. She tells Barbara Bodichon, for example: ". . . I have a deep sense of change within, and of a permanent closer relationship with death." Joyful though it is, the sonnet sequence appears to be a way in which Eliot was trying to postpone her own death, or thoughts of death: by returning to childhood before her adult cares swung her around toward mortality. Like Wordsworth, she could assume immortality through recollection, although when the sequence ends, she and her brother are moving toward their own end. There was a deepening of recognition, but accompanied by another level of resignation. If anything, she intensified the internal conflicts when she had hoped to relieve them.

Another dimension of this move into childhood, or, even in "Jubal," into other aspects of life, death, and art, is reflected in Eliot's need to return to something sacred. The relationship she expresses occurs in the Garden; it predates the fall from grace, and it could as well be Adam and Eve as well as Eliot and her brother. Implied in this return is an awareness, conscious or not, that the sacred has left her life, or that because of irregularities she is paying a price in loss of earlier joy. Although she never expresses a single word against her union with Lewes, the desire to move outside her life is manifest in these sonnets. And their sacredness is linked to family—we must not neglect that; whereas profanity—divorce, severance, parting of ways—is implicitly connected to her later life.

Writing to Mrs. Mark Pattison, she expressed that her grief was so intense Lewes had to take her into "country solitude" and gave orders no letters should be forwarded. She says she hopes to be at home by the end of November, without making their friends suffer through the distress of "sad haggard faces." On 13 November, they returned to the Priory, and the Sunday afternoons soon began again. Lewes's letter to John Blackwood catches some of their uncertainty, that mixture of grief, wonderment, anger, bewilderment, possibly guilt. Eliot, he says, had lavished "almost a mother's love on my dear boy," and while she expected a recovery, Lewes indicates he had little hope and was, therefore, better prepared for the end. Lewes's feelings ran deep, but, overall, he appears to have taken in stride this loss of a second son—in the way that nineteenth-century parents were conditioned to infant or child death. But the outward Lewes was merely covering up; inwardly, he would pay.

The drama played itself out. As a kind of compensation, Charles's wife, Gertrude, was expecting a child. Because of her condition, she could not accompany Charles, Eliot, and Lewes to the Unitarian service for Thornie at Rosslyn Church and then to Highgate Cemetery for the burial. Incidentally, it was not this child but a daughter born in 1877, Elinor Southwood Lewes Ouvry (her married name), who became the link with contemporary writers on Eliot (Ouvry died in 1974) and who also drew up a list of the books in Gertrude's house— books which came from Lewes's and Eliot's personal library. Charles and Gertrude would become the beneficiaries of the main part of Eliot's estate.

Eliot meanwhile told Sara Hennell how restorative the country stay was, a comfortable farmhouse, with three young sisters as their hostesses. "I was very much shaken in mind and body, and nothing but a deep calm of fields and woods would have had a beneficent effect on me. We both of us felt more than ever before the blessedness of being in the country. . . ." In her annual birthday letter to Sara, Eliot is back in form, dueling with her friend about the consolations of religion. She denies that individual sufferers can be consoled by the idea of a higher being; she calls it a false notion. For her, the "rest of a higher religion might be, that it should enable the believer to do without the consolations which his egoism would demand." The believer, Eliot suggests, feels that God speaks to him, or her, as someone special deserving of notice and consolation; "real" religion does not pamper the ego, not even the suffering ego straining for meaning.

The images and expressions of death in her letters should alert us to how death lies at the heart of *Middlemarch*: actual death, the death of hope, the sense of dashed plans, the frustration of desire, the thwarting of long-range goals. Youth must pass over into aging before it can accommodate life; there is little sheer joy except in the superficial characters. Values have deepened, shadows have intensified, and death hovers—not only in Casaubon, but in the way of the world. Will Ladislaw offers rays of sunshine in his appearance, but his "sun" is shadowed by a shady past: not his but his family's, its outcast status, the fact he is touched by morbid Casaubon (his money) and deceptive Bulstrode (his earlier fraudulent behavior). The novel is full of dry bones.

Well into December, with a long letter to Stowe on the 10th, Eliot was pondering not only the death of those near her, but death itself. "Death," she writes, "had never come near to us through the twenty years since I lost my Father [she forgets Chrissey], and this parting has entered very deeply into me." She says she writes to tell her friend how her "silence has been occupied," a silence akin to death. She touches all relevant bases: Stowe's husband, but especially her brother, the Reverend Beecher, whose recent sermon his sister had sent on. Eliot's response, within a context of encouragement, is curiously flat, even negative. "The great vocation of the preacher, which in your brother's case is, I believe, eminently effective, has a melancholy emptiness among us.

My soul is often vexed at the thought of the multitudinous pulpits, which are such a vast ground for teachers, and yet are for the most part filled with men who can say nothing to change the expression of the faces that are turned up towards them."

During this dismal period, *Middlemarch* went on hold. Eliot did complete "Jubal" in the early part of the new year (on 13 January), and sold it for £250. She entered one of her typical stalled periods, when she lay fallow—until early March 1870—and then reentered the novelistic arena with sustained application. If ever she was Persephone plumbing the underworld of her emotional life before emerging with fictional ideas, this was the time. Her correspondence began to pick up later in December 1869, and she welcomed several visitors to the Priory: Maria Congreve, Spencer, Trollope, the Arnolds, Mrs. Arthur Hugh Clough, Lady Colville, and the Burne-Joneses, now among her closest friends and confidants. What would eventually take the grieving couple out of themselves would be a trip to Germany, to visit old and new sites. But before this, they ventured forth to Rossetti's studio to view his paintings,* and also visited George Frederick Watts's studio. Dickens came to lunch just three months before he died, apparently of a heart depleted by overwork and strain. They attended the Saturday afternoon concerts at St. James's Hall and became acquainted with the violinist Mme. Norman Neruda, who came to the Priory. But despite the activity, there was slow recovery. Lewes was sickly—ringing in the ear, a propensity to faint, and severe headaches—clearly a response of the nervous system to the terrible strain of losing a second son. His mourning was on the edge of passing into deep melancholy. It was this feeling of ineptness and his inability to work (on his *Problems of Life and Mind*) which led to Germany, after he had tried a week on the Isle of Wight with Spencer. Although Spencer was sympathetic, a man so hypochondriacal was hardly fit company for someone heading toward deep depression.

On 7 March, she announces that her novel, "I suppose, will be finished some day; it creeps on." This is our first indication in 1870 that *Middlemarch* was reentering her plans, however dimly. Her chief concern before their departure, however, was not fiction but the state of Lewes's nervous system: ". . . he has had the wisdom to cease writing entirely on finding that it left him in a state of nervous exhaustion. An interesting journey in which we shall see many acquaintances and be within reach of amusements, will be the best thing for him." On 14 March they departed, with their first stop Berlin. It was tonic for Lewes in particular to be honored by old friends and seated at functions with the high and mighty of the academic and political worlds. Even the American ambassador, George Bancroft—he would complete his ten-volume *History of the United States* in 1874—came to call on Eliot and to invite the couple to dinner.

---

* Rossetti became friendly not only with the Leweses but with Barbara Bodichon, who offered him her place at Scalands as a residence. He lunched at the Priory on 9 January, then invited the Leweses to see his paintings, *Pandora*, *Mrs. Morris*, and several others. He saw the couple again on 7 February at Mme. Bodichon's. He sent Eliot some of his sonnets. There is the question whether Eliot in her poetry was influenced by some Rossetti / pre-Raphaelite mannerisms, grafted on to her basically Wordsworthian line. What is clear is that her poetic models were male.

The round of distinguished people went on and on, including Theodor Momm-sen, the German historian, and the chemist Robert Wilhelm Bunsen (of Bunsen burner fame). Never modest about his social activities, Lewes spells them out carefully in his letters. They heard *Tannhäuser,* and concluded it was not for them, feeling more at home with *Figaro,* Gluck's *Armida,* and "even Verdi." Amidst the glitter, Lewes did remember Eliot was the star, he the satellite. "It was very funny last night at a grand party," he wrote his mother, "to see Polly surrounded by adoring women, and a crowd of others all waiting their turn to say a word. She compared it to a flock of birds waiting each to have a peck at her."

Lewes did not miss the opportunity to spend considerable time with Dr. Karl Friedrich Otto Westphal, the specialist in nervous diseases. Eliot called his branch of study "Psychiatric," and characterized him as a "quiet, unpretending little man, who seems to have been delighted with George's sympathetic interest in this (to me) hideous branch of practice. I speak with all reverence: the world can't do without hideous studies."

Since the Berlin weather was poor, and with Eliot suffering from a sore throat and cold, the couple entrained for Prague,* where they stayed for two days before heading for Vienna. They reached Vienna on 8 April and remained for nine days. Lewes's diary carefully records their stay. Robert Lytton, first Earl of Lytton (not the novelist Bulwer-Lytton), a friend of Lewes's, met them at the station, and had secured for them a grand apartment. But Eliot's sore throat, cold, and general indisposition were alarming, and another old Lewes friend, Dr. Mortiz Fürstenberg, cautioned that she should remain in bed for three days.

Lewes rambled alone around the city, now so altered by new architecture he could barely recognize his old landmarks. He also found time to investigate the latest Austrian developments in pathology; conversations followed with Theodor Hermann Meynert, director of the Psychiatric Clinic, and the patholo-gist Salomon Stricker. Lewes was moving along the edges of a revolutionary new discipline, and while his investigations did not involve original research or clini-cal experience, he was alert to the latest developments through his extensive European contacts. As a side issue, Sigmund Freud in 1870 was still a Viennese schoolboy, but when he was moving toward his own forms of psychotherapy in the 1890s, his chief opposition came from neurologists like the above, who had themselves been pioneers in this still inchoate field.

The purpose of the trip had been to relieve Lewes's gloom and deepening nervous depression, and once he became caught up in good society and learned conversation, he seemed to bounce back. As for Eliot, the journey was also intended to dissipate gloom; she noticeably backed off from serious work and allowed daily events to carry her, but in her case, far more than in Lewes's, the intense social activity proved wearing, tedious, and ultimately unbearable. She recovered sufficiently from her sore throat for them to dine with the Lyttons, but by the time they left Vienna they had had enough, despite the kindness and generosity of friends and acquaintances.

---

* The synagogue, which turns up in *Daniel Deronda,* was of particular interest.

Salzburg acted as a restorative. Their quarters at the Melböck Hotel were comfortable, the food was to their liking, the weather excellent. They made an expedition to Berchtesgaden, which in its pre-Hitler days was dramatically glorious, and then went on to Munich before returning to the Priory via Paris. They were back in London on 6 May, tired and ready for a long rest at the Priory, although their social calendar was full. The Sunday afternoons began again, with visits from their usual crowd (Spencer, Lord and Lady Amberley, various scientists and professionals), and they dined out, meeting that combination of literary and scientific people who came together at Lord Houghton's (Annie Thackeray, Kinglake, Lecky, and Rossetti, among others). One matter pulled Eliot deeply back into the past, almost to the time in which *Middlemarch* was set, and that was Sara Hennell's republication of Charles Hennell's *An Inquiry into the Origins of Christianity*. Eliot expressed her own obligation to the book and said she hoped a cheap edition would reach "minds to whom it will bring a welcome light in studying the New Testament—sober, serious help towards a conception of the past, instead of stage lights and make-ups."

In the background, not forgotten, was work on the novel. In her journal, Eliot observed she was hopeful about future work. But she felt languid, and as a consequence her novel languished. John Blackwood spoke with her on 23 May and discovered she was not so far along as she intended to be. The publisher, nevertheless, was optimistic that it "promises to be something wonderful— English provincial life. . . ."

That languor or depression Eliot was experiencing is caught perfectly in "Armgart," which Eliot wrote mainly by the end of September and which expresses her general feelings over the last several months. A verse drama, "Armgart" differs from *The Spanish Gypsy* in having no stage directions, no indications of place or time, no authorial intrusions. It is simply an expression of pain and anguish from someone who can no longer perform. Armgart has lost her voice; a doctor, in "curing" her, made her voice woolly and unsuitable for opera. Armgart is now torn between her role as a woman and her role as a former diva. A year before, she had rejected the marriage proposal of the graf (a titled nobleman), who was interested in marrying the woman, not the career. Having insisted on her career, she rejected him. The graf argued that a woman's achievement lies in the "fulness of her womanhood," where she is royal. Armgart refuses to accept that women have to look only to men and to motherhood. She insists she is both an artist by birth and a woman, that the two cannot be separated. The graf leaves, and within a year Armgart loses her voice, but still insists she does not wish to be "prisoned in all the petty mimicries / Called woman's knowledge, that will fit the world / As doll-clothes fit a man."

But now that she cannot live to sing, Armgart must still learn to live. From her personal maid, the lame Walpurga, and from her singing master, Leo, she hears there is still life outside the magical world of opera and concert. With sorrow, with resignation, with a desire to pay back what in the past she has only taken, Armgart makes peace with herself by becoming a teacher of song instead of a practitioner.

The potentialities of this drama for Eliot are considerable. That they reflect her present state there is no question. She, too, has lost her voice, and she feels isolated from the rest of mankind without her gift. The latter had demonstrated her distinction from the rest of womanhood and justified her irregular life, her lack of children, her sacrifice of certain traditional womanly things for the right to pursue what was her birthright. The play also reveals a good deal of anger, that a woman has to choose so definitely between the graf, who desires a wife without a career, and the career itself; men do not make that choice. Further, the loss of her voice makes her commonplace. If we apply some of this to Eliot, we see someone who was beginning to lose her belief in herself as soon as she could no longer be distinguished from other women. It was now four years since her last long fiction, and *Middlemarch* was still quite uncertain. Although "Armgart" is hardly top-drawer Eliot, it does open up her life in ways that perhaps a more well-wrought effort might not.

In visiting the Pattisons, on 25 May for a four-night stay, Eliot enjoyed her first view of Oxford. At first disappointed, she quickly recognized the beauty of the place, especially as she walked along the river. Country sights picked her up. But the visit was also notable for the people she met, including the daughter of Thomas Arnold, Matthew Arnold's brother, a woman who later married T. Humphry Ward and became known as a novelist and reformer, Mrs. Humphry Ward. The latter was only eighteen when she met Eliot, but the memory was sufficiently intense that she wrote about her in detail a full forty-eight years later, in *A Writer's Recollections* (1918). Her portrayal of Eliot gives one of the few seemingly unprejudiced views of the novelist as she was about to resume work on *Middlemarch*. Chiefly, it reveals her generosity with young women and the appeal she had, her accessibility, uncondescending manner, and lack of affectation. We can understand why so many women, including those with much firmer public views on feminist issues than she, came to worship her.

Eliot had heard that Arnold's daughter was reading a good deal about Spain, and she talked with her for about twenty minutes, re-creating Zaragoza, Granada, the Escorial, and other places. From this, Mrs. Ward, forty-eight years later, wrote:

> . . . she talked with perfect ease and finish, without misplacing a word or dropping a sentence, and I realised at last that I was in the presence of a great writer. Not a *great talker*. It is clear that George Eliot was never that. Impossible for her to "talk" her books, or evolve her books from conversation, like Madame de Staël. She was too self-conscious, too desperately reflective, too rich in second-thoughts for that. But in tête-à-tête, and with time to choose her words, she could—in monologue, with just enough stimulus from a companion to keep it going—produce on a listener exactly the impressions of some of her best work.

She concludes: "When it was done the effect was there—the effect she had meant to produce. I shut my eyes, and it all comes back:—the darkened room, the long, pallid face, set in black lace, the evident wish to be kind to a young girl."

In a revelatory moment, Mrs. Ward noticed Mrs. Pattison as she looked out from the window of the rector's lodgings, at the corner of the quad. To the young woman, it is a privileged moment, an epiphany, and then she observes Eliot experiencing the same sensation, that something unusual had occurred even in this familiar situation. The younger woman sees the scene as a painting, by Greuze or Perronneau, a sudden moment in time caught forever by an artist on the lookout for such moments. But when she sees Eliot respond and go running to Lewes to draw his attention to the window, Mrs. Ward records a deep novelistic moment, not for herself but for Eliot. "If she had lived longer, some day, and somewhere in her books, that vision at the window, and the flower-laden garden would have reappeared. I seemed to see her consciously and deliberately committing them both to memory."

Eliot's own Oxford journal mentions only a passing chat with Miss Arnold. Her comments focus more on Lewes's world, especially their visit to the museum where Dr. George Rolleston (a professor of anatomy and physiology) dissected a brain for her. They were also shown instruments for measuring various elements. On the next day, 27 May, Eliot chatted with the two daughters of Mrs. Gaskell, the novelist, who had died in 1865.

At supper that night they enjoyed the company of Benjamin Jowett, the famous classicist,* and met Walter Pater for the first time, already well known for his article on Leonardo da Vinci (1869), which became the sixth piece in his *The Renaissance.* Jowett they liked and cultivated; Pater, not at all. Later, when Pater's *Studies in the History of the Renaissance* was published, Eliot spoke about it with the classicist R. C. Jebb. His misgivings gave her both comfort and strength, she said.

There is always the possibility that Eliot, and Lewes, noted a sexual ambiguity or effeminacy in Pater which they found, if not distasteful, then unsettling. We get some hint of that possible unease for the "other" from Eliot's response to women who fell at her feet, expressed everlasting love, like Edith Simcox, and appeared to be somewhat out of the heterosexual "norm" Eliot hewed to. This is a thorny question, since the incidence of so many women throwing themselves at her would appear to indicate they sensed some receptivity; but there is no indication she encouraged more than devotion and that her response was generous rather than sexually based.†

Despite the couple's desire to settle in at the Priory, Lewes's health seemed spooked there. All kinds of food products and derivatives were tried—cod liver

---

* In a long and productive career, Jowett was responsible for translations of Plato, Aristotle, and Thucydides, among many others, including biblical studies. In 1870, he was elected Master of Balliol College, Oxford.

† In an unpublished article on Eliot's relationship to Edith Simcox (" 'My Whole Soul Is a Longing Question': Edith Simcox and George Eliot"), Professor Bonnie Zimmerman suggests that "beneath the flirtation [the show of affection] lay a complex love affair between Edith Simcox and George Eliot." Zimmerman traces this to the romantic, chivalric tradition, where the love is unrequited. This is *not* to suggest that Eliot felt any physical desire for Simcox; the "affair" was played out in coded terms, with Simcox unable to break the magnetic pull she felt in Eliot, and the latter subtly encouraging this in one of her "spiritual daughters" while rejecting any further physical advances. Further comments on their relationship appear later in this book, when, in December 1872, Simcox first visited Eliot, and thereafter remained enthralled.

oil, the great cure-all for earlier generations, and phosphates—but it was concluded that only country air might help. They set out on 15 June for Cromer on the Norfolk coast. But before they departed, Dickens's sudden death on 9 June (1870) left everyone at the Priory shocked. Eliot recalled the prophetic story Dickens had told them at lunch on 6 March: "He lunched with us just before we went abroad and was telling us a story of President Lincoln having told the Council on the day he was shot, that something remarkable would happen, because he had just dreamt for the third time a dream which twice before had preceded events momentous to the nation. The dream was, that he was in a boat on a great river all alone—and he ended with the words 'I drift—I drift.' " Eliot thought Dickens looked "dreadfully shattered," and she conjectures that it is probable he never recovered from the effect of his railway accident (on 9 June 1865, when he was returning from Paris with Ellen Lawless Ternan, an actress and his mistress).

At Cromer, for a fortnight, the couple read a potpourri of materials: Trollope, Balzac, Rossetti, Mendelssohn's *Letters,* and Morris's *Earthly Paradise* in its most recent volume. From Cromer, they headed to Harrogate, where Lewes wanted to try the chalybeate waters. But the waters, which had helped in 1864, were only temporary relief.

Before leaving Harrogate, Lewes wrote Robert Lytton about their routine: familiar but also a form of doom. Nothing seemed to help Lewes more than briefly, and even that appeared to be as much psychological as physical. At Harrogate, they drank the waters, walked before breakfast, then Lewes smoked his morning cigar, while Eliot read; this was followed by a ramble along the fields, together or alone. They spoke of "lovely things that conquer death." Lewes asserted further that to be with Eliot "is a perpetual Banquet to which that of Plato would present but a flat rival." As the day progressed, they drank more water, listened to tepid music in the Spa Gardens, and observed a "rather unfashionable scene"; at two, they dined "copiously," then napped and went to an evening concert. After supper at nine, they read a French novel and were in bed by ten or ten-thirty. In these seaside resorts, they went unnoticed. It is remarkable how far removed Eliot was from writing, although she had in her head a book of considerable complications. We glean from this that when it came to priorities, Lewes's health and well-being preempted all else.

At Whitby, Eliot was pleased to find Mrs. Burne-Jones and her two children, and for the fortnight they spent there the friends were together, walking, talking, discussing Goethe's *Faust.* Like a large variety of women, Mrs. Burne-Jones was deeply moved by Eliot's presence; she revealed her feelings in a letter written on 2 August, the day after the couple returned to the Priory. She thanks Eliot for her kindness to her, and apologizes if she seemed to talk only about herself; she reflects "upon what a trap for egoism your unselfishness and tender thoughts for others is." "I think," she adds, "I need spend no more time on this looking back—the balance of everything is that you have won my grateful affection, and I hope you will accept it."

On her return to the Priory, Eliot began to write her rather drab but revealing little drama, "Armgart." Drab as it was, her name made it commercially viable, and she sold it for £300; £200 from *Macmillan's* and £100 from the *Atlantic Monthly*. By 8 August, the couple was off again, this time to Limpsfield, for three weeks, where Eliot almost finished "Armgart." If this drama is indeed an indication of current feeling, then it was a desperately uncertain time. While at Limpsfield, Eliot revealed great interest in the Franco-Prussian War, which was now entering a critical phase. Her feelings about the two countries were mixed: she admired German progress, but also respected French culture.

Her specific comments to Barbara Bodichon, obviously a supporter of the French because of her husband, are compelling. While she felt sorry for the sufferings of the French, she thought

> . . . the sufferings are better for the moral welfare of the people than vic-
> tory would have been. The war has been drawn down on them by an iniqui-
> tous government [Louis Napoleon, the discredited Petit Napoleon], but in
> a great proportion of the French people there has been nourished a wicked
> glorification of selfish pride, which like any other conceit is a sort of stupid-
> ity excluding any true conception of what lies outside their own vain
> wishes. . . . It was quite true that the war is in some respects the conflict
> of two differing forms of civilization. But whatever charm we may see in
> the Southern Latin races, this ought not to blind us to the great contribu-
> tion which the German energies have made in all sorts of ways to the
> common treasure of mankind.

Eliot's words about the merits of the French and Germans recall comparable talk in the late 1930s: French decadence against German energy and progressivism. What she missed—although shortly she admitted that the war was a personal sorrow for everyone—was that Prussian saber rattling was a malevolent kind of energy. She recalled German advances in the sciences, or German music, which she confused with other kinds of energy; and she condemned the French overall because their government was corrupt, laughable, insidious. This war led her to read Carlyle's *French Revolution,* which demonstrated how good ideas lead to bad practices.

The couple returned from Limpsfield on 29 August. Sometime during this month, Lewes was given the small portion of *Middlemarch* Eliot had written. She also turned down an offer from *Scribner's* to write a number of short stories, an indication she was contemplating a return to her long novel. In another area, Lewes's son Bertie had become engaged to an agreeable and well-educated young woman, Eliza Stevenson Harrison; and despite opposition from her father, but with Lewes's and Eliot's support, they were married in August 1871. They named their first child Marian Lewes. In September, "Armgart" was com-pleted. Lewes apparently was enjoying a recovery and was once again busy revis-ing his *History of Philosophy*. The war, meanwhile, occupied Eliot more intensely than any other political event, especially with the capture of Napoleon after the fall of Sedan on 1 September. With the Germans prepared to march on Paris, the Third Republic was finished, and the future of France was uncertain. As she told D'Albert-Durade in early 1871, the entire affair was a "great calamity" for the French, with whom she now sympathized. She was particularly upset at the weapons used in the field, weapons which could make eight wounds at once in a body, and she condemned it all as barbaric.

The fall of 1870 was conspicuous for its "lacks"—for anything approximating some sorting out of her priorities and any reordering of her present life. If we found a certain drift in the mid-1860s in and around *The Spanish Gypsy*, there was now a real failure of energy or will. "Armgart" was left-handed work, neither fine poetry nor meaningful drama. Not until December would *Middlemarch* reemerge, and that would be merely another attempt rather than accomplishment. Worry about Lewes could certainly account for some of this enervation, as could aging and an embrace of its pitfalls before they actually occurred; very probably change of life; and a certain passivity now that fame and money were hers. Eliot does report she is "continually suffering from headache and depression," which may have caused or resulted from her inability to work on her novel. "Armgart," she says, afforded her some comfort.

Age is unquestionably on her mind as she poured out her distaste for the sermon of Charles Haddon Spurgeon, whom Ruskin had highly praised. She felt it was a libel on Calvinism, with the feeblest examples offered up and with no sense of whether or not God is present in our souls. The entire performance sent her into a Hamletic discourse on life and death. "Oh how short life—how near death—seems to me!" she writes Sara. "But this is not an uncheerful thought. The only great dread is the protraction of life into imbecility, or the visitation of lingering pain." Of course, another dreaded birthday was looming, her fifty-first. She writes she had hoped that as she and Sara aged, they were more capable of "calm enjoyment," but that does not seem the case.

For her birthday, on 22 November, Lewes bought her a lock-up book for her autobiography, an item which has never been recovered. It is unfortunate for many reasons, but especially because in the lock-up she may have revealed some sense of progress on *Middlemarch*, or on other matters, which she held back from her more open journal or diary. In any event, her journal for 2 December 1870 mentions she was "experimenting in a story," which she began "without any very serious intention of carrying out lengthily." This was the material called "Miss Brooke." Writers on Eliot have eagerly grabbed hold of such tidbits, since so little about the early development of the novel is at hand. She says she is at page 44. Lewes also reports Eliot read aloud to him what she had written of "Miss Brooke," and then progress appeared to be in the offing, for her change of plans gave her about one hundred pages within the month. By the end of 1870, she appeared to be on her way.

If we consult the "Quarry," which is not dated for individual notations, we see a segment called "Relations to be developed." There are eleven items here, indicating a real sense of direction in the novel—Dorothea to Casaubon, Lydgate to Rosamond—and the listing of these in that order suggests the relationships were perceived as parallels, or as comparisons and contrasts. She

continues: Fred Vincy to Mary Garth, the Vincys to Old Featherstone, Doro-
thea to Will Ladislaw, Lydgate to Bulstrode, Bulstrode to John Raffles, Celia to
Sir James, Ladislaw to Mr. Brooke, Caleb Garth to Mr. Brooke, and, finally,
Mr. Farebrother to all, except Sir James and Mr. Brooke. This listing is followed
by "Private Dates," in which Eliot attempted to work through her chronology.
In this, Dorothea is married to Casaubon in 1827; Lydgate to Rosamond in 1830
(July or August); Mr. Brooke tries for Parliament in May 1831, just two months
after Casaubon's death; Dorothea's second marriage, to Will Ladislaw, is in January or February of 1832, with a child born in 1833. Bulstrode buys Stone Court
in June or July 1831, Raffles returns in July 1831, and the latter dies in August
1832, two years after Lydgate's marriage. *

This is by no means the total material in the "Quarry." Other material indicates a more detailed breakdown of scenes into subscenes, and discussions of
different characters' motives—in effect, almost a chapter-by-chapter outlining
of where the novel was to go. By the time she came to individual scenes, Eliot
had the novel well in hand conceptually. That slow start was indeed a period of
incubation, as her synthesizing powers brought together an immensely varied
amount of material toward the creation of a community or society.

One area the "Quarry" slights is that concerning Eliot's final disposition of
the novel's sexual matter. Although several critics have pointed to Casaubon's
impotence—critical in his relationship to Dorothea, besides its overall metaphorical impact—few have noted how asexual Dorothea herself is. Asexual,
that is, until she is saved or rescued from an emotional wasteland by Will, the
outsider who is a sexualized noble savage of sorts. She is "rescued into love," a
practice which extends from Richardson and Fielding in the previous century to
later writers like Hardy, Meredith, Lawrence, and Forster. Eliot, here, seems to
be playing with her own rescue by Lewes.

But there is more to it than this. As an outsider, albeit a a male one, Will
has something of the feminine in him, at least some of the social weakness

---

* Eliot then reiterates some of this information with alterations and additional connections. Dorothea is settled again at Lowick (after Casaubon's death) in June 1831; Bulstrode and Raffles are at
Stone Court now in June 1831; Fred Vincy's adventure and choices occur in July 1831; and Lydgate's
disclosure of his trouble to Rosamond comes in August of 1831. Eliot then lists the sequence in the
novel of Parts I, II, III, IV, and so on. But interspersed with these sections—for example, between
Parts III and IV—is a segment called "Motives." She provides a further breakdown of events, such
as Featherstone's burial and the arrival of Ladislaw; Ladislaw's relationship to Rosamond and Casaubon; the dismay of Sir James and the Cadwalladers concerning Will; the attacks on Mr. Brooke as
landlord; Lydgate's tortured relationship to Bulstrode and to the hospital. Another "Motives (in
general)" appears between Parts IV and V. Here, some of the above material is repeated—Casaubon
dies, Brooke stands and falls, Raffles appears, Lydgate is embarrassed, further scandal comes to the
hospital, Rosamond flirts with Ladislaw, Dorothea talks to Rosamond. Some of the motives do not
appear in the novel until later, although they are listed here. After Part VIII, there is a brief listing
of ages for the Garth family, including Mary, twenty-two; then also Bulstrode, fifty-eight; Raffles,
fifty-one; Joshua Rigg, thirty-two; his mother, fifty-six. After this comes a series of sketches all
devoted to Bulstrode and his background, his deceptions, the way in which Will is implicated by
way of his inheritance, and how he is further entangled with both Casaubon and Bulstrode. Other
elements include more connective tissue, especially with Lydgate—an indication of how significant
Eliot considered him in the final workings of the novel—and then follow listings of political dates.

Eliot associated with women. With his curious name, his exotic lineage (Polish, perhaps part Jewish), his scorn of the status quo, he serves as the kind of marginal figure Dorothea would like to be, a male double, as it were. If we view him this way, Dorothea's choice of him, and his choice of her, is inevitable, virtually a brother–sister rather than a husband–wife joining. That defuses the sexual in favor of the familial: Eliot as Isis finally united with her torn brother Osiris, or Maggie with her brother Tom in *Mill.*

On 10 December, Lewes's mother died peacefully at eighty-three. Once she was buried, the Leweses spent the Christmas holiday on the Isle of Wight, where Barbara Bodichon had leased Swanmore Parsonage at Hyde. It was a relaxing time, although there is some indication Eliot tried to work on her novel. Lewes had been attached to his mother, who showed a mature understanding of her son's life; but after her death, his attention did not have to be divided anymore. With Mrs. Lewes gone, Thornie dead, Bertie in Natal, and Charles well established, Lewes was now free of all other intimate relationships and entanglements. The last eight years of his life could be almost completely devoted to Eliot's needs. She was voracious in her requirements: someone to shield her, an audience who was uncritical and lavish in praise, a companion supportive of her mood swings, which often left her depressed and indisposed for days at a time.

In their relationship, we see the dim foreshadowing of still another couple, the famous pairing of Leonard and Virginia Woolf. Leonard Woolf performed heroically in his role as husband—although "husband," by mutual agreement, probably did not include sexual consummation—but he has been criticized for having cocooned his wife. During her periods of severe headache, depression, mood swings, and even bouts of madness, he cared for her needs, providing the kind of shield for her that Lewes provided for Eliot. Of course, Eliot was not mad, and her bouts of depression were not so profound as Woolf's; there is little question that the two women were different and had different requirements, physical and otherwise. But Lewes did cocoon his wife, and the question always arises whether or not the male figure has so preempted the larger world that the woman is circumscribed or kept infantile except in the one area where she can be herself, at her desk. According to this reasoning, by so shielding her, Leonard had not allowed Virginia her space; and he had no intrinsic right to assume she would fall apart without him. On a lesser scale, Lewes spent the next eight years isolating Eliot from anything that might upset her; supporting her work, even while we do not know what his real feelings were; and establishing a wall of protection that made life as special as it could be for a human being. He handled the business deals, negotiated with publishers, deposited the money, paid the expenses, and carried on an extensive correspondence in England and abroad over Eliot's affairs. He did everything except make the money. Under these cocooned circumstances, however, Eliot wrote two exceptional novels of very widely different points of view.

Although we have observed how *Middlemarch* had finally entered into her imagination, we must not lose sight of still another aspect of her life as it pertains to her fiction: her friendship with Emanuel Deutsch, and the influence his work on the Talmud had on her own growing desire to write about Jews and early forms of Zionism. Zionism was then known as "Jewish nationalism," and Deutsch—who died at forty-four—was a typical early believer, his life stretching from birth in Silesia, once part of the Austro-Hungarian Empire, to death in Alexandria, Egypt.* He had been a frequent caller at the Priory, and he also instructed Eliot in Hebrew. The relationship was solid and admiring on both sides, to the extent she referred to his commentary on the Talmud, in 1867, as that "glorious article," rare praise for her. She saw him at Oxford in 1870, heard a talk he gave at the Sheldonian Theatre on the Moabite Stone, and stored away in her head his exploration of the Talmud. This would come later, after *Middlemarch.*

What caught Eliot's eye in the Talmud article was Deutsch's argument that after the Babylonian captivity—the period of exile beginning in the late sixth century B.C.—Jews acquired a sense of nationalism about their race, their prayers, their songs. Deutsch could not explain why this occurred, and he could find no explanation in the exile itself to explain the transformation. But transformed they were into a communal love for their history, and out of this came the first stirrings of nationalism. Other elements also touched Eliot, one of them being the parallels and similarities between Talmudic thought and the New Testament. Deutsch took pains to point them out, including ideas of redemption, regeneration, and the structuring of a son of God. Once Eliot saw how meticulously Deutsch had worked out these patterns, she was able to embrace Talmudic thought not as some distant alien cultural form but as something she could equate to her own experience.

But possibly the presence of Deutsch went even further than the Talmudic writings and Eliot's recognition of the great intellectual abilities of a man still in his thirties. In 1869, he went into a deep depression, something Eliot could identify and sympathize with. He had overworked himself, that was clear, but he was also experiencing the first stages of illness which would lead to his death in 1873. He did not, however, surrender, and he continued to argue for the rapprochement of religions, not only Judaism and Christianity, but also Islam. George Eliot would be touched intellectually and ideologically by this desire for conciliation.

Whatever she was planning—and it may have been no more noticeable to her than a developing interest—would grow into an intense preoccupation with Judaism and Jewish life, not only in *Daniel Deronda* but in her later essay called "The Modern Hep! Hep! Hep!" In another respect, her attitudes in *Middlemarch* may have been affected; for example, Bulstrode's Christian-created venality confronted by simple right conduct in Caleb Garth, a small-scale Job.

On 20 December, Eliot and Lewes began their nine-day stay with Barbara

---

* Deutsch's "Jewish nationalism" was timely, since it coincided with Cardinal Manning's belief that when the Antichrist did appear, he would be a Jew. Ironically, when he appeared, he was a German Christian.

Bodichon on the Isle of Wight. Eliot even attended a high Anglican service with her friend on Christmas Eve, what she called "all sorts of Catholic ceremonial in a miniature way." The surface was one of real pleasure; subsurface was her recognition that she had written only a hundred pages, and her sense, further, that while she might appear happy, she was doing little for others. The old Calvinism still peeked through.

On 8 January of the new year (1871), the Russian writer Ivan Turgenev visited, one of many times he came to the Priory. Turgenev was precisely the kind of writer Eliot and Lewes could enjoy: his intelligence, sophistication, and Westernization made him quite welcome.* At the same time, the Lewes were seeking a country house where Eliot could have quiet for her novel while renovations on the Priory were undertaken. Since November of 1870, they had been on the lookout, but Eliot ominously expressed their vacillation as to how they should arrange their "short lives." Their options were to keep the home in London and seek a modest retreat in the country, or give up London altogether and move to a more countrified environ. Lewes says that in such a case their needs would not be modest, since they require space for books and "snugness suitable for rickety old people." But despite their hesitation, they did take possession of a house in Surrey called Brookbank, at Shottermill, near Haslemere, a house belonging to Mrs. Alexanger Gilchrist, whose now deceased husband had been a well-known writer and a biographer of William Blake. On 2 May, they moved in and stayed there for three months, leaving on 1 August, when another tenant claimed it. They then moved into Cherrimans, which lay across the road from Brookbank, and they stayed there for two months. On returning to the Priory, they found, among other alterations, a new bathroom.

Unquestionably, Lewes and Eliot, in the kind of symbiosis often characteristic of couples who do not have children of their own, were taking on each other's physical needs. Together, they had begun to consider themselves old, and they were arranging their lives around aging. Creature comforts had long since become essential; but there was more—the sense that only a few years were still allotted to them. They were preparing for death, although as in any symbiotic relationship neither could face who would go first. They competed in aging, suffering, recovering from illness. They both appeared to need the roles they were playing.

For the time being, Europe was more or less closed off to them because of the Franco-Prussian War and then its aftermath, the Paris Commune and the near state of anarchy in the city.† Before leaving for Shottermill, Eliot found herself picking up somewhat, her journal indicating 236 pages (of print) on her novel,

---

* Having met Turgenev at a party, Lewes told Mrs. William Cross (the mother of his successor) that the Russian author, now transplanted, was pleasing: "To see him is to like him." Lewes had originally encountered Turgenev in 1839, in Berlin.

† Rome, too, was in turmoil, although of a different kind. The Roman Catholic Church, in its eagerness to counter science and material progress, proclaimed, in 1870, papal infallibility in matters of faith and morals.

which she says she hoped to complete by November. Although the date was unrealistic, her progress was not at all meager. Her hesitation is part of her anguish at ill health and languor. That recurrence of languor would be more compelling if we could link it to something definite; but except for the ailments themselves, psychologically derived or not, and the fear of aging, the languor seems exaggerated in terms of the way Eliot's life was arranged. That she should suffer such periods, like anyone else, makes sense; but that she should emphasize the condition to such a degree while a major book was bubbling in her head suggests some psychological dimensions which elude us. We may speculate about an uncertainty, a sense of loss, an awareness of a lack of self-satisfying achievement given her high expectations, some kind of disappointment, possibly in Lewes, a possible sexual failure: all of these, none of these, or several. Or else she could not shake the continuing tension of her irregular relationship, or the trauma of her early fear she was wasting her life; but nothing in her letters or journal allows us to speak precisely.

Self-doubt plagued her, especially as she confronted such a huge task of a novel growing to four volumes.* For that, as we shall observe, something new on the publishing end had to be devised to maximize the kind of work *Middlemarch* was becoming—a strategy devised by none other than Eliot's manager and agent, Lewes. In the interim, Eliot may have complained about society as "oppressive," but nevertheless she could not do without it when she was in London. On Sunday, 23 April, she and Lewes entertained for lunch, among others, Turgenev, Trollope, and Emily Cross (John Cross's next-to-youngest sister), with seventeen people invited afterward, including the Burne-Joneses, Mrs. Arthur Hugh Clough, Lady Colville (of a distinguished family in service in India), and the famous soprano, now retired, Mme. Michelle Viardot. The latter sang "divinely" and entranced the audience. Even with considerable servant help, the planning and running of such a party took considerable time and energy. The event lasted until six o'clock, and then Lewes went to dinner at Mrs. Alexander Orr's—a sister of Frederick Leighton and biographer of Browning—where he encountered the famous scientist John Tyndall, as well as Dr. William Budd, an epidemiologist of great note (he charted how typhoid and Asiatic cholera were spread), and the editor William Hardman. The luncheon party was not exactly the activity of a woman who finds society oppressive, nor were the additional activities those of a man who is constantly ailing. Arriving home at 11:45, Lewes called it a "day of talk and excitement."

Once in Shottermill, with *Middlemarch* beginning to sort itself out into a long, slow development—what we can glean from the "Quarry"—it was clear

---

*Yet it should be emphasized that once Eliot linked the Dorothea and Lydgate segments the manuscript is strikingly clean. Despite some deletions, corrections, and insertions (especially in Chapter 19 on Fred Vincy, Chapter 51 on the election, and Chapters 64 and 74, respectively, on Lydgate and Rosamond and on Bulstrode in his fall), she revealed little hesitation in moving the massive machinery forward. The patterns of development are clear, notwithstanding the complications and tightness of the plot.

some fresh format would be necessary. Dickens had discovered a strategy for his very long novels, published in numbers, but Eliot's kind of clustered fictional shaping did not lend itself to the breakup into small parts which Dickens's more episodic procedure made possible. Lewes had wanted Eliot to consider weekly publication, for he saw that it was a great source of money, but when she balked and it became clear her novel was antithetical to this method, he devised another way of publishing *Middlemarch*.

Lewes wrote Blackwood from Shottermill, on 7 May, about what he thought would prove a wonderful solution. His remarks reveal he was the secret sharer of Eliot's needs: that he used his knowledge of publication to create precisely the correct form for publishing her novels. He says the story must not be ruined for lack of space. He proposes, as Blackwood had himself more than once suggested, that the circulating libraries be circumvented; that once their stranglehold was broken, books could then be bought rather than borrowed. By the 1870s, the libraries had outlived their function. They had always created a kind of censorship, especially the largest ones like Mudie's, which was puritanical and exclusionary—more Victorian than the Victorians were reputed to be. Now with a new generation of writers about ready to appear, with only Eliot and Trollope among the giants still alive and publishing, the time seemed appropriate for the libraries to be brought down.

This was precisely Lewes's plan. "I have devised," he wrote, "the following scheme, suggested by the plan Victor Hugo followed with his long *Misérables*—namely to publish it in *half-volume parts* either at intervals, or as I think better, two months. The eight parts at 5/- could yield the 2 £ for the four volumes, and at two month intervals would not be dearer than Maga. Each part would have a certain unity and completeness in itself with separate title. Thus the work is called *Middlemarch*. Part I will be *Miss Brooke*." This was exactly the format Eliot followed, with Book I appearing in December 1871, and the other books following at intervals, sometimes two months, but at one a month near the end of the novel.*

Lewes was also concerned with the book's appearance. He felt that a stiff paper cover—"attractive but not booksellish"—ought to "seduce purchasers, especially if Mudie were scant in supplies. It would be enough to furnish the town with talk for some time, and each part thus keep up and swell the general interest." *Tristram Shandy* you "may remember was published at irregular intervals; and great was the desire for the continuation. Considering how slowly the public mind is brought into motion, this spreading of the publication over 16

---

*As follows, after December 1871: Book II, February 1872; Book III, April 1872; Book IV, June 1872; Book V, August 1872; Book VI, October 1872; Book VII, November 1872; Book VIII, December 1872. The identical sheets were used for two further editions in four volumes, in 1872 and 1873. A one-volume edition appeared in 1874—a further indication of how the circulating libraries were being defied. The 1874 edition was the final one corrected by Eliot and usually stands as the version later reprinted. The most authoritative paper editions to date (Gordon Haight's in the Riverside edition and W. J. Harvey's in the Penguin edition) both derive from the 1874 one-volume edition.

months [actually 13] would be a decided advantage to the sale—especially as each part would contain as much as one ought to read at a time." *Tristram Shandy*, however, was a very different kind of book, episodic and more easily broken up.

In one respect, Lewes's remarks helped shape the novel from the outside, since once publication considerations were established—with Book I only seven months away—Eliot would write a novel that accommodated such specifications. The symbiotic relationship of Lewes to her career and indeed to her way of fictional thinking had rarely been closer, closer even than those days when he directed her toward a certain kind of realism which he said was essential to the English novel. She had, in time, departed from that formula and created her own terms for realism, but she had followed his dictates, his knowledge of the market, his efforts to help her focus her talents. As for Blackwood, he was open to such suggestions, although his earlier experiment with publishing Eliot in sixpenny weekly parts, in an illustrated edition, had not proven successful—and that was primarily because her work was not episodic enough to hold the reader's attention from one issue to the next. A good deal of chance resided in this proposal; it was not merely a publishing decision, but one relating to composition, to shaping, to patterning the novel.

Lewes's final words to Blackwood are that the publisher should ponder this, or "suggest a better plan!" From this point on, Eliot's months were characterized by submission of manuscript to her publisher, his responses, and then further work on the book, in a recurring cycle. She was also afflicted with an extremely painful condition, either neuralgia or something worse (Lewes called her condition *tic douloureux*), which she felt was caused by bad teeth. She suffered considerable pain, but tried to hold herself together with quinine, which provided only temporary relief. Since her surgeon, Sir Erasmus Wilson, was away, she had to do with hasty nostrums. Blackwood had in the meanwhile visited the Priory and come away with "Miss Brooke." On 2 June, he reported on it with great delight, as well he might. Spacious, expansive, unhurried, the book promised a great deal literarily. From the publisher's point of view, the excellence lay in the fact he would recognize so many of the types, especially "the old twaddler Brooke." But all characters, he says, stand out "clear and distinct."

While teeth kept Eliot in a state of pain and forbearance, she could not help but notice that Lewes flourished at Shottermill. "George is gloriously well," she wrote Barbara Bodichon, "studying, writing, walking, eating, and sleeping with equal vigour. He is enjoying life here immensely." Eliot is absolutely dithyrambic about the countryside, the undulating heath and copse and pure veins of water, all set amidst a pine wood. Clearly, once outside of London, they felt rejuvenated. In the meantime, she was progressing on *Middlemarch*, to the extent that on 27 June she read portions of Book II to Lewes. This was, apparently, a difficult and delicate stage, a difficulty which began possibly early in 1871, when she had to weld together the Lydgate and Dorothea segments to disguise the fact they were conceived of at different times. Lewes, as always, approved, and may have helped with some of the technical problems.

Eliot sent off what she had on 14 July,* and Blackwood responded with great dispatch and warm praise. He called it "a most wonderful study of human life and nature. You are," he wrote, "like a great giant walking about among us and fixing every one you meet upon your canvas. In all this life like gallery that you put before us every trait in every character finds an echo of recollection in the reader's mind that tells him how true it is to Nature." The publisher wondered how Eliot knew the way men talked—where did she learn it? And of course with this he had hit upon something very significant in her work, her ability to write about men—that gender crossover so difficult for many Victorian novelists. Even the hallowed Austen and Brontës created male figures that were, in the one instance, stiff or sources of mockery, or in the second, fantasy males derived from dominating figures in their juvenilia.

As we re-create the novel in the mind of its first independent reader, we try to see it freshly, and we perceive how much new ground *Middlemarch* broke to the degree that it defined a new kind of realism in English fiction, possibly in all of fiction with the exception of Tolstoy's major novels. It was a realism with several checks and balances: with the pull of social determinism which entraps everyone, especially women; with the sense of detail that still allowed imagination and speculative flights; with the ability to capture spirit as much as body; and finally, with the craft that recognized such fragmentation in human experience had made old-fashioned chronological narrative no longer possible—only clusters of events would do. When she was finished, the novel genre was becoming a different form.

Blackwood was convinced their method of publication in segments was correct; whatever the loss of continuity would be compensated by freshness. Each group, he felt, was a complete little book of its own; in fact, each "book" designation was almost a short novel in itself. The publisher, of course, could not see the connectedness of the plan, which undermined his assertion of complete individual books. Eliot indicated that the two books she submitted for reading would come to about one of the larger volumes of *Bede* or *Mill*. When Lewes spoke of some changes—to "take in a portion of Part II at the end of Part I"— she responded she was hesitant to leave anything out. Her design, she says, was very important to her, a design "which is to show the gradual action of ordinary causes rather than exceptional, and to show this in some directions which have not been from time immemorial the beaten path. . . . But the best intentions are good for nothing until execution has justified them. And you know I am always compassed about with fears."

*There is little paperwork to show how the firm received the book. From office memos, Blackwood clearly seemed eager to have the book even if it proved unprofitable. We know some of the submission dates, such as 14 July, from Eliot's diary. We do have Lewes's negotiations with an American publisher, Osgood, Tickner & Co., to publish the novel in weekly installments in *Every Saturday*, for £1,200. Osgood in time switched the copyright to *Harper's Weekly*, a much better known and more reputable publication, and *Middlemarch* started to appear there on 16 December 1871. As usual with Lewes's plan, profit was maximized, although Blackwood was made uneasy by what he considered backdoor trading.

Meanwhile, Eliot saw "Armgart" appear in both *Macmillan's* and the *Atlantic Monthly*. Also, the couple had to move, as it turned out, across the road, a move Eliot did not appreciate now that she was working well. But she consoled herself that it would not be too much trouble—although most of the work fell on her. They enjoyed their "secure solitude," which held, except for Tennyson, who lived three miles away and visited. Their first face-to-face meeting had come on 14 July; Eliot characterized the poet laureate as one of the "hill-folk."* She had in the meanwhile accepted an invitation to Edinburgh for ceremonies honoring Scott, whom she said she worships "devoutly,"† but was then gratified she could withdraw. "The journey and the fuss would have been intolerable to me," she told Cara, not to mention the interruption of her work.

The routine at Shottermill and Cherrimans was not much different from the one that the Leweses held to when they traveled. They preferred their solitude, and it took on a particular shape of quiet evenings reading serious matter. Eliot's mornings were passed in writing, her feet propped on a warm hot-water bottle; they dined at two, had tea at four; at twilight, they walked in the commons, and by dark they were back in their house. Everything in *Middlemarch* was deriving from memory or research, not from present experience. Eliot reshaped pastness, an act of retrieval, and she combined her perception of the past with historical events in and around the later 1820s and early 1830s, when she was herself coming into full observation.

It was on 21 August that Lewes made his proposal to Blackwood, £6,000 for *Middlemarch*, to be published in four volumes at 40 shillings for a four-year copyright.‡ The money could be payable in installments as Blackwood deemed fit. That way, however, would involve publisher risk. If the firm so chose, Lewes and Eliot would themselves take the risk and accept, instead, 2 shillings royalty per copy on each 5-shilling part sold in the original form. Accounting would be half-yearly. Lewes also asked for a comparable royalty on the cheaper editions.

Faced with such a huge outlay, Blackwood preferred the royalty arrangement. As we look over the receipts of *Middlemarch*, from Eliot's own account book, we note that the novel earned her £8,783.4.0 from 1872 to 1879 on sales of almost

---

*Tennyson showed up several times. On 26 August, he came and read "The Northern Farmer" and *Maud* aloud, a true test of friendship; and on the 31st he read, among others, "Tears, Idle Tears," "Northern Farmer New Style," and the segment "Guinevere" from *The Idylls of the King*. Eliot was apparently moved to tears at the latter. Mrs. Tennyson was present and noted the emotional scene in her journal, but pointedly omitted it in her memoir of Tennyson, in 1897. So much for George Eliot or Marian Evans as "Mrs. Lewes" even in the dying days of Victorianism.

†No other writer, she told Alexander Bain, an admirer, "would serve as a substitute for Scott, and my life at that time would have been much more difficult without him. It is a personal grief, a heart-wound to me when I hear a depreciating or slighting word about Scott." This is only one of numerous Eliot statements of praise for Scott, whose type of novel she very carefully avoided when she wrote her own; nevertheless, *The Heart of Midlothian* appears in *Adam Bede*, and even in *Romola* Scott surfaces.

‡Just so we don't forget proportions, that proposed advance of £6,000 was more than sixty times the annual income of the average working-class family. When an author at present receives, let us say, an advance of $250,000 on a book, that figure is about ten times the working man's annual family income.

34,000 copies in various editions. These monies did not derive from any single huge sale, but from several sources. The largest amount came initially with payments from Blackwood of £1,947 in September of 1872 and then £2,195 in December, followed by translations, American and Australian rights, cheaper editions, and the like. Only *Daniel Deronda* proved more profitable, bringing in £9,236.4.6 in three years, from 1876 to 1879. If Eliot, or Lewes, had been worried about her earning power even with complicated books, these two novels disproved that particular anxiety.

Blackwood was quite alarmed at Lewes's American deal, already made, because he felt extracts from the novel would leak into England and undermine sales there. He says he hopes Lewes gained a very large sum, to compensate for losses at home. Publisher and agent were playing a cat-and-mouse game. But Blackwood had nothing to fear; the extracts did not leak, publication was almost simultaneous, and Lewes's arrangement worked well. The publisher indicated that the eight 5-shilling parts sewn together would come to 42 shillings, not 40—but an amount in any event well beyond the average Englishman. He was, however, "very sanguine that we shall run a great coup." He repeated that he thought the novel "tremendously good," and he suggested a whispering campaign to help sales. Lewes responded that if the publisher felt the £1,200 from the American edition would hurt the English publication, he would sacrifice it; but he believed the contrary, that "a little tittilation of the public curiosity will do good rather than harm." Another idea of his was to include an "advertisement sheet"—paid-for advertisements—bound up with each part, like those found with Dickens and Thackeray, although he recommended that it not be on the covers. "This," he told Blackwood, "would not only bring in some hard cash, it would help to make the volume look bigger for the 5 / - which in British eyes is a consideration not to be neglected."

The start of publication on 1 December was still far off, but, unlike Dickens, Eliot could not bear to hang precariously in the fictional winds, writing a segment while the previous one was appearing. Since she could not fall back on new episodes or on new characters as a means of extending the serial, her kind of novel depended on pre-preparation of large chunks. Her work on her fiction, as already suggested, was like maneuvering for battle, with points of attack, salients to establish, allies to exhort, and, she hoped, victory.

In September, as the plans for the edition went forward, Eliot fell into one of her most serious ailments to date, a depression of spirit and a liver condition (or so diagnosed), which was followed later in the month by gastric fever, or some related digestive problem. Lewes for a time viewed her indisposed condition as possibly a spur to production of copy, on the assumption her illness made her even more eager to work. For his part, Langford, in the London office, was not sanguine about the way the new novel was to be published. He feared the parts would appear like halves of a thin ordinary novel and would discourage sales. He looked to some variation on the scheme, to publish perhaps in demy 8vo. (a book size of $5\frac{1}{2} \times 8\frac{3}{4}$ inches)—which would approximate Hugo's *Les Misérables*, with spongy paper to thicken the volume. The public, he said, wants quantity for its money, but might be willing to settle for the appearance of it, or for novelty of form.

The edition went ahead without heeding Langford's complaints, but from his remarks and from Lewes's we can see how new ideas were beginning to change the shape of book publishing. As the libraries lost their hold, even publishers as conservative as Blackwood's were seeking to break new ground; and from this we can perceive a new audience was also growing, one less concentrated on traditional forms, one more attuned to novels as entertainment than instruction, an audience more concerned with quantity than quality, and one that had more money to spend on marginal items such as cultural artifacts. George Gissing's *New Grub Street*, in 1891, would chart these gloomy waters. Eliot was working outside of this purview, but Lewes seemed aware of the changes, and attempted to incorporate them into a novel as centrally Victorian as *Middlemarch*.

While Langford's suggestion about spongy-texture paper was not pursued, Blackwood did agree to make each book look bulkier, and he also recognized that fewer words on the page would result in greater bulk. The first part would contain 214 pages, aimed at satisfying an audience looking for quantity as well as quality. Approving the appearance, Lewes did ask for more margin and for a slightly shorter line. But more than anything else he now was frightened by Eliot's latest illness. This time it seemed a close call, with the doctors "powerless," Dr. H. Hudson Rigg coming five times in two days and Sir Henry Holland once. At first it was believed the fresh paint at the newly renovated Priory could have caused her internal disturbance, but Holland diagnosed it as a colonic condition. On her own—given the primitive state of medication—Eliot began to rally, although she remained very weak.

By 26 September, she had rallied sufficiently to discuss with Lewes Alexander Main's proposal to publish a collection of "sayings" from Eliot's work. A young Scot admirer who had once studied for the ministry and was something of a mother worshipper, Main had sent on a specimen of four pages of quotations. Telling Main that Eliot was still too weak to respond, Lewes answered it would prove a treasure for readers and not an uncommercial project for publishers. With Blackwood's as publisher, Lewes proposed calling it "Thoughts and Sentences in Prose and Verse Selected from the Works of George Eliot." As he further mulled over a title, he came up with "Wise and Witty Sayings from George Eliot." The final title was more cloying: *Wise, Witty, and Tender Sayings in Prose and Verse Selected from the Works of George Eliot*, published in December. Lewes sent on a letter introducing Main to John Blackwood, and indicating that such a book would give Eliot considerable satisfaction.

To Lewes's surprise, Blackwood was at first not taken with the project and rejected it. Since he held the copyright, his cooperation became essential. Only after he met Main was the project reconsidered and accepted. Lewes was also busy with translation rights, especially one close to the couple's hearts, in German. He wanted to break Baron Tauchnitz's hold over English fictional reprints, since Tauchnitz paid niggling amounts, less than £100 for *Romola*. In order to maximize the profit from what Lewes perceived would be an extraordinary literary event, he went to Asher & Co in Berlin, and from that firm and its agent, Albert Cohn, he eventually derived £327. He was active in other deals as well, apparently giving up his own work to manage Eliot's immediate fortunes.

September proved a difficult month to get through. All the money and fame Eliot carried back with her to the Priory could not prevent the series of ailments, the annoyance at the smell of fresh paint, the disorder which existed with their books, furniture, and other possessions, and the anxiety she recorded about her work on such a long and intricate novel. While she required absolute peace and silence, she was undergoing quite the opposite, despite Lewes's efforts to seal off space for her.

Eliot's personal need for orderliness and organization intrudes into her fiction; her very principles of realism are based on the assumption there is order in the world and that fiction is its vehicle. The "Quarry"—with its lists of political developments, its itemization of relationships, and its working out of a pattern for the development of the novel—is, clearly, an indication of how intensely she required order while she proceeded. In this respect, her own personal philosophy, based on a rational universe filled with dutiful people, however tinged by determinism, suggests she perceived that elements would indeed fall into place if people hewed to a community of values. Sharing needed order; order ensured sharing. Such a community, while permitting individual foibles and irregularities—like her own—would have communal assumptions. Those people in her novels who destroy others or who are themselves destroyed—starting with Hetty Sorrel and Arthur Donnithorne near the beginning of her fictional career—fall outside of an ordered life, for they indulge appetites that deny the patterns which might fulfill them. Behind this desire for order is a woman whose own daring, audacious, adventurous choices in life have tested out those very limits of order.

18

Middlemarch

"For what we call illusions are often, in truth, a
wider vision of past and present realities—a willing
movement of a man's soul with the larger sweep of
the world's forces—a movement towards a more
assured end than the chances of a single life."

A lthough we don't normally associate Eliot with trivial affairs, she found
herself upon her return to the Priory confronted with quite mundane
choices. One of them was the hiring of servants since her previous two—servants of ten years' standing—gave a month's notice. The element that kept the
Eliot–Lewes household running smoothly was the presence of these two women,
now to be replaced by two others, plus a third whom the couple all along had
felt they needed. In a long letter to Cara Bray, Eliot speaks of the domestic
situation and how her two faithful servants—Grace and Amelia, sisters—dictated who could and could not work in the house, and how they had been
developing "oddities" that were getting stranger with the years. Eliot had nevertheless planned to retain them, and when they couldn't work any longer, to
pension them off; but once they left, she was pleased, since they had become
possessive, even territorial. They had made life difficult for the woman hired as
Thornie's nurse, and they were unable to tolerate any stranger in the house,
even one there to help them.

If we think Eliot removed herself from domestic details, the following note in
her hand suggests how carefully she supervised the servants. Here is what she
required from the downstairs crew:

Lay and light all fires and keep all stoves clean. Shake Mats, clean
Entrance. Empty all slops, clean Baths and Washing stands and open Beds.
Make beds and dust bedroom furniture. Wash up after lunch. Prepare tray
for dinner. Close dining and drawing room shutters and bring up lamps.
Light the Hall gas. Wash up after dinner. Turn down beds, etc. Bolt the
outer doors and put out the gas.

This was daily work. Weekly work was recorded on a calendar: sweeping the carpets, cleaning the plate, the doorsteps, the bell handle.

These duties are in addition to preparing meals and taking care of the Sunday afternoons when fifteen to twenty people might come, or lunches for six or eight. In September 1871, that difficult month when Eliot fell seriously ill and became "as thin as a medieval Christ," Lewes had to help with the household duties, especially with the turnover in servants: ". . . Mr. Lewes," she tells Cara, "is exerting his ingenuity to feed me up. He has been housekeeper, secretary and Nurse all in one—as good a nurse as if he had been trained in a hospital."

Behind the Priory door, there was a typical "upstairs–downstairs" arrangement. We assume Eliot was a kind taskmaster, but we must also assume she expected disciplined work. Since the Leweses traveled a good deal, their servants over the last ten years would have had an easy time while they were away. But Eliot's words indicate not everything was smooth: that with the two sisters demarcating their territory and insisting on their prerogatives, there were outbursts, disturbances, peevish acts in the household. Most of all, during the terrible time when Thornie was dying and Eliot and Lewes sensed their own deaths, the presence of the nurse created an unpleasant situation. Once the sisters were gone, Eliot used two servants from their friends, the Calls, and added a third. With that, *Middlemarch* could move along.

Eliot's severe September illness, with its gastric-digestive upset, cannot be separated completely from what she found upon her return to the Priory. The smell of fresh paint, the need to put their daily life back in order, the notice from the two sisters—all of this disorganization was sufficient to send her into illness *as a protection* against these incursions on her sensibilities. Such an ailment permitted her to become an invalid while things she did not wish to handle were arranged by others, including Lewes. In this respect, she could use illness as a shield against the kind of disorderliness she tried not to confront in her personal life. By the time of her recovery at the end of the month, all the other disagreeable elements were straightened out.

By early October, proofs were beginning to arrive at the Priory for the 1 December publication of Book I. Lewes arranged all the details—the delays, the omission of the Proem or prelude, and other related matters. He also agreed to handle Alexander Main's collection of Eliot's sayings when it appeared in manuscript or proof. He wrote to Blackwood that the publisher's encouraging response to "Miss Brooke" gave Eliot confidence to "shake the ever-present doubt of herself and her doing. . . ."* He says she is recovering well and is "burning with poetic fire to be at Dodo once more." As the go-between, Lewes now worked out arrangements with Main for length of manuscript, his classifications, and kinds of extracts to use. In one respect, Main's anthology became Lewes's.

---

*In the background of all this activity, we should not ignore Lewes's correspondence with Mrs. William Cross, so that the connection between Leweses and Crosses was maintained throughout Lewes's life, and his successor, John Cross, was in place when the former died.

As usual, Langford in the London office had his complaints, now with "Miss Brooke." He was unhappy that the construction led to the part ending with Dorothea's marriage to Casaubon. He felt new people should have been brought in sooner, and he would omit the "Prelude" given the choice. Langford, of course, dealt with the firm, not with Eliot, and did not have to tiptoe around the author's touchy feelings.

Eliot had recovered sufficiently by 20 October to console William Blackwood on the death of James Blackwood, John's last surviving brother. William, the nephew, was now heir apparent. She had by this time left her room and bed. Blackwood told her he appreciated her condolences about James; he too, like her, was acquainted with death, having seen all six of his brothers go down in the prime of life. This degree of mortality, of so many brothers all dying so young, was not lost on Eliot, who was now past the age of most of those six when they died. She was coming up to another birthday, her fifty-second.

Solicited to contribute to establish a hospital for women by Mrs. Elizabeth Garrett Anderson, one of the earliest women physicians, Eliot agreed to become an annual subscriber when the project became set. The Elizabeth Garrett Anderson Hospital opened on Euston Road in 1872. Eliot and Lewes contributed £5 (perhaps $200 in current monies) in that year, and £2.2 thereafter, with the contributions continuing after Lewes's death. Although Eliot hesitated to support larger or more politicized women's causes, she was particularly attuned to discreet causes like this or to those associated with women's education.

With her recovery, the couple spent four days in the country, and, as usual, they felt the experience as a tonic, only to begin to degenerate once they returned to London at the end of October. Lewes was still busy with Alexander Main's anthology, which was rapidly being concluded. Lewes was particularly careful that the public should not suppose Eliot had any more to do with it than the granting of permission.* In the background, Blackwood was attempting to arrange reviews for the first part of *Middlemarch*, especially with the man at the *Times*, Mowbray Morris; but his efforts failed, and Morris did not come through for more than a year, in March 1873. Incidentally, the English practice of reviewing was, and continues to be, more personalized than it is in the United States. In England, much of the hypocrisy was removed from the process: publishers courted reviewers, often knew ahead of time who the reviewer was, and took much of what might be secret into the open. Since the *Times* of London was the single most important review for an English book, it was quite ethical

---

* Her own response to Main was gratitude. "I have too long made no sign to you of the gratitude I feel towards a mind whose emotions and judgments have given me the encouraging response which I find both in your letters and in your selection of passages. Over the latter I have not done more than run my eyes hastily, but I believe that when your book appears I shall be almost like one of the public in making acquaintance with it. I have read my own books hardly at all [not true] after once giving them forth—dreading to find them other than I wish. And now I am haunted by the fear that I am only saying against what I have already said in better fashion. For we all of us have our little store—our two or three beliefs which are the outcome of our characters and experience; and there is equal danger of our harping on these too long, and of taking up other strains which are not at all our beliefs, but mere borrowing and echo." To this, she offers only the antidote of "Good Sense"—her classical balance—which can deliver us from fatuity.

for Blackwood to court the reviewer. The English assumption that, once the book was in hand, the reviewer would be impartial may have been a charade at which everyone winked.

Sara Hennell, meanwhile, was still turning out very weighty books which no longer interested Eliot; but the latter felt obliged to respond. The latest, published in October of 1871, was Sara's Volume II of her *Present Religion: as a Faith Owning Fellowship with Thought*. Such stuff made Eliot's head spin. She tells her friend she will send her a copy of *Middlemarch*, and she reports that Spencer seemed younger than ever. Spencer and Huxley, friends and supporter of Darwin in these turbulent post-*Origin* years, were disputing Spencer's assertion that the physical body of man can be compared to the body politic, and whether such analogies and parallels made sense. Their polemic was carried out in the November and December *Fortnightly*. When Eliot disparaged Huxley's point to Sara, we must not forget her loyalty to Spencer.

Sara was not the only recipient of presentation copies of Book I of *Middlemarch*. The others included Lewes's sons, Charles and Bertie, his sister-in-law Susanna, Eliot herself (three copies), Mrs. Maria Congreve, Owen Jones (the decorator), and Alexander Main.* Noticeable is the absence of famous people. As she usually tried to do, Eliot wrote Sara Hennell, on 22 November, hailing Sara's fifty-ninth birthday and her own fifty-second. She insists all her memories remain "very sunny," and says she is certainly the better for having been Sara's "Pollian," using the familiar, nostalgic name saved for her closest Coventry friends.

To celebrate the appearance of Book I on 1 December, the Leweses threw a party on 30 November. As the year closed out, it had been a most difficult period for Eliot, who spoke of having two months of her life "blotted out." Yet, as we have observed, in the past she used illness, enervation, and then rest as ways of gathering her forces for another fictional foray. Ailing as she was, she was also doing the most intense work of her career; and we can hardly say that her concentration faltered. Her enormous powers of synthesis allowed her to hang on, and she held to her plan once she saw how interconnected the Lydgate and Dorothea stories were.

None of this implies, however, that she escaped the anxieties of writing, or planning for imminent publication in segments. In a broad letter to John Blackwood, Eliot tells of "the terror of the unwritten." She informs him of great praise she has received, which is "wonderful" to her; but her overall feeling is fear she may suddenly stop writing while the wheels of publication roll on. Fortunately, at this stage (18 January 1872), Lewes was very pleased with Book IV, which would be published in June. She reported a diversion, attending the Tichborne trial, in which one Arthur Orton posed as Roger Charles Tichborne, the owner of large estates, who was lost at sea in 1854. Orton eventually was convicted of

---

* When Barbara Bodichon saw her copy, she complained of the jacket filled with crawling vines and scrolls as a design; even the paper, a yellowish green, was distasteful, creating a somewhat bilious appearance. Eliot found nothing objectionable here.

perjury and sentenced to fourteen years in prison. Eliot may have foreseen in this material some possible source for a future fictional effort. She considered it an experience "of great interest," although because Lewes succumbed to the poor courtroom air, she could not remain for the full day. Meanwhile, she perused Alexander Main's anthology, which she apparently found wanting. But she was fearful of hurting his feelings; she found him as "keenly sensitive" as she, and any negative comment from the woman he worshipped could prove devastating.

Middlemarch was now the central concern of both its author and her companion. Lewes was intent on making the segments workable; having planned to publish this way, he took responsibility for success or failure. He was afraid that Book II as written had too little of Dorothea and Casaubon, and he suggested that parts of what was now Book III be transposed to Book II. That would also mean material from Book II would have to be transferred forward, to Book III. About eighty pages were in question. * Lewes here is like a director who is shifting material to make the performance tighter and more accessible, or rearranging scenes for a more effective curtain; and so completely did Eliot believe in his taste and judgment, she acquiesced to what was, in effect, his restaging of her material.

While the novel marched forward, another literary event was also of note, John Forster's first volume of his life of Dickens. Forster's life, three volumes in all by 1874, became the basis for one stupendous piece of information Dickens had kept hidden from his wife, children, and closest friends, except for his future biographer, Forster. This was the episode, when Dickens was twelve, in the blacking warehouse or factory, a time when he felt victimized and lost to the world. He reproduced some of that in *David Copperfield*; but Forster's divulgation of it was the first time it appeared openly. Lewes eventually reviewed the biography less than enthusiastically and wrote a paper on Dickens for the *Fortnightly*. This piece appeared before Volume III of Forster's biography, which subsequently contained an attack on Lewes. Eliot was also reading the work, which she found most interesting for Dickens's early years and for its charting of his amazingly rapid development. As for the biography, she found it wanting in several respects: poorly organized, critically weak, full of excessive material.

---

* The chapters moved to Book II to give fullness to Dorothea and Casaubon were 19–22 of Book III; to make room for that material, Fred Vincy's problems were extricated from Book II and moved into the opening of Book III. The changes created more symmetry and parallelism in the novel. Besides the problems here and those of joining the two parts—the Lydgate and "Miss Brooke" segments written separately—Eliot moved laterally as well as sequentially. By 19 March 1871, as Jerome Beaty points out, she had in hand at least the initial eighteen chapters as well as Chapter 23, and had linked the two separate stories. But when Eliot decided, on 31 December 1870, to make the juncture, she was as yet unaware of how to do it. The story of that rethinking of her material is the subject of Beaty's detailed study, and it takes us into several problematic areas, some of them more of textual than biographical interest. All manuscript evidence points to the fact that once she experienced the revelation that Lydgate and "Miss Brooke" were one story, she felt her way very cautiously. Yet despite such caution, the manuscript—as noted above—contains long stretches that are clean, except for selected chapters already cited which appear to have given her trouble.

Nevertheless, she told Sara to read it for those childhood experiences and for the letters from America Forster reprinted.

Christmas for the Leweses was not a gala time, in fact was doleful. It was not for lack of things to do, but ill health, anxiety over the progress of Middlemarch, and Lewes's continued mourning for Thornie depleted their energies and made them downcast. Main's anthology was a source of only limited satisfaction. While Eliot said it "broke the clouds a little," she found it insufficiently "fastidious," not quite scrupulous enough, especially in the preface. Overall, she accepted it. The couple did get out, to see Henry Irving in The Bells, and they also visited Gertrude, Charles's wife, who was pregnant and in danger of miscarrying. Eliot's words to Blackwood indicate that as a couple she and Lewes were narrowing down and drawing in because of ill health and a generalized depression. She says they are among "the happiest of mortals," but follows with a lament that since they have no grandchildren "to get up a Christmas tree for, we had nothing to divide our attention to our headaches." She recognized they were entering a physical and emotional decline from which they could not extricate themselves. Yet on the other side was the complex, intricate novel on her desk.

Eliot rued that Forster's life of Dickens was selling better than Middlemarch, which she says was the result of a fickle British public willing to pay more for expensive biographies than fiction. She was, of course, omitting that this was Dickens and that it provided new evidence of his phenomenal development from street urchin to world figure—surely she could not have expected to compete here. In any event, Middlemarch held its own. Her remarks further indicate how competitive Eliot felt not only with biography but with Dickens; and possibly her rueful remark reveals displeasure that with Dickens dead at last the field should be hers—except for Forster and his tales from the tomb.

On 1 January 1872, the Leweses left for Weybridge, in Surrey, to stay with the Cross family. In their delightful three days there, they encountered, among others, Jowett and C. S. C. Bowen (junior counsel to the attorney general). When the Leweses threw a large dinner party at the Priory on the 27th of the month, Bowen and his wife came, along with Spencer, Frederic Harrison, Mrs. Mark Pattison, Charles Lewes, and other close friends who stayed on for music and singing until well after midnight. These parties and dinners were followed by lunches which included the usual array: Browning, Barbara Bodichon, Mrs. John Jay (descended from the famous American colonial Jays), the George Du Mauriers, and Frederic W. H. Myers, a Fellow of Trinity College.* With their wealth about to be increased by Middlemarch monies, Eliot began to dress more

---

* Myers, who described what became a famous conversation with Eliot (discussed in the next chapter), was, like Matthew Arnold, an inspector of schools, and later a founder of the Society for Psychical Research. Despite his attraction to questions of immortality, he was instrumental in introducing Freud to England and to an English public. He was an excellent example of an intelligent man caught between science and religion; a man who felt drawn to science but someone who could not forgo the idea that only immortality gave man's existence meaning. Eliot resisted him on this.

richly; we note that she purchased a silk dress at Heilbronner's, one of London's smartest stores. She would, in the future, begin to wear more lavish outfits, in an effort to match her appearance to the income pouring in, and, possibly, to offset what she perceived as excessive aging.

Blackwood wrote his expected letter, enthusiastically praising Book III as "beautiful all over." He understood that the three dramas going on at the Vincys', at Lowick Manor, and at Stone Court are contrasting scenes, that they were part of Eliot's effort to create a society not by its homogeneous elements but by virtue of those forces which might pull it apart. Eliot responded with suitable gratitude, emphasizing that her poor health made her feel duller than usual. She was cheered, however, by the arrival of a new dog, Dash, a dark-brown spaniel, a replacement for the pugs of former days. "You see what infantine innocence we live in!" she tells Maria Congreve. Unfortunately, Dash was lost a month later. On 1 February, Book II of *Middlemarch* appeared, while Eliot was writing Book V. In her regular report to Sara, she says she leads "rather a crawling life," the result of the weather, her indisposition, and, surely, her need to maintain a pace of two or three books ahead of publication. On 1 April, Book III would appear, and she only completed Book V on 8 May. In August, Book V was published.

All of this indicates she was not as far ahead of publication as she would have liked, and a serious indisposition could have proved disastrous. But whatever her valid fears, the novel had found its public. By 10 January, the figures had mounted to 4,750, which the firm estimated was about 1,000 more than would have been sold in the old form. As far as that "old form" was concerned, Mudie's had threatened to boycott the novel, but when sales proved so strong in the separate book version, the library relented and took 1,500 of Book I. It handled about the same number for each succeeding book. Eliot not only proved exceptionally strong in the cheaper version, she succeeded in cracking open the elitist idea behind Mudie's.

On 1 February, Eliot wrote to Mrs. Elma Stuart, the start of a correspondence with a woman who worshipped the writer, one of those women who locked into their deity and treated her as the center of their lives. Some of these women, like Mrs. Stuart, were or had been married; some were single. Elma Stuart, the widow of a lieutenant in the Black Watch, learned wood carving at Dinan, in Brittany, made a book slide, and sent it to Blackwood's asking Eliot to accept it. The latter wrote to thank her. Mrs. Stuart was a fervent reader of Eliot's works, and the gift was an offering of love. With this, a considerable correspondence began, in which the wood-carver wanted only to prostrate herself at Eliot's feet and stare up into her beloved's eyes. Strikingly, after her death, the widow's body was transported from Menton to London, where she was buried next to Eliot in Highgate Cemetery. Eliot's response to her was that, after her husband's love, there was no love more precious to her than that which lay in the minds of her readers. She spoke of their relationship as "our spiritual companionship," and in later letters she addressed her as "Daughter," their difference in age being eighteen years. Mrs. Stuart outlived Eliot by twenty-three years and became an author herself, of a self-help book: *What Must I Do to Get Well? and How Can I Keep So?*

Blackwood was very pleased with the way publication of *Middlemarch* was going, and he told Lewes the merit of the book was beyond description. Book II, he felt, would more than sustain Book I's considerable reputation, and Book III he considered transcendent. Yet Eliot was not buoyed by this near barrage of admiring notices. Lewes reports to Blackwood she was in one of her most depressed moods—this in mid-February of 1872.* "Reading 'Felix Holt' the other morning made her *thin* with misery," he writes, "so deeply impressed was she with the fact she could never write like that again, and that what is now at hand is rinsing of the cask! How battle," he asks, "against such an art of ingen-iously self tormentings?" Of course, one element even the observant Lewes might have missed is how Eliot spurred herself on through periods of despair, how she found strength by way of sinking and then recovering. It was a cycle which, we can assume, was deeply personal and not detectable to anyone, possi-bly not even to herself.

One is tempted to invoke a psychiatric use of the classical Nemesis, the agent of retribution or punishment and a favorite reference for Eliot. In this modern version, a person believes he (or she) will repeat in his life the pattern of an important other person's life which ended in tragedy—such an important person died or was hospitalized and usually is a parent or parental figure. The survivor sometimes feels responsible for the death of the person so doomed, and doomed also is the imitator. As far as we know, Eliot did not feel guilt at Robert Evans's death; nor did she feel his life ended in tragedy. But she periodically experienced the depths of depression which caring for him had meant to her, and *her illnesses were a repetition of the period when she felt her life was doomed by this significant person's illness.* By imitating the illness, she activated Nemesis. By repeating conditions of illness, she could approximate that period, feel defeated, and then gather her wits and emotions for the struggle to put it all behind her—only to fall back into it again because she was unconscious of what was occurring.

By the end of February or in early March, the Leweses were seeking a country retreat. The Priory had become a center, a salon, and although the couple had themselves brought it about, they also felt the need to drop out—especially with so much of *Middlemarch* yet to be written. They went to Redhill, Surrey, on 24 May, for three months, during which time Eliot tried to complete Book VI, two from the end. With her release from London, she managed the book in five weeks and submitted it to Blackwood on 2 July. Lewes, who knew more about her working habits than anyone else, recognized a productive cycle, so he sug-gested to Blackwood that instead of appearing at two-month intervals, books should appear in succeeding months, with Book VII in November and Book VIII in December. The publisher agreed, and Eliot, encouraged by her ability

---

* Ever on the alert for letters or words which could pick up Eliot's spirits, Lewes also wrote Mrs. Stuart, thanking her for the "exquisite pleasure" she has given both of them. With that, he sent on Main's volume of Eliot's sayings, which he says he knows the widow will like.

to work quietly, sailed through Book VII by 7 August and had most of Book VIII completed by 11 September. Redhill was exactly what she needed.

This does not imply all went smoothly. In biographical study, we tend to see periods in the subject's life—especially when work is being produced—as smoother than they actually were. Eliot worried about the shortness of the third book, for example, although she wanted to end it with the death of Peter Featherstone. Yet she feared that the public would be shortchanged if the firm asked for 5 shillings for less than usual length. Here, she was very much the daughter of Robert Evans, scrupulous about charging accurately. She tried to justify herself by measuring shorter segments against more effectiveness, and hoped there was balance. As always, Blackwood calmed her anxieties, saying that although Book III might run thin, there "is the matter of volumes in it." Besides, Simpson was bulking up the book with different paper.

After nearly two years, Harriet Beecher Stowe wrote again, with an apology for not having answered Eliot's letter. Stowe was now deeply involved in her own spiritual revival, and recommended two books by Robert Dale Owen: *Footfalls on the Boundary of Another World* and *The Debatable Land Between This World and the Next*. This put Eliot in a difficult situation, since while she liked Stowe, she could not abide such work. She asserted she would keep her mind open, but added "hitherto the various phenomena reported or attested in connexion with ideas of spirit-intercourse, 'psychism' and so on, have come before me here in the painful form of the lowest charlatanerie." She was not through, calling the audience for these displays "semi-idiots," which Stowe might have taken note of. Eliot ended by trying to soften the harshness of her attack; she praised Stowe for writing in such a way as to touch others in instances where she, Stowe, had been deeply impressed.

This and another letter to Stowe, on 24 June, came when Eliot was firming up her own rather apposite beliefs. Her mockery of Casaubon's effort to create a key to all mythologies was not only ridicule of this limited man writing that capacious book; it was also a scornful view of *any kind of overall design* which tried to explain human behavior.* It is not that Eliot disbelieved that myths had once served a useful function; it was now her belief that a synthesis of knowledge—even Spencer's monumental effort in this regard—was a betrayal of human experience. She voiced a typical Victorian dilemma: the recognition that proliferating subcultures undermined an organic society and yet the accompanying fear that any effort at synthesis was a denial of actual experience. Eliot's two letters to Stowe straddled the period when she was writing Book V of *Middlemarch* and beginning Book VI.

Book V is titled "The Dead Hand." The dead hand refers to several matters,

---

* In her review of Robert William Mackay's *The Progress of the Intellect* in the *Westminster Review*, Eliot mentioned Otfried Muller's *Prolegomena to a Scientific Mythology*, which ruled out the possibility of tracing diverse myths, etymologically, to a single Hebrew (or other) origin, Casaubon's project. This is what Will Ladislaw means when he says Casaubon is ignorant of German materials, since this book would have demonstrated to him that the Germans had exploded his thesis once and for all.

not merely to Casaubon's death. The "dead" aspect also relates to Lydgate, who is being sucked into unethical behavior by the need for money in his marriage and in his support of Bulstrode in order to gain the supervision of the New Hospital. There is, here, the death of his ideals. There is another "death," also, and that is Dorothea's suppression of herself. In trying to be what Casaubon wishes, she deadens whatever spark or vitality exists within herself. Their argument over his demand for blind obedience unsettles both of them; and when he dies suddenly after this, Dorothea attributes it to her refusal to promise what he requested. The "dead hand" lies heavily over the novel, and this particular book is the most morbid of all the longer segments.

Yet Eliot was careful not to spiritualize the material; she remained secular, pragmatic, empirical. Stowe's letters stirred her opposition. The American wrote about several things, not only about spiritualism, although responding to the latter dominated Eliot's answers. Stowe praised the first book of *Middlemarch* and cited its "web" design: Eliot's pattern of using a web as a way of gathering in her characters, holding them in place, and suggesting some dread deterministic scheme from which they must extricate themselves if they can. But it was Stowe's experience with the planchette at a séance which occupied much of Eliot's response on 24 June. Stowe claimed that through the planchette—a board which reveals messages through one's fingertips—she had heard the words of the spirit of Charlotte Brontë, a condition Eliot found "so enormously improbable that I could only accept it if every condition were laid bare, and every other demonstration to be impossible." She then devastates this entire attitude and the spiritualized world based, as she feels, on complete deception.

> If it were another spirit aping Charlotte Bronte—if here and there at rare spots and among people of a certain temperament, or even at many spots and among people of all temperaments, tricky spirits are liable to rise as a sort of earth-bubbles and set furniture in movement, and tell things which we either know already or should be as well without knowing—I must frankly confess that I have but a feeble interest in these doings, feeling my life very short of the supreme and awful revelations of a more orderly and intelligible kind which I shall die with an imperfect knowledge of.

She apologizes for not spending more time on this discussion, but says she is energyless after writing all morning and then reading aloud to Lewes for three hours a day. But feeling she may have been too dismissive, she says she has not had anything of the range of experience Stowe had suffered through, and the latter should "not misinterpret anything I say to you as being written in a flippant or critical spirit." For her part, Stowe told Eliot she was an artist for the few. Curiously, the American identified Casaubon with Lewes, telling Eliot she sympathizes with her as having a literary husband who goes on "forever getting ready to begin—absorbing learning like sponges—planning sublime literary enterprises which never have a *now* to them."

This was something Eliot could not accept—and we are leaping ahead a few months to when she responded. "But do not for a moment imagine that Dorothea's marriage experience is drawn from my own. Impossible to conceive any creature less like Mr. Casaubon than my warm, enthusiastic husband, who cares much more for my doing than for his own, and is a miracle of freedom from all author's jealousy and all suspicion. I fear that the Casaubon-tints are not quite foreign to my own mental complexion. At any rate I am very sorry for him." Stowe was not deflected by Eliot's denials, and she returned with much of the same in subsequent letters. She found Casaubon "dreadful," "cold and repulsive," and she could not surrender the idea he was someone close to Eliot.

While there is nothing of Lewes in Casaubon, there is the sense of fear in Eliot herself that *she* could still become Casaubon. The character, cold and repulsive as Stowe says he is, gains our sympathy by the degree of his failure to achieve his expectations. We accept him once we perceive he is helpless, as much trapped within the marriage as Dorothea is, and worse off, because he is old and ill and there can be no recovery. That degree of sympathy could be evinced only if Eliot had thrust some of her own fears onto Casaubon. Her very anxieties about *Middlemarch*—which was to be a synthesis of her ideas as much as the "key" was to be Casaubon's—remind us how Eliot dreaded she had not achieved her expectations, or even clearly defined them. The fear of failure which fills our nostrils when Casaubon appears could be the personal element Stowe picked up, not in Lewes, but in Eliot.

Back in March (1872), Lewes exhorted Blackwood to tell Eliot how much he appreciated Book IV. "Her magnificent powers of apprehension of all that can be interpreted into an unfavorable opinion of her work," Lewes writes, "make her convinced that you don't like Part IV and don't like saying so." By now well trained, Blackwood wrote the next day to tell Eliot everything stands out as clear and finished as it can be, that her touches are exquisite. She needed the encouragement, for the poor weather in late March—heavy snow and cold—took her from her desk with "hemicrania" (pain on one side of the head) and "intestinal malaise." She tells Main, on the 29th, she is depressed and "retarded by much bodily discomfort," but that fortunately Book IV was safely in print. She writes of having a week of headache and asks if in his young life he had ever suffered from that. Then she reveals some rather intimate ideas, especially to a young man barely over thirty. Main had apparently tried to forecast the direction Eliot would take with Dorothea, and she in turn opened up with some of her deepest feelings about life and art.

> Try to keep from forecast of Dorothea's lot, and that sort of construction beforehand which makes everything that actually happens a disappointment. I need not tell you that my book will not present my own feelings about human life if it produces on readers whose minds are really receptive the impression of blank melancholy and despair. I can't help wondering at the high estimate made of Middlemarch in proportion to my other books. I suppose the depressed state of my health makes my writing seem more than usually below the mark of my desires, and I am too anxious about its

completion—too fearful lest the impression which it might make (I mean for the good of those who read) should turn to nought—to look at it in mental sunshine.

Implied here is a strong heuristic component of her art; but one that is sub-verted, she says, by her anxiety about just completing the book. But her novel is clearly in the pedagogical tradition of Victorian thought—Carlyle, Ruskin, and Arnold, among others. Her impulses are the basically humanistic ones of trying to show people guidance, giving them sustenance to find their way, and then revealing to them certain inalienable truths about human experience. Crit-ics were beginning to assert that there was little space for joy in her novels; but the joy or pleasure they failed to see was implicit in her feeling she was creating a monument to human behavior. *There* lay satisfaction, in one's sense of duty, one's sense of accomplishment. Eliot was neither grim nor morbid, but she was solemn about life. Despite long passages of wit, sarcasm, and irony, *Middlemarch* is a solemn, stately procession of a novel, as befitting its heroine and her attach-ment to St. Theresa, Sir Thomas Browne, and Milton. Eliot here becomes one of Milton's daughters.

Blackwood came through with £500, the first installment of payment for *Mid-dlemarch.* On 24 May, as noted, the Leweses left the Priory for their three months in Redhill, Surrey—the time set aside to give Eliot the opportunity for a long drive on the novel. "I am very much in need," she told Mrs. William Augustus Tollemache (Marguerite Home Purvis, a new acquaintance), "men-tally as well as physically, of an absolute retreat from the 'world'—rather a mag-nificent phrase for my want of strength to enjoy the visits of friends new and old who are kind enough to wish to see me."

But in the first few days of the move, Eliot suffered bitterly from sore throat and inflamed gums. The conditions seemed to flare up at regular intervals, indi-cating some organic problem; or else they were the result of stress and anxiety she imposed on herself. The inflamed gums and poor tooth structure dogged her for the next eight years. She nevertheless felt more comfortable in the new quarters, having taken along two of her servants, and she was, after all, in the countryside. * By now she had sent on Book V to Blackwood's, and was working well on VI, completed a little more than a month after their arrival at the Surrey home.

She called it their "hiding place," and found both bodily and mental clarity there, although Lewes was now not well. The latter asserted that not a soul knew where they were, so they were not even bothered by letters—although

---

* If we think the Leweses lived high or anywhere up to their income, we need only compare their style of life with that of a slightly later contemporary, Mrs. Humphry Ward. The latter had consider-able success with her fiction, especially with *Robert Elsmere* in 1888. She and her husband lived on an estate in Hertfordshire, with shooting, tennis, and golfing parties, a total of eight general ser-vants, plus a driver who doubled as a gardener. They could also afford regular trips, first class, to the continent, as well as a town house in Grosvenor Place. Much of this was within reach of Eliot in her later years, if she so wished.

both he and Eliot did give out their address. There was little question that escaping from London had, once again, proved tonic; Eliot's color returned, her energy was closer to former times, and she gained weight, after a drastic loss which had left her gaunt. Of course, all this would prove temporary, since London was her fate.

Her reading at Redhill was curious. She and Lewes—she reading aloud—went through Alfred Russel Wallace's masterpiece *The Malay Archipelago: The Land of the Orang-Utan and the Bird of Paradise* (in two volumes, 1872). Wallace was the scientist who had developed the theory of evolution based on natural selection at the same time as Darwin, but lost the race to fame; later, he became a devout spiritualist, of the kind Eliot disavowed in her letters to Harriet Beecher Stowe. She also read Edward Tylor's *Primitive Culture: Researches into the Development of Mythology, Philosophy, Religion, Art and Custom* (in two volumes, 1871). This famous book was one of the landmark studies in the developing discipline of anthropology. Eliot's interest, if we can speculate, was to discover how diverse societies functioned, possibly as a way of reinforcing her own ideas of the social "web" which encircled and enveloped her characters in *Middlemarch*.

She was now a grandmother, by way of Charles and Gertrude, who finally had a healthy birth, a girl, after their first baby was born strangulated. At the end of July, Blackwood weighed in with one of his usual encomiums, commenting on Book VI and wondering what part was the "most perfect." He was particularly disturbed, still, by the "obstinate devil" (Rosamond) and suggested Lydgate might have taken a stick to her. What he failed to see is that just as Lydgate has married under false pretenses about his wife, so did Rosamond marry under a misapprehension about her husband. Eliot provides sufficient ammunition to give Rosamond a role characteristic of what women like her confront: desire for a comfortable, bourgeois existence, some hope of a husband providing rich and famous connections, a way of entering better society and achieving lifelong security through marriage.

This does not excuse her from selfish or wayward behavior, but Eliot's presentation does demonstrate what limited movement and choice such a woman has, especially since her upbringing has created certain expectations. Furthermore, Rosamond's juxtaposition to Mary Garth—by way of her brother Fred's love for Mary—highlights all those unpleasant characteristics of Rosamond which made Blackwood want to take a stick to her. Mary is the dark-haired embodiment of perfection, her lack of physical beauty making her, in Eliot's eyes, even more admirable. Anyone juxtaposed to her looks doubly poor, and Rosamond's fate is to be contrasted with the one near perfect creature in the book, and to be shadowed by another stalwart figure, Dorothea herself. She must lose, not only for those qualities in herself, but by way of the narrative pattern. Yet it is a mistake to judge Rosamond isolated from her background, from the expectations of a young woman brought up to be nothing but decorative, separated from any sustenance in her family except the drive to make a suitable marriage. Eliot may dislike her, but she is, for the author, a typical victim, even if she misbehaves, frets, pouts, and regresses; she is as much a victim in *her* way as Hetty Sorrel is in hers or as Gwendolen Harleth will be in hers.

On 9 August, after having read Part VII to Lewes, Eliot sent off the manuscript to Edinburgh. She was busy maneuvering material back and forth from Book VII to Book VIII, so as to introduce a more commodious development in the final part. She assures him there will be "no unredeemed tragedy in the solution of the story," this after Lewes told her the *Spectator* considers her "the most melancholy of authors." She repeats that Lewes deletes from newspapers, before she sees them, any criticisms "which refer to me, so as to save me from these spiritual chills—though, alas, he cannot save me from the physical chills which retard my work more seriously."

She appears satisfied with her work overall, and although she rues it is so long, she consoles herself it has not attained the length of *Vanity Fair* or *Pendennis. Vanity Fair,* of course, comes to mind as the direct precursor of *Middlemarch;* not because the two authors shared a common fictional ideology, but because each had chosen to create an anatomy of a society.* Both moved to historical periods, Thackeray to the era just before and after Waterloo in 1815, Eliot some fifteen years later; and both created a society which could either fall, as Thackeray's seems to do, or recover itself, as Eliot's does—but where, in both, there appear sufficient cracks in the body politic to warrant serious attention to its defects. Thackeray's novel is more biting, less compassionate, less sympathetic to human folly; but Eliot, in hers, is quite aware of folly, without the desire to devastate it. She is not, however, celebratory. Her Dorothea, in her desire to marry someone like Casaubon, is following in the footsteps of Thackeray's Dobbin, who wishes to marry Amelia; or to shift patterns, Amelia is a forerunner of Rosamond, and Lydgate's marriage to the latter proves as unfortunate as Dobbin's would have to Amelia early on. In both writers, marriage becomes the measuring rod of a society, the great Victorian subject. Marriage becomes the definition of one's intentions toward life, the degree of one's seriousness, even when marriage, as with Lydgate or Dorothea, is disguised as something other than what it proves to be.

On 8 August, as the Leweses were beginning to think of returning to the Priory and Eliot was closing in on the final book, Blackwood sent on his accounting: 19,342 copies of Books I through IV, with a royalty of £1,434.4. This was less than Lewes had figured on, but as we have observed, the sum mounted considerably during the decade. Remaining in stock were over 2,000 copies, although in time these and more would sell. Another £100 came from Australia, with an additional £100 to come for newspaper rights there. Somewhat disappointed, the publisher tried to soften the sales figures by speaking of the novel as a succès d'estime. In response, Lewes said the success had been as great as Eliot expected, but her own words to Mrs. William Cross ten days later indicate that neither success nor failure would have moved her. She speaks of

---

* Later, we will examine this effort at an overview, along with Dickens's "anatomy," *Bleak House.* Together, the three novels become a kind of Victorian saga of upper-, lower-, and middle-class life.

nothing but despair: "I dare not count on fulfilling any project, my life for the last year having been a sort of nightmare in which I have been scrambling on the slippery bank of a pool, just keeping my head above water."

It is difficult, once again, to pinpoint where Eliot's expression of despair confronts her considerable literary achievement and its sufficiently commercial popularity. She had achieved everything she started out to do, and when the reviews for *Middlemarch* poured in, there were few indeed Lewes had to hide from her. Appearing well past middle age was that divide between inner Eliot, full of fears and uncertainties which no amount of success could dissipate, and an even deeper Eliot who could gather her powers for an extended major effort. Just as there were triple names, there seemed to be several Eliots, including the public person.

While she thrived on London and its intellectual and cultural excitement in the post-Darwinian era, she nevertheless only felt emotionally liberated once she left the city for the countryside. Yet it had been the very countryside, when she was young, that nourished her fear she might be buried there, as a person unfulfilled in her deepest wishes; and now it was this very London that seemed to reinforce her disorders. Through London and her London experience, she had reshaped herself, and yet now London exacerbated her ailments. It was, all in all, a series of paradoxes for which *she* could find no resolution, as we can observe from her frequent trips in and out of the city seeking relief.

Eliot had two sets of character development: one that proceeded smoothly in a seeming procession of intellectual and artistic triumphs, onward from the *Westminster Review* and her years with John Chapman; but then there was the "other" Eliot, whom, perhaps, only Lewes perceived, and it is doubtful he saw all of her. That "otherness" was an Eliot who peered into the black hole, who saw doom rather than achievement, and if not doom, then the temporality of all success. This "other" Eliot never really recovered from her loss of faith; and she was too intelligent to believe she could actually find it elsewhere, whether in work, or artistic creation, or even in that reshaping of experience at which she was so masterful. Her recognition that she could never recoup what she had lost and that she could never compensate for those desperate years of uncertainty and lack of focus brought her down, giving the "other," the failure, the opportunity to share her life with the successful, famous, and now rich author.

Even when she was so successful, it is telling Lewes had to protect her. That she could not tolerate adversarial remarks without being thrown off course is a sign of how such comments reminded her of frailties she had never resolved. Lurking in that shield she demanded from Lewes was her fear of being just Marian Evans, but more than that, a fear of death—and, perhaps even more fearful to an artist, a confirmation she had, indeed, failed in her goals. Some of that— but not all—was a woman's recognition that the male world was only biding its time to submerge her.

This description of herself as being on a slippery slope which she could barely cling to, with drowning as her fate, came during one of her most productive times, near the end of her stay at Redhill. In nine days, on 28 August, she and

Lewes would return to the Priory, and possibly the experience of packing once again and then returning to London turned her so pessimistic. But we sense it went deeper than the moment, that she was defining a persistent attitude toward life. She may have wanted to feel more joy, but she found she could only bear it all, which was no laughing matter.

On 2 September, Lewes posted to Edinburgh ninety pages of manuscript of Book VIII. He asked for quick proofs as they were planning to be off for Hamburg, Germany, to take the waters. He promised the remainder of the manuscript rapidly—Eliot came through, depression and all, on 2 October—and reminded Blackwood that the firm should announce the change in publication, for November and December. Lewes was concerned with every detail, leaving Eliot free to write.

September would indeed be crowded, for besides the need to complete *Middlemarch* and to prepare for Hamburg (on the 18th), the couple also planned a long weekend starting the 13th at Six Mile Bottom, near Cambridge, with Henry Bullock-Hall, brother-in-law of John Cross. Once there, Eliot was in the presence of her future husband, as well as several siblings-in-law.

Blackwood poured on the encouragement. He says he skipped church in order to read the first hundred pages of "Sunset and Sunrise" (Book VIII), indicating that Dorothea "is better than any person that ever was preached by man. It is noble." He was also gratified that Dorothea planned to bail out Lydgate—this going back to the publisher's belief the doctor was trapped by the vile Rosamond, a misreading which fails to take into account that Lydgate was trapped by Lydgate. It was a cautionary tale; and the serpent in the doctor's garden was not Rosamond's golden curls, but his own character.

By the time of the couple's departure for Bullock-Hall's, Eliot was enervated and nervous, to the degree she says even the chirping of a grasshopper, if it were to be heard in their parts, would add to the sounds already irritating her. One incident sent her spinning: Mrs. Cross, with Eliot in tow, found her widow's streamers catching fire at the candle, and although the fire was soon extinguished, without any great damage, "Polly had a slight hysterical fit from the shock." The next day she awoke with such a "dreadful headache and sickness" they had to delay their departure until the midday train. When they arrived back at the Priory, after what should have been a relaxing time, Lewes makes it clear how close Eliot was to breakdown.

While *Middlemarch* can be read as mainly accommodating and balancing, Eliot was testing dangerous waters. She was trying out the limits of how individual behavior can undermine a society if ego and self are given their full empowerment. It was, for her, a test case. Then having given ego its full potential, she tried to find what was necessary to put self and society back into balance. In the process, she imagined herself at the edge of possible disorder, even anarchy; and this edginess intensifies if we see Dorothea's marriages as shadowy elements in Eliot's own life: as fear of being drowned with Casaubon, as romantic hope of being saved with Ladislaw.

She still had the "Finale" to complete, but that was only a few pages and did not require "invention," since it was merely the typical Victorian summing up. Readers assumed not only a happy ending, but an ENDING. The finality of the last page was a form of solace. It denied the rage of ego and confirmed stability. It is, nevertheless, ironic that a finale of such a pattern, with most characters satisfied with their lives, should have been written when Eliot was grappling so hard to remain on the slippery slope without drowning.

On 18 October, as planned, the couple set out for Hamburg, arriving on the 21st. At Hamburg, they took lodgings on the entire first floor of a house at 14 Obere Promenade. Their plan was to take the waters and enjoy the baths. Eliot, who was so negative about spiritualism as a fake "cure" for the mind, was not so suspicious about the curative powers of the waters, whose medicinal aid for those with real afflictions required suspension of disbelief. She perceived a possible help for her ailments, which were now revealing themselves more clearly as a digestive condition which could only become more pronounced as she aged.

The gambling at Hamburg disturbed her immensely. The disturbance went beyond the fact that gambling drew the kind of crowd she reviled. It seemed to point, as we read her words to Mrs. Cross, to the heart of a disorganized, patternless, uncertain world she drew back from with fear:

> . . . The air, the waters, the plantations are all perfect—"only man is vile."
> I am not fond of denouncing my fellow-sinners, but gambling being a vice
> I have no mind to, it stirs my disgust even more than my pity. The sight of
> the dull faces banding round the gambling tables, the raking up of the
> money, and the flinging of the coins towards the winners by the hard-faced
> croupiers, the hateful, hideous women staring at the board like monomani-
> acs—all this seems to me the most abject presentation of mortals grasping
> after something called a good that can be seen on the face of this little
> earth. Burglary is heroic compared with it. I get some satisfaction in look-
> ing on from the sense that the thing is going to be put down. Hell is the
> only right name for such places. *

She observed in the hellish gambling at the tables an attitude or idea which became fixed in her mind. She would reproduce it in *Daniel Deronda*, when

---

* Not content with this blast, she repeated much of it to John Blackwood the following week (on 4 October). Eliot's remarks were set off by her view of Byron's niece, Geraldine Amelia Leigh, at the gambling tables at the Kursaal: ". . . is only 26 years old, and is completely in the grasp of this mean, money-raking demon. It made me cry to see her young fresh face among the hags and brutally stupid men around her. Next year, when the gambling has vanished the place will be delight-ful. . . ." Gambling is implicitly the negation of art and nature, an area where Eliot was a Ruskinite. The ideas on art developed between Will Ladislaw and his friend Naumann or in discussions involv-ing Dorothea, for example, derive from Ruskin. As early as 1854 (June), Eliot reviewed, for the *Leader*, Ruskin's *Lectures on Architecture and Painting*, substituting for Lewes, who was ill. In the review and in her responses to Ruskin more generally, Eliot revealed how the language of art en-hances morality. Several notebook entries support her deference to Ruskin. Gambling was a total desecration of this and every other part of Eliot's "rational" world.

Deronda first catches sight of Gwendolen as she feverishly gambles in the hell-hole of such a den.

The Leweses were immediately picked up socially by people they had come to know through Mrs. Ernst Benzon, who kept an expensive salon in London. As a result their circle widened, in a replay of their previous trips to Germany. The couple's ill health and indisposition seemed to melt away, as they attended dinners, went on drives, or simply enjoyed undirected sightseeing. Their reacquaintanceship with the music of Wagner—this time through a piano run-through of *Tristan and Isolde* and *Lohengrin*—made Lewes comment that Wagner's language was simply one they did not understand. He included Eliot in this remark.

The couple's entrance into social activity served its fictional purposes, for with *Daniel Deronda,* Eliot was able to write a version of the international novel. Not only did she learn to write about foreign places, she gained knowledge of social levels which existed outside of English life. Since her other novels, before *Deronda,* were historical, her use of English class and caste was simplified: mainly upper class or squires and a lower working class, without the innumerable gradations which Europe afforded. Only in *Middlemarch* had she begun to explore these subdivisions, but by *Deronda,* her experience was far more varied.

The social activity in Hamburg finally did exhaust the couple, and on 13 October they moved on to Stuttgart and Karlsruhe for ten days of peaceful communion with nature, in beautiful autumnal weather. They continued on to Paris for what turned into an unpleasant stay. They made a night journey, which was a mistake, and when they arrived they suffered headaches and a kind of unnerving which turned their response to disgust. Eliot wrote Mrs. Cross that "George became quite rabid towards Paris, and only calmed down a few minutes when we found a comfortable knitted waistcoat with silk sleeves which is what we have been seeking for him these five years. The vices of great capitals are more tolerable when one gets just the thing one wants in them."

No question about it, the Leweses had become consumers. They could well afford it, * and we observe them becoming more and more entrenched in what money could buy and less interested in places for their own sake. They were getting older in that they were gradually losing their ability to observe freshly. They were also being spoiled. Eliot was now a great international celebrity. Wherever she went and revealed herself, the self-made rich, those born to money and family, and royalty itself all sought her company. Lewes was well known in scientific circles, although when he traveled with her, he was still, more or less, "Mrs. Eliot." Their response to their celebrity status was not unusual: they enjoyed it for a time, but they required long periods away from everything, preferably in natural quiet.

Back at the Priory on 31 October, Eliot awaited the *Middlemarch* notices. The

---

* An income that came to £5,000 a year, with investments in railways and utilities, guided and supervised by John Cross, who by now was their financial adviser and investment banker. This was more than fifty times the average worker's annual salary.

Spectator reviewer (anonymous, but R. H. Hutton) wrote a running commentary, picking up various books of the novel as they appeared. Hutton was insightful in that he had, like several others, become attuned to the Eliot type of fiction. He writes of her "large friendly way of letting the light fall on human weakness," and says that her sarcastic remarks are out of place, natural to a writer like Thackeray, but unnatural to her. The final judgment of Book I is "fascinating." Book II brought out that the entire novel, if it follows the earlier material, will be "full of a wisdom somewhat too acid at times for our taste, but always truthful, and full also of fine and delicate portraiture." By Book IV, Hutton was grumbling at the length, at the slow pace, but all in all he was forced to agree that "there is nothing to compare with it appearing at the present moment in the way of English literature. . . ." By Book VI—in what was now becoming a reviewing saga, with thousands of words expended on each book— Hutton was prepared to call *Middlemarch* "one of the greatest books of the world." He says this despite indicating there are tones and undertones not to his liking; but when someone aims as high as was Eliot, one must expect defeats. He contrasts her with Trollope, who moves broadly, he asserts, but who eschews the depth behind his characters. Here, Hutton is suggesting her great contribution to the Victorian novel, the psychological method.

On 7 September 1872, the *Spectator* continued with another immensely detailed review. The reviewer, still Hutton, questioned whether an author who aims as high as Eliot should permit publication before her entire work is completed. We observe in these and similar remarks a questioning of the world of Victorian publishing, which Eliot had acquiesced to: installment publication while the writing was still in progress. It put an almost overwhelming strain on her; it created problems for Thackeray, who often waited until the last minute and then supplied filler; and it made several of Dickens's longer fictions into episodic works which with more time might have been more tightly structured. What was remarkable about Eliot's achievement was how unepisodic her work proved and how tightly woven it became.

By the time of the four-volume publication, Hutton had begun to take it for granted that *Middlemarch* was "a great book." Warwickshire, he concluded, "has certainly given birth to the greatest forces of English literature, for we are indebted to it not only for the greatest of English authors [Shakespeare], but also for by far the greatest of English authoresses."* While implying that women writers rank second to male authors, he indicates, nevertheless, that Eliot will take her place in a firmament that contains Scott and Fielding, on a comparative level with all but Shakespeare. Eliot could accept that!

In the *Academy*, the reviewer was Edith Simcox, but her role in Eliot's life

---

* Although Edward Dowden—the first professor of English literature at Trinity College, Dublin, and a well-known Shakespearean scholar—did not write directly about *Middlemarch* (in an August 1872 piece), his remarks about Eliot set the stage for a complete evaluation of her body of fiction. Dowden wanted to dispel the notion that her novels were didactic treatises, as they had been called; he considered them "primarily works of art." He called her an artist as much as a teacher, a designation which pleased her when Lewes read aloud portions of this article to her.

went well beyond that of reviewing *Middlemarch*. Simcox in time threw herself at Eliot, addressed her as "Mother," and offered eternal love. Her lavish affection for Eliot, which on occasion embarrassed the subject, accompanied real accomplishments as a social reformer and a writer. She was not merely a troubled person seeking a guiding force. Simcox was a generalist, with an interest in moral questions, gender issues, and the legal apparatus, as her published titles indicate: *Natural Law: An Essay in Ethics* (1877); *Episodes in the Lives of Men, Women, and Lovers* (1882); and *Primitive Civilizations* (1894). She read widely, was feverishly energetic, but was also someone seeking a pillar of emotional support. Although highly charged and somewhat erratic, Simcox was not the near lunatic as she has often been portrayed.

She and Eliot first met on 13 December 1872, as Simcox was preparing her review for the *Academy*. It was clear to Eliot that Simcox was a kind of "secret sharer," not as a creative person but as a self-educated woman of considerable substance. Like Eliot, she had a solid grasp of classical languages, as well as better spoken French than the novelist and equal German. Her reading and knowledge were of a breadth which rivaled Eliot's, in law, folklore, economics, mythology, and interrelated fields. She was a dogged proponent of women's suffrage and other issues affecting women. She was also more socially committed than Eliot, in her concern for the poor and her advocacy for housing for the lower economic classes, and in her support of trades unions, and she was a pioneer in advocating equal employment opportunities for women. She was, as well, an entrepreneur, running a shirt-making factory with her friend Mary Hamilton, where women were employed under far better conditions than in other mills and factories in England. Had there been a Labour Party at the time, she would have been an avid member. She toyed with Marxism, but found it incompatible with English life; and she threw her remaining energies, which were formidable, into education for both sexes without ecclesiastical control. She was a freethinker, a secularist, but also someone much involved with "spiritual patterns" found in mythology and folklore. Although she appears a polymath, her learning went deep.

About six months after the meeting, Simcox—who returned to the Priory several times after that December—began to treat Eliot in special ways. Whether or not she felt an erotic passion for her "Mother" and "Madonna" is unclear. One can only speculate that Eliot became for her an obsessive object, and that the obsession soared well beyond eroticism or the desire for physical possession. In some old-fashioned way, Simcox seemed to want nothing less than Eliot's soul. She did attempt a physical rapprochement—kissing the writer's feet, trying to embrace her, making love to her on bended knees. It was a fierce courtship, and it clearly had erotic overtones, but it should not be viewed as solely that. Whatever Simcox's intentions to devour Eliot, the overriding consideration was a passion whose parallel we can find in several places, in writers who understood obsession. In Proust, Charles Swann's desire for Odette Crécy makes him wish to possess her without even wanting her physically;

his obsession makes her a need he cannot forgo because it leaves him incomplete. Simcox needed Eliot. And once she engaged Eliot through her brains, she tried bodily intimacy.

Eliot tolerated, enjoyed, and revelled in the attention, but rebuffed Simcox when the avowals became too insistent. We cannot tell if she reciprocated. Simcox was not the first to declare such love, or by any means the last. Earlier, Eliot had undergone something similar with Mrs. Richard Congreve. The extant letters to Maria Congreve are all excerpts, for Eliot's originals were destroyed by Congreve's niece—long before Gordon Haight could acquire them for his edition. What we do have of the correspondence comes from John Cross, with parts clearly expurgated. These are intensely compelling episodes because they open up the possibility of something in Eliot which brought forth female declarations of love, even passion.

In her unpublished autobiography, Simcox wrote of Maria's "passion for Eliot"—this after the writer's death, when Simcox and Congreve became close friends. Maria told Simcox "she had loved my Darling [Eliot] loverwise too—too much to repeat much of her words, but she [Maria] told me on seeing her [Eliot] again after an interval her heart was palpitating so violently that to avoid a painful breaking down she forced herself into a calm that seemed cold: she tried to talk in common fashion." Simcox continued that once when Lewes was away, Eliot—"the Darling, my sweet Darling"—rushed out of the room in tears. We have no explanation for this. She recorded several episodes of passionate feeling for Eliot, with expressions of "my own beautiful Love" as characteristic. She made these jottings on an almost daily basis, and from them, once we become accustomed to the overheated rhetoric, we see that Eliot and God— one of Simcox's mythical gods—were indeed merging in Simcox's mind. In some way, emotionally, physically, or otherwise, she had turned to Eliot as the guide in life we normally associate with a religious quest for the divine. She inscribed her book *Natural Law* with a passionate yearning for Eliot and an expression of "idolatrous love."

Eliot was not always amused, and she may have been disturbed as much by the excess as by the content. Her letters to Maria Congreve (except for excerpts, mentioned above) and to Edith Simcox do not remain, although they may have run into the hundreds. While we cannot speculate on what was in them, we do gather from Simcox's autobiography that Eliot turned away from extreme behavior. What seems common to both women, Congreve and Simcox, is that Eliot had become something or someone "beyond," the figure for worship they needed to fill a huge emotional gap in their lives.

Maria Congreve was not satisfied in her marriage, and as an intelligent woman she obviously felt her talents suppressed by a conventional union. Her sexual life, also, may have been depressing—although we cannot find such evidence—and from an uninterested husband wrapped up in positivism she may have turned to a woman. Simcox, who never married, was perhaps a lesbian, or possibly a woman who identified so strongly with other women socially, politically, and emotionally that she as a matter of course passed the gender line. We have no way of knowing. Her excessive display of passion for Eliot, manifest even when the beloved object hesitated to reciprocate, reveals that despite all her considerable achievements, she, too, had not found emotional satisfaction.

Simcox's review of *Middlemarch*, in the *Academy* (1 January 1873), was a love fest. Her main point is that Eliot marks "an epoch in the history of fiction" for her ability to trace incidents from the mind, for revelations of how the mind works on mind and character on character. She is quite acute: ". . . the material circumstances of the outer world are made subordinate and accessory to the artistic presentation of definite passage of mental experience, but chiefly as giving a background of perfect realistic truth to a profoundly imaginative psychological study." Significant here is not Simcox's dithyrambic approach to Eliot, but the fact she was helping to establish the way in which the writer's body of work would be fitted into the English novelist tradition. What Simcox began, F. R. Leavis completed. Her psychology, Simcox said, is more complex than Fielding's; her range contrasts with Austen's "scanty" knowledge of the world; her view of life is varied, as contrasted with Thackeray's one-sidedness. With this as a prologue, Simcox moved to particulars: provincial life, social complications, and other aspects of the *Middlemarch* web. She saw in Dorothea some of the dilemmas of women in general: ". . . that their beauty must always rest on a basis of illusions because there is no right place for their bestowal." This comment locates Dorothea's problems precisely: not that she has capitulated to marriages which are beneath her, but that even with beauty, money, and position she has little choice in life outside marriage.

Maga's review was expectedly congratulatory, as were those in the *Telegraph* (like Simcox, the reviewer felt Eliot's novel established another level of standard for English fiction) and even in the usually hostile *Edinburgh Review.* Journals of very different political persuasions all pointed to the achievement of the novel. In the *Fortnightly,* Sidney Colvin (later a close friend of Joseph Conrad and a man of letters as well as an art critic) extolled the fullness and ripeness of *Middlemarch.* "What she writes is so full of her time. It is observation, imagination, pathos, wit and humour, all of a high class in themselves; but what is more, all saturated with modern ideas and poured into a language of which every word bites home with peculiar sharpness to the contemporary consciousness." He says he will leave it to posterity to locate this great work of fiction, since she has brought into it "so many new elements, and gives it pregnancy and significance in so many unaccustomed directions, that it is presumptuousness to pronounce in that way as to the question of art."

When the *Times* review (7 March 1873) appeared, by Frederick Broome, the context for criticism of *Middlemarch* had been more or less set. While this review was always very important for a critical and even commercial success, *Middlemarch* had already passed into literary history. The *Times* came through enthusiastically, with the reviewer not only extolling his first reading of the novel, but suggesting that successive rereadings would be equally rewarding. Eliot could not have wished for anything more.

Middlemarch joins *Vanity Fair* and *Bleak House* as one of the longest novels of the Victorian era. While length alone would not be sufficient to provide a grouping for these novels, length is not to be discounted. For obvious reasons, all three are encompassing fictions, with each novelist using fiction as a means of both encapsulating his or her sense of the century and, at the same time, opening up its potentialities. Thackeray is the least "open," perhaps because his satire and cynicism preempt growth and development. Of the three, only Dickens was writing contemporaneously; Thackeray moved his novel back to the time of Waterloo, and Eliot maneuvered in and around the 1832 Reform Bill. Yet despite the historical distinctions among these three novels, they are clearly cautionary tales for the century. With her vantage point of the 1870s, Eliot had an additional quarter of a century to look back over Thackeray's and Dickens's mid-century novels; but even that temporal advantage for Eliot did not alter certain common factors. *

Once we set aside the obvious elements—the common assault on materialism, the attack on technological progress, the nostalgia for old values (embedded in Thackeray's Dobbin, Eliot's Caleb Garth, and Dickens's old soldier George, among others), the shared suspicion of the business and professional worlds as often little more than whorish enterprises—once we acknowledge these commonalites, we can look to more underlying factors which draw these fictions together. All are, in their way, "experimental" fictions, within the context of traditional forms for the mid-nineteenth century. They are experimental in that they expand realism, the dominant Victorian mode, while at the same time paradoxically holding everything up to a realistic light. Dickens's novel is clearly the most "unrealistic," an intense effort to create a phantasmagoria, a metaphor of Victorian instability underlying life as usual. For his part, Thackeray—with his cynical narrator, his puppet master, and his use of internal drama—creates a carnival of sorts, a nineteenth-century equivalent of Rabelais's Panurge in his attempt to seek out disorder, instability, subterranean forces of destruction. Since our focus is on *Middlemarch*, we must also try to see Eliot going literarily against her own precepts, her respect for order and social comity.

Middlemarch consistently pokes through to the disorder which lies at the heart of a seemingly orderly society. While it is not consciously subversive as is *Bleak House*, it nevertheless rebels against both social and religious stereotypes, and it reinforces those elements which emphasize free choice, the breaking away from expected forms, and the puncture of given notions. Dickens may find in his Dedlocks an indication of the older order's decay, but Eliot is not far behind in her condemnation of the electoral process, her often satirical handling of the clergy, and her reliance on value systems which lie outside authority, convention, and historical process. When she does touch on business or professional

---

* Although Eliot praised Thackeray—calling him in 1857 "the most powerful of living novelists"—we should not discount how heavily Dickens lay over her sense of large fictions. While she identified with Thackeray's realism, she did not reject completely Dickens's "magical realism," even when it made her uncomfortable. Dickens's use of mythical and fairy-tale elements is not that distant from her substantial use of biblical or classical mythical references.

life, she is strongly condemnatory, to the extent she cites how corruption—whether in medicine or in business—lies at the heart of all ostensible success. She surely does not pursue a Victorian convention of displaying wealth as a given and the wealthy person as someone who has earned and deserves his power. She views money, both its acquisition and its status as power, as a corrupting influence, and empowerment itself as a form of hypocrisy. She is concerned with how corruption seeps into nearly every important transaction, whether a hospital vote or the arrangements made for heirs; and how that corruption strangles love, good feeling, openness, and the possibility of reciprocity. Hers is a society not heading toward corruption, but already corrupted; and here she finds common ground with both Dickens and Thackeray. They were, all, doing no less than redefining the ground on which Victorians founded their beliefs and held to them; in that respect, they were morally and ethically experimental.

To some extent, all three were outsiders. Thackeray had had money, but allowed it to dribble away in gambling debts; and physically, since he was large and ungainly, he perceived himself as a stranger who now needed to earn his way. Dickens we know well, from his days in the blacking warehouse to his sense of himself as a lost soul, until he began his phenomenal rise with *Pickwick*. Eliot's outsider status we have discussed throughout, a status that remained despite her views, which attempted to make her seem conventional. She could not in fact be conventional, whatever her efforts, since as an intellectual woman involved in an irregular relationship, she was marked. Their respective views of themselves as individuals who did not fit reverberated through their works, unlike Trollope, who despite dire poverty as a child and young man saw himself as part of the great world. The subversive quality we pick up in all three, even in Eliot, the least subversive, must be attributed to their perceptions of themselves as marginal, even when they achieved great success and were suitably honored and admired.

Eliot went well beyond puncturing the professional and business worlds in *Middlemarch*. Although she remained a realist, she nevertheless flirted with several untraditional forms: heightened contrasts, fantasy or dream materials, elaborate parallel or counterpointed structures. And her view of society, while still based on the comity of a contract, allows for several contaminating elements to poke through. The political system is itself highly charged with irregularities and patterns of misbehavior, or simply stupidity; the economic system seems to work on the basis of deception and hypocrisy; religion is itself little more than a shield behind which hypocrisy can function; the family may be stalwart or, as with the Vincys, divisive and disruptive, based on class and caste ideas; the professions, as in medicine, are riddled with compromises, the desire for soft berths, distancing oneself from patients' concerns. The world of scholarship, as with Casaubon, is littered with presumption, lack of perspective, inability to function adequately. Marriage has its support in some instances, as with the Garths, but it is often, like religion, merely a shield for people's weaknesses. The parallel marriages, Dorothea with Casaubon, Lydgate with Rosamond, as well as the Garths, Vincys, and Bulstrodes—the very structure of the novel—indicate that behind closed doors the power game, not love, not mutual support or understanding, valorizes the relationship. *

If we list all the larger areas in the social-political-economic-personal contract which makes up society, then *Middlemarch* takes its place with *Vanity Fair* and *Bleak House.* All three condemn institutions and systems; all three observe, jejunely, cultures splitting into subcultures. Thackeray goes after the hallowed war itself, turning Waterloo, an English legend, into as much a social as a martial event. People are puppets caught in terrible events, and yet they dance away the final hours of their lives. In *Bleak House,* the holiest of the holiest, children, are victimized by inadequate parents, by parents who abandon them or who themselves must be parented by their children. Eliot is more benign, but her whip lashes other elements almost as fiercely. The breakdown in comity between Lydgate and Rosamond curves back to the divisiveness in the Vincy family, which almost permits Fred to fall through the cracks. Dorothea's mistakes, to some extent, can be attributed to the foolishness of her guardian. As we have observed before, except for the Garths, parental figures are either absent or emotionally and intellectually missing; they simply do not know their children, a theme Dickens pursued obsessively in *Bleak House* and which Thackeray handled intensely with the Osbornes in *Vanity Fair.* These malfunctioning elements preempt gender roles: that is, while women seem to suffer most from their placement in such families, men are penalized almost as much.

This inability of parents and children to communicate is a metaphor for the disorder lying below the surface of every apparent contract. Eliot was always probing for the weak points in what seemed a strong society or group; she sought out the places where disorder subverted what should be solid and continuous. With Eliot, as with Thackeray, there was an attempt through structure to create order. † Thackeray's puppet show was an ideal model, an artifact of order created by the author, an intrusion that serves as a locus of stability. For Eliot, structure came with bunching: the parallelism of the numerous marriages; the balancing of various professional activities, such as political life, medical practice, and the business and banking worlds; the pairing of characters for both contrast and comparison, cutting across gender and achievement; the yoking together of characters with various levels of disappointment—Casaubon, Lydgate, Dorothea, Rosamond, Farebrother, to name only five.

But perhaps more than any of this was Eliot's psychological suggestiveness, which helps create the density of the novel and serves as its own structural concept. She is full of subtexts, even as she provides the story line the Victorian

---

* The relative absence of active children also reinforces Eliot's view of marriage here not as reciprocity but as conflict. As a whole, she does not do much with children in her later novels, except perhaps to see them as victims, as we observe with Lydia Glasher's in *Daniel Deronda.* While not exactly divisive, children do not serve as peacemakers either. Few, indeed, are the happy families.

† In any discussion of order, Dickens does not fit, since his "order" is something that often seems artifically imposed on extreme disorder just to end his novel—*Bleak House* or others. Dickens's strength really lay in disorder or, to be Miltonic, in re-creating Pandemonium. The very episodic nature of his longer novels is a sign of disorder.

reader demanded. The subtexts are various, but the sexual ones dominate, in that what is unstated hovers over major parts of Middlemarch. Dorothea's unconsummated marriage to Casaubon becomes a metaphor for the entire sexual process in which Dorothea, not to speak of other characters, is involved. Her attraction to Will, and his to her, is clearly sexual; and as a consequence, he is not only a foil to Casaubon, he is a sexual threat. Casaubon's alteration of his will (with its play on "Will"), so that if Dorothea marries Ladislaw she forfeits the Casaubon income, is an admission the older man must use money as a substitute for sexual power. The husband who cannot consummate the marriage uses his money as a threat and as a form of empowerment; the suitor, who lacks money, offers sexuality, which Dorothea embraces and, as a consequence, forfeits the money.

Dorothea Brooke represents a perfect example of the sexual dilemma Eliot novelistically found herself in and a shaded version of her own earlier predicament. In marrying an impotent Casaubon, Dorothea fulfills the Victorian "ideal" of a woman above sexual desire. But by being attrached to Will Ladislaw, she reveals a dirty secret which might well cheapen her: that his maleness is irresistible and that beneath their bantering romance is little more than sex. One unconsummated marriage, a second marriage entered into for sexual attraction: Dorothea moves at the extremes, caught as she is in Victorian contradictions. In another respect, if she remained single, she would be considered incomplete, an aberration who was not fulfilling women's evolutionary role. Her movement, then, was dictated by such severe social restriction she could satisfy others' feelings only by suppressing her own. In this manner, Dorothea works out her female destiny. To gain any kind of personal power, she must flout larger social considerations. Marian Evans found herself in 1854 in a similar predicament.

A sexual ballet is played out also with Lydgate and Rosamond, in that the doctor's inability to support his wife in the way she expects makes him impotent in the marriage. It is inconceivable that he and Rosamond continue to have sexual relations while they bicker over furniture, income, and related matters. As Lydgate moves toward bankruptcy, Rosamond conspiratorily asks his baronet uncle, Sir Godwin, for assistance. The very act of Rosamond setting up someone more powerful than Lydgate who will service her needs has as its subtext a desexing of her husband.

Empowerment gets play throughout the novel. Lydgate's stature as a man depends on his ability to position himself by way of original science research. Dorothea seeks empowerment through plans for cottages and other improvements. Rosamond does it through her strategy for raising herself in terms of class and caste. Bulstrode has empowered himself through fraud and embezzlement in his earlier business practices. Casaubon seeks potency by means of scholarly success, which will compensate for the personal poverty he has experienced. This desire for empowerment extends even to Fred Vincy, who is not a "man" until Mary Garth accepts him. The theme puts Eliot right on the cutting edge of her society, for it demonstrates how desire for power undercuts humanity, subverts social comity, and destroys sexuality itself. The quest is not ennobling. It is not in the popular Samuel Smiles tradition of Victorian thought, wherein power means the lowly have risen, made their fortune, developed their abilities. Eliot was not buying any cheap remedies; she had gone well beyond popular nostrums to the very substrata of Victorian doubt about power, progress, and success. In this way, she has joined with Dickens and Thackeray in *their* mega-novels.

In another respect, Eliot's "bunched" segments create a dialogue with her individual characters—the way Thackeray does with his intrusions, and Dickens with his carefully placed contrasting characters. In *Middlemarch*, social concerns are played off against individual needs: the dialogue, then, moves between the bunched opinions of the group and the characters' thrust toward self-achievement. Through this complicated dialogue, Eliot could present her layered views of female concerns. She was able to track the boundaries of what was possible for a woman. Here she departs from Thackeray and Dickens, probing far more deeply *into the individual* than either of them.

Dorothea is truly daring, first in her desire for social improvements (when she is herself comfortably placed among the elite); then in her need for fulfillment through marriage to someone whose intellect she, unfortunately, overrates; and finally, in her attachment to someone like Will, whom everyone considers marginal, and even an interloper or an adventurer. In each instance, she plays off what is possible for the individual woman against what is socially sanctioned, and she barely remains within the boundaries established by the latter. Even in her decision to aid Lydgate she socially compromises herself.

In Rosamond's case, we also have something quite complicated. She experiences a fantasy life, a "family romance," which is an outgrowth of her beauty, her privilege, her lack of restraint. She seeks something higher than herself, and her marriage to Lydgate is, in actuality, a socially daring move. Doctors were not in themselves considered to be of great social stature, since their ability to cure was minimal. More often than not, doctors helped the patient die, not live. Rosamond's decision forgoes the more traditional one of marrying an up-and-coming local businessman, not an outsider, even one with aristocratic connections. Through that act of daring, she puts herself in jeopardy when her fantasy of upward social mobility is frustrated by lack of funds. She has, in this respect, tested out what is possible for a middle-class woman of her time, and in her way she has acted out, however dimly and on different grounds, something of the irregular arrangement Eliot herself made with Lewes.

Through these two examples alone, we observe Eliot on the cutting edge of change, in that she permitted her female characters to move the boundaries, and then withdraw only when social sanctions make it necessary. But even then, with social sanctions in the balance, someone like Dorothea makes her decision to marry Will Ladislaw. He may not satisfy us, and her decision to marry may not resolve the problem of her own identity, but the act is in itself daring. Eliot, Dickens, and Thackeray all found ways in which to test out social prohibitions in their mega-novels; but more than that, they played individuals off against society in ways that undercut communal ideas, and when their characters did succeed it was never within the progressive ways advocated by Samuel Smiles or other prophets of individual success. The three novelists made their characters carry out a dialogue with social needs and then go their own ways. As we chart Eliot's professed conservatism in social and political matters, we should not lose sight of the fact that in her most finely wrought and thoughtful novel, she challenged nearly every one of her personal positions,* as did Thackeray and Dickens in their respective novels. By working through her deepest doubts of how society and the individual intersect and by probing the period's most profound uncertainties, she consolidated her position as the voice of the century.

The discussion of Middlemarch among Eliot's reviewers and her friends led, inevitably, to attempts to identify various characters, with the search for Casaubon being the most intense. There is little question Mary Garth is a persona for Eliot herself, with sister Chrissey as Celia, Dorothea's sister. Mary is practical, just, not pretty, but witty and sharp, and simply more insightful than anyone else in the novel. Her wit sets her off from Dorothea, whose solemnity is often heavy; and her perception of others, especially Fred Vincy, makes her a psychological secret sharer of her creator. There is also something of Eliot in Dorothea: the desire to be and do good, the emphasis on duty and discipline, the attempt to define herself in moral and ethical terms. Dorothea's attraction to Will Ladislaw, furthermore, brings into fictional terms, however shaded, the relationship of Eliot and Lewes.

One of the few failures in the novel is Ladislaw,† and that was perhaps because Eliot was too close, too involved to turn Lewes into a complex fictional character; or possibly because his multidimensional character simply fell outside of what she could do. She attempts sprightliness, wit, breadth of learning—but little of it coheres. Because Will is comic relief to Dorothea's solemnity and somberness, he seems insubstantial when he is supposed to prove leavening. In

---

* This is not to say she satisfied feminist critics writing in the 1970s. Kate Millet (in Sexual Politics, 1972) castigated Dorothea as becoming no more than a secretary in marrying Will, while he is himself no more than a good companion. Ellen Moers (in Literary Women, 1977) called Dorothea good for nothing except to be admired, designating her spoiled, arrogant, and selfish. Later feminist critics viewed Dorothea differently, at times as ambiguous, on other occasions almost as a heroine.

What all ignored was Eliot's firmness in matters of female education. Perhaps the following passage will redress the problem: the penultimate paragraph, deleted from the 1874 edition of Middlemarch, reveals her fierceness in this area. "Among the many remarks passed on her [Dorothea's] mistakes, it was never said in the neighbourhood of Middlemarch that such mistakes could not have happened if the society into which she was born had not smiled on propositions of marriage from a sickly man to a girl less than half his own age—on modes of education which made a woman's knowledge another name for motley ignorance—on rules of conduct which are in flat contradiction with its own loudly-asserted beliefs."

† Efforts to link Ladislaw to Daniel Deronda based on Jewish backgrounds are speculative; the former's so-called Jewishness is no more than town gossip. Will is "foreign," not Jewish in origins, although "foreign" often meant Jews. Will comes up in another respect. After making her now famous remark that Middlemarch is one of the few English novels written for adults, Virginia Woolf commented on the young men (Philip and Stephen) in Mill; and to these she would add Will Ladislaw: that infirmity and fumbling shook Eliot's "hand when she had to conceive a fit mate for a heroine." As for the heroines, Woolf saw them as ending in tragedy or "in a compromise that is even more melancholy." She means marriage to someone like Will.

the fictional relationship, Eliot was clearly attempting to limn a couple who enjoyed each other's company—Eliot and Lewes, once again; but Will is caught more by Dorothea's beauty than her intelligence or gravity, at least at first, and she is caught by qualities Eliot cannot quite define. Will is a Jamesian "adventurer" who must become marriageable material; the transformation is never convincing.

As we have observed, a good deal of curiosity was expended on Edward Casaubon, since he seemed so evidently the demon of the early parts of the novel, and nearly everyone close to the Leweses' circle felt he could be identified. The leading candidate for this bilious but pitiful creature, as noted, was Mark Pattison, who, with his wife, had been well known to Eliot, although some friction between the couples developed in later years. One of Pattison's Casaubon-like characteristics was his interest in the French scholar Isaac Casaubon, whose life he published in 1875. Eliot had herself been interested in the French Casaubon, who had published, among other books, an edition of Theophrastus's *Characters*. Near the end of her life, Eliot published a collection of essays called *Theophrastus Such*. There are linkages by way of name and usages, and the fact that Pattison did indeed have a younger wife. The rumor that Pattison was the model picked up after his death in 1884, despite some warning in obituaries that he was a weak candidate for the character. Mrs. Pattison remarried, the well-known historian Charles Dilke, and Dilke found no real resemblance between his wife and Dorothea; but he muddied the waters considerably, in 1905, by indicating that Eliot used many passages from Mrs. Pattison's letters for the "religious side" of Dorothea. Evidence for this no longer remains.

Other candidates for the desiccated scholar have been put forth, and we must shoot them down as well. Casaubon may have had some real-life models in part: Dr. Brabant, * whom many saw as a bumbler, and Robert William Mackay, who married at forty-eight. We have already noted these. But the marriage of older men to younger women is not conclusive in any attempt at linkage, since the January–May wedding was a much-used convention in literature; and Eliot herself was not immune to the idea, since it was one way of blending father and husband. She saw it as a master–student relationship; and surely her treatment of Dorothea is in that tradition, one she had already probed in *Romola*, where her heroine is "wedded" to her father.

The search for Casaubon's original is futile. The character was surely a composite of qualities Eliot had observed in other writers, especially those who had grandiose plans they failed to carry out. And her line to Stowe that Casaubon's tints were not foreign to her own mental makeup is accurate. Casaubon represents that fearful underside to Eliot, which we have seen in her depressions and despair, in her description of herself as hanging on to slippery slopes so as not to slide into the "destructive element." Casaubon represents not only failure in

---

* He had planned a study which would destroy all religious dogma, all superstition, and replace it with a kind of early positivism. It was, in some respects, to be as grand as Casaubon's "Key to All Mythologies," and, like Casaubon, Brabant went no further than brief skirmishes into the material.

terms of his "key," but in life itself: he is that terrified half Eliot was never able to bury. She cast him as an older man who marries a young woman so as to highlight the contraries in herself. It is impossible to track exactly what psychological impact Casaubon made on her, or she on him; but what seems probable, if we accept this reading of her, is that Casaubon represents some deeper level of experience which kept her divided, doubtful, and uncertain of achievement.

Still another character in *Middlemarch* has something of Eliot's fear of failure: Lydgate, the medical man who hopes to make a great reputation as a research scientist. Lydgate has also been the source of much investigative reporting. Haight offers up Eliot's brother-in-law Edward Clarke as a likely prospect, in that Clarke (Chrissey's husband) was well-born and died bankrupt (in debt for more than £1,000). But there are no indications Clarke's ambitions went beyond a decent practice, solvency, and the ability to support a large family. We do not know of any intense yearnings for greatness through some grand discovery. Lydgate, after all, like Casaubon, wants to rise above all the rest, those country physicians and surgeons, and settle into a firmament of his own. Several other candidates put themselves forward as the model: the doctor Eliot had met at Leeds, Clifford Allbutt, nominated himself; and Oscar Browning saw himself in Lydgate, although he was not even a doctor. Such was Eliot's fame that people who knew her or who revolved in her circle were eager to identify even with her failures.

Inevitably, Lydgate and Casaubon both fail through their marriages. Eliot's attack here on marriage extends well into other areas: Mrs. Bulstrode is deceived by her husband, by a past of which she knows nothing. The Vincy marriage is based on accommodation, not on any mutuality of interests. Only the Garths have a stable give-and-take marriage, and their daughter, Mary, must be sure her marriage will be of the same kind before she accepts Fred Vincy. Even the Reverend Farebrother, a highly sympathetic character, cannot fully escape: unmarried, he watches his sole love slip away when Mary chooses Fred. Eliot's ambivalence about marriage contains the fears she reveals on a broader scale about failure.

By the early part of 1873, *Middlemarch* had turned Eliot from a successful and renowned novelist into an icon. It had penetrated into virtually every level of English society, first through its individual books and then as a surprisingly successful four-volume novel. Emily Dickinson, in Amherst, Massachusetts, commented on the book as containing the mysteries of human nature, and she wondered what kind of creator could have brought forth such a work. Harriet Martineau read it twice, commenting on its sense of poignancy. Eliot heard from people in England and from all over the world,* but nothing from her

---

* Among others, Frederic Myers, Fellow of Trinity College, Cambridge, wrote to say that now that there is no longer any God, one must turn to someone like George Eliot for noble and interesting comments. And Benjamin Jowett, the classicist and Master of Balliol, Oxford, congratulated her on her "great work." He says everyone is reading and speaking of it. On a paternal note, which he would not have directed at a male author, he says he hopes she is resting "after such a great intellectual effort," his remark directed at the Victorian notion women had only so much mental energy to expend.

family. Isaac was now fifty-six and still unforgiving, and Fanny was sixty-seven and invisible. Their opposition no longer had any basis, not even the hypocrisy of the age; for Lewes and Eliot had been accepted at many levels of English society (despite the hesitation of women like Mrs. Tennyson to be associated with her), and their relationship was now approaching the twenty-year mark.

The novel enervated her. As she informed Alexander Main, on 4 November 1872, just as she finished all of *Middlemarch* except the "Finale," she feels terrible once a subject begins to grow in her, "until it is wrought out." Her image is that of a fetus finally emerging as a baby. Once it becomes a "complete organism," it "seems to take wing and go away from me. That thing is not to be done again— that life has been lived. I could not rest with a number of unfinished works on my mind. When they—or, rather, when a conception has begun to shape itself in written words, I feel that it must go on to the end before I can be happy about it. Then I move away and look at it from a distance without any agitations." It is true Eliot did not leave loose ends. What she began in fiction she completed. This attitude, to complete something once started, was linked to her need for perfection, or her sense of herself as someone who could succeed in life only if she reached beyond herself. A "failed God" was hiding somewhere in this ideal.

She also told Main she and Lewes were very happy, especially when compared to so "many who are not at all happy." She indicates great interest in the reshaping of Europe, as she sees it, by the "new attitude of Common Labour" and foresees the center of gravity shifting, a change which "will not pause because people of taste object to the disturbance of their habits." Her tone is mixed: such shifts are harbingers of possible social betterment, but they also mean a potential lowering of taste. She could bend, but not too far.

Another birthday came, Eliot's fifty-third. She was being fêted, with invitations coming in from several areas, as her social circle widened. But behind all the glamour awaiting her if she wished to embrace it was her diffidence about giving too much of herself; her desire to read and to keep intellectually alive; and her feeling—the ever-abiding feeling—that somehow society and her role in it was the mirror of life, not the reality. The reality lay not only at her desk but in her awareness of the temporality of fame itself, her consciousness that the meaning of life—whatever that was!—lay outside the plaudits of others. Yet she did not resist the social call. She was not a hermit, although she often liked to think of herself and Lewes as retirees. *

Eliot responded to the *Maga* review of *Middlemarch* (by W. Lucas Collins, who had been carefully selected) with special appreciation of the reviewer's regard for Casaubon. "I am pleased with the writer's sensibility to the pathos in Mr. Casaubon's character and position"—an indication, surely, that her identification with the failed scholar went deep into his disappointment as well as his

---

* Meanwhile, Elma Stuart, who had sent a carved book slide at the beginning of 1872, was starting to present a series of sizable gifts, all carved from wood. The items included an oak table, a writing table, and the like, all decorated with birds and other figures, with her signature inscribed and intertwined with Eliot's. Mrs. Stuart abased herself at Eliot's feet, stating she wished to kiss her dress, and calling Eliot her "spiritual mother"—Simcox, we recall, did the same. Stuart had turned her friend into Hera, queen of the gods.

folly. She was particularly proud that Sir James Paget, surgeon to Queen Victoria and one of the men who had treated Thornie, found no erroneous medical detail. Paget wondered how someone not herself part of the medical establishment could have so much insight into its workings; but he was unaware of the "Quarry," which details her meticulous researches. He thought she had a biographical foundation for Lydgate's career, but Lewes told the doctor no such instance existed. Paget then said it was like "assisting at the creation—a universe formed out of nothing." Even an expert on drug usage chimed in, George Dransfield Brown, who asserted that Lydgate's use of opium would contract his pupils, not dilate or brighten them, as Eliot has it. Paget, however, assured her that Lydgate's excitement might widen his eyelids even while his pupils might contract. Such were the details which concerned her.

John Cross, whom Eliot now addressed as "My dear Nephew," had looked over a piece of property in Surrey, near Shere, which the Leweses had considered buying and building upon. But Eliot agreed it is easier to imagine other people doing wise things—such as buying and building—than doing them oneself. They eventually tried to lease a house called Blackwood, in Kent; but after a stay of two months in the fall of 1873, the deal fell through.

On 16 December 1872, the couple went for two days to Hastings, south of Dover and Rye, on the Channel, to seek the sun, but they found it windy and stormy. Although the ink was hardly dry on *Middlemarch,* Eliot complained of idleness, which for her, she said, means she will run down a good many streets because everything seems tempting to her. She spends hours with her feet at the fireplace reading a Lewes manuscript. She repeats that she flourishes "on this pasture very well"; but her language, while bovine, sounds ominous, that she is out to pasture, with its implied image of impending death. There would not be a new project for some time.

Their plans called for a few days at Weybridge, with Anna Cross, John Cross's younger sister, now Mrs. Albert Druce. Before they departed, John Blackwood gave Lewes a complete accounting to date of *Middlemarch,* which left a balance to be paid of £2,243.2 minus the £94.16.7 offered as an extra discount to Smith and Son. The separate books sold over 40,000 copies, and the four-volume edition sold 240, to which must be added what the circulating libraries took. As Blackwood indicates, the public was now full of the book, and the libraries were having a run on Book VIII because of people's eagerness to read the end. Lewes in response tried to squeeze the last pence from the novel by suggesting a cheap two-volume edition on very thin paper. Eventually, a one-volume *Middlemarch* would be issued. * Although Eliot had free time, all financial negotiations still went through Lewes, and all reviews and comments continued to be screened by him. On 24 December 1872, the couple began their five-day journey to Wey-

---

* Behind the scenes, the firm viewed the statistics less cheerfully. John Blackwood wrote to the Earl of Lytton that although the novel had reached the ear of the press and the public, its sales (of individual books) had barely reached an average of 5,000, and this he finds the limit of an expensive novel. He is gloomy about the libraries, which took the 31/6 novel at 18/-, a discount the firm opposed but was forced to capitulate to.

bridge, but it ended with Eliot feeling desperately ill with what Paget later diagnosed as neuralgia and indigestion. She was in for a siege, in which her health
fluctuated from bearable to considerable discomfort. Of some consolation was
Blackwood's end-of-the-year congratulations on her achievement, in which he
called Middlemarch one of the events by which 1872 would be remembered.
"The public mind," he wrote, "has been wonderfully exercised by the book and
exercised for good."

Eliot celebrated New Year's Day 1873 with a litany of complaints about her
health which, she says, more than balanced out the success she enjoyed with
her novel. "Hardly anything could have happened to me which I could regard
as a greater blessing than the growth of my spiritual satisfactions [in that her
novel was an influence for goodness on individual minds] when my bodily existence is decaying. The merely egoistic satisfactions of fame are easily nullified
by toothache, and that had made my chief consciousness for the last week." She
speaks of pain, of remaining in bed; in his diary, Lewes writes of the fluctuations
of her condition, and of Paget's attendance on her.

We have already commented at length on her guardedness, in which Lewes
served faithfully as either watchdog or knight who protected his mistress from
danger. Despite all of Eliot's acquiescence to the procedure, even her desire for
it, it is a strange process as it continued deep into her career. Lewes becomes
more than her knight protecting her while she cowers in her room or at her
desk. He has become in several respects a paternal figure who protects the delicate or weak daughter. In effect, she sought to be the weak female who had to
turn to the strong male as shield. In a way, she empowered him as her manager
and guardian, even as she disempowered him by making him financially dependent on her. The rhythms of their relationship were both strikingly Victorian
and strikingly un-Victorian.

We cannot calculate with precision how much the irregularities of her union
influenced and colored her practice of hiding behind Lewes, although we must
assume the "wound" was always present, and perhaps made her strengthen his
role. In a parallel case of some interest, the novelist Mary Elizabeth Braddon
(eighty-five books to her credit, from 1860 to 1916) went to live with the publisher John Maxwell when she was twenty-six. Maxwell had five children and a
wife, who was confined to a lunatic asylum—he could not, therefore, seek a
divorce and marry Braddon. Nevertheless, she bore him six children and finally
married him thirteen years later, in 1874, when his wife died. The point of the
comparison is that Braddon paid socially for her "transgression," for when her
kind of novel was literarily attacked—she wrote "sensational" fiction, in the
mode of Wilkie Collins—her personal life was dredged up as the reason for the
irregularities of her fiction. Like Eliot in her books, she touches in shadowy ways
on this condition, which made her pay even after she married Maxwell.

As Eliot's health continued to give her trouble in early January of 1873,
Blackwood kept coming back with plans for Middlemarch, suggesting a guinea
edition bound in one volume. This, he thought, would give the sales impetus,
and he was correct. He offered Lewes a "lordship" or royalty of 5 shillings per

volume, which comes to almost 25 percent, a lordly lordship. Lewes and Eliot accepted, with Lewes emphasizing it should be hurried out so as to take advantage "of the ground swell beginning which will rapidly affect the libraries and we ought to be ready for the top of the wave." He then lists some of the famous places where the book is being talked up, including among bishops and archbishops at the Academy dinner. He suggests that the guinea edition have something of the same format and same color as the uniform 12-shilling edition of other Eliot works. She was concerned she could not make corrections—Main was discovering errors—but the book was stereotyped and therefore closed for revisions.

By now, John Cross had interceded in the couple's life and was investing monies for Eliot and Lewes, at this time, £2,000–3,000, well over $150,000 in current spending power. As for Lewes, he had been working for some time on a mammoth study called *Problems of Life and Mind,* which would be published in several volumes and would provide alternate views to the religious life Blackwood himself adhered to. The latter accepted the project for future publication, but did express reservations, hoping that Lewes would say nothing to injure the cause of "real religion." He characterized it as Lewes's "Key to all the Mythologies." "If the lamented Casaubon had written it," Blackwood says, "I should have insisted on his publishing at his own risk." He adds he trusts Lewes to be clear and readable. Lewes sent on Volume I on 11 March, but the firm asked him to find another publisher. Lewes tried to reason with the publisher, but rather than disturb the relationship between Eliot and Blackwood, Lewes agreed to seek another outlet. It was the so-called heresies which turned the firm against the volume, what Lewes had possibly foreseen in its being "metafeesically shocked."

Eliot, meanwhile, was reading *Tristram Shandy* aloud, but not laughing too hard because of terrible suffering from tooth and gum pain. Paget recommended removal of the tooth, which was done on 23 January, and this mitigated somewhat the face-ache, but dental problems would recur. Nevertheless, she remained alert, and in a remarkable letter about women, addressed to Mrs. Nassau Senior, who had been appointed temporary inspector of workhouses,* Eliot ranged over how far women had come.

> The influence of one woman's life on the lot of other women is getting greater, with the quickening spread of all influences. One likes to think, though, that two thousand years ago Euripedes made Iphigenia count it a reason for facing her sacrifice bravely that thereby she might help to save Greek women (from a wrong like Helen's) in the time to come. There is no knife at your throat, happily. You have only got to be a good faithful woman such as you have always been, and then the very thought of you will help to mend things. Take it as a sign of that, when I tell you that you

---

*The first woman appointed to this position, and virtually the first woman in any position of authority among English institutions.

have entered into my more cheerful beliefs and made them stronger, because of the glimpses I have had of your character and life.

Eliot's use of the Iphigenia parallel suggests she saw women's efforts in a long historical sweep, so that no one act—not even her friend's appointment—would wipe away the still lowly situation of women.

An invitation to the Priory was now a celebrated event. Even though there was no overall social approval of Eliot's relationship with Lewes, women in increasing numbers accompanied their husbands: independent women who hoped to debate with Eliot on a variety of topics in literature, history, religion, and the like. As Haight points out, there was a certain irony in a couple who were not married and who were not conventional believers living in a house called the Priory. Many jokes were directed at this situation, including Dickens's having said that he had hoped one day to attend "services" at the Priory. But Eliot took it all in stride, including the fact that some people approached her as though she were reigning royalty. One such was Mrs. Frederick Ponsonby, herself solidly connected to the upper reaches of the aristocracy as wife of the queen's private secretary and a granddaughter of Earl Grey (a former prime minister). There was something hieratic in Eliot, something so composed and grave in her manner that she became for those visiting the Priory a combination of royal personage and religious icon. *

Eliot at times welcomed the intense social activity, and at others insisted on her privacy; but as she became more famous, after *Middlemarch*, she seemed to retreat, even wither. The onslaught of people who wanted to meet, touch, or worship made her aware that most of it was hollow. What was building in her mind, now more unconscious than conscious, was the material for *Daniel Deronda*. She had had a glimmer of her subject in the European panorama she had witnessed on the couple's last journey to Germany. Gamblers, aristocrats, common people with faith, arrivistes, and those still on the way up—all came under her eye, particularly at the gambling tables. What she needed for a novel was a firmer sense of subject in which she could contrast those who pursued wealth or enjoyed it as parasites with those who felt a higher calling or a greater sense of innerness.

In some way surely not yet clear to her, this book would become her summation. She would synthesize the social contexts of *Middlemarch*, the yearnings of a Romola-like figure, the social and political fallout from *Felix Holt*, and the faith she had portrayed in *Adam Bede*. In still more personal terms, *Deronda* would contain a shadowy Eliot, although not so intimately as in *Mill*. How all this would come together was a long process, abetted, however, by the unfortunate death in Alexandria on 12 May of Emanuel Deutsch, who became one of the sources for Deronda. She was now financially free to write anything she

* Yale possesses an extremely long letter from Mrs. Ponsonby to Eliot (dated October 1874), in which the former treated the author as a priest or father confessor. Mary Ponsonby's letter is an outpouring of her religious beliefs to someone who had, she felt, achieved perfect balance between science and faith. Like many others, she did not realize how precarious that balance actually was.

wished, and by the spring of 1873, some dim murmurings indicated she would write on a Jewish subject, and by June she began an intense study of Judaism and Judaica. As her idea developed, she thought of it as both a novel and a play. The play seemed to be Lewes's idea, but after her tortured grappling with *The Spanish Gypsy*, Eliot recognized drama was not her calling.

Financial freedom also enabled her to purchase whatever she wanted. The couple purchased a Broadwood piano, which they could have afforded before; and then, at the end of 1873, they indulged in what was the ultimate conspicuous consumption of the nouveau riche, a Morgan landau, a carriage of their own.* A description of Eliot in 1876, by one Mrs. S. M. Downes (who came armed with an introduction from Emerson), gives some sense of the new look: ". . . a slender, tallish woman, with an oval face, abundant hair, doubtless once fair, now almost gray, and questioning light eyes," wearing "a high-bodiced black velvet dress." The dress had simple sleeves and lace at the throat; Eliot wore lace also on top of her head.

Not all of Eliot's money, however, was going for vanity or for material goods commensurate with the couple's rise. The Leweses, in fact, were living quite modestly for their income, with a good deal of it going into investments managed by John Cross. Further, Eliot was helping several people, including Lewes's wife (her lover, Thornton Hunt, died in June of 1873) and her children. But she also tried to help the Brays, who refused, despite the failure of their factory, although she left Cara an annuity of £100. She did not forget Chrissey's children, who needed aid even now that they were adults. She sent sums to Bertie Lewes in Natal, who had named his oldest child after her. She donated other sums to Charlie's wife, Gertrude, and her sister, not for themselves but for charities they deemed worthy. Gertrude's sister, Octavia Hill, wished to devote all her time to housing reform (Dorothea Brooke's great concern), and Eliot contributed £200 to establish an annuity so Octavia could give up teaching. This was not an inconsiderable sum. Eliot also contributed to Girton College, which had been established solely for women, and to other women's causes, such as the Elizabeth Garrett Anderson Hospital and Women's College, as well as a small annual amount to the Comte Fund, to encourage the education of those interested in positivism and to help disseminate its message. But her largest overall contributions were to Agnes Lewes and her children, with Lewes contributing to Agnes's upkeep to the tune of £100 a year, which increased in the mid-1870s to over £150, plus sums for the children.†

One visit to the Priory, on 15 April 1874, that was particularly gratifying

---

* A fashionable two-seater, with a removable top, drawn by a single horse; the model was named after the town Landau in Germany where the design originated.

† In 1874, when Lewes gave Agnes £54, he earned precisely that; in 1875, he gave her £175 and earned £334 (£250 from the third edition of the *Life of Goethe*); in 1876, when he gave her £166, he earned £275; and in the last two years of his life, his earnings came to only £74 in 1877 and to less than £100 in 1878. After his death, Eliot contributed varying amounts. Agnes lived until 1902, and in addition to Eliot's contributions existed on insurance money from Hunt and donations from Charlie and his wife, which was money rerouted from Eliot.

came from her niece, Edith, Isaac's oldest daughter, who broke with her father's rigidity. Edith came with her husband, the vicar of St. Nicholas, and then sent on pictures of Griff House. By now, Eliot had turned her life at Griff into that romantic "hut dream" which people carry with them, in which they invest a former or fantasized dwelling with a certain sacred quality. The hut in their imagination, which they identify with some place where they hope to retreat, is the perfect place, where all experience was prelapsarian, and where, even after the fall from grace, there was no retribution. With human relationships at this place perfect, the individual finds balance, peace, a kind of Zen-like communion with sacred nature. Eliot had invested Griff House with these qualities, as we see in her letter to Edith on 9 May 1874:

> Many thanks for the photographs which I am delighted to have. Dear old Griff still smiles at me with a face which is more like than unlike its former self, and I seem to feel the air through the window of the attic above the drawing-room, from which when a little girl, I often looked towards the distant view of the Coton College [actually the workhouse]—thinking the view rather sublime.

We have jumped ahead somewhat because the letter indicates how desperately the couple wanted to find their perfect house in the woods, how they needed to fulfill her "hut dream," with the woods available for long walks, a solitudinous existence whereby they could sit by the fireplace, read, converse, and, possibly, continue to write.

Since the "hut dream" is an illusion, the dreamer throws off all unpleasantness. With the past as reality isolated, memory or reverie of the dreamlike place takes on qualities of the golden age, the Garden—all equally illusory. That Eliot would contain within herself this memory of the past, and that she could imbue it with such a sacred quality, indicates that for all her rationalism she still needed some faith-like hold on the past, something neither reason nor logic could explain. To the end, she believed there was a great mystery at the "center of it all," and that mystery could be found, in part, in the reveries one held about the perfect place.

Blackwood was always looking for ways in which he could make the best possible use of Eliot's properties, and one of his schemes in early 1873 was to reprint "The Lifted Veil" in a proposed new series of "Tales from Blackwood." He would not interfere, however, if Eliot wished to keep it for a volume of miscellanies. But he would like, he said, this "striking although horribly painful story" to help start the new series. In response, Eliot said she did not want it to be reprinted at present. Instead, she wrote some lines, a kind of motto, which would later be affixed to the story in the Cabinet edition, where it appeared sandwiched between *Silas Marner* and "Brother Jacob." The motto:

> *Give me no light, great heaven, but such as turns*
> *To energy of human fellowship;*

No powers save the growing heritage
That makes completer manhood.

Her reasoning was that the story should not appear in its "dismal loneliness," but in harness with other productions. "There are many things in it," she tells Blackwood, "which I would willingly say over again, and I shall never put them in any other form. But we must wait a little. The question is not in the least one of money, but of care for the best effect of writing, which often depends on circumstances much as pictures depend on light and juxtaposition." That Gothic terror evinced in the story would appear, altered, in *Daniel Deronda,* in the terror-filled dreams Gwendolen Harleth experiences. Eliot found there the things she would "willingly say over again."

19

Toward Deronda

"There are episodes in most men's lives in which their highest qualities can only cast a deferring shadow over the objects that fill their inward vision. . . ."

With *Middlemarch* now part of literary history and with *Deronda* still unshaped, Eliot fell back into that kind of idleness which meant she wished to see few people, except her closest friends. On Fridays, for example, she still saw Georgiana Burne-Jones. More often than not, Lewes engaged in solitary outings. One of the people he ran across on a regular basis at lunches and dinners was John Cross, along with the usual array of titled figures who had literary tastes and professionals who mixed with them. Once a circle like this had developed, as part of a kind of traveling salon, the class barriers were, at least temporarily, removed. But what was occurring in the larger sense was also a slow shift, from aristocratic rule—although aristocratic families still owned a huge, disproportionate chunk of British real estate—toward a gradual meritocracy. Money made some of the difference, but also eminence in a profession, as surgeon and physician (if well connected), as barrister, as research scientist, as social philosopher, and as classicist. Linkage to a top public school or to Oxford or Cambridge in some capacity helped, as did association with the Church of England. There were in this mixture few Catholics or Jews and few businessmen directly involved in making money, although the Benzons were an exception. Whether she attended such parties with Lewes or not, Eliot herself was part of that shift in power; and her novels, while not precisely socially progressive, helped to diminish the class and caste lines which had defined England earlier in the century.

As the couple began to seek a country house, Lewes—ill health to the contrary—used his city time for frequent social activity. When Eliot came along, he hovered over her, to make certain no one wearied her with insipid conversation. One observer mentions how tired and lined her face seemed—the result of tooth and gum ailments—but that nevertheless, she seemed eager and committed to all conversation. Even her "massive features," as they are described, became suffused with a kind of beauty as she was engaged in talk. Her voice, according to Frederic Myers, gave her a mysterious quality, as if her words were emanating from some unknown, unknowable source.

Several contemporaries commented on her "spiritual qualities." Part of it was, of course, her intense intellectuality, which gave her, in conversation, a certainty of her facts outside the scope of even the most educated. Another part was her certainty that life was a balance of pleasures and pains, that no single individual, including herself, could be free of pain and anguish no matter what his or her achievements. But the major point in her spiritualized presence was the way in which she could dramatize herself, so that she communicated an almost preternatural calm, while internally, as we know, she was still uncertain of her role. Even as Myers was remarking on her spirituality, she was telling Elizabeth Stuart Phelps, author of the religious novel *The Gates Ajar*, that the "responsibility of the writer becomes heavier and heavier." She adds that it is only through a new work, which "grows into imperious activity within one," that it is possible to "make a really needed contribution to the poetry of the world. . . ." These are the words of a woman whose external presentation of serenity and ultimate wisdom belies the struggles within.

Then there is the famous Myers commentary on Eliot, which resulted from his association with her and Lewes in May of 1873, when Myers, a Trinity College Fellow, invited the couple to Cambridge. He wrote these words later, in the November 1881 *Century Magazine*, after Eliot's death. The subject was ultimate matters, the great questions of whether or not there is a God and whether or not it was possible to support a moral and ethical individual or society without some absolute spiritual force, called God or the equivalent. The questions went to the very heart of Eliot's fictional work, as well as her personal beliefs. Myers reports, as though verbatim, what Eliot took as her text:

> . . . [her] three words which have been used so often as the inspiring trumpet-calls of men—the words, *God, Immortality, Duty*,—pronounced with terrible earnestness, how inconceivable was the *first*, how unbelievable the *second*, and yet how peremptory and absolute the *third*. Never, perhaps, have sterner accents affirmed the sovereignty of impersonal and unrecompensing Law. I listened, and night fell; her grave, majestic countenance turned toward me like a sibyl's in the gloom; it was as though she withdrew from my grasp, one by one, the two scrolls of promise, and left me the third scroll only, awful with inevitable fates. And when we stood at length and parted, amid that columnar circuit of the forest-trees, beneath the last twilight of starless skies, I seemed to be gazing, like Titus at Jerusalem [the apostle Paul's disciple], on vacant seats and empty halls,—on a sanctuary with no Presence to hallow it, and heaven left lonely of a God.

Myers makes Eliot sound like a spiritual leader, or else, to cite her favorite classical tragedian, Sophocles, like Tiresias. Her female form, her male name, her seeming ability to cut through deception, and her prophetic qualities, as Myers saw her, do recall Tiresias. Myers might dispute the message, but he cherished the moment as revelatory; and it has become one of the most quoted and descriptive passages in Eliot biography.

But before this visit to Cambridge in May, Eliot wrote quite movingly to the painter Edward Burne-Jones about the nature of his art, and, inevitably, about art itself. "It would be narrowness to suppose that an artist can only care for the impressions of those who know the methods of his art as well as feel its effects. Art works for all whom it can touch." We note the Tolstoyan appeal. She says that Burne-Jones's art makes life "larger and more beautiful to us," by which she means it communicates a moral dimension. "I mean that historical life of all the world in which our little personal share of her seems a mere standing room from which we can look all round, and chiefly backward." She notes something sad in it, even a sense of tragedy, in which outer forces urge us on against our inner impulses. She drives home the point that the mind of the artist is reflected in his work, not directly, but morally: a nasty mind makes nasty art, and a meager mind will "bring forth what is meagre."

A good many of these comments and pronouncements are part of a general summing up. With such remarks, Eliot was moving toward her final long statement in fiction, *Daniel Deronda*. For with all its faults of sentimentality, of longueurs and overresearch, the novel does serve as a capstone. As her health deteriorated and her will to write lessened, she needed one work which would include everything; and it was precisely this desire to be inclusive which made *Deronda* into such a supreme and yet problematic work.

In May 1873, Blackwood was beginning to let Lewes down about his manuscript of *Problems of Life and Mind*. Lewes, however, refused to go quietly and argued that the publisher misunderstood his position on religion. He accused Blackwood of taking the most radical explanation offered in the book, instead of seeing that he, Lewes, was offering two possibilities. It was a standoff: Blackwood affirming traditional values; Lewes offering an opening to a set of values which took into account Darwin, Huxley, and that entire generation of scientists. We have here, in miniature, the larger conflict between the religious faithful and the supporters of the "new science"; that struggle, among others, between Bishop Wilberforce—who argued a fundamentalist biblical explanation of the earth's beginnings—and the evolutionists. *

* Darwin, now a friend, had called at the Priory as recently as 23 March. On 8 May, the death of John Stuart Mill eliminated another strong force who could have supported Lewes's views. William Wilberforce (known unaffectionately as "Soapy Sam") was first Bishop of Oxford and then Bishop of Westminster, but made his reputation as an orator trying to hold the line between high-church and low-church factions among Anglicans, as an opponent of Catholicism, and, most particularly, as an adversary of evolution and evolutionary theory. A famous moment, known to generations of students, came in 1860 when Wilberforce squared off against Thomas Henry Huxley at the annual meeting of the British Association for the Advancement of Science. The bishop asked: "Was it from

In June, the couple spent a most pleasant weekend with Jowett in Oxford and met a varied group of visitors, including Mark Pattison and W. H. Thompson, Master of Trinity College. Jowett was enormously impressed with Eliot as a woman of the highest intelligence who "throws an interesting light on every subject on which she speaks. She seems to me just right about philosophy, quite clear on materialism, women's rights, idealism, etc." He added: "She wanted to have an ethical system founded upon altruism; and argued that there was no such thing as doing any action because it was right or reasonable, but only because it accorded with one's better feelings towards others." He concedes she does not condemn those who follow popular religion, inasmuch as life is so complex and one's own path so intricate and uncertain it was impossible to be condemnatory.

Jowett's view of Eliot's philosophical position is, obviously, reductive. But as she approached her final long fiction, she was still attempting to find some middle path through all the minefields of nineteenth-century beliefs: Comtean and Harrisonian positivism, religious orthodoxy of one kind or another, utilitarianism (Bentham's or John Stuart Mill's), Huxley's agnosticism, Darwin's evolutionism and determinism, Spencer's social Darwinism, and Marxism and its various offshoots. All of them in one respect or another appeared to her too mechanical, although nearly all had some appeal. Positivism, she felt, was becoming a religion of its own, and she could not follow. Utilitarianism, as she considered it, was neglectful of human foibles, anomalies, and uncertainties. It flourished too much on clear-cut choices and assumed too much reason. Huxley's agnosticism appealed to her, but she could not completely forgo the idea of something divine, which was not "beyond" but within the individual. What she wanted, also, was some philosophical position which represented her as a woman. All these other developments and ideas were male-oriented, devised by men, and, except for Mill's, based on a masculine outlook. Hers was a philosophy based on giving, on looking to others' needs, on self-denial when necessary, on creating in oneself the kind of behavior one would like to see throughout society.

After Oxford and Jowett, the Leweses spent several days with the Cross family at Weybridge. On 24 June, they left for a rambling trip to Europe; but, more important, just after this date, *Deronda* began to shape itself in Eliot's mind.

---

his grandfather or grandmother that Huxley claimed descent from a monkey?" The scientist's response carried the day. "I asserted—and I repeat—that a man has no reason to be ashamed of having an ape for his grandfather. If there was an ancestor whom I should feel shame in recalling, it would rather be a *man*, a man of restless and versatile intellect who, not content with an equivocal success in his own sphere of activity, plunges into scientific questions with which he has no real acquaintance, only to obscure them by an aimless rhetoric, and distract the attention of his hearers from the real point at issue by eloquent digressions and skilled appeals to religious prejudice." While Huxley won the moment, the controversy raged, and Eliot, as we know, was herself drawn in to both Darwinism and species determinism. Herbert Spencer, for his part, adapted Darwin, to fit what came to be known as social Darwinism, with the assertion that society, like nature, functions on natural selection; that the fittest survive; that a state of nature is the preferred basis for the best society. From this a laissez-faire economics flowed, and Eliot's social contract, her pleas for comity, would prove illusory.

She did not see it as two separate stories—one of Gwendolen Harleth and her unfortunate marriage and the other of Daniel Deronda and his discovery of his Jewish background—but as one story with two interdependent, intertwined elements. It is, nevertheless, difficult to read the novel as she intended, since the quality of the Gwendolen section is literarily so much more compelling than the Deronda part, however fervent Eliot meant his religious affiliation to be. *

Their plan in Europe was, as Eliot put it, no plan. One idea they had was to visit the D'Albert-Durades in Geneva, but heat drove them to the Vosges, to Plombières-les-Bains, twenty miles south of Épinal, the kind of spa they preferred. Once there, they hated to leave, quartered as they were in their own chalet, with a private garden, and splendid food, as well as the waters for bathing and for drinking. This usually led to a temporary alleviation of their ailments, and it certainly helped Eliot in the short run. Since what was developing in her now seemed to be a kidney ailment (as diagnosed from our point of view), the waters would be only helpful, not curative. Lewes, however, in their characteristic back-and-forth movement of ailments, turned up with a seriously infected ear resulting in partial deafness.

From the Vosges, they turned to Luxeuil (another Vosges spa, just south of Plombières), spending a week there, and then went on to Frankfurt before heading to Hamburg on 2 August. Although Hamburg was full of friends and admirers, this time they wanted to keep to themselves, and so they checked to see who was in town. When friends appeared, they started back, arriving at the Priory on 23 August. Travel was becoming increasingly difficult. Eliot commented that railway journeys "were too formidable for us old weak creatures," and the heat of the high summer also discouraged them. When they started out in June, she indicates, they were "both shattered, and needed quiet rather than the excitement of seeing friends and acquaintances." Writing to D'Albert-Durade, to explain why they curtailed their trip short of Geneva, she omitted her probable desire to get on with her new project, the fact that everything else began to recede.

Lewes revealed some of the background here: While in Fontainebleau, on 29 June, he and Eliot walked in the park and then sat and discussed "new projects for novel and play." On 30 July, while in Frankfurt, Lewes purchased books on Jewish subjects for Eliot; and on Friday, 1 August, they went to the Frankfurt synagogue, "for Mutter's purposes," he tells his son Charles. They were also reading, together, Leopold Kompert's stories of life in the ghetto. By the end of the trip, Eliot was filled with her new project.

The couple planned to stay at the Priory for one week and then spend some time at Blackbrook, the house near Bickley, in Kent, that they had rented on a

---

* Harriet Beecher Stowe, for one, wrote Eliot extensively about the novel, and she clearly distinguished between the two parts. She was stirred by the Deronda segment—Stowe's husband was a student of Jewish life and customs—but she found the Gwendolen sections "artistic gems." She finds the young woman an infinitely intriguing character, not only as an individual but as a reflection of a heathenish and selfish society. The American writer was, of course, seeking condemnation of a materialistic culture.

year's lease before they went abroad. But Blackbrook turned out to be a mixed experience, apparently in keeping with much in their present life. It contained little in the way of furnishings they could use—the furniture they had seen earlier had been removed—and they were forced to rely on what they had sent on, which did not arrive on schedule. They decided then and there, on their first day, to stay for only two months. As Eliot told Mrs. Cross, the house "is old and cold and wants rebuilding—in fact is too much like our own bodies. And, as usual, we were too precipitate in our considerations about practical matters—engaging ourselves without due examination into facts."

The house itself was well situated, with the kind of isolation they required. The lawn, trees, and relative seclusion once again reproduced Eliot's memories of Griff. Their visitors included John Cross, now known affectionately as their "tall nephew." It was a curious scene, with Cross already worshipful of Eliot, himself a bachelor in his thirties, handling the finances of the couple by way of Lewes, serving as Lewes's friend as well, being identified as "nephew," and, seemingly, less of kin than of kind. What Eliot suspected of Cross's feelings we cannot tell. She knew that Alexander Main, among others, fawned over her; but Cross seemed more masculine, very much a man of the world, and not simply a sycophant. In addition, she and Lewes were familiar with Mrs. Cross and with John's sisters. He appeared regularly now, becoming part of the Lewes household.

One advantage of Blackbrook was the easy access to Darwin, who lived nearby, at Downe. With the publication of *The Descent of Man* in 1871, Darwin was at the height of his fame and notoriety. Maria Congreve, more worshipful than ever, came down for a day visit, as did still another celebrant, the carver and gift-giver Elma Stuart. Sir John Lubbock, who shared scientific interests with Lewes, and his wife drew the couple into local life. But for the most part, Eliot wished to enjoy the solitude of the place, and she had, after all, her three servants with her for all the distasteful chores.

As she was moving toward her fifty-fourth birthday, she was aware of final things, especially since *Deronda* would be a synthesis of all she thought. She used the pretense of the 1865 portrait by Sir Frederic Burton, a kind of pre-Raphaelite Eliot, as a way of commenting upon herself to Elma Stuart. "I am now a bit like it. . . . Imagine a first cousin of the old Dante's—rather smoke-dried—a face with lines in it that seem a map of sorrows. These portraits seen beforehand are detestable introductions. . . ." Blackwood broke into questions of mortality with good news on *Middlemarch*, which, although it continued to sell in the 21-shilling edition, the publisher wanted to put into a one-volume edition at 7 / 6, on which he would pay a royalty of 1 / 6 on every copy sold beyond 2,000 (with a £50 honorarium up front). Eliot assented to this proposal, to be prepared at once but not published precipitately. She wished to make corrections of errors she had picked up in the four-volume edition, and wanted it to be called a "revised edition."

Concern about the one-volume *Middlemarch* may also have served another function, to revive her from what she considered her "feeble" condition and prepare her for her next long haul. *Deronda* would be of about the same length as *Middlemarch* and even more ambitious. Not only did it intertwine two stories (as did the earlier novel) but it took Eliot into unfamiliar religious and cultural areas. We do not have a "Quarry" for *Deronda*, but if we did, it would surely prove as ambitious as the one for *Middlemarch* and involve reading, as well, in several languages. Among other preparations, Eliot worked on Hebrew.

To Mrs. Cross, Eliot expressed regret that the house was so dilapidated they could not contemplate making it their sole home. She recognizes that these "troubles" are not meaningful in the larger scale of values; they are, in fact, "pitiable." But she rues the time and effort spent on them, nevertheless, and experiences guilt for indulging them. She mentions how favorably she views Henry Sidgwick, who kept the larger world in mind and acted out of conscience, not expedience. In 1869, Sidgwick petitioned for the abolition of Cambridge University's religious tests for Fellows (the famous Thirty-nine Articles); and when that was not forthcoming, he resigned his fellowship on personal grounds. He was permitted, however, to retain his lectureship, so respected was he by his colleagues. This brief vignette of Sidgwick's act and Eliot's approval—"a chief favorite of mine"—indicates how completely she located moral advocacy not in larger social movement but in individual behavior. Sidgwick could have been one of her literary heroes. *

The decision not to remain at Blackbrook did not discourage the Leweses entirely from seeking a country house, which they now planned to keep in addition to the Priory. What they still required was isolation and yet accessibility to conveniences, such as railways. By 31 October, they were back at the Priory with their health holding up.

In another area altogether, we get a view of Eliot and Lewes from a very different point of view, from one of Herbert Spencer's disciples, the American John Fiske. An assistant librarian at Harvard, a man with good connections, Fiske received an invitation to the Priory and came on Sunday afternoon, 23 November, the day after Eliot's fifty-fourth birthday. Fiske had a good deal to say. On Lewes, he mentions first his unprepossessing appearance: wizened, old, and feeble-looking, little, "ever so homely." Yet when he speaks, he is transformed, Fiske says. "His manners are *fascinating beyond all description* and he took my heart captive at once. I never before saw a man who seemed so full of the divine indescribable something that makes a man different from common man—and all this in spite of his homely and meagre and puny physique. I don't wonder that he captivated George Eliot; I think he is just the man that any woman who had an eye for the spirituelle would fall in love with."

At thirty-one, when he made the observation, Fiske describes Lewes as we

---

* To John Cross, she indicated how she honored the Hebraic and Christian traditions because they gave the individual the ability to rise against his, or her, "unregulated passion" into a sense of duty. And nonbelievers, she says, "may often more beneficially cherish the good within them and be better members of society by a conformity based on the recognized good in the public belief, than by a non-conformity which has nothing but negatives to offer." Conformity, however, must be sincere and without hypocrisy.

think Eliot saw him; and, we must remember, Fiske was observing Lewes in his decline, at fifty-six, only five years from his death. The key element is "transformation," not only for Lewes but also for Eliot, two physically unattractive people who became quite something else when they spoke, or became animated and interested. As for Eliot, Fiske became an immediate admirer, even a worshipper. Right off, he denies she is a "fright," which is what he was probably told to expect. Her observes her as a plain-looking woman, much better-looking, he says, than George Sand. While no "blooming beauty," she has a "good" nose, rich blue and expressive eyes, a very large mouth, hair that is light-colored and profuse. All of these features had been described before, but Fiske sees them as a pattern, not "ugly" or "horse-faced," but pleasing. He even sees her as a motherly type, perhaps because she demonstrated such concern for Lewes.

Fiske's physical panegyrics were only the beginning, for he fully appreciated Eliot's mental abilities. He asserted he had never before seen such "a clear-headed woman." Then in the tones of the day, he condescends but means praise: "She thinks just like a man, and can put her thoughts into clear and forcible language at a moment's notice." He found her knowledge "amazing." He says he had never found a man, except Spencer (at whose feet Fiske had placed himself), who could state a case equal to her. She knew as much about Homer, in the original Greek, as did Fiske, and this was one of his specialties. He was beside himself at her knowledge of Homer's poems, "knowing the ins and outs of the question, and *not putting on any airs*, but talking sincerely of the thing as a subject which has deeply interested her—this is, indeed, quite a new experience."

Fiske thinks she and Lewes are "a wonderful couple," and that Lewes is fortunate indeed to have such a "simple-hearted, honest, and keenly sympathetic wife." He agrees with Spencer, who thinks Eliot "is the greatest woman that has lived on the earth—the female Shakespeare, so to speak." Even allowing for Fiske's gushiness—he was writing to his wife in America and eager to impress her—there is quite a bit that rings true in his assessment. Eliot could effortlessly roll out the knowledge she had acquired from the kind of reading few Victorians were capable of; and she was able to translate complex ideas into fairly simple language—"no airs," as Fiske put it. As for Lewes, he still retained his liveliness, his ability to entertain, and his way of bringing forth wide knowledge in interesting conversation.

Just two and a half weeks before Fiske's visit, Eliot revealed to John Blackwood she had "slowly simmering" another big book, but she was worried that with so many people giving supremacy to Middlemarch they "are sure not to like any future book so well." At the same time, she was gratified the world could absorb so much of Middlemarch.

Although we should not make too much of the episode which follows, some of Eliot's uncertainties surface when we see her entering into a spiritualist séance, on 16 January 1874. Lewes found it amusing and a source of mockery, but Eliot attempted to experience what so many of her friends were trying—the séance had been arranged by Erasmus Darwin, Charles Darwin's brother. Lewes refused to participate, while Eliot tried, only for the couple to leave "in disgust," as Emma (Mrs. Charles) Darwin later described the event. Eliot entered into the episode as a way of investigation, and she had come out convinced, more firmly than ever, that it was degrading, farcical, an imposture. That she should try, even if pressured by friends, is a suggestive comment on how desperately she wanted to find some spiritual anchor in experience; but, at the same time, her rationalistic impulses would not permit her to accept what she perceived as something intellectually shoddy.

In a November 1873 policy statement to John Blackwood, she made it clear she was not to be represented by bits and pieces, even in the Main anthology of her sayings, which she had approved. She insisted on being seen whole. "Unless my readers," she writes, "are more moved towards the ends I seek by my works as a whole than by an assemblage of extracts, my writings are a mistake. I have always exercised a severe watch against anything that could be called preaching, and if I have ever allowed myself in dissertation or in dialogue [anything] which is not part of the *structure* of my books, I have there sinned against my own laws." She fears that Main's book of sayings will encourage just that possibility.

But the issue is broader. Eliot's care is connected to her recognition of how morality and ethics cannot be finalized in pieces, as they seem to be in formal religion. If she is to avoid traditional Christianity or Judaism, she must move between dictates, into those gray areas of behavior which characterized, for example, Lydgate's choices in *Middlemarch* and which foreshadow Gwendolen Harleth's decisions in *Daniel Deronda*. Eliot knew her strengths: if she were to have any psychological impact, if she were to delve beneath surfaces and types into individual behavior, then she could not, in her eyes, be categorized as advocating this or that type of behavior. Not unexpectedly, she expressed belated misgivings about Main's anthology, and his effort, now, to expand the preface to the collection. Frightened off, Main for his part retained the original preface in the second edition and added nothing from *Middlemarch*.

After the couple spent Christmas with the Crosses, Eliot's journal for the new year, on 1 January 1874, is typical, in that it mixed blessings with dire predictions. She does count her blessings, including admirable children, kind servants, the devotion of Lewes to her and she to him, abundant wealth that went well beyond immediate needs, but also the sense that her unspeakable joy in Lewes "must one day end in parting." She admits that Lewes's intellectual activities barely keep him going, and her assessment is the first real recognition she may lose him. He was thinner than ever, dyspeptic, carried by "wonderful elasticity and nervous energy." As for herself, she says she has been rendered virtually helpless for intellectual work "by constant headache and nausea." These recurring conditions suggest that her kidney ailment was now the governing force of her indisposition, although, of course, other factors could have been involved. Her main regret was that she could not regain "the uninterrupted power of work." With this, she welcomed in the next year.

The new book was also heralded in. *Daniel Deronda* was to reach the sketch stage in January and February of 1874. Some impetus was given the novel by

Emanuel Deutsch, the German-Jewish scholar who had been a frequent visitor at the Priory and who had given Eliot Hebrew lessons (which she continued to pursue on her own). Once he had journeyed to the Middle East and the Wailing Wall in Jerusalem, Deutsch became a passionate supporter of Palestine as a Jewish national home. He was also a doomed man, destined to die young of cancer; and his intense intellectual energies became obsessively focused on a homeland even as he saw his life slipping away. When Deutsch died, on 12 May 1873, Eliot had her tragic figure, in Mordecai, clearly based on Deutsch and his aspirations. *

By the time Deutsch died, Eliot was moving along on *Deronda,* and it is a sign of her own independence from the scholar and her research that she concentrated first on Gwendolen Harleth. Book I, consisting of ten chapters, is called "The Spoiled Child." Yet as she accumulated increasingly the material for the Jewish parts, she found her time wasted on indisposition, "incapacitating headache and other miserable sensations," as she told Alexander Main on 14 January. But the novel had, nevertheless, gained in firmness, with a basic plan, focus, and direction. Her reading intensified, despite ill health, and she referred to it as "dwelling among the tombs." That is why the Gwendolen segment became so important to her, removing her from the "tombs" and reintroducing her into the living.

But living was becoming more difficult. An ominous note was sounded in early February, for it was becoming clearer that Eliot's ailments were connected to what would eventually kill her. She had been "a sad invalid," she told Barbara Bodichon, and then suffered a new kind of attack, what she called a neuralgia above the left hip. The condition exhausted and drained her. She seemed to recover with temporary remedies, but an examination by Dr. Clark on 4 February indicated "concretion in the kidney"—kidney stones. Clark, however, was not quite certain of this diagnosis; but Eliot suffered another attack the next day. The succession of attacks and then withdrawal, leaving her enervated, was characteristic of a kidney malfunction. Nevertheless, visitors continued to arrive at the Priory, including Ruskin, Du Maurier, and Edith Simcox.

Eliot was also occupied with Spencer and Dickens. The latter's life was revealed in the fullness of its anguish by the publication of Forster's third volume of his biography, covering the years 1852 to 1870; including, as well, Forster's personal and professional attack on Lewes. But most of Eliot's commentary was saved for Spencer, who was under siege from several sources. Sara Hennell had written an article for the *Examiner* called "Mr. Spencer and the Women," an attack on his belittling of women as potential government leaders in his *Study of Sociology.* Sara had privately indicated to Eliot far more dislike of Spencer's

---

* The Pforzheimer Library Eliot Notebooks (especially the fourth volume, edited by William Baker, 1985) indicate how intense her work on background materials became. From emphases on the Hebrew language to statistics on the world's Jewish population to lists of further readings to accumulated comments on the history of the race, Eliot tried to find contexts for her novel. Although the story line was hers, her reading and notes suggest she was profoundly guided by her reading, as much as she had been for *Romola.*

position than she eventually put into print. Although Spencer fully deserved the barrage, Eliot deflected this criticism of her close friend and pointed out he was "running the gauntlet in rather a fatiguing way between Cambridge men who are criticising his physics and psychology, and historians who are criticising the 'Sociological Tables,' on which he has already spent £500 in the hope that he is doing the world a service." She cites still another attack, from John Fletcher Moulton, who carried on a journalistic give-and-take with Spencer. Eliot's tone indicates he does not need still another assault, this time from Sara, and that "philosophical celebrity" has opened him up to potshots from one and all. She remained loyal.

She also remained as constrained as ever in her political views. The 1867 Reform Bill had brought in many more (male) voters, and, like Blackwood, Eliot worried about the results.* "I who am no believer in Salvation by Ballot," she writes her publisher, "am rather tickled that the first experiment with it has turned against its adherents [Gladstone replaced Disraeli as prime minister and was himself replaced in 1874, after passage of the Secret Ballot Act of 1872]. And I heartily wish that with the outgoing of this ministry there might go out for ever the fashion of indulging an imbecile literary vanity in high places—as if it were not putting on a fool's cap instead of laurels for a man who has the most responsible business in the country to be turning the Shield of Achilles into doggerel of this sort—'Boötes, hight to boot the Wain.' " The man revealing "imbecile literary vanity" was William Gladstone, who published "The Shield of Achilles" in *Contemporary Review* (February 1874). What Eliot neglected to say is that his chief opponent for the last decade or more was another vain literary man, Benjamin Disraeli, whose beginnings were in fashionable novels and whose vanity extended to his manner of dress as well. Of course, Disraeli was a Tory, Gladstone a Liberal, and Eliot's tastes, like Blackwood's, ran conservative.

Very little in her chatter would indicate that, despite the discomfort of kidney stones, Eliot was sketching out *Deronda*, although it is unclear how far she went by the end of February. Her journals of 1861–77 mention "sketches towards Daniel Deronda," although her letters during the period of composition are curiously empty of references to the novel. She was reading, among other books, in that buildup of history and detail: Grätz's *Geschichte der Juden*, Milman's *History of the Jews*, Renan's *Histoire des langues sémitiques*, Stanley's *Böhmische Juden*, Erckmann-Chatrian's *Le Juif polonais*, Kompert's *Geschichte einer Gasse*. The chief danger for Eliot was that the Jewish element would be drowned in history, buried under detail and backgrounding.

Possibly because of the heaviness of her reading or the onerousness of her plans for *Deronda*, possibly for deep personal reasons, she felt the need to leaven the present. In any event, she brought together her poems, for a volume to be called *The Legend of Jubal, and Other Poems*. Not that these poems were

---

* Carlyle, in *Shooting Niagara: and After?*, also found the 1867 Reform Bill a dangerous act. Eliot seemed to agree with him that it pushed England "into the Niagara Rapids."

featherweight. Blackwood, in fact, asked Eliot if she had anything lighter. The poems had in the main been published in magazines, starting in 1865, but her most accomplished poem had not been published before and was thus "new"—"O May I Join the Choir Invisible." Also "new" were the "Brother and Sister" sonnets. Although we have commented on these poems earlier, when they were written, Eliot's timing is of interest. As she felt herself aging, and as she exaggerated what an old, decrepit couple she and Lewes were, the brother–sister relationship intensified in her mind as a remembrance of lost events, of spent time, of a period which could be recalled only prismatically.

The brother–sister relationship, in memory, somehow transcends whatever else had transpired. The terms of the relationship were marriage, now severed by separation and divorce. Eliot's imagery is not quite transcendent, but her longing for another kind of "marriage" is apparent. It is a marriage she and Lewes could not have had, since they met as experienced adults, not as pristine children. The sequence is fitting in that Eliot was embarking on a long novelistic journey in which childhood and background—Deronda's in particular—would center her work; and this contemplation may have brought her back to her own childhood, when the wedding of two siblings transcended all other experiences. She reveals a desire to return to fundamentals, to reassert family primacy—for this woman who never had children and, so far, did not have even a marriage. The poems published at this time suggest all the inner schisms and conflicts.

"O May I Join the Choir Invisible," which concludes the volume, is associated with the brother–sister sonnets. The final poem is an "ending," a conclusion which winds back to the beginning. Even as she enters her own particular novelistic summation in Deronda, she is contemplating final things. "O may I join the choir invisible / Of those immortal dead who live again / In minds made better by their presence. . . ." She was thinking of immortality—as a person, a novelist, and a woman who had defied convention—but she was unwilling to forsake those earlier memories, however painful. In the combined Deronda venture and the volume of poems, she reveals a circling around of her life, a circumlocution through which she can express whatever she has been and now is. That she was not a greater poet does not subvert the effort, which was to capture it all in the mid-1870s, as if she could then retire from the arena, as she indeed did.

Blackwood picked up the sadness of the poems, remarking on the "solemn cadence and power" and noting "almost a warning voice" about them. They are clearly didactic, nudging, imploring, moving readers toward some higher anagogic sense of themselves. Eliot had now polished her vision of how each individual transcended self in order to find the better self; a quest undertaken, incidentally, in parallel fashion by Matthew Arnold, and earlier by Carlyle. The "Choir Invisible" is just such an exhortation: to create an example of the sublime as a guide for those who might lead little lives. Her fiction had been from the first a vehicle for showing people how to reach into themselves for something better. Now she was repeating it in what is her most deeply felt poem, and then again lengthily in her novel to come. She viewed Deronda as part of a reassessment, almost forty years into the queen's rule, of what is valuable in life and what is dross. Through pain, anguish, and intense suffering, Gwendolen Harleth must recognize that her sense of Victorian comfort, an unearned comfort, could not suffice once she entered the real world; that she could not shield or buffer herself from the fate of a woman, which may be a horrendous marriage or some mysterious, dark fear.

Her linkage to Grandcourt is a sign Eliot was ratcheting up the connubial machine a few more notches, to a new level of pain. But the two marriages— Gwendolen and Grandcourt, Dorothea and Casaubon—are of the same kind. Casaubon's emotional abuse is not much different from Grandcourt's psychological cruelty; and both women marry because of advantages that prove illusory. Each in her pride and delusion thinks she will prevail—Dorothea through her intellect and desire to give, Gwendolen through her manipulative powers; and both come away crushed by the experience.

The Legend of Jubal, and Other Poems was published in early May 1874. The manuscript copy was inscribed to "my beloved Husband, George Henry Lewes," whose tenderness for twenty years, she says, "has alone made my work possible for me." She also added three lines from "The Legend of Jubal," a prophetic statement of her fears her marital situation was not to last long: "And the last parting now began to send / Diffusive dread through love and wedded bliss, / Thrilling them into finer tenderness." At this time, in early to middle 1874, there was enormous cross-referencing in Eliot's life. She was confronting death at several levels; in her own aging, in Lewes's illnesses (although for the time being he seemed to recover), in her awareness that twenty years marked a milestone in a relationship. And yet at still other levels, there was an equal awareness she was not finished with her work, that something large and spacious remained to be done, and *that* would possibly postpone final things. As she moved back and forth between *Jubal* and *Deronda* in its planning stages, she found she was not only shaping material, she was being reshaped by her attitudes toward that material. She was not yet finished with her own development. The poems and *Deronda* play off against each other, as though the collecting of one meant she had to write the other: the poems as emotion recollected in some kind of tranquillity, the novel as a positive furtherance of her personal philosophy.

Meanwhile, Jewish material poured in. Deutsch's friend and associate on his *Literary Remains*, Lady Emily Strangford, told Eliot of how the rabbis had warned that while those who returned to Palestine should be considered saints, they also should not work, but instead depend on charitable donations—part of Eliot's gathering of information. The latter was considering a journey to the Middle East with Lewes, and Lady Strangford cautioned that autumn was preferable to spring; from that, she outlined a strenuous regime which neither Eliot nor Lewes felt up to undertaking. *

Although Lady Strangford urged them to see the Middle East, what she

---

* Lady Strangford, incidentally, was a considerable woman: a published author of a serious book called *Egyptian Sepulchres and Syrian Shrines* and then, after the death of her husband, a trained nurse with an active interest in providing health care for the poor of England.

described as the land of the future, Eliot and Lewes chose a quite different course. At the beginning of June they would depart for a four-month sojourn just fifteen miles from the Priory, near Redhill, Surrey, staying in a cottage at Earlswood Common. For the first time, she recognized that reasons of health made it impossible for her to do research on the scene. *Deronda* is, in essence, a historical novel, although it takes place in her present, the sole Eliot novel which is contemporary. The Jewish material, and the concomitant background of the emerging Zionist question, brought her into areas where on-the-scene observation and research were possible, especially since she was learning Hebrew. Some of the staleness of the historical background can be traced to the fact that while Eliot had absorbed it intellectually, she did not assimilate it into her own thoughts; and, as a consequence, the experience is less than whole. Her health had become a factor in her creative process.

Presentation copies of *Jubal* were sent to Alexander Main, Anthony Trollope, Cara Bray, and others, as well as to Lewes's sister-in-law Susanna, to whom she signed off as from "her affectionate sister." This, too, was a departure for Eliot, who had forsworn presentation copies; but the poems quite possibly meant something special, catching up as they did the entire cycle of her life. She would appear to be sinking into solipsism, the result of poor health, surely, but also the consequence of her growing pessimism about amelioration, either societal or individual. Her "philosophy" of the transcendence of self, of self reaching toward higher achievement, of self enriched by way of suffering—all of these appear to have deserted her in the short run, even while she advocated them in the long.

Her opinion on the English Poor Laws—revealed by Dickens as scandalous— indicates how pessimistic she was about change. In writing to Mrs. Nassau Senior, Eliot argued that government organization of the poor, in poorhouses where they almost literally wasted away, must be bypassed in favor of individual initiative. She asserted that while she knew many poor in her youth (agricultural poor, quite different from urban poor), she had little practical experience; she felt incompetent to judge. But judge she does, castigating government efforts, but then pulling back because she does not feel strongly enough to intervene. She creates a vision of a typical pauper girl—"stubborn, apathetic, capable of violence," as Mrs. Senior describes the pauper—and wonders if she can be improved, or if she is any better than another pauper who might be more vicious and yet contain a "more human sort of passion in her." Eliot's position suggests weariness, not at direct action, but even at the subject. She says she favors some kind of home education which "teaches" emotions to interact with the "common needs of life, and create that interest in means and results which is the chief part of cleverness." Overall, she views the pauper system as "communistic," vitiating individual personal responsibility and activity, as though realistically someone within the system could be activated to perform along the lines she suggests. She does perceive, through it all, that the systemic evils of pauper treatment should be recognized, but she is unclear about where to go once recognition occurs.

Her remarks here do not mean that as an imaginative writer she must have views on every issue; but her comments do indicate a certain exhaustion meant she could not bring a meaningful philosophy to practical problems. For fictional purposes, this "confusion" might even be useful, since it allowed a single-minded focus: the need for individual action without hope of social support. The flip side, however, is less promising, for it suggests she was merely circling around. Implied is that the loss of religious direction meant a slithery path that led to inconclusive morality and ethics. It was a melancholy thought, for Eliot and others, that man needed a transcendental force to keep him in line, since she realized such a force was no longer credible.

John Blackwood, meanwhile, felt that both Lewes and Eliot were waxing, not waning, and he foresaw her novel "on the stocks." Lewes, he says, thinks Eliot would begin soon—it was now nearing the end of May—once her oppressive doubts at beginning anything lifted. The publisher makes light of such doubts, but they were indeed oppressive. *

In the meantime, the one-volume *Middlemarch* appeared and provided still another source of income. By 2 June, they were ready to start their four-month stay at Earlswood Common, in Surtey, a period which proved rewarding. Eliot worked steadily on *Deronda*, and Lewes, now temporarily rejuvenated, was able to concentrate on the second volume of his *Problems of Life and Mind*. All was not work, however, and they enjoyed drives in the countryside or long walks—all the time looking, still, for a permanent home outside London. They were not recluses, either. They welcomed Lewes's son Charles and his wife, and their daughter, Blanche. John Cross visited and stayed for dinner, as did Maria Congreve and her sister, as well as Elma Stuart—the contingent of devotees. The country experience made Eliot almost expansive, or so she tells Mrs. Cross. She speaks of their "happiness in the secure peace of the country, and the good we already experience in soul and body from the sweet breezes over hill and common, the delicious silence, and the unbroken spaces of the day." The country girl had come alive, despite the chill weather that made winter clothes necessary in the middle of June. She was enchanted with the area and told friends they would like to settle there permanently. They saw a house that seemed suitable, but were discouraged by a sign on an adjoining piece of land indicating it could be let for building.

To John Blackwood, she reported from Earlswood Common she was "brewing my future big book with more or less (generally less) belief in the quality of the liquor which will be drawn off." Eliot had noted in her journal that once in the country she hoped she could sink "deep shafts" into *Deronda*. It suddenly seemed to her that her amount of time was doubled, for, even with guests, the couple avoided heavy entertaining or socializing. Their compatability as a couple made

---

* Given her depression, James Thomson's gift of "The City of Dreadful Night" was not exactly a booster of spirits. But in acknowledging the poem to Thomson, Eliot praised it, and yet at the same time said she hoped the poet would enlarge his sense of human fellowship and write in more heroic strains. Eliot simply could not accept such a dour, pessimistic view of mankind, even while her view of herself was not that distant from a "dreadful night."

it possible for them to sink back into their lives and miss the outside world less
and less. Their life was of course rather easy, what with their full retinue of
servants to handle cooking, cleaning, and other mundane affairs, and even with
two dogs in attendance, a Skye terrier and a brown spaniel. The Skye, true to
its terrier pedigree, yapped so much Eliot was finding it an annoyance—the
extent of her complaints. Lewes referred to their stay as "our sweet monotony of
existence—never seeing a soul—but working like negros."

The interaction of the two creates a curious foreshadowing of another relationship, in the mid-twentieth century, in France, that between Simone de
Beauvoir and Jean-Paul Sartre. The influence on Beauvoir is well documented,
from the French writer's early reading of The Mill on the Floss and her identification with Maggie Tulliver to her plan late in life to do a television program on
Eliot. The parallels go much deeper than "influence," however. Both Eliot and
Beauvoir became marked women because of their efforts to live outside conventional constraints—Eliot very much the bourgeois despite her adventurous
moves, Beauvoir also a bourgeois despite her even more adventurous existence.
But the paradoxes are enormous. For while Beauvoir preached female equality
and wrote the twentieth-century primer on justice for the "second sex," she
was in effect Sartre's servant. Whatever the conditions of her own life and her
requirements, his needs came first, whether it was his manuscripts which
required reading and revision, his magazine (Les Temps Modernes) which called
for editing and supervising, or his health which demanded attention. For this
woman who advocated justice between the sexes, he was the primary object in
her life, and she enslaved herself to him, even while his infidelities wounded
her deeply. Eliot, who was hesitant to support any explicit female causes, on
the other hand, had attached herself to a man who played Beauvoir to her
Sartre. Like Beauvoir, although on a smaller scale, Lewes had his own estimable
career; but his main occupation during his twenty-four years with Eliot was to
ensure that her career remained primary. He gathered material for her, discussed
her manuscripts, read her work in various stages, served as her agent, handled
all the monies accruing from her books, and corresponded with publishers over
quality of paper and binding, publicity, and advertising. He protected and
shielded her, until his death remaining a buffer between her and the rest of life.
Like Beauvoir, he was "on call," and while there was reciprocity—more than
that between the French couple—the balance definitely tipped toward Eliot.

Resemblances go even further. For even as Beauvoir was importuned by
women, like Violette Leduc and others, who threw themselves emotionally at
her, Eliot was of course in much the same position with Edith Simcox, Elma
Stuart, and Maria Congreve. Each writer drew to herself the lavish attention of
women whose devotion and desire for discipleship suggested eroticism. Beauvoir
tried to dispel all talk of lesbian attachments, but they were apparently there,
and not infrequent; whereas for Eliot, as far as we can determine, such talk had
no basis in fact. That she attracted lesbian attention is unquestionable, but that
her sexual preference was heterosexual also seems unquestionable. Obviously,
the absence of the full Simcox and Congreve correspondence leaves a gap in

our assessment. Yet overall, these devoted disciples, whatever the extent and intensity of their attachment, become part of the Eliot–Beauvoir parallel, in that these women, young and old, formed circles. In Beauvoir's case, there was indeed an extended family, labeled and accepted as such; and there was a round-robin of sexual contact among the members, mainly heterosexual. For Eliot, the circle was held at a distance; she cherished her privacy too much to allow it to spiral out of control. But, nevertheless, the circle included visits from her disciples, and their presence became part of her personal world accepted by Lewes.

In both instances, the two women were able to carve out prominent and influential careers; and in each, we can see their lives and careers as pioneering. Eliot, obviously, was the more daring and adventurous. Without any slighting of Beauvoir's achievement, it is clear Eliot's mid-nineteenth-century England was less fluid and flexible than Beauvoir's mid-twentieth-century France, and surely less flexible than George Sand's contemporaneous France, where another parallel might be found. To do what Eliot did was nothing short of a radical breach of everything her society held to be normal, although beneath that surface a good deal of socially unsanctioned behavior went on.

Ready for travel, the Leweses left Earlswood Common at the end of September for the Priory and immediately departed from there for a four-day stay at Bullock-Hall's, at Six Mile Bottom; this was followed by a fortnight in Europe. On 3 October, they headed for Paris, where they stayed a week, and then spent another week, until 19 October, traveling to Brussels by way of Soissons, Reims, and Sedan. Sedan, in the Ardennes, almost against the Belgian border, had been the site of a great battle in the Franco-Prussian War, in which the French lost all. The couple's travels abroad immediately turned them into patients, suffering from sore throats, colds, and general indisposition. But their return to London on 19 October was short-lived, and they went on the move the next day, ailments and all, this time to find suitable locations for characters who would appear in *Deronda*. One curious point, as Haight points out, is that Eliot sought places in *her* Wessex at just the time Thomas Hardy was beginning to explore *his* Wessex for *Far from the Madding Crowd*. They did not meet.

Salisbury and the Stonehenge area proved unsatisfactory, and after a short return to London, she and Lewes set out again on 28 October, now to Wiltshire and Devizes just to the west of Bath, an area Eliot recalled from her visit thirty-one years before to see Dr. Brabant. They finally found what could be the source for Sir Hugo Mallinger's Topping Abbey, in Lacock Abbey. Such excursions were absolutely necessary for Eliot's kind of realism, which depended on factual detail she could then reconfigure into fiction. She even needed a stated geographical spot for the meeting of Deronda and Mirah, which she located along the Thames toward Richmond.

While still at Earlswood Common, in early August, Eliot responded to good sales of the one-volume *Middlemarch*—5,000 sold, another 2,100 in print—by citing how abysmal other novels were: "The effect was paralyzing, and certainly justifies me in that abstinence from novel-reading which, I fear, makes me seem supercilious or churlish to the many persons who send me their books or ask about their friends' books." * Whatever else, her remarks to Blackwood indicate a fervent sense of literature, but linked to her uncertainty of her own abilities. Given the low state of literature, in her eyes, she wonders if there is any justification in writing at all. She worries about writing indifferently after having written well; she poses this as a general hypothesis, but clearly means herself. She compares this to an eminent clergyman spoiling his reputation "by lapses and neutralizing all the good he did before." She recognizes she is just going on. "It is only a sample of the way in which depression works upon me."

This is the down side of her character. But the same attitude can be viewed as the way by which, as we have observed before, she could drive herself to achievement. Not unlike some of the saints whom Dorothea Brooke wished to emulate, Eliot was herself something of a self-flagellator. She now had John Blackwood as correspondent and confidant to whom she could pour out her fears and uncertainties: the fear of obstacles, the self-inflicted pain, the anguish of potential failure, the recognition of loss of powers. That such fears were part of a depressive personality seems clear; yet for this seemingly most resigned of women, depression served not as an end in itself but as a springboard into the deepest regions of herself which she could then transform into fiction. Such was her state of mind when she and Lewes left for the continent in October of 1874.

One of the few things which appeared to pick her up was the warm reception of her books, a warmth which translated into high sales. *Jubal* and *The Spanish Gypsy*, to everyone's surprise, were going well, along with the backlist of her other novels. What this meant to Eliot beyond sales was that there was continuity to her life, that her achievement was not isolated in a given book. There was the sweep of a great career, such as that enjoyed by Dickens and Trollope. It meant that, rightly or wrongly, she could feel her "message" was being heeded. She wanted people to be better, to transcend themselves, at the very time, in the 1860s and 1870s, when the more general cry was for social and political action. Eliot was working against the grain, for the social-political sphere called for the extension of the franchise; female empowerment in various areas (education, extension of the divorce laws, property rights); the growth of movements to improve workers' conditions (early forms of the Labour Party, the outlawing of infringements on people's rights); a justice system which served all classes; the creation of greater political liberties for those outside the system, especially in religious matters; and the weakening of the aristocracy, which nevertheless still owned most of England.†

---

* Trollope, with *The Prime Minister*, in 1876, was winding down. Gissing did not begin publishing novels until 1880. Yet George Meredith and Thomas Hardy published important novels in the 1870s.

† To isolate just one area, a political matter which Eliot only touched upon: in the 1870s, 7,500 families in England (out of 32 million people, including Scotland and Ireland) owned four-fifths of the land in the British Isles. The breakdown: in England proper, such ownership was 56 percent; in Scotland, where the aristocracy had enormous estates and castles, it was 93 percent. If we add squires, peers, and those who rose through making fortunes, the upper classes owned a hugely disproportionate part of English and Scottish real estate. To redress that was part of a growing political movement.

Once she had settled upon locations for her scenes in *Deronda,* Eliot once again consulted Frederic Harrison about legal questions, no less knotty in the new novel than they had been in *Felix Holt.* She was looking particularly for legal answers in the area of heirs, with properties entailed. She was now collecting information from all sides, including questions about what the terms of a scholarship involved (Deronda had wanted to win a scholarship but failed to do so); what life at Cambridge would be like, if Deronda had gone, information she asked of Leslie Stephen; and even what songs Mirah would sing, which she asked Charles Lewes about.

In a succession of letters to Elma Stuart—now the supplier of ever more expensive gifts—Eliot encourages the woman's devotion and offers advice. Stuart's health was poor, and Eliot warns her not to take valerian, opium, and other drugs, since they are temporary. She should work her way toward health through "right conduct of her body." Eliot admits she has not always practiced her own precepts, but she says she damaged her body not through neglect, but through "overwork and over-confidence, till it was too late to do more than patch and patch the old carcase. But I take as much pains," she writes, "not to get worse, as I should wish you to take not to destroy the fountain of spirits, energy, and love which still bubble in your somewhat damaged organism."

As a side issue—but perhaps not so marginal to Eliot as it may at first appear—she responded to Harriet Beecher Stowe about her brother's "unspeakable troubles." Even as Eliot indicated she hoped the troubles were at an end, Henry Ward Beecher was struck with a suit charging him with adultery and would go on trial (for six months) in January 1875. The question of adultery for Eliot, intermixed with the brother–sister relationship of Harriet and Henry, could not have gone unnoticed in her assessment of the issue. Lewes was in fact an adulterer, as was his wife, Agnes; and by becoming the third party, Eliot had become part of an adulterous ring, as it were. The brother–sister relationship—Harriet stood by her brother even when it became clear he was guilty—was not a small matter to Eliot, either, coming as it did just when she was reliving her own failed brother–sister relationship in *Jubal.*

Yet despite these interruptions, she was moving well with *Deronda.* She told Blackwood he should not despair of her, since she had settled down to produce "a thick slice" of manuscript while at Earlswood. It has been read aloud to her "private critic," Lewes, and "was immensely approved by him." She doubts if it is "up to the mark," but he vows it is. Anxieties permeate her journal entries. She was particularly worried that even if she completed the novel, it would not be worthy of "literature" and might become a mere addition to the heap of books. This seems to be almost an obsession for her now: her role in literature, her place among the greats, her desire not to write books—as she felt Trollope was doing—which revealed she was past her prime. As she edged toward 1875, she was coming up to Chapter 16, but still feared that the completed novel would be little better than those books she reviled as popular fiction, or those by "silly novelists."

John Cross showed up to accompany Eliot to the Lord Mayor's show on 9 November. Lewes was attending a London Library meeting. This was only the

first of several invitations from Cross: another was to an album show of autographs at the Bank of England, then one to Woolwich Arsenal, and finally to
the tennis courts to watch a celebrated match. She and Lewes also went to the
National Gallery and the South Kensington Museum—all of this activity in
middle November. They attended services twice at the Russian church, not for
the religious message but for the choral singing and the organ. Cross suggested
longer outings for the couple, including one of several days on a boat kept by
his brother-in-law, Albert Druce. Eliot declined, as ailments kept her in pain.

After this outburst of social activity, Eliot returned to her manuscript and
then wrote an enormously long letter to the Honorable Mrs. Henry Frederick
Ponsonby, who had written to her in October. Mrs. Ponsonby was another one
of those remarkable contemporary women who, without becoming well known
to us, took their lives courageously into their own control. Some broke out of
poverty, some out of wealth; they broke through class, caste, and educational
restrictions to be organizers, writers, and supporters. Ponsonby wrote Eliot
because she believed her to hold the secret to certain mysteries in life, where
science and morality crossed. She immediately threw herself at the writer,
although without the physical importuning of Edith Simcox.

Ponsonby had embraced the latest in scientific thought—molecular physics,
for example—and from this she had extrapolated that individual love and moral
action have lost their efficacy. Eliot will have none of this: "One might as well
hope to dissect one's own body and be merry in doing it, as take molecular
physics (in which you must banish from your field of view what is specifically
human) to be your dominant guide, your determiner of motives, in what is solely
human. That every study has its bearing on every other is true; but pain and
relief, love and sorrow, have their peculiar history which make an experience
and knowledge over and above the swing of atoms."

Eliot continues: "With regard to the pains and limitations of one's personal
lot, I suppose there is not a single man, or woman, who has not more or less
need of that stoical resignation which is often a hidden heroism, or who, in
considering his or her past history, is not aware that it has been cruelly affected
by the ignorant or selfish action of some fellow-being in a more or less close
relation of life. And to my mind, there can be no stronger motive, than this
perception, to an energetic effort that the lives nearest us shall not suffer in a
like manner from us." Eliot was, in fact, reverting to the very attitude she took
toward Dempster in "Janet's Repentance" in her first book. Her point has been
remarkably consistent: the saints' admonition to "turn the other cheek"; the
resignation that, she felt, gave woman their moral superiority over men; her
recognition that a society can be normalized only when individual egos and
needs are subservient to the larger need.

Her anxiety about the issues involved forbids her to let go, and, unusually for
her, she adds a postscript. She measures the individual's mortality against the
length of history, and suggests one must act as if one were immortal. "As to
duration, and the way in which it affects your views of the human history, what
is really the difference to your imagination between infinitude and billions,

when you have to consider the value of human experience? Will you say that since your life has a term of three-score and ten, it was really a matter of indifference whether you were a cripple with a wretched skin disease or an active creature with a mind at large for the enjoyment of knowledge and with a nature which has attracted others to you?"

Eliot's position fits well into Victorian beliefs in modified amelioration: what she found in Carlyle and Ruskin, for example, or among agnostics, such as Mill and Arnold. This was, in fact, the last burst of the ameliorative phase, for by the 1880s and surely by the 1890s, it would disperse into aestheticism, into attitudes favoring individual behavior, into disbelief in the saving qualities of human endeavor, into a distrust of "progress"—dispersed into writers as different as George Gissing, Thomas Hardy, Oscar Wilde, and Samuel Butler.

Meanwhile, while inching her way into *Deronda*, Eliot had quietly passed her fifty-fifth birthday. As she shaped that novel, we are struck by how much her writing of it shaped her: a reciprocity we observe in much of her fiction. Even as she wrote about real people and events which had to change themselves in order to become the people and events she wanted to write about, Eliot was learning about herself. With the novel her summation, she was careful to include all previous observations and transformations; but in Deronda himself, we sense something more. That "more" is a dimension of reshaping which has within it something of Freud's "family romance," in which the individual believes he or she belongs to a family better or higher than his birth indicates. In the planning stages, Eliot wavered about Deronda's background: Was he the illegitimate son of Sir Hugo Mallinger and, therefore, someone who could be legitimatized by an act of Parliament? Or could his birth indicate another source? She decided on the latter, establishing his Jewish origins. In Deronda, Eliot had material which cut sharply into her own sense of self. More than any other character, Deronda represents the shift of values, birth, attitudes, and matters of class and caste which force him to a radical change of perspective— comparable in several respects to the intellectual and emotional journey Eliot herself took. Both needed to be reborn and to emerge.

Early in 1875, she was pursuing Frederic Harrison's legal knowledge for matters involving entailed property, questions of legitimacy and inheritance laws, and related issues which sent him scurrying to his books. In the version Eliot settled upon, Deronda's inheritance is bypassed when his birth indicates he is a Jew, not connected by blood to Sir Hugo. But at this still early stage, Eliot was trying to wade through thickets of English precedent, thickets even Harrison was finding difficult to penetrate. Since her serious kidney attack of almost a year ago, her health had been fairly good, although headaches, colds, and other complaints continued. She was fitted with eyeglasses in 1875, although that did not relieve the headaches. As in the past, Eliot's ailments intensified when she concentrated on a book, and neither eyeglasses nor treatment of her teeth— which helped to alleviate real physical problems—could strike at the more profound character of her indisposition.

The kidney ailment was of another kind, and a painful and serious attack would recur on 2 March 1875, just thirteen months after the previous one. These were apparently kidney stone attacks, with some deterioration of kidney function. They were physical, probably inherited, not prompted by her work, and there was clearly damage. This March onset did not last hours, but days, and was repeated two months later, and then with frequency for the next five years. Heat, baths, and medication helped to lower the intensity of the pain; but we can say with assurance that during the writing of *Deronda* and for the remainder of her life, Eliot's periods of good health fell between excruciating attacks of stones and related ailments.

20

Summa:
Daniel Deronda

"He was at present too ill acquainted with disaster to enter into the pathos of a lot where everything is below the level of tragedy except the passionate egoism of the sufferer."

Eliot's problem in 1875 and 1876 was to maintain some mental stability while her body began its slow deterioration and she suffered from periodic attacks of considerable pain. The lack of work in the final four years of her life after *Deronda* can be attributed in large part to her loss of physical health, although we should not discount her sense that she had exhausted her resources in this "summa" fiction. Her life for the next year or more settled undramatically into generating manuscript pages. She kept to her desk for a good part of this time, except for periods in March and May, and thereafter, when she had to take to her bed. At those times, Lewes was most helpful. While there were servants to handle household matters, Lewes abandoned his own work to care personally for Eliot. *

One other source of enervation could, possibly, be attributed to a crisis of faith within Eliot as she moved from *Middlemarch* to *Deronda*. According to this reasoning, she felt that things were falling apart spiritually, and her emphasis on the Hebraic elements—influenced perhaps by Matthew Arnold and his Hebraism as well as by his *Literature and Dogma*—brought her to a reevaluation. Yet this view has several branches. *Deronda* is not concerned primarily with religion, but with community, with discovering where one belongs and consol-

---

* Eliot told Charles Ritter (a translator who learned English to read Eliot) early in 1875 that her husband knew "nothing of jealousy," and was "open as day to sympathy in the work of others. . . . He gets more pleasure out of any work of mine than I do. . . ." She adds that with her doubts about the novel she is writing, only Lewes's support and "firmness of opinion as to the worth of what is already written" enable her to carry out her intentions. "In this way he has always supported me— by his unreserved sympathy and the independence of his judgment."

idating self with the group. It contains more a social than a religious or racial idea. Like Arnold's Hebraism, it is informed by matters of conduct; and it is precisely here that she may have felt uncertain. Even as she argued right con-duct, she sensed a falling apart, a decline in behavior, a subversion of the social contract.

We catch her anxiety in her emphasis on music, especially on voice, which must evoke the spirit of community, not merely individual achievement. The use of voice—Eliot was possibly influenced by John Hullah, a music historian and conductor—reveals how that instrument defines character. Hullah argued for the "natural" voice which he felt English education and culture blocked. For him, choral singing was natural, a form of community; Gwendolen in seeking a major career defies this, while Mirah pursues it in social settings.

Blackwood, meanwhile, weighed in with one of his regular reports on sales, with *Middlemarch* bringing in for 1874 a total of £864.0.6; there were steady sales of *Jubal* (now in a second edition) and *The Spanish Gypsy* sold out in its fourth edition. These editions were rather small printings, so that "second" and "fourth" do not mean large figures, although any sale of poetry was encouraging. Eliot was gratified and turned to her journal for the first time in a year and a half. She tried to fill it with happiness, connected to Blackwood's check and general sales. Her entry is her usual year-end or new-year mixture of the bless-ings she has enjoyed with her private doubts as to the worth of what she was doing. She even fears she may not be able to complete *Deronda*.

Her worry about the manuscript of the novel and the frailty of her health made her pale and drawn, as Blackwood commented when he observed her at the Priory in May. Yet she continued to apply herself, on most mornings until lunch at one, a routine she held to unless she was in bed.* Her correspondence now takes on a tone of resignation: the feeling she had expressed whatever she had to say and her ideas were stale. Elma Stuart continued to send gifts, coincid-ing with Eliot's most recent attack on 2 March, and this required a response. It became a communiqué from the sickbed: she was suffering "a dulled sensibility," with a condition creeping over her body now diagnosed as "that admirable sub-stance called 'gravel' in the place where it is least wanted—even less than in one's boots." She may have called the attack "a mild one," but Lewes considered it quite serious, since it included blood in her urine and only opiates and fomen-

---

* She and Lewes, however, did break the routine by seeking out, still further, locations in Kew and Richmond for scenes in *Deronda*. As for naming, Gwendolen's Christian name, according to Eliot's notebook, derived from Charlotte Yonge's *History of Christian Names*, and is related to white-ness (Gwendolyn is Welsh for "white") or being "white browed." If we see parts of *Deronda* as allegory—especially in the role of Gwendolen / Guinevere as an avenging beauty—we may cite certain Arthurian legends, Tennyson's *Idylls* or others. In another respect, Eliot was rewriting Sam-uel Richardson, with Gwendolen based on Clarissa Harlowe (Grandcourt on Richard Lovelace) and Deronda taking on the role of Sir Charles Grandison, "Mr. Perfect," in Richardson's novel after *Clarissa*. Gwendolen even takes on Clarissa's extreme distaste for sex, telling young Rex how she hates his making love to her. Gwendolen dislikes even being touched. Chapter 12, the interchange between Gwendolen and Grandcourt, with her decision to be married or "sold," was not easy for Eliot. The manuscript reveals deletions and corrections in the exchange between the two "lovers," although the deletions are heavily barred and, therefore, illegible.

tation (the application of liquids or ointments to the body) would help during its duration of several days.

What she omits is the terrible depression or despair which remained after the great pain. We recall Emily Dickinson's "After a great pain, a formal feeling comes"—it is probably this psychic letdown Eliot describes as being "still out of health." Yet not all was waste, for in several ways her physical and mental condition appears in the book. We observe it in the wide swings of hope and despair which shape the themes; but, even further, in the use of contrasts between one character's move toward happiness, Gwendolen's, and another's gravitation toward utter disaster, Lydia Glasher's. We find comparable contrasts in Deronda's life.

We can find, still further, in Gwendolen's artistic aspirations some shadowy fears in Eliot's own life as she sought language and identity. Gwendolen is discouraged by Klesmer, a Jew, and this is paralleled by Deronda's mother, the Princess Halm-Eberstein, who is restrained from a stage career by her Jewish father. This refusal to permit women to define their own language not only recalls Eliot's own apprehension about emergence, but further intertwines that restraint with Jewish themes. Mirah, also Jewish, is allowed a career, but only on a small stage, in private homes, preparatory for her life as a wife. In this light the personal tensions in *Daniel Deronda* are almost unbearable.

Not unrelated to this, the two parts of the novel indicate Eliot's desire to "reinvent" history, by joining the two disparate elements of Jew and Gentile. She was personally trying to will herself into health through a fusion of parts. As the result of Deronda's hold over Gwendolen, from the beginning until she is transformed, the Jewish and Christian elements are linked as a historical, temporal unity. If we view the novel in this perspective, we can connect the two plot strands into a universal entity or into a generalized human struggle reaching for some transcendental level, a form of ultimate health. Eliot was establishing her "formal feeling."

Yet in another respect, even as she was reaching toward some cure for the Western world as for herself, Eliot overdetermines her moral point. Deronda has influenced her, even as he influences Gwendolen. Eliot reifies the Jew: Mordecai is heroized, Deronda is ennobled, a Jewish Parsifal, Mirah is an updated version of Scott's ideal Rebecca, the Cohens are cute. All of this was part of Eliot's effort to find community in England, even as she struggled to stabilize herself. Yet by permitting Deronda to drift into his calling without any real internal conflict, she makes the Jewish element relatively easy, whereas Gwendolen's path is thorny; she, not he, walks the path of sorrow. Eliot sees the male as the new force, the female as the traditional bearer of pain. Her identification with Deronda and *health* was so complete she could find no fault. *

Yet bad health and all, by 21 April, the first volume of *Deronda* was ready for perusal. On a luncheon visit, William Blackwood found both Lewes and Eliot "rather seedy," but Eliot especially shocked and distressed him when he saw

* In 1948, a street in Tel Aviv was named after Eliot.

her "looking so aged and haggard. . . ." As for the novel, she expressed it as "detestable," but Lewes, ever perky, pronounced it "perfectly charming." Blackwood suggested to Lewes that he take with him the first volume to show his uncle, John, who could then discuss it with the couple. They agreed it was a "capital idea," but then Eliot came in to express "horror and fright" and a "meek expression." "It was one of the most striking scenes I have ever seen," Blackwood observed; she responded as though he were taking her baby. He bowed to her wishes and left it behind. In a further effort to cheer up their now doubtful author, Blackwood pointed out how Queen Victoria was devoted to her works, particularly to *Adam Bede.* *

The Leweses did not stay completely put. They saw Calvini in *Othello*, twice in April; they dined at Lord Lytton's; and they made a three-day visit to Oxford, to see Jowett. On 3 May, while at Oxford, Eliot suffered another severely painful attack of kidney stones, and when she felt somewhat recovered the couple started for home. She remained unwell, Lewes notes, until 9 May, staying in bed, while he attended her.

At this time, Leslie Stephen responded to her inquiry about Deronda's resignation of his scholarship—part of her original plan for his early career. She backed off from this idea in her mental revision of the book, and instead of having him resign, she has him fail in his effort to gain a scholarship because of his attention to the needs of Hans Meyrick. This was not merely a random plot turn. It became an essential ingredient in Deronda's passage toward his destiny, and it helped solidify the two sides of the novel, Gwendolen's selfishness and self-centeredness and Deronda's altruism.

When John Blackwood lunched at the Priory on 19 May, he took back with him to the firm Volume I of *Deronda*, what had originally proven so difficult for Eliot to part with when William Blackwood visited earlier. As we can expect, the publisher became effusive, saying he spent the night reading her work. He went on with "leisurely enjoyment" until 3 A.M., with only half the volume read. This was one day after he received it, an indication of how a publisher catered to a favored author. To Eliot five days later—he had already told his nephew *Deronda* promised to be "a wonderful book"—he wrote enthusiastically about the entire first volume. He found Gwendolen a "fascinating witch," a quaint form of description. He saw Grandcourt as a remarkable creation and used effectively as a contrast to Deronda, although that was not really Eliot's use of him. Blackwood even liked the Jewish material, which was quite new to his experience.

The Leweses were once again house-hunting, and on 7 June they moved to the Elms, a house in Rickmansworth, Hertfordshire, just north of London.

---

* Haight cites a copy of *Adam Bede* in the Royal Library at Windsor Castle with the queen's note inside indicating she had read it in September and October of 1859. Also, a copy of *Romola* reveals that the queen probably read it while staying at the Villa Palmieri outside Florence. Victoria's intellect has often been attacked as soft, but it is hard to think of a U.S. president reading a serious novel by one of America's leading writers. In the social arena, Eliot over time was invited to attend royal functions by three of Victoria's daughters, although not by Victoria herself.

Lewes called the house "delightful," and it did provide a refuge, although not from Edith Simcox. She made one visit unannounced, was received coolly, and did not return uninvited.

Rickmansworth proved a three-and-a-half-month refuge, with Eliot interrupting the stretch only once, to see a London dentist on 28 July. He pulled a tooth, which seemed to relieve some of the neuralgia she suffered. For his part, Lewes returned to the Priory several times to oversee renovations. The move to the Elms proved very rewarding in terms of manuscript copy generated, for Eliot finished Volume II and struck out well into Volume III before their return on 23 September. Her concentration was, as in the old days, four or five hours of steady work. Her manuscript indicates how certain she was of direction and expression, and how little she needed to revise once she had things straight in her mind. *

Lewes's family had taken an upturn in May with the birth of a son to Bertie, who was now living in Durban, South Africa. It then took a tragic downturn on 29 June when Bertie died there. News did not reach the couple for over a month; but when it did they were so grief-stricken they told few people so as not to have to face condolences. What was particularly upsetting, apart from the death of Lewes's third son, was that they had been enjoying their Rickmansworth stay oblivious of all. Lewes had even in his ignorance accepted an invitation to meet the queen of Holland, at a party given by Lady Airlie, an invitation Eliot had declined. He recounted how a dotty queen (described as "somewhat feeble") confused him with someone else and had the place wrong where she claimed they had met. But he revelled in the well-known invitees, including Jenny Lind, P. T. Barnum's "Swedish Nightingale," as well as Robert Browning, Lady Stanhope, and so on, with a heavy emphasis on society rather than artistic people. In the mail, meanwhile, to make all this appear trifling, was the notice of Bertie's death.

The couple's stay in Hertfordshire was indeed companionable, quiet, retiring. After Eliot finished at her desk, they often rode around in the area or else rambled on foot. In the evening they read to each other, or discussed *Deronda.* Eliot relied heavily on what Lewes told her, although his advice was always gentle and mainly ambiguous for fear of hurting her feelings or impeding her progress. On 3 July, his *On Actors and the Art of Acting* was published, a primer for those aspiring to take up acting careers, and very possibly an influence on one career choice for Gwendolen Harleth. It was not a serious publication, but, rather, part of that intense interest in theater displayed by several literary figures, Dickens and Wilkie Collins among others.

* The manuscript at the British Museum Library (Add. No 34039-34042) reveals that not all was easy, however. Chapter 12 proved troublesome as Eliot attempted to get the exchange correct between Gwendolen and Grandcourt; Chapter 37, the first on Mordecai, contains insertions and deletions indicating that the Jewish material did not come easily; Chapter 40, the end of the Mordecai segment, also caused trouble, even to the motto, which Eliot changed to an excerpt from Wordsworth's *Excursion* (Book IV). For the most part, however, she moved along confidently, the shaping of the novel firmly set from the outset on contrasts.

On the eve of hearing about his son's death, Lewes told John Blackwood he and Eliot are hermits, seeing not a soul. And on 1 August, having not yet received word, Lewes went about his usual business. On 9 August, Eliot did not tell her correspondent, Mrs. Peter Taylor, anything about Bertie; and only on 13 August, in writing to Barbara Bodichon, did she go into detail. She reveals they knew Bertie was ill, suffering from a glandular disease, she says, which led as an adult to neuralgia (a Victorian catchall for ailments which defied diagnosis), then to bronchitis (probably pneumonia) which caused his death. Eliot's letter does not sound particularly sorrowful—she mentions importuning the Alfred Morrisons (wealthy art collectors) for contributions to Girton College for women—but we know from subsequent events how upsetting the news, even though possibly expected, proved to be.

It was to John Cross, on 14 August, that Eliot finally poured out her sorrow. In her remarks—and we must be cautious here to distinguish clearly—Eliot treated Cross more like one of her female friends than her male ones. She handled her information in an intimate, even chatty way; and although she did write to several women about serious matters, she tended to be open and conversational with them, as she is now with Cross. What this means is that she has accepted him as a confidant, like Barbara Bodichon, Mrs. Burne-Jones, or several others. She expresses herself easily, familiarly, without the reserve she displayed with male correspondents. She repeats that glandular disease brought Bertie down, after he seemed to have conquered it in childhood and grown into a healthy, strong adult. Durban was supposed to be the place where he would regain his health, but it turned out to be his graveyard. She feels additional sorrow for his wife and two small children, including an infant born only in May. Her assessment is pragmatic: "He was a sweet-natured creature—not clever, but diligent and well-judging about the things of daily life." She says, with some condescension, she and Lewes felt that with his qualities he could prosper best in the colonies. She adds they cannot feel self-reproach because it ended badly; they must be resigned. Nevertheless, she experiences guilt, and wonders if his condition might have been bettered by something closer to home.

To Mrs. Ponsonby, however, Eliot switched gears entirely and expressed her views, not on Bertie, but on drinking, especially on those "rich brewers in Parliament" who plant their "poison shops" (pubs) throughout every village, one public house to every six dwellings. She says they ply their "million-making trade" based on human misery, while probably they are philanthropists, or "devout evangelists and ritualists." Such sharp, caustic views rarely, if ever, turn up in Eliot's fiction, although in *Deronda* she was consumed with anger at gambling establishments. But while her fictional voice was on such hypocrisies as they bled into the public world, she was not blinded to them as personal attributes. *Felix Holt, Middlemarch,* and *Deronda* were textbooks in this area.

Yet this outburst of anger to Mrs. Ponsonby tells us something we may have somewhat skirted before, that Eliot in her fiction responded directly to few of the ills permeating England. She neglected not only the rich men in Parliament protecting their "poison shops," but the large holdings of real estate by the few, the extreme poverty of the lower half of the population, the lack of sufficient nutrition and sanitation among that disadvantaged half, the continuing lack of government interest in the people's general welfare (the Poor Laws, for example, which condemned people to lives of misery), and the imperialistic mission of the country which diverted attention from the insufficiency of the economic system to protect the majority of its people.* Eliot was aware of some of these abuses and injustices, but not primarily concerned with them; and if she was indeed England's "voice," then we see that someone as committed as she to moral justice forsook social reform. She took the high ground, which subsumed details of injustice, inequality, and insufficiency. *Deronda* is an immediate example of how she bypassed the question of poverty in order to emphasize a higher state, the Meyrick family, in which warmth and solidarity supersede their chronic lack of funds, their slippage into that lower half of society.

Except for a visit by Charles Lewes and his family, the couple remained retired, almost hermits. Charles had originally wished to go to Durban to bring back Bertie's widow and two children, but both Lewes and Eliot—perhaps fearing turmoil—convinced him to remain at home, with his own wife pregnant. In the meantime, Lewes sent money to Bertie's widow, Eliza, and Eliot continued the support in the years after Lewes's death.

Of compelling interest are the different roles Eliot was now playing with the people in her life. To John Cross, she was "aunt" and "auntie"; to Elma Stuart, she was "mother" or "spiritual mother"; to Lewes, she was "wife" (as ever, in quotation marks) and the ambiguous "Madonna"; to Charles's and Bertie's children she was "grandmother"; to Lewes's son(s) she was "Mutter," with the German designation a way of avoiding "mother" or "stepmother." She signed her name "G. E. Lewes," "Polly," or "M. E. L." People wrote to her as "Mrs. Lewes," but to Emily Clarke she was "Aunt Polly." Nobody called her "George." She referred to her "husband," often, as "Lewes." The proliferation of names involved several which were not legally established, and yet she expected them as forms of address or signs of affection. She had accumulated a family, Lewes's children and grandchildren; a "nephew," whom she would later marry; an adopted daughter, as it were, in Elma Stuart; a potential "lover" in Edith Simcox; and a "husband" whose legal wife would outlive the century—while the one close relative she did have, her brother, remained beyond communication and, seemingly, beyond interest.†

We seek meaning here, in a context of names and naming, identities sought,

---

* To cite only two areas: the British position in Africa and in India. In several campaigns, against the Zulus, for instance, thousands of British soldiers were sent out, the lower classes for the most part, with upper-class officers, to be killed, mutilated, or permanently disabled. In Afghanistan and India, periodic skirmishes and outbreaks led to a comparable loss of English life among those whom the economy could not support. Those who died for their country had least to gain from it.

† She did, however, respond to her nephew, Robert Evans, her half-brother's son, on 26 September 1874. She explains why she and her half-sister, Fanny, no longer communicate: ". . . years ago, she spoke of me with dislike and unkindness. . . ." Eliot says their split is final, despite her nephew's effort to reopen communication: ". . . I have," she says, "no store of nervous energy, no superfluous time, to make it right for me to encounter the excitement of reviving those memories [of past relations] actively in personal meetings. . . . My correspondence is very onerous to me, and I must not enlarge it in any way that does not wear the aspect of duty." She signs it an ambiguous "Your sincerely well-wishing Aunt M. E. Lewes."

roles to be played and replayed, a self both deconstructed and reconstructed. One way to read *Deronda* is to see in the main character's question of identity a transformed and imaginative use of Eliot's own position. Deronda was brought up to think he is the heir to an upper-class Gentile world, when he is in actuality a Jew and the heir to a considerably different tradition. The novel, in this segment, turns on questions of birth, naming, backgrounds, role-playing, profound issues of destinations and goals—all of which we can cite in Eliot's own confusion of naming.* Each of her names portends a different destination, a distinctive goal, an aspect of her personalities—dualities proliferate.

We cannot dismiss the psychological and emotional import of her assumption of so many different roles, and we cannot ignore the question of which roles she held for herself: some, all, others. In her conscious life, Eliot appeared to identify with all and to play them gracefully; but in her inner world, those doubts, uncertainties, and periods of despair about her work (or in general) could be attributed to this lack of proper definition, or, conversely, to an overloading of selves. Exactly what toll these numerous shifts of role and name meant remains speculative. But it is clear that Eliot, seemingly the most balanced and "located" of novelists, was in actuality caught in a spiral of elements she could deal with only by playing all the roles expected of her. In this respect, also, perhaps curiously, she was a Victorian voice, like Matthew Arnold's wanderers among several diverse worlds. As Arnold wrote: "And each half lives a hundred different lives," which is why he warns his scholar-gypsy to flee ever "deeper in the bowering wood." It was advice Eliot heeded; in that "bowering wood," she sought unity.

That unsettled sense of self, whatever surface defenses she raised, could not be completely disguised and had to be revealed in her fiction. Just as Dickens had manifested aspects of wildness almost akin to madness in his novels, while carrying on a seemingly ordered life, there was in Eliot, on a lesser scale, some of that same collision between a public self and the private self embedded in her fiction. This goes well beyond sadness or even that sense of melancholy readers and reviewers were alert to. The duality goes to the heart of her personality: not a natural one, but one created out of circumstances and then cobbled together by a willed self. Since she had tremendous intellectual ability as well as emotional control, she could create a personality which seemed integrated; but when the time came for the revelations of her fiction, she lost the shields and defenses. In her novels, she revelled in failures, in wandering female characters, in depicting poor choices, in cataloguing disastrous marriages. She was, like most of her contemporaries, bewildered by things which lacked their former coherence and continuity.

---

* More transformations: written at about the same time as *Daniel Deronda*, the poem "The Death of Moses" (late 1874) uses the transformation of Moses from leader into lawgiver as part of Eliot's own concern with the law. God insists on taking Moses' soul from his body, despite opposition from the angels Michael, Gabriel, and Zamaël, and then through the Invisible Will reasserts the leader as lawgiver. Through Moses, and indirectly through the Jewish material of *Deronda*, Eliot imposed her own views of duty, discipline, and obligation. The poem works on transformation, in much the way Deronda is transformed from a somewhat aimless young man into a future leader of his people, a lawgiver, a Moses.

Gwendolen's self-confident manner in *Deronda*, for example, is underscored by fits of violence, emblems of unconscious forces—from her strangling of her sister's canary to the panel episodes and to her horrible enjoyment as Grandcourt drowns. The canary episode recalls Maggie Tulliver's terrible vengeance on her "Fetish" doll, and then her orgiastic end with her brother, a love that fulfills only in violent death. One could argue that the preponderance of females in *Deronda*—three Mallinger daughters, three Meyrick daughters, Gwendolen's sisters, Lydia Glasher's three daughters, as well as some marginal women—is Eliot's final effort to work through women's chance-ridden and tentative destinies as they shadow aspects of her own unconscious fears and doubts.

When the Leweses returned to the Priory on 23 September, they found it in a still unfinished state, with the smell of paint too strong to bear, the wallpapering not completed, and even some items—like Lewes's cigars—stolen. But since they had money, they did what the rich always do: they left for another place, having given their servants their assignments to put the place into shape. Just one day after returning to the Priory, the couple headed for Wales, where they found a good deal of poor weather, which meant they had time for reading: Austen's *Emma*, Dickens's *Uncommercial Traveller*, Sterne's *Sentimental Journey*, and Turgenev's *Moscow Tales* (which they read in French). Somewhat refreshed, they returned to the Priory on 9 October, to find that the work was still unfinished; but this time they chose to settle in, so that Eliot could reestablish her routine.

By 20 October, she sent the first two of the three volumes of *Deronda* to Edinburgh, having agreed to a decision to publish the completed novel in eight monthly parts, between February and September 1876. The decision to start in February was Lewes's—December was too soon for American arrangements, and January, he felt, was a poor month for publishing anything. Even as Eliot informed Blackwood of this, she had to add that while she was not at all satisfied with the book and lacked a "comfortable sense" of what she was doing, she was moving along because Lewes was satisfied. But she was not happy about cutting her work up into pieces, opposing now, as she had before, publication in smaller parts; nevertheless, she acquiesced to Lewes's and Blackwood's prodding. She insisted on monthly episodes, however, feeling that weekly installments would destroy the sweep of her narrative. She indicated she had both sufficient public and money without undermining her work any further.[*]

By early November, proofs were ready for Eliot to peruse and revise. Terms duplicated those for *Middlemarch*: 40 percent on the 5-shilling book. With typical self-doubt, Eliot worried that charging 5 shillings for each book might shortchange the public. In response, Blackwood poured on praise, citing the enthusiasm of other members of his family, and assuring Eliot the work so far was "splendid," even "glorious." As for the division, Blackwood told her, "Divide as

---

[*] She was also very concerned about the actual division, especially whether parts would be too long; and she wondered how to make the division so as to maximize the novel's effectiveness. The arrangement was for Book I to end with Chapter 10; Book II, Chapter 18; Book III, Chapter 27; and Book IV, Chapter 34.

you think best without regard to the outward aspect of the volumes."

In addition to her artistic concerns, Eliot's edginess about the divisions and length could possibly be attributed to her upcoming fifty-sixth birthday, on 22 November 1875—birthdays lately being times when she became more aware than usual of the approach of her final years. Her extreme care about *Deronda* cannot be disconnected from an awareness of finality. Yet Lewes took over, and it was his words which would determine the final outcome. He insisted that monthly, not bimonthly, issues were better; and as for publication date, as we have noted, he had American rights in mind, especially since £1,700 from Harper's (in a cheap and an expensive edition) was at stake. *

The February date to start publication became the sole acceptable one. Lewes indicated he had read and reread the parts with a view toward the division and agreed that the present arrangement was best, although he suggested that the last five pages of Volume I be recast to make the opening of Volume II. This was done with Chapter 19 of the original Volume II, incorporating the final pages of Chapter 18. Lewes's suggestions were not only technical; they involved artistic matters as well, and Eliot bowed to him. For a time, they seemed on a collision course about the rearrangement of the material—Eliot's letter to Blackwood on this point has apparently been lost—but Lewes's argument held. He suggested, further, how he would like the novel advertised: "George Eliot's New Story of English Life—DANIEL DERONDA—will appear in Eight Monthly Parts. The first part to be published on February 1." Lewes left it to the firm to improve upon it.

As he read and reread proof, Blackwood kept up the momentum of praise. He wondered where she obtained knowledge of the Jews, and particularly praised that "Jew boy"—the six-year-old Jacob Alexander Cohen, son of the pawnbroker—as a little marvel. He adds he and his family have been trying to puzzle out what is going to happen and who Deronda is—as though the characters were living beings. The so-called split in the novel did not appear to concern him—a split which Eliot vehemently denied, since she saw the material as associative, reciprocal, and interlocked.

Lewes, incidentally, answered Blackwood's query about how Eliot learned so much about Jews—who, after all, lived in rather large numbers in England. Lewes says he is pleased the publisher feels she has done Jews so well, because he, Lewes, feared readers might not sympathize with that story element. But, he adds, if she could make readers love Methodists, "there was no reason why she should not conquer the prejudice against the Jews." He is quite eloquent on how her sympathetic treatment of the Jews, without disguising "the ludicrous and ugly aspects," will reveal the ideal side of "that strange life." He hopes Mordecai will rouse all the Jews of Europe to admiration, since Eliot's presentation is so authentic only learned rabbis are as well versed as she. His pride in

---

* Lewes was, in fact, busy on several fronts to gain as much from *Deronda* as was possible: in addition to the American money, £200 from Australia, £100 for German publication and £250 from Tauchnitz for German reprint rights, and £40 from the Dutch.

her achievement—he calls it "a stupendous genius"—is palpable. Blackwood could only agree she was writing one of the most remarkable books ever produced by man or woman. There is little question that if we look at the novel purely as a document, rather than as an aesthetic whole, it is indeed remarkable for its assimilation of late-nineteenth-century thought in terms of nationalism (Zionism as a form of nationalism); women's roles; marriage; the slippage of the upper classes; the emergence of new, disturbing forces; and the role of the artist in a basically hostile society.* As we shall see, the Jewish elements created the greatest stir, as anti-Jewish feeling from the critics rose up into overall criticism of the book.

Despite a cold, chills, and the usual ailments, Eliot moved along on Volume III; and as she told her publisher, she did not want to send any copy until the volume was completed. She indicates she cannot abide reading any other fiction while she is writing, and so informed Trollope when he sent on the first part of his *Prime Minister*. But she had already written off her friend as in decline. Her journal, however, reveals feelings she could not divulge to Blackwood. She thinks "very poorly" of her latest work. "Each part," she says, "as I see it before me *im Werden* [in the making] seems less likely to be anything else than a failure, but I see on looking back this morning—Christmas Day—that I really was in worse health and suffered equal depression about Romola—and so far as I have recorded, the same thing seems to be true of Middlemarch." She is not finished with self-doubt; having completed Book V, she has not moved along as well on Book VI as she wished, "the oppression under which I have been labouring having positively suspended my power of writing anything that I could feel satisfaction in."

Lewes was not unaware that a novel's popularity and reception depended on how well the first part was publicized and received. He especially wanted the *Times* to notice *Deronda*, but cites *Middlemarch*, which was not noticed until well into the novel's progress and came too late, he felt, for any good effect. Lewes's insistence had results, because Blackwood's devoted sixteen pages of advertisement for Books I and II.†

Eliot saw herself at this stage as a prisoner of her enterprise. She writes Lady Sebright (youngest daughter of Lord Castletown) that she and Lewes "rarely

---

* After the first installment in February, Henry James weighed in with an unsigned review in the *Nation* (24 February 1876). His view here would be qualified when the entire book appeared, but on the basis of this segment, he wrote, rather preciously: "It strikes us sometimes perhaps as rather conscious and over-cultivated; but it gives us the feeling that the threads of the narrative, as we gather them into our hands, are not of the usual commercial measurement, but long electric wires capable of transmitting messages from mysterious regions."

† Lewes saw a much larger public for *Deronda*, apparently from among Jews. "The Jews alone," he wrote Blackwood, "would constitute an energetic propagandist party, for never have they been idealized and realized so marvelously before." Quite possibly, Eliot had a Jewish audience in mind as she searched for authenticity. One of her notebooks (Folios 19 and 20 of the Pforzheimer Library Eliot Notebooks) lists not only the major Jewish festivals and feasts—Passover, Feast of Weeks, Yom Kippur, the New Year, the Feast of the Tabernacles, the Feast of Lights, Deliverance of the Israelites—but several of the more obscure ones linked to events in the Old Testament. Once again, her research into unfamiliar materials was mighty.

know anything of the world except through the stragglers from the crowd, who visit our cell." One interruption in this monastic life came with another visit to the dentist, with the extraction of several teeth relieving her neuralgia; but this was followed by "severe pains" in her stomach. She was now in that familiar cycle: depression, physical suffering, and achievement—back and forth—until the long project was completed and calmness itself seemed the result.

Through early January 1876, the correspondence between Blackwood and Lewes was extensive, with arrangements and counterarrangements for Deronda. As for Eliot, not only was she struggling with her doubts, she was still attempting to define the purposes of her fiction. She describes her writing as "a set of experiments in life—an endeavour to see what our thought and emotion may be capable of—what stores of motive, actual or hinted as possible, give promise of a better [life] after which we may strive—what gains from past revelations and discipline we must strive to keep hold of as something more sure than shifting theory." She adds that she fears to adopt any formula "which does not get itself clothed for me in some human figure and individual experience. . . ." She skirts aesthetic questions, or matters of shaping, transformation, imaginative re-creation, and the like, in favor of her moral message. And this is precisely the point in Deronda that one of Henry James's three conversationalists (in his December 1876 review article "Daniel Deronda: A Conversation") finds to critique in the novel. Constantius, the one who stands for moderation in the discussion, argues that there are two distinct elements in Eliot: the spontaneous and the artificial. He points out that the latter enables her to philosophize very sufficiently, "but meanwhile she has given a chill to her genius. She has come near spoiling an artist."

The remark, which runs through James's "Conversation," suggests there were warring elements in Eliot that she resolved insufficiently. The implication is that the urgency to provide details and moral argument blocked the flow of spontaneous creation. But James's point goes further. He recognizes at the same time that the very details and morality which war with imagination also make the novel stick with the reader. Deronda "becomes part of one's life; one lives in it or alongside of it. . . . it is so vast, so much-embracing! It has such a firm earth and such an ethereal sky. You can turn into it and lose yourself in it." These comments come from Theodora, who is an ardent defender of the novel. Pulcheria, the hostile reader, picks away at Jewish matters—to the extent of picking away at Deronda's "nose." "I am sure he had a nose, and I hold that the author has shown great pusillanimity in her treatment of it." As James knew, Jewish noses are always good for a laugh. *

But the most profound position is held by Constantius, the moderate reader. On Gwendolen, in particular, he is superb. "What is it [human life] made of but

---

* An early Eliot biographer, the father of Virginia Woolf, Leslie Stephen, was also put off by the Jewish material, not by noses but by the fact that Deronda would devote himself to something as Chimerical as a Jewish nation. Stephen's repeated concern with the almost farcical aspect of this quest borders on a barely controlled anti-Semitism, the very thing Daniel Deronda was attempting to combat.

the discovery by each of us that we are at the best but a rather ridiculous fifth wheel to the coach, after we have sat cracking our whip and believing that we are at least the coachman in person? We think we are the main hoop in the barrel, and we turn out to be but a very incidental splinter in one of the staves. The universe, forcing itself with a slow, inexorable sensitive mind, and making it ache with the pain of the process—that is Gwendolen's story." Constantius continues: "She is punished for being narrow and she is not allowed a chance to expand. Her finding Deronda pre-engaged to go to the East and stir up the race-feeling of the Jews strikes one as a wonderfully happy invention. The irony of the situation, for poor Gwendolen, is almost grotesque, and it makes one wonder whether the whole heavy structure of the Jewish question in the story was not built up by the author for the express purpose of giving its proper force to this particular stroke."

In this reading, the doubling structure of the narrative is perceived as architecturally solid. Deronda's story is not separate or parallel, but part of the intrusion into Gwendolen's life which reveals to her the shaky basis of her thought and feeling. The great passage in Constantius's remarks comes when he cites Gwendolen's awakening to herself not as part of some base passion, but as part of an exalted one which is going to be denied to her. The tragic dimension is there.

Blackwood indicated some hesitation in accepting Eliot's portrayal of Mordecai, a phase of the novel which puzzled him and caused him to delay writing to her. She was not surprised. She asked him to wait until the work was finished before he judges. She emphasized she was not writing about Sidonia, the romanticized Jew of Disraeli's *Coningsby;* which is her way of saying she is not presenting a deliberately attractive Jew in order to counter anti-Jewish attitudes in her readers. She says she is seeking a more complex character and "a higher strain of ideas." She touches on artistic matters: ". . . such an effect is just the most difficult thing in art—to give new elements—i.e. elements not already used up—in forms as vivid as those of long familiar types. Doubtless the wider public of novel-readers feel more interest in Sidonia than in Mordecai." Readers, in effect, prefer soap-opera types to more layered, disturbing figures.

The follow-up to this was predictable: Eliot fell into a depression over what she considered to be Blackwood's dislike of Mordecai in her treatment. Lewes wrote immediately to inform the publisher not to repeat anything like this and, at the same time, defended Mordecai as "one of the greatest of her creations." The atmosphere was now one of gloom, a dampening of "her already desponding mind; she feeling that the public will in general share your imperfect sympathy." Lewes says he has tried to dissuade her from assuming that even sophisticated readers will reject her vision of the Jewish ideal as embodied in Mordecai; and yet now with Blackwood's remarks, her negative view is reinforced. He adds that Eliot should be encouraged by the great success of the first part, but she is not. "She knows her gloom is foolish, but this knowledge can't displace the feeling. What a blessing a little of the author's self-satisfaction would be to her!"

Blackwood could not let go and answered Lewes, saying that Eliot's "wonderful Jew" was gaining much praise from those few in and around the office who had read as far as Book V. The amusing part of this was that very little in Blackwood's mind was linked to artistic matters. His view of Mordecai had its own agenda, which was that that kind of Jewishness—as apart, possibly, from Sidonia's more genteel type in the Disraeli work—was a source of great discomfort to him. In a follow-up letter, he refers to the character as "the marvellous Mordecai" and suggests that the "whole tribe of Israel should fall down and worship" Eliot for her portrayal of Mordecai and the Cohen family. One suspects the staid publisher of some irony.

Eliot was now in a race to complete a novel which apparently meant so much to her it was sending her into ever-deeper cycles of despondency and work. Blackwood, meanwhile, was writing enthusiastically about sales, for in early March it was clear that Book III would overtake Book I, which was itself moving well. This was intended as support. Eliot's eagerness to finish with the novel was intensified by her and Lewes's desire to travel to Europe in June as a way of calming down. The couple did take a break with twelve days, starting 12 March, at the Bullock-Halls', in Weybridge, one of their favorite spots. She did not stop writing while there. Any break from the Priory seemed to soothe her.

As Lewes moved toward his fifty-ninth birthday, he was asked to become a member of the council of the Physiological Society. His own forward work had slackened as he, too, showed signs of aging, along with his urgent need to protect Eliot. The profusion of letters going back and forth between Lewes and Blackwood over *Deronda* and related matters demonstrates to what extent Lewes's time and thought were given over to Eliot. Furthermore, he still had a strong taste for social activity, and he went out, alone, to many luncheons and dinners. His diary reveals the furious activity: lunches with psychologists and physiologists, meetings with Huxley, Humphry, and other scientists. Lewes had become, in lieu of a better term, a member of the establishment, and he seemed to love every minute of it. On 18 April, his birthday, he and Eliot went together to a production of Tennyson's *Queen Mary*, with Henry Irving and Kate Bateman. Lewes considered it hideously acted, but also the play was not really performable, being, like *The Spanish Gypsy*, one of those numerous closet dramas of the mid- and late-Victorian period, written to be read, not performed.

On 10 April, Eliot sent off Book VII, but with her usual misgivings, most of them associated with the "Jewish element," which she felt would satisfy nobody. Overall, she expressed doubt about every part of the enterprise, even as the novel's early success surpassed that of *Middlemarch*.

As we observe Eliot undergoing such agony over her work, feelings which are more intense than uncertainty or doubt—almost akin to paranoia—we speculate as to how much of that was attributable to her position as a woman and to her perception of that role in society. Despite her enormous success, to what extent was she suffering from the position she had put herself in, even though that position had enabled her to emerge and empower herself? According to this assessment, Eliot was caught in the trap awaiting all women. If they achieved according to their abilities, they still could not feel part of the order of things, and if they failed to achieve, their fate was equally dismal. Being "exposed" as Eliot felt she was—despite the profusion of names and roles—there was no place she could hide, not even in her fiction; and this condition could not be appeased by admirers, sales of books, or even support from Lewes.

An unusual controversy over the American poet Walt Whitman revealed some of Eliot's feelings about novelty and particularly about the new poetry, which fell so far from the kind of verse she wrote. In some vague way, she felt threatened. Having used a motto from Whitman's "Vocalism" in Book IV, she had second thoughts and wished it could be expunged: ". . . not because the motto itself is objectionable to me—it was one of the finer things which had clung to me from among his writings—but because since I quote so few poets, my selection of a motto from Walt Whitman might be taken as the sign of special admiration which I am very far from feeling." * Apparently, she and Lewes had missed it in reading the proofs. Unusual in the light of her hostile remark is the fact that Lewes's diary indicates a £2 donation to Whitman for 1876.

Not all was focused on *Deronda,* however. Writing to Alexander Main—in a correspondence that had remained steady since Main's anthology of sayings from Eliot's work—she reveals her dismay at the present state of letters.

> Are you not sometimes made rather desponding by the reading of newspapers and periodicals? One cannot escape seeing and hearing something of political and literary criticism in one's need to know what one's fellow-man are doing, and all information is given in a soup of comment. The ignorance and recklessness, the lack of any critical principles by which to distinguish what is matter of technical judgment and what of individual tastes, the ridiculous absence of fundamental comparison while hardly any judgment is passed without a futile and offensive comparison of one author with another—"Tired of all this," I sometimes shrink from every article that pretends to be critical. . . .

She omits that criticism of a very high level indeed was being written, by Matthew Arnold, among others; but her point is that in the popular press, there was no standard of excellence, no measure of taste, no objective use of knowledge. She adds that in her own case, she is "saved from getting my mind poisoned with print about myself" by her husband. She hopes that Main may do something to make periodical writing "a genuine contribution to culture. . . ."

Harriet Beecher Stowe had written a lengthy letter to Eliot in mid-March, mainly about the sordid affairs of her brother. Eliot's response, on 6 May, is curious, since it bypassed Stowe's duress and concerned itself with her own tra-

---

* She omitted it from the second edition but permitted it in the Cabinet. It reads: "Surely whoever speaks to me in the right voice, / him or her I shall follow, / as the water follows the moon, silently, / with fluid steps anywhere around the globe." Book IV of *Deronda* is titled "Gwendolen Gets Her Choice."

vails, with her latest "child." Possibly, the idea of adultery, the legal case ensuing from it, and the wide scandal that could be expected struck too close to
home; or else Eliot was quite simply following Stowe's injunction not to respond
directly to the situation. But then one wonders why Stowe mentioned it and
whether she had any idea of Eliot's true marital situation.

Lewes kept telling one and all how feeble Eliot was, and his strategy may have
been to use her indisposition as a way of controlling social invitations. They did
visit Jowett, on 20 May, for the weekend, where, as usual, they were lionized.
But Lewes's letters speak of her as "feeble, despondent and incredulous of being
able to finish effectively." She did pass up meeting with the king of Belgium,
Leopold II, who was shortly to mastermind the rape of the Congo. He met
Lewes instead, in another one of those vacuous social activities "Mrs. Eliot"
appeared to enjoy.

In early June, the end was finally in sight—by now an ordeal for Eliot which
tested not only her skill as a novelist but her sanity as a person. When Blackwood came with his son, on the 6th, she kept to her room. On the 7th, she
read the next-to-last chapter, on Deronda and Gwendolen, to Lewes, who left
the experience with "hot eyes and a sense of having been beaten"; and on the
8th, it was done and dispatched to Edinburgh. On the 10th, they were packed
and ready to depart for France and Switzerland. Her approach to *Deronda* in
these final months indicates she saw it as her most significant, and perhaps final,
statement in fictional terms. She had located all of her voices, all of her beliefs,
and all of her strategies for composition, especially in the juxtaposition of opposing elements; and she had resolved them in a renewal of spiritual belief: the
hope Deronda has of reclaiming a homeland for the Jews as part of his quest.
Such was Eliot's intensity here that we must view her interest in Deronda and
his quest as somehow linked to her own: his desire to make his dream come true
related to her desire to bring her novelistic art to another level. Although Judaism and Zionism were not personally attractive to her, the search for belief and
for certainty was; and we must never lose sight of her immersion in Deronda's
mission. The novel is something of an apologia.

During this trying time, Blackwood visited the Priory, on 18 May, when Eliot
was in full swing at her desk. He thought she looked worn and felt Lewes "fidgets
her in his anxiety both about her and her work and himself." That reciprocity
of anxiety, from Eliot to Lewes and then back to Eliot, had proven effective,
although the publisher apparently felt Lewes overdid it. He also indicates that
while Eliot says she never reads reviews, she has a good grasp of what everyone
was saying about *Deronda*.* She expressed sorrow that people were disappointed

---

*One element which recurred in the early reviews of individual books and in reviews of the
completed novel was a lament for a lack of humor, which had been abundant in *Adam Bede* and
Scenes of Clerical Life. Some critics, like A. V. Dicey in the *Nation*, saw humor in *Deronda*, but
without the proportions found earlier. Such critics failed to perceive that Eliot's fictional purposes
had deepened and that *Deronda* was at another level from those earlier and, in their view, more
successful works. They did not grant the largeness and sweep of her development as a writer, while
still honoring what they repeatedly called her "genius." Even a sympathetic reviewer like R. E.
Francillon, in *Gentleman's Magazine*, suggested that many readers of Eliot's new novel would have
some passing disappointment because it failed to be another *Adam Bede* or *Middlemarch*.

she did not develop her characters as they expected, rather than as she felt they had to be developed.

As in the past, their trip to the continent started in Paris, where they remained for several days, before moving on to Aix-les-Bains where they visited Rousseau's house in mid-June. At Aix, Eliot was felled by the oppressive heat and, more probably, by the excitement of finishing the novel and leaving so soon after. She fell ill repeatedly, some of her ailments directly attributable to her kidney condition. They stopped at Lausanne and Vevey, whose combined loveliness was lost on them as they felt quite poor. They moved on to Berne, Zurich, and Ragaz, where they began to recover with walks, baths, wholesome food, and relaxation. Eliot tried to put as good a face on it all as she could, telling Blackwood that despite their illness, they were enjoying the lovely scenery, "the combination of rich, well-cultivated land, friendly to man, and the grand outline and atmospheric effects of mountains near and distant."

Their regimen was one we would expect of an aging couple, with plenty of financial resources and nothing pressing—although we know that this particular couple was highly nervous, full of anxieties, anguish-ridden, and hardly relaxed even when they were relaxing. Their routine: rise at 5, drink a glass of warm water, walk until 6:45, breakfast, then walk from 8 to 11, rest, and some repetition of this pattern in the afternoon, with reading interspersed and then an early bedtime. With the inward-looking quality of people who have no one but themselves to look after, both Eliot and Lewes repeatedly described their regimen to several people, with Eliot going into it in greatest detail to Mrs. Nassau Senior. At one point, Eliot gave Lewes some Hebrew lessons as an amusing way they could converse with each other without being understood by the Swiss hotel personnel who knew all the mainstream languages.

They also enjoyed the music, up to three times a day, although most of it was of the thump-thump band variety. Despite their traveling, Eliot could still tell Mrs. Senior that she and Lewes were seeking a house in the country, not only for summers but for visits throughout the year. It had to be close to London, such as in Surrey or Kent, and comfortable for two "old people."

Hof Ragatz (Ragaz) in eastern Switzerland, just south of Liechtenstein, was the present place of choice, and the couple stayed there for five weeks. Then after a brief visit to the Black Forest in Germany, they were back at the Priory on 1 September. Blackwood's letter of 12 July with the figures for *Deronda* caught up with the couple in Switzerland, and it was gratifying news. On the sale of individual books, earnings came to £4,052.16, with Blackwood depositing £2,000 in Eliot's account and the remainder to be paid six months from 30 June. We also note that the firm had publicized the books with considerable ardor, handing out a total of 703 presentation and review copies, plus many gratis books. On hand were still 3,284 copies, the majority of them Book I and Book VI. The report was like a love fest for publisher and author, although Blackwood could not know that this was Eliot's last venture into fiction.

Lewes's reply indicated that Eliot was flourishing in the regimen away from the Priory, that the routine of "bathe, eat, read, and idle—'letting the world fleet by as in the golden time' " had proven quite effective in lowering her anxieties, banishing headaches, and postponing kidney stone attacks. They have eschewed all society, Lewes says, speaking to no one above the rank of shop-keeper or waiter.

With their return on 1 September, Eliot looked forward to the publication of Book VIII in that month, and then the four-volume edition priced at the exorbi-tant 42 / . But despite the price, over 300 such sets were sold by January of the next year. At a time when Lewes's income was drifting down to almost noth-ing—£275 in 1876 and then £74 the following year—Eliot's income for *Deronda* alone in 1876 was over £8,000, the equivalent in present-day buying power of over half a million dollars. The couple had achieved wealth, although their style of life remained relatively modest.

But despite all this healthy financial news, Eliot was not in a buoyant mood. She recognized, as she informs Blackwood, that she and Lewes "can't be made young again," and that even amidst all the loveliness of forest and mountain, they suffered headaches, with Lewes experiencing severe stomach cramps. To Barbara Bodichon, she was blunter. "We are both pretty well, but of course not cured of all infirmities. Death is the only physician, the shadow of his valley the only journeying that will cure us of age and the gathering fatigue of years." There was of course a birthday looming. Yet while she spoke of final things, in the great world she was being compared to the most significant of writers: Aus-ten, Dickens, Thackeray, and Fielding.

Letters arrived daily from Jewish leaders—Hermann Adler, the Bayswater Synagogue rabbi, and Haim Guedalla, a Jewish community head, among oth-ers—praising her handling of Jewish issues and thanking her for bringing to the world's attention something so sensitive. Even Blackwood was touched and recognized that despite the grumbling of "anti-Jews" in the country, Eliot had held her audience. He wonders if Disraeli will comment on the subject. Eliot tried to handle the bombardment of letters and requests even while settling in from her two-and-a-half-month trip. Despite her sense of doom, she felt that the journey overseas had proven ameliorative.

In an independent observation, Emily Davies* wrote to a friend, Annie Crow, about her 23 September visit to the Priory, a letter full of interesting comments on Eliot. Among other things, Davies mentions a new ailment, pain in the hip, which was not sciatica and which remained undiagnosed. The main part of the visit was not devoted to trivial conversation, but to heavy questions of morality and its teachings. Eliot revealed considerable ambiguity here and was not at all certain when truth should be spoken of or kept hidden. She suggested that one should avoid situations in which truth must be suppressed so as to obviate the telling of a lie. "She thinks," Davies writes, "you are not bound to say all that you think, but would use as a test, whether your silence would lead to action being taken under a false impression." The question then deep-ened into what life itself holds, and Eliot responded that as long as one didn't

---

* Emily Davies was one of those female reformers (Josephine Butler was another) who kept coming on in a society which attempted to frustrate them at every turn, in her case an effort to establish a women's college, which eventually became Girton (Eliot contributed £50 to the effort).

commit suicide one must admit there is a better life and a worse life and choose between them, a kind of throwback to early forms of utilitarianism. The question then arose of how an education, at what became Girton College, would approach political matters: "She hoped my friend [who was secretary of the Froebel Society and a teacher planning a course of study for young women] would explain to the girls that the state of insensibility in which we are not alive to high and generous emotions is stupidity, and spoke of the mistake of supposing that stupidity is only intellectual, not a thing of character—and of the consequent error of its being commonly assumed that goodness and cleverness don't go together. . . ." The views Eliot expressed are consistent with her position since her earliest fiction.

Although Davies reports that Eliot responded to all of these points—as did Lewes, now preparing Volume III of *Problems*—there was the unmistakable sense of fatigue, as though she had made these statements so repeatedly she need not go on further. But the very points which arose were unclear to her readers, since her secularity was still unfamiliar to readers of women's fiction. Dickens, Thackeray, Meredith, and even Trollope could contain large doses of secular thought: they were men. But for female writers, some deference to formal spiritual matters was expected, *even though* there was a solid tradition of secular female authors, in Austen and the Brontës, for example.

All this aside, Eliot was being bombarded with questions related to the Jewish material. This was, after all, something bizarre in serious English fiction, foreshadowing enormous political developments in Zionism as the result, later, of Theodor Herzl and his *Der Judenstaat (The Jewish State),* in 1896. It touched all kinds of nerves, Jewish and Gentile alike. Haim Guedalla wanted to publish in the *Jewish Chronicle,* in Hebrew, the club scene of Chapter 42. Eliot was truly moved by his tribute to her, but refused any piecemeal publication. Her explanation is compelling. She opposed any "introduction of my own personality to the public," she says, but beyond this she had a conviction "founded on dispassionate judgment, that any influence I may have as an author would be injured by the presentation of myself in print through any other medium than that of my books. False statements are frequently made both in British and American newspapers about my history and opinions, but I shall never break silence in an effort at contradiction until I perceive that some one else is being injured by those falsities in any way that my protest can hinder." Eliot has so far suggested that her function as a writer is heuristic; but in writing to Guedalla, she is not neglectful of her personal function. It is, if possible, to act

> . . . for good on the emotions and conceptions of my fellow men. But, as you are aware, when anyone who can be called a public person makes a casual speech or writes a letter that gets into print, his words are copied, served up in a work of commentary, misinterpreted, misquoted, and made matter of gossip for the emptiest minds. By giving occasion for more of this frivolous (if not vitiating) kind of comment than already exists in sickening abundance, I should be stepping out of my proper function and acting for what I think an evil result.

Her artistic purpose, we can say, was to demonstrate through myths, symbols, and extended images and metaphors those forms of behavior that can be productively followed. The myths may be watery (a constant in her fiction), her symbols may be connected to money (another constant), and the images may be linked to lights and darks (still another constant), yet all have a pedagogical function. She is mindful of how a public can be manipulated by a press; and, conversely, how a public makes demands on a press which lead to that manipulation. She fears that since she is a public person—especially so because of her personal life—she is in danger of being misquoted and misrepresented, her very artistic position distorted. Since she casts herself as a teacher of morals and ethics, she argues for an organic view of life. Judgments must be based on entities, and she rejects the handy quote, the superficial blurb, and the summary excerpt (the sound bite, as we call it now).

This organic view was part of her structuring of *Deronda,* in that interconnection and interlocking of the stories of Gwendolen Harleth and Daniel Deronda. She is particularly gratified, she told Barbara Bodichon, that both Jews and Christians have responded favorably to the religious elements, since that means they are reading the novel as more than merely Gwendolen, as she puts it. We get her more extensive views on this when, shortly, she writes to Harriet Beecher Stowe, a letter which reveals not only a good deal about Eliot but about English society. What her comments reveal is that she and Lewes, as they moved in the higher reaches of society, encountered a sporadic series of anti-Semitic remarks and slurs. English society was not virulent, certainly not so anti-Semitic as France and most of Europe (Bismarck's Germany, czarist Russia, the Slavic countries, and large parts of the Austro-Hungarian Empire). But English society was class driven, even as the aristocracy was beginning to lose power; and class and caste were part of the English view of Jews, who failed obviously in caste terms and most of the time in class terms, even when money permitted them to move up. Disraeli, who was once again prime minister (1874–80), and himself the product of a conversion to Christianity, was nevertheless always reminded of his Hebrew background, and not in complimentary terms. This least stereotypical of men was fitted into nearly every racial stereotype. Eliot and Lewes moved in these circles, heard remarks deriding the prime minister—she cites these—and other comments on noses, the eating of ham, and the like. This sequence of events evidently drove her, with Lewes's support, to protest through her novel. Of course, even Eliot vaunted the "right kind" of Jews; the others she saw stereotypically.

In her letter to Stowe,* Eliot stoutly defended her position on Jews, with the American quite supportive. Eliot says that at first she expected much stronger

---

* While all this was going on with the explanations of Judaism, Blackwood offered Eliot £4,000 for a ten-year renewal of copyright on her novels (*Scenes, Adam, Mill, Marner, Holt*), the present copyright being almost exhausted. To this, he would also add *Middlemarch, Romola,* and *Daniel Deronda,* with the monies to be paid out over a period of three years. Eliot said she needed time to consider the proposal, and finally concluded that a royalty arrangement was preferable. Lewes as usual handled the matter and found an error or blunder in Blackwood's figures, which the publisher freely admitted and apologized for. Eliot's and Lewes's decision on royalties proved a happy one for the author, since her future earnings soared well beyond Blackwood's £4,000.

resistance "and even repulsion than it has actually met with." She goes on: "But precisely because I felt that the usual attitude of Christians toward Jews is—I hardly know whether to say more impious or more stupid when viewed in the light of their professed principles, I therefore felt urged to treat Jews with such sympathy and understanding as my nature and knowledge could attain to." She notes that toward all Oriental peoples the English display "a spirit of arrogance and contemptuous dictatorialness" which she calls a national disgrace.

> There is nothing I should care more to do, if it were possible, than to rouse the imagination of men and women to a vision of human claims in those races of their fellow-men who most differ from them in customs and beliefs. But towards the Hebrews we western people who have been reared in Christianity, have a peculiar debt and whether we acknowledge it or not a peculiar thoroughness of fellowship in religious and moral sentiment. Can anything be more disgusting than to hear people called "educated" making small jokes about eating ham, and showing themselves empty of any real knowledge as to the relation of their own social and religious life to the history of the people they think themselves witty in insulting. They hardly know that Christ was a Jew. And I find men educated at Rugby supposing that Christ spoke Greek.

Could she have meant John Cross, Rugby educated?

With her next remarks, she sounds remarkably like Matthew Arnold of the 1860s and 1870s, although the outrage is clearly Eliot's.

> To my feeling, this deadness to the history which has prepared half of our world for us, this inability to find interest in any form of life that is not clad in the same coat-tails and flounces as our own lies very close to the worst kind of irreligion. The best that can be said of it is, that it is a sign of the intellectual narrowness—in plain English, the stupidity, which is still the average mark of our culture.

Eliot's remarks suggest much broader issues than English treatment of Jews, which was verbally contemptuous and socially condescending but otherwise tolerant. She observes there is a general lowering of the educated class into a narrow, constricted view of England and things English. She laments, as did Arnold, the lack of a broader culture, with excellence as its standard. She notes the slow slide that was occurring in English public life, even as England was moving, under Disraeli, toward greater achievements abroad. English culture was extending itself mightily—annexation of the Fiji Islands, the Zulu wars in Africa, the annexation of the Transvaal, wars also against the Afghans, the crowning of Victoria as Empress of India—but instead of broadening the educated Englishman, it turned him inward, toward nationalistic standards. The imperial sweep was toward breadth, but the mentality remained "Little England."

Eliot had already expressed her views about the precipitous fall in literature, the declining standards of reviewing and article writing, the diminished level of what had once been considered high culture. Implied in her remarks is her sense that as England became more democratic—ironically, under reforms initiated by Disraeli—there was a loss of real culture and it was being replaced by a veneer, influenced by those "barbarians" from below, as Arnold labeled them, and abetted by the middle class. If we applaud Eliot's desire to see higher standards prevail, we must not neglect her fear that the swell from below was contaminating all culture. She was not a ringing democrat or liberal in these respects, and like several of her aging contemporaries, such as Tennyson, she looked with disfavor on a democratic culture she saw as substandard and debased from below.

Eliot's response to Stowe was the result of the American author's long and sympathetic letter which divided *Deronda* into English and Jewish halves, * with the English half finding more favor. This is not to say Stowe opposed the Jewish element; her husband, Calvin, was a student of Jewish history and Stowe referred to him as "my Rabbi." Nevertheless, Stowe lauded Gwendolen, full of "uneasy instincts that point to soaring among the clouds of heaven." Yet she failed to observe that Gwendolen's "intrigue" gains much of its substance from juxtaposition, first to Klesmer and then to Deronda. She has substance, but still gains more by contrast. Stowe's emphasis on the English side was probably connected to her disapproval, in the Deronda segment, of Eliot's religion of humanity, which the American writer felt was a bastardized form of religious belief without real substance.

In still another respect, Stowe failed to perceive that Deronda is part of the thematic as well as structural unity of the novel. The Jewish world offers Gwendolen some hope of salvation, whereas the Gentile world traps her in hypocrisy and egomania. Her (mild) anti-Semitism—her stereotyping of Jews as avaricious, then her reminding Deronda she doesn't mind he is a Jew—is countered and finally contained by Deronda's message about self-fulfillment and community. It was clear, although not to Stowe, that the novel, by means of contrasts and parallels, needed both parts to work through Eliot's sense of human unity.

By downgrading the Jewish element—although without prejudicial feeling—Stowe pointed to Eliot's perceived shortcomings, not as a novelist, but as a thinker, philosopher, or theologian. The American believed Jesus Christ was

---

* The Jewish audience for the book obviously emphasized this split, with its fervent appreciation of Eliot's sympathetic portrayal of Jews and her intimate knowledge of racial and religious matters. Jews in English literature had almost always been portrayed vilely, or else as the opposite, as noble victims whose fate was to suffer. Whichever way, they were bent out of shape. Marlowe's vile Jew in *The Jew of Malta* should be contrasted with the patient Rebecca of *Ivanhoe*. In later literature, there was Dickens's saintly Riah in *Our Mutual Friend*. Trollope, however, showed traditional English anti-Semitism, as did Thackeray, with stereotypes of Jews rather than real people. The *Jewish Chronicle* was in the forefront of holding up Eliot as an antidote to the usual portrayal of Jews. In fact, there was such general admiration of her exaltation of Mordecai these readers seemed unaware of any other dimensions to the novel. *Deronda* criticism, then, passed through several phases, one in which the Jewish aspect was stressed, another in which the Jewish dimension was almost ignored, and a third in which some effort was made to see the "two sides" of the novel as complementary. What nearly everyone omitted, as we have observed, is how Eliot made snide remarks at the "wrong kind" of Jews, Jews who are stereotypically too Jewish, or where individual crudeness becomes characteristic of the race.

divine; Eliot accepted Jesus as a historical figure with a historical role to play. From Stowe's point of view, if Jesus is not considered divine, then there can be no belief, there cannot even be a Christian. Stowe believed in prayer, not as asking God for something, but as resting in his arms, listening to his voice, counting on his strength, seeking renewal in his example. Her God is, obviously, anthropomorphic: "his" arms, and so on. It was precisely that part of Christianity Eliot had long ago rejected; God's strength lay for her in the individual's striving to discover the "God" in himself and then to emerge strengthened. Eliot was a late Victorian intellectual with all the suspicions that had formed about Christian belief; Stowe was an earlier believer who found in God the assurance and support she needed for daily life. It is compelling to watch these two sympathetic women joust for position: Stowe through her letters, Eliot in her novels.

When Lewes wrote to Blackwood that a royalty arrangement for Eliot's copyrights was the most satisfactory for all parties, he indicated that in this way he and Eliot would have greater control of editions and prices. Along the way, he says that Jews seem quite grateful for *Deronda* and compensate for "the deadness of so many Christians to that part of the book which does not directly concern Gwendolen." Lewes hopes that when the cheap edition is issued, this Jewish sympathy will be turned into sales, on the analogy of the vast number of doctors who purchased the cheap edition of *Middlemarch.* As a marginal matter, it is interesting to note that Lewes, even while he and Eliot were quite well fixed, was still angling for the utmost sales—possibly not solely for the money but to fulfill Eliot's hopes of reaching a wider audience. When money came up, Eliot, too, was not shy, citing her numerous extended familial obligations.

Although reviews and notices of *Deronda* were hardly weak, she had the feeling she had received a poor press. She was reading into the reviews her own doubts and fears. "Certainly, if I had not very strong proofs to the contrary," she tells Blackwood, "I should conclude that my book was a failure and that nobody was grateful for it. . . . I am saved from concluding that I have exhibited my faculties in a state of decay by very delightful letters from unknown readers and reported judgments from considerable authorities." These people asserted that she widened their knowledge of other cultures, and she says that had been her intent: ". . . to widen the English vision a little in that direction and let in a little conscience and refinement."

She recognized that reviewers—often on the basis of the incomplete novel—compared *Middlemarch* with *Deronda* and found the latter wanting. R. H. Hutton, in the *Spectator,* cited *Deronda* as rising to greater heights than *Middlemarch* while lacking the average power of that novel, a view which appears close to the mark. But we know Eliot's negative perception of her venture would have remained regardless of the quality of the reviews. Her aim had been a perfect work: a deeply social and political statement as well as an aesthetic achievement. She had attempted linkage of more than she had ever attempted before, and this effort to reach out made her believe she had created her most significant statement.

Just as in Middlemarch there was a near frenzy to identify her "models," so in
Deronda. Klesmer, superficially, would seem to be based on Franz Liszt, whom
Eliot had met and admired many years ago when she and Lewes visited Weimar.
But Liszt was a poor guess for several reasons, among them the fact that Klesmer
is Jewish and Liszt was a lifelong anti-Semite, with a manner quite different from
Eliot's somewhat forbidding character. Haight is probably correct in locating a
partial model in Anton Rubinstein: German, Slav, Semite, as Eliot describes
Klesmer. Rubinstein, whom Eliot also met at Weimar, when he was twenty-
four, went on to have a large career as pianist and composer, although not on
Liszt's scale. Even physically, Klesmer recalled Rubinstein, and in manner they
shared a tart, caustic view of humanity. In terms of background (considerable
poverty), ethnic origins (Rubinstein had a Jewish mother, a Russian father),
and related matters, he seems the model; and when he came to London, in
1877, as if life were following art, he witnessed duets and tableaux from his
"Jewish opera," The Maccabees. Once all this is said, however, it must be added
that Klesmer belongs very much to Eliot, with her own strictures on artistic
standards, her refusal to bend to popular taste, and her derision of those who
thought being an artist was easy to achieve. Klesmer may have had Rubinstein
in the background, even some Liszt, but in the foreground he had Eliot.

Deronda himself seems a combination of several figures, not the least Emanuel Deutsch, the biblical scholar who so impressed Eliot. Haight makes Deutsch
a partial model for Mordecai, but the deceased Talmudic scholar also set off in
Eliot her interest in a Jewish subject which cannot be disentangled in her mind
from Deronda. A Colonel Albert Goldsmid claimed he was Deronda, but the
fit—except for some Jewish origins and Christian upbringing—was attenuated,
except in the colonel's mind. Other possible models offered themselves, but no
one substantial. Deronda represented in Eliot's mind not a real person on whom
she based him but a conglomeration of ideas, attitudes, and outlooks which had
characterized her fiction from the beginning. He is related, in some respects, to
the artisan Adam Bede, the fiery orator Felix Holt, the idealist Will Ladislaw,
and even the sacrificial Romola: in brief, an Eliot creation, with the exception
of Deutsch in the background.

For Mordecai, Deutsch comes up again, but Haight makes a good case for the
consumptive watchmaker Cohn, whom Lewes had known from the Philosophers Club of his youth. Lewes had himself shot down this connection when it
was presented to him. More likely, Mordecai was an original creation with some
resemblance to Baruch Spinoza, the philosopher whom Eliot had translated and
whom Lewes had written about in the Fortnightly, in 1866.

Mirah, similarly, had many interpreters, but all the models put forward seem
unlikely, including Phoebe Sarah Marks, Barbara Bodichon's protégée. Even
Bodichon denied the possibility. Like the other characters, Mirah has significance in Eliot's own work, deriving as she does from fictional creations far more
than from any possible real personages. Mirah recalls Dinah Morris, and the
contrast between Mirah and Gwendolen in Deronda recalls the contrast in Adam
Bede between Dinah and Hetty Sorrel, or in Romola between Romola and Tito

Melema's peasant mistress. In each instance, two contrasting women seek the soul of the male protagonist. Gwendolen is herself modeled on other Eliot fictional creations: Rosamond Vincy in *Middlemarch*, most obviously, but also Esther Lyon in *Felix Holt*, and in the shadows Hetty Sorrel.

The search for real personages behind Eliot's characters, which was a kind of parlor game among her contemporaries, may disguise a more salient point: that she drew on her characters repeatedly. Like a theater troupe which recycles actors and actresses according to the parts they fill, she created and re-created them, so that they recur and reemerge, transmogrified as need be, but nevertheless recognizable. In addition to the above, there is a line from Maggie Tulliver through Mary Garth and Dorothea Brooke and the transformed, chastened Gwendolen, with some Esther Lyon mixed in. Similarly, the male characters have their own lines of succession: Adam Bede and Felix Holt through Deronda; Tom Tulliver through Tito Melema and Lydgate; Arthur Donnithorne also through Tito; Felix Holt through Will Ladislaw, with Adam Bede in the background.* Only Grandcourt seems a new figure for Eliot, new in terms of his class and his isolation from anyone she had previously described, even Arthur Donnithorne. He would appear to be the product of the high society in which she and Lewes now moved. He was, all in all, part of the English society which remained narrow and ignorant of anything beyond, but was quite willing to insult what it did not know. This society ruled by threat.

The Jewish element would not go away—this had touched a nerve. Blackwood tried to be soothing: "I always knew that the strong Jew element ['Jew' became an adjective] would be unpopular, but your picture of the Jew family at home did wonders in overcoming the public distaste to a kindly view of the Jewish character." He also tells her not to be disturbed about the reviews, inasmuch as "people keep discussing the book like a great historical event about which there is a difference of opinion." More ominous than the less than perfect reviews were the signs of real physical decline, toothache, biliousness, general depression, and frequent kidney stone attacks. They were a sign, even to someone as resigned as Eliot, that something terminal was in the offing. They kept coming on, especially the attacks of stones. Was she, who wanted to be Antigone, now playacting Job?

Blackwood's extensive report on sales, including *Deronda* so far, would have cheered most authors; but Eliot was approaching another birthday, her fifty-seventh, on 22 November. As was her usual routine, she wrote Sara Hennell a

---

* Also recycled was Eliot's attitude toward parent–child relationships, one of the abiding Victorian themes. While there are functioning families in her fiction, malfunction dominates; and here, in *Daniel Deronda*, the protagonist's relationship with his mother, the Princess Halm-Eberstein, is compelling. The princess defines herself as a mother who refuses the material role in order to pursue an artistic career. But the career seems herself as a facade behind which she can hide her real distaste for motherhood, which she sees as a form of entrapment. We recall Armgart in that Eliot poem, torn between career and a suitable marriage, and also Erinna (in an unpublished poem), a young poet chained by her mother to a spinning-wheel, where she perishes. We think of others: Maggie's and Felix Holt's respective mothers, Dorothea's and Celia's uncle / guardian, Romola's "blind" father, and the like.

newsy letter, keying in on how bodily infirmity "spoils life even for those who have no other trouble." She describes her own feelings contradictorily, saying she has lost her "*personal* melancholy"; that while she feels sad about the destinies of others, "I am never in that mood of sadness which used to be my frequent visitant even in the midst of external happiness." This is followed by: "And this, notwithstanding a very vivid sense that life is declining and death close at hand."

She is, however, amused that Herbert Spencer, the opponent of biography and autobiography as unprofitable and unscientific, was now busily collecting materials concerning his family and personal history. Eliot here does not pick up on Spencer's obsessive secrecy about his autobiography, which was published after his death in 1903, or on his ambiguous desire to suppress as much as he was forced to reveal. He destroyed letters partially used in his book, and because of his secrecy made life extremely difficult for his biographer, David Duncan. It is unfortunate Eliot never tried to "do" Spencer, since he would have proved not only fascinating but a psychological study of considerable complexity, an entire menu of anxieties and mental gymnastics.

In bringing up the expectation of Harriet Martineau's own autobiography, Eliot makes several remarks which indicate her distaste for the possibility she would ever write her own memoir. The idea must have occurred to her, or to Lewes, since her story told with full intellectual breadth would have been, very possibly, the finest of revelations for the century, on a par with Mill's *Autobiography.* Instead, she published only one more book, *Impressions of Theophrastus Such* (1879), completed in November of 1878, just before Lewes's death. Although not a memoir in any sense, *Such* allowed Eliot to roam freely in subjects which interested her. Except for the final essay, called "The Modern Hep! Hep! Hep!," which touches on *Deronda,* it is one of the least satisfactory of Eliot's publications, perhaps because it fell between the memoir she disdained to write and the desire, near the end of her life, to write more freely about more personal things.

Hints in her notebooks suggest, however, that she may have been planning another novel, this one based on Napoleonic themes or set in Napoleon's days of conquest. In the Pforzheimer Library Notebook manuscripts, notations on her reading in history, biography, and private diaries suggest such a venture. But we have no further indication that she moved beyond the initial research into even a formulated outline, no less any manuscript pages. The direction of the intended novel, if it was that, remains unclear since her reading took her into legal matters, autobiographical memoirs, and social and political treatises: the kind of saturation reading she had done for *Romola* and *Daniel Deronda.* Nevertheless, the sketchy notebook entries reveal she was thinking of a novel mixing intrigue, a double agent, conspiracy, and spying—a foreshadowing of something on the order of Joseph Conrad's *The Secret Agent,* with her more familiar rural settings. One further fictional venture is indistinct and dim, but possible: a novel based on the life of Ferdinand Lassalle (1825–64), the German-Jewish social democrat. There is an extended reference to Lassalle in one of her notebooks (Folios 35–37, Pforzheimer), although little indication of a follow-up, not even any mention in her letters. But the notebook entry covering his career suggests Eliot's interest in the man and his work: a man who set his socialism in opposition to Marx's model (Marx called him a "Jewish Nigger"), went to prison for advocating resistance to taxes for a government he detested, and died in a duel (possibly a setup) with the fiancé of the woman he loved.

Eliot's diary now settled into noting small satisfactions; she was clearly reducing the size of her world in this post-*Deronda* period. Her brain was spinning, but without a subject. She was pleased that even while the Jewish element continued to create repugnance in some, * she had received many expressions of interest in *Deronda;* and the sales had been better than *Middlemarch* in the expensive four-volume form. The negatives were part of her fame, as Blackwood recognized, citing Dickens, Thackeray, and Bulwer-Lytton as those who suffered slings and arrows as their fame grew. She was, whether she confronted it or not, a target.

---

* As John Blackwood told Lewes: "The Jews should be the most interesting people in the world, but even *her* magic cannot *at once* make them a popular element in a Novel. The discussion however goes on and the power she has expended on the despised element will tell and force its way. The fact is that Mrs. Lewes stands on such a pinnacle that the Critics are (unconsciously perhaps) glad to fix on anything they can possibly mention as a flaw."

PART SEVEN

Entering the Valley of Bones

21

Post-Deronda

"He was conscious of that peculiar irritation which will sometimes befall the man whom others are inclined to trust as a mentor—the irritation of perceiving that he is supposed to be entirely off the same plane of desire and temptation as those who confess to him."

The post-*Deronda* Eliot was not focused clearly, and, as already noted, she was withdrawing. One thing she and Lewes finally accomplished on 6 December 1876, after years of trying, was to purchase a country house, called the Heights at Witley, in Surrey, within easy travel of London by rail. John Cross had taken them to see it, and they liked it sufficiently to offer a bid up to £5,000. They obtained the house for £4,950, not a small sum at that time, equal in purchasing power now to possibly a quarter of a million dollars. They knew Surrey well from their stay at Shottermill; and Weybridge, their destination on several occasions, was also familiar.

Eliot was now regarded as England's greatest living novelist; and even in those reviews which found negative things to say, she was respected as a national treasure. Time had dissipated much of the hostility toward her marital arrangement, and many even believed she and Lewes were now indeed married. Of course, her brother Isaac knew better. He required as evidence a marriage certificate. Agnes Lewes was still alive and well, destined to outlive Eliot by twenty-two years, her husband by twenty-four. She had grown into a fat, frumpy old lady; and looking at her in later photos, it is difficult to believe she was the siren who mothered four children by Thornton Hunt, as well as four by Lewes. Agnes lived on in Kensington, with her three daughters and one son by Hunt never too distant. Had she died, Lewes would have been free to marry Eliot; but Agnes refused to cooperate.

Eliot settled in. She had abundant money, a companion deeply devoted to her, and dependent upon her, a home in London, a country house in Surrey, a carriage and horse. Flatterers, hypocrites, as well as sincere admirers poured in letters and notes. She and Lewes received dozens of invitations for every one they accepted—and they accepted few. Fame seemed for the time to turn Eliot into more of a hermit, probably because of ill health and the knowledge she was at the end of her creative productivity, at fifty-seven. Dickens had died at virtually that age; Trollope, she felt, had seen better days; Thackeray was long dead; Bulwer-Lytton was not deemed a fully serious writer; Meredith does not seem to have impressed her. Hardy was just starting out. All other significant female writers—Mrs. Humphry Ward was not considered a major contender—had long since died. She lived now in her own world, really one of her own creations. She had reshaped Mary Anne Evans, Mary Ann Evans, Marian Evans into everything she dreamed of, and far beyond that. It was a curious world, a fame she indeed reached for but could not enjoy because she knew it was ephemeral, false, an artifact of an artificial life. To sustain it, she had buried herself personally as M. E. Lewes, which she was not, and professionally as George Eliot, under a man's name which denied her very gender. She had played games with names so repeatedly that her emergence involved roles, role-playing, and acting-out, which scrambled reality; and she was aware of the factitiousness of it all. With the creative drive gone, she increasingly sought out hiding places.

She and Lewes did continue their pattern of attending the concerts at St. James's Hall, on Saturday afternoons. She was observed, looking elderly, somewhat stooped, walking slowly and cautiously. The Sundays at home diminished in intensity and in size. Eliot occasionally saw her niece, Emily Clarke, and took her to a play based on *Silas Marner,* called *Dan'l Druce, Blacksmith,* by W. S. Gilbert (the librettist for the Gilbert and Sullivan operettas), with the young Forbes-Robertson. Lewes thought the whole thing rather awful. The Sundays also included visits by John Cross, who rarely came unattended. Lewes and Eliot spent a weekend at Six Mile Bottom. But aside from these occasional activities, they remained quiet, as though following through on Eliot's notion of "waiting for death."

Letters that poured in were increasingly from Eliot's female admirers who wished to throw themselves at her feet. Edith Simcox and Elma Stuart were only two among several, and we have commented on how they infiltrated into the couple's lives. Simcox remains one of the most interesting of these because she was so accomplished and was clearly not merely compensating for a wasted life. She had achieved in half a dozen ways, as author, reformer, organizer, entrepreneur. Coming forth now as "lover," in waves of idolatrous and emotional outpouring, she did not need Eliot the way Elma Stuart did, as compensation for a lackluster life. As we follow Simcox's actions, we observe she would have liked to devour Eliot, as though in some primitive ritual. Simcox was a fearful presence, almost a specter of destruction in her obsession with embracing, touching, kissing, or simply being close to her idol. And Eliot did not reject this: she could have told Simcox to stay away, or made certain Lewes refused her entrance to their home.

Yet there is no evidence in Eliot's life or work that she felt an erotic attachment to a woman. In her work, when women do reject men with hatred or disdain, as Gwendolen rejects Grandcourt, it is not purely for sexual reasons, but because men represent an empowerment that must be countered. Thus, Romola with Tito, Mary Garth at first with Fred Vincy, Rosamond with Lydgate, and the like. One reason Eliot permitted Simcox to make such advances was probably her recognition that her friend needed to find emotional outlets; and perhaps Eliot herself found solace here. Yet there are other possibilities as we assess her relationship to these idolatrous women, chiefly her fascination with outrageous or extreme behavior, elements we do not normally associate with her or her work.

Eliot is always characterized as our novelist of moderation and balance. But her novels often bespeak morbidity, death, and forms of extreme behavior: in *Romola*, Florence as a city of death, the Arno as the River Styx; in *Silas Marner*, a context of evildoing, self-destructive behavior; in "The Lifted Veil," poison and would-be murder; in *Deronda*, Gwendolen's situational "murder" of Grandcourt; in *Mill*, water as doom and an implied incestuous pattern; in *Adam Bede*, a desperate would-be infant killer in Hetty and a near murderous Adam. Even *Middlemarch* has a "murder," in Bulstrode's permitting his old antagonist to die. There is a fascination with aberrations and socially unacceptable forms of behavior. Grandcourt contains within himself so many perverted feelings he is a kind of nineteenth-century version of the serial murderer whose victims are women, himself a throwback to the sinister Gothic male. Killers and near killers abound. Dempster in "Janet's Repentance," at the very beginning of Eliot's career, is a murderously dangerous drunkard, capable of wife-killing. Tom Tulliver, in *Mill*, would "kill" Philip Wakem, and in *Romola*, Baldassarre does kill his adopted son, Tito. In "Mr. Gilfil's Love-Story," the romantically thwarted Caterina prepares to kill Captain Wybrow; and back in *Deronda*, Lydia Glasher (pronounced "glacier") becomes a Medea-like figure in her desire for revenge on both Gwendolen and Grandcourt. Felix Holt is accused of murder, and even Maggie Tulliver disguises her wish to kill by driving nails into her "Fetish" doll. These are not the images and scenes of a "moderate" novelist. Eliot's behavior with Simcox, her tolerance of the latter's frenzied idolatry, fits well within these patterns of extremes. Only when Simcox became particularly desperate did Eliot step back and warn her friend to desist.

For deeply personal reasons, Eliot resisted the idea of anyone writing a biography of her—her dislike of that deriving from the same desire not to write her memoirs. She was horrified at the revelations in Harriet Martineau's *Autobiography*, published in 1877 in three volumes the year after her death. What set Eliot off were comments from Blackwood, in October 1876, when he pointed out that someone who has risen as high as she will inevitably be the subject of "idle gossip," something for which the public has a "depraved appetite." But Eliot's distaste for a personal memoir went further than that, into the kind of secrecy reflected amply in her novels. And beyond that, a secrecy she desired because she feared her personal philosophy, held up to scrutiny, did not really cohere. A memoir would expose her.

On the one hand, she wanted to show how people can reshape themselves, how the individual can find fulfillment here and now; on the other, she feared too much individuality because it threatened the social and political comity— her opposition to the female franchise can be viewed in this light. She found herself in the typical Victorian dilemma; for even as she believed in individual will, force, and determination, she also held to a society based on justice and order, a contract. John Stuart Mill in *On Liberty* (1849) had argued this very point. It was a subject worked over by the great prose writers of the century: Carlyle, Newman, Ruskin, and Arnold, among others. The two parts, individual and society, did not quite fit, nor could they be resolved philosophically, surely not fictionally. What Eliot suggested, inevitably, was that everyone be like her: achieve, fulfill, work through one's own needs; then halt, become part of the larger comity, maintain order, rein in one's desire for power and accomplishment. It was, all in all, a futile quest.

Reviewers and critics had already picked at seeming inconsistencies, but had gone on to praise her because fiction did not have to be philosophy or be socially correct. A biographical study or an autobiographical memoir, on the other hand, might not only reveal too much of her personal life—a real fear—but also dismantle some of her fictional building blocks. Nineteenth-century criticism, with only a little encouragement, tended to separate out beliefs and ideas from their artistic forms, as if fictions or poems were moral essays. A memoir would provide this impetus. We can also speculate that some of Eliot's depression and anguish in the later years are the consequence of her recognition that her fictional philosophy would not make much social or political difference. This is a recognition that strikes every major creative writer; but with Eliot it was particularly intense and severe because she had brought so much of her self to this "resolution" and had been so single-minded about it. She had determined to make herself a voice, *the* voice. Too much scrutiny, her own or others', might subvert it all.

Yet alongside her fears, her secretiveness, her desire for a passive life was her real joy in the Heights at Witley. It was a veritable country estate, a red-brick house on eight and a half acres—all of it reminiscent of the red-brick farmhouse at Griff. It had good prospects from nearly all windows, several fireplaces, a high-gabled roof, and a railway station only minutes away. In the distance were the towns of Haslemere, Hindhead, and Blackdown (Tennyson's home). They had a friend in the next house, the son of Sir Henry Holland, their former physician. Renovations were called for, almost an inevitability wherever the couple lived. The kitchen was to be enlarged, the plumbing modernized. What is striking is how niggardly they had become, for when the architect offered to do the major renovations for £640 or else minor, minimum ones for half the price, they thought of selling the house and then decided on the minimum renovations when clearly they could have afforded to redo the entire place.

Their pleasure in the Heights, which seemed to offer so much, was short-lived, however, because of a sequence of ailments.* During the Christmas holidays, spent with the Crosses at Weybridge, Eliot fell ill, and then in February 1877 she suffered a recurrence of her kidney stones. For his part, Lewes was attacked by what was called rheumatic gout, probably a hereditary ailment which had been dogging him for years and had gone undiagnosed. Yet even with this, they were not socially inactive, although selective. The farm girl from Nuneaton had become the central figure in groups that included Browning, Tennyson, Arnold (who was present at the 26 December Boxing Day dinner), Clara Schumann, Joseph Joachim (the famous violinist), and Burne-Jones. Several portraits of Eliot were made at this time, including one by Princess Louise, another by Mrs. Alma-Tadema† (now at the National Portrait Gallery), and a third by the painter Lowes Dickinson.

Eliot's public life now became structured by fame and celebrity. Her reputation was at its highest point, but the acme was reached at a time when she had nothing left to say in fiction. She was playing a familiar role—Matthew Arnold had sketched it out in his caustic poem "Growing Old." At the moment when the writer recognizes he or she has nothing left, the world applauds. The praise fills a vacuum. Eliot now, until Lewes's death in less than two years, had emptied out personally.

We have little sense of her internal world, since she did not reveal much and seemed to accept homage as her right, although celebrity status did not make her preen. The pattern of her life was really set: an effort to keep as healthy as possible even while suffering intimations of death; fears about Lewes's continuing poor health; an awareness she had reached the end of that spectacular curve of achievement begun only twenty years before; dismay at current events and political developments; uncertainties about the course of English life as it began to disintegrate into subcultures and incoherence; and a more generalized sense of a growing social disorder, both perceived and imagined.

Most of these were the fears of any intelligent person in the late 1870s, although different observers reacted differently. Matthew Arnold, for example, expressed the apprehensiveness of those who saw the breakup of an organic society, with the concomitant fear that the lower or middle classes were going to be empowered. Much of the apprehension about disorder derived from this observation: that previously disenfranchised and disempowered groups were

---

* Balanced to some degree by the continued outpouring from Jewish admirers. When Abraham Benisch, a Bohemian Jew and editor of the *Jewish Chronicle*, wrote, Eliot's response was heartfelt. She says that she expected to offend most people. "But I did not expect the cordial encouragement which you and other instructed men have given me to believe that my anxious effort at a true presentation is not a failure, and may even touch the feeling of your people to welcome issues." It is interesting that in writing to Elizabeth Stuart Phelps (author of the religious novel *The Gates Ajar*, 1868) on the same day, Eliot emphasized that her Christian point of view has never changed and that what she said about Dinah Morris is "equally at the root of my effort to paint Mordecai."

† Princess Louise—Marchioness of Lorne—was an accomplished sculptress, and an educator with special attention to the training and education of women. She never became another Simcox in her relationship to Eliot, but she did insist on getting to know the writer, which resulted eventually in the portrait she sketched of Eliot. Mrs. Alma-Tadema (the former Laura Epps) was married to the famous and fashionable Sir Lawrence Alma-Tadema.

poised to assume control, and from this would develop a second-rate, un-English culture, lacking in substance and characterized as vulgar. Eliot's idea had been to bring people up, and now she feared vast groups would bring the rest down, or at least be encouraged to do so. All of this maneuvering was of course a test of true democracy; yet England in the Victorian era was not a democracy, but an aristocracy with sharp class distinctions working alongside several nascent democratic institutions. It had more or less excluded the lower working and agricultural classes; privilege prevailed, while the urban and rural poor barely held on.

Once her fiction was done, Eliot found herself forced to confront a morass of contradictions. She moved in high social circles without having full regard for upper society; she felt democratic impulses, in which every individual had the right to self-fulfillment, but feared disorder and foresaw chaos; she argued for individual justice and even equality, but observed that that could lead to social breakup; she supported women in her fiction—strong, formidable women in some instances—but argued that in life women were not yet ripe for such responsibility; she sanctioned female sacrifice and suffering, but knew that in her own life with her father she felt only desperation. She saw, finally, that there was a huge gap between what she argued for in her fiction and what she found outside it; and she attempted to ignore the inconsistencies by throwing herself into London and Surrey social activity, or, alternately, into a hermitic existence.

One of those social activities involved the May concerts in Albert Hall, the Richard Wagner concerts, at which Wagner conducted. Franz Liszt had given his daughter, Cosima, a letter of introduction to Lewes; Cosima was now Wagner's wife. She came to the Priory to meet Eliot, * and sat in the Lewes–Eliot box at the concerts Wagner conducted. The couples became friends, entertaining each other on numerous occasions and creating an amusing side-light. The woman who had just written a strongly pro-Semitic novel was seated with another woman whose anti-Semitism made the anti-Semitism of her fabled husband seem like the garden variety. Yet whatever was said and whatever was ignored, the couples were close, with Wagner, at one dinner, reading aloud from his *Parsifal*. Wagner also appeared eager to speak to Eliot. In his diary of these events, Lewes left no record of what was said, although another amusing sidelight was that Lewes did not particularly appreciate Wagner's operas and only attended because of Cosima's introduction.

In the background, Blackwood was moving along with the Cabinet edition of Eliot's works: the final accolade, an edition. Eliot had earlier told John Black-wood she was impressed with a fine octavo page (6 × 9 inches) of an edition of Henry Fielding, and it occurred to her she would like to be published in eight volumes of similar size, with fine type and paper. She suggested that the six long novels would each make a volume; then another volume would come from

---

* In her diary entry for 6 May 1877, Cosima notes "made the acquaintance of George Eliot, the famous woman writer, who makes a noble and pleasant impression."

Scenes of Clerical Life, Silas Marner, "The Lifted Veil," and "Brother Jacob," with the final volume made up of *The Spanish Gypsy* and the occasional poems. The price for each could be anywhere from the 7 / 6 suggested by Lewes to 10 / - in her own plan.

By April 1877, Lewes had seen the third volume of his *Problems of Life and Mind* through the press, and on the 17th, it was published. Like Eliot's *Deronda,* it was a summation, his effort to consolidate his studies in psychology and physiology toward some resolution of man's dualism; an effort, incidentally, that more or less died with the nineteenth century, with Freud as one of the last major researchers in this area. Lewes's diary continued to reveal his enjoyment of social activity, and he and Eliot went together to Oxford, to stay with Jowett; dinner parties for sixteen on successive nights followed. Haight quotes at length from observations left by Adolphus G. C. Liddell, a barrister who had entered into a long conversation with Eliot. He describes her in the standard way, as having "a noble face of the equine type," with fine, gray eyes. Liddell's comments, however, suggest the awe with which people approached her, for he is astonished she would even spend this amount of time with him. "I felt," he wrote, "that she had been very good-natured to talk so much to an 'ordinary mortal,' and to look so kindly out of her gray eyes." When someone else came up, the talk turned to a theoretical problem in mathematics and geometry, and Eliot glided easily into that.

Still leading up to this somewhat frenetic social activity, Eliot was working through the possibilities of the Cabinet edition of her entire works. She now saw value in Blackwood's suggestion for a more expansive edition. The publisher offered not eight volumes but nineteen or twenty—which would include wider margins, finer, tinted paper, and some landscape illustrations in each volume. The edition was moving toward a suitable memorial, and Eliot was quite taken with something that would prove a monument. Also, she agreed that the volumes, of different lengths, need not be priced the same. She even suggested a color, what she called the "Abode of Snow." *

The end of May saw the move to the Heights, with the servants doing the nasty business of packing up and handling the shift. Lewes and Eliot spent five days with the Sidgwicks (he was a Fellow of Trinity College) at Cambridge, while the house was put in order. This led to a veritable orgy of social engagements, not only dinners but lunches and breakfasts with Conservative M. P. Arthur Balfour, the classical scholar R. C. Jebb, Sidney Colvin, lords and ladies; and included a visit to Girton College, where Eliot went despite having been invited by a student (Frances Müller) rather than by the headmistress (Marianne Frances Bernard).

---

* Although we can be certain Eliot consulted with Lewes about every aspect of the edition, he hardly stood still. His diary (for 30 March and 20–25 April) is full of events, belying a man slowly declining. In just the latter six-day period, he made notes on the work of the physiologist Pierre Jean George Cabanis, attended a morning concert, had dinner at Lord Charlemont's, lunched with Tennyson, saw the architect about work at the Heights, met John Cross, carried on extensive correspondence, went to the Royal Society, talked with Darwin, Tyndall, Harrison, and others, all the while hosting Charles and his family and caring for Eliot, who was ill and out of sorts.

Eliot had perused the Harriet Martineau autobiography, revolted by the idea of someone revealing herself to others. Eliot could not tolerate that with Martineau now dead, she had left remarks about people she knew and correspondents still living. There was, in effect, no redress for those who were treated unkindly or rudely. The public split between Martineau and her brother James was another source of Eliot's dismay, obviously striking her in a particularly sensitive way given her own rupture with Isaac. Eliot surmises that James was moved by jealousy of his sister's success, and his attack on her (going back to an 1851 review in *Prospective Review*) was a show of envy. This, too, is revealing, suggesting that Eliot read Isaac's motives as based not on public morality, as he intimated, but on pure and simple jealousy at his sister's enormous success. Her words to Sara Hennell are especially acute here, since they strike at the heart of her kind of society.

> But however the blame may be distributed, it remains a grievously pitiable thing to me that man or woman who has cared about a future life in the minds of a coming generation or generations should have deliberately, persistently mingled with that prospect the ignoble desire to perpetuate personal animosities, which can never be rightly judged by those immediately engaged in them.

But as Eliot read Martineau's account of her brother, James, she thought of Harriet Beecher Stowe's defense of her brother, the Reverend Henry Ward Beecher, when he was charged by Victoria Woodhull with adultery with a member of his congregation, Elizabeth Tilton. Although a civil jury voted nine to three for his acquittal, evidence seems to prove Beecher was guilty. Stowe's support of her brother had been particularly fierce in her letter to Eliot of 20 August 1874, the very day Elizabeth Tilton's husband, Theodore, swore out the complaint against Beecher. Stowe mounted a multileveled defense, but one point stood out, that her brother's fame and celebrity as a preacher left him vulnerable to attack. He was a target for many different kinds of people, but mainly because he was "advanced." The parallels with Eliot and Isaac, in which the gender roles are reversed and she becomes the advanced one, were remarkable, at least in her mind. The case fascinated and repelled her, as we observe in her letter to Sara Hennell almost three years later, when she conflated Harriet Martineau and her brother with Stowe and hers. Stowe's letter really reached into Eliot's world, for the American writer included an attack on Tilton himself, citing family letters in which he was compared to Tito Melema, Romola's philandering husband.

Whatever else she felt, Eliot saw herself being sucked into a case three thousand miles away, one subtly penetrating into her own psychological needs. Although she remained friendly and sympathetic to Stowe, the case entrapped her. Another level of the Stowe argument revealed that while she was eager to condemn Byron of incest on flimsy evidence—on the word of Lady Byron—she was just as eager to acquit her brother on equally weak evidence. This letter, in 1874, was Stowe's last for two years, perhaps because in her response Eliot tried to finesse the question and concentrate on other matters. Stowe, however, when the correspondence resumed, did not let Eliot go. She hammered away at her brother's nobility, citing his involvement in anti-slavery activities, his support for women's rights, his attempt to reform the church and its teachings, his progressive theological positions, his support for social amelioration, and his immense popularity as a man and as a preacher. Stowe constructs a veritable hero, Carlyle's "hero as priest." She also does not slight how her brother supported her own efforts to end slavery and other injustices.

Then she comments on the virulence of the trial, its expense (the huge sum of $18,000 for Beecher), the efforts at bribery of the jury foreman, and other sordid details Eliot surely did not want to hear. She defends Beecher's purity and innocence. Stowe says she is certain her brother is blessed with all the beatitudes. In the background, however, the Beecher family did not stand firm; a sister, Isabella, was convinced of her brother's guilt, and the Beechers—like the Evans clan—fell apart over adultery. Although Isabella was not completely reliable—she heard God's voice that she was his vice-regent in a society governed by women—she did have impeccable credentials on women's issues; and Stowe was put into a profound quandary: caught between her own principles, which she shared with Isabella, and defense of her brother, who in the trial represented male chauvinism and opportunism. She had no way to resolve the dilemma, and, like Eliot, she gradually became more closed as she aged. But while Eliot hesitated, uncertain and doubtful, Stowe used spiritualism as a form of certainty; nevertheless, both writers believed women should not jeopardize their spiritual advantage by thrusting themselves into public activities.

Another dimension emerges in this Stowe–Eliot correspondence and the Beecher case, a dimension we have not touched upon because it remains without clear evidence. We do not know to what extent this case deeply disturbed Eliot—although we do know it certainly aroused her—because it struck close to home. The entire question of Beecher's adultery, whether validated or not, opened up the possibility of whether Lewes had been completely faithful. *We are here immersed in intimations and suggestions, not in hard evidence.* As the politicians say, there is no smoking gun. There is, however, some combination of details which suggests the possibility that in all that social activity Lewes indulged in without Eliot, he may have slipped. However speculative, we should attempt to follow the trail.

After Lewes's death in November of 1878, Eliot had full access to his papers, his journal and diary, his daily jottings. She went through them carefully, especially since she had time on her hands. The tone in her letters suddenly changes, with the abrupt change coming in mid-April of 1879, when she had time to contemplate what she was reading. Her diary for 16 May indicates "Crisis." But before that, on 3 May, she had written to Mrs. Edward Burne-Jones if she could ask her husband to spare a half hour to see her—a mysterious request, possibly connected to the increased attention Cross was paying her, possibly not. Henceforth, her references to Lewes are respectful and cool, and few. One explanation could be that she was seeing a good deal of John Cross, and Lewes was settling into memory; but the changeover is rather rapid, and Eliot was not someone who would relegate her companion of twenty-four years to oblivion so fast unless she had reason. We are, nevertheless, still pursuing a shadowy trail, which adultery, real or suspected, usually creates.

Eliot also added lines from Wordsworth's *The Excursion* to the section on remorse in the fourth part of Lewes's *Problems* (a segment published as *The Study of Psychology*), and these lines suggest infidelity: a wife and mother "pitifully fixing Tender reproaches, insupportable!" This is not evidence, but it does have its strange side, especially when we read it as part of an entire passage of *The Excursion*. * So far, then, we have several seemingly discrete pieces of material: the sudden call for Burne-Jones; the cooling off in her letters of references to Lewes; the possibility she had seen something suspicious in Lewes's assorted notes; the strange inclusion of the lines from Wordsworth, with their intimations of infidelity; the single mention of "Crisis" in her diary. It could all mean something, or perhaps nothing but a certain kind of depression over the loss; or else a quandary about Cross. There is another intimation, and this is reaching far: and that is how Eliot treated Romola's soured, hostile feeling for Tito when she recognized his infidelity—a feeling which suggests Eliot would cut herself off from Lewes if she ever discovered unfaithfulness; that such an occasion occurred in mid-April of 1879 is tentatively possible.

At the time of her correspondence with Stowe, Eliot had not come to any of these conclusions, if we can even call them that. But the entire Beecher case could have proven so sensitive to her because of the personal potential: suspicions, no certainties, nothing more than shadowy feelings she might not have even admitted to herself. Or else, she was simply touched by the case because it had entrapped her friend, Stowe, in its virulence, and recalled her own scandal. There is no way of knowing. In her letter to Sara (15 May 1877), cited above, Eliot's language is particularly strong, so strong in fact it may well have suggested the Beecher case as well as the charges Stowe made against Byron. "We poor mortals," she writes, "can hardly escape these sins of passion. But I have no pity to spare for the rancour that corrects its proofs and revises and lays it by, chuckling with the sense of its future publicity." She admits she had "glided on" from Stowe to Martineau, as though the two instances were combined, because they involved brothers, fidelities, secrets revealed, and publicity given to personal and private matters.

All these responses to the revelations of secret selves preceded the move to Witley. But even with servants moving furniture and their personal things, Eliot

---

* For, like a plague, will memory break out;
And, in the blank and solitude of things,
Upon his spirit, with a fever's strength,
Will conscience prey. Feebly must they have felt
Who, in old time, attired with snakes and whips
The vengeful Furies. Beautiful regards
Were turned on me—the face of her I loved;
The Wife and Mother pitifully fixing
Tender reproaches, insupportable!

turned the event into something challenging. As she told Elma Stuart, they would camp at Witley "experimentally," to see if they liked it. If so, they would empty it out again and make the necessary renovations cited above, the minimum needed. She inveighs against such activities, the coming and going, the moving in and out of furniture, the need to relocate books. "I wish we never had to think of these outside things. The small remainder of our lives seems all too little for the emotion and ideas which are aloof from our own chairs and tables, dinner-service and paper-hanging." We invest too much in things.

Her apprehension about Witley and what awaited them seemed borne out. Neither she nor Lewes was well at first, and then one thing after another went wrong: furniture arrived late, their bedroom looked too spare, the water pipes malfunctioned, even groceries were difficult to get hold of. Yet she did appreciate the lovely setting, the good weather, the long walks, the evening reading. Her remarks nevertheless suggest final things, her inability to bounce back and her willingness to accept the fact that nothing functions smoothly. They also suggest a slight imperiousness, as though she expected everything, at this late stage, to fall into place for her; and when it failed to do so, she found herself helpless.

Despite its shortcomings, Witley was a magnificent home, "ravishing," Lewes called it. The would-be hermits ended up seeing a succession of people, especially since the rail trip from London took only an hour. A regular visitor was, of course, John Cross. This was the perfect situation for the banker, since it allowed him to worship Eliot from a suitable distance. Cross made himself helpful in several ways, easing their problems with the functioning of Witley and even arranging for fish to be delivered twice a week. He was a kind of super errand boy, but also a man of considerable financial knowledge, handsome, youthful, solid. He was the son Eliot might have liked, although not a man of large intelligence. He was, however, an eager learner, especially under the influence of two such highly charged individuals. But on the debit side, he carried with him very conventional ideas, a traditionalist in social and political areas, and on the question of women's rights, very much a mid to late Victorian—in brief, harmless, pleasant to have around, no threat, on the contrary comforting. It was a splendid arrangement for all concerned, even though it would have a comic-book ending. Lewes felt no hostility, since Cross, ever a bachelor now coming up toward forty, seemed sexless, something of a momma's boy, in fact. Eliot could keep him at a distance—no Simcox, he—as "nephew"; and he for his part could play the roles designated for him while worshipping her.

The couple saw a good deal of the Hollands, and they entertained John Blackwood down from Scotland or London. He, too, was almost family. They also saw Jowett on several occasions, Elma Stuart and Alice Helps, their neighbor Birket Foster, an artist, and the Frederic Harrisons. To Harrison, during the second week at Witley, Eliot wrote a pathetic passage thanking him for his letter. "It has done something towards rousing me from what I will not call self-despair, but resignation of being of no use." This will become a regular theme.

She cites how she wasted "three years in writing (what I do not mean to print) a poetic dialogue embodying or rather shadowing very imperfectly the actual content of ideas." This was "A College Breakfast-Party," finished in 1874 but not published until July of 1878.*

The couple read. Lewes packed books, and they went through several volumes they already knew, like Richardson's *Sir Charles Grandison*, Scott's *The Heart of Midlothian* and *The Legend of Montrose*, *The Three Musketeers*, plus some new novels, such as Trollope's *The American Senator*, Charles Reade's *A Woman Hater*, Turgenev's *Virgin Soil* (in French), Zola's *L'Assommoir*, a good deal of Tennyson, including his *Idylls*, also Daudet, Sainte-Beuve, and others. Gradually, their life settled into their regular routine, although it lacked the intense morning writing sessions Eliot was accustomed to. In June, Eliot read R. M. Milnes's *Life, Letters, and Literary Remains of John Keats* and seemed to have recovered some equilibrium. Lewes worked on Volume 4 of *Problems*, which was left unfinished at his death the next year. They walked or drove around the lovely area and apparently felt more at peace, or so John Blackwood reported after spending a day at Witley. Strikingly, however, there is no mention of new work, no solicitation of a new book, no offering up of an idea. In early July, a warning signal came when Lewes reported that Eliot's renal troubles "are incessant," that she never has two days of consecutive quiet; "not often great pain, but constant uneasiness with headache, sickness and inability to work." Her sole new labor would be to put together the essays for *Theophrastus Such*, a miscellany.

The region gradually began to take hold of Eliot's imagination; it was, she says, more beautiful than she had assumed, "having both wildness and culture in delightful alternation." Lewes called the new home "a small paradise" and indicated they were in "perpetual delight." He relates a story that at dinner the other day "Madonna" was asked by the politician and writer John Bright about women's suffrage. Princess Louise interrupted with the question to Eliot whether she believed in the superiority of women, and Thomas Henry Huxley answered that "Mrs. Lewes rather teaches *the inferiority of men*." Lewes felt this was amusing and not at all hostile or threatening. And although Huxley's remark is a little off center, revealing some unease on his part, it has enough truth in it that we wonder at the response of "Madonna." Lewes does not offer that.

When Frederic Harrison came for a visit on 31 July, he and Eliot—with Lewes, we assume, contributing—discussed the present direction of positivism.

---

*Reprinted in the *Jubal* volume, this poem lies dead in the water, although it has some interest as coming at the same time as *Deronda*, plus the fact that Eliot expended three years on it. It is an attempt, through Platonic dialogue, to forge some kind of belief in a world disintegrating into units or subcultures. Eliot uses the characters in *Hamlet* to express different views on science, progress, religion, the individual, an organic society, the role of art. Her conclusion, expressed through Hamlet himself, is surprisingly Paterian: that poesy has a "transfigured realm," that art is freed from the practical and grosser world, that it "rises beauteous / As voice of water-drops in sapphire caves. . . ." Like Pater, Eliot exalts art as transformational and transfigurative. "For you will grant," says Hamlet, "The ideal has discoveries which ask / No test, no faith, save that we joy in them: / A new-found continent with spreading lands / Where pleasure charters all."

Harrison had written to Eliot (on 12 June) asking for her present views on Comte's "Religion of Humanity." Her positivist friend fully acknowledged she had departed from orthodoxy, but he wanted to know to what degree she disagreed or still accepted some of Comte's polity, and to what extent she saw any future for positivism in its present form. Harrison indicates her readers are eager to learn where Eliot stands—which meant *he* was eager. He suggests that Eliot answer the large questions not by art but by philosophy, with a broadly based paper outlining her relationship to positivism and its implications for humanity.

Eliot's response, touched upon above, was that she wasted three years in writing a poetic dialogue shadowing such ideas, and she is now unable to put together such a large-scale statement. She indicates it is beyond her powers, but suggests her fiction has said everything. Harrison recognized this, but hoped that a personage like Eliot, with her command of both fact and breadth, could create believers in Comte. The 31 July session at Witley was an attempt to gather material for some statement, but Eliot refused. Harrison particularly feared that positivism was being led into religious fervor, by Richard Congreve, among others seeking spiritual guidance. It was with this in mind that Eliot dug out "A Symposium," which she retitled "A College Breakfast-Party," sold to *Macmillan's* for £250 when Blackwood rejected it for *Maga.* *

How did Eliot manage to fill her time now that she was not working on a long project? The Cabinet edition was going forward, of course, and she was correcting copies of her books for inclusion there. She agreed on two volumes for each long novel, at 7 / 6 each, plus the inclusion of *Romola* in the 3 / 6 edition as well. In August, in what seems unlikely for a woman whose chief exercise had been walking, Eliot learned lawn tennis under John Cross, a sport she enjoyed immensely, not the least when taught by a handsome, attentive admirer. When her health permitted, she played frequently, although we lack precise information about her serve or backhand. Shortly after, Cross introduced her to badminton. The Witley "experiment" was proving very rewarding, with that mixture of "wildness and culture" acting as a tonic. Yet even with this, there were almost constant reminders of the couple's physical deterioration, a regular drumbeat in their ears. There was, also, the drift, the lack of commitment to a long-term project, the failure or inability to focus on steady work. Even the contemplation of an edition was a mopping-up exercise, not a foray into new territory. As Eliot was consolidating by rereading her books, she was revisiting the past and reassessing her achievements, all of which carried home the point that the past was all she could consider. Under these circumstances, it is not unusual that *Theophrastus Such* is filled with pastness.

To Elma Stuart, who had sent on another gift, a silver clasp, Eliot told of the pleasures of lawn tennis, which she was now playing almost daily. "Should you not be amazed to see your mother using the bat and running after the vagrant

---

* Macmillan was the logical choice for the poem since the publishing house had hoped she would write, for its "English Men of Letters" series, a life of Shakespeare. John Morley, who had reviewed her books, was overall editor of the project, but Eliot would not undertake it. Later, she would herself appear in the series as subject of a biography by Leslie Stephen, in 1902.

balls?" Then taking another tack, she thanked David Kaufmann for his article, in German, "George Eliot and Judaism: An Attempt to Appreciate *Daniel Deronda,*" now available in English; and with that, she reimmersed herself in Hebrew and Jewish matters.* This, too, was part of a pastness.

On 25 September, the Leweses left for five days with the Bullock-Halls at Six Mile Bottom, while the servants began the transferral of furniture and other goods from Witley to the Priory, a move completed by the 29th. Once back in their London home, the couple went from lawn tennis to badminton, which required far less space. They used the drawing room for their games. When they were not playing badminton, the drawing room was rearranged for their usual Sunday afternoons, invitations to which were now more prized than ever. Eliot was pleased by the publication of the one-volume *Daniel Deronda,* in itself a kind of completion. Priced at 7 / 6, it was uniform with the one-volume edition of *Middlemarch.*

However much an author is honored by a partial or complete edition, it is not an unalloyed joy. It speaks a death sentence in its way, since it indicates one is "done," relegated to the ages—what the Nobel Prize has done in our century. Few authors have much left to say after an edition, inasmuch as it has spoken for them. In the background, as we shall see, publisher and author are on different courses, despite the generous words they exchange. The publisher wants to honor himself by honoring a valuable author, but nevertheless worries about profits and losses. The author must, somehow, fight against being buried by the glory of it all. As John Blackwood tells his nephew, William, another reason for having such an edition is to provide a focus "round which I hope to see the more popular editions cluster and flourish." He hoped, nonetheless, to provide "a permanent and creditable presentment of George Eliot's works." Such an edition was incumbent upon a publisher who knew he had a national treasure in hand; but in point of fact, the firm had not made inordinate amounts of money on Eliot. She had done quite well, as we have observed, from Lewes's astute management, but the firm's profits had been relatively slim. As a prestige item, then, Eliot needed to be given a monument, one which *preceded* death and burial.

Blackwood's breakdown of terms for the edition was for it to be in nineteen volumes, to sell at 5 / - a volume. Of the seventeen prose volumes, the royalty would be 1/2½ on each copy of every book sold after the first 500—in effect, a royalty of about 30 percent once the firm could recoup on the initial 500 copies. For the two volumes of poetry (*The Spanish Gypsy* and *Jubal*), the royalty would be slightly higher—since sales would be lower—1/6 and 1/8, respectively, after the first 500. Notified that these were the best terms Blackwood's could offer, Lewes and Eliot accepted.

---

*She also thanked Kaufmann for sending on Hebrew translations of Lessing and a collection of Hebrew poems. She expresses great fear at events in Eastern Europe, as a widespread Balkan war was shaping up, and Hungary—Kaufmann was a Hungarian Jew—seemed in a particularly exposed position, especially for its Jewish population. Blood libel accusations against Jews were not far in the future, not only in Hungary but throughout the entire area.

Edith Simcox was permitted to call, in connection with her new book, *Natural Law*, though she found Eliot dissatisfied with it, despite the dedication to her. But just being close to Eliot made Simcox feel better, and her gloom lifted. Yet her excitability and efforts to display affection (she went for her idol's cheeks and feet) made Eliot dole out her visits, and we receive the impression the latter found some of the conversations painful. When Simcox vaunted women and attacked men, Eliot either was silent or else defended men and brought women to another level, the spiritual level Simcox could not accept. At this point, the two had little to offer each other, except for Simcox's devotion and Eliot's continued receptivity.

Eliot's friendship with Tennyson, on the other hand, deepened, either alone or in company, and in February 1878 the couple attended the marriage of Tennyson's younger son, Lionel, to Eleanor Locker, in Westminster Abbey. Tennyson visited frequently at the Priory and saw Lewes at lunches. At one level it was a strange relationship, the poet who had mocked women in *The Princess*, and then treated women as whores or madonnas in his *Idylls*, with the famed writer whose fictional sympathies made her see women as victims of men or as great spiritual forces.

But both Tennyson and Eliot had grown increasingly conservative, suspicious of reform and supportive of governmental measures which ensured stability in the short run even while they perpetuated injustice and inequality in the long run. Eliot did not share Tennyson's eager colonialism and imperialism, and she rejected his simplistic views of the superiority of English ways to life in so-called backward countries; but she was curiously passive. She might rue the conflicts in Eastern Europe or in Africa, but she was not angered, or drawn to any kind of protest.

The 1870s, in any case, were a curious time of incoherence, of extremes which did not link up. Disraeli was putting together an empire that would last until 1914, and in some instances until the end of World War II. The sun never set . . . , and all that, while the red on the map indicated England's reach. The military was an arm of government policy, and while it suffered huge casualties in the Afghan, Zulu, and other African wars, they were all far from home. The writers were quiet on most of this, except for jingoists like Tennyson, and later Kipling. Carlyle, another believer in England first but disenchanted by progress itself, was now old and ineffective, a Jeremiah gone sour, as was Browning. Mill was dead. Ruskin was beginning to show his insanity. By mid-decade, Eliot had pulled back, and only Hardy remained, but he was still almost unknown. The scientists prevailed. The post-Darwinians, Huxley and Spencer (living, respectively, to 1895 and 1903), were voices, but they were concerned with the ways in which evolution and progress could be combined. What made the 1870s so problematic was that the decade lacked a salient voice. Only Matthew Arnold kept up his warnings, but he was speaking of English culture as a whole, without directing concern for the details that affected people's daily lives. The population appeared to move along passively, with the government making all the claims, carrying out all the action, and becoming almost impenetrable to criti-

cism. Governmental industrial successes—despite downturns in the economy—
and extension of the empire carried the day and undercut criticism of poor
domestic conditions. *

On 10 November, as her fifty-eighth birthday approached, Eliot rejected
Macmillan "English Men of Letters" series editor John Morley's plan for her to
write a volume on Shakespeare. Eliot was not Morley's first choice—Arnold had
already turned down the same offer—but possibly his third. In the background,
Macmillan had spoken of Eliot as "our Prima Donna" who must be paid three to
five times what anyone else would get. But neither money nor the topic
attracted her, and it is doubtful if any project would have. When we observe
her enervation, we must not see it as chiefly psychological—although that was
a factor—but physical, worn down as she was by the intense pain of the renal
attacks. She was attuned to illness, a hostage to pain.

Several letters attest to this "closing down." After telling Sara Hennell how
grief-stricken she was at Barbara Bodichon's deteriorating condition, Eliot
speaks of herself as someone who lives in a world that "has grown around me in
these later years. . . ." Writing to Frederic Myers, a Trinity College Fellow,
Eliot probed more deeply. She has come to a tragic sense of life, hoping to find
something positive to cheer up her correspondent. Yet even as she makes the
effort, she acknowledges how depression and mournfulness can block out all
hopeful interest.

> I only long, if it were possible to me, to help in satisfying the need of
> those who want a reason for living in the absence of what has been called
> consolatory belief. But all the while I gather a sort of strength from the
> certainty that there must be limits or negations in my own moral powers
> and life-experience which may screen from me many possibilities of bless-
> edness for our suffering human nature. The most melancholy thought
> surely would be that we in our own persons had measured and exhausted
> the sources of spiritual good.

Seemingly offhand, these lines become very significant, not only for Eliot but
for the drift of Victorian thought in the late 1870s and into the 1880s and even
1890s. Having carried her humanitarian philosophy as far as it can go, Eliot
recognizes it may not suffice for those who do not share her life experience, or,

---

* This is not to say reform was dead: the religious test at universities was abolished; the secret
ballot (for men) was introduced in 1872; a workman's act addressed conditions and hours in 1875
and was further modified in the Factory and Workshop Act of 1878; compulsory education became
law, although it was only sporadically enforced; but there were also a depression, unemployment,
and bread lines. While average wages rose, by 1870 about 50 percent over 1815, nevertheless governmental services did little for those living in hovels or experiencing daily danger in factories or
mines. The huge population increases—fourfold in the century—were not met by commensurate
ways of dealing with so many people. The point is not that England was going under—quite the
contrary, it was thriving—but that by the late 1870s it was clear that social and political coherence
was lost as "progress" became the shibboleth. As Dickens had observed, a permanent underclass was
established; and as Disraeli had predicted, England was "two nations."

she might have added, her intellectual powers. She realizes, then, that people may need a different kind of belief, which is unacceptable for her, but which she sees as still meaningful. "Spiritual good," as she calls it, *might* come from sources other than oneself. As she reaches the limits of her philosophical position and observes it may not accommodate alternative lives, she enters into that Victorian crisis of belief and, in her way, becomes its voice of both yearning and doubt.

This "crisis" differs from what happened to those like John Stuart Mill who became agnostics or atheists, or those scientists like Huxley whose arguments made scientific truth superior to biblical or theological explanations. The crisis existed more broadly, on theological, social, and political grounds. It included those who responded on several levels: to the religious confusion created by the German Higher Criticism of the Bible and the scientific attack on the biblical explanation of man's beginnings, to the evident hypocrisy of the church in its neglect of social conditions, to the condescension of the Anglican bishops toward the lower or working classes, to the benign neglect of the government or state as a whole; as well as those who, as a consequence, sought direction from other sources, whether societal as in Comte or Marx, or individual as in Mill or Eliot. The crisis could not be shrugged off, for part of it was the abiding Victorian fear that chaos and even anarchy would prevail if traditional religion failed to make the parts cohere: that is, contain the dissatisfied, disaffected classes.

Eliot's position, then, to move outside formal religion and to attempt an alternative faith or belief, without forsaking Christian principles, was a dangerous and daring act; and even she was awed in later life by what she had tried to do. She tells Sara they "are greatly changed in spiritual as well as bodily matters" and observes how far they have moved from each other, with Sara writing books that try to find religious answers to the big metaphysical questions, with Eliot having forsworn not the questions, but the standard answers. All she could say was "Trust me."

She recognized the tremendous burden she had placed on herself and her books. She had not offered simplistic entertainment, nor was she content to be merely heuristic. As she awaited the Cabinet edition, her apotheosis, she hoped her message—more art than pedagogy—would come through. Hoarding her talent, she was incensed that Alexander Main, having already compiled an anthology of excerpts from her works, now wanted to do *The George Eliot Birthday Book*, which Blackwood said he was willing to publish if she agreed. Main's plan, apparently, was to create a "diary" of short excerpts from Eliot's works, with space left for the names of friends to be written in, we assume, for each extract. Eliot called these birthday books (one on Tennyson had just been published, compiled by Emily Shakespear, and others existed on Burns and Shakespeare) "the vulgarest things in the book stalls. . . ." She says she can offer no opinion until she sees the Tennyson; but everything in her is chilled by the prospect of the "puffing, gaudy, clap-trappy" forms of publication. But Lewes suggested it might be a way of spreading her views to new readers, and she put herself in Blackwood's hands as to whether he thought it would be advantageous for circulation of her works overall.

Despite her misgivings, Eliot did get caught up in this jejune undertaking (*The George Eliot Birthday Book* appeared in 1878). She tells Main on 4 December that she has now seen the Tennyson volume and considers it "exceedingly ill done." The extracts, she says, are far too numerous and too brief. "The effect is dolting and feeble." She says "our beloved Tennyson" deserves something better. She hopes that Main will improve on it, and insists she wants extracts from her poems as well as fiction. Her tone is one of wariness that she was being exploited, but became swayed by Lewes's suggestion her sales would pick up. On 17 December, she wrote Main again, after she had examined his selection of extracts. She feels that the brief passages create a sameness, what she calls "a disadvantageous effect of recurrence." She cautions, also, that the selections from *Deronda* seem inadequate and unrepresentative, an indication of how much she valued that novel. She fears that too much of the present volume sounds like a redistribution of the previous *Sayings*. Although her tone is hectoring, based on her sense she was being co-opted, even railroaded, she tries to spare Main's feelings.

Eliot's first response to the Main venture had come on 22 November, her fifty-eighth birthday and perhaps the reason for her acerbic tone. She was fitful and unsettled, as she told D'Albert-Durade. "London," she writes, "in spite of our utmost efforts to ward off visits and other engagements, is a place of continued unrest and interruption. Letters and other small claims eat away much time and leave no corresponding benefit." In this mood, she suspended plans to spend Christmas with the Burne-Joneses. She says she and Lewes are "dull old persons" and unsuitable company for the two young children, who "ought to find Christmas a bright bead to string on their memory, whereas to spend the time with us would be to string on a dark shrivelled berry."

On 11 December, Edith Simcox visited, at Eliot's request. She, not Eliot, left a record, replete with every affectionate gesture that occurred, or else took place in her imagination. "She [Eliot] kissed me at length." The discussion turned on marrying late, for a woman, and what this meant. Simcox felt that by twenty-seven—the age of a friend's daughter—a woman might not have any further chances and should grab whatever opportunities she does have. Eliot firmly disagreed, arguing that late marriages have a better chance to succeed because people go on developing, especially after thirty, surely with herself in mind. Simcox writes: ". . . she was so beautiful, and I was so fond of her that I wasn't angry when she proceeded to affirm that I had never been so fit to marry as now—I answered 'that wasn't saying much'—to which with a sweet laugh and a still sweeter gesticulation—that brought her hand within reach of my lips—that she didn't pretend that her speeches amounted to much—it was enough if they came to a little."

Then in a very different area of discourse, Eliot warned Simcox not to let her name become associated with Charles Bradlaugh and Annie Besant, active in reviving the International Working Men's Association, or with Mrs. Harriet

Law, a supporter of atheism. Bradlaugh was also an atheist who insisted on being admitted to Parliament, to which he had been elected, without taking the traditional oath; and Mrs. Besant was active in women's causes. Eliot's warning was that the "dread of Pharisaism" could undermine Simcox's own social reform efforts, a warning more fearful to Eliot than to her friend.

With the end of 1877, Eliot put aside her journal, which she had kept for over sixteen years. What she wrote was morbid:

> . . . as the years advance there is a new rational ground for the expectation that my life may become less fruitful. The difficulty is, to decide how far resolution should set in the direction of activity rather than the acceptance of a more negative state. Many conceptions of works to be carried out present themselves, but confidence in my own fitness to complete them worthily is all the more wanting because it is reasonable to argue that I must have already done my best. In fact, my mind is embarrassed by the wide variety of subjects that attract me, and the enlarging vista that each brings with it.

She closes by saying that henceforth she will keep a more businesslike diary, but no such diary has turned up.

These somewhat despondent sentiments which ended 1877 would become realities in 1878. Despite the supportive Cabinet edition, a volume of which appeared each month, the year would see Lewes's death, the end of a twenty-four-year relationship that coincided with nearly everything Eliot had achieved in her professional life. The year was marked not only by Lewes's death, but by months of steady deterioration before the end came on 30 November. His symptoms of enteritis, intestinal pains, and excruciating suffering were finally diagnosed in June as intestinal cancer. But well before that, according to John Cross, Lewes was aware of something more serious than digestive troubles or a nervous stomach. Nevertheless, he hid his suffering, and when the pain ceased (probably with doses of morphine or some other opiate), he would reenter his life as a raconteur, as someone still youthful in spirit. When Henry James saw him on 10 April,* he found him repulsive but clever; and yet the cleverness was tempered by the American's observation that Lewes was a piffler, a "professional raconteur." Yet despite Lewes's agility and powers of disguise, he could not hide from Eliot that something terminal was working its way through him.

James, incidentally, returned to the Priory on 28 April 1878, and after that he considered himself a Sunday regular. "The great G. E.," he wrote, "herself is both sweet and superior, and has a delightful expression in her large, long, pale,

---

* At a dinner hosted by John Cross at the Devonshire Club. James, who was then living on Bolton Street, had last seen Lewes at the Priory, when he arrived to find Thornie writhing in agony on the floor.

equine face." He finds no fault with her, although even in this brief glimpse of their talk together, we observe James turning her into one of his novelistic characters.

Early in the year, renovations were undertaken at Witley: building, papering, painting, creating an upset which made it impossible for furniture to be moved in until the end of March. On 18 January, Blackwood sent on to Lewes the sum of £1,006.17.7 covering sales of Eliot's novels for the year. He adds that the subscription to the first volume of the Cabinet edition, *Romola* (divided into two volumes), was not very cheering, with a printing of 1,050, but with only 611 copies subscribed. Lewes responded that while the check surpassed their expectations, he was surprised that *Silas Marner* lagged and the poems showed strong staying power. Eliot was herself reading steadily in English history, including books by John Richard Green and William E. H. Lecky, then ranging far to a book on Blaise Pascal by John Tulloch. A copy of Pascal's *Pensées* had been given to her as a school prize when she was fourteen, and his ideas had remained with her.*

From now on, each month would see another volume in the edition, with Volume II of *Romola* in February. The month of February also found Edith Simcox visiting, and her record of these meetings, in her unpublished autobiography, is characteristically highly charged. Images of near hysteria when she is in Eliot's presence dominate. Hers is more than simply nineteenth-century rhetoric; it is the nun enjoying a vision of her god: ". . . I did nothing but make reckless love to her." Or: "I threw my arms around her," or there was "no one as adorable as herself," or "I had told her of my ambition to be allowed to lie silently at her feet as she pursued her occupations," or her references to Eliot as "divinity." One particular visit so affected Simcox she left "choked with tears."

A week later, Eliot visited her friend, an act which suggests they had reached a kind of truce. Eliot, after all, did value Simcox's extraordinary intelligence and her energy for social responsibilities, and very possibly the adoration. They discussed ethical questions, especially as they applied to utilitarianism, and Eliot latched on to one of the weaknesses of that powerful position, its avoidance of questions of motive and, by implication, its mechanical nature. Much of Eliot's argument was angled so as to give credence to Herbert Spencer's argument. His use of evolutionary theory led him to a synthesis of all knowledge, in his ongoing *Synthetic Philosophy* (1855–93), a combination of biology, sociology, psychology, ethics, and even the hard sciences. If one gives credence to Spencer, then the utilitarian version of ethics must give way to a much broader application,

---

*Ultimately, Pascal could not prove acceptable to her philosophically or theologically. His linkage of morality to spirituality, while attractive, was the very element Eliot had abandoned. But she could enjoy his rationalism, his irony, his scientific learning, his efforts at a syncretic philosophy. How could she resist the following "thought"? "We sail within a vast sphere, ever drifting in uncertainty, driven from end to end. When we think to attach ourselves to any point and to fasten to it, it wavers and leaves us; and if we follow it, it eludes our grasp, slips past us, and vanishes for ever" (No. 72). For some thirty years, Eliot had come close to believing this.

in which ethics cannot be considered apart from evolutionary development, biological change, individual psychology, social criteria, and the rest. Eliot was profoundly affected by this effort at synthesis, even when she felt Spencer was insufficiently responsive to individuals and their motives, aspirations, and need for transformation.

None of this suggests she was giving way on her own views; on the contrary, she remained consistent. But she did recognize that new theories, especially Spencer's, were opening up possibilities which, while they did not threaten her, did force her to restate her position. For all her immersion in philosophical questions, Eliot's ideas about individuals and society could have derived from a less complex mind. Unquestionably, her reading had led her to certain conclusions, but in another sense, her attitudes were shaped by her own feelings as much as by study; and there is little point in claiming objectivity for her, as she herself recognized when she was confronted by competing theories. *

The owners of the Priory may have been sick, queasy, and depressed, but social activity during the winter and early spring of 1878 was heavy. They met with Victoria's fourth daughter, Princess Helena, and then with the Royal Princess herself, Victoria's oldest daughter and the Crown Princess of Germany. They attended dinners where the guest list included Trollope, Dean Stanley, J. A. Froude, Kinglake, John Morley, and their like. They attended the Royal Academy of Music, to hear, among others, Joseph Joachim, the great Hungarian violinist, for whom Brahms wrote his concerto. They entertained Tennyson at dinner, and then themselves attended a musical soiree given by Mrs. Ignaz Moscheles, the composer's widow. One thing Eliot did reject, and that was the pleas of visiting interviewers, such as the American poet and journalist Louise Chandler Moulton. Eliot had met her at Lord Houghton's on 12 February, but she resisted Houghton's efforts to have her receive the American: ". . . I have a horror of being interviewed and written about," she wrote, "and though I would not impute an intention of that sort to Mrs. M, my experience in relation to other American ladies has confirmed me in my churlish habits."

Lewes's diary for 10 April through 21 April reveals a virtual orgy of social activity, including the Devonshire Club lunch with Henry James. In early May, Eliot's niece, Emily Clarke, came for a brief visit. She and Lewes took her to see Henry Irving in Dion Boucicault's *Louis XI*, then to the Royal Academy exhibition.

In the course of inviting the couple to Oxford, Jowett touched on Eliot's

---

* In a parallel view, a contemporary critic demonstrates Eliot's "resolute resistance to many aspects of Spencer's biological determinism, especially as it found expression in his developing analysis of female sexuality and motherhood [perhaps an unexpected precursor of Freud]. Moreover, by understanding Eliot's acceptance of some tenets of Spencerian—as opposed to Darwinian—evolutionism, we can begin to understand the conservative force that Victorian science and evolutionary theory exerted in containing the debate on what Victorians called the Woman Question." But if Eliot's ideas were touched by Spencer's, she influenced him, as we observe in his *Autobiography*, even to his reversal on several questions concerning female evolutionary potential. Yet when all is said and done, Eliot's fundamental positions were set *before* she met Spencer and Lewes.

hesitation to accept fully Spencer's theories. The Master of Balliol pointed out he agreed with her emphasis that the abiding interest of philosophy is human motive, the very weakness or lack in the Spencerian sociology. Jowett, however, went further than Eliot and saw in a philosophy of human motives an opening for religion, when, in fact, Eliot saw the application of ethical questions to human motives as sufficient religion in itself. Ideas, however, became secondary to friendship.

William Blackwood's new report on the Cabinet edition was quite satisfactory for him and for Lewes. England was now undergoing a dip in sales of all products, a form of economic depression which affected trade, including publishing; and yet Eliot's books were moving well. In all, *Romola* had now sold over 1,300 copies, *Silas Marner* over 800, and *Adam Bede*—just issued in its second volume—663. Blackwood's real purpose, however, was to inquire when the firm would receive or hear about "another fascinating book from Mrs. Lewes to give the series of her books another fresh start as well as delighting the public with something to read and think over." Lewes's response did not address this, but he complained that nobody really knew of the Cabinet edition because it had been inadequately publicized. He asked for additional advertising, especially in the publisher's column of the *Times*.

Since Witley needed furniture, now that renovations were winding down, Lewes and Eliot at the end of May and beginning of June went shopping, before joining Jowett in Oxford on 8 June. They even purchased a billiard table. Their search for the right pieces brought them to regular furniture outlets as well as to auction houses, in London and Guildford. The Oxford sojourn, for its part, did not prove satisfactory. The Whitsun holiday created large crowds at the railway, and after a two-hour delay, the couple also lost their portmanteau. It finally arrived much later. But once the rigors of the journey were over, Lewes attempted to enter into the constant round of social activity, with the usual procession of the learned, wise, and famous. His eagerness to immerse himself in all this—and in good conversation—soon turned to ashes when severe intestinal pain laid him low, a sign of the cancer spreading. Turning down a Monday luncheon, with the Princess Eugénie, the couple left, eager now to find peace and quiet.

On 21 June, they returned to Witley. The servants had prepared the house, so that the couple entered into a calm, ordered place. There was little to do except admire the woods, enjoy the quiet, read, and spend uninterrupted time together. It was the perfect retirement scene, although Nemesis was lurking in the form of Lewes's advanced stage of intestinal cancer. As late as 27 June, Eliot could still say he was under treatment for gout, which was causing nightly attacks of cramps and inward malaise. * Very possibly unconsciously deceiving

---

* To Elma Stuart (27 June), her words are more poignant. "My only real trouble is, that my Little Man is sadly out of health, racked with cramps from suppressed gout and feeling his inward economy all wrong." She grasps at one detail, that after a morning walk he felt and ate better.

herself, she complained that the food was being inadequately prepared, which she in part blamed for Lewes's indisposition. Her remarks suggest a whining tone, her feeling she deserved everything to be perfect, and it was not working out.

Alone at Witley until John Cross came on 14 July, the couple established a regimen consisting of walks before breakfast—especially for Lewes—pills to relieve headaches and other ills, walks later in the day, reading, and little more than tennis when they felt up to it. Lewes reports himself as gouty and dyspeptic, and Eliot as laid up with an assortment of ills which made leaving her bed impossible. When she recovered, he encouraged her to get some sun by playing tennis or by going for drives in the afternoon. Although these are details of small moment, they indicate how Eliot's world had shrunk, almost in this respect a replica of her early life at Griff. Instead of Robert Evans declining, she had Lewes, but she had duplicated that early life in similar rural surroundings, the relative isolation, the quiet and peace, the opportunities for long stretches for reading. Having accomplished everything she had set out to do, she was now completing the circle. She had written some of the essays that would appear in *Theophrastus Such*, which because of Lewes's death would not be published until May of 1879. These essays were the result of her seasons at Witley, but they are in a minor key, except for "The Modern Hep! Hep! Hep!"*

While working on *Such*, Eliot did not encourage guests, although the Congreves and Mrs. James Geddes (Maria Congreve's sister) came for dinner on 21 July. Congreve was still pursuing positivism, seeking religious reinforcement there, and his wife still adored Eliot. Lewes was rapidly deteriorating: there was no denying that, even for Eliot. Walks early in the day seemed to relieve the cramps, but nights were torturous. Simcox remarked how awful Lewes looked, as he was losing pounds from an already slim frame; and yet she found in his paleness and ill health a certain beauty because he did not display any ill temper at his condition.

Eliot was still being importuned, this time by Mrs. Peter Taylor (a woman of wealth and an energetic educator), to speak out on public topics: the economic plight of the poor, the sorry state of education, the minimal role of women in social and political life, the creation of a permanent poverty class, and the like; but Eliot firmly declined. She says not even her best friend, not even Lewes, could make her speak when she had decided to remain silent. "My function," she wrote, "is that of the *aesthetic*, not the doctrinal teacher—the rousing of the nobler emotions, which make mankind desire the social right, not the prescribing of special measures, concerning which the artistic mind, however strongly

---

* On 26 January 1878, Eliot wrote John Blackwood that La Bruyère (*Les Caractères de Théophraste*) cannot "be done justice to by any merely English presentation." The germ of *Theophrastus Such* is here, as it is in her notebooks (Pforzheimer Folio 64), where she quotes, from La Bruyère, "Le plaisir de la critique nous ôte celui d'être vivement touchés de très belles choses." Her goal is to probe as deeply into the "character" of Such as she possibly can, on the order of the seventeenth-century French writer.

moved by social sympathy, is often not the best judge. It is one thing to feel keenly for one's fellow-beings; another to say, 'This step, and this alone, will be the best to take for the removal of particular calamities.' "

There is another side to this. Eliot's social activities in themselves speak volumes for her later attitudes: the people she met, and who desired to meet her, all had a huge stake in a settled, ordered, stable society. Except for Simcox, she had little or no contact with those who were marginal socially or outside the political structure, or who advocated radical change in what they perceived as inequities. As a consequence, Eliot's outlook was rooted in an existing social context which, with all its shortcomings and injustices, had served to keep England stable. This did not make her insensitive or irresponsible. It made her both passive and representative, in that she was voicing what most intelligent people felt. Dissent, such as it was, came from only a few groups, middle- to upper-class women, socialists and supporters of labor unions, some aristocrats who had little to lose. English "progress" had created its own peculiar energies, and few indeed were eager to attack it, unless the attack came from those like Carlyle, who wanted to roll it all back to the Middle Ages.

That there was some movement at all, in prison reforms, in Poor Laws, in education, and even in the role of women in divorce settlements and related matters, was left to those inside government who saw such change as unthreatening: Disraeli, for example, who could hide social reforms behind the drumbeat of colonial expansionism. Such changes, then, occurred within a very safe context, so that basic ills remained despite marginal amelioration. Well into the last quarter of the century, justice was quite different for each individual, depending on class and caste, financial ability, and family connections. Education was also heavily weighted in favor of the privileged, as were all positions of influence in government and finance—weighted toward those who had come through a privileged educational system, when the correct public school meant that a university degree was unnecessary. While there were some openings in the social hierarchy, it was fundamentally a society still perceived as closed. Eliot had broken through in one of the few ways an outsider and woman could, through her pen. Lewes, also, had come through with his pen and his association with Eliot. Despite their intellect, they would otherwise have remained fringe people, disempowered because of lack of the privileges that came with birth.

With Lewes sinking at the Priory—Fanny Kemble remarked he looked as if he had been gnawed by rats—Eliot tried nevertheless to keep an equable appearance, and the two continued with their social activities. They saw Thomas Trollope and his new wife (the sister of Ellen Lawless Ternan, Dickens's mistress), as well as the Du Mauriers. Lewes dissembled as best he could, often becoming the life of the party as he sang through operatic roles, with Eliot accompanying him on the piano. None of this could disguise his condition; it simply pointed to his courage in going on in the face of ever-increasing bouts of agonizing cramps. What he could not hide was his inability to travel. When John Blackwood invited the couple to Strathyrum, Eliot was forced to beg off because of Lewes's growing incapacitation and her own lack of "daring" to support his needs away from home. In making much the same report to D'Albert-Durade, she also roved into a political settlement arranged by Disraeli on the "Eastern Question."* She attacks Gladstone and his Liberal Party for not agreeing to the settlement, and then states how her position has altered since she was living with the D'Albert-Durades in Geneva. "You remember me as much less of a conservative than I have now become. I care as much for the interests of the people, but I believe less in the help they will get from democrats."

The Leweses, even now, were hardly the recluses that Eliot's letters made them seem. People did visit, and the couple made occasional forays in the area. And once they returned to the Priory, after 11 November, they entertained on a modest scale. One frequent visitor was the Russian novelist Turgenev, whose company gave both Lewes and Eliot great pleasure. Also, his overwhelming admiration for Eliot did not hurt; he considered her, he told Lewes, the greatest living novelist—this at a time when Lewes had called the Russian the greatest. Turgenev said he was not himself in the same fictional class as Dickens, George Sand, or George Eliot—Sand being a strange example here, an indication of how her contemporaries overrated her fictional abilities, as apart from her courage as a woman and a rebel.

Mrs. Richard Greville visited frequently. She was an elocutionist who without much urging recited poems, and when she came to the Priory she had large chunks of Eliot's poetry committed to memory. She considered every setting a stage, and for some reason she became almost an intimate of the Leweses. Henry James thought she was a "fool," and she may well have been; but in a compelling way she was entertaining, devoted, and zany. At one point, on 1 November, she arrived at the Heights with James, who had just published *The Europeans*. The Leweses, however, were too preoccupied with their own miseries and paid no attention to the novel. James felt he was welcomed into the house merely as a way of shortening the time before he could be ushered out. He had arrived, of course, hoping his novel would attract the attention of the great woman whom he truly admired, despite the waspish criticism he made of her work. But Eliot was uncommunicative, and Lewes went even further, asking Mrs. Greville to take back with her the two volumes of *The Europeans* given her by James and which she had brought two weeks earlier. It was a considerable breach of etiquette and an indication of Lewes's indisposition. He clearly had not considered it important and was not even prepared to have it in his house. James was

---

* Among other disorders were Turkish atrocities in the Balkans against the Bulgarians and, more important, a Russo-Turkish war which might have drawn in the Western powers, as in the Crimean War. Disraeli opposed Gladstone's Russian policy and supported Turkish diplomacy as a way of protecting British interests in the Mediterranean and minimizing Russian influence. The Congress of Berlin in 1878 reduced Russian power in the Balkans. All of this was, of course, foreplay for World War I.

profoundly wounded.* He was so preoccupied with his own needs—not an unusual condition for him—he failed to note the disintegration of the household: none of the amenities, no tea offered or served, disregard of visitors and their wishes, no interest in the latest publications.

Even Lewes recognized he was sinking. When he told John Blackwood that a visit to his home was out of the question, he also indicated, in early August of 1878, that he had been forced to avoid all intercourse with friends and had not had even his children for a visit. He was unable to go up to London for the marriage of a friend, and he let important business slide. He admitted that his imaginary maladies were now proving real, and he especially feared that the excitement of traveling and visiting friends, even seeing people, would accelerate his pains. With this admission, Lewes could no longer dissemble before Eliot that he would eventually become well.

We note that at this period, in the late 1870s, there were no cures for any of these internal disorders, and the sole means of alleviating intense suffering was through morphine or some derivative. Exploratory surgery was possible—anesthesia was available—but in most cases, it killed far more than it helped; and, in any event, Lewes's condition was too far advanced. Diagnosis, moreover, was still primitive. Cancer was known, but not how and to what extent it worked; techniques for dealing with it had not, of course, been put into place. Eliot's renal condition was also unresolvable; once again, exploratory surgery might have removed stones, but if she survived the operation there was already serious kidney damage. Both she and Lewes were being worn out by incessant, regular, expected attacks of one thing or another. They could expect only temporary relief.

Even the monthly appearance of a new volume in the Cabinet edition—for which Eliot was making minor corrections—could not relieve the heavy gloom descending on the Priory. Eliot was certain this edition would be her memorial and cautioned William Blackwood that her revisions and corrections should be made accurately: ". . . this edition is to last." She seemed particularly upset about *Deronda*, wanting to make certain it was exactly right, a further indication of how much she valued this novel. But she was also concerned with the appearance of *The Spanish Gypsy*, perhaps because it was such a departure for her at a time when fiction was not forthcoming. The edition gave Eliot some anxiety, but it did provide focus for her at an age when she was doing little other writing, except for the *Such* essays. She tried to sound "bright" for John Cross, whose

---

* His response in *The Middle Years*, the final volume of his *Autobiography*, is witty, waspish, full of punctured pride, a scene from one of his novels. "The bruise inflicted there I remember feeling for the moment only as sharp, such a mixture of delightful small questions at once salved it over and such a charm in particular for me to my recognising that this particular wrong—inflicted all unawares, which exactly made it sublime—was the only rightness of our visit. Our hosts hadn't so much as connected book with author, or author with visitor, or visitor with anything but the convenience of his ridding them of an unconsidered trifle; grudging as they so justifiedly did the impingement of such matters on their consciousness. The vivid demonstration of one's failure to penetrate there had been in the sweep of Lewes's gesture [thrusting the books at James], which could scarce have been bettered by his actually wielding a broom." For the couple, James at this time was no higher up the ladder than the chattering Mrs. Greville.

relative youth made him perhaps less sympathetic to constant illness than her other, aging friends. In word and person, however, he was never less than discreet.

After the couple closed the Heights and waited for the servants to prepare the Priory, they had sufficient energy left to visit Brighton. They met Emily Clarke there, and spent their time walking the main promenade, like any daytripper down from London. This was prior to their return to the city when Lewes received, in effect, his death sentence, a diagnosis from Sir James Paget on 18 November, (just four days before Eliot's fifty-ninth birthday) that he was suffering from a "thickening of the mucous membrane." Lewes had thought he was suffering from piles, although that would not explain the intestinal cramps. A thickening of the mucous membrane indicated that something was rampaging within him and creating a malfunction of immense proportions, a closing up of his entire intestinal tract. He was now in constant pain, which only morphine would partially relieve. Paget came daily to the Priory, although no hope was held out even for a remission. As late as October, Eliot's letters had still spoken of cramps and gout, without any intimation of something terminal. She saw Lewes as being "as joyous as ever," and said they were "intensely happy" in their bit of country at Witley.

Edith Simcox stopped in often to inquire after Lewes, but was not seen. John Cross came on 29 November, at a time when his mother was near death. The meeting of "deaths" here is compelling: both Cross and Eliot went into deep mourning at the same time. In Cross's case, his mother had been a strong woman with a significant influence on him—at close to forty he was still unmarried. He had behaved in every way which would conform to his mother's plans for him. He had been successful in business without bringing a competitive woman into the family. Only with his mother dead did he feel he could marry, and then to a woman born only a few years later than Mrs. Cross. As for Eliot, Lewes has served as a shield, as much maternal as it was paternal. Once he was dead, she needed a protector: there is little question that Eliot, with all her feelings about female independence, could not face life without a strong male relationship—Robert Evans, Bray, Brabant, Chapman, Lewes, and now Cross. The two, then, found themselves in comparable situations, exposed and isolated from their usual support.

On 21 November, Lewes penned his final letter, to John Blackwood, and sent on the first part of the *Such* manuscript. In commenting on his condition, he did not yet know of Paget's diagnosis, but indicated a "nasty attack" and said he felt "the storm has now passed by." On the 18th, Eliot told Mrs. Edward Burne-Jones that Lewes was "grievously ailing." On the 25th, she commented to Barbara Bodichon: ". . . I have a deep sense of change within, and of a permanently closer companionship with death." By now she had decided not to disguise, to others or herself, her "deep anxiety" and her unhappiness, with Lewes "sadly ill" and herself absorbed in nursing him. The doctors on the 25th told her Lewes seemed better, this five days before his death, in that temporary recovery terminally ill patients often experience before the end.

This is the foreground. In the background was a back-and-forth correspondence over *Such* (it would be published as *Impressions of Theophrastus Such*). John Blackwood characteristically praised what he had so far read, singling out the first chapter, a piece of autobiography called "Looking Inward." Eliot obviously gained some satisfaction from the firm's enjoyment of the manuscript and responded on business matters concerning publication that Lewes once handled. She discussed advertising the book as well as questions involving American and German rights. Blackwood agreed to all suggestions, evidently pleased with a volume in which the essays "seemed desperately good, full of wit and wisdom." Eliot then wrote on 25 November that she could not think of the book and did not wish it published under present circumstances. With the death of Lewes on 30 November,* she fell silent.

The funeral took place at Highgate Cemetery in London, on 4 December, with Eliot not present.† John Cross and Charles Lewes were the chief mourners among not many more than a dozen altogether. That group included the Burne-Joneses, the Harrisons, and Spencer, who accompanied Charles Lewes. Edith Simcox was not aware of the funeral service and did not attend. Agnes Lewes may or may not have been at the graveside. Their friends wrote letters of consolation: among others, John Blackwood, of course; Herbert Spencer—who said he grieved with Eliot; Alfred Tennyson; Robert Browning; Robert Williams Buchanan; Ivan Turgenev; Benjamin Jowett—who called Lewes "one of the first literary men of the day‡; Emily Clarke; Mrs. Isaac Pearson Evans; John Morley; Edward Burne-Jones. Eliot's first extant letter after her bereavement was to Barbara Bodichon: ". . . I am a bruised creature, and shrink even from the tenderest touch." To John Blackwood, she indicated she had not even read any letters sent to her, although we do know she tried to console herself by reading Tennyson's *In Memoriam*, some Shakespeare, and John Donne. She admitted that writing now seemed "all trivial stuff"—this in connection with her completion of *Theophrastus Such;* but she says Lewes wanted her to finish and print the book, citing his request to see a specimen page only two days before he died. Blackwood assured her that under the circumstances there was no reason to hurry. He did not yet understand that Eliot's physical condition made "hurry" a necessity.

---

*Cross incorrectly gave Lewes's death as the 28th. The death is recorded at Somerset House as 30 November. As Haight indicates, Charles Lewes read proof for Cross and missed the dating error. Paget gave the reason for death as enteritis, which covered a multiple of ills.

†Simcox communicated how Eliot saw it: "She cannot bear it. There have been unendurable sorrows, but I do not see how any can equal hers—who can feel as she does, who could have so much to love? . . . what does anything matter—would God the grief might kill her even now. But whether she lives or dies—there is no comfort for her left on earth but this; to know that their love and life have not been in vain for others, that the happiness which is dead and the sorrow that endures bind us for evermore to love and service of the sorrowing and the glad.—But oh! to think of that sweet frame shaken with the unconsolable anguish!" This was, we emphasize, Simcox's perception of Eliot.

‡Thomas Clifford Allbutt, whom we encountered earlier as the inventor of the clinical thermometer, told of the lasting effect Lewes had on other scientists. He quotes one young biologist who said physiology never became vital to him until he read Lewes on the subject. Allbutt predicted that Lewes would live with his followers.

22

After
George Henry Lewes

"... pride only helps us to be generous; it never
makes us so, any more than vanity makes us witty."

F or Eliot, there was the matter of putting a life in order which had already
suffered heavy blows of physical decline, depression, forewarnings of the
end—a death watch for herself—and now abandonment.* Her failure to appear
at the funeral could have been excessive grief, or else the old problem that
everybody would be reminded she was not Lewes's wife, however much she and
he had believed she was. For all she knew, Agnes Lewes might have been there.
The funeral opened up all the old wounds, and not to confront them in their
complexity kept her away. As she sat in the Priory, she was heard to scream
out. Only Charles Lewes and her maid Brett were her companions. The poems
of John Donne were a particular consolation, especially his own grief at his
wife's death.

John Cross soon became a visitor, two companions in grief, his mother having
died on 10 December, less than two weeks after Lewes. Eliot did start to arrange
her life by putting in order Lewes's remaining volume of *Problems of Life and
Mind*. But even this proved a hard lot, because each contact with the manuscript recalled a passage from Shakespeare's *King John* which she copied into her
diary: "Never to taste the pleasures of the world, / Never to be infected with

---

* We would need more clinical evidence to see if Eliot's mourning had turned to melancholia. In
Freud's formulation of this, in his important 1917 paper "Mourning and Melancholia," the latter
occurs when mourning becomes self-destructive. The melancholic individual is filled with guilt, loss
of self-esteem, and self-loathing in extreme cases, leading to a lack of interest in external affairs and
almost complete loss of personal focus. One way this works is that the ambivalence the individual
feels toward the lost object (for abandonment, among other things) is transformed into self-hatred
and, thus, justified. That Eliot did not fall into full melancholia was probably because of John Cross's
presence and support.

delight / Nor conversant with ease and idleness . . ." (IV, iii, 68–9). She would not see anyone after the funeral, and she could barely deal with Charles, who faithfully served as a respondent for the mail pouring in. By 5 January 1879, she had gotten through the manuscript, and then wrote her first letter, to Barbara Bodichon, two days later.

Once she broke through with that letter, she began to handle her affairs. Her references to Lewes are reverential, and this devotional sense now raises the question why in mid-April she became more businesslike in her remarks about him—possibly to justify her growing involvement with Cross, or as part of something unexpected she discovered in Lewes's life. Or else, she was gaining control over herself and becoming, once more, self-possessed. Her dealings with Blackwood over financial matters, in late January, suggest she had recovered sufficiently to handle her affairs, although in several areas of investment and related matters Cross helped. In a plaintive letter to Cross on 30 January—addressed as "Dearest Nephew"—she indicates she is trying to "live a little while that I may do certain things for his sake." She says she takes care of her diet and attempts to keep up her strength; she works "as much as I can to save my mind from imbecility." Yet, she admits, it is hardly easy: ". . . what used to be joy is joy no longer, and what is pain is easier because he has not to bear it." She asks Cross to be silent that she wrote asking to see him, suggesting with this some uncertainty about propriety. The letter is signed "M. E. L." The mode of address is compelling, for Eliot maintained the age difference by referring to Cross as "nephew," when in fact the correspondence would bring them together as quite something else.

In a follow-up letter, on 7 February, also addressed to "Dearest Nephew," Eliot restated her need for his response: "Every sign of care for me from the beings I respect and love is a help to me." She says that in a week or so, she will be ready to see him. "And my sense of desolation increases. Each day seems a very beginning—a new acquaintance with grief." To Barbara Bodichon the previous day, she had complained of her own ailing condition, but she says that even if she were well, she could not bear to forsake the things Lewes used and looked upon. She indicates she is entirely absorbed with his manuscripts, as though his lasting reputation now depended on her putting everything in order. There is something of Dorothea Brooke in this, eager to give herself over to a task beyond the self; or else a recognition that her own abilities having wound down, she can work through her mourning by bringing Lewes's manuscripts into order and print.

Edith Simcox and Cross met outside the Priory (Eliot was still not seeing her), and he told her he feared Eliot's isolation would prove fatal if prolonged. Quite possibly at this point, with his mother and Lewes dead within ten days of each other, he realized he could create the circumstances whereby Eliot would view him as a suitor. Simcox's remarks, while not directed to this point, suggest that Cross was hovering, as she was also—each of course with different agendas. It was an anguished time, with a particularly cold winter which Eliot said she felt in her heart, along with sharp pains in her hip. Paget gave her sedatives but the attacks became frequent, nearly always featuring nausea, headache, and acute pain, all from her renal ailment. Barbara Bodichon attempted to draw her out of what seemed like a self-inflicted cycle of pain and anguish, but Eliot felt she could not travel, not even to staunch Barbara, herself quite ill.

While there was a real physical condition of great seriousness for Eliot, there was also a wallowing in pain, a desire to indulge it. It was curious and not so curious: Curious because she had argued that death was final and should not be rejected; it was part of life. Lewes would live on in her and others' minds. But not so curious because, nearing sixty, she was alone, despite fame, literary reputation, and riches. Creating a cycle of pain in some sense would reunite her with Lewes; for in their last years they had indeed wallowed in pain, in a kind of symbiotic, reciprocal give-and-take. She had this need to be taken care of, and in turn to care for another.

By early February, however, she had recovered sufficiently to take out the carriage for a drive. On the 23rd, she saw Cross; Spencer called but was not asked to stay. The toll showed in her physically, "incredibly thin," she told Barbara Bodichon; she was down to $103\frac{1}{2}$ pounds on what had once been a slim but sturdy five-foot-five-inch frame. Two books awaited her, Lewes's and her own. Having gotten what she called *The Study of Psychology* in order, she arranged for it to be printed. As for her book, "Characters and Characteristics," she read proof and sent it on to Blackwood. She recognized soon that *Theophrastus Such* would be a more literary title.

Although she was going ahead with its preparation for publication, as late as 25 February she told John Blackwood it "would be intolerable to my feelings to have a book of my writing brought out for a long while to come. What I wish to do is, to correct the sheets thoroughly and then have them struck off and laid by till the time of publication comes." She feels she can wait since her doctors have advised her there was nothing the matter to create urgency other than "the common uncertainty" life exerts on us all.

The essays themselves are of mixed quality. Eliot's narrator is Such, male, a bachelor who in some respects recalls Herbert Spencer. He is self-centered, someone who, while drawing others into telling their intimate stories, turns to writing his own impressions only if they can be revealed posthumously. Despite the cross-gendering—Marian Evans as George Eliot now burying herself further in another male disguise—the essays are also full of Eliot's own perspectives: her "bachelor" status, her distaste for autobiography, her feeling that the form itself is incomplete and, therefore, false, her fears of failure as an author, her belief that her philosophy is not "the formula" of her personality, her awareness that the true judge of one's value must be left to posterity.

One salient characteristic of the essays, except for the final one on Jews,* is

---

* "The Modern Hep! Hep! Hep!" should be read with *Daniel Deronda* in mind, as Eliot's attempt to deal with social and folk theories now running rampant in Europe. She sees the Jews as a race who, despite persecution and alienism, "have escaped with less of abjectness and less of hard hostility towards the nations whose hand has been against them, than could have happened in the case of a people who had neither their adhesion to a separate religion founded on historic memories, nor their characteristic family affectionateness." The title, incidentally, derives from the Latin *Hierosolyma est Perdita* (Hep, Jerusalem is lost), once a call for the murder of Jews during the Crusades.

that while they purport to be autobiographical, they are concerned with secrets, Such's and others'. Such speaks of an "incompleteness" as a given in autobiography, and to be incomplete is, in reality, to bury or secrete the self or information. Such explains he is a failure (his one published work failed), not rich, and lacking high connections. Other people, in fact, use him, but he has gained a moral though cynical perspective of some precision: ". . . the illusions that began for us when we were less acquainted with evil have not lost their value when we discern them to be illusions." This is an older person's view of life as full of secrets, role-playing, illusions, and deceptions.

Eliot believed that if the form proved sound—by which she meant popular and literarily satisfactory—she would do a second series. Such would prove salutary, since it revealed to her that she was capable of writing, however much it was a pale shadow of her former work. But fiction as an expression of her deepest feelings was no longer possible. Short of an autobiography or a personal memoir, those feelings now went into hiding.

While working on Such, Eliot was trying to make sense of Lewes's manuscripts and in so doing became acquainted with Dr. Michael Foster, a physiologist whom Lewes had held in high regard. Through Foster, and with the help of other advisers, she conceived of establishing the George Henry Lewes Studentship in Physiology, whose trustees included Thomas Henry Huxley, Henry Sidgwick, Francis Balfour, and others of almost similar achievement. The idea was to give a young student the opportunity to train formally in a field where Lewes had worked somewhat hit-and-miss. For this fellowship, she gave over £5,000, whose annual interest would support the winning candidate; the first was C. S. Roy, and later ones included Sir Charles Sherrington and a succession of distinguished scientists.

Lewes's will created several problems, in that it left all his other property except his copyrights to the "spinster" Mary Anne Evans. This involved several legal tangles, since Eliot's money was commingled with his, in his name, and she had to extract it. But the largest element of this was the revelation, for all who cared, of her spinster state. The copyrights were left to his then three sons, in the 1859 will; now at his death, one son, Charles, was his heir. To Eliot, he left less than £2,000, whereas her part of the will, her money, involved £30,000 in securities and bank accounts, plus the two houses which she owned. Her part of the estate was over £50,000, which in current spending power would be well over $2 million. She needed a complicated legal maneuver to extricate the £5,000 for the Lewes Studentship and the remainder of her money. The funds were first transferred to Mary Anne Evans, spinster; then she was deeded the name Mary Ann Evans Lewes—deeded, not given her in the way she had been using it; then the money was finally transferred to her account. Having passed through this, with all the dreaded name changes, she was in possession of her own money.

The witnesses for these transactions were Charles Lewes, who of course knew that virtually everything except his father's copyrights belonged to Eliot, and John Cross, who was her monetary and legal adviser. Cross also counseled her to remove some investments from American stocks—the San Francisco Bank, for example, which he deemed volatile—and to reinvest in English funds, in London and Northwestern debentures, which were more solid. She also remade her will, on 18 March, an indication that by March she had been convinced to give up her seclusion and reenter her life. All her financial dealings went through Cross, who advised her devotedly. The personal situation had developed in ways even he, ever worshipful, might have only imagined.[*]

Eliot began to emerge. Not only did she go for drives and start to correspond, she also saw friends: Cross, as noted, also Henry Sidgwick about the Lewes Studentship, then Maria Congreve, Mrs. Edward Burne-Jones, Spencer (who finally made it through the door), Elma Stuart, and even Edith Simcox, who turned up unannounced, as she had done nearly every day since Lewes's death. On 12 April, she was finally admitted. What Eliot feared was the extreme emotionalism Simcox brought to each situation. Simcox fought back tears, sought a kiss, but generally was so delighted to be in Eliot's company she restrained herself. Simcox found her friend removed from "morbid sensibility," in fact rather voluble as she chatted on about Lewes's manuscripts. In early April, Eliot felt secure enough to visit Charles Lewes's house for the first time since his father's death.

But March also brought with it a radical change of mind about *Such*, still connected to appearances. On reading the revision, she decided to suppress the book altogether in its present form, and "regenerate it whenever—if ever—I recover the power to do so." She changed her mind yet again, but she still felt guilt about publishing so soon after Lewes's death. A further point is that on rereading her work she recognized it fell beneath her usual level of accomplishment, and she preferred to be remembered by *Deronda*. Her comment is cryptic, and we cannot be certain of her motivation, but we must assume part was her sense of herself as a "broken-spirited creature."

On 5 April, she reversed her position on *Such* and told Blackwood to proceed with publication in May. She was trying to apply logic to her inner uncertainties. Our suspicion that she found something in Lewes's papers that possibly turned her mind from *Such* and created the "Crisis" is countered by her desire to get on with the Lewes Studentship. But then we have her peremptory request to Frederic Harrison to call, again about a matter she does not indicate. This was on 8 April and had nothing to do with her will, which was already settled. The record is unclear. She appeared to be acting strangely, even irrationally, and yet we have no evidence she had found anything conclusive, or even damaging. In her long letter to Stowe, on 10 April, she speaks of her bereavement, two old warriors now bending under defeat. Stowe and her husband were undergoing illness, and Eliot commiserated. "Joy and sorrow are both my perpetual

---

[*] By early March, Eliot was making decisions on the appearance of *Such*, including margins, print, and paper. She was worried that her handwriting had been misread, and she was fearful of typographical errors. She also wished for a notice to be printed on the flyleaf of the book indicating she had submitted it last November—that is, before Lewes's death, to avoid any appearance of impropriety. In another area, Alexander Main's *George Eliot Birthday Book*—in a plain binding as well as in a more elaborate brown leather one—sold 9,400 copies, which astonished everyone in the firm. In still another aspect of her work, *Romola* was now available in D'Albert-Durade's translation, but she tells her friend she has not looked into it, "finding no interest in my own work at present."

companions, but the joy is called Past and the sorrow Present." The occasion for Eliot's letter was that Stowe had sent on an illustrated 1879 edition of *Uncle Tom's Cabin*. She praises Stowe for her great effort on behalf of the American nation, then adds a comment about England's "wicked war" in South Africa, by which she means "wicked on *our* part," although it is not clear how that should be taken. That "wicked war" did result in Lewes's widowed daughter-in-law and two grandchildren returning from Natal on April 28.

Eliot's letter to Stowe indulges in bathos, a kind of moral repulsion that she continues to live: ". . . it is difficult to feel that there is anything which would not *now* be done as well if I were gone away. While He [sic] was here I never had to ask whether my continuing life was of any use." She indicates that soon she will be leaving for Witley, but doubts if she can survive there without Lewes. "Now everything seems difficult." Yet even that confession does not satisfy her, because she feels she is desecrating the past, subverting memory. She still feels some rebellious spirit, especially when she observes empty lives going on "in vigorous uselessness," but she recognizes that spirit returns slowly.

Although Eliot had apparently acquiesced to John Blackwood's depreciating reference to the Zulus as "ourang outangs"—when the publisher wrote about the British attacks on Zululand in 1878—she concluded that the war in southern Africa was "unjustifiable." She also says, to David Kaufmann, who was interested in Jewish matters, that industry was languishing and "the best part of our nation is indignant." To Simcox, she would speak of the support she was receiving from servants, in particular, but to others she began to see the world in dark, shadowed terms.

Sympathetic women showed up regularly at the Priory. Anne Thackeray Ritchie was followed by Lucy Clifford (widow of Dr. William Kingdon Clifford), and on one occasion—Clifford reports—Eliot "put her wonderful hands" on her hair and "sent a thrill through me." The chief caller, however, was not a woman, but John Cross. On 22 April, Eliot had written she was "in dreadful need of your counsel. Pray come to me when you can—morning, afternoon, or evening. I shall dismiss anyone else." The request, so peremptory, seems unnatural. We do not know what Eliot had in mind, unless it was something she had come across in Lewes's papers, or a sudden need for personal or financial support.* Cross did note in his life of Eliot that he now saw her constantly. With his mother dead, he was himself unfocused, and in a move toward redirecting himself he started to work on his Italian, taking up Carlyle's translation of Dante's *Inferno* as guide. When Eliot heard of this, she exclaimed, "Oh I must read that with you." Cross reports that for the next year they read through the *Inferno* and *Purgatorio* with great care and attention to detail. Cross says he felt this diversion distracted Eliot's mind from her sorrowful memories. "The divine poet took us into a new world. It was a renovation of life." Possibly they saved *Paradiso* for their honeymoon.

---

* The argument for finance is that she was being importuned for loans, with Bessie Parkes (now Mrs. Belloc), among others, asking for £500, which was declined, apparently, on Cross's advice.

The relationship with Cross was cemented at this stage, although whether it would lead to marriage was another consideration. His fantasy of being close to Eliot was now being realized, with her need for advice and support stronger than ever. The question of "love" cannot be satisfactorily answered, since Cross worshipped Eliot, and she found in him the right man at the right time. At close to sixty, she may not have been capable of romantic love, especially in such poor health; whereas he, at forty, may have been so overwhelmed by worship he could not accommodate love. His own sexual predilections, moreover, seemed low-keyed. Although he was said to have had women friends, he may still have been a virgin. Several commentators have suggested, without any hard supportive evidence, that Cross was possibly a latent homosexual. But more likely his unmarried state resulted from his closeness to his mother and a low-keyed sexual drive, although the homosexual possibility cannot be entirely ruled out. But to be more precise about how we should structure his sexual life from this distance, always a tempting question, is essentially beside the point. We are concerned, ultimately, with Eliot, not Cross, and from her point of view he was masculine enough.*

By the end of April, Eliot was awaiting the arrival of Eliza Lewes and her two children from Africa. Because of this, she could not decide when to leave for Witley, which, in any event, now seemed a hollow place, inhabited only by herself and the servants. The arrival of Bertie's widow and children would turn out to be less than satisfactory, since each, Eliot and Eliza, had different ideas of what was due the other. Also, at this time, Eliot told Simcox she had struggled through a period when "the springs of affection" had dried up, but with that strange and horrible experience having passed, love and tenderness were as precious as ever. The "morbid time for repression was over for ever" were either her words or Simcox's sense of them.

The arrival of Eliza and the children on 28 April occupied Eliot to the point she felt "a little oppressed just now with the claims on my time and thoughts and can long for nothing except to get away to my country home." She indicates she intends to live as bravely as she can; in the meantime, friends were crowding in on her before she was prepared. One of the things that may have pressed on her was Swinburne's savage attack on her and her work, in his piece on Charlotte Brontë. The attack came in 1877, but Lewes kept it from her; she eventually read it and was appalled, especially since she had once praised Swinburne's poetry. Among other things, the poet called her "an Amazon," whatever that meant, but with a tone of suggested lesbianism; and then he embroidered upon it, "an Amazon thrown sprawling over the crupper of her spavined and spurgalled Pegasus." Either he meant Lewes here or something far more cryptic; but

* Another dimension remains, but to pursue it we would need evidence we do not possess. That is, Eliot was drawn to Cross precisely because he was lacking in sexual drive; that her attraction to women meant that she, too, had confused or bisexual leanings; and that, as a result, Cross with his own confused or bisexual leanings would be particularly appealing. This or some version of it can be offered, but it must be withdrawn for lack of documentation, witnesses, or anything else to support it.

he also indicated she plagiarized parts of *The Mill on the Floss* from a Gaskell novel Eliot had not even read. As she learned, fame meant it was open season.

Spencer had come, on 20 April, but was more concerned with himself than with Eliot. He sought advice on his autobiography, on whose composition he was now concentrating his considerable ego. With Spencer now reentering, it is compelling to see Eliot attempting to pick up the pieces, trying to recompose some sense of her life. The requests for loans, among other things, revealed to her how exposed she was, as a widow and without Lewes's protection. She had lived, as she recognized, in a cocoon. In that respect, she had cut herself off from a world of objects (and people) to experience only what Lewes deemed least damaging. Now, as she emerged, she encouraged experiences she might not even have known about if Lewes had lived.

One such roughening experience was her encounter with Bertie's widow, Eliza, and her children. Eliot was appalled by the "uncivilized" children, in contrast with the well-brought-up offspring of Charles; Eliza for her part became aware she was considered inferior because of her colonial background. The encounter revealed there was no rapport here, although Eliot was more than willing to continue her support of the family, to the tune of at least £200 a year, more if we include gifts. Thoughtfully, she placed dolls around the sitting room for the children; but she did this as well for Charles's children, whom she clearly preferred. Eliza considered herself special, and her expectations were both huge and unrealistic. Dissatisfied with Eliot's contribution to her support, she even considered asking for a sizable loan. Later, in July, she threatened to return to Natal unless Eliot came across more generously. The latter was clearly upset by events which had now piled on to her own sense of pain. "The news about Eliza," she tells Charles Lewes, "is of the dreariest—especially the untruthfulness. I am alarmed still more to find that she has a notion of borrowing money; and since she seems disposed to throw the blame on you [Eliza conceived of Charles as a competitor for 'Mutter's' money], would it not be better after all for me to write to her? The worst of it is, that in my present mood I could hardly help writing to her very severely. Don't take a tone of dissuasion about her going back to Natal or remaining. That effects nothing but harm." Eliot was evidently struggling to remain civil.

But this was still in the immediate future. In the foreground was a good deal of anguish, muttering, possibly cross words. None of this was helped by the fact that at about the time Eliza arrived, the almost traumatized Eliot had finally agreed on the ornament for Lewes's grave, a simple piece of granite for the headstone with the inscription:

GEORGE HENRY LEWES
BORN 18th APRIL 1817
DIED 30th NOVEMBER 1878

Eliot would herself be buried next to him.

On 19 May, there was some brightening of what had been mainly gloom when she received a copy of *Theophrastus Such* and Volume IV of Lewes's *Prob-*

lems of Body and Mind, a suitable twinning of publications. The bad news was that John Blackwood was falling ill, first with bronchitis, and then with complications leading to his retirement from the firm and, on 29 October, his death. At first, Eliot did not remark the seriousness of Blackwood's case, possibly because of her own bereavement; but once his condition penetrated, she was seriously concerned. Next to Lewes, the publisher and his brother William had been perhaps the most reliable friends she had had since leaving Chapman. When we read her later words, we recognize how much faith she had placed in this man of contrasts: deeply conservative and traditional and yet more than willing to embrace this woman who had broken so many conventional rules. He had let her dictate the terms of her career, and he had put all the resources of the firm behind her. She needed someone honest and forthright in her dealings, and Blackwood proved he could be trusted. For someone as sensitive as Eliot, so easily thrown off her concentration, the firm proved a marvel of consistency and support. Her words upon his death bear this out, for as she told Charles Lewes, Blackwood had been bound up for twenty years with what she cared most for in her life; his good qualities, she says, made many difficult things easy for her. It was, all in all, an "odd couple": the rigid, socially correct Scotsman, and a woman who started out at the opposite from him. Strikingly, as the relationship developed, the publisher moved closer to the center, and Eliot, as we have observed, moved closer to the right, or what passed for it in the 1870s.

All business transactions were now going directly from the firm to Eliot. Translations of *Such* were proceeding, for German and Dutch markets, among others. Eliot noted in her diary that she suffered a severe attack of pain on 20 May, and another on the 26th. She stayed in bed, but the attacks were slowly wasting her frame; she had lost nearly twenty pounds to date. On the 22nd, after the first attack but before the second, she left for Witley, the servants having prepared the way. She took to the piano for the first time since Lewes's death, and she saw *Such* go into a second impression. On 18 May, before her departure for Witley, Simcox saw that Eliot's face had a "deathlike expression of pain." She likened it to Paolo's in Dante's Paolo and Francesca story as painted by George Frederick Watts. Simcox feels her friend has exhausted her energies in trying to do too much for her daughter-in-law, something Eliot denied. She found Eliot receptive to caresses and comforting. "It is so sweet of her," she wrote, "to endure to be loved."

Once Eliot was exposed to the silence of her country home, she felt some sense of recovery. Within easy distance was John Cross, and he probably influenced her to return to the piano. "Nephew" came often, once at least with his sister Mary, but usually alone. The visits were becoming more than sessions in reading Dante and conjugating Italian verbs, although that remained the pretense. Eliot had come to depend on Cross increasingly for all matters, large and small, even for food orders. As prescribed by Paget to cleanse out her system, she was to drink a pint of champagne every day, which perhaps kept her slightly tipsy. The frequent meetings with Cross, the fact they were in private, and the further fact that he was helping to bring her back into the world all led up to one decisive question. Probably at some point in August, he proposed that their relationship proceed to its next, natural stage, marriage.

Eliot recorded "Decisive conversation" in her diary on 21 August, and then something of a lull settled in with Cross. He had made his move too soon. Eliot was attached to him, supported by him, and grateful; but the timing was wrong. They backed off, became more formal, and waited, although for what we cannot be certain. Her dilemma was clear. She was a seriously ill woman; she was losing weight, and her condition could hardly improve. The difference of twenty years could possibly have made less difference if she were robust. Yet she desperately wanted marriage, so that she could be accepted back into the family fold; however much she may have dismissed Isaac and his narrow views, even at this late stage she still wanted acceptance and respectability. At close to sixty, she was not the young rebel, nor was she willing to continue to flout convention.

She was playing out, with suitable differences, the role she had written for Dorothea Brooke. She was now Casaubon to Cross's Dorothea, in one of those cross-gender and cross-age transformations we have often noted in her life and fiction. Unlike Casaubon, she had achieved a great deal, but in terms of her worn-out, somewhat desiccated, enervated condition, she was no match for the healthy, youthful-looking Cross.* Like Dorothea, in this cross-referencing, the young suitor worshipped someone whose destiny he wished to link himself to; and like Dorothea, he saw himself as offering youth, energy, and health to the reclamation and preservation of someone great. Did Eliot recognize the irony of her situation? We cannot tell, unless we see in her initial rejection of Cross in August a realization she would be going from a socially unacceptable relationship to a socially scandalous marriage. Did she recall Sir James Chettam's remark, "He is no better than a mummy," and Mrs. Cadwallader's reply: "For this marriage to Casaubon is as good as going to a nunnery"? Yet once she had set out on her rebellious course, she was inevitably put in situations outside conventional boundaries.

Meanwhile, in the months leading up to the August proposal, Eliot reported attacks, indisposition, and discomfort from an unusually cold and drippy spring. Amidst all this, she was nevertheless eager to make certain Lewes's record as a writer was kept straight, even while her references to him seem formal, more attuned to his reputation than to the man. She was pleased that Frederic Harrison was to read a paper at the prestigious Metaphysical Society starting out with a quotation from Lewes's *The Study of Psychology*. Cheeringly, the *Times* review of *Such* was excellent,† and the book as of 11 June had sold almost 4,000 copies. Her reply to William Blackwood (now taking over the firm as his uncle, John, declined) indicates she hung on good news, and even expresses the view

---

* A drawing of Cross in about 1878 reveals the enormous physical difference between the two. It shows a healthy-looking individual, going slightly bald, full-bearded and robust in the Victorian manner, handsome in a slightly weak way, and well turned out. In some respects, he looks like a fleshier Lewes, handsomer of course, but soft around the edges. The face has no depth.

† Somewhat balanced out by the poor notice in the *Athenaeum*, which cited Eliot for being didactic and unsympathetic to her own creations, whom it called puppets. No Lewes could protect her against this. In any event, a third printing of the book occurred in June, another 1,050 copies.

that books can succeed without universal praise. She was already building up a defensive position against future onslaughts. But this temporary brightness was offset by another attack on 17 June, putting her in bed and leading her to tell John Blackwood she "was in more acute pain than I have ever known in my life before."

We assume Cross was coming and going frequently. Eliot told Mrs. Edward Burne-Jones she was being watched over by "a very comfortable country practitioner" and there was "a devoted friend who is backwards and forwards continually to see that I lack nothing." This means that Cross saw Eliot ill, in bed, in pain, surely not at her best. What he saw was what she was, a woman of almost sixty who was slowly melting away. His worshipful attitude overrode sexual attraction: the woman he admired almost to the point of a divinity was Lewes's "Madonna." The Eliot whom he courted was a sick woman he wanted to protect and shield, more mother than fiancée.

By 30 June, she was well enough to contemplate inviting Charles and his family, along with Eliza and hers—four adults, five children, plus one of their servants—for a weekend. She looked forward to the children eating the strawberries which would be in abundance by then. Although her plan was to have them down on 12 July, a sudden severe relapse made her so weak she postponed the event until the 19th. Also, the weather was so exceptionally poor she called it "a greater calamity even than the Zulu War." Her report to Charles Lewes is an effort to seem lighthearted about something which was dragging her down. After indicating she is wasting her spiritual substance in riotous living—the daily pint of champagne—she adds, "my bodily substance in the shape of flesh is wasting also. . . . To counterbalance other pains I have had no headache to speak of." She adds that, even so, she has been able to do some letter writing and proofreading, and even some piano playing.

What we observe is how much of each letter she writes—to John Blackwood, Charles Lewes, Barbara Bodichon, and others—is now given over to communiqués from the sickbed. As with most ill people, she was consumed by her own condition; and if not directly, then indirectly she linked her illness to the world's or society's ills. She was becoming fascinated by the progress of her decline—this even as Cross was moving toward his declaration. She could not stop describing the champagne tippling, the headaches receding or intensifying, the chills, the renal pain, the hours spent in bed, the temporary recoveries. As friends inquired, she responded that she had little but disagreeable news to communicate. In this context, there was an inevitability to her linkage with Cross. For if she could think of little outside herself, she found the perfect mate, who could think of little but her. Furthermore, while the servants surrounding her, especially Brett, were supportive, in all areas generated by her fame she needed help. All Cross had to do, in this scenario, was await the right moment.

Toward the end of July, she was well enough to go for drives and walks. While her energy was depleted, she did have good days. Meanwhile, John Blackwood was temporarily well enough to answer correspondence, although the running of the firm was now in William's ("Willie's") hands. In August, both the weather and Eliot's various conditions seemed to pick up. In writing to Charles Lewes, she shows an unusual degree of anger at a letter addressed to her, by an "impertinent American," as "Miss Marian Evans." She tells Charles to respond by saying that Mrs. Lewes has no photograph to send and "systematically abstains from giving her autograph." The tone of outrage is directed at "Miss Marian Evans," which she had ceased to acknowledge. In the same letter, she does indicate how she is momentarily cheered by the sale of her books, which in various editions and at different prices continued to find buyers; but that show of pleasure quickly became silence. There is a break in her correspondence for two weeks, except for the diary entry on 21 August of "Decisive conversation." The break could indicate several matters, illness among them; but more likely it was the consequence of perplexity, shock, uncertainty, confused feelings, and a host of other possibilities which remained disguised both to her and to those who attempt to read her situation.

As we grapple for clues to Eliot's inner life, we do know that a quartz-like formality shaped itself in her references to John Cross. "Johnnie" becomes "Mr. Cross"; Eleanor Cross came with a person designated by Eliot as "her brother," the erstwhile Johnnie. Tears followed, although even here Eliot does not specify. Her diary is as much disguise as revelation, as though she feared that words themselves might define feelings she wished to keep hidden from herself. She wrote cryptically on 8 October that "Joy" arrived in the evening; but is "Joy" Johnnie Cross? Or something we do not know about? Another entry is equally cryptic: "Choice of Hercules." Was she locating herself in Hercules' "choice," which involved pleasure and self on the one hand, virtue on the other? It is not as if she had lived like a hermit during this time—Barbara Bodichon had come for several days in September, at the time "Mr. Cross" came for dinner. The diary itself gives little else away, with only the entry of "Tears, tears" on 3 October suggestive of anything dramatic.

Except for these entries, her life seemed uneventful. Her reading was Plato's *Republic,* and then Dante's *Purgatorio.* Her diary entries also reveal she was still studying Hebrew as well as algebra. On 14 October, she wrote to Elma Stuart, indicating she was trying to cultivate "hopefulness," which, whatever the circumstances, Lewes had always encouraged. But there is nothing else in this letter, or on that day, to suggest a huge change in her life. And yet it was apparently occurring, between the 14th and 16th, when she wrote Cross a delicate, carefully conceived love letter. This was not the letter of mother to son, or aunt to nephew, but of a woman who had been courted and won over. The change in her attitude was probably a slow process, in which, having recovered from the August proposal, she weighed the possibilities, kept them all to herself (as far as we know), was not even certain by the 14th of October, and then made a decision based on still emerging feelings about marriage. At this stage, Eliot had to be careful not to appear a fool, an elderly, sick, weak-looking woman marrying someone so obviously her junior. But the letter is unmistakable; she was his.

Best loved and loving one—the sun it shines so, so cold, when there are no eyes to look love on me. I cannot bear to sadden one moment when we are together, but wenn Du bist nicht da [when you are not there] I have often a bad time. It *is* a solemn time, dearest. And why should I complain if it is a painful time: What I call my pain is almost a joy seen in the wide array of the world's cruel suffering. Thou seest I am grumbling today—got a chill yesterday and have a headache. All which, as a wise doctor would say, is not of the least consequence, my dear Madam.

Through everything else, dear tender one, there is the blessing of trusting in thy goodness. Thou dost not know anything of verbs Hiphil or Hophal or the history of metaphysics or the position of Kepler in science, but thou knowest best things of another sort, such as belong to the manly heart—secrets of lovingness and rectitude. O I am flattering. Consider what thou was a little time ago in pantaloons and back hair.

. . . Why should I compliment myself at the end of my letter and say that I am faithful, loving, more anxious for thy life than mine? I will run no risks of being "inexact"—so I will only say "varium and mutabile semper" but at this particular moment thy tender

Beatrice

Dante's beloved in the *Inferno!* There is a certain coyness in this, something suggesting a virginal being held in waiting for Cross's embrace. She had given herself over—Lewes's "Madonna" was now Cross's "Beatrice."

Coinciding with this dramatic event in Eliot's personal life was a parallel event. John Blackwood's condition suddenly worsened when he suffered a second heart attack, and his daily life now became a struggle to survive. Eliot indicates his "want of breath" in the clear sunshine, a reference probably to his inability to play his favorite game, golf. But in responding to this, to William, Eliot made no mention of her own news. William had indicated an increase in her royalty on *Such*, which was selling unexpectedly well, 6,000 copies in four months. And she made no mention to those closest to her, Mrs. Edward Burne-Jones, Charles Lewes, or Barbara Bodichon. Her failure to tell Charles is itself strange, since she considered him a son, his children her grandchildren, and he considered her "Mutter." Possibly, she feared an adverse response from "Mother" marrying someone young enough to be her son. When she wrote to Barbara, the crux of her letter is objective news, that a candidate had been designated for the Lewes Studentship, an Edinburgh student named Dr. Charles Roy, a promising young physiologist. *

Letters that followed did not mention anything personal, either. Meanwhile, John Blackwood's condition worsened and on the 29th of October he died.† All

---

* Although not so well known as some of the succeeding Lewes Studentship winners, Roy had a distinguished career, even within a short life span, culminating in his appointment as professor of pathology at Cambridge University.

† For his part, Blackwood thought of Eliot in his final hours and spoke of publishing a supplementary volume to the *Sayings* with the poetry in it or not, according to her wishes in the matter. This plan, incidentally, she rejected, and suggested that additional sayings from *Deronda* and *Such* could be added without making the volume too large if thinner paper could be substituted. This was done, with a volume of 462 pages, longer than the original but much thinner.

of this coincided with Eliot's plan to move back to the Priory, which she did on
1 November, after a visit to the Crosses at Weybridge. Once back at the Priory,
she entertained Cross almost constantly, although their pattern did not alter.
They spent evenings reading together, from a variety of literature: Shakespeare,
Wordsworth, Chaucer, Dante, Sainte-Beuve (his *Causeries*). It was what she had
enjoyed with Lewes, although here she was in the role of tutor with pupil. Whatever their personal arrangements, Cross and Eliot would not marry until the following May, and there were some ripples to come. Eliot was now reaching her
sixtieth birthday, and in her usual birthday letter to Sara Hennell, she speaks of
feeling much stronger than she had ever expected to feel again. Yet despite this
note, she adds a sentiment that hardly signifies a woman about to marry: ". . . I
am exceptionally blessed in many ways, but more blessed are the dead who rest
from their labours and have not to dread a barren useless survival."

Such sentiments evidently derive from a very deep part of Eliot's life, and yet
we cannot quite account for them at this time. We speculate. Was she reconsidering marriage? Was Cross's mind too trivial for her? Was she reconsidering the
whole drift of her life, where mistakes outnumbered achievement? Was this part
of some dance of death which she indulged? Was it a response to illness and
pain, the desire to get it all over with? Was it, as seems more probable, a sign
of her feelings of uselessness—her knowledge that as a writer she was too enervated to produce anything? Was she, like many writers, equating the end of her
writing with death itself, in that *Deronda* had effectively served as the final stage
of her fictional life?

Yet shortly after this, on 6 December, she invited the entire family to lunch:
the five children, Charles, Gertrude, and Eliza. Before that, she drove into the
city in the morning to buy books and toys for the children, this entry in her
diary being followed by one indicating a visit to the cemetery, and that one
succeeded by her measurement of her loneliness. All of this indicates an up-
and-down emotional life, a cycle of moods from a real effort to reclaim her life
and a desire, perhaps equally powerful, to succumb.

Lewes hovered over her study at the Priory and over her thoughts. Although
a large photograph of him stared down at her from over the fireplace, she told
Elma Stuart she did not want any visible evidence; she had memories. Stuart
was arranging to have a bust of Lewes made, which she planned to present to
Eliot. But the latter demurred in quite unmistakable terms.

Any portrait or bust of Him that others considered good I should be glad
to have placed in any public institution. But for *myself* I would rather have
neither portrait nor bust. My inward representation even of comparatively
indifferent faces is so vivid as to make portraits of them unsatisfactory to
me. And I am bitterly repenting now that I was led into buying Mayall's
enlarged copy of the photograph you mention [the one over the fireplace
in the Priory study]. It is smoothed down and altered, and each time I look
at it I feel *its* unlikeness more. *Himself as he was* is what I see inwardly, and
I am afraid of outward images lest they should corrupt the inward.

Linked to this was Eliot's wish to have no biography of Lewes. Mrs. Thomas Trollope, Anthony Trollope's sister-in-law, inquired if she were writing a biography of Lewes—Mrs. Trollope had been asked this by Dr. Ludwig Haller, Eliot's friend from Berlin, who also wanted to know if there was already in existence a Lewes biography. Eliot mentions an article in the *New Quarterly Magazine* (she mistakenly identifies it as *New London Quarterly*) called "George Henry Lewes," but she judges it not very strong. What she wanted to see was certainly not a deep probing into the life—for obvious reasons—but some just assessment of the work. She had always felt Lewes was underestimated, or even dismissed as a witty but shallow amateur. Along the way, she expresses distaste not only for a biography of Lewes but for all such work: "Biographies generally are a disease of English literature."

Her rancor here may or may not be connected to a further cryptic entry in her diary, for 25 November: "Another turning point." Nothing more. It comes after a brief entry, "Wrote to Dr. Roy," this in connection with the Lewes Studentship; but the cryptic remark could not be associated with Roy, whom Eliot did not even know. Whether it had anything to do with Lewes, his private life, her general disdain for biography, her particular distaste for any biography of him we cannot tell. We do know that Eliot was reading Lewes's letters at this time; further, that she bundled them together to be buried with her. Once again, the question arises whether these letters led her to say "Another turning point," or whether in some guarded way the whole matter is connected to Cross.

Now that she was back at the Priory, Simcox came calling. The latter is often our source for how frequently Cross came and related matters. Ailments and all, Eliot was clearly no hermit. Spencer dropped in (and then left for Egypt), as did the Harrisons, William Blackwood, the Darwins, Jowett, the Burne-Joneses, Maria Congreve, Leslie Stephen, and several others. She was, all in all, a kind of legendary figure, the last of the great Victorian novelists; after Victoria herself and perhaps Florence Nightingale, she was the most famous woman in England. Yet she spent Christmas Day alone at the Priory. Cross was with his sister in Lincolnshire, and the Lewes children and grandchildren had come on Christmas Eve. She wrote to Cross to commemorate the holiday, but her letter is curiously lacking in romantic sentiment, as though once she had expressed herself earlier she did not need to repeat endearments. The sole possible warmth came in the salutation, "Bester Mann." Increasingly, she saw the servants as friends, telling Cross that although she would be alone on Christmas Day, she would smell the servants' goose and hope that "a fraction of this world's inhabitants are enjoying themselves." She adds she is content to be alone, inasmuch as she is out of pain.

Simcox turned up the day after Christmas, finding Eliot alone. In what had become a kind of ballet, in which each pranced around the other, she apologized for intruding and offered to leave once she had received a kiss on the cheek. But Eliot asked her to remain, as she was not tired. They discussed politics, and Eliot showed strong support for Disraeli and vehement hostility to the Liberal speeches of Gladstone. Simcox would have none of that, attacking Disraeli for showing indifference to women and children in the mines, in his novel *Sybil.*

Eliot agreed, but countered by saying Simcox should make only specific charges against Disraeli and not attack the whole man. The two roved back and forth into history, using Louis Napoleon as their next focus—Simcox attacking him for the weak, featureless man he had been, Eliot agreeing, but not quite in her friend's camp. In their exchanges, their different political ideologies become clear. Simcox was always seeking just causes and attacking those who subverted them. Eliot was more accepting, more willing to tolerate human frailties as long as the social contract was not threatened. Louis Napoleon, once, had been all negative to her; now she could find some force for good in him—although she was not specific about what it was. Granted, the former emperor of France was complex, but while he advocated some reforms and liberalization, as the nephew of Bonaparte he was self-serving, ruthless, and authoritarian. Miscalculating Bismarck, he led France into crushing defeat in the Franco-Prussian War, which had caught Eliot's sympathies on both sides.

On a more amusing note, Eliot asked Simcox to stop calling her "mother." Most probably, as she moved toward marriage, she did not want "mother" coming from a woman of Simcox's age, only five years younger than Cross. Her explanation was that her feeling for her friend was not that of a mother. This could also have been a way of cementing the friendship, rather than keeping them as mistress and disciple.

As December closed out, Eliot received the kind of letter, from Benjamin Jowett, that every author cherishes. Jowett told her that her gift was too great for it to terminate, and he encouraged her to continue writing. What he was ignorant of was her lack of energy, her loss of will and focus. She simply had little desire but to hold on, and that barely; even letter writing was becoming more a duty than a pleasure. Whereas earlier Lewes had handled the correspondence that remained marginal to Eliot's interests, now she was inundated with mail. Most people knew she had made considerable money on her books, and that resulted in appeals for a variety of causes, including, as we have noted, lining the pockets of individuals. Even her Sunday afternoons, which continued, were becoming too onerous for her to handle: too much talk, movement, expectation. Both Charles and Cross attempted to help, relieving her when someone proved fatiguing.

One interesting visitor—and not someone we would ordinarily think of as so sympathetic—was the American "frontier writer" Bret Harte, now serving as consul in Glasgow. Unlike Henry James's malicious touches, his words on Eliot are particularly apt. Having heard of her plainness of features, he found her face not only intelligent but strong and noble, a grand face, he called it. "It expresses elevation of thought, kindness, power and *humour*." He describes her eyes as neither large nor beautiful, but sympathetic. He says her face lights up when she smiles, and at that point "all thought of heaviness vanishes. She reminds you continually of a man—a bright, gentle, lovable, philosophical man—without being a bit *masculine*." Of course, as a man of his times, Harte fell into that cliché, that a bright, intellectual woman "thought like a man." But he was, nevertheless, truly generous, saying she revealed many fine things to him about his work and even asked him to return to see her, a privilege in his eyes.

That first visit came on 4 January 1880. The early part of the year would be marked by Eliot's closeness with Cross, as they read together, visited museums, * and went for walks. They were replicating her life with Lewes. The marriage would be, in Cross's eyes, a continuation of this, an older couple as companions, he sitting at the feet of the divinity. Eliot's diary for the first days of January indicates a social schedule: dinner with Cross, the return of Harte on 9 January, visits by Edith Simcox and Charles Lewes, some driving out to see other friends and to visit Eliza, plus considerable letter writing. When she was not in actual pain, Eliot found a reservoir of energy or will, but not of the kind leading to concentrated writing.

Money poured in, £400 for *Theophrastus Such*. There is little question, Simcox observed, that Eliot's spirits had risen somewhat as the result of Cross's attention and presence. Simcox sounds envious that her friend has gained a spring in her step which, at times, makes her more vibrant than the much younger Simcox herself. Eliot was considerably cheered when George Smith— her publisher for *Romola*—said he was reissuing that novel in an elegant luxury edition. It was limited, printed on fine paper, with India paper illustrations, and an eye-catching binding. Smith said he was doing it because Lewes had wished it, and he sent on an honorarium of £100. Eliot was quite gratified at Lewes's suggestion being carried out and at the unexpected money.†

In his biography of Eliot, Cross writes of her loneliness, a loneliness which she once experienced *à deux*, but which now she had to undergo alone. He hoped his presence would allay some of her sense of solitude. One other activity gave Eliot emotional reinforcement: she played the piano at the Priory, chiefly for Cross. She may have been partially hidden away from the public, choosing a shadowy role, but her books in various editions were keeping her name well before readers. One volume or another was appearing, or going into a new edition, or else being transformed into "sayings." While nowhere to be seen except by a small circle, she was everywhere. In mid-February, William Blackwood, now the firm's director, sent on £784.10.3 accrued from these various editions: the Cabinet, the cheap edition, even colonial sales. His accounting, however, was not clear to Eliot, who admitted "stupidity" in her inability to disentangle total number of books distributed from those on which royalties were paid, and apologized for having an unclear head. Near the end of March, she spent the weekend at Weybridge with the Crosses, then returned to the Priory for the sixth birthday of Charles's daughter Maud.

Early April seemed a good period for her, as she kept busy with visits and visitors. And on 9 April, her diary is definitive: "Sir James Paget came to see me. My marriage decided." This was based on still another proposal by Cross,

---

* A considerable assortment: Dulwich, South Kensington, the British Museum (now Library), Old Masters, the Grosvenor Gallery.

† This edition of *Romola* (limited to 1,000 copies) appeared on 15 October 1880, shortly after the new edition of *Sayings*, edited by Alexander Main, with additional material from *Deronda* and *Such*.

his third. According to Charles Lewes as relayed by Edith Simcox, Eliot had apparently broken off after the second proposal, or postponed the possibility of marriage, based probably on her uncertain health.* But we should not discount other factors: foremost, her fear of appearing foolish and her sense that her reputation as a serious novelist might suffer. In any event, Paget gave her the go-ahead based on her current health, possibly to give her spirits a boost. With Paget's approval, plans for a May ceremony went ahead. Earlier in March, Simcox had come, and their talk moved in and out of quite intimate things. The younger woman made one of her most evident pitches for female love, apparently, and Eliot felt she had to answer, but without rejecting her friend. Simcox's concern was surely linked to the imminence of Eliot's marriage.

They dueled over the question of whether or not one should seek pleasantness in the inner life, wherever it led. Simcox insisted that all normal appetites were sane and lawful in themselves. From this, they moved, physically, to a place near the hearth, where Simcox knelt at the feet of her beloved. Eliot felt she had spoken harshly, but Simcox, so grateful to be there, said it all sounded like consolation. She then kissed Eliot repeatedly "and murmured broken words of love," according to Simcox. This led to a delicate discussion of the nature of love, and Eliot's words have become well known: ". . . that the love of men and women for each other must always be more and better than any other and bade me not wish to be wiser than 'God who made me'. . . ." She was not through, however: "Perhaps it would shock me [Simcox]—she had never all her life cared very much for women—it must seem monstrous to me. I said I had always known it. She went on to say, what I also knew, that she cared for the womanly ideal, sympathised with women and liked them to come to her in their troubles, but while feeling near to them in one way, she felt far off in another; the friendship and intimacy of men was more to her." Eliot's explanation was that when she was young, girls and women looked on her as "uncanny," whereas men "were always kind." Simcox says she did not mind the sentiment as long as Eliot did not mind the kisses, which would burn a hole in her cheek. Their farewell was emotional: ". . . I asked if she would never say anything kind to me. I asked her to kiss me. Let a trembling lover tell of the intense consciousness of the first deliberate touch of the dear one's lips. I returned the kiss to the lips that gave it and started to go—she waved me a farewell."

We have, of course, only Simcox's version. Her words suggest she was trying to insinuate herself as an equal mate between Eliot and Cross. In these expressions of love and in her gestures of affection, she perceived herself as the third person in the triangle, someone not to be neglected or ignored in what she thought might be an attenuated relationship, a marriage of convenience perhaps. Although there is no reason to disbelieve Simcox, she may, however,

---

* Our source is Simcox's unpublished autobiography. "Charles said she had twice broken it off as impossible—had thought of all the difficulties—the effect upon her influence and all the rest; then she had consulted Sir James Paget, as a friend, her physician and impartial. He said there was no reason why she should not. Charles thought it would be well for the world, as she might write again now."

have exaggerated, in order to display her role as larger than it actually was, or to make herself a more singular player in Eliot's life than she proved to be. More obviously, she seemed eager to take on Cross as a personal competitor and to establish her own claim to Eliot territory, at least some portion of that dear one's cheek.

23

Eliot and Cross:
Liebestod

> "I can just now grasp nothing as truth but the princi-
> ple that that which is best in ethics is the only means
> of subjective happiness, that perfect love and purity
> must be the goal of my race, that only while reaching
> after them I can feel myself in harmony with the
> tendencies of creation."

Once the decision was made, Eliot was forced into furious activity. She and Cross chose 4 Cheyne Walk, in Chelsea, as their residence, except for the summer months spent at Witley.* The Priory would be put up for sale. Eliot also needed clothes, not only to replace her widow's weeds, but for traveling and, in some instances, as a means of looking a little younger. She shopped at very fashionable places, and she may have been aware of background gossip that her appearance could hardly be enhanced sufficiently to disguise the difference in age between herself and Cross. She had to worry, furthermore, about the reception of the Cross sisters: going from companion of their brother to wife was a huge step. To her friends, she was circumspect, even to Maria Congreve and Elma Stuart. She asked Elma if her love for her was sufficient to satisfy her even if she, Eliot, acted in some unexpected way. To Mrs. Burne-Jones—to complete the circle of her most loyal friends—she seemed hesitant and unable to express herself.

Clearly, as with Lewes, Eliot was entering into a relationship that gave her apprehension and made her fear for appearances. The woman who had to live down public distaste for her arrangement with Lewes now felt she might appear ridiculous, or worse, in marrying Cross. She might be considered an elderly

---

*Cheyne Walk was one of the most famous areas of London, consisting of a group of Queen Anne mansions overlooking the Thames. Some residents included Dante Gabriel Rossetti (at No. 16), Carlyle (No. 5), and Whistler (No. 21). Before Eliot, the painter Daniel Maclise lived and died at No. 4. At the extreme western end of Cheyne Walk, the painter J. M. W. Turner spent his last years, and Mrs. Gaskell was born there. Henry Fielding and Tobias Smollett had lived nearby at Monmouth House on Lawrence Street, and Gay wrote *The Beggar's Opera* there.

woman besotted with sexual desire. Moreover, in Eliot's circle, Cross had the reputation of possessing only average intelligence. He was not the kind of high-powered man Eliot meant when she told Simcox she preferred the company of men to women. To do him justice, Cross was accomplished, and eager to learn; but he was very much a conventional man of his period, as his biography of his wife reveals. It is also clear that from his point of view he was marrying a monument of English literature, a Madonna figure whom he, suitably, worshipped, very possibly a woman who replaced his own recently dead mother. The psychology on both sides seems muddied: he with his dead mother, his worshipful attitude; she with her desire for respectability, her need for marriage at some point in her life; and yet for both, apprehension about the difference in age and, not to be neglected, the difference in intellect. Compared with Eliot, Cross intellectually simply did not exist; nor could he be measured against Lewes, Jowett, Spencer, or, earlier, Bray, Brabant, and Chapman. Her own words in her declaration of love, in which she lists some of the things he does *not* know, indicate how aware she was of the disparity.

The Crosses, however, were supportive. They truly liked Eliot, who was a very warm human being if one met her under the right circumstances. And she liked the Crosses and was grateful for their support. They welcomed her into their large number as "sister." She told them, with pleasure, she had not been called that for many, many years. And her words are heartfelt: "Without your [Eleanor's, but all the Crosses'] tenderness I do not believe it would have been possible for me to accept this wonderful renewal of my life. Nothing less than the prospect of being loved and welcomed by you could have sustained me. But now I cherish the thought that the family life will be the richer and not the poorer through your Brother's great gift of love to me."

In Eliot's failure to notify her closest friends, it seems she did not see the union as an unqualified pleasure until the eve of the wedding. "Yet I quail a little," she wrote Eleanor Cross in April, "in facing what has to be gone through—the hurting of many whom I care for. You are doing everything you can to help me, and I am full of gratitude to you all for his sake as well as my own." The "hurting of many" is curious. Actual hurt would be only for Simcox; but implied hurt derives from Eliot's perception of her own weakness in carrying out something she needed, to open herself up to the "springs of affection," as she called it.

In a follow-up letter, she writes of the inward struggle, the doubt—"all has been a trial, and I have often wished that my life had ended a year ago." These are indeed strange words to write to the sister of the man she is marrying, implying it would be better for all if she had died before the ceremony became possible. With a foreboding that she does not have long to live—although marrying!—Eliot says that "what remains of it [her life] must have a new consecration in gratitude for the miracle of his love." The implication is that his love has brought her back from the dead, her death as a writer of fiction and as the result of Lewes's end and her own physical decline. She says she hopes she will bring "an added love that you will not despise in union with his." These words repeat how she perceived the negative aspect of the marriage in others' eyes. So heavy was all this she did not write to anyone until the ceremony was absolutely settled, and then she wrote on the same day to William Blackwood, Cara Bray, Maria Congreve, and Barbara Bodichon, but not Sara Hennell. She also informed Georgiana Burne-Jones.* Simcox was told after the event by Charles Lewes, but indicated she had expected it.

On 24 April, with the way now cleared and the atmosphere as open as it would ever be, Eliot went for a three-day visit to Weybridge and the Crosses. She had not, as yet, told Charles Lewes of her plans, and in fact she could not face the prospect. She asked Cross to inform him, and Charles responded perfectly. He went to the Priory, where he and Eliot had a long interview, with clear understanding on his part—so she thought—of what she was doing: ". . . have been greatly comforted by the perfectly beautiful feeling he has shown." Charles was possibly relieved his beloved "Mutter" was being passed into someone else's able hands; for as much as he was devoted to her, she was becoming a burden to a man with a family of his own.

Eliot asked Albert Druce, Cross's brother-in-law, to accompany her from her house to the church, and in effect give her away. This is a role that normally would have fallen to Isaac Evans. She tells Druce that since he is the man to whom Cross was most attached, it was their wish "that you should have this part in the act that binds us together. . . ." Druce accepted graciously and warm-heartedly. Then came Eliot's series of letters to William Blackwood and to her friends, on 5 May. To Blackwood, Eliot set the tone: it was a huge surprise—"a great surprize" are her repeated words—to each correspondent. She also indicated she and Cross would head for the continent immediately after the ceremony, for two or three months, and then settle into Witley and, finally, Cheyne Walk.

To Barbara Bodichon she was very delicate in breaking the news, calling on their friendship in the event she found the marriage "incomprehensible." This letter, incidentally, was not mailed; it was misplaced, either consciously or not. Barbara learned of the marriage three days later only indirectly. Eliot's language to her is striking: she is marrying this friend of Lewes's because he, seeing her alone, decided his happiness lay "in the dedication of his life to me."

To Mrs. Burne-Jones, almost the same words: ". . . now that I am alone, he sees his only longed-for happiness in dedicating his life to me." She had taken up a defensive position, clearly, in order to validate the type of marriage she was making. By casting it in terms of Cross's dedication of his life to her—shades of Dorothea Brooke with Casaubon, that recurring nightmare in Eliot's life!—Eliot could subvert any suspicions it was a romantic or love marriage, or that physical passion was part of the equation. By defusing what might make her look ridiculous, she could justify her position as a serious woman securing a disciple. That

---

* In Eliot's visit to her friend on 23 April, for a sitting with Burne-Jones, Georgiana observed how weary Eliot seemed, how unfitted for life—this only two weeks before her marriage. Eliot also expressed her concern that she was tired "of being set on a pedestal and expected to vent wisdom."

this disciple was prepared to marry her only meant he considered her life more important than his own. In this respect, consciously or not, she was devaluing Cross: he is not a lover so much as a saint devoting his life to the reverence of a deity. Along the way, Eliot assured her friends none of this would make any difference in her attitude toward the Lewes family, either during her life or after. She assures everyone Cross cannot be a fortune hunter because he has a sufficient fortune of his own.

All in all, Eliot was playing still another role in the most subtle way she could. She obviously felt she needed a "presentation" of the marriage and of herself in order to make the act look palatable. But this playing of roles was not solely for others; it was apparently for herself as well. Each time she offered explanations, she was seeking reasons for what she was doing. Emotionally, she was lonely and, after Lewes's shielding of her, unable to handle the constant incursions on her time and dwindling energy. Not negligible were how illness, pain, and aging had reduced her defenses against life. She was not Mary Anne or Mary Ann or Marian becoming George Eliot or Marian Evans Lewes; she was George Eliot declining, and for that Cross offered support.

The written response from her friends was exemplary. Barbara Bodichon said that Cross did what she would have done herself if "you would have let me and I had been a man."* Georgiana Burne-Jones was a little more ambiguous about her feelings, although she did send on her love. In any event, these all arrived after the ceremony, which took place at 10:15 A.M. on 6 May 1880 at St. George's Church, Hanover Square,† with Charles Lewes her only close member of the family present. He, not Albert Druce, gave her away. The Druces were present, as were the Crosses and Bullock-Hall. It was a considered, low-key affair, as befitting two senior people making their "first" marriage. After signing their wills, following the ceremony, George Eliot, now Mrs. John Walter Cross, headed with her husband for Dover and a long European holiday. It was as though they had set the Furies in motion.

This was, of course, still another name change, in that process of name changing which had characterized Mary Anne Evans from early adulthood. Most significantly, she went from Marian Evans Lewes or Marian Lewes, a name she had appropriated, to Mrs. John Walter Cross, in effect her first "legal" name since birth. Not only a legal but a gender role was regularized; she who had been woman turned "man," was now woman. In the process, she submerged George Eliot, and the attendant fame and fortune, into her role as the wife of Cross. She was no longer writing fiction, and thus in the course of merely a couple of

---

* These cross-gendering romantic sentiments were echoed by Maria Congreve, who was not at all happy with the arrangement—she was informed of it by Charles Lewes. Maria Congreve, like Simcox, loved Eliot passionately, seeing in her, again like Simcox, a lover as well as a friend. Further, she believed in uninterrupted widowhood, part of her positivistic beliefs. It took Maria three weeks to write a congratulatory letter; and in return Eliot begged off not having told her directly with the excuse she didn't want to upset her friend, whose brother-in-law had recently died.

† St. George's in Hanover Square was noted for its fashionable marriages: the remarriage of Shelley and Harriet Westbrook in 1814; the marriage of Disraeli and Mrs. Wyndham Lews in 1839; of Theodore Roosevelt and Edith Carow in 1888; of H. H. Asquith and Margaret Tennant in 1894.

years she had finally become that singular Victorian person, a married woman with her husband's name as her legal name.*

Yet the biggest events after the wedding were yet to come, events curiously connected to name changes. When Lewes died, Isaac Evans's wife—and not Isaac—offered condolences to Eliot for her loss. The latter responded, acknowledging the sentiment and sending her love to her brother. That "love" was not feeling so much as symbol, a plea for acceptance. Now, Isaac was informed of the marriage to Cross by Holbeche, the joint trustee of Robert Evans's bequest to Eliot. Isaac was not exactly effusive, but he did acknowledge his sister existed for him:

My dear Sister

I have much pleasure in availing myself of the present opportunity to break a long silence which has existed between us, by offering our united and sincere congratulations to you and Mr. Cross, upon the happy event of which Mr. Holbeche has informed me. My wife joins me in sincerely hoping it will afford you much happiness and comfort. She and the younger branches unite with me in kind love and every good wish. Believe me

Your affectionate brother
Isaac P. Evans

The letter is dated 17 May, and it sounds as though it were packed in dry ice.

When the letter caught up with her in Milan, Eliot answered, nine days later. Her letter, too, is icy; but the coldness of tone is mitigated by her remembrances of when they were young and meant a good deal to each other. The reconciliation in her letter is reminiscent of that moment at the end of *Mill*, when Maggie and Tom can finally meet, although it is brief enough.

My dear Brother

Your letter was forwarded to me here, and it was a great joy to me to have your kind words of sympathy, our long silence has never broken the affection for you which began when we were little ones. My Husband too was much pleased to read your letter. I have known his family for nine years, and they have received me amongst them very lovingly [unlike Isaac]. He is of most solid, well tried character and has had a good deal of experience. The only point to be regretted in our marriage is that I am much older than he, but his affection has made him choose this lot of caring for me rather than any other of the various lots open to him.

Always your affectionate Sister
Mary Ann Cross

---

* A man of propriety who was never too happy with women who lived outside traditional roles, Henry James sent wedding congratulations on the 14th.

Defensive as in her other letters, Eliot repeats the point that Cross has decided to devote his life to caring for her. It is not clear whether Isaac knew the full extent of the age difference. There is little of Cross himself in the letter which might have made Isaac acknowledge how well she had married; simply that he was solid and "well tried." She might have mentioned his financial success, his perfect breeding as an English gentleman (something of a Sir James Chettam, perhaps), his interest in sports, his immersion in English upper-class life as a result of his Rugby education, all of which made him, for better or worse, a member of the establishment. Eliot's letter, instead, is tentative, as though family form alone dictated the need for this reportage. It was all a matter of retrieving memory, a replay of the earlier "Brother and Sister" sonnet sequence, those indelible images of the two playing together and her admiration, even worship, of the slightly older brother. No such exchange occurred with her half-sister, Fanny Houghton, who was now an old seventy-five. That relationship remained shrouded in distaste and suspicion.

Eliot's report to Cross's sister Eleanor of her first married days sounds idyllic. She speaks of "our happy married life three days long," much of it the result of the fact that all the Crosses are interwoven "into the pattern of my thoughts." In the background, Charles Lewes was delegated to inform the people whom Eliot had not told of her marriage, like Mrs. Pattison and Anne Thackeray Ritchie.

The background "noise" was by no means all supportive, as we shall see. Eliot had written only to those she felt would be completely sympathetic. And some of those visited by Charles were upset, for different reasons. We recognize how people had different stakes in Eliot. Some admired her for her rebelliousness against convention and thus were appalled at her church wedding, some were hostile to the sharp age difference, and some considered her their own, not to be shared with this interloper. Spencer remained solid. Since for him marriage was something that happened only to other people, he had no negative feelings about Eliot and Cross, whatever his reservations about the man. Benjamin Jowett was exceptionally supportive and showed great feeling, indicating that since Eliot was a celebrated author she could expect people to talk. He said she would be foolish to forsake actual affection for the sake of what people might say. Anne Thackeray Ritchie, also, was generally supportive, but only because Charles Lewes made such a strong case for Eliot, asserting he owed everything to her.[*] He indicated that his father, not a jealous man, would have wanted her to be happy. Charles also showed considerable insight when he said that Eliot recognized human failings so strongly she could write about them—implying that such failings in herself might explain the marriage.

The negatives were quite insistent. Mrs. Peter Taylor, who never took

---

[*] When Charles said that Dr. Paget felt Eliot's influence would not be affected by the marriage, Anne Ritchie countered by saying that sometimes it was better to be genuine than to have influence, surely an indication of the reservations she held even within a supportive stance.

umbrage at Eliot's relationship with Lewes, was appalled by her conventional marriage. Mrs. Taylor was part of the group which had cast Eliot in their own image. Richard Congreve, the fervent Comtist and positivist, felt that Eliot's "peculiar position" made her desire a marriage ceremony in St. George's, although she was hardly an Anglican believer. For Cross, it obviously made no difference. The comments, mainly as gossip, went back and forth, with several people wondering how Eliot could have settled on someone so intellectually inferior to her—the implication here being that she fell, at her unseemly age, for a pretty face and a young body.

The fallout from the marriage was an indication of several factors coming together. As a famous and celebrated woman, she was expected to exhibit a certain decorum, but it is clear that no matter what she did she would disappoint those who saw her success as a reflection of their own needs. Marriage is an excellent way of measuring later Victorian thought, and especially marriage for a woman who had flouted its very conventions. The unease people felt with anything that broke with standard behavior can be observed even in those who considered themselves liberated from trivial ideas about society. Even those sensed some breach of propriety, based on the conventions a sixty-year-old woman was expected to honor. Furthermore, those who recognized her desire for a private life were nevertheless dismayed she was not keeping to the high standards of her fiction, that high ground she had insisted upon. That, too, was a factor, that the woman was not so virtuous as the writer. Richard Congreve's remark, that as a positivist she owed more to her readers than she was showing, indicates how even a sophisticated man could harbor reservations.

But men such as Congreve were hardly the only objectors. Although Eliot's social position was not impregnable, that level had been achieved not by the morality of her private life but by the insistence of her fame. She was welcomed nearly everywhere not as Mary Ann Lewes but as George Eliot, an enormous distinction. All those houses which eventually opened to her recognized the writer, not the woman. Now that the woman had reasserted herself, all the old stories resurfaced; they had not really been silenced, merely relocated in the shadows. Marriage meant so much more to the Victorian than to the present-day reader that we cannot overestimate how marriage, or lack of it, became the standard for the individual, almost akin to soul. Any woman—including Eliot—who played hard and fast with marriage was labeled a "sexual delinquent." The model for this unregenerate behavior in the 1860s was Catherine Walters, known as Skittles, who became the great love of Wilfred Scawen Blunt. Such a woman would be well known to Lewes and, indirectly, to Eliot. Skittles was the measuring rod for all those women who broke from conventional behavior.

There was other gossip as well. The forty-year-old Cross was not excluded. Why would a healthy man, it was asked, wait until he was forty to marry? The same question was asked of Spencer, but he was so clearly wedded to his ideas and his books, he could be let off. But Cross had followed a different calling, as banker and investment counselor, and such men married and had children. He was deemed, by some, to be a mama's boy who only married once his mother died. And then the question arose why a healthy man would marry someone as physically wasted as Eliot, celebrated though she was. A further development became significant: Had Cross taken advantage of his closeness to Eliot and Lewes so as to gain proximity to her considerable fortune? Was he a gigolo, a fortune hunter, a homosexual adventurer preying on an older woman to get hold of her money? Sexual innuendo ran through everything, from Cross's possible homosexuality to Eliot's rampant sensuality and desire for a young man. Such a marriage was a feast for gossip.

The trip to the continent was leisurely and served as a restorative in its earlier phases. As in the past, Eliot came alive when she left London, as though the very presence of her difficult choices there had permanently poisoned the atmosphere. Paris was the obvious first stop, followed by a ramble through Grenoble on their way to Italy, precisely the way she and Lewes had traveled. From Lyons, she told Elma Stuart she was "wonderfully well and able to take a great deal of exercise without fatigue. . . ." Her letter to Charles Lewes from Grenoble is quite sparkling, to the extent the couple congratulated themselves on altering their original plan, which was to reach Italy through the Grand Corniche. Her sole regret in seeing "the sublime beauty of the Grand Chartreuse" was that Lewes had not seen it, she tells his son. "I would still give up my own life willingly if he could have the happiness instead of me. But marriage has seemed to restore me to my old self. I was getting hard, and if I had decided differently I think I should have become very selfish. To feel daily the loveliness of a nature close to me, and to be grateful to it, is the fountain of tenderness and strength to endure."

The Crosses were slowly working their way toward Venice, where the terrible incident would occur. It so dominated Eliot's wedding trip that as we examine it in retrospect we attempt to discover further clues as to what happened, or why it happened. Eliot's letters offer only affirmatives. To Florence Nightingale Cross, her husband's youngest sister, she says she is well, although Cross indicated a headache which incapacitated Eliot for a while. She repeats she feels "quite strong with all sorts of strength except strong-mindedness." This was from Milan, where they stayed for several days to rest, collect their mail, and answer what correspondence required a response (including Isaac Evans). They attended a performance of Ernesto Rossi in *Hamlet,* a role in which Eliot had seen him before, in London, and from which she had carried away the worst of impressions. If anything, she said this one was worse—calling it a "drunken" performance. "One would be prepared to enjoy Irving after seeing Rossi," she told Charles Lewes.

By 1 June, in their slow journey toward Venice, they were in Verona. The next stop would be Padua and then, finally, Venice, where they arrived by 2 June, for a three-week stay. Eliot's letter to Barbara Bodichon of 1 June is curious, however, and may offer a clue to at least some of the trouble which lay ahead. Our interest centers on her early remarks to her close friend. She tries to explain why she did not tell her friends sooner of her intention to change the course of her life, as she puts it. "But I really did not finally, absolutely decide—

I was in a state of doubt and struggle until only a fortnight before the event took place and for a week of that time I was ill with influenza, so that at last everything was done in the utmost haste."

We cannot pinpoint how much Eliot's hesitation resulted in Cross's aberrant behavior. We do know he had suffered from depression or depressive symptoms before. According to Barbara Bodichon and Edith Simcox, Eliot herself knew of some such episodes, what Simcox called an "impending cloud." Cross apparently had an aberrant or disturbed brother, and there may have been some hereditary imbalance. But whether that depressive element was fueled by Eliot's pronounced hesitation—forcing Cross eventually into three separate proposals—we cannot be certain. Most likely, as this episode began to shape up, several factors contributed to his period of instability, which lasted, in varying degrees and stages, for at least three weeks. One factor—and we are speculating—could have been a sudden sexual demand made on him by Eliot; in this view, the relationship went from friendship and companionship to real marriage. Or else, as a corollary, there was more general recognition of sexual failure, leading to the grand seizure which Cross could no longer deal with. But added to this, perhaps, was the juxtaposition, in his mind, between his mother, recently dead, and Eliot, old enough to be his mother. To what extent, if any, this can be considered we do not know, although if it were a factor, it would of course immobilize his sexual energies. A related point might be a low sexual energy in Cross, apart from other pressures: simply a desire to protect Eliot, like the knights of old did with their ladies, but not to consummate a physical relationship with her.

A still further dimension, already suggested, is how he was affected by Eliot's own apprehensions, her fear of seeming ridiculous because of age differences, her hesitation about forgoing her influence as a writer for the sake of personal gratification. In still another way, it is possible Cross did not recognize beforehand what was expected of him in this relationship, whether as companion and shield, or lover; and when the two of them followed Eliot's earlier path with Lewes, he found himself in an unresolvable situation, being forced to compete with Lewes and finding himself impotent.

We do not know, of course, if the Venice incident even overtly involved sex, or if it was the first time, although we know Eliot craved affection and was by now quite experienced. How this affected a man already prone to depressive spells, or to depressive symptoms, we cannot tell. What we have, in any event, is a response to something in his relationship to Eliot, to Venice, to his honeymoon and to marriage, possibly to his dead mother, possibly to his cohabitation with a woman of maternal age, possibly to demands made on him he could not fulfill, possibly to his recognition of impotence or even disgust.

As Eliot and Cross positioned themselves for this traumatic event, we search her diary for clues. Up to the 16th of June, there is nothing to go on, simply a sketchy listing of activities, such as visiting the Accademia to see the Bellinis or going with friends to the Manfrini Palace. Then on the 16th comes the cryptic notation: "Dr. Ricchetti called." Nothing on the 17th. On the 18th:

"Dr. Cesare Vigna called. Came at 10:30 p.m. Willie arrived in the evening."
All this requires explanation. On 16 June, Cross fell ill, an account of which he
left in his *George Eliot's Life*. He writes:

> We thought too little of the heat, and rather laughed at English people's
> dread of the sun. But the mode of life at Venice has its peculiar dangers. It
> is one thing to enjoy heat when leading an active life, getting plenty of
> exercise in riding or rowing in the evening; it is another thing to spend all
> one's day in a gondola—a delicious, dreamy existence—going from one
> church to another—from palaces to picture-galleries—sight-seeing of the
> most exhaustively interesting kind—traversing constantly the *piccoli rei*,
> which are nothing more than drains, and with bedroom-windows open on
> the great drain of the Grand Canal. The effect of this continual bad air,
> and the complete and sudden deprivation of all bodily exercise, made me
> thoroughly ill.

Cross indicates they left Venice within the week, and he quickly regained
strength in the purer air of Innsbruck.

Eliot's review of the episode came in a letter to Barbara Bodichon on 1
August, well after matters were in hand. "Mr. Cross had a sharp but brief attack
at Venice—due to the unsanitary influences of that wondrous city in the later
weeks of June. We stayed a little too long there with a continuous Sirocco
blowing and with smells under the window of the Hôtel de l'Europe, and these
conditions found him a little below par from long protracted anxiety and excitement before our marriage." She adds that as soon as they left Venice he gained
strength. Of some interest is Eliot's statement about Cross's "anxiety" concerning the marriage. That is, very possibly, the only element of truth in her statement. The rest of her letter descends into trivialities, so that Cross's condition
seems to become one of those minor tourist annoyances, an upset stomach, a
headache, a bout of diarrhea.

If we return to the diary entry of "Dr. Ricchetti called," on 16 June, the
situation was quite different. Cross was not under the weather, but caught by
some sudden seizure, or else some nervous collapse, a form of madness, which
led to his jumping from their window into the Grand Canal, where he was
pulled out by gondoliers. He was less in danger of drowning than of catching a
deadly disease. Dr. Giacomo Ricchetti was called—he was probably recommended by the hotel staff as an excellent physician—and he brought in Dr.
Cesare Vigna, the doctor mentioned in Eliot's diary entry of 18 June, an indication it was not a simple case of exhaustion, or poisoning. The "Willie" also
mentioned in that entry was William Cross, John's brother. Eliot had telegraphed to him, and he arrived on the 18th or 19th. The presence of Willie
clearly reinforced the contention that the case was not indisposition caused by
lack of exercise or fumes from the canal, but something far more serious and
family related. Eliot was, apparently, horrified—although, as we have observed,
she seemed to know there was mental illness in the Cross family.

Haight provides a very useful note, from Lord Acton, who said in no uncertain terms that Eliot thought Cross was mad, and that this knowledge sent her into a deep depression from which she never recovered. Acton also indicates Eliot told Dr. Ricchetti that Cross had a mad brother and she confirmed the jump into the canal. What is of further interest is that Cross did not seem to suffer recurrences.* Once Eliot died, he led a quiet life, without any display of madness (as far as we know), and continued on to 1924, when he was eighty-four, a full forty-four years after Eliot's death. He never ceased to worship at the shrine. What this suggests—and once again we enter into speculation—is a psychological condition in which a latent morbidity or depression is present, but which does not emerge except under extraordinary circumstances. This could well be the "madness" lying deep in the Cross family, or the anxiety and excitement Eliot mentioned, which created a "cloud." Then when something did occur in that hotel room—possibly a sexual situation Cross could not deal with—the situation triggered something which put him out of control. Under these conditions, the sole thing he could do was to alleviate the pressure or dissipate the cloud, and in that respect, even death was preferable to the immediate suffering or humiliation.

In retrospect, there is something somewhat amusing about the situation—amusing, that is, for those who hear the story told in a certain way. For Eliot, as well as for Cross, it was devastating. But for the reader, it does in part sound ridiculous: a younger man on his honeymoon, finding himself in the footsteps of his predecessor, with a fixation on a woman he worships as a divine presence, is confronted by this woman perhaps in a state of undress, or naked, and all his inhibitions, anxieties, confusions come to haunt him in a sudden expression of impotence. Unable to face the pressure on him, he leaps into the Grand Canal, that most romantic of places, but in actuality one of the most pestilent places on earth. The honeymoon turns into a nightmare. The amusing part—if we put on hold the pain of the participants—comes from our laughter at sexual failure, the standard fare of comic drama, the basis of the mock-heroic.

Eliot was frantic. The diary entry for 19 June mentions Dr. Vigna twice, and the arrival of Willie Cross; but she had already noted Willie had arrived on the 18th, an indication of her confusion. On the 19th, she announces Cross is "Better," also that she wrote to the girls, meaning his sisters. On the 20th, she reports "Better on the whole"; Dr. Vigna came again, twice. On the 21st, Cross was quiet and did not need chloral, which was the sedative of choice; Dr. Vigna came still again, for the sixth time. On the 23rd, the patient was sufficiently recovered for the couple to leave Venice early in the morning. On 27 June, Eliot made her first explanation of the illness, well before the fuller reply to Barbara Bodichon. She told Elma Stuart what was now becoming standard,

---

*History and literature are full of instances of such single bouts. For example, when Joseph Conrad was twenty, he attempted suicide, shooting himself directly through the chest with a pistol; he missed all vital organs, recovered, and, while depressed and despondent throughout most of his life, was never actively suicidal again.

about the lack of exercise and the influence of poor climate. This explanation fits, of course, into Cross's own brief treatment of the episode, where he speaks of a condition typhoid-like in its symptoms.

Eliot now not only had a sick man on her hands, she was trying to effect damage control. Fortunately, her own health during this period was reasonably sound, although we cannot measure to what extent her terror, anxiety, and fear led to her final breakdown and terminal illness. All the old splits, uncertainties, and doubts came to the surface: Cross was supposed to shield her, and now she was shielding him, not only physically, but also in terms of potential scandal that could make both of them appear ridiculous. She was quite possibly never more aware of how a January–May marriage (here with gender reversal) is perceived as worthy of little but mockery. Even as she reestablished contact with her self-righteous brother, she now had a forty-year-old "son" whose behavior had spiraled out of control.

Eliot's letters up to this episode had been affirmative, full of praise for sights, sounds, colors, and climate. She even told Maria Congreve—one of those not too pleased with the marriage—that she felt herself in a kind of "miracle-legend," an idyll. She indicates, as she had to others, that the relationship has prevented her feelings from drying up, that she has recovered her "loving sympathy," not only for Cross but for all her old friends, like Maria. A letter to Mary, Eleanor, and Florence Cross is upbeat, amusing, charitable, generous. Cara Bray wrote that Eliot seemed "as rather in a dream-land."

Then came the event, followed by a move to Verona, on 23 June, which would start the couple's departure from Italy. On the 27th, they were in Innsbruck, and Cross was beginning to rally. All official information suggests that the change of climate altered his condition. In still another respect, his condition now would ensure that if the trigger point was indeed sexual, then Cross would not be called upon to perform again. That may have helped recovery more than climate. On 7 July, they were in Stuttgart, and on the 8th in Wildbad, where they stayed until the 17th. Bordering on the Black Forest, Wildbad was a spa of the kind Eliot used to visit with Lewes. The baths were restorative, temporarily. In Eliot's letter to Elma Stuart, on the 11th, there is no mention of Cross's condition.

In her long letter to Charles Lewes, on the 13th–14th, she indicates Willie has left them, so that we learn she had taken along Cross's brother in the event of a relapse. She mentions that Johnnie is "quite well again." Charles had received the official explanation. The rest of this lengthy letter is taken up with trivia, no more about Johnnie; nor was there anything more in another letter, this time from Luxembourg, on the 21st. By the 26th, Eliot and Cross were back at Witley. As though nothing unusual had occurred, Eliot reentered her Surrey life. Regular visitors included Lady Holland, Cross's sisters, and Charles and Gertrude Lewes. A good deal of the couple's social life revolved around the Cross family. No further mention of the episode in Venice comes up in Eliot's correspondence. She writes now not as a ferocious intellectual, or as a famous author, or as a woman who has helped to redefine the role of women, but as a devoted sister-in-law or friend, basically just a nice, pleasant, aging human being.

To the Cross sisters, she signed "Your loving Sister." To others, she was M. A. Cross—having buried George Eliot and Mrs. Lewes in the married name. She seems occupied with a new coachman, with visiting cards, and the need for family visits. She sounds, all in all, like any good burgher married to a successful man, and without a real worry in the world. As she told Charles, ". . . our life has had no more important events than calls from neighbors and our calls in return." Cross, meanwhile, was taking the opportunity to get in some lawn tennis—the exercise that he so sorely lacked in Venice!

But there was talk just beyond their ears. On one visit to the Bullock-Halls at Six Mile Bottom, the Richard Jebbs—he was the classical scholar, then professor of Greek at Glasgow University—were there, and they found the display of happiness between Eliot and Cross a little too much to bear. What follows could simply be gossip or else some sharp observation. Eliot is described as old-looking and ugly, although sweet and winning despite this physical impression. But Mrs. Jebb's chief observation is based on age: there was not, she says, a person in the room whose mother Eliot could not have been. She says she felt Eliot was depressed at her age and at the fact that everyone else was of another generation—the Jebbs themselves were still in their thirties. Mrs. Jebb picks up what she thinks is jealousy, in the fact that when Cross spoke so much to her (Mrs. Jebb), Eliot seemed possessive, adoring of her husband. She says she sensed snappishness in Eliot's irritation, something for which, Mrs. Jebb insists, there can be no remedy. Yet at the same time *she* may have been irritated that her husband, possibly, was paying too much attention to Eliot. But the observer is not finished. The final remarks are vicious, in that Mrs. Jebb points out that Eliot's attention to men has made her try to appear more attractive when her ugliness has convinced her it is impossible. Mrs. Jebb was no friend, obviously, but we should not dismiss the substance of her remarks: that Eliot was possessive, that in company she became far more conscious of the age difference, and that, finally, she could not hide her sixty years with rich clothing or fashionable hair styles.* Comparably, in company—as we recall in *Middlemarch*—while Dorothea glowed, Casaubon withered.

Although we lack hard evidence, it would not be an unusual observation: that the famous writer had become silly over the younger man and was jealous when anyone looked at him too long. This was the history of January–May marriages. Whether the charge of Eliot's jealousy was valid we cannot know, since in the months remaining she did not reveal any such feeling. That she had some sense of possessiveness is possible, but that she feared Cross would be "stolen away" is unlikely. He was a worshipper, not a lover. He seemed happiest

---

* Lady Jebb (Jebb was subsequently knighted) comments acidulously on Eliot's outfit as an expensively cut and tailored costume intended to show off her slenderness and to disguise her age. The remarks suggest that for wishing to appear at her best the author has committed a crime.

in his reading with Eliot (most recently Daudet and George Sand) and while exercising. He laid out a full tennis court at Witley and himself helped to clear away some of the foliage and trees which obscured the view. As for Eliot, Lewes had vanished from her letters, and she was completely taken up with her new life at the Heights, introducing Cross to the pleasures of her favorite country house. Her reports are almost always of him—he exercises, he cuts trees, he plays lawn tennis—or of visits to his family. Her relationships with other close friends began to decline slightly—still very warm and generous, but lacking eagerness. Simcox fumed that she had seen Eliot for only five minutes in the last eight months, "an utter, barren blank." She felt closeness "is now over." She indicates she has answered Eliot's letter, but it is likely the latter "will feel no impulse to write again." Simcox recognized that the kissing and physical play were finished; Cross would not be so tolerant as Lewes. In her fantasy, she felt Eliot would no longer wait anxiously for her knock.

This would be, in effect, the last period in Eliot's life when she was not encumbered by pain and indisposition, leading to the inevitable decline. Witley, plus the latter parts of the European trip, after Venice, had picked her up somewhat; but there was no calculating to what degree Cross's behavior accelerated what was already a deteriorating physical condition. So much of her life was now invested in Johnnie, in making sure he could get something out of their time together. It is surely that objective Lady Jebb picked up on in her snide remarks: Eliot's concern that the Venice episode did not recur. She had kept it secret.

By early September, Eliot's condition showed a good deal of fraying around the edges. She was suffering from a cold, but was coughing and sneezing heavily, an attack on what she called her "poor person." Nevertheless, she was well enough to visit Lincolnshire and Cambridgeshire, the first for the Otters (Cross's sister Emily and her husband) and the second for the Bullock-Halls. Now a squire, Otter recalled to Eliot a good deal of her early life, when Robert Evans was an estate manager. She admired both the Otters and the Bullock-Halls for improving their properties, helping their tenants lead a better life, building healthier cottages, and "in general doing whatever opportunity allows towards slowly improving this confused world."

Even as she wrote on 14 September that "we are just now living in an oasis of peace and content," she was on the edge of a severe renal attack, with intense pains that could not be alleviated. Yet her remarks to Elma Stuart are poignant: "My (Scotch) husband looks better and feels stronger every day, and acts more and more completely as my guardian angel." She then engages in an amusing debate over whether the best Scots were not better than the best English; and she realizes she is on delicate ground inasmuch as she is comparing Cross and Lewes. Her solution: the Scots are generally better, but one has to be aware of particular Englishmen, especially those who have been best to oneself.

She was in good enough spirits to tell Charles Lewes, on 19 September, about Cross's activity with indoor battledore and shuttlecock, which the couple played for lack of regular lawn tennis. She is pleased that Cross is putting on some flesh. But three days later, her diary records the grim facts of life: her ailments were not improving, and on the 29th, she and Cross went to Brighton, hoping the sea air might lead to improvement. But the diary records that they returned, on 9 October, with Eliot feeling no better. The remainder of October, as revealed in very brief diary entries, records a litany of recurring attacks, some recovery, then relapse. While Charles and Gertrude were visiting, Eliot became very ill, and needed an opiate to relieve the pain. Doctors became routine.

By the end of the month she recorded some recovery. But these successive attacks and the severe pain from kidney stones and inflammation made her very weak; and as fast as Cross was gaining weight, she was losing it. Her weight at this time must have fallen below 100 pounds. The age difference between her and Cross never seemed greater—he becoming more robust, she beginning to wither as she approached her sixty-first birthday. She ignored that birthday, as she had other recent ones. Aging now meant little more than deterioration.

In her remarks to Charles Lewes, she downgraded the intensity of her attacks. In these last months, he became her mainstay, the "son" who never disappointed her. By the end of October, Cross had gone back and forth to London several times, trying to prepare their new residence at 4 Cheyne Walk, taking furniture, books, and other items from the Priory. Since the move was imminent, this brought Eliot into touch with many remains of her relationship with Lewes, relics which had meant something to them, but whose moment had passed. She considered that burning such effects was "desecrating fate," because with her belief in the presentness of the past, she felt that items held in memory remained living things, not objects. But she was feeble and not completely focused.

With Cross and the servants working almost daily to get things in order, Eliot had little to do, and little energy to do it. Her mind kept whirling, however; her reading was still of the highest order—Spencer's *Sociology*, for example. But she was locked in herself, in cycles of pain and debilities. By 3 November, she observed some improvement, once again fully recognizing the attacks would reappear. She jokes about being clear of her "main element," but with it went half her "bodily self." It is evident none of her close friends recognized how serious her condition was, since when she wrote she almost always indicated a recovery, or a remission from whatever the attack was. Only Simcox seemed to have some idea, since after Eliot died, she said she knew her friend suffered from Bright's disease, which was fatal.*

To D'Albert-Durade, Eliot revealed, more openly, some of her feelings, for this old friend from Geneva reported that his wife, in poor health for years, had died. Sounding like Romola, Eliot wrote, "Blessed are the dead who rest from the struggles of this difficult life. The pitiable are those who survive in loneliness. . . ." These are lines concerning final things, and she was not finished.

---

* Named after Richard Bright, an English physician, a condition recognized by the late 1820s; described as an inflammation and a degeneration of the kidneys, a form of nephritis; also characterized by albumin in the urine, leading to a complete malfunction of the kidneys.

She says that this loneliness will increase in direct proportion to the devoted care given another, clearly directing the pointed remark to herself as someone who nursed Lewes while being unwell. She appears fascinated by her condition, her dwindling body, and to Elma Stuart she speaks of needing to regain the weight and strength lost in midsummer attacks.

From the 15th to the 25th of November her diary does not reveal any severe attacks. She was clearly looking forward to setting up house at 4 Cheyne Walk, the first house she and Cross could call their own, without lingering memories of Lewes. Having finished Spencer's *Sociology,* she began reading Max Müller's *Lectures on the Science of Language,* such reading an indication of how alive her brain still was, and her continued eagerness for knowledge. She also read Comte, whose work had remained as a kind of leitmotif in her life even as she rejected his "religion of humanity" as being more religion than humanity. This ten-day period seemed settled, as her birthday passed, and her health, while not good, did not further deteriorate.

Concerned with daily events, not eternity or spiritual communication, Eliot emphasized to everyone how hardworking Cross was, with particular attention to the removal of the books from the Priory. As long as her energy held up, she was herself helping. Before they moved into 4 Cheyne Walk on 3 December, she and Cross spent four days at Bailey's Hotel on Gloucester Road, while the servants put the finishing touches on their new home. Writing to Cara Bray— in a correspondence that had slackened on both sides—Eliot painted a romantic picture of connubial bliss. She described herself as surrounded and cherished by family love, by brothers and sisters who were her friends before they became her family, accompanied by a husband who is both father and brother to this family. She pictures herself and him as the two of them sitting by their hearth in "dual companionship." It was, all in all, a portrait of a couple interchangeable with Eliot and Lewes in their retirement and part of her need for a "family romance." She clearly needed to leave with her dear friend from those early days an image of a Mary Ann Evans who had discovered the ultimate stage of personal happiness.

At Bailey's Hotel, from 29 November to 3 December, Eliot read almost continually—Tennyson's new volume, *Ballads and Other Poems,* Goethe's *Hermann und Dorothea,* more Comte, and a selection by Mrs. Oliphant in the *Cornhill*— and once she finished unpacking at Cheyne Walk, she began Duffield's translation of *Don Quixote* and Myers's *Wordsworth.* On 3 December, the couple made their move into their new home, and soon they felt comfortable enough to ask friends to call. Ironically, with this move, Eliot had achieved the final stage of respectability: marriage and a home that belonged jointly to her and a husband; moreover, it was a London house that was located in a literarily famous area. At first, her health did not seem poor; and she speaks of herself as "a mended piece of antique furniture." She did not go out much, although she and Cross attended the concerts in St. James's Hall. Cross, however, came down with some malady: ". . . robust as he looks," she writes, "[he] is obliged to be very careful as to temperature and is at the moment in bed with a feverish cold which has caused me a very anxious night. . . ." Two days later the doctor came and declared Cross's ailment to be a bilious attack.

Exactly what this was we cannot of course pinpoint, but we recall how Eliot and Lewes interchanged one ailment or another: she was sick, he nursed; he became sick, she nursed. Some of them were physically based (her renal attacks in later years), but many were of mysterious origin: the cycles of headaches, the nausea and stomach upset (before the onset of his final and fatal condition), the general enervation and indisposition. The pattern of dependence gave each the other's undivided attention, or caused the other to leave his or her desk. In the early stages of the Eliot–Cross relationship, this pattern seems renewed. She was the really ill one, but Cross began to take on the kinds of ailments severe enough to create anxiety in his wife and to force her intense attention.

When the end came, it was quite sudden. On 17 December, Eliot was well enough to attend an Oxford undergraduate performance of Aeschylus's *Agamemnon*, in Greek. Enthusiastic about what she saw, she intended to reread it with Cross, in English. The next day they attended the regular popular concert in the park. On 17 December, she had invited Mme. Louis Belloc (Bessie Parkes) to lunch on Monday, 20 December, or some other suitable date. Her worries focused on Cross's biliousness, while her description of herself was simply "rickety." When Spencer came to visit on 19 December, Sunday afternoon, he did not consider her to be unduly ill. Edith Simcox followed him, but missed the hints that Eliot was not well. As usual, she kissed her beloved "again and again." Cross's manner, however, seemed attuned to final things, suggesting he knew Eliot's condition could not be reversed or even remitted for long.

She wrote letters (nine, as far as we know) up to 19 December, three days before her death, the last to lady Richard Strachey. But the letter breaks off suddenly, and Cross completed the sentiments in it (consolation for the loss of Lady Strachey's sister's husband), now that Eliot's hand was stilled. The rest we learn from Cross. On Monday morning, 20 December—the day Mme. Belloc was scheduled to come to lunch—Cross went for help to Dr. Andrew Clark. He was referred to a general practitioner, Dr. George Mackenzie, who was in the neighborhood. He showed little concern, although had the full story of Eliot's renal problems been known, there may have been greater anxiety. In Mackenzie's diagnosis, her sore throat, noted by Simcox, became acute laryngitis. But her pulse and temperature were "neither very high—in fact little more than normal and he was not in the least anxious about the case." The next day, Mackenzie's lack of concern seemed borne out as she appeared decidedly better, with pulse and temperature lower. He was now certain it was a three-day laryngitis: troublesome and painful, but no cause for anxiety. He came again on Tuesday night and found her unchanged; Eliot had a bath and went to sleep soon after eleven. But her night was disturbed, and the condition worsened, with a severe attack of pain in her right kidney.

Mackenzie returned on Wednesday morning and found considerable change in her vital signs, an elevated pulse rate, her strength reduced considerably. He came again at 2 P.M. and found her still weak. He recommended cold beef jelly and an egg beaten up with brandy, nourishments suitable for a heavy cold, not for a woman dying of kidney failure. Eliot dozed heavily, and when Clark finally came at 6 P.M. she was on her deathbed. He put the stethoscope to her heart and heard a loud irregularity; he noted that "the heart was struck." He feared she now had no power of resistance. Cross in his biography says that while the doctors were at her side, she said, "Tell them I have great pain in the left side"; she then relapsed into unconsciousness and died at 10 P.M. on 22 December 1880. She had passed her sixty-first birthday by one month. Cross wrote: "And I am left alone in this new House we meant to be so happy in." He adds, in a letter to Elma Stuart, "And your hearts too will know the void there is no filling. All the world is an infinite loser by this most untimely catastrophe. . . . I am stunned. I cannot write more."

Controversy did not end with Eliot's death, however. She may have been England's finest woman novelist, with Dickens perhaps England's greatest novelist, but many had not forgotten her 1854 elopement with the married Lewes, or the circumstances of her twenty-four-year relationship with a man who "tainted" everything he touched. The controversy started when Cross, in speaking to Spencer, suggested that Eliot should be buried at Westminster Abbey, which was the resting place of great English writers, but also a church first and foremost. Spencer telegraphed to the dean of Westminster, Stanley, who was not opposed if there could be demonstrated strong support for the burial there. He asked for marked representation from the famous, to give strength to his petition. But when the campaign began, divisions showed almost immediately, as old wounds were opened. Henry Sidgwick and C. S. C. Bowen collected signatures, and Edward Burne-Jones pitched in to obtain a distinguished list of supporters. Spencer was quite enthusiastic and helpful. He believed wholeheartedly that Eliot belonged in the famous Poets' Corner. The scientist John Tyndall was the most enthusiastic of all, and he attempted to cut through the obvious problem by writing Dean Stanley that she should be enshrined as a "woman whose achievements were without parallel in the previous history of womankind."

Thomas Henry Huxley, a friend of Eliot's and a sometime supporter of Lewes, knew otherwise: that her selection, while just, would lead to extreme controversy which might becloud her considerable achievements. She would be neglected as a great writer and calumniated as a scarlet woman. He said that Eliot's life and work all argued against enshrinement in what was, after all, a holy place. She was opposed, Huxley argued, to Christian marriage practices and to Christian theory. He emphasized that it would be unjust to Eliot, although he did not recognize that the heat of her earlier positions had softened and the Poets' Corner would probably have suited her. She would, we speculate, have perceived the Corner not as part of a church, but as a segment of a literary tradition in which she filled a large place. Huxley, however, knew what he was talking about. Some of the most famous names—such as Browning, Arnold, and Tennyson, who might have proved decisive—were missing from the petition. And the influential historian and journalist John Morley agreed it would be better not to rake over the past. Cross became convinced that the scandal attending her enshrinement was not in anyone's best interests. *

With Westminster Abbey no longer a possibility, Eliot was buried in a place that was thoroughly appropriate, next to Lewes, in the unconsecrated (Dissenters) portion of Highgate Cemetery in London. † Despite the inclement weather, Eliot's enormous fame and reputation drew a large crowd. On 29 December, family mourners were joined by the overlapping groups who frequented her Sunday afternoons, which came to be a brilliant cross section of writers, scientists, aristocrats with literary interests, successful men of business, painters, and the like. The family mourners included Isaac Evans, who had been informed on the 22nd by Cross in a most touching letter. The Crosses showed up in abundance, brothers-in-law as well as sisters. The lifelong friends were there: Spencer, Congreve, Browning, Harrison, William Blackwood, Langford, Pigott, and others. Among notables observed in the procession were Huxley, Du Maurier, Millais, Yates, Lord Arthur Russell, Lionel Tennyson (not Alfred Lord), Sir Henry Maine, Sir Charles Dilke, John Morley, and several women who did not make it into the listing; only Alice Helps and Lady Colville are mentioned. The absence of women in the newspapers was probably linked to their lack of fame: their husbands were the names to catch the reader's eye. Along these lines, Cross came to be called George Eliot's widow, put into the same position as many of the women she knew who had married famous men.

The service was conducted by Dr. Thomas Sadler, and he used the prayer book, as he had before with Lewes, but he did not stress the Unitarian sense of God. The inscription on the coffin has Eliot's birthdate incorrect, giving 1820, not 1819. Her gravestone got it right.

Cross did not fade away—he would do that later—but became quite active. In his letter to Isaac Evans, he tried to suggest what Evans had missed in his sister all these years: ". . . your noble sister and my wife died this night a little before 10 o'clock. I can scarcely realize yet that the crown of my life is gone." The remainder of the letter details matters already cited above in his letter to Elma Stuart.

The final words should rightfully belong to Edith Simcox. It is doubtful if either Lewes or Cross revered Eliot more than did this devoted woman. She recalled the scene in her autobiography, the entry on the very day of the funeral.

. . . In the cemetery I found the new grave was in the place I had feebly coveted—nearer the path than his and one step further south. Then I laid my violets at the head of Mr. Lewes's solitary grave and left the already gathering crowd to ask which way the entrance would be. Then I drifted towards the chapel—standing first for a while under the colonnade where

---

* A tablet commemorating Hardy, along with his ashes, was not forbidden, but despite his controversial views on religion Hardy died in a more open era, in 1928. Dickens made it, despite his having kept a mistress; as did Thackeray, not the most spiritual of men. In death, Eliot was punished as a woman.

† Elma Stuart was buried nearby, in 1903.

a child asked me, "Was it the late George Eliot's wife was going to be buried?"—I think I said Yes. Then I waited on the skirts of the group gathered in the porch between the church and chapel sanctuaries. Then some one claimed a passage through the thickening crowd and I followed in his wake and found myself without effort in a sort of vestibule past the door which kept back the crowd. . . . The coffin bearers passed in the very doorway, I pressed a kiss upon the pall and trembled violently as I stood motionless else, in the still silence with nothing to mar the realization of that intense moment's awe. . . . White wreaths lay thick upon the velvet pall—it was not painful to think of her last sleep so guarded. I saw her husband's face, pale and still; he forced himself aloof from the unbearable world in sight. . . . I was standing between his [Lewes's] grave and hers and heard the last words said: the grave was deep and narrow—the flowers filled all the level space. I turned away with the first—Charles Lewes pressed my hand as we gave the last look. Then I turned up the hill and walked through the rain by a road unknown before to Hampstead and a station. Then through the twilight I cried and moaned aloud.

> *This is life to come,*
> *Which martyred men have made more glorious*
> *For us who strive to follow. May I reach*
> *That purest heaven; be to other souls*
> *The cup of strength in some great agony,*
> *Enkindle generous ardour, feed pure love,*
> *Beget the smiles that have no cruelty—*
> *Be the sweet presence of a good diffused,*
> *And in diffusion ever more intense.*
> *So shall I join the choir invisible*
> *Whose music is the gladness of the world. [final stanza]*

In his funeral oration, in which he recited this poem, "O May I Join the Choir Invisible," Dr. Sadler altered the second line, "Of those immortal dead who live again," to the less mellifluous "who still live on." But the message, like the poem, was clear. Although she did not join the other greats in the Poets' Corner, Eliot became an integral part of England's great tradition.

Epilogue

During her lifetime, while Eliot did take her place as England's greatest novelist after Dickens's death and its most representative voice, not all other writers, or readers, were enchanted with her. Some had even dismissed her and Dickens and considered Thackeray the most compelling novelist of the century. More specifically, Wilkie Collins, Dickens's close friend, traveling companion, and fellow actor in amateur theatricals, mocked Eliot's looks in Marian Halcombe in *The Woman in White*. Marian is ugly, with the protruding jaw, the large-featured face, the trace of masculinity all ascribed to Eliot. In Florence Wilford's *Nigel Bartram's Ideal*, the protagonist Marian Hilliard (the "Marians" proliferate) is modeled on Eliot and Charlotte Brontë. Eliot is not treated well. We have already noted Alice James, Henry's and William's invalid sister, who equated Eliot with a fungus-like growth. Elizabeth Robins's *George Mandeville's Husband* uses the "George" of George Eliot and is not kind.

The medley of comments suggests how controversial Eliot remained for female, as well as male, novelists during and after her death, a figure whom they could not conveniently pigeonhole. Their resentment seemed to derive from her holding herself so far above the fray; her sibylline qualities—often a derogatory designation; her presentation of herself as superior—not so much in what she said as in her bodily movements, her gestures, her assumption she was different from others. Eliot's own comments in "Silly Novels by Lady Novelists" did not help her, since it attacked many of the very kinds of novels her critics would be writing. She was too ready, they thought, to accept masculine precepts of what made fictional enterprises significant; and her emphasis, inevitably, on maternal or traditional values did not endear her to women writers who felt themselves different from domestic women. Further, her companion, Lewes, had not built a reputation for sympathy to female novelists who strayed from conventional fictional paths. His categorization of "women novelists," for example, in his review of Charlotte Brontë's iconoclastic *Shirley* (in the *Edinburgh Review,* January 1850) deeply upset the novelist, since she felt he was holding women to a lesser degree of accomplishment than he would men.

We are omitting from the equation how much envy there was at Eliot's literary and financial achievements, since, except for the vitriolic Alice James, we lack direct evidence of such feelings. We also omit here the undertone of resentment at her domestic arrangement, its heavy presence during the entire twenty-four years, and the fact she was able to ride it out. She confounded her critics at every turn, especially those soon after her death who ridiculed or underestimated her achievements. Since 1930, the George Eliot Fellowship, located in Coventry, has promoted interest in her life and works, and has made certain through its international membership that Eliot retains her high position among English novelists. In 1980, in marking the centenary of Eliot's death, the fellowship with the aid of the membership placed a memorial stone in the Poets' Corner of Westminster Abbey—in one respect, at least, compensating for a censorious public and church that disallowed her burial there. In 1986, the fellowship made possible the placement of a bronze statue of Eliot, by the Warwickshire sculptor John Letts, in the center of Nuneaton. The president of the fellowship at present is Jonathan Ouvry, the great-great-grandson of George Henry Lewes; and the patron of the fellowship is the Viscount Daventry, of Arbury, where Robert Evans was agent for the estate.

It is fitting that a descendant of Lewes is president of the fellowship and was the person to unveil the statue of Eliot in Nuneaton, for Charles Lewes was the beneficiary of most of Eliot's estate. In 1882, two years after her death, he gave many of his father's and Eliot's books, about 2,405 items, to Dr. Williams's Library in London. Some of the remaining books were disposed of in two sales after the death of Charles's widow, Gertrude. The two sales were by Foster's in May 1923 and Sotheby's in June 1923. Mrs. Elinor Southwood Ouvry (now deceased), daughter of Charles and Gertrude, drew up a list of the books in Gertrude's house, which she showed to Gordon Haight. Many items consisted of several volumes, so that up to 10,000 books were left by Lewes and Eliot, 10 percent or so being Lewes's philosophical and scientific library. Numerous volumes contain comments by Eliot or Lewes, so that the collection at Dr. Williams's Library has become a virtual treasure trove.

When Eliot died, there remained Matthew Arnold, Tennyson, Browning, Carlyle, and Trollope, the last four old and shadows of themselves, plus a now mad Ruskin and a nonfunctioning Swinburne. Long dead were the great mid-century Victorians: Dickens, Thackeray, Mrs. Gaskell, the Brontës, Mill. There was the sense of an ending, but also a beginning, with Hardy, Gissing, Butler, the birth of Joyce, Woolf, Lawrence, the movement toward literary maturity of Joseph Conrad, the early poetry of William Butler Yeats. At the time of her death, despite her detractors, Eliot was something of a cult figure, a legend, and it was upon this fame John Cross hoped to build in his idolatrous biography, in three volumes in 1885. Not only did he not make any startling disclosures, as we have seen he papered over several episodes in Eliot's life which, he felt, would tarnish the legend. His intent was less accuracy than protection. Eliot's relationship with Chapman, for example, vanished; and Charles Bray gave way to the much safer Cara. Cross wanted to rely completely on Isaac Evans for his sister's background and, while Evans did not encourage Cross, he did come through when he saw it was better for him to provide information than to permit speculation and whatever else might ensue. In a sense, everything that Cross wrote about Eliot's younger years went through the critical pen of Isaac. The entire episode at Griff, which was so ambiguous for Eliot even as in memory she burnished its image, became for Cross celebratory, not psychologically divisive. In several ways, that high Victorian image is preserved in Gordon Haight's far more authoritative, detailed, and impressive biography of Eliot, published in 1968. But despite the meticulous scholarship, the angle of vision, as in Cross, is narrow, squeezed, protective, and carefully conventional.

As for Eliot's intimates after her death in 1880, many lived well into the twentieth century, which must have bewildered them. Charles Bray, however, died in 1884, D'Albert-Durade in 1886, Burne-Jones in 1886 (Georgiana in 1920), Barbara Leigh Smith Bodichon in 1891, Chapman in 1894, Sara Hennell in 1899. Others lived into a changing scene: Simcox to 1901, Agnes Lewes to 1902, Herbert Spencer and Elma Stuart to 1903, Cara Bray to 1905, William Blackwood (John's nephew) to 1912, Maria Congreve to 1915, Alexander Main to 1918. John Cross passed an almost invisible life and died in 1924.

The Eliot–Lewes–Stuart triangle of tombs in Highgate Cemetery is not easy to locate. Most visitors rush by to find the burial site of Karl Marx. Eliot might have found that ironic.

At the peak of her achievement, she was one of the three most famous women in England, along with Queen Victoria and Florence Nightingale. Victoria gave her name to the century and Nightingale to the Crimean War, but Eliot gave the era its intellectual sweep, offered it moral stability, and gave voice to the huge forces contesting one another. Her sense of a "higher calling" for women was not solely gender based, but a call for both sexes to transcend themselves, become better, and create a more equitable and just society. By the turn of the century, with a world war a distinct possibility, her voice was stilled; but her novels remain. No war can efface that fact.

Credits

South Farm *(Dolores Karl)*

George Eliot's baptismal entry *(Warwickshire County Record Office; Chilvers Coton Baptism Register: DR374/1)*

Arbury Hall *(Dolores Karl)*

Griff House, the Eliot corner *(Dolores Karl)*

Griff House, front view *(Dolores Karl)*

Chilvers Coton *(Dolores Karl)*

Robert Evans *(Coventry City Libraries)*

Charles Bray, two photos *(Coventry City Libraries)*

Sara Hennell and Cara Bray *(Coventry City Libraries)*

George Eliot in 1850 *(National Portrait Gallery)*

John Chapman *(Nottingham Museum and Art Gallery)*

Herbert Spencer in 1855 *(Picture Collection, The Branch Libraries, The New York Public Library)*

George Eliot in 1858 *(The George Eliot Fellowship)*

Emma Gwyther's grave *(Warwickshire County Council, Nuneaton Library)*

George Henry Lewes in 1859 *(Gordon Haight)*

Isaac Pearson Evans *(Warwickshire County Council, Nuneaton Library)*

George Eliot in 1860 *(Mistress and Fellows, Girton College)*

Barbara Bodichon *(Mistress and Fellows, Girton College)*

The Heights at Witley *(The George Eliot Fellowship)*

George Henry Lewes's tombstone *(Dolores Karl)*

George Eliot's grave *(Dolores Karl)*

Two views of the George Eliot memorial *(Dolores Karl)*

I wish to express special thanks to Howard Ross and Dolores Karl for their indispensable help in preparing these photographs.

APPENDIX A

The Westminster Review
Prospectus

"The newly-appointed editors will endeavour to confirm and extend the influence of the *Review* as an instrument for the development and guidance of earnest thought on Politics, Social Philosophy, Religion, and General Literature; and to this end they will seek to render it the organ of the most able and independent minds of the day." The editors outline their fundamental principle, which will be "the recognition of the Law of Progress," but without forsaking the past: "the actual" and "the possible" will always serve as guidelines. Controversial questions will be examined with the aim of "the conciliation of divergent views." Toward this end, "Independent Contributors" will be sought out, so that ideas at variance with the general spirit of the *Review* may be aired. The *Review* expects to focus especially on "that wide range of topics which may be included under the term 'Social Philosophy.' " It will try to make sense of the diverse, "chaotic mass of thought now prevalent" concerning social thought. This means, in practice, an attempt to reconcile Comte's positivism from France, the Manchester school of laissez-faire economics, the revitalized utilitarianism of John Stuart Mill, the discontent of workers and their efforts at trades unions, the emerging concerns of middle-class merchants, the threat of revolution, both political and social, from the continent, and several other converging elements. In politics, the *Review* will present the "vital questions" without party distinctions, although aspects of the quarterly were in the main Liberal or Radical. As for particular focuses: a progressive extension of the suffrage, "with a view to its ultimate universality"; a stress on the correct balance between individual liberties (we recall England has no Bill of Rights, no written protections) and the needs of the central government; an emphasis on an equitable distribution of power between local governments in the colonies and the mother country; an advocacy of "Free Trade in every department of Commerce"; a radical reform of the Court of Chancery, including the "simplification and expediting of all legal processes" (Chancery grievances as the basis of Dickens's *Bleak House* shortly after); a revision of ecclesiastical revenues, with an idea

toward reform, so as to promote the interests of the people; a program of national education, and a new policy of university and public schools so as to "render them available
irrespective of the distinctions of sect." In areas of religion, the wording is most careful:
"In the treatment of Religious Questions the *Review* will unite a spirit of reverential
sympathy for the cherished association of pure and elevated minds with an uncompromis-
ing pursuit of truth." Elements of ecclasiastical authority and dogma "will be fearlessly
examined, and the results of the most advanced biblical criticism will be discussed without reservation. . . ." In effect, secularism and agnosticism will prevail. In the area of
general literature, Eliot's private preserve, "the criticism will be animated by desire to
elevate the standard of the public taste, in relation both to artistic perfection and moral
purity. . . ." Coverage will be afforded historical and critical sketches of contemporary
literature, and notice will be paid to the most remarkable books from the continent as
well as from England. All in all, it was to be a liberal journal, liberal in our terms and in
nineteenth-century terms.

APPENDIX B

The Westminster Review

APPENDIX C

——— •◦◦• ———

George Eliot's Works

Strauss's *The Life of Jesus*, translated from the German, 1846
Feuerbach's *The Essence of Christianity*, translated from the German, 1854
Scenes of Clerical Life ("Amos Barton," "Mr. Gilfil's Love-Story," "Janet's Repentance"), 1858
Adam Bede, 1859
"The Lifted Veil," 1859
The Mill on the Floss, 1860
Silas Marner, 1861
Romola, 1863
"Brother Jacob," 1864
Felix Holt, the Radical, 1866
The Spanish Gypsy, 1868
Middlemarch, 1871–72 (completion of monthly installments)
The Legend of Jubal and Other Poems, 1874
Daniel Deronda, 1876 (completion of monthly installments)
Impressions of Theophrastus Such, 1879

Eliot's essays can be found in selected editions: *Essays of George Eliot*, ed. Thomas Pinney, 1963; *George Eliot: Selected Essays, Poems and Other Writings*, ed. A. S. Byatt and Nicholas Warren, 1990; *Essays and Uncollected Papers*, Volume 22 of the Cabinet edition. The Cabinet edition of Eliot's works began publication in 1878, starting with Volume I of *Romola* and continuing with one volume per month.

The Evans, Cross, Hennell, and Lewes Families

The Evans Family

George Evans (1740–1830) m. Mary Leech and had eight children: Mary (1765–?); George (1766–?); William (1769–1847); Thomas (1771–1847); Ann (1775–1860); Samuel (1777–1858); Susannah (1781–1811); **Robert** (1773–1849), **father of George Eliot.**

In 1801, Robert Evans m. Harriet Poynton (d. 1809) and had two children: Robert and Frances Lucy. In 1813, Robert Evans married Christiana Pearson (d. 1836) and had three children: Christiana ("Chrissey," 1814–1859) m. Edward Clarke and had nine children; Isaac Pearson (1816–1890) m. Sarah Rawlins and had four children; **Mary Anne** (later spelled Mary Ann, Marian; then George Eliot: 1819–1880) m. John Walter Cross, 1880.

The Lewes Family

George Henry Lewes (1817–1878) m. Agnes Jervis (1822–1902) in 1841 and had four children: Charles Lee (1842–1891); m. Gertrude Hill), Eliot's favorite—this line continues to the present; Thornton Arnott ("Thornie," 1844–1869); Herbert Arthur ("Bertie," 1846–1875; m. Eliza Stevenson Harrison); St. Vincent Arthy (1848–1850). Agnes Lewes also bore Thornton Hunt, son of the poet Leigh Hunt, four children.

The Cross Family

Anna Chalmers Wood (1813–1878) m. William Cross and had ten children: Elizabeth, m. William Henry Bullock, later Bullock-Hall, friends of Eliot's; William ("Willie"); **John Walter** (1840–1924), **m. George Eliot, 1880;** Anna Bowling Buchanan, m. Albert

Druce, friends of Eliot's; Mary Finlay; Richard James; Eleanor (friend of Eliot's); Emily Helen, m. Francis Otter; Alexander; Florence Nightingale.

The Hennell Family

James Hennell (1782–1816) m. Elizabeth Marshall and had eight children: Mary; Eliza; Harriet; Lucy; Charles Christian; James; **Sara Sophia** (1812–1899), close friend of Eliot's; **Caroline** ("Cara," 1814–1905), m. Charles Bray (1811–1884), close friends of Eliot's.

Notes*

1: The Youngest

p. 7 **came through the economy itself**—Fear of change could take many shapes, of course. In an early poem, "Supposed Confessions of a Second-Rate Sensitive Mind," the very young Tennyson revealed how the loss of traditional beliefs could send him reeling through the halls of nihilism and despair. "O weary life! O weary death! / O spirit and heart made desolate! / O damned vacillating state!" he concludes.

p. 8 **it meant a life of drudgery**—Alongside drudgery was, often, hope, since from 1815 to 1890, some 12 million Britons emigrated (many returned) to settle new lands as pioneers, investors, colonists and imperialists, scoundrels, missionaries, and the like (data from A. H. Imlah, *Economic Elements in the Pax Britannica* [Cambridge: Harvard University Press, 1958]). The British depended on a self-proclaimed ladder of progress based on capacity for freedom and enterprise: British at the top, then Americans and other Anglo-Saxons; Latins next, but well down the ladder; then the Oriental societies of Asia and North Africa; at the bottom, aborigines, so-called savages and tribes, who were disdained for their inability to make themselves into a state. Until the 1880s, when these assumptions began to fall apart, the British government acted on the acquisition of power and then protecting it with troops.

p. 11 **is rarely a significant factor**—In *Adam Bede* (Book IV, Chapter 33), when Mrs. Poyser speaks her mind to old Squire Donnithorne, she expresses the rights of the tenant farmer. But pure subsistence is not at stake; the right to a decent life is. Like most landowners, Donnithorne squeezed his properties and tenants and was niggardly about repairs. Even Mrs. Poyser's well-kept establishment suffers from a cellar full of water, frogs and toads hopping around, rotten floors, and rats and mice gnawing at the cheese her dairy produces.

p. 17 **she always sought in later life**—Gordon Haight, *George Eliot* (New York: Oxford University Press, 1968), is representative of this point of view. See p. 5, for example.

p. 17 **"very clever"**—British Library manuscript of *Mill on the Floss*.

p. 19 **"fiercer stroke than usual"**—*Mill*, Riverside ed. (Boston: Houghton Mifflin, 1961, ed. Gordon Haight), pp. 26–27.

* Source notes are keyed to pertinent passages in the text.

2: Finding Herself Outside

p. 22 **in Eliot's fiction**—When it comes to epigraphs, as apart from references, the overwhelming preponderance in Eliot's work derives from herself (about one hundred), with Shakespeare next and Wordsworth a distant third. After that, only Chaucer, Dante, Heine, and Sir Thomas Browne appear more than once or twice. Given her pleasure in reading the classic Greek authors, the paucity of epigraphs from classical literature (two from Sophocles, one from Homer, one from Theocritus) is striking. Possibly, she felt any given passage suffers too much from losing its context.

p. 22 **"to talk to grown-up people"**—*The George Eliot Letters,* ed. Gordon Haight (New Haven: Yale University Press, 1954–78), I, 41n. Henceforth referred to as *Letters.*

p. 24 **"more vicious than my Milby"**—*Letters,* II, 347, also 347n. (MS: National Library of Scotland.)

p. 25 **education was in order**—It is impossible to estimate how many intelligent young women were frustrated by lack of educational opportunities. Some, however, through sheer will and determination, broke through. Mary Somerville (née Fairfax), daughter of an admiral, is an excellent example of a girl whose father, unlike Evans, gave her no encouragement, and, in fact, kept her out of school until she was ten. But on her own she turned herself into a learning machine—classical languages, music, mathematics—and became a leading scientist in botany, geography, and astronomy. Born two generations before Eliot, Somerville was finally recognized by her male colleagues as someone accomplished in the sciences.

pp. 25–26 **"the envy of the other"**—George Eliot's School Notebook (Yale's Beinecke), from the section called "Affectation and Conceit." Also, the following quotations.

p. 28 **the "Captain Swing" phenomenon**—See *Captain Swing: A Social History of the Great English Agricultural Uprising of 1830,* Eric Hobsbawm and George Rude (New York: Pantheon, 1968). The study reveals that the uprising had spread to virtually every county in the country, although the incidence of it in Eliot's area was slight—one or two outbreaks compared with sixty-one, twenty-three, fifteen, and eighteen in the south and southeast. But to the east of her region, we find twenty-eight and nineteen incidents registered. Arson was the greatest source of destruction, far more than the destruction of property. Since Eliot's regions were identified more with industry than purely with farming, they seemed to escape—not because their farmers and landowners were more benevolent. "Swing" became the generic name for all those who operated as incendiarists and destroyers of machinery.

p. 29 **Tour of Monmouthshire**—Haight, p. 17.

p. 31 **pursuit of the golden calf**—In *The Mill on the Floss,* even the secular Maggie Tulliver is caught by the need for purification, and she experiences, as Eliot writes, the "awful visitation" of the God her father once talked of.

p. 32 **copied into her notebook**—School Notebook,

p. 34 **"Braham (a Jew too!)"**—*Letters,* I, 13. (MS: Yale.)

p. 35 **"honey from his pages"**—To Maria Lewis, *Letters,* I, 22, 16 March 1838. (MS: Yale.) The letter is misdated in MS as 16 February. Following quotation, same source.

p. 35 **"specimens of human nature"**—*Letters,* I, 23. (MS: Yale.)

p. 35 **"and leaves no record"**—*Mill,* p. 174; also, following quotation.

p. 35 **"conception, predominate still"**—*Mill,* p. 174.

p. 35 **"as soon as born"**—*Letters,* I, 23, still to Maria Lewis. Also, for following quotation.

p. 37 **"to be binding on Christians"**—*Letters,* I, 25, 20 May 1839. (MS: Yale.) Following quotation, p. 26.

p. 37 **"in a shattering violent manner"**—*Mill,* p. 208n. (MS: British Museum / Library.)

p. 37 **"come near to her"**—*Mill,* p. 208.

p. 37 **she sent on to Maria Lewis**—*Letters,* I, 27–28. (MS: Yale.)

p .38 **"uninteresting but useful stone"**—*Letters,* I, 29, 4 September. (MS: Yale.) Also, following quotation.

p. 39 **"anything but uninteresting"**—*Letters,* I, 31, 26 May. (MS: Yale.) Also, following quotation.

p. 40 **"never seek a better portion"**—*Letters,* I, 70, 20 October 1840. (MS: unknown; text from *Bookman,* 3 December 1892, p. 83, via Haight.)

p. 40 **"all our hopes imperfectly"**—*Letters,* I, 56, 6 July 1840. (MS: Yale.)

p. 40 **"the exercise of conversation"**—*Letters,* I, 47, 6? April 1840.

p. 40 **"I regularly disgraced myself"**—*Letters,* I, 41, 13 March 1840, to Maria Lewis. (MS: Yale.) Also, following quotation.

p. 41 **"allusive and elliptical"**—*Letters,* I, 34, 22 November 1839, to Maria Lewis. (MS: Yale.)

p. 42 **"for ever closed behind them"**—*Mill*, p. 171.

p. 43 **twenty years earlier**—*Silas Marner* (London: Penguin Classics, 1944), p. 129. "But in reality [before the loss of Marner's gold coins] it had been an eager life, filled with immediate purpose which fenced him in from the wide, cheerless unknown. It had been a clinging life; and though the object round which its fibres had clung was a dead disrupted thing, it satisfied the need for clinging." Once the gold is gone, Marner finds his life "a blank like that which meets a plodding ant when the earth has broken away on its homeward path." That broken line between the immediate past and the blank present, between focus and loss of all certainty, between support and failure of all support systems, characterizes not only Marner in his loss of gold but Mary Ann in her fears she was like that ant plodding home when the earth has broken away.

p. 45 **"would have them to be"**—*Mill*, p. 252; following quotations, pp. 254, 255.

p. 45 **not to fulfillment**—*Mill*, p. 286.

p. 47 **"very threshold of her youth"**—See Chapter VI of Book 6 of *Mill*, "Illustrating the Laws of Attraction." For quotation, p. 336.

3: Discovering Herself

p. 49 **"course of an unmapped river"**—*Mill*, p.. 351. In his *System of Logic* (1843), John Stuart Mill had asked a similar question: "Are the actions of human beings, like all other natural events, subject to invariable laws? Does that constancy of succession, which is the foundation of every scientific theory of successive phenomena really obtain among them?" (Book VI, Chapter 1, Section 2). Since the question opens up the question of individual freedom, Mill hovered around it for his entire professional life.

p. 51 **noted in his journal**—The journal is in private hands. For immediate reference, see Haight, p. 40.

p. 52 **dissuade her from her course**—*Letters*, I, 124, 28 January 1842. (MS: Tinker Collection, Yale.) Following quotations, pp. 125, 125–26.

p. 53 **"individual and social happiness"**—*Letters*, I, 128. (MS in private hands.) Following quotations from pp. 129, 129–30.

p. 54 **"leaving my Dear Father"**—*Letters*, I, 131, 12 March 1842, to Mrs. Pears. (MS: Yale.) Following quotation, p. 134.

p. 55 **"our self-catechizing afresh"**—*Letters*, I, 133, 31 March 1842. (MS: Tinker Collection, Yale.)

p. 55 **"and the sublimest resignation"**—*Letters*, I, 136, 11 April 1842. (MS: Yale.)

p. 56 **"instead of an integral part"**—*Letters*, I, 138, 20 April 1842, to Cara Bray. (MS: Parish Collection, Princeton.)

p. 58 **could deploy later on**—For example, from *Adam Bede* (Riverside ed., p. 148): "Our mental business is carried on much in the same way as the business of the State: a great deal of hard work is done by agents who are not acknowledged. In a piece of machinery, too, I believe there is often a small unnoticeable wheel which has a great deal to do with the action of the large obvious ones. Possibly there was some such unrecognised agent secretly busy in Arthur's mind at this moment. . . ."

p. 58 **"and refining the spirit"**—*Letters*, I, 140, 27 May 1842, to Maria Lewis. (MS: Yale.)

p. 59 **"tendencies of creation"**—*Letters*, I, 143, 3 August 1842. (TS: National Library of Scotland.) Following quotation, p. 144.

p. 61 **"in this world of egotists"**—*Letters*, I, 145. (MS: Yale.)

p. 61 **"as well as my character"**—*Letters*, I, 147. (MS: Yale.)

4: Who Was She?

p. 66 **"related the circumstances to me"**—Chapman's diary. See also *George Eliot and John Chapman, with Chapman's Diaries*, Gordon Haight (New Haven: Yale University Press, 1940; also Archon Books, 1969), p. 186. (Diaries: Yale.)

p. 69 **eventually into social policy**—See Charles Bray, *Phases of Opinion and Experiences During a Long Life* (London: Longmans, 1884). This was published four years after Eliot's death.

p. 72 **were only recently broken**—For some views of this, see Gordon Haight's essay "George Eliot's Bastards," *George Eliot: A Centenary Tribute*, eds. Gordon Haight and Rosemary Vanarsdel (New York: Macmillan, 1892).

p. 73 **Jacob Bright**—Although John Bright was the more famous, his brother Jacob, as a Radical member of Parliament for Manchester, was a fierce advocate of women's rights and far more a defender of the poor than John. Jacob Bright while in Parliament strongly asserted women's rights in marriage, divorce, questions of property and wills, decision-making after marriage, and a host of related subjects. His wife was equally an advocate, putting her energies into social issues, especially the establishment of Mechanics' Institutes for working people in Manchester.

p. 74 **"one's friends to be"**—*Letters*, I, 167, 30 November 1843. (MS: Yale.)

p. 75 **"which is a great thing"**—*Letters*, I, 171, January 1844. (Tinker Collection, Yale.) Also, see Haight's note, *Letters*, I, 171n.

p. 75 **"peeps through microscopes"**—*Adam Bede*, p. 429. Also, following quotations. See also p. 412.

p. 77 **"to correct the sheets for Strauss"**—*Letters*, I, 176, April 1844. (MS: Yale.)

p .78 **"but to all the fine arts"**—*Letters*, I, 177, 18 June 1844. (MS: Yale.)

p. 78 **But it failed to work**—Cara Bray tips her hand in stopping off at Manchester, writing her mother about her effort at matchmaking: ". . . for she [Mary Ann] was tired and unwell, and I thought looked her very worst, but you know we were only there one night and neither Frank nor Philip paid her special attention. I wish friend Philip would fall in love with her, but there certainly were no symptoms of it." *Letters*, I, 178, 21 August 1844. (MS: Tinker Collection, Yale.)

p. 79 **"you ever being understood"**—John Cross, one-volume edition of his three-volume life of Eliot, *George Eliot's Life as Related in Her Letters and Journals* (Edinburgh & London: Blackwood, 1885), p. 58.

p. 79 **"to meet at Baginton"**—*Letters*, I, 183, 30 March 1845. (MS: Tinker Collection, Yale.) Following quotations, p. 184.

p. 80 **"did not become one 'du coeur' "**—*Letters*, I, 185–86, 6 April 1845. (MS: Yale.)

p. 80 **"at least for the present"**—"*Letters*, I, 188. Following quotation, p. 189. Also, following quotation.

p. 81 **"leaves me the power of thinking"**—*Letters*, I, 199, September 1845. (MS: Yale.)

p. 81 **Cara, Sara, and Mary Ann**—Haight (*Letters*, I, 200n) reproduces the itinerary which was given in Cara Bray's diary for October 1845. Joined by the Rathbones and Martineaus, the group set out on 14 October and returned on the 28th, with stops at all the familiar spots, Scott's Abbotsford, Loch Lomond, Trosach's Inn, Glasgow, and Edinburgh.

p. 82 **"at times with her work"**—*Letters*, I, 206, 14 February 1846. (MS: Tinker Collection, Yale.)

p. 82 **"uninteresting to me"**—*Letters*, I, 207, 4 March 1846, to Sara Hennell. (MS: Yale.)

p. 82 **"careless of mankind"**—*Letters*, I, 209, March ? 1846, to Sara Hennell. (MS: Yale.)

p. 83 **"from a French pen"**—*Letters*, I, 235, 10 May 1847, to Mary Sibree. (MS: Yale.)

p. 83 **"in my soul"**—*Letters*, I, 277, 9 February 1849, to Sara Hennell. (MS: Yale.) Following quotations, pp. 277–78.

p. 83 **even as a beacon**—In *George Sand and the Victorians* (1977), Patricia Thomson asserts that Eliot took a number of scenes and situations from Sand's novels, especially in her *Mill on the Floss*. Thomson argues that Eliot did not only learn from her own background and reproduced it, but that she used her reading from Sand. Thomson sees Sand's *Histoire de ma vie* as a direct influence on *Mill*, with Aurore preceding Maggie in terms of her conversion at fifteen and general adolescence. ". . . Maggie's resemblance to both Consuelo and Aurore Dupin should finally scotch the belief" that Maggie is essentially the young Mary Ann Evans (p. 169). A more cogent argument, however, is that both Sand and Eliot drew on materials common and familiar to all nineteenth-century novelists. Resemblances became inevitable.

5: Limbo

p. 87 **"must be writing her novel"**—Bray–Hennell Extracts, Yale. (Also, Haight, p. 61.)

p. 88 **mid-September letter**—The 14th? (MS: Yale.)

p. 89 **"as well as proud"**—*Letters*, I, 225, 5 November 1846. (MS: Yale.)

p. 90 **"comes up to my ideal"**—Addressed to Charles Bray, *Letters*, VIII, 13, 21 October 1846. (MS: Yale.) Following quotation, p. 14.

p. 91 **"a fine poetical genius"**—*Letters*, I, 231, 28 February 1847, to Sara Hennell. (MS: Yale.)

p. 91 **"intellectually and morally stronger"**—*Letters*, I, 237, 16 September 1847, to Sara Hennell. (MS: Yale.)

p. 91 **"at the roof and arches"**—*Letters*, I, 229, 20 December 1847. (MS: Yale.)

p. 92 **"to those of (so-called) religion"**—*Letters*, I, 240, 15 October 1847, to Sara Hennell. (MS: Yale.)

p. 92 **"wisdom and divine enthusiasm"**—*Letters*, I, 241, 27 November 1847, to Sara Hennell. (MS: Yale.) Also, following quotation.

p. 93 **"for physical and moral ends"**—*Letters*, I, 246, 11 February 1848, to John Sibree. (MS: Berg Collection, New York Public Library.) Also, following quotations, pp. 246, 247. *Daniel Deronda* would be a refutation of many of these remarks, although she was not happy with the manners and style of Eastern European Jews.

p. 94 **"to their own destruction"**—*Letters*, I, 251, February 1848. (Copy: Yale.)

p. 95 **"underlie our everyday existence"**—*Letters*, I, 253, 8 March 1848. (Copy: Yale.) Following quotations, pp. 254, 255.

p. 95 **working-class movements, like the Chartists**—The Chartists' Six Points, established in 1838, called for universal male suffrage, elimination of property qualifications for members of Parliament, payment of members, annual general elections, for more direct representation and equally divided electoral districts (to replace the unequal county and borough sectioning), and the secret ballot. While threatening to the ruling classes and particularly the landed aristocracy, Chartism was a peaceful movement.

p. 95 **"we English are slow crawlers"**—*Letters*, I, 254, continuation of 8 March 1848 letter to John Sibree. Following quotation, p. 255.

p. 96 **"a mere echo of another"**—Ibid. Also, following quotations.

p. 96 **"never think of self again"**—*Letters*, I, 261, 14? May 1848, to John Sibree. (Copy: Yale.) These copies of Eliot's letters to John Sibree were made by his sister, Mary Sibree Cash, in most instances. In this letter, Eliot applauded Sibree's decision to give up the ministry. "I sincerely rejoice," she wrote, "in the step you have taken—it is an absolutely necessary condition for any true development of your nature. It was impossible to think of your career with hope while you tacitly subscribed to the miserable etiquette (it deserves no better or more spiritual name) of sectarianism. Only persevere—be true, firm and loving—not too anxious about immediate usefulness to others—that can only be a result of justice to yourself." (I, 261.)

p. 96 **"heroines of police reports"**—*Letters*, I, 268, 11 June 1848. (MS: Yale.)

p. 97 **"I unconscious of length or breadth"**—*Letters*, I, 264, 4 June 1848. (MS: Yale.)

p. 97 **"in the valley of Dolour"**—*Letters*, I, 265, 5 June 1848. (MS: Yale.)

p. 97 **"reign of Mammon shall end"**—*Letters*, I, 267, 8 June 1848, to the Brays and the Hennells. (MS: Yale.)

p. 97 **"as badly as ever"**—*Letters*, I, 269–70, remarks made to both Mary Sibree and Sara Hennell, respectively, 13 June 1848 and 23 June 1848. (MS: in private hands for the Sibree, Yale for the Hennell.) Also, following quotation, p. 186.

p. 97 **"I have ever seen"**—*Letters*, I, 270, 14 July 1848, to Sara Hennell. (MS: Yale.) See *Letters*, I, 271, n. 6, for Gordon Haight's details of the encounter. Following quotation, p. 271.

p. 98 **"looks like a ghost"**—*Letters*, I, 272, 11 September 1848, Cara Bray to Sara Hennell. (Tinker Collection, Yale.)

p. 98 **"to think and to love"**—*Letters*, I, 272–73, 23 November 1848, to Sara Hennell, for all four quotations. (MS: Yale.)

p. 99 **"the energy to do"**—*Letters*, I, 276–77, 9 February 1849, to Sara Hennell. (MS: Yale.)

p. 99 **"every day of my life"**—*Letters*, I, 279, March ? 1849. (MS: Yale.) Also, following quotation.

p. 100 the **"worship for mortals"**—*Letters*, I, 283–84, for both quotations, May 1849. (MS: Yale.)

p. 100 **"purifying restraining influence"**—*Letters*, I, 284, 30 May 1849, to the Brays. (MS: Yale.)

p. 101 **a hasty departure**—Cara Bray's diary or commonplace book, located in Coventry, lists the itinerary. The Nuneaton Museum and Art Gallery, incidentally, contains early specimens of fiction by the Hennell sisters, with Sara's watercolor illustrations. Nearly everyone in the group wrote, publicly or privately, so that Mary Ann had numerous examples.

p. 101 **"has proved able to do"**—*Letters*, I, 289, 23 July 1849. (MS: in private hands.)

p. 101 **The Campagne Plongeon**—For details, see *Letters*, I, 290, n. 3, 4, 5.

p. 102 **"society of superior people"**—*Letters*, I, 290, 27 July 1849, to Charles Bray. (MS: Yale.) Following quotations, pp. 290–91.

p. 103 **"a proud silence on such matters"**—*Letters*, I, 292, 5 August 1849, to the Brays and Sara Hennell. (MS: Yale.) Her letters now to the Brays, or together with Sara Hennell, are very long and detailed, suggesting some loneliness or homesickness despite the adventure of her new life.

p. 103 **"feelings of others towards me"**—*Letters*, I, 296, 20 August 1849, to the Brays and Sara Hennell. (MS: Yale.) Following quotation, p. 297.

p. 104 **"my books, etc."**—*Letters*, I, 298, still 20 August 1849. Also, following quotations.

p. 104 **"my strength and spirit"**—*Letters*, I, 302, 28 August 1849, to the Brays. (MS: Yale.) Also, following quotations.

p. 105 **"since I came"**—*Letters*, I, 305, 13 September 1849, to the Brays. (MS: Yale.)

p. 105 **"know so well in another person"**—*Letters*, I, 308, 20 September 1849, to the Brays. (MS: Yale.) Following quotations, pp. 308, 309. This is one of the longest letters Eliot wrote, another indication, possibly, of homesickness and loneliness.

p. 106 **prepared to seize happiness**—*Middlemarch*, Chapter 10.

p. 107 **"truth will permit"**—*Letters*, I, 312, 4 October 1849. (MS: Yale.) Following quotation, Cross, III, p. 240.

p. 107 **"the equality of human destinies"**—Letters, I, 313–14, 4 October 1849, to Mrs. Henry Houghton (Fanny). (Cross, pp. 228–30, no MS of letter.)

p. 108 **"worth talking to"**—*Letters*, I, 315, 11 October 1849, to the Brays. (MS: Yale.) Also, following quotation.

p. 108 **"when he is present"**—*Letters*, I, 316–37, 24 October 1849, to the Brays. (MS: Yale.) Following quotations, pp. 317, 316.

p. 109 **"the principle of vitality"**—*Letters*, I, 318, same letter as above. Comment on food, Cross, I, p. 150.

p. 109 **"pleasure of seeing it"**—*Letters*, I, 319, 26 October 1849, to Bray. (MS: Yale.) Also, following quotation. The reference to "nest-making" foreruns her fictional references to snug, warm accommodations, with the hearth turned into an almost sacred place.

p. 110 **"from becoming quite soft"**—*Letters*, I, 321, 4 December 1849, to the Brays. (MS: Yale.) Following quotations, pp. 321, 322.

p. 111 **"she is no beauty"**—Haight, p. 77. For more on the lectures, see *Letters*, I, 325, n. 1.

p. 111 **"have a real interest in me"**—*Letters*, I, 328, 9 February 1850, to Mrs. Henry Houghton. (Cross, I, pp. 244–46.) Eliot's assessment of Alboni as "a very fat syren" neglects the contralto's well-deserved fame and reputation.

p. 112 **"to that alternative"**—*Letters*, I, 329, 15 February 1850. (MS: Yale.)

p. 112 **"an idle wretch"**—*Letters*, I, 332, 26 March 1850, to Sara Hennell. (MS: Yale.) Also, following quotation.

6: *London at Mid-Century, and the* Westminster Review

p. 113 **"since we met"**—*Letters*, I, 334, 4 April 1850, to Martha Jackson. (MS: British Museum.) Also, following quotation.

p. 114 **of a private residence**—*Letters*, I, 335, n. 1, for details of charges.

p. 115 **Edward Casaubon**—Haight (p. 80) draws some similarities between Mackay and Casaubon, and others have pointed to him more directly as a model for the desiccated pseudo-scholar.

p. 115 **Chapman asked Marian**—Anyone writing about Marian and Chapman is deeply indebted to Gordon Haight's *George Eliot and John Chapman*, to his transcription of Chapman's *Diary*, and to his Chapter III of *George Eliot*.

p. 116 **than he could comprehend**—Following another course was Thomas Henry Huxley, the biologist and theorist whose early ideas were appealing in part to Eliot, although she had to fault them for a certain mechanical quality. In "A Liberal Education and Where to Find It," in *Science and Education*, Huxley in a famous passage formulated his equation of man and the universe. "The chess board is the world, the pieces are the phenomena of the universe, the rules of the game are what we call the laws of Nature. The player on the other side is hidden from us. We know that his play is always fair, just and patient. But also we know, to our cost, that he never overlooks a mistake, or makes the smallest allowance for ignorance. To the man who plays well, the highest stakes are paid with that sort of overflowing generosity with which the strong shows delight in strength. And one who plays ill is checkmated—without haste, but without remorse" (New York: Appleton, 1897, p. 82).

p. 119 **"that she dislikes her"**—Entry for 18 February 1851 (Yale); also available in Haight, *George Eliot and John Chapman*, p. 142. Besides the diaries for 1851, Yale also possesses Chapman's diaries for 1860 and 1863; unfortunately, several pages are torn out, apparently by Chapman himself. Subsequent quotations are from the 1851 diary, extending through 5 April, "I begged her to be calm. . . ."

p. 121 **"duly exorcised"**—*Letters*, I, 354, 20 June 1851, to John Chapman. (MS: Parrish Collection, Princeton.) While Susanna Chapman was away, she wrote her husband about his relationship with Marian, some of which is reproduced in Chapman's *Diary* for 8 April–5 May 1851.

p. 123 **"or to any house in London"**—Entry for Thursday, 29 May 1851. Following quotation, from the *Diary*, for 30 May 1851.

p. 123 **"could make her happy!"**—*Diary* entry for Saturday, 31 May 1851.

p. 124 **to many famous and interesting people**—In a curious paralleling and overlapping of careers, the very popular novelist Eliza Lynn Linton was preparing herself in much the same way as Eliot, although in all instances on a lesser scale. Without real talent, she willed herself into a successful career. Once she left home for London, she used the reading room of the British Museum as her education; then by 1851, she was a full-time journalist at the *Morning Chronicle* earning a considerable twenty guineas a month—while Eliot earned room and board. Linton contributed reviews, travel reports, and various articles to Dickens's *Household Words.* In religious terms, she went from orthodoxy through all the Victorian "isms," ending up as a Comtist, a humanitarian, and a social ameliorist. She also tried to learn languages, with mixed results: Latin, Greek, Hebrew, German, French, Italian, and Spanish, Eliot's own seven. She disliked George Henry Lewes, whose path she crossed, and defended Thornton Hunt in that triangle. She resented Eliot's eminence, while agreeing to her excellence. Like Eliot later, she wanted to be published by Blackwood, and wrote a pleading letter that she would let him guide her fiction if the firm accepted her. Blackwood refused, whereas he welcomed Eliot. At this point, Linton's career as a novelist was a mere shadow of Eliot's.

p. 124 **"I may do otherwise"**—*Diary,* entry for 21 September 1851.

p. 125 **"the best of them all"**—*Letters,* I, 355, 20 June 1851. (MS: Parrish Collection, Princeton.)

p. 127 **"in your time of distress"**—Haight, p. 95. Also, following quotations.

p. 128 **"since I came"**—*Letters,* I, 364, 4 October 1851, to Bray. (MS: Yale.)

p. 128 **"her teeth horrid"**—*Letters,* I, 365, 6 October 1851, to Bray. (MS: Yale.)

p. 129 **"really Freda Bremer"**—*Letters,* I, 366, 8 October 1851, to Bray. (MS: Columbia.)

p. 129 **"fat purses both"**—*Letters,* I, 371, October 1851, to Cara Bray. (MS: Columbia.) Also, following quotations.

p. 130 **"Merry Wives of Windsor"**—*Letters,* I, 376, 24 November 1851, to Sara Hennell. (MS: Yale.)

p. 130 **"working the hardest"**—*Letters,* I, 377, 20 December 1851. (MS: Yale.)

p. 130 **"to stay till Saturday"**—*Letters,* I, 378, 23 December 1851. (MS: Yale.)

p. 132 **the first seven issues**—See literary receipts for Lewes, in a notebook he kept, at the Berg Collection of the New York Public Library; also *Letters,* VII, 365–83.

p. 132 **"real Life"**—*Westminster Review,* January 1852; more accessible in *Selected Essays, Poems, and Other Writings* (of Eliot), ed. A. S. Byatt and Nicholas Warren (London: Penguin, 1990), pp. 297–301.

p. 134 **looked forward to his contributions**—*Letters,* II, 5, 2 January 1852, to Sara Hennell. (MS: Yale.)

p. 134 **"soundness of judgment"**—National Library of Scotland.

p. 135 **"almost serpentine grace"**—Haight, p. 103.

p. 135 **into Parkes's face**—See *Letters,* II, 138, 21 January 1854. (MS: in private hands.) Also, following quotation.

p. 136 **"bad influence"**—*Letters,* II, 44, 15 July 1852. (MS: in private hands.)

p. 136 **"Marian is so great"**—Haight, p. 87, Bessie Parkes to Barbara Leigh Smith.

p. 137 **like Barbara Leigh Smith**—Two excellent books on women's issues, from mid-century on, which also describe Barbara Leigh Smith's role, are *Feminism, Marriage, and the Law in Victorian England, 1850–1895* by Mary Lyndon Shanley (Princeton: Princeton University Press, 1989), and *A Mid-Victorian Feminist, Barbara Leigh Smith Bodichon* by Sheila R. Herstein (New Haven: Yale University Press, 1985).

p. 137 **a passage canceled**—In the manuscript at the Morgan Library.

p. 139 **"self-interest"**—Eliot wrote Chapman at great length from Broadstairs (II, 47–50, 24–25 July 1852, in the Parrish Collection, Princeton). Following quotations, pp. 47–50.

p. 140 **"let him write a fresh Prospectus"**—In her attempt at a summational novel, *Middlemarch,* Eliot presents numerous "web" images or passages, all of them illuminating her belief in necessity and interconnectedness. Among other things, she characterizes the fate of Rosamond Vincy and Lydgate as caught by necessity, caught in a "gossamer web." (See Riverside ed., p. 253.) Because the young people are ignorant of each other and of themselves, the web entraps; but it has the possibility also of joining.

p. 141 **"neither tall nor short"**—*Letters,* II, 23, 5 May 1852, to the Brays. (MS: Yale.)

7: *Herbert and George: The Two Voices*

p. 143 **"sentimentality all through"**—*Letters,* II, 18, 15 April 1852. (MS: Yale.)

p. 144 **"as we like"**—*Letters,* II, 22, 27 April 1852, to the Brays, but addressed mainly to Cara. (MS: Yale.) Also, following quotation.

p. 144 **"the better I like you"**—*Letters*, VIII, 42, 21 April 1852. (MS: British Museum.) This series of plaintive letters which Eliot wrote to Spencer at and around this time was unavailable to Haight when he wrote his biography of Eliot in 1968. They were available when he added two further volumes to his edition of Eliot's letters.

p. 145 **"instincts would not respond"**—See *Letters*, VIII, 42–43, n. 5. Also, following quotation.

p. 145 **"for the sea-breezes"**—*Letters*, VIII, 50–51, probably 8 July 1852. (MS: British Museum) Also, following quotations.

p. 146 **"might think of me"**—*Letters*, VIII, 56–57, probably 16 July 1852. (MS: British Museum.) Several of these Eliot letters to Spencer were published previously, in 1976, but with numerous errors; and of course Cross in his biography of Eliot had ignored them, as did Spencer in his *Autobiography*.

p. 147 **"untroubled by painful emotions"**—*Letters*, VIII, 61, probably 29 July 1852. (MS: British Museum.)

p. 148 **"for general inspection"**—*Letters*, II, 35, 14 June 1852. (MS: Yale.)

p. 148 **"the fields and hedgerows"**—*Letters*, II, 37, 23 June 1852, to Bray. (MS: Yale.)

p. 149 **"influence of blue devils"**—*Letters*, II, 53, 30 August 1852, to Sara Hennell. (MS: Yale.) Also, following quotation, 2 September, 1852.

p. 150 **Spencer's letter**—At Yale. Also, following quotation.

p. 150 **Spencer's 21 October 1884**—At Yale. Also, the 2 February 1885 letter.

p.151 **"in Plato's dialogues"**—*Letters*, II, 59, 7 October 1852. (MS: Yale.)

p. 152 **"I am resigned"**—*Letters*, II, 65, 30 October 1852. (MS: in private hands.)

p. 152 **"keep my eyes open"**—*Letters*, II, 68, 22 November 1852. (MS: Yale.) Also, following quotation.

p. 153 **"a kindness from him"**—*Letters*, II, 75, 31 December 1852, to the Brays and Sara Hennell. (MS: Yale.)

p. 154 **a life of reason**—Spencer appeared to fall into the kind of neurasthenia which took on almost epidemic proportions among accomplished Victorians: Darwin (the most famous), Tennyson, Florence Nightingale, and Beatrice Webb, among others. Characteristic were exhaustion, inability to function, and lack of interest in the very activities that were making them famous. It was a middle-class disease, and that it struck so many renowned people indicates they had lost balance between inner and outer, between self and culture. Repression led to withdrawal. The conditions seem both individual and societal. Although Eliot did not appear to suffer from neurasthenia as such, her recurring ailments and headaches suggest she was a borderline case. Neurasthenia can be called by other names, such as depression, nervous collapse, and even what we now label manic-depression or bipolar disorder. The cure lay with rest and hydropathy, the water cure at spas which Eliot and Lewes frequented whenever they went abroad. In retrospect, we can see that hydropathy became therapeutic because it removed the individual from work and created some still point. It was, of course, temporary.

p. 155 **"moral asphyxia"**—*Letters*, II, 97, 16 April 1853, to Cara Bray. (MS: Yale.) Also, following quotations.

p. 156 **"mask of flippancy"**—*Letters*, II, 98, 16 April 1853, to Cara Bray. (MS: Yale.)

p. 156 **"my hollow tooth"**—*Letters*, II, 103, 17 June 1853, to Cara Bray and Sara Hennell. (MS: Yale.)

p. 156 **"not fit for a Strand life"**—*Letters*, II, 109, 12 July 1853, to Bessie Parkes. (MS: in private hands.)

p. 157 **"state of convulsive change"**—*Middlemarch* (Riverside ed.), p. 359.

p. 160 **the child of Thornton Hunt**—Victorian gossip had it that the Leweses and their growing family lived in a cooperative household with the Hunts, the Gliddons (Hunt's wife was a niece of Arthur Gliddon), and the Laurences. As Haight points out (p. 130), no evidence has surfaced that they all shared quarters, or mates. The fact that the Lewes and Hunt lives so intertwined had given rise to talk of a harem.

p. 160n **Haight quotes**—P. 329.

p. 160 **costly and elaborate procedure**—By now, it was clear that Lewes could not obtain a divorce from Agnes, since to petition Parliament would cost, in present monies, $10,000 or more.

p. 162 **"for my only view"**—*Letters*, II, 111–12, 3 August 1853, to Cara Bray. (MS: Yale.)

p. 163 **"as I can get"**—*Letters*, II, 117, 19 September 1853. (MS: Yale.)

p. 163 **"little dinners for me"**—*Letters*, II, 119, 20 October 1853. (MS: Yale.)

p. 163 **"physically by my change"**—*Letters*, II, 123, 5 November 1853. (MS: Yale.)

p. 164 **"Father's hair in it"**—MS: Yale.

p. 164 **"moral and intellectual weakness"**—*Letters*, II, 127, 25 November 1853. (MS: Yale.)

p. 165 **"services which I render"**—*Letters*, II, 128, 25 November 1853. (MS: Yale.)

p. 165 **"other agglomeration of cells"**—*Letters*, II, 129, 2 December 1853, to Cara Bray. (MS: Yale.)

p. 166 **"self-sufficing, complete being"**—Ludwig Feuerbach, *The Essence of Christianity*, translated by George Eliot (New York: Harper, 1957), p. 6.

p. 166n **Barbara needing it**—See Barbara Bodichon to Bessie Rayner Parkes, V, 178. (MS: Girton.)

p. 167 **"an instrument by others"**—Feuerbach, p. 39. Following quotation, p. 47.

8: One George, One to Go

p. 171n **Haight quotes**—Haight, p. 138.

p. 172 **"and our pockets after"**—*Letters*, II, 130–31, 2 December 1853. (MS: Huntington Library.)

p. 173 **"flavour any good result"**—*Letters*, VIII, 90, 28 November 1853. These letters to Combe, as well as Combe's and Chapman's to each other, were not available to Haight when he wrote his biography. Eliot's to Combe are, in the main, at the National Library of Scotland, as this one is.

p. 174 **"new book and the public"**—*Letters*, II, 137, 18 January 1854, to Sara. (MS: Yale.)

p. 174 **"truly representing German"**—*Letters*, II, 141, 6 February 1854, to Sara. (MS: Yale.)

p. 175 **"compensating improvement"**—*Letters*, II, 156, 19 May 1854. (MS: Yale.)

p. 176 **"to me every day"**—*Letters*, II, 156, 19 May 1854. (MS: Yale.)

p. 177 **"take into account"**—*Letters*, II, 158, 27 May 1854. (MS: Yale.)

p. 177 **"it must be learned"**—*Letters*, II, 160, 3 June 1854. (MS: Yale.)

p. 177 **"and other evils"**—*Letters*, II, 161, 12 June 1854, to Sara Hennell. (MS: Yale.)

p. 178 **"mode of statement"**—*Letters*, II, 164, 10 July 1854, to Sara Hennell. (MS: Yale.)

p. 179 **"better left to imagination"**—*Letters*, II, 171, 16 August 1854. (MS: Coventry City Libraries.) The meeting with Brabant took place on 30 July.

p. 180 **"names at their doors"**—Ibid.

p. 181 **"my ideas and feelings"**—*Letters*, II, 171, 18 August 1854. Continuation of above letter.

p. 181 **"mar the picture"**—Journal (Yale), 10 August 1854. Reproduced by Haight, 155–56.

p. 182 **"am looking forward"**—*Letters*, II, 173, 10 September 1854, to Bessie Parkes. (MS: in private hands.) Also, following quotations.

p. 183 **"of the masculine style"**—*Essays of George Eliot*, ed. T. Pinney (London: Routledge & Kegan Paul, 1963), p. 53. Following quotations, pp. 53, 54, 55, 56, 57, 58 (all in Pinney).

p. 184 **"harvest of human happiness"**—Pinney, pp. 80–81.

p. 185 **"intellectual sympathy deepen"**—*Letters*, II, 173, 30 August 1854, to John Chapman.

p. 185 **"stink pots of humanity"**—*Letters*, II, 176, 4 October 1854. (MS: in private hands.)

p. 186 **"but that is all"**—*Letters*, II, 177, 19? October 1854. (MS: Parrish Collection, Princeton.)

p. 186 **Combe wrote to Bray**—*Letters*, VIII, 129–30. (Copy in National Library of Scotland.) Following quotations from this letter.

p. 187 **Bray defended Marian**—*Letters*, VIII, 130, 19 November 1854, Bray to Combe. (MS: National Library of Scotland.)

p. 187 **"my only answer is *silence*"**—*Letters*, II, 177, 19 October 1854, cited above.

p. 187 **"I am entirely indifferent"**—*Letters*, VIII, 123, 15 October 1854, to Chapman. (MS: Yale.) Also, following quotations, pp. 123, 124, 125.

p. 189 **"not to obtrude myself"**—*Letters*, II, 179, 23 October 1854. (MS: Parrish Collection, Princeton.)

p. 189 **"sympathy from his wife"**—*Letters*, VIII, 122. (MS: National Library of Scotland.)

p. 189 **"in privacy and loneliness"**—*Letters*, VIII, 128, 28 October 1854. (MS: National Library of Scotland.)

p. 189 **"the infidel esprit forte"**—Amusingly, Kingsley was on Eliot's mailing list for at least *Adam Bede*. See Robert Bernard Martin, *The Dust of Combat: A Life of Charles Kingsley* (1959), p. 181.

p. 191 **"groaning on the margin"**—*Middlemarch* (Riverside ed.), p. 574.

p. 192 **"and thwarted his purposes"**—*Middlemarch*, p. 540. Also, following quotation.

p. 193 **" 'speaking proudly' etc."**—*Letters*, II, 181, 31 October 1854, to Sara Hennell. (MS: Yale.)

p. 193 **"you may act towards me"**—*Letters*, II, 182, 31 October 1854, cited above.

p. 193 **"I mean nothing unkind"**—*Letters*, II, 186, 15 November 1854. (MS: Yale.)

p. 194 **himself unfaithful to his wife**—According to his daughter, Bessie, and his granddaughter, Mrs. Belloc Lowndes; see Haight, p. 166, n. 2.

p. 195 **"disinclination to accommodate me"**—*Letters*, II, 184, 12 November 1854. (MS: Parrish Collection, Princeton.) Also, following quotation.

p. 195 **"make the pit rise in horror"**—*Letters*, II, 185, 15 November 1854, cited above. Also, following quotation.

p. 196 **"in its own country"**—*Letters*, II, 187, 15 November 1854, Sara Hennell to Marian, n. 8. (MS: Yale.)

p. 197 **"by an agreement with Bohn"**—*Letters*, II, 189, 22 November 1854. (MS: Yale.)

9: Facing Up

p. 200 **send her love**—*Letters*, II, 191, 9 January 1855. (MS: Yale.)

p. 200 **"more refined cousins"**—See Eliot's Journal, "Recollections of Berlin"; also, Haight, p. 175.

p. 200 **"are sympathetic ones"**—*Letters*, II, 196, 16 March 1855, to Bessie Parkes. (MS: in private hands.)

p. 202 **"fairly through the press"**—*Letters*, II, 197, 4 April 1855. (MS: Parrish Collection, Princeton.)

p. 203 **"he returned from consciousness"**—*Letters*, II, 199, 1 May 1855. (MS: Yale.)

p. 204n **"expression of disapprobation"**—*Letters*, II, 199, 1 May 1855. (MS: Yale.)

p. 206 **"reputation for sanctity"**—*Westminster Review*, October 1855, but more accessible in Pinney, p. 160. Following quotation, Pinney, p. 189.

p. 207 **"reduced by evaporation"**—*Letters*, II, 206, 25 June 1855. (MS: Berg Collection, New York Public Library.) Following quotation, p. 207.

p. 207 **"personal and intellectual sympathy"**—*Letters*, II, 209, 27 June 1855. (MS: Berg Collection, New York Public Library.)

p. 208 **"entertainment I gave you"**—*Letters*, II, 209, 16 July 1855. (MS: Parrish Collection, Princeton.) Following quotations, p. 210. The review is unrelenting and ferocious: "If we had found these *Lives of Men of Letters* [by Brougham] in a biographical dictionary, we should perhaps have thought them up to the average of the piecework usually to be met with in such compilations; finding them, as we did more than ten years ago, in an *édition de luxe* adorned with portraits and with Lord Brougham's name on the title-page, we felt some simmering indignation at such gratuitous mediocrities in a pretentious garb; and now that we see them in a cheaper reissue—as if there were any demand for these clumsy superfluities, these amateur locks and pokers—our indignation fairly boils over" (*Leader*, 7 July 1855). The remainder of the review is no less hostile.

p. 209 **"quite an affecting fact to me"**—*Letters*, II, 211, 21 July 1855. (MS: Yale.)

p. 210 **"believing the same of me"**—*Letters*, II, 214, 4 September 1855, to Cara Bray. (MS: Yale.) Following quotations, pp. 214, 215.

p. 211 **"would be a misfortune"**—*Letters*, II, 232, 22 March 1856. (MS: in private hands.)

p. 212 **for the authorship to be kept secret**—Eliot told Bray that a strong impression "would be counteracted if the author were known to be a woman." *Letters*, II, 218, 15 October 1855. (MS: Yale.)

p. 212 **"the fine gold of art"**—Pinney, p. 223.

p. 213 **"master of the house"**—*Letters*, II, 224, 1 January 1856. (MS: Yale.)

p. 214 **"Mrs. Gaskell, Harriet Martineau," and many others**—*Letters*, II, 225, 18 January 1856, to Sara Hennell. (MS: Yale.)

p. 215 **"as to morals and religion"**—*Letters*, II, 231, 15 March 1856. Also, following quotation.

p. 216 **"a temple or palace"**—Journal, 8 May–26 June 1856; Haight, p. 242. Also, following quotation. (MS: Yale.) The segment is titled "Recollections of Ilfracombe 1856," and runs over 7,000 words.

p. 217 **"distinct, vivid ideas"**—Ibid. Also, following quotation.

p. 218 **"than of the sturdy countryman"**—*Westminster Review* (July 1856), p. 54, and Pinney, p. 268. Following quotation, Pinney, p. 269.

p. 218 **"would be of great contribution"**—*Westminster Review*, p. 55, and Pinney, p. 271. (This essay is also available in the Penguin edition.) Following quotation, Pinney, p. 271.

p. 219 **"and no one for himself"**—Pinney, p. 272. Also, following quotation. In his *Fortnightly Review* (XVII, February 1872) article on Dickens, Lewes capitulates to Eliot's 1856 remarks in her Riehl review. Lewes had long been a friend of Dickens—since 1838, after the latter's striking success with *Pickwick*—but he had distinct reservations about the kind of novel Dickens wrote: primarily that this great writer had little or no psychological sense. Although we know that this was a misreading of Dickens—he had profound psychological insights, both individual and social—Lewes emphasized his imagination and exploration of the unreal in visions and hallucinations. "Dickens sees and feels, but the logic of feeling seems the only logic he can manage. . . . Compared with that of Fielding or Thackeray, his was merely an *animal* intelligence, *i.e.*, restricted to perceptions." (For a discussion of this and other aspects of Lewes's relationship to Dickens, see Haight, "Dickens and Lewes," *Publications of the Modern Language Association of America*, LXXI, March 1956, pp. 166–79.)

p. 221 **"give me much trouble"**—Journal (Yale); Cross, I, p. 296.

p. 221 **"in my future life"**—Journal; also Haight, p. 206.

p. 221 **"descriptive parts of a novel"**—Journal; also Haight, p. 206. Following quotations, Journal; Haight, p. 206.

p. 222 **"the fashion of a volcano"**—*Scenes of Clerical Life* (Penguin ed.), p. 81. Also, following quotations.

p. 224 **"masculine aptitudes and experience"**—Pinney, p. 324. Following quotations, Pinney, pp. 323, 322.

p. 224 **"as well as some amusement"**—*Letters*, II, 258, 20 July 1856, from Tenby. (Haight reproduces the letter from a Magg Bros. Catalogue, No. 314, item 2816.)

p. 225 **"my writing time to the minimum"**—*Letters*, II, 261, 1 September 1856, from Richmond. (MS: Yale.)

10: Becoming George Eliot

p. 226 **Marian's journal**—Journal (Yale.).

p. 228 **"elevations, and sections"**—*Scenes* (Penguin ed.), p. 41. Following quotation, p. 42. Implied here is a firm opposition to Benthamism and to James Mill's views of a "scientific" society and even the utilitarianism developed by John Stuart Mill, whose other stands on individual liberties and women's issues Eliot would find sympathetic. All of the above she would deem uncalculatingly ameliorist, although, later, positivism attracted her.

p. 229 **" 'I think your pathos is better than your fun' "**—Journal, 6 December 1857. (MS: Yale.) Also, *Letters*, II, 407, and Haight, p. 212.

p. 230 **"into the most respectable society"**—*Scenes* (Penguin ed.), pp. 78–79.

p. 231 **"an image of death"**—*Scenes* (Penguin ed.), p. 114.

p. 231 **by Thackeray and others**—Some of the popular novels were really popular, like Mrs. Henry Wood's *East Lynne* (1860–61), the 1850s fictions of G. J. Whyte-Melville and James Grant, with their historical novels (*The Scottish Cavalier, Bothwell*, and others), and Thomas Hughes's immensely successful *Tom Brown's School Days* (1857).

p. 232 **"troubles of other men"**—*Letters*, II, 269, 6 November 1856. (MS: National Library of Scotland.) Also, following quotation.

p. 233 **"very humourous and good"**—*Letters*, II, 272, 12 November 1856, from Edinburgh. (MS: National Library of Scotland.) Amusingly, while Lewes was conducting business matters with Blackwood, Eliot was analyzing theological questions in her correspondence with Sara Hennell, who had no idea her "Marian" was now becoming George Eliot. The topic in question was "design" and what this signified in terms of a God-like being in a natural theology. Following quotations, p. 272.

p. 233 **"are English clergymen"**—*Letters*, II, 275, 18 November 1856. (MS: National Library of Scotland.)

p. 234 **"so high is his ambition"**—*Letters*, II, 276, 22 November 1856—on Eliot's thirty-seventh birthday. (MS: National Library of Scotland.) Following quotations, p. 277.

p. 235 **"prefers the Almighty"**—Pinney, p. 337; *Selected Essays*, p. 165.

p. 236 **"anything so fresh"**—*Letters*, II, 283, 29 December 1856. (MS: National Library of Scotland.)

p. 237 **"passion and the poetry of his life"**—*Scenes* (Penguin ed.), p. 130.

p. 237 **"anything of real merit"**—*Letters*, II, 290, 30 January 1857. (MS: National Library of Scotland.) Also, following quotation.

p. 238 **"will be really profitable"**—*Letters*, II, 292, 4 February 1857. (MS: National Library of Scotland.)

p. 238 **"it was their family history"**—*Letters*, II, 298, 16 February 1857, from London to Edinburgh. (MS: National Library of Scotland.)

p. 239 **"now fairly raised"**—*Letters*, II, 293, 10 February 1857. (MS: National Library of Scotland.) Also, following quotation.

p. 239 **"and so may you"**—*Letters*, II, 295, 11 February 1857. (MS: National Library of Scotland.)

p. 239 **"still predominate over hope"**—Journal (Yale).

p. 240 **"in both these stories"**—*Letters*, II, 297, 16 February 1857. (MS: National Library of Scotland.) Also, following quotation.

p. 240 **the ultimate accolade**—Blackwood referred to Thackeray as "the wandering 'puller down of Kings' " (*Letters*, II, 300, 23 February 1857). Eliot had insisted that her stories "always grow out of my psychological conception of the dramatis personae" (*Letters*, II, 299, 18 February 1857). (Both MSS at the National Library of Scotland.)

p. 241 **"and thin lips"**—*Scenes* (Penguin ed.), p. 169.

p. 242 **"or *against* an enemy"**—*Letters*, II, 301, 24 February 1857. (MS: Yale.)

p. 243 **"done in that way"**—*Letters*, II, 307, 9 March 1857. (MS: National Library of Scotland.)

p. 243 **"of the lethal weapon"**—*Letters*, II, 308, 11 March 1857. (MS: National Library of Scotland.)

p. 243 **"in actual life"**—*Letters*, II, 309, 14 March 1857. (MS: Yale.) Following quotation, pp. 309–10.

p. 243 **Lewes's journal**—For 15–18 March 1857, at Yale.

p. 243 **"with yielding back etc."**—Lewes's Journal (Yale); also, *Letters*, II, 311.

p. 244 **"to place above it"**—*Letters*, II, 315, 15 April 1857, from Scilly Isles. (MS: John Rylands Library.) Also, following quotation.

p. 245 **"with magnificent eyes"**—*Letters*, II, 319, 16 April 1857, from Scilly Isles (St. Mary's). (MS: Yale.) Also, following quotation, p. 320.

p. 246 **"Jesuitical interloper"**—*Scenes* (Penguin ed.), p. 282. Also, following quotations.

p. 247 **take a walk with his old mother**—"It was rather sad and yet pretty to see that little group passing out of the shadow into the sunshine, and out of the sunshine into the shadow again; sad, because this tenderness of the son for the mother was hardly more than a nucleus of healthy life in an organ hardening by disease, because the man who was linked in this way with an innocent past had become callous in worldliness, fevered by sensuality, enslaved by chance impulses; pretty, because it showed how hard it is to kill the deep-down fibrous roots of human love and goodness— how the man from whom we make it our pride to shrink, has yet a close brotherhood with us through some of our most sacred feelings" (*Scenes*, Penguin ed., p. 299).

p. 247 **"finger-shadow of advancing death"**—*Scenes* (Penguin ed.), p. 318.

p. 248 **"but a puppet-show copy"**—*Scenes* (Penguin ed.), p. 357.

p. 248 **"felt the sunshine melancholy"**—*Scenes* (Penguin ed.), p. 394.

p. 249 **"I think first rate"**—*Letters*, II, 328, 22 May 1857. (MS: National Library of Scotland.)

p. 250 **"and one in England"**—*Letters*, II, 331–32, 20 May 1857. (MS: Parrish Collection, Princeton.)

p. 250 **degree from St. Andrews University**—For details of his degree, see Haight, *George Eliot and John Chapman*, pp. 93–94.

p. 251 **"accept it without reserve"**—*Letters*, II, 342, 5 June 1857. (MS: Yale.) Also, following quotation.

p. 251 **"who knows Coton stories"**—*Letters*, II, 337, 2 June 1857. (MS: in private hands.)

p. 252 **"love and gratitude"**—*Letters*, II, 340, 5 June 1857. (MS: Yale.)

p. 252 **"a resource as beer"**—*Letters*, II, 344, 8 June 1857. (MS: National Library of Scotland.) Also, following quotation.

p. 252 **"under your Father's Will"**—*Letters*, II, 346, 9 June 1857. (MS: Parrish Collection, Princeton.) The letter is reproduced from a copy Isaac Evans kept.

p. 253 **"eight-and-twenty years ago"**—*Letters*, II, 347, 11 June 1857. (MS: National Library of Scotland.) Also, following quotations, pp. 347, 348. This exceptionally long letter, from Gorey in Jersey, indicates a critical point in Eliot's professional career, since an insensitive response from Blackwood might have turned her from fiction.

p. 253 **"is not legally divorced"**—*Letters*, II, 349, 13 June 1857. (MS: Parrish Collection, Princeton.) Following quotations, pp. 349, 350. Holbeche's brief letter to Isaac Evans, forwarding Marian's to him, is dated 17 June 1857 and is in the Parrish Collection, Princeton.

p. 254 **"contributor considerably modified"**—*Letters*, II, 351, 14 June 1857. (MS: National Library of Scotland.)

p. 256 **"did poison the beast"**—*Letters*, II, 360, 7 July 1857. (MS: National Library of Scotland.)

p. 256 **"miserable mental states"**—*Letters*, II, 362, 12 July 1857. (MS: National Library of Scotland.)

p. 257 **"hideous sound in my ears"**—*Letters*, II, 363, 12 July 1857. (MS: National Library of Scotland.) Following quotation, p. 364.

p. 258 **"to false rumours"**—*Letters*, II, 364, 14 July 1857. (MS: Yale.)

p. 258 **of Jersey in her journal**—at Yale; also *Letters*, II, 367ff.

11: Becoming an Author

p. 262 **"who have lived before us"**—*Letters*, II, 376, 18 August 1857, to Sara Hennell. (MS: Yale.)

p. 262 **"those admirable figures"**—*Letters*, II, 378, 23 August 1857. (MS: National Library of Scotland.)

p. 262 **"newspapers as a hard duty"**—*Letters*, II, 379, 1 September 1857. (MS: in private hands.)

p. 263 **"of a future mistake"**—*Letters*, II, 384, 24 September 1857, to Bessie Parkes. (MS: in private hands.)

p. 264n **"eyes of the librarians"**—*Letters*, II, 400, 7 November 1857, to John Blackwood. (MS: National Library of Scotland.) Mudie's did best with multi-volumes, taking 2,400 copies of Volumes 3 and 4 of Macaulay's *History of England;* in the years from 1853 to 1862, Mudie added almost a million volumes to his stock (half of them novels). See Richard D. Altick, *The English Common Reader* (Chicago: University of Chicago Press, 1957), Chapter 13, "The Book Trade, 1851–1900."

p. 265 **"during the year"**—Journal (Yale); also, Haight, p. 247. Also, following quotation.

p. 265 **"and very poor stories"**—*Letters*, II, 419, 9 January 1858. (MS: National Library of Scotland.)

p. 265 **"long time to come"**—*Letters*, II, 419, 9 January 1858, to John Blackwood. (MS: National Library of Scotland.)

p. 267 **"in a promising way"**—*Letters*, II, 422, 17 January 1858, to Sara Hennell. (MS: Yale.) Following quotation, p. 223.

p. 267 **"I am a woman myself"**—*Letters*, II, 424n, Dickens writing to Joseph Langford.

p. 267 **"since the world began"**—*Letters*, II, 424, 18 January 1858. (MS: British Museum.)

p. 267 **"has been appreciated"**—*Letters*, II, 424, 21 January 1858. (MS: National Library of Scotland.)

p. 268 **"ears in History"**—*Letters*, II, 426, 21 January 1858, Jane Carlyle to Eliot. (MS: in private hands.) Following quotations, pp. 426, 427.

p. 269 **"immediately to be corrected"**—*Letters*, II, 428, 27 January 1858. (Copy: Blackwood.)

p. 269 **"but a good expression"**—*Letters*, II, 436, 1 March 1858. (Copy: Blackwood.) Also, following quotation.

p. 270 **"data for such guesses"**—*Letters*, II, 443–44, 31 March 1858. (MS: Yale.) Also, following quotation. Previous quotation, II, 443, 29 March 1858.

p. 270 **"usual sad catastrophe!"**—*Letters*, II, 446, 31 March 1858, John Blackwood to Eliot. (MS: National Library of Scotland.)

p. 272 **"the prettier she looked"**—*Adam Bede*, Riverside ed. (Boston: Houghton Mifflin, 1968), pp. 72–73.

p. 272 **prettily like a flower**—*Adam Bede*, p. 73.

p. 274 **not the least Dickens**—In the famous Governor Eyre case on the island of Jamaica, in 1865, Dickens sided with the most reactionary elements in English society who supported Eyre's bloody, and unreasonable, massacre of innocent protestors. When Eyre came up on charges of misconduct, Dickens signed a petition supporting him. John Stuart Mill was on the other side. Eliot did not sign, but we suspect she would have agreed with Dickens. The case split Victorian intellectual society, with the so-called humanists siding with Eyre—not only Dickens but Carlyle, Ruskin, and Tennyson; the scientists and rationalists (empiricists, materialists, utilitarians)—Mill, Huxley, Spencer—found Eyre's behavior outrageous and criminal.

p. 275 **"yoke of traditional impressions"**—*Adam Bede*, p. 347.

p. 276 **"of some great wrong"**—*Adam Bede*, p. 355.

p. 276 **"into a new state"**—*Adam Bede*, p. 357.

p. 278 **"cries in our loneliness"**—*Adam Bede*, p. 407.

p. 278 **into the subject of a novel**—Journal (Yale); also, Cross, II, pp. 48–49.

p. 279 **"than Dinah is my aunt"**—Ibid. Following quotations, Cross, pp. 49–50, 50.

p. 280 **"dreary, wasted period"**—Cross, II, p. 55. Following quotation, p. 56.

p. 280 **"to love and admire"**—*Letters*, VIII, 199–200, 27 March 1858. (Copy: Coventry *Herald.*) Following quotations, p. 200.

p. 280n **on a particular subject**—*Letters*, II, 447, 2 April 1858. (MS: National Library of Scotland.)

12: Arrival

p. 282 **Physiology of Common Life**—Haight provides a most interesting footnote on Lewes's book, as a study which influenced the great Russian physiologist Pavlov to enter the field; Pavlov had a copy of the book in the German translation. Haight also cites a reference to Lewes's study in Dostoyevsky's *Crime and Punishment,* where it is noted, in rather unlikely fashion, that the prostitute Sonia has read Lewes's *Physiology* (Haight, p. 255, n. 5).

p. 283 **"life of the animal"**—*Letters,* II, 451, 17 April 1858, to Sara Hennell. (MS: Yale.)

p. 284 **"barren of propositions"**—*Letters,* II, 454, 10–13 May 1858, to Sara Hennell. (MS: Yale.)

p. 286 **"unspeakable journey"**—*Letters,* II, 471, 28 July 1858, to Sara Hennell. (MS: Yale.) Following quotation, Eliot's Journal; also, Cross, II, p. 34.

p. 286 **"splendid city in Germany"**—That is, in the Austro-Hungarian Empire; *Letters,* II, 470, 23 July 1858, to John Chapman. (MS: Yale.)

p. 286 **"lamp forever burning"**—Journal.

p. 287 **"the affections engaged"**—*Letters,* II, 474, 16 August 1858. (MS: National Library of Scotland.)

p. 287 **noted in her journal**—20 July 1858.

p. 288 **"little villain"**—*Letters,* II, 484, 4 October 1858. (MS: National Library of Scotland.)

p. 289 **"as it is arbitrary"**—*George Eliot: The Critical Heritage,* ed. David Carroll (New York: Barnes and Noble, 1971), p. 75.

p. 289n **Eliot finally grounds her**—For perceptive discussions of collateral points about Hetty's centrality, see Susan Horgan's *Sisters in Time: Imagining Gender in 19th Century British Fiction* (New York: Oxford University Press, 1989).

p. 290 **"guess at authorship"**—*Letters,* II, 486, 6 October 1858, to Sara Hennell. (MS: Yale.)

p. 291 **"secure all adventitious aids"**—*Letters,* II, 506, 2 December 1858. (MS: National Library of Scotland.)

p. 292 **"extreme aversion to disclose?"**—*Letters,* II, 494, 5 November 1858. (Copy: Magg Bros. Catalogue, No. 330, item 141.) As indicated, the original of this letter has not turned up, and in printing it from the Magg Brothers Catalogue, Haight was forced to accept the omissions. The fierceness of Eliot's position, nevertheless, is quite apparent, although she never denies authorship outright.

p. 292 **"not the author of 'Adam Bede' "**—*Letters,* III, 13, 12 February 1859. (MS: Parrish Collection, Princeton.)

p. 292n **"holly and laurel"**—*Letters,* III, 14. (MS: Yale.)

p. 293 **"covering a fermenting heap"**—Cabinet ed., XVII, p. 270.

p. 295n **course she was following**—For a compelling examination of "The Lifted Veil" and how it fits into traditional female-oriented fiction, see *The Madwoman in the Attic : The Woman Writer and the Nineteenth Century Literary Imagination* by Sandra Gilbert and Susan Gubar (New Haven: Yale University Press, 1979), Chapter 13.

p. 296 **rise, achieve, emerge**—For an argument about Hetty as "demonic," see Nina Auerbach's perceptive study, *Woman and the Demon: The Life of a Victorian Myth* (Cambridge: Harvard University Press, 1982).

p. 296 **"sake of wreaking itself"**—Cabinet ed., p. 296.

p. 297 **"arguing with myself"**—*Letters,* II, 501, 26 November 1858, to Cara Bray. (MS: Yale.)

p. 297 **"before my novels"**—*Letters,* II, 509, 22 December 1858, to John Blackwood. (MS: National Library of Scotland.) Following quotation, *Letters,* II, 509–10, 25 December 1858, Blackwood to Eliot.

p. 298 **"I distrusted my own opinion"**—*Letters,* II, 512, 28 December 1858. (MS: National Library of Scotland.)

p. 298 **"people whom I know"**—*Letters,* III, 6, 29 January 1859. (MS: National Library of Scotland.)

p. 299 **"of this desire"**—Lewes's Journal, 9 February 1859.

p. 299 **"laid it down"**—*Letters,* III, 17–19, 20 February 1859, for this and following comment. (MS: Tinker Collection, Yale.)

p. 299 **"myself on this paper"**—*Letters,* III, 115, 10 July 1859. (MS: Parrish Collection, Princeton.)

p. 300 **"masters of the art"**—*Critical Heritage,* p. 77. Following quotation, p. 84.

p. 300 **"assent and sympathy"**—*Critical Heritage,* p. 88.

p. 301 **"keeping simple accounts"**—*Letters,* III, 22, 24 February 1859. (MS: Yale.) Following quotation, pp. 22–23.

p. 302 **"and care for her"**—*Letters,* III, 26, 26 February 1859. (MS: Yale.)

p. 302 **"ploughed my heart"**—*Letters,* III, 23, 24 February 1859. (MS: Yale.)

p. 302 **"for the last half hour"**—*Letters,* III, 34, 17 March 1859, to John Blackwood. (MS: National Library of Scotland.)

13: *There*

p. 305 **"I mention it"**—*Letters*, III, 41, 31 March 1859. (MS: National Library of Scotland.)

p. 306 *"which is a shame"*—*Letters*, III, 44, 10 April 1859, Eliot to John Blackwood. (MS: National Library of Scotland.)

p. 306 **"with the Spring tide"**—*Letters*, III, 46, 11 April 1859. (MS: Yale.)

p. 306 **"melt out of me"**—*Letters*, III, 56, 26 April 1859. (MS: Tinker Collection, Yale.)

p. 306 **"my heart of hearts"**—*Letters*, III, 63, 5 May 1859. (MS: in private hands.) Following quotations, p. 64.

p. 306 **"usual among gentlemen"**—*Letters*, III, 50, 15 April 1859. (Copy: the *Times*.)

p. 307 **"Resquiescat in pace"**—*Letters*, III, 147, 7 September 1859. (MS: Yale.)

p. 307n **"a Molière-comedy"**—*Letters*, III, 76, 6 June 1859, Eliot to William Blackwood. (MS: National Library of Scotland.)

p. 308 **"books can be written"**—*Letters*, III, 99, 27 June 1859, to the Brays and Sara Hennell. (MS: Yale.)

p. 308 **"declare myself the author"**—*Letters*, III, 102, 28 June 1859. (MS: National Library of Scotland.)

p. 309 **"he is a swindler"**—*Letters*, III, 93, 25 June 1859. (MS: National Library of Scotland.)

p. 309 **"cannot be put straight"**—*Letters*, III, 94, 25 June 1859. (MS: National Library of Scotland.)

p. 309 **"go on with my work"**—*Letters*, III, 99, 27 June 1859. (MS: Yale.)

p. 310 **"helped by such a trick"**—*Athenaeum*, 2 July 1859, p. 2.

p. 310 **"no sympathy with it"**—*Letters*, III, 109, 2 July 1859. (MS: in private hands.)

p. 311 **"wistfully and very lonely"**—*Letters*, III, 96. (MS: Yale.)

p. 311 **"to see the end of"**—Lewes's Journal, 24 March 1859. (Yale.)

p. 311 **"to the world generally"**—*Letters*, III, 111, 5 July 1859. (MS: Yale.) Following quotation, p. 110.

p. 312 **"in my chagrin"**—*Letters*, III, 124, 30 July 1859, Eliot to John Blackwood. (Copy, from Cross, II, p. 123.)

p. 312n **"and petty egoism"**—*Letters*, III, 119, 23 July 1859. (MS: in private hands.)

p. 313 **"loving mother"**—*Letters*, III, 127, 30 July 1859, Eliot to Charles Lee Lewes. (MS: in private hands.)

p. 313 **"was born into the world"**—26 July 1859; Cross, II, p. 89.

p. 314 **"from all she most values"**—MS: Bodleian Library, Oxford; also, Haight, p. 299. Also, following quotation.

p. 315 **"that people love you"**—1 May 1859. (MS: Yale.)

p. 316 **"off the lazy British tongue"**—*Letters*, III, 240. (MS: National Library of Scotland.)

p. 317 **"brave clearness and honesty"**—5 December 1859, to Barbara Bodichon; Cross, II, p. 108. Also, in *Letters*, III, 227; also, following quotations.

p. 318 **in a ducal family**—See J. A. Sutherland, *Victorian Novelists & Publishers* (Chicago: University of Chicago Press, 1976).

p. 318 **"to write only for money"**—*Letters*, III, 152, 13 September 1859. (MS: National Library of Scotland.)

p. 319 **"as to the author's life"**—*Letters*, III, 161, 21 September 1859. (MS: National Library of Scotland.) Also, following quotation.

p. 319 **"that risk myself"**—*Letters*, III, 162, 22 September 1859. (MS: National Library of Scotland.) Also, following quotation.

p. 319 **"throughout the Kingdom"**—*Letters*, III, 163–64, 26 September 1859. (MS: Yale.)

p. 320 **"through several counties"**—*Letters*, III, 168, 30 September 1859. (MS: Yale.) For other background activity on this matter, see *Letters*, III, 164–65 (26 September 1859); 165–67 (28 September 1859); 167–68 (29 September 1859), Lewes to Bracebridge.

p. 321 **deteriorated into calculation**—*Letters*, III, 172–73, 5 October 1859, William to John Blackwood. (MS: National Library of Scotland.)

p. 321 **"were fused together"**—*Letters*, III, 175, 7 October 1859.

p. 321 **"be a transient agitation"**—*Letters*, III, 179, 10 October 1859. (MS: Yale.)

p. 322 **"most thoroughly hood-winked"**—*Letters*, III, 194, 3 November 1859, George Simpson to Joseph Munt Langford. (MS: National Library of Scotland.)

p. 323 **"a mere daylight fact"**—*Letters*, III, 198, 11 November 1859. (MS: John Rylands Library.)

p. 323n **"like her to fancy"**—Haight, p. 312.

p. 323 **"of George Eliot's sex"**—*Critical Heritage*, p. 141.

p. 325 **"interest and pleasure to me"**—*Letters*, III, 203, 14 November 1859. (MS: Berg.)

p. 325 **"with hardly thanks"**—*Letters*, III, 206, 18 November 1859. (MS: National Library of Scotland.) Also, following quotation.

p. 325 **Langford replied to John Blackwood**—*Letters*, III, 207, 18 November 1859. (MS: National Library of Scotland.)

p. 325 **"author of *Adam Bede*"**—*Letters*, III, 18 November 1859, n. 10. (MS: National Library of Scotland.)

p. 326 **"understanding in the matter"**—*Letters*, III, 215, 26 November 1859. (MS: National Library of Scotland.)

p. 326 **"so far taken place"**—*Letters*, III, 217, 28 November 1859. (MS: National Library of Scotland.) Previous quotations, pp. 216, 217.

p. 327 **"generosity of your tone"**—*Letters*, III, 218, 30 November 1859. (MS: National Library of Scotland.) Following quotations, pp. 218, 219.

p. 327 **the fact that the manuscript**—British Library Add. MS 34023-34025.

p. 327 **"of any future work"**—*Letters*, III, 221, 1 December 1859, William to John Blackwood. (MS: National Library of Scotland.) Also, following quotation.

p. 328 **"I did in explanation"**—*Letters*, III, 222, 2–4 December 1859. (MS: National Library of Scotland.) Following quotation, p. 223.

p. 329 **"history of mankind"**—*Letters*, III, 231, 6 December 1859. (MS: British Museum.) Following quotations, pp. 231, 232.

p. 329 **"of a taking narrative"**—*Letters*, III, 233, 12 December 1859. (MS: National Library of Scotland.)

p. 329 **successful 1857 novel**—Sales of 11,000 in nine months, fewer copies than Dickens but more than Eliot.

p. 330 **another £1,000 at nine months after publication**—Plus retaining copyright, an act which brought additional hundreds of pounds as the book continued to sell.

p. 334 **he was "enchanted"**—*Letters*, III, 259, 9 February 1860. (MS: National Library of Scotland.) The follow-up letter came on 10 February 1860, acknowledging receipt of the manuscript of the second volume.

p. 334 **"than give up either"**—*Letters*, III, 264, 23 February 1860, to John Blackwood. (MS: National Library of Scotland.)

p. 335 **"to go through *that*"**—*Letters*, III, 270, 6 March 1860. (MS: in private hands.)

p. 335 **"difference to us"**—*Letters*, III, 273, 15 March 1860, Lewes to William Blackwood. (MS: National Library of Scotland.)

p. 335 **"only dispute himself"**—*Letters*, III, 277, 22 March 1860. (MS: Yale.)

p. 336 **"about himself the better"**—*Letters*, III, 405. (MS: Yale.)

p. 337 **"dirty, uninteresting streets"**—Journal (Yale); Cross, II, p. 126. Following quotation, *Letters*, III, 284, 3 April 1860, to John Blackwood. (MS: National Library of Scotland.) Eliot also wrote at considerable length to Maria Congreve (Mrs. Richard Congreve), 4–6 April 1860, from Rome. This would be followed, on 4–5 May, by a long segment on Naples.

p. 337 **"be the more welcome"**—*Letters*, III, 285, 3 April 1860. (MS: National Library of Scotland.)

p. 338 **"widening psychology"**—*Letters*, III, 317–18, 9 July 1860, Eliot to John Blackwood. (MS: National Library of Scotland.)

p. 339n **them during her trip**—The unsigned review in the *Spectator* (7 April) was not altogether favorable—citing the inferiority of the characters to those in *Adam Bede*—but concluded that it was superior as a work of art to the previous novel, with a higher aim and that aim more profoundly worked out. The unsigned notice in the *Saturday Review* (14 April) stated there was no falling off in power from *Adam Bede*—although the reviewer showed surprise to discover the author was a woman—but felt there was too much pain in *Mill*. As we examine the reviews, including the one in the *Times* (19 May), we observe how a strict moral standard was entering into so-called literary criticism. It tended to support Tom Tulliver and condemn Maggie. The *Westminster* (July 1860) used the review as a land mine, citing Charlotte Brontë as a weapon with which to explode the author of *Mill*.

p. 339 **observed the similarities**—What follows are two assessments by leading literary figures, Swinburne in 1877 and Ruskin in 1881, shortly after Eliot's death. Having turned Maggie into a Madonna-like figure, Swinburne finds it totally inexcusable that Eliot would have such a young woman tempted by the likes of Stephen Guest. Swinburne is tempted to call him out. He sees the episodes as more than a blemish, more like a cancer, "in the very bosom, a gangrene in the very flesh. It is a radical and mortal plague-spot, corrosive and insurable. . . ." Ruskin's attack is on all fronts. The characters are commonplace (Maggie), loutish (Tom), without the slightest importance to anybody in the world. He calls this "Cockney literature," that which will appeal to brick houses that are forming in every manufacturing town. In such a literature, "which consummates itself in George Eliot," the characters derive from the counter and the gutter. By now, Ruskin was mad. In one respect it is fortunate Eliot could not read the words of a man whose wisdom she had once respected and admired.

p. 341 **"French journals or reviews"**—*Letters*, III, 302, 7 June 1860, from Venice. (MS: unknown, copy at Tinker Collection, Yale.) Following quotation, p. 302.

p. 341n **Haight indicates that the *Punch* circle**—Haight, p. 327, n. 3.

p. 342 **Lewes was pleased**—Lewes's Journal for Geneva and Paris, 26–28 June 1860; also, *Letters*, III, 308–309. (MS: Yale.)

p. 344 **"big boy Charley"**—*Letters*, III, 324, 14 July 1860. (MS: Yale.)

p. 344n **"each other's self"**—*Letters*, III, 336. (MS: Yale.) Following quotation, p. 338.

p. 344 **"remarkable sense of duty"**—*Letters*, III, 324, 14 July 1860. (MS: Yale.)

p. 344 **"like the rest of us"**—*Letters*, III, 329, 6 August 1860, to Sara Hennell. (MS: Yale.)

p. 346 **"my maiden name"**—*Letters*, III, 398. Following quotation, *Letters*, III, 397. (These letters derive from Cross, II, pp. 294–95, 296–97.)

p. 346 **Eliot decided to tip her hand**—*Letters*, III, 339. (MS: National Library of Scotland.)

p. 347 **"the author's resources"**—*Letters*, III, 355, 1 November 1860. (MS: National Library of Scotland.)

p. 347 **not bother herself with doubts**—As per custom, Lewes protected her from hostile reviews, from the one in the *Quarterly Review*, for example, although he did report one aspect of it to her. She is amused at the attack on the classical quotations in her work as lacking accuracy, when, in fact, there is only one such quotation, from Sophocles' *Philoctetes*, in "Amos Barton." She sees this as the false pedantry befitting reviewers.

p. 347 **"except my niece Emily"**—*Letters*, III, 358, 13 November 1860. (MS: Yale.) This should be compared to the invitation to Maria Congreve to spend the night: "There is a bed ready for you" (19 October 1860).

p. 347 **"working well again"**—Journal (Yale).

p. 348 **"frivolous women would do"**—*Letters*, III, 367, 26 December 1860. (MS: in private hands.)

p. 349 **"popular stories going"**—*Letters*, III, 371, 12 January 1861, Eliot to John Blackwood. (MS: National Library of Scotland.)

p. 349 **wedded to Eliot herself**—In one of those curious historical parallels, the Polish novelist Józef Ignacy Kraszewski (1812–87) wrote a novel called *Jermola, the Potter*. Jermola, a despairing, solitary type, lives alone in a remote house, but when he finds an infant under an oak tree, his despondency is relieved. He becomes a potter and makes a living for himself and the boy. When the parents turn up, they reclaim their son, only to have Jermola and the boy run off into the woods. The boy dies of hardship, and Jermola ends up as a hermit. Although the Eliot and Kraszewski versions differ, they both offer the chance of recovery through an act of nature, the wonder of a small child. Eliot's sense of redemption is triumphant, however, whereas Kraszewski saw destiny differently.

p. 351 **"perfect studies in fact"**—*Letters*, III, 379, 19 February 1861. (MS: National Library of Scotland.) Following quotation, p. 380.

p. 351 **"natural human relations"**—*Letters*, III, 382, 24 February 1861. (MS: National Library of Scotland.) Also, following quotation. This latter quotation firmly connects Eliot's recollection to Wordsworth's poem "Resolution and Independence," where the narrator gains confidence in himself when he sees the proud independence of a poor wanderer.

p. 355 **"something worth reading"**—*Critical Heritage*, p. 179. Following quotation, p. 185.

14: *The Question of* Romola

p. 360 **"a dread of failure"**—Cross, II, p. 222. Following quotation, p. 224.

p. 360 **"for a new edition"**—Cross, II, p. 229. Following quotation, p. 242.

p. 360 **"increase the depression"**—Cross, II, p. 249.

p. 360 **"not yet done"**—Cross, II, p. 252; also, Eliot's Journal (Yale).

p. 361 **impeded by ill health**—Even on the trip out, from Nice, she wrote Charles Lewes about the couple's mutual ill health. But, she says, "I happen to be the stronger man of the two today—poor Pater being headachy and bilious" (*Letters*, III, 408, 25 April 1861). Yet she then launches into aspects of their travels which describe two adolescents out for a frolic.

p. 362n **"life to the picture"**—*Letters*, III, 427, 15 June 1861. (MS: National Library of Scotland.) Earlier comment about Italian, *Letters*, III, 430, 28 June 1861. (MS: National Library of Scotland.)

p. 364 **"disturbing his rest"**—*Letters*, III, 8 July 1861. (MS: Yale.) Also, preceding quotation.

p. 366 **"other outside enjoyments"**—*Letters*, III, 449, 26 August 1861. (MS: Yale.)

p. 367 **She explained to the firm**—*Letters*, VIII, 292, 17 October 1861. (MS: National Library of Scotland.)

p. 368 **"yet made for a novel"**—Lewes's Journal (Yale), 27 February 1862.

p. 368 **"quite a secret"**—*Letters*, IV, 15, 22 February 1962.

p. 368 **"on the subject"**—*Letters*, IV, 18. (MS: National Library of Scotland.)

p. 369n **"ever offered for fiction"**—*Letters*, IV, 28, 1 May 1862. (MS: Coventry City Libraries.)

p. 369 **"slow, and inefficient"**—*Letters*, IV, 34, 17 May 1862. (Lewes's Journal, Yale.)

p. 369 **"my books to you"**—*Letters*, IV, 35, 19 May 1862. (Copy: National Library of Scotland.)

p. 370 **"have much more"**—*Letters*, IV, 36, 20 May 1862. (MS: National Library of Scotland.)

p. 370n **"ones are vulgar"**—*Letters*, IV, 38, 25 May 1862. (MS: National Library of Scotland.) Also following quotation.

p. 370 **"shall like very much"**—Haight, pp. 356–57.

p. 370 **"and of execution"**—Eliot's Journal (Yale), 10 June 1862; also, *Letters*, IV, 42.

p. 371 **"and came away"**—*Letters*, IV, 44, 18 June 1862, John to William Blackwood. (MS: National Library of Scotland.)

p. 371 **"for the same public"**—*Letters*, IV, 49, 14 July 1862. (MS: Carl Pforzheimer Library.) Also, following quotation.

p. 372 **"our fire-side affections"**—*Letters*, IV, 68, 28 November 1862. (Copy: Tinker Collection, Yale.) Also, following quotation.

p. 372 **Cross reports her later remark**—Cross, II, p. 265.

p. 372 **"the slightest provocation"**—*Letters*, IV, 75, 2 February 1863, to Sara Hennell. (MS: Yale.)

p. 373 **"ill and alarmed"**—See Eliot's Journal (Yale), 16 March–16 April 1863, for these statements of malaise for her and Lewes.

p. 373 **"in great excitement" she has killed Tito**—Eliot's Journal (Yale), 6–18 May 1863.

p. 373n **in Latin and Italian**—For a discussion of the unused epigraphs to *Romola*, see the Penguin edition, edited by Andrew Sanders, pp. 682–85.

p. 376 **"figure in the book"**—*Critical Heritage*, p. 204. Also, following quotation.

p. 376 **defends her concentration on details**—One such area of detail: The classical allusions in *Romola* become a parade of learning—and mislearning—for Eliot. One example of classical use, as mentioned above, came in her original plan to use Latin and Italian, also possibly Greek, quotations as epigraphs for each chapter, after the Proem and up to Chapter 9. Once the serial started, however, she realized that such epigraphs served no function and she abandoned the plan. Some of the quotations she dropped derived from Machiavelli, the historian Benedetto Varchi (whom she drew upon heavily), Dante, Pulci, Tacitus, and others. The study of Greek plays through Tito's speech, and it is of course the basis for Baldassarre's credentials as a scholar. Her use of the Greek background gets her into difficulty because, as Richard Jenkyns observes, her descriptions are more Byronic or mid-nineteenth century than ancient Greece. Her larger error in this passion for detail came in her failure to recognize the mystical nature of the period—its neo-Platonism, the presence of Pico della Mirandello and Ficino—while she pursued rational, logical arguments from her own age. Jenkyns says Bardo sounds like "a Victorian free-thinker," whose son has become a friar and been disowned for having rejected "the clear light of reason and philosophy. . . ." (Richard Jenkyns, *The Victorians and Ancient Greeks;* Cambridge: Harvard University Press, 1980.)

p. 376 **"to find a voice"**—*Letters*, IV, 97. (Cross, II, pp. 360–63.)

p. 376 **"not on the public"**—*Letters*, IV, 58, 12 September 1862. (MS: Coventry City Libraries.)

p. 377 **Browning now became a visitor**—Browning wrote to Eliot (2 August) to eulogize *Romola:* ". . . to express my gratitude for the noblest and most heroic-prose-poem [cf. his *The Ring and the Book* later in the decade] that I have ever read." He says he regrets having to go away without being able to finish the book (*Letters*, IV, 96, 2 August 1863; MS: Tinker Collection, Yale).

p. 377 **"are settled again"**—*Letters*, IV, 94, 30 July 1863. (Cross, II, pp. 359–60.)

p. 378 **"and possible practice"**—*Letters*, IV, 106, 1 September 1863. (MS: Yale.)

p. 378 **"apart from the upholstery"**—*Letters*, IV, 113, 14 November 1863, to Cara Bray. (MS: Yale.)

p. 379 **Eliot wrote to his son**—*Letters*, IV, 133–34. (MS: in private hands.) All quotations from that.

p. 379 **"two thousand years hence"**—*Letters*, IV, 139, 23 March 1864. (Cross, II, pp. 380–81.)

p. 381 **"expectation of marriage"**—Cross, III, pp. 42–43.

p. 382 **"to be fulfilled there"**—*Letters*, IV, 154, 24 June 1864. (Copy: Tinker Collection, Yale.)

p. 382 **"we may never see"**—Ibid., p. 155.

p. 382 **"bit of human goodness"**—*Letters*, IV, 156, 25 June 1864, to Sara Hennell. (MS: Yale.)

p. 384 **"swamp of miseries"**—Journal (Yale), 23 November–15 December 1864.

p. 384 **"mode of their action"**—*Selected Essays*, p. 393.

p. 385n **"Ordering and Creating God"**—Quoted in Paul Kennedy, *The Rise and Fall of the Great Powers* (New York: Random House, 1992), p. 158.

p. 385 **"their lives respectable"**—Pinney, p. 396.

p. 385n **written before the novel**—The argument in favor of "before" derives from "The Genesis of *Felix Holt*" by Fred G. Thompson, *Publications of the Modern Language Association of America* (December 1959). The argument that it may have come much later is held by Peter Coveney in his Penguin edition of *Felix Holt* (Middlesex, England, 1972), pp. 639–40.

15: *Out of the Valley with* Felix

p. 388 ***being* a salvation"**—*Letters*, IV, 183, 18 March 1865. (MS: Yale.)

p. 389 **"with brass buttons"**—*Felix Holt* (Penguin ed.), pp. 77–78.

p. 391 **as a valuable source**—See Haight, p. 382n.

p. 391 **"small money subscription"**—*Letters*, IV, 200, 1 June 1865. (Cross, II, pp. 406–408.)

p. 392 **a flurry of letters**—Beginning with one on 14 September 1865, there are ten in about a three-month period. All this occurred while she was going to sources for *Felix Holt*, to the blue books making up *Reports from the Select Committee on Bribery at Elections*, published in 1835. Several Victorian novelists used blue books as research materials—including Charles Reade, Dickens, Wilkie Collins—but none worked over election bribery the way Eliot did. Whereas she used the material for research purposes, Dickens often used it for parody, as in *Bleak House* and *Hard Times*.

p. 395 **"making her any happier"**—*Felix Holt*, p. 97. Following quotation, pp. 106–107.

p. 397 **"from a bilious attack"**—*Letters*, IV, 219, 12 January 1866. (MS: Tinker Collection, Yale.)

p. 398 **"most memorable drama"**—*Letters*, IV, 221, 18 January 1866. (MS: Tinker Collection, Yale.)

p. 398 **"precious and strengthening"**—*Letters*, IV, 221. (MS: Tinker Collection, Yale.) Following quotations, pp. 221, 222.

p. 398 **"sighed for as unattainable"**—*Letters*, IV, 231, 31 January 1866. (MS: Tinker Collection, Yale.)

p. 399 **"from bodily malaise"**—*Letters*, IV, 232, 12 February 1866. (MS: Yale.)

p. 399 **"and uninterrupted companionship"**—Journal (Yale), 7–8 March 1866.

p. 399 **"been more perfect"**—*Letters*, IV, 235, 9 April 1866, to Sara Hennell. (MS: Yale.)

p. 399 **"worse than either"**—*Letters*, IV, 236, 10 April 1866. (MS: in private hands.)

p. 400 **"how good your politics are"**—*Letters*, IV, 246, 26 April 1866. (MS: National Library of Scotland.) Previous quotations, pp. 244, 245.

p. 400n **"ordinary Novel interest"**—*Letters*, IV, 243, 24 April 1866, to Lewes. (MS: in private hands.)

p. 401 **"strictly a secret"**—*Letters*, IV, 247, 26 April 1866. (MS: National Library of Scotland.)

p. 401 **"serious and sincere"**—*Letters*, IV, 247–48, 27 April 1866. (MS: National Library of Scotland.)

p. 401 **"terrible fidget"**—*Letters*, IV, 251, 31 April 1866. (MS: National Library of Scotland.)

p. 401 **if she wishes it**—In a further letter, Blackwood amusingly reveals his social sensibilities, that if something is unpleasant, it is better to sweep it under the carpet. He says the historian John Hill Burton told him that no prisoner escaped hard labor, and the general picture of convict life "is something too horrible to think of, so that the best way is touch as lightly as possible upon it" (*Letters*, IV, 257, 9 May 1866). Burton further said that if Eliot made mistakes, no one would know it—just as no one picked up the absurd errors made by Charles Reade in his account of prison life in the highly acclaimed *It's Never Too Late to Mend*. As a rule, Eliot muted extreme unpleasantness, although in "Janet's Repentance" she had revealed drunkenness leading to domestic brutality and violence.

p. 402 **"disadvantage of his reprint"**—*Letters*, IV, 258, 10 May 1866, to John Blackwood. (MS: National Library of Scotland.)

p. 403 **"writing a serious matter"**—Lewes's Journal (Yale), 1–7 June 1866; also, *Letters*, IV, 265. Following quotation, p. 267.

p. 403n **James finally meet Eliot**—James's remarks come in a letter to his father, Henry James, Sr., 10 May 1869. (MS: Harvard.)

p. 404 **In faulting the political aspects**—For James's remarks on *Felix Holt*, see *Critical Heritage*, pp. 273ff. His emphasis on her as a feminine writer comes on page 277.

p. 405 **To cap the spate of fine reviews**—John Morley, in the *Saturday Review*, and himself a Radical (Liberal) politician at the beginning of his career, saw Eliot as an excellent genre artist, like the Dutch painter Teniers. Morley, however, went further than this and perceived in her work as a whole "the evil usage which women receive at the hands of men." Like Maggie and Romola, Mrs. Transome illustrates "the curse which a man can be to a woman." R. H. Hutton, in the *Spectator*, found this the least melancholy of Eliot's novels. In the influential *Times*, E. F. Dallas said that whereas Jane Austen has had first place among "lady novelists," a greater one has now arisen in George Eliot. Dallas places her firmly among "women novelists." Yet once he left the gender issue, he was quite perceptive in seeing that *Felix Holt*, while occurring in the immediate Reform Bill period, was less concerned with political events than with "the exhibition of men as they conduct themselves in a political struggle. . . ." (See *Critical Heritage*, pp. 265ff.)

p. 405 **"throbbing and palpitation"**—*Letters*, IV, 267, 5 June 1866, to Cara Bray. (MS: Yale.)

p. 407 **"but to shun base joy"**—*The Spanish Gypsy*, Book I, in *Collected Poems*, ed. Lucien Jenkins (London: Skoob Books, 1989), pp. 313ff.

p. 408 **"stock of health"**—*Letters*, IV, 277, 23 June 1866, to John Blackwood. (MS: National Library of Scotland.)

p. 408 **"at the monster speedily"**—*Letters*, IV, 279. (MS: National Library of Scotland.) Also, previous and following quotations.

p. 409 **In his letter to Charles**—*Letters*, IV, 283–84, 15 July 1866, to Charles and his wife. Also, following quotation about Frankfurt.

p. 409 **"but in measure—a drama"**—*Letters*, IV, 286, 19 July 1866. (MS: Tinker Collection, Yale.) Also, following quotations.

p. 410 **"of our familiar life"**—Ibid., p. 287. Also, following quotation.

p. 410 **"and half by priests"**—*The Spanish Gypsy*, Book I, in *Collected Poems*, pp. 337–38.

p. 411n **"growing out of barbarism"**—*Letters*, IV, 292, 25 July 1866, to John Blackwood. (MS: National Library of Scotland.)

p. 412 **"hidden waters lie"**—*The Spanish Gypsy*, Book I, in *Collected Poems*, p. 360. Also, following quotations.

p. 412 **"issue very doubtfully"**—*Letters*, IV, 301. (MS: Tinker Collection, Yale.)

p. 413 **"Spanish history and literature"**—*Letters*, IV, 305, 6 September 1866, to John Blackwood. (MS: National Library of Scotland.)

p. 413 **need for intense concentration**—For a sympathetic and perceptive discussion of Eliot's relationship to her stepsons, see Rosemarie Bodenheimer's *The Real Life of Mary Ann Evans: George Eliot, Her Letters and Fiction* (Ithaca: Cornell University Press, 1994), Chapter 7, "George Eliot's Stepsons," pp. 189–231.

p. 414 **"theories of politics"**—*Letters*, IV, 313, 2 November 1866, to John Blackwood. (MS: National Library of Scotland.)

p. 416 **"strive to get it"**—*Letters*, IV, 316, 7 December 1866. (MS: Yale.)

p. 417 **Lewes apparently was not impressed**—Remarks from Lewes's Journal (Yale), from Paris, 29–31 December 1866; also, *Letters*, IV, 327ff.

p. 417 **"contributed to my life"**—*Letters*, IV, 333, 16 January 1867.

p. 418 **"lost his old spirits"**—*Letters*, IV, 335, 22 January 1867, to Frederick Lehmann, her husband. Following quotation, p. 336.

p. 418 **"shadows of an exquisite blue"**—*Letters*, IV, 338, 2 February 1867, to Barbara Bodichon. (MS: in private hands.)

p. 419 **"very near my heart"**—*Letters*, IV, 347, 21 February 1867, to John Blackwood. (MS: Parrish Collection, Princeton.) Her identification of the work came on 21 March 1867 (*Letters*, IV, 354); following quotations are from that letter, pp. 354, 355.

p. 420 **"in looking at it"**—*Letters*, IV, 357. (MS: National Library of Scotland.)

p. 420 **"privileged creatures"**—*Letters*, IV, 358, 12 April 1867, to D'Albert-Durade. (Copy: Tinker Collection, Yale.)

16: *Maturity*

p. 422 **"tenderness in man"**—*Letters*, IV, 364, 14 May 1867. Following quotation, p. 365.

p. 423 **"unrighteous power"**—*Letters*, IV, 366, 30 May 1867. Also, following quotations.

p. 423 **"or done wretchedly"**—*Letters*, IV, 425, 28? March 1868, to Barbara Bodichon. (MS: in private hands.) Also, following quotations.

p. 423 **"Address to Working Men"**—This is most accessible in the Penguin edition of *Felix Holt*, or in Pinney's edition of her essays.

p. 424 **"in preventing injury"**—Pinney, pp. 416–17. For following quotations, see Pinney, pp. 418ff; *Selected Essays*, pp. 607–27.

p. 428 **"to take into account"**—*Letters*, IV, 377, 26 July 1867. (MS: in private hands.) Also, following quotation.

p. 428 **"by the feminine character"**—*Letters*, IV, 468, 8 August 1868. Also, following quotation.

p. 429 **"as it subsides"**—The notebook is at Yale, but the material is more accessible in *Selected Essays* and in Pinney. This and following quotations, Pinney, 433ff.

p. 431 **"after-dinner political speeches"**—*Letters*, IV, 385, 13 August 1867, to Emanuel Deutsch. (MS: Clark Memorial Library, California.) All immediate quotations from this letter.

p. 431 **"would be less important"**—*Letters*, IV, 396, 9 November 1867. (MS: National Library of Scotland.)

p. 432 **"care most to influence"**—Ibid., p. 397.

p. 432 **"more on that head"**—*Letters*, IV, 403, 6 December 1867. (MS: National Library of Scotland.)

p. 432 **"the well-meaning Radical"**—*Letters*, IV, 404, 7 December 1867. (MS: National Library of Scotland.)

p. 433 **"we could become"**—*Letters*, IV, 411, 28 December 1867. (MS: National Library of Scotland.)

p. 433 **"under the leaden sky"**—*Letters*, IV, 413, 30 December 1867. Also, following quotation.

p. 433 **"state of delight"**—*Letters*, IV, 30 December 1867, to John Blackwood. (MS: National Library of Scotland.) Also, following quotations.

p. 434 **"be divined by outsiders"**—*Letters*, IV, 413, 30 December 1867. See also Haight, p. 415n.

p. 435 **the firm should first announce it**—*Letters*, IV, 428, 4? April 1868, to John Blackwood. (MS: National Library of Scotland.) For further comments on the dramatic poem, see Eliot's letter to Blackwood for 21 April, *Letters*, IV, 431.

p. 437 **"readable and debatable"**—Letters, IV, 438, 7 May 1868. (MS: Yale.)

p. 437 **her personal stake in *Gypsy***—As the book was going through production, Richard Simpson, the brother of a Blackwood's clerk, and a cabinetmaker interested in design, told William Blackwood (John's nephew) repeatedly that the binding of *Gypsy* was full of tasteless ornamentation. He found fault with the gilt side, and criticized the back as suitable, perhaps, for a volume on the architecture of Spain. He felt something light and graceful was called for. "The sight of this," he writes, "would I suspect give George Eliot a sick headache." Letters, IV, 439, 9 May 1868, George Simpson to William Blackwood. (MS: National Library of Scotland.) Simpson's remarks bore results, because the bookbinder, James Frederick Burn, eventually designed a quite tasteful binding, and one that satisfied Eliot.

p. 438 **"do not exactly know"**—Harrison's remarks here and elsewhere derive mainly from his lengthy letter of 11 November 1868, *Letters*, IV, 483ff.

p. 439 **"dispositions and motives"**—*Letters*, IV, 472, August 1868. Also, following quotations. Her reference to a "shifting compromise" recalls the monumental theological struggles in the Oxford Movement in the 1830s and early 1840s which resulted in Newman leaving the Anglican Church for the Roman Catholic faith. The movement continued to reverberate at the level of distinctions between one theological position and others in the subsequent conversion of Henry Edward Manning, archdeacon of the Anglican Church, who went over to Catholicism and became a cardinal. His career is amusingly unrolled by Lytton Strachey as the first of his *Eminent Victorians* (1918).

p. 441 **"no social position to maintain"**—*Letters*, V, 7, 29 January 1869, Norton to George William Curtis.

p. 441 **"social morals in England"**—Ibid., p. 8. Also, following quotation on Lewes.

p. 442 **"dull eyes, heavy features"**—Ibid., p. 9. Also, following quotation.

p. 443 **"what is to follow after"**—Notebook (Berg).

p. 444 **"will not be barren"**—*Letters*, IV, 481, 21 October 1868, to John Blackwood. (MS: National Library of Scotland.) Also, following quotation.

p. 444 **"real outcome of life"**—*Letters*, IV, 488, 16 November 1868, to Barbara Bodichon. (MS: in private hands.)

p. 444n **"the point to you"**—*Letters*, IV, 492, 12 December 1868. (MS: National Library of Scotland.)

p. 445 **"unworthy of them"**—*Letters*, IV, 501, 31 December 1868. (MS: National Library of Scotland.)

p. 445 **"at present be very rare"**—*Letters*, IV, 499, 30 December 1868. (MS: Fitzwilliam Museum, Cambridge, England.)

p. 446 **"damp to the touch"**—*The Diary of Alice James*, ed. Leon Edel (New York: Dodd, Mead & Co., 1964), p. 116.

17: *Toward* Middlemarch

p. 452 **"for a complete embodiment"**—*Letters*, V, 16, 19 February 1869, to John Blackwood. (MS: National Library of Scotland.)

p. 454 **"used to our trouble"**—*Letters*, V, 35, 11 May 1869, to John Blackwood. (MS: Yale.)

p. 454 **"broken into small fragments"**—*Letters*, V, 44, 13 June 1869. (MS: Yale.)

p. 454 **"in the development"**—Eliot's Journal (Yale), 2 December 1870; see also Journal for 31 December 1870; also, *Letters*, V, 124, 127.

p. 456 **"difficulty of the human lot"**—*Letters*, V, 31, 8 May 1869. (MS: in private hands.) Also, following quotation.

p. 457 **the matter ends there**—See Haight, p. 39n.

p. 458 **"as impudent imposture"**—*Letters*, V, 48–49, 11 July 1869. (MS: in private hands.) Also following quotation.

p. 459n **The phrase derives from Goethe**—Ibid., p. 49, n. 2.

p. 459 **"visible danger"**—*Letters*, V, 51, 5 August 1869, to John Blackwood. (MS: Nuneaton Public Library.)

p. 459n **"influence of a plan"**—*A Century of George Eliot Criticism*, ed. Gordon Haight (Boston: Houghton Mifflin, 1965), p. 81.

p. 460 **"rapid assimilation"**—*Letters*, V, 57, 4 October 1869. (MS: in private hands.)

p. 461 **"new passion and new joy"**—*Collected Poems*, p. 114; previous quotation, p. 111.

p. 461 **"amid their poverty"**—*Collected Poems*, p. 114.

p. 462 **"make manhood whole"**—*Collected Poems*, p. 86.

p. 463 **"when my brother came"**—*Collected Poems*, p. 89.

p. 463 **"relationship with death"**—*Letters*, V, 70, 25 November 1869. (MS: Huntington Library.)

p. 463 **"love on my dear boy"**—*Letters*, V, 66, 14 November 1869. (MS: National Library of Scotland.)

p. 464 **"being in the country"**—*Letters*, V, 67, 15 November 1869. (MS: Yale.)

p. 464 **"his egoism would demand"**—*Letters*, V, 69, 22 November 1869.

p. 464 **"very deeply into me"**—*Letters*, V, 71, 10 December 1869. (Copy: Tinker Collection, Yale.) Following quotations, pp. 71–72.

p. 465 **"it creeps on"**—*Letters*, V, 81, 7 March 1870, to John Blackwood. (MS: National Library of Scotland.) Also, following quotation.

p. 466 **"to have a peck at her"**—*Letters*, V, 83, 28 March 1870, Lewes to Mrs. John Willim. (MS: in private hands.)

p. 466 **"without hideous studies"**—*Letters*, V, 86, 3 April 1870, to Maria Congreve.

p. 467 **"English provincial life"**—*Letters*, V, 99, 23 May 1870, John Blackwood to nephew William Blackwood. (MS: National Library of Scotland.)

p. 467 **"As doll-clothes fit a man"**—*Collected Poems*, p. 144.

p. 468 **"some of her best work"**—Mrs. Humphrey word *A Writer's Recollections* (1918), pp. 107–10; also, Haight, pp. 426–8. Following quotation, *Recollections*, pp. 109–10.

p. 469 **Eliot's own Oxford journal**—Journal (Yale), 25–28 May 1870.

p. 470 **"with the words 'I drift—I drift' "**—*Letters*, V, 102, 13 June 1870, to Sara Hennell. (MS: Yale.)

p. 470 **"that conquer death"**—*Letters*, VIII, 481, 15 July 1870, Lewes to Robert Lytton. (MS: in private hands.) Following quotation, p. 482.

p. 470 **"you will accept it"**—*Letters*, VIII, 482–83, 2 August 1870. (MS: Yale.) Also, previous quotation.

p. 471 **"common treasure of mankind"**—*Letters*, V, 113, 25 August 1870, from Limpsfield. (MS: in private hands.)

p. 472 **"headache and depression"**—Journal (Yale), 27 October 1870.

p. 472 **"of lingering pain"**—*Letters*, V, 122, 18 November 1870, to Sara Hennell. (MS: Yale.)

p. 472 **If we consult the "Quarry"**—The "Quarry" was purchased by Amy Lowell and left to Harvard University. See Anna Theresa Kitchel, *George Eliot's Quarry for "Middlemarch"* (Los Angeles: University of California Press, 1950).

p. 476 **"in a miniature way"**—*Letters*, V, 131, 2 January 1871, to Sara Hennell. (MS: Yale.)

p. 476 **"short lives"**—*Letters*, V, 120, 15 November 1870, to Mrs. Mark Pattison. (MS: British Museum.)

p. 476n **"is to like him"**—*Letters*, IX, 21, 24 July 1871. (MS: Yale.)

p. 477 **"talk and excitement"**—*Letters*, V, 144, 26 April 1871, to Charles Lewes. (MS: in private hands.)

p. 478 **"will be *Miss Brooke"***—*Letters*, V, 146, 7 May 1871, to John Blackwood. (MS: National Library of Scotland.) Also, following quotations.

p. 479 **"clear and distinct"**—*Letters*, V, 148, 2 June 1871, John Blackwood to Eliot. (Draft: National Library of Scotland.)

p. 479 **"enjoying life here immensely"**—*Letters*, V, 153, 17 June 1871. (MS: in private hands.)

p. 480 **"is to Nature"**—*Letters*, V, 167, 20 July 1871. (MS: National Library of Scotland.)

p. 480 **"compassed about with fears"**—*Letters*, V, 168–69, 24 July 1871. (MS: National Library of Scotland.)

p. 481n **"slighting word about Scott"**—*Letters*, V, 175, 9 August 1871. (MS: Yale.)

p. 482 **"run a great coup"**—*Letters*, V, 183, 6 September 1871, John Blackwood to Lewes. (MS: National Library of Scotland.)

p. 482 **"not to be neglected"**—*Letters*, V, 184, 7 September 1871, Lewes to John Blackwood.

18: Middlemarch

p. 485 **"put out the gas"**—Haight reproduces this note, p. 440, n. 4.

p. 486 **"trained in a hospital"**—*Letters*, V, 197, 6 October 1871, to Cara Bray. (MS: Yale.)

p. 486 **"at Dodo once more"**—*Letters*, V, 201, 12 October 1871.

p. 487 **omit the "Prelude" given the choice**—*Letters*, V, 207, 25 October 1871, to John Blackwood. (MS: National Library of Scotland.)

p. 487 **"mere borrowing and echo"**—*Letters*, V, 212, 9 November 1871.

p. 488 **analogies and parallels made sense**—For this and related matters, see *George Eliot and Herbert Spencer: Feminism, Evolutionism, and the Reconstruction of Gender* (Princeton, N.J.: Princeton University Press, 1991).

p. 488 **"terror of the *unwritten"***—*Letters*, V, 237, 18 January 1872. (MS: National Library of Scotland.) Also, following quotation.

p. 489n **as Jerome Beaty points out**—In his study *Middlemarch from Notebook to Novel* (Urbana: University of Illinois Press, 1960).

p. 490 **Eliot's words to Blackwood**—*Letters*, V, 231, 1 January 1872. (MS: National Library of Scotland.) All quotations about Christmas.

p. 491 **"beautiful all over"**—*Letters*, V, 235, 17 January 1872. (MS: National Library of Scotland.)

p. 491 **"we live in!"**—*Letters*, V, 238, 22 January 1872.

p. 491 **"a crawling life"**—*Letters*, V, 242, 29 January 1872. (MS: Yale.)

p. 491 **"our spiritual companionship"**—*Letters*, V, 244, 1 February 1872. (MS: British Museum.)

p. 492 **"ingeniously self tormentings"**—*Letters*, V, 246, 13 February 1872. (MS: National Library of Scotland.)

p. 493 **"the lowest charlatanerie"**—*Letters*, V, 253, 4 March 1872. Also, following quotation.

p. 494 **"to be impossible"**—*Letters*, V, 280, 24 June 1872. Following quotations, pp. 281–82.

p. 495 **"very sorry for him"**—*Letters*, V, 332, ? October 1872. (Copy: Yale.)

p. 495 **"like saying so"**—*Letters*, V, 254–55, 12 March 1872. (MS: National Library of Scotland.)

p. 496 **"in mental sunshine"**—*Letters*, V, 261, 29 March 1872. (MS: in private hands.) Also, previous quotations.

p. 496 **"wish to see me"**—*Letters*, V, 273, 21 May 1872. (MS: in private hands.)

p. 497 **"obstinate devil"**—*Letters*, V, 293, 29 July 1872. (MS: National Library of Scotland.)

p. 498 **"my work more seriously"**—*Letters*, V, 296, 4 August 1872. Also, previous quotations. The "unredeemed tragedy" Eliot refers to could be located in Casaubon and Lydgate. For an excellent discussion of this and related points, see W. J. Harvey, "The Intellectual Background of the Novel: Casaubon and Lydgate," in *Middlemarch: Critical Approaches to the Novel*, ed. Barbara Hardy (London: Athlone Press, 1967), pp. 25–37.

p. 499 **"my head above water"**—*Letters*, V, 301, 19? August 1872. (MS: Tinker Collection, Yale.)

p. 500 **"It is noble"**—*Letters*, V, 307, 6 September 1872. (MS: National Library of Scotland.)

p. 500 **"hysterical fit from the shock"**—Lewes's Diary (Yale), 13–17 September 1872. Also, following quotation.

p. 501 **"name for such places"**—*Letters*, V, 312, 25 September 1872. (MS: Tinker Collection, Yale.)

p. 501n **"place will be delightful"**—*Letters*, V, 314, 4 October 1872. (MS: Parrish Collection, Princeton.)

p. 502 **"one wants in them"**—*Letters*, V, 318, 27 October 1872. (MS: Tinker Collection, Yale.)

p. 503 **"fall on human weakness"**—All quotations from *Critical Heritage*, pp. 294ff. For the later *Spectator* review, see p. 314.

p. 503n **"primarily works of art"**—*Critical Heritage*, p. 321.

p. 505 **"in common fashion"**—18 January 1881, Folio 88. (MS: Bodleian Library, Oxford.)

p. 506 **"imaginative psychological study"**—*Critical Heritage*, p. 323. Following quotations, p. 326.

p. 506 **"contemporary consciousness"**—*Critical Heritage*, p. 332. Also, following quotation.

p. 512n **"loudly-asserted beliefs"**—Henry James, in one respect, updated *Middlemarch* in his *The Portrait of a Lady*, with Isabel Archer making a similar mistake with Gilbert Osmond. In both novels, images abound of imprisonment and coldness, of shadows and darkness, of stiflement of self.

p. 512n **"even more melancholy"**—Virginia Woolf, *The Common Reader* (New York: Harcourt, 1925), p. 174.

p. 514 **could have brought forth such a work**—Haight, p. 445.

p. 514 **"great intellectual effort"**—14 August 1872, Haight, p. 451.

p. 515 **"it is wrought out"**—*Letters*, V, 324, 4 November 1872. (MS: Yale.) Also, following quotations.

p. 515 **"not at all happy"**—*Letters*, V, 326, 14 November 1872. Also, following quotations.

p. 515 **"character and position"**—*Letters*, V, 334, 1 December 1872, to John Blackwood. (MS: National Library of Scotland.)

p. 516 **"formed out of nothing"**—*Letters*, V, 338, 5 December 1872, Lewes to Alexander Main.

p. 516 **"My dear Nephew"**—*Letters*, V, 340, 11 December 1872. (MS: Yale.)

p. 516 **"pasture very well"**—*Letters*, V, 344, 16 December 1872, to Mrs. Mark Pattison. (MS: British Museum.)

p. 517 **"exercised for good"**—*Letters*, V, 353, 31 December 1872, from John Blackwood.

p. 517 **"for the last week"**—Journal (Yale), 1 January 1873; also, *Letters*, V, 357.

p. 518 **"top of the wave"**—*Letters*, V, 365, 8 January 1873, Lewes to John Blackwood. (MS: National Library of Scotland.)

p. 518 **"at his own risk"**—*Letters*, V, 369, 17 January 1873. (MS: National Library of Scotland.)

p. 519 **"your character and life"**—*Letters*, V, 372, 24 January 1873.

p. 520 **lace also on top of her head**—Haight, p. 461; originally in the New York *Tribune*, 25 March 1876.

p. 520 **Octavia Hill, wished to devote all her time**—See Haight, p. 460.

p. 521 **"the view rather sublime"**—*Letters*, VI, 46, 9 May 1874.

p. 521 **"horribly painful story"**—*Letters*, V, 379, 26 February 1873. Eliot's response: *Letters*, V, 380, 28 February 1873. (MS: National Library of Scotland.) Quotation that follows from there.

19: *Toward* Deronda

p. 524 **"poetry of the world"**—*Letters*, V, 388, 18 March 1873. (MS: in private hands.)

p. 524 **"lonely of a God"**—*Century Magazine*, XXIII (November 1881), 62–63; also, Haight, p. 464.

p. 525 **"whom it can touch"**—*Letters*, V, 391, 20 March 1873. (MS: Yale.) Also, following quotations.

p. 525 **Blackwood was beginning to let Lewes down**—For this exchange between Blackwood and Lewes, *Letters*, V, 400, 14 April 1873: John Blackwood to Lewes, where he accuses the latter of casting "mankind adrift without religion of any kind," something he cannot imagine any man with "a real head on his shoulders" wishing to do; Blackwood once more to Lewes, *Letters*, V, 410, 24 May 1873; Lewes to Blackwood, *Letters*, V, 413, 25 May 1873.

p. 526 **"women's rights, idealism, etc."**—Haight, p. 465; also, following quotation.

p. 527 **"seeing friends and acquaintances"**—*Letters*, V, 426, 9 August 1873, to Maria Congreve. Also, previous quotation.

p. 527 **Writing to D'Albert-Durade**—On 9 August 1873; *Letters*, V, 427.

p. 528 **"due examination into facts"**—*Letters*, V, 436, 17 September 1873. (MS: Yale.)

p. 528 **"are detestable introductions"**—*Letters*, V, 437, 17 September 1873. (MS: British Museum.) Eliot sent on a "shabby little lock of hair," along with the sentiment that she loved her friend the better for having seen her in the flesh (on 3 October). She signs off, "Yours maternally."

p. 529 **To Mrs. Cross, Eliot expressed**—*Letters*, V, 435, 17 September 1873. (MS: Yale.)

p. 529n **"but negatives to offer"**—*Letters*, V, 448, 19 October 1873. (MS: Yale.)

p. 529 **"would fall in love with"**—*The Letters of John Fiske*, ed. Ethel Fiske (New York: Macmillan, 1940), pp. 277–79, for this and following quotations; also Haight, p. 453; also *Letters*, V, 463–65, 23 November 1873.

p. 530 **"future book so well"**—*Letters*, V, 454, 5 November 1873. (MS: National Library of Scotland.)

p. 531 **"against my own laws"**—*Letters*, V, 459, 12 November 1873. (MS: National Library of Scotland.)

p. 531 **"end in parting"**—Journal (Yale); also, *Letters*, VI, 3, 1 January 1874.

p. 533 **"doing the world a service"**—*Letters*, VI, 15, 10 February 1874, to Sara Hennell. (MS: Yale.)

p. 533 **" 'Boötes, hight to boot the Wain' "**—*Letters*, VI, 22, 20 February 1874. (MS: National Library of Scotland.)

p. 533 **She was reading**—Grätz, *History of the Jews*; Renan, *History of the Semitic Languages*; Stanley, *Bohemian Jews*; Erckmann-Chatrian, *The Polish Jews*; Kompert, *History of a Street*.

p. 536 **"sort of passion in her"**—*Letters*, VI, 47, May 1874. (MS: Parrish Collection, Princeton.) Also, following quotation.

p. 537n **But in acknowledging the poem to Thomson**—*Letters*, VI, 53, 30 May 1874. (MS: Fitzwilliam, Cambridge.)

p. 537 **"unbroken spaces of the day"**—*Letters*, VI, 55, 14 June 1874. (MS: Tinker Collection, Yale.)

p. 537 **"will be drawn off"**—*Letters*, VI, 58, 16 June 1874. (MS: National Library of Scotland.)

p. 538 **"but working like negros"**—*Letters*, VI, 61, 23 June 1874, Lewes to John Blackwood. (MS: National Library of Scotland.)

p. 540 **"their friends' books"**—*Letters*, VI, 76, 8 August 1874, to John Blackwood. (MS: National Library of Scotland.) Also, following quotations.

p. 541 **"somewhat damaged organism"**—*Letters*, VI, 85–86, 26 October 1874. (MS: British Museum.)

p. 541 **"approved by him"**—*Letters*, IX, 138, 11 November 1874. (MS: National Library of Scotland.)

p. 542 **"the swing of atoms"**—*Letters*, VI, 98, 10 December 1874. (MS: Cross, III, 245–50.) Following quotations, pp. 99, 100.

p. 543 **legitimatized by an act of Parliament**—*Letters*, VI, 100, 30 December 1874, Eliot to Frederic Harrison. (MS: Tinker Collection, Yale.)

20: *Summa:* Daniel Deronda

p. 545n **"independence of this judgment"**—*Letters*, VI, 3 January 1875. Also, previous quotations.

p. 546 **"than in one's boots"**—*Letters*, VI, 127, 4 March 1875, to Elma Stuart. (MS: British Museum.)

p. 547 **"still out of health"**—*Letters*, VI, 130, 20 March 1875, to D'Albert-Durade. (Copy: Tinker Collection, Yale.)

p. 548 **"aged and haggard"**—*Letters*, VI, 135, 21 April 1875, William to John Blackwood. (MS: National Library of Scotland.) Also, following quotations.

p. 548n **Haight cites a copy of *Adam Bede***—*Letters*, VI, 137, n. 9.

p. 548 **"leisurely enjoyment"**—*Letters*, VI, 143, 20 May 1875. (MS: National Library of Scotland.)

p. 548 **"fascinating witch"**—*Letters*, VI, 144, 25 May 1875. (MS: National Library of Scotland.) In subsequent letters, John Blackwood dances around the Jewish elements, not too certain what his ground is or should be.

p. 549 **notice of Bertie's death**—Lewes's Diary, 8 July 1875; also, *Letters*, VI, 154, Lewes to Mary Finlay Cross.

p. 550 **"things of daily life"**—*Letters*, VI, 165, 14 August 1875. (MS: Yale.)

p. 550 **"evangelists and ritualists"**—*Letters*, VI, 166, 19 August 1875.

p. 551n **"dislike and unkindness"**—*Letters*, IX, 134–35. This letter was not available to Haight when he wrote his biography, and it points up how her distancing of herself from her family led to her assumption of so many identities.

p. 553 **"comfortable sense"**—*Letters*, VI, 172, 10 October 1875. (MS: National Library of Scotland.)

p. 554 **"aspect of the volumes"**—*Letters*, VI, 186, 17 November 1875. (MS: National Library of Scotland.)

p. 554 **"to be published on February 1"**—*Letters*, VI, 192, 22 November 1875. (MS: National Library of Scotland.)

p. 554 **"Jew boy"**—*Letters*, VI, 195, 30 November 1875. (MS: National Library of Scotland.)

p. 554 **"prejudice against the Jews"**—*Letters*, VI, 196, 1 December 1875. (MS: National Library of Scotland.) Also, following quotations.

p. 555 **"from mysterious regions"**—*Critical Heritage*, p. 363.

p. 555 **"to be true of Middlemarch"**—Journal (Tinker Collection, Yale), 25 December 1875. Also, following quotation. Christmas always brought out her worst doubts about herself and her achievement (see also *Letters*, VI, 201).

p. 555n **"so marvellously before"**—*Letters*, VI, 205, 29 December 1875. (MS: National Library of Scotland.)

p. 556 **"who visit our cell"**—*Letters*, VI, 209, 1 January 1876. (MS: in private hands.)

p. 556 **"than shifting theory"**—*Letters*, VI, 216, 25 January 1876, to Dr. Joseph Frank Payne on the death of his mother. (MS: in private hands.)

p. 556 **"and individual experience"**—Ibid., p. 217.

p. 556 **"near spoiling an artist"**—*Critical Heritage*, p. 428. Following quotations, pp. 420ff. The review article appeared in the *Atlantic Monthly* (December 1876).

p. 557 **"higher strain of ideas"**—*Letters*, VI, 223, 25 February 1876. (MS: National Library of Scotland.) Also, following quotation.

p. 557 **"would be to her!"**—*Letters*, VI, 224, 27 February 1876. (MS: National Library of Scotland.) Also, previous quotations.

p. 559 **"very far from feeling"**—*Letters*, VI, 241, 18 April 1876, to John Blackwood. (MS: National Library of Scotland.)

p. 559 **"pretends to be critical"**—*Letters*, VI, 244–45, 2 May 1876. (MS: Parrish Collection, Princeton.) Also, following quotations.

p. 560 **"to finish effectively"**—*Letters*, VI, 247, 9 May 1876, to John Blackwood. (MS: National Library of Scotland.)

p. 560 **"her work and himself"**—*Letters*, VI, 253, 18 May 1876, John to William Blackwood. (MS: National Library of Scotland.)

p. 561 **"mountains near and distant"**—*Letters*, VI, 265, 6 July 1876, to John Blackwood. (MS: National Library of Scotland.)

p. 561 **Their routine**—Ibid., p. 266. Both Eliot and Lewes wore their routine as a kind of badge of honor. They repeated much the same information to several correspondents; their time of rising differed from account to account, but basic details remained.

p. 561 **Lewes's reply indicated that Eliot**—*Letters*, VI, 274, 17 July 1876, from Hof Ragatz.

p. 562 **"fatigue of years"**—*Letters*, VI, 280, 6 September 1876. (MS: in private hands.)

p. 562 **bombardment of letters**—Also from Jewish figures such as Abram Samuel Isaacs, of the Theological Seminary in Breslau, and Abraham Benisch, editor of the *Jewish Chronicle*.

p. 562 **"under a false impression"**—*Letters*, VI, 286, 24 September 1876, Davies to Annie Crow. Following quotation, p. 287.

p. 563 **"my protest can hinder"**—*Letters*, VI, 289, 2 October 1876. (MS: Jewish Museum, London.) Also, following quotation.

p. 565 **"it has actually met with"**—*Letters*, VI, 301, 29 October 1876. (MS: in private hands.) Following quotations, pp. 301, 302.

p. 566 **"among the clouds of heaven"**—See Marlene Springer's "Stowe and Eliot: An Epistolary Friendship," *Biography* (Winter 1986), IX, 66. The letter is dated 25 September 1876. A good part of the letter is concerned with Stowe's exhortation to Eliot to enjoy "a more positive communion with Him who is immortal youth health strength and vitality" (p. 68).

p. 567 **"not directly concern Gwendolen"**—*Letters*, VI, 303, 29 October 1876. (MS: National Library of Scotland.)

p. 567 **"conscience and refinement"**—*Letters*, VI, 304, 3 November 1876. (MS: National Library of Scotland.) Also, previous quotation.

p. 568 **Haight makes a good case**—Haight, p. 489.

p. 569 **"view of the Jewish character"**—*Letters*, VI, 305, 5 November 1876. (MS: National Library of Scotland.) Also, following quotation.

p. 570 **"have no other trouble"**—*Letters*, VI, 310, 22 November 1876. (MS: Yale.) Also, following quotations.

p. 571n **"mention as a flaw"**—*Letters*, VI, 313, 25 November 1876. (MS: National Library of Scotland.) A further instance of Eliot's interest in Jewish material is found in seven leaves of written material bearing on the Lassalle project, mentioned above, in the Parrish Collection at Princeton. The Pforzheimer Notebooks contain two reading lists, and parts of them serve as background material for the possible project.

21: *Post*-Deronda

p. 577 **"depraved appetite"**—*Letters*, VI, 295, 12 October 1876. (MS: National Library of Scotland.) Edward Dowden, among others, had considered a book on Eliot, but abandoned it. Also, see Eliot's letter to John Blackwood, *Letters*, VI, 350ff., 20 March 1877, for her horror at the revelations in Harriet Martineau's *Autobiography* (3 vols., published 1 March 1877).

p. 579n **"to welcome issues"**—*Letters*, VI, 317, 16 December 1876. (MS: Jewish Museum, London.)

p. 580n **"and pleasant impression"**—*Cosima Wagner's Diaries 1869–1877*, Vol. I (New York: Harcourt Brace Jovanovich, 1976), p. 962.

p. 581 **"out of her gray eyes"**—Haight, p. 504.

p. 581 **"Abode of Snow"**—*Letters*, VI, 358–59, 29 March 1877. (MS: National Library of Scotland.)

p. 582 **"engaged in them"**—*Letters*, VI, 371, 15 May 1877, to Sara Hennell. (MS: Yale.)

p. 584 **"its future publicity"**—Ibid., p. 372.

p. 585 **"dinner-service and paper-hanging"**—*Letters*, VI, 378, 27 May 1877. (MS: British Museum.)

p. 585 **"of being of no use"**—*Letters*, VI, 387, 14 June 1877. (MS: Tinker Collection, Yale.) Following quotation, p. 388.

p. 586n **"Where pleasure charters all"**—*Collected Poems*, p. 183.

p. 586 **"sickness and inability to work"**—*Letters*, VI, 391, 9 July 1877, to John Blackwood. (MS: National Library of Scotland.)

p. 586 **"in delightful alternation"**—*Letters*, VI, 392, 10 July 1877, to Mme. Louis Belloc. (MS: in private hands.)

p. 586 **"perpetual delight"**—*Letters*, VI, 393, 12 July 1877, to Elma Stuart. (MS: British Museum.) Following quotation, p. 394.

p. 588 **"of George Eliot's works"**—*Letters*, VI, 410, 25 October 1877. (National Library of Scotland.) Also, see John to William Blackwood, *Letters*, VI, 405, 15 October 1877. Blackwood's calculations on royalties come in a letter to Lewes, 25 October 1877 (*Letters*, VI, 412).

p. 590 **"in these later years"**—*Letters*, VI, 420, 16 November 1877. (MS: Yale.)

p. 590 **"sources of spiritual good"**—*Letters*, IX, 201, 16 November 1877. (MS: Trinity College, Cambridge.)

p. 591 **"in the book stalls"**—*Letters*, VI, 423, 22 November 1877, to John Blackwood. (MS: National Library of Scotland.) Also, following quotation.

p. 592 **"dolting and feeble"**—*Letters*, VI, 431. (MS: Morgan Library.) Also, previous quotation.

p. 592 **"effect of recurrence"**—*Letters*, VI, 433.

p. 592 **"no corresponding benefit"**—*Letters*, VI, 428, 27 November 1877. (Copy: Tinker Collection, Yale.)

p. 592 **"dark shrivelled berry"**—*Letters*, VI, 430, 3 December 1877, to Mrs. Edward Burne-Jones. (MS: Yale.)

p. 592 **"came to a little"**—Simcox's Autobiography, 12 December 1877, for all quotations.

p. 593 **"each brings with it"**—Eliot's Journal (Yale), 31 December 1877; also, *Letters*, VI, 439–40.

pp. 593–94 **"pale, equine face"**—Cited above.

p. 594 **had remained with her**—She writes of his *Pensées* as reviving "my sense of their deep though broken wisdom" (*Letters*, VII, 11, 26 January 1878).

p. 594 **"as adorable as herself"**—Simcox's Autobiography, entries for 6 and 13 February 1878.

p. 595n **In a parallel view**—See Nancy L. Paxton, *George Eliot and Herbert Spencer* (Princeton, N.J.: Princeton University Press, 1991); also, for related matters, Cynthia Eagle Russett, *Sexual Science: The Victorian Construction of Womanhood* (Cambridge: Harvard University Press, 1989).

p. 595 **"in my churlish habits"**—*Letters*, VII, 19, 9 April 1878, to Lord Houghton.

p. 596 **"read and think over"**—*Letters*, VII, 26, 16 May 1878, to Lewes.

p. 596n **"inward economy all wrong"**—*Letters*, VII, 34, 27 June 1878. (MS: British Museum.)

p. 597n **"merely English presentation"**—*Letters*, VII, 11. (MS: Yale.)

p. 598 **"removal of particular calamities"**—*Letters*, VII, 44, 18 July 1878.

p. 598 **gnawed by rats**—Haight, p. 512.

p. 599 **"will get from democrats"**—*Letters*, VII, 47, 1 August 1878.

p. 600n **"wielding a broom"**—Henry James, *Autobiography*, ed. Frederick W. Dupee (New York: Criterion Books, 1956), pp. 583–84.

p. 600 **"edition is to last"**—*Letters*, VII, 55, 8 August 1878. (MS: National Library of Scotland.)

p. 601 **"intensely happy"**—*Letters*, VII, 15 October 1878, to Barbara Bodichon. (MS: Huntington Library.)

p. 601 **"has now passed by"**—*Letters*, VII, 78, 21 November 1878, to John Blackwood. (MS: National Library of Scotland.)

p. 601 **"grievously ailing"**—*Letters*, VII, 78, 18 November 1878. (MS: Yale.) She adds that "nobody ever committed suicide because the world was full of suffering, unless he felt the fact through some misery of his own."

p. 601 **"companionship with death"**—*Letters*, VII, 84.

p. 602 **"full of wit and wisdom"**—*Letters*, VII, 82, 24 November 1878, John Blackwood to Langford. (MS: National Library of Scotland.)

p. 602 **"first literary men of the day"**—*Letters*, IX, 246, 3 December 1878, Jowett to Eliot. (MS: Balliol, Oxford.)

p. 602n **"with the unconsolable anguish"**—Simcox's Autobiography, 30 November 1878; also, *Letters*, IX, 243.

p. 602 **"from the tenderest touch"**—*Letters*, VII, 93, 7 January 1879. (MS: in private hands.)

p. 602 **"all trivial stuff"**—*Letters*, VII, 93, 13 January 1879. (MS: Yale.)

22: After George Henry Lewes

p. 604 **"things for his sake"**—*Letters*, VII, 99, 30 January 1878. (MS: Yale.) Also, following quotations.

p. 604 **"is a help to me"**—*Letters*, VII, 101. (MS: Yale.) Following quotation, p. 102.

p. 605 **"time of publication comes"**—*Letters*, VII, 108–109, 25 February 1879. (MS: National Library of Scotland.) Also, following quotation.

p. 605n **"characteristic family affectionateness"**—*Such* (Cabinet ed.), p. 253.

p. 606 **"discern them to be illusions"**—*Such*, p. 38.

p. 607n **"my own work at present"**—*Letters*, VII, 115, 9 March 1879. (Copy: Tinker Collection, Yale.)

p. 607 **"the power to do so"**—*Letters*, VII, 122, 25 March 1879, to William Blackwood.

p. 607 **"broken-spirited creature"**—*Letters*, VII, 122, 30 March 1879, to Lydia Maria Child, a Boston abolitionist. (MS: in private hands.)

p. 608 **"Past and the sorrow Present"**—*Letters*, VII, 132, 10 April 1879. (Copy: Yale.) Also, following quotations.

p. 608 **"our nation is indignant"**—*Letters*, VII, 138, 17 April 1879.

p. 608 **"a thrill through me"**—Haight, p. 525.

p. 608 **"dismiss anyone else"**—*Letters*, VII, 138. (MS: Yale.) See also Cross, III, pp. 359–60. The passage on Dante comes from his life of Eliot.

p. 609 **"was over for ever"**—Simcox's Autobiography, 29 April 1879.

p. 609 **"to my country home"**—*Letters*, VII, 143, 28 April 1879, to Barbara Bodichon. (MS: in private hands.)

p. 610 **"nothing but harm"**—*Letters*, VII, 185, 23 July 1879. (MS: in private hands.)

p. 611 **"endure to be loved"**—Simcox's Autobiography, 22 May 1879; also, *Letters*, IX, 269.

p. 612 **"going to a nunnery"**—*Middlemarch*, p. 43.

p. 613 **"in my life before"**—*Letters*, VII, 170, 20 June 1879. (MS: National Library of Scotland.)

p. 613 **"that I lack nothing"**—*Letters*, VII, 174, 29 June 1879. (MS: Yale.)

p. 613 **"even than the Zulu War"**—*Letters*, VII, 183, 16 July 1879, to John Blackwood. (MS: National Library of Scotland.)

p. 613 **"no headache to speak of"**—*Letters*, VII, 179, 7 July 1879. (MS: Yale.)

p. 614 **"from giving her autograph"**—*Letters*, VII, 193, 12 August 1879. (MS: Yale.)

p. 614 **references to John Cross**—Eliot's Diary (Berg Collection) gives some indication of her state of mind at this critical time.

p. 615 **"particular moment thy tender / Beatrice"**—*Letters*, VII, 211–12, 16 October 1879. (MS: Yale.)

p. 616 **"a barren useless survival"**—*Letters*, VII, 225, 22 November 1879. (MS: Yale.)

p. 616 **"should corrupt the inward"**—*Letters*, VII, 233, 24 December 1879, to Elma Stuart. (MS: British Museum.)

p. 617 **"disease of English literature"**—*Letters*, VII, 230, 19 December 1879, to Mrs. Thomas Trollope. (MS: Berg Collection.)

p. 617 **"are enjoying themselves"**—*Letters*, VII, 254, 24 December 1879. (MS: Yale.) She signs off: "Your obliged ex-shareholder of A and C Gaslight and Coke," shares she had sold off two days earlier. Cross is now less than lover, more than banker.

p. 618 **"power and *humour*"**—Haight, p. 534, for this and following quotations; from *Letters of Bret Harte*, ed. G. B. Harte (Boston, 1926), p. 168.

p. 620n **"might write again now"**—Simcox's Autobiography, 7 May 1880; also, *Letters*, IX, 308.

p. 620 **"broken words of love"**—Simcox's Autobiography, 9 March 1880, for this and subsequent quotations; also, *Letters*, IX, 299.

23: *Eliot and Cross:* Liebestod

p. 623 **"gift of love to me"**—*Letters*, VII, 259, 13 April 1880, to Eleanor Cross. (MS: Yale.) Also, following quotation.

p. 623 **"ended a year ago"**—*Letters*, VII, 260, 14? April 1880, to Eleanor Cross. (MS: Yale.) Also, following quotations.

p. 624 **"feeling he has shown"**—*Letters*, VII, 267, 30 April 1880, to Eleanor Cross. (MS: Yale.)

p. 624n **"expected to vent wisdom"**—Haight, p. 537.

p. 624 **"that binds us together"**—*Letters*, VII, 266, 27 April 1880. (MS: in private hands.)

p. 624 **"his life to me"**—*Letters*, VII, 268, 5 May 1880. (MS: in private hands.) Following quotation, *Letters*, VII, 269, 5 May 1880 (MS: Yale). Eliot assures Mrs. Burne-Jones that "this will make no difference in my care for my lost one's family either during or after my life. Mr. Cross has a sufficient fortune of his own." She had written the identical sentiment to Barbara Bodichon, in the identical words.

p. 625 **"I had been a man"**—*Letters*, VII, 273, 8 May 1880. (MS: Tinker Collection, Yale.)

p. 626 **"and every good wish"**—*Letters*, VII, 280, 17 May 1880. (MS: Yale.)

p. 626 **"various lots open to him"**—*Letters*, VII, 287, 26. May 1880. (MS: in private hands.)

p. 627 **"pattern of my thoughts"**—*Letters*, VII, 274, 9 May, from Paris. (MS: Tinker Collection, Yale.) The letter indicates that Eliot had embraced Eleanor as family.

p. 629 **"exercise without fatigue"**—*Letters*, VII, 281, 18 May 1880. (MS: British Museum.)

p. 629 **"strength to endure"**—*Letters*, VII, 283, 21 May 1880. (MS: Yale.)

p. 629 **"except strong-mindedness"**—*Letters*, VII, 286, 25 May 1880. (MS: Yale.)

p. 629 **"after seeing Rossi"**—*Letters*, VII, 289, 28 May 1880. (MS: Yale.)

p. 630 **"in the utmost haste"**—*Letters*, VII, 290, 29 May–1 June 1880. (MS: in private hands.)

p. 630 **"impending cloud"**—Simcox's Autobiography, 5 February 1882, an assessment made well after Eliot's death.

p. 630 **search her diary for clues**—At Yale, for 14–26 June 1880.

p. 631 **"made me thoroughly ill"**—Cross, III, pp. 293–94.

p. 631 **"excitement before our marriage"**—*Letters*, VII, 307–308, 1 August 1880. (MS: Parrish Collection, Princeton.)

p. 632 **confirmed the jump into the canal**—Haight, p. 544, n. 3.

p. 633 **"in a dream-land"**—*Letters*, VII, 300, 17 June 1880. (MS: Berg Collection, New York Public Library.)

p. 633 **long letter to Charles Lewes**—*Letters*, VII, 304–306, from Wildbad.

p. 634 **"our calls in return"**—*Letters*, VII, 312, 12 August 1880. (MS: in private hands.)

p. 635 **"utter, barren blank"**—Simcox's Autobiography, 29 July 1880. Also, following quotations.

p. 635 **"improving this confused world"**—*Letters*, VII, 322, 14 September 1880, to Barbara Bodichon. (MS: Parrish Collection, Princeton.)

p. 635 **"as my guardian angel"**—*Letters*, VII, 323, 14–15 September 1880. (MS: British Museum.) Also, previous quotation.

p. 636 **"bodily self"**—*Letters*, VII, 332, 3 November 1880, to Maria Congreve.

p. 636 **"those who survive in loneliness"**—*Letters*, VII, 333, 15 November 1880. (MS: Harvard.)

p. 638 **"a very anxious night"**—*Letters*, VII, 345, 9 December 1880, to Mrs. Lionel Tennyson. (MS: Parrish Collection, Princeton.) Eliot's diary for 29 November–4 December 1880 does not read like that of a woman only a few weeks from death; it sounds active and hopeful.

p. 638 **"anxious about the case"**—*Letters*, VII, 351, 23 December 1880, Cross to Elma Stuart. (MS: British Museum.) Also, following quotations.

p. 639 **"history of womankind"**—25 December 1880 (MS: Yale).

p. 640 **"crown of my life is gone"**—*Letters*, IX, 321, 22 December 1880. (MS: British Museum.)

p. 641 **"I cried and moaned aloud"**—Simcox's Autobiography, 29 December 1880. Also, *Letters*, IX, 323–24.

Index